Analyzing American Democracy

Praise for *Analyzing American Democracy*

The new edition of Bond and Smith's revered text threads the needle by adding several exciting touches—most notably, the thoroughly updated content and thematically integrated boxes—without sacrificing the features that so many devoted instructors have long loved—most notably, the unapologetically scientific approach and the vivid, deeply engaging writing style.

John Hibbing, *University of Nebraska–Lincoln*

From its focus on the principles of democracy to the actual practice of democracy in the United States, Bond and Smith's introductory text provides university students with the necessary tools to critically analyze American politics. The authors effectively apply political science research in a way that is fresh and accessible to students and do so in a way that will make students think well beyond their preconceptions about politics. The chapter on elections is the most thorough and engaging treatment of presidential elections you will find in an introductory American politics textbook.

Jeffrey S. Peake, *Clemson University*

Jon Bond and Kevin Smith's *Analyzing American Democracy* provides the most comprehensive and nuanced treatment of American political institutions and behavior to date. By drawing upon the most recent political science literature, the text encourages students to see American politics through a theoretical lens, and promotes a more generalized understanding of political concepts that transcend time and space. With stimulating real-world examples of the trade-offs, paradoxes, and competing ethical perspectives that are negotiated in a modern representative democracy, students become conversant and critically-engaged in the challenges confronting the country, and thus, become better citizens.

Sarah A. Fulton, *Texas A&M University*

Analyzing American Democracy is one of the best American Government books on the market. Not only is it comprehensive in covering material across the vast spectrum of American politics, but it also has an interesting point of view: the idea that our expectations of government and its performance may not be entirely realistic. Bond and Smith have written a book that is accessible to undergraduate students, yet provides sufficient detail for professors to examine the nuances of American politics today.

Richard W. Waterman, *University of Kentucky*

Nobody does a better job than Bond and Smith of integrating modern political science with a thoroughly up-to-date introduction to American government. Most of my students have already been exposed to an AP-style high school American government survey, and a text that is clearly more science than civics is exactly what they need at the college level. On top of that the writing has the wit, snap, and drive that keeps students reading and thinking in spite of themselves.

John R. Alford, *Rice University*

Teaching a broad survey course that covers the breadth of American politics can be a daunting task for both instructors and students. Bond and Smith have organized what could be an overwhelming amount of information into a logical structure coupled with a straightforward, journalistic writing style that incorporates cutting-edge political science research with key political concepts. The result is a textbook that is truly an introduction to political science, not just civics or popular politics.

Amanda Friesen, *Indiana University–Purdue University Indianapolis*

Analyzing American Democracy
Politics and Political Science

Third Edition

Jon R. Bond
Texas A&M University

Kevin B. Smith
University of Nebraska–Lincoln

Third edition published 2019
by Routledge
52 Vanderbilt Avenue, New York, NY 10017

and by Routledge
2 Park Square, Milton Park, Abingdon, Oxon, OX14 4RN

Routledge is an imprint of the Taylor & Francis Group, an informa business

© 2019 Taylor & Francis

The right of Jon R. Bond and Kevin B. Smith to be identified as authors of this work has been asserted by them in accordance with sections 77 and 78 of the Copyright, Designs and Patents Act 1988.

All rights reserved. No part of this book may be reprinted or reproduced or utilized in any form or by any electronic, mechanical, or other means, now known or hereafter invented, including photocopying and recording, or in any information storage or retrieval system, without permission in writing from the publishers. Printed in Canada.

Trademark notice: Product or corporate names may be trademarks or registered trademarks, and are used only for identification and explanation without intent to infringe.

First edition published by Routledge 2013
Second edition published by Routledge 2016

Library of Congress Cataloging-in-Publication Data
Names: Bond, Jon R., author. | Smith, Kevin B., 1963- author.
Title: Analyzing American democracy : politics and political science /
   Jon R. Bond, Texas A&M University, Kevin B. Smith, University of Nebraska-Lincoln.
Description: Third Edition. | New York : Routledge, 2019. | Previous edition: 2015.
Identifiers: LCCN 2018029421 | ISBN 9781138345188 (hardback) |
   ISBN 9781138345195 (paperback) | ISBN 9780429438035 (ebook)
Subjects: LCSH: United States—Politics and government. |
   Democracy—United States.
Classification: LCC JK276 .B65 2019 | DDC 320.473—dc23
LC record available at https://lccn.loc.gov/2018029421

ISBN: 978-1-138-34518-8 (hbk)
ISBN: 978-1-138-34519-5 (pbk)
ISBN: 978-0-429-43803-5 (ebk)

Typeset in Minion Pro
by Apex CoVantage, LLC

Visit the eResources: www.routledge.com/9781138345195

BRIEF CONTENTS

Preface   xix

CHAPTER 1   The Basics of Democracy   2

PART I: THE CONSTITUTIONAL FRAMEWORK

CHAPTER 2   The American Constitution   40
CHAPTER 3   Federalism   77
CHAPTER 4   Civil Liberties   112
CHAPTER 5   Civil Rights   146

PART II: CONNECTING CITIZENS TO GOVERNMENT

CHAPTER 6   Interest Groups   184
CHAPTER 7   Political Parties   221
CHAPTER 8   The Mass Media and Politics   258
CHAPTER 9   Public Opinion and Political Socialization   291
CHAPTER 10   Elections   324
CHAPTER 11   Political Participation and Voting Behavior   386

PART III: OFFICIAL DECISION MAKING

CHAPTER 12   Congress   422
CHAPTER 13   The Presidency   468
CHAPTER 14   The Bureaucracy   522
CHAPTER 15   The Federal Judiciary   556

PART IV: CONCLUSION

CHAPTER 16 Core Democratic Principles and Public Policy 608

Appendix A	The Declaration of Independence	A1-633
Appendix B	The Articles of the Confederation (1781)	A2-636
Appendix C	Constitution of the United States	A3-642
Appendix D	*Federalist* Number 10	A4-655
	Federalist Number 51	A4-660
Appendix E	Partisan Control of the Presidency, Congress, and the Supreme Court	A5-663
References		R-667
Glossary		G-687
Cases Index		I-701
Name Index		I-703
Subject Index		I-707

DETAILED CONTENTS

Preface   xix

Chapter 1   **The Basics of Democracy**   2

Key Concepts: Politics, Government, and Popular Sovereignty   5
- Politics and Government   5
- Popular Sovereignty   6
- Process and Substance   7
- Core Democratic Principles   8

Two Basic Forms of Democracy   11
- Direct Democracy   12
- Representative Democracy   13

Representative Systems and Core Democratic Principles   13
- Elections   14
- Political Parties   14
- Interest Groups   15

Representative Democracy in the United States   15
- Central Beliefs of Democracy in America   16
- Fallacies Associated With Democracy in America   16

The Challenge of American Democracy   17
- Diversity and Difference   18
- Dynamics   18
- Ideology and Partisanship   20
- False Consensus   21

Meeting the Challenge?   22
- The Case for American Democracy   22
- Major Criticisms of American Democracy   23

Making Sense of Politics: Political Science   25
- The Roots of Political Science   25
- The Scientific Method   26
- Thinking Analytically   30
- Theoretical Frameworks in Political Science   31

General Approach and Organization of the Book   36

Top 10 Takeaway Points   37

Key Terms and Cases   38

PART I: THE CONSTITUTIONAL FRAMEWORK

Chapter 2 The American Constitution — 40

The Concept of a Constitution — 42
Circumstances That Led to the Creation of the Constitution — 43
- Historical Antecedents of the Constitution — 43
- Economic Conditions — 46
- Group Rivalries and the Movement for a Convention — 47

The Constitutional Convention — 49
- The Founders — 50
- Agreement, Disagreement, and Compromise at the Convention — 51
- The Limited Role of Religion — 52
- The Ratification Campaign — 53

Constitutional Principles — 57
- Written Constitution — 61
- Representative Government — 62
- Fragmentation of Power — 62
- Mixed Government — 65

Changing the American Constitution — 66
- Formal Amendments — 66
- Constitutional Change Through Custom and Usage — 72
- Executive Interpretation — 73
- Legislative Interpretation — 74
- Judicial Interpretation — 74

Top 10 Takeaway Points — 75
Key Terms and Cases — 76

Chapter 3 Federalism — 77

The Concept of Federalism in Context: Confederal, Unitary, and Federal Systems — 79
- Confederation — 80
- Unitary Government — 81
- Federalism — 81

Why Federalism? — 83
- Advantages of Federalism — 83
- Disadvantages of Federalism — 86

Division of Powers in the American Federal System — 87
- The Powers of the National Government — 87

The Powers, Rights, and Obligations of State Governments	89
Refereeing Power Conflicts	95
The Evolution of Federalism	**96**
Dual Federalism	98
Cooperative Federalism	100
New Federalism	103
Federalism and the Future of State–Federal Relations	108
Top 10 Takeaway Points	**109**
Key Terms and Cases	**111**

Chapter 4   Civil Liberties   112

The Concept of Civil Liberties	**115**
Liberty and Authority	115
Restrictions on the Government	**118**
The Bill of Rights	118
Restrictions on State Violations of Civil Liberties	119
Freedom of Religion	**122**
Prohibition Against the Establishment of Religion	123
Free Exercise of Religion	126
Freedom of Expression	**127**
General Approaches	128
Specific Tests	128
Unprotected Speech	131
The Right to Privacy	**134**
Criminal Procedure	**136**
Exclusionary Rule	138
Right to Counsel	138
Right Against Self-Incrimination	139
Capital Punishment	140
Top 10 Takeaway Points	**143**
Key Terms and Cases	**145**

Chapter 5   Civil Rights   146

The Concept of Civil Rights	**149**
African Americans	**150**
Racial Segregation	152
The Judicial Strategy to End Segregation	152
The Revolution in Race Relations	153

Government's Response to the Race Revolution	155
Affirmative Action	156
Latinos	**161**
Native Americans	**165**
Women	**167**
Historical Background	168
The Reemergence of Women's Rights	170
People With Disabilities	**175**
LGBTQ Citizens	**178**
Top 10 Takeaway Points	**179**
Key Terms and Cases	**181**

PART II: CONNECTING CITIZENS TO GOVERNMENT

Chapter 6 Interest Groups — 184

The Concept of Interest Groups	**187**
Interest Group Goals	188
Interest Group Membership	189
Why People Join Interest Groups	**190**
The Benefits and Costs of Group Membership	190
Collective Action, Public Goods, and Free Riders	192
Overcoming the Free Rider Problem	193
The Origins and Growth of Interest Groups	**194**
Theoretical Perspectives on the Formation of Interest Groups	194
The Growth of Interest Groups	196
Interest Group Resources and Activities	**201**
Political Resources	201
Political Tactics	203
The Power and Regulation of Interest Groups	**209**
Interest Group Power and Influence	210
Regulation of Interest Group Activity	216
Top 10 Takeaway Points	**218**
Key Terms and Cases	**220**

Chapter 7 Political Parties — 221

The Concept of Political Parties	**223**
The Challenge of Defining American Political Parties	223

        Comparison of Political Parties and Other Political Groupings   223
        Membership in American Political Parties   224
        Incentives for Associating With Political Parties   226

Two-Party Competition in American Politics   229
        The General Types of Party Systems   231
        American Party Competition at the National Level   231
        Minor Political Parties   237

What Political Parties Do   241
        Facilitate Participation   241
        Promote Government Responsiveness   243
        Promote Government Accountability   244
        Promote Stability and Peaceful Resolution of Conflict   244
        The Responsible Party Model   245

The Strength of Political Parties   246
        The Strength of Party in the Electorate   246
        The Strength of Party in Government   250
        The Strength of Party Organizations   253
        Cycles of Party Strength   255

Top 10 Takeaway Points   255
Key Terms and Cases   257

Chapter 8   The Mass Media and Politics   258

The Concept of a Free Press   261
        Information and Education   262
        Agenda Setting   271
        Watchdog and Public Advocate   272

Threats to a Free Press   273
        Government Control   274
        Private Control   275

Media Bias   277
        Political Bias   278
        Racial and Gender Bias   283
        Negativity Bias   284

Changes in the Public Sphere   285
        The Decline of the Gatekeepers   285
        Information and Civic Engagement   287

Top 10 Takeaway Points   289
Key Terms and Cases   290

Chapter 9 Public Opinion and Political Socialization — 291

The Concept of Public Opinion — 294
- Direction — 294
- Stability — 294
- Intensity — 296
- Salience — 297

The Competence of Public Opinion — 299
Elite Opinion and Issue Publics — 300
Interpreting Public Opinion Polls — 301
- Did the Poll Ask the Right People? — 302
- What Is the Poll's Margin of Error? — 304
- What Was the Question? — 305
- Which Question Came First? — 307

The Bases of Public Opinion — 308
- Political Culture — 309
- Ideology — 310
- Political Socialization — 311
- Biological Models of Public Opinion — 317

Public Opinion and Participation — 320
Top 10 Takeaway Points — 321
Key Terms and Cases — 323

Chapter 10 Elections — 324

The Concept of Elections — 326
Methods of Nominating Candidates — 327
- Legislative Caucus — 327
- Convention — 327
- Direct Primary — 328

Nominating Presidential Candidates — 329
- The Allocation of National Convention Delegates — 329
- The Method and Timing of Delegate Selection — 329
- The Nomination Campaign — 332

Electing the President — 351
- The Electoral College — 351
- The Campaign — 360
- Financing the Presidential Election — 362

Nominating Candidates for Congress — 364
- Primary Laws — 364
- The Politics of Choosing Congressional Candidates — 364

Electing Members of Congress	**366**
Apportionment	367
Congressional Districts	367
Overlapping Terms and Staggered Elections	371
Incumbency Advantage in Congressional Elections	374
Financing Congressional Elections	380
Top 10 Takeaway Points	**383**
Key Terms and Cases	**385**

Chapter 11 Political Participation and Voting Behavior — 386

The Concept of Political Participation	**389**
Forms of Political Participation	389
The Theoretical Basis of Political Participation	389
Is Political Participation in America High or Low?	391
The Right to Vote	**392**
Voter Turnout	394
The Political System and Turnout	395
Individual Desire and Ability to Participate	401
Voting and Democracy	407
Models of Voting Behavior	**408**
The Sociological Model	408
The Social-Psychological Model	410
The Rational Choice Model	411
Explaining Voter Choice	**412**
Party Identification	413
Candidate Image	415
Issues	416
Voting Behavior and the Operation of the American Political System	**417**
Contemporary Realignment?	418
Top 10 Takeaway Points	**419**
Key Terms and Cases	**420**

PART III: OFFICIAL DECISION MAKING

Chapter 12 Congress — 422

The Concept of the U.S. Congress	**425**
Responsibilities of Congress	**426**

Primary Responsibilities	426
Secondary Responsibilities	432

Members of Congress and Their World — 436
Backgrounds of National Legislators	436
Tenure and Career Patterns	438
Daily Life of a Member of Congress	439
Congressional Pay and Perquisites	441

Bicameralism in the American Congress — 444
Leadership in the U.S. Senate	446
Leadership in the U.S. House of Representatives	447
The Committee System	449

Running the Legislative Obstacle Course — 456
Bill Introduction and Committee Referral	457
Committee Consideration and Action	458
From Committee to the Floor	459
Resolving House–Senate Differences	463

Top 10 Takeaway Points — 465
Key Terms and Cases — 467

Chapter 13 The Presidency — 468

The Concept of the U.S. Presidency — 471

The Development of the Presidency — 473
A Single Executive	473
Broad Constitutional Provisions	474
Public Acceptance of Positive Government	474
Congressional Delegation of Power	475
Contemporary Expectations of the President	476

The President and the Presidency — 476
The President as an Individual	477
The Presidency as an Organization	479
Organization of the Presidency and Presidential Effectiveness	486

The President's Primary Constitutional Responsibilities — 489
Chief Executive	489
Commander in Chief	490
Chief Diplomat	492

The President as Party Leader — 494
Limitations on the President as Party Leader	495
The President and Party Organization	495
The President and Electoral Activities	496

The President as Public Opinion Leader	**498**
Going Public	499
Presidential Approval Ratings	503
The President and Congress	**505**
Messages and Recommendations	505
The Veto	506
Presidential Success in Congress	507
Unilateral Powers	515
Top 10 Takeaway Points	**519**
Key Terms and Cases	**521**

Chapter 14 The Bureaucracy — 522

The Concept of Bureaucracy	**524**
The Characteristics of Bureaucracy	**526**
The Weberian Model of Bureaucracy	526
The Merit System	527
Neutral Competence	529
The Bureaucrats	530
The Structure of American Bureaucracies	**532**
The Executive Office of the President	533
Cabinet Departments	533
Independent Agencies	534
Regulatory Agencies and Commissions	534
Government Corporations	535
Other Bureaus	535
The Politics of Organization	536
The Power of Bureaucracy	**537**
Rulemaking	538
Adjudication	539
Bureaucratic Lobbying	539
Controlling the Bureaucracy	**541**
Theories of Bureaucratic Behavior	542
Monitoring Bureaucracy	546
Influencing Bureaucracy	548
Reforming Bureaucracy	**551**
Running Government Like a Business	551
Businesses Running Government	552
Top 10 Takeaway Points	**554**
Key Terms and Cases	**555**

Chapter 15 The Federal Judiciary — 556

The Concept of the Federal Judiciary — 559
The Jurisdiction of Federal Courts — 559
- Jurisdiction Defined in the Constitution — 560
- Original and Appellate Jurisdiction — 561
- The Power of Congress to Define Jurisdiction of Federal Courts — 561
- Jurisdiction Determined by Judicial Interpretation — 561

The Structure and Organization of Federal Courts — 562
- The District Courts — 562
- The Courts of Appeals — 564
- The U.S. Supreme Court — 565

The Selection and Background of Federal Judges — 570
- Party Affiliation and Philosophy — 571
- Balancing the Representativeness of the Court — 574
- Judicial Experience and Merit — 576
- Confirmation Politics in the Senate — 577

Judicial Decision Making — 584
- Models of Judicial Decision Making — 584
- Evidence of Political Influence on Judicial Decision Making — 586

Judicial Review in a Democratic Society — 591
- The Origins of Judicial Review — 592
- Concepts of Judicial Review — 594
- Patterns in the Exercise of Judicial Review — 596
- Constraints on the Exercise of Judicial Review — 599

Top 10 Takeaway Points — 604
Key Terms and Cases — 606

PART IV: CONCLUSION

Chapter 16 Core Democratic Principles and Public Policy — 608

The Concept of Public Policy — 611
The Stages of Policymaking — 612
- Agenda Setting — 613
- Policy Formulation and Adoption — 617
- Policy Implementation — 621
- Policy Evaluation — 625

Public Policy and Core Democratic Values — 627

	Majority Rule	627
	Political Freedom	628
	Political Equality	628
	Conclusion	**630**
	Top 10 Takeaway Points	**630**
	Key Terms and Cases	**632**

Appendix A	The Declaration of Independence	A1-633
Appendix B	The Articles of the Confederation (1781)	A2-636
Appendix C	Constitution of the United States	A3-642
Appendix D	*Federalist* Number 10	A4-655
	Federalist Number 51	A4-660
Appendix E	Partisan Control of the Presidency, Congress, and the Supreme Court	A5-663
References		R-667
Glossary		G-687
Cases Index		I-701
Name Index		I-703
Subject Index		I-707

PREFACE

We are political scientists, so almost by definition we are fascinated by politics and believe the best way to understand the political world is through the scientific method. Between us we also have decades of teaching experience, so we are acutely aware that the typical undergraduate shares neither our passion for politics nor a familiarity with the scientific method. The central mission of the third edition of *Analyzing American Democracy*, like its predecessors, is not simply to educate students about the political and policy world, but also to teach them two general lessons. First, as citizens of the republic and citizens of the world, as individuals pursuing an education, a career, and a fulfilling life, they have a lot of extremely good, self-interested reasons to know more about politics. Second, if they want to know more about politics, approaching it scientifically is the most systematic and useful way to do so.

That, we fully realize, can be a tough sell, especially in an era of alt-facts and roll-your-own reality. We live in a polarized and partisan world, and most of what undergraduates know and learn about politics comes from friends, family, and social media, not from political science or political scientists. Indeed, most undergraduates are likely to take only one class and read only one textbook on American politics during their college career. Precisely because our chances to contribute to their education are so limited, we believe that a textbook needs to pursue three fundamental goals. First, at the most basic level, it must be comprehensive. The content between the covers of this single volume should capture a soup-to-nuts overview of the context, rules, processes, and institutions of the American political system. Second, it must not only introduce students to the basic mechanics of American politics but also present in an accessible way the basics of political science and how political scientists explain why politics works the way it does. Third, and most importantly, it must provide students with some basic intellectual tools necessary to promote independent analytic thought about the often confusing and always changing world of American politics. The third edition of *Analyzing American Democracy: Politics and Political Science* seeks to achieve these three goals.

First, the book is comprehensive. It begins by providing students a historical and constitutional framework for understanding American politics. This means introducing students to the concept of democracy, the values democracy represents, and how these values are expressed in the structure and evolution of governance in America. It means a comprehensive examination of the linkage mechanisms that connect citizens to government and how those mechanisms express—or fail to express—the core democratic principles embodied in the American political system. It means systematically covering the key policymaking institutions of national government, not just the decision-making institutions established by the Constitution—

the legislative, executive, and judicial branches—but also bureaucracy, one of the most important and least understood institutions of American politics. Finally, it means giving an overview of how all these elements come together in making and implementing public policy. Of course, we can't cover everything, and we hope students reading this textbook might be intrigued enough by some of the topics that they will continue with additional upper-division courses in American politics. But we aim to include enough of the raw material to help students understand the workings of contemporary American politics such that they can become engaged members of the polity.

Second, this book aims not simply to cover the basics of the American political system but also to demonstrate how politics can be usefully and systematically studied generally. It is valuable for students to have the basic details down and even better for them to begin understanding how the pieces fit together. Our goal is to put into your hands a book that is about not just politics, but political *science*. We take seriously the charge implied in the book's title: A central goal here is to teach students how to think analytically about the complexities of political conflict, processes, institutions, behavior, and policies. We introduce students to the science and craft of political science in Chapter 1 and use the frameworks and scholarship of the discipline to organize and explain all aspects of the American political system. In particular, we introduce students to three theoretical frameworks that illustrate the scientific study of politics—rational choice models, behavioral models, and evolutionary/biological models—and repeatedly return to these frameworks as explanatory aids throughout the book. Because we believe that the text used in political science courses should show students how political scientists report the results of their research, we continue to use the American Political Science Association style of in-text citations, with a comprehensive list of references. More generally, we lean heavily on political science scholarship in all of our explanatory accounts—our aim is to show students political science in action. We particularly want to do this because an Introduction to American Politics class may be the only political science course many students take in their undergraduate career. We want them to leave that class knowing something about what political scientists do and why it is important, just as students taking introductory economics or biology come away knowing something about the core theories and perspectives of those disciplines. In our view, too few introductory American politics textbooks achieve this, and too few members of the population see the value of political science compared to punditry and sound bites.

Third, the book seeks to be accessible but not "dumbed down." In our experience, students get the most out of this course not just by mastering the facts and theories covered, but when they further develop the tools of analytical thought. All our chapters begin with a story, written magazine-style, that provides a quick and easy introduction to the core themes of the chapter. The next section highlights the core concepts associated with the topic: What principles guide the creation and practice of a federal system? What role does public opinion, which is often ambiguous or divided, play in governance? How does political participation uphold the core principles of American democracy? What purpose does Congress serve as the national legislative institution? From there, chapters progressively build on these foundations to present the most important concepts, theories, and tools for understanding the great complexity of American politics. Undergraduate students could never hope to know everything about politics in America. Indeed, even if they did, such knowledge would quickly become outdated as new media emerge, rules change, and outcomes of public policies evolve to face new challenges among the citizenry. Students are best served by their textbook and by their undergraduate education if they also learn how to apply core principles and tools to future challenges. For example, the rapidly fragmenting and increasingly partisan media landscape feeds worries about media bias in many citizens. Understanding the core principle of political freedom puts a more partisan press into perspective—a functioning and healthy democracy does not need an unbiased press; what it needs is a *free* press. Or consider that many citizens are frustrated with the increasingly polarized nature of American politics and that elections increasingly seem to represent a choice between partisan extremes. Understanding the core principle of political equality and how the nomination process makes some more equal than others in deciding the general election ballot can help students understand why polarization exists and stimulate thinking on paths to reduce political polarization. American politics and the scholarship of political science tell an interesting and fascinating story; the task of telling that story in an engaging and accessible manner, we treated as both a challenge and an important responsibility.

NEW TO THE THIRD EDITION

Updated coverage throughout includes:

- 2016 and 2018 election updates and analysis of their political and policy impact
- Social media's growing influence on politics
- The impact of the alt-right and rising populism on elections and policy
- New trends in public opinion
- Weakening of the Voting Rights Act
- Campaign finance upheaval
- The changing congressional landscape
- Updated tables, figures, and photos present the empirical details of American politics, helping students gain quantitative literacy
- Landmark court cases, now highlighted and linked to key concepts
- Refreshed feature boxes reinforce the book's dedication to helping students understand the scientific approach to politics, incorporating intriguing new topics including genetics and public opinion, the biology of political participation, and evolution and the bureaucracy

PEDAGOGICAL FEATURES

We have devised a number of learning tools in this text to help students master the goals of their course. First, before students get immersed in the details of a chapter, they will find at the start a list of key questions to help frame the objectives of that chapter. These questions will help form a conceptual map of what comes next.

Next, every chapter has at least two themed features—"Thinking Analytically" and "Applying the Frameworks"—specifically crafted to show students how the concepts and theories covered in the main body of the chapter are translated into promoting systematic understanding of politics and to prompt them to put that systemic approach to thinking analytically into practice. The framework for doing this is established in the first chapter, where we provide students with a basic framework on the scientific method and what it means to think analytically. The features in each chapter are designed not just to report how that method is put into action, but to get students to do it themselves. The idea is to present them with questions—How do we measure media bias? Does business experience make a better president?—and give them applied practice in systematically thinking their way to their own answers.

In keeping with our focus on political science, we try to graphically illustrate researchers' findings and general concepts as much as we can. In these pages you will find a rich assortment of tables, figures, charts, and maps to present the empirical details of American politics. These are designed to support and parallel the primary themes of each chapter and help reach students with diverse learning styles.

At the end of each chapter, students might rightly ask themselves what were the most important points covered. We present the "Top 10 Takeaway Points" to answer just such a question. These lists are a handy reference for students reviewing their reading and preparing for quizzes and tests. They also further our goal of helping students see the forest through the trees, discerning the general principles that make sense of the numerous factual details.

ACKNOWLEDGMENTS

Like all books, this is a collaborative undertaking. The authors would like to extend thanks to all the good folks on the Routledge editorial team who contributed so much to what you hold in your hands, in particular: Jennifer Knerr, Ze'ev Sudry, Olivia Hatt, Nikky Twyman, and Dean Drake. We also thank James B. Cottrill, Byron D'Andra Orey, Scott Granberg-Rademacker, and Rebecca Hannagan for their past work on the online eResource materials and add special thanks to Katelyn Abraham who updated these materials for the third edition.

We appreciate it.

Thanks are also due to the distinguished team of teacher-scholars who have provided reviewed drafts of this book and given invaluable feedback and input for revisions. These reviewers included David Connelly, Don Dugi, Lawrence Friedman, Mike Gruszczynski, Rebecca Hannagan, Richard Krupa, Douglas Kuberski, Jason Frederick Lambacher, Adam Myers, Joanna Mosser, Geoffrey Peterson, Geoffrey Rogal, Joseph Stewart, Richard Waterman, and additional anonymous individuals.

As always, we must also recognize Ken Meier, who made the original phone call that brought the two authors together on this project. In spite of all the hard work that phone call led to, the authors are still speaking to him—well, most of the time.

Jon Bond is grateful to numerous friends and colleagues. Rich Fleisher at Fordham University deserves special thanks. Although Rich is not a collaborator on this project, he has continued to offer cogent insights and advice that have made this a better book. Current and former colleagues at Texas A&M University who shared their expertise on various topics include George Edwards, Roy Flemming, Bob Harmel, Kim Hill, Pat Hurley, Paul Kellstedt, Norm Luttbeg, Dave Peterson, Eric Godwin, and Jim Rogers. Several current and former graduate students helped with background research, provided technical support, and contributed in many other ways (yes, students, "many" is the appropriate adjective here). I am grateful to Lydia Andrade, Kristi Campbell, Michelle Chin, Jim Cottrill, Nathan Ilderton, Glen Krutz, Jose Villalobos, Leslie McDonald, and Garrett Vande Kamp. I am grateful to Gary Jacobson at the University of California, San Diego, and George Edwards at Texas A&M University, for sharing their data that helped me update some key sections so that we can compete more effectively with their books. Larry Baum at Ohio State University, Frank Baumgartner at the University of North Carolina at Chapel Hill, Beth Leech at Rutgers University, and John Bibby of the University of Wisconsin–Milwaukee also offered helpful comments and advice. Finally, I am most grateful for the love and support of my wife, Karon, and my daughters, Lynne, Mika, and Monika.

Kevin Smith would like to thank colleagues at the University of Nebraska–Lincoln, especially Beth Theiss-Morse and John Hibbing. A very special thanks also goes to Emily Johnson, who put in a lot of hours and made numerous important contributions to what follows—"research assistant" is a title that just doesn't convey the credit she deserves. Finally, to the Dallas Cowboys, thanks for, well, uh, not being the Cleveland Browns, I guess.

SUPPORT MATERIALS FOR STUDENTS AND INSTRUCTORS

Analyzing American Democracy is accompanied by a number of useful resources designed to aid in student learning and foster the instructional goals of faculty.

Online eResources

Analyzing American Democracy offers an online eResource for both students and instructors at **www.routledge.com/9781138345195**.

Test Bank

A full test bank, written by James Cottrill (St. Cloud State University) and updated by Katelyn Abraham, covers each chapter with multiple choice, short answer, and essay questions. It is available to professors in a password-protected Word file for easy editing.

Powerpoint Lecture Slides

Written by Scott Granberg-Rademacker (Minnesota State University, Mankato) and Rebecca Hannagan (Northern Illinois University) and updated by Katelyn Abraham, these PowerPoint slides feature concise lecture outlines as well as all the figures and tables from the text.

Jon R. Bond
Kevin B. Smith

Analyzing American Democracy

1 THE BASICS OF DEMOCRACY

KEY QUESTIONS

What is politics? What is government? What is a democracy?

What are the core principles of democracy?

How does a representative democracy uphold these core principles?

How can we make sense of democracy and politics in America?

© J. David Ake/AP Photo

PRESIDENT GEORGE W. BUSH'S first administration was not happy with political reporter Ron Suskind's White House coverage. That's why, in summer 2002, he was on the receiving end of a scolding from a senior advisor to the president. Nothing hugely unusual about that. Irritating government officials is an occupational hazard if you write about politics for a living, and you can hardly blame those smarting from the sting of a reporter's pen for trying to blunt some of its sharp edges. This was not a typical off-the-record clearing of the air, though. Suskind was getting a presidential finger-wagging for being a card-carrying member of the reality-based community, an accusation almost calculated to baffle a reporter for the mainstream media. To start with, what, exactly, is the "reality-based community"? The advisor described them as people who believed that the best way to figure out solutions to political and policy problems was through "the judicious study of discernible reality." And, that's supposed to be a bad thing? Certainly not for Suskind; he responded by talking about the importance of Enlightenment values—empiricism, rational, analytical and scientific thinking—but the advisor cut him off. "That's not the way the world really works," the advisor said; "when we act, we create our own reality" (quoted in Suskind 2004).

Suskind was taken aback. Was a senior official in the United States government really suggesting that politicians and policymakers inhabited some sort of post-modern universe where facts were a matter of perspective and comforting "realities" could just be made up? Fast-forward a decade and a half and there's plenty of grounds for arguing the answer to that question is yes. What were once just plain and simple falsehoods can now be "alternative facts," and truthiness—believing something to be true because it feels true, even if it is demonstrably not—is an actual thing (Bradner 2017). If anyone says something that contradicts our comforting self-created "realities", especially if it comes from some know-it-all reporter or academic, you don't have to worry about taking it seriously. Just call it fake news. Tom Nichols, a political scientist who wrote a book about "the death of expertise," describes a contemporary America where, "policy debates sound increasingly like fights between groups of ill-informed people who all manage to be wrong," where debate does not distinguish between "you're wrong" and "you're stupid," and where "to refuse to acknowledge all views as worthy of consideration, no matter how fantastic or inane they are, is to be close-minded" (Nichols 2017, 25).

That's kind of a depressing picture. And if it's even half-way accurate, you need to know from the beginning that this book is going to be swimming hard against the tide. We not only belong to the reality-based community; we also want you to join us. What follows is premised on the idea that whatever we want the world to be, and regardless of how hard we believe it is exactly that, it just ain't necessarily so. We believe the world is more than the sum of our own preferences and biases, whatever they are, and that to act otherwise is not only to deny reality but to potentially put democracy at risk. We believe the world, including the political world, is real. It can be prodded and poked, observed and measured, patterns can be identified, outcome probabilities calculated, and cause and effect systematically assessed. We believe that some perspectives—those emerging from serious study and empirical analysis—are simply better than others. And by better, we mean better informed, better thought-out, and better at dealing with the often uncomfortable reality—and it is *reality*—that our political world presents us with.

Fair warning: This sort of analytical thinking, especially about a subject like politics, can be hard work. Most people think politics is, or at least should be, easy. It's just applied common sense, right? Well, no. Turns out that most people have it dead wrong. Americans know remarkably little about politics and government other than that they hold pretty much all of it in disdain. We think the fundamental reason for this is that Americans really do not understand what a democracy is and what a democracy does. Their judgments of politics and government are not based on hard-nosed assessments of the realities of democracy. Much of the frustration that Americans express about their government is anchored in a misunderstanding of what democracy is supposed to do, an unrealistic expectation of what it can do, and a failure to comprehend the dangers of pursuing undemocratic alternatives to solving problems.

This is not too surprising. Democratic politics is messy and contradictory; making reasoned sense of it is never going to be easy and there are other

Analytical thinking is not always easy, but if you want to understand politics it's worth the effort.
© Alain Pitton/NurPhoto/Sipa/AP Photo

options that require a lot less effort. For example, it takes a lot less effort to simply see and understand the political world through our biases and predispositions, our ideology and our preferences. Putting those aside and trying to rationally and analytically understand politics requires some intellectual sweat and labor. But it's not rocket science. We have no doubt the vast majority of citizens—and that definitely includes you—possess the ability to think cogently and logically about politics. Doing so requires knowing something about the machinery of democracy, its institutions and its operating principles. But that's not enough. If citizens are to really understand how the parts of a democracy fit together and whether they are working properly, they need to learn how to think analytically about politics. And that's exactly what this book is going to try and teach you to do.

Welcome to the reality-based community.

KEY CONCEPTS:
POLITICS, GOVERNMENT, AND POPULAR SOVEREIGNTY

This book is about understanding how democracy works in the United States. We examine what a democracy is, examine what it is supposed to do, and seek to explain how the institutions and processes of the American political system operate in theory and in practice. We also aim to help readers learn how to think systematically about politics, to employ reasoned analysis—as opposed to ideology, personal preference, or wishful thinking—to make their own independent judgments about what is happening in the political system, why it is happening, and whether it is compatible with the core principles of democracy. This first means gaining a firm understanding of three crucial concepts—politics, government, and popular sovereignty—and what their combination means in the American context.

Politics and Government

For many people, the word "politics" is derogatory. To call others "political" is to accuse them of being manipulative and self-serving. Scholars, however, tend to view politics in more neutral terms. Here are probably the two best-known scholarly definitions of **politics**.

1. According to Harold D. Lasswell (1938), politics is "who gets what, when, and how."
2. According to David Easton (1953), politics is the "authoritative allocation of values."

Both definitions say the same thing: All groups must have some way to make collective decisions, and the process of making those decisions is called politics. Politics is thus the process of coming to some definitive understanding of who is going to get what or whose values everyone is going to live by. Because individuals often disagree about who should get what or whose values should be binding on everyone, politics is a process of conflict management and resolution: It is a natural outcome of human interaction, not just something in which politicians and governments engage. Three friends arguing over what movie to watch are engaging in a small-scale form of politics; they are figuring out whose values (in this case, taste in movies) will be binding on the group.

Although disagreements among friends over what movie to watch usually can be resolved without the group resorting to formal decision-making institutions and processes, this is not the case for large groups such as nations. How can we decide what to do as a society? Who or what gets to decide which values are binding on everyone? The institution that has the authority to make such decisions is generally referred to as **government**.

Government is not the only institution that seeks to manage conflict and make authoritative decisions about who gets what. Churches, for example, make decisions about what behaviors are right and wrong and urge their members to follow church teachings. What makes government different from other decision-making institutions is coercion. Churches can coerce members of their congregation through threats of excommunication and the like, but they cannot extend that power over nonmembers and other organizations. Governments can. A church that decides that abortion or alcohol consumption is wrong can attempt to make such values binding on its congregation. A government can make such values binding on everyone. Act in defiance of government decisions—that is, break the law—and the government can take your property, your liberty, and even your life. Government is the only institution in society that can legitimately use such coercion on all individuals and organizations, making it the ultimate decider of who gets what (Downs 1957, 23).

Popular Sovereignty

The authority to legally wield this coercive power to allocate values is called **sovereignty** (this is why monarchs are sometimes called "sovereigns," reflecting the historical role of kings and queens as absolute rulers). Governments can be categorized into three basic forms based on who wields sovereign powers. Vesting sovereignty in a single person creates a form of government called an **autocracy**. Autocrats rule as absolute monarchs or dictators, personally deciding who gets what. Nazi Germany under Adolf Hitler and the Soviet Union under Joseph Stalin are examples of autocracies. A second option is to vest power in a small group of people, a government called an **oligarchy**. A military junta (a group of generals) is an example of an oligarchy. The third option is to broadly share power among all citizens, a form of government called a **democracy**. The word "democracy" is derived from two Greek roots: *demos*, which means "people," and *kratia*, which means "rule." Literally, democracy means "rule by the people."

---

politics The process of making binding decisions about who gets what or whose values everyone is going to live by.

government The institution that has the authority to make binding decisions for all of society.

sovereignty The legitimate authority in a government to wield coercive power to authoritatively allocate values.

autocracy A form of government in which the power to make authoritative decisions and allocate resources is vested in one person.

oligarchy A form of government in which the power to make authoritative decisions and allocate resources is vested in a small group of people.

democracy A form of government in which all the citizens have the opportunity to participate in the process of making authoritative decisions and allocating resources.

Thus, in an autocracy a single person is sovereign, and in an oligarchy a small elite is sovereign. In contrast, in a democracy, sovereignty belongs to *all citizens*, a distribution of political power known as **popular sovereignty**. Popular sovereignty gets to the core of what a democracy is: a form of government where all citizens have the right to participate in the process of deciding who gets what. What this means is that democracy is primarily about *process*, or how decisions are made. But a democratic decision-making process does not guarantee that the *substance* of those decisions will be democratic.

Process and Substance

Democracy as Process

In a democracy, how decisions are made is as important as what those decisions are. Indeed, some scholars view democracy as much more about means than ends (Schumpeter 1942). The means of democracy—the institutions and rules that organize and operate the political system—create a decision-making process that is typically slow and inefficient. Because all citizens have a right to participate, democratic decision making demands patience, tolerance of opposing viewpoints, and a willingness to compromise.

Ironically, it is this basic nature of a democratic process—inefficiency, gridlock, and lots of conflict—that Americans find most objectionable (Hibbing and Theiss-Morse 1995, 147). Given these distasteful features, it's worth asking whether a democratic decision-making process is the best approach to politics in the United States. Why opt for a form of government all but guaranteed to be slow, inefficient, and constantly embroiled in conflict? The short answer is that a system based on popular sovereignty tends to be more equitable and just. As one astute observer put it, "democracy is the worst form of government. It is the most inefficient, the most clumsy, the most unpractical … Yet democracy is the only form of social order admissible because it is the only one consistent with justice" (Briffault 1930, quoted in Thomsett and Thomsett 1994, 37). A democratic process is rarely marked by efficiency, agreement, clarity, or speed. Instead, the characteristics of a democratic process include the right to vote, to publicly disagree with government decisions and other citizens, to petition an elected representative, to sue, to form an organization with policy goals, to engage in a political campaign, and to support a political party.

Democratic Substance

Though the heart of democracy is about process, substance counts too. Paradoxically, a democratic process can produce an undemocratic outcome. For example, in the United States, majorities historically have supported policies to deny voting rights and educational and economic opportunities to citizens based on gender, ethnicity, and race. Legislatures responded to these preferences with laws systematically denying civil rights and liberties to certain citizens. The process of making

popular sovereignty The idea that the highest political authority in a democracy is the will of the people.

those policies could be considered democratic—elections were held, legislators debated, and the majority preference became law. The substance of those decisions, though, systematically stripped large numbers of citizens of their ability to participate fully in political life. The end result was not just unfair, but undemocratic. By taking away the rights of certain citizens to participate in the process of deciding who gets what, the democratic process had made America less democratic.

This is one of the central problems of a democratic system: how to ensure popular sovereignty when people want to use their ability to authoritatively allocate values to limit the rights of others. As U.S. history amply demonstrates, those in power have been tempted to limit the political participation of those who disagree with them. How does democracy uphold the concept of popular sovereignty when some want to use that power to limit the rights of others?

Core Democratic Principles

Popular sovereignty helps ensure a system where everyone is a political equal and free to participate in making binding decisions. In practice, popular sovereignty rests on the extent to which the process and outcomes of a political system are consistent with three core principles: majority rule, political freedom, and political equality. To be democratic, the process of making decisions *and* the outcomes of those decisions must be compatible with these core principles.

Majority Rule

In a democracy, popular sovereignty means government decisions should reflect the will of the people and that citizens hold the government accountable for its actions. While this sounds fine in theory, citizens often have very different ideas of what the government should or should not do. Government cannot respond to the preferences of all citizens, because citizens want government to do contradictory things. Consider differences in public opinion on issues ranging from immigration to tax cuts. The government cannot provide a path to legal residence for the undocumented while simultaneously seeking to deport them as illegal immigrants any more than it can cut taxes by raising tax rates. How can popular sovereignty be meaningful when people have such profoundly different notions about how values should be authoritatively allocated?

Democracies seek to exercise popular sovereignty through **majority rule**, which means that government follows the course of action preferred by most people. The preferred alternative does not necessarily have to be an **absolute majority**, defined as 50 percent plus one of all eligible citizens, or even a **simple majority**, defined as 50 percent plus one of those who actually vote. If voters' preferences are divided among three or more courses of action, so that none have more than 50 percent support, the choice with the greatest support is called a **plurality**.

Though majority rule is the basic guideline for translating popular sovereignty into political decisions in democracies, it has to be balanced with **minority rights**.

---

majority rule The principle under which government follows the course of action preferred by most people.

absolute majority Fifty percent plus one of all members or all eligible voters.

simple majority Fifty percent plus one of those participating or of those who vote.

plurality The largest percentage of a vote, when no one has a majority.

minority rights The full rights of democratic citizenship held by any group numerically inferior to the majority. These fundamental democratic rights cannot be taken away—even if a majority wishes to do so—without breaking the promise of democracy.

A minority is any group numerically smaller than a majority, and it retains the full rights of democratic citizenship. In democracies, minority viewpoints are permitted to be heard and to be critical of the majority's views and actions. In the theory of democracy, the rights of minorities—their political freedom—cannot be taken away, even if the majority prefers this course of action. In practice, as we shall see, majorities often have succeeded in depriving minorities of their democratic rights.

Political Freedom

Government cannot respond to the will of the people if people are not free to express their wants and demands. To uphold the notion of popular sovereignty, minorities—even if they consist of one or two people with repugnant views—must have the right to participate and express those views. The necessary ingredients for political freedom are the right to criticize governmental leaders and policies, the right to propose new courses of government action, the right to form and join interest groups, the right to discuss political issues free from government censorship, and the right of citizens to seek and hold public office.

Note that the objects of free expression are plural. If all the people have the right to express their wants, demands, and preferences, they will rarely express the *same wants*, demands, and preferences. In the United States, political freedom means a lot of different wants, demands, and preferences, which makes it difficult for government to respond to the people. The central reason democratic governments do not respond to the will of the people is not that they fail to listen. On the contrary, it is that they are listening all too well to a set of vague, conflicting, and contradictory preferences.

Political freedom also means a basic guarantee of individual liberty. Individual citizens are free to make their own choices and to select their own goals and the means to achieve them. However, there are limits on individual liberty. Society, for example, will not sanction an individual's desire to become a skillful thief. Yet democracies keep limits on individual freedom to a minimum. Political freedom bestows on the individual the right to choose, advocate, or follow different political, social, and economic ideas, paths, and plans.

Political Equality

Ensuring popular sovereignty also means giving all citizens the same opportunities to influence the process of deciding who gets what. This idea is captured in the concept of **political equality**, which means individual preferences are given equal weight. For example, when citizens vote, each vote should count the same. Wealth, partisanship, or ideology cannot make one person's vote count more than any other. This notion of political equality not only refers to participation in influencing governmental decisions; it also involves being subject to those decisions. Everyone is entitled to **equality under the law**. The law is applied impartially without regard to the identity or status of the individual involved. In a democracy,

political equality The idea that individual preferences should be given equal weight.

equality under the law The idea that the law is supposed to be applied impartially, without regard for the identity or status of the individual involved.

wealth, fame, and power are not supposed to exempt anyone from the sanction of law. Few quarrel with these notions and their importance to upholding popular sovereignty, but political equality is a complicated concept because of its relationship to social and economic equality. **Social equality** is the idea that people should be free from class or social barriers and discrimination. Many view social equality as a desirable ideal but disagree on what, if anything, the government should do to achieve it. The long battle over racial equality in the United States, for example, reflects different attitudes on race as well as different views about government's responsibility to deal with racial differences in social, political, or economic opportunities or outcomes. Under its strictest interpretation, **economic equality** means each individual should receive the same amount of material goods regardless of his or her contribution to society. Equal distribution of wealth, especially as a coercive government policy, is unlikely to be considered compatible with the core principles of American democracy. Redistributing power and wealth from the well-off to the less well-off is always controversial—and for good reason: It limits the freedom of individuals to decide how to use their economic and social resources.

Yet social and economic equality are inevitably tied to political equality because social and economic resources can be translated into political influence. People with wealth and status can participate in politics more easily and effectively than others. Since democratic government responds to the preferences of those who participate—those who actually exercise the right to express their preferences—government policy tends to benefit those with wealth and status. This upper-class bias in turn gives upper-class citizens a greater ability to influence government in the future and thus brings into question the basic notion of popular sovereignty.

The issue of how to handle the conundrum connecting political equality with social and economic equality is largely unresolved. At a minimum, democracies must preserve political equality by guaranteeing that everyone has an equal right to express their preferences. Yet, inequitable distribution of wealth also gives certain individuals more forceful and effective ways to express their preferences. A wealthy campaign contributor is much more likely to get the attention of a legislator than a busy single parent who can hardly find the time to vote. If accused of a crime, a rich individual can hire a top-notch attorney, a private investigator, and an independent set of experts for the defense. A poor person accused of the same crime may have to rely on a single overworked public defender.

Political equality is generally reconciled with social and economic equality through the concept of **equality of opportunity**, meaning the right of all people to develop their abilities to the fullest extent. In other words, all individuals should have the opportunity to go as far in life as their desires, talents, and efforts allow. If people differ in abilities, desires, and work ethic, some will acquire more social status and economic wealth than others. In the United States, democracy thus aims to give individuals the paradoxical right of an equal opportunity to become unequal. This sounds good, but does everyone really have the same opportunity to "become unequal" in practice? Those who are born into wealth, who live in neighborhoods

---

social equality The idea that people should be free of class or social barriers and discrimination.

economic equality The idea that each individual should receive the same amount of material goods, regardless of his or her contribution to society.

equality of opportunity The idea that every individual has the right to develop to the fullest extent of his or her abilities.

with good schools, and who have nurturing parents have advantages and opportunities that those born into poverty, trapped in subpar schools, and suffering from abusive or neglectful parents do not. This disparity raises the question of whether government is required to level the playing field by guaranteeing a set of services (such as adequate nutrition, housing, education, and healthcare) considered essential to individual development. Equal opportunity to become unequal suggests that although a democratic society is not required to guarantee equality at the end of the individual's developmental process, it should ensure equality at the beginning. What constitutes equality at the beginning—what level of educational, health, and social services provides a roughly equal set of opportunities for all to develop to the fullest extent of their abilities—is a matter of constant controversy and debate.

Conflicting Values: A Delicate Balancing Act

To sum up, democracy is a form of government where the power to authoritatively allocate values is held by all citizens (popular sovereignty), which in turn rests on a commitment to three core principles: majority rule, political freedom, and political equality. One of these principles by itself is not enough to make a government democratic. At least in theory, all three must be reflected in the process and the outcomes of government decisions. In practice, achieving all three simultaneously is a difficult balancing act because these principles can conflict. Maximizing freedom may lead to less equality; achieving more equality may require placing limitations on someone's freedom; the majorities may use their power to rob minorities of their political freedom and their political equality.

TWO BASIC FORMS OF DEMOCRACY

All democracies share the basic traits described in the previous section, but all democracies are not the same. Democracy can take different forms depending on how popular sovereignty is put into practice. For example, consider the core principle of majority rule. Just how much control do citizens need to exercise over government decisions to uphold this principle? Is it sufficient that majorities choose decision makers, or must majorities approve specific government decisions? Do citizens need to be capable of determining for themselves what kind of policy is needed to preserve and advance liberty and equality in society, or is judging policies that are suggested by others sufficient?

These questions have no definitive answers. Reasonable people equally committed to democratic values may disagree on them. Thus, although a general theory of democracy rests on a core set of principles relating to popular sovereignty, there are different theories about the specific procedures, ideals, and assumptions associated with a democratic society. These differences can be divided into two broad categories: direct democracy and representative democracy.

Direct Democracy

In a **direct democracy**, citizens are the principal political decision makers. Direct democracy was first practiced in certain ancient Greek city-states, notably Athens. Direct democracy is used in the United States today, though in pretty limited forms. For example, the New England town meeting, where all citizens in the community are eligible to participate in making local government policy decisions, is a form of direct democracy. The **initiative** and **referendum** are other forms of direct democracy in which citizens vote on policy decisions. About half of the states allow ballot initiatives, which in the past 30 years have increasingly been used to make major policy decisions on everything from setting tax rates to approving—or rejecting—same-sex marriage.

Successful direct democratic systems are rare because inherent problems lead to instability and poor policy decisions. These include the unwieldy decision-making machinery of direct democracy (imagine setting tuition rates by inviting all taxpayers in the state to a series of meetings to decide what a college education should cost). More serious are the demands that direct democracy places on the individual. Sound decision making in a direct democracy requires a huge commitment to public life on the part of average citizens. At a minimum, it requires citizens to understand the nuts and bolts of government and politics, to be fully informed of the issues on which they vote, and to be actively and continuously engaged in public life. Citizens lacking these traits cannot grasp the consequences of their decisions for the government or society, and they can be misled or manipulated by well-funded groups with a stake in seeing one side prevail. When this happens, direct democracy is prone to producing bad policy decisions. Critics argue that this is the problem with modern forms of direct democracy such as the ballot initiative, which some see more as a tool for well-heeled interest groups than as a means to ensure the will of the people is reflected in public policy. The Founders explicitly rejected direct democracy as a desirable basis of governance for just these sorts of reasons.

Even with well-informed and fully engaged citizens, direct democracies are vulnerable to tyranny of the majority or mob rule, situations where the core values of political equality and political freedom are readily violated. Policy can quickly be shaped by whatever passions incite a majority of the citizens. Those who advocate unpopular minority viewpoints in a direct democracy and incur the displeasure of the majority may face some unpleasant consequences. These risks are acute in a large and diverse society with social fault lines—such as race, religion, and ideology—separating the majority from the minority. In a direct democracy, abiding by the core principles of democracy is the majority's responsibility. Thus, to live up to the promise of democracy, the majority must consist of individuals who understand and are deeply committed to all those principles, not just the principle of majority rule. Yet a constant temptation for the majority is to abandon those principles and benefit themselves by using democratic processes to make decisions that are undemocratic in substance, since those decisions discriminate or persecute a minority. For these reasons, the history of direct democracies is often one of instability and failure (Broder 2000).

direct democracy A form of democracy in which ordinary citizens, rather than representatives, collectively make government decisions.

initiative An election in which ordinary citizens circulate a petition to put a proposed law on the ballot for the voters to approve.

referendum An election in which a state legislature refers a proposed law to the voters for their approval.

Representative Democracy

Because direct democracy is simply not a stable or practical basis for government in large, diverse societies, an alternate form of democracy developed in Western nations. The form of democracy practiced in nations such as the United Kingdom and the United States is called **representative democracy**, defined as a system of government where ordinary citizens do not make governmental decisions themselves but choose public officials—representatives of the people—to make decisions for them. Representative democracy is based on popular sovereignty, but it is achieved indirectly by the people's representatives rather than by the people themselves, as in a direct democracy. Representative democracies such as the United Kingdom and the United States are sometimes called **liberal democracies** because of their concern for individual liberty. In liberal democracies, the rule of law and a constitution constrain elected representatives and the will of the majority from using their power to take away the rights of minorities. Thus, liberal representative democracies embody the three basic principles of democracy, but they use different institutions and slightly different ideals than direct democracies to accomplish these goals. In representative democracies, only a tiny fraction of citizens hold policymaking positions. For example, each member of the U.S. House of Representatives has a constituency of over 700,000 people, which means a single individual represents the interests of nearly three-quarters of a million citizens.

The form of liberal representative democracy we know today first developed in three Western nations: the United Kingdom, Switzerland, and the United States. In the late eighteenth and early nineteenth centuries, a large number of people in these countries began to select their own political leaders. From this narrow base, liberal democracy spread to other nations of Western Europe and the British Commonwealth. Thus, liberal representative democracy is a relatively new form of government, originally practiced by just a handful of nations. In fact, if genuine democracy requires that *all* citizens have the right to affect governmental decisions by choosing the government's leaders, then this type of government is a modern phenomenon. In the United States, male citizens did not gain universal voting rights until the latter part of the nineteenth century, and women had to wait until the 1920s. Ethnic minorities were systematically excluded from political participation up until the early 1960s. One can reasonably argue that the core principles of democracy were not securely embedded in representative democratic systems until the past half-century.

REPRESENTATIVE SYSTEMS AND CORE DEMOCRATIC PRINCIPLES

Because citizens do not govern directly in a representative democracy, ensuring that basic democratic principles are protected and advanced rests on a set of political

representative democracy Defined as a system of government where ordinary citizens do not make governmental decisions themselves but choose public officials—representatives of the people—to make decisions for them.

liberal democracy A representative democracy, such as the United Kingdom or the United States, that has a particular concern for individual liberty. The rule of law and a constitution constrain elected representatives and the will of the majority from using their power to take away the rights of minorities.

techniques and institutions different from those used in a direct democracy. Representative democracy means the many watching the few, but it is not just the few who rule who are important. The many who select and hold those rulers accountable are where we find out whether popular sovereignty is actually practiced. At a minimum, the many must be able to implement their observations through political action, and there must be an incentive for representatives to be responsive to the wishes of the people. To make this happen, representative democracy is heavily dependent on the institutions used to organize the political system and the values that underpin its operation. A number of democratic institutions are common in representative democracies. Three of the most central are elections, political parties, and interest groups.

Elections

Elections are the most obvious mechanism employed by representative democracies to incorporate democratic principles into the political system. Through elections, representative democracies deliberately create job insecurity for major officeholders. Those who hold office exercise power for a fixed term, so that citizens have periodic opportunities to determine whether the officeholders should continue exercising power. If citizens are displeased with the performance of those in public office, the remedy is to replace them. In this fashion, the rulers have an incentive to be responsive to the needs and demands of the ruled, and the citizens can hold the rulers accountable if they fail to be responsive. Elections are the central mechanism for achieving majority rule in representative democracies. Though representatives are often chosen by plurality rather than outright majorities, in principle all citizens retain the power to decide whether representatives will continue for another term.

If the country is going to pot, at least some of the blame goes to ballot initiatives. In 2016, voters used such initiatives to legalize marijuana in California and Nevada.

© Jeff Chiu/AP Photo

Political Parties

For elections to truly hold representatives accountable, a democratic system must offer citizens meaningful choices. The institution that typically fills this need is the political party, defined as an organization that puts forward candidates for public office. To provide an element of choice, at least two competing parties must propose candidates. With competition, voters can choose the party that best represents their preferences. Political parties must accept one another's existence as a necessity for a functioning representative democracy. Accordingly, the party (or parties) in control of the government must allow the opposition party (or parties) to criticize what current government leaders are doing and to propose alternative courses of action for the consideration of voters. That is, the party in control of government must recognize the political freedom of those out of power.

Interest Groups

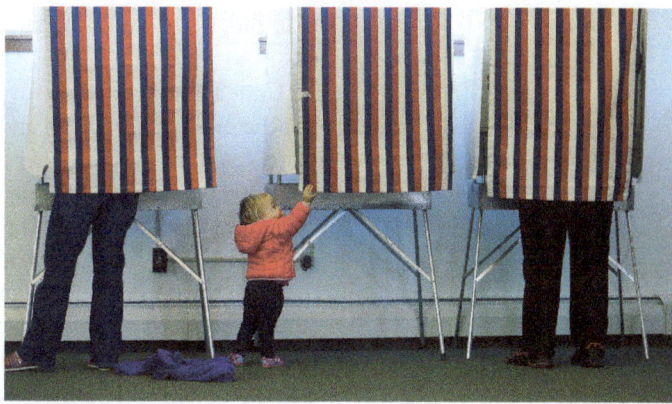

In a democracy every citizen has a right to vote and thus a direct voice in choosing elected officials. By creating insecurity of tenure for major officeholders, elections create incentives for the elected to respond to the needs of the electors and also provide recourse for the electors if the elected are not being responsive.

© Ted S. Warren/AP Photo

Continuous communication between representatives and citizens is critical to ensuring that citizens' views are incorporated in political decision making. Political parties fulfill this function to some extent; decisive election results can send a clear message to government. But elections occur only once every few years, and citizens need ways to communicate their changing needs between elections. Although citizens have the freedom to express their opinions individually, communication is more effective if diverse individual views are aggregated and transmitted in a coherent way. Citizens in a democracy also have the freedom to organize around common interests and communicate those interests to government.

An institution that has emerged to promote such communication is the interest group. Interest groups aggregate the interests of like-minded individuals and organize to press their common views on government decision makers. Interest groups are likely to contain only a small proportion of the total population, but they enable elected officials to gain some understanding of how a number of people in a common situation—for example, students, businesspeople, or farmers—feel about matters, such as student loan programs, taxes, or farm price supports. Moreover, because communication is a two-way process, interest groups not only press demands on decision makers; they also transmit proposals by political leaders back to their memberships. Just as parties compete to place their candidates in public office, interest groups vie to influence public policy. If the system is operating properly, these groups check and balance one another's efforts, and no one group or small collection of groups dominates the political process.

REPRESENTATIVE DEMOCRACY IN THE UNITED STATES

Although these institutions and principles characterize all representative democracies, there is considerable variation in how they are implemented in different nations.

Central Beliefs of Democracy in America

In the United States, popular sovereignty is anchored in a core belief that people are, for the most part, rational and capable of deciding what is good for them personally. Even if the average person is often incorrect, no elite group is assumed to be wise enough or unselfish enough to rule in the interests of all members of society. To ensure that the interests of everyone will be taken into account, the bulk of the population has the right to influence decisions that affect their lives through mechanisms such as elections, and government has the obligation to make this possible by protecting individual rights to liberty and free expression.

These central beliefs underpinning American democracy—that fundamental individual rights are inviolate and there is a universal prerogative to participate in collective decisions—constitute a general commitment to popular sovereignty. Accordingly, we expect the American political system, in process and substance, to reflect and uphold the three core principles of democracy. Yet no political system produced by human beings completely lives up to its ideals; a gap always occurs between the ideals and the operation of the political institutions designed to embody them. To better understand how the American system lives up to the ideals embedded in the core principles of democracy, it is important to understand not just what a democracy is, but also what it is not.

Fallacies Associated With Democracy in America

In practice, a political system based on popular sovereignty contrasts sharply with a number of popularly held fallacies, or incorrect beliefs, about democracy. One fallacy is that democracy promises the best policy decisions. It does not. Democracies in general, and certainly the democracy in America, make no promises to produce the most effective, efficient, or fair policy decisions. Representative democracy handles disagreements about what we ought to do by allowing everyone to get involved in the conflict. The result is often untidy, confusing decisions with which few are wholly satisfied. The outcomes, in other words, are frequently less than optimal. What we end up with is usually not what we want, but rather what we can, however grudgingly, live with. Such outcomes do not represent the failure of democracy. The whole point of a democratic system is to broker compromises among competing points of view and arrive at decisions that the majority supports and the minority can tolerate.

A second fallacy is a belief that democracy boils down to majority rule, that the American system is predicated on the majority always getting what it wants. The Founders of the American form of democracy placed no particular trust in the majority, and in the United States the majority has never been given the freedom to decide all matters that affect people's lives. If people have fundamental rights, as the Founders believed, then the majority must be kept from depriving the minority of those rights. Liberal representative democracy is founded on the notion that although government should respond to the wishes of the majority, the majority is limited. Certain fundamental rights cannot be taken away, even by majority vote. For example, in the United States and the United Kingdom, majorities of the population are Protestant, but they are not allowed to tell people of Catholic, Jewish, or other faiths how to worship. Likewise in Western democratic nations, the individual's right to private property is respected, and personal goods cannot be taken for public use without compensation. It is precisely such limitations on the scope of government that distinguish democratic societies from totalitarian ones. Majority rule, in other words, does not outrank political freedom or political equality.

A third fallacy is that social conflict is caused by the institutions of representative democracy and the people who occupy them. Representative institutions reflect rather than cause social conflict. Indeed, if the diverse views and conflicting interests that exist in society as a whole did not show up in our representative institutions, then they would not be representative. Political scientist Benjamin Barber argues that we must realize that in democracies, "representative institutions do not steal our liberties from us, [but rather] they are the precious medium through which we secure those liberties" (1996, 20). In other words, representative institutions help ensure that the people's often conflicting views are expressed and dealt with. They are designed not to make these conflicts disappear but to provide an arena and a set of ground rules where they can clash.

Exposing these fallacies is not intended to paint a cynical portrait of American democracy but rather to paint a more realistic one. Representative democracy is first and foremost about process, in how decisions are made. The system of representative democracy seeks to embody core democratic principles by instilling them into the institutions and mechanisms that organize the political system and by embedding a set of beliefs about individual liberty in the principles that operate it. For the whole system to be judged democratic, the outcomes, not just the process, must also reflect core democratic principles. Outcomes, though, are secondary; as long as they respect the core principles, outcomes do not have to be wise or effective to be democratic. Decisions made by representative institutions can be irritating, ineffective, silly, or even downright wrong but still uphold the core principles of democracy. A messy, less than optimal policy in which all views and rights are taken into account is not a failure of democracy. A failure is a fast, efficient policy where the dissent is ignored or, worse, quashed.

THE CHALLENGE OF AMERICAN DEMOCRACY

The practice of democratic politics is always going to be messy. Conflict, confusion, and compromise are a central part of the package even in democratic societies where citizens share ethnicity, religious beliefs, and cultural roots. In a large, diverse society such as the United States, the practice of democracy is even more challenging.

Diversity and Difference

The United States is one of the most populous countries on the planet and geographically one of the largest. Its people are highly mobile and come from diverse religious, cultural, demographic, geographic, racial, ethnic, and socioeconomic backgrounds. The astonishing diversity in these characteristics produces a wide range of different political interests and preferences. Blacks and whites may hold broadly different views about the merits of affirmative action. Latinos and blacks may have different ideas about what rights, if any, should be granted to undocumented immigrants. An urban city dweller in New York, Chicago, or Los Angeles likely has little interest in farm subsidies; those same subsidies may be the central topic of conversation in the coffee shop of a rural agricultural community in Nebraska, Kansas, or Iowa. Conservative Christians may view the posting of the Ten Commandments in public buildings and on public monuments with pride and approval; Muslims and agnostics may view such actions with trepidation or even fear. A wealthy individual may view the capital gains tax as unjust; a poor individual may not know what the capital gains tax is and may not care. For a college student at a public university, there may be no more important issue than government support for higher education, at least as it affects tuition; for senior citizens, Social Security may be much more important than subsidizing the studies of teenagers at the local state college.

This vast diversity in the backgrounds and interests of American citizens leads to different ideas of what we should do and who should get what. A big challenge for American democracy is to manage all these differences within a democratic framework, to make sure the process and the substance of collective decisions respects the rights of all. Given that many of these differences seem unbridgeable—for example, differences on abortion, immigration, and budget deficits—this is an enormously ambitious undertaking for a democratic system.

Dynamics

Getting a firm handle on American politics is sometimes difficult because the conflicts processed by democracy are shaped by a constantly changing backdrop. This changing context continually shapes and reshapes questions of what we ought to do.

Consider that the first census of the United States, taken in 1790, indicated that the 13 original colonies accounted for 900,000 square miles of land, forming a relatively narrow corridor along the eastern seaboard. Within this narrow corridor were fewer than 4 million people. Both of these basic characteristics have changed almost beyond recognition. Geographically, the United States grew west, steadily pushing its boundaries to the Pacific and beyond. Today, the 50 states include roughly 3.6 million square miles and a population of about 323 million. Population and geographic growth have a profound effect on politics. States, for example, do not grow at the same rate (see Figure 1.1), and because the number of representatives a state sends to Congress is based on population, population shifts can alter the size of a state's congressional delegation. Presently, power in the

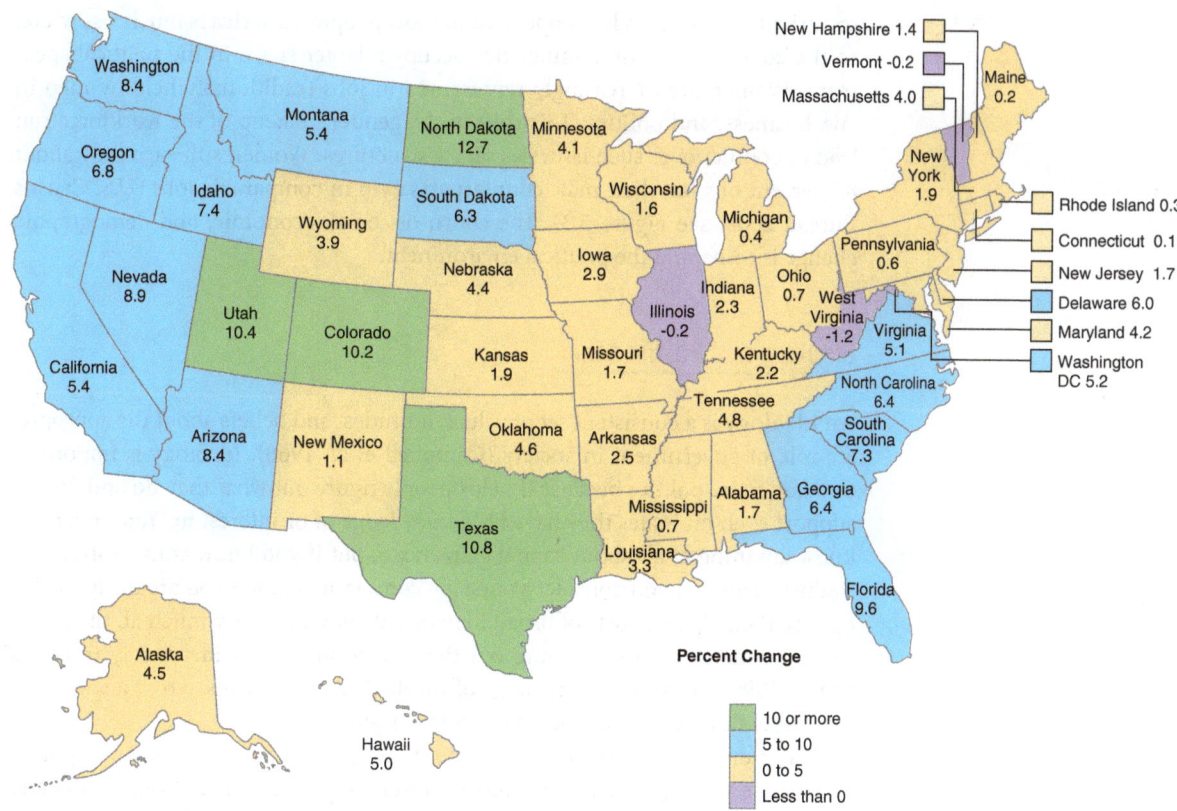

FIGURE 1.1 Population Growth in the United States, 2010–2016

Source: Data from U.S. Census Bureau, Population Division. Table 2, Cumulative Estimates of Resident Population Change for the United States, Regions, States, and Puerto Rico and Region and State Rankings: April 1, 2010 to July 1, 2016 (NST-EST2016-02).

Congress is following population trends and shifting south and west. What New Yorkers and Wisconsinites want the government to do is becoming less important than what Californians and Texans want.

It is not just overall growth that presents a challenge. The population is becoming more diverse ethnically and economically. Hispanics and Latinos now make up roughly 18 percent of the nation's population, African Americans account for 13 percent, and while Asians only account for about 6 percent they have been the fastest-growing racial group since 2000 (Holland 2016). The nation is also seeing shifts economically, with those at the highest income levels increasing their share of the nation's wealth over the past few decades, while those at the bottom see incomes flatline or even decline (Center on Budget and Policy Priorities 2016). As America becomes more urban, more racially and ethnically diverse, and as the gap between the poorest and wealthiest citizens grows, political interests and ideas about what we should do change. America is no longer a nation of farmers, so agriculture policy is less important to most people. America is much less white, so the concerns of ethnic minorities occupy a larger space in the political spectrum. Women are increasingly represented in jobs traditionally held by men in law, business, and politics. This shift in the gender makeup of the workforce can lead to conflict over such issues as salary structures. Women still earn only about 80 percent of what their male counterparts earn in comparable jobs (U.S. Census Bureau 2008; see Figure 5.3). The churn of social, economic, and demographic change is reshaping the political environment.

Ideology and Partisanship

An **ideology** is a consistent set of values, attitudes, and beliefs about the appropriate role of government in society (Campbell et al. 1960). Ideology is important to democratic politics because it helps people figure out what they do and do not support even on issues they have little knowledge of or interest in. You might not know anything at all about capital gains taxes, but if you know conservatives are against them and you consider yourself a conservative, then you are likely to also oppose them. These sorts of broad ideological cues are pretty much all the information Americans use to figure out their positions on a wide variety of issues (Bawn 1999). In America the range of ideological beliefs runs across a spectrum from liberals (the left) to conservatives (the right).

Traditionally, conservatives favor the status quo and want any social or political change to respect the laws and traditions of society. Traditionally, liberals believe that individual liberty is the most important political value and that people should be free to express their views and live their lives as they please with minimal limitations from government or from traditional values. Generically, conservatives are more likely to oppose regulating individual economic choices and more likely to support regulating individual moral choices. Liberals do the opposite. However, ideological labels in the United States are, at best, only rough guides to how individuals orient themselves to political issues. Some readers of this text will support gay rights yet consider themselves conservative, and other readers will oppose gay rights yet consider themselves liberal.

ideology A consistent set of values, attitudes, and beliefs about the appropriate role of government in society.

America is a diverse society, and responding to the variety of perspectives and goals of such a highly diverse population is a challenge for elected officials. Although elected officials cannot satisfy all of these demands, a core principle of democracy is that the rights of all will be upheld in both the process and the outputs of democratic decision making.

© Ariel Skelley/Getty Images

Over the past couple of decades, public opinion data shows that, generally speaking, Americans are consistently center-right in their ideology. A bit less than 40 percent of Americans call themselves conservative, and roughly the same number consider themselves

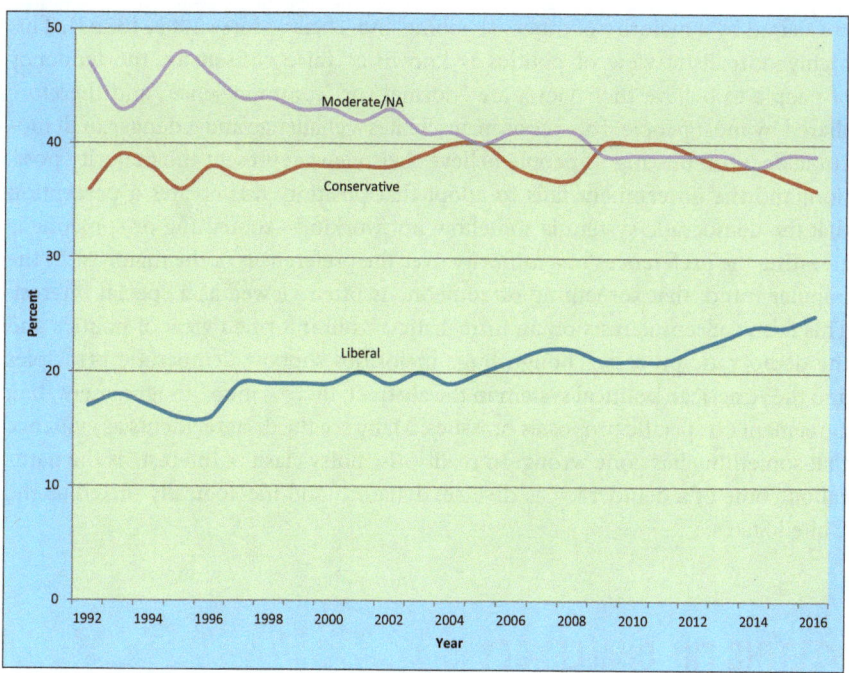

FIGURE 1.2 Ideological Self-Identification of Americans

Source: Data from the Gallup Poll, January 3, 2017. www.gallup.com/poll/201152/conservative-liberal-gap-continues-narrow-tuesday.aspx

political moderates (neither conservative nor liberal). About 20 to 25 percent self-identify as liberals (see Figure 1.2).

Many Americans wed their ideological beliefs to their support for a political party. **Partisanship** in American politics is viewed as a psychological attachment to a political party (Campbell et al. 1960). This means that most people view one of the parties as standing for their "brand" of politics. Broadly speaking, Republicans represent the conservative and Democrats the liberal brand of politics. According to one poll, in 2015 roughly a quarter of Americans considered themselves Republicans, about 30 percent called themselves Democrats, and the remainder aligned with neither of the two major political parties (Jones 2016). Political parties (as we discuss in Chapter 7) are the dominant organizing force of American politics: They provide coherence to elections, mobilize voters, and organize the government. Because neither party has the support of a commanding majority and because many citizens either have weak party ties or shuttle their support between the parties, parties are more likely to reflect the differences of Americans rather than bridge them.

False Consensus

Despite the huge variation in everything from ideology to ethnicity, religion, geography, wealth, and partisanship, Americans by and large believe their views

partisanship A psychological attachment to a political party.

are shared by a majority of others (Hibbing and Theiss-Morse 2003, 132n3). This highly unrealistic view of politics is known as **false consensus**, the tendency of people to believe their views are "normal" or "common sense" and therefore shared by most people. False consensus creates a challenge and a danger to democratic decision making. If people believe their views represent the majority position, and the government fails to adopt that position, this creates a perception that the democratic system is somehow not working—something or someone is elevating the preferences of a minority over the preferences of the majority. In the popular mind, that something or someone is often viewed as a special interest. This false consensus rests on an unrealistic and uninformed view of politics and the democratic process. Though huge majorities support democratic principles and the American political system in the abstract, there is more disagreement than agreement on specific proposals or issues. Many see the disagreements as evidence that something has gone wrong. In reality, the noisy clash of interests is the natural outcome of a democracy as diverse, dynamic, and ideologically mixed as the United States.

MEETING THE CHALLENGE?

Now that we have some sense of what a democracy is, what it is supposed to do, what it is not supposed to do, and some ideas of the challenges to democracy in the American context, it's worth raising the question of whether the U.S. political system manages to live up to these democratic ideals. Does its organization and operation account for diversity and change in a way that upholds core democratic principles in both the process and substance of resolving questions of who gets what? As we shall see, there is more than one answer to this question. The purpose of this book is not to reveal which answer is correct, but to give you the tools to make an independent analysis and make up your own mind. If your answer, in a general sense or on a specific issue, differs from your classmates' answers, do not be surprised. Reasonable people have long disagreed about how the concept of democracy translates into the practice of democracy in the American political system.

The Case for American Democracy

The case for American democracy rests on the assessment that our political techniques and institutions operate, for the most part, according to core democratic principles. This perspective views the American political system as highly **pluralistic,** where power is fragmented and distributed widely among diverse groups and interests. Businesspeople, laborers, farmers, African Americans, Latinos, students, the elderly, gays—virtually every conceivable group and interest has

---

false consensus The tendency of people to believe their views are normal or represent common sense and therefore are shared by most people.

pluralistic A term used to describe a society in which power is widely distributed among diverse groups and interests.

access to the political process. Although some may have more political assets—money, numbers, and campaign and propaganda skills—all have at least some political resources. At a minimum, citizens have the vote, but even non-citizens can participate by exercising First Amendment rights of free speech, press, and association.

Although some citizens may be more active in the political process than others—so-called political elites, activists, or influentials—those who are engaged ultimately represent a wide-ranging set of interests from the entire polity. The political moves and countermoves of this broad variety of political elites produce the energy for the American political system to work. They compete vigorously with one another but abide by the democratic rules of the game. They remain committed to the core principles of a democratic society, and they respect the fundamental rights and freedoms associated with majority rule, political equality, and political freedom—individual liberty, freedom of expression, the right to privacy, and the like. Indeed, these political activists are counted on to defend these principles when other less politically aware and less educated individuals oppose them. In the final analysis, supporters of the pluralistic view feel that American democracy serves the interests of a wide variety of individuals and groups. Although competing elites may take the initiative in public affairs, they must also take into account the interests of ordinary citizens. The elites require these ordinary citizens to provide support for public policy and to win elections.

Major Criticisms of American Democracy

Other analyses of American democracy reach considerably more critical conclusions than the pluralist perspective. Indeed, one of the major criticisms of American democracy is that it is not nearly as pluralistic or inclusive as its supporters claim. Many Americans believe that candidates and officeholders are more interested in manipulating public attitudes than in understanding and acting on them. Republicans and Democrats are charged with standing for little more than the acquisition of power and with robbing voters of meaningful choices rather than providing alternatives.

Some critics argue that significant minorities—including African Americans, Latinos, Native Americans, the poor, the young, and women[1]—are poorly served by the American political process. These groups are proportionally underrepresented in major political institutions, such as Congress, the executive branch, and the Supreme Court, and none are as effectively organized as the more dominant affluent groups, which casts an unflattering shadow across the sunny pluralist portrait. Moreover, organized groups do not check and balance one another as pluralist orthodoxy claims. Instead, each concentrates on getting what it wants

---

1 Women are not technically a minority. They constitute more than half of both eligible voters and the population as a whole. They may be considered a social minority in the sense that they have historically been both economically and politically disadvantaged compared to men.

from government: Business interests are served by the Department of Commerce, farmers by the Department of Agriculture, unions by the Department of Labor, and so on. Instead of regulating these groups in the public interest, government is organized to dole out favors to those with political muscle at the expense of the general taxpayer.

Such criticisms are supported by a good deal of systematic analysis. For example, a study by political scientist Morris Fiorina (2006) concludes that the intense party-based differences in American politics is evidence that government is not responsive to citizens. He argues that ideological extremists on the left and right have captured control of the parties' nominating process. The result is that in order to win party nominations, politicians must take extreme positions to appeal to these ideologues. Although most voters are not strongly ideological and prefer moderate, common-sense policies, party elites serve up two extreme candidates, and voters are forced to choose the one who is the least distasteful. "The result," according to Fiorina, "is a disconnect between the American people and those who purport to represent them" (2006, 51–52).

For such critics, the American system is not pluralistic, but **elitist**, in the sense that the political system is dominated by a set of organized, influential interests that are checked neither by one another nor by the general populace. These political elites are like professional athletes; they are devoted to the game they play, they are highly trained, they know all the rules and inside tricks, and they have access to a wide range of resources devoted solely to helping them win. When the rest of us try to get involved in politics, it's like 11 spectators coming out of the crowd to take on the Dallas Cowboys—even if the spectators manage to get on the field, the scoreboard will still end up reflecting the interest of the elite athletes. Critics of an elitist state of affairs thus offer a different picture of the American political system. The privileged status of elites and their overrepresentation in government enables them to set the public agenda and to determine which issues government considers of legitimate concern and which it does not. The result is a biased system that favors the status quo and provides an advantage to established groups over unorganized ones.

The contrasting overviews of American democracy represented by the positive pluralistic portrait and the negative elitist critique are not absolutes. Leading advocates of both lines of thought recognize elements of the other perspective in the reality of American political life. Pluralists acknowledge that some groups have greater control over the outcomes of political decision making than others; elitists observe that although a handful of organized interests control many major political decisions, they do not control all of them.

We bring up the pluralist and elitist perspectives to make the point that making systematic sense of politics, especially in a large, dynamic country such as the United States, is not easy. Coming to any kind of systematic and logically supported conclusion about the political system in general, or specific issues within it, is a tough analytical challenge. To reach those sorts of conclusions, to make systematic sense of the messy and often contradictory world of American democracy, it helps to know the analytical tools of political science and how to use them.

elitist A term used to describe a society in which organized, influential minority interests dominate the political process.

MAKING SENSE OF POLITICS: POLITICAL SCIENCE

Political science is the academic discipline dedicated to the study of government, political institutions, processes, and behavior (Isaak 1985). It is the job of political scientists to explain the how and why of the authoritative allocation of values—who gets what and why. Political scientists are interested in these sorts of questions: Who has power? Is it elites, or is sovereignty broadly shared? What determines power and power relationships in society? Is it class, ethnicity, socioeconomic status, or the will of the people? Who votes? Is it rich people or poor people, the young or the old? Why do they vote the way they do? Is it ideology, loyalty to a party, or something else? Why are some people conservatives and others liberal? Why are some people Democrats and others Republicans?

Answers to these and similar questions clearly have direct bearing on the main goals of this book. Understanding who votes and why, for example, can help us better form a judgment of the political system. If certain groups disproportionately participate in politics, this raises questions about the true extent of majority rule and minority rights. If certain laws and rules—for example, voter registration requirements—let some groups gain more power and influence than others, this raises questions about political equality. If other laws—for example, campaign finance laws—limit the ability of groups to get their message out to citizens and to government, this raises questions about political freedom.

The Roots of Political Science

Political science is both a very old and a very new academic discipline. Its roots are in philosophy, law, history, and economics; political science claims thinkers such as Plato, Aristotle, Thomas Hobbes, John Locke, James Madison, and John Stuart Mill as its intellectual forebears. All were serious students of politics and are mostly remembered as normative political philosophers. Asking **normative** questions means seeking to prescribe how things should be valued, what should be, and what is good or just, better or worse. As normative political philosophers, these individuals were interested in these sorts of questions: What is the *best* form of government—democracy, autocracy, or oligarchy? What constitutes the legitimate and *just* use of power? What are the *fundamental rights* of man? What are the *best* means to serve the public interest?

Political scientists continue to pursue these questions with vigor, but the study of politics is also focused on describing and explaining institutions, processes, attitudes, and behavior as they *are* rather than as they *should* be. This sort of empirical approach to studying politics has a long history. Five hundred years ago, Niccolò Machiavelli became a champion of realist political theory, an approach that seeks to objectively record politics and to understand how it works

---

political science The systematic study of government, political institutions, processes, and behavior.

normative Theories or statements that seek to prescribe how things should be valued, what should be, what is good or just, and what is better or worse.

in practice rather than figure out how it should work in theory. It was not until the last 75 years or so, however, that this sort of approach came to dominate the study of politics and to shape the modern discipline of political science. Rather than asking, "Is democracy the best form of government?" modern political scientists are more likely to ask, "Why do interest groups form?" or "Why does government pay attention to some issues and not others?" These latter sorts of questions are **empirical**, meaning they can be answered by careful observation. Using the scientific method to answer these empirical questions not only puts the "science" in political science, it provides a ready-made framework for thinking analytically about politics. Indeed, when we say "thinking analytically," what we mostly mean is "thinking scientifically." But what does it mean to think scientifically about politics?

The Scientific Method

Science is a method or a system of acquiring knowledge about something. You can think of it as a rigorous and systematic procedure to answer questions about our world, and that includes the political world. Of course, there are plenty of other ways besides science for answering questions about politics. What should the government do about issue X? Why does public opinion favor candidate Y? Does the political system uphold core democratic values? These sorts of questions can be answered using everything from the "revealed" knowledge of religious teachings, to knowledge gained from intuition or the insight of experts. Citizens can and often do try to make sense of politics by using their religious beliefs, adopting the perspectives of those they trust or admire, applying ideological rules of thumb, or simply coming to a conclusion because it "feels" right. Science, though, differs in important ways from these other methods.

Thinking analytically about politics using a scientific approach, at a minimum, involves four basic steps: asking a question, formulating a testable answer to that question, getting the measures and data necessary for that test, and conducting that test in a specific way.

Scientists ask particular types of questions. A **research question** is simply a statement of the information or knowledge being sought. Importantly, it is assumed that there is no known universally correct answer to this question and alternative answers need to be given fair consideration. Generating good questions is at least as important to analytical thinking as coming up with answers. A classic research question in political science is, "Why do people vote the way they do?" This clearly defines the objectives of research—we want to know why people support particular parties, ideologies, or candidates with their ballots. It also raises an important issue: Who gets what in representative democracies is determined in large part by how these choices are made in the voting booth. It is also far from comprehensively answered. Political science research has certainly helped us understand a lot more about why people vote the way they do, yet lots of people cast ballots for reasons we still do not fully understand. In other words, it remains a question worth asking.

---

empirical Questions and debates that can be answered by careful observation. Systematic empirical observation is the foundation of science and the scientific method.

science A method of acquiring knowledge through the formulation of hypotheses that can be tested through empirical observation in order to make claims about how the world works and why.

research question a statement of information or knowledge being sought. A research question assumes there is no known universally correct answer and that alternative answers need to be given fair consideration.

THINKING ANALYTICALLY

CRACKING THE CODE OF SCIENTIFIC RESEARCH

Scientific research has its own language, but you really only need to understand a few terms to make sense of the studies we will be highlighting in this text. Below are some key concepts that will come up from time to time, and if you familiarize yourself with these you should have the basic information necessary to decode the material.

Hypothesis: An "educated guess" or proposition that there is a relationship between variables. A hypothesis is a declarative statement that logically must be true or false and must also be *testable* and *falsifiable*. Testable means that a hypothesis must make predictions that can be supported or refuted through careful observation. Falsifiable means that it is possible to conceive of observable evidence that would disprove the hypothesis. An example of a hypothesis is: "Tax cuts increase economic performance." Logically, this statement must be true or false (tax cuts either do or do not increase economic performance), it can be tested by observing the impact of tax cuts on economic performance measures, and it is falsifiable because those performance measures will not increase (they will stay the same or decrease) if the hypothesis is false.

Variable: Something that takes on different values across a particular thing. For example, age, income, and political party affiliation vary from one person to another; election turnout varies across states; and the turnout rate in the nation varies over time.

Dependent Variable: In the context of a hypothesis, the dependent variable is something that is caused by another variable (or variables)—for example, whether you vote or not (the dependent variable) might *depend* on several other factors. It is what the research is trying to explain.

Independent Variable: If the dependent variable is what we are looking to explain, the independent variable is what we are using for the explanation. In the context of a hypothesis, we expect changes in the independent variable (e.g., education levels) to systematically predict changes in the dependent variable (e.g., probability of voting).

Operationalize: This is the process of taking an abstract concept and turning it into something that is observable. For example, *civic participation* is an abstract concept that can mean a lot of things. A set of survey questions might operationalize this concept by asking respondents whether they participated in different activities—voted in a recent election, donated to a campaign, put up a yard sign, or contacted a public official. This process operationalizes civic participation by giving us a set of data that we can observe and analyze.

Measurement: The process of systematically capturing and quantifying the values in a variable is called measurement. A yardstick is an instrument to measure linear distance; it provides a quantitative reading in inches or centimeters. A grading scale measures how well students perform on a test—pass/fail; A/B/C/D/F. A Wilson–Patterson Index is an instrument to measure ideology; it codes responses to a wide variety of questions about political issues to provide a numerical value of how conservative someone is.

Relationship: How the value of the dependent variable changes with a change in value of the independent variable. A hypothesis should indicate the nature of the expected relationship. We might expect more in one category than another—for example, women vote more Democratic than men. Or if we expect a relationship between two continuous variables, we should specify a direction. A *direct* relationship is one in which high values in one variable are associated with high values in the other—for example, as education increases, income increases. In an *inverse* relationship, high values in one variable are associated with low values in the other—for example, as the price of gasoline increases, the number of miles people drive decreases.

Strength of a Relationship: The relationship between two variables can be strong or weak. How can we tell how strong a relationship is? What does a strong or weak relationship look like? Two useful statistical indicators of the strength of a relationship are *correlation* and *slope*—both are used throughout this text, especially in the figures.

Correlation: A correlation is a measure of association between two variables. It is a number that ranges between −1.0 and +1.0. A −1.0 is a perfect inverse correlation; as the independent variable goes up, the dependent variable has a symmetrical decline. A +1.0 is a perfect direct correlation; as the independent variable goes up, the dependent variable has a symmetrical increase. A correlation of zero (0) means the variables have no relationship with each other.

Slope of a Regression Line: Don't be put off if this term seems unfamiliar or overly technical. Regression analysis is simply a way to estimate the relationship between two or more variables. This is done with the slope of a regression line, which simply shows how much y (the dependent variable) changes for a given change in x (the independent variable). A steep slope means that a small change in x is associated with a larger change in y, indicating that x has a strong effect on y. A shallow slope means that a large change in x is associated with a smaller change in y, indicating that x must change a lot to have an effect on y.

Consider the following scatterplots of two variables. The first plots age and reading score, the second proximity to a polling place and voting participation (the data in both cases are purely hypothetical). In Plot 1, we see a positive relationship, which is what you would expect—as children get older, they get better at reading. The correlation between these two variables is .70. The regression equation used to draw the solid line in Plot 1 is: Reading Score = .357 + .66(Age). This suggests that for every one unit increase across the horizontal or X axis—in other words, for every increase of one year in age—there is an associated .66 unit increase up the vertical or Y axis. In other words, it says that on average for every year they age, children's reading scores go up by .66 points. In Plot 2 we see a negative relationship—the farther away from a polling place you live, the fewer elections you vote in. The correlation between these two variables is −.80. The regression equation for the solid line is: Voting = 8.47 − .73(proximity). In other words, for every mile you live from a polling place, the regression equation

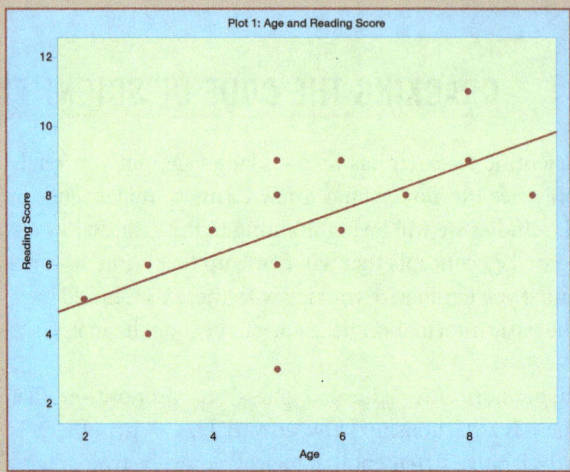

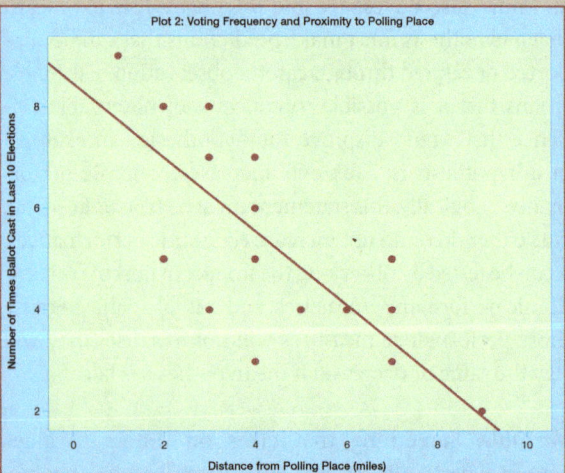

is estimating that participation in the past 10 elections declines, on average, by .73.

Discussion Questions

1. Think of three different ways to operationalize each of the following two concepts: political participation and ideology.
2. Formulate a hypothesis about politics and identify the dependent and independent variables that would be needed to test this hypothesis. Remember: to be a scientific hypothesis, you must have a declarative statement that logically must be true or false, and is testable and falsifiable.

Science seeks to answer research questions by creating and testing causal models or **theories**, which are potential explanations of how the world works. A number of theories have been developed to answer the question, "Why do people vote the way they do?" One of the best-known is the social-psychological model of voting behavior (also known as the Michigan model). This theory posits that people vote the way they do because they form psychological attachments to political parties at an early age. This attachment results in a strong tendency to vote on the basis of partisan loyalty even if a voter disagrees with most of the policies a particular party's candidate supports. (For a more in-depth discussion of this model, see Chapter 11.) This theory suggests a **hypothesis**, or an "educated guess" that logically must be either true or false and can be empirically tested. In this case, the research hypothesis is: Citizens who self-identify with a political party will vote for that political party. This may seem obvious, but note that the model suggests that citizens will vote their partisan loyalties even when they personally disagree with the policies being championed by their party's candidate. What makes the Michigan model so interesting to political scientists is that it rejects the classic understanding of how citizens behave in a democracy. Rather than citizens carefully weighing the pros and cons of issues and candidates in each election as classic democratic theory suggests, this theory suggests voters do no such thing. They have a "brand loyalty" and stick to it even when it does not benefit their personal interests.

To test the hypothesis proposed by the Michigan model, we would first need to define what it means to self-identify with a political party, and also what it means to vote for that party. Again, this sounds obvious, but defining even such simple-sounding concepts can be quite a challenge. What does it mean to vote for a party? Does it mean voting for all of a party's candidates in all elections? What if voters do this for some races, but not others? Does it mean voting for all of a party's candidates in a single election? This process of defining and deciding how to measure concepts can be critically important because they can influence the results of your hypothesis test. For example, measuring party voting as casting a ballot for all party nominees in a presidential election year is a tougher test of the hypothesis than measuring party voting by just using the vote cast for president.

Once you have a question, an answer (i.e., a theory and a hypothesis), and the necessary empirical measures, the final step is actually testing the hypothesis. This step is critically important because it largely defines whether an analysis can be thought of as scientific. *Scientists begin by assuming their research hypothesis is false and require overwhelming evidence to reject that assumption.* The opposite of the research hypothesis is the **null hypothesis**. A hallmark of a scientific analysis is that it is not looking for evidence that the research hypothesis is true, but rather it is looking for evidence that the null hypothesis is false beyond any reasonable doubt. The process is similar to Sherlock Holmes's approach to solving mysteries: "eliminate all other factors, and the one which remains must be the truth" (Doyle 1890, chap. 1). A scientific test never proves the research hypothesis: it "rejects the null."

theory A potential explanation of how the world works.

hypothesis An "educated guess" that logically must be either true or false and can be empirically tested.

null hypothesis A statement positing that there is no relationship between the variables being observed. It is the opposite of the research hypothesis.

There have been lots of studies testing the Michigan model. The most famous was put into a book called *The American Voter* (Campbell et al. 1960). The authors formulated the Michigan model, and to test their theory, they conducted some of the first extensive scientific surveys of voting behavior. These surveys asked lots of questions about who respondents voted for and their party loyalties. The researchers found convincing evidence to reject the null: People with strong party identification rarely voted against their party, and people with weak or nonexistent party loyalties didn't vote much at all.

Thinking Analytically

The scientific method might help make systematic sense of politics, but the description in the previous section might seem a bit too daunting to put into practice. It is one thing for research teams staffed with PhDs to approach political questions like this, but is it reasonable to expect the average citizen to do the same? Most people are not in a position to conduct their own scientific surveys and lack the skillset to subject them to sophisticated statistical analysis. However, some common-sense rules drawn from the scientific approach can be used to systematically think through pretty much any question about politics by pretty much anyone. Here's what a set of those rules might look like:

Question the Question

When you want to know anything about politics, try to think of the question you are asking, and then question the question. A good question points you toward something you do not know and is open to whatever answer can muster the best empirical and logical support. Questions along the lines of, "Why are conservatives so wrong on policy X?" or "How can I prove the liberal stand on policy X is correct?" are not analytical. These sorts of questions are all too common in how people approach politics, and they reflect sloppy and lazy thinking. It is okay to have an ideological or partisan perspective, but assuming a personal preference or feeling is correct and focusing on ways to support that preference regardless of evidence to the contrary is a poor substitute for critical thinking. In other words, be sure you are asking something that looks more like a research question rather than something that is just an excuse to confirm your own pre-existing beliefs.

Think Theoretically

People often equate "theory" with a "hunch" or "speculation." Theory means something completely different to a scientist; it is an explanation of how the world works. Theories with empirical support are the basis of knowledge in all scientific disciplines. Does this mean you need to create a full-blown causal model for every political question you pose? No. At a minimum, though, you need to think through reasonable potential answers to your question and what might make those answers empirically supportable. Personal preference, partisan or ideological leanings might make one answer more palatable to our questions than others. The reflexively pleasing answers thrown up by these sorts of beliefs, though, are poor substitutes for more reasoned and empirically supportable explanations about how the world of politics works and why it works that way.

Question the Answer

Take the null hypothesis seriously. This does not necessarily mean doing formal statistical tests. It does mean seriously looking at your answer and asking yourself: How would I know if this answer was wrong? It also means going one step further and seeing if there's a reasonable case that those conditions exist. *The hallmark of an analytical thinker is being less interested in figuring out how to find things that show they are right, and more interested in figuring out how they would know if they were wrong.*

Theoretical Frameworks in Political Science

Thinking analytically takes practice to do well. When it comes to politics, it also requires some discipline; it is always tempting to substitute individual ideological and political preference or the wisdom of an experienced commentator for a fair and systematic analysis. Many introductory textbooks on American politics try to nurture analytical thinking by organizing the subject matter around a single theoretical framework. We think this is a mistake, but not because it places too much emphasis on using theory. Rather, it is because politics has a lot of moving parts, and while one theory may explain parts of politics really well, it is unlikely to explain everything.

To provide a sense of how political science uses theory to make sense of the political world and to help us make sense of politics in America, in this book we often use and contrast different models from not one, but three of the most prominent theoretical frameworks. Two of these—rational choice models and behavioral models—have a long history in political science. The third—evolutionary and biological models—is a more recent and cutting-edge development that is seeking to integrate political science with large sectors of the life sciences, such as biology, genetics, and neuroscience. These theories do not appear in every chapter of the book. Some topics—civil liberties and civil rights, for example, both important for understanding the full picture of American politics—have not been extensively analyzed using the scientific method, so they are understood less through empirically testable theory than through interpretation of legal and historical evidence. While we will not apply all three models in all chapters in the book, in most chapters at least one will show up somewhere. The purpose of repeatedly returning to these models is not to convince you that they offer the "best" explanation, but rather to get you in the habit of thinking analytically, of getting a sense of how research questions are generated and answered, which is the big job of theories. To help prepare you to start thinking about politics like a political scientist, and to give you a sense of how political science is constantly seeking to generate and investigate new systematic explanations of the political world, we give a brief introduction to these three theoretical models.

APPLYING THE FRAMEWORKS

THE RATIONALITY, BEHAVIOR, AND BIOLOGY OF POLITICAL INTEREST

Politics is interesting to some people. Others can take it or leave it. Still others prefer to avoid the subject altogether; the thought of discussing politics makes them queasy.

There are not just three distinct categories of political interest, of course. People are scattered across a continuum anchored by political junkies on one end to political avoiders on the other. One of the great puzzles of political science is figuring out what explains that variation. Why are some people interested and engaged in politics, while others are disinterested and disengaged?

Thinking theoretically can help develop systematic answers to this question. Let's apply the three frameworks highlighted in this book and see what sorts of answers they might come up with. The rational model will construct an answer to this question by focusing on the costs and benefits of acquiring political information and participating in politics. Boning up on political candidates and issues takes time and effort. So does going to the polls. From a rational perspective, the big issue is whether it is all worth it. What's the payoff from knowing more about politics? For some people, maybe a lot of them, the answer is "not much," so why bother?

Getting involved in politics, doing stuff like donating a campaign contribution, sending an e-mail, or going to the polls, costs a lot in terms of time, effort, and maybe even money. The benefits that you get for those investments, though, are not clear. If you write a check for 10 bucks, chances are the cause or candidate you back is not going to drop everything to pay attention to your concerns when you want to discuss them. And 10 bucks might be a lot to you. For other people, 10,000 dollars might be chump change. In that case, spending the money is a minimal effort and it's a lot more likely to get you the ear of a candidate if you want to share your opinions. Why are some people interested and engaged, while others are not? The answer from the rational model is that people are, well, rational.

Tackling the question from a behavioral model perspective is likely to result in a different answer. Social-psychological theorists are likely to point out that a lot of people participate in politics when the costs clearly outweigh the benefits. An awful lot of people do write those 10-dollar checks, diligently keep up with the political news, and routinely show up to the polls knowing that their one vote will not make a lick of difference to the outcome. Why are they doing this?

A likely answer from the behavioral perspective is that they have been socialized to be interested and involved in politics. Their families, churches, or schools emphasized the importance of civic duty, of being an informed and engaged citizen. This created a sense of duty that forms an important part of their psychology. Of course, families, churches, and schools may socialize others differently. Some families may not discuss politics at the dinner table, or if they do, they condemn it as a snake pit of thieves and fools that is best avoided. Churches may caution against getting involved in petty earthly squabbles. Schools may be more interested in socializing good test prep habits than the habits of citizenship. Why are some people interested and engaged, while others are not? The answer from the behavioral model is that different patterns of socialization lead to different levels of political interest and engagement.

The biological model would argue that political interest and engagement is more than environmental conditioning. Some people are simply more comfortable in socially stressful situations than others. Some people like confrontation, and others do not. Comfort levels with confrontation and socially stressful situations are known to correlate with certain biological markers. For example, individuals with naturally occurring high cortisol levels (cortisol is the so-called "stress hormone") are more likely to go out of their way to avoid social confrontation. Individuals with lower cortisol levels seem to be much more comfortable with that sort of give and take.

Politics is all about social stress and confrontation; indeed, democratic politics is characterized by clashes of organized interests battling it out in a public arena. If you are physiologically primed to find such situations uncomfortable—perhaps because your genes predispose you to high cortisol levels—it makes sense that you would not be interested in that sort of thing and would go out of your way to avoid participating in such activities. Why are some people interested and engaged, while others are not? The answer from the biological model is that differences in our physiology either arouse or dampen the attraction of politics.

Thinking theoretically, then, gives us at least three systematic answers to the question of interest and engagement. Each can generate testable hypotheses: When costs outweigh benefits, people will not seek to acquire information (rational), individuals higher on measures of civic duty are more likely to participate (behavioral), individuals with higher levels of cortisol are less likely to participate (biological).

It is important to note that all of these hypotheses could conceivably be supported by empirical tests. You can be rationally interested, socialized to be engaged, and biologically primed to both. By the same token, all of these hypotheses may muster little backing at all in empirical tests. It may be the case that just one of these answers is correct, that all are at least partially correct, or that none of them are the real answer to our question. If the latter is the case, it may mean that we have to refine or rethink our theory to come up with an empirically supportable answer to our question.

Not finding strong evidence for a hypothesis should not be thought of as a failure. Think of it this way: We might not know what the answer is, but at least we will know what the answer is not. This process of asking questions, generating answers (theory), empirically testing those answers, and using the results to revisit and revise answers is what science, and that includes political science, is all about.

Discussion Questions

1. What is your level of interest and participation in politics? What do you think determines that level of interest and participation, and what would make it change?
2. If our biology is at least partially determining our levels of political interest and engagement, does that mean that getting people more interested and involved in politics is harder or easier? Why or why not?

Rational Choice Models of Politics

Rational choice models of politics borrow from economic theories that assume people do what they do primarily out of self-interest. The basic idea is that humans are goal-oriented, have preferences, and can rank their preferences from most to least desired based on the amount of **utility**—that is, satisfaction or enjoyment derived from each one. People make choices rationally by doing or choosing what they believe will give them the most satisfaction for the least cost in a given situation (this is said to maximize their utility). For example, when you go to a restaurant, you pick from the menu the meal that achieves your ultimate goal (satisfying your hunger) and maximizes your utility (you may enjoy a hamburger more than broccoli). So how does this help us understand politics?

Well, to begin with, the simple assumptions at the heart of rational choice actually do a surprisingly good job of explaining big chunks of democratic politics. For example, as strange as it seems today, in the middle of the twentieth

utility The amount of enjoyment an individual receives from a given situation or outcome.

century, one of the things that Americans found most frustrating about politics was the tendency of the Republican and Democratic parties to sound more alike than different on many major policy issues. This was not just irritating to voters who couldn't perceive a meaningful choice, but a real puzzle for political scientists as well. Why would political parties not offer more meaningful policy choices in a democratic system? In his classic work *An Economic Theory of Democracy* (1957), Anthony Downs tried to, among other things, figure out exactly that. Starting from the assumption that all people are utility maximizers, Downs reasoned that if the primary goal is to win an election, a party or candidate needs to take policy positions that will appeal to more voters than those espoused by the competition. If most voters prefer moderate policy positions, then in a two-candidate election both candidates will appeal to this center (Downs 1957, 117–118). Downs's theory, in other words, describes and explains the relatively middle-of-the-road politics that long typified the U.S. system.

Rational choice theory can also help us form judgments about how democracy and politics are practiced. Consider majority rule. If the political system works according to Downs's theory, American democracy is in pretty good shape. The government is going to reflect majority preferences because that's where all the votes are. But what about minority rights? If the major parties ignore minority voices or, worse, appeal to the majority by pushing policies that limit the political freedom of minorities, then the assessment of American democracy is less rosy. The point is, Downs's theory provides an explanation of how politics works, and that theory can be empirically tested. If observation shows the explanation is correct, we know something about how politics in the American system works and can use that knowledge to form judgments about how that performance reflects the basic principles of democracy.

Behavioral Models of Politics

In contrast to rational choice, behavioral models of politics draw from psychology and sociology rather than economics. At their root is the assumption that humans behave not according to a self-interested cost–benefit calculation, but as a response to an environmental stimulus. The Michigan model is a behavioral model (Greenstein 1965). It posits that we develop partisan attachments because Mom and Dad called Democrats one thing and Republicans another at the dinner table, or because we admired a particular leader at a formative time in our lives and transferred those feelings to his or her party. That socialization process leads us to respond to the stimulus of an election by voting our party affiliation.

Behavioral models have been enormously influential in all of the social sciences and are generically labeled the "standard social science model" because of the widespread assumption that people respond in predictable ways to particular environmental situations (Tooby and Cosmides 1992). How do behavioral models help us understand politics? Consider the implications for majority rule if significant proportions of Americans are socialized to be apathetic about politics.

What if at the dinner table Mom and Dad disparage politics as a worthless enterprise and politicians as corrupt and self-serving? What if the social environment teaches that politics is a dirty business that's best avoided altogether? It's hard to see how majority rule can be exercised if most people can't be bothered with politics. Again, the larger point is that the behavioral approach helps us know more about how politics works and puts us in a better position to systematically judge the performance of American democracy on the basis of the core principles.

Evolutionary and Biological Models

Evolutionary and biological models are increasingly being used to make sense of politics. It may seem a little odd for political scientists to be turning to evolution and biology, but the reasons for doing so are straightforward. As one scholar put it, "evolutionary biology underlies all behavioral disciplines because *Homo sapiens* is an evolved species whose characteristics are the product of its particular evolutionary history" (Gintis 2007). Humans, in other words, are animals too. It makes sense, therefore, to use theories that have proven themselves capable of explaining much of what goes on in the animal world and apply them to human affairs. Evolutionary frameworks have been used for decades to explain the social structure and behavior of species from bees to chimpanzees.

Economists, anthropologists, psychologists, and, yes, political scientists are beginning to understand that these same evolutionary theories provide a powerful set of tools to make sense of everything from consumer behavior to voting behavior. Evolutionary frameworks suggest that at least some of our attitudes toward politics and government; our preferences for particular types of policies, institutional arrangements, and political leaders; and our reasons for engaging in certain types of political behavior are partially inherited or shaped by evolutionary forces. Some of this may sound surprising, but social scientists have tested a number of hypotheses along these lines and have found strong evidence to support them.

For example, research by political scientists shows that at least some of our political attitudes are inherited (Alford, Funk, and Hibbing 2005). Other research using brain imaging techniques found distinct differences in how Democrats and Republicans look at candidates (Tierney 2004). The evolutionary and biological approach is a new method for building models of political attitudes and behavior that helps us think about and understand politics in new and different ways. For one thing, it suggests that liberals and conservatives see, experience, and react to the world from different perspectives, and no amount of informed debate is going to change those perspectives (Hibbing, Smith, and Alford 2014). The rational choice, behavioral, and biological models do not always agree—sometimes they have competing and contradicting explanations of why people vote the way they do, hold the attitudes they have, and so on. Political scientists are busily conducting empirical studies to assess which does the better job of explaining particular elements of politics, and in some cases, there is fierce debate over what model the current evidence supports.

GENERAL APPROACH AND ORGANIZATION OF THE BOOK

With the basic concepts of politics, government, and democracy in hand, as well as a little historical perspective on democracy in the American context, and a basic notion of the toolkit necessary for studying politics analytically, you should be in a good position to tackle the rest of this book. In what follows we present the information and analytic tools that will allow you to make your own reasoned judgments about politics and democracy in America.

The book is divided into four parts. Part I consists of four chapters analyzing the constitutional framework. Chapter 2 looks at the political forces that led to the drafting and ratification of the U.S. Constitution and analyzes the values and assumptions underlying that framework. Chapter 3 focuses on one major element of this framework and a dominant feature of American politics—federalism, a system that divides power between state and national governments. Chapters 4 and 5 examine the liberties and rights guaranteed by the Constitution and how they have (or have not) been extended to various groups.

Part II addresses the general subject of connecting citizens to government—that is, how citizens encourage those in power to be responsive to their needs and how citizens hold them accountable for their actions. Chapter 6 focuses on the major institutional mechanism for connecting citizens to government between elections—the interest group. Chapter 7 examines the role that political parties play in organizing politics and translating public preferences into coherent policy agendas. Chapter 8 looks at the mass media's role in shaping opinions and structuring the public agenda. Chapter 9 explores the general nature of Americans' political views, how those views are acquired, and the various outlets for expressing those views in the political process. Chapters 10 and 11 examine elections by reviewing the processes of nominating and electing candidates and analyzing voting behavior, as well as other forms of political participation.

Part III focuses on the institutions involved in official decision making in government. These institutions are Congress (Chapter 12), the presidency (Chapter 13), the bureaucracy (Chapter 14), and the courts (Chapter 15). We examine these institutions in terms of the kinds of people who serve in them and how they got there, the institutions' general structure, and the procedures that each utilizes to carry out its activities. In addition, we analyze the relationships and interactions among the officials who serve in these separate institutions.

Part IV concludes the book. In Chapter 16, we examine how the processes and institutions of the American political system combine to make public policy.

The appendices contain important supplemental information and documents. We include: the Declaration of Independence, the Constitution of the United States, and two frequently used *Federalist* Papers (Numbers 10 and 51), and a glossary of all terms used in the book.

CHAPTER ONE
Top 10 Takeaway Points

1. Politics is the authoritative allocation of values; government is the institution that can legitimately use coercion to allocate values for all people in a society.

2. Democracy is a form of government characterized by popular sovereignty, which means that the power to authoritatively allocate values is shared by all citizens. Popular sovereignty is dependent on a political system's commitment to upholding three core democratic principles: majority rule, political freedom, and political equality.

3. For a political system to be considered truly democratic, both the process and outcomes of the system must abide by the three core principles.

4. Democracy has two basic forms: direct democracy and representative democracy. The political system of the United States includes elements of both but is primarily a representative democratic system.

5. Representative democracies have common elements to their political systems, including elections, political parties, and interest groups.

6. The American political system gets mixed reviews on how well it abides by the core principles of democracy. Some see a pluralist system that does a good job of upholding the core principles. Others see an elitist system that routinely violates the core principles.

7. Politics in the United States is complex. The country is large, with a diverse population characterized by constant change.

8. Political science is the academic discipline that systematically seeks to describe and explain politics using the scientific method. Thinking analytically requires asking careful questions, considering alternate answers, and employing empirical evidence to figure out not just why a particular answer is correct, but why competing answers are incorrect.

9. Systematic explanations of the how and why of politics include rational choice, behavioral, and biological models. Each can be used to provide a deeper understanding of how and why politics works the way it does.

10. The purpose of this book is to provide an analytical toolkit and sufficient information to allow the reader to make informed, independent judgments about the politics and practice of democracy in the American political system.

CHAPTER ONE
Key Terms and Cases

absolute majority, 8
autocracy, 6
democracy, 6
direct democracy, 12
economic equality, 10
elitist, 24
empirical, 26
equality of opportunity, 10
equality under the law, 9
false consensus, 22
government, 6
hypothesis, 29
ideology, 20
initiative, 12
liberal democracy, 13
majority rule, 8
minority rights, 8
normative, 25
null hypothesis, 29
oligarchy, 6
partisanship, 21
pluralistic, 22
plurality, 8
political equality, 9
political science, 25
politics, 6
popular sovereignty, 7
referendum, 12
representative democracy, 13
research question, 26
science, 26
simple majority, 8
social equality, 10
sovereignty, 6
theory, 29
utility, 33

PART I

The Constitutional Framework

2 THE AMERICAN CONSTITUTION

KEY QUESTIONS

Why did Federalists want a new constitution to replace the Articles of Confederation?

What is the Madisonian dilemma, and how does the U.S. Constitution try to solve this dilemma?

How does the meaning of the U.S. Constitution change?

The Signing of the Constitution of the United States in 1787

© The Signing of the Constitution of the United States in 1787, 1940 (oil on canvas), Christy, Howard Chandler (1873–1952)/ Hall of Representatives, Washington, DC, USA/The Bridgeman Art Library

AMERICAN CITIZENS have an odd—and, it must be said, a not completely honest—relationship with the U.S. Constitution. On the one hand, Americans tend to imbue the Constitution with an almost religious reverence. Louis Marshall, a well-known civil liberties lawyer of the early twentieth century, described the Constitution as "our holy of holies, an instrument of sacred import. It has been the guiding principle of the freest Government on earth. Let no unhallowed hand be laid upon it" (Klarman 2016, 1). That quote neatly captures popular sentiment. The Constitution is widely viewed as a sort of secular scripture, something that provides not just the legal framework of the political system, but a divine bequest of universally agreed-on democratic wisdom from the nation's Founding Fathers.

Yet while vast numbers of Americans express an abiding faith in and support for the Constitution, not many have actually read it and few have even a passing familiarity with the politics that produced it. In short, while Americans have a deep reverence for the iconic notion of the Constitution, that image often bears only a passing resemblance to its reality. The idea of the Constitution as some sort of revealed democratic truth, for example, would have seemed very odd to those actually involved in deciding whether to adopt it as the basis of government. Indeed, at the time it wasn't particularly popular, and for good reason. The document itself was the product of a bare-knuckled political fight waged in secret by a small elite seeking to vastly expand the power of the national government. Its authors arguably acted illegally in writing the Constitution, and many were dissatisfied with its final form. Reading it for the first time, many citizens saw it as a not particularly democratic power grab. Once circulated for ratification it ran into a storm of opposition from many citizens and elected officials who stoutly (and sometimes violently) opposed its ratification. In the one state (Rhode Island) where ratification of the Constitution was submitted to a popular vote, it was overwhelmingly rejected.

None of this is to suggest that the Constitution is anything other than a brilliant piece of political engineering. It is. The point is that many of the ideas Americans hold about the Constitution are based more on feel-good mythology than any real understanding of what constitutes the historical and legal basis of the republic. In reality, the Constitution is less a sacred text and more of rulebook, a rulebook for the political system of the United States. If you do not understand the rulebook and how it came to be, the bottom line is that you cannot understand American government and politics. To ensure you have that understanding, this chapter examines what a constitution is, and provides a basic primer on the political history of the U.S. Constitution and the basic goals and purposes of democratic politics that it articulates.

THE CONCEPT OF A CONSTITUTION

A **constitution** is the basic framework of government that defines the nature and conduct of public authority. A constitution consists of three essential elements:

1. The *functions* of government: the powers and responsibilities that reside in the public rather than in the private sphere
2. The *structure* of government: the institutions and mechanisms that constitute the framework of government
3. The *procedures* of government: the manner in which government carries out the powers and responsibilities entrusted to it

Together, these elements provide the basic rules and guidelines for the exercise of political authority. Note that this is a definition of constitutions in general. The functions, structure, and procedures specified by a particular constitution determine whether the government is an autocracy, oligarchy, or democracy.

Thus, a democratic constitution spells out how the core principles of democracy are to be upheld. Consider, for example, the powerful role of public officials and institutions in a representative democracy. They have the authority and power to make binding decisions regulating individual and group behavior. A constitution performs a similarly powerful role in relation to the public officials themselves; it determines what they can and cannot do and the nature of their relationship with other officeholders and the general populace. A state of mutual dependence and influence, therefore, characterizes a representative form of government. The people grant public officials the power to enact laws and decrees, but ordinary citizens ultimately control how that power is exercised. A democratic constitution

constitution A document or unwritten set of basic rules that provides the basic principles that determine the conduct of political affairs.

spells out that popular sovereignty is the basis of political authority and constrains those who exercise that power from limiting the political freedom of others.

A constitution, then, establishes a set of legal relationships between leaders and the led. It is the heart of a nation's political process, and it shapes the process by determining the rules for accessing and exercising political power. The content and form of a constitution are in turn shaped by a political process as groups struggle to write the rules to favor their own interests.

CIRCUMSTANCES THAT LED TO THE CREATION OF THE CONSTITUTION

To understand the U.S. Constitution, we need to appreciate two sets of contemporary circumstances that led to its creation. The first is the historical antecedents—the Declaration of Independence, the Articles of Confederation, and the various state constitutions—that provided a basic philosophy of governance. The second is the economic and social conditions that created dissatisfaction with the forms of governance established by these earlier frameworks.

Historical Antecedents of the Constitution

The Declaration of Independence

The **Declaration of Independence** lays the foundation of American constitutional theory. Technically, a committee established by the Second Continental Congress wrote it, though its primary author was Thomas Jefferson.[1] The declaration justifies the struggle for independence with a republican theory of government based on the concept of natural rights. Borrowing from the ideas of John Locke, Jefferson's elegant prose asserts that "all men are created equal" and that they enjoy "unalienable rights" that include "life, liberty and the pursuit of happiness." These statements reject ideas of philosophers such as Thomas Hobbes who argued that people surrender certain natural rights when they leave the state of nature. The Declaration of Independence provides the basis of republican government, declaring that people create governments to secure these rights, and governments derive their "just Powers from the Consent of the Governed." If a government fails to protect these rights, "it is the Right of the People to alter or to abolish it, and to institute new Government." Together, these ideas can be viewed as a comprehensive conception of popular sovereignty (Becker 1922; Wiecek 1992).

The legal status of the Declaration of Independence is somewhat ambiguous. Although Congress placed it in the U.S. Code under the heading "Organic Laws of

Declaration of Independence A document written by Thomas Jefferson that lays the foundation of American constitutional theory. Jefferson justifies the struggle for independence with a republican theory of government based on the concepts of natural rights and popular sovereignty.

---

1 The committee included John Adams, Benjamin Franklin, Roger Sherman, and Robert Livingston.

Thomas Jefferson wrote the Declaration of Independence, and John Hancock was the first to sign it in July 1776. In the document, Jefferson presents a comprehensive idea of popular sovereignty, one that laid the foundation for the Constitution's major principles.

© Signing the Declaration of Independence, July 4, 1776 (oil on canvas), Trumbull, John (1756–1843)/Yale University Art Gallery, New Haven, CT, USA/The Bridgeman Art Library

the United States of America," the Supreme Court has rarely interpreted it to have binding legal force. Some legal authorities even deny that there is a constitutional right of revolution. Nonetheless, the Declaration of Independence is a basic statement of constitutional principles and lays the foundation for American constitutional order (Wiecek 1992).

The Articles of Confederation

The **Articles of Confederation** served as the first constitution of the United States. A committee of the Continental Congress began drafting this constitution in June 1776—even before independence had been declared—though bickering and political divisions meant that the document was not submitted for approval by the states until November 1777.

The Articles of Confederation established a national government consisting of a **unicameral** (one-house) legislature; there was no independent executive or judicial branch. Under the Articles, the national government's powers were limited primarily to raising an army and navy, entering into treaties and alliances, and sending and receiving diplomatic representatives—matters of war and peace that wartime experience indicated should be vested in the nation. The national government had no authority to regulate interstate and foreign commerce, which the Confederation's Framers associated with the Acts of Trade and Navigation passed by the British Parliament that helped spark the Revolution.

The national government also lacked the power to levy taxes, so it had no control over its revenues. Although the national government could requisition funds from the states for expenses, it had no authority to compel payment.

Articles of Confederation The first constitution of the United States.

unicameral A legislature with one chamber.

Instead, the states themselves had to levy the taxes to pay these requisitions, and they often refused to do so. The authority to provide troops for the national military also resided with the states. Lacking the authority to make the states meet their obligations, and bereft of the power to tax or conscript individuals, the national government lacked the means to fulfill the basic governmental responsibilities entrusted to it. Moreover, there was little chance of changing these arrangements because any alteration of the document required unanimous consent of all the states.

State Constitutions as Models of Government

While the national government was off to a fragile start, the states were busy asserting their independence not only from Great Britain but also from one another and from any national government that might be formed.

Principal features of the national government established under the Articles of Confederation—for example, a dominant legislature and weak (or nonexistent) executive and judiciary—reflected institutional arrangements already included in several state constitutions. In most states, for example, the governor was chosen by the legislature; only four states had a popularly elected executive. There were, however, some notable exceptions to this general pattern. New York, for example, had a strong governor system. State judiciaries were also weak and largely subservient to their legislatures, which frequently appointed judicial officials and gave them only limited powers.

Terms of legislators were short—only one year in most of the states. Rhode Islanders were even more wary, allowing their representatives only six months. Most state constitutions (and the Articles of Confederation) put term limits on legislators and allowed the recall of unpopular elected officials at any time.

State constitutions and the Articles of Confederation clearly went to some lengths to uphold at least some of the core principles of democracy. Recall provisions and the dominance of legislatures, for example, reinforced majority rule by giving the people frequent opportunities to hold their representatives accountable. Yet whatever their democratic elements, state constitutions and the Articles of Confederation shared a common weakness: They produced weak and ineffective governments. The overriding concern reflected in these constitutions was a distrust of centralized power. The colonists' experience with British governance had led them to see a strong, centralized government as a threat to the core democratic principle of political freedom. The Revolution, after all, had been fought in no small part because of the colonists' resentment of taxes imposed by a legislature to which they sent no delegates and in which they had no voice. This certainly seemed to violate the democratic principle of political freedom.

Yet state constitutions (and the Articles of Confederation) focused too much on limiting governmental power. Rather than being too powerful, the state and national governments of the early United States were often too weak to do much at all. This weakness carried enormous risks—including the very real potential that the United States would fail as a political system.

Hard-won experience at the state level led to constitutional innovations that later served as examples for the Framers of the U.S. Constitution to follow. For example, New York developed a strong governorship free of legislative dominance in order to handle military and civilian affairs. This experience showed the worth of an independent executive and demonstrated that such an executive was not necessarily a threat to political freedom. Encouraged by John Adams, voters in Massachusetts adopted a constitution that included a popularly elected house of representatives and an "aristocratic" senate apportioned on the basis of taxable wealth. It also included a popularly elected governor vested with considerable powers (such as a veto) who was eligible for reelection, and an independent judiciary. Both the New York and Massachusetts constitutions would help shape the deliberations at the Constitutional Convention.

Economic Conditions

The United States in the 1780s faced a period of major adjustment following its successful revolt against Great Britain. Within a few years of the end of the Revolutionary War in 1781, America was plunged into a depression. Accounts differ as to how serious it was. Some claim the critical period was brief, and the corner turned by the time the Constitutional Convention met in mid-1787. Others claim it was serious enough to threaten the existence of the new nation. There is general agreement that the economic downturn affected groups differently; small farmers and the few hired laborers of the day experienced little of the effect, but people in commerce and finance were hit hard.

Domestic rivalries worsened the economic problems. Fierce economic protectionism developed as states levied duties to raise revenue and to protect local interests against out-of-state competitors. Lacking the authority to regulate interstate commerce, the national government was powerless to remove the obstacles to free trade within the nation. Adding to the economic woes were the worsening fortunes of the creditors who financed both public and private ventures in the young nation. Debtors often used the political process at the state level to lighten their financial obligations. For example, some states enacted "stay" laws that postponed the due dates of promissory notes. Another type of law allowed a debtor to declare bankruptcy, pay off his obligation at less than face value, and begin his financial life anew with a clean slate. Another advantage for debtors was the issuance of cheap paper money by state legislatures. This practice fueled inflation, meaning that the face value of debt was worth far less than the money originally borrowed.

Even more financially frustrated were those who had lent the nation money to fight the Revolution. They had no way to collect on public securities issued by a government that lacked the financial ability to pay its debts. Similarly affected were veterans of the war, who had volunteered their services on the promise of compensation via proceeds from government bonds. Given the precarious financial situation facing the new nation, there was a risk that the government would default on its debts.

Although the United States had theoretically achieved an independent status in the family of nations, its sovereignty was vulnerable even after the guns had fallen silent. The structure of government lent itself to internal divisions and united the states in little more than name. Economic strife pitted one group against another, and the world's major powers remained active on the North American continent. Spain closed the mouth of the Mississippi to all shipping. The supposedly vanquished British troops refused to withdraw from some northwestern forts until the claims of British creditors were honored. The new nation tottered on the uncertain economic and political legs of its newfound independence. George Washington, the Revolutionary War's great hero, observed that something had to change in order "to avert the humiliating and contemptible figure [they were] about to make on the annals of mankind" (Collier and Collier 1986, 3).

Group Rivalries and the Movement for a Convention

The groups particularly aggrieved in the postwar period were manufacturers, merchants, shipowners, and creditors. The professional classes—lawyers, doctors, newspaper editors, and so on—sympathized with their clients, as did former soldiers who felt cheated out of their rightful claims for services rendered in the cause of nationhood. Combined, they composed a potent group that wanted change. After the Constitution had been drafted, they were to come together to support its adoption under the name of **Federalists**.

Federalist interests were for the most part concentrated in the cities, but some rural Americans also found their interests jeopardized by postwar conditions, including commercial farmers who produced a surplus of crops that they wanted to sell in interstate and foreign markets. Most were large landholders who ran agricultural operations dependent on slave labor; they found common cause with merchants whose futures were also linked to commerce.

Opposing the Federalists were people who did not depend on trade for their livelihoods. At the core of this opposition were small subsistence farmers, small businessmen, artisans, mechanics (the small laboring class of that time), and debtors who welcomed government assistance in their perennial struggle to keep one step ahead of creditors. This coalition of interests, labeled **Anti-Federalists**, resisted ratification of the Constitution.

As a group, the Federalists were wealthier and better educated, and they worked in higher-status occupations. Anti-Federalists tended to be lower-class, obscure individuals of modest means. Although the leadership of the Anti-Federalists did include a number of prominent Revolutionary-era

Federalists The group of people who supported the adoption of the Constitution and favored a stronger national government.

Anti-Federalists The group of people who opposed a stronger national government than what existed under the Articles of Confederation and opposed the ratification of the Constitution.

Patrick Henry, a lawyer from Virginia and a controversial member of the Continental Congress, made the first speech when it convened. Despite being a well-known representative for the Anti-Federalists, who did not support the idea of a strong central government, Henry did not attend the Constitutional Convention.

© North Wind Picture Archives

APPLYING THE FRAMEWORKS

A RATIONAL CHOICE EXPLANATION OF THE U.S. CONSTITUTION

What motivated the Founders to scrap the Articles of Confederation and write a whole new Constitution? The prevailing popular historical interpretation is that the Founders were selfless patriots, men seeking nothing more than to provide the basis for a stable republic that balanced strong, effective government with a respect for individual rights. As comforting as this view might be, it is not a scientific explanation. Rather it is based on idiosyncratic factors—the individual personalities and events—of the time. But scientists—including political scientists—seek broader explanations based on some general theory.

Several scholars have sought to explain the individual motivations behind the authors of the Constitution using a rational choice framework, and those analyses suggest more than selfless patriotism was motivating those who authored the Constitution. Probably the most famous of the rational choice analyses is more than a century old, Charles A. Beard's *An Economic Interpretation of the Constitution of the United States* (1913).

Beard's central hypothesis was that the Founders were motivated largely by economic self-interest. As he put it, the majority of the Constitutional Convention's participants "were immediately, directly, and personally interested in the outcome of their labors ... and were to a greater or lesser extent economic beneficiaries from the adoption of the Constitution" (1913, 149).

Beard tested his hypothesis empirically—he used records from the United States Treasury Department to survey economic interests in the United States as of 1787. This identified two broad classes of economic interests, one based on real property (land and buildings), and one based on personal property that is moveable (e.g., cash and securities). Beard's analysis concluded that the people who wrote the Constitution and advocated for its adoption belonged to the latter set of economic interests, and that the adoption of the Constitution tended to benefit those interests.

Beard's analysis has long been controversial, but it's important to note that when first published rational choice theory was not well developed, and modern statistical techniques to test hypotheses were still in their infancy. A century later, Robert McGuire (2003) picked up on Beard's general framework to offer "a new economic interpretation of United States Constitution" that takes advantage of these innovations. McGuire's interpretation is not so much new, but rather a recasting of Beard's basic theory in terms of the modern, more general conception of rational choice—namely, the assumption that humans are rational actors who make choices to maximize utility. Remember, *utility* refers to the relative benefits—satisfaction or enjoyment—derived from each of the alternatives. Utility certainly encompasses the notion of economic interests at the heart of Beard's analysis, i.e., tangible, pecuniary benefits. But it also includes intangible, nonpecuniary benefits such as political principles, ideology, and constituents' interests. McGuire tested this more developed rational choice framework using multivariate statistical models that allowed him to estimate the effects of particular variables—e.g., financial circumstances—while holding constant the effects of other variables that might influence choices.

He analyzed how economic and non-economic variables influenced delegates' votes on several specific clauses coded as either pro-nationalism or pro-confederation at the convention. He used similar statistical models to analyze how these variables influenced votes to support or oppose the Constitution at the state ratifying conventions. This analysis indicates that the Founders' choices were consistent with self-interested and partisan behavior. McGuire presents evidence that partisan economic (pecuniary) interests and partisan ideological (nonpecuniary) interests influenced vote choices at the Philadelphia convention and at state ratifying conventions in ways that are consistent with Beard's interpretation. *Ceteris paribus*, delegates with merchant and commercial interests who held public or private securities were more likely to support a strong national government and the Constitution, while delegates with agricultural interests with debt were less likely to support a stronger national government.

In short, what McGuire's analysis revealed was that the Founders were self-interested, but their interests—the things that gave them utility—were not just limited to whatever helped them line their own pockets, as Beard seemed to suggest. And, McGuire suggested, we probably should not be too surprised by this. He concludes that because human beings are naturally self-interested, "it is unlikely that *any* real-world constitution would ever be drafted or ratified through a disinterested and nonpartisan process" (2003, 8).

Discussion Questions

1. If scientific theories are neutral, objective explanations of some real-world phenomenon, why is popular reaction to them often normative?
2. Are normative reactions to scientific research the result of the values we associate with the phenomenon being studied, or do you think scientific theories have inherent biases?

luminaries—such as Richard Henry Lee, Patrick Henry, and George Clinton—the Anti-Federalists could not match either in numbers or in fame those who lent their skill and prestige to the Federalist cause, such as George Washington, Alexander Hamilton, and James Madison.

Two events in the fall of 1786 enabled the Federalists to act on their desires for a stronger national government. One was a meeting at Annapolis, Maryland, convened to discuss problems of interstate trade and the possibility of adopting a uniform system of commercial regulations. Delegates from only a few states showed up, and most had Federalist sympathies. The Federalist majority, notably Hamilton and Madison, seized the opportunity to issue a report to the Continental Congress suggesting that a commission be assembled the following May to revise the Articles of Confederation.

The second event was an armed revolt in western Massachusetts by farmers who were resisting state efforts to seize their property for failure to pay taxes and debts. **Shays' Rebellion**—named for its leader, Daniel Shays—was put down, but some Americans regarded it as a threat to the very existence of the United States. Among those concerned was George Washington, the most popular American of all. Appalled by the news that a former officer in his army had brought the state of Massachusetts to the brink of civil war, Washington lent his great prestige to the movement for a convention.

THE CONSTITUTIONAL CONVENTION

Pushed by these two events, in February 1787 Congress called on the states to send delegates to a convention in Philadelphia to revise the Articles of Confederation. All except Rhode Island, which was dominated by debtor interests, eventually responded, though some states responded more quickly than others.

Shays' Rebellion An armed revolt by farmers in western Massachusetts who were resisting state efforts to seize their property for failure to pay taxes and debts.

The convention was supposed to open on May 14, 1787, but a quorum was not achieved until May 25. The New Hampshire delegation did not arrive until July 1787, some two months after the deliberations began.

The Founders

The most important feature of the Constitutional Convention was that an overwhelming proportion of the delegates were Federalists. As soon as the convention assembled, it made two important decisions: It named George Washington the presiding officer, and it bound the delegates to secrecy. Naming Washington as presiding officer gave the convention immediate credibility, and the Federalist majority could exercise a larger degree of influence behind closed doors than in open public debate.

Anti-Federalists matched and perhaps exceeded their opponents as a proportion of the general populace. Given their numbers, it is somewhat puzzling that more Anti-Federalists did not attend the convention, especially since the state legislatures that selected delegates had strong Anti-Federalist sentiments. There are two possible explanations. One is that some Anti-Federalists did not want to dignify the convention with their presence. The best-known instance was Patrick Henry, whose oft-quoted reason for staying away was that he "smelt a rat." The second possible explanation is that Anti-Federalists thought attendance was unnecessary because the convention's legal mandate was limited to revising the Articles of Confederation. The Anti-Federalists believed they could block anything contrary to their interests because any changes had to be approved by all states. As it turned out, the convention quickly abandoned its assignment of reworking the Articles of Confederation and secretly began drafting a blueprint for a new government.

Anti-Federalists were represented in this enterprise (examples included Elbridge Gerry and Luther Martin), but they were outnumbered. And most Anti-Federalists who were in attendance belonged to the social, political, and economic elite; the nation's subsistence farmers, who constituted the rank and file of the Anti-Federalist cause and who were the most numerous economic group in the nation, were hardly represented at all. All 55 delegates, Federalist or otherwise, were decidedly unrepresentative of American life and interests. Most were lawyers, most were college-educated, and most had political experience. Three-quarters had served in the Continental Congress, eight had signed the Declaration of Independence, and most were dominant figures in the political lives of their states. Although unrepresentative, they were a gathering of political talent of the highest order, a collection with few historical comparisons.

Often called the father of the Constitution because of his huge contribution to its writing and ratification, Madison also collaborated in the writing of the *Federalist* Papers, which described the justifications for the political institutions and processes the Constitution established. He was elected to the first national Congress, and after serving as secretary of state under Jefferson, he served two terms as the fourth president of the United States.

© James Madison (1751–1836) (color litho), Stuart, Charles Gilbert (c. 1787–1813)/Private Collection/Peter Newark American Pictures/The Bridgeman Art Library

Most delegates took an active role in the proceedings, but a few emerged as dominant figures. The most influential was James Madison of Virginia. Madison was hardly a dashing Revolutionary hero, as were some of his contemporaries. Short, frail, and uncomfortable with public speaking, he nevertheless possessed a towering intellect. He spent months preparing for the convention, poring over treatises on government and historical accounts of the ancient Greek city-states, and he arrived at the convention with a well-defined plan for a new government. Called the **Virginia plan**, it was the first major proposal presented to the convention, and it formed the basis of the Constitution. Madison's contributions went far beyond his labors at the convention. He was a key figure both before and after the convention, and his diary constitutes the main historical record of the four-month proceedings. Because of these efforts, Madison is remembered as the father of the Constitution.

Ranking only slightly below Madison in importance were the two delegates from Pennsylvania: James Wilson and Gouverneur Morris. Wilson was a Scotsman in his mid-forties; a lawyer known for his penetrating logical mind, he placed great faith in the common people. Morris, 11 years Wilson's junior, was a swashbuckling figure. Tall, handsome, and known for his biting wit, Morris viewed the common people with aristocratic mistrust. Despite their differences, both advocated a strong federal government with a powerful executive, and through their service on influential committees at the convention, they shaped both the content and the phraseology of the document that ultimately emerged.

Two of the most famous figures present were George Washington and Benjamin Franklin, both of whom made significant contributions to the convention. Washington did not play an active role in shaping the Constitution, but his enormous national prestige and the assumption that he would be the nation's first chief executive provided the convention and the document it produced with a crucial air of legitimacy. Franklin was past his peak of political creativity in 1787, but his justly famed wit served to cool tempers. These two renowned and revered figures played key roles in the fight for ratification simply by lending the Constitution their approval.

Agreement, Disagreement, and Compromise at the Convention

There was a good deal of common ground among the delegates at the convention. Key among these agreements was the consensus on the need for a stronger national government with the power to fulfill the responsibilities entrusted to it. The dilemma was how to achieve this goal. How could a government be powerful enough to protect and serve the common good without tempting tyranny by placing power into too few hands? This conundrum was complicated by the delicate question of relations between state and national governments. The states would have to approve the Constitution, and it was universally recognized that the states had a legitimate interest in defending their sovereignty. So although there was broad agreement on the need for a stronger central government, differences over specifics often divided the convention into shifting and competing groups: large

Virginia plan The first major proposal presented at the 1787 Constitutional Convention that formed the basis of the Constitution. It called for a bicameral legislature with a popularly elected lower house and an upper house nominated by state legislatures.

state versus small state, North versus South, and of course, Federalist versus Anti-Federalist.

Thus, the proposed structure of the new government percolated through several proposals. For example, Madison's Virginia plan called for a **bicameral**, or two-house, legislature with a popularly elected lower house and an upper house nominated by state legislatures. Representation in each was to be based on the financial contributions or population of the state. Large states, whose representatives would dominate the national legislature, supported this plan, while small states opposed it. A rival proposal, the **New Jersey plan**, proposed a one-house legislature with equal state representation, similar to that established by the Articles of Confederation. This favored small states, which would wield equal power with their more populous neighbors. The conflict was resolved by the **Connecticut Compromise** or Great Compromise, so called because delegates from Connecticut worked hard for its acceptance. It proposed a two-house legislature, with a House of Representatives apportioned on the basis of population and a Senate representing the states on an equal basis. Similar battles were fought over the composition and selection of the executive branch (these are detailed in Chapter 13).

Such political compromises are a notable feature of the document produced by the convention. Some of these compromises are unsavory, and others left fundamental issues unresolved. For example, northern and southern states split over the question of slavery. The South wanted slaves counted for purposes of representation (even though there was no thought of allowing slaves to vote) but not for purposes of taxation. Northern states favored the reverse. A bargain struck was to count each slave as three-fifths of a person for both representation and taxation. As for the very controversial question of ending the slave trade, the convention simply put it off for the future with a provision that barred Congress from outlawing it before 1808. The unresolved question of slavery perpetuated a problem that neither the bloody Civil War in the nineteenth century nor an extended battle for civil rights in the twentieth has fully resolved.

A number of factors contributed to the willingness of delegates to accommodate their sometimes sharp differences. Many believed that the nation was on the brink of dissolution and that this was the last chance to secure a government that united the states into a single country. Since most of the delegates were Federalists, they were in broad agreement on the need to create a much stronger national government, and on the essential structure of that government, though they sometimes disagreed strongly on the details. This underlying consensus permitted the delegates to find ways to compromise on how to apply these principles. The secrecy of the proceedings also fostered compromise. Free of public scrutiny and pressures, the delegates could change their minds and modify their stands as they groped for answers to the nation's most difficult problems.

The Limited Role of Religion

Of the values and motivations that influenced the delegates to the Constitutional Convention, religion played a limited role. Although the delegates were Christian

---

bicameral A legislature with two chambers.

New Jersey plan A proposal presented at the Constitutional Convention that called for a one-house legislature with equal representation for each state.

Connecticut Compromise (Great Compromise) A proposal at the Constitutional Convention that called for a two-house legislature with a House of Representatives apportioned on the basis of population and a Senate representing each state on an equal basis.

(except for a few Deists), a review of notes on the debate at the Constitutional Convention reveals few references to religion or God (see Benton 1986). The few references that were made do not suggest that the Founders attempted to base the Constitution on an explicitly Judeo-Christian belief system. On the contrary, they viewed religion as belonging to the private rather than public sphere. Their primary concern was to protect the individual's religious beliefs from the government, not to base a government on a particular set of religious principles.

It is this latter concern that is expressed in the one direct reference to religion in the text of the Constitution.[2] Article VI, Section 3 states that members of the legislative, executive, and judicial branches of both federal and state governments "shall be bound by oath or affirmation, to support this Constitution; but no religious test shall ever be required as a qualification to any office or public trust under the United States." In effect, this provision prevents government at all levels in the United States from requiring its members to be Christian or Protestant or even to believe in God. Such a requirement would in effect establish an official state religion and thereby use the coercive power of government to persecute those with different beliefs. The practice of requiring religious tests as a qualification for civil and military officers was common in England during the reign of Charles II, a practice explicitly referred to—and roundly condemned—in the ratification debates. For example, Oliver Ellsworth, a delegate from Connecticut, argued, "the sole purpose and effect of [prohibiting religious tests] is to exclude persecution, and to secure ... the right of religious liberty" (Ellsworth [1787] 1986, 522).

There is also indirect evidence that the Founders wanted government to be neutral with respect to religion. For example, the presidential oath of office allows the president to "swear *or affirm* allegiance to the Constitution" (Article II, Section 1, emphasis added). Article VI offers other government officials the same option to indicate their support for the Constitution by "oath or *affirmation.*" Permitting "affirmation" to substitute for an oath accommodates religious beliefs that forbid swearing and imposes the same level of personal responsibility on someone who is not religious as affirmation does for a religious person (Mount 2006b).

Thus, the convention proposed a new governmental structure intended to correct the defects of the Articles of Confederation (see Table 2.1). Yet when 39 of the 55 delegates signed the Constitution on September 17, 1787, their work had not ended. Actually, it had only just begun. They now faced the task of persuading their fellow citizens to approve what they had done.

The Ratification Campaign

Ironically, some of the conditions that promoted agreement and compromise at the convention made the subsequent ratification process difficult. Anti-Federalists

---

[2] The Constitution concludes, "done in Convention by the Unanimous Consent of the States present the Seventeenth Day of September in the Year of our Lord one thousand seven hundred and Eighty seven." This was a standard way of writing dates at the time rather than a reference to binding religious principles.

TABLE 2.1 SIDE-BY-SIDE COMPARISON: THE ARTICLES OF CONFEDERATION AND THE CONSTITUTION

Provision	Articles of Confederation	U.S. Constitution
Name	The United States of America	The United States of America
Creator of the Constitution	Sovereign States agree to form a Perpetual Union	The People of the United States in order to form a more perfect union
FUNCTIONS		
Major Powers		
Declare war	Congress	Congress
Army	Congress decides size of force and requisitions troops from each state according to population	Congress authorized to raise and support armies
Navy	Congress authorized to build a navy; states authorized to equip warships to counter piracy	Congress authorized to build a navy; states not allowed to keep ships of war
Treaties	Congress	President, subject to ratification by the two-thirds vote in the Senate
Taxes	Apportioned by Congress, collected by the states; no power to compel states to pay	Laid and collected by Congress
Coin money	Both states and the United States	United States only
Regulation of interstate commerce	No power to regulate interstate commerce	Congress
Staffing government	Congress authorized to appoint ambassadors, maritime judges, and other "civil officers"	President appoints executive branch officials and federal judges, with advice and consent of the Senate
Powers Prohibited		
Bills of attainder	Not prohibited	Prohibited to both states and Congress
Ex post facto laws	Not prohibited	Prohibited to both states and Congress
Religious test to hold office	Not prohibited	Prohibited to both states and Congress
STRUCTURE		
Governmental Structure		
Form of government	Representative; confederation	Representative; federation
National–state power relationship	States required to abide by acts of Congress, but each state retains sovereignty and all powers not expressly delegated to the United States	U.S. Constitution, federal laws, and treaties are the "supreme law of the land," and take precedence over state constitutions and laws that conflict
Legislature		
Structure and name	Unicameral, called Congress	Bicameral, called Congress: House of Representatives and Senate
Presiding officer in Congress	President of Congress	Speaker of the House of Representatives; vice president is president of the Senate
Representation in Congress	Between two and seven delegates per state	Two senators per state; representatives apportioned according to state population

TABLE 2.1 *continued*

Provision	Articles of Confederation	U.S. Constitution
Executive power	None specified; Congress authorized to appoint civil officers to manage affairs of the United States	President
Commander in chief	Appointed by Congress	President
JUDICIARY		
National judiciary	Only maritime judiciary	Established one Supreme Court; Congress authorized to create inferior courts
PROCEDURES		
SELECTION OF REPRESENTATIVES		
Members of Congress	Delegates appointed by state legislatures in the manner directed by each legislature	Representatives elected by popular vote; senators appointed by state legislatures
Qualifications for office	None; determined by the state legislatures	U.S. citizen, resident of state, at least 25 years old for House and 30 years old for Senate
Term of legislative office	One year	Two years for representatives, six for senators
Term limits	No more than three out of every six years	None
Recall members of Congress	State may recall its delegates at any time	None
Congressional pay	Paid by states	Paid by the U.S. government
LEGISLATIVE PROCEDURES		
Voting in Congress	One vote per state	One vote per representative or senator
Vote required to enact legislation	Nine (of 13) states	Simple majority in both House and Senate; some actions require two-thirds
When Congress is not in session	Committee of states has the powers of Congress	President can call Congress into session
INTERGOVERNMENTAL		
New states	Admitted upon agreement of nine states, with open invitation to Canada to join	Admitted upon agreement of Congress
Adjudicate disputes between states	Congress	Supreme Court
Extradition of criminals	Accused criminals who flee to another state shall be returned to the state having jurisdiction upon demand of the Governor	Same provision
Full faith and credit	States must grant "full faith and credit" to other states' records, acts, and judicial proceedings	Same provision
AMENDMENT AND RATIFICATION		
Amendment	When agreed to by all states	Proposed by two-thirds of states or two-thirds vote in Congress; ratified by three-fourths of states
Ratification	Consent of all states	Consent of nine states

Source: Adapted and expanded by the authors from Mount, (2006a). "Comparing the Articles and the Constitution." March 15, 2006. http://www.usconstitution.net/constconart.html (accessed March 14, 2018).

did not see national disintegration as imminent, and they believed that the difficulties attributed to the Articles of Confederation were manageable or temporary. Although they constituted a minority of convention delegates, Anti-Federalists were well represented in state legislatures and the general populace. The secrecy that had promoted cooperation at the convention invited suspicion and resentment among those denied information about the proceedings.

Before the convention dissolved, the delegates made some decisions designed to facilitate the adoption of the proposed Constitution. They ignored the unanimous consent required by the Articles of Confederation and specified that ratification could be secured with the approval of nine states. This provision meant that a single state such as Rhode Island, which had no representatives at the convention, would not be able to block the entire enterprise. Aware of the Anti-Federalist sentiments in state legislatures, the delegates also specified that elected state conventions were to be the ratifying bodies. The Federalists could influence the selection of representatives to these conventions, as well as shape the broader course of deliberations. Ratification was also given a boost by the Continental Congress. This body, which the new Constitution proposed to put out of business, somewhat surprisingly forwarded the convention's instructions to the states.

Having slanted the rules to favor ratification, the Federalists set out to transform their opportunity into reality. They labored to get themselves and their sympathizers elected as state convention delegates, and 25 of the Constitution's 39 signatories were so chosen. They developed strategies for convention proceedings, and they began a campaign to win public support for the new Constitution.

The Federalists had some notable political advantages, including the endorsements of Washington and Franklin, which were worth thousands of votes in and of themselves. Trading on the important contacts of such luminaries also provided an important communications network for the various state and local campaigns. And the Federalists had a vital asset that their opponents lacked—a positive program to sell. The Anti-Federalists had been maneuvered into the position of favoring some changes in the Articles of Confederation but having no concrete plans to make them. Lacking a viable alternative, Anti-Federalists were forced to adopt a negative, defensive stance in the ratification battle, while the Federalists argued that rejection of the Constitution would lead to a return of the chaos promoted under the Articles.

Still, even with such advantages, ratification was no sure thing. Although the Constitution held obvious appeal to states such as Delaware and New Jersey that were burdened with heavy taxes and debts and squeezed by high interstate duties, other states, such as Rhode Island, saw little to like. There was genuine and fierce opposition to the Constitution in other states, as well. Four states were crucial because of their size and political strength: Massachusetts, New York, Pennsylvania, and Virginia. If one of these major states failed to ratify, even a legally constituted union of nine or more states would be shaky.

Federalist activities in these key states reveal the efforts they were willing to make to get support for the Constitution. The Pennsylvania state legislature had been in session in the upstairs chamber of the Philadelphia State House even as the convention was finishing its work on the Constitution downstairs. The day after the convention adjourned, the state assembly obtained an unofficial copy of the document. The day after that, the document was printed in the newspapers, and within a week, a rising tide of public opposition threatened to engulf the chances of ratification in the state. The Pennsylvania legislature threatened to swing to the Anti-Federalists in upcoming elections, even before the assembly had summoned a state ratifying convention. Realizing the danger of allowing a legislature dominated by Anti-Federalists to set up the procedures for electing the ratifying convention, the Federalists pushed a motion calling for a ratification convention, even though the Continental Congress had yet to officially present the Constitution to the states for approval. Sensing their opportunity, 19 Anti-Federalists bolted from the chamber during a noon recess on September 29, denying the legislature a quorum and hence the legal ability to pass the motion. In response, the sergeant at arms of the Philadelphia legislature assembled a Federalist mob that physically carried two of the recalcitrant representatives back to the chamber, forced them into their seats, and barred the doors! The two captives were enough to muster a quorum, and the Federalists passed the necessary motions to secure a ratifying convention (Morgan 1992, 150–151).

Even in relatively open and free debate, the Federalists often faced tough opposition. In Virginia, James Madison—with the able assistance of future Supreme Court Justice John Marshall—had to take on the formidable opposition of Patrick Henry and future president James Monroe. Although George Washington was not a participant at the state convention, his influence was evident in Virginia's 89–79 vote for approval. The vote in New York was even closer—30 to 27 in favor of ratification.

With the major states in the fold, the Federalists had won, and the other states eventually fell in line to make approval unanimous. The struggle of the formation and adoption were over.

CONSTITUTIONAL PRINCIPLES

What had the Federalists created? What were the underlying objectives of the Constitution, and what democratic ideals and purposes did it embody? Embedded in the document is a set of values and goals shared by the delegates to the Constitutional Convention. These values were most clearly articulated by Madison, who—along with Hamilton and John Jay—wrote the best-known explanation and defense of the Constitution. The *Federalist* **Papers** were originally a series of political essays published under the pseudonym Publius with the express purpose of persuading New Yorkers to ratify the proposed Constitution. They were subsequently published together as the *Federalist*. They remain the single best source for understanding the justifications for the political institutions and processes the Constitution established. In a real sense, they constitute the theory that lies behind the practice of American politics.

Federalist **Papers** A series of 85 political essays written by James Madison, Alexander Hamilton, and John Jay with the intent of persuading New Yorkers to ratify the proposed Constitution. They remain the single best source for understanding the justifications for the political institutions and processes the Constitution established.

Madison wrote 30 of the 85 essays, and his contributions make clear that the democratic principle he cherished most was liberty: the individual's right to choose reasonable goals and exercise the means to reach those goals. Madison also recognized that unchecked liberty could cause problems. Freedom to pursue individual goals and the means to achieve them meant there would be an uneven distribution of wealth; some people would be better at acquiring worldly goods than others.

Madison was very much attached to the notion of private property rights, which he saw as the cornerstone of political freedom. Yet he also reasoned that the unequal distribution of property could cause problems. In *Federalist* Number 10 (all essays in the *Federalist* are titled by the order of their original publication; see Appendix D for *Federalist* Number 10), he observed that societies naturally divide into various factions. He defined **faction** as

> a number of citizens, whether amounting to a majority or a minority of the whole, who are united and actuated by some common impulse of passion, or of interests, adverse to the right of other citizens, or to the permanent and aggregate interests of the community.

The causes of factions are numerous and can include religious and political differences. But Madison argued that

> the most common and durable source of factions has been the ... unequal distribution of property. Those who hold and those who are without property have ever formed distinct interests in society. Those who are creditors and those who are debtors, fall under a like discrimination.

Yet Madison did not divide the world into two simple classes, the rich and the poor. He viewed property as a distinguishing characteristic of a variety of groups, all willing to act in their own self-interest to the detriment of the interests of others.

The existence of factions sets up a difficult problem that is sometimes called the **Madisonian dilemma**: How can self-interested individuals administering strong governmental powers be prevented from using those powers to destroy the freedoms that government is supposed to protect? Madison and his contemporaries were under no illusions about the civic altruism of their fellow citizens. They assumed the rich would use political power to exploit the poor, and the poor to plunder the rich; those attached to one religious belief or partisan agenda would use power to force their beliefs on others, without regard for individual liberties.

To avoid these ugly consequences, Madison saw two options: either remove the cause of factions or control the effects. He rejected the first option as not only impossible but also repellent. The only way to remove the cause of factions was to eliminate individual differences and give everyone the same "common impulse of passion, or of interests." Individual differences were rooted in human nature, and nothing, least of all government, could make them disappear. So Madison turned to the other option—controlling the effect of factions. He believed minority factions posed little threat because the majority could protect its interest by voting them down. The more serious threats were factions that constituted a majority.

faction In James Madison's terms, "a number of citizens, whether amounting to a majority or a minority of the whole, who are united and actuated by some common impulse of passion, or of interests, adverse to the right of other citizens, or to the permanent and aggregate interests of the community."

Madisonian dilemma The problem of limiting self-interested individuals who administer stronger governmental powers from using those powers to destroy the freedoms that government is supposed to protect.

THINKING ANALYTICALLY

WHAT WERE THE MAJOR DEFICIENCIES IN THE ARTICLES OF CONFEDERATION, AND HOW DID THE DRAFT CONSTITUTION CORRECT THEM?

How can we think analytically about constitutions? Well, in general, analysis involves breaking a complex substance or phenomenon into its constituent parts to understand what they do and the relationships among them. We can use the three essential elements of a constitution discussed earlier to analyze the two U.S. constitutions and see how the Constitution of 1789 corrected deficiencies in the Articles of Confederation. Recall that the three essential elements of a constitution include: (1) the *functions* and powers of government, (2) the *structure*—that is, the institutions and mechanisms—of government, and (3) the *procedures* through which government carries out its powers and responsibilities. The Articles of Confederation were inadequate on all three dimensions. (The side-by-side comparison in Table 2.1 illustrates this.)

Notice first that the Articles and the Constitution have some important features in common. For example, both set up a representative government based on the notion of governance with the consent of the governed, and Congress is the principal representative institution in both. Governing with the consent of the governed is an essential aspect of democracy, but neither the Articles nor the Constitution established a true representative democracy. Representation in Congress under both systems is based on states rather than on individuals, which gives small states disproportionate power in violation of the democratic principle of political equality. Yet, while sovereign states are key components of both systems, the Constitution fundamentally altered the relationship between states and the national government.

The overarching weakness in the Articles of Confederation was the lack of centralized power adequate to govern a nation. We see a big difference right at the beginning. The Preamble is a broad statement of the origin, scope, and purpose of the new government. Under the Articles, the national government was created by the unanimous agreement of sovereign states. Under the Constitution, the national government is created by "the people of the United States of America." It is significant that this wording replaced an earlier draft that referred to "the people of the States of New Hampshire, Massachusetts, [etc.]," rather than to "the People of the United States" (Benton 1986, 161–168). The Supreme Court has interpreted the preamble to mean that the Constitution was created by the people, rather than an act of sovereign states as in the Articles (see *McCulloch v. Maryland*, 1819, and *Chisholm v. Georgia*, 1793).

The Constitution altered the functions of government by enhancing the major powers of the national government. Under the Articles, Congress had the authority to declare war and to raise and equip an army and navy, but it had to rely on state governments to supply the armed forces. Although Congress had the power to apportion taxes among the states, the states collected the taxes, and there was no power to compel states to pay their portion. The states and the national government both had the power to coin money, making the nation's money supply insecure. And Congress had no authority to regulate interstate commerce. The Constitution gives Congress sole authority to raise an army and navy, levy and collect taxes, coin money, and regulate interstate commerce.

The proposed expansion of national government powers raised concerns about protecting individual liberty. A major objection to the Constitution was the absence of a bill of rights. Because the Articles granted such limited power to the national government, there was little concern that it would threaten individual liberty. States retained the bulk of governmental power, and a number of state constitutions contained bills of rights. But these protections varied across states, and the national government had no authority to protect individual liberties from encroachment by the states. Although most explicit protections of individual rights in the Constitution were added later in the Bill of Rights, the delegates at the convention were concerned about limiting certain abuses of government power. The proposed Constitution included important limitations on governmental power—both state and national—that were absent in the Articles. For instance, the Constitution expressly prohibits passing ex post facto laws or bills of attainder, and it prohibits religious tests as a requirement to hold public office.

The Constitution also modified the structure of government. Perhaps the most significant structural change was replacing the confederation with a federal system (see Chapter 3). Although states retain sovereignty over their internal affairs in a federal system, the Constitution, federal laws, and treaties are the "supreme law of the land" and take precedence over state constitutions and laws if there is conflict (Article IV). Establishing separate executive and judicial institutions also overcame a key structural deficiency that aggravated the national government's ability to exercise what limited powers it had.

The Constitution made some important changes to governmental procedures as well. Representatives to Congress under the Articles were appointed by state legislatures, so representation was indirect. Under the Constitution, members of the House are directly elected, so ordinary citizens have direct control over part of the national government. But notice that the Articles set short terms (one year) for representatives, and they were subject to recall and term limits. Terms are longer under the Constitution (two years for House, six years for Senate), and there are no term limits or provisions for recall. Government decision making under the Articles required a supermajority—nine of 13 states, with each state having one vote. Although the Constitution requires a two-thirds majority for certain actions—overriding presidential vetoes, proposing amendments to the Constitution, expelling members of Congress, ratifying treaties in the Senate—most actions require only a simple majority in each chamber.

Discussion Questions

1. What are the deficiencies of the current constitution (with amendments)?
2. Why do you view them as deficiencies?
3. How would you correct them? Could they be corrected with a few amendments, or would we need to write a whole new constitution?

Madison realized that a majority of his fellow citizens were capable of quashing or persecuting a minority to serve their own interests. As Madison put it, the grand objective of the constitutional undertaking was "to secure the public good and private rights against the danger of such a faction, and at the same time to preserve the spirit and form of popular government."

To achieve this goal, Madison rejected morals or religion as an effective check on the self-interested appetites of humans. Since "men are not angels," society itself would have to take on the job of blunting and controlling the opinions and wishes of a majority that threatened private rights and the public good. He argued that this restraint could be best accomplished through a **republican form of government**, defined primarily as representative government.[3] The two primary goals of republican government are to create a government that governs with the consent of the governed, and at the same time limit a tyrannical majority from using the government power to infringe on personal liberty. Thus, a republic can be distinguished from a monarchy in that representatives who exercise power are responsible to the people either directly through election or indirectly through appointment by elected representatives. Yet it differs from pure or direct

republican form of government
A form of government in which the government operates with the consent of the governed through some type of representative institution.

---

[3] This discussion describes the Founders' view of republican government and does not refer to the platforms and principles of any contemporary political party that may use the name.

democracy in that representatives make decisions on behalf of the people rather than allowing the people to make binding decisions directly by majority rule.

In essence, Madison was making an argument for how the U.S. Constitution would uphold the core values of democracy. Popular sovereignty would be achieved through a representative form of government but with limits on those who hold power. Majority rule was accepted, but Madison placed special emphasis on the rights of the minority. Political freedom and political equality were tied to the notion of individual property rights and the right of like-minded people to pursue their own interests as they saw fit.

The Constitution includes a number of features designed to incorporate and uphold these basic principles, outlined in the following pages.

Written Constitution

The first notable feature of the U.S. Constitution is that it is a written document. Although we tend to take this for granted, at the time of America's founding, a written constitution was quite innovative. Before the American and French Revolutions, a constitution was conceived as something that evolved from a nation's history and practice. The notion that a constitution could be "drafted" was met with contempt in England. English writer Arthur Young ridiculed the American and French idea of a written constitution as "a new term they have adopted; and which they use as if a constitution was a pudding to be made by a recipe" (quoted in Pritchett 1976, 2; Zink 2009, 442).

A written constitution essentially reverses the traditional view. As political scientist C. Herman Pritchett explains, the Founders' view was that a

> constitution was a formal written instrument, a "social contract" drafted by a representative assembly and ratified by a special procedure for determining public assent. ... The constitution brought the government into existence and was the source of its authority. The government was the creature of the constitution. (1976, 2)

Recall that a constitution defines the fundamental rules and powers under which government operates. It also establishes the "rule of law" so that no one, not even the lawmakers, is above the law. The discussion and debate at the Constitutional Convention focused on creating a stronger central government that would protect individual liberty. James Wilson, one of the most influential delegates, offered a comprehensive theory of the written American Constitution. An analysis of Wilson's writings (Zink 2009) shows that he agreed that the primary purpose of the Constitution was to secure individual liberty based on natural rights. Yet Wilson recognized the inherent tension between the notion of inalienable natural rights and the need to establish a common identity in the new nation. He believed that the written Constitution would minimize this tension "by cultivating within each citizen a refined understanding of the complex interdependence of liberty and law" (Zink 2009, 448).

Governmental powers can be established and limited in ways other than through a written document. Great Britain, for example, is among the few nations that still has an unwritten constitution. Nonetheless, writing down the basic rules and processes of government for everyone to see is one way to establish limits on governmental power: If what government can and cannot do is written down on parchment, then it will be more apparent if government exceeds its legitimate authority. Yet words on parchment alone cannot prevent abuse of power. Traffic lights, for example, are generally effective in regulating the safe flow of traffic through a busy intersection. But just as a red light cannot prevent someone from running the light and crashing into crossing traffic, writing down powers and limitations on government cannot prevent self-interested individuals from abusing those powers to infringe on liberty. Thus, while the Founders provided a written constitution to create a stronger government that would also remain limited, they included a number of other features to protect liberty.

Representative Government

One of the most important republican principles incorporated into the American Constitution is representative government. This system operates with the consent of the governed without establishing a direct democracy. A representative system allows deliberation and refinement of public views by passing the views through a body of citizens whose knowledge of the public good is superior to that of the general populace. In addition, representative government permits effective popular rule over a much larger area than direct democracy does, bringing under its control a greater variety of people and interests than direct democracy. Representative democracy also makes it difficult for groups with diverse interests to band together into a majority that could threaten the basic rights of minorities or the general public.

Fragmentation of Power

Another way to protect liberty is to divide power among a number of different institutions and offices so that no single individual has absolute power (as under a monarchy), and no single class or faction is able to control government. The Constitution fragments power in two ways.

Separation of Powers

A major feature of the Constitution aimed at pitting leaders against one another is the principle of **separation of powers**. The concept is borrowed from the French political philosopher Charles Montesquieu, who argued that liberty is associated with the dispersal of power and tyranny with its concentration. As framed by the Constitution, separation of powers might more accurately be termed as separation of processes. Each of the three branches of government is authorized to exercise a

separation of powers The idea that each branch of government is authorized to carry out a separate part of the political process.

different type of governmental power: The legislature makes the laws, the executive implements them, and the judiciary interprets them.

These processes are not wholly independent of one another. Although each of the branches is assigned the major responsibility for one of these processes, each to some degree also participates in the principal activities of the others. For example, Congress has the primary responsibility for enacting legislation, but the president is authorized to recommend measures to Congress and to veto laws passed by that body. Similarly, Congress can decline to appropriate money to fund the operation of executive branch departments, and the Senate can affect the president's execution of laws by failing to approve his nominees for major positions in the executive branch. Congress can influence the courts' interpretations of the laws through its power to define their jurisdiction—that is, the kinds of cases they are entitled to hear.

The three branches can thus **check and balance** one another's influence and political power. One branch can assert and protect its own rights by withholding its support for the essential activities of another. But because the three branches are also dependent on one another, the system of shared processes also requires them to cooperate. In this fashion, the separation of processes and checks and balances complement each other to achieve the desired effect in the political system. The first prevents one branch from usurping the responsibilities of another; the second allows each branch to counteract the influence of the others. The result is a fragmentation of political power. Figure 2.1 illustrates the separation and overlap of processes among the branches of government.

The separation of powers calls for more than just separation of process; it also requires separation of personnel. People who serve in one branch of government are not allowed to concurrently serve in another branch. For example, an individual may not hold a congressional office and a position in the executive branch at the same time. Allowing such a practice would obviously permit power to concentrate.

Another aspect of the separation-of-powers doctrine reflected in the American system is the separation of **constituency**. That is, different groups with different interests choose the personnel of the three branches. As originally envisaged in the Constitution, the president would be selected by the electoral college, an independent group of electors chosen by means specified by each state legislature, none of whom could be a member of Congress. Senators also were chosen by state legislatures, whereas members of the House of Representatives were popularly elected from smaller political districts. Members of the national courts were to be nominated by the president and confirmed by the Senate, so that a single branch of government did not choose them. Once appointed and confirmed, judges serve for a term of good behavior, which amounts to life tenure. Thus, the personnel of the three branches have largely separate and independent bases of political support and power.

Federalism

Madison conceived of another check on the majority, which we examine in detail in the next chapter. **Federalism** is the constitutional division of powers between

check and balance The idea that each branch of the federal government should assert and protect its own rights but must also cooperate with the other branches. Each branch is to serve as a limit on the others' powers, balancing the overall distribution of power.

constituency The group of people served by an elected official or branch of government.

federalism A political system in which regional governments share power with a central or national government, but each level of government has legal powers that are independent of the other. This division of power between the national and state governments attempts to balance power by giving independent sources of authority to each and allowing one level of government to serve as a check on the other.

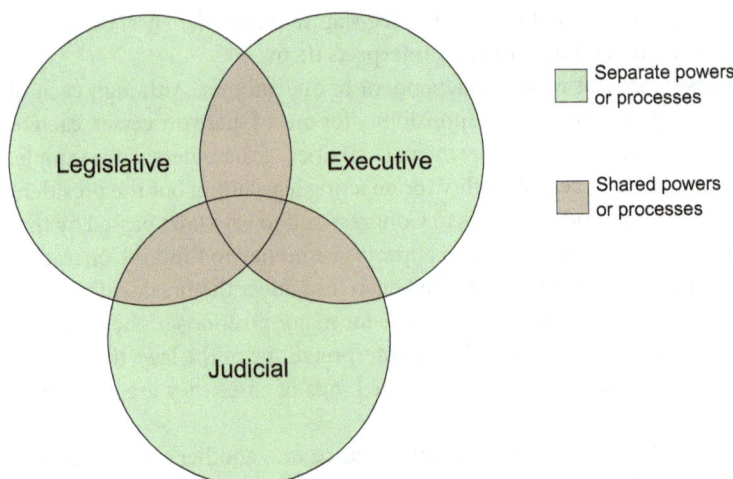

FIGURE 2.1 Separation and Overlap of Government Powers

the national government and the states. In *Federalist* Number 10, Madison argues that such a division of powers limits the threat of faction: "the influence of factious leaders may kindle a flame within the particular states, but they will be unable to spread a conflagration through the other states."

Madison's system for checking the evils of factionalism was to create a series of dikes to interfere with the free flow of majority will. First, majority interests are filtered by the actions of their elected representatives, who are expected to have more refined views of the public good than the voters themselves. Second, the wishes of the majority are diluted because republicanism allows government to take in a wide variety of interests. And finally, the majority will is directed into many channels by the joint effects of federalism and the separation of powers. Madison wrote in *Federalist* Number 51,

> In the compound republic of America, the power surrendered by the people is first divided between two distinct governments, and then the portion allotted to each subdivided among distinct and separate governments. Hence a double security arises to the rights of the people. The different governments will control each other, at the same time that each will be controlled by itself.

Grasping the importance of this idea is fundamental to understanding the American political system. The system was designed to make it difficult for any faction, even a majority, to wield broad political power. The Constitution essentially divides the various elements of sovereignty, divides them again, and then parcels off the pieces to different institutional actors governed by different processes and characterized by different constraints. This means that, by design, it will be enormously difficult for the government to do anything opposed by even a relatively small portion of the electorate. American government is often slow, conflict-riddled, and able to produce only brokered compromises because it was designed to be exactly that way. The idea is to make it so difficult to bring together all those pieces the Constitution carefully distributes that government is likely to take action only in those rare circumstances when the public will and the public good are so unified as to be indistinguishable.

Mixed Government

There is good reason to believe that the Founders provided separate constituencies not only to preserve the independence of the different branches of the national government but also because they wanted them to represent different social and economic interests. The idea of **mixed government** is that it should represent both property and the number of people. The Constitution did not mandate property qualifications for officeholders or voters, but it is significant that originally only the House of Representatives was popularly elected. Direct election of senators was not authorized until adoption of the Seventeenth Amendment in 1913.

Other offices were more insulated from popular influence. As Figure 2.2 illustrates, members of the Senate were two steps, the president was three steps, and

mixed government The idea that government should represent both property and the number of people.

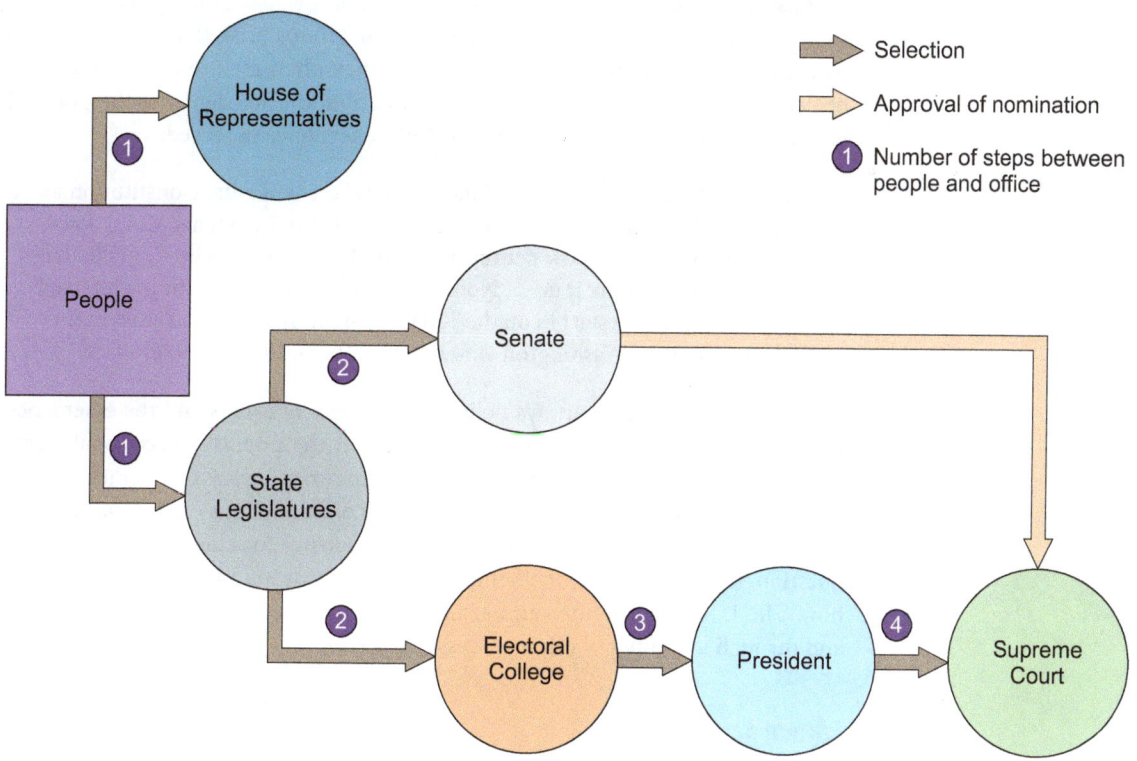

FIGURE 2.2 **Relationship Between the People and the Selection of Officeholders Under the Original Constitution**

the Supreme Court was four steps removed from the direct control of the people. Furthermore, the longer terms of senators (six years), the president (four years), and Supreme Court members (life) would make them less subject to public pressures than members of the House of Representatives. Because fewer people were chosen for these three political bodies, they would be more prestigious than the lower house of the national legislature. This greater prestige in turn would attract better-qualified people to these bodies, and because property ownership was considered a reflection of natural ability, the individuals chosen would be those of economic substance from the upper social classes. Thus, in all probability the Founders expected the House of Representatives to represent the interests of the common people who owned no private property of consequence. The Senate—with its smaller, more prestigious membership, insulated from popular control by its longer terms of office and (then) indirect method of selection—would constitute the more aristocratic division of the legislature.

CHANGING THE AMERICAN CONSTITUTION

A constitution necessarily reflects the interests and values of the groups responsible for its original formulation. In time, new groups arise that are dissatisfied with the existing distribution of values, and they often seek to rewrite the rules of democratic governance to change this distribution. Recognizing the political motivations of such changes, humorist Will Rogers once observed,

> See where there is a bill up in Congress now to change the Constitution all around … It seems the men who drew up this thing years ago didn't know much and we are just now getting a bunch of real fellows who can take that old parchment and fix it up … Now when they get the Constitution all fixed up they are going to start in on the Ten Commandments, just as soon as they find somebody in Washington who has read them. (Rogers 1974, 14)

Constitutional change is always political. The press of events and the emergence of different attitudes on the part of leaders and the populace occasionally create a need to alter a nation's fundamental framework. Every democratic system must provide a mechanism to achieve such accommodations or run the risk that frustrated individuals and groups will turn to violence to achieve their goals. The question, therefore, is not whether a democratic constitution will be changed, but how. The U.S. Constitution can be changed through a formal amending process and through a number of other processes as well.

Formal Amendments

One important method of changing the Constitution is the process of formal amendment. This consists of two distinct stages: (1) the proposal of the amendment, and (2) the ratification of the amendment. The Constitution provides two options for each stage.

The two methods of proposing amendments are: a two-thirds vote in both houses of Congress, and a national convention called by Congress at the request of two-thirds of the states (34 of the 50 states). To date, the only method used to propose any amendment is the first, a two-thirds vote in Congress.[4] The authority to propose amendments under this method rests exclusively with Congress; the president has neither the responsibility to sign amendments nor the authority to veto them. But the president is not prohibited from politically supporting or opposing proposed amendments. During his administration, for example, President Clinton actively lobbied members of Congress to defeat a balanced budget amendment and urged them to propose an amendment granting Washington, DC, full representation in Congress.

Since ratification of the Constitution in 1789, there have been more than 400 applications from states to call a convention to propose amendments. More than 90 percent of all requests were made in the last half of the twentieth century, motivated almost exclusively by conservatives outraged by liberal Supreme Court decisions on such issues as busing to achieve integration of public schools, reapportionment of congressional districts, school prayer, and abortion. Usually, only a handful of state legislatures pass resolutions requesting a convention. Given the difficulties of coordinating political action across a large number of state legislatures, it is perhaps not surprising that Congress has proposed all of the amendments to date. Some issues, however, have come close to mustering requests from the required number of states. One is the movement to call a convention to propose an amendment requiring a balanced federal budget. Indiana was the first state to call for a convention on a balanced budget amendment in 1957. Subsequently, 31 other states submitted similar applications, just three states short of the 34 required (Weber and Perry 1989).

Since the convention method has never been used, no one is really sure how this process would work. Do two-thirds of the state legislatures have to pass resolutions with exactly the same wording, or are similar resolutions on the same issue sufficient? Is there a time limit on how long it can take for two-thirds of the states to request a convention? If a convention is called, how many delegates will attend the convention, and how will they be apportioned among the states? How will delegates be selected? Will they be popularly elected, appointed by state legislatures, or selected by state governors? Will the convention require a simple majority or a supermajority (two-thirds or three-fourths) to propose amendments? Is the convention limited to proposing the amendment for which it was called, or can delegates propose additional amendments—or perhaps even become a runaway convention and rewrite the Constitution entirely, as happened in 1787?

Congress has the constitutional authority to resolve these issues, and the answers will inevitably involve political choices, not strictly legal or constitutional

---

[4] The requirement is two-thirds of those present and voting, not two-thirds of the chamber's entire membership. Since amendments typically involve very important issues, however, few members miss these votes.

President Richard Nixon signs the Twenty-Sixth Amendment, which guarantees 18-year-olds the right to vote, July 5, 1971.

© Charles Tasnadi/AP Photo

ones. Although the convention method of proposing amendments has never been used, it is important because the Constitution provides states with the means to initiate the formal amending process. Even if an effort falls short, if the number of states calling for a convention nears the required two-thirds mark, Congress may feel pressure to act. For example, Congress proposed the amendment to allow for the direct election of senators in response to the pressure of states requesting a convention. Moreover, such calls have been instrumental in raising public consciousness about issues and have increased the pressure on politicians to propose remedies other than constitutional amendments. Yet Congress retains considerable authority to determine exactly how a convention would be called and how it would operate. Thus, proposing amendments is ultimately a political process, and Congress plays a key role regardless of the method used.

Ratification is also a political process, and states determine whether a proposed amendment will be ratified. After an amendment has been proposed, it must be ratified by three-fourths of states (38 of the 50 states) before it can become part of the Constitution. The Constitution provides two ways for states to ratify amendments: by votes of state legislatures, and by conventions held in the states. Congress specifies which ratification method is to be used. The only amendment ratified by state conventions was the Twenty-First (repeal of prohibition). There was concern that forces favoring prohibition controlled key leadership positions in state legislatures and might be able to thwart popular support for repeal. Congress specified state conventions, perhaps in the hope that they would more accurately reflect popular sentiment.

Most successful amendments have been ratified within about two years of being proposed—the median number of months is 25 (see Table 2.2). Although three amendments lingered substantially longer, in most cases if there is not sufficient support in the states to ratify within two or three years, the amendment is likely to die. The Constitution does not specify a time limit for states to act on proposed amendments. Beginning with the Eighteenth Amendment (proposed in 1917), Congress instituted a seven-year deadline on ratification.[5] Amendments proposed

---

5 Initially, Congress placed the time limit in the body of the amendment. With the proposal of the Twenty-Third Amendment in 1960, the deadline was placed in a separate submission resolution. The importance of the change is that resolutions require only a simple majority to be passed because they are not a formal part of the amendment. Thus, when the seven-year limit on the Equal Rights Amendment (proposed in 1971) was about to expire, Congress extended it for three more years on a simple majority vote. In 1978, when Congress proposed an amendment to treat Washington, DC, as if it were a state for purposes of representation, it reverted to the practice of placing the time limit in the body of the amendment.

TABLE 2.2 LENGTH OF TIME BETWEEN CONGRESSIONAL APPROVAL AND ACTUAL RATIFICATION OF THE 27 AMENDMENTS TO THE U.S. CONSTITUTION

Amendment		Time Required for Ratification	Year Ratified
I–X	Bill of Rights	26.5 months	1791
XI	Lawsuits against states	11 months	1795
XII	Presidential elections	6.5 months	1804
XIII	Abolition of slavery	10 months	1865
XIV	Civil rights	25 months	1868
XV	Suffrage for all races	11 months	1870
XVI	Income tax	42.5 months	1913
XVII	Senatorial elections	11 months	1913
XVIII	Prohibition	13 months	1919
XIX	Women's suffrage	14 months	1920
XX	Terms of office	11 months	1933
XXI	Repeal of prohibition	9.5 months	1933
XXII	Limit on presidential terms	47 months	1951
XXIII	Washington, DC, vote	9 months	1961
XXIV	Abolition of poll taxes	16 months	1964
XXV	Presidential succession	22 months	1967
XXVI	Eighteen-year-old suffrage	3 months	1971
XXVII	Congressional salaries	2,438 months	1992
Median		**25 months**	

Sources: Congressional Research Service, *The Constitution of the United States: Analysis and Interpretation* (Washington, DC: U.S. Government Printing office, 1973), 23–44 (92d cong., 2d sess., S. Doc. 92–82); *Congressional Quarterly Weekly Report* (1992), 1423. Table adapted from Harold W. Stanley and Richard G. Niemi, *Vital Statistics on American Politics 1999–2000* (Washington, DC: CQ Press, 2000), 303.

before 1917 had no time limits; it was generally assumed that these proposals died if the states did not act within a reasonable time so that the decision would reflect a "contemporaneous consensus."

The absence of a deadline presented an interesting political dilemma in one case. Reacting to a political furor over congressional pay hikes in the 1990s, Michigan and New Jersey dusted off an old proposal and became the thirty-eighth and thirty-ninth states to approve the Twenty-Seventh Amendment, which requires an election to intervene before a congressional pay raise can take effect. This amendment was originally submitted to the states along with others that became the Bill of Rights. Its May 7, 1992, ratification came 203 years after its proposal!

Though it is highly unlikely, there are four proposals with no time limit that theoretically could be ratified. These proposals concerned apportionment of U.S. representatives, the issue of titles of nobility for citizens, slavery, and child labor. The first of these was one of 12 proposals submitted by the First Congress. It dealt with apportionment of House districts, providing one representative for every 30,000 people. When the House grew to 100 members, Congress would regulate the proportion until the size reached 200 members, at which time Congress could increase the size beyond 200 so that each representative would represent no more than 50,000 people. To date, only 12 states have ratified the proposal; the last recorded action was ratification by Connecticut and Georgia in 1939. Today, membership in the House is capped at 435 by a statute passed by Congress. As of 2018, each member represents a district containing more than 700,000 people. If the proposed limit of 50,000 constituents per member of Congress were followed, the House would need roughly 6,500 members to represent a population of close to 325 million.

Another amendment proposed in 1810 without a time limit would have denationalized any U.S. citizen who accepted honors or titles of nobility without prior congressional approval. Twelve states ratified this amendment, one short of the 13 required at the time it was submitted. As more states were admitted to the Union, the number required to validate the amendment increased: Louisiana became the eighteenth state in 1812, increasing the required number to 14. The issue has subsequently been dealt with by statute.

Congress proposed another constitutional amendment with no time limit on March 2, 1861. Proposed as a gesture of compromise in an effort to avert the secession of southern states, it stated that no constitutional amendments could authorize Congress to interfere with state laws regarding slavery. Only three states ratified it. It was rendered moot by the conclusion of the Civil War and the ratification of the Thirteenth Amendment abolishing slavery.

The last amendment with no time limit was proposed on June 2, 1924. It would have given Congress power to regulate child labor. Although Congress had established the practice of attaching time limits in 1917, it did not attach a time limit to this proposal. Only 28 states have ratified the proposal. The ratification process provoked controversy that ended up in the Supreme Court when the state of Kansas first rejected the amendment in 1925 but then reconsidered and ratified it 12 years later. In the case of *Coleman v. Miller* (1939), the Supreme Court held that Congress has the ultimate authority to decide whether there will be a time limit and whether the requisite number of states has properly ratified a proposed amendment. Both state and federal statutes now regulate child labor.

In addition, two proposals failed when the time limit set by Congress expired. One of these, known as the Equal Rights Amendment (ERA), was submitted to the states in 1972 with a seven-year time limit. The core provision was a mere 22 words: "Equality of rights under the law shall not be denied by the United States or by any State on account of sex." The proposal had wide initial support, and 22 of the necessary 38 states ratified it in the first year after it was proposed. But momentum stalled as opponents organized, and only 13 more states had ratified the amendment when the time limit expired in 1979, three short of the necessary number. Some states that had ratified the amendment passed resolutions rescinding their earlier action, although given the ruling in *Coleman v. Miller*, it is not clear that states may retract ratification. Just as time was about to expire, Congress extended the limit to 1982, but no additional states ratified the proposal.

The final proposal that failed to gain support from 38 states concerned representation for Washington, DC. Since the citizens of Washington, DC, are not part of any state, they have no voting representatives in Congress. The House allows the citizens of the nation's capital to send a nonvoting delegate, but they have neither voice nor vote in the Senate. The amendment proposed in 1978 would have treated the District of Columbia as if it were a state for purposes of representation and in voting for president and vice president. This means that the residents would have had two senators, at least one representative, and the same number of electoral votes as states with similar populations. When the time limit expired in 1985, only a handful of states had ratified the amendment. Congress had inserted the time limit in the amendment itself, rather than putting it in a separate transmittal resolution, as was done with the ERA. Any extension of the time, therefore, would require a two-thirds vote.

James Madison was primarily responsible for the first 10 amendments (Klarman 2016, 566–590). As a member of the First Congress, he became the primary advocate and author of a set of proposed amendments designed to address Anti-Federalist criticisms of the Constitution. A number of these objections focused on the Constitution's lack of guarantees for the individual of political freedom and political equity, and in drafting a set of amendments Madison deliberately sought to address those concerns. Accordingly, we generally refer to these first 10 amendments as the Bill of Rights because most are concerned with **civil liberties**—protecting individuals against arbitrary government action. Many of the subsequent amendments revolve around the central democratic principle of equality. The Thirteenth, Fourteenth, and Fifteenth Amendments relate to race; the Nineteenth, Twenty-Third, Twenty-Fourth, and Twenty-Sixth govern the voting rights of women, residents of the District of Columbia, people who live in jurisdictions where a poll tax is levied, and citizens between the ages of 18 and 21. These amendments were designed to safeguard disadvantaged groups' access to the political process and the social and economic life of the United States. Unlike the Bill of Rights that originally applied only to the federal government, these amendments primarily affect the states.

The Seventeenth and Twenty-Second Amendments also relate to political participation, but they deal with the suffrage rights of all voters, not particular groups. The Seventeenth Amendment provides for direct election of senators, thus allowing all voters to choose members of the upper house of the national legislature. The Twenty-Second Amendment limits the length of presidential terms by preventing voters from choosing the same person more than twice. The two amendments are based on somewhat different assumptions about human capacities: The Seventeenth expresses faith in the electorate's ability to choose good senators; the Twenty-Second reflects a fear that voters may fall victim to the entreaties of a demagogue.

Four amendments—the Eleventh, Twelfth, Twentieth, and Twenty-Fifth—bear no particular imprint of group influence or political philosophy. Rather, these amendments relate to changes brought about by the press of particular historical events, and they primarily deal with the structure and procedures of government. For example, the Twelfth Amendment specifies that members of the electoral

civil liberties The freedoms and protections against arbitrary governmental actions given to the people in a democratic society.

college must cast separate ballots for president and vice president; this amendment was a direct result of the election of 1800, in which Thomas Jefferson and Aaron Burr—the presidential and vice presidential candidates of the same party—received the same number of electoral votes. The Twentieth Amendment reduces the time between the election and inauguration of the president and vice president.

Two other amendments altered powers and procedures of the national government. The Sixteenth allows the federal government to levy an income tax, and as already discussed, the Twenty-Seventh limits the authority of members of Congress to give themselves a pay raise by requiring an election to intervene before the raise can go into effect. The remaining two amendments—the Eighteenth establishing prohibition of alcohol and Twenty-First repealing it—resulted in no net change.

Although amendments have produced important changes in the Constitution, only 27 amendments have made it past the hurdles embedded in the process, and of these, 10 came at once, and two counteract each other. Thus, in more than two centuries, the Constitution has undergone lasting formal alteration on only 15 occasions. But formal amendments to the Constitution are responsible for only a portion of the vast changes that have occurred in the functions, procedures, and structure of the American political system over this period. Other constitutional changes have been a result of other processes—specifically, of custom and usage and of interpretation by officials of the three branches of the national government.

Constitutional Change Through Custom and Usage

Constitutional change through **custom and usage** occurs when practices and institutions not mentioned in the written document evolve in response to political needs and alter the structure, functions, or procedures of the political system. For example, political parties as we understand them are not mentioned at all in the Constitution. Nonetheless, political parties developed soon after ratification in response to the demands of electoral politics. Although parties are not government institutions, they have fundamentally altered the structure and procedures of government. For example, members of Congress are chosen in partisan elections, and Congress itself is organized along party lines.

Political parties have also changed the way the electoral college operates. The Founders created the electoral college in part because they did not trust ordinary citizens to exercise sound judgment in choosing a president. The Constitution mandates that "each state shall appoint, in such manner as the Legislature thereof may direct," a number of electors equal to its number of senators and representatives (Article II, Section 1). Each state originally appointed one slate of electors. As political parties developed, they began nominating slates of partisan electors, and the popular vote in a state now determines which party's electors cast that state's electoral votes for president. Thus, although the constitutional provisions governing the electoral college have not been significantly altered by formal amendment,[6]

custom and usage The term used to describe constitutional change that occurs when practices and institutions not specifically mentioned in the Constitution evolve in response to political needs and alter the structure, functions, or procedures of the political system.

---

6 The Twelfth Amendment specified that electors were to cast separate votes for president and vice president, but this provision did not change the goal of removing selection of the president from direct popular control.

the operation of the electoral college has changed significantly from the original intent of the Founders; it has become more democratic through a process of custom and usage.

Executive Interpretation

The Constitution contains three types of powers. **Enumerated powers** are powers explicitly granted to government or to a particular institution. Article I, Section 8, for example, lists the powers of Congress (power to declare war, raise an army and navy, coin money, regulate interstate commerce, and so on); Article II enumerates specific powers of the chief executive (the power of commander in chief of the army and navy, to make treaties with the advice and consent of the Senate, to see that the laws are faithfully executed, to receive ambassadors, and so forth). **Implied powers** are not formally specified by the Constitution but rather inferred from the powers that are formally specified. Implied powers flow from the "necessary and proper" clause in Article I, Section 8, which empowers Congress to make other laws that are "necessary and proper for carrying into Execution … all other Powers vested by this Constitution in the Government of the United States."

Inherent powers (or prerogative powers) are not derived from either enumerated or implied powers but are those that are essential to the functioning of government or a particular office. Federal courts, for example, issue fines and incarceration for contempt of court on the grounds that courts cannot perform their judicial functions without the ability to control courtroom misbehavior. Similarly, presidents periodically claim certain inherent powers as chief executive or commander in chief. In 2006, President George W. Bush authorized the National Security Agency (NSA) to engage in electronic eavesdropping on American citizens without a warrant, although warrants are required by the Foreign Intelligence Surveillance Act (FISA). President Bush argued that as commander in chief, he had the inherent power to protect America from terrorist attacks and that Congress does not have the authority to limit the president's espionage power during wartime.

Although the formal powers of the president have changed little since George Washington first exercised them, the political powers of the presidency have expanded significantly through executive interpretation. Such interpretation derives mainly from the concept of inherent or prerogative powers; presidents have claimed them as an essential characteristic of the executive office. An early example of executive interpretation occurred when George Washington interpreted the power to "receive ambassadors and other public ministers" to mean that the president also had the authority to recognize foreign governments. This interpretation significantly expanded presidential powers beyond those specifically enumerated. Perhaps the best-known example is **executive privilege**, the power of the president to withhold confidential communications from Congress and the courts if disclosure would violate separation of powers or interfere with the president's ability to discharge the powers and duties of the executive branch. For example, in the early years of the George W. Bush administration, some members

enumerated powers The powers specifically listed in the Constitution as belonging to the national government.

implied powers Those powers belonging to the national government that are suggested in the Constitution's "necessary and proper" clause.

inherent powers (prerogative powers) Powers that are not listed or implied by the Constitution but that rather have been claimed as essential to the functioning of government or a particular office.

executive privilege An inherent power of the president to withhold confidential communications from Congress and the courts if disclosure would violate separation of powers or interfere with the president's ability to discharge the powers and duties of the executive branch.

of Congress wanted to know who was meeting with Vice President Cheney to help develop national energy policy. President Bush refused to provide this information, arguing that getting candid advice required protecting the confidentiality of those actually tapped to give it. Another example is the president's ability to dismiss high-ranking members of the executive branch. There is nothing in the Constitution about the procedure for removing executive branch officials. Does the president have the power to do this unilaterally as part of his power as chief executive, or is the Senate's approval also required? That issue surfaced as a factor in the impeachment action against President Andrew Johnson shortly after the Civil War and eventually led to a number of court decisions after Presidents Woodrow Wilson and Franklin Roosevelt also removed key executive officials from their positions.

Legislative Interpretation

Each time Congress enacts legislation, it must interpret the Constitution. Some laws passed by Congress are so far-reaching that they fundamentally alter the responsibility and functions of the government. For example, the Social Security Act of 1935 involved the federal government in basic social welfare services, and the Employment Act of 1946 gave the national government responsibility to use its power to promote economic prosperity and full employment. Both laws were highly controversial when first enacted, and opponents argued that they were beyond the constitutional scope of government. Congress's interpretation prevailed. Today, the government's responsibility in these areas is generally accepted.

Judicial Interpretation

Judicial review refers to the power of courts to declare the acts and actions of legislatures and executives unconstitutional. It is an extraordinary power that seems to challenge the democratic principle of majority rule. And nowhere does the Constitution explicitly grant courts the authority to nullify the actions of elected officials. In a prime example of constitutional change through judicial interpretation, the Supreme Court itself claimed the power of judicial review in the case of *Marbury v. Madison* (1803), which is discussed in detail in Chapter 15.

It is hard to overstate the importance of judicial interpretation in the American political process. For example, Supreme Court interpretations of the "equal protection of the laws" clause of the Fourteenth Amendment altered the composition of both the House of Representatives and state legislatures, and revolutionized race relations in this nation. The words remain unchanged, but judicial interpretation changed what the words mean.

judicial review The power to review decisions of the lower courts and to determine the constitutionality of laws and actions of public officials.

CHAPTER TWO
Top 10 Takeaway Points

1. A constitution establishes the basic principles on which government operates by defining (1) the *functions* and powers of government, (2) the *structure*—that is, the institutions and mechanisms—of government, and (3) the *procedures* through which government carries its powers and responsibilities. In defining these basic principles, constitutions establish a set of legal relationships between the leaders and the led by determining the rules for accessing and exercising political power.

2. The Declaration of Independence, the Articles of Confederation, and state constitutions provided the philosophical foundations on which the Constitution is based. In these historical antecedents is a commitment to popular sovereignty through representative government, limited powers for the central government, and dominant legislatures.

3. The major deficiency of the Articles of Confederation, the first constitution of the United States, was the central government's lack of sufficient power to govern. Civil unrest and the inability of the national government to respond to economic priorities fueled a movement to create a stronger national government. Those who favored a new constitution giving more power to the national government were called Federalists; those opposed were known as Anti-Federalists.

4. In February 1787, the Continental Congress called on the states to send delegates to a convention in Philadelphia for the purpose of amending the Articles of Confederation. Although there was considerable support in the general populace for the Anti-Federalists' opposition to a strong central government, few Anti-Federalists attended the convention.

5. Federalists, who agreed that the national government should be more powerful, dominated the convention. The delegates quickly abandoned the charge to revise the Articles of Confederation and decided to write a new constitution.

6. Although the Federalists who dominated the convention favored a stronger central government, they also wanted a limited government that would protect natural rights. These conflicting goals posed what is called the Madisonian dilemma (because of James Madison's role in framing the issue): How can self-interested individuals administering strong governmental powers be prevented from using those powers to destroy the freedoms that government is supposed to protect?

7. The Constitution corrected the major deficiencies in the structure, function, and procedures of government under the Articles of Confederation. The stronger central government it created achieved popular sovereignty through representative government, while limiting the power of government to infringe on individual liberty, by fragmenting governmental power.

8. Although the Constitution created a stronger national government, power was divided among three coequal branches. The legislative, executive, and judicial branches each had some ability to check abuses of power by the other branches.

9. Power was also decentralized through creation of a federal system in which the national government was granted limited powers and states retained sovereignty in other jurisdictions. The Constitution had to be approved by nine states to be ratified. The ratification battle was a bruising political contest. The Federalists just managed to pull out majorities in several key states. Rhode Island was the last state to ratify in May 1790, and the Constitution was officially ratified and took force in May 1791.

10. There are several ways to change the Constitution. In addition to changes by formal amendment, the Constitution has been changed by custom and usage and through legislative, executive, and judicial interpretation.

CHAPTER TWO
Key Terms and Cases

Anti-Federalists, 47
Articles of Confederation, 44
bicameral, 52
check and balance, 63
civil liberties, 71
Connecticut Compromise (Great Compromise), 52
constituency, 63
constitution, 42
custom and usage, 72
Declaration of Independence, 43
enumerated powers, 73
executive privilege, 73
faction, 58
federalism, 63
Federalist Papers, 57
Federalists, 47
implied powers, 73
inherent powers (prerogative powers), 73
judicial review, 74
Madisonian dilemma, 58
mixed government, 65
New Jersey plan, 52
republican form of government, 60
separation of powers, 62
Shays' Rebellion, 49
unicameral, 44
Virginia plan, 51

3 FEDERALISM

KEY QUESTIONS

Why does the United States use a federal system to divide power between different levels of government?

What are the advantages and disadvantages of federalism?

How are state–federal relations changing?

© Robert F. Bukaty/AP Photo

GREGG ABBOTT'S job as Texas' attorney general was pretty simple: "I go into the office, I sue the federal government and I go home" (Owen 2013). He wasn't kidding. As the Lone Star State's chief lawyer, he sued President Barack Obama's administration early and often. During the eight years of the Obama presidency, the state of Texas filed no fewer than 48 law suits, 31 of them coming on Abbott's watch as attorney general (Satija 2017). Abbott stopped regularly suing the federal government only when he was elected governor in 2015.

Abbott, like a number of other Republican state attorneys general, made no secret that they mounted legal campaigns against the federal government because they didn't like a range of policies being pursued by the Obama administration. The GOP enthusiasm for hauling the federal government into court cooled when a fellow Republican, Donald J. Trump, was elected president in 2016. The policies of the Trump administration, however, lit a fire under Democratic state attorneys general who were plotting to adopt the Republican strategy of suing the federal government early and often within days of Trump's inauguration (Burns 2017).

What's going here? Why are some states suing the federal government with such regularity? And why does that set of states shift with whoever is in the White House? The short answer to these questions is that what the federal government wants is often very different from what a particular state government wants. The more liberal-leaning Obama administration backed regulations and policies that supported its progressive preferences on issues like clean energy and expanding Medicaid. Those policies and regulations were often very unpopular in conservative states like Texas. In contrast, the Trump administration's support for things like refugee bans and immigration restrictions often had high levels of support in those states, but ran into a wall of opposition in more liberal-leaning states like Washington and California.

Those sorts of political differences can lead to heated legal conflict between state and federal governments because both sets of government are sovereign. State governments are not the underlings of the federal government, but coequals who draw much of their power from their own citizens and constitutions. The upshot of this political arrangement is that whatever domestic policies are being pursued by the federal government, they are likely to run into headwinds in at least some states. As a general rule, states want to be free to make their own policies and not be forced to follow the federal government's lead. Those differences can be strong enough that states, quite literally, will make a federal case out of them.

At the heart of these conflicts is a simple question: Who has the power to do what, and who has to pay for it? Indeed, this is the fundamental question of American federalism. In a real sense, the debate about the appropriate roles of state and national governments that lay at the heart of the struggle between Federalists and Anti-Federalists has never been fully resolved. Defining those roles is at the center of many important political struggles. States still seek to protect their independence from one another and from federal encroachment, and the federal government still struggles to provide the regulatory uniformity that characterizes a nation-state.

Conservatives and liberals take one side or the other of the issue, depending on what is at stake. Some conservatives often echo Anti-Federalist arguments championing states' rights—this is clearly what happened when Abbott and his colleagues in other states sued to stop the federal government implementing regulations in areas such as renewable energy and Medicaid expansion. Yet support or opposition for federal or state government primacy in a particular policy arena is often based more on the policy at hand than on any consistent commitment to state rights or national government supremacy. On some issues—medical marijuana, for example—the same conservatives are quick to support sweeping legal intervention by the federal government. Similarly, liberals turn to the federal government to provide uniform solutions to important issues such as civil rights, but prefer leaving other issues, such as medical marijuana, with the states.

An important prerequisite to making analytical sense of the complicated nature of American politics is understanding the division of power between different levels of government. This chapter provides a basic grounding in federalism by outlining the concept of federalism and its relation to other ways of distributing governmental power, detailing the federal system adopted in the United States, tracing the evolution of state–federal relationships, and examining the consequences of these arrangements.

THE CONCEPT OF FEDERALISM IN CONTEXT: CONFEDERAL, UNITARY, AND FEDERAL SYSTEMS

All political systems divide and delegate power. What distinguishes one system from another is where sovereignty resides. In Chapter 1 we identified three forms of government—autocracy, oligarchy, and democracy—based on whether one, few, or many exercise power. Another way to classify governments is based on *how* sovereignty is divided between a central (national) government and regional (state) governments. This approach identifies three distinct types of political systems: confederal, unitary, and federal.

Confederation

In a **confederation**, regional (state) governments are sovereign, and the central (national) government is created by—and can exercise only the authority granted to it by—unanimous agreement of regional governments. Powers of the weak central government extend exclusively to foreign policy or issues confronting the entire collection of states, and the national government has no direct power over the citizens of the sovereign states. Two other features typically associated with a confederation include the right of a component government to withdraw from the larger union and a requirement that all members of the union consent to any change in the division of powers between the two levels of government. Figure 3.1 illustrates relationships in a confederation.

A familiar example of a confederal system is the United States under the Articles of Confederation. The original Congress could not exercise direct control over people or states to enforce its authority. It had to rely on state governments to provide money and troops for the Revolutionary War, and it needed state courts to enforce its laws. A modern-day example of a confederation is the United Nations (UN). In this body, 193 nation-states—such as the United States, China, Mexico, and Kenya—are the component governments, and the UN itself is the central political unit. Member nation-states remain sovereign, and the UN exercises only those powers granted to it by its members: It depends on voluntary contributions of money and military forces for its operations, it cannot force its provisions on individual members, and nations are free to withdraw from it at any time.

confederation A political system in which the central government receives no direct grant of power from the people and can exercise only the power granted to it by the regional governments.

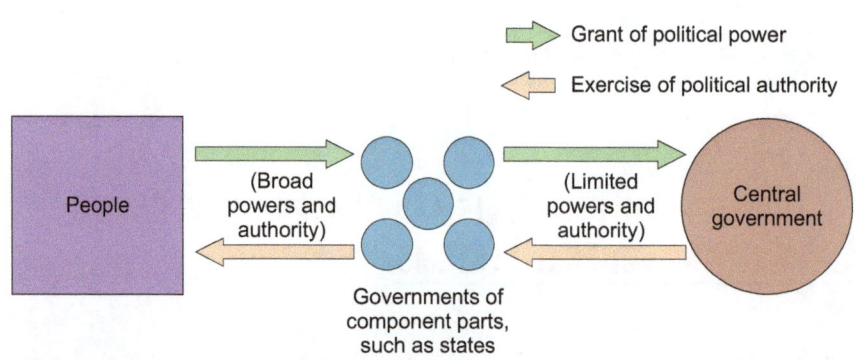

FIGURE 3.1 Confederation

Unitary Government

In a **unitary system**, sovereignty resides wholly in the central government. The central government may (and usually does) create regional governments, but these local units can exercise only the powers delegated and authorized by the central government (Figure 3.2). The central government retains the most extensive and important powers, and it may reduce or take back any powers it grants to the lower political units.

Most countries have unitary governments. An example of a unitary relationship in the United States is the relationship between every state government and its local governments. In this case, the state (central) government is sovereign over its villages, cities, counties, and school districts. These local governments exercise only the powers given to them by the state government, and they do not have the power to block any changes in state–local relationships, nor can they legally withdraw from the jurisdiction of a state government.

Federalism

Standing somewhere between the confederate and unitary options is **federalism**, a system in which central and regional governments share sovereignty. Each level of government has its own jurisdiction and set of responsibilities. In the American system, for example, neither the national government nor any individual state is dependent on the other for its political power. The same is true of other federal systems. Provinces in Canada, cantons in Sweden, and *Länder* in Germany have power bases independent of their national governments. Figure 3.3 illustrates federal relationships.

The two essential features of a federal system are (1) that each level of government is granted power directly by the Constitution and (2) that each level possesses and exercises some powers that are legally independent of the other. A federal system has two other important characteristics. First, both levels of government must participate in any decision to change the division of powers between them.

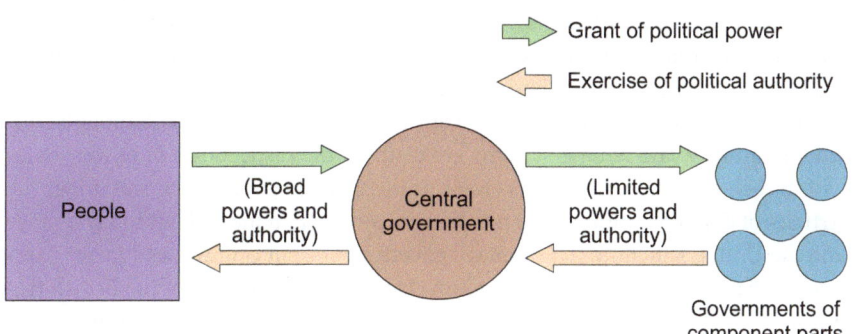

FIGURE 3.2 Unitary System

unitary system A political system in which the power is concentrated in the national government, and the regional governments can exercise only those powers granted them by the central government.

federalism A political system in which regional governments share power with a central or national government, but each level of government has legal powers that are independent of the other. This division of power between the national and state governments attempts to balance power by giving independent sources of authority to each and allowing one level of government to serve as a check on the other.

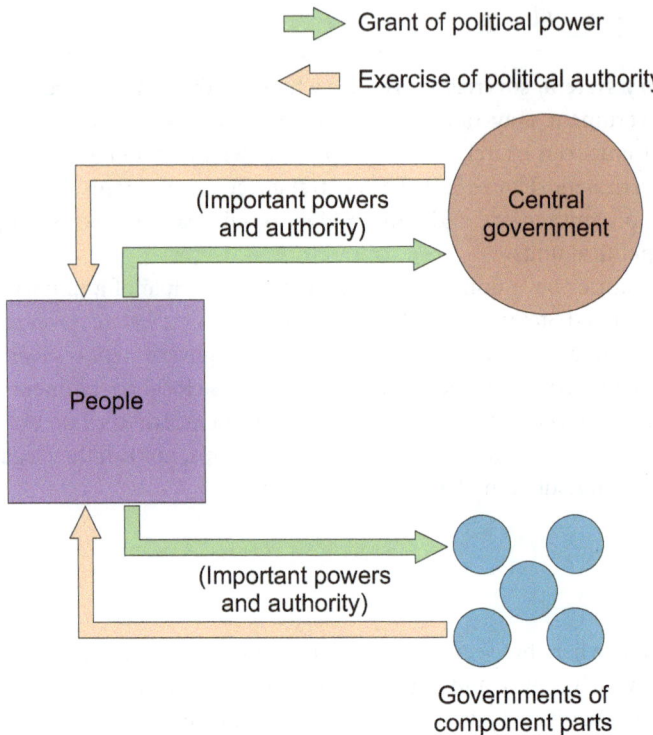

FIGURE 3.3 Federalism

For example, in the United States, the states play a role in amending the federal Constitution. Second, the component parts are not free to leave the Union. This was the major legal issue underlying the American Civil War. The southern states claimed that they had the right to secede from the Union, and the northern states disagreed. The question was decided in favor of the North on the battlefield and in the courtroom.

Notice that all three types of government involve a division of power. What keeps the categories distinct is *how* the power is divided: In confederations, the regional governments decide how to divide power; in unitary systems, the central government decides how to divide power; in federal systems, a constitution divides power so that each level has some power independent of the other. Although confederal, unitary, and federal systems are distinct, the distribution of power varies within each of these categories. As weak as the national government was under the Articles of Confederation, it had much more power than the UN has today. France and the United Kingdom have unitary governments, but counties and towns exercise more power in the United Kingdom than in France because of the British tradition of local self-government. In federal systems, the relative power of states and the national government varies. For example, in the United States, all states have equal sovereignty, whereas in India and Russia, some states have more autonomy than others; overall, power is more centralized in the Russian Federation than in the United States (Zhuravskaya 2010).

WHY FEDERALISM?

Federalism is the primary institutional feature of the U.S. Constitution. It is also an innovative feature of the Constitution. The Founders rejected the forms of government familiar to them—unitary and confederal—and invented federalism. Why did they invent a new type of government? We can see practical political and philosophical motivations.

Federalism was the only option that made sense given the political environment. The experience with the Articles of Confederation had made clear to them that a confederacy was not strong enough to govern a nation, and as colonists, they had learned how the concentrated power of unitary government threatened liberty. Furthermore, because Anti-Federalist sentiments ran high in many states, politically the Constitution stood no chance of ratification unless the states retained a good deal of independence from the central government.

In opting for a federal system, however, the Founders were doing more than bowing to the demands of their political environment. A federal system was compatible with a guiding philosophical principle of the Constitution—fragmentation of power. They made a conscious choice to create a political system that trades off some goals for others.

Advantages of Federalism

Dispersal of Power

A primary objective for the Founders was to disperse power. Federalism preserves the right of the states to be autonomous governments accountable to their own citizens rather than to the national government. A key reason the Founders wanted states to share this responsibility—to be partners of the federal government rather than its subordinates—was the idea that having strong and independent states would prevent the federal government from gaining too much power and threatening the rights of citizens. Americans have always feared concentrations of power, and dividing power between the states and the federal government was an attempt to provide balance. If the states remained sovereign governments, power remained closer to the people and thus would less likely be used against their will. Federalism thus institutionalizes and safeguards the division of powers that the Founders believed to be so critical to a well-constructed republic.

THINKING ANALYTICALLY

STATES AND THE COMPARATIVE METHOD

For political scientists, one of the key advantages of the American system of federalism is its contribution to thinking analytically. This contribution was almost certainly not on the minds of the Founders when they were organizing the republic on the basis of multiple sovereign governments, but that contribution is nonetheless very real.

How does federalism help political scientists think analytically? Well, lots of questions about politics deal with policy, institutions, or behavior at the aggregate level of the political system. Will term limits increase electoral competition? Will lowering income taxes increase economic output? Are political systems dominated by a single party less representative? There is a virtually endless list of important questions like this, but it is tough to answer them empirically if you only have one government to study and collect data from. You can't really figure out if, say, term limits increase electoral competition unless you can compare different political systems with different levels of electoral competition, some of them with term limits and some of them without. Ideally, what you would like, in order to address these sorts of questions, is a lot of governments with two crucial properties.

First, you want these governments to be genuinely comparable. Doing comparative studies across countries is challenging because these nations will have independent histories, culture, and unique traits in terms of political organization and political process. Let's say that you are interested in trying to figure out what explains why people do (or do not) bother to vote. This is clearly an important question to address; representative democratic governments respond to elections, and government is more likely to pay attention to the preferences and interests of those who actually show up to the polls.

Let's say you are specifically interested in the hypothesis that higher education levels lead to higher turnout. The basic idea is that groups with higher levels of education are more likely to be knowledgeable about politics, to recognize the importance of civic participation, and to be better equipped to navigate the bureaucratic requirements of registering to vote and actually casting a ballot. So, you gather data from a couple of dozen democratic countries and, sure enough, voter turnout in countries with higher overall levels of education is higher than in countries with lower education levels. While this seems to confirm your hypothesis, there are clearly a lot of potential caveats to consider here. Maybe it's not education levels at all, but something idiosyncratic about the history, culture, or political systems of the countries you've selected to study. Ideally, you'd like to remove those as potential counter-arguments to your hypothesis.

Second, you want a lot of variation on your key independent and dependent variables. A dependent variable, remember, is what you are trying to explain, and an independent variable is what, at least in theory, causes changes in the dependent variable. So if our hypothesis is that higher education levels lead to higher voter turnout, our dependent variable is voter turnout. Our independent variable is educational attainment. Measuring the concept of voter turnout is relatively easy; you can just take the number of people who actually cast ballots as a proportion of the population that was eligible to vote. On this measure then, "50 percent turnout" means that half of those who were eligible to vote showed up at the polls. But what about educational attainment—how could we measure that?

One option would be to simply measure some yardstick of educational achievement. We can do this by measuring the percentage of a given population that has a college degree. Given our hypothesis, then, we would expect that increases in the percentage of a population with a college degree (the independent variable) will lead to higher numbers on our measure of turnout (the dependent variable).

For a careful and convincing test of that hypothesis, we'd ideally want a lot of sovereign political units that have lots of variation on education levels and a lot of sovereign political units where voter turnout is very different. And, keeping in mind our first concern, we want these units to be truly comparable—we want some assurance that if we see evidence for or against our hypothesis it is not coming from some idiosyncratic difference of culture or history, institution or process.

This is where federalism provides such a boon to political scientists. The system of federalism in the United States gives scholars 50 truly comparable, sovereign governments—in other words, the states. They share a common national history, culture, and basic political philosophies, institutions, and processes thanks to the strictures of the United States Constitution. Yet they are also truly sovereign governments that, among other things, control voter registration deadlines and have very different voter turnout rates.

In the figure below, the horizontal axis represents what percentage of each state's population has a college degree, and the vertical axis represents what percent of eligible voters cast a ballot in the 2016 presidential election. In this sort of graph, which is called a scatterplot, the horizontal axis is typically called the "X" axis, and "X" is a shorthand way of referring to an independent variable. The dependent variable is typically plotted on the vertical or "Y" axis, and—you guessed it—"Y" is shorthand for a dependent variable.

There are 50 dots plotted in the two-dimensional space created by the X and Y axis, and these tell us where each state is in relation to the percent of its population with a college degree and its voter turnout in the 2016 presidential election. Eyeballing the dots is enough to show a definite pattern; generally speaking, as more of a state's population has a college degree, the higher a state's voter turnout. The red line going through the dots makes this clear and provides a more precise estimate of this relationship. This is a *regression line*. It simply represents the linear relationship between X and Y and makes clear that the relationship between education levels and turnout is indeed positive. Presto, we've tested our hypothesis using 50 sovereign governments and found it is empirically supported.

As mentioned above, there is virtually an endless set of questions that can be approached analytically using states and the same basic comparative, X/Y system used in the graph—everything from the impact of partisan control of legislatures on expenditure levels, to whether legally mandated curricular improve or worsen graduation rates. Bottom line: The states have proven a boon to systematic and analytical thinking in political science.

Discussion Questions

1. What other variables might help explain voter turnout in the states? If you plotted these on the X axis of the graph, rather than state education levels, what do you think the regression line would look like?
2. Besides voter turnout, what other dependent variables measured at the state level might be interesting for political scientists to analyze?

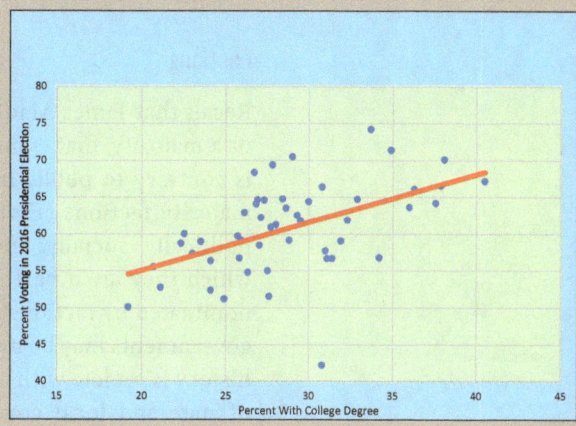

State Voter Turnout and State Education Levels, 2016

Source: Constructed by the authors using data from the United States Election Project (http://www.electproject.org) and state education levels compiled by the U.S. Census Bureau (https://factfinder.census.gov/faces/tableservices/jsf/pages/productview.xhtml?pid=ACS_15_5YR_S1501USA.gov).

Accommodation of Diverse Interests

With independent political power granted to states, local interests and political priorities are respected and represented. States have broad latitude to pursue their own policy paths, allowing them to respond to the wishes of their citizens rather than to the dictates of the federal government.

Policy Experimentation

Variation in laws and public policy across states is one of the most commonly cited advantages of federalism. As Supreme Court Justice Louis Brandeis observed, state governments are the "laboratories of democracy." Public policy experimentation provides important lessons not only for other states but also for the national government. Expansion of the vote to women is one example of a policy implemented in some states before it became a national policy.

Disadvantages of Federalism

Institutionalizing a division of power, accommodating diverse interests, and allowing state and local experimentation are clear advantages of the American system of federalism. But there are also some disadvantages.

Factions

Recall that James Madison defined a faction as any group, either a minority or a majority, that is motivated to act in a way that harms individual rights or is contrary to public interest in general. He was especially concerned about majority factions (*Federalist* Number 10). Smaller political units tend to be politically, socially, and economically more alike than the larger nation of which they are a part. As a result, these political units are more likely to be dominated by factions, and because of their sensitivity to local interests, state governments may be more vulnerable to a tyranny of the majority. The nation's history is replete with examples of dominant factions appropriating the power of state and local governments and denying minority groups equal rights, precisely the sort of behavior Madison feared. One example is the systematic disenfranchisement of African Americans following the Civil War, especially in southern states. Whites in many of these states used their majority status to enact Jim Crow laws to deny blacks equal political, social, and economic opportunities.

Complexity and Inefficiency

Though experimentation in public policy has advantages, it leads to a bewildering variation in state laws. In Nebraska, the speed limit is 75 miles per hour. Cross into neighboring Iowa or Kansas at that velocity, and you immediately break the law. In other words, crossing a state line means entering a different political jurisdiction with different legal standards. All this variation makes coordinating intergovernmental action difficult, creates headaches for those who engage in interstate business and must deal with a patchwork of regulatory requirements, and can catch even a conscientiously law-abiding citizen unaware. Your status as a traffic scofflaw depends not only on what you do but also on what state you do it in.

Accountability

The variation can also make it harder for the citizen to hold government accountable. For example, who gets the blame or credit for the policies and programs funded at least in part by the federal government—the federal government, because it put up the cash and insisted on some general rules about how it was spent, or the states, which also kicked in a lot of dollars, implemented and administered most of these programs, and independently created programs of their own? Or both? When popular public services get slashed, who gets the blame: the states that will not raise taxes or the federal government that is cutting grants? Such questions can be frustratingly hard to answer in a federal system.

DIVISION OF POWERS IN THE AMERICAN FEDERAL SYSTEM

Federations differ on the particular methods they use to divide political power. The United States uses a written constitution to divide political power, with specific grants of authority going to the national government and the rest being reserved for the states. As a result, the central operative questions in politics include not just "Who gets what?" but also "What level of government gets to decide who gets what?" The answer to the second question often determines the answer to the first. To formulate an answer to this second question, you need to know how the Constitution divides power between state and federal governments.

The Powers of the National Government

Article I, Section 8 of the U.S. Constitution spells out certain powers given to Congress. These include the power to levy and collect taxes, to borrow money, to regulate interstate commerce, to coin money, to declare war, and to raise and support an army and a navy. The specific grants of power given to the national government are called enumerated powers. But the national government's powers are not limited to these. Included in Article I, Section 8 is a vague and sweeping grant giving Congress the power "to make all laws which shall be necessary and proper for carrying into execution the foregoing powers" (often called the "elastic" clause of the Constitution). With this statement, the Founders expanded the authority of the national government beyond its enumerated powers by giving it implied powers. Madison strongly favored implied powers. The logic behind these powers is the impossibility of listing in detail every specific power the national government would be authorized to take in every conceivable situation.

Enumerated powers make it clear that the power of the national government is meant to be limited, yet the potential for increasing central government's influence through the doctrine of implied powers is hard to overestimate. The scope of this potential was first tested in the case of **McCulloch v. Maryland** (1819), which involved a dispute over whether the central government had the power to create a national bank. The national bank was originally created as part of a broad economic program formulated by Secretary of the Treasury Alexander Hamilton. President George Washington had some doubts about the constitutionality of this proposal and got conflicting advice from two key members of his cabinet—Hamilton and Thomas Jefferson.

Hamilton acknowledged that establishing a bank was not one of the national government's enumerated powers but argued that the "necessary and proper" clause gave it the implied power to do so because the bank would be a convenient way to keep and administer the revenues Congress raised by taxing and borrowing. Hamilton interpreted *necessary* as "convenient" or "appropriate." Jefferson, in contrast, interpreted *necessary* as "indispensable." A national bank was not indispensable to safeguarding federal funds (they could be deposited in state banks, for instance) and was accordingly beyond the authority of the national government. Washington sided with Hamilton and signed the national bank bill into law. A quarter of a century later, the bank became the center of a constitutional controversy when the state of Maryland taxed a branch of the national bank located within its borders. On instructions from his superiors, the bank's cashier, James McCulloch, refused to pay the tax on the grounds that it constituted state interference with a legitimate activity of the national government. In deciding this case, the Supreme Court affirmed Hamilton's interpretation that *necessary* meant "appropriate," not "indispensable."

This early judicial test opened the door to the expansion of federal government activities through the use of implied powers. Yet enumerated powers have been broadly interpreted and have, if anything, given the federal government greater opportunities for expanding its influence. This is especially true of the power to regulate interstate commerce and the power to tax and spend for the general welfare.

The constitutional issue boils down to the same thing in both instances: how narrow or broad an interpretation to give the applicable phrases. The Supreme Court has interpreted the interstate commerce clause to give the national government the power to license the operation of boats on New York State waters (*Gibbons v. Ogden* 1824), to regulate what farmers can feed chickens (*Wickard v. Filburn* 1942), and to prohibit private acts of racial discrimination (*Heart of Atlanta Motel v. United States* 1964 and *Katzenbach v. McClung* 1964). Passenger vessels are considered interstate commerce even if they are not directly engaged in the buying and selling of goods; what farmers feed chickens affects the interstate market for wheat; and individuals who racially discriminate while serving substantial numbers of interstate travelers or while relying on interstate commerce for their supplies are held to interfere with the rights of minorities to travel and engage in interstate commerce.

The general pattern of court decisions led some students of constitutional law to conclude that, given the interdependent nature of American economic and social

McCulloch v. Maryland An 1819 court case involving a dispute over whether the central government had the power to create a national bank.

activities, the Supreme Court would consider almost no activity beyond the scope of the interstate commerce power. In recent decades, however, the Supreme Court has shown a willingness to limit the use of the commerce clause. For example, in *United States v. Morrison* (2000), the Supreme Court ruled that the federal government did not have the power to provide a civil remedy for sexual assault. The case turned on the Violence against Women Act of 1994, which gave rape victims the right to sue their attackers in federal court. Congress justified its intrusion into what is traditionally an area of law left wholly to the states by using the interstate commerce clause. The argument was that fear of violence prevented women from such activities as traveling alone and going out at night. Because these actions are often associated with work obligations and may involve crossing state lines, Congress could invoke the interstate commerce clause. The Supreme Court disagreed and, for the first time since the 1930s, rejected a congressional argument that a popular activity constituted interstate commerce.

As was the case with the "necessary and proper" clause, the power of the national government to tax and spend for the general welfare provoked a debate between two of the nation's early leaders: Hamilton and Madison. These coauthors of *The Federalist* disagreed about what the national government had the power to tax and spend money on. Madison argued that the national government could tax and spend only for the activities it was specifically authorized to undertake. Hamilton held that the power to tax and spend was independent of the other enumerated powers. In other words, in Hamilton's view, Congress had the power to tax and spend for functions it could not otherwise control.

Again, a series of Supreme Court decisions decided the issue on Hamilton's terms. The implications for the expansion of federal power are considerable; this means Congress can use its taxing power as an indirect method of regulating an activity, such as by taxing gambling. Since the meaning of "the general welfare" has undergone a similarly broad interpretation, the taxing and spending power of Congress has evolved into a powerful tool.

Regulation of interstate commerce and taxation, the two powers the Founders thought most crucial to the operation of a national government, have become the major bases for the constitutional expansion of national government. The federal government has significantly expanded its power since its founding.

The Powers, Rights, and Obligations of State Governments

The Constitution focuses more on the national government than on states. Nonetheless, states are granted certain powers and rights under the Constitution, and states are required to fulfill certain obligations to one another.

State Powers

In contrast to the federal government, state governments receive no specific grant of powers from the Constitution. In fact, in its original form the Constitution made no mention at all of state prerogatives. The Federalists argued that all powers not

In a federal system of shared powers, policy jurisdictions and responsibilities can overlap government levels. This means agencies from different levels of government often have to work together. Here a U.S. Immigration and Customs Enforcement (ICE) agent and a local law enforcement officer take a suspected illegal immigrant into custody.

© Charles Reed/U.S. Immigration and Customs Enforcement/AP Photo

granted to the national government would remain with the states. But because the lack of explicit guarantees was a sore point with Anti-Federalists, the Federalists promised that if the Constitution was adopted, it would be amended to include a guarantee of states' rights. This promise was kept with the Tenth Amendment pledge that "the powers not delegated to the United States by the Constitution, nor prohibited by it to the states, are reserved to the states respectively, or to the people."

The constitutional questions raised by the Tenth Amendment center on the scope of national powers. Advocates of states' rights argue that the amendment is an important check on the expansion of the federal government into state prerogatives. For much of the twentieth century, however, judicial interpretation tended to provide legal support for almost any activity the federal government wished to undertake. This interpretation provided an important nationalizing influence on American federalism. A shift in the stance of the Supreme Court during the 1990s reversed the trend. For example, in *United States v. Lopez* (1995), the Supreme Court ruled the Gun-Free School Zones Act of 1990 unconstitutional. The Court reasoned that this federal law banning possession of firearms within 1,000 feet of any school had nothing to do with commerce and therefore exceeded the federal government's authority. In other words, the states had jurisdiction, not the federal government.

Although such court decisions show that the Tenth Amendment still provides important protections for state independence, the general source of political authority for the states comes from their own constitutions, which specify each state's powers and limitations. As long as these constitutions do not contravene the U.S. Constitution or conflict with legitimate federal statutes and treaties, states are generally free to establish their own form of government and responsibilities. This means that, unlike their federal counterpart, state legislatures exercise plenary, or comprehensive, power (Tarr 2000, 7). You can think of the constitutional difference between state and federal governments like this: Congress needs authorization from the U.S. Constitution to do anything, whereas states can do anything they want as long as it is not expressly forbidden by the U.S. Constitution or their own state constitution.

State powers include **police power**, or the authority to pass laws for the health, safety, and morals of their citizens. This grant of political authority is in many ways much broader than any given to the national government. States also have **concurrent powers**, or powers that the national and state governments can exercise. For

police power The authority of the states to pass laws for the health, safety, and morals of their citizens.

concurrent powers The powers listed in the Constitution as belonging to both the national and state governments.

example, both levels of government have the authority to tax and to borrow money. The large jurisdictional overlap of concurrent powers and the vaguely defined divisions between state and federal authority arising from the Tenth Amendment, the "necessary and proper" clause, and the broad interpretation of enumerated powers mean that federal–state relations are often marked by tension. Who has the authority to do what? The ability and authority to answer that question is the key to power in the American political system. Given the wide range of possible interpretations of national and state constitutions, the question is often frustratingly hard to answer.

States' Rights

The Constitution guarantees the states certain rights in the American federal system. First, the Constitution guarantees the states that the central government will protect them from invasion and insurrection. National defense is a responsibility of the central government, and Article IV, Section 4 declares that the invasion of any state is an invasion of the United States. States are thus freed from the obligation of maintaining standing military forces. If local authorities are unable to maintain law and order, the governor may ask the president to send federal military troops to assist.

Second, the Constitution guarantees the states a republican form of government. The term is not precisely defined by the Constitution but is generally taken to mean a government based on the consent of the governed and representative institutions—in other words, a representative democracy founded on the notion of popular sovereignty. The enforcement of this constitutional guarantee is political rather than legal. The federal courts generally have declined jurisdiction and have deferred to Congress to determine whether a state has a republican government. Senator Charles Sumner (D-MA) once expressed concern that this clause is a "sleeping giant" because it potentially gives Congress authority to intervene (some might say meddle) in local affairs. Politics, rather than legal limitations, constrain this type of congressional intrusion.

A third constitutional guarantee to the states is equal representation in the Senate. This system of representation is inconsistent with the principle of political equality because sparsely populated states have more than their fair share of representation in the Senate, and the most populous states have less than their fair share. For example, in 2016, the least populous state, Wyoming, had roughly 0.18 percent of the nation's population, whereas the most populous, California, had 12.1 percent, but each state had two U.S. senators (or 2.0 percent). Thus, Wyoming's representation is about 11 times greater than its share of the population, and California's is only one-sixth of its share. Equal representation in the Senate is a constitutional recognition that states are units of government that have special status not possessed by other units of local government such as counties or cities.

Fourth, under the Constitution all states are equal after admission. Every state has the same degree of sovereignty, with the same rights and powers. The president or Congress has occasionally tried to mandate certain conditions of statehood, but such requirements are unenforceable if they would give the new state more or less power than other states. For example, President William Howard Taft vetoed legislation admitting Arizona as a state because he objected to a provision in the proposed state constitution permitting voters to recall state judges. Once the offending clause was deleted, Taft signed the act, and Arizona became the forty-eighth state in 1912. The new state promptly restored the recall provision (Peltason 1982, 122). Similarly, in 1907, Congress attached a provision to the enabling act passed prior to Oklahoma's admission as a state, prohibiting Oklahoma from moving its state capital from Guthrie for 10 years. Two years later, the voters of the state approved a referendum to move the capital to Oklahoma City. When the residents of Guthrie sued in federal court to enforce the provision of the enabling act, the Supreme Court held that the provision could not be enforced because once Oklahoma had become a state, it was on equal footing with all other states and thus had control over the location of the seat of government (*Coyle v. Smith* 1911). There is no seniority when it comes to state power and sovereignty: Once a territory achieves the constitutional status of statehood, it is equal to all other states.

Finally, states have the right to decide how or whether the Constitution is to be changed. Three-fourths (38) of the states must agree to any changes in the Constitution. This requirement is a major protection of states' rights and sovereignty because amendments must be approved by the states acting as governmental units through either state legislatures or state conventions. In other words, the Constitution gives the states, not the people, the power to approve amendments. This means that the 13 least populous states, which represent about 4 percent of the nation's population, can block a change favored by the other 37 states, which represent the other 96 percent of the nation's people.

"full faith and credit" The provision in the Constitution that requires states to honor the civil obligations (wills, birth certificates, and other public documents) generated by other states.

Federal troops were called in to help desegregate Central High School in Little Rock, Arkansas, in 1957 (as shown here). Desegregation was opposed by many at the local and state levels. When segregation was ruled unconstitutional by the U.S. Supreme Court, however, state laws mandating racially separate schools were invalidated. State laws cannot violate the U.S. Constitution, which is the law of the land.

© Paul Slade/Hulton Archive/Getty Images

Obligations of States

The Constitution imposes certain obligations on the states. Article IV, Section 1 requires states to grant **"full faith and credit"** to one another's public acts and records. This provision ensures that important civil obligations, such as property rights, wills, and marriages, will be valid and honored in all states.

This provision applies only to civil proceedings. Because states have the right to establish their own criminal laws and punishments, a state is precluded from enforcing the criminal laws of another state. The constitutional obligation of one state to another in the area of criminal law is limited to **interstate rendition**. If a person accused of a crime flees across state lines, Article IV, Section 2 says that the governor of the state to which the criminal has fled shall deliver the criminal back to the state with jurisdiction over the crime.

The Addition of New States

New states were added to the original 13 states by congressional action as specified in Article IV, Section 3. New states cannot be formed by combining or dividing existing states without their consent.[1] Once admitted, states have equal sovereignty and powers with all other states.

The typical procedure for adding states to the Union is as follows:

- Congress forms an incorporated territory.
- Residents of the territory petition Congress for admission as a state.
- Congress passes a resolution called an **enabling act**, authorizing the residents of the territory to draft a state constitution and hold a referendum to approve it. The resolution must be approved by the president.
- When the proposed state constitution is approved by the majority vote of both houses of Congress and signed by the president, the territory becomes a state on equal footing with all other states.

Texas is a special case because it began as an independent nation, the Republic of Texas, and then negotiated with Congress for statehood. The congressional resolution admitting Texas as a state contains a provision authorizing Texas to divide itself into five states if the state legislature desires. Although some Texans claim this could be done unilaterally without congressional approval, the Civil War and Supreme Court rulings have established that Texas has the same rights, powers, and limitations as other states, so such action would require consent of Congress as well.

The most recent discussion about adding a new state involves Puerto Rico. Puerto Rico is an unincorporated territory of the United States. Its residents are U.S. citizens, but they pay no federal income tax. Puerto Rico's special commonwealth status gives it greater control over local matters than territories such as Guam, American Samoa, and the Virgin Islands. At 3.5 million, Puerto Rico's population is similar to Oklahoma's 3.5 million, and it is bigger than roughly half the states. Yet citizens of Puerto Rico cannot vote in presidential elections, and they have no voting representatives in Congress. They do have a nonvoting delegate to

interstate rendition The obligation of states to return people accused of a crime to the state from which they fled.

enabling act A resolution passed by Congress authorizing residents of a territory to draft a state constitution as part of the process of adding new states to the Union.

---

[1] Five states were formed from other states with the consent of Congress and the legislatures of the affected states: Vermont from New York in 1791, Kentucky from Virginia in 1792, Tennessee from North Carolina in 1796, Maine from Massachusetts in 1820, and West Virginia from Virginia in 1863 (Peltason 1982, 122). The West Virginia case is a little different from the others. The Virginia legislature voted to secede and join the Confederacy. Several counties wanted to remain in the Union, and representatives from those counties formed a new Virginia legislature that approved the formation of West Virginia during the Civil War.

the House but have no voice at all in the Senate. Over the years there have been periodic attempts to move Puerto Rico toward statehood. For example, in a nonbinding referendum in 2012 a majority of voters indicated a preferences for seeking statehood, and a political party, the New Progressive Party (NPP), advocates statehood as part of its platform. In 2016, the NPP won a majority in the Puerto Rican National Assembly as well as capturing the governor's office. In 2017 the NPP backed a nonbinding referendum where 97 percent of those who cast ballots supported statehood. That result is less overwhelming that it sounds, as groups opposing statehood called for a boycott of the referendum and turnout was less than a quarter of eligible voters. In addition to the questionable popular support, any effort to make Puerto Rico a state anytime soon is also likely to be hobbled by the commonwealth's severe financial problems. The Puerto Rican government's inability to meet its debt obligations led it to declare a form of bankruptcy in 2017 (Walsh 2017). Washington, DC, also poses difficult issues relating to statehood and representation. Since the passage of the Twenty-Third Amendment, U.S. citizens who reside in the nation's capital have voted for president, but they have no voting representation in Congress. Like Puerto Rico and the territories, they have a nonvoting delegate in the House and none in the Senate. Yet about 680,000 people live in the District of Columbia, about 100,000 more than the population of Wyoming. Because the Constitution establishes Washington, DC, as the seat of the national government, it is neither a state nor a part of a state. Technically it is a federal city, a unique political jurisdiction that is not sovereign in the same way as a state. Local government in DC is completely dependent on the power it is granted from the federal government, which can take away that power whenever it wants.

Admitting new states has always been an inherently political process. In the early years of the republic, the politics of gaining admission to the Union revolved around the issue of slavery. The Civil War resolved this issue, but it did nothing to end the intensely political conflicts that surround application for statehood. For example, Utah's struggle for statehood dragged out for nearly half a century because of a political fight over the definition of marriage. From the first request in 1849 to 1896, when statehood was finally achieved, the political obstacles centered largely on suspicion about the Mormon Church's practice of plural marriage. In effect, the federal government required the church to alter its views on marriage as a condition of statehood, thus regulating intimate relationships a century before the question of same-sex marriages arose (Lyman 1986, 1–5).

The admissions of the last two states, Hawaii and Alaska, amply demonstrate the politics surrounding statehood. Hawaii's statehood was long delayed, partly because of suspicion of the traditional political, social, and economic systems of a Polynesian culture. Granting Hawaii statehood presented Congress "with an unprecedented dilemma: … the question of equality under the nation's Constitution for a non-contiguous area with an essentially nonwhite population" (Bell 1984, 5). Hawaii finally gained statehood in 1959. Alaska was admitted the same year after a political struggle of more than a decade that involved concerns about the indigenous nonwhite population and some partisan bickering.

Refereeing Power Conflicts

The Constitution makes some provisions for settling conflicts between state and federal operations. Article VI declares that the U.S. Constitution, laws passed by Congress, and treaties made by the national government shall be the **"supreme law of the land."** State constitutions and laws are subordinate to the supreme law, and if there is a conflict between a state provision and a federal provision, the latter is enforced. The Constitution thus establishes a hierarchy of law; the U.S. Constitution is superior to both national laws and state laws and constitutions, and national laws and treaties are superior to state constitutions and laws. Given the vague and broad constitutional language, this means that the ultimate umpire in the federal system is the Supreme Court, which has the final say on how to interpret the Constitution.

The Supreme Court has historically tended to favor the federal government in apportioning powers, but the states are far from helpless in these conflicts. For example, the federal system ensures that state interests play an important role in the national government. Although Congress is the lawmaking branch of the national government, members of Congress are elected to represent state and local—not necessarily national—interests. Most members of Congress, at least those interested in reelection, have a fundamental interest in ensuring that national legislation either positively benefits their constituents or, at least, does not harm them. For example, in 2009, the Republican leaders in Charleston County, South Carolina, formally censured their state's senior U.S. senator and fellow Republican, Lindsey Graham. The Charleston County GOP was upset with Graham's willingness to work with Democrats on several issues, especially on climate legislation that Graham saw as a key national and international priority. Charleston County Republicans obviously did not see it as such and sought a censure by the state party organization to go with the rebuke issued by the county party (Associated Press 2009). Graham, in short, faced a conflict between the preferences of local and state interests and his beliefs about what was in the best interests of the nation. These conflicts have no easy solution, but elected officials who consistently choose the latter over the former run the real risk of being replaced by someone willing to reverse the order of priority.

"supreme law of the land" The idea that the U.S. Constitution, laws passed by Congress, and the treaties made by the federal government are supreme, and state constitutions and laws are subordinate to them.

Muriel Bowser holds a unique elected position in the American political system. As the mayor of Washington, DC, she is the chief executive office of the nation's only federal city.

© Bill Clark/CQ Roll Call/AP Photo

THE EVOLUTION OF FEDERALISM

A historical analysis of governmental development in the United States points to one overriding pattern: the growth of activities at *all levels* of the political system. Though the fortunes of state and federal governments have waxed and waned in their relationship to each other, taken as a whole, local, state, and national governments all provide more services and regulate the actions of their citizens to a greater extent today than at any time in the past. Government expenditures tell this story clearly: At the beginning of the twentieth century, the total expenditure of all levels of government was less than $2 billion; in 2017, the federal expenditures alone were more than $4 trillion (that's a four followed by 12 zeros), a staggering sum that accounts for outlays at only one level of government.

One of the key reasons for this increase is the expanded role of the federal government. While government spending at all levels has risen, the proportion of total government expenditures accounted for by the federal government has increased, while the proportion accounted for by states has decreased. At the beginning of the twentieth century, state governments spent more than the federal government. Those spending patterns have reversed—currently the federal government spends more than state and local governments combined. Three historical events that occurred between 1916 and 1950 help explain the reversal of these trends: World War I and its aftermath (roughly 1917 to 1922); the Great Depression and New Deal response (roughly 1929 to 1940); and the buildup and aftermath of World War II (roughly 1941 to 1948).

State and federal spending as a percentage of the nation's gross domestic product (GDP) is a good indicator of government activity. Figure 3.4 shows federal and state government expenditures as a percentage of GDP from 1900 to 2015. This chart shows long-term increases in both state and federal government expenditures. It also shows the abrupt increases in federal activity during these crises. War and economic depression meant the growth in the federal government's spending was, to some extent, expansion by default. Military matters have always been the primary concern of the national government, and World Wars I and II required harnessing a large portion of the nation's resources to the military effort. Government activity at the state and federal levels increased in response to the Great Depression in the 1930s. The federal government was in a better position to respond to this crisis than state or local governments because it had power over currency, the banking system, and the regulation of interstate economic activities. It also had a superior tax base, since the Sixteenth Amendment, ratified in 1913, gave Congress the authority to levy an income tax. This chart also illustrates what's known as a *ratchet effect*: Government activity spikes in response to a crisis, and recedes when the crisis ends. But like a ratchet, government activity does not fall all the way down to the pre-crisis level. Federal spending spiked to about 24

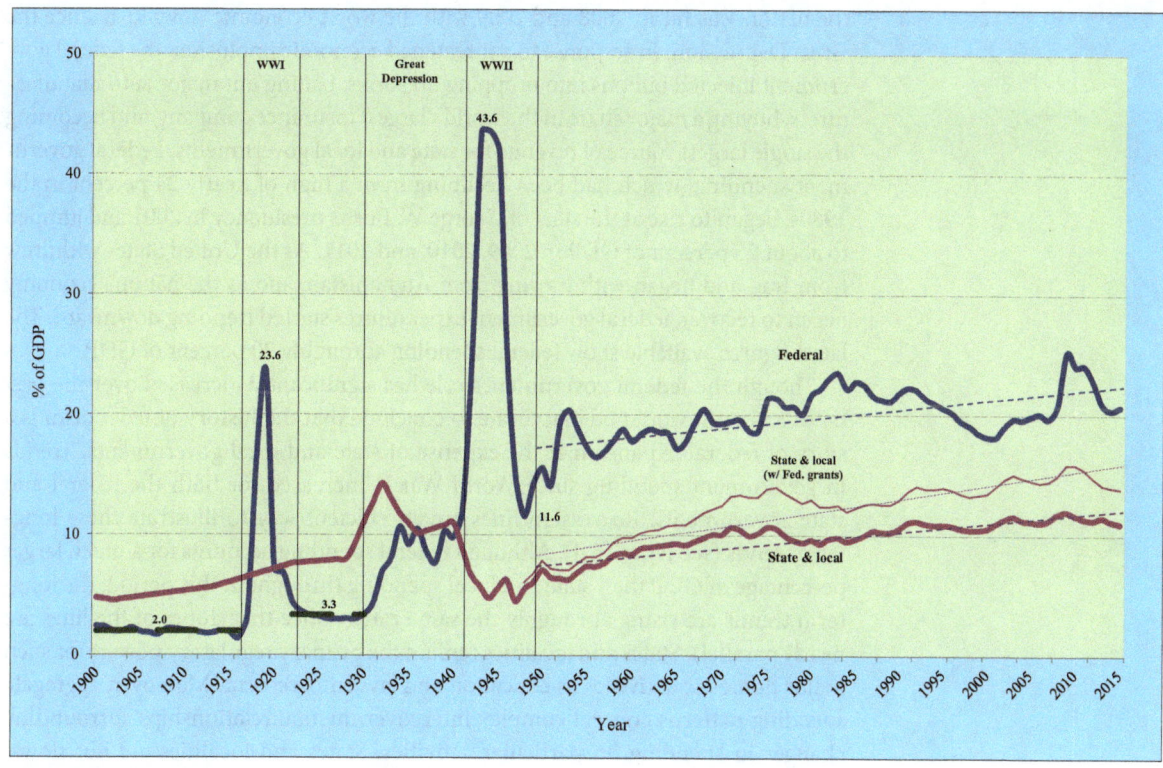

FIGURE 3.4 Federal and State Expenditures as a Percent of GDP, 1900–2015

Technical Note: State and local government expenditures reported in the Federal Budget is expenditures from own sources (NIPA Basis) net of interest. State and local government expenditures reported in Historical Statistics of the United States, U.S. Census includes expenditures from all sources including intergovernmental transfers and interest on debt. The difference in the two time series is trivial before 1948, but from 1948 to the present, state and local spending including intergovernmental transfers from the federal government and interest on debt increases more rapidly than do federal expenditures so that by the 1990s state and local expenditures are about equal to federal expenditures. Excluding intergovernmental transfers and interest on debt from state and local spending reported in Census documents closely matches the time trend from the Budget document.

Sources: Data from "Table Ea276–286 State and local government expenditure, by character and object: 1902–1996," *Historical Statistics of the United States, Earliest Times to the Present: Millennial Edition*, edited by Susan B. Carter, Scott Sigmund Gartner, Michael R. Haines, Alan L. Olmstead, Richard Sutch, and Gavin Wright. New York: Cambridge University Press, 2006, http://hsus.cambridge.org/HSUSWeb/table/expandtable.do?id=Ea276–286; and the Budget of the United States Government, Table 15.3, "Historical Tables: Total Government Expenditures As Percentages of GDP1948–2012," http://www.gpo.gov/fdsys/browse/collection.action?collectionCodo=BUDGET&browsePath=Fiscal+Year+2014&searchPath=Fiscal+Year+2014&leafLevelBrowse=false&isCollapsed=false&is Open=true&packageid=BUDGET-2014-TAB&ycord=430; Office of Management and Budget, Historical Tables, Table 14.3, "Total Government Expenditures As Percentages of GDP: 1948-2015." https://obamawhitehouse.archives.gov/omb/budget/Historicals.

percent of GDP during World War I, but when the war ended it fell to 3.3 percent of GDP, which is slightly higher than the 2 percent before World War I. We see a larger effect in response to World War II—federal spending spiked to almost 44 percent of GDP, but fell back to about 12 percent of GDP after the war, which is considerably higher than pre-World War II levels.

Federal spending as a percentage of GDP began rising again in 2008 because of a new set of historical events. While it was fighting two wars in Iraq and Afghanistan, the nation was hit in 2008 and 2009 with the worst economic downturn since the Great Depression. In response to a threatened economic implosion, the federal government injected billions into propping up banks, bailing out major auto manufacturers, buying a major share in the world's largest insurance company, and becoming the single largest source of revenue for state and local governments. Federal government spending, which had been declining from a high of nearly 24 percent in the 1980s, began to rise at the start of George W. Bush's presidency in 2001 and jumped to about 25 percent of GDP in 2009, 2010, and 2011. As the United States withdrew from Iraq and began withdrawing from Afghanistan, and as the nation's economy began to recover, federal government expenditures started trending downward. The latest figures available show federal spending at roughly 20 percent of GDP.

Though the federal government's role has significantly increased over the past half-century, it would be inaccurate to conclude that the history of federalism is a story of federal expansion at the expense of state and local governments. Trends in government spending since World War II increased for both the federal and state governments. Regression lines are an efficient way to illustrate these long-term trends (see Figure 3.4). Although federal spending accounts for a much larger percentage of GDP than state and local spending throughout this period, the long-term trends are rising at roughly the same rate (notice that slopes of the lines are nearly parallel). States and localities remain the primary regulatory powers for such major domestic activities as education and law enforcement. Moreover, aggregate spending patterns conceal complex intergovernmental relationships surrounding changes in spending on particular activities. States and localities are not slowly disappearing into the shadows cast by the federal government's fiscal power. Their capabilities and responsibilities have increased dramatically during the nation's history, and they have not by any means evolved into supplicants of the federal government. Indeed, a significant part of the increase in federal spending is in the form of federal grants to state and local governments (more on this below). The trend in state and local spending is based on money raised from their own sources. If federal grants are included, the trend in state and local spending increased at a faster rate than federal spending (see the trend line for state and local spending including federal grants). At times, states have fiercely fought to maintain independence from the federal government, and states have established a broad set of working relationships with the federal government that account for a great deal of the domestic policy we take for granted. Roads, schools, utilities, and much more are built and maintained as a result of combined federal, state, and local policies.

Although attempting to systematically describe the evolution of federalism is likely to provoke some debate, federalism can be categorized into three reasonably distinct eras. Each is characterized by a different model of federalism: dual federalism, cooperative federalism, and new federalism.

Dual Federalism

dual federalism The idea that federal and state governments are sovereign, with separate and distinct jurisdictions.

Dual federalism views federal and state governments as independent sovereign powers with separate and distinct jurisdictions. The central government has jurisdiction over national concerns: conducting national defense, coining money, and regulating interstate and foreign commerce. The states have responsibility for local concerns: exercising "police powers," including public safety, and managing education, health, and welfare.

In theory, national and state responsibilities are clearly divided. Each level of government is supreme in its own policy arena, and the other level has no constitutional basis to enter that arena uninvited. During the nineteenth century, the Supreme Court adopted dual federalism as the guiding principle to referee conflicts between state and federal governments. Compared to contemporary times, dual federalism was practiced to some extent. The federal government, for example, was less involved in the daily lives of its citizens during the formative years of the republic than it is today.

Still, intense controversies have always marked federalism. As discussed earlier, the ink was barely dry on the Constitution before Hamilton, one of its authors, began to loosely interpret its provisions to expand the federal government's power. In the first few decades after the adoption of the Constitution, Federalist sentiments dominated politics, and the federal government established itself as a central force.

This early expansion of national government fortunes underwent a sharp decline when Andrew Jackson became president in 1829 and set about resurrecting the Anti-Federalist states' rights platform. Jackson appointed Roger B. Taney as chief justice of the Supreme Court. Taney is generally acknowledged as the author of the dual federalism doctrine, and his rulings represented a clear philosophical break from those of his predecessor, John Marshall, who had been much more receptive to Federalist arguments.

Even though the federal government may have been less involved in the daily lives of its citizens, it was often involved in standoffs with state governments. These conflicts sometimes became so intense that even Jackson found himself on the nationalist side. For example, in the 1830s, states' rights advocates favored the doctrine of **nullification**, the act of declaring a national law null and void within a state's borders. In 1832, South Carolina nullified a set of national tariffs and threatened to secede from the Union. Jackson responded by threatening to use federal troops, and South Carolina dropped its secessionist stand.

Other states threatened to leave the Union because of disagreements with federal policy. The New England states threatened to secede en masse during the War of 1812 in response to a federally ordered trade embargo. The most notable of these disagreements was, of course, the Civil War, when 11 southern states broke away and formed the Confederate States of America (CSA). The CSA's defeat in the subsequent American Civil War settled the lingering questions of nullification and secession, and for a time power came back to the federal government. Three amendments—the Thirteenth Amendment outlawing slavery, the Fourteenth Amendment guaranteeing due process and equal protection of the laws, and the Fifteenth Amendment prohibiting denial of the right of citizens to vote on the basis of "race, color, or previous condition of servitude"—served to limit state power in these areas. During Reconstruction, the federal government became the dominant partner in the politics of many southern states.

nullification The act of declaring a national law null and void within a state's borders.

Toward the end of the nineteenth century, the country entered a period of explosive economic growth, sometimes referred to as the Gilded Age, fueled by freewheeling capitalism. During this era, the doctrine of dual federalism strongly reasserted itself, even in areas traditionally considered the domain of the national government. The dominant industrial capitalists of the day did not support strong central government regulation of business, interstate or otherwise. These sentiments were often reflected by the Supreme Court, which declared unconstitutional federal laws establishing a minimum wage and regulating the use of child labor. Still, the newly industrialized economy provided the impetus for greater federal regulatory powers, and World War I accelerated the movement to give the national government a more prominent role. Although this expansion of federal power blurred the line separating state and federal jurisdictions, dual federalism lingered as the operative model until a severe economic crisis pushed the federal government into a more central role.

Cooperative Federalism

In contrast to dual federalism, **cooperative federalism** recognizes an overlap in state and national responsibilities. Accordingly, state and federal governments have to work together, coordinating their actions to serve and respond to the needs of citizens.

The impetus for the cooperative model of federalism was the Great Depression, although it had been practiced in rudimentary form even before the Constitutional Convention. For example, in 1785, Congress passed a statute, supplemented by the Northwest Ordinance of 1787, giving states large sections of public lands to be developed for educational purposes. The basic form of this legislation—a grant from the central government so that the states could achieve a desired policy end—remains the basic mechanism of cooperative federalism.

Initially, federal grant programs to the states mostly involved land, a resource that the national government had in abundance. Toward the end of the nineteenth century, the form of grants shifted from land to cash, and instead of being once-only gifts, the grants came in the form of continuing appropriations. This new form of subsidy became known as **grants-in-aid**, and it is the reason cooperative federalism is sometimes called *fiscal federalism,* recognizing that cooperation among the levels of government is often characterized by financial relationships.

Grants-in-aid became more common in the early twentieth century as the federal government tapped the lucrative new revenue source of the income tax and became more willing to involve itself in regulating the economy. Federal grants-in-aid expenditures jumped from $5 million in 1912 to almost $34 million in 1920. Most of these funds went to education, highways, and agricultural extension programs, but Congress laid the basis for modern assistance programs by providing money for maternal and child healthcare.

During the New Deal, the use of grants-in-aid exploded and became perhaps the central characteristic of American federalism. State and local governments were ill prepared to deal with the massive economic dislocation of the 1930s.

---

cooperative federalism The idea that the distinction between state and national responsibilities is unclear and that the different levels of government share responsibilities in many areas.

grants-in-aid A form of national subsidy to the states designed to help them pay for policies and programs that are the responsibility of states rather than the national government.

Facing a social disaster of unprecedented proportions, the federal government stepped into the breach. Between 1932 and 1935, grants-in-aid expenditures swelled from $200 million to more than $2 billion. Instead of having the federal government administer burgeoning new programs in welfare, health, employment security, and public housing, President Franklin D. Roosevelt chose to funnel the money and much of the program responsibility through state and local governments.

The outbreak of World War II temporarily slowed grants-in-aid programs, as the national government conserved its resources for the military effort. But the war propelled the federal government into an unprecedented centralization of power. Among other things, the federal government regulated wages, prices, and industrial production. Beginning in 1948, grant expenditures began to rise again, and by 1954, they had reached their prewar level of $3 billion. During the administration of President Dwight D. Eisenhower in the 1950s, the amount of grants-in-aid money increased as an explicit attempt to counter the centralization of domestic programs in Washington.

The 1960s and early 1970s witnessed a major surge in grants-in-aid programs similar to the surges of the 1930s. As part of President Lyndon Johnson's Great Society initiative, roughly two dozen grants-in-aid programs were enacted in 1964 and 1965 alone. During the next two presidential administrations, more than 100 grant programs were created. These programs tended to concentrate on the problems of large metropolitan areas and covered a broad range of policy issues dealing with economic development, education, and race relations. They brought another important feature to the evolution of grants-in-aid: Some grants went directly to private groups, bypassing state and local governments.

By the early 1980s, the federal government was funneling huge amounts of money to states and localities, which in turn used the funds to finance an enormous expansion of the programs and policies they provided to citizens. Federalism was now characterized by the politics of grants-in-aid—a struggle between state and national government not over whether the federal government *should* be involved in policy areas that were traditionally the responsibility of the states but over *how* the involvement should be conducted.

The political battles over grants-in-aid reflect changing policy priorities over the past half-century. In the 1940s and 1950s federal assistance for health programs accounted for less than 10 percent of all federal grants to states and communities. Since the mid-1990s, healthcare programs have been the largest single category, accounting for close to 50 percent of federal grants-in-aid in recent years (see Figure 3.5). Federal grants to state and local governments currently account for 16 percent of all federal expenditures.

Given a choice, state policymakers tend to favor **general revenue sharing**, a type of grant that originated in the early 1970s and that comes with no strings attached. In general revenue sharing, the federal government gives money to states and localities to use as they wish. Federal policymakers, however, tend to favor **categorical grants**, programs that provide funds for a defined area of activity, such as education or public housing, but that also specify how the programs are to be carried out. Categorical grants allow the federal government to use the power of

general revenue sharing A type of federal grant that returns money to state and local governments with no requirements as to how it is spent.

categorical grants A type of federal grant that provides money for a specific policy activity and details how the programs are to be carried out.

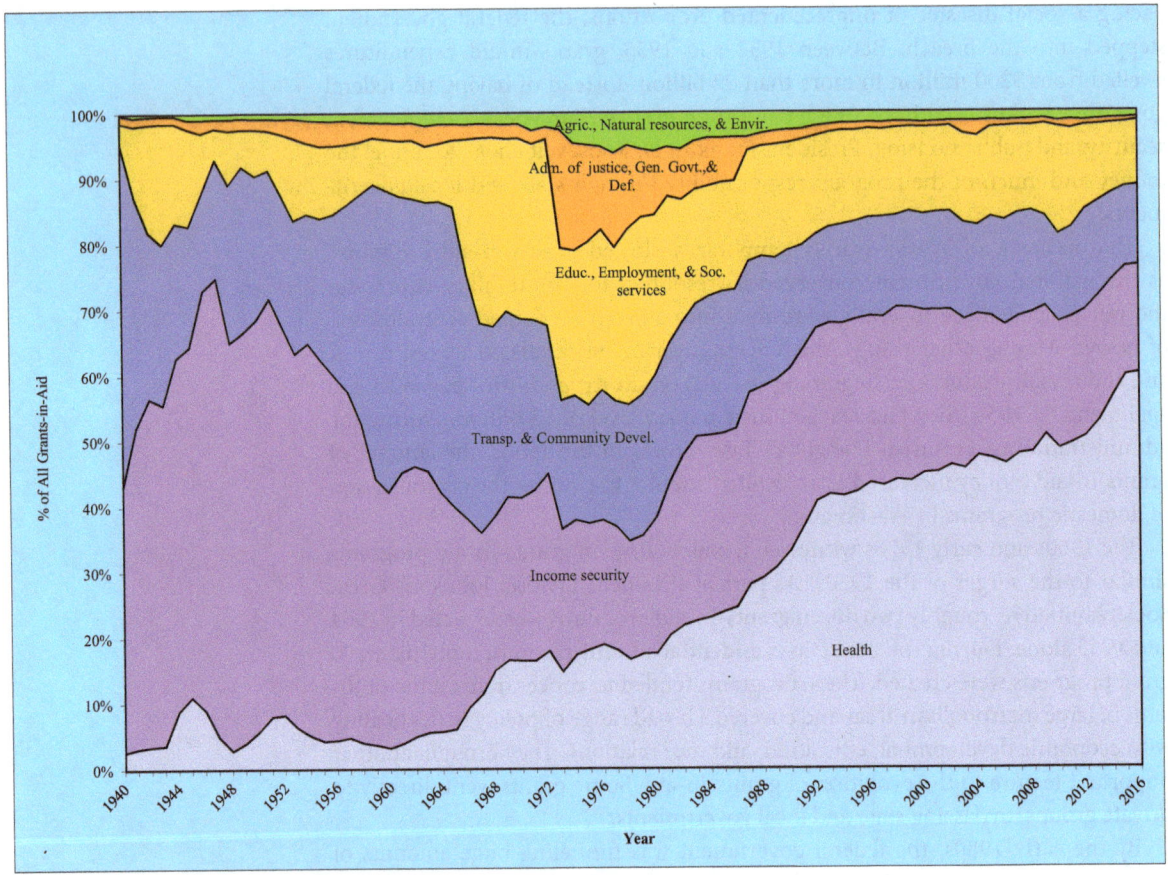

FIGURE 3.5 Changing Priorities in Grants-in-Aid, 1940–2016

Source: Data from Budget of the United States Government, Federal Budget, FY 2017, Table 12.2—Total outlays for Grants to State and Local Governments by Function and Fund Group: 1940–2021 (in millions of dollars), https://www.gpo.gov/fdsys/granule/BUDGET-2017-TAB/BUDGET-2017-TAB-15.

the purse to exercise maximum control over various policy responsibilities of state and local governments. Somewhere between general revenue sharing and categorical grants are **block grants**. Block grants provide funds for a general policy area, but they allow states and localities greater discretion than categorical grants in designing the programs being funded.

As grants-in-aid programs multiplied, they produced major problems of coordination and control for all government levels. No single, centralized mechanism manages grants-in-aid. Instead, they are controlled piecemeal by a dizzying array of departments and bureaus, many of which operate according to their own rules and regulations. The compartmentalization of hundreds of programs sometimes means the federal left hand does not know what the federal right hand is doing. The Department of Transportation, for example, might help develop a highway that displaces low-income urban residents, creating a shortage of low-income housing that ultimately becomes a major concern of officials in the Department of Housing

block grants A type of federal grant that provides funds for a general policy area but offers state and local governments' discretion in designing the specific programs.

and Urban Development. Legislators, governors, mayors, council members, and other officials charged with tracking overall public needs find it difficult to control the activities of specialized agencies and establish priorities among them.

Though these problems are significant, the two central drawbacks associated with cooperative federalism are its expense and its tendency to concentrate power in the hands of the federal government. State and local government revenues from income, sales, and property taxes nosedived during the recession of 2008–2009, and federal grants-in-aid became the largest single source of revenue for states and localities in 2009 and 2010. Those federal dollars come with strings attached. Grants-in-aid may require matching funds, which means that states must put up part of the money for a project, which the federal government then matches dollar for dollar (or sometimes three or four dollars for a dollar). Some complain that this matching requirement distorts states' authority to set priorities because states have an incentive to shift their tax revenue away from high-priority problems to get the federal subsidy that deals with a lower-priority problem. Other strings attached to federal grants-in-aid are aimed at quality control and at ensuring that the money is spent honestly and efficiently. For example, the American Recovery and Reinvestment Act (ARRA) did not just send billions in federal aid to states and localities; it required those governments to meet strict reporting and accountability requirements. By far the most controversial string attached to federal grants-in-aid is the so-called **crossover sanction**. Crossover sanctions are conditions placed on the receipt of grant money that have nothing to do with the original purpose of the grant. They are, in effect, the fee exacted for access to the federal treasury, and that fee is state acquiescence to the federal government's policy preferences. For example, the national government effectively set the national minimum drinking age at 21 by threatening to withhold highway funds from states that did not adopt this policy. Constitutionally speaking, setting the legal drinking age is the legislative province of the states. But the Supreme Court ruled that the federal government was allowed to place conditions on offers of financial aid as long as the states had the right to refuse the aid. The other options, such as raising taxes or going without the federal funds, were largely unpalatable to state politicians and the electorate. So the states accepted the conditions and the money. There has been a uniform drinking age of 21 in all states since the mid-1980s.

New Federalism

New federalism was a movement to take power from the federal government and return it to the states. Just as the era of cooperative federalism overlapped the era of dual federalism, no clear date marks the beginning of new federalism. The term *new federalism* was first used by President Richard Nixon to describe an early 1970s plan to reverse the trend of federal government expansion triggered by the Great Society programs of the 1960s. Nixon had mixed success. The main policy associated with Nixon's new federalism was general revenue sharing, which was popular with state and local governments but which hardly promoted their independence from the federal government.

crossover sanction Conditions placed on grant money that have nothing to do with the original purpose of the grant.

new federalism A movement to take power away from the federal government and return it to the states.

The first president to attempt a systematic reversal of cooperative federalism was Ronald Reagan. In the 1980 presidential election, Reagan campaigned vigorously against the concentration of power in Washington and promised to cut states free from the regulatory thicket that bound them to federal government dictates. President Reagan had some success in this effort. Federal grants-in-aid had increased from less than 1 percent of GDP in the 1940s to about 3.4 percent when Reagan took office in 1981. When he left office in 1989, spending on grants had fallen to 2.3 percent of GDP (see Figure 3.6).

But President Reagan's push to make federalism more state-centered quickly ran into several problems. First, cutting regulations and federal grants (including eliminating general revenue sharing entirely) did not simply cut the federal budget. It also shifted policy power and responsibility to the states, a process termed **devolution**. In essence, Reagan was proposing a radical restructuring of program and funding responsibilities between national and state governments, and this was

devolution The return of policy power and responsibility to the states from the national government.

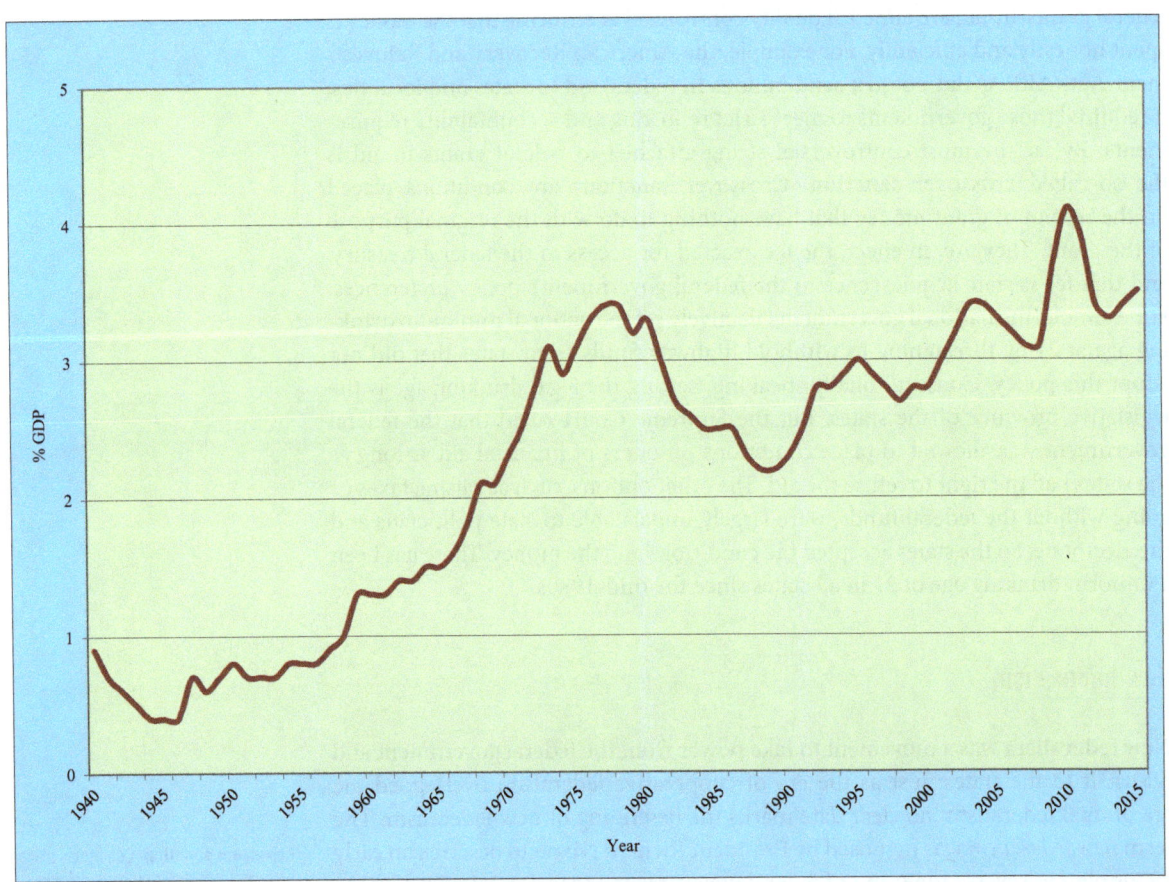

FIGURE 3.6 Grants-in-Aid as a Percent of GDP, 1940–2015

Source: Data from Budget of the United States Government, Fiscal Year 2017, Table 12.1—Summary Comparison of Total Outlays for Grants to State and Local Governments: 1940–2021, https://www.gpo.gov/fdsys/search/pagedetails.action?collectionCode=BUDGET&granuleId=BUDGET-2017-TAB-12-1&packageId=BUDGET-2017-TAB&fromBrowse=true.

opposed by Congress, which feared diminished influence over federal policy priorities, and by state officials who feared the loss of federal dollars that were now a critical revenue source. Thus, given the opposition, reducing federal grants (and their attendant regulations) was a hit-and-miss affair. When Reagan's successor, President George H. W. Bush, left office in 1993, federal spending on grants-in-aid had climbed to around 3 percent of GDP, and it remained at about that level through the 1990s. Second, many of Reagan's supporters began to realize that there were advantages to federal (as opposed to state) regulation, and they started to oppose the effort to turn regulatory power over to the states. Such reconsideration was especially true of business groups. Facing the prospect of 50 systems of regulation in areas such as consumer product safety and the environment, businesses began lobbying Congress for uniform and standardized federal laws.

New federalism picked up steam in the 1990s with the election of Bill Clinton, a former Democratic governor sympathetic to state interests, and a Republican Congress that made taking power away from Washington its campaign battle cry. The most dramatic of the new federalism initiatives of this era was the 1996 welfare reform law that ended the Aid to Families with Dependent Children (AFDC) program and gave states more flexibility to design and run their own welfare programs. The drive by Congress and the president to push more responsibilities toward the states was supported by a series of Supreme Court decisions that put more teeth into the Tenth Amendment. Among other things, the Supreme Court ruled that the federal government could not force local law enforcement agencies to perform criminal background checks (*Printz v. United States* 1997) and that citizens could not use a federal law to sue a state in a state court (*Alden v. Maine* 1999).

New federalism represented a rethinking of which level of government should bear primary responsibility for a particular policy area and which level of government should pay for the programs in that area. Many saw this as potentially constructive; the give-and-take over program and funding responsibility would result in policy responsibilities evolving to their "natural" level of government. For example, because of its broader tax base and national reach, the federal government was seen as better suited to manage redistributive policies (policies that take something from one group and give it to another, such as Social Security and welfare programs). State governments, on the other hand, were seen as better suited to handle developmental policies (roads, education, and the like) (Peterson 1995).

Though a good idea in theory, in practice the new federalism movement never managed to get federal and state governments to agree to such a neat (and perhaps sensible) division of policy responsibilities. States took on big redistributive policy responsibilities. Welfare, for example, is a redistributive policy where responsibility has shifted significantly away from the federal and toward the state level. This raised concerns that states would adopt stingier welfare programs because generous welfare programs might attract disadvantaged people from less generous states. This is good for the states they leave because it reduces states' welfare costs. It is bad for the states they move to because it forces taxpayers in those states to shoulder a disproportionate share of the burden in providing a social safety net. The obvious way to avoid being the sucker in this scenario is for a state to slash its welfare benefits. Doing so then encourages surrounding states to do the same, and the net result is a "race to the bottom" (Peterson and Rom 1990; Rom, Peterson, and Scheve 1998).

By the beginning of President George W. Bush's administration, it was clear that governmental commitment to the philosophical underpinnings of new federalism was suspect, especially at the federal level. The federal government continued to pass **unfunded mandates**—provisions in federal statutes requiring states and localities to take on certain responsibilities without covering any of the associated expenses. For example, the signature domestic policy of Bush's first term was the No Child Left Behind (NCLB) law. This law required state and local governments to pay for large portions of a federally mandated program, but also shifts power over education—constitutionally a responsibility of state governments—toward the national government. Bush was a former governor, and he came to office as a strong supporter, at least rhetorically, of the new federalist philosophy. Yet the first years of his presidency were marked by a sagging economy and devastating terrorist attacks in New York City and Washington, DC; early military successes in Afghanistan and Iraq were followed by unexpectedly difficult guerilla campaigns, and the economy took the biggest downturn since the Great Depression during his last year in office. Recession and war traditionally focus power on the national government because it can better deal with such challenges. Here, this was the case: States and localities followed the lead of the federal government.

State–federal relations during the Clinton and George W. Bush years were sometimes described as **ad hoc federalism**, in which a state-centered or nation-centered view of federalism is adopted on the basis of political ideology (Baybeck and Lowry 2000; Smith, Buntin, and Greenblatt 2004, 52). Rather than a commitment to a particular vision of what state and federal governments should or should not do, the issue at hand (and who supported it) determined whether federal policymakers employed the states' rights or federal supremacy argument.

The new federalism movement stumbled at the beginning of the twenty-first century because of the unusual strength and coherence of a single political party, which for much of the Bush presidency controlled the White House, both houses of Congress, and a majority of governorships and state legislative chambers. Ironically, this was the Republican Party in control, traditionally the party of states' rights and of limited federal government. A centralized and coherent Republican Party structure seemed to help overcome the fragmented nature of the federal system and allow at least some party policy preferences to be achieved in a more national, top-down fashion (Krane and Koenig 2005). **Preemption**, in which Congress expressly gives national laws precedence over state laws, was a hallmark of several important policy areas during the Bush administration (examples include the No Child Left Behind law, which mandated that states follow federal education policies, and the Real ID Act, which set federal requirements for state-issued drivers' licenses and identification cards). Certainly by the end of the Bush presidency, state and local governments saw the federal government as having largely abandoned the ideals of new federalism.

The basic lack of a guiding philosophy or principle in shaping state–federal relations continued through the Obama administration, though Bush's successor found it increasingly hard to push a top-down policy agenda onto the states.

unfunded mandates Federal mandates for which the federal government does not pay any associated costs.

ad hoc federalism The process of adopting a state- or nation-centered view of federalism on the basis of political convenience.

preemption Congress expressly giving national laws precedence over state and local laws.

APPLYING THE FRAMEWORKS

IS IT RATIONAL TO CUT WELFARE BENEFITS?

States have a good deal of leeway in determining how much of a social safety net to place beneath their citizens. Unsurprisingly, the generosity of that net varies a good deal across states. According to one study by the Cato Institute, a libertarian-leaning think tank, you'd need a job paying $29 an hour to equal the welfare package you can get in Hawaii. In Idaho, on the other hand, welfare benefits are more miserly, equaling an hourly wage of $5.36 (Tanner and Hughes 2013). That's less than the minimum pay you'd get operating a fry machine at the local burger joint.

So, why not move to Hawaii? Great weather, great beaches, and you can live high on the $29-an-hour hog without working a lick. If you are scraping by on Idaho's chintzy welfare checks, wouldn't it be rational to move to Hawaii?

According to the rational choice framework, variation in welfare benefits across states might indeed create incentives for welfare recipients to move. Thus we might expect those rational, but less well-off citizens to flock to states with generous welfare benefits. This is the "magnet hypothesis," the idea that states with higher welfare benefits will become magnets for the needy. There's a catch here, though. Rational choice theory can actually help explain why this might not happen.

State policymakers might have a different set of incentives than the poor. From their perspective it might be rational to decrease welfare benefits to dissuade the less well-off from moving to the state, and to increase incentives for the unemployed to seek out a job. This will keep government expenditures lower and increase revenues—the cost–benefit there is pretty clear.

If people are rational, then it would suggest less that some states will become welfare magnets than that states should engage in a "race to the bottom." Recognizing that welfare recipients are rational and will shop for the best benefit deal, state policymakers will rationally decide to lower their benefit levels to avoid the possibility of their state picking up more than its fair share of the nation's welfare tab.

This all sounds like a reasonable enough hypothesis, intuitive even, but does it actually happen? In contrast to the magnet hypothesis, research suggests that states do not actively undercut each other to avoid attracting welfare recipients, and welfare recipients do not move from state to state looking for a better benefit package (Allard and Danziger 2000; Berry, Fording, and Hanson 2003).

What's going on? Are people—welfare recipients and state policymakers—not rational? Well, if there's no influx of benefit seekers swelling welfare rolls, policymakers have less rational incentive to cut benefits. As for welfare recipients, consider that moving to Hawaii from Idaho is not cheap, and the cost of living is higher there, so the benefits are not directly comparable on a dollar-for-dollar basis. Just gathering all the information to make a good rational decision on the costs versus benefits of going on the dole in Hawaii versus Idaho could be a pretty big headache in and of itself. It might be more rational just to stay put.

Discussion Questions

1. Is it rational to decide to enroll in an out-of-state university where tuition is higher compared to an equivalent in-state university with lower tuition?
2. Imagine two friends trying to decide where to go to college and facing the same sort of scenario laid out in question 1. These friends are neighbors, their families have similar incomes, and they are equivalent in academic interests and qualifications. Is it possible for one friend to decide to go to the out-of-state university and the other to go to the in-state university and for both decisions to be rational? Why or why not?

A number of states, notably those under conservative Republican leadership, fought against Obama's policy priorities ranging from environmental regulation to Medicaid expansion. In the Obama era, big partisan and ideological differences on a range of policies opened up between the states, as well as between some states and the national government. As a result state–federal relations developed into what some called "two-speed federalism" (Posner and Conlon 2014). This described the ground reality that, while some conservative states like Texas resisted the Obama administration's policy agenda, other more progressive-leaning states like California were much more in tune with Obama's policy preferences. To deal with these yawning gaps in state-level policy preferences, the federal government started giving some states opt-outs, which allowed them to avoid participating in some federal programs. Other states were given waivers that allowed them to go far beyond the federal minimum requirements in areas like environmental regulation. Thus the "two-speeds"—more conservative states employed opt-outs to slow or even halt federal government initiatives within their borders, while more progressive states sought waivers to speed up or surpass those same initiatives.

Federalism and the Future of State–Federal Relations

For much of the twenty-first century, state–federal relations have been characterized by increasing partisan and ideological polarization. In the first decade or so of the century, gridlock and inertia by the federal government on a range of policy issues important to the states—everything from immigration to environmental regulation—pushed the states into stepping into the policy vacuum. For example, states mounted a serious attempt to take the lead in pursuing immigration reform, a policy arena traditionally considered in the jurisdiction of the federal government. Arizona passed a law allowing the state to revoke the licenses of businesses knowingly hiring undocumented immigrants. Oklahoma passed laws requiring people to demonstrate proof of citizenship or legal immigration status to receive certain government benefits.

This growing policy independence from the federal government was slowed sharply as a result of the Great Recession of 2008–2009. The economic contraction severely squeezed state revenues, and the federal government responded by pumping billions of dollars into programs critical to state and local governments. Taking the federal government's money, however, also meant prioritizing the federal government's policy priorities, something that many states did not want to do. As their economies and finances stabilized, state governments once again began asserting their independence, though during the Obama administration this increasingly became characterized by ideological and partisan divisions, rather than by any core philosophy of an appropriate division of state–federal policy responsibilities.

Contemporary scholarship tends to characterize current state–federal relations as increasingly ideological and partisan (Rose and Bowling 2015). This was brought into particularly sharp relief during the Obama administration as governors and attorneys general in conservative states—like Gregg Abbott in Texas—aggressively sought to unhitch their wagons from the federal policy train. Indeed, the relationship became so fractious that some conservative states resurrected what amounted to nullification laws during the Obama administration. As discussed above, the issue of nullification—declaring federal laws null and void within states' borders—was settled by the Civil War. Yet several states tested the limits of that settlement. For example, Montana, Missouri, and Kansas experimented with laws that exempt from federal regulations all firearms manufactured in-state. When legally challenged, these laws failed to pass constitutional muster in federal court (basically, the courts have ruled a state cannot ignore federal regulations). Still, just the fact that states actively sought to revive a legal basis for nullification—an issue, remember, that helped trigger the Civil War—shows just how antagonistic state-federal relationships became during the Obama administration.

The election of Donald Trump in 2016 brought the policy preferences of such conservative states much closer to those of the federal government, but prompted more Democratic and progressive states to pick up the mantle of resistance to federal policy priorities. In other words, the most recent presidential election seems to have done little to reduce the stark ideological and partisan divisions between state and federal governments. It has just prompted states to switch sides, flipping from resistance to cooperation or vice versa based on the partisan and ideological leanings of state leadership.

Though certainly increasingly fractious, it is also important to note that state–federal relations are not uniformly antagonistic. For example, even the most conservative states and the Obama administration showed a willingness to give and take on some issues. For example, many states asked to be exempted from the regulatory requirements of the federal No Child Left Behind law, requirements that the states argued to be unrealistic and impose undue budgetary burdens. In nearly all cases, the Obama administration granted these waivers. So, while the federal and state governments are clearly not happy with each other on some issues, both continue to recognize that, like it or not, they need each other to get things done. What they disagree on is who has the power to decide what should be done and who should pay for it. That disagreement, though, is nothing new. It is a debate as old as the constitution, and an argument state and federal governments will vociferously engage in for the foreseeable future.

CHAPTER THREE
Top 10 Takeaway Points

1. Federalism is a political system in which regional governments share power with the national government. In the system established by the U.S. Constitution, states are sovereign powers and are partners of, rather than subordinates to, the federal government. Federalism was adopted because the Founders saw it as both philosophically pleasing and politically feasible.

2. Two other primary means of dividing power in a political system exist. In a confederation, the central government is subordinate to the regional governments. In a unitary system, power is concentrated in the central government, and regional governments can exercise only the power granted to them by central authority.

3. Federalism offers some general advantages. It allows experimentation and gives regional governments the ability to tailor policy more closely to local preferences. It has disadvantages, such as creating an often confusing patchwork of laws and regulations across a nation.

4. The Constitution grants the national government enumerated and implied powers. Enumerated powers are specified in the Constitution. Implied powers come from broad constitutional clauses such as the power to "make all laws which shall be necessary and proper" (Article I, Section 8). Enumerated and implied powers have been interpreted broadly and have allowed the constitutional expansion of the national government.

5. The Constitution gives no specific powers to state governments. The Tenth Amendment says that the powers not given to the national government or prohibited to the states "are reserved to the states respectively, or to the people." The general source of political authority for the states is their own constitutions, which specify each state's powers and limitations.

6. The Constitution spells out certain rights and obligations of the states. Rights include a republican form of government, equal representation in the Senate, equality with other states, and the right to approve any changes to the U.S. Constitution. Obligations include extending "full faith and credit" to the public acts and records of other states and returning criminals who cross state lines to the state with jurisdiction over the crime.

7. All state and federal laws, including state constitutions, are subordinate to the U.S. Constitution, in effect making the Supreme Court the ultimate umpire of the federal system.

8. Federal and state governments and the relationship between them have evolved considerably in the two centuries the Constitution has been in force. All levels of government have become larger and have played a more prominent role in the lives of citizens.

9. State–federal relations can be roughly categorized into three eras: dual federalism, cooperative federalism, and new federalism.

10. State–federal power relationships are currently fractious and unstable. States have different ideological and partisan policy preferences on a range of issues,

and those preferences can bring states into direct conflict with the policy agenda of the federal government.

CHAPTER THREE
Key Terms and Cases

ad hoc federalism, 106
block grants, 102
categorical grants, 101
concurrent powers, 90
confederation, 80
cooperative federalism, 100
crossover sanction, 103
devolution, 104

dual federalism, 98
enabling act, 93
federalism, 81
"full faith and credit", 92
general revenue sharing, 101
grants-in-aid, 100
interstate rendition, 93
McCulloch v. Maryland, 88

new federalism, 103
nullification, 99
police power, 90
preemption, 106
"supreme law of the land", 95
unfunded mandates, 106
unitary system, 81

4 CIVIL LIBERTIES

KEY QUESTIONS

What are civil liberties?

How can civil liberties be balanced with the need to maintain social order?

What individual freedoms are guaranteed by the Bill of Rights?

© John Rudoff/Sipa/AP Photo

HAMEED KHALID DARWEESH repeatedly put his life in danger for the United States of America. He spent a decade working for America's military in Iraq, a job that made him very unpopular with some very dangerous people. When the all-too-real death threats made against him and his family became too much, he immigrated to the United States with his family. At least, he tried to.

Darweesh was not welcomed by the country he had faithfully served for so many years at great personal risk. Indeed, when he landed at Kennedy International Airport in January 2017, government officials handcuffed and detained him, then threatened to send him back to Iraq. Soldiers who had worked with Darweesh were appalled at how the United States government was treating their former comrade. "We have a moral obligation to protect and repay these people who risked their lives for U.S. troops," said former 101st Airborne Division infantry officer Brandon Friedman, who had worked with Darweesh during a tour of Iraq (Kulish 2017).

Darweesh was just one of hundreds of people caught up in an immigration ban triggered by an executive order signed by President Donald Trump shortly after he took office in early 2017. This barred people from seven predominantly Muslim countries (Iran, Iraq, Libya, Somalia, Sudan, Syria, and Yemen) from entering the United States for 90 days, and prevented the admission of all refugees for 120 days. The order was politically explosive because it was widely interpreted as a "Muslim ban" and was quickly and successfully challenged in federal court. Darweesh was, eventually, allowed entry into the country.

At the center of this controversy was a question of whether the president had overstepped his constitutional authority by effectively putting a religious test on entry into the United States. The Trump administration claimed it was doing no such thing, that its motivation was solely a concern for national security and that the policy was aimed at keeping terrorists out of the country, not Muslims. The sweeping nature of the executive order—and Trump's own campaign rhetoric—raised enough skepticism about this reasoning that implementation of the order was quickly blocked by a series of federal judges. The Trump administration returned to the drawing board to try and craft a more narrowly tailored set of immigration restrictions.

This controversy highlights one of the central tensions in democratic societies: the need to balance individual freedom with social order. Few people believe that banning people from the United States based on nothing more than their religious beliefs serves the broader interests of society. Yet most people also believe that the government needs enough power to go after bad guys who mean us harm, maybe even when the evidence that the "bad" guy is really bad is not wrapped up in a nice neat package. On the campaign trail, Trump repeatedly played up the need to tighten border security in the name of national security. Part of that was doing a better job of figuring out how to prevent terrorists from slipping into the country by camouflaging themselves as one of the thousands of completely innocent immigrants and refugees who, like Darweesh, were simply trying to flee turmoil in their homeland and start a new life in America. The big question was whether the potential guilt of a few overwhelmed the rights of the many, whether national security trumped individual civil liberties. The basic issue in this whole controversy was whether the government should have the power to sweep aside the rights of certain individuals in the name of protecting the common good.

There are no universally approved answers to this sort of question. The problem of balancing the freedom of the individual with the need for social order is a dilemma that raises big questions about the core democratic principle of political freedom. It is a balancing act that requires facing the Madisonian dilemma discussed in Chapter 2: How do you give government enough authority to preserve social order and communal values, but not so much that it places unfair and inappropriate limits on individual freedom of choice? In this chapter, we explore how the United States has struggled with this question by examining civil liberties—the freedom of individual citizens—and the constitutional principles that protect them.

Hameed Khalid Darweesh repeatedly put his life in danger working for America's military in Iraq. He immigrated to the United States to escape threats against him and his family. But when he landed at Kennedy International Airport in January 2017, government officials detained him and threatened to send him back to Iraq. Darweesh was just one of hundreds of people caught up in an immigration ban triggered by President Donald Trump's executive order that barred people from seven predominantly Muslim countries from entering the U.S. Darweesh was allowed to enter the country after a federal court overturned the order. Here Darweesh addresses the media after his release.
© Andrew Kelly/Reuters

THE CONCEPT OF CIVIL LIBERTIES

Civil liberties are the freedoms enjoyed by individuals in a democratic society. They constitute the choices individuals are free to make with minimal interference from governmental authority. Examples of freedoms that the Constitution guarantees to Americans include choosing and practicing religious beliefs, speaking our minds, forming associations of like-minded people, and due process of law before government can take one's life, liberty, or property. Civil liberties thus boil down to the core democratic principle of political freedom: They represent a basic guarantee that individual citizens are free to make their own choices and to select their own goals and the means to achieve them.

Yet civil liberties are not absolute. Even democratic governments impose restrictions on individual liberties in the name of the public interest. Consider the First Amendment rights of free speech and assembly, for example. You cannot use speech to incite a riot, and before you exercise your right to assemble by organizing a mass demonstration, government authorities may require you to obtain permits and to satisfy health, safety, and sanitary regulations. Such restrictions seek to balance individual freedoms with the need to maintain social order.

Liberty and Authority

Striking the right balance between individual liberty and the government authority necessary to maintain social order is not an easy task. Championing the freedom of the individual over the need for social order (or vice versa) is not just a philosophical choice, but a perspective that can change depending on particular time and circumstance. For example, in the immediate aftermath of the terrorist attacks of September 11, 2001, government authority took precedence over individual liberty as citizens sought assurances of personal safety and national security. Just 45 days after 9/11, Congress passed the PATRIOT Act, legislation that gave the government sweeping new powers to spy on its own citizens. This aggressive response to ensure security and social order was popular, at least initially. Yet it soon became clear that the aggressive efforts to tighten national security ran into, and sometimes over, civil liberties. Under the provisions of the PATRIOT Act, government agencies can secretly search your house or even your library records. Compare these powers with the individual freedoms guaranteed by the Fourth Amendment, which gives individual citizens the right to be secure in their "persons, houses, papers, and effects" and free from "unreasonable searches and seizures." If the government is conducting a "sneak and peak" search of your records to make sure you are not taking an unhealthy interest in extremist religious groups and is doing it without your knowledge, do you still have all the liberties guaranteed by the Constitution?

civil liberties The freedoms and protections against arbitrary governmental actions given to the people in a democratic society.

As 9/11 passed into history, the basic justification for the PATRIOT Act—that the government needs the power to snoop on Americans to help keep Americans safe—came under increasing scrutiny. The original legislation passed overwhelmingly; the only U.S. senator to cast a nay vote in 2001 was Senator Russ Feingold (D-WI), who waged a lonely battle against giving the federal government the power to infringe on the civil liberties of its citizens. In 2006, 10 senators—nine Democrats and one independent—voted against reauthorizing the PATRIOT Act. In 2011, when key provisions of the PATRIOT Act came up for renewal, 12 senators—including two Republicans—cast nay votes. In 2015, Republican senators cast 30 of 32 nay votes. In other words, despite consistent passage of the law by large majorities, opposition in Congress began to grow, from a single senator to a small cadre of Democrats to a larger core dominated by Republicans. This growing concern about the power given by the PATRIOT Act to the federal government reflected increasingly mixed views about whether the law appropriately balanced individual freedoms with the need for social order. In 2011, public support was split, with roughly 40 percent of people supporting the law as a tool for catching terrorists and about a third seeing it as a threat to civil liberties (Pew Research Center 2011). In 2013, stories of widespread surveillance of phone records and even e-mails by the National Security Agency (NSA) began cropping up in the media, and support for this sort of snooping became even more mixed. Majorities favored such intrusions of privacy if it helped catch terrorists, but majorities also opposed giving the federal government license to monitor citizens' online activities (Pew Research Center 2015b). In 2015, about two-thirds of Americans said they believed that limits on the kinds of phone and Internet data the government can collect from them were not adequate (Pew Research Center 2015a).

These shifting views on the PATRIOT Act and the federal government's justifications for sifting through phone records and e-mails reflect the difficulty of coming up with definitive answers to questions about how the American political system can best balance individual liberty and the authority of government. How much of our civil liberties are we willing to give up for greater assurances of security? Should the government be able to detain people indefinitely without charges? Conduct secret searches? Target groups for surveillance based on their religious or political beliefs?

These questions are hard to answer because the issue is not whether we pick liberty *or* authority, but rather figuring out the right mix of liberty *and* authority. Government must have some authority to set and enforce limits on individual freedom to maintain social order because without social order, that freedom ceases to exist. Without that authority, one individual's freedoms extend only to the willingness of the next individual to respect those freedoms. Inevitably, some will use their freedom to deprive others of their liberties, their property, or even their lives. Without a central authority, social order is replaced by anarchy. Yet democracy does not require complete social order, because this would mean that the state could dictate individual behavior, and this too would threaten individual freedom. The government, for example, could make the country more secure from the threat of terrorism by increasing the monitoring of individual activities, restricting the freedom to travel, and outlawing certain political groups or beliefs.

APPLYING THE FRAMEWORKS

BIOLOGY AND CIVIL LIBERTIES

The United States was founded on the concept of natural or inalienable rights, or the idea that rights cannot be taken away from the individuals who possess them. This is the idea embedded in the Declaration of Independence, which states that "all men are created equal" and endowed by their creator "with certain inalienable rights."

Yet it is also clear that a person's civil liberties depend critically on the legal, political, and economic system they happen to find themselves in. In the newly independent United States many African Americans did not get the right to speak their minds or even own the rights to their own bodies. So does this mean the concept of universal, inalienable rights—the very idea on which America was founded—is just so much bunk?

The problem for empirical researchers in dealing with questions like, "What are civil rights? Where do they come from?" is that they seem unavoidably normative. They seem like subjective questions about what is right and what is wrong; more the realm of philosophers and theorists rather than empirical social scientists.

Jonathan Haidt is a psychologist who wanted to understand the long running puzzle of why moral reasoning varies across human cultures. In some societies it's acceptable for individuals to do their own thing and it is considered immoral to limit their freedoms, while in others it's considered perfectly ethical to limit or even deny those freedoms in the name of social order.

Haidt and his colleagues began asking people questions about various moral dilemmas. For example, they asked what people took into consideration when they were deciding if something was right or wrong: Did someone suffer emotionally? Was someone treated differently? The answers suggested people took five distinct concerns into consideration when making decisions about right and wrong. Two reflected concerns about treating individuals fairly and preventing individual harm. Three reflected concerns more about the group than the individual: respect for authority, violations of social taboos, and group loyalty. Haidt (2012) called these five concerns "Moral Foundations."

What differs across societies and individuals is which of the five Moral Foundations are given emphasis. Those who base their moral judgments more on concerns about the group are more willing to restrict the rights or freedoms of individuals. Those who focus more on concerns about the individual tend to be more willing to let people make their own choices even if it upsets the group.

Think of the Moral Foundations as five dials. The settings on those dials vary a lot across societies and a lot across individuals. That variation correlates with how people and societies view civil liberties. Haidt and his colleagues argue that what settings we get on these dials is partially embedded in our DNA, the basic idea being that our psychology was shaped by evolutionary forces acting on repeated social dilemmas. These dilemmas included what to do with people who broke accepted norms or rules, and how much to trust outside groups. Given enough time, these evolutionary selection forces were strong enough to shape a set of human psychological modules—the Moral Foundations—in much the same way evolutionary forces shaped our physical characteristics. The society and situation we are born into also moves the dials based on whether we are in a culture that prizes individual freedom or group cohesion.

So where do civil liberties come from? Are we born with them, or are they gifts of a particular political, legal, economic, and social system? Moral Foundations research implies the answer to this last question might be a bit of both.

Discussion Questions

1. Take the Moral Foundations survey at http://www.yourmorals.org/. How do you think the results relate to your attitudes on civil liberties?
2. How would you go about testing whether scores on the Moral Foundation survey predict attitudes toward civil liberties? How would you measure these attitudes?

Doing so, however, would destroy political freedom. The crux of the issue is how a free and secure society can achieve an acceptable balance between the values of individual freedom and the authority needed to maintain social order.

Resolving the conflicts that arise over these two values is difficult and complex, especially when individual liberties conflict. One group or individual exercising its rights may infringe on the rights and liberties of others. You have probably heard the old cliché that you can exercise your rights only as long as doing so does not interfere with someone else's rights. That's wrong. When an individual exercises a right, it inevitably comes into conflict with someone else's right. A classic case is a newspaper editor who exercises freedom of the press by publishing information about a crime that consequently jeopardizes the right of the accused to a fair trial. Is freedom of the press more important than a fair trial? Or does the right to a fair trial justify limiting freedom of the press? In such cases, the authority of government has to choose, in effect, whose freedoms are more important. How does a democratic society go about choosing which individual freedoms take precedence over others?

RESTRICTIONS ON THE GOVERNMENT

The basic approach to dealing with civil liberties in the United States begins with the belief that citizens should have as much freedom as possible to make individual choices. The Bill of Rights provides a starting point for establishing what individuals are free to do without government meddling. These freedoms have evolved considerably over the past two centuries.

The Bill of Rights

A central concern among those who took the initiative in calling the Constitutional Convention was the protection of individual property rights from state governments. But the convention's participants gave almost no consideration to safeguarding civil liberties from the actions of national authorities. Although one of the main reasons for splitting from the United Kingdom was the lack of guaranteed individual rights, the notion of formally including such rights in the Constitution was brought up only toward the end of the convention, and even then in a half-hearted way. As originally written, the Constitution contained virtually no mention of guaranteed civil liberties (Collier and Collier 1986, 338).

The absence of a guaranteed set of civil liberties—a Bill of Rights—became one of the central issues raised by opponents to the Constitution during the ratification campaign. Even leaders such as Thomas Jefferson, who favored the adoption of the Constitution, were unhappy that the convention had not included a statement of rights. The absence of a Bill of Rights "nearly sank the Constitution" (Collier and Collier 1986, 342). In response, the Federalists backing adoption of the Constitution agreed to make fashioning a Bill of Rights one of the first orders of business of the new government formed after ratification. Acting under a moral rather than a legal obligation, George Washington, in his inaugural address, asked Congress to give careful attention to the demands to amend the Constitution to include a statement of rights.

James Madison took the lead in coordinating the suggestions of state ratifying conventions and introduced the amendments into the House of Representatives. Congress pared the list down to 12, and 10 of the resulting amendments were ratified relatively quickly. These first 10 amendments constitute the Bill of Rights, which became the legal basis of civil liberties in the United States. Both the Anti-Federalists and the Federalists gained from the process. The former saw their initial support for a Bill of Rights vindicated, and the latter gained additional popular support for the Constitution they authored.

Restrictions on State Violations of Civil Liberties

The Bill of Rights originally applied only to the federal government, not to state governments. In the early years of the republic, this made sense for the simple reason that states were well ahead of the federal government in guaranteeing basic civil liberties. For example, Virginia's Declaration of Rights, passed years before the Constitutional Convention, guaranteed its citizens basic freedoms of press and religion and the right to a trial by jury. In fact, all the early state constitutions either contained a separate Bill of Rights or incorporated similar provisions as part of the basic document.

Since state governments already had basic guarantees of civil liberties in their constitutions, it is not surprising that Congress focused on the national government when developing the Bill of Rights. Nowhere did Congress specifically state that the amendments in the Bill of Rights applied only to the national government, but this was likely the intention of those who drafted them in the early 1790s.[1] The Supreme Court explicitly confirmed that the Bill of Rights applied only to the national government in the case of *Barron v. Baltimore* (1833).

The application of the Bill of Rights to state governments, however, gradually became an increasingly important question in guaranteeing civil liberties. This issue was especially important in the South during much of the nineteenth and twentieth centuries, when a number of state governments passed laws systematically denying civil liberties to racial minorities. The Civil War had ended slavery, thus freeing African Americans from involuntary servitude, but state laws prevented many from enjoying the full rights and freedoms of citizenship. Following the Civil War, the Thirteenth, Fourteenth, and Fifteenth Amendments seemed to take a large step toward making the Bill of Rights apply to state governments as well as the federal government. Of particular importance is the Fourteenth Amendment, which reads in part, "No state shall make or enforce any law which

Barron v. Baltimore The 1833 Supreme Court case that explicitly confirmed that the Bill of Rights applied only to the national government.

---

[1] The First Amendment states that "Congress shall make no law," and presumably this phrase is read into the amendments that follow, although this is never clarified.

shall ... deprive any person of life, liberty, or property, without due process of law." The Fifth Amendment contains a "due process of law" clause that applies to the national government, and the same clause in the Fourteenth Amendment applies to the states. The same clause appearing in both amendments implies that at least part—and perhaps all—of the Bill of Rights is binding on state governments.

These parallel provisions sparked a running debate over what is known as the **incorporation doctrine**, the notion that the Bill of Rights applies to state governments as well as the federal government through the due process clause of the Fourteenth Amendment. Some argued that the Fourteenth Amendment applied the entire Bill of Rights to state governments. Others disagreed, arguing that the due process clause applied the Bill of Rights more selectively to the states, and the applications and limitations should be worked out on a case-by-case basis. The Supreme Court followed the latter course and slowly began using the Fourteenth Amendment's due process clause to apply the Bill of Rights to the states.

An important early example of this piecemeal approach to the incorporation doctrine came in the 1925 case of *Gitlow v. New York*. Here the Supreme Court ruled that the freedoms of speech and the press are such fundamental rights that the Fourteenth Amendment prevents states from unduly limiting these freedoms. Using similar reasoning in other cases, the Court added the other First Amendment freedoms to the liberties so protected. Over the years, much of the Bill of Rights has, provision by provision, been applied to the states. Table 4.1 lists provisions in the Bill of Rights that have been incorporated. Today most, but not all, of the limitations on government in the Bill of Rights apply to the states as well as to the national government. Some of the rights guaranteed by the Bill of Rights that the U.S. Supreme Court has not yet applied to state governments through the due process clause of the Fourteenth Amendment include the Fifth Amendment right to indictment by grand jury and the Seventh Amendment guarantee of a jury trial in civil suits.

The most recent amendment to be incorporated is the Second Amendment's right to keep and bear arms (*McDonald v. Chicago* 2010). In full, the Second Amendment states, "A well regulated Militia, being necessary to the security of a free State, the right of the people to keep and bear Arms, shall not be infringed." There has been considerable disagreement over what this provision means. Some argue that it guarantees individuals the right to own and carry firearms with minimal regulation by government. Others argue that the amendment refers to citizen militias—citizen-based military organizations formed for the purpose of common defense that were common during the founding era—but provides no individual right to own firearms (Williams 2003). The few existing precedents supported the latter interpretation. This position was most clearly expressed in *U.S. v. Miller* (1939), in which the Supreme Court held that the Second Amendment's "obvious purpose" was to ensure the effectiveness of a well-regulated militia and not to guarantee an individual's right to gun ownership. The Court reaffirmed this interpretation in *Lewis v. United States* (1980).

In the case of **District of Columbia v. Heller** (2008), striking down the Washington, DC, ban on the possession of handguns, the Supreme Court overturned these precedents and for the first time held that the Second Amendment protects

---

incorporation doctrine The idea that the specific protections provided in the U.S. Bill of Rights are binding on the states through the "due process" clause of the Fourteenth Amendment.

District of Columbia v. Heller The 2008 case in which the Supreme Court struck down the Washington, DC, ban on the possession of handguns and for the first time held that the Second Amendment protects an individual's right to possess a firearm for lawful purposes such as self-defense.

TABLE 4.1 INCORPORATION OF THE BILL OF RIGHTS TO APPLY TO STATE GOVERNMENTS

Year	Amend.	Issue	Supreme Court Case	Vote
1868	XIV	Fourteenth Amendment ratified		
1897	V	Just compensation in taking of private property by government	*Chicago, Burlington & Quincy RR v. Chicago* 166 U.S. 266	9:0
1925	I	Freedom of speech & press	*Gitlow v. New York* 268 U.S. 652	7:2
1927	I	Freedom of speech	*Fiske v. Kansas* 274 U.S. 380	9:0
1931	I	Freedom of press	*Near v. Minnesota* 283 U.S. 697	5:4
1932	VI	Counsel in capital criminal cases	*Powell v. Alabama* 287 U.S. 45	7:2
1934	I	Free exercise of religion	*Hamilton v. Regents of the U. of California* 293 U.S. 245	9:0
1937	I	Freedom of assembly & petition	*De Jonge v. Oregon* 299 U.S. 253	8:0
1940	I	Free exercise of religion	*Cantwell v. Connecticut* 310 U.S. 296	9:0
1947	I	Separation of church & state	*Everson v. Board of Education* 330 U.S. 1	5:4
1948	VI	Public trial	*In re Oliver* 33 U.S. 257	7:2
1949	IV	Unreasonable searches & seizures	*Wolf v. Colorado* 338 U.S. 25	6:3
1961	IV	Exclusionary rule of evidence from unreasonable searches & seizures	*Mapp v. Ohio* 367 U.S. 643	6:3
1962	VIII	Cruel & unusual punishment	*Robinson v. California* 370 U.S. 660	6:2
1963	VI	Counsel in all criminal cases	*Gideon v. Wainwright* 372 U.S. 335	9:0
1964	V	Self-incrimination	*Malloy v. Hogan* 378 U.S. 1	5:4
			Murphy v. Waterfront Commission 378 U.S. 52	9:0
1965	VI	Right to confront adverse witnesses	*Pointer v. Texas* 380 U.S. 400	7:2
1965	IX	Right to privacy	*Griswold v. Connecticut* 381 U.S. 479	7:2
1967	VI	Impartial jury	*Parker v. Gladden* 385 U.S. 363	8:1
1967	VI	Obtaining & confronting favorable witnesses	*Washington v. Texas* 388 U.S. 14	9:0
1967	VI	Speedy trial	*Klopfer v. North Carolina* 386 U.S. 213	9:0
1968	VI	Jury trial in non-petty criminal cases	*Duncan v. Louisiana* 391 U.S. 145	7:2
1969	V	Double jeopardy	*Benton v. Maryland* 395 U.S. 784	7:2
2010	II	Individual right to keep and bear arms	*McDonald v. Chicago,* 561 U.S.___	5:4

Sources: Stanley and Niemi (2011, 295); Supreme Court of the United States, "2009 Term Opinions of the Court," http://www.supremecourt.gov/opinions/slipopinions.aspx?Term=09 (accessed July 3, 2010).

an individual's right to possess a firearm for lawful purposes such as self-defense. Justice Scalia noted, however, that "the right secured by the Second Amendment is not unlimited" and that the ruling should not be interpreted as preventing reasonable restrictions such as prohibitions against possession of firearms by felons and the mentally ill or laws banning firearms in sensitive places such as schools.

Because this case involved Washington, DC, it limited federal, not state, power (remember from Chapter 3 that the District of Columbia is a federal city). In **McDonald v. Chicago** (2010), the Supreme Court ruled that the Second Amendment right of an individual to "keep and bear arms" applies to the states as well as the federal government. The city of Chicago had a ban on possession of handguns similar to the one voided in Washington, DC. The Court reaffirmed, however, that although an outright ban on handguns is unconstitutional, reasonable restrictions such as those mentioned in *District of Columbia v. Heller* are permissible.

Even if a right has not been incorporated and made binding on states, states may extend that right to their residents. The Nebraska constitution, for example, guaranteed rights of firearms ownership to all citizens of that state long before *McDonald v. Chicago* applied the Second Amendment to all states. The right to keep and bear arms is a good example of how states frequently offer broader rights and liberties than those guaranteed by the U.S. Constitution. The Bill of Rights can be thought of as a minimum set of guarantees; states can and often do go well beyond those minimums.

Because most of the liberties guaranteed by the Bill of Rights have been incorporated, in practical terms they provide a common yardstick to judge the minimal set of civil liberties shared by all citizens. This means that the most important dilemmas pitting liberty against authority, or liberty against liberty, are resolved by the Supreme Court interpreting and applying the Bill of Rights in specific cases. The next sections discuss controversies and Supreme Court decisions addressing freedoms and rights guaranteed by the Bill of Rights and considered fundamental civil liberties: freedom of religion, freedom of expression, the right to privacy, and the protections offered to people accused of committing crimes.

FREEDOM OF RELIGION

Many Americans assume that freedom from government interference in religious matters is a right that predates the founding of the republic. Tradition tells us that Puritans fled England in the early 1620s to escape the dictates of the official Anglican Church and that the right of individuals to worship as they saw fit was a characteristic of the Massachusetts Bay Colony. In reality, the Puritans wanted only the freedom to impose their own religious views on others. They quickly established the Congregational Church and forced all inhabitants under their jurisdiction to follow its religious precepts. Other colonies followed similar practices, and as late as the Revolutionary War, most of them had what were known as established churches, or a particular set of religious beliefs that were favored by the government.

For the most part, these established churches did not survive the Revolutionary period. Rather than a single established church, some of the Founders (notably George Washington) wanted all Christian churches to be state religions of

McDonald v. Chicago A 2010 case in which the Supreme Court ruled that the Second Amendment right of an individual to "keep and bear arms" applies to the states as well as the federal government.

equal standing and to be supported by taxation. This notion was opposed by others who thought it unwise to mix church and state and who sought an official separation of the two (those favoring this position included James Madison, Thomas Jefferson, and George Mason). The Virginia Statute for Religious Freedom adopted in 1786 mandated that state government could force no one to frequent or support any religion or religious practice. Other states adopted this perspective about church–state relations. Two sections of the Constitution made separation of church and state national policy. Article VI prohibits a religious test as a requirement for public office, and the First Amendment mandates that "Congress shall make no law respecting an establishment of religion, or prohibiting the free exercise thereof." In *Cantwell v. Connecticut* (1940), the Supreme Court ruled that the establishment clause of the First Amendment represented a fundamental liberty, applicable to state governments through the due process clause of the Fourteenth Amendment.

In making the religious provisions of the First Amendment apply to all governments, the Supreme Court incorporated two separate guarantees. First, the **establishment clause** prohibits government authorities from showing a preference for one set of religious beliefs over others, or for religious beliefs in general over nonreligious beliefs. Second, government cannot prohibit the **free exercise of religion**, which means that individuals are free to choose religious beliefs and practice them as they see fit or to not practice any religion at all. These two guarantees, of course, are related—if government uses its power to establish a religion, then it also prevents the free exercise of other religious beliefs. They are two different ideas, however, and the Supreme Court has made a point of keeping them distinct.

The free exercise of religion is a constitutional right familiar to Americans, but the interpretations of how to uphold that right are often controversial, especially with regard to religion in schools. The Supreme Court has consistently ruled that when a public authority supports an activity with religious content (such as prayer in public schools), it is favoring a belief system, which is prohibited by the First Amendment. On the other hand, it has also ruled that government support of secular activities by parochial schools is legal if it does not promote excessive relations between church and state and does not impede or promote religion. Here, U.S. Secretary of Education Betsy DeVos reads to kindergarteners during a visit to St. Mary's Catholic School, Thursday morning, September 14, 2017, in Lincoln, Nebraska. What difficulties do you see in comparing these types of rulings?

© Eric Gregory/The Journal-Star/AP Photo

Prohibition Against the Establishment of Religion

Controversies over the establishment clause deal with whether public authorities can sanction religious activities or favor a particular religious group or belief. The Supreme Court has generally said public authorities cannot do this directly, although it has allowed public authorities considerable leeway in indirectly supporting secular activities undertaken by religious organizations. Public education provides an excellent case study of how these issues have evolved over the past century.

An early case involving public education and the establishment clause was ***Everson v. Board of Education*** (1947). This case involved a New Jersey law that authorized local school boards to reimburse parents for costs incurred in transporting their children to parochial schools. The key question was whether the

establishment clause A clause in the First Amendment of the Constitution that states that government cannot establish a religion.

free exercise of religion The First Amendment guarantee that individuals are free to choose religious beliefs and practice them as they see fit or to not practice any religion at all.

Everson v. Board of Education The 1947 case in which the Court for the first time directly articulated the principle of separation of church and state, concluding that transportation expenditures to parochial schools did not support any religious activity but rather assisted families and were therefore allowable.

expenditures showed favoritism that constituted an establishment of religion. The Court for the first time directly articulated the principle of **separation of church and state**, meaning that neither federal nor state government could pass any law supporting one religion or all religions or any law preferring one religion over another. Although the *Everson* ruling called for a sharp separation between church and state, the Court concluded that the transportation expenditures did not support any religious activity, but rather assisted families and were therefore allowable. In directly articulating the concept of separation of church and state, however, the Court laid the foundation for several other cases that had a much broader and more controversial impact on education.

One of the most significant cases was *Engel v. Vitale* (1962), which held that public schools could not officially sanction prayer. The heart of the case involved a prayer written by New York State officials that was read aloud by teachers and students in public schools: "Almighty God, we acknowledge our dependence upon Thee, and we beg Thy blessings upon us, our parents, our teachers, and our country." In a blunt majority opinion, the Court declared,

> The constitutional prohibition against laws respecting an establishment of religion must at least mean that in this country it is no part of the business of government to compose official prayers for any group of the American people to recite as part of a religious program carried on by government.

In *Abington Township v. Schempp* (1963), the Court extended this principle by prohibiting states from requiring Bible reading or recitation of the Lord's Prayer in public schools.

The Supreme Court has struck down state- or school-sanctioned religious activities in most subsequent cases. In *Stone v. Graham* (1980), a Kentucky statute requiring the Ten Commandments to be posted in every public school classroom was ruled unconstitutional. An Alabama statute authorizing a one-minute period of silence in public schools for "meditation or voluntary prayer" met a similar fate in *Wallace v. Jaffree* (1985). In *Lee v. Weisman* (1992), the court ruled that having clergy offer prayers at public school ceremonies that students were required to attend was a violation of the establishment clause.

What all these cases have in common is some form of governmental authority (state law, school district, public official) sanctioning or supporting some form of religious expression, belief, or activity. The Court has consistently ruled that when a public authority organizes, requires, or officially approves any activity with religious content, it is favoring a particular belief system. This favoritism, the Supreme Court has ruled, constitutes establishment of religion and is prohibited by the First Amendment's establishment clause. This ban has been extended to prevent everything from drawing school district boundaries to create public schools with a particular religious majority (*Board of Education Kiryas Joel Village v. Grumet* 1994) to student-led prayer at high school football games (*Santa Fe Independent School District v. Doe* 2000). More recently, a federal court (though not the Supreme Court) struck down a requirement enacted by a Pennsylvania school district that intelligent design be taught as an alternative to evolution. A group of parents objected to this requirement,

---

separation of church and state The idea that neither national nor state governments may pass laws that support one religion or all religions or give preference to one religion over others.

arguing that intelligent design—the notion that life was created by an intelligent force rather than by natural selection—was cover for a religion-based creationist belief system that had no place in a public school science curriculum. In *Kitzmiller et al. v. Dover School District* (2005), U.S. District Court Judge John E. Jones III agreed, ruling that the requirement was an unconstitutional violation of the establishment clause.

These cases address what government cannot do without running afoul of the First Amendment: It cannot establish a religion. But what *can* the government do? The First Amendment is much less clear on this point. Parochial schools engage in a wide range of educational activities that have no direct religious component. Can government support some of these activities, even though that support would indirectly benefit an organization that promotes a particular religion? That indirect support is permissible was the implication of the *Everson* case, which allowed reimbursement for the costs of traveling to a religious school, even as the ruling affirmed the separation of church and state. The Supreme Court has generally ruled that as long as an activity at a religious school has a secular purpose, does not impede or promote religion, and does not promote excessive entanglement between church and state, government may support that activity without violating the establishment.

Even so, using public money or other resources to support activities at religious schools is controversial. Behind these disputes is a more fundamental debate about the role that schools, especially parochial schools, should play in a democratic society. Those who support public expenditures for parochial schools argue that they educate a lot of children, which saves the public school system a good deal of money. Furthermore, say proponents, it is not fair to tax parents for the public schools while they are paying parochial school tuition; these parents are in effect paying twice to educate their children. Finally, supporters of parochial schools argue that such schools do not raise serious religious problems in American society because they devote most of their activities to educating students in secular rather than sectarian subjects.

Opponents argue that sending children to separate schools on the basis of religion is democratically undesirable. A primary advantage of public schools is their democratizing influence, and this includes bringing children of various religious backgrounds together during their formative years. This diversity is particularly important because religious differences are often associated with differences in ethnicity and socioeconomic background. Opponents, therefore, do not want to see government take any action that would foster parochial schools at the expense of public ones. If parents wish to send their children to church-supported schools rather than to public schools, then that is their prerogative. But they must assume the financial burden of that choice and not expect the rest of society to assist them. Just as those who choose to hire private security firms are not exempt from paying taxes to support local law enforcement, those who choose to send their children to private schools are still required to contribute to public schools. Finally, opponents believe that it is not possible to draw clear distinctions between sectarian and secular matters and that religious points of view have an effect on the way that many nonreligious subjects are taught.

Recent Supreme Court rulings on this issue sided with proponents of programs that result in tax dollars going to religious schools. *Zelman v. Simmons-Harris* (2002) considered the constitutionality of a school voucher program in Cleveland, Ohio. The publicly funded vouchers were given to disadvantaged students, who could use them to pay for tuition at private schools. The overwhelming majority of vouchers (more than 90 percent) were redeemed at religiously affiliated schools. Opponents argued that the vouchers represented little more than a way to subsidize religious institutions. Proponents argued that the program was designed to help underprivileged students by giving them the means to leave failing public schools and did not constitute government favoring religion. The financial boon to religious schools was therefore not a policy goal but simply a by-product of individual choice neither required nor encouraged by government. In a 5–4 decision, the Court sided with proponents of vouchers. *Arizona Christian School Tuition Org v. Winn* (2011) tackled a similar issue to that considered in *Zelman*. This case was brought by a group of taxpayers who objected to an Arizona law that provided tax credits to people underwriting scholarships for students attending private, primarily religious schools. Again, the argument was that this amounted to little more than a legal ruse to provide indirect public subsidies for religious schools. In another 5–4 decision, the Supreme Court dismissed the suit on the grounds that the taxpayers had no standing—there was no direct government expenditure, and therefore taxpayers suffered no damages or harm. In these two rulings the Supreme Court seems to be saying that indirect subsidies of religious educational institutions such as vouchers and tax credits can be (and in some cases are) prohibited by state constitutions, but they do not violate the separation of church and state mandated by the First Amendment.

Free Exercise of Religion

Controversies involving the free exercise of religion deal with the extent to which the state can regulate individual religious practices. In the late 1870s, the Supreme Court had to decide whether a federal law banning polygamy in the territories violated the First Amendment rights of Mormons who practiced plural marriages. In *Reynolds v. United States* (1879), the Court made a clear distinction between religious beliefs and actions stemming from those beliefs. The justices reasoned that Mormons had every right to believe that God permits men to have as many wives as possible, but that Mormons had no right to implement this belief because it violated social duty and order.

As *Reynolds* indicates, the free exercise of religion is a liberty subject to some restrictions by government. Nonetheless, the Court has frequently acted to protect individual religious choices from government restrictions. For example, a series of cases in the 1930s and 1940s dealt with Jehovah's Witnesses who acted on their belief that each member of the group is a minister with a duty to spread the gospel. In distributing religious literature in the public streets, Jehovah's Witnesses ran afoul of state and local laws relating to permits, fees, and taxes. The Court ruled that Jehovah's Witnesses had the right to pass out tracts in residential areas. The Court in effect had to balance the right of Jehovah's Witnesses to propagate their faith with the right of individuals to privacy—in this case, to not be bothered by people seeking to convert them (*Cantwell v. Connecticut* 1940; *Minersville School District v. Gobitis* 1940; *West Virginia State Board of Education v. Barnette* 1943).

Few issues better highlight the delicate balance between the right to free exercise of religion and the broader interests of society than religious exercises in state-supported schools. This issue actually spans both the establishment and free exercise clauses. Since its initial ruling banning mandatory prayer in public schools in 1962, the Supreme Court has consistently ruled that because public schools are government institutions, the Constitution prohibits state and local authorities from commanding schoolchildren to pray aloud or silently or to engage in other activities that could be construed as having a religious purpose. Yet none of these decisions prevent an individual from praying in school. The government has no right—and, as a practical matter, no ability—to interfere with such practices. Nor can public authorities prevent religious groups from using public facilities if such access is available to others (*Lamb's Chapel v. Center Moriches School District* 1993; *Good News Club v. Milford Central School District* 2001).

Although the government cannot limit individuals or groups from practicing their religious beliefs, the Supreme Court has also ruled that public authorities are not obligated to subsidize how individuals choose to exercise those rights. In *Locke v. Davey* (2004), the Supreme Court decided that state governments are allowed to withhold taxpayer-funded scholarships for those who choose to study for the ministry. At issue in this case was the constitutionality of Washington State's so-called Blaine amendment. Blaine amendments (named for the congressman who tried, and failed, to add his amendment to the U.S. Constitution) are included in some state constitutions, and they specifically prohibit state governments from funding religious activities. Joshua Davey was a college student who won a publicly funded scholarship and decided to study for the ministry. The state rescinded the scholarship on the grounds that paying to train someone to lead a congregation constituted support of a religious activity. Davey sued, arguing that withholding a scholarship available to students studying in any other field amounted to religious discrimination. The Supreme Court held that Washington State was under no First Amendment obligation to provide the scholarship.

Davey makes an interesting companion case to the *Zelman v. Simmons-Harris* (2002) and *Arizona Christian School Tuition Organization v. Winn* (2011) rulings. In the latter cases, the Supreme Court said state governments could, at least indirectly, support activities undertaken by religious organizations. In *Davey*, the Court ruled that even though state governments *could* support such activities, they were not *obligated* to do so. Withholding financial support from religious education imposes no criminal or civil limitations on the free exercise of religion, and states are free to mandate that tax dollars not be used to support any religious activity.

FREEDOM OF EXPRESSION

In addition to freedom of religion, the First Amendment spells out a number of other liberties that government may not interfere with: freedom of speech and the press, the right of peaceful assembly, and the right to petition the government for redress of grievances. Together, these constitute means by which individuals and groups can express their views and communicate them to one another, as well as to public officials. Like religious freedom, the First Amendment liberties relating to expression did not become a matter of major concern for the Supreme Court until the twentieth century. It was not until the 1950s that social and political changes prompted the Supreme Court to rule on a series of vital First Amendment issues.

General Approaches

There are several basic approaches to dealing with issues of freedom of expression. One is to treat this freedom as absolute. This **absolutist approach** argues that the Founders wanted the words of the First Amendment to be taken literally; in other words, the language "Congress shall make no law" means that government cannot take any action that interferes with the free expression of views, no matter how offensive, hurtful, or even harmful they may be. Absolutists generally recognize that society does have a right to place limits on the freedom of expression, but they want those limits kept to an absolute minimum.

Other approaches to freedom of expression issues differ from the absolutist position in degree rather than kind. Some justices have adopted the **preferred freedoms doctrine** approach to freedom of expression. According to this doctrine, First Amendment rights are so fundamental to achieving a free society that courts have a greater obligation to protect these freedoms than other rights. Justice Oliver Wendell Holmes Jr. first expressed this view in the early 1900s. This doctrine supports an argument that courts should take a more active role in First Amendment controversies rather than defer to Congress and the president.

Other justices have avoided trying to treat freedom of expression issues with a universal philosophy. For example, Justice Felix Frankfurter was known for a pragmatic **balancing test** approach to free expression. Essentially, this approach called for weighing competing values on a case-by-case basis to determine when restrictions on freedom of expression were warranted in order to protect society or the rights of individuals or groups. The significant difference between the balancing test approach and the absolutist and preferred freedoms approaches is that the former rejects the idea that freedom of expression is an absolute value that ought to take precedence over other legitimate concerns.

absolutist approach The view of the First Amendment that states that the Founders wanted it to be interpreted literally so that Congress should make "no laws" about the expression of views.

preferred freedoms doctrine The idea that the rights provided in the First Amendment are fundamental and as such the courts have a greater obligation to protect those rights than others.

balancing test The view of freedom of expression that states the obligation to protect rights must be balanced with the impact on society of the action in question.

Specific Tests

Although the general judicial approaches to freedom of expression reflect important basic attitudes, in practice none have been particularly helpful in dealing with the wide variety of freedom of expression issues the Supreme Court has faced in the past half-century or so. The basic problem is that although most justices advocate the greatest degree of freedom possible in matters of individual expression, it has proven difficult to balance that freedom with society's need for order and authority. The Supreme Court has devised various tests to provide a basic rule about when freedom of expression can legitimately be regulated.

The **"clear and present danger" test**, articulated by Justice Oliver Wendell Holmes Jr. in *Schenck v. United States* (1919), follows from his preferred freedoms doctrine. The case involved a socialist convicted of violating the Espionage Act by circulating antiwar leaflets to members of the armed forces. According to Holmes, the central issue was whether the leaflets constituted a "clear and present danger" of bringing about "substantive evils" that Congress had a right to prevent. Schenck's activities were deemed to meet this test; the possibility of soldiers refusing to fight was considered a substantive evil, and his conviction was upheld.

The **bad tendency rule** was articulated just a year after the *Schenck* case in *Pierce v. United States* (1920). This case also involved socialists distributing antiwar pamphlets, though there was no indication that any of this literature reached members of the armed forces or had an immediate effect on the war. The case is notable because it eased the "clear and present danger" test for restricting freedom of speech. Instead of requiring that speech raise the probability of an immediate evil before it could be restricted, the bad tendency rule allowed restrictions if speech simply might tend to bring about an evil at some time in the future.

This ruling raised the question of when to use the "clear and present danger" test and when to use the bad tendency rule, a question the Court sought to answer in *Dennis v. United States* (1951). This case revolved around Communists charged with conspiring to overthrow the government. In deciding whether expression advocating the overthrow of the government was protected by the First Amendment, the Supreme Court indicated that the nature of the evil to be avoided had to be taken into account. If the evil was grave enough—such as the violent overthrow of the government—then it was not necessary to demonstrate that the expression would probably result in the immediate occurrence of the evil. But if the evil was less grave, such as a local disturbance, then those seeking to regulate expression must meet the thresholds established earlier. In this case, the Court seemed to say that if the evil is serious enough, the bad tendency test should be employed; if the evil is less serious, the "clear and present danger" standard is applicable.

The difficulty with all these tests, as well as with those applied to other areas of free expression, is that verbal formulas cannot possibly capture all the complexities of social situations. In other words, judges ultimately exercise considerable discretion in deciding freedom of expression issues. This discretion is sometimes used to defend individual liberty against the authority of the state. For example, in *Texas v. Johnson* (1989), the Supreme Court ruled that burning the American flag was a form of expression that had constitutional protection. Despite widespread support for laws outlawing desecration of the flag, the Court ruled that a "bedrock principle" of the First Amendment is that the government has no authority to prevent the expression of an idea simply because it is offensive. This basic idea was reaffirmed in *Snyder v. Phelps* (2011). Fred Phelps and members of his family are the driving force behind the Westboro Baptist Church (WBC), a fundamentalist congregation militantly opposed to homosexual rights. WBC members believed military casualties in Iraq and Afghanistan were God's punishment for America's tolerance of homosexuality. They demonstrated at military funerals, including

"clear and present danger" test An approach to determining whether an action should be protected under the First Amendment that considers "whether the words used are used in such circumstances and are of such a nature as to create a clear and present danger that they will bring about the substantive evils that Congress has a right to prevent."

Schenck v. United States The 1919 case that articulated the "clear and present danger" test.

bad tendency rule An approach to determining whether an action should be protected under the First Amendment that considers whether the action would have a tendency to produce a negative consequence.

Texas v. Johnson The 1989 case in which the Supreme Court ruled that burning the American flag was a form of expression that had constitutional protection.

that of Lance Corporal Matthew Snyder, holding up signs that read, for example, "Thank God for Dead Soldiers" and "You're Going to Hell." Lance Corporal Snyder's father, Albert Snyder, sued the WBC for millions in damages, claiming emotional and psychological harm. Yet in an eight-to-one decision, the Supreme Court said the First Amendment gave WBC a right to picket and express their views at a military funeral, however repugnant or disturbing those views might be to grieving family and friends. In short, the Court once more reaffirmed that the purpose of the First Amendment is to protect the expression of ideas and views that others find disagreeable.

One of the most famous cases of the Supreme Court upholding the right to free speech, even though that speech was considered offensive to many, came in ***Brandenburg v. Ohio*** (1969). Clarence Brandenburg was a member of the Ku Klux Klan (KKK) who was filmed by a television crew giving speeches that alluded to gaining "revengeance" against blacks and Jews, castigated the government for oppressing whites, and called for a march on Washington, DC. Brandenburg was convicted for inciting people to break the law. The Supreme Court, however, overturned his conviction, ruling in a unanimous decision that Brandenburg's speech, though supportive of lawbreaking in the abstract, contained no incitement to commit an "imminent or specific" crime. This **imminent lawless action test** replaced the old "clear and present danger" test and protects a broader range of speech.

Although the Court ruled that burning flags is protected speech, in *Virginia v. Black* (2003) it ruled that burning crosses is not. The key issue in this case was a Virginia law that made it a felony to burn a cross for the purpose of intimidating any person or group. The Supreme Court rejected the argument that cross burning with the intent of racial intimidation was constitutionally protected free speech. In this case, the Supreme Court used its discretionary power to limit the freedom of the individual in the name of protecting security and social order.

In *McConnell v. Federal Election Commission* (2003), the Supreme Court upheld Congress's right to limit some forms of political speech immediately before an election. The issue here was not what was said or how, but where and when it was said. The McCain-Feingold Act of 2002 banned special interest groups from running issue ads within 60 days of a federal election. Opponents of the law sued, arguing that the law violated First Amendment rights in a way that was particularly offensive; in effect, the law served to weaken the voices of citizens when they were most likely to be heard—that is, right before an election. The Court disagreed, ruling that the money underlying these ad campaigns raised the possibility of perceived or actual corruption and that the government had a basic interest in preventing both. That interest overrode the right of special interest groups to speak loudly in an election.

Yet in ***Citizens United v. Federal Election Commission*** (2010), the Court overturned its decision in *McConnell v. Federal Election Commission* and struck down a provision of the McCain-Feingold Act that prohibited all corporations and unions from broadcasting "electioneering communications" that mentioned a candidate within 60 days of a general election or 30 days of a primary. This ruling effectively prevented Congress from limiting independent campaign spending, on the grounds that such expenditures reflected political speech protected by

Brandenburg v. Ohio The 1969 case that upheld a KKK member's right to controversial speech, which supported lawbreaking in the abstract, because it contained no incitement to commit an "imminent or specific" crime, establishing the imminent lawless action test.

imminent lawless action test As decided in *Brandenburg v. Ohio*, speech is protected if it contains no incitement to commit an "imminent or specific" crime. This test replaced the old "clear and present danger" test and protects a broader range of speech.

Citizens United v. Federal Election Commission A 2010 Supreme Court case holding that a provision of the McCain-Feingold Act prohibiting corporations and unions from broadcasting "electioneering communications" within 60 days of a general election is an unconstitutional limitation on the First Amendment guarantee of free speech. It also held that corporations and labor unions can spend unlimited amounts of money in campaigns.

the First Amendment. The decision was enormously controversial for its potential to increase the political influence of those with deep pockets. The ruling cleared the way for independent-expenditure political action committees dubbed "Super PACs," which can accept unlimited donations and spend as much as they want. These Super PACs were used to funnel massive amounts of money into the 2012 and 2016 elections, much of it spent in the form of negative advertising. The experience thus far has done little to diminish the fears of the ruling's critics who worried it would increase the influence of those with fat check books and make already negative electoral environments even more cynical and sharp-tongued.

It is probably fair to say that over the years, the Supreme Court has shown more than a little inconsistency in its rulings on freedom of expression (e.g., it is legal to burn a flag but not a cross). The point to keep in mind is what the Court is striving for in each of these cases: to balance the right of individual expression with the need to preserve social order. The simple fact is that there is no generally agreed-upon standard that applies to every specific case.

Unprotected Speech

The Supreme Court has ruled that some forms of expression are always beyond constitutional protection and can be outlawed or strictly regulated by the government. Yet even in these cases, the Court has struggled to strike an appropriate balance of competing values and clear standards that both government and individuals can understand and follow.

Obscenity

Few civil liberty issues have given the Supreme Court more difficulty than obscenity. Rulings in two 1957 cases, *Roth v. United States* and *Alberts v. California*, held that obscenity was not protected speech but was instead a form of expression that government could outlaw. Yet while government can ban obscenity, neither case produced a clear definition of obscenity.

In *Roth*, the test of obscenity was whether an "average person, applying contemporary community standards," would find that the dominant theme of the material in question would appeal to prurient interest. The ruling made clear that isolated passages from a film or a literary work could not be used to judge whether the work was obscene; the dominant theme of the entire work had to be judged. The test caused enormous problems in application. There was huge variation in what people considered obscene, and this variation existed not simply from community to community but also from state to state and even from court to court.

Justice Potter Stewart most famously articulated the frustration caused by the Court's inability to provide a clear and universally applicable definition of obscenity. In *Jacobellis v. Ohio* (1964), Stewart wrote, "Perhaps I could never succeed in intelligibly [defining obscenity]. But I know it when I see it." Stewart's statement points out a basic problem with enforcing restrictions on sexually explicit expression: Those who engage in such expression often do not know whether they are breaking the law because of the elasticity of the definition of obscenity.

In *Miller v. California* (1973), the Supreme Court set three criteria for judging whether a work was obscene:

1. The average person applying contemporary standards finds that the work as a whole appeals to prurient interests (the *Roth* test).
2. The work "depicts or describes, in a patently offensive way, sexual conduct specifically defined by the applicable state law."
3. The work lacks any "serious literary, artistic, political or scientific value."

These guidelines have subsequently been incorporated into federal and state statutes, but thus far, they have not surmounted the problem articulated by Stewart. Frequently, the enforcement of obscenity statutes seems to have been driven by the subjective moral judgments of policymakers and politically active groups rather than by any objective standard of obscenity (K. Smith 1999). The problem is that if government is going to be given the authority to completely outlaw some forms of expression, citizens must know exactly what the forms of expression are. If the state has the authority to arbitrarily or inconsistently declare some forms of expression to be beyond constitutional protection, this clearly threatens individual liberty.

The advent of the Internet and the World Wide Web—where pornographic material is just a mouse click away for anyone with an Internet connection—has given new relevance to the debate over sexually explicit materials and free speech. In *Reno v. ACLU* (1997), the Supreme Court found key provisions of the Communications Decency Act, a law passed by Congress that sought to define and regulate the Internet as a broadcast rather than a print medium, to be unconstitutional. The law argued that even sexually explicit materials constitutionally protected as free speech could not be legally sold to minors. In the name of protecting minors, television networks are not allowed to broadcast X-rated movies over the open airwaves. Why, proponents of the law argued, should the Internet be any different? The Supreme Court saw things differently. Who is going to decide what is indecent and therefore illegal to post on the Web? Rather than create another endless definitional debate about what is or is not "indecent," "pornographic," or "obscene," the Court ruled the Internet to be the equivalent of a print medium or public forum. Thus, the Court was obligated to provide that medium the broadest First Amendment protection, and it struck down the Communications Decency Act. Yet the Court has also ruled that government can seek to limit minors' access to sexually explicit materials on the Internet. In *United States v. American Library Association* (2004), the Court ruled that Congress was not unduly restricting free speech rights by requiring libraries to install filtering software on computers as a condition of receiving federal funds.

One form of expression that is universally considered obscene is child pornography. To protect children, both federal and state governments prohibit distributing or possessing sexually explicit images of children. Yet even here, there has been controversy. The Child Pornography Prevention Act passed by Congress in 1996 banned sexually explicit material that appears to depict minors but that was produced using youthful-looking adults or computer-imaging technology rather than real children. In *Ashcroft v. Free Speech Coalition* (2002), the Supreme Court held that this attempt to prohibit what is sometimes called "virtual child pornography" was overbroad because it bans materials that would not be considered obscene under the *Miller* standards and are not produced by exploiting real children. Again, we see the Supreme Court engaged in a delicate balancing act, on the one hand trying to maximize liberty and restrict government interference with individual choices, and on the other trying to allow government enough authority to ensure that the free exercise of those liberties does not threaten social order.

Libel and Slander

Other forms of unprotected speech have run into the same problem. Making false and defaming statements about someone is **slander** when the statement is spoken and **libel** when it is made in print or other media. The Court has ruled that an individual's right to free speech does not extend to using that right to harm others, so slander and libel do not have constitutional protection. This principle has raised concerns about the First Amendment's guarantee of freedom of the press.

The basic requirements for proving libel are as follows:

1. Publication—the statements must be communicated in such a way that third parties can observe them.
2. Identification—the aggrieved party must be clearly specified.
3. Harm—the aggrieved party must suffer as a result of the libel.

The basic defense in a libel suit is truth. If a communication is defamatory but also completely factual, the aggrieved party generally does not have the basis for a successful libel suit. The problem for the press is that the news media often report on issues that portray public figures in an unfavorable light, and under the pressure of deadlines or because they are not privy to crucial information, they could unwittingly libel someone.

The standards for winning libel cases are higher for public officials than for private citizens who are not in the spotlight. In *New York Times Co. v. Sullivan* (1964),

slander To make false or defamatory oral statements about someone.

libel To make false or defaming statements about someone in print or the media.

Donald Trump in a cabinet meeting where he announces proposed changes to libel laws and threatens to sue media that publish embarrassing information. Such suits would be difficult to win, especially when published information is demonstrably true.

© Evan Vucci/AP Photo

the Supreme Court ruled that in order to win a libel suit, a public official who is defamed in press reports must prove not only that a report was false and defamatory but also that it was issued with "actual malice." In other words, false and harmful reports about public officials are not libelous unless it can be proved that the reports were known to be false when they were published or were published with a "reckless disregard" for the truth. However, public officials have discovered that proving malice is a legal hurdle comparable to defining obscenity. In later rulings, the Supreme Court extended the principle in *Sullivan* to include public figures such as movie stars, athletes, and other celebrities (*Associated Press v. Walker* 1967; *Curtis Publishing Company v. Butts* 1967). As a result, this standard gives the press broad liberties to report on public figures in order to inform the public, but public figures have limited recourse if this freedom is used to issue false and misleading statements about them.

THE RIGHT TO PRIVACY

Nowhere does the Constitution explicitly articulate a **right to privacy**. Yet there is nothing new about privacy as a fundamental civil liberty. The Constitution does include numerous amendments and clauses upholding an individual's right to be free of government interference without due cause or due process. Combined, these establish a right to be left alone.

Privacy became the focus of controversy in the latter half of the twentieth century, when the Supreme Court expanded the right of privacy beyond traditional protections actually spelled out in the Constitution and granted it independent status. Over a series of decisions, the right to privacy, in essence, became a part of the Bill of Rights. The lead case in this movement was ***Griswold v. Connecticut*** (1965). In ruling that Connecticut could not prohibit the use of contraceptives by married couples, the Court enumerated a right of marital privacy, even though no such right was spelled out in the Constitution. Lacking a specific constitutional provision, the Court argued that various guarantees in the First, Third, Fourth, Fifth, and Ninth Amendments create "zones of privacy" that the government has no right to invade.

In the years following *Griswold*, the Court signaled a willingness to expand this right to privacy. In *Eisenstadt v. Baird* (1972), the Court ruled that it was unconstitutional to prevent the dissemination of birth control information and devices to unmarried people. "If the right of privacy means anything," wrote Justice William J. Brennan Jr. for the majority, "it is the right of the individual, married or single, to be free from unwarranted governmental intrusion into matters so fundamentally affecting a person as the decision to whether to bear or beget a child."

A controversial expansion of the right to privacy came in two 1973 decisions, ***Roe v. Wade*** and *Doe v. Bolton*, invalidating laws in Texas and Georgia regulating abortions. The Court reaffirmed the right of privacy enumerated in *Griswold*, balancing the woman's right to privacy against the state's interest in protecting

right to privacy An individual's right to be free of government interference without due cause or due process.

Griswold v. Connecticut The 1965 case ruling that Connecticut could not prohibit the use of contraceptives by married couples, enumerating a right of privacy. Although the Constitution contains no explicit right of privacy, the Court argued that various guarantees in the First, Third, Fourth, Fifth, and Ninth Amendments create "zones of privacy" that the government has no right to invade.

Roe v. Wade The 1973 case in which the Court reaffirmed the right of privacy enumerated in *Griswold*, balancing the mother's right to privacy against the state's interest in protecting an unborn fetus.

the unborn fetus. Justice Harry Blackmun's decision divided pregnancy into three periods. During the first trimester, the decision about whether to have an abortion is between the woman and her physician without interference from the state. During the second trimester, when abortion poses a greater risk to a woman's health, states can enact regulations to protect the health of the mother. Only during the final stage of pregnancy is the state's interest in protecting the fetus great enough to warrant severe restrictions on abortion, and even then the state must allow exceptions to save the life of the mother.

Since *Roe*, the Court has ruled on a number of restrictions on abortion rights enacted by states and municipalities. It has invalidated those requiring the consent of the father and those that require the abortion be performed only in a hospital. Since the 1980s, however, the Court has signaled a willingness to permit restrictions on abortion rights. In *Webster v. Reproductive Health Services* (1989), the Court upheld a Missouri law that prohibited abortion in a publicly funded facility. In *Planned Parenthood v. Casey* (1992), the Court upheld a Pennsylvania law that mandated counseling and a 24-hour waiting period prior to an abortion and also required that minors obtain parental or judicial permission in order to get an abortion. Although these decisions seemed to chip away at the broad privacy rights articulated in *Roe*, the Court has thus far declined to overturn the substance of that ruling.

Although the Court has extended the right to privacy to cover some personal areas of an individual's life, it has also ruled that other behaviors are beyond this protection. For example, it struck down a Georgia law allowing news reporters to be sued for publishing or broadcasting the names of rape victims, ruling that states may not impose sanctions for the publication of truthful information contained in court records that are open to the public (*Cox Broadcasting v. Cohn* 1975). In balancing individual liberties, the Court has generally favored the right to free expression over the right to privacy. Yet the Court has chosen government authority over individual privacy on certain issues. In *United States v. Miller* (1976), the Court refused to extend the right of privacy to individual bank accounts, ruling that the government has the right to obtain records of checks and other transactions. Similarly, the Court ruled that state laws prohibiting physician-assisted suicide are constitutional (*Washington v. Glucksberg* 1997).

Advances in surveillance and tracking technology have also raised questions about privacy. In *United States v. Jones* (2012), the Supreme Court ruled that law enforcement's use of GPS tracking devices could constitute a search that falls under the protections of the First Amendment. The case involved District of Columbia police officers who, without a warrant and without consent, attached a tracking device to a suspect's car and used it to record the suspect's movements for nearly a month. The Supreme Court unanimously ruled that this violated Fourth Amendment protections, but the justices were split on the reasons. Some justices argued that attaching the tracking device amounted to trespass on private property without a warrant. Other justices, however, argued that the key violation was not trespass on private property, but a citizen's right to a reasonable expectation of privacy.

Other controversial questions about an individual's right to privacy have focused on state laws outlawing consensual sodomy between members of the same sex. In effect, these cases try to decide the question of whether the government has the right to regulate what consenting adults do in the privacy of their own bedrooms. In *Bowers v. Hardwick* (1986), the Court upheld a Georgia law that made it a crime to engage in homosexual sex. In **Lawrence v. Texas** (2003), however, the Court overturned this decision and ruled that the government had no right to regulate or control consensual personal relationships. In both *Bowers* and *Lawrence,* police officers had entered the homes of gay men and caught them having sex. In the former case, the Court ruled that state bans against homosexual acts had deep cultural roots and that the government had the right to enforce these bans in the name of social order. In *Lawrence,* the Court rejected that reasoning and came down firmly on the side of individual liberty, justifying its shift on the grounds that the government has no legitimate reason to intrude into the personal and private lives of individuals. Harvard law professor Laurence Tribe (2004) suggests that *Lawrence* "may well be remembered as the *Brown v. Board* of gay and lesbian America."

Although the right to privacy has been greatly expanded and refined since the *Griswold* decision, broader social movements continually pressure this right. Wendy Kaminer (1999) observed that such individual liberties as freedom of expression and the right to privacy are quickly subordinated when they conflict with other values central to a particular ideological point of view. On the left, some feminists want individual freedom of expression limited when it is sexually explicit because they believe that sexually explicit material objectifies women and encourages violent crimes against women. On the right, some conservatives back the "imposition of moral absolutes," such as making homosexual acts a crime, even in the most private realm of individual behavior.

Polls show that large numbers of Americans are willing to give up some of their rights to privacy under some circumstances in exchange for greater security (Pew Research Center 2011). Yet the revelation in 2013 of the National Security Agency's large scale surveillance of telephone and e-mail communication made similar numbers of Americans uneasy about potential invasions of their privacy. Many expressed approval of reports that the NSA was tracking and considering publishing the porn-viewing habits of Muslim radicals as means of discrediting their fundamentalist appeals. Others pointed out, however, that if the NSA can collect such information on one group, it has the capability to do it for others, and maybe already has. Chances are that many Americans would object if the NSA started publishing Internet porn-viewing habits more broadly (Oremus 2013). This illustrates yet again that balancing an individual's right to privacy and society's broader interests is difficult and often contentious.

CRIMINAL PROCEDURE

Lawrence v. Texas The 2003 case ruling that the government had no right to regulate or control consensual personal relationships. This case overruled *Bowers v. Hardwick*, which had allowed states to make engaging in homosexual sex a crime.

One area in which privacy rights are usually respected is criminal procedure. Democracies generally go out of their way to protect individuals from the state because the power of government is so much greater than that of the individual in criminal cases. The state can marshal vast resources against a single person accused of having committed a wrong against society. To ensure that government does not abuse this power, a person's rights to privacy and to freedom from arbitrary governmental action are basic values in American society. It has long been a central feature of Anglo-American legal systems that an individual cannot be subject to criminal sanctions arbitrarily. As early as the fourteenth century, English courts provided that no one could be imprisoned or put to death except by "due process of law." English settlers in America brought with them a concern for the rights of the accused and a determination to protect those rights in criminal procedures.

This solicitude for the rights of the accused in criminal cases is explicitly codified in the Constitution and in subsequent court rulings. The government is prohibited from violating the privacy of the individual through unreasonable searches and seizures of home or person. The government is also prohibited from arbitrarily arresting people, and in a trial, the burden is on government to prove the charges against the individual "beyond a reasonable doubt." Such requirements deliberately make it difficult for government to deprive any citizen of property, freedom of movement, or the right to life itself. Such protections favor the accused in order to protect the innocent; to lessen the chances that government will punish an innocent person, the Constitution establishes rules and procedures that make it difficult to punish anyone.

The federal system in the United States establishes separate legal systems with separate lists of criminal offenses and trial procedures for the federal government and for each of the 50 states. Most "major crimes"—murder, rape, assault, robbery, burglary, and the like—are violations of state rather than federal law and are thus tried in the state courts. Criminal violations of federal law include certain drug-trafficking activities, transporting stolen property across state lines, and plotting to assassinate federal officials, among others.

The rules governing criminal procedure and the rights of the accused in federal cases spring from several sources. The most important is the Constitution, particularly the Fourth, Fifth, Sixth, and Eighth Amendments:

- The Fourth Amendment protects individuals from unreasonable searches and seizures of personal property.
- The Fifth Amendment contains the historic English guarantee that a person cannot be denied life, liberty, or property without due process of law and also includes specific protections from coerced confessions and from being tried twice for the same offense.
- The Sixth Amendment lays down specific guidelines for a fair trial, requiring a speedy and public trial by a jury of one's peers, the right to confront witnesses, and the right to be represented by counsel.
- The Eighth Amendment prohibits cruel and unusual punishment.

Through various cases, most of these rights have been applied to state as well as federal trials.[2] Thus, regardless of which level of government charges an individual with a crime, it must abide by a set of basic safeguards and guarantees in these constitutional clauses.

---

2 The Fifth Amendment's provision requiring indictment by a grand jury and the Eighth Amendment's prohibition of excessive bail have not been applied to trials in state courts.

These rights were the source of significant controversy in the twentieth century. A series of rulings expanded the rights of the accused and imposed increased burdens and responsibilities on the government. In general, the Court has expanded rights through interpretation of the Constitution, has applied the rights to the states through the due process clause of the Fourteenth Amendment, and in later rulings has placed limitations on the expanded rights. The swing of the judicial pendulum demonstrates that achieving the "right" balance between individual liberties and social order is an extraordinarily difficult objective that periodically must be reconsidered in a process that is political.

Exclusionary Rule

One of the most controversial interpretations of the Fourth Amendment's protections against unreasonable searches and seizures is the **exclusionary rule** first articulated in *Weeks v. United States* in 1914. This ruling held that evidence obtained through an unreasonable search and seizure cannot be used as evidence in federal trials. The case of *Mapp v. Ohio* (1961) extended the exclusionary rule to state trials. Excluding evidence of a crime is a controversial way to protect individuals' rights against unreasonable search and seizure. The goal is to deter police from infringing on the rights of innocent people, but it is frustrating to be prevented from using evidence to punish guilty people.

The courts have been unable to find a better way to protect the innocent from overzealous police, but court rulings in recent decades have backed away from the exclusionary rule. In *Nix v. Williams* (1984), the Supreme Court granted an **inevitable discovery exception**, ruling that illegally acquired evidence can be used in court if it would have been discovered eventually through legal means. In *United States v. Leon* (1984), the Court granted another significant exception to the exclusionary rule, the so-called **good faith exception**. As long as a law officer believes that the warrant authorizing a search is valid, the good faith exception makes evidence obtained in the search admissible even if the warrant is later found to be flawed. This ruling is viewed as a significant weakening of the exclusionary rule because what constitutes good faith is open to broad interpretation.

According to the Fourth Amendment, "probable cause" is required before law enforcement officers or agencies can make any arrest or obtain any search warrant. In other words, before any evidence is collected, and before anyone is taken into custody, there must be some reasonable basis for believing criminal activity has occurred. However, there has been considerable debate and controversy over exactly what constitutes probable cause. In *Illinois v. Gates* (1984), the Supreme Court defined probable cause as a "fair probability" that some criminal activity has taken place. Like the good faith exception, such rulings are controversial because what constitutes a "fair probability" is often in the eye of the beholder.

Right to Counsel

One of the rights to the guarantee of a fair trial is the Sixth Amendment right to assistance of counsel in mounting a defense against a criminal charge. As early as 1790, Congress passed a law providing legal counsel for all people charged with

---

exclusionary rule The rule derived from the Fourth and Fourteenth Amendments that states that evidence obtained from an unreasonable search or seizure cannot be used in federal trials.

Weeks v. United States The 1914 case that said that evidence obtained through an unreasonable search and seizure cannot be used in federal trials.

Mapp v. Ohio The 1961 case that extended the exclusionary rule to state trials.

inevitable discovery exception An exception to the exclusionary rule that states that evidence obtained from an illegal search may be used in court if the evidence eventually would have been discovered through legal means.

good faith exception An exception to the exclusionary rule that allows evidence obtained in a search with a flawed warrant to be admissible as long as the law officer believed the warrant was valid at the time of the search.

capital crimes (those punishable by death), but generally speaking, the ability to exercise this right was limited to people who could afford it. This practice changed in federal cases in 1938, when the Court required provision of counsel to anyone accused of a federal crime (*Johnson v. Zerbst*).

The obligation of state governments to provide an attorney was not firmly established until almost 30 years later. In **Gideon v. Wainwright** (1963), the Supreme Court ruled that the right to counsel is a fundamental part of a fair system of criminal justice, reasoning that without the assistance of counsel, a trial is stacked in favor of the government. *Gideon* was a landmark case that opened the door to a series of specific questions involving the right to counsel. Most fundamental was what kind of criminal cases initiated the state's obligation to provide a lawyer. In a series of later rulings, notably *Argersinger v. Hamlin* (1972) and *Scott v. Illinois* (1979), the Supreme Court ruled that any charge that carried a potential loss of liberty was serious enough to trigger the state obligation under *Gideon*.

Right Against Self-Incrimination

Probably the most famous expansion of the Fifth Amendment right against self-incrimination came in **Miranda v. Arizona** (1966). At issue was a confession to the crimes of kidnapping and rape that Ernesto Miranda made to police officers during a two-hour interrogation. The Court ruled the confession inadmissible on the grounds that once Miranda had been taken into custody or deprived of his freedom in any significant way, the police had an obligation to inform him that he had the right to remain silent, and that if he gave up this right, anything he said could be used against him in court. This ruling also shifted the Sixth Amendment right to counsel from the trial stage to the police station: *Miranda* required police to inform suspects of their rights to counsel and to have an attorney appointed if they could not afford one.

The basic reasoning behind the *Miranda* ruling was that confessions can be coerced in ways other than beatings. Just being questioned by police while in custody in a strange environment is a psychologically coercive situation. Furthermore, criminal laws are often complex, and an accused individual may unwittingly admit to criminal acts. Individuals cannot exercise their constitutional right against self-incrimination if they are unaware of it, and they need the help of an attorney to protect their rights.

The *Miranda* decision provoked a storm of protest. Law enforcement officials complained that it would handcuff them in dealing with criminals. The ruling seemed to be placing the rights of criminals above the public interest. Subsequent rulings have placed some limits on the Miranda decision. For example, in *Michigan v. Mosley* (1975), the Court ruled that if a defendant exercises the right to be silent when originally questioned about a crime, but voluntarily makes statements about a different crime during a subsequent interrogation, later statements are not protected by the original decision to remain silent and can be used as evidence in a trial. In *New York v. Quarles* (1984), the Court ruled that the police are allowed to interrogate a suspect before advising him or her of rights if "public safety" is at risk; this was considered a significant erosion of the rights established by earlier rulings. The Court narrowed the Miranda protections further in 2010. The case of

Gideon v. Wainwright The 1963 case in which the Supreme Court ruled that state courts are required under the Sixth and Fourteenth Amendments of the Constitution to provide counsel in criminal cases for defendants who cannot afford to hire their own lawyer.

Miranda v. Arizona The 1966 case that established a criminal suspect's right against self-incrimination and right to counsel during police interrogation.

Ernesto Miranda (right) and his attorney John Flynn leaving the U.S. Supreme Court in June 1966 after it overturned the Arizona State court's decision of guilt and a jail sentence of 20 years.
© Bettmann/CORBIS

Berghuis v. Thompkins (2010) involved a suspect who did not explicitly invoke or waive his right to remain silent. After remaining silent through nearly three hours of questioning, the suspect made an incriminating statement that was used as evidence in his trial. The Court held that a suspect must make an explicit, unambiguous statement that he or she wishes to remain silent. Even after lengthy silence, any voluntary statements made imply that the suspect waives the right to remain silent.

Although having to let a guilty person go free on a legal technicality is frustrating, *Miranda*'s role in adding to such frustrations is debatable. Ernesto Miranda, for example, was retried and convicted of rape on the basis of evidence other than the coerced confession.

Capital Punishment

Capital punishment is one of the most divisive controversies in American jurisprudence. At one time, it appeared that the death penalty would be ruled a violation of the Eighth Amendment's protection against "cruel and unusual punishment." In *Furman v. Georgia* (1972), the Supreme Court outlawed the death penalty as it was then implemented by the states. But only Justices William Brennan and Thurgood Marshall stated that the death penalty was inherently unconstitutional. Other justices claimed that the problem was not the penalty itself but rather how it was applied; it seemed to be applied arbitrarily and was disproportionately used on defendants who were socioeconomically disadvantaged.

Furman thus left open the possibility that death penalty statutes could pass constitutional muster if they avoided imposing the sentence in a capricious manner. Between 1972 and 1975, some 30 states passed new statutes that did exactly that. These states used one of two basic approaches. One was to make the death penalty mandatory for certain offenses, such as the murder of a police officer. The second was to essentially hold two trials: one to determine guilt or innocence and the other to determine whether to apply the death penalty.

In 1976, the Supreme Court heard five related cases involving the constitutionality of death penalty laws in Georgia, Texas, Florida, North Carolina, and Louisiana. It upheld the laws of the first three states and invalidated those of the latter two. Laws that contained a two-part procedure for determining guilt and sentencing passed constitutional muster, whereas the two that set mandatory death penalties did not. In *Gregg v. Georgia* (1976), the most important of these cases, the Court

THINKING ANALYTICALLY

THE VARIABLES THAT LEAD TO DEATH ROW

Since the Supreme Court's 1976 decision in *Gregg v. Georgia*, states have executed more than 1,450 people. Most of these have been killed using lethal injection, though a sizable number (roughly 160) have been electrocuted, while 11 died in a gas chamber, 3 were hung, and 3 were executed by firing squad.

Yet not all convicted murderers end up strapped to a gurney awaiting lethal injection or sent to a gas chamber. In some cases this is because the crime is committed in a state that either no longer has a death penalty or rarely uses it. But even in states that continue to use the death penalty with some regularity, capital punishment is not always imposed on those convicted of capital crimes. What explains why some people get the death penalty while those convicted of seemingly equally wicked crimes do not?

This is a big question that has attracted the interests of political scientists for some time. If we take the imposition of the death penalty as the dependent variable, what independent variables might explain when it is or is not used? Isaac Unah (2012), a political scientist at the University of North Carolina at Chapel Hill, examined this question by looking at three different causal models.

The first model he considered is what's termed the *theory of formal legal rationality*, which assumes a decision to impose the death penalty is based on a set of legal rules. For example, several states have statutes listing aggravating and mitigating circumstances. An aggravating factor might be whether the victim of a murder is a law enforcement officer. Mitigating factors might include the convict's mental impairment or long history as a law-abiding citizen.

Socio-structural theory argues that the socio-demographics of the criminals and their victims make a difference. As mentioned in the text, historically minorities, especially African Americans, have been more likely to get the death penalty. This is especially the case if the victim is white. Socio-structural theory, though, is not just about race. For example, it also posits that age plays a role, with the elderly and the very young less likely to be given the death penalty because they are seen as frail or not fully in control of their emotions.

Institutional theory treats the death penalty as an outcome of the political process. So, for example, a staunch conservative prosecutor who favors the death penalty is more likely to successfully pursue capital sentences, especially if there is an upcoming election in a constituency that also favors the death penalty.

Unah examined hundreds of recent murder trials in North Carolina, creating variables to represent the key arguments of each theory. He put all of these independent variables into a single statistical model to see which were better at predicting whether the death penalty was imposed.

Perhaps the most disappointing findings were those related to socio-structural theory—not because those variables did a poor job of explaining death penalty decisions, but because of precisely the opposite. The race, age, and social status of defendants and victims seem to play a big role in influencing whether the death penalty is imposed. The quick summary of Unah's study is this: In modern capital cases, the facts of a case have more to do with whether a death penalty is imposed than politics. Yet the death penalty continues to be decided on more than the facts of the case. Age, sex, and especially race continue to influence who ends up on death row and who does not.

Source

Death Penalty Information Center. *Methods of Execution*. http://www.deathpenaltyinfo.org/methods-execution.

Discussion Questions

1. Why do you think race continues to be a factor in death penalty decisions?
2. Unah's study looks at three theories or causal models: the theory of formal legal rationality, socio-structural theory, and institutional theory. Try to come up with another causal model to explain the death penalty. What variables would you use to test that theory?

ruled that the death penalty does not, by itself, violate the Constitution. It was not considered cruel and unusual punishment as long as death sentences were not automatically imposed upon conviction, but instead came after due deliberation.

Even though the Supreme Court ruled the death penalty constitutional, its application has continued to raise controversy and concern. The case for the death penalty rests on the argument that some crimes are so repugnant and heinous that, in the name of the greater good, society has a right to assess the ultimate penalty and take someone's life. Yet for a system that tries to maximize individual liberty and minimize government authority, the basic problem with the death penalty is the potential for executing the innocent. In such cases, the state completely and irrevocably squashes individual liberty. Hence, democracies are much less likely to employ the death penalty than are nondemocratic nations. Figure 4.1 shows that 79 percent of nondemocratic nations employ the death penalty, whereas only 32 percent of democratic nations do so. Among Western representative democracies, typically thought of as the U.S. peer group—democracies with highly developed economies that originated in Western Europe or the British Commonwealth—only the United States still enforces the death penalty.

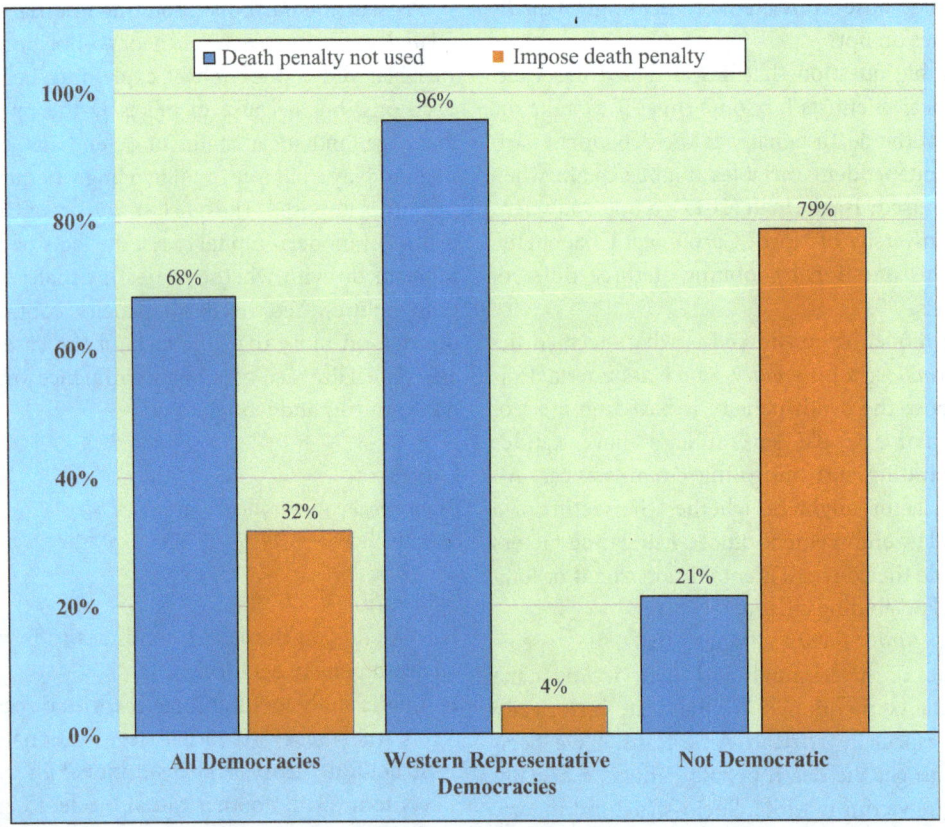

FIGURE 4.1 **Most Democracies Do Not Employ the Death Penalty**

Source: Data from Freedom House (2006) and Amnesty International (2006).

A second objection to the death penalty is that its application is racially biased—minorities tend to be disproportionately represented on death row, and numerous studies indicate that death penalty sentences are more likely when the victim is white (Death Penalty Information Center 2012). These concerns have driven a long-running battle between opponents and proponents of the death penalty. In 2003, Illinois governor George Ryan, citing a system "fraught with error," commuted the death sentences of 167 death row inmates. Ryan's decision came after investigations showed at least 13 men convicted and sentenced to death were later exonerated and set free. His decision was celebrated by death penalty opponents and harshly criticized by proponents, who argued that the net result of the action was to literally let people get away with murder while trampling the rights of victims.

CHAPTER FOUR
Top 10 Takeaway Points

1. Civil liberties are the freedoms enjoyed by individuals in a democratic society. They constitute the choices individuals are free to make with little or no interference from governmental authority.

2. Civil liberties are not absolute, and there remains a need for constraints on them to preserve social order. Balancing liberty and authority is difficult, and finding an appropriate balance is one of the central dilemmas of democratic societies.

3. The Bill of Rights originally applied only to the federal government, not to state governments. The Fourteenth Amendment added after the Civil War contains a "due process of law" clause that applies to the states, and the same clause appears in the Fifth Amendment, which applies to the national government. The same clause in both amendments sparked a debate over the incorporation doctrine—the notion that the Bill of Rights had been made binding on state governments as well as the federal government through the due process clause of the Fourteenth Amendment.

4. Although some argued that the Fourteenth Amendment made the entire Bill of Rights binding on state governments, the Supreme Court adopted a piecemeal approach and applied specific provisions in the Bill of Rights to the states on a case-by-case basis. Today, all but a few of the limitations on government in the Bill of Rights apply to the states as well as to the national government. The most recent right made binding on states is the Second Amendment right of individuals to keep and bear arms.

5. The First Amendment contains two distinct guarantees to protect religious freedom: First, government cannot establish a religion, which means that public authorities cannot show preference for one set of religious beliefs over another, or for religious beliefs in general over nonreligious beliefs. Second, government cannot prohibit the free exercise of religion, which means that individuals are free to choose which religious beliefs to practice or to not practice any religion at all. These two guarantees are related because if government uses its power to establish a religion, then it also prevents the free exercise of some religious beliefs. These guarantees of religious freedom call for the separation of church and state.

6. The First Amendment's specific guarantees of freedom of speech and the press, of the right of peaceful assembly, and of the right to petition the government for redress of grievances establish a general right to freedom of expression. Freedom of expression is the means by which individuals and groups can express their views and communicate them to one another as well as to public officials. Freedom of expression is not absolute and can be limited in some circumstances, and some forms of expression such as libel and slander and obscenity are not protected forms of expression.

7. Although the Constitution does not explicitly articulate a right to privacy, the Supreme Court has held that various guarantees in the First, Third, Fourth, Fifth, and Ninth Amendments create "zones of privacy" that the government has no right to invade.

8. The rules governing criminal procedure and the rights of the accused are found in the Fourth, Fifth, Sixth, Eighth, and Fourteenth Amendments.

9. The exclusionary rule prohibits the use of evidence and confessions obtained in violation of constitutional rights in federal or state trials. This practice is controversial, but the courts have been unable to find a better way to protect individuals' rights from unreasonable illegal government action.

10. The Eighth Amendment prohibits "cruel and unusual punishment." Few Supreme Court justices have taken the position that capital punishment is inherently unconstitutional. Recent challenges have focused on whether the death penalty is applied in ways that satisfy constitutional rights.

CHAPTER FOUR
Key Terms and Cases

absolutist approach, 128
bad tendency rule, 129
balancing test, 128
Barron v. Baltimore, 119
Brandenburg v. Ohio, 130
Citizens United v. Federal Election Commission, 130
civil liberties, 115
"clear and present danger" test, 129
District of Columbia v. Heller, 120
establishment clause, 123
Everson v. Board of Education, 123
exclusionary rule, 138
free exercise of religion, 123
Gideon v. Wainwright, 139
good faith exception, 138
Griswold v. Connecticut, 134
imminent lawless action test, 130
incorporation doctrine, 120
inevitable discovery exception, 138
Lawrence v. Texas, 136
libel, 133
Mapp v. Ohio, 138
McDonald v. Chicago, 122
Miranda v. Arizona, 139
preferred freedoms doctrine, 128
right to privacy, 134
Roe v. Wade, 134
Schenck v. United States, 129
separation of church and state, 124
slander, 133
Texas v. Johnson, 129
Weeks v. United States, 138

5 CIVIL RIGHTS

KEY QUESTIONS

What are civil rights?

What is the difference between civil rights and civil liberties?

What groups have historically been denied civil rights?

© Robert Cohen/St. Louis Post-Dispatch/AP Photo

MAH'RIA PRUITT-MARTIN was a star student in Normandy, Missouri, when her school district lost its accreditation. The news wasn't exactly a shocker—the Normandy School District had been on state probation for 15 years. For students like Pruitt-Martin it was actually a good thing to have the state pull the district's accreditation because it opened up an opportunity to attend a better school.

Under Missouri law an unaccredited school does not have to close, but its students automatically get the right to transfer to an accredited school for free and the school district even has to cover transportation costs. The academic demise of Normandy's schools thus gave Mah'Ria a ticket to the neighboring Frances Howell School District, which was not only fully accredited, but had much better facilities than the school Mah'Ria was leaving. "I was elated," said Mah'Ria's mother Nedra Martin. "I was just so excited."

Parents at Frances Howell did not share that enthusiasm. Roughly a thousand students wanted to opt out of Normandy and go to Frances Howell, and they were not met with open arms. Parents at Frances Howell were worried. About the potential impact of this influx of students on their schools' accreditation. About the possibility of importing violence into their schools. About the costs their school district might have to bear. Meanwhile, the sudden rush to the doors in Normandy was pushing that district towards financial disaster. Roughly a quarter of its students had decided to take advantage of their opt-out right and were not only bussing out to other districts but also taking state-aid dollars with them. This put an unsustainable strain on the budget of the already struggling district. And if the Normandy district went belly-up, thousands more students would have to be absorbed into neighboring districts.

Alarmed, the state intervened. In kind of a strange way. It re-named the Normandy School District the "Normandy Schools Collaborative," and while the school district was unaccredited, the state declared the collaborative "non-accredited." The reason for the semantic tap-dancing update quickly became clear—it was designed to get around the law giving students the right to opt out of an unaccredited school. Students who had transferred to Frances Howell were told they had to go back to Normandy. To say this was a shocker for Mah'Ria and her mother is an understatement. Mah'Ria was an honors student at Frances Howell. She did not want to go back to a struggling school and the potentially negative impact on her future educational and economic opportunities (This American Life 2015).

Here's the kicker to this story. Normandy, the underperforming, underfunded school district overwhelmingly served black students, while Frances Howell, the high-performing, well-funded school district served mostly white students. Thus the state's response to mostly African American students like Mah'Ria getting a shot to attend a better school primarily populated by whites was to figure out a way to take that opportunity away for them. Stories like this are controversial because they suggest that certain groups in American society are being systematically denied opportunities that are granted to others.

The United States has a long history of just this sort of unequal treatment of social groups, especially racial minorities. For example, schools were racially segregated by law in many states well into the middle of the twentieth century. Today most people accept that government should not actively discriminate on the basis of race and that everyone has a right to equality of educational opportunity. Yet what happened to Mah'Ria and her Normandy School District (sorry, Collaborative) classmates seems to suggest that whatever the law says, there's still plenty of inequality in the public education system.

Government has historically tried to address this sort of inequality through affirmative action, or actions designed to help minorities overcome the effects of past discrimination and compete on an equal basis with the majority. In recent years, however, the Supreme Court has become increasingly skeptical of these sorts of policies. For example, in *Schuette v. Coalition to Defend Affirmative Action* (2014) the court effectively ruled that people can vote away affirmative action programs. At the heart of that case were affirmative action admission policies at Michigan universities designed to give underrepresented minorities—students like Mah'Ria—a little help in college admission decisions. Michigan's affirmative action program was eliminated by a ballot initiative, and the Supreme Court ruling upheld the outcome.

Regardless of the larger fate of affirmative action policies, what happened in Normandy continues to raise the question of whether certain groups in American society are being systematically denied rights and liberties enjoyed by other citizens. In this chapter, we explore the struggles undertaken by several groups to achieve equality.

THE CONCEPT OF CIVIL RIGHTS

Civil rights are the rights of all citizens to legal, social, and economic equality. The key word here is *all*. The liberties granted by the First Amendment, for example, are supposed to apply equally to all citizens. Your race, socioeconomic status, age, or sexual orientation is not supposed to matter. As civil rights, these liberties belong to all in society, not just to those who have a certain skin pigment or sexual preference. Yet these factors have mattered and in some cases still do. Certain liberties and freedoms are denied to some simply because they belong to a particular group. If and how civil liberties are guaranteed to all groups and what government should do when those rights are denied to specific groups cuts to the heart of the core democratic principle of political equality. It is this group aspect and the government's responsibility to act or not to act that distinguishes civil rights from civil liberties.

In Chapter 4, we learned that individual citizens have civil liberties, or the freedom to make individual decisions. In order to ensure they enjoy those freedoms, limits are placed on the coercive power of government to prevent government from using its power to arbitrarily deny individuals the right to exercise their civil liberties. Civil rights, in contrast, impose an obligation on government to use its coercive power to ensure that those freedoms are not arbitrarily denied to certain categories of citizens. The metaphor of the "shield and sword" (*Pollock v. Williams* 1944) serves to clarify the distinction between civil liberties and civil rights. Questions of civil liberties—the shield—center on the issue of protecting individual freedom from government interference. Questions of civil rights—the sword—center on the issue of the government's obligation to take action to protect individual freedoms from other outside interference. The shield, or civil liberty, is a negative safeguard: "it enables a person whose freedom is endangered to invoke the Constitution" to invalidate government action (Carr 1947, 3). The sword, or civil rights, is a "positive weapon wielded by the federal government, which takes the initiative in protecting helpless individuals by bringing criminal charges against persons who are encroaching upon their rights" (Carr 1947, 5).

Historically, both federal and state governments have tolerated unequal treatment of citizens based on characteristics such as race, gender, and religion. The most notorious example is the treatment of African Americans. In the name of political pragmatism, the Founders accepted the institution of slavery and enshrined in the Constitution the value of slaves (referred to as "other persons") as three-fifths of a person for purposes of taxation and representation (Article I, Section 2). Since most blacks were slaves at the time, the Constitution itself violated the civil rights of a large section of the population on the basis of race. Even for free African Americans and even after the abolition of slavery, basic liberties such as the right to vote were systematically denied on the basis of race.

African Americans are not the only group to wage an extended battle over the federal government's duty to prevent their freedoms from being arbitrarily denied.

civil rights The obligations placed on government to protect the freedom of the people.

Other racial and ethnic minorities, including Native Americans and Latinos, have suffered like discrimination and faced similar obstacles. It is not just racial and ethnic groups that have been systematically denied rights and liberties. Other groups include women, people with disabilities, and LGBTQ individuals. Age has also been a battleground for civil rights. During the Vietnam War, young people were angry that their government could send them to fight in a war but would not allow them to vote and have input on the decision to wage the war in the first place. This concern was the driving force behind the Twenty-Sixth Amendment, adopted in 1971, that guarantees all citizens aged 18 or older the right to vote. On the other end of the spectrum, advocates for the elderly have fought mandatory retirement and age discrimination in employment. Other groups with civil rights agendas range from welfare recipients to smokers.

In short, the list of groups that have fought or are fighting extensive civil rights campaigns is long, and to do them all justice would require a book unto itself. Although we cannot examine every struggle to gain equal access to the rights and privileges of citizenship in one chapter of a textbook, we can examine some representative cases to give a sense of how groups denied civil liberties have sought to get government to act not just as a shield, but as a sword.

AFRICAN AMERICANS

Slavery systematically denied civil rights to large numbers of African Americans for almost the entire first century of the republic's history. The end of the Civil War brought with it a constitutional ban on slavery. In the postwar period, the federal government embarked on a program to bring liberated slaves, who were concentrated in the South, into the mainstream of American life. Congress passed legislation granting African Americans the right to sue, to give evidence in court, and to buy, sell, and inherit property. New federal laws also outlawed segregation in transportation, schools, and public accommodations. The Fifteenth Amendment specifically prohibited states from denying any adult male the right to vote on the basis of race, color, or previous condition of servitude.

Benefiting from the newfound political rights guaranteed by the federal government, African Americans made significant gains toward political equality. African Americans were elected to Congress and to numerous state and local offices. These advances were made possible by federal occupation forces that remained in Confederate states following the Civil War. This federal presence helped ensure that the new constitutional protections were enforced. Those federal forces, and the protection they represented, withdrew following the disputed election of 1876. Southern Democrats acquiesced in the selection of Republican Rutherford B. Hayes over their candidate, Samuel J. Tilden, in return for Hayes's agreement to withdraw troops from the South when he came to office.

(MIS)APPLYING THE FRAMEWORKS

SOCIAL DARWINISM, EUGENICS, AND CIVIL RIGHTS

The application of evolutionary and biological theories is a relatively recent and novel scientific approach to studying politics and policy. The *misapplication* of evolutionary and biological theories, on the other hand, has a long and dark history in the United States, one with devastating consequences for civil liberties and civil rights.

Two of the best known of such movements are Social Darwinism and eugenics. Social Darwinism argued that people's political, social, and economic position was dictated by "survival of the fittest." In other words, people at the top of the political, social, and economic hierarchy were there because they were somehow better than those at the bottom. The eugenics movement sought to improve society by ensuring the heritable traits of the "fittest" were passed on and the traits of the weak and social undesirables were not.

Social Darwinism and, especially, the eugenics movement gained a remarkably broad degree of scholarly and popular support in the first half of the twentieth century. They were used to justify removing the sword and shield governmental protections of individual freedoms. In other words, they were mostly racist, sexist, and classist pseudo-science used to strip citizens of their civil liberties and groups of their civil rights.

Social Darwinism and eugenics enthusiasts provided a scientific fig leaf to justify racial discrimination and segregation, anti-miscegenation laws banning interracial marriage, and more broadly to maintain existing social hierarchies that were headed by white males and consigned females and nonwhites to inferior positions. Eugenics advocates successfully lobbied Congress to limit immigration from "inferior" racial and ethnic groups and state governments to pass compulsory sterilization laws that targeted the mentally and physically disabled and those considered socially degenerate or immoral.

Tens of thousands of people were sterilized under such laws, which the Supreme Court ruled were constitutional (*Buck v. Bell* 1927). It was not until after World War II that the eugenics movement really started to recede from public prominence, partly because atrocities carried out by Nazi Germany had been justified by similar arguments. Even so, in America the impact on civil rights and liberties of eugenic and Social Darwinian ideas continued to linger. States carried out enforced sterilizations into the 1970s, and studies of racial differences in intelligence (which is partially heritable) continued to spark controversy into the 1990s.

One of the truly astonishing things about this shameful record is that Social Darwinism and eugenics stood on such poor scientific, not to mention moral, ethical, and democratic, foundations. The "survival of the fittest" of Social Darwinism was based largely on a misunderstanding of natural selection, which posits that organisms best suited to their local environments are more likely to reproduce, not that the strongest get to rule at the top of the social hierarchy. Eugenicists incorrectly—and against the weight of much empirical evidence—downplayed the importance of environment in shaping desirable social traits, and misunderstood and misrepresented the complex genetic influences on those same traits.

Ideas like Social Darwinism and eugenics also imposed a high cost on the (truly) scientific study of how biology shapes attitudes and behavior. One reason why political scientists, economists, and other social sciences have been slow to investigate biological influences on our preferences and choices is because of the long shadow of Social Darwinism and eugenics and their devastating effects on civil liberties and civil rights.

Discussion Questions

1. Does studying how biology influences social traits inevitably lead to concerns about civil liberties and civil rights? Why or why not?
2. Given the history of Social Darwinism and the eugenics movement, do you think political scientists should continue to investigate how biology influences attitudes and behavior? Why or why not?

Racial Segregation

With the federal government's protection removed, the systematic denial of African Americans' civil and political rights spread throughout the South. Initially, racial segregation, or the separation of people based on their race, was based on tradition. Gradually, however, state laws mandated segregation of public schools, transportation, and accommodations by race. Other laws politically disenfranchised African Americans with legal techniques such as **poll taxes** (fees required for casting a ballot), **literacy tests** (a requirement that citizens demonstrate their fitness to vote by passing a reading or comprehension test), and the exclusion of African Americans from Democratic Party primaries. In the last two decades of the nineteenth century, lynching was used to deter African Americans from exercising their constitutional rights. By the early years of the twentieth century, segregation of African Americans through intimidation and disenfranchisement was complete in the southern states.

At about the same time, however, the locus of race problems began to shift. While the overwhelming proportion of African Americans had been concentrated in the rural South, millions began migrating to urban areas in the North to escape oppression and improve their lives economically. Northern cities were less than welcoming. African Americans were often shut out of white neighborhoods by residential segregation ordinances and restrictive covenants forbidding the sale of property to nonwhites. These legal means of oppression were sometimes augmented by beatings and bombings. The end result was that African Americans were often concentrated in low-rent, racially exclusive ghettoes. In terms of day-to-day life, northern ghettoes may have been better than southern plantations, but discrimination and segregation remained a central fact of life in the North as well as the South.

African Americans' reaction to being systematically denied their civil rights varied. Some, such as Booker T. Washington, urged accommodation. Others, especially a group of northern intellectuals, argued for a more active pursuit of political equality. Among the best known of this latter group was W. E. B. Du Bois, who in 1909 joined with prominent white intellectuals such as philosopher John Dewey and lawyer Clarence Darrow, among others, to form the National Association for the Advancement of Colored People (NAACP).

The Judicial Strategy to End Segregation

Because African Americans were often prevented from exercising their right to vote, elected officials in the state legislatures and governors' mansions were unresponsive and even hostile to demands for racial equality. Excluded from the electoral process, African Americans turned to the federal courts for help in securing fundamental constitutional rights.

The NAACP became the major group fighting for civil rights and led the way in court battles to end segregation and disenfranchisement. Soon after its founding, the NAACP filed a series of test cases on several legal fronts. Its initial victory came in *Guinn v. United States* (1915), in which the Supreme Court invalidated the **grandfather clause** of the Oklahoma constitution, a clause that exempted people

---

poll taxes A technique used to keep certain groups from voting by charging a fee to vote.

literacy tests Reading or comprehension tests that citizens are required to pass to demonstrate their fitness to vote.

grandfather clause A provision in election laws used in conjunction with literacy tests to prevent African Americans from voting. People whose ancestors were entitled to vote in 1866 (i.e., whites) were exempt from passing the literacy test, but African Americans, whose ancestors were slaves, had to pass the literacy test in order to vote. This clause was ruled unconstitutional in 1915.

whose ancestors were entitled to vote in 1866 from the literacy test. Only whites had the right to vote that year.

In the three decades following *Guinn,* the NAACP scored a number of other notable victories. The most significant was the fight to get equal treatment in public facilities such as schools. The Fourteenth Amendment prohibits states from passing or enforcing any law that would deny "any person within its jurisdiction the equal protection of the laws." Southern states responded by passing laws requiring **separate but equal** accommodations for blacks and whites in public facilities such as public transportation. An 1896 Supreme Court decision, ***Plessy v. Ferguson,*** ruled that separate public facilities for people of different races satisfied the Fourteenth Amendment's equal protection clause, provided they were "equal."

Initially, the NAACP tried to chip away at the "separate but equal" doctrine on a case-by-case basis. The first big victory came in *Missouri ex rel. Gaines v. Canada* (1938). The University of Missouri had refused to admit a qualified African American student to its law school, but the state offered to pay his expenses at a school in a neighboring state that admitted blacks. The Supreme Court ruled that this policy did not satisfy the state's constitutional responsibilities. "Separate but equal," in other words, meant separate but equal within the state.

After this case, the Supreme Court began to pay closer attention to whether separate facilities were actually equal. In the early 1950s, NAACP lawyers decided to abandon the policy of chipping away at the "separate but equal" doctrine and to advance the argument that separate facilities for different races in and of themselves violated the equal protection of the law clause of the Fourteenth Amendment. The strategy was vindicated in ***Brown v. Board of Education*** (1954), one of the Supreme Court's most important civil rights decisions. A unanimous Court overturned the "separate but equal" precedent set by *Plessy.* To give added weight to the ruling, Chief Justice Earl Warren wrote the opinion declaring that separate educational facilities are inherently unequal. Even if all the tangible characteristics of schools—such as classrooms, libraries, curricula, teachers' salaries, and teachers' qualifications—are equal, wrote Warren, the intangible quality of education is not equal in racially segregated schools. Racial segregation of public schools deprives African American children of equal protection of the laws because "to separate them from others of similar age and qualifications solely because of their race generates a feeling of inferiority … that may affect their hearts and minds in a way unlikely ever to be undone." The following year, the Court ordered states to dismantle the system of segregated schools "with all deliberate speed" and entrusted the federal district courts to require local school boards to comply. There was resistance to integration of the schools throughout the Deep South, and the federal judges entrusted with enforcing the Constitution were at the center of legal battles for more than a decade to follow (Peltason 1961).

The Revolution in Race Relations

Although the NAACP scored significant victories in court, the legislative and executive branches of government initially did little to secure the rights of African

separate but equal A practice in southern states to comply with the Fourteenth Amendment's "equal protection" clause by passing laws requiring separate but equal accommodations for blacks and whites in public facilities. The Supreme Court ruled such laws unconstitutional in 1954.

Plessy v. Ferguson An 1896 Supreme Court decision ruling that separate public facilities for people of different races satisfied the Fourteenth Amendment's equal protection clause, provided the facilities were "equal."

Brown v. Board of Education The 1954 case in which a unanimous Court overturned the "separate but equal" precedent set by *Plessy v. Ferguson* and declared that separate educational facilities are inherently unequal.

Americans. Southern senators successfully filibustered an attempt to enact anti-lynching legislation, and even liberal presidents of the first half of the twentieth century showed little commitment to the civil rights of African Americans. Franklin Roosevelt, for example, introduced no major civil rights legislation; he established a Committee on Fair Employment Practices in 1941 only after being threatened with a march on Washington to secure job opportunities for minorities.

The first significant steps for racial equality were taken shortly after World War II, when President Harry Truman ended segregation of the armed services and of civilian jobs in national government and mandated that the federal government would do business only with firms that did not discriminate in hiring. Truman also proposed a broad civil rights program to Congress and appointed a committee to study race relations. Truman's successor, Dwight Eisenhower, followed up on the process of desegregating the armed forces and pushed to end segregation in the District of Columbia. The Civil Rights Act of 1957 created the U.S. Civil Rights Commission and was the first civil rights law to be passed by the federal government since the Reconstruction period following the Civil War.

By the mid-1950s, then, the judicial, executive, and legislative branches of the federal government finally had begun to take proactive steps to uphold the civil rights of African Americans. At about the same time, a large segment of the African American community started to aggressively challenge the status quo in race relations, and refused to accept the inferior position imposed on them. Civil rights activists engaged in acts of **civil disobedience**, or deliberately disobeying laws viewed as morally repugnant. An event that energized this development was the December 1955 arrest of Rosa Parks, an African American seamstress who refused to move to the back of a municipal bus in Montgomery, Alabama. The arrest sparked a bus boycott led by a young minister, Dr. Martin Luther King Jr., and ultimately led to government action to outlaw racial segregation.

What had been a battle waged by a relatively few well-educated, middle-class African Americans became a broad movement that cut across social and economic lines. The legal battles and conciliatory negotiations with government and white leaders that had been used by groups such as the NAACP and the National Urban League came in for sharp criticism. According to Dr. Martin Luther King Jr. and others of a new generation of civil rights leaders, what was needed was direct action by the masses, including peaceful boycotts, sit-ins, and protest marches. African Americans were no longer willing to wait for the outcome of lengthy courtroom campaigns to win rights for their children. The reasons for this sudden shift are varied. In World War II many African Americans serving in the armed forces had the novel experience of being treated with respect by white people in France and the United Kingdom who gave them a social acceptance they had never enjoyed in their own country. Coming back from military service, they naturally resented returning to an inferior position in civilian life and desired to do something about it. Furthermore, many were keenly aware of the irony of a country's fighting a war against the racist philosophy of Nazi Germany while at the same time practicing its own brand of racism at home.

The attitudes of whites, though far from uniform, also began to change. Supreme Court decisions and executive actions indicated that the political system was either responding to or promoting more tolerant racial attitudes in the white mainstream.

civil disobedience Deliberately disobeying laws viewed as morally repugnant.

Capitalizing on these changes, leaders such as King began to push for full integration in all aspects of American life. Adopting the technique used successfully by Mahatma Gandhi to obtain India's independence from Britain, Dr. King urged **passive resistance**, a technique of civil disobedience where individuals peacefully submit to arrest for refusing to obey laws they consider immoral. A broad coalition of new groups emerged, including the Southern Christian Leadership Conference, the Student Nonviolent Coordinating Committee, and the Congress of Racial Equality. Sympathetic whites lent support, particularly college students who went to the South to assist in registering African American voters and integrating public facilities.

By the mid-1960s, some African Americans concluded that nonviolent direct action also was too slow, and some advocated pursuing change through violence. Leaders of the Black Muslims, a group founded in the 1930s, and the Black Panthers, an organization founded in 1966 in Oakland, California, to protect African Americans from police brutality, openly advocated violent revolution. Race riots in Los Angeles, Detroit, Washington, DC, and other major cities in the late 1960s seemed to be spontaneous mass reactions to police brutality or to the assassination of Dr. Martin Luther King Jr., not organized actions coordinated with a particular group's agenda.

passive resistance A nonviolent technique of protest that entails resisting government laws or practices that are believed to be unjust.

Civil Rights Act of 1964 The landmark law that outlawed racial segregation in schools and public places and barred discrimination in employment based on sex.

On August 28, 1963, Martin Luther King Jr. delivered his "I Have a Dream" speech to over 200,000 people who marched on Washington, DC, that summer.

© AP Photo

Government's Response to the Race Revolution

Although the social turmoil of race relations in the 1950s and 1960s was not pretty, it did seem to affect the political system. In the summer of 1963, more than 200,000 people marched on Washington, where Dr. Martin Luther King Jr. delivered his "I Have a Dream" speech, one of the most eloquent declarations of the moral force behind calls for racial equity in the United States. This march pressured the Kennedy administration into supporting the expansion of the 1957 Civil Rights Act. After Kennedy was assassinated in November 1963, President Lyndon Johnson, acting with the moral authority bestowed by the shadow of the slain president, picked up Kennedy's civil rights bill, strengthened it, and submitted it to Congress. The **Civil Rights Act of 1964** is a landmark law that outlawed racial segregation in schools and public places and barred discrimination in employment based on sex. Title II of the law barred racial segregation in public accommodations; Title

VI outlawed racial discrimination in any program that received assistance from the federal government; and Title VII banned discrimination by employers and unions based on race, religion, sex, or national origin. That same year also saw the ratification of the Twenty-Fourth Amendment, which made poll taxes unconstitutional and strengthened the voting rights of African Americans.

A year later, Johnson signed the 1965 Voting Rights Act into law. This act targeted **Jim Crow laws** used mainly by southern states to establish racial segregation in all public facilities (such as schools, public buildings, and transportation) and to disenfranchise African Americans by requiring them to pass literacy tests, pay poll taxes, and be of "good moral character," among other things, as prerequisites to voting. Significantly, the **Voting Rights Act of 1965** authorized the federal government to ensure that eligible voters were not denied access to the ballot. For the first time since the end of Reconstruction, the federal government started to actively enforce the Fifteenth Amendment's promise of voting rights for African Americans. In the wake of the Voting Rights Act, millions of African Americans registered to vote, making it harder for elected officials to ignore their concerns and pressuring the political system to provide them with full political equality. And the number of black elected officials has increased. In 1965, only five members of Congress were black. As of 2017, there were 49 black members, including U.S. Senators Tim Scott (R-SC), Cory Booker (D-NJ), and Kamala Harris (D-CA). Although three senators does not sound like a lot, it is nonetheless a historical high for the number of African Americans concurrently serving in the Senate.

While racial equality has improved since the Jim Crow era, representation for African Americans continues to be a source of conflict in American politics. The Supreme Court, for example, gutted key aspects of the Voting Rights Act in a controversial 5–4 decision in *Shelby v. Holder* (2013). At stake was a part of the law that required state and local governments with past histories of denying ballot access to minorities to gain federal approval for any changes in their election laws. The majority opinion (written by Chief Justice John Roberts) argued that while this rule might have been necessary at one time, that historical era had passed. The law, argued Roberts, "is based on 40-year-old facts having no logical relationship to the present day." Some criticized this reasoning, arguing that events after the decision highlighted exactly why the law was enacted in the first place and why the law was still needed. For example, Texas, one of the affected states, promptly announced that a state voter identification law and a contested redistricting plan would immediately be put into effect. Both the ID law and the redistricting had been bitterly opposed on the grounds they undercut ballot access and equal representation to minorities (Liptak 2013).

Affirmative Action

Americans generally agree that no one should be denied political equality or the rights of citizenship because of race. Accepting these values, however, has not ended the civil rights movement for African Americans. If nothing else, the controversy surrounding the *Shelby* decision clearly demonstrates that significant disagreements still exist over the extent of racial barriers to political equality. The issue of **affirmative action**, in particular, has generated a second, long-running

Jim Crow laws Laws designed to prevent African Americans from voting.

Voting Rights Act of 1965 Act authorizing the federal government to ensure that eligible voters were not denied access to the ballot, actively protecting the Fifteenth Amendment's promise of voting rights for African Americans.

affirmative action Governmental actions designed to help minorities compete on an equal basis and overcome the effects of discrimination in the past.

political dispute. Affirmative action programs began in the 1970s, signaling a shift from eliminating the legal obstacles to political equality to pursuing programs that actively seek to counter past or present effects of discrimination.

The basic argument for affirmative action policies is that inequality cannot be wiped out by removing **de jure discrimination**, or discrimination by law. The effects of discrimination linger long past their official sanction in law. As President Lyndon Johnson put it,

> You do not wipe away the scars of centuries by saying: Now you are free to go where you want, do as you desire, and choose the leaders you please … We seek not just freedom but opportunity. We seek not just legal equity but human ability, not just equality as a right and a theory, but equality as a fact and equality as a result. (Americans United for Affirmative Action 1999)

In other words, equality before the law is not enough. To combat the lasting effects of discrimination—in hiring, college admissions, and promotions—government needs to take proactive steps to help those excluded from the full rights and privileges of citizenship overcome the enduring effects of discrimination.

The argument against affirmative action is that it replaces one form of discrimination with another. Rather than promote equality, opponents argue, affirmative action actually promotes political inequality because it amounts to "reverse discrimination," namely punishing whites because of their race. Critics argue that if any race is discriminated against, equality suffers.

The Supreme Court has tried to strike a balance that allows policies to promote diversity in the name of the greater social good, without promoting outright quotas. A key early case was *Regents of the University of California v. Bakke* (1978). Allan Bakke was denied admission to medical school at the University of California, Davis, which had designated a set-aside quota for minority students. Bakke's academic record was superior to that of all of the students admitted under the quota, and he sued, claiming the school violated his Fourteenth Amendment right to equal protection of the law. The Court agreed, ruling that racial quotas violated federal law. The Court, nonetheless, upheld the basic legitimacy of affirmative action, ruling that race could be used as a factor in deciding admissions, but it could not be the sole criterion.

In later cases, the Court ruled that racial set-asides were constitutional under some circumstances. For example, in *United Steelworkers of America v. Weber* (1979), the Court upheld an affirmative action plan voluntarily agreed to by Kaiser Aluminum Chemical Corporation and a union representing its employees. The plan guaranteed a certain number of jobs to African Americans until the racial makeup of the company's employees reflected the racial breakdown of the local labor force. The Court said that this plan did not violate federal statute because its purpose was to redress the effects of past discrimination.

Critics charge that affirmative action programs provide unfair advantages to minorities and unduly downgrade merit as the basis of social economic opportunities. This view has spawned several movements to eliminate race as a basis for preferential treatment. In 1996, a majority of California voters approved Proposition 209, which effectively eliminated the state's affirmative action policy. Other states, including Washington, Michigan, and Nebraska, have passed similar propositions in subsequent years. During the same period, the Supreme Court also

de jure discrimination Discrimination that is set forth in law.

began chipping away at affirmative action. The Court let stand a lower court ruling in *Hopwood v. Texas* (1994) prohibiting the use of race and gender in public college admissions policies in Texas, Louisiana, and Mississippi. In *Ricci v. DeStefano* (2009) the Supreme Court ruled that the city of New Haven could not invalidate promotion exams in the fire department because no black firefighters had passed the exam. And, as discussed in the opening section of this chapter, in 2014 the court ruled in *Schuette v. Coalition to Defend Affirmative Action* that anti-affirmation action ballot initiatives are constitutional.

Opponents of affirmative action have received an increasingly sympathetic hearing in the political and legal arenas. Proponents counter that affirmative action is needed because African Americans still are not on an even playing field. Four decades after the federal government first took such steps to address historical discrimination in the 1970s, African Americans still lag behind the white majority on average income to educational achievement. African Americans' earnings relative to whites has improved only slightly over the last 35 years—from around 75 percent of white workers' earnings in the 1970s and 1980s to about 80 percent in the 2000s. The trend line with an essentially flat slope summarizes this interpretation (see Figure 5.1). And blacks lag even further behind whites in getting a

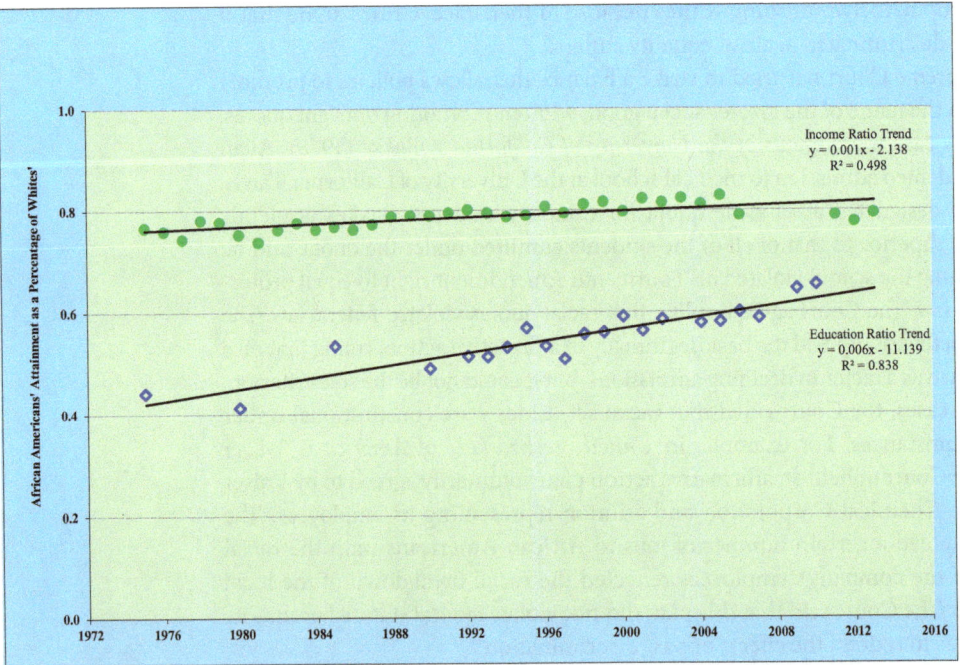

FIGURE 5.1 **African Americans' Earnings and College Education Relative to Whites**

Sources: Data from U.S. Census Bureau, Current Population Survey, Annual Social and Economic Supplements Table P-43: Full-Time, Year-Round All Workers by Median Earnings and Sex: 1960 to 2006. (Workers 15 years old and over with earnings beginning with March 1980, and workers 14 years old and over with earnings as of March of the following year for previous years. Before 1989 earnings are for civilian workers only.) Bureau of Labor Statistics, "Median Usual Weekly Earnings of Full-Time Wage and Salary Workers by Age, Race, Hispanic or Latino Ethnicity, and Sex," http://www.bls.gov/news.release/wkyeng.t02.htm and http://www.bls.gov/news.release/wkyeng.t03.htm.

THINKING ANALYTICALLY

HOW DO YOU MEASURE RACIAL ATTITUDES?

There are two basic reasons to oppose affirmative action policies designed to benefit minority racial groups. The first is a principled objection to the notion of government treating citizens differently on the basis of their membership in any racial group. The second is racial prejudice. So which is it? Is opposition to affirmative action primarily rooted in perfectly defensible political principles, or considerably less defensible racial prejudice? Opponents and supporters of affirmative action frequently give different responses, and it has proven frustratingly difficult to come up with a reliable empirical answer to this question.

The key problem is figuring out how to measure racial attitudes. The primary means used by political scientists (and social scientists generally) to measure racial attitudes is through surveys. In other words, we just ask people their opinions and attitudes about race and trust them to give an honest answer. There are two big drawbacks to this approach. First, people may be less than honest in answering. Over the past 50 years it has become increasingly socially unacceptable to express openly racist views, and people are increasingly reluctant to report racial biases even when they have them. Second, some people may have unconscious biases. Humans often reflexively favor their in-group, and race is often used as a marker of a social in- or out-group. There may be no conscious ill will to those in the out-group, yet an implicit positive bias toward the in-group may remain, and that bias may subconsciously influence our attitudes on issues like affirmative action.

So, let's think about this analytically. How can you measure racial attitudes if people may deliberately give misleading answers to survey questions about race and may even be unaware that they have biases toward an in-group or against an out-group?

One approach is not to ask direct questions about racial attitudes or support for affirmative action, but try to measure how strongly people link particular concepts. Are positive concepts more likely to be linked with one racial group and negative concepts linked to another? And if so, how could you measure the strength of that link without asking direct questions?

One possibility is the Implicit Association Test (IAT), developed by psychologist Anthony Greenwald (Greenwald, McGhee, and Schwartz 1998) to measure the strength of implicit, or automatic, associations between two concepts. The basic idea is simple: In an IAT test people look at a computer screen with two categories listed, one in the top left corner, and one in the top right. A series of stimuli appear in the middle of the screen, and subjects have to put that stimulus into one of the two categories as quickly as possible by pressing computer keys. Importantly, subjects periodically have to reverse the categorization of the concepts.

So, for example, in a race IAT the two categories might be "white" and "black," and the concepts might be a series of positive and negative words. On some trials, subjects will be told to classify positive words as white and negative words as black. On other trials, they will be told to classify positive words as black and negative words as white. The idea is that differences in how long it takes to classify these words measures implicit biases. So, if someone is quicker to classify positive words when they are associated with "white" compared to when they are associated with "black," it suggests they automatically associate positive concepts more with white than with black. In other words, they have an implicit bias toward whites.

Race IATs have been revealing ... and extremely controversial. Race IATs are only weakly correlated with more explicit (survey question) measures of racial attitudes, but show pretty strong implicit preferences for whites among whites (McConnell and Leibold 2001). Indeed, some studies have even shown that some nonwhites have this bias toward whites. What all this suggests is that if the IAT is indeed meaningfully tapping into racial attitudes, there still exists a fairly strong bias by whites toward whites. Other studies using the IAT suggest that such biases lead to real-world consequences such as employment discrimination (Ziegert and Hanges 2005). If that's the case—in other words, that social and economic opportunity is still at least partially tied to membership in a particular racial group—it strengthens the argument for keeping affirmative action.

Others are not convinced by such indirect measures of racial attitudes. Some argue the IAT is not a particularly good measure of subconscious racial preferences, and even if it is, this does not outweigh the conscious racial preferences embodied in affirmative action policies.

To be sure, many people do have legitimate, principled objections to affirmative action policies. Nonetheless, results from the IAT studies suggest that affirmative action policies are still needed because bias against minority groups still exists and has important consequences for social and economic opportunity, and thus civil rights.

Discussion Questions

There are many IAT tests available online at Project Implicit (https://implicit.harvard.edu/implicit/). These include tests for implicit attitudes toward many of the groups discussed in this chapter—blacks, Native Americans, women, gays, the disabled. Take some of these tests, examine the results, and answer the following:

1. Do you think these results accurately represent your views toward groups you do not belong to? Do you think these results say something about your attitudes that would not have been captured if you were asked standard survey questions about these groups?
2. Do these results line up with your attitudes on political issues like affirmative action, gay marriage, and access for the disabled?

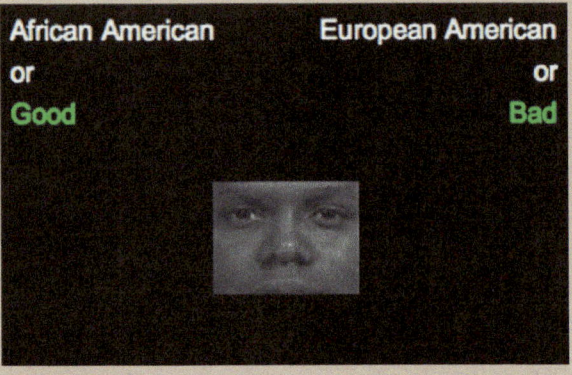

Screenshot of an IAT test. As soon as the image appears on the screen, the test-taker has to press buttons indicating "Good" or "Bad" as rapidly as possible.

---

college education, though the positive slope of the trend line indicates that the gap has narrowed somewhat over time. In the 1970s, the proportion of blacks with a college education was less than half the proportion of whites, increasing to about two-thirds that of whites by the early twenty-first century.

Do these disparities reflect inequality of opportunity that lingers as a result of discrimination? Do they reflect continued **de facto discrimination** (discrimination "by fact")—patterns of segregation and social opportunity? Or are the issues more complex? There are no easy answers, and the struggle for the civil rights of African Americans will continue.

Perhaps there is no better example of this continuing struggle than the **#BlackLivesMatter movement**, a modern civil rights movement formed to publicize and protest police brutality and killings of African Americans. Noteworthy features include: effective use of Twitter's hashtags and other social media, inclusion of those who were marginalized in earlier black liberation movements (women, lesbian, gay, bisexual, transgender, and queer), and a localized organizational structure with no single recognizable leader who speaks for the movement (https://blacklivesmatter.com/). The movement began in 2013 after a Florida jury acquitted George Zimmerman, a neighborhood watch volunteer, of shooting and killing an unarmed African American teen, Trayvon Martin. Alicia Garza, a young

de facto discrimination Discrimination that exists in fact, in real life, or in practice.

#BlackLivesMatter movement A modern civil rights movement formed to protest police brutality and killings of African Americans. Noteworthy features include: effective use of Twitter's hashtags, inclusion of those who were marginalized in earlier black liberation movements (women, lesbian, gay, bisexual, transgender, and queer), and a localized organizational structure with no recognizable leader who speaks for the movement.

black activist in Oakland, posted an impassioned message on Facebook: "Black people. I love you. I love us. Our lives matter." A close friend, Patrisse Cullors, read the post and shared the words online using #blacklivesmatter. Thus, a new type of civil rights movement began (Day 2015). The hashtag resurfaced about a year later when protests broke out in Ferguson, Missouri, in response to the shooting of Michael Brown, an unarmed African American teenager, by Darren Wilson, a white police officer. Protesters chanting "Black lives matter" captured the deeply held perception that white elected officials did not represent or treat the city's majority black population equitably.

The movement continued to grow through 2017 as it protested numerous incidents of violence against African Americans. Whatever the advances in race relations, and these have been considerable, the recurrence of such incidents serves as a stark reminder that race continues to be a factor in determining social, economic, or political equality.

African Americans are not the only group to have been denied the full rights and privileges of citizenship because of race and ethnicity. Though no other group has suffered the wholesale indignity of being reduced to property or counted as only three-fifths of a person in the Constitution, other racial and ethnic minorities have long struggled for political equality. Two notable groups are Latinos, the largest ethnic minority in the United States, and Native Americans.

LATINOS

Latinos, or people who came from or whose ancestors came from Spanish-speaking nations or Latin America, are the largest ethnic minority in the United States. In 2016, the U.S. Census Bureau estimated that 17.8 percent of the population was Hispanic, compared to 13.3 percent African Americans. Latinos account for roughly half of all population growth in the United States (U.S. Census Bureau 2011). Mexican Americans are the most numerous, and their political power has been increasing in many states, particularly in the Southwest.

The initial experience of Mexican Americans with American society was as a conquered people. The Treaty of Guadalupe Hidalgo, which ended the Mexican–American War in 1848, ceded parts of what are now seven southwestern and western states to the United States. The treaty guaranteed Mexican Americans living in these areas citizenship and certain land grants and rights. But these rights were rapidly abrogated as land was seized by both legal and illegal means by cotton plantation owners, cattle and sheep ranchers, miners, and farmers. Some Mexican Americans struck back with armed raids, and even after the violence subsided, the divisions remained well into the twentieth century.

During the Great Depression, the government succeeded in deporting some Mexican Americans, and groups such as the League of United Latin American Citizens (LULAC) had to work hard to gain even a semblance of integration into mainstream American life. About a million Mexican Americans fought in World War II, and Mexican American combat units were often highly decorated. The industrial war effort drew many others into urban centers, where for the first time they obtained high-paying skilled jobs. The GI Bill of Rights enabled Mexican American veterans to go to college and receive other benefits, such as housing and expanded economic opportunities. As a result, Mexican Americans, along with Latinos in general, increasingly refused to accept second-class status and, like African Americans, began to demand social equality. Significant progress has been made, but even after decades of civil rights progress, Latinos still lag behind whites in income and education, and they often face the additional burden of language barriers. Indeed, the slope of the trend line for income is negative (see Figure 5.2), indicating that Latinos have lost ground over the last three decades. Latinos earned about three-fourths the earnings of whites in the mid-1970s, and by 2011, Latino earnings had fallen to about two-thirds of white earnings. The gap in getting a college education is even bigger, and the trend is flat—from 1975 to the 2000s, the proportion of Latinos with a college education remained at only about 40 percent the proportion of whites. Although relative earnings and education show improvement in recent years, it is too early to tell if this marks a change in the trend.

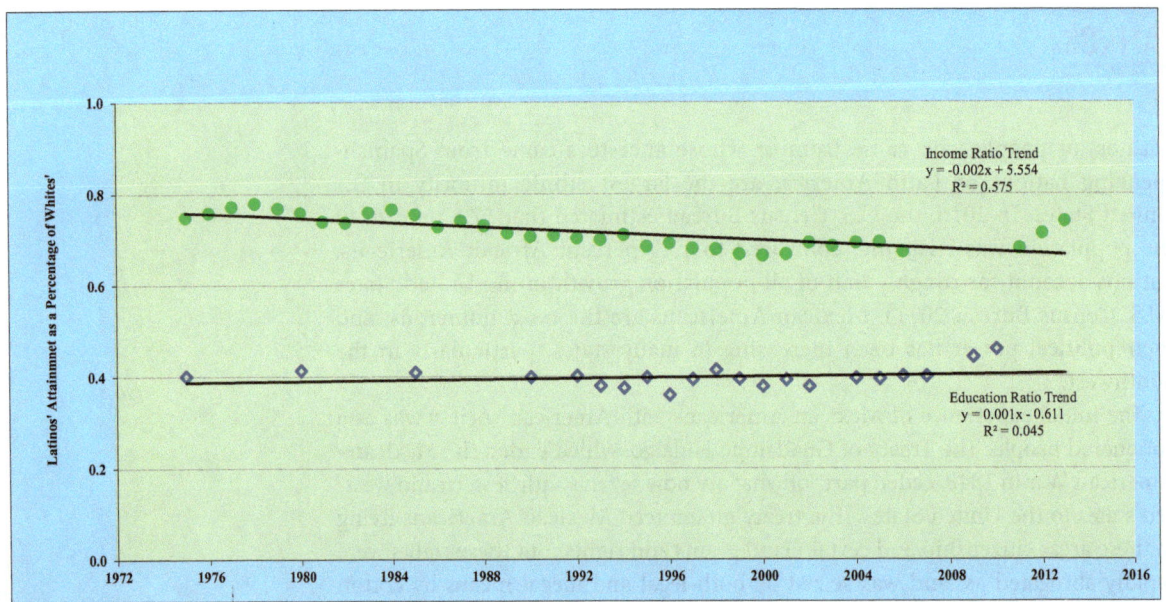

FIGURE 5.2 **Latinos' Earnings and College Education Relative to Whites**

Sources: Data from U.S. Census Bureau, Current Population Survey, Annual Social and Economic Supplements Table P-43: Full-Time, Year-Round All Workers by Median Earnings and Sex: 1960 to 2006. (Workers 15 years old and over with earnings beginning with March 1980, and workers 14 years old and over with earnings as of March of the following year for previous years. Before 1989 earnings are for civilian workers only.) Bureau of Labor Statistics, "Median Usual Weekly Earnings of Full-Time Wage and Salary Workers by Age, Race, Hispanic or Latino Ethnicity, and Sex," http://www.bls.gov/news.release/wkyeng.t02.htm and http://www.bls.gov/news.release/wkyeng.t03.htm.

The civil rights struggle of Latinos combines litigation and political activism. Among the groups spearheading these efforts during the past four decades have been the Mexican American Legal Defense and Educational Fund (MALDEF) and the Puerto Rican Legal Defense and Education Fund (PRLDEF). These groups often model their tactics on the litigation pursued by the NAACP, and they have focused their efforts on issues related to education. They have scored notable successes in lawsuits seeking more equitable distribution of resources for schools, implementation of bilingual programs, and equal access to higher education. They have also fought aggressively to protect Latinos' voting rights and to increase their representation in the political process. For example, in *White v. Register* (1973), a test case brought by MALDEF, the Supreme Court overturned multimember electoral districts in Texas, agreeing with arguments that such districts unfairly stacked the deck by making it harder for minority candidates to win a majority.

These sorts of victories, combined with their numbers, have made Latinos an important political force in recent decades, especially in the Southwest. Yet their representation in elected and appointive office still does not reflect their relative proportion of the voting-age population. The number of Latino members in Congress, for example, increased from four in 1965 to 46—a record high—in 2017 (41 in the House, which includes one nonvoting delegate, and five U.S. senators). But this level of representation in Congress is only about one-third as large as the Latino voting-age population. Consequently, issues that resonate in Latino communities, such as bilingual programs and access to educational opportunities, are not always fully represented in the policymaking process.

Even when these issues are pushed into the political process, they are often perceived as attempts to limit the rights of Latinos rather than expand them. Immigrant access to public services is a notable example of this. Much of the growth in the Latino population is being driven by immigration, and Latino immigrants—especially undocumented, or "illegal," Latino immigrants—have faced a backlash. This backlash is ironic because the United States views itself as a nation of immigrants, evidenced by the inscription on the base of the Statue of Liberty welcoming prospective Americans: "Give me your tired, your poor, your huddled masses." Political developments over the past decade or two have sent a clear message that the welcome does not apply to undocumented immigrants (who often end up existing on the margins of the economy and are thus often tired and almost always poor).

An Arizona law passed in 2010 made it a state crime (not just a federal crime) to be an undocumented immigrant. The law cracks down on those who hire, transport, or shelter undocumented immigrants, and obliges law enforcement officers to check for immigration status and to arrest individuals if there is probable cause to believe they are undocumented. Several other states enacted similar laws: Utah, Indiana, South Carolina, Georgia, and Alabama. These laws sparked fierce debate. Opponents saw them as enshrining racial profiling into law and unfairly—and unconstitutionally—targeting the civil rights of Latinos. Supporters argue that states were all but forced to act on illegal immigration because of the federal government's continued inaction on the issue.

A number of groups, including the Mexican American Legal Defense Fund, the NAACP, and the National Coalition of Latino Clergy and Christian Leaders, challenged the Arizona law. In *Arizona v. United States* (2012) the Supreme Court upheld the centerpiece of the law, ruling its "show me your papers" provision constitutional, in effect, allowing state law enforcement officers to investigate the immigration status of anyone they stop or arrest. However, the Court struck down a number of other provisions in the Arizona law—for example, its imposition of criminal penalties for undocumented immigrants who seek work in the state.

The fate of a highly sympathetic group of undocumented immigrants led to the **Dream Movement**. "Dreamers" are undocumented immigrants mostly from Latin America who arrived in the US as children. Dreamers have grown up in the United States, but they generally did not realize the costs of undocumented status until near the end of high school when they applied for a driver's license or admission to college. Because activism posed a risk of deportation to a country foreign to them, Dreamers remained mostly in the background until recently. As their numbers grew and more and more revealed their status in public coming-out ceremonies, they realized that their personal struggles to achieve the American dream could generate public support. The movement gained momentum as they began to use traditional activists' tactics, including marches, sit-ins, and civil disobedience. By late 2010, the Dreamers' struggle for citizenship had become a full-fledged civil rights movement. Senator Richard Durbin (D-IL) has called it "the civil rights issue of our time" (quoted in Gambino 2018).

The Dream Act to provide a pathway to citizenship for young undocumented immigrants was first introduced in 2001, but the bill stalled, as did several bills introduced over the next decade. The defeat of a bipartisan bill in December of 2010 led competing factions within the movement to coalesce and focus their frustrations on President Barack Obama, who had failed to deliver on his campaign promises to protect immigrants' civil rights. The protests and lobbying paid off during a tough reelection campaign in 2012 (Preston 2017). Months before the election, President Obama used executive power to create the Deferred Action for Childhood Arrivals (DACA) program that protected nearly 800,000 Dreamers from deportation. Those who met the requirements (e.g., entered the United States by sixteenth birthday, currently in school or graduated, or veteran of the armed forces, no felony convictions) could register and receive a work permit and Social Security for two-year renewable terms. But unilateral executive action provides only temporary legal status. A future president can rescind it, as President Donald Trump did in 2017.

Measures aimed at illegal immigration have proved popular with voters, and opposition to illegal immigration was a

Dream Movement A civil rights movement to protect "Dreamers," undocumented immigrants mostly from Latin America who arrived in the United States as children and have known no other country.

The Trump Administration put an end to the Deferred Action for Childhood Arrivals (DACA) immigration policy, prompting protests on behalf of Dreamers—undocumented immigrants who were brought into the United States illegally as children and who, until recently, could dream of a path to citizenship.
© Alan Diaz/AP Photo

major issue in Trump's presidential campaign in 2016. Although President Trump claimed to be fulfilling a campaign promise when he rescinded DACA, he has urged Congress to enact permanent legislation to protect Dreamers. The Dream Movement has continued to push for civil rights, but the issue continues to be debated in the courts and in Congress. Yet, as a significant and growing portion of the population, Latinos represent a potential powerful political force.

NATIVE AMERICANS

Native Americans, or American Indians, are the original inhabitants of the land that became the United States. As the European settlers moved westward, tribe after tribe was chased off its land, and the remaining tribes were moved onto reservations, mostly in the West. Some scholars and critics have equated the treatment of Native Americans by the U.S. government with **genocide**, which is the deliberate destruction of a population.

Historically, native tribes were considered independent nations, and the U.S. government's legal relationship with Native Americans operated through the tribal governments. The Constitution (Article I, Section 8) specifically grants Congress "the power to regulate commerce with foreign nations, among the several states, and with the Indian tribes."

These relationships were codified in a confusing legal tangle of hundreds of treaties made with different tribal authorities. This government-to-government relationship differentiates the struggle for civil rights for Native Americans from that of other racial and ethnic minorities. The rights of Native Americans derive from their legal status as members or descendants of a tribe that is a separate nation rather than from their race (Strickland 1992).

Government policies toward Native Americans have changed repeatedly. The nineteenth century saw organized campaigns to rob Native Americans of their traditional ways of life. These campaigns repeatedly demonstrated that Native Americans were being systematically denied rights and protections taken for granted by most U.S. citizens, including basic property rights, freedom of movement, and voting rights. Indeed, it was not until near the end of the nineteenth century that Native Americans were formally recognized as persons who were entitled to the rights and protections of the law.

This question was addressed in the landmark case of *Standing Bear v. Crook* (1879). Standing Bear was a chief of the Ponca, a tribe that the federal government relocated from its traditional homeland in Nebraska to Oklahoma. The relocation was devastating to the tribe, which suffered from disease and starvation. Among the fatalities was Standing Bear's son, Bear Shield. Honoring a promise to his son, Standing Bear took Bear Shield back to Nebraska to be buried in his ancestral home. On orders from Secretary of the Interior Carl Schurz, Standing Bear was arrested for leaving the reservation in Oklahoma. With the aid of a sympathetic attorney and some government officials, Standing Bear sued for a writ of habeas

genocide The killing of an entire race of people.

corpus, a legal action that requires whoever is holding a prisoner to bring him before a court and demonstrate that he is being detained legally. In May 1879, U.S. District Court Judge Elmer Dundy ruled in Standing Bear's favor, finding that he was being held illegally by federal authorities. More importantly, Dundy set the precedent that "an Indian is a person" and therefore entitled to the rights and protections of the law. This was a critical step in establishing the civil rights of Indians; until Dundy's decision, federal authorities had been able to treat Native Americans in whatever way was politically expedient, regardless of whether it violated their rights.

The decision stopped well short of fully protecting Native Americans, however. For example, Dundy's ruling never explicitly addressed the question of citizenship and left intact constraints on Native Americans that did not apply to U.S. citizens. For example, even though Standing Bear was set free, the federal government retained the power to arrest Native Americans who left reservations without permission. Native Americans were not formally incorporated as full U.S. citizens with universal voting rights until Congress passed the American Indian Citizenship Act in 1924—54 years after ratification of the Fifteenth Amendment (1870) that formally enfranchised African American men and four years after ratification of the Nineteenth Amendment (1920) extending the franchise to women.

Although this federal law clearly says that "Indians [are] citizens of the United States," several, mostly western, states perpetuated legal barriers to prevent Native Americans from exercising their right to vote, parallel to the Jim Crow laws used against African Americans in the South, long after 1924. But "Jim Crow, Indian style" (Svingen 1987; Wolfley 1991) was different in that these laws relied on Native Americans' unique legal status as members of a separate nation under the guardianship of the federal government. Some claimed that Native Americans who lived on reservations were not eligible to vote because they were not "residents" of the state. Others claimed that because state taxes did not apply on the reservation, Native Americans would not have to obey the laws these taxes helped produce. Others refused to give Indians citizenship rights unless they became "civilized" by severing their tribal ties (Berman and Salant 1998; McCool 1985; Wolfley 1991). The Voting Rights Act of 1965 and amendments in 1975 and 1982 helped Native Americans secure their voting rights. Nonetheless, government officials and non-Indian citizens in some states continued to discriminate against Native Americans and prevent them from voting (Svingen 1987).

Because of this continuing discrimination, like African Americans, Native Americans turned to the courts in their fight for civil rights, and they have scored a number of important victories regarding treaty violations, including rulings granting hunting and fishing rights and awarding substantial financial compensation for past wrongs. Congress has passed laws guaranteeing First Amendment rights and criminal due process protection to Native Americans living in federally supported housing and has also provided welfare, education, and food-stamp programs, community development grants, and federal funds for tribally controlled colleges.

Native Americans' struggle to create a coordinated, broad-scale civil rights movement has been hindered by separate tribal identities, the geographical separation of tribes, and the hundreds of separate treaties governing tribal relationships with the federal government. It was not until the 1960s that Native Americans began to take coordinated action. In 1970, the Native American Rights Fund (NARF) was founded to pursue the litigation tactics proven successful by the NAACP and MALDEF. The NARF's legal advocates, who are Native Americans with expertise in Indian law, have successfully used the courts to secure fishing and hunting rights, support tribal land claims, and advance Native American rights in a broad variety of areas.

Other Native American groups have engaged in more radical activities. The best-known incident to focus national attention on the plight of Native Americans was the 71-day occupation of Wounded Knee, South Dakota, in 1973 by 200 members of the American Indian Movement (AIM). The AIM wanted, among other things, a federal investigation into the condition of Native American tribal communities and a review of the 300 treaties between tribes and the federal government. Although this incident did not lead to any major reforms, it served to raise awareness of the grievances of some Native Americans, particularly those who wanted to follow a more traditional form of tribal governance.

Native American groups have had numerous important successes, particularly in reclaiming lands confiscated by the federal government in treaty violations or legitimized by one-sided agreements. However, Native Americans still face a number of challenges. Litigation to protect sacred sites and to gain the right to engage in religious practices involving, for example, ceremonial consumption of peyote has frequently been unsuccessful. A movement to fight negative stereotyping by challenging the practice of using epithets and tribal names as sports teams' names and mascots also has met with mixed success. Some schools have renamed their teams, but others have refused to do so. There have also been vigorous legal challenges over trademark disputes with the National Football League's Washington Redskins and Major League Baseball's Atlanta Braves and Cleveland Indians. Native Americans also continue to receive relatively little representation in the political process. In 2017, just two Native Americans served in Congress, Rep. Tom Cole and Rep. Markwayne Mullin, both Republicans from Oklahoma.

WOMEN

Women differ significantly from the other groups discussed in this chapter—they are not a minority in terms of numbers. Females make up slightly more than 50 percent of the U.S. population, more than 50 percent of college graduates since 1985, and in recent elections more than 50 percent of voters. But this apparent advantage in numbers has failed to protect women from many of the same types of discrimination suffered by minorities. In the past, women were prevented from voting and owning property and denied political, social, educational, and economic opportunities. Although numerous barriers have fallen, significant obstacles remain.

Historical Background

The struggle for women's rights in the United States has been tied to the cause of equality for African Americans. Women made significant contributions to the abolitionist movement that sought to end slavery, but ironically, they discovered that many men who were vehemently opposed to slavery did not extend such passion to the rights of women.

Women were refused the right to participate in the 1833 Philadelphia convention to form the American Anti-Slavery Society, a snub that was repeated at the 1840 World Anti-Slavery Convention in London. Among the women in the American delegation to the latter were Lucretia Mott and Elizabeth Cady Stanton. Outraged at being denied participation on the basis of their gender, Mott and Stanton organized a women's rights convention in 1848 at Seneca Falls, New York. The 300 delegates at this meeting approved a Declaration of Sentiments modeled after the Declaration of Independence: "We hold these truths to be self-evident, that all men and women are created equal; that they are endowed by their Creator with certain inalienable rights; that among these are life, liberty, and the pursuit of happiness" (quoted in McGlen and O'Connor 1983, 389). The convention marked the beginning of the women's rights movement in the United States.

Conventions similar to Seneca Falls met in different cities in the East and Midwest nearly every year until the Civil War. Although Susan B. Anthony and others argued that the struggle for the rights of African Americans and the rights of women were inseparable, the women's rights movement was temporarily suspended during the Civil War. When the movement recommenced shortly after the war, it became clear that although African Americans and women shared a number of mutual interests, they would fight separate battles. Some feminists wanted to add the word "sex" to the statement in the Fifteenth Amendment about "race, color, or previous condition of servitude." Frederick Douglass and other African American leaders opposed linking **suffrage** (the right to vote) for women and African Americans, fearing this would make it easier to defeat the amendment. Some in the women's movement agreed. They argued that if African American men were given voting rights first, it would make gaining the vote for women easier. Ultimately this argument prevailed, and the women's rights movement separated itself from the cause of racial equality.

The women's rights movement was hampered by division. Advocates

suffrage The right to vote.

Though still proportionally underrepresented in all levels of government, females frequently serve in high government office. Hillary Clinton twice won election to the U.S. Senate, made a strong run for the Democratic presidential nomination in 2008, and served as U.S. secretary of state in President Obama's first administration. She made history in 2016 by becoming the first woman to win a major party nomination for president. Here she makes her acceptance speech for the nomination to be president at the Democratic National Convention in Philadelphia on Thursday, July 28, 2016.

© Bill Clark/CQ Roll Call/AP Photo

agreed that female suffrage was necessary, but disagreed about broader goals. In 1869, Anthony and Stanton organized the National Woman Suffrage Association, which advocated the broad cause of women's rights and regarded the vote as the means to a general improvement of women's place in society. The same year, Lucy Stone helped form the American Woman Suffrage Association to concentrate on suffrage as an end rather than a means and to seek change on a state-by-state basis. The National Woman Suffrage Association was more militant, advocating an amendment to the federal Constitution. The American Woman Suffrage Association tried to appear "respectable" and avoided taking stands on controversial issues involving marriage and religion. Over time, Stone's more conservative organization gained supporters, and the women's rights movement increasingly focused on the suffrage issue. In 1890, the two groups merged into the National American Woman Suffrage Association, which evolved into a single-issue organization pursuing suffrage. In 1890, Wyoming gave women the right to vote, and by 1918, 15 states allowed women to vote (see Figure 5.3).

In time, a new generation of women suffragists threw off the conservative constraints of the National American Woman Suffrage Association. Particularly

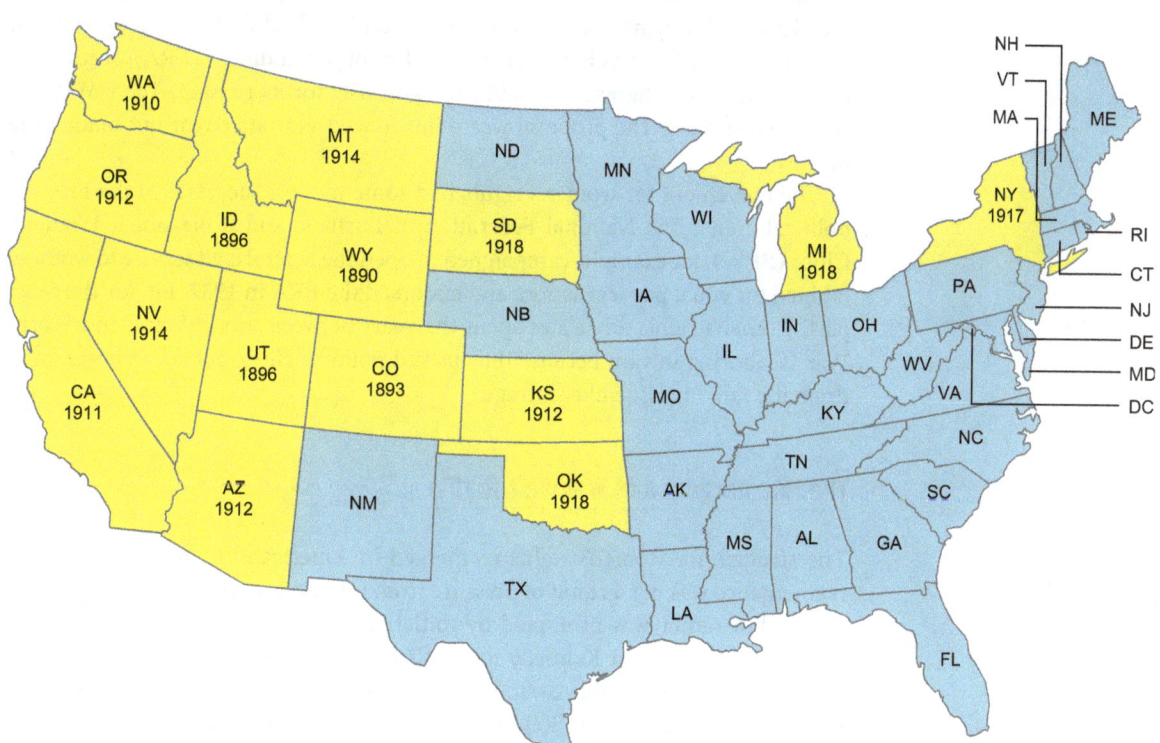

FIGURE 5.3 States (in Yellow) That Allowed Women to Vote Before the Nineteenth Amendment

Source: The States Where Women Voted Long Before the 19th Amendment. History.com. http://www.history.com/news/the-state-where-women-voted-longbefore-the-19th-amendment.

important was Alice Paul, a militant feminist who formed a small radical group called the Congressional Union in 1913. Its members were generally dissatisfied with the slow and uneven progress in the state-by-state strategy. They sought an amendment to the Constitution and used unorthodox means to achieve it, including parades, picketing of the White House, mass demonstrations, and hunger strikes. Some were willing to be jailed in order to get the issue onto the public agenda.

World War I helped promote the arguments of the Congressional Union. Women made critical contributions to the war effort, and women's rights advocates argued that they had earned the right to vote. Responding to this pressure, Congress proposed an amendment giving women the vote in 1919. It was ratified a year later and officially became the Nineteenth Amendment. More than 70 years after the Seneca Falls convention, the Constitution finally guaranteed that citizens' right to vote could not be "denied or abridged" on the basis of sex.

The cause of women's rights won some important victories in the years immediately following passage of the Nineteenth Amendment, including notably a federal law granting women citizenship independent of their husbands. But the broad-based coalition that had grown around the suffrage issue dissolved. Only a few groups continued to actively push for women's rights. Key among them was the National Women's Party (NWP), which had evolved from the Congressional Union. In 1923, the NWP drafted an equal rights amendment (ERA), secured its introduction to Congress, and lobbied vigorously for its passage. The NWP met with little success. The proposal was reintroduced year after year but made little headway.

The movement for women's rights had some modest successes in the broader political arena. The National Federation of Business and Professional Women's Clubs (BPW), for example, campaigned to open the federal civil service to women, lobbied for equal pay legislation, and endorsed the ERA in 1937. But for the most part, women's rights advocates spent the years between World War I and World War II laboring in vain because they lacked political allies, public support, and a dramatic rallying issue like suffrage.

The Reemergence of Women's Rights

The struggle for women's rights reemerged in American life in the 1960s. This reemergence was not a result of pressure from interest groups outside the political system but rather was prompted by initiatives from within the federal government. When President Kennedy took office in 1961, he appointed Esther Peterson, a longtime labor lobbyist, to head the Women's Bureau in the Department of Labor. Peterson convinced Kennedy to establish the President's Commission on the Status of Women, a body consisting of 13 women and 11 men and headed by Eleanor Roosevelt. In October 1962, the commission issued *American Women*, a factual report on the status of women in employment and education that also contained recommendations for government action. The report was moderate in tone and achieved some concrete results. President Kennedy revised an 1870 law that had banned women from high-level federal employment, and in 1963, Congress passed the Equal Pay Act, which mandated equal pay for equal work performed under equal conditions. Both actions had been recommended by the commission.

Although these represented significant advances, some feminists had serious doubts about the way the reforms were achieved and the slow pace toward ensuring broader equality for women. The Commission on the Status of Women was seen as an easy way for Kennedy to repay his political obligations to the women who had been active in his campaign. Some feminists even suggested that Kennedy's actions were meant to take any remaining political steam out of the drive for an ERA, which the commission opposed in its final report. The 1963 Equal Pay Act was interpreted by some critics as increasing the job security of men by preventing their replacement with lower-paid women.

In the mid-1960s, a series of events converged to stimulate the formation of a new type of interest group to press for women's rights. Betty Friedan's *The Feminine Mystique* (1963) led many women to begin questioning their general situation in society. While commuting to Washington to gather material for a second book, Friedan began talking with women who worked in Congress, the executive branch, and the Citizen's Advisory Council. Many of these women wanted the Equal Employment Opportunity Commission (EEOC) to take sex discrimination in private employment as seriously as it took racial discrimination. A number of them were frustrated with groups such as the National Federation of Business and Professional Women's Clubs and the League of Women Voters, which had refused to launch campaigns against sex discrimination for fear of being labeled "militant" or "feminist."

Within this atmosphere, a specific issue and a particular event combined to spur the creation of a new feminist interest group. The issue was the EEOC's failure to prevent newspapers from running separate job listings for men and women; the event was the third annual conference of State Commissions on the Status of Women. When the latter met in June 1966, many women wanted the group to pass a strongly worded resolution condemning sex discrimination in employment, but they were informed that the conference was not allowed to pass resolutions or take action. Outraged by the failure of the EEOC to act and disappointed in existing organizations, a group of women formed the National Organization for Women (NOW).

Incorporated in October 1966 with Betty Friedan as its first elected president, the NOW passed a strongly worded resolution calling for action to bring women into the mainstream of American society. Instead of shrinking from the feminist label, this group embraced it. The NOW pressured the EEOC for favorable rulings, opposed confirmation of Supreme Court nominee G. Harrold Carswell for his anti-feminist positions, filed suit against the nation's largest corporations for sex discrimination, lobbied for funds for child care centers, and picketed all-male bars.

Women's rights advocates scored several important victories in the 1960s and the 1970s:

- The 1964 Civil Rights Act barred discrimination in employment based on sex.
- The Equal Opportunity Act of 1972 extended the coverage of the anti-discrimination provisions of the 1964 Civil Rights Act to educational institutions and state and local governments.

- The Education Amendment Act, also passed in 1972, prohibited sex discrimination in all federally aided education programs.
- A 1974 law extended the jurisdiction of the U.S. Commission on Civil Rights, which was originally set up to study problems of minorities, to include sex discrimination.

The most dramatic congressional victory was the passage of a proposal that had been doggedly building support for a half-century—the Equal Rights Amendment. After the original introduction of the amendment in 1923, it took two decades before first the Republicans and then the Democrats endorsed the measure as part of their party platforms. In the 1950s, the amendment twice passed the Senate but failed to gain approval in the House. By the 1970s, pressure to pass the ERA had become overwhelming. The amendment was backed by virtually every women's rights group, President Richard Nixon, and a bipartisan group of members of Congress. In March 1972, the ERA finally received the required two-thirds vote in both the House and the Senate and was ready for ratification by three-fourths of the states.

Initially, the ERA had easy sailing at the state level, and 28 state legislatures ratified the amendment in the first year. But in 1973, the Stop ERA campaign began a national drive against the measure. Led by Phyllis Schlafly, an articulate spokeswoman for conservative causes, the campaign drew support from a number of right-leaning organizations, including the John Birch Society, the Christian Crusade, and Young Americans for Freedom. Opponents claimed that the ERA would make women eligible for the draft, deny wives the support of their husbands, and remove children from the custody of their mothers. State legislatures soon felt serious pressure to oppose the ERA, and the ratification movement lost momentum. The deadline for ratification expired in 1979, but women's groups persuaded Congress to extend it until 1982. The extra time did not help, and the ERA movement was halted just three states short of the 38 needed for ratification.

Although the ERA failed, women's rights advanced significantly in the 1980s and 1990s. Among changes made in 1972 to the 1964 Civil Rights Act were the denial of federal funds to any public or private program that discriminated on the basis of sex and the inclusion of Title IX, which required that women's athletics be given equal standing with men's athletics in schools. In 1984, Representative Geraldine A. Ferraro became the first woman to run for the vice presidency on a major-party ticket. The courts became more open to claims of sex discrimination. In 1994, Congress passed the Violence against Women Act. In 1996, the Virginia Military Institute was required to admit women or lose state funding, ending more than 150 years as an all-male, state-supported college. In 2002, Representative Nancy Pelosi (D-CA) became minority party whip and then, later that same year, minority party leader. In 2005, she became the first female Speaker of the House. These are the highest offices ever held by a woman in the U.S. Congress. These examples are suggestive of a political system responsive to concerns of sex-based discrimination.

During the same period, women also began to play a greater role in the political, social, and economic life of the nation. Only two senators and 11 members of the House of Representatives in the 89th Congress (1965–1966) were women. The 115th Congress (2017–2018) included 111 women, 22 in the Senate and 89 in the House (including four nonvoting delegates). Women also increasingly occupy high-ranking positions in the judicial and executive branch of government. Examples include Madeleine Albright, Condoleezza Rice, and Hillary Rodham Clinton, all of whom served as secretary of state, and Supreme Court Justices Sandra Day O'Connor, Ruth Bader Ginsberg, Sonia Sotomayor, and Elena Kagan. Women continue to fall far short of political equality relative to the voting-age population, but the days when a female in a high-ranking public office was a novelty have passed.

Women have also made advances in the economic arena. Women make up roughly half of the U.S. labor force, and nearly 70 percent of women work full-time. Women have made significant inroads into traditionally male-dominated career fields. In 2016, for example, women reached parity with men in the study of medicine (49.8 percent women) and law (50.3 percent women) (Association of American Medical Colleges 2016; Olson 2016).

Nevertheless, full equality between the sexes remains an elusive goal. Men still dominate national political institutions; women are more likely to live below the poverty line than men; and some career fields remain largely segregated by sex. A persistent pay gap between males and females remains, with women earning about 80 percent of what men earn, though the overall trend is positive (see Figure 5.4). Much of this gap can be explained by work patterns; women, for example, tend to work fewer hours per year and have less full-time work experience than men. These factors cannot account for the entire gap, however, and some experts suggest that discrimination still plays a role in gender-based wage differences (General Accounting Office 2003). The potential for gender-based wage discrimination was acknowledged by Congress in 2009 when it passed the Lilly Ledbetter Fair Pay Act. Lilly Ledbetter was a longtime employee of the Goodyear Tire and Rubber Company who sued her employer for wage discrimination. After 20 years on the job, Ledbetter was receiving significantly less pay than male colleagues with similar experience. Although no one disagreed that Ledbetter was getting less money than comparable males, there was a big disagreement over whether the disparity reflected gender discrimination or job performance. (Ledbetter's pay, like that of her male colleagues, was determined in large part by performance reviews.) What constituted wage discrimination was never fully defined in this case because in *Ledbetter v. Goodyear Tire and Rubber Co.* (2007), the Supreme Court sidestepped the core issue and ruled against Ledbetter on technical grounds. Under the provisions of civil rights laws at the time, there was a 180-day statute of limitations to file a claim for pay discrimination. In other words, if an employer engaged in wage discrimination, the injured party had six months to sue from the first paycheck issued. Ledbetter's claim fell outside of that six-month window, and the Court said that was enough to nullify her suit. Recognizing that such technicalities ignored very real issues of discrimination that should be addressed, Congress passed the Lilly Ledbetter Fair Pay Act to make it easier for workers to sue employers for wage discrimination. Essentially, the new law says an individual has six months to sue after every unfair paycheck, not just the first one. This nullified the Supreme Court ruling and cleared the way for women to sue whenever they discover their employers engaging in wage discrimination.

Women have made greater progress toward equity with men in getting a college education. There have been more females than males enrolling in college since the 1970s, women have been earning a majority of college degrees since the 1980s, and the proportion of the female population with a college education has climbed dramatically in the past four decades. Within the past few years the proportion of women holding a college degree exceeded the proportion of men holding a college degree for the first time (see Figure 5.4). And women also earn a majority of Master's and PhD degrees.

To some extent, the broad-based movement promoting women's rights has been a victim of its own success. As one report put it, after decades of tearing down barriers in employment, education, sports, and other areas of social life, many women are increasingly skeptical of the activism that did so much to achieve these breakthroughs. Indeed, many women now reject the label "feminist" because "they fear being stereotyped as strident, humorless and anti-male, or worry that feminists downgrade the importance of motherhood" (C. Clark 1997, 169).

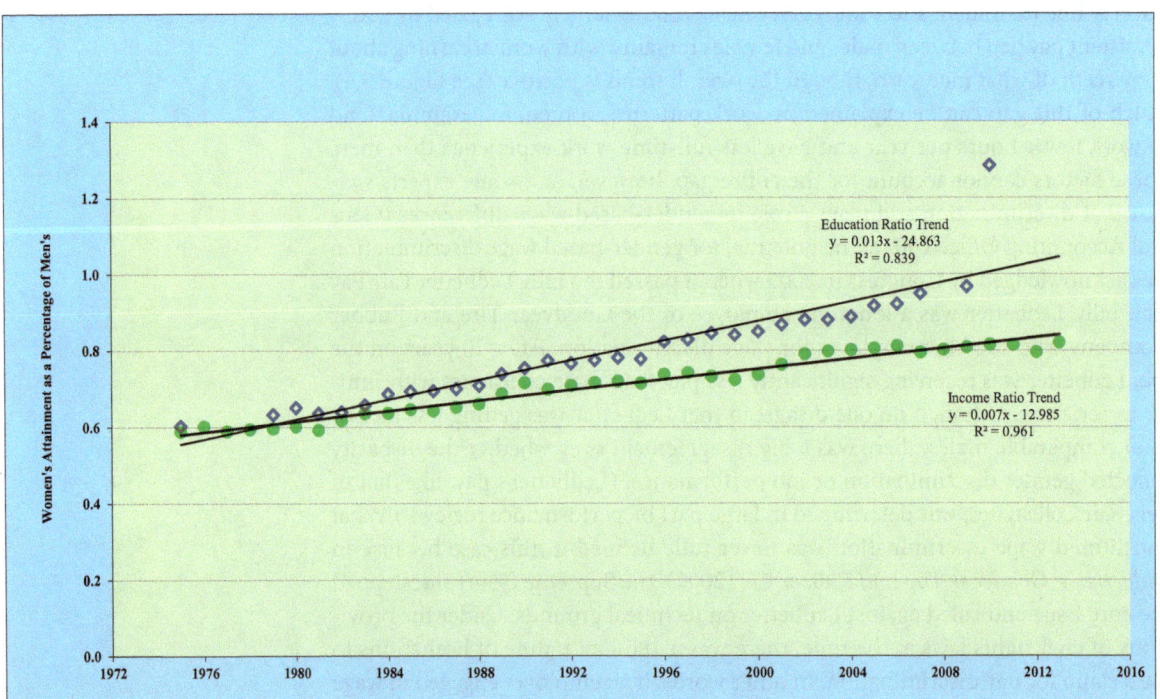

FIGURE 5.4 Women's Earnings and College Education Relative to Men

Sources: Data from U.S. Census Bureau, Current Population Survey, Annual Social and Economic Supplements Table P-38: Full-Time, Year-Round All Workers by Median Earnings and Sex: 1960 to 2006. (Workers 15 years old and over with earnings beginning with March 1980, and workers 14 years old and over with earnings as of March of the following year for previous years. Before 1989 earnings are for civilian workers only.) http://www.census.gov/hhes/www/income/histinc/incpertoc.html; and Bureau of Labor Statistics, "Median Usual Weekly Earnings of Full-Time Wage and Salary Workers by Age, Race, Hispanic or Latino Ethnicity, and Sex," http://www.bls.gov/news.release/archives/wkyeng_01242012.pdf, http://www.bls.gov/news.release/wkyeng.t01.htm, http://www.bls.gov/news.release/wkyeng.t03.htm and http://nces.ed.gov/programs/digest/d10/tables/dt10_008.asp.

Yet, an innovative use of social media in 2017 helped overcome women's reticence to speak out about remaining barriers and energized the struggle for equal rights. Tarana Burke, a community organizer, founded the "Me Too movement" in 2006 to "help survivors of sexual violence … know they're not alone in their journey." The goal was "to de-stigmatize survivors" by "bringing vital conversations about sexual violence into the mainstream," and highlight "the breadth and impact sexual violence has on thousands of women" (https://metoomvmt.org/). But a tweet in response to a *New York Times* report in October 2017 that more than a dozen women accused movie producer Harvey Weinstein of sexual harassment, assault, and rape energized the movement. Actor Alyssa Milano tweeted to her followers, "If you've been sexually harassed or assaulted write 'me too' as a reply to this tweet." Twitter confirmed that the hashtag had been tweeted nearly half a million times within 24 hours (Gilbert 2017). Facebook indicated that there were more than 12 million posts, comments, and reactions in less than 24 hours. Thus, **#MeToo Movement** helped achieve a primary goal of the original movement—to de-stigmatize survivors, and highlight the prevalence of sexual harassment and assault in society. Increased awareness of the prevalence of sexual violence has led to numerous resignations of powerful men in fields outside the entertainment industry, including state legislators and members of Congress. Rep. Jackie Speier (D-CA) introduced the Member and Employee Training and Oversight on Congress Act (ME TOO Congress) Act 2017 to provide congressional staff greater protection and recourse for reporting sexual harassment from members of Congress.

PEOPLE WITH DISABILITIES

People with mental or physical disabilities have often been the target of particularly virulent forms of discrimination. Their disabilities have been viewed as divine retribution for the sins of families or individuals or as a sign of spiritual uncleanliness. Prior to the twentieth century, they were marked for persecution, and many were prevented from fully participating in social, political, and economic life (Humphries and Wright 1992). In the United States, basic care for people with disabilities was seen largely as the responsibility of family and private initiative, and the government made little effort to overcome the barriers that physical or mental disabilities presented to citizens seeking to exercise their rights.

Wounded war veterans were the first group of disabled citizens targeted for assistance from the federal government. The Smith-Sears Veterans' Rehabilitation Act was passed in 1918 to help veterans disabled in World War I. In 1920, it was followed by the Smith-Fess Act, which was the first law to provide broad-based government assistance to disabled citizens. The federal government provided grants to state vocational rehabilitation programs, and states were required to match the funds on a dollar-for-dollar basis. These programs, which were aimed at boosting the economic self-sufficiency of military veterans disabled as a result of their service, had a limited effect. Nonetheless, assistance programs for people

#MeToo Movement A movement using social media to de-stigmatize survivors of sexual violence, and highlight the prevalence of sexual harassment and assault in society.

with disabilities slowly began to expand. All states had vocational rehabilitation operations by the end of the 1930s, and the Social Security Act of 1935 made the federal government's role in supporting these programs permanent. The reach of government policy began to expand to include medical assistance to those with mental disabilities and broader support for the families of disabled citizens. The range of services and people covered by such programs was expanded even further by the Barden-LaFollette Act of 1943.

World War II created more pressure for the federal government to increase its involvement in assisting citizens with disabilities. In 1947, President Harry Truman helped establish the President's Commission on the Handicapped, which became a vocal advocate for disabled people. In 1954, the Vocational Rehabilitation Act substantially expanded the government's involvement in assisting people with disabilities, providing support for a wide range of physical and mental disorders. Such initiatives were significant, but they were not part of a cohesive civil rights agenda. Rather, they were viewed as extensions of moral obligations.

This view began to change in the late 1950s, when the government began to seriously examine the problems of access for the first time. Access is the ability to get into and make use of public facilities, and it became a focal point for the development of a true civil rights campaign for people with disabilities. Advocacy groups for the disabled point out that they were being segregated from the broader society and denied equal opportunity. A report by the National Commission on Architectural Barriers issued in 1968 estimated that more than 20 million Americans were "built out of normal living by unnecessary barriers: a stairway, a too-narrow door, a too-high telephone" (Percy 1989, 50). Pressure began to build for the federal government to take action to ensure access to public facilities to the greatest extent possible. This pressure resulted in the Architectural Barriers Act of 1968, a law that mandated designing public buildings to allow access for those with disabilities. This law shifted public policy from a service orientation to a focus on rights.

The Americans with Disabilities Act (ADA) extended to people with disabilities formal recognition of their civil rights and protections. It also highlighted issues of access in the private sector, not just in the public sector. Here a volunteer who works for the city of Jacksonville, Florida, writes a citation for an SUV parked in a space reserved for disabled drivers.

© Bob Self/The Florida Times-Union/AP Photo

The new focus on the civil rights of people with disabilities began to bear fruit in the 1970s. First were two important legal victories. *Pennsylvania Association for Retarded Children (PARC) v. Pennsylvania* (1971) contended that the state was arbitrarily denying students with mental disabilities a right to an education because state law assumed that children with mental disabilities were incapable of being educated, and it did not provide due process in excluding mentally disabled students from the public school system. As part of an agreement to settle the suit in 1972, the state acknowledged that it had an obligation to provide a free and appropriate education to students with mental disabilities. In *Mills v. Board of Education of the District of Columbia* (1972), parents of mentally disabled students sued the education authorities in the nation's capital using a similar argument. The court ruled in the plaintiffs' favor and ordered school authorities to provide "a free and suitable publicly supported education regardless of the child's mental, physical, or emotional disability or impairment." Although neither case reached the Supreme Court, both were important civil rights victories for people with disabilities because they established a legal precedent for civil rights action (Percy 1989, 56–57).

The legal victories were followed by important legislation. The 1973 Rehabilitation Act provided some of the same protections to people with disabilities that had earlier been granted to minorities and women, including a prohibition on discrimination on the basis of disability by any program receiving federal funds. The legislation was complex and controversial. It was passed during the tenure of President Richard Nixon but was not implemented by either Nixon or his successor, Gerald Ford. When President Jimmy Carter also sought to delay implementation, his foot-dragging prompted a public outcry. The regulations putting the law into practice were finally signed by Secretary of Health, Education, and Welfare Joseph Califano Jr. in April 1977. Califano said that the law represented "the first federal civil rights law protecting the rights of handicapped persons and reflects a national commitment to end discrimination on the basis of handicap" (Worsnop 1996).

In 1975, Congress approved the Education for All Handicapped Children Act, which required all states to provide a "free appropriate public education" to children with disabilities, thus writing into law the decisions in *PARC* and *Mills*. Like the Rehabilitation Act, this legislation was controversial because of its cost and complexity and its increased federal preemption of what traditionally had been an area under state and local government control. President Ford threatened to veto the bill, but it passed Congress with enough votes to override a veto. The Education for All Handicapped Children Act evolved into the Individuals with Disabilities Education Act in 1992. In essence, this law guaranteed people with disabilities the right to a public education and obligated schools to protect and support that right regardless of the costs they incur in doing so (Biskupic 1999).

The costs associated with the Rehabilitation Act and the Education for All Handicapped Children Act were particularly worrisome to institutions such as schools. They had to invest in physical improvements such as installation of elevators and wheelchair ramps to make their facilities accessible, and they had to make a greater commitment to special education programs. Although federal funds were available to help cover some of these costs, it quickly became apparent that part of the financial burden was being passed on to local governments.

The federal government expanded the civil rights protection of disabled individuals in 1988 with the Fair Housing Amendments Act, which was aimed at preventing discrimination in housing. Then, in 1990, Congress passed the **Americans with Disabilities Act (ADA)**, which specifically extended to disabled citizens the civil rights and protections that were the cornerstone of the 1964 Civil Rights Act. Although a landmark victory, the law "was notable more for its sweep than its novelty" (Worsnop 1996, 1118). It largely codified existing laws and regulations and extended them to the private sector.

Like the laws it superseded, the ADA was controversial. It required private companies to assume "reasonable" expenditures to meet the legislation's requirements.

Americans with Disabilities Act (ADA) Specifically extended to citizens with disabilities, the civil rights and protections that were the cornerstone of the 1964 Civil Rights Act. It largely codified existing laws and regulations and extended them to the private sector.

Businesses complained that the federal government was now able to dictate the width of hallways in a private office building, where a store could display its merchandise, and much more. Although the federal government had the power to make such mandates, it assumed little or none of the cost of actually following through on them (Ferguson 1995).

In enforcing the ADA, the government has tended to concentrate on guaranteeing access to public and civic life and has preferred to negotiate compliance with public and private organizations that have been the target of complaints. For example, the city of Waukesha, Wisconsin, responded to pressure from the federal government to make its city hall accessible. The complaint was initiated by a city alderman who used a wheelchair and had difficulty getting into city facilities, including the room where the council held closed meetings (U.S. Department of Justice 2000). The Supreme Court, however, has signaled a willingness to set limits on the rights of people with disabilities. For example, in *Board of Trustees v. Garrett* (2001), the court ruled that employees of state agencies cannot pursue discrimination claims by using the ADA to sue their employers in federal court. In this case, the Supreme Court ruled against the civil rights of people with disabilities and upheld the sovereign immunity of states, which restricts the rights of individuals to sue states in federal court.

LGBTQ CITIZENS

Ethnicity, gender, and disability are far from the only classifications used to arbitrarily deny American citizens full participation in political life. Sexual orientation has also served as a basis for systematic discrimination. Lesbian, gay, bisexual, transgender, and questioning/queer (LGBTQ) citizens have fought to get state and local governments to enact policies preventing systematic discrimination against LGBTQ individuals and to get the federal government to prohibit denying them employment opportunities for the same reason.

The fight over LGBTQ rights has been partisan and extremely controversial. On one side, many Americans have historically perceived homosexuality as a threat to mainstream family values and strongly opposed legalizing same-sex acts, let alone same-sex unions (Haider-Markel and Meier 1996). The adoption of policies prohibiting discrimination on the basis of sexual orientation provoked a political backlash from such constituencies, succeeding in some states and localities, failing in others. In *Lawrence v. Texas* (2003) the Supreme Court ruled unconstitutional state laws criminalizing homosexual sex conducted between consenting adults in the privacy of their own bedrooms. This represented a significant step forward for the gay rights movement because, in essence, it said that gay citizens have the same right to privacy as everyone else. Yet in upholding this right, the Court stopped considerably short of granting LGBTQ individuals full political equality. Nowhere was this more apparent—or more controversial—than in the long-running conflict over same-sex marriage.

In 1996 President Bill Clinton signed into law the Defense of Marriage Act (DOMA). Key elements of this law stipulated that states would not be obligated to recognize same-sex marriages, and prevented same-sex marriages from being recognized by federal law. Legally, however, marriage remained a civil contract entered into under state rather than federal law, so individual states had leeway to approve same-sex unions even if they were not recognized by federal laws or by other states. The upshot of this strange situation was a patchwork of laws and court rulings at the state level that accumulated over the following two decades. Some states approved same-sex marriage by passing laws or ballot initiatives, or state supreme courts issued rulings affirming that state constitutions granted same-sex couples the same right to marry as heterosexuals. Other states passed laws defining marriage as a union between a man and a woman, explicitly outlawing same-sex marriage. By 2014, roughly 40 percent of states had legalized same-sex marriage in some form, with the rest outlawing same-sex marriage through statute or constitutional amendments. Whether a same-sex couple could get married or have a marriage legally recognized thus depended on geography.

DOMA's critics had questioned its constitutionality from the beginning, arguing that it violated the due process and equal protection clauses of the Fourteenth Amendment. Though the conflict over same-sex marriage was fought mainly at the state level for two decades following the passage of DOMA, it was clear that ultimately the issue would have to be resolved by the United States Supreme Court. The first significant blow to DOMA came in *United States v. Windsor* (2013), where the Supreme Court ruled that it was unconstitutional for DOMA to define marriage for purposes of federal law as a heterosexual union. This was broadly seen as a huge victory for proponents of legalizing same-sex marriage, but it did not make same-sex marriage legal everywhere; it merely meant that the federal government could not discriminate against LGBTQ married couples.

The Supreme Court legalized same-sex marriage in 2015 in a landmark case, ***Obergefell v. Hodges***. The case centered on a same-sex couple, James Obergefell and John Arthur, who sued because the state they lived in, Ohio, would not recognize their marriage license. The case presented two basic questions to the Court: Does the Fourteenth Amendment require a state to issue marriage licenses to same-sex couples? Do all states have to recognize same-sex marriages? In a 5–4 decision, the court ruled the answer to both questions was yes, effectively sweeping away the patchwork of state laws and legalizing same-sex marriage nationwide.

CHAPTER FIVE
Top 10 Takeaway Points

Obergefell v. Hodges A 2015 Supreme Court ruling that marriage is a fundamental right protected by the Constitution that must be extended to same-sex couples.

1. Civil rights are the obligations placed on government to protect the freedom of people. Civil rights are conceptually different from civil liberties. Civil liberties ensure that government does not use its coercive power to arbitrarily

limit individuals' freedom to make the choices they please. Civil rights ensure that government will use its coercive power to prevent those freedoms from being arbitrarily denied to certain categories of citizens.

2. Over the course of American history, numerous minorities have been systematically excluded from the political and social mainstream. Unequal treatment of citizens has been based, among other things, on race, ethnicity, gender, physical disabilities, and sexual orientation.

3. Minorities have engaged in long struggles to get the government to ensure that they enjoy rights equal to those enjoyed by the majority. Each group's struggle has elements unique to that group, though all seek to force the government to uphold the democratic principle of political equality.

4. Affirmative action involves governmental actions designed to help minorities overcome the effects of past discrimination and compete on an equal basis with the majority. Affirmative action is controversial. Opponents argue that it replaces one form of discrimination with another.

5. The most notorious example of government tolerance of inequality is the historical treatment of African Americans. The Constitution set the value of slaves as three-fifths of a person. It took the better part of two centuries to get the federal government to guarantee African Americans civil rights, and this remains a contentious political issue today.

6. Latinos are the largest ethnic minority in the United States. Latinos' struggle for equality has focused on issues related to bilingual education, the protection of voting rights, and increased representation in the political process.

7. Native Americans are members of tribes that are considered independent nations. The U.S. government's legal relationship with individuals has operated through the tribal governments. This government-to-government relationship differentiates Native Americans' struggle for civil rights from the struggles of other racial and ethnic minorities. Native Americans did not gain full citizenship rights until 1924, but even after they were granted citizenship, some states erected legal barriers to prevent them from participating in the political process.

8. Women differ from other groups that had to struggle to overcome discrimination in that they are not a minority in population numbers. After gaining the right to vote, women still had to engage in a protracted political struggle for equality in employment, education, and the political process.

9. In 1990, Congress passed the Americans with Disabilities Act (ADA), which extended to citizens with disabilities the civil rights and protections that were the cornerstone of the 1964 Civil Rights Act, which prohibited discrimination in employment and education based on race, ethnicity, sex, or religion.

10. Lesbian, gay, bisexual, transgender, and questioning/queer (LGBTQ) citizens have fought to get state and local governments to enact policies preventing systematic discrimination against them and to get the federal government to prohibit denying them employment opportunities for the same reason. Recent controversy has focused on marriage of same-sex couples, which was finally legalized nationwide with a 2015 Supreme Court decision.

CHAPTER FIVE
Key Terms and Cases

affirmative action, 156
Americans with Disabilities Act, 177
#BlackLivesMatter movement, 160
Brown v. Board of Education, 153
civil disobedience, 154
civil rights, 149
Civil Rights Act of 1964, 155
de facto discrimination, 160
de jure discrimination, 157
Dream Movement, 164
genocide, 165
grandfather clause, 152
Jim Crow laws, 156
literacy tests, 152
#MeToo Movement, 175
Obergefell v. Hodges, 179
passive resistance, 155
Plessy v. Ferguson, 153
poll taxes, 152
separate but equal, 153
suffrage, 168
Voting Rights Act of 1965, 156

PART II
Connecting Citizens to Government

6 INTEREST GROUPS

KEY QUESTIONS

Why do people form and join interest groups?

What do interest groups do?

Why is it so hard to regulate interest groups?

What influence and power do interest groups have?

© Matt York/AP Photo

IN 2016, DONALD TRUMP campaigned for the presidency on promises to "drain the swamp" and eliminate the influence of special interests on the federal government. He broke that promise more or less immediately. Even before taking office, Trump staffed his transition team with exactly the sort of corporate influence merchants he had railed against on the campaign trail (Lipton 2016). And after taking power the Trump administration not only staffed the White House and lots of other federal agencies with dozens of lobbyists, it initially refused to provide the Office of Government Ethics with their names and copies of the waivers that special interest group advocates must secure to be employed by the federal government (Lipton 2017).

While the numbers and the secrecy were unusual, Trump is hardly the first president to find that it is easier to rail against special interests on the campaign trail than it is to govern without the policy expertise and savvy of lobbyists. Citizens are likely to be suspicious of any claims that lobbyists might provide useful contributions to public service. Most Americans think special interests have too much influence, influence that is somehow undermining popular sovereignty because government responds to these special interests rather than to ordinary citizens. Actually, that's not the case at all. In fact, quite the opposite is true. Granted, the Trump administration's embrace of lobbyists raised more than a few eyebrows, but if President Trump or any other federal official actually managed to deliver on the promise of banishing the influence of special interests, that would undermine popular sovereignty.

How do we figure that? Well, as former *Newsweek* editor Robert J. Samuelson (2008) observes, we as a democracy constitute a collection of special interests. According to Samuelson, "the only way to eliminate lobbying and special interests is to eliminate government." At least, we'd have to get rid of a democratic form of government. Give citizens free speech, freedom of association, the right to petition government to redress grievances—in a nutshell, give them the First Amendment—and the inevitable result is special interests and lobbying. In short, pretty much the only way to get rid of special interest influence is to get rid of political freedom—in other words, to deliberately violate a core principle of democracy.

This might seem like something of a strange argument given the popular image of lobbying and special interests. Americans generally see special interests as a corrosive, corrupting influence on democracy, conjuring images of fat-cat elites buying votes and favors with campaign contributions. Some of that does happen, and when it does, it tends to get a lot of media attention and reinforce the collective notion of lobbying as seedy and unbecoming. Those running for public office tend to be some of the loudest denouncing this negative influence, rhetorically whipping special interests even as they quietly acknowledge that special interests are an unavoidable part of the democratic system.

What seems to bother people the most about the influence of special interests is the idea that the rich and the powerful are doing their level best to get the government to do what they want it to do. And truth be told, they are. Bankers, lawyers, CEOs, unions—you name a powerful special interest group, and chances are they are lobbying for government to see things their way. Here's the deal, though: They're not the only ones lobbying government. So are hospitals, advocates for the poor, child welfare organizations, and believe it or not, universities, colleges, and people trying to keep your tuition costs down. Shouldn't abused kids, the sick, and college students get to petition government for redress of their grievances?

The answer, of course, is yes, they should. But this is a right shared equally with Wall Street bankers, the National Rifle Association (NRA), labor unions, business groups, farmers, and so on. The pluralist nature of American politics means every group and every interest has an equal right to pester, cajole, plead, and bargain with the government—just as they all have an equal right to make their views known to the public. That's what political freedom is all about.

We must remember that the First Amendment guarantees the "right of the people peaceably to assemble, and to petition the Government for a redress of grievances." This is a forthright expression of the core democratic principle of political freedom. Political freedom means, in part, having the right to join with others to pursue shared interests. Americans enthusiastically embrace this right. Alexis de Tocqueville, a French aristocrat and political thinker, noted in the early nineteenth century that Americans exercise the right to form associations more often than their counterparts in other nations. Even today, Americans are still joiners.

We must also keep in mind, though, that these freedoms bring no guarantees that everyone's views will be heard or accounted for in the making of public policy. There is certainly no guarantee that the "right" or "just" or "best" view will prevail. There is not even a guarantee that the most popular or best-known view will come out on top.

Why would a government that's supposed to govern with the consent of the governed fail to adopt the most popular view? The answer is that, in general, the American political system is not designed to detect the will of the people and translate it into government action. The government responds less to the will of the people than to the people who are involved in the process; motivated and well-organized groups can be more effectively involved than individuals or less well-organized interests. As political scientist E. E. Schattschneider observed, "What [300] million people can do spontaneously, on their own initiative, is not much more than a locomotive can do without rails" (1960, 139).

The American political system is characterized by a variety of interest groups battling for government action and public support and employing a number of different techniques to achieve their goals. Groups' abilities to achieve their objectives depend not only on having political resources but also on how well they use the resources. Hiring a lobbyist to advocate on your behalf is one effective way to influence government. Yet there are other options, which include everything from making campaign donations to running public education campaigns. The point is that having a grievance, an opinion, a point of view, or a demand is not enough if you want the government to respond to your concerns. You must get involved in the political process, and doing that means dealing with the fact that a lot of people who hold opinions and points of view that do not necessarily match yours are also involved. It may not matter that justice, logic, common sense, and the facts are on your side. If a group cannot effectively engage in the political system, government is unlikely to respond. Providing understanding of how groups go about achieving their goals and how and why the government responds to these efforts is the purpose of this chapter. The chapter thus examines what interest groups are, who joins them and why, their sources of power and influence, and their place in American politics.

THE CONCEPT OF INTEREST GROUPS

Political scientists have long recognized that the formation and mobilization of interest groups is the natural result of like-minded individuals coming together to pursue a common goal (Truman 1951). Yet there is debate over exactly what an interest group is and how to define it (see Baumgartner and Leech 1998, 22–33). For our purposes, an **interest group** is an organization of people who share a common concern or value and who engage in collective action to make demands on others in society with respect to those interests.

interest group A group organized around a set of views or preferences and who engage in collective action to influence others in order to promote or protect those preferences.

Not every group fits this definition. People who have red hair or who are college students share certain characteristics but have different interests. They make up what sociologists call *categorical groups*. The first basic requirement of an interest group is a shared interest, not simply a common characteristic.

This definition also excludes groups that are not political in nature. Some groups do not make demands on society or seek to influence collective decisions about who gets what. For example, people who share a common interest in classical music may meet to listen to recordings, attend concerts, or sponsor a touring orchestra. But such a group is not an interest group. If that same group demands that a rock music radio station devote an hour a day to Mozart and Beethoven, then the group meets the second requirement to be defined as an interest group because its members work together to make demands on others in society.

The preceding example illustrates that groups can engage in political action without involving government. For example, though labor unions exert extensive influence in and on government, they also make demands on employers and the general public through strikes and picketing. Other groups also seek to satisfy their demands by dealing directly with private individuals and organizations. Students, for example, have sought to bring about major changes in universities through negotiation and confrontation with school officials.

Political action, nonetheless, frequently does involve government. Getting the government involved offers significant advantages because government has coercive power. If, for example, the classical music lovers are unsuccessful in convincing the owners of radio stations to play classical music, they might ask the Federal Communications Commission (FCC), the federal agency that grants licenses to radio stations, to require stations to devote a certain percentage of airtime to serve the public interest in order to keep their broadcast licenses. The harassed radio station owner may decide that it is easier to cooperate with the music lovers than to defend the station's programming decisions before the FCC. Furthermore, the classical music interest group might persuade the city council to subsidize a local orchestra with public funds so that its performances can be broadcast. This politically savvy set of Mozart and Beethoven lovers would thus have taken advantage of the government's ability to require radio stations to conform to certain rules and would have gained tax money taken from people who do not necessarily like classical music.

Interest Group Goals

Political interest groups pursue two general objectives:

1. They seek new positive benefits to *promote* the group's interest.
2. They defend current benefits to *protect* the group's interest.

Engaging in political action to persuade a radio station to play classical music and trying to convince a city council to subsidize a local orchestra are examples of seeking new benefits. Groups that are satisfied with the present distribution of resources take defensive actions in the political arena to preserve the status quo. Interest groups thus attempt to achieve their objectives by trying to get their group and its goals to be the answer to the question of who gets what.

Interest Group Membership

Political activity in the United States has always been shaped by organized group activity. James Madison was fully cognizant of the role interest groups played in American politics; the groups he called "factions" in *Federalist* Number 10 fit our definition of political interest groups quite well. As Figure 6.1 illustrates, most Americans belong to some form of voluntary organization—about 79 percent in one study. Although many organizations are not political interest groups as we define them in this chapter, on average, 61 percent of the members of these organizations reported that their organization took stands on political issues (Verba, Schlozman, and Brady 1995, 62–65).

At the very least, the vast majority of Americans are not far removed from an interest group. For example, many are members of, or have parents or grandparents in, the American Association of Retired Persons (AARP), one of the largest

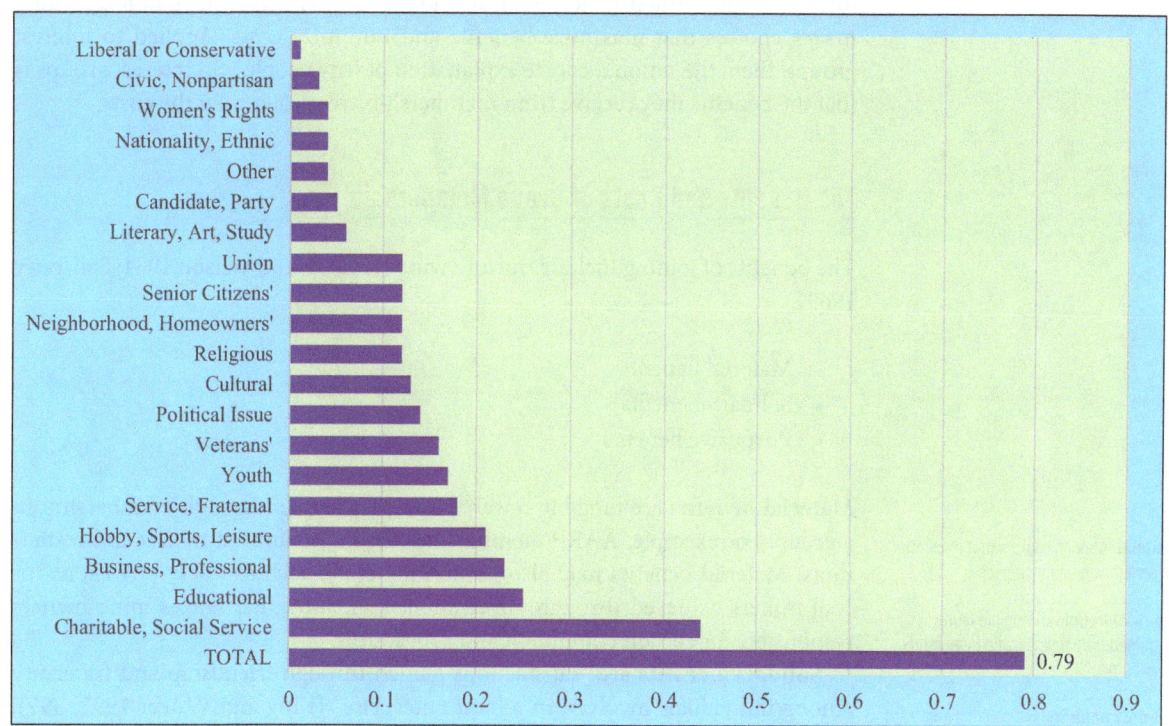

FIGURE 6.1 **Percentage of Americans Affiliated with Voluntary Organizations**

Source: Data from Verba, Schlozman, and Brady (1995, 62–65); figure format adapted from Lowery and Brasher (2004, 33).

and most powerful interest groups in the nation. The AARP has around 38 million members—roughly one out of every two Americans over the age of 50—with revenues of more than a billion dollars. Among the many issues it addresses are laws to protect pensions, laws to fight age discrimination, and laws to provide healthcare coverage. Other Americans are members or are related to members of labor or teachers' unions, the American Bar Association, the American Medical Association, or other business or professional groups that lobby some level of government on behalf of their members. Students may be involved in campus or school organizations that make demands on the university for facilities, funding, or recognition. It is likely that some students who read this text are members of the NRA or the Brady Campaign to Prevent Gun Violence, or another group that shares a common interest and makes demands on others with respect to that interest.

WHY PEOPLE JOIN INTEREST GROUPS

For the most part, political scientists explain why people join interest groups using rational choice models of behavior. This explanation assumes that individuals join and participate in interest groups because it is **rational** to do so (Olson 1965). Rationality is defined in terms of an individual's self-interest: A rational being makes choices that maximize benefits and minimize costs. Applied to interest groups, then, the rational choice explanation of why people join interest groups is that the benefits they receive from membership are greater than the costs.

The Benefits and Costs of Group Membership

The benefits of joining include the following (P. Clark and Wilson 1961; Salisbury 1969):

- Material benefits
- Solidary benefits
- Purposive benefits

Material benefits are tangible rewards that people gain through membership in a group. For example, AARP membership offers discounts at motels and restaurants. Material benefits may also be nonmonetary, such as safety provisions for coal miners achieved through government regulation that makes mine owners responsible for certain equipment and procedures.

Solidary benefits are "satisfactions gained through friendship and fraternity among individuals involved in a joint enterprise" (King and Walker 1992, 397). Farmers may join a farm organization mainly to socialize with others involved in agricultural work. Recreational shooters may join the NRA because it brings them into contact with others who enjoy marksmanship competitions. The sense

---

rational Making choices that maximize benefits and minimize costs.

material benefits Tangible rewards gained from membership in an interest group.

solidary benefits Satisfaction gained from membership in interest groups such as friendship and a sense of belonging to a group or meeting people with similar interests.

of membership and identification, and perhaps even having fun, are important incentives for joining a group. Even though there appears to be nothing tangible here, this still fits comfortably within the rational choice of theoretical framework mentioned in Chapter 1. Imagine someone who gains *utility* (satisfaction or enjoyment) from saving money and from the companionship of gun owners. If companionship brings greater satisfaction than saving money, it is rational to pay the membership dues and join the NRA because the benefits outweigh the costs. That is, trading the cost of membership dues for the benefit of interacting with other gun owners brings more satisfaction and enjoyment than keeping the money and forgoing the pleasure of belonging to the group.

Established in 1980, the special interest nonprofit group Mothers Against Drunk Driving (MADD) has grown to more than 600 affiliates and 2 million members nationwide, and it has successfully sponsored more than 2,300 antidrunk-driving laws. MADD works closely with the National Highway Traffic Safety Administration (NHTSA) to expand programs with the goal of saving lives. MADD President Colleen Sheehey-Church speaks about her support for DWI courts at the 2017 NADCP Training Conference Closing Ceremony at the Gaylord National Resort and Convention Center on Wednesday, July 12, 2017 in Oxon Hill, Maryland.

© Paul Morigi/NADCP/AP Photo

Purposive benefits transcend an individual's own material or solidary interests; they are benefits derived from feeling good about contributing to a worthy cause. Public-interest groups such as the government watchdog group Common Cause are often largely concerned with purposive benefits. They channel the desire of members to improve the lot of society in general, not just the individual concerns of the group's members. Again, this makes sense from a rational choice perspective—it is perfectly rational to join an interest group if the purposive benefits maximize utility. If someone has an individual preference to serve the greater good over improving his or her own lot in life, it is rational for that person to give up time and money for a group and a cause that will provide no material or solidary benefits to the individual.

Material, solidary, and purposive benefits are not mutually exclusive. An interest group may provide all three. For example, the United Automobile Workers (UAW) union provides material benefits to its members in the form of higher wages obtained through contract negotiations, sponsors recreational and other activities, and may push for social and economic reforms to benefit groups beyond its membership. Thus, the UAW provides different kinds of incentives to appeal to the different interests or requirements of its members.

The most obvious cost of participating in an interest group is membership dues. More important than monetary costs, however, are the costs of collective action—the time spent in meetings, in maintaining the organization, and in planning and participating in activities in pursuit of the group's goals. Thus, we generally assume that people form and join interest groups when the benefits (material, solidary,

purposive benefits Benefits that interest group members derive from feeling good about contributing to a worthy cause in an effort to improve the lot of society in general, not just the individual concerns of the group's members.

and purposive) outweigh the costs of participating (dues, time, and the effort involved with working with others).

Collective Action, Public Goods, and Free Riders

Although the assumption of rational action is at the heart of mainstream explanations of why people join interest groups, Mancur Olson (1965) points out a fundamental problem: It is not rational to join an interest group if the benefit it produces is a public good. If the benefits of a public good are greater than the costs, then why is it not rational to pony up your share? The answer has to do with the nature of public goods. A **public good** is a benefit that cannot be withheld from anyone—even those who do not contribute to the cost of providing the good. For example, an environmental group that pushes for clean air laws is seeking a public good—pleasant outdoor activities, better health, lower medical costs—that will be available to everyone. A rational actor who supports these goals may decline to join the group because he or she will get the benefits of the group's activities without paying any of the costs. In other words, if a group is providing a public good that is available to everyone, it is rational to be a **free rider** and get the benefit without paying anything for it. The term *free rider* is not intended to be pejorative, as the term *free loader* would. The concept of a free rider simply describes a rational choice to enjoy the benefits of group activity without incurring any of the costs.

The paradox is that securing a public good requires **collective action**—that is, a lot of people have to work together to make demands on others in society to actually produce the public good. It makes sense from a cost–benefit perspective to engage in collective action and produce public goods. Everyone is better off if we have clean air and clean water and if everyone pays their taxes, volunteers for community projects, and generally plays by the rules. And if lots of people work to produce the public good, the cost to each individual is likely to be much less than the benefits gained. If all the Sierra Club members work hard to get clean air laws, you can take as much as you want of the product of all that hard work whether you belong to the Sierra Club or not (breathe in a lungful—it's free!). But even if you are a member of the Sierra Club and are committed to clean air laws, it is not likely that your individual dues are going to make that much difference to the outcome; nor will your presence at a rally or your signature on a petition. The collective action problem presents something of a catch-22: Producing a public good requires organized collective group action, but each individual contribution is such a small part of the total cost that nonparticipation won't be noticed. Because everyone receives the benefits, it's rational to get a free ride and save the costs; but if everyone makes the rational choice, there won't be enough people engaging in the collective action to produce the benefits of the public good.

Some suggest that the notion of purposive benefits helps solve this puzzle. If we observe people making choices that do not seem to maximize benefits, there must be some psychological satisfaction from "doing the right thing" that maximizes utility; either that or people are irrational. Even if we accept the idea that a preference to do the right thing will persuade some to shoulder considerable individual

public good A benefit that is provided to everyone and cannot be withheld from those who did not participate in its provision.

free rider A person who makes the strictly rational choice to enjoy the benefits of public goods without incurring the costs of providing them, thus presenting a dilemma to the community as a whole.

collective action Action in which a group of people work together for the provision of public goods.

costs simply for the satisfaction of being part of a worthy cause, this idea does not solve the free rider problem because purposive benefits are essentially public goods. In effect, the argument is circular: People join an interest group and engage in collective action to produce a public good because they have a purposive desire to see the public good provided (King and Walker 1992, 397).

Thus, we need to look elsewhere for a solution to this puzzle. Interest groups that can overcome the collective action problem and persuade potential free riders to join are more likely to play a significant role in deciding who gets what. The challenge is to make it more attractive to join than to ride for free.

Overcoming the Free Rider Problem

Groups have several ways to overcome the free rider problem. One is to get government to require membership. For example, workers in some states are required to join a union if a majority of workers vote to let the union represent them. This arrangement is called a *union shop* or *closed shop*. But federal law also permits states to legislate an open shop so that workers are not required to join a union. Not surprisingly, labor unions in open-shop states are weaker than are those in closed-shop states because of the free rider problem. Why join the union if everyone gets the benefits regardless? The problem is that because the unions are smaller and weaker in open-shop states, they lack the political muscle to achieve their collective goals. Open-shop states with weak unions tend to have lower wages and less job security—the very benefits the free riders may want the most.

Labor unions are not the only group that seeks to use the government to overcome the free rider problem. Many universities require students to pay fees to support student government and other student organizations. Some students have objected when the money supports organizations that espouse social or political views they find objectionable or speech they find offensive. Supporters of the general activity fee counter by pointing out that colleges should support the free and open exchange of ideas, even objectionable ideas, because this contributes to the growth of knowledge—a public good. Using government coercion to overcome the free rider problem, however, is relatively unusual and can be used only if the conditions are right.

Another way to discourage free riding is to use peer pressure to persuade others to do their part in achieving group goals—in other words, the group can threaten to ostracize people who do not join in. Ostracizing people who do not contribute tends to be more effective in small populations in which individuals have frequent face-to-face contact. In small groups, an individual's failure to contribute is more likely to be noticed because each individual contribution is a relatively large part of the collective group effort. In such settings, ostracism can be a powerful behavioral influence. Most people desire a sense of identification with a group, and group disapproval is an important counter to the temptation to free-ride. In other words, small groups can use the pejorative term "free loader" to discourage free riders.

The third and most common approach to entice people to join an organization is to offer **selective benefits**, or material benefits that are available only to

selective benefits Benefits provided by interest groups that are available to members only.

members. These incentives include low-cost life insurance and health plans for union members and technical journals and newsletters for professionals. Selective benefits make perfect sense from a rational choice perspective; they provide a benefit unique to group membership and thus offset the costs of joining. The selective benefits available to AARP members, for example, include everything from hotel and restaurant discounts and discounts on insurance and healthcare products to complimentary magazine subscriptions (check out the selective benefits of AARP membership at www.aarp.org/benefits-discounts/). These selective benefits alone can easily outweigh the annual membership dues ($16.00 a year in 2018 for AARP). By using selective benefits to encourage membership, groups can overcome the free rider problem and secure a large enough base to engage in collective action to secure public benefits.

THE ORIGINS AND GROWTH OF INTEREST GROUPS

Interest groups have long played an important role in the American political system. For example, the Chamber of Commerce of the United States, an organization designed to advance the interests of the nation's business community, was formed in 1912. A related group, the National Association of Manufacturers, was established in 1895. The American Farm Bureau Federation dates back to 1919, currently one of the largest agricultural interest groups in the nation with a membership of more than 6 million. These groups and others like them have been actively making demands on others in society through government action for the better part of a century. But what drives people to form interest groups?

Theoretical Perspectives on the Formation of Interest Groups

Political scientists have suggested several other explanations for why interest groups form.

Pluralist Theory

The **pluralist explanation** is that interest groups are a natural extension of a democratic system that guarantees freedom of expression and association. An early advocate of this perspective is David Truman, who argued that changes in the political environment encouraged formation of new groups (Truman 1951). Because people will coalesce around a common cause more readily when they feel threatened, new groups are especially likely to emerge when changes adversely affect their interests. There are numerous examples of this kind of interest group formation. For example, the National Association of Manufacturers—the largest industrial trade association in America—formed in response to widespread concerns about

pluralist explanation (of interest groups) The idea that interest groups form in reaction to problems created by particular social or economic events.

the effects of an economic depression. Sometimes government activity precipitates group formation; in some cases, government explicitly encourages it. Theodore Lowi (1969) argues that the Departments of Agriculture, Commerce, and Labor are examples of government delegating the power to formulate and administer public policy to particular clienteles. In other cases, groups form in response to governmental action that is unpopular with a particular interest. The antiabortion group, the National Right to Life Committee (NRLC), for example, formed in 1973 in response to the Supreme Court ruling to legalize abortions in *Roe v. Wade*.

By-Product Theory and Exchange Theory

A drawback of the pluralist theory is that it does not explain how latent groups—groups of people who share common interests but are not organized or perhaps even aware of their common circumstances—overcome the free rider problem. Exchange theory and by-product theory address this puzzle. The central problem is this: If taking the free ride (not joining the group) is the rational choice, how do groups manage to form in the first place?

Viewed from this perspective, the formation of so many interest groups seems less like a natural outgrowth of a pluralistic democracy than the product of mass irrationality. Mancur Olson (1965) provided a simple answer to this puzzle: **by-product theory**. In a nutshell, by-product theory argues that group leaders overcome the free rider problem either by offering selective benefits—material, social, or recreational benefits available only to members, as described previously—or by creating coercive incentives such as mandatory membership in a professional organization. Whereas pluralist theory suggests that groups form because of a spontaneous coalescing of common interests around a common goal, by-product theory argues that special interest groups exist because they have overcome the free rider problem by attracting members using some other means. Any pursuit of a public good—NARAL's (National Abortion and Reproductive Rights Action League) pursuit of pro-choice laws, the NRA's opposition to an assault weapons ban—is not the main reason the group exists but is in reality a by-product of a successful strategy to recruit members.

Political scientist Robert Salisbury (1969) refined this general argument into an **exchange theory** of interest groups. Exchange theory explains the formation of interest groups as a rational quid pro quo between supplier and consumer. The basic idea is that groups form as a result of a deal—an exchange—between a **group entrepreneur** and an unorganized interest that may be underrepresented or not represented at all. The group entrepreneur invests resources (such as time, money, and organizational skill) to create and build an organization that offers various types of selective benefits (material and solidary) to entice others to join the group. Individuals with a common but unorganized interest join the group in exchange for the benefits of membership. Exchange theory is similar to by-product theory in that it is based on an assumption of rational actors: Groups form because they provide a set of benefits available only to members that outweigh the costs of membership. Exchange theory, though, views interest groups as essentially suppliers in

by-product theory The theory that most people will not engage in collective action with the sole aim of producing public goods. Instead, groups build membership by offering selective benefits available only to group members.

exchange theory The theory that interest groups form as a result of a deal—an exchange—between a group entrepreneur and an unorganized interest that may be underrepresented or not represented at all.

group entrepreneur Someone who invests resources (such as time, money, and organizational skill) to create and build an organization that offers various types of benefits (material, solidary, and purposive) to entice others to join the group.

a market. Groups form to "sell" a particular benefit package to induce people with certain interests to join (King and Walker 1992; Lowry 1997).

Niche Theory

Another theoretical approach applies biological concepts such as population ecology (the study of how animals interact with their environment) and carrying capacity (the maximum number of animals a given environment can sustain indefinitely without deterioration) to interest groups. Political scientists Virginia Gray and David Lowery (1996a) reasoned that just as a biological environment has a certain carrying capacity to support the various species that compete for its resources (such as food and nesting space), a political environment has a certain carrying capacity to support the interest groups that compete for its resources (such as members and financial contributions). The carrying capacity of an environment—biological or political—can be expanded if it is partitioned into small niches, or spaces that contain an array of resources necessary for survival (Lowery and Brasher 2004).

Niche theory explains the explosive growth of interest groups as the partitioning of policy niches into segments representing narrower and narrower interests to reduce direct competition among groups with similar goals. For example, general environmentalist groups such as the Sierra Club once dominated the environmental policy niche. The generalist organizations, though, left opportunities for specialized groups to cater to specialized environmental niches (e.g., Ducks Unlimited, a group that focuses on policies related to wetlands and waterfowl). Specific groups can fill such specialized niches because new techniques and technologies, in effect, increased the carrying capacity of America's political environment. For example, changes in communications technology and the growing importance of money in mounting competitive political campaigns have provided opportunities for entrepreneurs to identify and reach particular constituencies, to make their interests widely known, and to make them a potent political force through fundraising activities. Emily's List, the nationwide network of political donors that backs pro-choice female Democratic candidates, is a good example of how such niche organizations have grown. ("Emily," by the way, is an acronym rather than a person. It stands for "Early Money Is Like Yeast"—it raises dough.) Emily's List was started in 1985 by 25 women, many of them already office holders, who operated mostly out of group founder Ellen Malcolm's basement. Within three years, Emily's List was raising nearly a million dollars to support pro-choice candidates. Five years after that its membership topped 20,000, and nowadays Emily's List can raise and distribute tens of millions of dollars per election cycle (see www.emilyslist.org/who/history/ and www.opensecrets.org).

The Growth of Interest Groups

Although niche theory helps explain why the number of interest groups has increased, the growth is not uniform across all types of groups. Growth of some categories of interest groups has been spectacular (see Table 6.1). Overall, from

TABLE 6.1 UNEVEN PATTERNS OF GROWTH OF INTEREST GROUPS

	Number of Associations			Percentage Change	
	1959	1990	2008	1959–1990	1990–2008
Public affairs	117	2,249	1,966	1822.2%	-12.6%
Social welfare	241	1,705	2,320	607.5%	36.1%
Recreational (hobby, athletic, social, fan clubs)	539	3,206	3,251	494.8%	1.4%
Educational (engineering, science, arts and humanities)	857	4,595	3,570	436.2%	-22.3%
Health and medical	433	2,227	3,391	414.3%	52.3%
Legal, governmental, military, veterans	273	1,254	1,720	359.3%	37.2%
Cultural (religious, nationality, ethnic)	417	1,744	1,891	318.2%	8.4%
Environmental and agricultural	331	940	1,355	184.0%	44.1%
Business (trade, commerce, tourism)	2,409	4,086	4,086	69.6%	0.0%
Labor unions, associations, and federations	226	253	239	11.9%	-5.5%
Total	5,843	22,259	23,789	281.0%	6.9

Sources: Data from Baumgartner and Leech (1998), *Encyclopedia of Associations* (Detroit, MI: Gale).

1959 to 1990 the total number of interest groups increased by 281 percent (from 5,843 to 22,259). Over this same period, several categories experienced similar growth rates, but the increase in the number of public affairs associations was 1,822 percent (from 117 to 2,249). In contrast, business and labor groups grew at much slower rates. Since the 1990s, growth in the number of associations has leveled off and even declined in some categories. The health and medical category has grown the fastest since the 1990s, but the 52 percent increase is considerably less than the 414 percent increase in the earlier period. Public affairs, educational, and labor groups experienced negative growth.

Furthermore, groups are active across a broad range of issues, but some interests are more prominent than are others. Research consistently shows that business interests are the dominant force in both numbers and spending, and labor unions and other citizens' interests are much less prominent. A study of Washington lobbying groups by Frank Baumgartner and Beth Leech (2001), for example, found that over 59 percent of registered lobbyists were from business and trade associations, whereas unions accounted for less than 2 percent, and nonprofit citizens' groups accounted for less than 10 percent. An update of this analysis shows that these findings still hold. More than 60 percent of lobbyists in Washington in 2017 represented various business interests (49 percent from financial, construction, communications, and electronics industries and 14 percent from agribusiness, energy, and natural resources); 2 percent represented labor and 11 percent represented educational, nonprofit, civil servant, and religious interests (see Figure 6.2a). We see the same pattern in spending. Of the $3.3 billion spent on lobbying in 2017, 70 percent ($2.3 billion) came from business and related interests (energy, agriculture, natural resources), compared to 1.4 percent (about $46 million) from labor and 7 percent (about $231 million) from education and nonprofits (see Figure 6.2b).

Activity and competition across issues also is highly skewed. Only a small number of issues attract the attention of a large number of groups presenting opposing views, and on many issues there is only one group actively lobbying. Differential success in overcoming the collective action problem may account for some of the differences in activity. Another likely explanation for uneven group activity is that groups successfully stake out their own little niche partitioned from other groups. Baumgartner and Leech (2001, 1204) found that business groups, trade associations, and representatives of state and local governments were active on all types of issues, but on issues "where only one or two groups were active, participation was almost exclusively limited to" these interests. Unions, nonprofits, and citizens' groups were likely to be active on highly visible issues in competition with many other groups, including business.

Thus, group influence tends to be greatest on issues that attract little attention and controversy because there is no one to present an opposing point of view. Those big, controversial issues where we see intense conflict from opposing groups are the issues that Americans see on TV or that are debated in political campaigns.

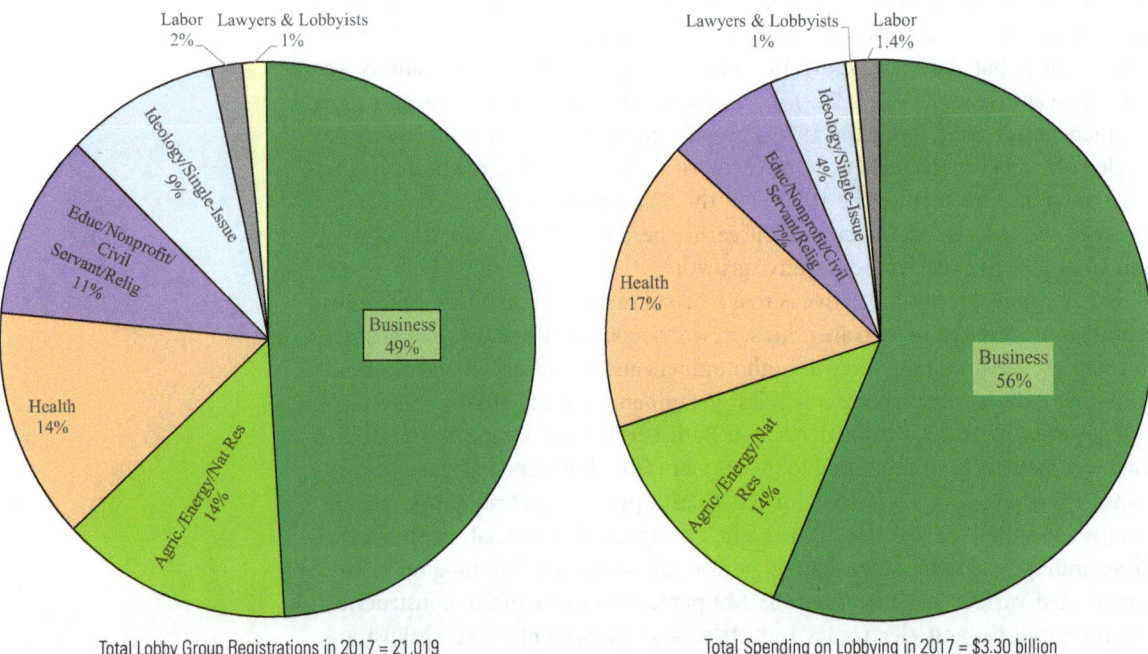

FIGURE 6.2 (a) Lobby Group Registrations; (b) Spending on Lobbying

Source: Data from the Center for Responsive Politics, at https://www.opensecrets.org/lobby/top.php?showYear=2017&indexType=c (accessed March 10, 2017).

APPLYING THE FRAMEWORKS

HOW BIOLOGY HELPS EXPLAIN WHY INTEREST GROUPS LOBBY

Why do interest groups lobby? Rational choice models assume that interest groups lobby to get government benefits, and that those benefits outweigh the costs of lobbying. Interest groups hire thousands of lobbyists and spend enormous sums of money on lobbying (see Figures 6.2a and 6.2b), and we assume these groups must be getting something for their money. Indeed, the popular perception is that these powerful organizations use their wealth as if they were going into a policy supermarket and filling their shopping carts with the policies they want.

Yet numerous studies show that lobbying just doesn't work that way. The basic takeaway from this research is that lobbyists win some and lose some (Baumgartner and Leech 1998, 134), and they are more likely to win under pretty narrow circumstances. Special interest groups are most likely to be successful when lobbying on a narrow, technical issue that arouses little public interest; they are least successful when lobbying on big, high-profile issues, exactly the sort of efforts that typically require a huge investment of resources (Lowery 2007). If anything, the existing research suggests that the more interest groups lobby and the more resources they devote to lobbying, the less they win. That doesn't seem rational.

So what explains this "lobbying paradox"? Why would a rational, utility-maximizing interest group ever lobby when the costs so frequently seem to outweigh the benefits? The surprising answer is that the goal of lobbying may not always be to influence policy. Political scientists Virginia Gray and David Lowery employed niche theory adapted from the field of population biology to show that the primary motivation to lobby is more basic—survival (Gray and Lowery 1996a, 1996b, 1997; Lowery 2007). Population biologists developed niche theory to understand how a population interacts with resources in the environment to survive. The array of resources in an environment that bear on a species' survival is called the "fundamental niche," or the space in which it might survive. Similar species compete for survival in a portion of this niche (Hutchinson 1957). The result of this competition, however, is not overt conflict, but rather the partitioning of resources to avoid overt conflict. For example, if two similar bird species have overlapping niches, "partitioning may entail segregating territories, feeding at different times of the day, specializing in foods initially available to both, or partitioning of any other shared resource" that will sustain viable niches (Gray and Lowery 1996b, 94).

Population biologists, then, emphasize competition but focus on competition between similar groups fighting for the same resources. Applying this basic idea to interest groups means that watching monumental, public battles between opposing interests (e.g., manufacturers vs. environmentalists) is analogous to watching clashes between predator and prey—sometimes the cat catches her dinner; sometimes the bird gets away. It's great drama, but it doesn't teach us about the much bigger question of survival—cats don't threaten *the survival of an entire species* of birds. A key insight from niche theory is that to develop a more general understanding of interest group behavior, we need to analyze competition *within* the same species of groups for the resources to survive—e.g., competition among environmental groups, rather than between environmental groups and manufacturers.

So, what are the resources similar interests compete for? Gray and Lowery (1996b) identify five essential resources for a viable interest group niche: (1) members, (2) selective benefits to mobilize potential members, (3) finances to support operation of the organization, (4) access to the policymaking process, and (5) existing or proposed policy of concern to the interest group. Several important insights emerge from niche theory. First, lack of overt conflict does not necessarily mean lack of competition. It may mean the absence of competition, but it can also indicate a successful partitioning of the fundamental niche to avoid overt conflict.

Second, multiple resource arrays mean that organizations lobby in pursuit of multiple goals. Achieving favorable policies is certainly one goal of lobbying; it's just not the only one, or even the primary motivation. The choice of goals and lobbying targets depends on which of the resource arrays is most threatened by competitors. For example, if a group is losing members or lacks adequate finances, it may lobby on some hot-button issue with no hope of winning in order to retain old members and attract new members, or to secure financial support from a wealthy patron. Or if an organization lacks public opinion support, it may shift from inside lobbying on narrow issues of great concern to its members to fuzzier outside lobbying in pursuit of a longer-term strategy to create a more favorable public opinion environment.

Third, niche theory provides insight about how and why external actors who control vital resources can leverage those resources to influence the behavior of organizations. The central hypothesis of most studies of interest group influence is whether lobbying causes policymakers to support the policies favored by the group. But policymakers control a vital resource for interest groups—access to the policymaking process. They can use the threat of withholding that to mobilize organized interests to lobby on behalf of the elites' preferred policy agenda.

Thus, applying lessons from population biology to the behavior of organized interests, we learn that organizations lobby in pursuit of multiple goals, most of which concern payoffs other than just adoption of policy favorable to the group. Interest groups pursue these other goals when they involve scarce resources essential to the organization's survival. A key implication is that we need to redefine the meaning of success. Although costly lobbying often fails to achieve policy benefits, there's a lobbying paradox only from the rational choice model's narrow definition of payoffs. When organized interests engage in costly lobbying, it

> may be about maintaining membership rolls *or* securing access from political elites on other issues … *or* changing the salience and popularity of the issue over the long haul *or* blocking rival organizations from relying on a shared issue agenda, membership base, or patrons *or* any number of other goals, all of which help the organization survive. If lobbying secures these other goals, it must be counted as successful irrespective of the outcome of a final policy vote (Lowery 2007, 53).

Discussion Questions

1. An important insight from niche theory is that political elites can manipulate proposals on the agenda to mobilize organized interests to support what the agenda setter wants. Does this mean that elected representatives are looking out for our interests?
2. Can you think of some goals other than policy that elected elites might want interest groups to help with?

As important as these issues are, they are just a tiny fraction of the issues on which groups seek to influence who gets what. The most common type of group influence occurs on small, noncontroversial issues where only one perspective is presented and that are outside the view of the media and most citizens.

Growth in numbers has also been accompanied by a shift in the nature of interest groups. One matter of concern is the rapid rise of **single-issue groups**—groups that take positions and are active on only one specific issue (such as abortion, guns, homosexuality, or the environment). There are often single-issue groups on both sides of an issue. For example, antiabortion National Right to Life Committee and pro-choice NARAL have opposite goals on abortion, but these groups are similar in that they tend to take extreme, uncompromising positions on a single issue. Critics argue that single-issue groups undermine the democratic process by polarizing the issues and blocking efforts to find common ground. Others respond

single-issue groups Groups that take extreme, uncompromising positions on only one specific issue (e.g., abortion, guns, LGBTQ rights, the environment).

that these groups just provide a different type of representation. Traditional interest groups represent some economic or occupational interest (such as farmers, businesspeople, or lawyers), whereas these so-called single-interest groups represent ideas about a specific issue (such as protecting the environment, promoting peace, or achieving racial equality). These issues are not necessarily narrow, and such groups are not new to American politics (Tesh 1984). Groups advocating abolition of slavery, the prohibition of alcohol, and women's suffrage were active early in our nation's history. The intense conflict over abortion in contemporary politics is not nearly as divisive, or as violent, as the slavery issue was in the 1860s.

Another troubling form of interest group activity is the rise of so-called think tanks that blur the line between research and advocacy. Traditionally, think tanks have been institutions dedicated to the scholarly examination of policy issues of national importance. Although some have a partisan perspective, organizations such as the Brookings Institution and the American Enterprise Institute have reputations as sources of creative and independent thinking on policy matters of national importance and not as advocates of a narrow set of interests.

The new generation of think tanks is much more ideological and partisan and much more aggressive in trying to influence policy decisions. Some depend financially on organizations with a vested interest in the outcome of their research and have been accused of providing a scholarly facade to blatantly self-interested agendas (L. Jacobson 1995). Think tanks with a clear ideological slant are disproportionately, but not exclusively, conservative. Examples of prominent conservative think tanks include the Heritage Foundation and the Cato Institute. Prominent liberal think tanks include the Urban Institute and the Center for American Progress.

INTEREST GROUP RESOURCES AND ACTIVITIES

Understanding the role of interest groups in the democratic process requires consideration of the sources of their political power and how it is exercised. The sources of interest group power can be divided into two broad categories: political resources and political tactics.

Political Resources

Political resources are the tools interest groups have at their disposal to influence the political process. They include membership, money, leadership, and expertise.

Membership

The most basic political resource of an interest group is its membership. Several aspects of group membership can provide muscle in the political arena. One is sheer size. Groups that can potentially shift large blocks of voters behind a candidate or a policy proposal often have an advantage. A group such as the AARP, representing millions of senior citizens who are likely to turn out to vote, has a good deal of clout from size alone.

Numbers are not everything, however. The geographic distribution of the membership is also important. Groups with members spread out over the entire country are likely to have an advantage over groups with members largely confined to a single region. One reason teachers' unions are formidable political players is the wide geographic distribution of their membership. Schools are a recognizable and central component of nearly every community in the nation. Collective action by teachers can bring pressure on the government from all points simply because every congressional representative has a large number of teachers as constituents.

In addition to size and geographic distribution, the status of a group's membership is also a valuable political resource. The American Medical Association and the National Academy of Sciences, for example, do not represent huge blocks of voters, but physicians and scientists have high social status and respect, so their collective voice is treated with deference.

Money

Perhaps the most popularly recognized political resource of interest groups is money. A well-financed group no doubt has an advantage in the political arena. But money is a tool, not a guarantee. It is not just how much money a group has but what the group does with the money. Spending money on an unpopular campaign, for example, can diminish a group's political clout rather than enhance it. Such was the case in April 1995, when the NRA mailed a fundraising letter signed by NRA Executive Vice President Wayne LaPierre describing federal agents as fascist thugs who wore "Nazi bucket helmets and black storm trooper uniforms" and who "harass, intimidate, and even murder law-abiding citizens." Former president George H. W. Bush was outraged and called the letter a "vicious slander on good people." Bush turned in his lifetime NRA membership (Spitzer 1998). The letter designed to bolster support for the NRA's position turned out to be a public relations disaster.

In order to spend money, groups first have to raise it, and this can be hard work. Interest groups get their money from a variety of sources, including membership dues, fundraising campaigns, special events, endowments, and returns on investments, to mention just a few. All of these sources require a significant investment. Even a stable membership base requires careful tending. For a national organization, staying in contact with members can be expensive. Setting dues that are high enough to defray costs but low enough to retain existing members and attract new ones is a delicate balancing act.

Leadership and Expertise

The most important sources of political clout are a group's leadership and expertise. With dynamic and forceful leadership, clear objectives, and a well-prepared plan on how to achieve those objectives, a small group operating on a shoestring can be as effective as a much larger and well-financed operation lacking such leadership. When these assets are combined with a large membership and operating budget, the group can be a potent political force. Groups such as the Sierra Club and the NOW enroll less than 1 percent of the adult population as members, but they have committed leaders, chapters operating in all 50 states, and an active membership base (Skocpol 1999). Combined, these assets give them influence in the political arena beyond that provided by membership or money alone.

Emma Gonzalez, a student and survivor of the Parkland shooting speaks at the first ever March for Our Lives to demand stricter gun control laws on March 24, 2018 in Washington, DC.

© Olivier Douliery/Abaca/Sipa/AP Photo

Perhaps the most commonly overlooked source of interest group power is the knowledge and expertise of a group. On matters of health policy, for example, the American Medical Association often has clout not only because of its members' status but also because it represents the collective voice of medical experts. Interest groups are not shy about using their expertise as a political tool. A primary objective of interest group lobbying is to provide policymakers with information they can use in decision making. For example, the American Bar Association routinely issues ratings of nominees to the federal judiciary.

Political Tactics

It is one thing to have political resources; it is quite another to exercise political influence or power. Tactics are the ways groups use their political resources to achieve their goals. In order to influence public policy, a political interest group must have access to official decision makers. That is, it must have some means of presenting its point of view to them.

Access is more than just the ability to contact decision makers; it also implies willingness on the part of a decision maker to consider the group's views, whether or not the official ultimately decides to adopt them. To successfully make demands on others in society through government action, a political interest group deploys its resources to gain access to decision makers. The generic term for this process is **lobbying**. The term originated from an actual lobby, the entrance hall to the House of Commons, where citizens could meet and discuss their concerns with members of Parliament. Today, lobbying refers to any activity in which a person or group attempts to influence public policymaking on behalf of themselves or other people or groups (Baumgartner and Leech 1998, 33–34). Lobbying takes on a number of forms, uses a number of tactics, and is aimed at a number of targets.

lobbying Activity of a group or person that attempts to influence public policymaking on behalf of the individual or the group.

Professional Lobbyists

A common approach is to hire a **lobbyist**, an individual whose job it is to contact government officials on behalf of someone else. Some groups—such as unions, large trade associations, and corporations with offices in Washington—use their own executives as lobbyists. But many others hire a professional lobbyist to look after their interests in the nation's capital. Professional lobbyists often work for several clients. Some Washington law firms not only carry on standard legal practices but also represent clients on political matters before legislative and executive officials. And although some firms tend to be associated with a particular political party, some large lobbying firms hire highly visible lobbyists from both parties to increase access for whomever their client might be. The Livingston Group, for example, is a high-profile lobbying organization founded by former Republican congressman Bob Livingston. One of his partners is former Democratic Assistant Secretary of Commerce Lauri Fitz-Pegado (you can get a pretty good idea of what a top-level lobbying firm does by exploring the Livingston Group's website: www.livingstongroupdc.com). Other lobbyist-entrepreneurs specialize in matters that do not require legal expertise and that provide services on a fee basis. Often the founders and leaders of groups with purposive goals, such as eliminating handguns, serve as lobbyists for their organizations.

Interest groups look for people who possess the information, skills, and access that make them effective in transmitting group views to decision makers. Former members of Congress are especially sought after as lobbyists because they understand the complexities of legislation, have contacts among former colleagues and staff, and have the right to go onto the floor of the legislative chambers—a privilege that may give them a special type of access to policymakers. However, more lobbyists come from the executive branch than from the legislative branch. There are more former executive branch employees to draw from, and many crucial decisions are made by administrative agencies. It may be more important for an interest group to have a conduit to an agency that implements a law than to the legislature that passes it.

Direct and Indirect Lobbying

Interest groups and their lobbyists employ a variety of approaches to communicate their viewpoints to decision makers. Some involve direct contacts with public officials—called **direct lobbying**. Others use intermediaries to make the contact, which is **indirect lobbying**.

Lobbyists trying to influence Congress have a number of direct lobbying options. Because the fate of legislative proposals largely depends on the committees that initially consider them, lobbyists routinely appear before these committees to express their groups' viewpoints on pending legislation. Speaking before a congressional committee allows a lobbyist to have direct contact with more than one legislator and makes the group's views a matter of record in the transcripts of committee hearings that are routinely distributed to interested parties. One-on-one contact with

---

lobbyists Individuals whose job it is to contact and attempt to influence governmental officials on behalf of others.

direct lobbying Direct contact by lobbyists with government officials in an effort to influence policy.

indirect lobbying The use of intermediaries by lobbyists to speak to government officials, with the intent to influence policy.

individual representatives is usually more effective than an appearance before a committee. Members of Congress are frequently absent from committee meetings and may be distracted by other business when they are present. A personal visit ensures attention and conveys the impression that the representative is important enough to merit special consultation.

Lobbyists often find it advantageous to work through others who enjoy special relationships with a decision maker they hope to influence. Personal friends or relatives of officials, of course, may provide an entree. One of the most effective ways to reach senators and representatives is through their constituents, especially constituents who can affect their political careers. If a lobbyist can convince, say, a major campaign contributor or a newspaper editor in a legislator's home state to present the group's point in a favorable light, the message is likely to be well received.

Another effective way to use the indirect approach is to draw on a group's membership. Members of Congress take note of letters, phone calls, and e-mails about issues, and enough contacts—especially from a member's own constituents—can gain a legislator's attention. A flood of mail and calls can alert a decision maker to the importance of an issue. Such tactics are sometimes ineffective, however, because legislators can usually detect a contrived campaign that is pretending to be a grassroots effort (i.e., a spontaneous outpouring of sentiment from voters). Letters that contain the same wording, that were sent on the same day, and that disproportionately come from a few zip codes indicate that constituents' expressions of concern are not spontaneous. Some political consulting firms specialize in such campaigns, which are called AstroTurf to distinguish them from true grassroots campaigns.

A subtler form of indirect lobbying is to inform voters about a legislator's votes, rather than informing the legislator about voter preferences. Interest groups frequently provide their members with "report cards" on legislators. The report lists the percentage of the time a legislator opposed or supported the group's preferences. Table 6.2 shows how several different groups rated some prominent members of Congress. Groups in the first four columns support liberal, labor, civil liberties and environmental positions; groups in the last four columns support business, low taxes, social conservative, and conservative positions. Notice that Democrats tend to have high scores from liberal groups and low scores from the conservative groups, whereas Republicans score high with conservative groups and low with liberal groups. For example, the two major contenders for the Democratic presidential nomination in 2008, Senators Hillary Clinton and Barack Obama, had nearly identical liberal voting records during their last year in the Senate. There are a few outliers, however. Relative to other Democrats, Texas Rep. Henry Cuellar and West Virginia Sen. Joe Manchin received lower scores from liberal groups. And Washington Rep. Jaime Herrera Beutler and Maine Sen. Susan Collins have less conservative records than do most Republicans.

Other possibilities for effective indirect lobbying include having group members talk to their representatives when the politicians are back home campaigning or visiting, having group members who are visiting Washington call on their legislators, and holding a conference in the nation's capital to let lawmakers know firsthand how concerned individuals and groups are about an issue. A less frequently used

TABLE 6.2 INTEREST GROUP RATINGS FOR SOME MEMBERS OF CONGRESS

	ADA	ACLU	AFL-CIO	LCV	COC	CFG	FRC	ACU
DEMOCRATS								
Rep. Nancy Pelosi (CA-12), Minority Leader	80	88	90	91	38	4	0	4
Rep. Steny Hoyer (MD-5), Minority Whip	70	77	90	91	50	2	0	0
Rep. John Lewis (GA-5), Chief Deputy Whip	85	72	95	91	25	15	0	11
Rep. Henry Cuellar (TX-28)	15	27	76	31	89	18	75	36
Sen. Charles Schumer (NY), Minority Leader	90	100	100	80	50	0	0	0
Sen. Richard Durbin (IL), Minority Whip	100	92	100	100	12	0	0	45
Sen. Barack Obama (IL)	95	83	100	100	55	7	0	8
Sen. Hillary Clinton (NY)	95	83	100	71	67	8	0	8
Sen. Joe Manchin (WV)	80	73	89	20	13	20	40	32
REPUBLICANS								
Rep. Paul Ryan (WI-1), Speaker of the House	0	0	14	3	79	69	88	80
Rep. Kevin McCarthy (CA-23), Majority Leader	0	0	19	0	100	43	88	76
Rep. Jaime Herrera Beutler (WA-3)	5	5	25	11	93	52	88	60
Rep. Kevin Brady (TX-8)	0	0	10	0	92	67	100	87
Sen. Mitch McConnell (KY), Majority Leader	5	6	17	20	100	55	100	84
Sen. John Cornyn (TX) Assist. Majority Leader	5	0	6	20	100	72	93	92
Sen. John McCain (AZ)	5	53	33	20	86	88	79	91
Sen. Marco Rubio (FL)	5	40	6	0	75	92	100	96
Sen. Susan Collins (ME)	35	60	56	69	88	34	36	44

Data: Data from Barone and McCutcheon (2011) and Barone and Cohen (2007; 2015).

Notes: Entries are the percentage of the time that the member voted in agreement with the group's position. Scores are from 2014; party leaders are those serving in the 114th Congress when Republicans were the majority in both House and Senate. Scores for individuals who did not serve in the 114th Congress (Obama and Clinton) are from the last year they served.

ADA: Americans for Democratic Action (liberal)
ACLU: American Civil Liberties Union (pro–individual liberties)
AFL-CIO: American Federation of Labor Congress of Industrial Organizations (liberal labor)
LCV: League of Conservation Voters (environmental)
COC: Chamber of Commerce of the United States (conservative pro-business)
CFG: Club for Growth (conservative pro-tax limitation)
FRC: Family Research Council (social conservative)
ACU: American Conservative Union (conservative)

method is to stage a dramatic demonstration in Washington. This tactic was used by civil rights and antiwar groups in the 1960s, by members of the American Agricultural Movement in the 1970s, and by groups involved on both sides of the abortion debate from the 1980s to the 2000s.

Coalition Building

coalition building A means of expanding an interest group's influence that involves working with other groups.

One effective way to extend a group's political influence is to join forces with other groups. This process of **coalition building** is a form of indirect lobbying that signals to politicians that a particular issue is of concern to more than just an isolated segment of the public.

One basis for forming a coalition is to focus on common and overlapping interests. Even groups that oppose each other occasionally find common interests. The major automobile manufacturers, for example, banded together with the United Auto Workers to delay the imposition of emission standards. Despite their differing positions on labor-management issues, all feared that the timetable favored by environmental groups would impose harmful economic costs on the automobile industry.

A second basis for coalition building comes through a process called **logrolling**. Groups propose an exchange, "You support me on my issue, and I'll support you on yours." Logrolling often results from a coalition of uncommon interests—that is, a coalition of groups whose interests do not necessarily overlap but neither are they in opposition. For example, the Chamber of Commerce of the United States typically sides with the American Farm Bureau Federation on agricultural policy issues, and the Farm Bureau takes the chamber's side on business issues.

logrolling The exchange of support on issues between groups that do not have common interests in order to gain mutual advantage.

Shaping Public Opinion

Perhaps the most appealing coalition is the public itself. If an interest group can make enough people sympathetic to its desires and persuade them to convey their sentiments to those in public office, it achieves a major strategic objective: Other people are lobbying on its behalf. Efforts to shape public attitudes have become an increasingly important tactic.

A group's membership can be one vehicle to shape public opinion. For example, to mobilize opposition to healthcare proposals that it considered to be "socialized medicine," the American Medical Association got doctors to distribute literature and talk to patients about the issue. This activity capitalized on patients' tendency to respect their own physicians and to view them as experts. Another tactic is to use well-regarded experts or trusted figures to persuade the public to support a group's cause. For example, NRA members elected Charlton Heston president in 1998. Heston had a long record of Second Amendment activism prior to this election, but Heston is most famous as an actor, especially for his portrayal of Moses in the 1956 movie *The Ten Commandments*. He gave up the NRA presidency in 2003, but Heston's name recognition and the moral authority identified with the characters he played in movies gave the NRA a powerful public champion.

Ultimately, though, probably the most powerful way to shape public opinion and attitude is through the mass media. Appeals through the mass media can camouflage the partisan self-interest that is their source. For example, letters to the

Well-known public figures can bring considerable public attention to interest groups and garner public support for them. Alyssa Milano's tweet launched the #MeToo hashtag: "If you've been sexually harassed or assaulted write 'me too' as a reply to this tweet." Here she speaks at the Anita Hill and Fatima Goss Graves Discussion on Harassment at United Talent Agency on Friday, December 8, 2017, in Beverly Hills, California.

© Willy Sanjuan/Invision/AP Photo

editor may be statements drafted by lobbyists for individual signatures. And public service announcements broadcast on television touting a company's commitment to the environment, for example, might counter a negative corporate image being portrayed by environmentalist groups. Campaigns through the traditional mass media, however, have been replaced by savvy use of social media. Setting up a Facebook page or a Twitter account is fast, cheap, and capable of pushing out precisely targeted messages instantaneously to a potential audience of millions.

Campaign Support

The most basic support an interest group can provide any public official is help winning office. If the candidate seeks an appointive office, the group's representatives can use their influence to see to it that those responsible for making the appointment are aware of the nominee's qualifications and the high esteem in which the nominee is held. Many interest groups become involved in appointments to major executive posts and seats on the federal bench.

Interest groups also provide campaign support to candidates running for elective office. Examples include financial contributions, providing information for political speeches and audiences to hear the speeches, favorable coverage in the organization's newsletter, and helping to register and mobilize voters. The earlier a group provides political support and the more extensive that support, the more likely the public official is to grant the access that is all-important to the organization (Austin-Smith 1995; Grier, Munger, and Roberts 1994).

There are also risks if a group irrevocably commits to a single party's candidates. The group is unlikely to have much influence if the candidate it supports loses. To minimize this risk, groups frequently contribute to both major political parties. The presumption is that, regardless of the outcome, the group will have lent enough support to gain the access it desires.

Lobbying in Court

Interest groups also use the judicial process to further their interests. This claim may seem odd because Americans widely accept the "myth of judicial objectivity"—namely, that courts and judges are above politics, impartial referees to resolve legal disputes. Yet political scientists have found evidence that courts are political institutions that make public policy (see Chapter 15). For example, when the Supreme Court ruled that states could not ban abortion early in a pregnancy (*Roe v. Wade* 1973), it was binding public policy about who gets what. The rules for lobbying the judiciary, however, differ from efforts to influence the legislative or executive branches. Lobbyists cannot go to a judge's office and try to persuade the judge to give them a favorable ruling in an important case. Nonetheless, interest groups can influence judicial policymaking in two legal and legitimate ways: filing test cases and filing *amicus curiae* briefs.

A **test case** is a lawsuit filed to test the constitutionality of some government policy. The lawsuit must be filed by someone who has actually been injured by

test case A lawsuit filed to test the constitutionality of some government policy.

the policy, and the court's ruling technically applies only to the parties involved in the suit. But because judicial rulings serve as precedents to guide rulings in future cases, some cases represent major policy victories for certain interests. Perhaps the most famous test case is *Brown v. Board of Education* (1954). The Reverend Oliver Brown filed suit on behalf of his seven-year-old daughter, Linda, challenging the constitutionality of the Topeka, Kansas, school board's policy requiring her to attend an all-black school. The *Brown* case was one of several similar suits posing the same question: Do racially segregated schools violate the equal protection clause of the Fourteenth Amendment? Where did these citizens of modest means get the huge sums of money required to take this case through the judicial system all the way to the Supreme Court, and how was it that they filed such similar suits all at the same time? An interest group—the National Association for the Advancement of Colored People (NAACP)—provided the resources and the strategy to challenge the segregation policy in the courts. Although the NAACP was not a party in this case (the parties were the plaintiff, Reverend Brown, and the defendant, the Board of Education), the interest group made this suit a test case as part of a political strategy. Since the *Brown* decision, other interest groups have pursued a judicial strategy to promote their interests.

Interest groups can also try to influence judicial decisions by filing an **amicus curiae brief**, which is a legal brief filed by someone or some organization who has an interest in a case but is not an actual party to it. In a lawsuit, the plaintiff and the defendant each file legal briefs making arguments about how the case should be decided. Sometimes other organizations present arguments even though they are not a party in the suit. This procedure is a way for interest groups to present arguments and information as *amicus curiae* (Latin for "friend of the court"). The Supreme Court sometimes quotes from these briefs in their written opinions, indicating that sometimes the arguments in *amicus curiae* briefs can be persuasive.

THE POWER AND REGULATION OF INTEREST GROUPS

Understanding what interest groups are, who joins them, and what they do is important. The central concern most citizens have about interest groups, however, is the extent of their influence on political decision making. Are they too powerful? Do they make a positive or negative contribution to the democratic process? In exploring the answers to these questions, keep in mind that interest groups, as Madison recognized, are a natural by-product of a free and open democratic process. Interest group activity, in essence, is the core principle of political freedom being put into practice: In a free and democratic society, people with shared interests have the freedom and opportunity to band together in order to advance their common preferences. A system of divided powers as in the United States, with multiple venues in which to seek a response from the government, is especially conducive to group action. In theory, this group activity contributes to

***amicus curiae* brief** A legal brief filed by someone or some organization who holds an interest in a case but is not an actual party.

greater democratic responsiveness. Government has a hard time responding to an individual vote in a presidential or congressional election. Responding to collective input such as an endorsement from the multimillion-member AARP is much easier. So interest group activities make a positive contribution to the performance of democracy by helping the government make good on the promise to act on the will of the people.

Some political scientists argue that interest groups act as a more general stimulant to political involvement and activity by giving individuals an opportunity to develop the skills necessary for political participation. This contribution is called *unintentional mobilization* because it is an unintended by-product of group involvement (Leighley 1996). Also, organized group action on one side of an issue often spawns another interest group taking the opposite position, so interest groups can be seen as promoting pluralism. Thus, interest groups may contribute to a healthy democratic system.

Other observe that interest groups are exactly what Madison had in mind in his discussion of factions in *Federalist* Number 10. All the dangers Madison associated with factions potentially apply to interest groups. Some may seek to advance their agendas by suppressing the preferences of others. This activity may contribute to low levels of satisfaction with democracy. It is important to realize that not all interest groups are equal. Some have more resources and more influence. Some interest groups exercise power in very specific policy niches where they do not have to compete with other interests to influence who gets what.

Interest Group Power and Influence

Have interest groups become too powerful? Do a handful of groups exercise undue influence? Is the result a political process that is elitist rather than pluralist? Researchers have found evidence to support affirmative answers to such questions.

It is clear that well-organized, well-financed groups have enough political muscle to hinder adoption of visible, controversial policies they oppose. Furthermore, the groups themselves may be dominated by a small number of elites who are less concerned with compromise than are other members. Although most interest groups look democratic in the sense that rank-and-file members have some say over policy decisions and the election of officers, in practice an active minority usually runs the organization. Attendance at an annual convention by rank-and-file members who have limited knowledge of the group's operations does not place a meaningful check on the actions of the group's leadership. There is no group of officeholders to counter the ruling clique, so rarely is there any organized opposition to the current leadership. Unlike the broader political arena, the internal operation of interest groups is not governed by a system of checks and balances.

Of particular concern is the organized collection and disbursement of enormous sums of money into the political arena. More than 50 years ago, Will Rogers quipped, "America has the best politicians money can buy" (quoted in Sterling 1979, 63). Corporations and labor unions have long been prohibited from making campaign contributions directly to candidates. To get around this ban, interest groups connected to various economic sectors (e.g., business, trade organizations, and labor, as defined in Figure 6.2) use **political action committees (PACs)** to raise funds and make political contributions to candidates and parties on a group's behalf. Over the last several decades, the number of PACs and the amount of money they pump into the electoral process have exploded. Currently thousands of PACs spend hundreds of millions of dollars every national election cycle.

Even more troubling than activities of traditional PACs connected to various economic sectors is the growth of non-connected PACs. These organizations incorporate under various sections of the Internal Revenue Code that regulate tax-exempt organizations, and they are known as Super PACs. A **Super PAC** is a type of political committee that can raise unlimited sums of money from corporations, unions, associations, and individuals to independently support or oppose political candidates or issues. Unlike traditional PACs, Super PACs may not contribute directly to or coordinate with political candidates' campaigns (Center for Responsive Politics 2012a, 2012b; Levinthal 2012). Rather than promoting some general economic interest, Super PACs operate on behalf of strongly ideological, single-issue groups. These groups contribute to the intense polarization in contemporary politics because they pursue a narrow, ideological mission, and support candidates who are less willing to compromise. Particularly troubling is that some Super PACs can keep their donors and members secret. This lack of transparency prevents voters from discovering the groups' underlying motivation.

Figure 6.3 documents the explosive growth in spending of single-issue groups. Until the 2002 election cycle, each of the four general PAC categories—corporate, trade, labor, and single-issue—spent similar amounts on campaigns. Between 2004 and 2010, spending by single-issue PACs was slightly higher than that of other PACs. In the 2012 election cycle, spending by single-issue PACs increased sharply to about $1.3 billion, and then skyrocketed to nearly $3.0 billion in 2016.

The activities of PACs and lobbyists certainly can create the impression that the political process, or at least significant parts of it, is for sale to the highest bidder. Political science research, however, suggests that such impressions do not reflect reality. For example, lobbyists are typically pictured as stealthy figures carrying satchels stuffed with money with which to bribe government officials. Although there certainly are instances of public officials taking bribes, such corruption is the exception rather than the rule. If relationships between interest groups and public officials have changed over time, they have probably become less corrupt.

Political scientists studying this issue have generally found a remarkably weak connection between financial contributions and decision making. A systematic review of numerous studies looking for a correlation between campaign contributions and roll call votes found little evidence that votes in Congress are purchased (Baumgartner and Leech 1998, 14–15). However, drawing firm conclusions about overall interest group influence—or rather lack of influence—is difficult because most of these studies focused on one issue, and they did not use a common set of measures so that the findings could cumulate (Leech 2010). But a comprehensive study of the lobbying activities of more than 1,000 groups on a random sample of nearly 100 issues found no relationship between groups' monetary resources and getting what they wanted (Baumgartner et al. 2009).

political action committees (PACs) Organizations specifically created to raise money and make political contributions on behalf of an interest group.

Super PAC A type of political committee that can raise unlimited sums of money from corporations, unions, associations, and wealthy individuals to independently support or oppose political candidates. Unlike traditional PACs, Super PACs may not contribute directly to or coordinate with political candidates' campaigns.

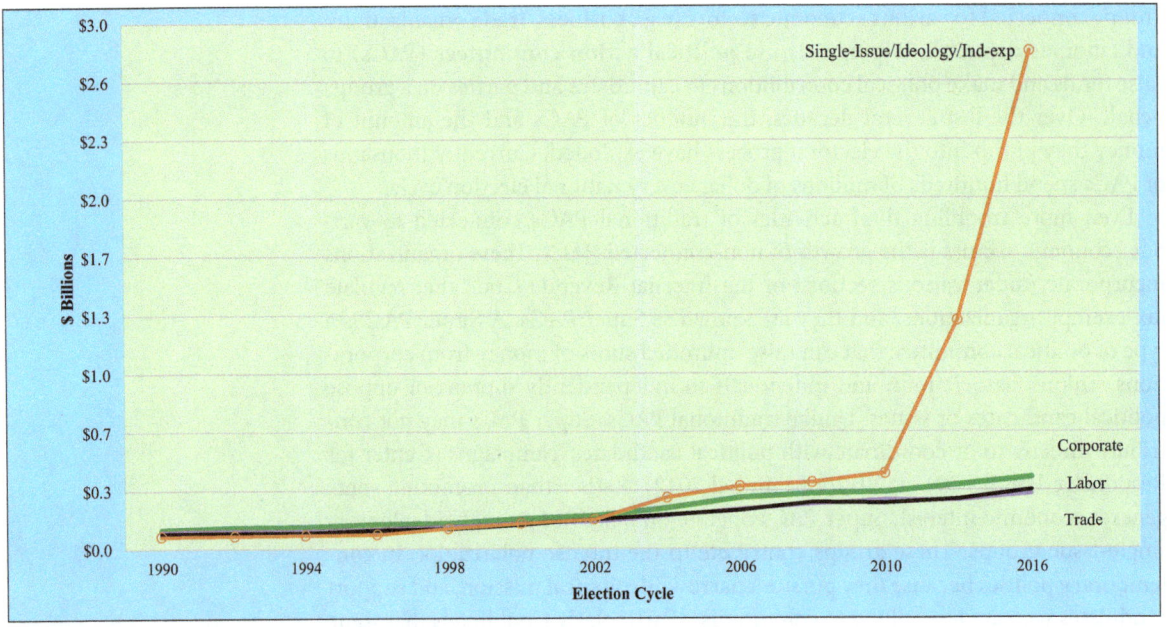

FIGURE 6.3 PAC Spending, 1990–2016

Source: Data from Federal Election Commission reports, http://www.fec.gov/press/bkgnd/cf_summary_info/2010pac_fullsum/4sumhistory2010.xls, http://www.fec.gov/press/summaries/2012/ElectionCycle/PACYE.shtml, and https://www.fec.gov/updates/statistical-summary-24-month-campaign-activity-2015-2016-election-cycle/.

Even if there is no direct connection between money and votes, the primary goal of interest groups is to gain access, and some studies find evidence that contributions do help groups get a foot in the door (Austin-Smith 1995; Grier, Munger, and Roberts 1994; Wright 1990). But other research shows that groups associated with PACs do not have an advantage over constituents in gaining access to elected representatives. A study of who gets appointments with members of the House of Representatives found that "members give priority to constituent requests over PACs" (Chin, Bond, and Geva 2000, 545).

Another common view is that interest groups use their access to pressure elected officials to do their bidding. Indeed, interest groups are often referred to as "pressure groups." Yet systematic research has found very little evidence of group lobbyists pressuring policymakers into doing something they don't want to do. Instead, we find that interest groups spend most of their time talking to friends and allies (Baumgartner et al. 2009; Hojnacki and Kimball 1998). And what do they talk about? Basically, groups provide policymakers with information and political support to help them pursue goals they already agree with (Ainsworth 1997).

Researchers studying the details of how bills are crafted in committee have found evidence that interest group activity does influence public policymaking. This influence, however, turns out to be much less clear-cut than the quid pro quo, or money-for-favors, process often imagined by the general public (R. Smith

THINKING ANALYTICALLY

DOES MONEY BUY ACCESS TO MEMBERS OF CONGRESS?

The growing number of Political Action Committees (PACs) channeling enormous sums of money into the political process raises legitimate concerns about how well representative democracy works in America. Of particular concern is the impression that our representatives pay more attention to rich and powerful interests than to us ordinary folks—their constituents—who elected them. We assume that members of Congress are rational actors who, when presented with choice, will choose the alternative that maximizes their own self-interest. PACs give representatives thousands of dollars to persuade them to look out for some narrow, special interest; all we have to offer in exchange for looking out for our interest is our vote.

What should we look at in order to determine if elected representatives pay more attention to PACs than to constituents? Political scientists' first instinct was to look at how members vote. Yet after dozens of good empirical studies, the evidence that campaign contributions directly influence the votes of elected representatives is mixed and unconvincing. But how representatives vote is not the relevant behavior to study. Lobbyists consistently claim that they just want *access* in order to present their case. Making campaign contributions is a way to establish a relationship with elected representatives and increase the chances that they will get to present their case. So PAC money is not trying to buy votes; it's trying to buy access? If so, that suggests that the really important question is: Do PACs have an advantage over constituents in gaining access to members of Congress?

Analyzing the relationship between money and access using the scientific method is extraordinarily difficult. The basis of the scientific method is systematic observation of some real-world phenomenon. In the study of money and votes, both variables are available in the public record—members must report PAC contributions to the Federal Election Commission, and how they vote is recorded in the Congressional Record. In contrast, meetings take place behind closed doors, so we can't observe who gets to meet with members of Congress or what they talked about. We might be able to get copies of members' schedules to see who they met with and when. But even if we found lots of meetings with PACs, we still wouldn't be able to figure out if PAC requests were granted over those of constituents.

A properly designed field experiment can model the essential elements of the access-granting process. An experiment allows the researcher to manipulate the variables of interest, hold other things constant that might influence choices, and directly observe whether PACs or constituents are more likely to get a meeting. What features of a field experiment would accurately model the access-granting process in Congress and allow a reasonable inference about causation? First, we would need a sample of members that is not significantly different from the membership of Congress on key political factors—Democrats and Republicans, liberals and conservatives, junior and senior members—that might affect decisions to grant access. The sample needs to be large enough to have a reasonable number of cases in each experimental condition.

Second, we would want requests from PACs or constituents to speak to the member about low-visibility, business-oriented issues that could be of interest to any representative, rather than highly charged ideological issues that divide members by party and ideology. Highly visible ideological issues may be the most interesting, but they do not pose the biggest threat to the representation of constituents' interests. Highly charged issues tend to have big money lobbying on both sides, so constituents have a voice regardless of their preference. It's the low visibility issues with lobbying on only one side that pose the biggest threat to PACs pushing constituents out. Third, and most important, the participants need to be actual decision makers, in other words people who actually make choices that determine access to members of Congress. To generalize the findings of this experiment to other members of Congress, we need actual congressional schedulers to participate in the study.

Recruiting political elites like congressional schedulers to take time out of their busy day to participate in an academic study of how they do their job is unusual. But a team of political scientists with contacts to congressional staff members recruited actual schedulers in 69 House offices to participate in an "in-basket" exercise that closely simulated their decision-making situation (Chin, Bond, and Geva 2000). The sample did not differ significantly from the House membership on party, ideology, or seniority. Each in-basket had a partially filled-out schedule for a member of Congress. There were 16 possible requests (13 placebo requests plus the three target requests from either a PAC or a constituent) and only eight available time slots. Each request had a 0.5 probability of being accepted or rejected. The schedulers had to decide whether to accept or deny each request and how to fit accepted requests into the schedule. Participants were randomly assigned to one of the "treatment conditions"—PAC request or constituent request. Random assignment ensures that potentially confounding influences are held constant.

If PAC status affects access, then the mean number of PAC requests granted will be higher than those from non-PAC requests. If constituents have an advantage, then the mean number of constituent requests granted will be significantly higher than those from non-constituents. The figure shows the results of the experiment. The mean number of requests granted was 1.06 for PAC and 1.08 for non-PAC (see panel A); the difference between the two groups is not distinguishable [$F (1, 65) < 1.0$, $p = 0.86$]. There is, however, significant difference for the constituency treatment. Congressional schedulers are more likely to approve requests from constituents (mean 1.63) than similar requests from non-constituents (mean 0.60); the difference is statistically significant [$F (1, 65) = 15.75$, $p = 0.0002$].

Thus, contrary to the perception that PACs buy access to representatives at the expense of constituents, these results suggest that constituency is a more important influence on approval of scheduling requests than is PAC status.

Discussion Questions

1. If someone offered you a scholarship, but required you to take classes and major in something that you really didn't like, what would you do? Does your answer make you more or less likely to believe special interest contributions "buy votes"?
2. Try to come up with another research design to test the hypothesis that PAC contributions influence voting. Assume you have unlimited resources, and try to come up with a design that has good external validity.

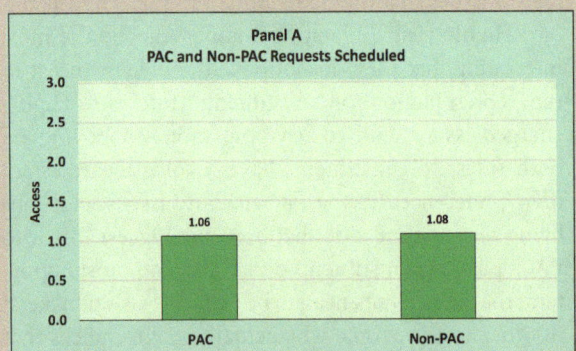
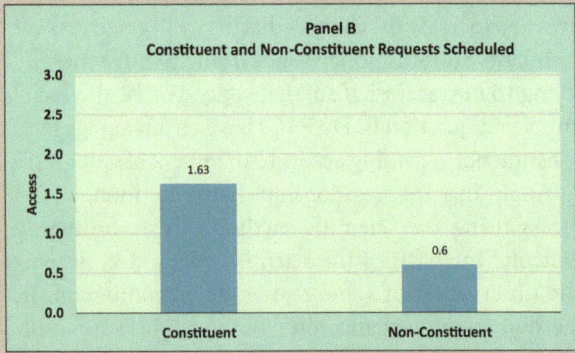

1995). Contributions, direct lobbying, and the various other tactics employed by interest groups can indeed influence what sort of bill comes out of a committee (Hall 1996). But an interest group's chance of getting what it wants depends much more on opposing interest group activity than on the money given to a campaign and the number of direct contacts with an official. A clash of interests and their associated lobbying efforts puts a significant constraint on group influence.

Indeed, a clash of interests can elevate the role of public officials as independent decision makers. Groups opposed to gun control, for example, were able to block or defeat legislation in Congress for many years in part because there was no organized group supporting the legislation. Passage of the Brady Law in 1993, requiring a five-day waiting period to purchase a handgun, came about at least to some extent because lobbying by Handgun Control, Inc., countered efforts by the NRA (Spitzer 1995, chap. 4). Political scientist Diana Evans (1996, 301) concludes that "Far from viewing members of Congress as their pawns, a stereotype evidently cherished by much of the public, lobbyists saw committee leaders as powerful decision-makers, especially in cases of conflict." Though the NRA appears to have regained its clout. After a number of mass shootings since 2010, several killing dozens of schoolchildren, Congress failed to enact any meaningful legislation to reduce such incidents.

But unlike gun control or abortion, most issues do not attract attention and controversy from opposing interests. Rather, most issues draw the attention of a tiny number of groups that may not disagree; on these issues, well-heeled groups use their access to quietly push through specific policy provisions favorable to their interest (Baumgartner and Leech 2001).

Furthermore, interest group success is affected by whether the group is trying to get some new benefit from government or trying to protect benefits it already has. Because governmental power is fragmented and policymaking requires not one but many decisions, groups defending the status quo have an advantage over groups pushing for new benefits. A proposal to provide new benefits must survive multiple decision points in Congress, a possible presidential veto, a likely legal challenge, and numerous smaller decisions in the bureaucracy that will implement the policy. In contrast, groups that would be harmed by the change can defeat, or at least delay, the new policy if they prevail at just one of the many decision points in the process. Research by Frank Baumgartner and his associates replicates the long-known power of the status quo—they found no change at all in about two-thirds of the issues they studied over a four-year period. But an important insight of this research is that when policy change does occur, it tends to be large and substantial rather than incremental (Baumgartner et al. 2009).

A discussion of power in a democratic society also needs to recognize that the relationship between interest groups and public officials is a two-way process: Private groups not only make demands on officials but also serve as potential bases of support for the officials. In other words, interest groups and their lobbyists act as an effective communications vehicle between the broader electorate and government officials. They provide a way for citizens with similar interests to make sure that the government is aware of and responds to their preferences. Interest groups often perform important services for those who are in office, including providing

The NAACP (National Association for the Advancement of Colored People) has served as a communication vehicle between minority groups and government officials for more than 100 years. Because of its long history, the group seeks to protect the advances it has already achieved while still working to eliminate the current adverse effects of racial prejudice and discrimination. Here Rev. Dr. Portia Rochelle, President of the Raleigh-Apex NAACP chapter, speaks before helping to lead a march as part of the Souls to the Polls movement, sponsored by local chapters of the NAACP, to an early voting site in Raleigh, North Carolina, Sunday, March 6, 2016.

© Al Drago/CQ Roll Call/AP Photo

Regulation of Interest Group Activity

Despite concerns about potential corruption, interest groups are only lightly regulated. Because lobbying is part of the rights of free speech, assembly, and petition protected by the First and Fourteenth Amendments, government's ability to regulate interest groups is limited. Congress has placed two types of restrictions on lobbying: (1) limits on the kinds of activities in which interest groups may engage, and (2) requirements that lobbyists and organizations disclose their identity and certain basic facts about their operations. Neither has been effective.

Federal law prohibits bribery; it is unlawful to offer a member of Congress "anything of value" for the purpose of buying a vote or otherwise trying to influence his or her official actions. Legislators who sell their votes are subject to criminal charges. Although the law prohibiting such activity is clear, in practice it is hard to enforce. It is difficult to prove that a favor was tendered for the purposes forbidden by law. For example, it does not constitute bribery for a lobbyist to promise future political support in an attempt to influence how a member of Congress votes. Informing a politician that group members will be happy if the politician votes a particular way is an act of free speech protected by the First Amendment.

In the 1970s, Congress passed legislation requiring lobbyists and interest groups with business before the national legislature to make their financial arrangements a matter of public record. That is, Congress took the approach of illuminating lobbying activities rather than prohibiting them. The **Federal Election Campaign Act (FECA)** in 1971 allowed unions and corporations to form political action committees to raise and contribute campaign funds to candidates. In 1974, Congress amended FECA to create the Federal Election Commission (FEC) to collect and report information on campaign contributions. These amendments limited individual contributions to $1,000 and PAC contributions to $5,000 in each election. The law also tried to place limits on how much a candidate could spend, but the Supreme Court held that mandatory limits on candidate spending violated the First Amendment (*Buckley v. Valeo* 1976). In 1979, campaign finance laws were changed to permit unlimited contributions to political parties for "party-building" activities.

Thus, individual and PAC contributions to candidates were limited; these direct contributions to candidates are known as **hard money**. But candidates—

Federal Election Campaign Act (FECA) A 1971 act that allowed unions and corporations to form political action committees to raise and contribute campaign funds to candidates.

hard money Campaign contributions made directly to candidates and regulated by law.

millionaires, for example—could spend as much of their own money as they wanted, and candidates were free to raise unlimited amounts of hard money as long as it was from individuals and groups that had not already given the maximum. And contributions to political parties for party building were unlimited; such unregulated contributions are called **soft money**.

These efforts to reduce the amount of money spent on campaigns were largely ineffective. Soft money contributions soared in the 1980s and 1990s, and the total amount of hard money contributions also went up as candidates used new techniques, such as direct mail solicitations, to raise huge amounts of money from many small contributions. The most effective feature of FECA was the disclosure requirements: Contributions had to be reported to the FEC, and campaign spending by interest groups and political parties also had to be reported.

Concern over the potentially corrupting influence of all this money in the political arena led to the **Bipartisan Campaign Reform Act (BCRA)** of 2002, better known as the McCain–Feingold Act for its main Senate sponsors, John McCain (R-AZ) and Russell Feingold (D-WI). This law raised limits on hard money contributions during each election cycle to $2,000 from individuals and $5,000 from PACs, but banned soft money. It also restricted "issue ads" run immediately before an election. Issue ads are political commercials run by interest groups that support or oppose some issue (such as abortion, gun rights, or protecting the environment). Numerous interest groups on both the left and the right strongly opposed this provision.

A strange coalition of interests (including the NRA, the NRLC, the American Civil Liberties Union, the AFL-CIO, the Republican National Committee, and the California Democratic Party) challenged the law in court, arguing that it unconstitutionally infringed on basic First Amendment rights of free speech and association. In 2007, the Supreme Court held that restriction on issue ads was an unconstitutional restriction on free speech (*Federal Election Commission v. Wisconsin Right to Life*).

This decision opened legal loopholes that interest groups quickly identified and exploited. One effective way to get around spending limits was the formation of a new type of campaign committee that spent money on issue advocacy, which was not limited, rather than spending to directly advocate the election or defeat of a candidate, which was limited. In 2010, another court decision allowed the formation of Super PACs discussed earlier that raise and spend unlimited amounts of money to support or oppose political candidates. In ***Citizens United v. Federal Election Commission*** (2010), the Supreme Court ruled that corporations, labor unions, and mega-wealthy individuals have a First Amendment right to spend unlimited amounts of money from their general treasuries to convince people to vote for or against some candidate. Although these groups cannot coordinate expenditures with candidates or parties, what does and does not constitute "coordination" is a matter of dispute. Furthermore, campaign staff members often leave the campaign to run a Super PAC, and many of the same individuals donate the maximum amount permitted to the campaign and much larger, unlimited amounts to Super PACs (Kesler, Vance, and Novak 2012; Maguire 2012).

The *Citizens United* decision accounts for the explosive growth in spending by single-issue groups in the 2012 and 2016 elections (see Figure 6.3). These

soft money Campaign contributions given to political parties rather than directly to candidates.

Bipartisan Campaign Reform Act (BCRA) A law that limited hard-money contributions during each election cycle to $2,000 from individuals and $5,000 from PACs, and banned soft money.

Citizens United v. Federal Election Commission A 2010 Supreme Court case holding that corporations, labor unions, and mega-wealthy individuals have a First Amendment right to spend unlimited amounts of money from their general treasuries to convince people to vote for or against some candidate.

independent groups have created the political equivalent of bare-knuckle brawling in high-profile elections. Yet lobbyists who work for special interest groups have incentives to exercise restraint in their attempts to influence policymakers. Despite the lack of effective legal regulation of lobbying, there are informal norms of behavior that most lobbyists follow. Lobbyists desire to protect their reputations with their colleagues and, more importantly, with public officials. Lobbyists who provide false or misleading information to public officials quickly lose the very thing they have worked so hard to achieve: access to those officials. Denial of access is a powerful deterrent to lobbyists who may be tempted to engage in improper activities in order to influence public officials. Lobbyists without access are of no use to their clients.

CHAPTER SIX
Top 10 Takeaway Points

1. An interest group is a politically oriented organization of people who share common attitudes on some matter *and* make demands on society with respect to that matter.

2. Political interest groups pursue two basic objectives: (1) they seek new benefits to promote the group's interest, and (2) they defend current benefits from outside threats to protect the group's interest.

3. People join interest groups for (1) material benefits, which are tangible benefits such as discounts on goods or services; (2) solidary benefits, which are intangible benefits such as the pleasure of socializing with like-minded people; and (3) purposive benefits, which are benefits that transcend the individual and the group and are aimed at others.

4. Many of the benefits that interest groups pursue are "public goods." Once they are provided, public goods are available to everyone and cannot be withheld from those who do not contribute to the cost of providing the good. Interest groups that seek public goods face the problem of free riders. People can receive the benefits of group activity without joining the group or contributing to its operation. Groups seek to avoid free riders through laws that require group membership, selective benefits provided only to group members, and social pressure.

5. Interest groups form in reaction to social or economic events because of the activities of organization entrepreneurs and in response to the carrying capacity of the political environment.

6. The large increase in the number of interest groups in recent years may be a result of the partitioning of a policy niche into groups representing narrower and narrower interests. The partitioning of policy niches increases the carrying capacity of a political environment so that it can support more interest groups competing for the resources they need to survive (such as members and financial contributions).

7. The ability of interest groups to achieve their objectives depends on political resources (membership size, geographical distribution, status, financial capacity, leadership, and expertise) and the success of political tactics (directly lobbying public officials, indirectly lobbying through third parties, mobilizing membership and voter education campaigns, coalition building, shaping public opinion, and involvement in electoral campaigns).

8. Many citizens are concerned about the power of interest groups, and there is a widespread perception that well-organized and well-funded interest groups have undue influence over lawmakers. Most academic research finds little evidence of a quid pro quo, or money-for-votes, relationship between interest groups and policymakers. What powerful interest groups want is to gain access to policymakers and the opportunity to argue their cases.

9. It is difficult to regulate interest group activity, and the regulations that do exist are ineffective. Constitutional guarantees of freedom of speech, freedom of assembly, and the right to petition government for redress of grievances virtually invite organized interest group activity and provide strong protections for it.

10. Rather than preventing or constraining certain actions or behaviors, laws regulating interest groups generally seek to make interest group activity a matter of public record through rules such as financial disclosure requirements. Informal rather than formal regulation tends to restrain flagrantly unethical behavior such as offering bribes to public officials or providing false or misleading information. Such behavior is as likely to result in reducing access to public officials as it is in guaranteeing it.

CHAPTER SIX
Key Terms and Cases

amicus curiae brief, 209
Bipartisan Campaign Reform Act (BCRA), 217
by-product theory, 195
Citizens United v. Federal Election Commission, 217
coalition building, 206
collective action, 192
direct lobbying, 204
exchange theory, 195
Federal Election Campaign Act (FECA), 216
free rider, 192
group entrepreneur, 195
hard money, 216
indirect lobbying, 204
interest group, 187
lobbying, 203
lobbyists, 204
logrolling, 207
material benefits, 190
pluralist explanation, 194
political action committees (PACs), 211
public good, 192
purposive benefits, 191
rational, 190
selective benefits, 193
single-issue groups, 200
soft money, 217
solidary benefits, 190
Super PAC, 211
test case, 208

7 POLITICAL PARTIES

KEY QUESTIONS

What is a political party?

Why are there political parties?

What do parties do, how do they do it, and why?

Do political parties contribute to or undermine representative democracy?

AMERICANS DON'T LIKE POLITICAL PARTIES very much. And we never have. In September 1796, six months before the end of his second term as president, George Washington announced that he would not be a candidate in the upcoming election. In what became known as his Farewell Address (Washington 1796), he set forth his hopes and fears for the young republic. Washington was especially concerned that the nation would be destroyed by the "baneful effects of the spirit of party." He acknowledged that parties might help preserve liberty "in Governments of a Monarchical cast," but "in Governments purely elective, it is a spirit not to be encouraged." He feared that "the spirit of party" in the new American republic would agitate "the community with ill-founded jealousies and false alarms," spread animosity between groups, and foment "occasionally riot and insurrection."

Washington's plea for the political system to turn away from parties went unheeded. As early as the Second Congress (1791–1793), officeholders had splintered into two factions. The Federalists coalesced around the political ideas and agenda of Alexander Hamilton and the Democratic-Republicans gathered around the ideas and agenda of Thomas Jefferson and James Madison. Midway into Washington's second term, both factions were sufficiently organized "to coordinate presidential elections, extend their concern over issues, and capture the affiliation of essentially all national politicians" (Aldrich 2011, 83). By the start of Jefferson's first term, the Federalists and the Democratic-Republicans had transformed themselves from loosely identifiable factions into the progenitors of modern political parties.

Historically, public sentiment about political parties in the United States has largely reflected Washington's initial suspicion and distrust. Scholars and professional political observers, however, argue that in organizing the first recognizable parties, Hamilton, Jefferson, and Madison contributed to the long-term health of the democratic process. Political scientists in particular have largely accepted that parties are a central, and probably necessary, democratic institution. Morris Fiorina (1980) argues that the only way collective responsibility can exist in a democratic political system such as the United States is through political parties. E. E. Schattschneider, one of the best-known political party scholars, put the matter more bluntly: "democracy is unthinkable save in terms of parties" (1942, 1).

THE CONCEPT OF POLITICAL PARTIES

The Challenge of Defining American Political Parties

An immediate problem in studying political parties, especially in the context of American politics, is deciding what exactly is being studied. Students of government have experienced much difficulty defining a political party. Particularly problematic is identifying the features of a political party that distinguish it from related concepts that also help connect citizens to government, such as interest groups.

The definition problem is not new. In *Federalist* Number 10, Madison used three different terms to describe divisions in society. One is *faction,* a concept explored in Chapter 2. Another is *interest,* which Madison calls the most durable source of factions, using as illustrations a manufacturing interest, a mercantile interest, and so on. Madison also refers to the conflict of *parties.* Washington's Farewell Address is similarly vague; his condemnation of the "spirit of party" seems to reflect a general unhappiness with the divisiveness and bickering among citizens rather than a criticism of a particular kind of political organization.

A way to distinguish parties from other political groupings is to define a **political party** as an organization that nominates and runs candidates for office under a party label in pursuit of two goals: (1) to win governmental offices, and (2) to enact policies favored by the party. While political parties sometimes coalesce around an ideology and propose policies consistent with ideological principles, the relative emphasis placed on winning office or enacting policies varies across party systems and over time within party systems. Anthony Downs (1957) viewed parties as teams competing for governmental power. For the two major parties in the United States, winning office is paramount. As Downs observed, "parties formulate policies in order to win elections, rather than win elections in order to formulate policies" (1957, 28).

Comparison of Political Parties and Other Political Groupings

Political parties are similar to interest groups in that both are organizations that engage in political action in pursuit of policy goals. Political parties, however, are not just a type of interest group.

The most important difference distinguishing parties from interest groups is that they use fundamentally different methods to influence the political process. Political parties nominate and run candidates for office under a party label. Interest groups do not run candidates for office but instead use a variety of lobbying techniques, including supporting the election of candidates sympathetic to the group's particular interest.

political party An organization that nominates and runs candidates for office under its own label.

A second difference is that political parties address a broad range of issues, whereas the focus of interest groups is narrower. In order to appeal to a broad electorate, political parties and their candidates must address the full range of large and small issues of concern to voters—foreign affairs, the economy, abortion, gun control, support for classical music, and so on. In contrast, interest groups are more effective if they limit their attention to the few concerns of their members. Individuals participate in interest groups because they share a set of attitudes on some specific matter, such as classical music. Group members agree on their love for classical music and they will support group activities to promote it. But classical music lovers do not necessarily agree on gun control, and if the group takes a position on such an issue, it risks splintering the group.

A third difference is that interest groups are private organizations, whereas parties are quasi-public. This distinction is important because private organizations can establish whatever membership requirements they wish. As private organizations, interest groups can restrict membership by income, professional qualifications, or even gender or race. Public organizations are legally prohibited from enacting such restrictions. Although political parties are not part of government, the U.S. Supreme Court has held that they are quasi-public organizations because they perform a "state function." Thus, according to the Court, the Texas Democratic Party could not declare itself a private club and limit participation in its primaries to white voters (as it once attempted to do), because such action prevented citizens of other races from effective participation in the political process (*Smith v. Allwright* 1944).

Parties also differ from factions. Historically, factions preceded political parties; they were groups of people who joined together on an ad hoc basis to win some political advantage. In the days of a restricted electorate and relatively few elective offices, factions formed around candidates, and they were able to control elections fairly effectively. As the right to vote expanded to include a greater diversity of social groups, more inclusive and permanent organizations became necessary. Particularly important was the task of making clear to voters which candidate represented which group. The crucial step that turned factions into political parties was running candidates for office under a common label.

Today, the term *faction* refers to an informal group that is part of a larger political entity. The term often identifies a segment within a political party based on a personality, a philosophy, or a geographical region. Thus, people speak of the Tea Party faction of the Republican Party or the southern faction of the Democratic Party. In this sense, *faction* is synonymous with *wing* or *division*.

Membership in American Political Parties

Another difficulty in studying parties in the United States is identifying the membership. In contrast to interest groups and political parties in other countries, most Americans do not formally join a political party and pay dues. The French Socialist Party and the American Farm Bureau Federation can quantify with fairly rigorous accuracy their membership; the Republican and Democratic parties in the United States cannot.

THINKING ANALYTICALLY

PARTY ON. AND ON. AND ON: WHY IS IT SO HARD TO GET RID OF POLITICAL PARTIES?

By pretty much any measure, Americans are fed up with political parties. Less than 40 percent of Americans think the two major parties do even an adequate job, and nearly 60 percent would like a viable third choice (Gallup 2016). Not surprisingly, proposals to limit the reach of political parties tend to be pretty popular with the public.

Yet despite the best efforts of many to find alternatives to the existing political party structure, or at least rein in various forms of partisan advocacy, political parties endure. Why? If Americans really do not like political parties that much, or at least do not like the hyper-partisan politics they seem to encourage, what's the best way to reduce the influence of political parties?

That's a tough question to answer. It's not like no one has tried. Especially at the state level, a wide range of reforms with the goal of reducing partisanship in politics has been tried. These include everything from term limits, to limiting party campaign spending, to getting rid of partisan primary elections, to going the whole hog and actually eliminating political parties from the state legislature (Nebraska currently has a nonpartisan legislature, and Minnesota had a nonpartisan legislature for much of the twentieth century).

None of it worked. Political parties just adapt to whatever reform comes down the pike and continue their role as central organizers of American politics. Even in the one still extant nonpartisan state legislature, political parties are active in supporting and bankrolling candidates and many of the legislators make no secret of their partisan affiliations or their pursuit of partisan goals.

What's going on? If Americans genuinely are lukewarm about parties—and arguably plain anti-party—why do parties keep chugging along as the dominant organizational feature of politics? Why on earth is it so hard to chase parties out of the political system?

Well, let's think analytically about this. More specifically, let's question that question. Rather than asking what's the best way to get rid of parties, or at least limit their influence, let's ask what political parties do that is so valuable. After all, parties must be doing something for somebody given that pretty much every attempt to get rid of them has failed.

Political parties clearly provide important services to representative democratic political systems, and you can read about those contributions in-depth in the main text (see the section on "What Political Parties Do"). But let's try to go a bit further than just listing the functions of political party, and get to what political parties are. They are organizations that run people for office under their own label. Who has a real and immediate stake in keeping organizations like that going?

One answer is "policy demanders" (Cohen et al. 2008a). Policy demanders are people who want government to do something—to raise or lower taxes, to increase or decrease regulation, or to spend more money or less money. The range of actions that people want from the government is virtually endless, but the specifics of what actions are being demanded is less important than the demand itself. If you wanted government to do something, what's the best way to go about that? Well, the obvious answer is to get the right people elected to office.

How can you do that? Well, if you've got resources—money, contacts, knowledge, and expertise—the obvious answer is to influence who gets nominated for office. That's important, because if whoever gets elected doesn't get the government action you have the pull to influence their nomination for the next election. Given that elected lawmakers want to be reelected, that gives you leverage to get government to do what you want to do.

It is easier for policy demanders to wield influence through political parties' prepacked nomination processes and, let's not forget, actually run the government. Political parties, in short, are pretty useful for policy demanders. Indeed, some political scientists say policy demanders effectively *are* political parties: "Whoever can credibly claim to have determined a nomination, be it a legislative caucus or the attendees at a convention or a shadowy group of business elites, is the party for all intents and purposes" (Masket 2016, p. 21).

If that's the case, it becomes clearer why political parties are so resilient and resistant to attempts to limit their role in politics. As long as representative democracy exists, there are always going to be coalitions of like concerns with the interest and resources to seek influence over who gets nominated to office. That's getting pretty close to the definition of what a political party is, which helps explain why political parties are so, so hard to get rid of.

Discussion Questions

1. Most Americans favor the creation of a third major party. Assuming this is possible, what are the advantages and disadvantages of having a competitive third party? Would this make politics more or less partisan? Why or why not?
2. How would you identify the policy demanders in your state or congressional district? Who is recruiting and providing major support for candidates? How much influence do they have over nominations?

Political scientist V. O. Key (1964) suggested a way to overcome this problem. Key defined political parties in terms of three distinct elements associated with different activities:

1. Party in the electorate
2. Party in government
3. Party organization

The **party in the electorate** consists of ordinary citizens who identify with the party and who usually support the party's candidates with votes and occasionally with campaign contributions. Although these partisan supporters are most active at election time, they tend to hold similar views on many political issues in periods between elections.

The **party in government** is the elected and appointed officeholders at the national, state, and local levels who are considered representatives of the party. Because partisans in different branches and levels of government share a party label and have similar views on many issues, they often use their official powers to pursue common policies.

The **party organization** refers to more or less professional party officials and workers, including those who hold a party office (e.g., convention delegates and national, state, and county party chairs and party committee members), and party activists (e.g., professional campaign consultants, financial donors, and unpaid volunteers) who provide a variety of essential resources to the party organization and candidates mostly during elections.

Incentives for Associating With Political Parties

The incentives for associating with political parties are similar to those for interest groups: material benefits, solidary benefits, and purposive benefits. Political

---

party in the electorate The component of a political party that is made up of the people in the public who identify with a political party.

party in government The component of a political party that is made up of elected and appointed government officeholders who are associated with a political party.

party organization The component of a political party that is composed of the party professionals who hold official positions in the party.

scientists classify people who participate in party activities into two major categories based on their primary motivation: (1) **party professionals**, whose incentives for participating are primarily material and social in nature (J. Wilson 1962), and (2) **policy-motivated activists** (Aldrich 2011, 187–188), whose incentives are primarily purposive and social. These two types of party activists hold different views about compromise, political patronage, and the internal governance of the party.

The material incentives that motivate party professionals to participate in politics include tangible rewards, such as patronage jobs and government contracts. These individuals are also motivated by social incentives. In general, they get satisfaction from the game of politics for its own sake—the quest for victory, the maneuvering for advantage, and the camaraderie of working and socializing with other party members. They like the exercise of political power and the deference paid to them because of the positions they hold and the influence they wield.

The professionals tend to place great emphasis on winning elections, mainly because their jobs and livelihood depend on it. Although they may personally favor a particular program, party professionals evaluate policy primarily in terms of whether it can attract political support. If a policy threatens to cost the party an electoral victory, professionals will work to moderate the party's position or even abandon the policy altogether. Professionals understand the importance of compromise in politics and are tolerant of people who differ on political matters. As for the internal operation of the political party, professionals expect it to be an oligarchy in which the people in top positions make the decisions (Aldrich 2011; J. Wilson 1962).

The prototype of a party organization run by professionals was the old-time political machine. A **political machine** is a party organization headed by a "party boss"; political machines and party bosses maintained power and control over government offices with such techniques as control over nominations, patronage, graft and bribery, vote buying, and rigging elections (Plano and Greenberg 2002, 111). The political organization also sponsored picnics, beer parties, and other events for supporters, many of whom were immigrants looking for new friends and social outlets. In return, the boss received votes from the recipients of this largess, political contributions from those on the public payroll (usually a set percentage of their salary known as a "lug"), and kickbacks from those with government contracts.

In contrast, policy-motivated activists are less concerned with using political parties to further their own interests; instead, they want to use parties to help other individuals or groups or society in general. They believe in certain principles and are dedicated to implementing those principles in public policies—for example, banning abortion or protecting the environment. Party activists of this kind are also referred to as "amateurs" (J. Wilson 1962), "purists" (Polsby and Wildavsky 2000, 44; Wildavsky 1965), and "intense policy demanders" (Cohen et al. 2008a). Unlike the "professionals," who must win in order to get the material benefits that motivate them (government jobs and contracts), these activists get satisfaction from doing the right thing as they see it and supporting candidates who agree with their policy goals. All else being equal, policy-motivated activists prefer to be on the winning side, but they would rather support a loser who espouses their principles

party professionals Party activists whose incentives for participating in party activities are primarily material and social in nature.

policy-motivated activists Party activists whose incentives for participating in party activities are primarily purposive and social. They are dedicated to implementing certain principles in public policies, and they are less willing to compromise those principles than are party professionals.

political machine A political organization characterized by a reciprocal relationship between voters and office holders. Political support is given in exchange for government jobs and services. Headed by a "party boss," political machines and party bosses maintain their power and control over government offices with techniques such as control over nominations, patronage, graft and bribery, vote buying, and election-rigging.

role theory A behavioral model of politics based on the assumption that human beings have a psychological need for predictability in their relations with each other.

APPLYING THE FRAMEWORKS

WHY PARTIES?

If the Founders of American representative democracy loathed parties so much, why did they form them? Were they just a bunch of unprincipled hypocrites? Perhaps they were, but making that determination is based on value judgments, not science. How can science explain the formation of political parties and the distinct party systems just described?

Political scientists turned first to sociology. V. O. Key's explanation of political parties suggests an answer based on *functionalism* and *role theory*. Functionalism is a broad framework that seeks to explain how entire societies achieve stability. The general idea is that various elements of complex societies—norms, customs, and institutions—each perform a function and work together to promote stability. **Role theory** is a model of individual behavior based on the assumption that human beings have a psychological need for predictability in their relations with each other. This need for predictability leads to the creation of roles—patterns of behavior that society generally expects of particular individuals based on their role.

Key's theory is that political parties perform a number of roles—recruit candidates, engage in activities to mobilize and influence voters, and coordinate the actions of those who get elected to office. As parties perform these roles, they develop into institutions that serve an important social function that makes popular government possible. In particular, Key (1964, 201) argued that popular government "compelled deference to popular views, but it also required the development of organization to communicate with and to manage the electorate." Functionalism has been criticized as overly concerned with stability. The focus on stability cannot explain the different party systems observed in America.

More recently, political scientists have turned to rational choice theory to explain political parties. John Aldrich's (2011, 19) answer to the "Why parties?" question is that ambitious politicians create political parties "to solve problems that current institutional arrangements do not solve." Collective action problems are the most pervasive. Aldrich identifies three distinct party systems in American history that evolved to address different problems.

The first party system—Federalists vs. Jeffersonian Democratic-Republicans—was created by ambitious politicians to solve the instability of voting in the early Congresses. The collective action problem that political parties solved was organizing government in the pursuit and adoption of particular policy agendas. The driving force behind the Federalists agenda was Hamilton, and Washington was its popular leader. Madison, who was serving in Congress, and Jefferson, who resigned from the Washington administration in 1793 over the national bank issue, organized the Democratic-Republican opposition.[1]

The second party system—one of mass electoral parties—was created to help mobilize a diverse and expanding electorate. It worked. In the election of 1824, voter turnout was less than 30 percent. Andrew Jackson won a popular vote plurality but failed to win a majority of electoral votes. Four years later, with the help of the new mass-based Democratic Party, voter turnout rose to over 50 percent and Jackson won the presidency. This success bred competition. The Whigs emerged as a competing mass-based party to the Democrats, and in 1840 voter turnout climbed to over 78 percent (Aldrich 2011, 104) as the Whig candidate, William Henry Harrison, won the presidency. The Whigs success was short-lived; they were replaced by yet another mass-based party, the Republican Party. The Republican Party ran its first presidential candidate, General John Fremont, in 1856. Since then, the Democratic and

---

[1] The label "Democratic-Republican" may be somewhat confusing. The party has also been referred to as the Anti-Federalist Party, the Jeffersonian Republican Party, and the Republican Party. The label used here is traced to a later incarnation of the Democratic Party during the Jackson administration that claimed to resurrect the Republican principles of Jefferson and Madison (Aldrich 2011, 331n10).

Republican parties have dominated American politics in the oldest continuous two-party competition in the world.

The third party system is candidate-centered. Although the party names remain the same and competition is still between two major parties, changes in the nature of the Republican and Democratic parties in the 1960s resulted in a different type of party system. In this system, parties do not dominate the candidates, but rather the party machinery has been taken over by policy-motivated activists who use the party to serve their needs. Although technological innovations make it possible for candidates to run their own campaigns, party organizations continue to provide resources and services candidates need. It's much less costly for ambitious politicians to take over existing party machinery than to create their own new machinery, and policy-oriented activists assist in this takeover (Aldrich 2011, chap. 6).

Thus, rather than viewing parties as a system of roles that constrain behavior and perform certain functions for society, rational choice theory explains parties as the result of the rational choices that ambitious politicians make to solve collective action problems. From this perspective, the Framers were pragmatic politicians who made choices to solve collective action problems so the new republic could work.

Discussion Questions

1. Does role theory or rational choice theory better explain the formation of parties? Why?
2. Can role theory and rational choice theory be complementary? In other words, is it rational to create roles?

than a winner who does not. Compared to professionals, policy-motivated activists are less willing to compromise their principles and the policies that follow from them (Cohen et al. 2008a). In actual party organizations, few individuals perfectly fit either category. So-called political professionals, for example, care about ideology and policy, and policy-motivated activists will compromise, especially if the choice is achieving part of their goals or nothing. In addition, the tools and activities of party professionals have changed over the years. Machine politics have waned as a result of reform movements. Modern party leaders continue to focus on winning elections, but they use public polling, computer technology, modern fundraising techniques, and media campaigns to build and maintain party organizations. And just as parties change, so do individuals: Policy-motivated activists evolve into professionals of sorts, though they are a different kind of professional than those old machine politicians (Aldrich 2011).

Nonetheless, the primary political orientation of many people and organizations can be characterized as essentially professional or policy-motivated in nature. Assessments of American political parties often turn on whether they are judged by the standards of a political professional or a policy-motivated activist.

TWO-PARTY COMPETITION IN AMERICAN POLITICS

Figure 7.1 provides an overview of American party competition since 1789. Except for Federalist dominance under George Washington and Democratic-Republican dominance during the era of good feeling in the 1820s, American politics has been

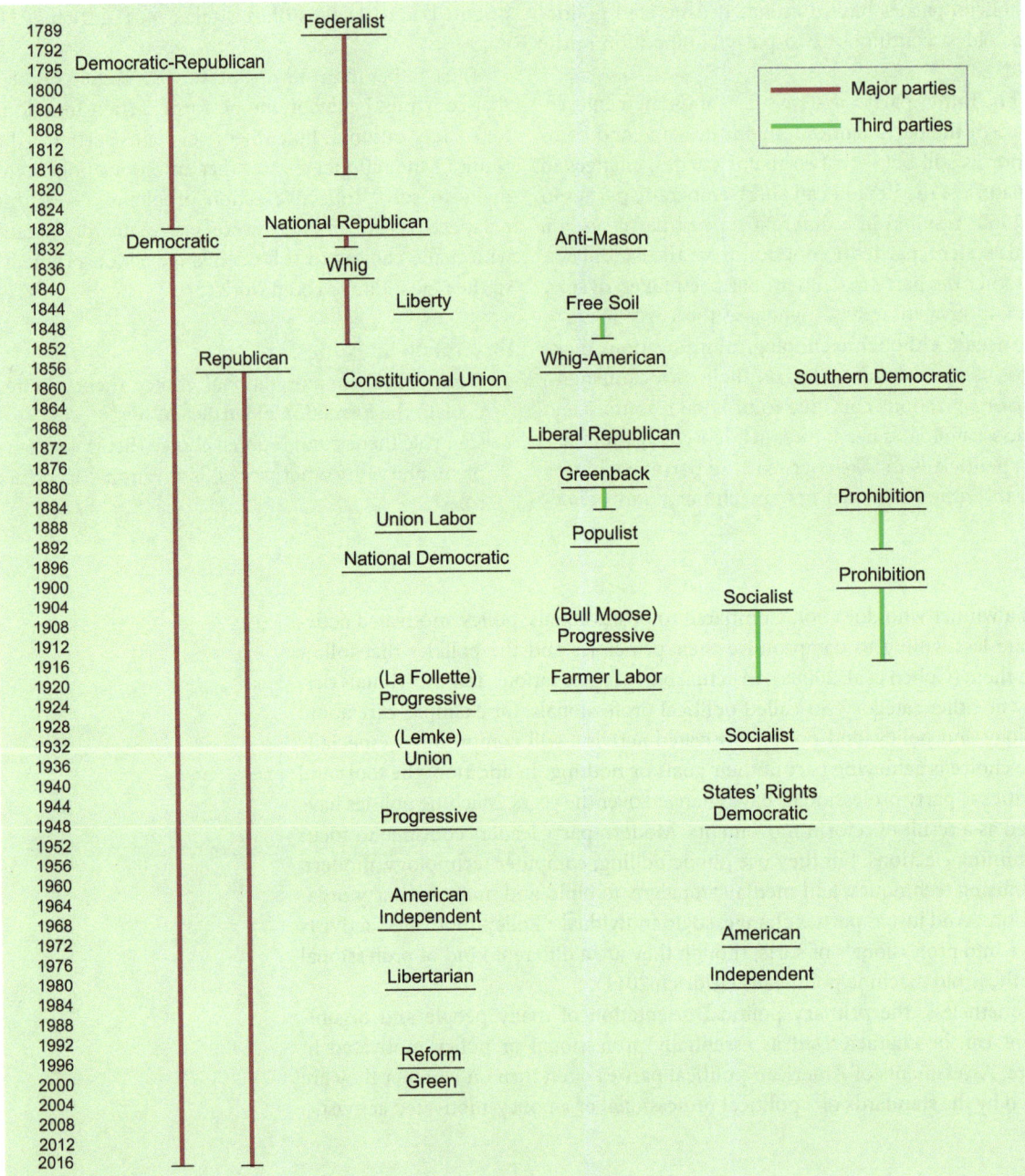

FIGURE 7.1 American Political Parties Since 1789

Note: In 1824 and later, the chart indicates the years in which the presidential candidate of a political party received 1 percent or more of the popular vote. Minor parties are not included if the minor party candidate is also the candidate of one of the two major parties (as happened in 1896, when the Populists endorsed William Jennings Bryan, the Democratic candidate). Party candidates sometimes run under different designations in different states (in 1968 George C. Wallace ran for president under at least 10 party labels). In such cases the vote totals for the candidate were aggregated under a single party designation. Sometimes candidates run under no party label, as H. Ross Perot did in 1992. (In 1996, Perot ran under the Reform Party label.)

Source: Stanley and Niemi (2013, figs 1–3, 10), adapted and updated by the authors.

characterized by competition between two major parties. Although minor parties have run candidates and have occasionally had an important influence, none has seriously threatened to replace a major party.

The General Types of Party Systems

Political scientists distinguish three types of party systems based on the number of parties—one party, two parties, or multiple parties—that effectively compete for power. In a **one-party system**, representatives of a single political party hold all or almost all of the major offices in government. This condition may prevail where only one party is legally permitted to run candidates, as in Nazi Germany and fascist Italy in the 1930s. Political systems that prevent opposition parties from competing for power are not democratic. There have been political systems in which opposition parties are legally recognized, but one party dominates electoral contests. In Mexico, for example, the Institutional Revolutionary Party (PRI) won election after election against weak opposition for about 70 years until Vicente Fox Quesada of the National Action Party (PAN) won the presidency in 2000. Democrats enjoyed the same sort of electoral dominance in southern states from the end of Reconstruction until the 1970s. Electoral competition in one-party democracies tends to be among factions within the dominant party.

Most contemporary democracies are **multiparty systems**, in which three or more parties effectively compete for political offices, and no single party can win sole control of the government. Multiparty systems are common in parliamentary systems in which the legislature chooses the leaders of the executive branch. These political systems typically have ruling coalitions. In other words, parties combine to form a government and divide up cabinet seats among parties in the governing coalition. Examples include Germany, Japan, and Israel.

Under a **two-party system**, only two political parties have a realistic chance of winning a significant number of major political offices. Each party is capable of capturing enough offices to govern, but the opposition party continues to obtain a sufficiently large enough vote to threaten the tenure of the majority party. As a result, public officials of both stripes must take public wishes into account or risk losing to the opposition party in the next election. Such a system works best if the opposition threat is at least occasionally successful, so that the parties alternate in governing. Two-party competition characterizes fewer than 30 percent of the world's democracies. In a comparative study of political parties, Arend Lijphart (1984) found that only six of the 21 nations that have been continuously democratic since the end of World War II have two-party systems: Australia, Austria, Canada, the United Kingdom, New Zealand, and the United States. The tendency of democracies to have multiparty systems continues to hold today, though it may have weakened somewhat since Lijphart's analysis.

American Party Competition at the National Level

The long-term rivalry between the Republican and Democratic parties clearly meets the requirements of two-party competition. From 1856 to the present, each

one-party system A political system in which representatives of one political party hold all or almost all of the major offices in government.

multiparty system A political system in which three or more political parties effectively compete for political office, and no one party can win control of all.

two-party system A political system in which only two political parties have a realistic chance of controlling the major offices of government.

of these two parties, and only these two, has won control of the major institutions of the national government—the presidency, the House, and the Senate. Figure 7.2 illustrates this close competition with plots of the percentage of presidential and congressional elections each party won during each decade of this period.[2] In presidential elections, Republicans were successful in 59 percent of the elections and Democrats in 41 percent. The figure clearly shows the Republican advantage in competition for the presidency. Nonetheless, Democrats show up as competitive players throughout the period.

The competition every two years for control of Congress has been even closer. In congressional elections since 1856, Democrats have won control of both the House and Senate in 34 elections (44.6 percent), and Republicans have won both in 31 elections (39.7 percent); in 13 elections (16.7 percent), Republicans have controlled one chamber, and Democrats have controlled the other. Thus, both Republicans and Democrats have been able to win political power in both the executive and legislative branches of government.

Even in defeat, the major parties still muster substantial political support. Landslide presidential elections (those in which the winner gets at least 60 percent of the vote) were rare in the twentieth century. There were only four: Warren Harding in 1920, Franklin Roosevelt in 1936, Lyndon Johnson in 1964, and Richard Nixon in 1972.[3] The popular vote for control of the House has been even closer. The losing party received less than 40 percent of the vote only twice—in 1920, when the Democrats lost, and in 1936, when the Republicans lost.

Although Democrats and Republicans have been able to oust each other from office at fairly frequent intervals, there have been notable periods of one-party dominance. Republicans largely dominated the executive from 1860 to 1932, with only two Democrats, Grover Cleveland and Woodrow Wilson, winning the presidency during that period (see Figure 7.2a). For the next 20 years, Democrats held the presidency. Similar one-party eras have occurred in Congress. Most notably, the Democrats had majorities in the House of Representatives from 1955 to 1995. On balance, however, the roughly equal division of major party victories over 150 years of competition, the close split of popular votes, and the relatively frequent alternation in power place the United States squarely in the two-party category.

If most democracies are multiparty systems, why does the United States have a two-party system? Scholars have identified several possible causes.

Historical Factors

One reason for the formation of a two-party system in the United States is the early division of political loyalties into two broad groups. As discussed in Chapter 2,

---

2 We define decades in terms of congressional apportionment periods. The end point of a decade is the year in which the decennial census is taken—that is, years ending in "0"—and the beginning of the next decade is the year ending in "2," the first election after reapportionment. The first period is less than 10 years because the Republican Party did not compete in all the elections between 1852 and 1860. The most recent decade ended in 2010, and 2012 is the start of the current one that will end in 2020.
3 Ronald Reagan came close with 59.2 percent in 1984, and that election is sometimes considered a landslide.

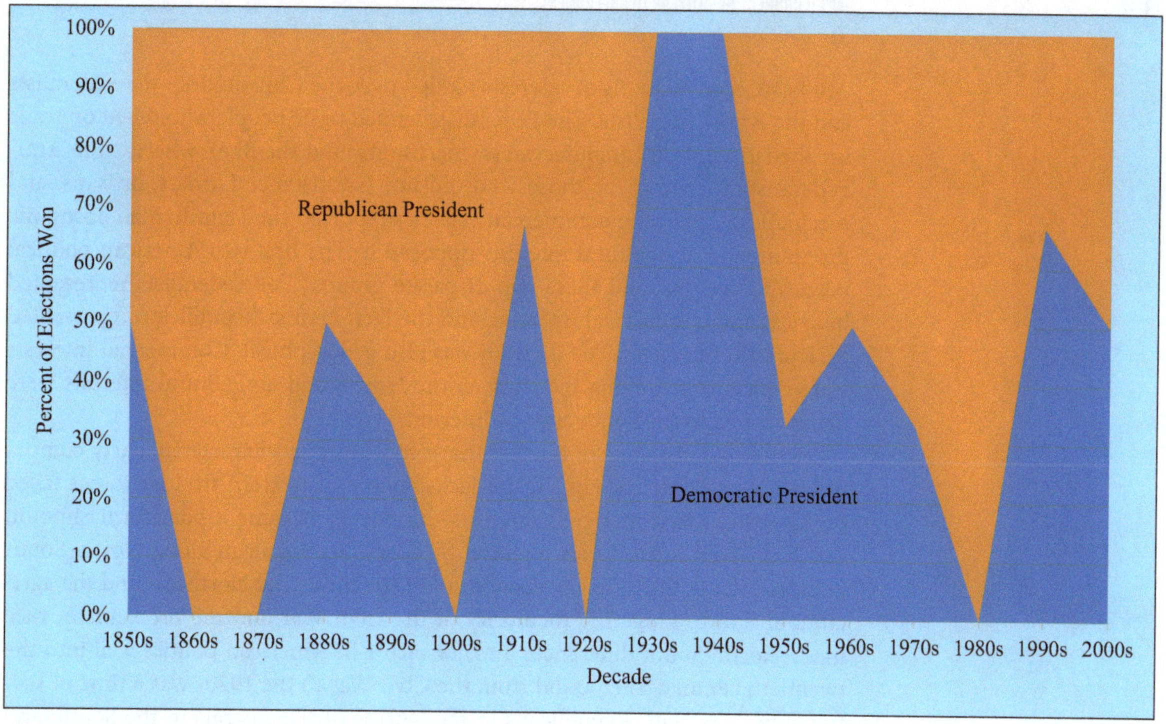

FIGURE 7.2a Competition for Presidency

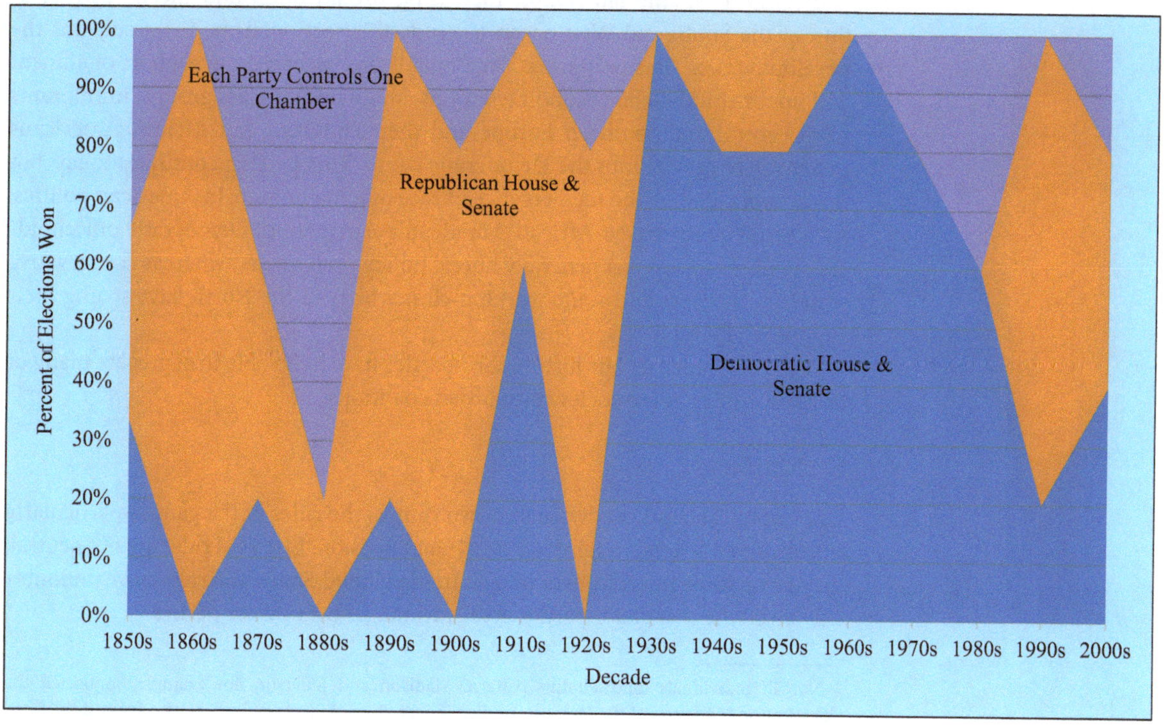

FIGURE 7.2b Competition for Congress

two basic constellations of interests battled over the Constitution: the Federalists and the Anti-Federalists. The Federalists tended to be people who relied on trade for their livelihood (manufacturers, merchants, and the like), whereas the Anti-Federalists tended to be those who did not (subsistence farmers, artisans, and mechanics). Later, the commercial classes supported the Hamiltonian economic program, and agricultural interests opposed it. The first two American political parties formed around these two disparate groups: The Federalists represented business and commercial interests, and the Democratic-Republicans represented agricultural interests.[4] The division was also geographical: Commercial interests were concentrated along the coast in the North, and agricultural interests were concentrated in the South and the interior.

Two broad divisions of interests have continued to characterize party competition in the United States. In the Jacksonian era, western frontier forces faced off against eastern moneyed interests. As slavery became a political flashpoint, this East–West schism was replaced by a new sectionalism along North–South lines, reflecting the differing economies of the industrial Northeast and the agricultural South. Lingering memories of the Civil War and the problems of race made North–South differences a major factor in American politics well into the twentieth century. The period from the Civil War to the 1920s was a time of sectional politics, with Republicans in the Northeast, Democrats in the South, and both vying for support in the West and Midwest, regions that held the balance of political power between the two parties.

Beginning in the late 1920s, increasing urbanization and the industrialization of the South and West began to erode this sectionalism. The result was the development of class politics, as the Republicans gathered the support of affluent and upper-middle-class economic groups, and working-class groups, immigrants from central and southern Europe and their children, and African Americans increasingly moved into the Democratic camp. This pattern continues today, but it is complicated by the reemergence of race as a major issue in American politics. As a result of increased African American participation, Democratic officeholders are likely to support generally liberal policy preferences, whereas conservative white southerners and some working-class whites in the North have swung their support to Republicans.

Thus, for much of our history, two parties have been able to aggregate many of the major interests in society into broad coalitions.

Electoral Rules

Once political conflicts divide into two camps, the rules of the game—particularly electoral rules—tend to reinforce that initial division. Electoral rules are not neutral; they favor some interests over others. In the United States, the rules have undoubtedly given the two major parties great advantages over minor parties.

---

4 Not all individuals followed this pattern. Madison and Jefferson, for example, supported the Constitution but founded the Democratic-Republican Party. Still, most leaders who favored the Constitution associated with the Federalist Party, whereas Anti-Federalists typically became Democratic-Republicans.

French sociologist Maurice Duverger documented a strong connection between the electoral system and the number of parties. Most liberal democracies use multimember constituencies and **proportional representation**, in which parties win seats in the legislature in proportion to their share of the popular vote. The United States uses the **single-member district plurality (SMDP) system**, in which the candidate with the most votes wins the seat and other parties get none. Proportional representation fosters many parties because parties can win some seats with a small proportion of votes, whereas a plurality winner-take-all system favors a two-party system because parties that consistently come in second win no seats (Duverger 1972, 23–32). This relationship is known as **Duverger's Law**.

Political scientists have found evidence that democracies using proportional representation tend to have multiparty systems, whereas democracies that use the plurality winner-take-all method tend to have two-party systems (e.g., Lijphart 1984), but there is not a law-like one-to-one relationship. Furthermore, Josep Colomer argues that Duverger's Law has the causal direction upside down. He argues that because political parties exist before elections, rational actors choose the electoral system that maximizes their chance of winning. If one party has sufficient support to get a majority, then a plurality electoral system is the rational choice. On the other hand, if support is distributed so that no party can be sure of winning a majority, then proportional representation makes the most sense. Thus, "it is the number of parties that can explain the choice of electoral systems, rather than the other way round" (Colomer 2005, 1).

The method of choosing the chief executive also influences the number of parties. The **parliamentary system** typical of other representative democracies encourages multiple parties. In a parliamentary system, the party that controls the majority of legislative seats chooses the chief executive (usually called the prime minister or premier). The prime minister then forms a government by appointing individuals to run the various government departments or ministries—secretary of defense, foreign secretary, interior secretary, and so on. Since minor parties often win seats in parliament, sometimes no party controls a majority of the seats. When no party has a majority of the seats, the leader of one of the parties will try to form a coalition government by offering cabinet seats to other parties in return for their support. As partners in majority coalitions, minor party representatives can end up in posts of central importance in running the government.

In contrast, the United States uses a **presidential system**, in which the chief executive and the legislature are elected independently. The system used to choose the U.S. president provides a distinct advantage to the two major parties. As we explain in Chapter 10, the president is not chosen directly by the popular vote but by the electoral college. The Constitution allocates each state one electoral vote for each of its representatives in Congress; a candidate must receive a majority (270) to win the presidency.[5] The state legislature decides how electors will be chosen

proportional representation A method of selecting representatives in which representation is given to political parties based on the proportion of the vote obtained. This method facilitates the emergence of multiple parties.

single-member district plurality (SMDP) system A method of selecting representatives in which a nation or state is divided into separate election districts and voters in each district choose one representative. The candidate in each district with a plurality of the vote wins the seat. This winner-take-all method tends to hinder the development of third parties.

Duverger's Law The tendency, as documented by French sociologist Maurice Duverger, for the single-member district plurality system to favor a two-party system.

parliamentary system An electoral system in which the party holding the majority of seats in the legislature selects the chief executive.

presidential system A political system in which the chief executive and the legislature are elected independently.

---

5 There are 538 electoral votes: one for each senator (100), one for each House seat (435), and 3 for Washington, DC.

(currently by popular vote in all states). Parties nominate partisan slates of electors, and the slate that gets the most votes casts all of the state's electoral votes for the party's nominee. Thus, electoral votes are allocated on a winner-take-all basis to the candidate who wins a plurality of the votes in the state. Although third party and independent candidates occasionally attract significant popular support nationwide, they often receive no electoral votes because they do not win a plurality in any state. For example, Ross Perot received roughly 19 percent of the popular vote in 1992, but not a single electoral vote. A party that has no chance of winning the nation's highest office is unlikely to be an enduring force in the nation's politics.

In addition, state laws regulating access to the ballot are a considerable obstacle to minor parties. Candidates of the two major parties automatically appear on the ballot in every state. Minor parties do not get automatic access. To appear on the ballot, minor parties typically must submit a petition signed by a number of registered voters equal to 2 or 3 percent of votes cast in the last election. This procedure requires considerable organizational and financial resources. If a minor party does qualify for ballot access in a state, it may have to repeat this arduous process if it fails to draw a minimum percentage of the vote (usually 5 percent). Laws regulating who is listed on the ballot are thus a significant handicap for third parties.[6]

The legal obstacles facing minor parties are typically justified as means for protecting the electoral process from frivolous candidates and parties. Many Americans do not consider making it difficult for "nuts and crackpots" to get on the ballot to be a serious threat to political freedom. Giving free ballot access to anyone who wants to run for office would increase the costs of administering elections and confuse voters rather than offer real choices. But since most Americans identify with one of the two major parties, this view can be seen as self-interested. Supporters of minor party candidates do not consider their proposals frivolous. They claim that Democrats and Republicans, who control the institutions that write the rules, have used that power to limit competition in order to protect themselves.

Natural Perpetuation of the Two-Party System

Another cause of the two-party system is a set of mechanisms that tend to make it self-perpetuating. As we will see in Chapter 9, people often develop an attachment to a political party at an early age, and the attachment deepens during their adult lives. In a society where two parties have been dominant for more than a century, it is natural for most citizens to think of themselves as Republican or Democrat. In other words, traditional party patterns embedded in the political socialization process perpetuate the two-party system.

Although minor parties regularly nominate candidates in federal and state elections, only the Republican and Democratic parties have a realistic chance of winning any offices. Ambitious politicians who aspire to political office realize that

---

6 A party that fails to qualify to have its candidates listed on the ballot can encourage write-in votes, but it is hard to get voters to support candidates who are not listed on the ballot.

without one of these labels, their chances of fulfilling their ambitions are small. Not surprisingly, political talent gravitates toward the two major parties rather than to minor parties.

The two-party system also perpetuates itself by channeling political conflict into two major outlets: the organization in power and the one out of power. Support for and opposition to the government thus coalesce into two distinct groups. Citizens unhappy with the status quo vote not only against present officeholders but also for candidates of the other major party because that is the only viable alternative to replace the party in power.

Minor Political Parties

Although America is clearly a two-party system, minor or **third parties**[7] have appeared often throughout our history (as Figure 7.1 illustrates). Despite never capturing a significant number of offices, third parties have occasionally had a considerable effect on American politics.

As political scientists John Bibby and L. Sandy Maisel point out, two-party politics is not mandated by the Constitution, and public opinion polls consistently find that "voters express a distaste for the major parties" and want an alternative (1998, 3–4). In the 1990s, voters awarded independent presidential candidate Ross Perot significant portions of the popular vote in two consecutive elections, and they elected independent and minor party governors in Maine (Angus King), Connecticut (Lowell Weicker), Alaska (Walter Hickel), and Minnesota (Jesse Ventura). In 2012 there was a concerted attempt to challenge the two-party system. Americans Elect was a nonprofit organization dedicated to running an online presidential primary, with the winner gaining ballot access in all 50 states. The effort was backed by some serious money—tens of millions of dollars were spent— and the idea seemed like it should appeal to an electorate supposedly craving an end to two-party politics. The effort fizzled; dozens of candidates were drafted, but none could reach the minimum levels of support the organization required to get onto the online primary ballot. Unable to hold a primary, Americans Elect could not field a candidate.

American political history is littered with minor parties and independent candidacies. Some, such as the Anti-Masonic Party of the 1830s, contested a single presidential election and disappeared almost immediately. Others, such as the Socialist Party, have fielded candidates in a hopeless electoral cause for a number of years. The Prohibition Party began running presidential candidates in 1872 and was still contesting the nation's highest office in the mid-1990s. The Communist Party of the 1920s sought a radical overhaul of the entire economic and political structure. The Libertarian Party seeks a drastic reduction of the level of governmental involvement in the economy and in individual lives. Although seldom

---

7 Although minor parties are commonly referred to by this term, there are typically more than three parties with candidates on the ballot. It would be more precise to label them "third," "fourth," or "fifth" parties depending on their relative electoral strength.

third parties Minor political parties that periodically appear but have little success in winning office.

getting more than 1 percent of the popular vote, the Libertarian candidate has been on the ballot in all 50 states in every presidential election since 1972.

The most notable recent third party movement sprang from Ross Perot's independent presidential bid in 1992. The organizational effort associated with this candidacy served as the genesis of a genuine third party—the Reform Party—that backed Perot's run for the presidency in 1996, and it ran 22 congressional candidates in the 1998 elections. It did not elect any members to Congress, but former professional wrestler Jesse Ventura was elected governor of Minnesota under its label. The Reform Party's promise to be an alternative to the major parties fizzled. Its major issue—a growing budget deficit—evaporated with the appearance of a balanced federal budget, and its "angry middle" constituency disappeared in the economic good times of the mid-1990s (Sifry 1998). Nonetheless, the Reform Party illustrates a common complaint of minor parties in American politics: a feeling that the two major parties are not adequately addressing some key concerns and frustrations of voters.

Goals and Types of Minor Parties

Some minor parties have introduced ideologies from Europe that challenge America's traditional commitment to free-enterprise economics. These include the Socialist Party, which has advocated public ownership of basic industries; the Socialist Labor Party, which sought to eliminate the capitalist system through essentially peaceful means; and the Communist Party, a group founded in 1919 that had close ties to the now-defunct Soviet Union. Of the three, the Socialist Labor Party was the longest-lived, running a presidential candidate in every election between 1896 and 1976. The Socialist Party has been the biggest vote-getter, pulling in 6 percent of the popular vote in 1912. The Communist Party's electoral forays have been sporadic and uniformly hopeless. The party's highest vote total was 100,000 in 1932, but this pales in comparison to the 23 million voters who chose the Democratic candidate, Franklin Roosevelt.

The most successful minor parties have protested economic injustices, but they promoted an ideology indigenous to America rather than imported from Europe. The Populists, for example, emerged during the 1890s, proposing free and unlimited coinage of silver, a graduated income tax, public ownership of railroads, an expansion of the money supply, and other measures designed to break the financial hold of the industrial East over the producers of raw materials. In 1892, the Populists received 8.5 percent of the popular vote and 22 electoral votes.

The Progressives were perhaps the most successful third party movement of the twentieth century. The Progressive movement, best known for attacks on abuses of both economic and political power, emerged from the liberal wing of the Republican Party. It proposed government regulation of monopolies and championed direct democracy reforms such as the initiative (a way for citizens to propose and enact legislation), the referendum (referring proposed laws to the electorate for the ultimate decision), and the recall (permitting citizens to oust unsatisfactory officeholders between elections). A second Progressive movement focused on the farmer and echoed the earlier Populist movement. Both Theodore Roosevelt (1912) and Robert La Follette (1924) ran for president under the Progressive label with some success. Roosevelt came in second with 27.4 percent of the popular vote and received 88 electoral votes; La Follette picked up 16.6 percent of the popular vote and got 13 electoral votes.

Racial conflict spawned intra-party competition in the decades following World War II. In 1948, a group of dissident Democrats bolted from their party's national nominating convention over the issue of civil rights. They formed the States' Rights Democratic Party, widely known as the Dixiecrat Party, and nominated J. Strom Thurmond of South Carolina and Fielding Wright of Mississippi as candidates for president and vice president. Twenty years later, a third party with similar racial views, headed by former Alabama governor George Wallace, ran candidates under the label of the American Independent Party. Both of these minor parties carried several southern states in presidential elections. The Dixiecrat ticket received only 2.4 percent of the popular vote nationally, but the party won four southern states with 39 electoral votes in 1948. Wallace's 13.5 percent of the popular vote was concentrated in five southern states giving him 46 electoral votes in 1968.

Effects of Minor Parties

It may appear that third parties have been of little significance in American politics. The most successful minor party foray into presidential politics—Theodore Roosevelt's 1912 run as a Progressive—attracted little more than a quarter of the popular vote and nowhere near enough electoral votes to be considered a serious threat to the two-party hold over the White House. Third parties have not only failed to capture the main prize in American politics; they have also had little success in attaining other national offices.

The significance of minor parties lies not in winning offices, but in their effects on the two major parties. Judged from this perspective, some third party movements precipitated seismic shifts in the American political landscape, including deciding the fate of the presidency. For example, Theodore Roosevelt's Progressive candidacy in 1912 contributed to Republican William Howard Taft's loss in his bid for a second term and helped elect Democrat Woodrow Wilson. The Progressives split Republican loyalties between the traditional party structure and its radical offshoot. George Wallace's strategy in his presidential bid in 1968 was not to win outright; he was a savvy politician who knew that his appeal was largely regional and that his chances of ending up in the White House were slim. His objective was to get enough electoral votes from the South to prevent either the Democrat Hubert Humphrey or the Republican Richard Nixon from winning the majority of electoral votes. This would allow him to be the king-maker who would instruct his electors to vote for the candidate he favored. The idea was to negotiate with Humphrey and Nixon for policy positions in return for the presidency. Although Nixon got a majority of electoral votes, Wallace's strategy was considered plausible (Bibby and Maisel 1998, 96–97).

Even if they do not decide who ends up in the White House, minor parties have played a major role in deciding who gets the electoral votes of particular states. Rather than take the laborious third party route of gaining ballot access, the 1948 Dixiecrats presented Thurmond and Wright as the official Democratic nominees in Alabama, Louisiana, Mississippi, and South Carolina. They carried these four states and received 39 electoral votes. In 2000, Green Party candidate Ralph Nader received more than 97,000 votes in Florida, where a margin of a few hundred votes gave Republican George W. Bush the state's 25 electoral votes that made him president. Had Nader not been on the ballot, challenger Al Gore probably would have received enough support from Nader voters to win Florida and the presidency. Several prominent Democrats and even some of those who had voted for Nader in 2000 begged him not to run in 2004 and risk helping to reelect President George W. Bush. Nader ignored these pleas and ran again, but he polled fewer than 500,000 votes and had no apparent effect on the outcome.

The effects of minor parties show up not only in vote totals. They help shape the policy orientation of the major parties if they adopt the minor parties' ideas as a way to attract more voters. The Democrats did this in 1896, when William Jennings Bryan adopted the Populists' call for free and unlimited coinage of silver. This position pushed the Democratic Party to the left and separated it from the "sound money" policies of the Republicans. In the aftermath of strong Progressive showings in 1912 and 1924, the Democratic Party absorbed some of the central campaign themes of Roosevelt and La Follette, such as the regulation of large corporations and the promotion of labor interests, which held little attraction for Republicans. The Republicans under Nixon embraced some of Wallace's American Independent Party's civil rights positions, distinguishing itself on racial issues from the Democratic Party.

This process of absorbing some appealing minor party themes has often led to the demise of the organizations that initially espoused them. The Populists were essentially assimilated by the Democrats; the Progressives eventually trudged home to the Republican Party; and the Dixiecrats returned to the Democratic fold or became Republicans (Dixiecrat Strom Thurmond, for example, switched to the Republican Party).

Thus, rather than serving as viable alternatives to the major parties, minor parties have had a more lasting effect by helping shape the composition of the major parties. Factions within a major party that believe they are losing internal conflicts over key issues may defect to the other major party or begin an independent movement. These movements can have important electoral consequences that prompt a response from the major party. Third party supporters

Minor parties have played a major role in deciding who gets the electoral votes of certain states. Many believe that Ralph Nader's Green Party campaign in 2000 cost Al Gore the presidential election. Despite being asked not to run in 2004, Nader again put in his bid for the presidency.

© Peter Pereira/AP Photo

who are motivated mainly by a policy goal may not regret the demise of their movement if a major party has adopted key policy positions and is better able to get it enacted.

Students of political parties see few signs that two-party dominance will end in the near future. Minor parties are likely to have important political roles from time to time. If nothing else, they can signal dissatisfaction with the performance or policy stands of the two major parties. If this signal is strong enough, the major parties will respond.

WHAT POLITICAL PARTIES DO

Defining political parties and knowing why and how they developed are important to understanding their place in American democracy. But what, exactly, do political parties *do*, and what do these activities contribute to the democratic process? Recall that political parties are organizations that run candidates for office under a common label. As they run candidates for office, parties engage in a number of activities—they recruit and nominate candidates, develop party positions on issues, disseminate party "propaganda," provide campaign support to their candidates, and sponsor get-out-the-vote drives to encourage potential supporters to vote, among other activities. Note that parties engage in these activities for selfish reasons—to recruit candidates who will appeal to voters, to win office, and to control or influence policy. Yet as parties pursue their own political self-interest, these activities produce by-products that contribute to the democratic process. Political scientists have identified four contributions political parties make to democratic governance:

1. Facilitate participation of large numbers of people
2. Promote government responsiveness
3. Promote government accountability
4. Promote stability and the peaceful resolution of conflict

Facilitate Participation

Democratic government relies on the participation of ordinary people. But from a rational choice perspective, participating in democratic politics involves costs, among which the largest are the time and effort required to gather necessary information regarding the issues facing government and to sort out which policies and which candidates serve an individual's interests. Political parties reduce these costs by doing the research and sorting out the issues ahead of time, making it possible for large numbers of people to participate in politics in effective and meaningful ways. In essence, political parties provide a way to overcome collective action problems (Aldrich 2011). Party activities facilitate participation in several ways.

Aggregating Interests

First, political parties facilitate participation because they aggregate interests and act as intermediaries between citizens and government. Parties seek to put together broad coalitions of different interests for purely selfish reasons—they want people to vote for their candidates. But as parties put these electoral coalitions together, they also aggregate individual preferences into coherent policy agendas that can serve as a plan of action for government (Bibby 1996).

This aggregation of interests provides a more or less organized way to resolve differences about what we ought to do. Like interest groups, political parties channel the views and demands of individuals and groups to public officials. But unlike interest groups that transmit relatively narrow positions, parties aggregate multiple and often conflicting demands into broader, more coherent messages by combining shared and overlapping interests and accommodating differences through compromise. Aggregating diverse interests into a party coalition helps ordinary people participate in politics in a meaningful way.

Simplifying Alternatives

Second, parties facilitate participation by simplifying alternatives for voters. Parties run candidates for public office under their label. To have a realistic chance of winning elected office, a candidate must run either as a Democrat or Republican.[8] Although party leaders sometimes actively recruit candidates, candidates for national offices (the presidency and Congress) are mostly self-starters who decide on their own to become candidates. To win a major party nomination, a candidate must survive an often grueling nomination contest (discussed in more depth in Chapter 10) that chooses a single party standard-bearer from among several candidates seeking the party's nomination. These nominating contests winnow out weaker candidates so that on election day voters choose between, at most, two viable candidates—one Democrat and one Republican—for the various offices.

Although some citizens complain about the limited choice, for many it serves a useful purpose: It reduces the amount of information necessary to decide which candidate is most likely to serve their interest. It is much easier to keep up with the issues and positions of two candidates than those of ten candidates. Suppose that in the 2016 election for president, rather than choosing either Republican Donald Trump or Democrat Hillary Clinton, voters could choose from among all who seriously considered running. Some voters would welcome the opportunity to sort out the qualifications and issue positions of dozens of candidates and find the one closest to their interest. Most Americans, however, would not invest the time and effort to dig up the information necessary to make a rational choice. Without relevant

---

8 Independent and minor party candidates do compete in elections, and they occasionally win seats in Congress, though this is rare. Socialist Bernie Sanders, for example, won Vermont's single House seat running as an independent in 1992, and in 1996, he was elected to the Senate as an independent. Former Maine governor Angus King was elected to the Senate as an independent in 2012. With rare exceptions, only major party nominees have a realistic chance of winning a seat in Congress.

information about the candidates, many citizens would be confused and deterred from voting.[9] Moreover, because most voters identify with one of the two major parties, some very useful information is printed right on the ballot—namely, each candidate's party affiliation. Simplifying the alternatives reduces information costs and helps many voters—over 137 million in the 2016 presidential election—to participate in the electoral process in a meaningful way.

Stimulating Interest in Politics and Government

Third, the parties' campaign activities facilitate participation by stimulating interest in politics. Parties contest elections and mobilize voters. They fund candidates, engage in media campaigns promoting partisan agendas, and help get their supporters registered and to the polls. That is, political parties have a fundamental interest in promoting political participation among their supporters. Although these activities are self-serving, as parties engage in these campaigns, they raise awareness and interest in politics among mostly disinterested citizens.

Supporters fill out volunteer forms at a newly opened organizing office for Democratic presidential candidate Hillary Clinton in the Roselawn neighborhood of Cincinnati, Tuesday, October, 4, 2016.

© John Minchillo/AP Photo

Promote Government Responsiveness

Promoting government responsiveness is another important contribution that parties make to democratic governance. To satisfy the core democratic value of popular sovereignty, government must be responsive to the demands of ordinary citizens. Parties help achieve this goal as they organize government and seek to pass a policy agenda (Bibby 1996).

Parties organize and operate the national government. Representatives in Congress split into majority party and minority party members. Members of the majority party hold the major leadership positions in Congress (for example, the Speaker of the House), and they chair and have a majority of the seats in all standing committees. This organizational control gives the majority party leverage to advance its agenda and block the minority party's agenda. The president is also an important policymaker who pursues a partisan agenda. Success in enacting this agenda is greatly influenced by whether the president's party controls Congress (referred to as unified government) or the opposition party controls it (divided government).

---

9 Local elections are often nonpartisan with no labels on the ballot. The intent is to remove politics from the election process, though removing party labels changes politics rather than eliminates it. Specifically, interest groups and the media have greater influence on voters' decisions. And turnout in nonpartisan elections tends to be low, at least in part because voters have a more difficult time distinguishing among the candidates.

Voter choices determine which party wins control of the institutions of government. Because voters base their choices at least in part on party agendas, as officeholders seek to advance a party agenda they are responding to citizens' preferences. Although government responsiveness may be somewhat clearer under unified government, even divided government may be a reflection of voters' preferences. Morris Fiorina (1996, 72–81) suggests that at least some voters prefer divided government, to check and moderate the extremes of each party's agenda.

Promote Government Accountability

Popular sovereignty requires not only responsiveness but also the means to hold government officials accountable if they are not responsive. Parties act as agents of accountability (Bibby 1996). Particularly important here is the role of the minority party in keeping an eye on the majority. The primary motivation to perform this watchdog function, of course, is partisan self-interest rather than a desire to promote the public good. Uncovering and publicizing questionable actions or broken campaign promises of the party in power may produce electoral benefits for the minority party in future elections. Democrats in Congress certainly tried to exploit the incompetence and numerous scandals of the Trump administration into a campaign issue in the 2018 midterm elections. But this self-interested scrutiny also serves a broader civic function in that the minority party helps to check any abuse of power by the majority, and it aids citizens in holding unresponsive policymakers accountable.

Promote Stability and Peaceful Resolution of Conflict

Finally, some scholars suggest that political parties promote stability and the peaceful resolution of conflict. The process of reconciling and accommodating a broad spectrum of views assists in settling social conflict and developing significant areas of agreement among citizens of diverse backgrounds and perspectives. The creation of such a consensus contributes to a basic feature of a democracy: the pursuit and maintenance of political power by peaceful means and, when the populace so desires, the peaceful transfer of that power into other hands. For example, after a bitter campaign in the 2016 election, former Secretary of State Hillary Clinton expressed disappointment but accepted her stunning upset with grace:

> Last night I congratulated Donald Trump and offered to work with him on behalf of our country. I hope that he will be a successful president … This is not the outcome we wanted … I know how disappointed you feel, because I feel it too … But I want you to remember this. Our campaign was never about one person, or even one election. It was about the country we love and building an America that is hopeful, inclusive, and big-hearted. We have seen that our nation is more deeply divided than we thought. But I still believe in America, and I always will. And if you do, then we must accept this result and then look to the future. Donald Trump is going to be our

president. We owe him an open mind and the chance to lead. Our constitutional democracy enshrines the peaceful transfer of power. We don't just respect that. We cherish it.

This argument is based more on the sociological theory of roles and functions than on rational choice theory. The argument that certain roles in society—in this example, the role of a "good loser" who patriotically places the national interest above her own—reduce conflict and promote stability is debatable. Even if there is a correlation between democratic norms and stability, determining the direction of causation is problematic. Some scholars argue that a stable democratic nation may actually produce "good losers," rather than the good losers producing a stable democracy. It is, after all, a lot less risky to be a gracious loser in a society that does not have a history of putting the political opponents of governmental leaders in jail.

The Responsible Party Model

The extent to which political parties promote these democratic benefits varies across different political systems. Political scientists use the phrase "**responsible party model**" to describe democracies with strong, competitive parties in which one party wins control of the government based on its policy proposals, enacts those proposals once it is in control, and stands or falls in the next election based on its performance in delivering on its promises. The party out of power (sometimes referred to as the loyal opposition) notes every policy failure and every action at odds with popular sentiment, and exploits those failures to provide points of contrast and debate in the next electoral cycle. The disciplined political parties of the United Kingdom are a close approximation of the responsible party model. The parliamentary system unifies control of the executive and legislative branches of government under the prime minister, who is the majority party leader. When the prime minister presents legislation to Parliament, members of the governing party are expected to support it, and members of the loyal opposition are expected to oppose it. Party members who do not vote along party lines may face sanctions including losing their seat.

In theory, competition between disciplined parties over policy promotes government responsiveness and accountability. Offering clear policy choices and making it easy to assign credit or blame gives voters the means to hold an unresponsive government accountable.

Although some political scientists proposed reforms to establish "responsible parties" in the United States (Committee on Political Parties 1950), American political parties do not operate as this idealized model suggests. In the American system of separation of powers and federalism, national parties have no centralized organization, and party leaders have few tools for enforcing **party discipline**—that is, the means to require party members to support a partisan agenda and to punish those who do not toe the party line. Party leaders,

responsible party model A concept that describes democracies with competitive parties in which one party wins control of the government based on its policy proposals, enacts those proposals once it is in control, and stands or falls in the next election based on its performance in delivering on its promises.

party discipline Requiring political party members in public office to promote or carry out the party's agenda and punishing those who do not.

for example, do not pick party nominees. Instead, voters in states and districts choose party nominees in direct primaries. If national party positions conflict with preferences of the voters back home, elected officials often side with constituents. Moreover, the American electoral system frequently results in **divided government**—when one party wins the presidency and another party wins a majority in Congress. Divided government makes it hard for voters to assign responsibility and to hold public officials accountable. As a result, the U.S. party system falls far short of the party discipline required by the responsible party model. Nonetheless, party strength in America has varied considerably over time.

THE STRENGTH OF POLITICAL PARTIES

To understand how party strength has varied over time, we need to measure the degree to which party structures behavior. The specific indicators are different for each of the three elements that define political parties in America—party in the electorate, party in government, and party organization. We will see that from the 1960s to the 1980s, partisanship—especially in the electorate and in government—was in a period of decline. The decades before and after, in contrast, are characterized by much greater partisanship.

The Strength of Party in the Electorate

Strength of party in the electorate refers to the degree to which party identification structures voters' attitudes and behavior. Party identification (PID) is a long-term, affective attachment to a political party (Campbell et al. 1960). Political scientists use two questions on public opinion surveys to measure an individual's PID. The first question asks, "Generally speaking, do you think of yourself as a Republican, a Democrat, an Independent, or what?" If Republican or Democrat, the follow-up question asks respondents if they would call themselves "a strong Republican/Democrat or a not very strong Republican/Democrat." If Independent, the follow-up asks if they think of themselves "as closer to the Republican or to the Democratic Party." Independents who feel closer to a party are referred to as "leaners." Researchers use these questions to place individuals on a seven-point PID scale: strong Democrat, weak Democrat, lean Democrat, independent, lean Republican, weak Republican, or strong Republican.

How strongly party identification structures the attitudes and behavior of the electorate is indicated by the percentage of strong partisans, the percentage of independents, and the percentage of straight-ticket voters (voting for the same party's candidates for president and Congress). All three indicators show that the strength of partisanship in the electorate declined from the 1950s to the 1970s but then reversed and increased since the 1980s.

---

divided government When one party controls the presidency and another controls Congress.

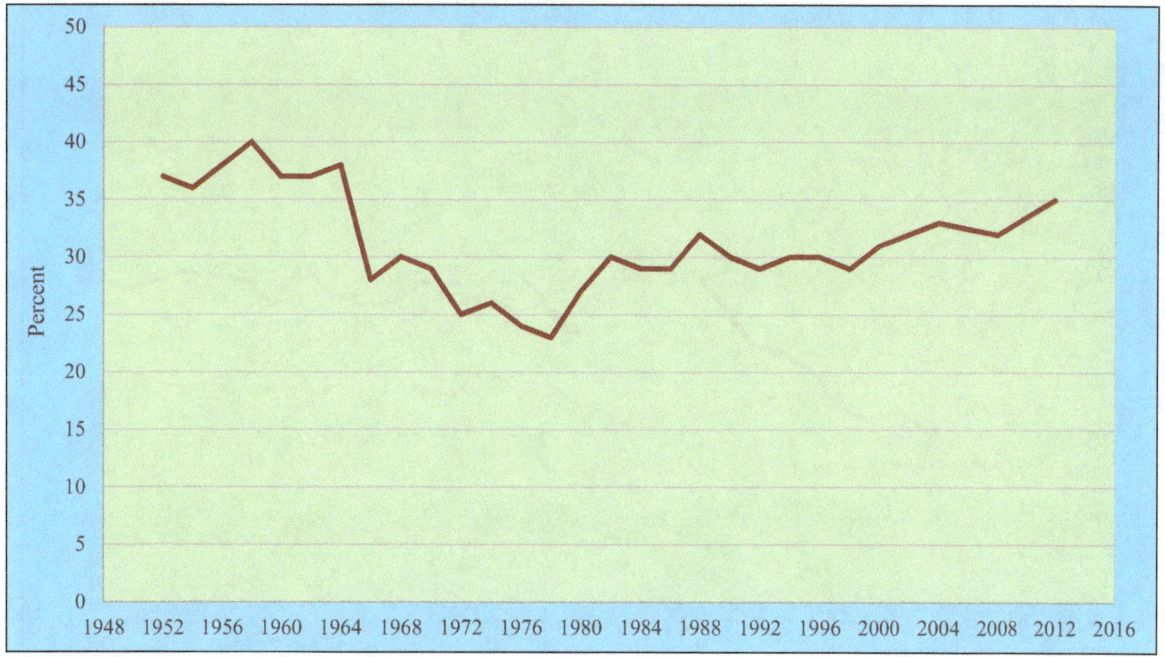

FIGURE 7.3 Strong Partisans in the Electorate

Sources: Data from American National Election Studies, *The ANES Guide to Public Opinion and Electoral Behavior* (Ann Arbor: University of Michigan, Center for Political Studies, 2006).

Figure 7.3 shows the percentage of strong partisans (that is, strong Democrats plus strong Republicans) since 1952. The percentage of strong partisans declined from around 37 percent in the 1950s to around 26 percent in the 1970s. But "the slide toward weaker partisanship … stalled" (Fleisher and Bond 2000b), and the strong partisans began to increase. By 2012, the percentage of strong partisans had rebounded to 35 percent, near the highs of the 1950s.

Another measure of party in the electorate focuses on independents—a growing number of independents suggests that the electorate is becoming less partisan. Figure 7.4 plots the percentage of Democrats, independents, and Republicans in the electorate. To interpret this evidence, however, we need to consider exactly who should count as independent. An average of about two-thirds of individuals who initially claim to be "independent" admit that they "lean" toward one party or the other. Should we count leaners as independents or as partisans? The choice makes a big difference in whether we find a growing number of independents.

Figure 7.4a (overleaf) shows the trends if independent leaners count as independents and if partisans include only those who express a party preference (strong plus weak partisans in each party). Using this definition, there appears to be a gradual long-term decline in the percentage of Democrats and Republicans and a concurrent increase in the percentage of independents. Indeed, there appears to have been more independents than Republicans since 1966 and more independents than Democrats since 2000.

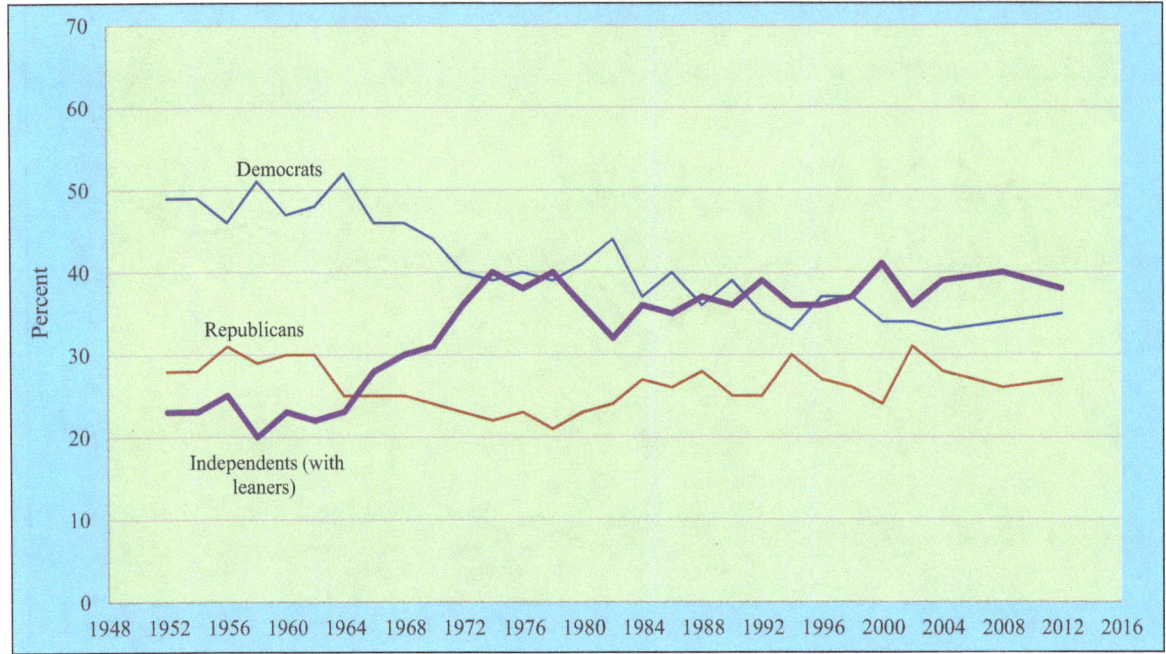

FIGURE 7.4a Party Identification in the Electorate: Independent Includes Leaners

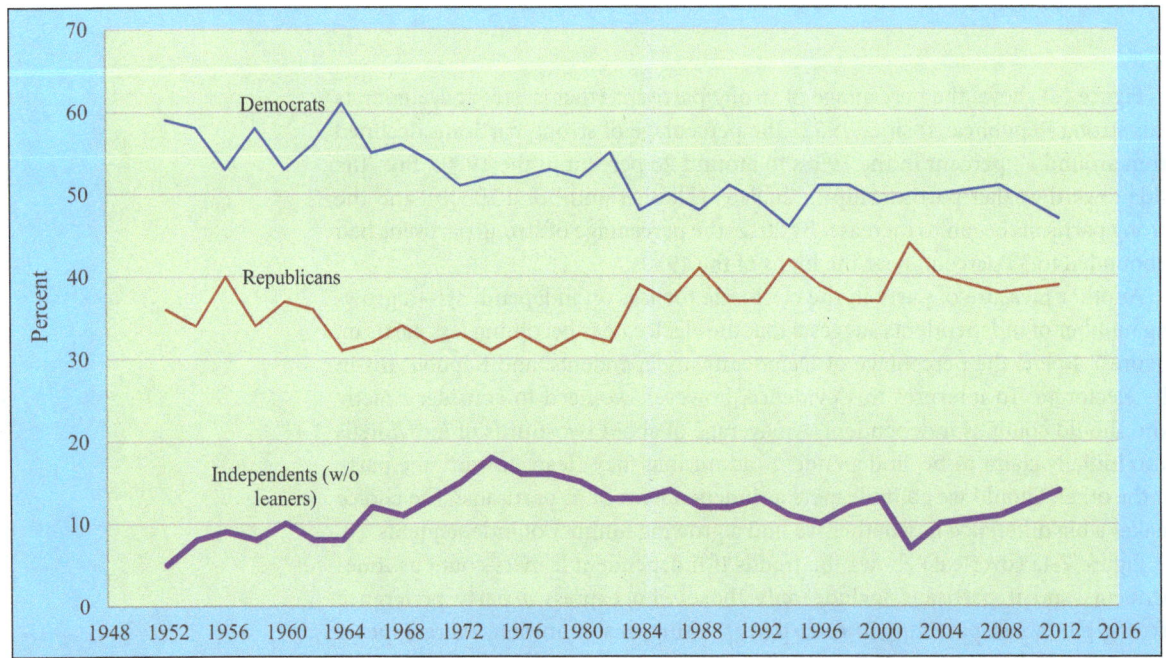

FIGURE 7.4b Party Identification in the Electorate: Independent Excludes Leaners

Source: American National Election Studies, *The ANES Guide to Public Opinion and Electoral Behavior* (Ann Arbor: University of Michigan, Center for Political Studies, 2006).

But this definition may overstate the rise of independents in the electorate. In presidential elections since 1952, independents who lean toward the Democrats or the Republicans voted for the candidate of the party they favor at slightly higher rates than did weak partisans—an average of 4.8 percent higher for independents leaning Democrat and 1.3 percent higher for independents leaning Republican. Because these results are based on surveys with a margin of error of plus-or-minus 3 percent, it is more accurate to conclude that there is no significant difference in the voting behavior of leaners and weak partisans. Nevertheless, this evidence suggests that leaners are more accurately viewed as partisans rather than as independents.

Figure 7.4b shows the trends if independents include only those who do not favor one party or the other (pure independents) and if partisans include independent leaners along with strong and weak partisans. With this definition, almost 90 percent of the electorate identify as either Democrats or Republicans, and the percentage of pure independents has increased only slightly. In the 1950s and 1960s, about 8 percent of the electorate identified as independent; the number of independents doubled to about 15 percent in the 1970s but then declined slightly, hovering around 12 percent since the 1980s.

Another indicator of partisanship in the electorate is the percentage of **straight-ticket voters**—that is, voting for the same party's candidates across different offices. A large number of straight-ticket voters suggests that party identification has a strong effect on vote choice. Figure 7.5 shows the percentage

straight-ticket voters People who vote for the same party's candidates across different offices.

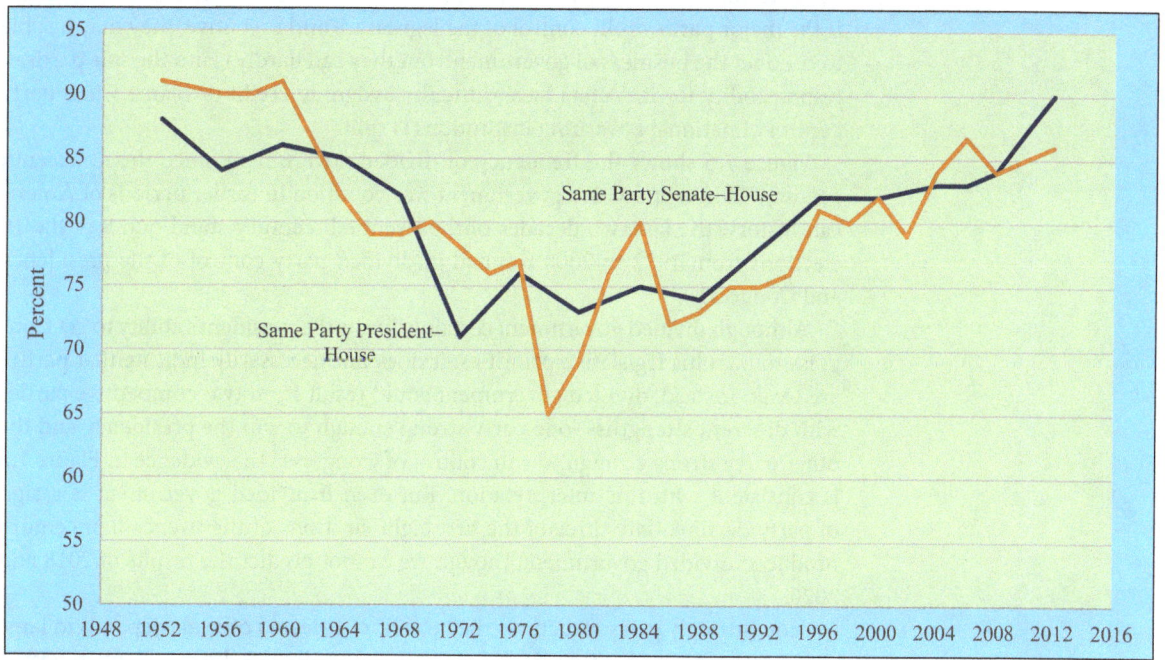

FIGURE 7.5 Straight-Ticket Voting

Sources: Data from American National Election Studies, *The ANES Guide to Public Opinion and Electoral Behavior* (Ann Arbor: University of Michigan, Center for Political Studies, 2006); Stanley and Niemi (2013). Information for 2006 provided by Gary Jacobson from Cooperative Congressional Election Study.

of straight-ticket voters for president–House, and House–Senate. During the 1950s and 1960s, over 85 percent of voters supported the same party for president, House, and Senate. Straight-ticket voting decreased considerably from the 1960s through the 1970s, but then started climbing back up; by the 2000s straight-ticket voting had rebounded to around 85 percent.

Partisan identification, therefore, remains a significant predictor of vote choice and helps shape how voters perceive candidates and issues. As Morris Fiorina observed, arguments about "issue voting" versus "party voting" miss the point: "the 'issues' are in party identification" (1981, 200). Democrats and Republicans tend to express different issue positions, and the level of distance between partisans (even weak and independent partisans) increased in the 1990s (Fleisher and Bond 2000b). Thus, the trend toward declining partisanship from the 1950s to the 1970s turned around, and the electorate became more partisan from the 1980s to the present.

The Strength of Party in Government

The strength of party in government also varies considerably over time. Some scholars see divided government as a symptom of weak parties because it hinders the exercise of coordinated government action (G. Jacobson 2001). In order to approach the responsible party model, parties must exercise enough control to get government to at least attempt to follow through on partisan policy agendas. If the major parties split control of the legislature and executive, they may be able to conduct the business of government, but they can hardly claim the sole partisan responsibility for it. Voters have difficulty assigning credit or blame when party control of national governing institutions is split.

Figure 7.6 shows the frequency of divided government since the nineteenth century. Although divided government was common in earlier periods of American history, the last two decades of the twentieth century stand out: 8 of the 10 elections from 1982 to 2000 resulted in divided party control of the presidency and Congress.

Although divided government certainly limits the president's ability to get Congress to pass his legislative priorities, it does not necessarily indicate that parties are weak. Instead, divided government could result from two competitive parties with different strengths—one party strong enough to win the presidency and the other party strong enough to win control of Congress. The evidence in Figure 7.2 is consistent with this interpretation. But even if divided government is a sign of party decline, only three of the first eight elections of the twenty-first century produced divided government, though we cannot predict the results of 2018 and 2020.

How strongly party structures the behavior of elected officials depends in large part on the strength of partisanship in the electorate. Political scientists David Brady, Joseph Cooper, and Patricia Hurley (1979), present evidence that a partisan electorate is a key requirement for partisan voting in Congress. When voters elect representatives on the basis of partisanship, members of Congress are more likely

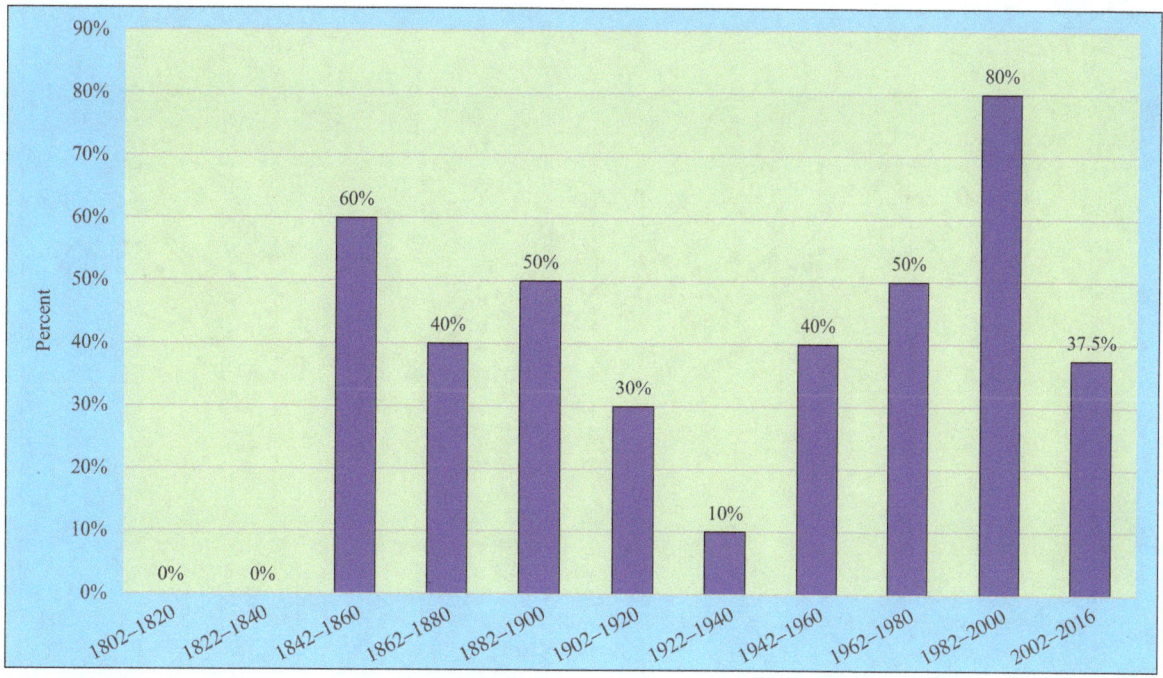

FIGURE 7.6 Elections Producing Divided Government

to be tied to a common party-centered electoral fate. When the electorate attaches its loyalties to individual candidates rather than to parties, officeholders have more leeway to resist the party line when it conflicts with constituent preferences. Thus, declining partisanship in the electorate erodes the party in government.

While partisanship in the U.S. Congress has never reached the levels common in most parliamentary democracies, there have been periods when party voting in Congress has been relatively high. A **party vote** is one on which a majority of Democrats vote on one side of an issue and a majority of Republicans on the other. Figure 7.7 shows that party votes were common in both the House and Senate from the 1870s to the early 1900s, occurring 80 to 90 percent of the time in some years. The party votes declined somewhat in the early twentieth century, rebounded briefly during the New Deal years of the 1930s, and then began a long-term slide, reaching a low point in the late 1960s. Party voting in both the House and Senate started to rise in the mid-1970s, reaching levels near the highs observed in the nineteenth century in recent decades. Partisanship has increased to the point that political scientists refer to the U.S. Congress as highly polarized (Fleisher and Bond 2000a).

Party polarization is defined as a distribution of preferences in which party means diverge toward opposite poles with little or no overlap in the center (DiMaggio, Evans, and Bryson 1996; Fiorina, Abrams, and Pope 2008; Fiorina and Levendusky 2006; Fleisher and Bond 2004). The contemporary Congress certainly

party vote A vote in which a majority of Democrats vote on one side and a majority of Republicans vote on the other.

party polarization A distribution of preferences in which party means diverge toward opposite poles with little or no overlap in the center.

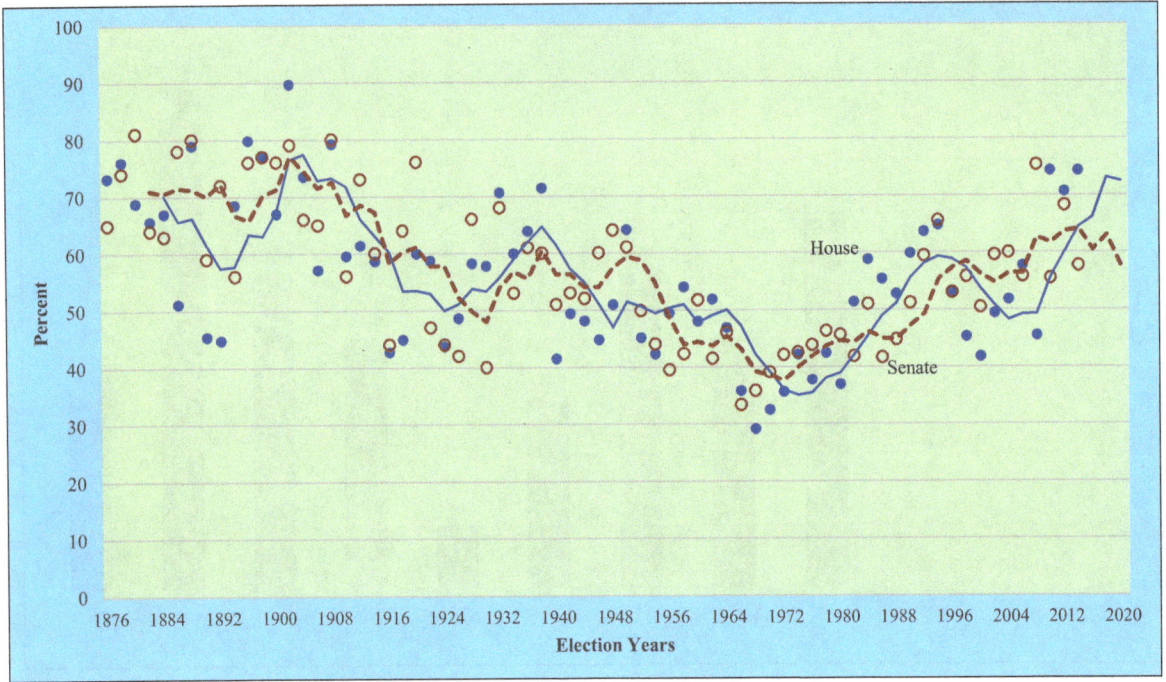

FIGURE 7.7 Party Votes in Congress

Note: A "party vote" is defined as one in which a majority of Democrats vote against a majority of Republicans. Markers indicate the percentage of party votes in the House and Senate during a two-year Congress. Trendlines are a four-period moving average.

Source: Data from 1877 to 1952 were generously provided by Patricia Hurley; data for 1953 forward are from various issues of *CQ Weekly*.

fits this definition—Democrats on the left, Republicans on the right, and few if any moderates in the middle.

Although parties in Congress have not been this polarized since the late nineteenth century, they do not satisfy the responsible party model. David Rohde and John Aldrich, however, have developed a theory of **conditional party government** (CPG) (Aldrich 2011; Aldrich and Rohde 2000; Rohde 1991) to explain the polarization of Congress since the 1970s. They suggest that "party government" depends, or is *conditional*, on high levels of ideological agreement among members of the majority party. When members of the majority party caucus achieve consensus on policy issues, they adopt reforms that strengthen party leaders' ability to promote party unity to enact the party's legislative agenda on which there is a consensus. Whether party members have similar ideology depends on what voters in their constituencies want. If partisan constituencies in different parts of the country have different preferences, members of the party caucus will reflect that diversity. From the 1940s to the 1970s, for example, Democrats in Congress were sharply divided between liberal northern Democrats and conservative southern Democrats. Implementation of the 1965 Voting Rights Act brought large numbers of African Americans with liberal preferences into the electorate, almost exclusively

conditional party government When members of the majority party caucus in Congress achieve consensus on policy issues, they adopt reforms that strengthened party leaders' ability to promote party unity to enact the party's legislative agenda on which there is a consensus.

in support of Democrats. As a result, southern Democratic constituencies became more liberal and southern Democrats in Congress began voting more like their northern colleagues (Fleisher 1993; Rohde 1991). At the same time, conservative white southern voters began voting for Republicans, contributing to the election of conservative southern Republicans to Congress. Thus, the parties diverged, moderates disappeared, and Congress polarized along party lines.

Another factor contributing to elevated partisanship in the 1980s and 1990s was the election of Ronald Reagan and the Republican takeover of the Senate in the 1980 elections. Republicans interpreted their electoral victory as a mandate to enact a conservative agenda. When House Democrats began to use the rules to prevent votes on the Republican agenda, Republicans turned to conservative activists such as Newt Gingrich. Under Gingrich's leadership, the Republican Party campaigned on the "Contract with America," a coherent policy agenda, in the 1994 elections. Republicans won control of both houses of Congress for the first time in 40 years. As Speaker of the House, Gingrich continued the aggressive use of House rules to enforce party discipline. These actions in the House may have contributed to the rise in partisanship in the Senate. Recent research suggests that Republican senators who served in the House during the Gingrich years—the "Gingrich Senators"—are responsible for much of the increased partisanship in the Senate (Theriault 2013; Theriault and Rohde 2011).

Republican electoral success in winning House seats was aided by redistricting after the 1990 census. States were encouraged to draw **majority–minority districts**—districts in which a majority of the population is composed of ethnic or racial minorities—to increase the number of African Americans elected to Congress. These efforts removed large blocs of reliably Democratic voters from the constituencies of white southern Democratic incumbents. A side effect of drawing districts to elect more African American representatives was the defeat of several moderate white Democrats by conservative Republicans in 1992 and 1994 (Kevin Hill 1995). The resulting large turnover of members created large freshman classes that were more likely to vote the party line than were the members they replaced (Hurley and Kerr 1997).

Thus, electoral changes, rules, and leadership of Congress have all contributed to more partisan voting behavior. Although party discipline in the United States has never attained the levels typical of parliamentary systems, parties remain the primary mechanism for organizing Congress, and party unity remains relatively high even in the face of divided government.

The Strength of Party Organizations

The strength of party organizations refers to the degree to which party officials can control who can run for office under the party label and discipline members who fail to support the party. Before the 1890s, political machines led by party "bosses" dominated politics in numerous cities and states. Most notorious was William M. Tweed, "Boss" of the Tammany Hall machine that dominated Democratic Party nominations for New York City and state offices in the 1860s and 1870s. "Boss" Tweed

majority–minority districts Districts in which the majority of the population is composed of ethnic or racial minorities.

famously explained, "I don't care who does the electing, so long as I get to do the nominating." Political machines maintained power through graft and corruption.

Part of the social activism of the Progressive Era from the 1890s to the 1920s were reforms designed to weaken party organizations and stop political corruption. One such reform was nonpartisan elections. Numerous cities and one state (Nebraska) adopted nonpartisan elections. The absence of party labels on the ballot made it more difficult for party bosses to mobilize voters in support of their candidates, though it did not completely eliminate partisan influence.

Another successful reform reduced **political patronage**—that is, government jobs and contracts that elected officeholders handed out to those who supported the party. Reformers advocated a **merit system**—hiring government workers based on their skills and qualifications to do the job rather than on party loyalty. In place of awarding government contracts to party supporters (who inflated the cost of doing the job and gave kickbacks to the party machine), reformers proposed a system of competitive bids to award government contracts to the lowest bidder qualified to do the job. Losing control of patronage diminished the role of parties in voters' political, social, and economic lives. No longer could parties use government jobs and contracts to recruit supporters and maintain their loyalty.

Two important election reforms were the direct primary and secret ballot. The **direct primary**—an election in which rank-and-file voters choose the party's nominees for various offices—transferred the key power for determining who has the right to use the party label in an election from party bosses to voters. Before the direct primary, elected officials would toe the party line or face the threat that party leaders would withhold the party label from them in the next election. Before 1890, the parties printed ballots with only their nominees listed. Party workers would entice voters to the polls (sometimes a bar) and watch while they placed the ballot into the box. In contrast, government prints secret ballots with all parties' candidates listed. Voters mark their choices in the privacy of a voting booth. This reform reduced intimidation and vote buying.

There is evidence, however, that although they differ from the old political machines, modern party organizations are alive and well. A group of political scientists undertook an extensive analysis of party organizations at local, state, and national levels in the 1960s, 1970s, and 1980s (Cotter et al. 1989; Gibson et al. 1989; Huckshorn et al. 1986). Contrary to those who forecast imminent party demise, these researchers saw active organizations busily reinventing themselves as central players in American politics. They found that party organizations at all levels had become more professional. Parties were key sources of funding and logistical support for candidates running under their labels, and they linked party members in differing levels of government and different offices. The research also found that parties remain capable of coherent policy platforms. Furthermore, party organization influences party in the electorate. John Coleman (1996, 821) finds that "strong, competitive party organizations contribute to generalized support for parties" among ordinary citizens.

These scholars do not deny that the reforms adopted around the turn of the twentieth century affected party organization. The reforms, however, did not

political patronage The giving of government jobs to people based on their party affiliation and loyalty.

merit system A system of governing in which jobs are given based on relevant technical expertise and the ability to perform.

direct primary The selection of a political party's candidate for the general election by vote of ordinary citizens.

permanently diminish the relevance of parties but rather obliged them to deal with a new political environment. Parties responded not by collapsing, but by adapting. For example, the new electoral environment may make candidates more independent, but they still need campaign funds, a clear message, a way to get the message to the voters, and the host of administrative and logistical services required to run a successful modern campaign. Parties provide all of this and more. By strategically deploying these resources, parties make themselves central players in electoral politics. Indeed, Cotter and his associates conclude that parties operate in "a framework of public regulation and support which protects more than weakens the existing parties" (1989, 168).

Cycles of Party Strength

Thus, we see that party strength rises and falls in cycles over time. At some points, parties have played prominent roles in structuring citizens' vote choice and in making public policy; at other times, their influence has waned. Rather than steadily declining over time, political parties have adapted to changes in the political landscape and have retained a central, albeit altered, place in the political system (Aldrich 2011). As long as political parties continue to attract adherents, they remain viable institutions central to the democratic process, and they have the potential to fulfill their broader functions in the political system.

Chapters 9, 10, and 11 focus on the role of parties in the electoral process. In subsequent chapters, we analyze the role of the party in the government in making public policy.

CHAPTER SEVEN

Top 10 Takeaway Points

1. The Founders did not incorporate political parties into the Constitution, and parties have been viewed with suspicion and distrust since their emergence in the early days of the republic, but political scientists tend to view them as essential organizations in promoting the long-term health and stability of the democratic process.

2. A political party is an organization that nominates and runs candidates for public office under its own label. This characteristic sets parties apart from interest groups, which often try to influence policy but do not run candidates for office under their own labels.

3. Parties can be thought of as consisting of three overlapping elements: (1) the party in the electorate, consisting of ordinary citizens who identify with the party; (2) the party in government, consisting of the elected and appointed officeholders who share a party label; and (3) the party organization, consisting of the party professionals who hold official positions in the party.

4. Political parties' activities produce by-products that contribute to the democratic process. Most importantly, political parties link citizens and government by facilitating participation. Parties facilitate participation in three ways: (1) they aggregate individual policy preferences into coherent policy agendas; (2) they structure and simplify alternatives for voters; and (3) their campaign activities stimulate interest in politics and government.

5. Political parties contribute to the democratic process in other ways as well: (1) they promote government responsiveness as they organize government and seek to pass a policy agenda; (2) they promote accountability when parties out of power scrutinize activities of the party in power and report mistakes and abuses; and (3) they promote stability and the peaceful resolution of conflict as they reconcile and accommodate a diverse spectrum of views to build broad coalitions.

6. Party systems are classified according to the number of parties that effectively compete for power: one-party, multiparty, or two-party. American politics has been characterized by two-party competition throughout most of its history. Democrats and Republicans have dominated political competition in the United States from 1856 to the present in the oldest continuous two-party competition in the world.

7. Reasons for the two-party system in the United States include: historical factors; electoral rules (including the single-member district plurality system, the electoral college, state laws regulating access to the ballot, and public financing of presidential elections); and a set of mechanisms that tend to make it self-perpetuating.

8. Minor or third parties do exist in the United States and have periodically had an important effect on American politics. By siphoning off votes from the major parties, minor parties sometimes influence who wins an election. Minor party issues that attract significant support tend to be absorbed by the major parties.

9. Political parties in the United States are not as strong and disciplined as parties in parliamentary democracies, and they fall far short of the responsible party model.

10 The power and importance of political parties in American politics has varied over time. There was a general decline in the strength of parties in the electorate and in government from the 1950s to the 1970s. Since the 1980s, partisanship in the electorate and in government has been increasing. Party organizations have remained active and vibrant as they have adapted to changes in the political environment.

CHAPTER SEVEN
Key Terms and Cases

conditional party government, 252
direct primary, 254
divided government, 246
Duverger's Law, 235
majority–minority districts, 253
merit system, 254
multiparty system, 231
one-party system, 231
parliamentary system, 235
party discipline, 245
party in the electorate, 226
party in government, 226
party organization, 226
party polarization, 251
party professionals, 227
party vote, 251
policy-motivated activists, 227
political machine, 227
political party, 223
political patronage, 254
presidential system, 235
proportional representation, 235
responsible party model, 245
role theory, 227
single-member district plurality (SMDP) system, 235
straight-ticket voters, 249
third parties, 237
two-party system, 231

8 THE MASS MEDIA AND POLITICS

KEY QUESTIONS

How does a free press help support the key democratic value of political freedom?

What are the primary threats to a free press?

Are the news media biased?

© Patrick Pleul/picture-alliance/dpa/AP Photo

ON NOVEMBER 9, 2016, 35-year-old businessman Eric Tucker Tweeted a picture of a line of buses parked on a street in Austin, Texas. Well, ho hum, you might say, not exactly something calculated to jump out from your social media feed. It was not the buses that got people's attention, though. It was Tucker's claim that they were being used to bring paid anti-Donald Trump protesters into town. Now that's the sort of information that does have social media pop. And, boy, did it. The story immediately rocketed beyond Tucker's 40-odd Twitter followers as pro-Trump and conservative social media platforms quickly began reposting. Those links were soon racking up hundreds of thousands of views and shares. The next day, Donald Trump was Tweeting to his millions of followers that "professional protesters, incited by the media, are protesting. Very unfair!" The story went viral not just on social media; it more or less dominated the mainstream news cycle for a day or two (Maheshwari 2016).

The big problem with this story is that there was not a lick of truth to it. None. Nada. Zilch. In fact, it was convincingly debunked within hours of being posted. The buses were not hired to bring in anti-Trump protesters, they were hired by a company called Tableau Software to shuttle people to and from a large conference it was hosting. Tucker admitted he had not checked the facts, and as it rapidly became clear there was no evidence to back up his claim, he first deleted his Tweet, then reposted it with a large, red "FALSE" stamp superimposed on top. It didn't seem to matter. His retraction got only 29 retweets, while his original (false) claim continued to light up the blogosphere. It was as if the truth of the claim, or more accurately the lack thereof, just didn't seem to matter. It affirmed what many people believed and that seemed to be more important than the original Tweet's accuracy, or lack thereof.

This story illustrates the concept of so-called "alternative facts," a term coined by Presidential Counselor Kellyanne Conway to describe demonstrable falsehoods that are advocated and/or accepted because they confirm or comfort a particular political belief. The notion of alternative facts was widely mocked, but it also worried a lot of people. We live in an era of fake news and politically polarized media consumption, a time where many are increasingly convinced that the media is biased against their political viewpoint, whatever that viewpoint happens to be. The worry is that if millions trust alternative facts more than they trust the media there might be negative consequences for democracy. It's hard to be realistic about governing, the argument goes, if politics and governing is not going to be based on reality.

Are alternative facts bad for democracy? If the press is irresponsible and politically biased, does that threaten democracy? Doesn't pushing a particular ideological or partisan point of view—especially if it is demonstrably false—represent at least some sort of ethical lapse? Isn't the media supposed to be neutral and unbiased? Does all of this threaten the foundations of the Republic? There's a short answer to these sorts of questions: No.

What is crucial to the functioning of a healthy democracy is not a neutral media, or a responsible media, or a fact-focused media, but a free and independent media. A free press means exactly that—that it is free and unregulated. Free does not mean fair, unbiased, or even accurate, and it certainly doesn't mean a media that avoids providing a megaphone for dubious news items guaranteed to gin up attention. It simply means free of government control. How people use that freedom, with few exceptions, is up to them. People can set up fake news sites, they can report alternative facts. As information consumers, people are free to prefer media outlets that consistently confirm their beliefs even if that means embracing what amounts to an alternative reality. The result of all this freedom is not always pretty; at times, it can be downright infuriating. Yet as soon as you start limiting the freedom of the media, you start limiting democracy.

We live in a media-soaked culture, with virtually unlimited access to information. Supplying that information is the **mass media**, a term describing all the means used to transmit information to masses of people. These means include the **print media**, which consist of newspapers, magazines, and books, and the **electronic media**, which consist of television, radio, movies, recordings, and the Internet. An increasingly important element of the electronic media are **social media**, which are websites and applications that allow users to share content and participate in virtual social networks. Of particular importance to politics

---

mass media All the means used to transmit information to masses of people.

print media Media consisting of newspapers, magazines, and books.

electronic media Consist of television, radio, movies, video and audio recordings, and the Internet.

social media Websites and computer applications that allow users to share content and participate in virtual social networks.

are the **news media**: organizations and journalists that cover the news. **News** is defined as accounts of timely and specific events. The print and electronic media partially or wholly devoted to collecting and reporting news in the United States consist of roughly 1,300 daily newspapers; 6,700 weekly newspapers; 1,700 television stations; 15,000 radio stations; hundreds of magazines; and the various publications' and stations' Internet-based counterparts (Barthel 2016; Newspaper Association of America 2010; Federal Communications Commission 2012). Generically, these are all known as the **press**.

In this chapter, we explore the role of the press in a democratic society. As it turns out, the freedom of the media—not its fairness or accuracy—is most critical to democracy.

news media Organizations and journalists that cover the news.

news Accounts of timely and specific events.

press The print and electronic media that are partially or wholly devoted to collecting and reporting news in the United States.

THE CONCEPT OF A FREE PRESS

A free press is just that—free. Free to say what it wants, investigate what it wants, and report what it wants without government interference or control. Allowing the press to investigate and criticize government, to promote a diverse set of perspectives and viewpoints, and to collect and distribute information with little government censorship or regulation is considered a central characteristic of a democratic society. A free press promotes the core democratic value of political freedom.

The media support political freedom by helping to create what Jürgen Habermas (1991) termed a **public sphere**, a forum where information on matters important to civic life can be freely accessed and exchanged. A free marketplace of perspectives and ideas is critically important because a healthy democracy requires that citizens not only be able to express their opinions and preferences but also be knowledgeable and informed when they make political choices.

For example, in a representative democracy elections are the primary way to connect the preferences of citizens to the actions of government. Elections cannot achieve this goal if citizens have no information about what their government is doing, what issues are important, and what options exist to address those issues. It is difficult, after all, to have preferences about issues, proposals, or candidates if you are unaware that they exist. In any society with a free press, it is easy to find out what the government is doing, identify the important issues of the day, and get a broad sense of what actions have been proposed to address those issues. All this

public sphere A forum where information on matters important to civic life can be freely accessed and exchanged.

information and much more is available with the click of a mouse, a swipe across a smart phone, or with the flick of a switch pretty much any hour of the day.

That free flow of information is critical to a functioning democracy not only because it helps inform voters but also because it serves as an important check on government officials. Public officeholders are aware that their proposals and their actions will be recorded and transmitted through the mass—and increasingly through the more individualized social—media, and they also know there are consequences if that information makes a negative impression on their constituents. Thomas Jefferson (1823) wrote, "The only security of all is in a free press. The force of public opinion cannot be resisted when permitted freely to be expressed."

The media create a public sphere and help uphold the core value of political freedom by serving a number of specific roles in democratic societies. These functions include information dissemination and education, agenda setting, and watchdog and public advocacy.

Information and Education

The traditional news media see their primary role as one of informing and educating the public. They monitor what the government is doing, report its activities to the public, and try to put these activities into context by seeking to explain the meaning and significance of government decisions or actions.

Processing Information

The news media's role in providing information and education is much more complex than simply providing the raw materials for neutral observers to make up their minds on whether they support a particular candidate or oppose a particular policy. For one thing, people are not neutral consumers of information; they filter what they read, hear, or watch through their own perspectives and biases. People are resistant to messages they do not want to hear and are eager to seek out sources of information that support their own opinions. This makes sense from all of the broad theoretical perspectives we are highlighting in this book. It makes sense from a social-psychological perspective to be more receptive to positive information about the groups you either belong to or view positively and to be equally receptive to negative information about groups you view negatively. Psychological experiments have repeatedly found that people readily accept information that confirms their own views but are much quicker to find fault with information that conflicts with their own views (Vedantam 2006).

It also is perfectly rational to seek out information that supports your preferred point of view. A number of academic studies view the media's information role through the prism of rational choice and conclude not only that it makes sense for utility maximizers to seek information that supports their own preferences, but also that it is rational for the media to serve those preferences. If a large audience shares a particular set of beliefs, it is rational for media outlets to provide information confirming those beliefs. Why? Well, because providing such information serves the rational interests of the media providers—it boosts circulation, viewership, and ultimately advertising revenue and profits (Mullainathan and Schleifer 2005). These findings raise important questions about bias in the media, an issue that is discussed in more detail later in this chapter.

Recent research shows that there is almost certainly a biological basis for how political information is processed. What seems to drive how we process political information is not the reasoning part of our brains, but the emotional part of our brains. One study used brain scans of 10 Republicans and 10 Democrats to study brain activity when people are exposed to information that supports or opposes their partisan viewpoints (in this case, pictures of candidates from the 2004 presidential election). The study found that people tend to react emotionally to the candidates they support; in effect we feel "warm fuzzies" when we see our "favorite." When people are exposed to pictures of the opposing candidate, however, they experience negative emotions that seem to suppress the more rational parts of the brain. In effect, although people accept the candidate they support based on passion and emotion, they pick the "other guy" over, looking for fault (Kaplan, Freedman, and Iacoboni 2007). Biologically, this is what we'd expect to find from the social-psychological framework. People invest themselves psychologically, for whatever reason, in a candidate or a cause. They tend to be relatively immune to rational arguments to dissuade them of that support because their support is based on emotion rather than a conventional cost–benefit calculus. On the other hand, they are quick to pick up on, or independently develop, rationalizations for why the candidates and causes they do not support are wrong.

Importance of the Information and Education Role

How people acquire and process political information from the mass media is an important research topic for social scientists because this is how most people learn about government and politics. The mass media's central importance as a source of political information has steadily increased as technological advances have made it increasingly easy to communicate to large audiences. In the past seven decades, network television has made its way into virtually every home in the United States; the advent of cable television introduced the constant news cycle; the Internet and the World Wide Web gave individuals the ability to not only instantly access news but also report it on websites and blogs; and, most recently, the rise of social media and the ubiquity of smart phones now allow us to stay connected to a limitless source of information pretty much 24 hours a day, wherever we are.

This radical and rapid development of communications technology has reshaped not just how people get political information, but also the very institutions and processes of politics. For example, the media have assumed some of the roles traditionally held by political parties. Prior to the widespread adoption of primary elections, the job of nominating candidates for office was controlled by relatively small groups of party elites. The rise of the direct primary took the power to nominate

APPLYING THE FRAMEWORKS

CHOOSING YOUR NEWS RATIONALLY

Historically, figuring out where to get your news basically boiled down to choosing an information source. That meant picking a newspaper, a news magazine, or a network television newscast and using that outlet to supply the news stories you consumed.

The arrival of social media has, at least partially, blown up that model. Consumers no longer have to pick an information source to package news stories for them. Rather than picking a particular source of information, today we can pick individual stories from multiple sources. Social media makes this easy. Individual news stories pop up regularly in social media feeds on platforms like Twitter and Facebook and people post shares and links to stories from a huge variety of different media outlets.

If the advent of social media has made it possible to pick individual stories rather than particular information sources, how do we go about picking which news stories to pay attention to? After all, social media is awash in news stories fighting to claim our attention and even the most addicted social media maven cannot consume them all. So how do we pick our political news from the information buffet social media presents us with?

One answer to this is that we pick on the basis of information utility, or our perception of how a particular news story is likely to support our preferences. That's just another way of saying that we are rational in selecting from the news stories that pop up in our social media platforms. That all sounds reasonable enough, but if your social media feeds are anything like ours there are a lot of those sorts of choices to be made. How do we go about deciding which links to follow and which to ignore?

Rational choice can help explain some of those choices right away. For example, you are more likely to follow stories clearly flagged as coming from a news source seen as more supportive of your political viewpoints. So, for example, if you are a conservative or a Republican, it is more rational to follow a story clearly flagged as originating with Fox News because it is a media outlet widely seen as more friendly and supportive of right-leaning political beliefs. Thus, Fox News stories are more likely to provide you with information utility than, say, stories from MSNBC, which is perceived to be more left-leaning. Academic research confirms this—partisan information consumers tend to follow stories in their social media feeds on the basis of anticipated agreement with their political views, which makes perfect sense from a rational choice point of view (Messing and Westwood 2014).

There are a lot of choices to be made in deciding which news threads to follow in social media platforms, though, and the sources and their perceived partisan leanings are not always easy to discern. If that is the case, how do you know if that juicy-sounding headline that just showed up in your Twitter feed is going to maximize your information utility? It might actually reduce your information utility—it could contradict your preferences or just be annoying clickbait.

Researchers studying news information consumption patterns on social media have found that a big influence on those choices are personal recommendations. We might not be sure of a source—or even care what it is—but if a story comes recommended by someone we know and trust, we are much more likely to follow it. Again, this makes perfect sense from a rational choice point of view. If we know someone and know that we have reasonably similar preferences, then we are more likely to trust that person to point us toward news stories that increase our information utility. Rather than relying on a news organization's judgment to put together an entire package of stories in a newspaper or a newscast or a website, we rely on individuals we trust to recommend stories from multiple sources that are more likely to increase our information utility.

A study conducted by political scientist Nicholas Anspach demonstrated this by creating two mock Facebook news feeds and varying the sorts of posts that showed up on them. This included the type of news stories (politics or entertainment), the perceived partisan basis of the news source (Fox News, Huffington Post), and most crucially, whether the story in a Facebook post either had likes and comments or did not have likes and comments. He found that, absent any likes or comments, people following these feeds tended to select political stories on the basis of partisan preference—conservatives were more likely to pick Fox News stories, liberals more likely to pick stories from the Huffington Post. So far, so rational.

Anspach also found "that social media users are more likely to select political news when their friends and family post it, irrespective of its ideological slant" (2017, 11). What that means is we tend to trust our friends and family to point us towards greater gains in information utility than news organizations. In short, we rationally use a fairly simple set of rules of thumb to select news stories about politics. Specifically, prioritize stories first on the basis of recommendations by friends or family, and second on the basis of the perceived partisan leanings of the news source.

The bottom line is that, while social media seems to offer a pretty chaotic buffet of potential news stories, we are pretty rational in picking which of those stories to follow.

Discussion Questions
1. How do you or your friends who are active on social media platforms decide what news stories to follow? Do those choices seem systematically rational? Why or why or not?
2. What other cues to potential information utility might we use to rationally choose whether to follow a news story?

---

candidates from party leaders and placed it in the hands of the voting public.[1] Because voters largely rely on the mass media for information about candidates, this shift in nomination procedures thrust the media into a more prominent role in connecting citizens to government.

The mass media have also taken over some of the traditional party roles for candidates. Historically, candidates relied on party organizations to connect with voters. To reach voters during campaigns, teams of party volunteers banged on doors, organized rallies where candidates gave speeches, and handed out campaign literature. Yet even the most dedicated party machine is an ineffective means of communication compared with the mass media. A television speaks to voters every day, right in their living rooms. Smart phones put a communication channel into a voter's pocket.

The net effect of these changes is "a new form of campaigning in which the mass media have replaced the political party as the main intermediary between voters and candidates" (Iyengar 1997, 144). Rather than through political parties, most voters now connect with candidates through television screens, newspapers, radios, and the Internet. Candidates now communicate with large numbers of people through the press, and sophisticated media marketing campaigns have been a centerpiece of election strategy for decades (Patterson 1984). More recently, social media have also become an increasingly important element of political campaigns, which allows candidates to bypass the news media and communicate directly with voters through texts or dedicated platforms like Facebook, Twitter, and Snapchat.

---

[1] The direct primary is discussed in more detail in Chapter 10.

Although there is little doubt that these media strategies can reach a much larger percentage of the electorate than even the most dedicated party effort, their impact on the information and education role of the media is mixed. In terms of quantity, the shift to media-based campaigns undoubtedly led to the availability of more information to citizens and gave candidates more opportunities to get their message to larger numbers of voters. The content of those messages, however, is no less partisan than that of the door-to-door campaigner's. Rather than seeking to educate citizens with civil debate, candidates for office often use their media campaigns to point out the faults of their opponents. There is nothing new about this; as long as there have been elections in the United States, candidates have engaged in mudslinging. The rise of the mass media, especially the electronic media, however, provided the opportunity to do this on a grand scale.

If anything, mass media campaigns have provided a boon for the negative electioneering that has always been part and parcel of democratic politics in America. As one political scientist observed, "more often than not, candidates use their media opportunities to criticize, discredit, or ridicule their opponents rather than to promote their own ideas and programs" (Iyengar 1997, 145). Such has been the case since the nation's founding, but mass literacy and the rise of daily newspapers, not to mention radio, television, and the Internet, make it easier than ever to sling more mud over a wider audience. Many bemoan the attack ads and scathing sound bites, but there is a simple reason for such negativity: it works. Tearing down your opponent can create doubt among voters, making it less likely they will vote in his or her favor. It may make them less likely to vote, period.

There is also a concern about information quality that accompanies the rise of mass media. Sound bites and Tweet storms can certainly reach huge audiences, but are these forms of communication really a good way to deliberate and debate on important issues and political differences? In addition to worries of political discourse becoming a high-tech barrage of bumper sticker negativity, there are also worries that the impersonal (and often anonymous) nature of modern communication methods undermines civility and negatively influences public opinion (Anderson et al. 2013).

Different Media, Different Information

Given the media's increasingly important role as a central connection between voters and government, the job of informing and educating the public has emerged as a fundamental service to the democratic process. The political freedom of citizens—their freedom to make choices—is tied to the information they have about government officials, actions, and issues. This connection raises the question of how well the media do this all-important job. It turns out that not all media are equal in terms of their ability to convey political information, and not all are equal in their ability to convey political information accurately. Much of this has to do with access.

Though increasingly challenged by the Internet, television remains the dominant mass medium in the United States. Access to television is nearly universal—

virtually every household has a TV—and the potential audience for television news encompasses just about every single citizen. Roughly half of Americans regularly watch TV news, and even more rely on television as a primary source of information about elections and political campaigns. Figure 8.1 reports the results of a survey asking people where they went to get their news in 2016 (note the figures add up to more than 100 percent because respondents could report going to more than one news source). Television is clearly the main news source for Americans, with close to 60 percent of adults saying they often used television to get news. Nearly 40 percent reported frequently getting news from the Internet, which could mean websites, social media, or specialized apps. Trailing far behind as news sources were legacy technologies, radio, television and newspapers, with no more than a quarter reporting they used these as regular news sources. This is a little misleading, however, as radio and, especially, newspaper content is migrating online. Rather than getting a newspaper delivered, people are increasingly just reading newspaper websites. Indeed, in 2017 three of the five most visited news websites were newspapers—nytimes.com, theguardian.com, and washingtonpost.com (Alexa 2017).

There are also clearly generational differences in information sources. For people aged 18–33 social media clearly play a more dominant role as a news source. Roughly 60 percent of this age group reports getting political news from Facebook in a given week, while only 37 percent get political news from television. Those numbers get flipped for people over 50, with 39 percent reporting getting political news from Facebook and 60 percent from television (Mitchell, Gottfried, and Matsa 2015). If those trends hold it seems only a matter of time before online sources edge out television as the primary information source for voters.

These shifts in news media consumption are important because different media have different capabilities to convey information. Television is a passive medium; it requires little effort or active involvement on the part of the viewer to get information. You do not even have to be literate to follow a television news broadcast. Yet although television makes it easy to access information, it also has drawbacks. Most importantly, television has tight limits on the amount and depth of information it can convey. One full minute of airtime, for example, constitutes a major story on a national network newscast. Even a longer report, such as those found on shows like *60 Minutes*, cannot contain the same amount of information as an in-depth article in a newspaper or news magazine. The print media and their Internet equivalents are less accessible because they require literacy, and the reader must be willing to follow

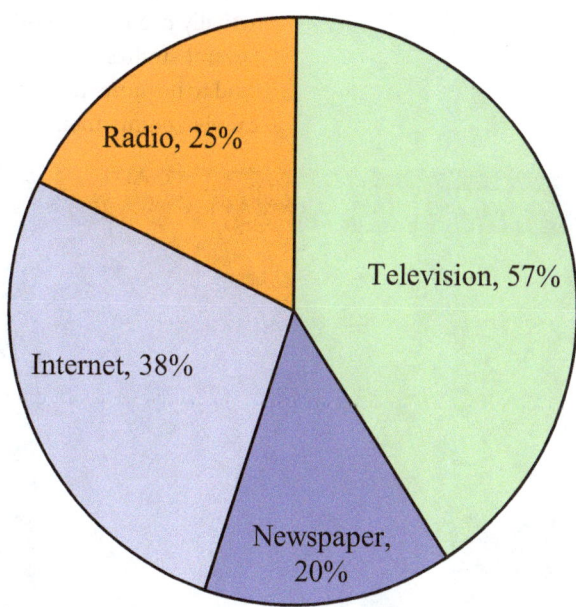

FIGURE 8.1 Primary News Sources for American Adults in 2016: Percent Who Often Get News From Each Media Platform

Source: Data from Mitchell, Amy, Jeffrey Gottfried, Miachel Barthel, and Elisa Shearer. Pew Research Center, 2016. "Pathways to News." http://www.journalism.org/2016/07/07/pathways-to-news/.

stories as they jump from page to page (or link to link), but these media can convey not only larger quantities of information but also more detailed information.

Surveys show that people who rely more on newspapers for their information tend to be better informed and more knowledgeable about politics than those who rely more on television. For example, in early 2012 the Pew Research Center conducted a survey designed to assess public knowledge about the candidates running in the Republican presidential primary. Of the four questions asked, 40 percent who relied on newspapers as a main news source got at least three answers correct; that number jumped to 73 percent for those who relied on the websites of major national newspapers such as the *New York Times*. In contrast, only 35 percent of those who relied on television as a major news source got three or more answers correct. The poor scores of the television viewers were about the same as the scores of those who relied on general Internet portals such as Yahoo, Google, or AOL as their main news source (Pew Research Center 2012). This finding is something of a concern because it means some people will be better informed—and thus in a better position to make informed political choices—than others. Young people, immigrants, the less educated, and the poor tend to be more reliant on television as a primary source of political news; these are also groups that tend to be less politically informed and less politically active (Chaffee and Frank 1996).

It is not just that some media do a better job of informing voters; some media actually produce **misinformation**, or the belief that incorrect information is true. Several studies have found that heavy consumers of political talk radio not only tend to be more misinformed; they also tend to have more confidence in the political viewpoints their misinformation supports. In other words, they are not only more likely to have inaccurate information about politics and government, but they are also more likely to base their political beliefs and actions on that misinformation (Hofstetter et al. 1999).

misinformation The belief that incorrect information is true.

President Donald Trump gives a televised news conference in the East Room of the White House. Despite paying a good deal of attention to the news, Americans remain politically uninformed, possibly due to their primary news sources, television and social media, which are less effective at conveying information than newspapers.

© Pablo Martinez Monsivais/AP Photo

It is not just conservative radio talk show hosts, though, who have a questionable impact on the quality of civic debate. Television programs that blur the lines between news and entertainment have become very popular. These include cable television shows hosted by the likes of Trevor Noah, Samantha Bee, and John Oliver that mimic many of the aspects of traditional newscasts, but play politics mostly for laughs. Following the election of Donald Trump it also includes a number of late night talk shows that picked up on this format, notably CBS' *The Late Show* with

Stephen Colbert and NBC's *Late Night* with Seth Meyers. The popularity of these sort of shows has created what has been termed the "*Daily Show* effect," named after the show that pioneered the basic format under its former host Jon Stewart. Basically the *Daily Show* effect describes a general increase in cynicism towards politics as people—especially young people—increasingly rely on "soft" infotainment shows like the *Daily Show* as primary sources of political information (Baumgartner and Morris 2006). The audiences of such shows tend to be pretty well informed, but the satire and sarcasm of the shows seems to contribute to more negative attitudes about candidates and a general contempt of politics and government.

An even greater source of concern to the erosion of the quality of civic debate is the rise of **fake news**, or stories presented as news articles that are intentionally and verifiably false. This became a particular concern during and after the 2016 presidential election as fake news stories flooded social media feeds. These often were links to stories on impressive-looking "news" sites that in reality were little more than propaganda platforms. One study estimated 115 pro-Trump fake news stories were shared on social media 30 million times during the 2016 campaign, and another 41 pro-Hillary Clinton fake news stories were shared 7.6 million times (Allcott and Gentzkow 2017). The study concluded that the impact of fake news on the election in terms of shifting votes was small and probably not decisive. Still, the fact that millions of Americans are consuming fake news during a presidential election campaign is a significant concern. The quality of civic debate can hardly be improved if citizens are turning to news sources that are verifiably and demonstrably not factual.

Trust and Information

Americans tend to be skeptical about the quality of information they get from the mass media. About two-thirds believe that news organizations often print or broadcast stories that are factually inaccurate. Roughly the same proportion also believes that the press covers up their mistakes rather than admitting to them (Pew Research Center 2009).

The credibility of news sources is often as much in the eye of the beholder as in the format or medium itself. The audiences for news sources are increasingly polarized along partisan and ideological lines, and these partisan differences play a large role in determining both media consumption patterns and perceptions of credibility. Generally speaking, those who say they are liberal or lean liberal draw information from a variety of mainstream news sources. In contrast, those who say they are conservative or lean conservative overwhelmingly rely on a single news source—Fox News—for their political information. These differences are reflected in the audiences of major news organizations. Most of those audiences tend to skew liberal, with one big exception: Fox News, whose audience is predominantly conservative (see Figure 8.2).

It is not just that people on different ends of the ideological spectrum are increasingly getting their political information from different sources, they also

fake news Stories presented as real news articles that are intentionally and verifiably false.

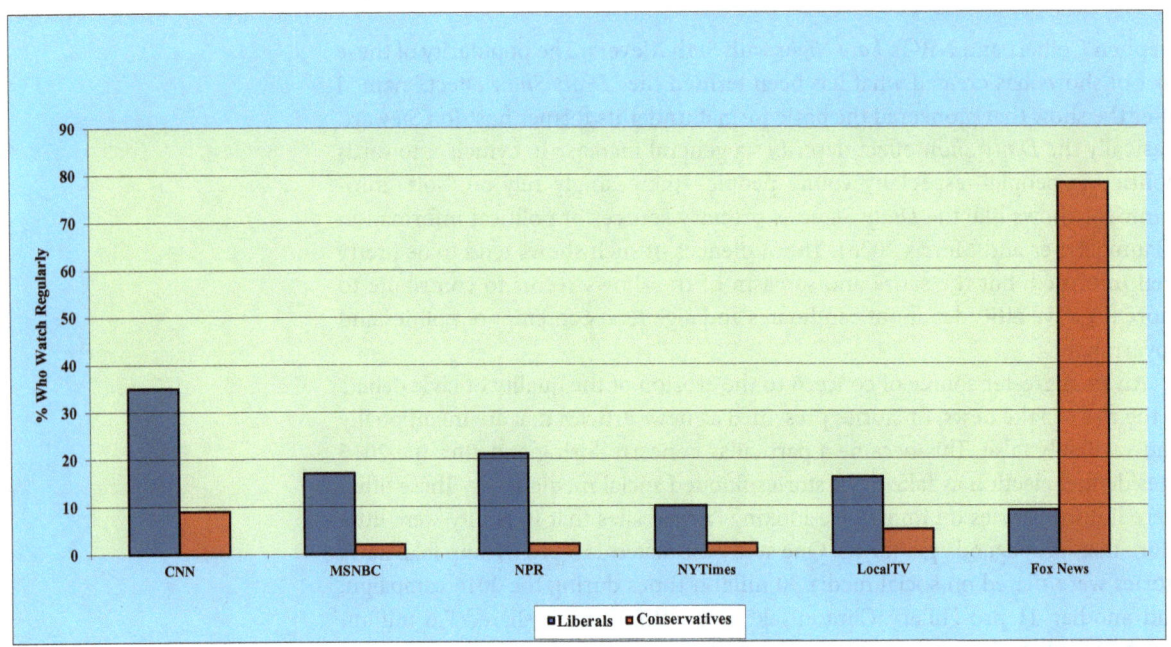

FIGURE 8.2a Ideological Differences in News Sources

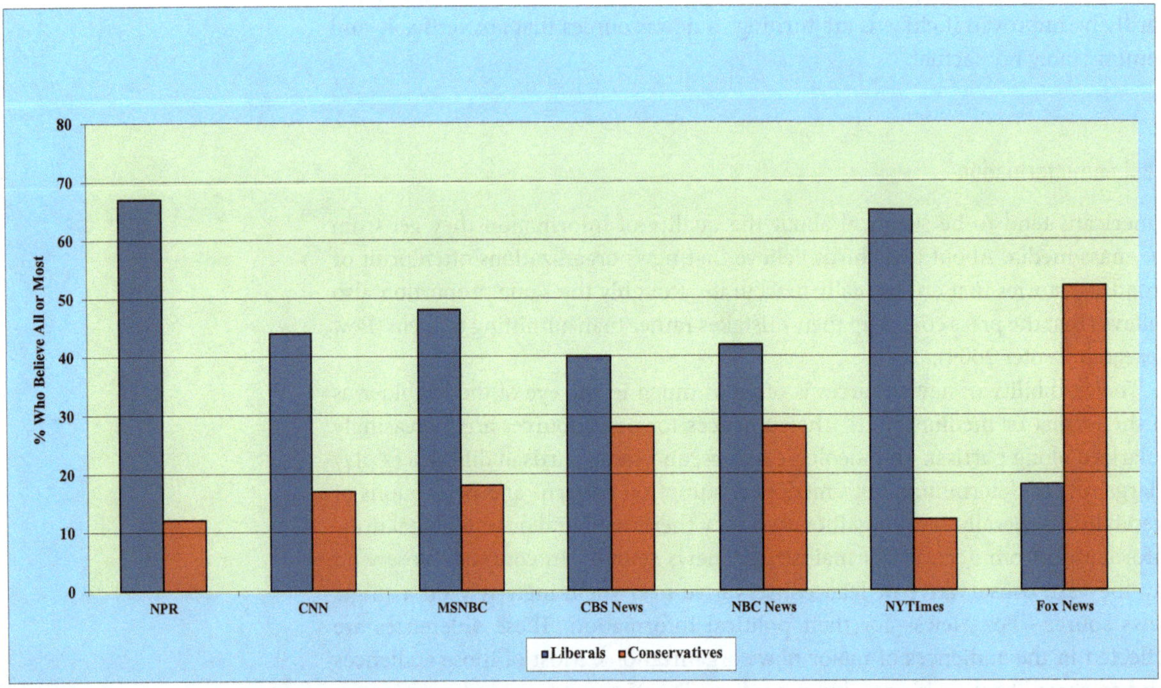

FIGURE 8.2b Ideological Differences in News Media Audiences

Sources: Pew Research Center, "Political Polarization and Media Habits," 2014, http://www.journalism.org/2014/10/21/political-polarization-media-habits/; and Pew Research Center, "Where News Audiences Fit on the Political Spectrum," 2014, http://www.journalism.org/interactives/media-polarization/outlet/rush-limbaugh-show/.

tend to trust their own sources and be more skeptical about the news sources used by the other side. Conservatives, for example, tend to express fairly high levels of distrust towards news sources like CNN and the *New York Times*, but 78 percent of conservatives say they trust Fox News (Mitchell et al. 2014). These patterns of information consumption and trust translate into differing views of the mass media's role in politics. Democrats tend to view the media as performing an important role in keeping politicians honest. Republicans increasingly view the media as an obstacle that prevents politicians from getting things done (Barthel and Mitchell 2017).

Americans, then, give the media mixed grades for the media's information and education role. On the one hand, Americans consume enormous amounts of information from lots of different sources: newspapers, radio, television, the Internet, and social media. Yet the information consumed is viewed as being of mixed quality. Mainstream media outlets are seen as less trustworthy than they were in the past, and the ideology and the partisanship of the viewer determine in no small part what he or she views as a credible information source. Seeing, reading, or hearing is not necessarily believing. These are just the sorts of findings we'd expect given the earlier-discussed theoretical frameworks on how individuals process information. All things being equal, people prefer to have their established beliefs confirmed and therefore seek out news sources that are more likely to do exactly that. News sources that do not provide such confirmation consistently—and this includes virtually all mainstream news media—find their credibility eroding.

Agenda Setting

Media scholar Bernard Cohen famously observed that the press is not very good at telling people what to think but that "it is stunningly successful in telling them what to think about" (1963, 13). This quote sums up the media's powerful role in shaping the public agenda. Simply put, the issues that make the front page of national newspapers and the stories that lead television news broadcasts are the issues that get the most attention from the public and the government. The government cannot pay attention to every single problem at once—it simply does not have the time or the resources. The media's agenda-setting role means it helps the government and the public to focus and prioritize issues and problems.

The media's power to determine the public agenda was confirmed in a study by Maxwell McCombs and Donald Shaw (1972). McCombs and Shaw measured the attention the media were paying to different issues and then asked a group of independent voters what they thought were the most important issues in an ongoing presidential election. What they found was a remarkably strong correlation; in fact, there was virtually no way to statistically distinguish between the prominence of an issue's coverage in the media and how important the issue was ranked by voters.

Yet, although McCombs and Shaw showed that Cohen was essentially correct, other studies have shown that this view of **agenda setting** underestimates the impact of the media. Although news reports are unlikely to make us change our

agenda setting The process of selecting the issues or problems that government will pay attention to.

fundamental political beliefs, it turns out that the media do play a more complex—and in some ways more influential—role than Bernard Cohen implies.

The media's agenda-setting role goes beyond simply identifying and ordering the list of topics that make up the public agenda. Media outlets also frame these issues for the public. **Framing** means emphasizing certain aspects of a story to make them more important (Iyengar and Kinder 1987). The theory behind framing assumes that our attitudes about any given thing—the president, the deficit, the price of gas, the guy sitting next to us in class—are made up of various characteristics associated with that thing. How much someone approves of the job the president is doing, for example, is a product of such characteristics as the president's ideology and partisanship, the president's personal likability, the state of the economy, and a whole lot more. The media frame an issue by emphasizing particular characteristics. For example, if a media story emphasizes a president's likable personality, that characteristic gets more weight. If a story emphasizes the president's failure to reduce the deficit, that characteristic gets more weight. Framing thus influences how we think about issues or topics by shifting what characteristics relevant to those issues or topics are or are not emphasized (see Chong and Druckman 2007). This clearly goes beyond agenda setting. Framing does not simply influence *what* we think about; it also helps shape *how* we think about issues or topics. What issues are emphasized in media coverage and how these issues are framed help us form what Walter Lippman (1922) called "the pictures in our heads."

Some of the most recent scholarship suggests that social media is starting to change the traditional agenda-setting role of the media. It is not that social media is taking over the agenda-setting role, but that the mainstream media has evolved a reciprocal relationship with the new communication platforms. In other words, sometimes Twitter amplifies the news from the mainstream media, increasing its agenda-setting role. Sometimes, however, the information flow can go the other way—something blows up on Twitter, gains the attention of the mainstream media and becomes the basis of news stories (Gruszczynski and Wagner 2017). The classic contemporary example of this is President Donald Trump, whose tweets frequently prompt coverage and analysis by mainstream news outlets.

Watchdog and Public Advocate

Representative democracy is a form of government where the many watch the few. Yet few citizens in modern representative democracies can afford to devote much time to watching government officials. Similarly, not many people have the time or resources to monitor whether the public interest is represented when government decides who gets what, when they get it, and how. If citizens are not watching, who watches to see if government officials are competent and truthful, and who blows the whistle if they are not? Who makes sure that the public interest, not just special interests, is represented in official decision making? The press has traditionally embraced the role of government watchdog, monitoring government officials for

framing Emphasizing certain aspects of a story to make them more important.

signs of corruption or deceit. Increasingly, the press has also taken on the role of public advocate and representative. As *Washington Post* writers Leonard Downie and Robert Kaiser put it, "anyone tempted to abuse power looks over his or her shoulder to see if someone else is watching. Ideally, there should be a reporter in the rearview mirror" (2002, 8).

Journalists not only keep an eye on government, but also see themselves as representatives of the public interest. The public does not send delegates to presidential press conferences, and the public galleries in legislatures are empty much of the time. Reporters, though, are invariably there. One of the roles the press takes upon itself is to use its unique presence and access to stand in for the public, asking questions and probing officials on behalf of the public interest.

There has always been an intense debate both within and outside the journalism community on how the press performs its watchdog function. For example, critics of President Barack Obama argued he got too much of a "free ride" from the media, a perspective that Obama took issue with, saying, "I've got one television station (he was clearly referring to Fox News) that is entirely devoted to attacking my administration" (Stelter 2009). While more positive about Fox News, President Donald Trump has repeatedly claimed the mainstream news media is unfairly critical of his administration.

These differing perspectives demonstrate the complexities of the watchdog function. Is the news media's coverage of the Trump administration good, tough journalism, or is there an element of ideologically motivated spin to it? The answer, of course, is that it depends. It depends not just on the particular story or issue at hand, but also on how the issue or story is viewed. Whether the news media are being principled watchdogs, partisan attack dogs, or gullible government stooges turns out to be very much in the eye of the beholder.

THREATS TO A FREE PRESS

Democracy presumes the existence of a public sphere where information can be freely accessed and transmitted. Without a public sphere, the core values of political freedom and popular sovereignty are difficult to uphold: Unless the people have the means to inform and develop their opinions and points of view, they cannot be truly free, and the will of the people cannot be the highest political authority. The need to maintain a public sphere makes keeping the press free of regulation and censorship a critical issue for democracy.

Yet it is often tempting to place limits on the free access of information. Government officials do not want their secret spying programs publicized; entrenched special interests would rather not have the negative side of their agendas broadcast and publicly dissected. Even though the press is seen as a primary defense of political freedom, most Americans seem to favor at least some form of media censorship. For example, during the initial stages of the war in Afghanistan, one survey showed that roughly 60 percent of Americans favored giving the military more power to control how the press reported operations in that theater (Pew Research Center 2001).

Given that majority sentiment may favor some government regulation of the mass media, protecting the public sphere and keeping the media free of government regulation can be difficult. Majority rule is also a core democratic value, and as we learned in Chapter 1, democracy requires a balancing act when these values come into conflict. Majority sentiment can threaten a free press in two ways: government control and private control. Either threat is capable of shrinking the public sphere, reducing the effectiveness of the media's democratic roles and thus limiting political freedom.

Government Control

In the United States, government's authority to control the press is limited. The primary limitation is the First Amendment, which states in part that "Congress shall make no law … abridging the freedom of speech, or of the press." The courts have consistently interpreted this provision to mean that the news media have great freedom to report on politics as they choose.

A governmental order to prohibit or censor a news story prior to publication or broadcast is known as **prior restraint**, and the Supreme Court has consistently ruled that, except in extraordinary circumstances, prior constraint violates the First Amendment. The only basis on which the government can prevent publication or broadcast of a news story is if the government can convince a court that the story would harm national security, an exception that is exceedingly rare.

Perhaps the best-known court case dealing with prior restraint is *New York Times v. United States* (1971), which dealt with what became known as the Pentagon Papers. The Pentagon Papers referred to a secret government study of U.S. involvement in Southeast Asia that revealed, among other things, that the government had deliberately deceived the public about the impact and success of military operations in Vietnam. In 1971, a copy of the study was leaked to the *New York Times*. A **leak** is a revelation of information that officials want kept secret.

President Richard Nixon sought—and received—a court order preventing the newspaper from publishing its stories about the study. The administration argued that publication of the study would threaten national security by undermining the war effort. But the Supreme Court ruled that this potential threat to national security was not serious enough to justify a prior restraint order, and the story was published.

prior restraint The prohibition or censoring of a news story prior to publication or broadcast.

leak The revealing of information that officials want kept secret.

The federal government did not want pictures of the coffins of U.S. servicemen killed in Iraq and Afghanistan publicized. The First Amendment, however, meant they could not prevent the press from publishing these pictures.

© Bloomberg/Getty Images

Congress has occasionally attempted to place some legal restraints on the freedom of the press, but these attempts are notable more for their failures than for their successes. For example, in 1798, Congress passed the Alien and Sedition Acts, which in part made publishing any "false, scandalous, and malicious writing" a crime. This law was mainly used as a legal tool by the Federalist Party to intimidate and silence critical newspaper editors. Opposition to the law was widespread, and after the Federalists were swept from office in the election of 1800, the law was repealed, those convicted of breaking the law were pardoned, and fines were repaid with interest.

However, the federal government has been given considerably more leeway in regulating broadcast media than in regulating print media. The reason is that broadcast media, unlike print media, rely on a public good to transmit information: the airwaves. There are a limited number of broadcast frequencies, and government began regulating their use in 1934 with the passage of the Communications Act.

Prior to this law, something akin to anarchy prevailed on the nation's radio airwaves, with stations broadcasting on the same frequencies and drowning out one another's transmissions. In the name of the public interest, the Communications Act regulated the nation's airwaves, required broadcast licenses, and established a set of performance standards as prerequisites for obtaining or maintaining a license.

The law also established the Federal Communications Commission (FCC), an independent agency that was empowered to enforce the Communications Act. Today, the FCC is charged with regulating interstate and international communications by radio, television, wire, satellite, and cable. There is no print equivalent of the FCC, and the primary justification for regulating the electronic media is that the industry is heavily based on a limited, public resource: broadcast frequencies.

There has been heated debate over whether the Internet should be treated as a broadcast or print medium. The Communications Decency Act, passed by the 104th Congress, sought to regulate the Internet as a broadcast medium by placing restrictions on indecent content. In *Reno v. ACLU* (1997), the Supreme Court rejected this approach by striking down key provisions of the law. The Court characterized the Internet as a print medium and extended to it the full protections of the First Amendment.

In practice, the regulations imposed on the electronic media are not particularly onerous, though in theory the FCC has the power to revoke licenses and to shut down television and radio stations. Such drastic action is rarely even considered, mainly because such a move would almost certainly provoke a public outcry. Freedom of the press is so embedded as a fundamental value of American society that the government is wary of restricting that freedom even when it has the legal power to do so.

Private Control

Although there are well-established limits on government control of the press, freedom of the press can be limited by private control as well. Left unchecked,

Facebook founder and CEO Mark Zuckerberg. Facebook is arguably the most powerful and influential social media platform in existence and has been criticized for facilitating the spread of fake news.

© Eliot Blondet/Abaca/Sipa/AP Photo

market forces also can limit the free flow of information. This restriction occurs in two basic ways.

The first is concentration of ownership. The public sphere presumes a marketplace of ideas, where numerous interests and points of view compete for attention. But what if the mass media are largely in the hands of a few narrow interests? If control of the news media belongs to only a specific few, what prevents them from censoring or distorting information that harms their interests?

The concentration of media ownership into a small number of powerful hands is not just idle speculation. Since the 1980s, there has been a significant change in the patterns of ownership in the mass media industry. Spurred on by new laws that deregulated the telecommunications industry and the widespread adoption of new technologies such as cable television and the Internet, mass media companies began to recognize and pursue multimedia strategies that allowed them to take advantage of shared resources and economies of scale. In 1983, 50 companies owned an estimated 90 percent of the media outlets in the United States. Thirty years later, only five companies owned 90 percent of the media (Business Insider 2012). Most everyone has heard of those companies, but not everyone realizes the extent of their media holdings. For example, CBS probably brings to mind the television network and its various divisions—CBS News, CBS Sports, and the like. Yet CBS also owns dozens of radio stations, the publishing giant Simon & Schuster, and a slew of online companies, including NFL.com and CNET. Rupert Murdoch's News Corporation owns not just Fox Broadcasting Company and Fox News but also the *Wall Street Journal,* the *New York Post,* and HarperCollins book publishers. Disney is way beyond Mickey Mouse; besides the studio that made it an icon, it owns ABC, ESPN, a radio network, Movies.com, and its own recording and book publishing operations. You can check out for yourself what companies own what media companies at http://www.cjr.org/resources/, a resource provided on the website of the *Columbia Journalism Review.* This concentration of so many media outlets into so few corporate families sets off alarm bells for critics concerned with the impact on the public sphere. For example, would a news organization vigorously pursue a story that reflected negatively on its corporate owner?

The second reason private control may limit the free flow of information is money. Giant media conglomerates such as News Corporation and Time Warner are not in business to promote the public interest or to help realize the core value of political freedom. Like most other businesses, they exist to make money. Profits in the print and electronic media industries are driven largely by advertising, and the larger the audience delivered to advertisers, the more money it is possible to make. Minority and marginalized voices get little attention from corporate media giants—not because big business wants their viewpoints silenced but because there is simply less money in a smaller audience. Some advertisers go beyond simply being interested in media that reach the largest audience: They actually try to influence the information carried by those media. For example, some advertisers have strict policies against buying advertising from media companies whose programming presents their sponsors in a negative light (Herman and McChesney 1997, 7).

The net product of these shifts in the media landscape over the past 20 years is that news itself has become a commodity—a product that is shaped by the forces of supply and demand and packaged to appeal to certain audiences (Hamilton 2004, 7).

Hard news, stories that focus on factual information about important decisions or events, is increasingly deemphasized in favor of **soft news**, stories characterized by opinion, human interest, and even entertainment value. Why? Soft news sells. News has become less focused on the give-and-take of politics or the major events of the day and more on whatever will appeal to audience interests. Ratings and circulation, after all, drive advertising revenues.

Among those who are worried about the impact of the profit motive on news gathering are journalists. Most reporters, especially those working for television or radio, believe that the quality of news coverage is being diluted by profit pressures. Opinions among journalists are notable for their contrast with the executives who handle the business side of news organizations. The latter acknowledge that the profit motive is changing what news organizations do and what they report, but they do not see this as a bad thing (Johnson 2004). Political scientists are not so sure. For example, newspapers have been reducing the number of reporters covering state legislatures, even as their importance as key policymaking institutions is increasing. Why cut coverage of an increasingly important part of government? Budgets and marketing. As political scientist Alan Rosenthal put it, "papers want to find stuff that connects with their audience … news that is more entertainment-oriented" (quoted in Boulard 1999). The fact is that covering state government does not pad the bottom line the way covering Hollywood does.

Ultimately, the danger of private control to the public sphere is not that voices will be legally censored or dissent outlawed, or that there will be government regulation of what can be broadcast or printed. The danger is that the information and messages that cannot attract a profit-making audience will simply be ignored.

MEDIA BIAS

Most people do not perceive government censorship or corporate ownership to be the biggest problem with the mass media. Most people believe the biggest problem is media bias. **Media bias** is the tendency to present an unbalanced perspective so that information is conveyed in such a way that consistently favors one set of interests over another.

hard news Stories that focus on factual information about important decisions or events.

soft news Stories characterized by opinion, human interest, and often entertainment value.

media bias The tendency to present an unbalanced perspective so that information is conveyed in a way that consistently favors one set of interests over another.

Virtually everyone believes at least some media outlets are biased, though there is a lot of disagreement on which outlets and the nature of the bias. This perspective was not always the case. Several decades ago, most people regarded the news media as trustworthy and regarded journalists as professionals who did their best to present information in a fair and balanced manner (Erskine 1970). The high regard that Americans once had for the news media has greatly eroded. In the first decade of the twenty-first century, the vast majority of people—as many as 70 percent—believed that stories in the media were often inaccurate, and 60 percent believed that stories were politically biased (Pew Research Center 2009). There is no single or universally accepted answer to why this change has occurred. In general, though, trust in society's institutions has fallen across the board, and the media have shown no immunity to this trend.

Although most people see the media as biased, they see bias in different ways. There are indeed different sorts of media bias, and the evidence on whether bias exists—and if it does, whether it has any negative impact on civic life—varies according to the type of bias being considered.

Political Bias

When most people discuss media bias, they are usually referring to **political bias**, or the tendency to favor a political party or ideological point of view. Political bias has a long history in the American media.

Prior to the advent of electronic media, most print media were openly partisan. For the first hundred years of the republic, newspapers were often little more than propaganda organs for political parties or other organized interests. The Framers, for example, endured scathing attacks in the press that make the most negative contemporary news stories look mild in comparison.

Consider the career of James Callender, a newspaper editor who made no secret of his political preferences. Writing in the *Richmond Examiner*, Callender called President George Washington a traitor, a liar, and a robber. He referred in print to Washington's successor, John Adams, as a "repulsive pedant," a "gross hypocrite," and a "strange compound of ignorance and ferocity, of deceit and weakness." Callender was put up to some of these character assassinations by none other than Thomas Jefferson, who not only reviewed and approved some of these stories but also probably paid their author to write them (Daniels 1965, 62–67; McCullough 2001, 537).

The partisan press gradually yielded to the vision of **objective journalism**, which seeks to report facts rather than promote a partisan point of view and seeks balance by reporting both sides of any given story (Alger 1996, 122–123). An early promoter of objective journalism was Albert Ochs, publisher of the *New York Times*, who made it the basis for his paper's news coverage at the turn of the twentieth century. This approach gradually became the standard for the mainstream print press and was adopted by the news organizations of the electronic media.

What objective journalism does not take into account is that people themselves are not objective. As discussed earlier, virtually every theory of how people

political bias The tendency to favor a political party or ideological point of view.

objective journalism An approach to journalism that places emphasis on reporting facts rather than on analysis or a partisan point of view.

process information suggests that people will not be neutral consumers of news, regardless of how objective or even-handed those news reports are. Research by political scientists has consistently found that people have a *disconfirmation bias*, or the tendency to dismiss or denigrate information contrary to their own political beliefs, and also an *attitude congruency bias*, or the tendency to uncritically accept information that supports their political beliefs. Alarmingly, researchers have also found that these information-processing biases lead to attitude polarization. This means that people with differing beliefs on a political issue will become further apart on that issue when they consume the same information, regardless of the subjective or objective content of that information (Taber, Cann, and Kucsova 2009).

Few people stop to consider that they might be biased in how they process political information supplied by the media; instead, most are convinced that the news media are presenting information in a biased way. Yet although most people agree that the press has a distinct partisan and ideological tilt, they disagree on which party or ideology the media actually favor. Conservatives tend to make the most consistent and loudest complaints of media bias, and they see the media as distinctly favoring Democrats and a liberal point of view. This claim is buttressed by research finding that reporters tend to be more liberal and more likely to self-identify as Democrats than the average American. Interestingly, journalists seem to have become a bit more conservative over the past decade or two, though they are still clearly more liberal than the general public. This does not mean the ranks of reporters are dominated by left-wingers. About a third of journalists report they are political centrists, a third say they are a little to the left, and about a quarter lean to the right. Only a small fraction—about 10 percent—characterize their politics as very liberal. When it comes to partisanship, about a third of journalists describe themselves as Democrats and about a fifth as Republicans (Weaver et al. 2006).

Liberals reject the notion of a liberal slant in the media; indeed, they see quite the opposite: a media so cowed and intimidated by conservative critics that it is afraid to give right-leaning issues and candidates the same tough scrutiny it gives to the left. Liberals point not to reporters, but to the owners of the dominant media outlets. As we have already seen, these are mostly giant media corporations headed by conservative-leaning business executives.

The problem with political bias in the media, of course, is that it is critics with a liberal or conservative bias of their own who make the charges. Although both the left and the right are convinced that the media

The line between news and entertainment is increasingly blurred, as even traditional news outlets focus more on soft news, or stories characterize by human interest or their entertainment value. Celebrity couples like Jay-Z and Beyonce can make "news" just by watching a basketball game.

© Marcio Jose Sanchez/AP Photo

systematically favor their ideological and partisan opponents, academic studies have been unable to substantiate these claims, at least not in any universal sense. Part of the problem is measuring media bias; two people can read the same story and come to very different views about whether it has a particular ideological or partisan slant. It has proven very hard to develop an objective measure that can sort out what subjective views of media bias might actually have merit.

Political scientist Tim Groseclose developed one of the better-known measures of media bias by looking at how many times a media outlet cited think tanks and policy groups in news stories compared to how many times those same groups were cited by liberal or conservative members of Congress. Using this measure, Groseclose's studies find media outlets to have a distinct leftward tilt (see Groseclose and Milyo 2005; Groseclose 2011). Yet this measure is far from perfect and has been criticized for making even conservative-leaning media outlets look liberal. For example, using Groseclose's measure, Fox News, the *Drudge Report,* and the *Washington Times* are all at least slightly left-leaning, even though these media outlets are generally seen as right-leaning.

One of the most systematic investigations of political bias in recent decades was undertaken by David Niven (2002), who examined the tone and type of coverage of specific issues to see whether they changed based on whether they involved Democratic or Republican officeholders. His conclusion was that no such systematic differences existed. There have been numerous other scholarly studies on political bias in the media and no general conclusion has emerged. Some studies find a bias towards Republicans/conservatives, others toward Democrats/liberals and others no systematic bias at all. Many of these studies have struggled even to define what bias is because it is such a subjective concept (Groeling 2013).

The **propaganda model** suggests that because most mainstream media are corporately owned, the media will be most consistently biased toward corporate interests. Corporate interests mean profit, not neutrality, so according to this model, the media will supply the news (1) that people want to consume and that advertisers are willing to pay for and (2) that supports social agendas that favor corporate interests—for example, by giving more attention and credibility to pro-capitalist viewpoints than those skeptical of capitalist systems. Evidence for the propaganda model is mixed, but it does make a certain amount of rational sense that media outlets would tend to favor—or at least not bite—the hands that feed them (Herman and Chomsky 2002; Puglisi 2008). The propaganda model suggests that if there's a big enough audience and a big enough profit to be made in partisan bias, corporately owned media outlets will be tempted to engage in such bias. It is the profit rather than the politics that is key, though.

Though the most supportable conclusion to draw from all the research is that the press has no general, systematic partisan or ideological bias, there is a growing sense that individual press outlets are increasingly drifting from the objective journalism model. Consistent with the propaganda model, this drift seems to be driven less by ideological commitment than by the corporate bottom line. For much of the twentieth century, the mass media, be it the print or the electronic media, were oriented toward assembling the biggest audience possible. Practically, that meant appealing to the broad middle of America. When there were only three

propaganda model The idea that mainstream media are biased toward corporate and conservative interests because most mainstream media are corporately owned.

THINKING ANALYTICALLY

HOW DO YOU MEASURE MEDIA BIAS?

Public opinion polls tell us that large majorities of Americans believe that the news media tends to play political favorites, fibbing to benefit one side or being unduly influenced by people in power (Center for People and the Press 2011). The media, in short, are seen as biased.

As discussed in the text, though, there isn't much agreement on the nature of that bias or even which specific news outlets are guilty of it. People tend to trust their favorite news sources, and distrust those they do not use. Liberals see conservative bias. Conservatives tend to see liberal bias. Which side has it right? That's a tough question to tackle because the answer requires being able to measure bias. How do you measure media bias? Nobody really knows. Thus far no one has come up with a valid, reliable, and broadly accepted measure of political bias in the media.

This is not for lack of trying. There are actually lots of measures of bias out there, just none that have proven to be universal objective indicators of the media's political leanings. To understand why it is so tough to measure media bias, let's think about this analytically. How can you measure the concept of bias? Keep in mind we are trying to measure the bias of an institution—the media—not the bias of individual people. Think of it like this. Perceptions of height differ among individuals. If you are 5 feet 2 inches, you might perceive someone who is 5 foot 8 inches as tall. If you are 6 feet 8 inches, you might see that same 5 foot 8 inch someone as short. Yet while two people may call the same 5 foot 8 inch person tall or short, there's no denying that objectively this person is 5 feet 8 inches tall. What we're after is a measure of bias that is equivalent to feet and inches. What would that measure look like?

One option suggested by Tim Groseclose and Jeffrey Milyo (2005) is to count the sources cited by a news outlet and compare them to how many times those same sources are mentioned by members of Congress. The basic idea is if conservatives in Congress cite one set of think tanks and policy groups to support their agenda while liberals cite another set, media bias can be detected by looking at which set of think tanks and policy groups are cited more in a news outlet. If the groups cited are disproportionately the same as those cited by conservatives in Congress, the argument goes, that news outlet has a conservative bias, and if the sources line up with those favored by liberals in Congress, then it's got a liberal bent.

Based on their measure, Groseclose and Milyo found a distinct liberal media bias. Their measure, though, leaves a lot of people unconvinced. For example, they find the *Wall Street Journal*—generally considered the national newspaper of conservative-leaning business—is more liberal than National Public Radio and the *New York Times*, which are both routinely accused of liberal bias by conservative business types.

Another option for measuring bias is to use news content rather than news sources. Tim Groeling (2008) opted for this approach in his analysis of how television news broadcasts reported public opinion polls on presidential job performance between 1997 and 2008. If there was bias, Groeling reasoned, outlets were more likely to report increases or decreases in presidential approval based on the political leanings of the president in office. He found ABC, NBC, and CBS were more likely to report increases in presidential approval when Bill Clinton (a Democrat) was in office, and more likely to report decreases in presidential approval when George W. Bush (a Republican) was in office. Fox News did the reverse. Does this show bias? Well, maybe, maybe not. Perhaps ABC, NBC, and CBS weren't wild about George W. Bush, but does that necessary generalize to a dislike of all things Republican or conservative? Does Fox's tendency to emphasize the negative about Bill Clinton translate into a bias against Democrats or liberals in general? The short answer is we simply do not know.

Ceren Budak, Sharad Goel and Justin Rao (2016) took yet a different approach. They crowdsourced the problem by getting roughly 750 people of all different political persuasions to evaluate more than 10,000 political news stories taken from 13 major news outlets.

The basic idea was that if there was any bias a consistent signal should emerge from that many judgements on that many news stories. The only real consistent signal they found was that there is not much political bias in media coverage. Mainstream outlets like the *New York Times*, the *Washington Post*, and the major TV networks, all play things pretty much right down the middle. While there are some detectable differences—between the *New York Times* and Fox News, for example—these were so small as to border on trivial. The traditional mainstream media comes off looking as pretty unbiased in this study.

Yet another approach was taken by Dave D'Alessio and Mike Allen (2000), who did what's known as a meta-analysis of media bias research, which is essentially a research study of research studies. They looked at 59 quantitative studies of media bias in presidential campaigns. What are the common findings on media bias from these dozens and dozens of studies? Well, basically that there isn't any bias. These researchers found slight hints here and there—news magazines seemed a tad more pro-Republican, TV news seemed a tad more pro-Democrat—but these differences were small and pretty insubstantial.

The studies reviewed here are pretty representative of the overall research on this issue. Some studies find the media has a slight general political bias, others find different news outlets have competing political biases, while still other studies find not much evidence of political bias at all. This is a huge contrast to the empirical evidence on whether we as individuals are biased consumers of information. That's a slam dunk: we are. The evidence for bias in the media as an institution is very, very different—it's all over the place. Why? Because it turns out to be incredibly difficult to objectively measure media bias, and without such a measure we cannot definitively say one way or the other if the media is biased.

Discussion Questions

1. What is a better measure of media bias than the measures discussed in the text? How does your measure better capture the concept of bias than these other measures?
2. Why is political bias in the media a problem? Does democracy really need a non-biased press?

television networks, for example, none of them could afford to play political or ideological favorites because catering to the political preferences of one segment of the potential audience meant going against the preferences of another. That risked losing those viewers and the ad revenue they represented. The smart play was to not show any obvious partisan favoritism and to structure news presentations that could appeal to the moderate middle. This was a model that lent itself to objective journalism and to making the mass media a vehicle for producing consensus.

That model started to come under pressure about three decades ago. First, we saw the rise of cable television and with it a proliferation of options other than major networks. Then we saw a massive contraction of the print media as people migrated to the Internet, which offered a seemingly endless variety of options for getting news and information. The net result of this proliferation of choices was a destabilization of the mass media model centered on a broad, middle-of-the-road audience, a model that had lent itself to the practice of objective journalism. Although the holdovers from the previous era—major network news, print publications such as the *New York Times,* and National Public Radio—still more or less operate on that model, other outlets such as cable news operations (MSNBC, Fox News), Internet sites (the *Huffington Post,* the *Drudge Report, Daily Kos, Free Republic*), and talk radio (Rush Limbaugh, Michael Savage) are much more likely to frame politics with a distinct ideological or partisan spin (see Baum and Groeling 2008). From a market point of view, this makes sense; in a world with endless options for information, it makes sense to play to the biases of how people process information rather than try to ignore or override those biases. The upshot is that we may be seeing something of a return to the partisan origins of the press. Taken as a whole, the press is still not distinctly liberal or conservative. Individual press outlets, however, are increasingly less shy about adopting a partisan perspective as a means to appeal to a particular audience segment (Starr 2010).

Thus, although television news overall may have no systematic partisan tilt, Fox News is viewed as the conservative news channel, and CNN and MSNBC are considered liberal news channels. Ironically, news outlets committed to the objective model are increasingly seen as untrustworthy by both sides. It is important to note, however, that this bias is at least as much perceived as real; in other words, it is the people who consume and process information that provide the political bias in the press at least as much as the suppliers of that information (Turner 2007).

Racial and Gender Bias

Although it receives considerably less attention, there is actually a better case for racial and gender bias, rather than partisan bias, in the press. For example, academic studies have consistently found that female candidates for elective office are covered differently in the news media than male candidates. Compared to their male counterparts, females tend to get less news coverage. The coverage female candidates do receive tends to disproportionately focus on "women's issues" such as abortion and education, and it places less emphasis on professional experience and accomplishments than it does on personality, appearance, and fashion decisions (Heldman, Carroll, and Olson 2005; Kahn 1992, 1996).

Academic studies have also found a systematic imbalance in the portrayals of African Americans compared to their white counterparts. Press coverage of Hurricane Katrina's 2005 devastation of New Orleans sparked a running debate on the language used in media stories to describe whites versus blacks. The predominantly black victims of Katrina were often described as "refugees." Victims of hurricane disasters that hit proportionately whiter populations were more likely to be described as "evacuees." Widely distributed photos of Katrina victims taking supplies from grocery stores were captioned differently, with whites "finding food" and African Americans "looting" (Sommers et al. 2006).

Communications scholars believe that these imbalances are at least partially the product of the demographic makeup of newsrooms. Conservatives complain that reporters are too liberal, and liberals complain that media owners are too conservative, but both sides ignore what the majority of reporters, anchors, editors, producers, owners, and shareholders have in common: They are overwhelmingly white males.

For example, historically, stories written by male reporters and published in the *New York Times* outnumber the stories written by females by a ratio of roughly 5–1 (Mills 1997). The most popular politically oriented talk shows are hosted by white males, and the vast majority of these male hosts are self-described conservatives, libertarians, and Republicans (Numbers USA 2002).

Negativity Bias

Perhaps the most open and obvious bias of the media is a tendency to favor stories that emphasize the negative aspects of politics and government. In presidential campaigns, for example, the large majority of candidates' comments are devoted to making a positive case for their candidacies. The large majority of the media's coverage of presidential campaigns, however, focuses on the negative attacks the candidates make on each other (Morin 2000).

In the media's defense, there are some good reasons for the bias toward negativity. The watchdog function of the press discussed earlier tends to promote an emphasis on reporting incompetence or wrongdoing in government. The press believes that it is the press's responsibility, at least in part, to alert the public to government misconduct, and the logical consequence is that stories emphasizing the negative get more coverage and more prominence. According to one study, approximately 80 percent of the news stories on President Trump's first 100 days in office were negative in tone (Patterson 2017). Some took this as evidence of media bias against Trump, but the patterns uncovered by the study make that unlikely. For example, 65 percent of the talking about Trump in television news coverage came from Donald Trump himself. Another 11 percent of the talk time was from administration officials, and another 4 percent was from various representatives of the Republican Party. Only 6 percent of the talk content in television news stories came from Democrats, and only 3 percent from protests. If there was any bias in the media it seemed to be towards giving the president and his spokespeople a disproportionate amount of time to get their side of the story out on national television.

What seemed to be driving the unusually strong media focus on the Trump administration was a series of attention-grabbing issues that largely reflected negatively on the president. This included Russian interference in the election, a string of controversial appointments, and a range of provocative statements from the president himself. It is just these sort of unusual and extreme stories that get the media's attention. Most of what government does is rarely considered news by journalists and editors. A front-page story headlined "Government Agency Run Pretty Competently, Does Job Reasonably Well" accurately describes the typical humdrum day-to-day reality of government, but it is not considered news. It is the exception to this general rule that gets the attention of the press. The Trump administration provided a steady string of those exceptions and the media avidly covered them.

The media's bias toward the negative may prompt people to be negative and cynical about politics. For example, the media tend to emphasize **strategic framing**, which means the story emphasizes which candidate or partisan side is winning or losing. This focus can create a cynical view of the political process, even when the people involved in that process are not being adversarial.

---

strategic framing Giving prominence in media stories to who is gaining or losing on an issue.

CHANGES IN THE PUBLIC SPHERE

Why has public trust in the media eroded, and why are so many Americans convinced that the media are biased? These are complicated questions that have a number of answers. As mentioned previously, there has been a general decline in trust in most of society's major institutions during the past three or four decades, and the media are no exception to this overall trend.

Yet the revolution in communications technology has had a particularly notable impact on the media. This revolution occurred at the same time as a number of broad-reaching changes in the political environment. The net result is that compared to the media of the 1990s, not to mention the 1960s, today very different media are shaping a very different public sphere.

As discussed previously, the technological changes include the rise of cable television, the introduction and widespread use of the Internet, and especially the rise of social media. Combined, these destabilized a long period during which political news had been dominated by three major television network news organizations, daily newspapers, news magazines such as *Time* and *Newsweek,* and radio news organizations such as National Public Radio. Generally, all practiced the objective journalism model.

These technological changes were accompanied by significant developments in the broader social and political environment. For example, the information revolution helped foster the rise of multinational corporations, organizations that defied traditional political boundaries. Japanese companies now make cars in America with components imported from China and Mexico. Multinationals may have tremendous economic clout in a single state or country, but they are not bound to the laws of any single nation; profit, not patriotism or ideology or the canon of journalistic values, is their guiding force. Media companies were not excluded from this trend. Companies such as Time Warner and News Corporation are international conglomerates.

The past 20 years have also seen the rapid expansion of single-issue interest groups (as discussed in Chapter 6), which have taken advantage of the new communications opportunities to aggressively promote narrowly focused agendas. Groups such as the National Rifle Association can (and do) raise and spend millions backing candidates who support their policy preferences. Many of those millions are poured into sophisticated media campaigns that focus on narrowly targeted interests. These sorts of developments have had important consequences for the public sphere. Notably, they have resulted in the decline of the media as gatekeepers and the potential for new technology to reshape civic engagement.

The Decline of the Gatekeepers

A **gatekeeper** is someone or some institution that controls access to something. In the mass media, the people who actually make decisions about what to print or

gatekeeper A person or institution that controls access to something.

what to broadcast (journalists, editors, and producers) and the organizations they work for have traditionally been considered gatekeepers of information. Thirty or forty years ago, editors and producers at major news organizations could realistically be viewed as society's information gatekeepers—a relatively small group of people decided what political information reached a mass audience. That is no longer the case. Control over information has been pushed downward and made more diverse.

Individuals now have numerous choices for obtaining very specialized and specific information. Cable television and, especially, the Internet and social media give individuals enormous control over the sorts of information they gather and consume. In some respects, this development has a positive impact on promoting the public sphere. Citizens now have virtually unlimited access to information, and they are much less reliant on a small number of gatekeepers to decide what information they will or will not get. Because the new technology is often social and highly interactive (think Facebook, Twitter, Snapchat), some political scientists are optimistic that the technology will make it easier for the average citizen to participate meaningfully in the exchange of ideas and opinions that make up the public sphere (Krueger 2002).

Yet there is also clearly a downside to these developments. The rise of cable television, the Internet, and social media has also fueled fierce competition among media organizations, which now have to fight harder to attract and maintain an audience that has an abundance of information options. Some see this cutthroat competition as having profoundly negative effects on the quality of information produced by news organizations. Political scientist David Swanson, for example, argues that the intense competition to find an audience "has led to a loosening of commitments to traditional journalistic values and canons of practice, resulting in news that is more sensationalized ... and less governed by serious news values" (2000, 411). This argument is backed up in a study by Matthew Baum and Tim Groeling (2008), which finds that traditional gatekeepers are increasingly being replaced with nontraditional alternatives, including not just cable news and talk radio, but even amateur bloggers. On social media it's not even clear that there are any gatekeepers as individuals follow stories not because professional journalists and editors have vetted them, but because friends or family recommend them (Anspach 2017). Platforms like Facebook not only have a more the merrier approach to information sharing; they also have a hard time filtering out fake news and propaganda. The standards of what qualifies as news and how that news is presented are very different between traditional and nontraditional gatekeepers. The former is much more likely to stick to the values embedded in the model of objective journalism; the latter is much more likely to pick and present stories with a clear partisan or ideological slant.

Historically, the mass media filtered information on the basis of quality as well as its ability to attract an audience. As new media shoulder aside traditional gatekeepers, the quality of information is given much less weight; the focus is squarely on whatever story will attract an audience. News has become a commodity, "a product shaped by the forces of supply and demand" (Hamilton 2004, 8). The result is a public sphere that is at least as dominated by celebrity profiles or the latest diet fad as by important policy issues. Media organizations have discovered that entertaining, rather than educating and informing, gets the bigger audiences and thus the bigger profits.

Information and Civic Engagement

Whatever the negative consequences of changes in communications technology, political scientists are increasingly interested in the potential impact on civic engagement. Social media and the Internet dramatically lower the cost of exchanging information. Will lowering the barriers and costs of exchanging information expand the public sphere in a positive way? Perhaps not.

In theory, new information technologies hold the potential to draw more citizens into the public sphere. At the dawn of the Internet era, scholars were hopeful that computer-based communication options would provide "an inviting opportunity for democratic dialogue" (T. Benson 1996, 61). By creating a virtual commons where people could exchange ideas and opinions in a "spirit of community and civility," the Internet was expected to provide a unique way to expand and improve the public sphere (T. Benson 1996, 61).

But the new communications technology clearly has not lived up to such idealistic hopes. People rarely surf the Web or check a social media feed to have their opinions and beliefs challenged; they tend to seek out sites and forums that fit their interests and preferences. Interactive forums do not automatically promote civil exchange. One study's conclusions about online media forums are succinctly summed up by a quote taken directly from a forum post: "destroy the scum, and then neuter their families" (Coffey and Woolworth 2003). Internet trolls and Tweet storms rarely promote reasoned civil debate.

There are clearly tradeoffs in the rise of new media and how they are employed by a changing democratic society. On one hand, "more citizens have more ready access to more information and opinion than ever before ... concerning more topics of both public and personal interest" (Swanson 2000, 412). On the other hand, "the Internet is filled with advocacy masked as information, with rumor and innuendo, and with the simply outrageous" (Swanson 2000, 412). The burden of judging information for its reliability and importance to the public sphere has clearly shifted toward the individual citizen and away from gatekeepers who served the old media model using a set of professional standards. The new media platforms seem less interested in facts and building civic community than in using outrage to grab audience share, capturing attention "with edgy content that shocks the audience while simultaneously flattering them for their moral and intellectual superiority, as demonstrated by their ability to see through the manipulative smoke, mirrors, and buffoonery offered by the other side" (Sobieraj and Berry 2011).

Some argue that these developments are a good thing, because they expand the political freedom of the individual. If unlimited access to information and access to a virtual press is within the grasp of every citizen, this is a good thing for democracy. Some research supports this positive view of the impact of new information technology on the public sphere. One study, for example, suggests that the

The freedoms of speech and of the press provide a wide-open opportunity to express views and exchange information, but they offer no guarantees of civility or civic debate. In the 2016 election, some opponents of Hillary Clinton did not just oppose her presidential candidacy, they openly called for her to be jailed.

© Evan Vucci/AP Photo

Internet significantly enhances voter information about candidates and elections and in doing so plays an increasingly important role in mobilizing voters and encouraging political participation (Tolbert and McNeal 2003). Many public officials, for example, have embraced Twitter. U.S. Senator Chuck Schumer (D-NY), for example, has more than a million followers on Twitter, giving him near-instant ability to share his political views with a very large audience.

Others are not so sure. Rather than building democratic community, some see the new media environment as dividing the public sphere. Consider the rising prominence of blogs in politics. There are many political blogs, some of which attract tens of thousands of regular readers and are a part of the daily information consumption patterns of political junkies. Examples include the *Daily Kos* (http://www.dailykos.com), a blog aimed at Democrats and liberals, and *Instapundit* (http://instapundit.com/), a blog with a libertarian slant. Blogs such as these not only disseminate the views and opinions of their authors but also can have a more direct impact on politics. The *Daily Kos,* for example, has helped raise and distribute to Democratic candidates hundreds of thousands of dollars in campaign contributions.

There is little doubt that blogs are here to stay or that their influence will continue to increase. High-profile electoral campaigns attract competing blogs; indeed, sometimes they are covert operations of the campaigns themselves (Kuhn 2004). Although few doubt that blogs and their offshoots, like Twitter, are an increasingly influential information source in the political world, there are mixed opinions on whether their overall contribution is positive or negative. Blogs typically make no pretensions to objectivity, and some spew ruthless—and not particularly well-sourced—attacks on perspectives and people from the opposite end of the partisan or ideological spectrum. In some ways, blogs are an unrepentant return to the partisan press of the past. Were he alive today, James Callender would almost certainly have a political blog, most likely a very popular one. Whether the contributions of the contemporary cyberspace Callenders are good or bad undoubtedly very much depends on whether you share their political opinions.

CHAPTER EIGHT
Top 10 Takeaway Points

1. The mass media are the means used to transmit information to masses of people. The mass media include the print media, the electronic media, and the news media. Generically, all are known as the press.

2. The press plays an important role in supporting the key democratic value of political freedom by helping to create a public sphere, a forum where information on issues important to civic life can be freely accessed and exchanged. It performs this role by giving us the information necessary to effectively and responsibly criticize governmental policies and leaders, propose new courses of action, and discuss political issues.

3. Different types of media provide different types of information. Citizens who rely more on newspapers tend to be more knowledgeable about politics than those who rely on other media.

4. The media have several specific roles in a democratic society that help promote the core value of political freedom. These roles include providing information and education, setting agendas, and acting as a watchdog and public advocate.

5. Most theories of how information is processed suggest that people are not neutral consumers of news. Our partisan and ideological viewpoints help determine what information and news sources we consider credible.

6. The media have taken over several of the traditional roles of political parties and are now a primary connection between citizens and government.

7. There are two basic threats to a free press: government control and private control. In the United States, government has always had a limited ability to control the press because of the First Amendment. Private control is more of a concern because profit pressures lead the mass media to ignore opinions and issues that will not attract large audiences.

8. Most people believe the media are biased, though scholarly evidence supporting these beliefs is inconclusive. There is little evidence of an overall systematic political bias in the media, though specific outlets do seem to be more willing than in the past to employ partisan frames. There is considerable evidence to support the idea of racial and gender bias. Negativity bias is confirmed by most systematic research.

9 A biased press is not necessarily a threat to democracy. Most important is a free press.

10 Changes in communications technology coupled with changes in the broader social, political, and economic environment have changed the mass media in important ways. Technology has increased the size of the public sphere and lowered the costs of participation. Competitive pressures, concentration of ownership, and other trends have diluted the media's gatekeeper function, and some critics argue that the quality of news reporting has been lowered as well.

CHAPTER EIGHT
Key Terms and Cases

agenda setting, 271
electronic media, 260
fake news, 269
framing, 272
gatekeeper, 285
hard news, 277
leak, 274
mass media, 260

media bias, 277
misinformation, 268
news, 261
news media, 261
objective journalism, 278
political bias, 278
press, 261
print media, 260

prior restraint, 274
propaganda model, 280
public sphere, 261
social media, 260
soft news, 277
strategic framing, 284

9 PUBLIC OPINION AND POLITICAL SOCIALIZATION

KEY QUESTIONS

Why is public opinion so important to policymaking in the United States?

Does public opinion really reflect the will of the people?

Where do political opinions come from?

© Jose Luis Magana/AP Photo

ABRAHAM LINCOLN ONCE SAID, "What I want to get done is what the people desire to have done, and the question for me is how to find that out exactly" (Crispi 1989, 1–2). Although many people would consider this a worthy and democratic sentiment, others might consider it naive, foolish, and perhaps even dangerous. It is all of these.

Given what we learned in Chapter 1, the democratic appeal of Lincoln's words should be obvious. Lincoln is expressing a straightforward desire to uphold the key democratic principle of majority rule. Yet Lincoln's desire to have the government do the people's bidding raises two problems. The first is practical: How do you find out what the people want? This problem is far from trivial. In most democracies, and certainly in the United States, citizens are rarely of one mind about anything. The people want government to do different things about everything from budget deficits to military operations in the Middle East. Ask the people whether they support Policy X to address Problem A, and the answer will almost always be yes. And no. And maybe. It all depends on what particular group of people you talk to.

How is it possible to add up the disagreements and different attitudes into a clear expression of the people's will? Lincoln had no systematic answer to this question. Seventy years after Lincoln's death, Elmo Roper, George Gallup, and Archibald Crossley proposed such a systematic answer. These individuals—a journalism professor, a jewelry salesman, and a market researcher—pioneered scientific public opinion polling (Crispi 1989). Scientific polling provided the first reliable way to assess public opinion on a particular issue or question. As such, public opinion polling is viewed by some as an expression of the will of the people and as a means to measure the preferences of the majority.

The second problem with fulfilling Lincoln's goal to follow the popular will is philosophical: Should the government really do what the people want? Public opinion turns out to be an unreliable basis for making policy because responses to survey questions are often uninformed, contradictory, and quick to change (Zaller 1992). Thus, the advent of scientific public opinion polling created a conundrum: On one hand, citizens rightfully expect government to act on their preferences; this cuts to the heart of the core democratic principle of majority rule. On the other hand, simply translating public opinion into policy can lead to ineffective, irresponsible, and even undemocratic answers to the question of who gets what.

The Founders had no knowledge of scientific polling, but they clearly felt that the whims of the masses—what we would call public opinion—should not guide government decision making. Accordingly, the Constitution deliberately avoided establishing a government to quickly translate the will of the people into public policy. Indeed, as discussed in Chapters 2 and 3, the Constitution does exactly the opposite. By design, it provides checks on the will of a majority to minimize threats to the rights of the minority and keeps key policymakers at arm's length from popular passions. In doing so, the Constitution seeks to uphold the core democratic principles of political freedom and political equality.

Yet the Founders did not renounce the principle of majority rule; they wanted a system that would govern with the consent of the governed. Popular governments existed long before scientific polling. In these early popular governments, the preferences of the citizens were communicated to government leaders through direct political participation rather than through surveys and opinion polls. Political participation has multiple forms, including voting, lobbying, circulating petitions, and e-mailing public officials. The Founders were very clear about protecting citizen rights to participate in this fashion, to petition government and speak their mind about public policy; that's what the First Amendment to the Constitution is all about. Yet clearly there is friction and contradiction between the core democratic principles and the system established by the Founders. The Founders wanted the government to be responsive to the preferences of citizens (to uphold the principle of majority rule), but not too responsive because they feared the majority might seek to trample the political equality and freedom of a minority.

The Founders tried to balance the inherent conflicts between these core principles by creating a system of government that would respond to the public will but act in the public interest. They did this by deliberately insulating much of government from the stormy winds of public opinion but also making clear that the government's authority and legitimacy rested on the will of the people. This is a tough balancing act to pull off without shorting at least one of the core principles.

In this chapter, we examine how well the American political system achieves this difficult balancing act by looking at what public opinion is, how it is measured, where it comes from, and the central role it plays in the American political system. This analysis provides a context for an examination of how political participation translates individual opinions, attitudes, and beliefs into action to influence public policy.

THE CONCEPT OF PUBLIC OPINION

Public opinion is the sum of individual attitudes or beliefs about an issue or question. Although this basic definition is simple, straightforward, and mostly accurate, it oversimplifies what is, in fact, a complex concept. What citizens think or feel about an issue depends on a variety of factors, most of which can change quickly. Measuring and understanding public opinion on any given issue is more than just a problem of arithmetic, or simply adding up who is for or against a proposed policy. To fully appreciate what public opinion is, it is useful to break it down into its basic elements: direction, stability, intensity, and salience.

Direction

The term **direction** refers to whether public opinion is positive or negative (favorable or unfavorable) about a given issue. On some issues, public opinion has no clear direction. Consider abortion, for example. Public policy on abortion is a controversial issue, and the government is frequently pressured to defend or restrict abortion rights. What should the government do in order to follow the will of the people on this issue?

As it turns out, public opinion is of little help in finding a clear answer to this question. As Figure 9.1 shows, positive and negative attitudes about abortion are more or less evenly balanced, with a slight majority favoring some limits but opposing an outright ban. This division leaves government with no clear signal from public opinion, with each specific proposal to place limits on abortion the subject of its own controversial debate.

Stability

The element of **stability** is the likelihood of changes in the direction of public opinion. On some issues, public opinion retains a clear direction (or lack of direction) over long periods of time. Strongly pro-choice and pro-life attitudes, for example, have remained relatively stable in the U.S. population for the last quarter-century. During this time, roughly a quarter of Americans believed abortion should be legal in all circumstances, and a slightly smaller proportion believed it should be illegal in all circumstances. The majority of Americans consistently put themselves between these two extremes. Notice that the trend lines of opinions for all three positions in Figure 9.1 are essentially flat (the slopes of the trend lines and the correlation coefficients are close to zero). The trends for the extreme positions diverge somewhat in the mid-1990s, but neither position has tended to greatly increase or decrease over more than a quarter-century.

---

public opinion The sum of individual attitudes or beliefs about an issue or question.

direction The idea of public opinion being either positive or negative (favorable or unfavorable) on an issue.

stability The likelihood of changes in the direction of public opinion.

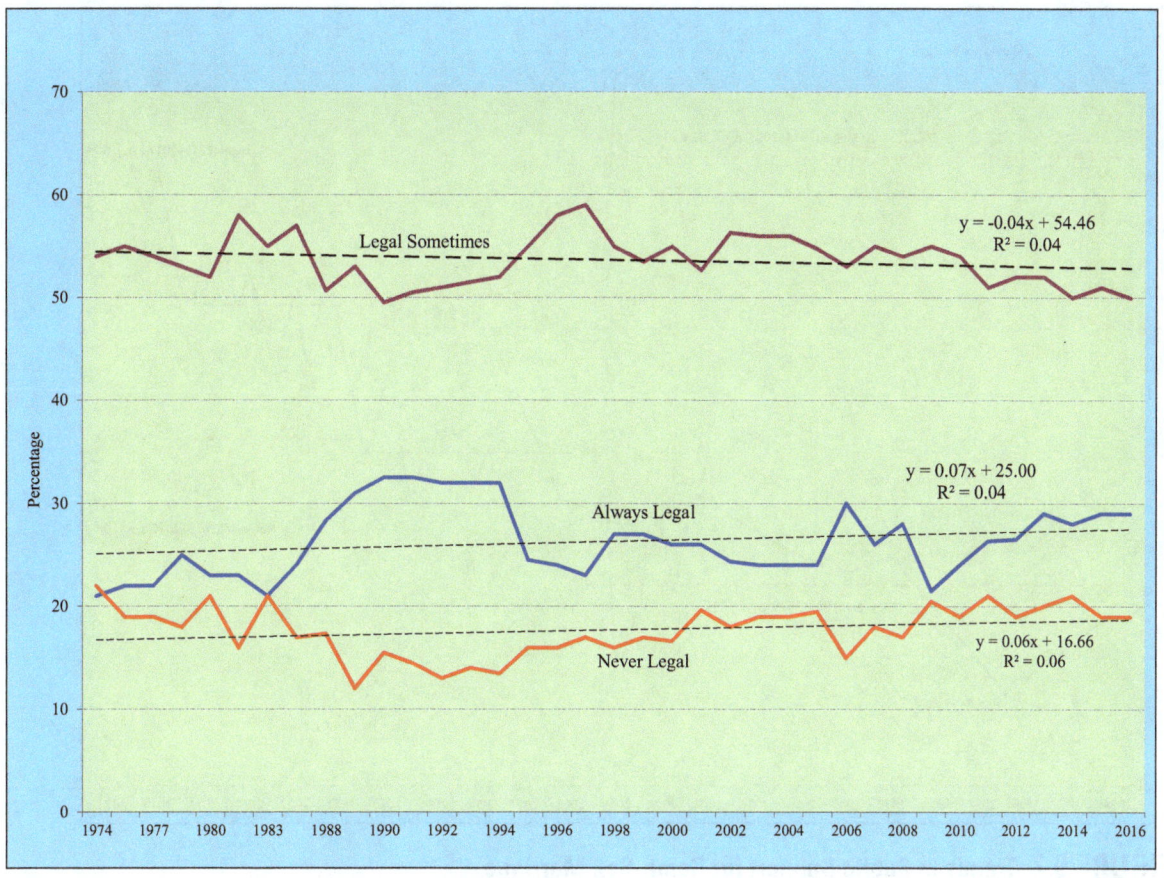

FIGURE 9.1 Trends in Public Opinion on Abortion

Source: Data from Gallup polls asking, "Do you think abortions should be legal under any circumstances, legal only under certain circumstances, or illegal in all circumstances?" http://www.gallup.com/poll/1576/Abortion.aspx (accessed May 22, 2017).

On other issues, however, attitudes and beliefs are more volatile, with the direction of public opinion subject to shifts because of new information or experiences. Contrast the stability of abortion attitudes with public opinion on another controversial social issue—whether gay and lesbian couples should be allowed to marry. Figure 9.2 shows a remarkable turnaround in public opinion on same-sex marriage. From 1994 to 2005, an average of just 33 percent of Americans supported the right of gay men and lesbians to marry, while 61 percent opposed. Public opinion over the next decade was closely divided, with a bare majority opposed from 2006 to 2010, and a bare majority supporting from 2011 to 2014. By June of 2015, on the eve of the Supreme Court decision legalizing same-sex marriage, public support had climbed to 60 percent, and opposition fell to 37 percent. Unlike the solid majority of Americans who support legalizing same-sex marriage, the Court's decision (*Obergefell v. Hodges,* 2015) was decided by a 5–4 vote. Thus, over the course of a decade, public opinion completely reversed itself on this controversial

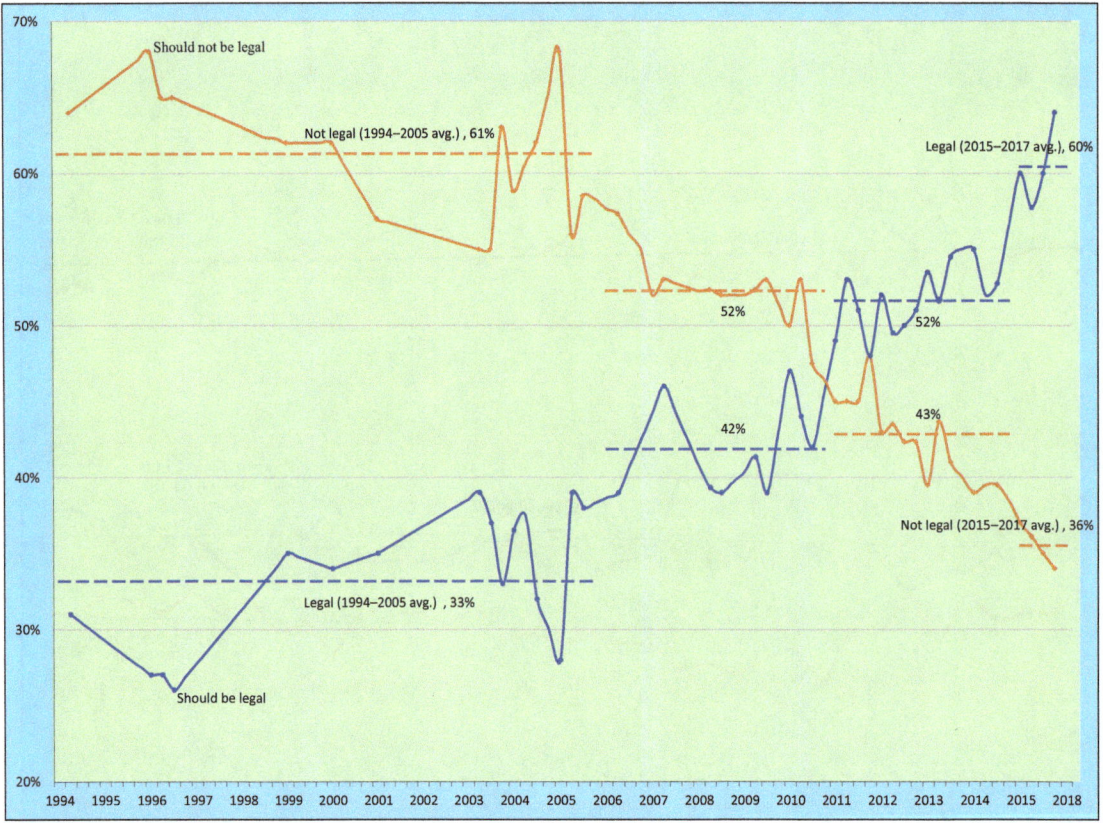

FIGURE 9.2 Trends in Public Support for Same-Sex Marriage

Source: Data from polls by various organizations (Gallup Poll, Pew Research Center, ABC/WP, CBS News/NYT, and Time/CNN) reported on PollingReport.com, http://pollingreport.com/civil.htm (accessed June 21, 2017). Question wording (with slight variation) was, "Do you think it should be legal or illegal for gay and lesbian couples to get married?"

social issue. Since the Supreme Court ruled that the Constitution protects the right of gay men and lesbians to marry, public support has ticked upward. In 2017, roughly two-thirds of Americans supported legalized same-sex marriage, and only a third were in opposition. Reversals of opinion on social issues, especially on this scale, are rare. Recall that public opinion on abortion has remained highly stable over more than four decades (see Figure 9.1). And support for capital punishment has been highly stable over seven decades. Except for a brief period in the 1960s, large majorities (typically more than 60 percent) of Americans express support for the death penalty (Jones 2014).

Intensity

intensity How strongly people hold the beliefs or attitudes that comprise public opinion.

How strongly people hold the attitudes and beliefs is the **intensity** of public opinion. Low intensity tends to make public opinion less stable, given that people are more willing to change their minds if they are not strongly attached to one point of view. Public opinion on issues where large numbers of people have intensely held views tends to be more stable. People with strong pro-choice or pro-life views, for example, tend to be very firm in their beliefs and are resistant to arguments or information coming from the other side.

Salience

Salience refers to the prominence and visibility of an issue and how important that issue is to the public. Individuals differ in their opinions about what issues are most important—or salient. Although salience and intensity may seem to be essentially the same thing, they are different concepts. Some citizens may have very intense views on abortion, but they may view economic problems or war as more important in terms of what affects their daily lives. If we add up all the differing opinions about which issues are most important, we get an indication of which issues are most salient to the public in general at a given point in time. Abortion may be salient periodically if a proposal to limit abortion rights or a court case on the subject is prominently covered by the news media. For much of the time, however, few people view abortion as one of the most important issues facing the nation. Instead, the economy and crime consistently show up as two of the most important issues.

Public opinion does not provide the government with clear guidance for making decisions related to abortion. Although attitudes and intensity have remained strong and stable, direction has been evenly balanced between those for and those against for many years, and the topic's salience wanes unless a specific issue becomes prominent.

© Paul J. Richards/AFP/Getty Images

Other issues, such as civil rights or healthcare, sometimes gain in salience if there is a great deal of media attention or political debate among policymakers. For example, in polls taken during the civil rights movement in the 1960s, civil rights consistently appeared among the most important issues facing the nation, and healthcare appeared toward the top in 1993–1994 when President Bill Clinton made it a legislative priority, and again in more recent years as Obamacare became a central point of conflict between Democrats and Republicans. When the nation is at war, war becomes more salient, as was the case with Vietnam from the mid-1960s to the mid-1970s and with the wars in Iraq and Afghanistan. An economic recession can also make certain issues more salient, and this was certainly the case as the United States sought to recover from the great recession of 2008–2009. In recent years, most polls indicated that Americans thought the economy, national security, and healthcare were the most important issues facing the nation (see Figure 9.3).

To provide the government with a clear signal on what it is expected to do in response to a particular question or issue, the elements of public opinion must come together in a particular way. Public opinion needs to have a clear direction

salience The prominence or visibility of an issue or question and how important the issue is to the public.

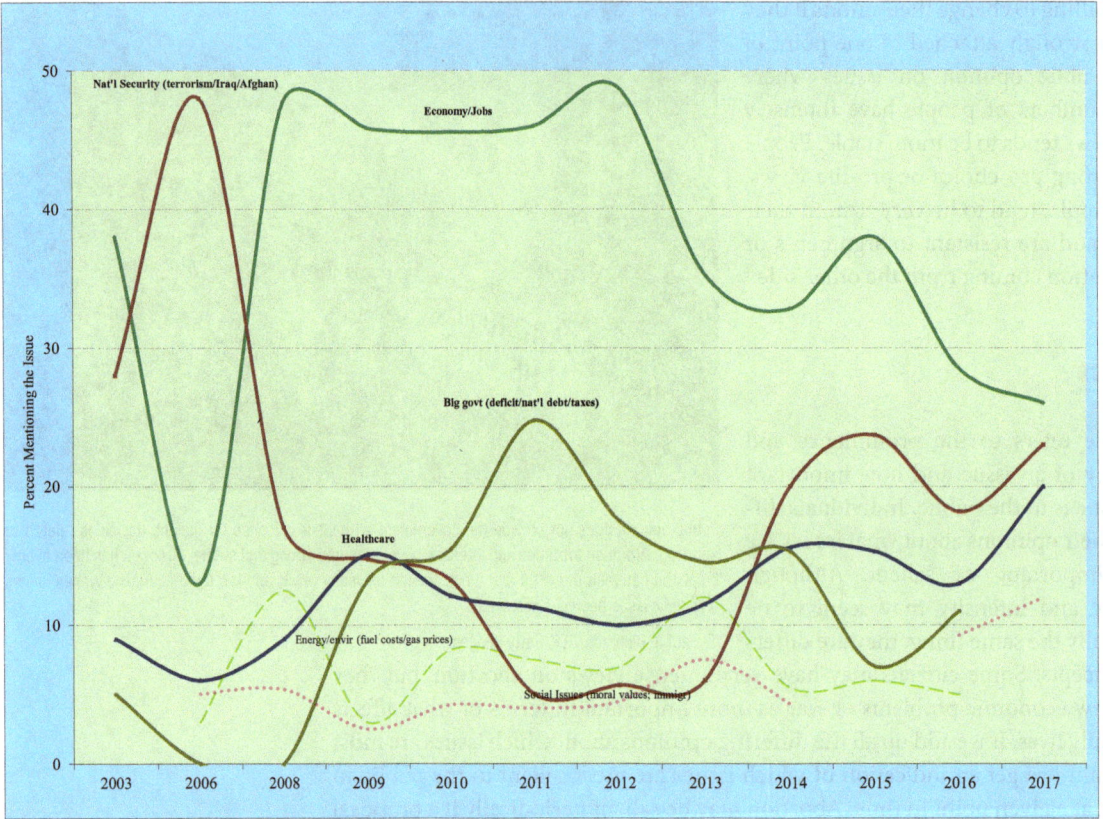

FIGURE 9.3 Public Opinion on Most-Salient Issues

Source: Data from polls by Bloomberg, CBS News/*New York Times*, CNN, Fox News, NBC News/*Wall Street Journal*, ORC, and Quinnipiac University reported at http://pollingreport.com/prioriti.htm (accessed June 21, 2017). Entries are annual averages of responses to questions asking "the most important issue for the federal government to address today."

and reflect high levels of intensity, be stable across a reasonable period of time, and concern an issue of high salience. The concurrence of all four elements is rare. On most issues facing the government, one or more elements are missing: Public opinion is divided or unstable, attitudes are not strongly held, or the issue is of low interest to most people.

Thus, rather than offering clear guidance, public opinion can often create difficult choices for government leaders. If the public knows little about a complex issue, considers it of little importance, and has no strong feelings one way or the other, public opinion can be a poor basis for deciding questions of who gets what. Public ignorance or indifference creates an obvious problem for a system with a strong preference for the delegate model. If public opinion cannot provide a competent basis for sound decision making, a system premised on following the dictates of public opinion is going to reflect that incompetence.

THE COMPETENCE OF PUBLIC OPINION

The appropriate role of public opinion in democratic government has been the subject of debate for a long time. Some, like George Gallup, believe that public opinion is a scientifically valid measure of the will of the people. As a direct measure of the will of the people, Gallup viewed public opinion polling as a means to uphold the core principle of majority rule; if scientific opinion polls can accurately gauge the will of the majority, then they should play an important role in guiding political decisions. This reflects a **delegate model of representative democracy**, which holds that the job of elected officials is not to act independently, making whatever decisions they feel are in the best interests of the community or society. Rather, their job is to translate the views of the majority, whatever those views may be, into government action. Others strongly disagree with Gallup's perspective, arguing that his view is not only naïve but even dangerous.

Walter Lippmann, a contemporary of Gallup, expressed this contrary view. He argued that public opinion is little more than a collection of individual biases that rest as much on ignorance and prejudice as on knowledge and rational thought. His great fear was that unless citizens were well informed about political issues, public opinion could be easily manipulated by groups promoting narrow interests. Prejudice, ignorance, and the self-interested campaigns of interest groups are hardly the best basis for making policy that serves the public interest. Lippmann argued that rather than a delegate model of democracy, the political system would be better served by a **trustee system of democracy**. In a trustee system, public officials are expected to be experts on the issues, and they make decisions they believe to be in the public interest, whether or not those decisions are supported by public opinion. In effect, Lippmann argued that public opinion was too ill-informed and too biased to be a guide for policies and laws that needed to both be effective and serve the public interest. Governing was best left to an elite that was knowledgeable enough to see beyond its own interests (Lippmann 1949, 195).

Political scientists have found a good deal of evidence to support Lippmann's criticisms of public opinion. People often express strong opinions about issues, candidates, and parties even though they have little factual information about these matters (Sears and Valentino 1997). Political scientist John Zaller found that "most people aren't sure what their opinions are on most political matters, including even such completely personal matters as their level of interest in politics" (1992, 76). Some studies have found that many voters are so uninformed on political issues they cannot accurately translate their policy preferences into a vote choice. In other words, ignorance of basic political facts means many citizens end up voting against their own policy preferences and personal interests (Fowler and Margolis 2014).

Low levels of political knowledge also make it easier to manipulate public opinion, at least as it is reflected in a given poll. Students of public opinion have long

delegate model of representative democracy The idea that the job of elected leaders is to make decisions solely based on the views of the majority of the people.

trustee system of democracy The idea that the job of elected leaders is to make decisions based on their own expertise and judgment, and not just make decisions based on the wishes and preferences of constituents.

known that responses to public opinion polls are influenced by the wording and the order of the questions. This knowledge can lead to attempts to distort public opinion to support a particular issue or candidate. For example, a **push poll** deliberately feeds respondents misleading information or leading questions in an effort to "push" them into favoring a particular candidate or issue. In a push poll, the interviewer might ask the respondent which candidate he or she favors in an upcoming election. If the response is "wrong"—in other words, if the respondent favors the candidate opposed by whoever is backing the push poll—there will be a follow-up question designed to push support away from this candidate. For example, the next question might be "Would you still support this candidate if you knew he favored tax increases?"

The broader question here is that if public opinion is so ill-informed and easily manipulated, can it really serve as a competent guide for making public policy?

ELITE OPINION AND ISSUE PUBLICS

The argument that public opinion is a poor basis for answering questions of who gets what obviously has some merit. Yet it can also be argued that, in at least some ways, public opinion is an informed and reliable basis for guiding government action.

Public opinion can be reasonably judged as informed and reliable in two basic ways, both involving the opinions of smaller, more select groups rather than of the public as a whole. One group that typically has high levels of information backing their opinions is elites, or people with influential positions within society. **Elite opinion** refers to the attitudes of people with large measures of political influence or expertise.

There is convincing evidence that the opinions of elites are more informed than those of the general public (Erikson and Tedin 2014). It is also clear that the opinions of some help shape the opinions of others. For example, I may have little information about an issue, but if an official I admire, or my priest or my boss or a prominent member of my peer group, is against it, I may be willing to follow their lead. Yet despite acknowledgment that elite opinion is more informed and serves as a guide for the opinions of others, using it as the primary basis for political decision making presents a clear conflict with the core principles of political equality and majority rule. The principles, remember, are supposed to reflect the idea of popular sovereignty, or the idea that the power to authoritatively allocate values is shared by all. This idea is hard to square with the notion that the will of the "people" is really the will of a small minority of elites.

The second approach to viewing public opinion as more competent than its critics suggest is to divide opinions by issue, rather than looking at opinions of elites or opinions of the general public. Although most Americans know little about the details of lawmaking and have low levels of information about most issues, many

push poll A type of public opinion poll that intentionally uses leading or biased questions in order to manipulate the responses.

elite opinion The attitudes or beliefs of those people with influential positions within society.

have clear preferences about the issues that are most salient to them. People tend to have higher levels of information on the issues about which they care the most.

Recognizing that people have well-informed opinions only on the issues that are most salient to them suggests that there is not just one general public opinion, but rather opinions held by numerous issue publics. An **issue public** is simply the section of the population with a strong interest in a particular issue. Issue publics tend to be well informed about the policy area in question and are capable of making sophisticated choices, even if the issue is complex. They are much more likely to be knowledgeable about the voting records of elected officials and the positions of candidates on the issues with which they are concerned. Armed with this base level of information, citizens can effectively monitor their representatives and the policy actions of government. They do not have to keep up with every decision and action by all elected officials, all of the time. All they need to do is keep alert to any actions related to the issues that interest them. For example, citizens involved on either side of the gay rights debate do not have to keep up with all the votes and decisions of their representatives. Knowing when representatives vote contrary to their views on same-sex marriage provides an informed basis for political opinion that is sufficient to keep government accountable (Hutchings 2003). The big problem with issue publics is that they may not represent the interests and preferences of the public as a whole. Indeed, some research has found that compared to the general public, issue publics tend to have more extreme views (Claasen and Nicholson 2013).

While recognizing their flaws, most political scholars believe public opinion polls can make a positive contribution to democratic governance. Many agree with "the common-sense view that when effective public opinion polls came on stream they positively added to the other modes of citizen expression" (Converse 1996, 649). Even the confusion created by the muddled and mixed messages that opinion polls often provide is not necessarily a bad thing. Instability and mixed direction show political leaders that the policy choices are not as clear, or the stakes as high, as they are often portrayed to be in partisan debate. Low levels of intensity and salience can demonstrate the need to transmit a clear and understandable message to the voters.

In short, even if they lack clarity, polls can still serve a positive democratic purpose by prodding politicians into making a better case for their policy agendas. The backing of public opinion provides a large measure of legitimacy to government action. If polling does nothing else, it forces public officials to fight for and justify that legitimacy rather than simply assume it exists.

INTERPRETING PUBLIC OPINION POLLS

Obviously, public opinion is complex and contradictory, and many groups seek to measure and influence the public mood by putting a particular spin on everything from the president's job performance to whether or not same-sex marriage should

issue public A section of the public with a strong interest in a particular issue.

Major public opinion polls all predicted that President Harry Truman would lose his bid to be elected to a full term in 1948. Relying on these polls, the *Chicago Tribune* went to press reporting a Republican victory before election returns were reported in many states. The polls turned out to be wrong because they were based on what was known as a "quota sample." In this infamous photo, President-elect Truman displays the embarrassing result of polls that do not use a random sample.

© W. Eugene Smith/Time Life Pictures/Getty Images

be legal. The net result is that public opinion often produces more confusion than clarity about the preferences of the majority. This raises questions about whether public opinion can ever be fully and objectively understood.

The short answer is no—assessing public opinion is an interpretive art, and on most issues, there is plenty of room for disagreement about the real state of the public's preferences. It is possible, however, to have an understanding of how public opinion polls work. This knowledge is essential to being an informed and effective participant in contemporary civic life. A straightforward approach to figuring out whether a poll is a reliable indicator of public opinion is to try to answer four basic questions (Edmondson 1996):

1. Did the poll ask the right people?
2. What is the poll's margin of error?
3. What was the question?
4. Which question came first?

Did the Poll Ask the Right People?

The validity of a poll, or its ability to accurately represent what it claims, is tied to the people who answered the questions. It is not possible to ask all Americans their opinion of a particular candidate or issue. When a poll finds that a certain percentage of Americans are for or against something, that percentage is an estimate. Pollsters make that estimate by selecting a relatively small group of people, called a sample, to represent the entire population.

There are many ways to go about getting a sample, and the poll's accuracy depends on the sample type. Scientific polls are based on the concept of random sampling. Although the mathematics used to calculate a random sample can get complicated, the concept itself is easy to understand: In order to use a small group to figure out the opinions and attitudes of a large group, everyone in the large group must have an equal chance of being in the small group. A **random sample** is thus one in which every person in the target population has an equal chance of being a poll respondent. If the target population is, say, Republican women, then the target population includes every woman who is a Republican. A random sample of Republican women would be a small group randomly chosen from the entire target population of Republican women. With random sampling, it is possible to get a reasonably accurate assessment of the opinions and attitudes of hundreds of millions of people—the entire population of the country—using a group that consists of a thousand or less.

random sample A method of selecting a sample (subset of the population) in which every person in the target population has an equal chance of being selected.

Other ways to select a group of poll respondents run the risk of creating a **biased sample**, which is a group that does not accurately represent the target population and thus provides inaccurate estimates of the true opinions and attitudes of the target population. Common examples of polls based on biased samples are radio and television surveys based on viewers who are asked to call or e-mail or vote online in response to a particular question. Such polls reflect the views of only those who were tuned into the television or radio program and felt strongly enough about the question to register their views. Because people who were not tuned in had no chance of expressing their views, such polls are not based on a random sample, and they are unlikely to produce an accurate picture of broader public opinion. Polls based on nonrandom samples are often referred to as **straw polls**, which also include "man on the street" interviews and mail-in surveys placed in magazines.

Even a very large nonrandom sample can produce misleading results. The classic example is a 1936 poll conducted by the editors of *Literary Digest* on the presidential contest between incumbent President Franklin Roosevelt, the Democratic candidate, and Alf Landon, the Republican nominee. The sample for this survey was put together using telephone books and automobile registrations, and more than 10 million ballots were sent out by the magazine. The resulting sample was huge—more than 2 million people responded to the survey. The survey results indicated the winner would be Alf Landon, and the magazine used the poll to predict a Landon victory. Never heard of President Alf Landon? Not surprising—Roosevelt won the election by a landslide, and Landon barely mustered a third of the popular vote.

Why was a poll based on a sample of 2 million so wrong? However large the sample, it was a biased sample. In the mid-1930s, the country was still in the grip of the Great Depression, and only the relatively prosperous had an automobile or a telephone. The well-off were much more likely to be Republicans. *Literary Digest* had essentially taken a massive straw poll of Republicans about who they were going to vote for. Not surprisingly, Republicans responded that they were going to vote for the Republican candidate. Underrepresented in the sample were Democrats, who tended to be less well-off but much more numerous. Though fewer Democrats were asked their opinion, this did not stop them from voting.

Getting good random samples in the modern era has become more of a challenge even for the most scrupulous and conscientious pollsters. A big reason is the replacement of landlines with cell phones. Not so long ago landline telephones were ubiquitous—pretty much every home and business had one. This allowed pollsters to get high quality samples through a process known as random digit dialing. In essence, this just meant randomly dialing telephone numbers in a particular city, district, state, or even the whole nation. As most people answered the phone when it rang, this was a highly reliable basis to get random samples. That reliability started to erode with the rise of telemarketers, which made people less likely to answer the phone, and the rise of the cell phone. Cell phones have portable numbers—in other words, they are less tied to a specific geographic location than landlines—and people are less likely to answer an incoming call on a cell

biased sample A group of poll respondents that does not accurately represent the target population and provides inaccurate estimates of the true opinions and attitudes of the target population.

straw polls Unscientific polls based on nonrandom samples.

phone from a number or person they do not recognize. This has made random digit dialing, long the primary sampling technique underlying scientific public polling, a less reliable basis for getting truly representative samples. It may also be part of the reason why public opinion polls have made some high-profile errors in predicting election outcomes in recent years (see the Thinking Analytically box "Are Polls Getting Less Accurate?").

What Is the Poll's Margin of Error?

Even a scientifically selected random sample will not perfectly reflect the views of a larger population. A well-selected sample approximates the target population's opinions, but it is almost always a little bit off. Fortunately, another useful feature of random samples is that statisticians can calculate the margin of error. The **margin of error** (sometimes called the *sampling error*) is the amount by which the sample responses are likely to differ from those of the population within very tight boundaries that are known as the confidence level of a survey.

Reputable and reliable surveys always report a margin of error and a confidence level. Although the math behind them may seem complicated, margin of error and confidence levels are easy and intuitive to interpret. A poll with a margin of error of 5 percentage points and a confidence level of 95 percent means that there is a 95 percent chance that the sample responses are within plus or minus 5 percentage points of the target population's real opinions.

The size of the random sample determines how large the margin of error is: The larger the random sample, the smaller the margin of error. A useful guide to determining the approximate error of a random sample is shown in Table 9.1. Note that it is the size of the random sample and not the size of the population that is important. A random sample of 1,000 will have a margin of error of plus or minus 3 percentage points in any large population, regardless of whether the sample is drawn from a population of 2 million, 20 million, or even 200 million.

There are two important points to keep in mind. First, the margin of error means that pinpoint precision about public opinion is unlikely; even a well-constructed poll can show only the likely range of public opinion. For example, a poll showing 47 percent of likely voters supporting candidate A and 44 percent supporting candidate B does not necessarily mean that candidate A is ahead. If the margin of error is 3 percent, this means candidate A's support ranges somewhere between 44 percent and 50 percent, and candidate B's support is somewhere between 41 percent and 47 percent. In other words, it is possible that candidate B has more support than candidate A.

The second point deals with the **confidence level**. As discussed earlier, a 95 percent confidence level means that there is a 95 percent chance that the true opinion of the population falls somewhere within the boundaries set by the margin of error. That means there is a 5 percent probability that the true opinion of the population falls outside that range. In other words, there is a 1 in 20 chance that the results of the poll are wrong and that the true opinion of the population is outside the margin of error.

margin of error The amount that sample responses are likely to differ from those of the population within very tight boundaries that are known as the confidence level.

confidence level The chance, measured in percent, that the results of a survey will fall within the boundaries set by the margin of error.

TABLE 9.1 GUIDE FOR DETERMINING MARGIN OF ERROR

Sampling Size	Margin of Error (%)
250	±6.0
500	±4.5
1,000	±3.0
2,000	±2.0

Source: Data from Michael W. Traugott and Paul J. Lavrakas. 2000. *The Voter's Guide to Election Polls*. 2nd ed. New York: Seven Bridges Press. 123.

These odds mean the probability of a well-constructed poll being wrong is very low, but the possibility cannot be completely dismissed. To make a reasoned judgment on what a poll says about public preferences, it is important, at a minimum, to know the margin of error. Any poll that does not report a margin of error should be treated with skepticism. Without the margin of error, it is hard to judge whether a poll is an accurate barometer of broader opinion.

What Was the Question?

In order to judge the validity of a poll, it is important to know not only the sample on which it was based and the associated margin of error but also the wording of the questions asked. Pollsters have long known that how a question is worded can help determine how a question is answered. Consider this example taken from a real survey: "Do you want union officials in effect to decide how many municipal employees you, the taxpayer, must support?" (Edmondson 1996, 14). This is a leading question, meaning it is worded so as to prompt a particular answer or opinion—in this case, opposition to municipal unions. Such questions do not produce accurate estimates of true opinions.

The process of designing survey questionnaires is known as **instrumentation**. Reputable pollsters are aware of the potential pitfalls of writing questions that mislead, confuse, or prompt off-topic responses. Technical wording that is hard to understand or questions that provoke strong negative or positive biases can easily threaten the validity of a survey. For example, asking whether people support welfare is likely to elicit a more negative response than asking whether people support programs to help the needy. The word *welfare* tends to prompt a negative image of individuals working the system and looking for handouts. The phrase *help the needy* conjures up an image of people in genuine distress through no fault of their own. These sorts of wording issues can determine whether a poll shows support or opposition to a particular issue or candidate.

Instrumentation involves not just the wording of questions but also how they are structured. Many surveys rely on closed-ended questions or multiple-choice questions. The advantage of closed-ended questions is that they ensure a degree of uniformity in responses, which makes data processing and analysis easier. Their disadvantage is that they prevent respondents from answering in their own words.

instrumentation The process of designing survey questionnaires.

THINKING ANALYTICALLY

ARE POLLS GETTING LESS ACCURATE?

Polling expert Sam Wang was so confident of a Hillary Clinton victory in the 2016 presidential election he said he would "eat a bug" on live television if Donald Trump received more than 240 votes in the Electoral College. Trump actually won 304. Say what you like about Sam Wang's ability to handicap an election, but he's a man of his word. After the election, Wang went on CNN and scarfed down a cricket.

Wang might have been the only polling expert eating bugs after the 2016 election, but he had plenty of company in eating crow. No major polling operation gave Trump much of a chance. Based on election-eve surveys, pollsters were rating the probability of a Clinton victory as somewhere between 70 percent and 95 percent. Needless to say, forecasts of a Clinton win turned out to be 100 percent wrong.

Polls have seemed a little off in more than just the 2016 presidential election. In the past few years a number of high-profile missed calls have called into question the accuracy of public polling. For example, Barack Obama beat Mitt Romney by a much bigger margin than polls forecast in 2012, Republicans won by bigger margins than expected in the 2014 midterms, and polls spectacularly failed to predict the United Kingdom's vote to leave the European Union in 2016.

Now any poll—even one scrupulously adhering to all the guidelines of scientific polling—can be inaccurate. A polling result with a 95 percent confidence level, don't forget, means there is a 1 in 20 chance that the true level of public opinion is outside the margin of error. This is why forecasting experts like Wang and Nate Silver, founder of fivethirtyeight.com, rarely rely on a single poll when they estimate the probabilities of who is or is not likely to win an election. Instead, they create sophisticated models that aggregate lots of different polls. But aggregation models can't help much if they are based on lots of surveys that are not accurately estimating true public opinion, and that certainly seemed to be the case in 2016.

What the heck is going on? Are public opinion polls really becoming less accurate? Well, let's think about this analytically. What would make a public opinion poll less accurate? Well, as we learned in the text, there are a number of possibilities, but we can probably eliminate some of these right away. It's doubtful major polling organizations are all writing poor questions and consistently getting question order wrong. While anyone can make a mistake, these organizations have a massive stake in getting things right—it's their reputation on the line—and they not only have instrumentation specialists, but also often trial run the questions.

The obvious question to ask is whether the samples are biased. As the text explains, scientific polling—in other words, valid probabilistic estimates of true public opinion—requires random sampling. Are pollsters not getting good random samples? That's a distinct possibility. The bottom line is that it has become harder and harder to get random samples. There are a number of reasons for this.

First, there's the steady replacement of landlines by cell phones. The more or less universal presence of landlines made it relatively easy to get a random sample; basically, it was just a matter of randomly dialing numbers in the area codes of the target population. Cell phones upend that, because their numbers—not to mention the people who use them—are not nearly as tied to a particular geographic area. There are also clear generational differences that accompany the technology; older people are much more likely to have a landline than younger people.

Second, it is not just what type of phone people have, but who bothers to answer it. Pollsters are increasingly worried about what is known as "non-response bias." Basically, what this means is that the people who do answer phone surveys, be it on a landline or a cell phone, are systematically different from those who do not answer. If, say, older Democrats are more likely to answer, the survey automatically becomes more biased towards the opinions of older Democrats.

Third, even a perfectly random sample can be systematically biased if respondents do not answer questions truthfully. Survey experts put a lot of thought into writing questions that do not inadvertently introduce bias, but these are no protection against survey respondents who simply do not want to answer accurately. One explanation floated for polling inaccuracy in 2016 was the so-called "shy Trump voter," someone who was planning on voting for Donald Trump but was reluctant to say so on a survey. Post-election analyses suggested this did not really explain polling inaccuracies, but the general possibility of deliberately inaccurate responses is a big concern to pollsters.

Does this mean that representative samples are no longer possible, polls are doomed to be inaccurate and therefore should not be trusted? Hardly. First of all, it's not like the polls, even in their high-profile misses, are completely off the mark. For example, national polls called the outcome of the popular vote in 2016 pretty accurately, i.e., they forecast Clinton would win the popular vote by a few percentage points and that was pretty much on the money. The mistake in forecasting an electoral win was mostly made because of polls in a handful of states that forecast a narrow victory for Clinton that in reality became narrow victories for Trump.

Pollsters are well aware of all of these problems and are trying to adjust in ways that make surveys more accurate and reliable. These include everything from weighting—basically over- or under-counting certain groups to correct for response bias—to moving away from the traditional telephone survey format entirely. For example, some polling companies now conduct surveys online using special panels of people constructed to produce accurate, representative samples. Some scholars have even started experimenting with "big data" approaches that mine Google searches and tweets for systematic indicators of public opinion (Beauchamp 2016).

Has any of this completely solved the problem of sample bias? No, not completely. But a well-done scientific poll is still the best measure available of public opinion on a given topic at a given time.

Discussion Questions

1. What would make you more likely to respond to a survey if you were contacted by cell phone? Would it help to have the caller identified as a recognized reputable organization like Gallup or Pew? What if the caller identification was anonymous or a media source you disliked—would that make you less likely to answer?

2. Are there any political opinions you would be reluctant to share on a survey? Are you more likely to accurately share those opinions with a live interviewer over the telephone or through a more impersonal medium like an Internet survey or a robo-call? Given your answers, what do you think is the best survey method to use if the objective is to get an accurate, representative sample?

By limiting the response options, a survey may miss important information and unanticipated trends (Manheim and Rich 1991, 115–123). For example, limiting respondents to the major-party presidential candidates in a presidential election poll will fail to gauge support for minor party candidates.

Which Question Came First?

The order of questions in a survey can also affect answers. Edmondson (1996) looks at two polls taken at virtually the same time that used almost identical questions about tax cuts and the federal deficit. One poll reported that 55 percent of Americans believed tax cuts and deficit reduction could be accomplished simultaneously, whereas the other poll reported that only 46 percent of Americans believed this to be possible. This difference, which is well outside the margin of error of the surveys, has to do with the order in which the questions were asked.

One poll first asked whether respondents favored a tax cut and then asked whether they would still favor a tax cut if it meant no deficit reduction, and only then were respondents asked whether a tax cut and deficit reduction could be achieved at the same time. The other poll asked only the latter question—that is, whether they thought tax cuts and deficit reduction could happen simultaneously.

What is probably going on here is that respondents in the first poll expressed support for a tax cut in the first question and then were reluctant to back away from that position when questions about the deficit were introduced, even if they favored deficit reduction. Respondents in the second poll had no question setting up a specific position on tax cuts and so were less boxed in by their own previously expressed preferences when the question of tax cuts and deficits came up. This example shows that the order of questions is critical; without knowing the order in which questions were asked, it is hard to form a solid judgment about the validity of the results.

Getting satisfactory answers to the four questions suggested by Edmondson can help determine whether a poll is providing a real reflection of public opinion or is simply a collection of largely meaningless numbers. Of course, it is often hard to get the information required to answer all these questions. Few news reports include all the technical details of polls, especially on matters such as question order. At a minimum, however, it is critical to get answers to the first two questions (whether a random sample was used and what the margin of error is); without this information, it is wise not to invest any faith in poll numbers.

THE BASES OF PUBLIC OPINION

Where do people get their opinions? Are they simply random thoughts plucked from whatever is foremost on people's minds when they are asked a question? If so, the consequences for a delegate model of democratic governance are harsh. Deciding who gets what on what is essentially random impulse can hardly be considered a good basis for effective governance.

The central theoretical models used to explain political attitudes and behavior generally assume opinions are more systematic, but they offer mixed help in explaining where those opinions come from. Rational choice theories are of little help. Rational choice takes preferences—and the opinions, attitudes, and biases behind them—as givens. In other words, rational choice accepts that people have strong beliefs and preferences but makes little attempt to explain *why* they have those beliefs and preferences.

Explanations of the origins of public opinion and political beliefs have largely been carried out using behavioral or social-psychological approaches. From these perspectives, public opinion is a complex product of numerous forces. The social-psychological framework suggests that our attitudes and opinions are products of our environments. They are formed as reactions and adaptations to everything from the political leanings of our immediate family members to the broader values expressed in the political system as a whole. These complex forces can be classified into three broad categories: political culture, ideology, and political socialization.

A more recent explanation of the origins of public opinion suggests that there is an innate component to our beliefs. Following the lead of behavioral geneticists, political scientists have found good evidence that beliefs on a broad variety of issues are partially hereditary. These evolutionary and biological models of public opinion show that the complex environmental forces championed by behavioral models are important, but also that they are incomplete explanations of how we come to our beliefs and opinions. What we believe is significantly shaped by who we are.

Political Culture

A stable political system rests on a set of shared beliefs that include a broad agreement about basic political values and the legitimacy of political institutions and broad acceptance of the process government uses to make policy. These shared beliefs constitute **political culture**.

Political culture helps tie a polity together by providing a basic sense of what the nation is, what it stands for, and what political actions will be considered acceptable. A consensus on fundamentals does not mean people agree on specific outcomes. It means that people share a general sense of how those outcomes should be achieved and what those outcomes should not include. Most Americans, for example, express a strong "tribal loyalty" to the political system. At least in the abstract, Americans believe in the democratic process and believe that the political system set up by the Constitution is the best way to run things. Support for our system does not mean that everyone likes particular officeholders or that we all approve of how particular parts of the system (Congress, the courts, etc.) are doing their jobs. Americans may dislike—even loathe—officeholders and the policies they produce, but the people generally accept the officeholders as legitimate as long as the latter are perceived as holding their positions and passing laws in accordance with the basic principles of the democratic process.

This broad agreement on how decisions should be made has important implications for public opinion. One of the significant characteristics about the beliefs that make up political culture is that they are stable and enduring: Direction, stability, intensity, and saliency are no problem at this level. Although Americans have occasionally quarreled over specifics, in general they have maintained a strong belief in and commitment to democratic institutions and processes as the appropriate means to political order. Anything that smacks of authoritarianism or oligarchy tends to find itself on the wrong side of public opinion. Well-heeled special interest groups, for example, are widely believed to wield too much influence, and Americans tend to have negative attitudes toward them—even though many belong to such organizations.

Political culture, then, acts as a unifying force. It sets the boundaries for what opinions, attitudes, and beliefs are considered legitimate. Positive or negative opinions of presidential performance, for example, are "in bounds" even though

political culture A set of shared beliefs that includes broad agreement about basic political values, agreement about the legitimacy of political institutions, and general acceptance of the process government uses to make policy.

these attitudes reflect fundamental disagreements among citizens. The notion of getting rid of the presidency and replacing the system of divided powers with a parliamentary system would likely be considered out of bounds because this attitude does not fit with the political culture's broad commitment as expressed by the Constitution.

Policies and actions that contradict the beliefs central to political culture tend to be rejected quickly, if they are considered at all. Political culture is the more or less stable channel through which the changing currents of public opinion flow.

Ideology

ideology A consistent set of values, attitudes, and beliefs about the appropriate role of government in society.

Although political culture can help explain very broad patterns in public opinion, it does little to help us understand where opinions on specific issues come from. Abortion rights and the war in Iraq evoke conflicting responses from people who share the same fundamental beliefs that make up political culture. Young people tend to have different views than older people. What is the source of these differing attitudes?

One answer is ideology. As discussed in Chapter 1, **ideology** is a consistent set of values, attitudes, and beliefs about the appropriate role of government in society (Campbell et al. 1960). Ideology is critical to understanding public opinion because it gives people preferences about issues even if they have no individual stake in them. Heterosexuals, for example, may have strong opinions about same-sex marriage. Males may have strong opinions about abortion rights. The opinions produced by ideology have important political consequences: They help drive political participation by prompting people to vote, join interest groups, and contact public officials (Bawn 1999).

Although political scientists have convincingly demonstrated that ideology plays an important role in determining individual opinions on a wide range of issues, this knowledge redefines rather than answers the question of where public opinion comes from. If opinion comes from ideology, where does ideology come from?

Young voters tend to be less conservative than older voters. In 2016 Bernie Sanders drew broad support from college-aged voters as he sought the Democratic Party's nomination for president.

© Elizabeth Robertson/The Philadelphia Inquirer/AP Photo

There is no unanimous answer to this question. Some argue that ideology is an outgrowth of national traditions and political culture. Others argue that it is a product of electoral systems, group interests, historical events, religious beliefs, family background, life experience, or some combination of these factors (Gerring 1997). Others argue that ideology is part of our individual psychology; some people are just more conservative or liberal than others, just as some people are more trusting, neurotic, or open to new experiences than others (Jost 2006).

Regardless of where ideology comes from, there is little doubt of its powerful role in shaping individual opinions. On many issues, all you need to form an opinion is your self-identity as a liberal or a conservative. This is because the key characteristic of ideology is a consistent, stable, and interconnected set of beliefs about politics and government. Individuals who view politics ideologically tend to have very coherent and consistent views on political matters, adopting regular and predictable patterns on issue positions, regardless of their levels of information.

Americans tend to lean to the right—that is, toward the conservative end of the ideological spectrum. This is not an overwhelming tendency, though. In 2016 about 37 percent of Americans self-identified as conservative, 35 percent saw themselves as moderates and 24 percent said they were liberals. There are clear generational differences in ideological self-identification. Younger adults tend to be much less conservative and much more liberal than older generations (see Figure 9.4).

Political Socialization

Most political scientists see ideology as a product of a broader process called **political socialization**, which is the process of acquiring political values. More precisely, political socialization is the process through which a younger generation learns political values from previous generations. Political socialization thus involves the transmission of values from one generation to another. These values help determine not only our ideology but also our opinions on specific issues. Traditionally, political scientists have organized the major agents of political socialization into five general categories: family, schools, peers, events and experiences, and the media (Erikson and Luttbeg 1973).

Some of these agents, including family, have an effect early in life. Others, such as coworkers or fellow students, can influence political opinions in a person's adulthood. Some of these agents involve groups where there are face-to-face relationships over long periods of time (family or church, for example). Others involve secondary groups such as labor unions or professional associations, where contact among members is more limited and involves different people across time. The broader point is that political socialization is a lifelong process—the agents of political socialization can shape our opinions about political matters at any age. Understanding the agents of political socialization offers a way to understand where public opinion comes from.

Family

The family is the most influential agent in shaping individual political attitudes, and it exercises its major effect during the individual's most impressionable years. For most people, the family enjoys a near monopoly over a person's political attention during the early years of life, and children often learn to orient themselves toward politics and government by imitating their parents. For example, if parents think and speak well of the president, children tend to echo that support. If parents are cynical

political socialization The process through which a younger generation learns political values from previous generations.

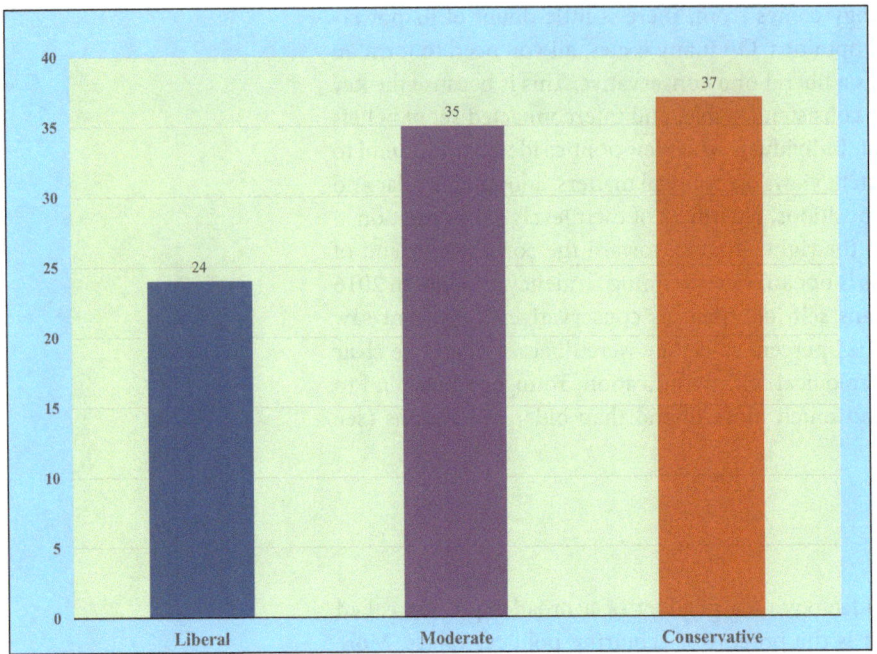

FIGURE 9.4a Political Ideology, 2016

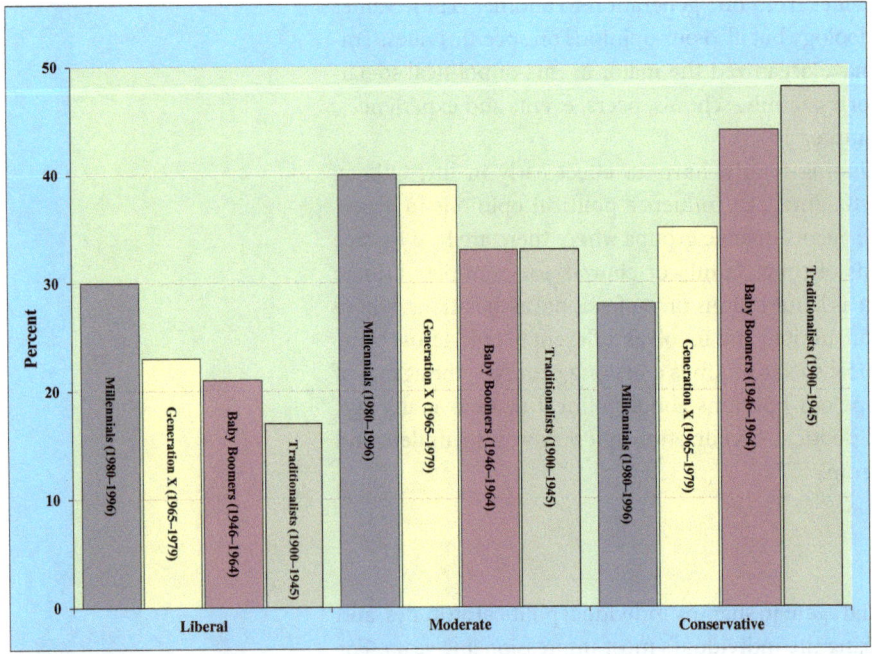

FIGURE 9.4b Political Ideology by Age, 2014

Source: Data from Gallup Polls, http://www.gallup.com/poll/188129/conservatives-hang-ideology-lead-thread.aspx?g_source=IDEOLOGY&g_medium=topic&g_campaign=tiles, http://www.gallup.com/poll/188129/conservatives-hang-ideology-lead-thread.aspx?g_source=IDEOLOGY&g_medium=topic&g_campaign=tiles, and http://www.gallup.com/poll/152021/Conservatives-Remain-Largest-Ideological-Group.aspx.

about government and politics, believing that politics and politicians are corrupt, their children tend to adopt those beliefs. Additionally, children tend to espouse the political party affiliation of their parents.

Political scientists have long recognized that the family's influence becomes less monopolistic as people are exposed to other agents of political socialization, but political attitudes do tend to persist across generations within families (Jennings and Niemi 1975). How a child is politically socialized by the family generally has a lasting effect on his or her opinions.

Schools

Schools also play a major role in shaping political attitudes. Like family, schools are an important part of a child's life. In fact, one of the reasons for establishing public school systems is to ensure the transmission of the "right" political values to the next generation. Yet there are important differences between schools and family as agents of political socialization.

A major difference is that schools have less influence on fundamental political orientations such as ideology and partisanship. In the United States, there has always "existed a tradition of strong dissent to a public system of education that teaches political doctrines" (Spring 1998, 10). And although any number of groups and individuals may try to use public schools to promote their political agendas, the ability of schools to actually influence specific ideological or partisan political opinions of students seems limited.

Rather than instilling particular attitudes about particular issues, candidates, or parties, schools play a more central role in reinforcing the broader set of beliefs that make up political culture. For example, in school children learn to salute the flag, recite the pledge of allegiance, sing patriotic songs, and honor the nation's heroes. The very notion of public school systems in the United States was based, at least in part, on the desire to promote democratic attributes such as a tolerance of different opinions. This sort of socialization is more likely to promote positive feelings about the nation and its system of government than it is to turn children into fervent Democrats, Republicans, or supporters of abortion rights or gun control.

Schools do play a direct role in opinion formation, but this is because they are places where people from different backgrounds and different ideas come into frequent contact with one another. Postsecondary education in particular exposes young adults to political and cultural diversity. Exposure to diverse ideas is a central characteristic of higher education, and students often change their attitudes and opinions about political issues while in college. This change is at least partially due to college faculties and student populations that tend to be more politically, ethnically, and socially diverse than their counterparts in high schools. Change of opinion in college tends to have less to do with professors brainwashing easily swayed undergraduates than with exposure to different peer groups with different political perspectives. Physical proximity to people with different attitudes—coupled with the feeling of many students that they have broken with the past—helps

Political socialization involves the transmission of values from one generation to another. By reinforcing a commitment to the United States and its political system, pledging allegiance to the flag is a form of political socialization familiar to most children who attend school in America.

© Dennis MacDonald/Alamy

promote the formation of new political attitudes and new ways of looking at the political world.

Peers

Peer groups are important agents of political socialization, not just in school but throughout life. The political attitudes of adults can be influenced by peers from formal or informal networks where common interests are shared. These networks include churches, clubs, ethnic groups, neighborhoods, and professional and recreational associations. Peer influence on political attitudes depends on how important political concerns are within the group, the extent of agreement on such matters among group members, and how closely an individual identifies with the group.

Individuals' political attitudes may also be shaped by groups to which they do not belong, at least not in any formal sense. Such groups are called **reference groups** because they provide signals that people use to get their social and psychological bearings. For example, a white liberal may identify with the National Association for the Advancement of Colored People (NAACP), which promotes policies designed to help African Americans, without personally joining the group or receiving any material benefits from the policies the group supports. Reference groups can provide negative as well as positive symbols. A candidate's association with radical groups, such as the Ku Klux Klan or fundamentalist groups that refuse to condemn acts of terrorism, may be enough to turn opinions and votes away.

Events and Experiences

Our own experiences and the larger political context in which they take place can have a powerful effect on our opinions and attitudes. Someone who has just been mugged, for example, is unlikely to be convinced by statistics that show crime is declining.

Presidential elections are cyclical events that periodically shape public opinion. Following the inauguration of a new president, the new executive typically enjoys a honeymoon period. The conflict of the election is past, and most Americans are willing to give the new president a chance to do the job. Initial job approval ratings of our three most recent presidents are depicted in Figure 9.5. Both President George W. Bush and President Barack Obama came into office with approval ratings in the mid-60 percent range. Donald Trump, in contrast, had historically low job approval during his first year in office. He began his term in office with an approval

reference groups Groups that influence the political attitudes of non-group members.

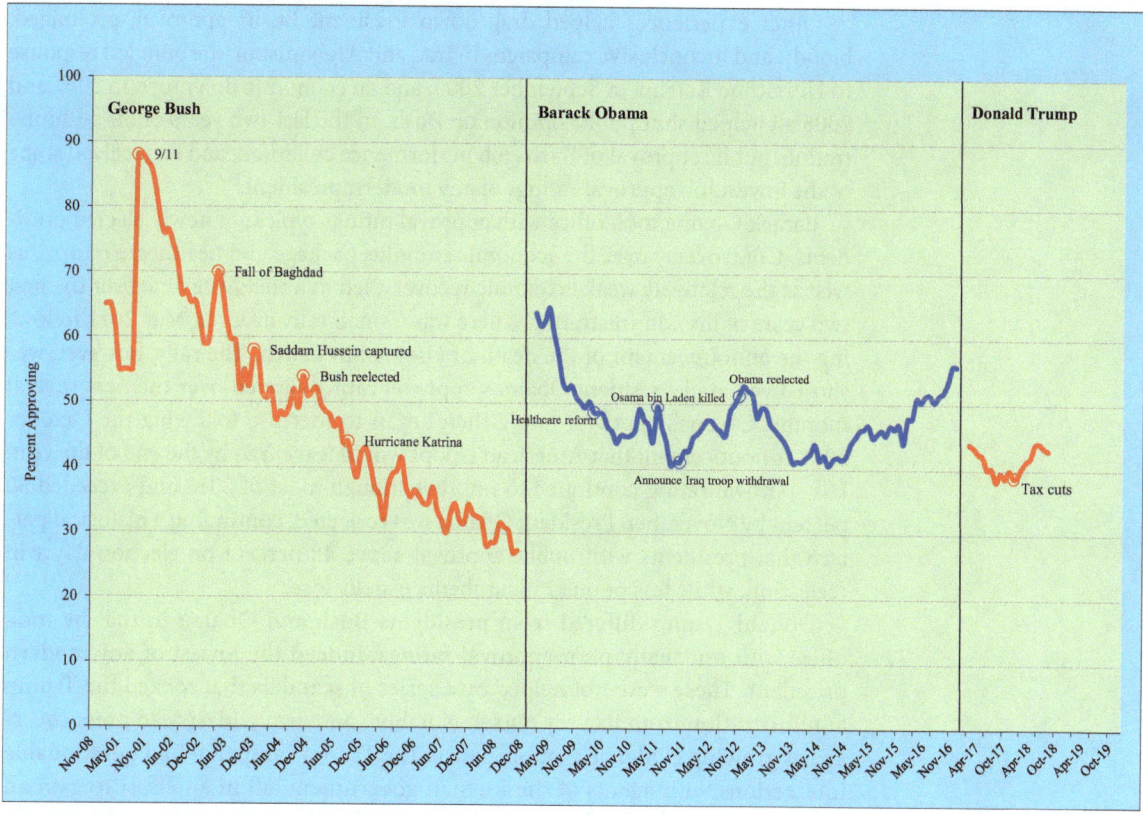

FIGURE 9.5 Presidential Job Approval

Source: Data from Gallup Polls reported at http://pollingreport.com/. Entries are monthly averages of responses to the question asking, "Do you approve or disapprove of the way [George W. Bush/Barack Obama/Donald Trump] is handling his job as president?"

rating barely over 40 percent and declined steadily to the mid-30 percent range where it remained throughout 2017. Regardless of where a president starts in terms of popular support, after the inauguration public opinion of the president can be driven up or down by other events. The terrorist attacks of September 11, 2001, were a powerful example of how an event can shape public opinion. Prior to the attacks, President George W. Bush had middling job approval ratings from the public, and opinion polls showed little evidence that the public considered a sustained campaign against terrorism a policy priority. Following the attacks, opinions of the president's job performance became overwhelmingly positive as people reflexively drew together and backed the nation's leader in a time of crisis. This effect is known as a "rally 'round the flag" response of public opinion. Rally events occur following dramatic presidential actions in response to international and military crises (Mueller 1973). For example, there was a much smaller rally in President Bush's job approval after the invasion of Iraq in March 2003 and the fall of Baghdad in April.

Other experiences helped drag down President Bush's approval; prolonged, bloody, and inconclusive campaigns in Iraq and Afghanistan, the bungled response to Hurricane Katrina in September 2005, and an economic downturn in 2007 and 2008 all helped shift public opinion on Bush. In the last two years of his administration, public approval of Bush's job performance collapsed, and he received some of the lowest job approval ratings of any modern president.

Barack Obama took office with approval ratings typical of newly elected presidents. Controversy over the economic stimulus package and healthcare reform, as well as the relatively weak economic recovery, led to a steady decline over the first two years of his administration. There was a small rally event in May 2011 following the announcement of the death of Osama bin Laden. The rally, however, was short-lived, and President Obama's approval rating slipped over the next several months. Obama's approval rating then began to increase following the October 2011 announcement that American troops would leave Iraq by the end of the year. His approval rating continued to improve though most of 2012 and exceeded 50 percent by November. President Obama was reelected, continuing a historical pattern that presidents with public approval above 48 percent on election day win reelection, while less popular incumbents usually lose.

Donald Trump differed from presidents Bush and Obama in that he took office with unusually poor approval ratings, indeed the lowest of any modern president. These were not helped by a series of scandals that rocked the Trump administration from its very outset. Notably, there was widespread press coverage of growing evidence that officials in the Trump campaign had questionable interactions with agents of the Russian government, all in an effort to gain an advantage in the 2016 election. Allegations of collusion with a foreign government to influence an election outcome, especially with a government widely perceived as antagonistic to the interests of the United States, is not exactly a story calculated to improve a president's image. Trump's approval numbers began falling almost immediately after he took office. After Congress passed the tax cut bill in December 2017, Trump's approval rebounded back up to near 40 percent.

The Mass Media

Another way to influence political opinion is through the mass media—television, radio, newspapers, magazines, and the Internet. The Internet has become an increasingly important tool of political and partisan persuasion (Browning 1996; Hill and Hughes 1997), yet television (just) remains the most important source of political information for most Americans (Stanley and Niemi 2013, 162).

Regardless of the media form, a number of scholars have expressed concern that media outlets shape public opinion in a negative way. The concern rests on the media's potential to make people skeptical and cynical about politics and government in general. Scandal, corruption, and incompetence are a staple of media reports on politicians and government. Some believe that the strong focus on the negative makes Americans more distrustful of government and more cynical about politics, even though federal officeholders operate under strict ethical guidelines and almost certainly engage in less unethical behavior than in other historical periods (Harris 1995, 61–62). Although studies indicate that the media only reinforce what people already believe to be true, the negative tone about politics, especially in television news programs and on various social media platforms, tends to promote negative opinions about government institutions, and these opinions persist even when more objective measures of government's job performance are positive (Hibbing and Theiss-Morse 1998).

Political campaigns may take advantage of the negative socialization effects of television by running negative ads. Viewers of these ads become more cynical about the political system and the ability of an average citizen to influence the democratic process (Ansolabehere et al. 1994). This increased cynicism makes people less likely to vote. A political campaign can exploit this socialization effect by aiming its ads at an opponent's supporters. Rather than trying to persuade voters to support a particular candidate or set of issues, the objective is to cut into the opponent's support by making those supporters less likely to vote. Of course, most candidates will not let an opponent run attack ads without replying in kind. The net effect of all the carefully crafted mud-slinging in 30-second television ads is to create a very troubling socialization effect: increased cynicism, apathy, and even anger.

The mass media also play another important socialization role by helping to create shared perceptions of social trends. On many issues there is a disconnect between what people experience personally and the perceptions of broader social trends generated by news reports. The latter are often more negative than the former, and they play an important role in shaping opinions. For example, consider that most Americans express satisfaction with their local schools, with most people grading them highly. News reports on public education, however, are almost always negative, stressing the worst of the educational system. As a result, although most people see their own public schools as doing well, they view public schools generally as performing poorly. There is a similar disconnect on many other issues: Americans are generally satisfied with their own families, communities, and workplaces but also believe that these institutions are in trouble nationally; people rate the U.S. healthcare system poorly, even though they rate their own healthcare positively (Loveless 1997).

Biological Models of Public Opinion

Biological models of public opinion argue that attitudes and opinions also have a genetic component. In this framework, beliefs and attitudes are seen as products of an interaction between inherited predispositions and the complex environmental factors championed by the behavioral approach.

There is actually good evidence, from research done on twins, to support these claims. As most people know, there are two kinds of twins: (1) identical twins (called monozygotic twins), who share 100 percent of their genetic material, and (2) fraternal twins (called dizygotic twins), who like most siblings share only 50

APPLYING THE FRAMEWORKS

HOW DO YOU GET OPINIONS OUT OF YOUR GENES?

One of the fundamental challenges of public opinion scholars is trying to figure out exactly where political attitudes come from. As discussed in the text, public opinion has multiple causes, with everything from what mom and dad espouse at the dinner table to current events news stories playing a role. This all makes intuitive sense. Less intuitive is the notion that our political opinions are, at least partially, influenced by our genes.

At this point, the evidence that political opinions are indeed genetically influenced is quite strong and is not limited to the twin studies discussed in the text. Adoption studies provide additional support for a biological influence on political attitudes and behaviors. The basic idea here is that if an adopted individual is more similar to his or her adoptive family on a given trait than their biological family, that trait is more socially than biologically influenced. However, if they are more similar to their biological family than their adoptive family it provides evidence that biology is influencing that trait. When it comes to political attitudes and behaviors, studies do indeed show adoptees tend to be more like their biological than their adoptive families.

Finally, a handful of studies have actually used measures of individual-level genetic variation (these are called genome-wide association studies, or GWAS) to see if people who are more genetically similar are more politically similar. The short answer is yes; people who are closer genetically tend to be more alike politically.

While the evidence of a genetic influence on political attitudes and opinions is pretty strong, it raises a big challenge for biological models. How exactly do you get from a gene to an attitude on, say, same-sex marriage or illegal immigration? No one is seriously suggesting anyone has a "same-sex marriage gene" or an "immigration gene," so how the heck do genes manage to influence these sorts of opinions?

One widely accepted explanation is that genes only indirectly influence things like political opinion. What genes do is help determine the structure and operation of things like your central and peripheral nervous systems. In other words, genes might not directly influence a political opinion, but they undeniably provide the basic blueprint and operating parameters for biological information processing systems that we use to form political opinions. An obvious hypothesis that springs from this theory is that differences in political attitudes and behavior should systematically correlate with individual differences in things like brain structure, neural activation patterns, and similar physiological differences.

A growing number of studies have tested this hypothesis empirically. Some of the most interesting look at disgust reactions. Humans have a well-known physiological response to disgust; for example, we involuntarily wrinkle our noses and activate our sympathetic nervous system (this helps biologically prepare us for action—it is sometimes called the "fight or flight" system). Yet some people are more easily disgusted than others. Show a random group of subjects the same picture of someone tossing their cookies or give them a whiff of the same stinky smell, and some will gag and some will shrug it off. Those individual differences in disgust sensitivity are known to be at least partially biological in origin, and researchers can measure these physiological responses.

Several studies show that individual differences in physiological disgust responses correlate with a particular set of political attitudes, specifically attitudes dealing with sex-related issues. Most notably, disgust sensitivity seems to align with attitudes on same-sex marriage. Basically, people who are more easily disgusted are also more likely to oppose same-sex marriage. Note that these studies are not testing whether people disgusted by homosexual sex are uncomfortable with same-sex marriage—that's almost true by definition. What they are finding is that physiological responses to disgust stimuli that are seemingly utterly irrelevant to politics (e.g., a picture of feces) nonetheless predict political attitudes.

What does all this mean? It connects a biologically based information processing system to a political opinion. Disgust reactions are largely reflexive—we don't think about the pros and cons of whether something is disgusting: The sight/smell/feel is automatically registered as disgusting and kicks in as an automatic physiological response. In the case of disgust, that response is typically negative—we want to avoid or reject these sorts of stimuli. It makes sense then, if you feel a flash of automatic disgust when you get a political stimulus—same-sex marriage, abortion, illegal immigration, whatever—your "gut" tells you to respond negatively. Thus you can have a negative opinion on these sorts of issues, all without ever consciously realizing that opinion is at least partially rooted in a physiological process that is genetically influenced.

Discussion Questions

1. If issue attitudes are at least partially biologically influenced, does this make it harder to persuade someone to change their political opinion? Why or why not?
2. Are some issue attitudes more likely to be biologically influenced than others? If an opinion is biologically influenced, does this mean that socialization is not important to political opinions?

percent of their genetic material. As siblings, twins are usually raised in the same environment (same family, same schools, same political culture, etc.). Yet like some other siblings, twins are sometimes raised apart because of divorce, adoption, or other events. Twins raised separately obviously have different environments: different family, different schools, and sometimes even different political cultures. Twins thus make an excellent basis for trying to sort out whether genes shape opinions and beliefs. There is a certain amount of variation on genetics and environment, and using statistical techniques, researchers can quite accurately sort out how much of the variation in a given attitude or belief is being driven by genetics or environment.

When researchers examined political opinions and beliefs using data sets based on twins, they found that a surprisingly large component of the variation in these beliefs could be attributed to genetics. One of the original studies to take this approach was done more than 30 years ago by a team of researchers headed by Nick Martin, an Australian behavioral geneticist (1986). They found a strong genetic component to political beliefs such as support for the death penalty. More recently, a team of political scientists focused on this issue using a large twin data set and found that on issues such as school prayer and property taxes, a third or more of the variation in expressed opinions was the result of genetics rather than the environment (Alford, Funk, and Hibbing 2005).

Does this mean there is a gene that determines what your opinion will be on school prayer or abortion? No. What it means is that your genes influence your opinions in combination with the environment. Take, for example, religiosity, or the extent to which an individual is religiously devout. Twin research has found a strong genetic component to religiosity; in other words, people do seem to inherit a predisposition to be religiously devout. Yet how that devotion is expressed seems to be almost wholly environmental. Whether you are a devout Methodist, Catholic, Jew, Muslim, or member of any other faith is more a product of the environment you find yourself in than any genetic predisposition. Political attitudes and beliefs are similar. You may inherit a predisposition toward being more politically oriented than someone else, but whether that heightened political intensity leads you to be a fervent Republican or Democrat—or to hold the range of opinions those partisan labels imply—is shaped more by the environment than anything else.

This research, in other words, does not support the notion of genetic determinism, or the idea that your genes automatically determine what you believe and how you behave. What it supports is the idea that there is a biological component to our opinions and behaviors. The origins of our opinions and beliefs, in other words, rest partly in the predispositions we inherit through our genes and partly in the broader political and social environment, but mostly through a combination of the two.

PUBLIC OPINION AND PARTICIPATION

Neither the government nor citizens have to rely on confusing public opinion polls to assess the will of the people. The attitudes and beliefs that make up public opinion can also be expressed through **political participation**, or the translation of a personal preference into a voluntary action designed to influence public policy. In other words, political participation is the process of turning an opinion into a direct contribution to the process of determining who gets what.

Rather than wait for a pollster to ask their opinion, trust that the poll is well constructed and fairly represents their views, and then sit back and hope that government acts on the results, people can express their will directly through involvement in the political system. The causes and consequences of political participation are addressed in Chapter 11. What is important for the purposes of this chapter is recognition that public opinion polls are not the only way to connect the attitudes and preferences of citizens to the actions of government.

Political participation involves everything from voting to writing letters or e-mails to government officials to joining an interest group. These activities may seem like a better guide to the will of the people than a public opinion poll. If an attitude or belief provides enough motivation to get someone to go vote or join an interest group, this certainly seems to indicate that an issue is salient and that an attitude is intensely held. The problem with participation is that not all people participate equally. As a result, some groups and their preferences exert a disproportionate influence on the political process. Some Americans do not participate at all, others limit their participation to occasionally casting a ballot, and still others concentrate on specific types of political involvement.

Scholars who study political participation as a means to connect the will of the people to the actions of government have raised persistent concerns that varying rates of participation across racial, ethnic, and socioeconomic lines mean that some preferences will be given more weight than others. This concern is consistent with the elitist perspective of the American political system.

political participation The translation of personal preference into a voluntary action designed to influence public policy.

Political scientists have found strong evidence that the voting rates of particular groups can determine election outcomes (R. Jackson 1997) and that disproportionate participation of those higher on the socioeconomic scale results in policies that favor their interests at the expense of those on the lower end of the scale (Bennett and Resnick 1990; Gant and Lyons 1993; Hill and Leighley 1992). But not all research findings support this elitist perspective on participation. There is some systematic evidence that government can and does manage to respond to the broader currents of public opinion, and not just to those who participate (Erikson, Wright, and McIver 1993).

Thus, participation may or may not be an accurate indicator of "what the people desire to have done," as Lincoln suggested. It indicates what the people who participate desire to have done, but even in a presidential election, that adds up to little more than half of eligible voters. Moreover, those who do participate tend to be distinct from the broader electorate in a number of important ways: They are older, better educated, and more prosperous; they are less racially and ethnically diverse than the public at large; and they are more likely to be dissatisfied with the status quo, distrustful of government, more partisan, and more confident that their views not only deserve to be respected but should receive a satisfactory response from the government (Verba, Schlozman, and Brady 1995).

We have come full circle, right back to the lament of Lincoln that opened the chapter. Varying rates of participation mean that elections cannot be counted on to reveal what the people—all of the people—really want. Although estimated turnout in the 1860 presidential election was a remarkable 82 percent of eligible voters, Lincoln won the presidency with less than 40 percent of the popular vote. Even with near-universal participation, how could Lincoln respond to the preferences of "all the people" when over 60 percent of them expressed a preference for one of his three opponents? If scientific polling had been available then, Lincoln still would have found it difficult to determine what "the people" wanted done. Public opinion turns out to be more complex than Lincoln imagined.

CHAPTER NINE
Top 10 Takeaway Points

1. Public opinion is the sum of attitudes or beliefs about an issue or question and is seen as one expression of the will of the people.

2. Public opinion has four elements: direction, stability, intensity, and salience.

3. Most people believe public opinion should play a significant role in guiding government decision making, a belief that reflects a commitment to the core

democratic principle of majority rule and to the delegate model of representative democracy.

4. The problem with public opinion is that it is often ill-informed, fragmented, and subject to rapid change. Because of this, the government of the United States is deliberately designed to shield policymakers from the excesses of public opinion.

5. Opinions are typically not the product of rational or knowledgeable analysis. They tend to be products of ideology, socialization, and political culture. Recent research also suggests that there is a biological component to opinions, with people inheriting predispositions toward certain political beliefs.

6. Understanding the reliability and validity of public opinion polls is an important civic skill. Getting answers to four questions is usually enough to discern the worth and accuracy of a poll: Did the poll ask the right people? What is the poll's margin of error? What was the question? Which question came first?

7. There is disagreement about the appropriate role of public opinion. Some believe public opinion is too poorly informed to contribute to competent judgments about complex issues. Others argue that public opinion has a rightful place in the broader democratic debate and is more informed and sophisticated than its critics give it credit for.

8. Issue publics, or people with a strong interest in a particular issue, tend to be well informed about that particular policy area and capable of making sophisticated choices.

9. Public opinion polls are not the only way the people can make their will known to the government. Political participation sends a direct message by translating personal preference into voluntary action.

10. Political participation is an imperfect reflection of the will of the people because different groups participate at different rates. Generally speaking, the well-off, the better-educated, and the middle-aged are more likely to participate than the poor, the poorly educated, and the young.

CHAPTER NINE
Key Terms and Cases

biased sample, 303
confidence level, 304
delegate model of representative
  democracy, 299
direction, 294
elite opinion, 300
ideology, 310
instrumentation, 305
intensity, 296
issue public, 301
margin of error, 304
political culture, 309
political participation, 320
political socialization, 311
public opinion, 294
push poll, 300
random sample, 302
reference groups, 314
salience, 297
stability, 294
straw polls, 303
trustee system of democracy, 299

10 ELECTIONS

KEY QUESTIONS

What features must be present to make elections effective?

Why is the process of nominating candidates as important as the process of electing them?

How does the process of nominating and electing the president differ from the nomination and election of members of Congress?

© Patrick Semansky/AP Photo

At least from a national perspective, presidential elections over the past couple of decades have looked pretty competitive. Winners routinely struggled to get 50 percent of the popular vote, election eve polls often forecast a tight race, and the major party candidates always campaigned furiously right down to the polling day wire. Since 1992, the victor's average winning margin in the popular vote is just 3.6 percentage points—not exactly a landslide. So it's with good reason that presidential campaigns often seem to end with election night nail biters.

Look a little closer, though, and things do not seem so competitive. The presidency (as we shall see) is a race for states, not a race for the national popular vote. And down at that level, only a handful of states are really in play in any given presidential election. For example, in 2016 Donald Trump won the presidency, but actually lost the popular vote. Roughly 3 million more people voted for the Democratic nominee Hillary Clinton than for Trump. But Trump won more states. The 2016 race seemed incredibly close because Trump won by razor-thin margins in just a few states—just a percentage point or so in Pennsylvania, Michigan, and Wisconsin. The race was indeed on a knife's edge in those states. For most of the country, though, the outcomes were anything but competitive. Clinton stomped Trump in California, getting more than 60 percent of the vote. Trump whomped Clinton in Tennessee with an equally lopsided win. In reality, there were only a dozen or so states where there was any real doubt about who was going to walk away the winner. A competitive presidential election, in other words, means there are a smattering of states where both major party candidates have a shot at winning. In four-fifths of the states the winner is pretty much a foregone conclusion.

Yet at least the presidential elections are vigorously contested and interesting, even if only in a limited number of geographic pockets. Congressional contests, on the other hand, are snoozers—more than 80 percent of House members typically coast to victory with more than 60 percent of the vote. In 2016, for example, 380 of the 393 incumbents running for reelection to the U.S. House of Representatives won and did so with an average margin of victory of 37.1 percent. That is a landslide. While this general pattern is occasionally shaken up, it is a pretty rare electoral cycle where more than a quarter of House incumbents fail to win reelection and where even half the seats being contested in the United States Senate are truly competitive.

This is important because competitive elections play a critical role in the achievement of popular sovereignty—without vigorous competition that gives voters a choice between at least two viable alternatives, representatives have less incentive to be responsive to the voters, and elections do not provide a realistic chance to hold unresponsive representatives accountable. Elections amount to choosing the decision makers, and these are the most critical choices citizens make in terms of shaping government policy and holding it accountable for its actions. Yet for decades elections in the United States, with few exceptions, have been mostly one-sided affairs. Where is the choice if the outcome is in the bag before a vote is cast?

In this chapter, we explore how candidates are elected to office. To fully understand the crucial role of elections in a democracy, we first need to understand the rules and procedures that structure the electoral process.

THE CONCEPT OF ELECTIONS

An **election** is a collective decision-making process in which citizens choose an individual to hold and exercise the powers of public office. Elections are the primary mechanism that representative democracies use to achieve popular sovereignty—that is, to make government responsive and accountable to the will of the people.

Elections to choose the president and members of Congress consist of two steps: nomination and the general election. **Nomination** is the process through which political parties winnow down a field of candidates to a single one who will be the party's standard-bearer in the general election. In the **general election**, voters choose their representatives from among the parties' nominees.[1]

election A collective decision-making process in which citizens choose an individual to hold and exercise the powers of public office. Elections are the primary mechanism that representative democracies use to achieve popular sovereignty.

nomination The process through which political parties winnow down a field of candidates to a single one who will be the party's standard-bearer in the general election.

general election The process by which voters choose their representatives from among the parties' nominees.

---

1 Although independent and minor party candidates may appear on the general election ballot, in the United States only the major party candidates—Democrats and Republicans—have a realistic chance of winning office.

METHODS OF NOMINATING CANDIDATES

How candidates are selected has important consequences for the operation of democracy. William Magear "Boss" Tweed, who headed the powerful Tammany machine in New York during the 1850s and 1860s, once said, "I don't care who does the electing as long as I do the nominating" (Thomsett and Thomsett 1994, 14). A sure way to influence a general election is to determine the choices available to voters. Parties in the United States have used three methods of nominating candidates—legislative caucus, conventions, and direct primaries. The method of nominating candidates has changed over time and differs for president and Congress.

Legislative Caucus

The need for a mechanism to choose who would carry party labels into the electoral arena arose with the development of political parties. Races for local offices, state legislatures, and even the House of Representatives presented no great difficulty. These elections involved a limited number of voters living in a reasonably compact political district. Parties simply held meetings, called **caucuses**, of their most active supporters to nominate candidates.

Selecting candidates for statewide offices presented more of a challenge. Transportation and communication were primitive, and it was no easy task to assemble party activists from all over a state. Nominating candidates for president and vice president presented the same difficulty on an even larger scale. The initial solution to this problem was to give the **legislative caucus** responsibility for choosing nominees for state and national offices. The party's members in a state legislature assembled to select candidates for statewide office, and party members in the House of Representatives caucused to select candidates for president and vice president. In short, members of the party in government chose candidates for offices representing large constituencies.[2]

Although convenient, allowing members of Congress to select presidential and vice presidential nominees presented several problems: It violated separation of powers; it did not represent elements of the party in states where the party had lost; and party activists who were not members of Congress had no voice in choosing the party's nominee for president.

Convention

The nomination method that emerged to tackle the drawbacks of the caucus approach to nominations was the **national party convention**, a meeting composed

---

caucus A meeting of members of a political party.

legislative caucus A method of selecting political party candidates that calls for party members in the state legislature to select candidates for statewide office and party members in the House of Representatives to select a party's candidates for president and vice president.

national party convention A nomination method in which delegates selected from each state attend a national party meeting to choose the party's candidates for president and vice president.

---

2 Chapter 7 explains the three elements of a political party: party in electorate, party in government, and party organization.

of delegates from various states. In 1832, the Democratic Party under Andrew Jackson became the first major party to use the national convention.[3] The convention quickly evolved into the dominant means of choosing candidates at both the state and national levels. Delegates to state conventions were sometimes chosen directly by local party members. But more commonly, delegates were selected by county conventions, whose delegates had in turn been selected by party members in smaller political units. The state convention then chose candidates for statewide office and the delegates to the national presidential convention. This system allowed rank-and-file party members to participate in choosing delegates, but the delegates, not the rank and file, made the key decisions. Candidate selection, in other words, shifted from party in government to the party organization, but it still excluded the party in the electorate.

Disillusionment with the convention began to grow in the early twentieth century as powerful party insiders manipulated the system to their own advantage. Meetings to choose delegates were often called without notice to all interested people and were packed with ineligible participants. Disputes between rival delegations from the same area were common, and the procedure used to decide which delegation to seat was often unfair and manipulated by party insiders who made the rules. Foes of the convention began advocating a way to nominate candidates that would shift power from the party organization to the party in the electorate.

Direct Primary

The direct primary allows voters to choose party nominees for public office. In the convention system, voters' influence is indirect—they choose the delegates who choose the nominee. In a direct primary, voters choose the nominee. Wisconsin passed the first law for a statewide direct primary in 1903. Today, all 50 states use the direct primary for some, if not all, nominations.

Primary laws vary from state to state. Some states hold **closed primaries** in which only registered Democrats may vote in the Democratic primary and only registered Republicans in the Republican primary; voters who register as independents may vote in the general election, but they cannot participate in party primaries. Other states hold **open primaries** in which independents—and in some cases voters from other parties—participate in a party's primary.

Direct primaries increase the influence of rank-and-file voters at the expense of party leaders. Party leaders retain somewhat more power in closed primaries than in open ones. Proponents of open primaries argue that they are more democratic because they allow all interested citizens to participate in the selection of candidates, and they criticize closed primaries as infringing on citizens' ability

closed primaries Elections to choose a party's nominees for the general election that are open only to party members.

open primaries Elections to select a party's candidate for the general election that are open to independents and, in some cases, to members of other parties.

---

[3] A minor party, the Anti-Masons, was actually first to employ a national convention in 1831. The Anti-Masons had no appreciable representation in Congress and could not use the legislative caucus effectively.

to participate in the electoral process. Defenders of closed primaries argue that participation by independents and supporters of the opposing party may undermine a party's chances by supporting candidates who are unacceptable to most party members or nominating weak candidates that will be easier to defeat in the general election.

NOMINATING PRESIDENTIAL CANDIDATES

Both major parties nominate their candidates for president and vice president in national party conventions composed of delegates from the states. To win a party's nomination, a candidate must get the support of a majority of delegates at the convention. The rules that govern the nominating contests that choose the delegates influence the participants' strategies and tactics. Rules are not neutral. Because rules inevitably advantage some interests at the expense of others, they can determine outcomes.

The Allocation of National Convention Delegates

Both parties use similar criteria to decide how many delegates each state party sends to the convention: state population and support for the party's candidates in the state. Table 10.1 shows the number of delegates each state party sent to the national conventions in 2016. Population is the most important determinant of the size of a state's delegation—large states get more delegates than small states get. For example, California, the most populous state, had the largest delegations at both party conventions, whereas the delegations of the least populous states, Wyoming and Vermont, were among the smallest. In addition, both parties give extra delegates to states with a record of supporting their candidates. Democrats use votes cast for the Democratic presidential candidate to award these extra delegates, whereas the Republicans reward states for electing a Republican governor, congressional delegation, and presidential electors. Oklahoma and Oregon, for example, are about equal in population, but strongly Republican Oklahoma has a larger delegation at the Republican convention, whereas strongly Democratic Oregon has a larger delegation at the Democratic convention.

The Method and Timing of Delegate Selection

State law determines the method state parties use to select delegates, whether the process will be open or closed, and the date when the parties select delegates. The

TABLE 10.1 SIZE OF STATE DELEGATIONS AT THE 2016 NATIONAL PARTY CONVENTIONS

State	Democratic Convention	Republican Convention	State	Democratic Convention	Republican Convention
California	551	172	Oregon	74	28
Texas	251	155	Oklahoma	42	43
New York	291	95	Connecticut	71	28
Florida	246	99	Iowa	51	30
Illinois	183	69	Mississippi	41	40
Pennsylvania	208	71	Arkansas	37	40
Ohio	160	66	Kansas	37	40
Michigan	147	59	Utah	37	40
Georgia	117	76	Nevada	43	30
North Carolina	120	72	New Mexico	43	24
New Jersey	142	51	West Virginia	37	34
Virginia	108	49	Nebraska	30	36
Washington	118	44	Idaho	27	32
Massachusetts	115	42	Hawaii	34	19
Indiana	92	57	Maine	30	23
Arizona	85	58	New Hampshire	32	23
Tennessee	75	58	Rhode Island	33	19
Missouri	84	52	Montana	27	27
Maryland	120	38	Delaware	32	16
Wisconsin	96	42	South Dakota	25	29
Minnesota	93	38	Alaska	20	28
Colorado	78	37	North Dakota	23	28
Alabama	60	50	Vermont	26	16
South Carolina	59	50	Wyoming	18	29
Louisiana	59	46	Other (DC; Terr.)	175	78
Kentucky	60	46			
			Totals	4,763	2,472

Note: States sorted from largest to smallest.

Source: Data from The Green Papers, http://www.thegreenpapers.com/P16/D-Del.phtml and http://www.thegreenpapers.com/P16/R-Del.phtml.

parties select national convention delegates in two basic ways:[4] (1) the **caucus method**, in which national convention delegates are chosen at a state convention; and (2) a **state presidential primary**, in which voters directly elect delegates.

Over time, there has been a trend of increasing use of primaries to choose national convention delegates. Figure 10.1 shows the percentage of national convention delegates chosen in primaries. The first time presidential primaries were a major part of a nomination strategy was in 1912. Although relatively few delegates were chosen in primaries over the next 50 years, states began switching to primaries in the 1970s. In the last several elections, more than two-thirds of delegates at party conventions were chosen in primaries. The rise of the direct primary shifted power over nominations away from professionals and toward amateurs.

This shift in power has had a profound effect on nomination campaigns. First, the nomination calendar is now critically important. To attract media attention and the broader support necessary to be serious contenders, presidential candidates must do well in the early competitions for delegates. The first two nominating contests are the Iowa caucuses and the New Hampshire primary. Despite having only a handful of delegates, these contests are widely perceived to have enormous influence on who wins a party nomination. The winner of these initial contests often does not win nomination, but a poor showing can cripple a campaign.

The perceived importance of these early contests has led to **frontloading**, in which states leapfrog their delegate selection contests to earlier dates in the process in an effort to gain more influence in the choice of a presidential nominee. Frontloading crams the selection of a disproportionate number of delegates into a few weeks at the beginning of the process.

Frontloading has several undesirable consequences. First, to have any chance, candidates must lay the groundwork early. A serious candidate must be familiar with the relevant laws and selection methods in all 50 states and understand the political situation in each. This requires political expertise, a well-administered national organization, time, and lots and lots of money.

Second, candidates need to raise a lot of money early. Having money does not guarantee victory, but the absence of money guarantees a loss. Frontloading has so shortened the time available to select delegates that candidates who do not have national name recognition, a national organization, and enormous sums of money at the start of the nominating contests have little chance of winning the nomination.

Third, the shortened time "degrades campaign quality." William Mayer and Andrew Busch observe that the almost insurmountable advantage of front-runners "substantially reduces the field of viable candidates" (2004, 3). When so many delegates are chosen in just a few weeks, early primary voters do not have

caucus method A method of selecting the delegates to a political party's national convention by permitting the state conventions to select representatives from their states.

state presidential primary A method of selecting delegates to a political party's national convention in which the voters directly elect delegates.

frontloading The tendency of states to move their primaries earlier in the season in order to gain more influence over the presidential selection process.

---

[4] Delegates were once handpicked by party officials, but this method has largely disappeared. Although the Democratic Party continues to set aside a number of delegate slots for party leaders and elected officials (PLEOs)—governors, members of Congress, and party officials—these constitute a small proportion of delegates at the Democratic National Convention. These delegates are popularly known as "super delegates." In the 2016 campaign for the Democratic nomination, Sen. Bernie Sanders (I-VT) complained that these super delegates rigged the nomination contest in favor of Hillary Clinton. Independent analyses indicate Clinton would have won the nomination without them.

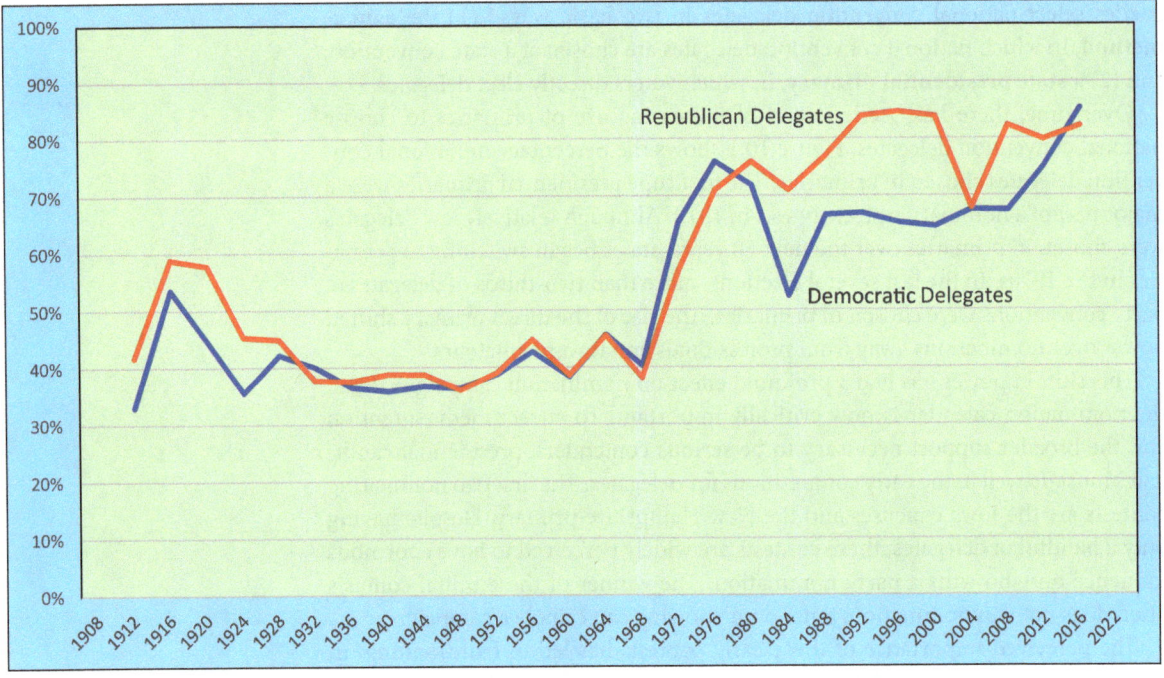

FIGURE 10.1 Percent of Convention Delegates Chosen in Primaries

Source: Data from Stanley and Niemi (2013, 43), Berg-Andersson (2016), and The Green Papers, http://www.thegreenpapers.com/.

adequate time to get to know the field of candidates in order to make a "deliberate choice," and late primary voters are deprived "of any meaningful choice."

Figure 10.2 illustrates how frontloading affects how long it has taken candidates to essentially clinch a party's presidential nomination. By the time two-thirds of delegates have been chosen, it is unlikely that any candidate will be able to win enough delegates in the remaining contests to stop the front-runner. In 1976, delegate selection was spread out over about 16 weeks, and two-thirds of delegates had not been chosen until the thirteenth week. By 2008, two-thirds of delegates to both major party conventions were selected in six or seven weeks. Both parties attempted (without success) to persuade states to spread out the process.

Nomination contests were less frontloaded in 2012. Primaries and caucuses were spread out over 26 weeks, and two-thirds of delegates were not selected until the seventeenth week. In 2016, however, the Republican calendar was again frontloaded with two-thirds of delegates chosen by week eight, while the Democrat's calendar remained much less frontloaded.

The Nomination Campaign

To win a party's nomination, a candidate must get the support of an absolute majority of the delegates at the convention—that is, 50 percent plus one of all delegates. The number of delegate votes needed to win is called the **magic number**.

magic number The number of delegates needed at a political party's national convention for a candidate to be nominated as the party's candidate for the presidency; this number equals 50 percent plus one of all delegates at the convention.

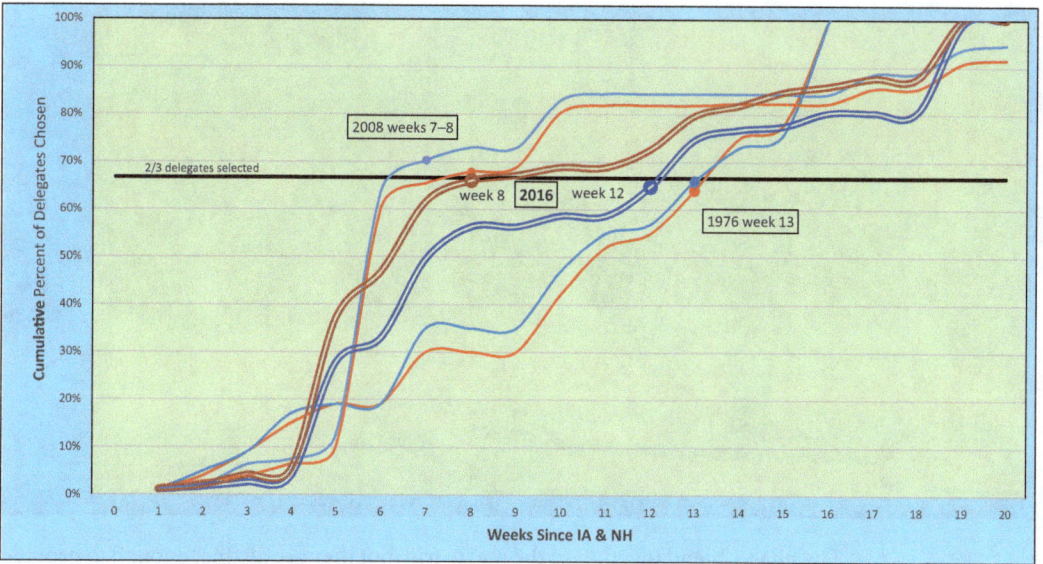

FIGURE 10.2 Frontloading of Delegate Selection

Source: Data for 1976 from Mayer and Busch (2004); data for 2008 and 2016 from The Green Papers, http://www.thegreenpapers.com/.

In 2016, the Republican National Convention was composed of 2,472 delegates, so the magic number needed to win the nomination was 1,237. The Democratic convention was larger, consisting of 4,763 delegates, and the magic number to win the Democratic nomination was 2,382. Candidates compete for delegates in the caucuses and primaries, hoping to win the magic number of delegates.

The nomination campaign is a winnowing process to determine which one of several candidates will win enough delegates to be a party's presidential nominee. As Table 10.2 illustrates, sitting presidents running for reelection typically have few if any challengers for the nomination. George W. Bush in 2004, and Barack Obama in 2012, had no opposition for their party nominations. The party not in power, however, will have numerous candidates competing for the nomination. In 2004, at least nine Democrats contested to challenge President Bush's bid for reelection. The 2012 Republican contest was wide open, with about a dozen Republicans actively competing to challenge President Obama's bid for reelection. The 2008 election was unusual because neither party had a sitting president or vice president running, so there was open competition for both party nominations.

This winnowing process has a number of filter points that weed out weaker candidates. There are four phases of presidential nomination campaigns (Hadley 1976; Kessel 1992):

1. Invisible primary
2. Initial contests
3. Mist clearing
4. National convention

Republican presidential candidates, from left, John Kasich, Carly Fiorina, Marco Rubio, Ben Carson, Donald Trump, Ted Cruz, Jeb Bush, Chris Christie, and Rand Paul share the stage with debate moderator Wolf Blitzer during the CNN Republican presidential debate at the Venetian Hotel & Casino on Tuesday, December 15, 2015, in Las Vegas.

© John Locher/AP Photo

The phases blend together in the real world, but they are distinct enough to provide analytic clarity to aid understanding of how a nomination campaign progresses.

Invisible Primary

An unofficial process begins long before the first official contests to select delegates. The period between the election of a president and the first official contests to pick the next one is called the **invisible primary** (Hadley 1976). The invisible primary takes place largely behind the scenes—there are no delegates chosen and few if any formal rules. During this period, potential candidates test the waters and decide whether to enter the race. They begin raising funds, putting together an organization, seeking endorsements, and maneuvering for political advantage. Although party organizations have no official authority at this stage, party insiders have considerable influence. Political scientists Marty Cohen and his associates (Cohen et al. 2008a, 2008b) describe the invisible primary as a "long-running national conversation" among party officeholders and other political notables about which candidate can unite the diverse and sometimes competing parts of the party coalition and win the next presidential election.

Speculation about the potential Democratic nominee in 2020 started just days after Donald Trump's inauguration. By May 2018 pundits had already begun speculating and looking for signs about who might run. And breaking with past tradition, President Trump officially filed for reelection on January 20, 2017, the day of his inauguration. Trump's unorthodox style also increases speculation about Republicans who might challenge him.

The invisible primary serves to sort out and begin solidifying the field of serious contenders who will wage the battle for delegates. The chief criteria for assessing

invisible primary The period of time between the election of one president and the first contest to nominate candidates to run in the general election to select the next president.

TABLE 10.2 CANDIDATES FOR PARTY PRESIDENTIAL NOMINATIONS, 2004–2016

Democrats	Republicans
2004	
Sen. John Kerry	**Pres. George W. Bush**
Sen. John Edwards	Unchallenged
Gov. Howard Dean	
Gephardt, Clark, Lieberman, Kucinich, Mosele-Braun, Sharpton	
2008	
Sen. Barack Obama	**Sen. John McCain**
Sen. Hillary Clinton	Fmr. Gov. Mike Huckabee
Fmr. Sen. John Edwards	Fmr. Gov. Mitt Romney
Biden, Richardson, Dodd, Kucinich, Bayh, Gravel, Vilsack	Fmr. Mayor Rudy Giuliani
	Fmr. Sen. Fred Thompson
	Brownback, Paul, Gilmore, Hunter, Tancredo, T. Thompson
2012	
Pres. Barack Obama	**Fmr. Gov. Mitt Romney**
Unchallenged	Fmr. Sen. Rick Santorum
	Fmr. Rep. Newt Gingrich
	Rep. Ron Paul
	Gov. Rick Perry
	Rep. Michelle Bachmann
	Herman Cain
	Donald Trump
	Palin, Huckabee, Huntsman, Christie, Barbour, Pawlenty, Pence, Daniels, Thune, Johnson, DeMint, Jeb Bush
2016	
Fmr. Secy. of State Hillary Clinton	**Donald Trump**
Sen. Bernie Sanders	Sen. Ted Cruz
Fmr. Gov. Martin O'Malley	Sen. Marco Rubio
Fmr. Sen. Jim Webb, Fmr. Sen. Lincoln Chafee	Gov. John Kasich
	Fmr. Gov. "Jeb" Bush
	Sen. Rand Paul
	Gov. Chris Christie
	Dr. Ben Carson
	Carly Fiorina, Mike Huckabee, Sen. Lindsey Graham, Sen. Rick Santorum, Gov. Scott Walker, Gov. Rick Perry, others

Note: Party nominees listed first in bold. Entries in *italics* are potential candidates who were high in the polls at some point but did not officially enter the race, and candidates who ran for their party nomination but were consistently low in preference polls, did not raise significant campaign funds, and never won a caucus or primary.

the strength of the potential candidates are money, standing in the polls, and endorsements.

The first indicator of which candidates are likely to emerge as major contenders is money. Money to finance a campaign is such an important indicator of a candidate's strength that political observers sometimes refer to this aspect of the contest as the "money primary." Yet the invisible primary involves more than money. Although having enough money to run a national campaign may be necessary, it is not sufficient to win a major party nomination.

Table 10.3 shows how candidates stacked up in the money primary in the 2008, 2012, and 2016 nomination contests. In the 2008 election cycle, fundraising success identified the major contenders in both parties, but not the eventual nominees—Obama and McCain finished second and third, respectively, in the money race. In the 2012 election cycle, only the Republican nomination was contested.[5] Mitt Romney led the Republican field with about $33 million raised and went on to win the nomination. Romney's path to the nomination, however, was not an easy one, and standing in the money race did not identify the strongest contenders. Texas governor Rick Perry, a distant second in fundraising, was briefly considered a strong alternative to Romney, who could appeal to divergent factions of the Republican Party—economic conservatives, and Tea Party Republicans who did not trust Romney because he had taken moderate positions on healthcare, abortion, and taxes as governor of Massachusetts. Yet Perry failed to emerge as a serious contender for the nomination, while Newt Gingrich and Rick Santorum (who ranked last) were able to hang on to compete in upcoming primaries and caucuses.

What does this example tell us about who will be serious candidates? Money is still crucial, but a new source of enormous sums of money emerged in the 2012 campaign—Super PACs. Recall from Chapter 6 that Super PACs may raise unlimited sums of money from corporations, unions, and wealthy individuals, but they may not contribute directly to or coordinate with candidates' campaigns. Because Super PACs cannot coordinate with candidates (and much of the spending occurs after the invisible primary), it is not appropriate to add this money to the money raised by the candidates. Spending by Super PACs, however, helps explain why candidates such as Gingrich and Santorum who would have been dismissed as weak in previous elections managed to stay the contest much longer than expected this time (Hartranft 2012). Thus, raising lots of money is important, but it does not guarantee success. To be a serious contender, a candidate must have a message and run a competent campaign that appeals to voters, as the example of Rick Perry's failed campaign in 2012 aptly demonstrates.

The 2016 nomination contests challenged much of what we have learned about the invisible primary. Hillary Clinton's path to the Democratic nomination was contested, but generally consistent with expectations. In the money primary (see

---

5 Although President Obama was unopposed for renomination, he raised nearly $100 million—more than for his nomination battle in 2008 and more than all Republican candidates combined in 2012. Obama was able to use this money in the general election campaign.

TABLE 10.3 PRESIDENTIAL NOMINATION CANDIDATES' STANDINGS IN THE "MONEY PRIMARY"

Democratic Candidates	Campaign Funds 3rd Quarter (millions)*	Republican Candidates	Campaign Funds 3rd Quarter (millions)*
2008			
Hillary Clinton	$90.96	Mitt Romney	$62.83
Barack Obama	**$80.28**	Rudy Giuliani	$47.25
John Edwards	$30.36	**John McCain**	**$32.12**
Bill Richardson	$18.70	Fred Thompson	$12.83
Chris Dodd	$13.60	Ron Paul	$8.27
5 others	$11.76	7 others	$13.58
2012			
Barack Obama	$99.6	Mitt Romney	**$32.83**
Unchallenged		Rick Perry	$17.20
		Ron Paul	$12.81
		6 others	$27.11
2016			
Hillary Clinton	**$77.47**	Ben Carson	$31.41
Bernie Sanders	$41.46	Ted Cruz	$26.57
3 others	$1.98	Marco Rubio	$14.60
		Jeb Bush	$13.38
		4 others (LT $10 each)	$24.48
		Donald Trump*	$3.93
		7 others (LT $4m each)	$9.75

Notes: Money raised as of the end of the third quarter of 2007, 2011, and 2015. Although Donald Trump raised about $4m dollars from his formal announcement in mid-June through the end of the reporting period on June 30, 2015, he has a personal net worth in the billions of dollars, and stated he would self-finance his campaign. Party nominee in bold.

Source: Federal Election Commission (2007; 2011; 2015).

Table 10.3), Clinton was far ahead of the lone serious challenger, Sen. Bernie Sanders (I-VT).[6]

The Republican contest, in contrast, surprised party professionals and political scientists alike. Donald Trump, a celebrity billionaire with no governmental experience, won the Republican nomination against a deep field of experienced politicians (including eight governors and five senators) while breaking all conventional campaign norms. The leader of the money primary was another political outsider, Dr. Ben Carson, followed by two sitting senators (Ted Cruz and Marco Rubio) and former Florida Governor Jeb Bush. Although he ranked fourth in fundraising, Bush,

---

[6] Sanders calls himself a Democratic Socialist, but was elected as an Independent. He caucuses with Democrats in the Senate. Although he ran in Democratic presidential primaries in 2016, he has not explicitly stated that he is a Democrat.

a successful governor of a large swing state and the son and brother of two former presidents, was favored to win the nomination. Yet while raising very little money, Trump dominated news coverage with a controversial campaign that tapped into frustrations of mostly white, working-class voters who felt left behind by globalization and forgotten by establishment politicians and the mass media.

A second early indicator of who the major contenders will be is standing in the polls. These polls ask Republican and Democratic voters whom they would like to see win their party's presidential nomination. Preferences expressed in polls taken years before the election reflect mostly name recognition, giving nationally prominent individuals an advantage. But early favorites often decide not to run, and lesser-known candidates engage in activities to get mentioned in the media and emerge as strong contenders.

Figure 10.3 shows how the major candidates stacked up in polls taken during the invisible primaries in 2012 and 2016. There was vigorous competition only for the Republican nomination in 2012. Mitt Romney led a crowded field in most of the 15 months before the Iowa caucuses and New Hampshire primary in January 2012, but his approval hovered below 25 percent, with the preferences of most Republicans divided among several others. Social conservatives and Tea Party Republicans were concerned that Romney was not reliably conservative on key issues, but there was no obvious alternative. Some commentators described the campaign as a contest between Romney and "Not Romney"—and at least six candidates auditioned for the role of "Not Romney." Figure 10.3a shows when the potential Romney alternatives climbed and then fell in the polls. Donald Trump surged in the polls in April, but his popularity faded quickly, and he never formally entered the race. Michelle Bachman's standing started to climb in July after some strong debate performances and her win in the Iowa straw poll, but Rick Perry's announcement of his candidacy in July eclipsed Bachman's rise. After a surge into first place, Perry's popularity peaked in September and started a rapid slide after lackluster debate performances and gaffes. As Perry's standing declined in November, Herman Cain climbed in the polls, only to have his candidacy collapse in November amid accusations of sexual harassment and an extramarital affair. Then it was Newt Gingrich's turn to audition. He climbed into first place in December, but Rick Santorum started to rise in the polls as well. On the eve of the first official contests to begin selecting delegates, it appeared that Gingrich and possibly Santorum could be serious contenders.

Both parties' nomination contests in 2016 were competitive. Early poll standings for the Republican nomination appeared consistent with past races. Jeb Bush and Wisconsin Gov. Scott Walker were near the top of a crowded field with support in the 15 percent range. Other politically experienced candidates and outsider Ben Carson were bunched together at 10 percent or less. Despite Trump's celebrity and brief spurt of popularity in the 2012 invisible primary, he entered the race in March 2015 with less than 2 percent support from Republican voters. Few political observers viewed him as a serious candidate. His campaign consisted of a series of gaffs (insults and ignorance of major policy issues), any one of which would have ended a political campaign in a typical year. Yet what the political establishment

CHAPTER 10 ELECTIONS   339

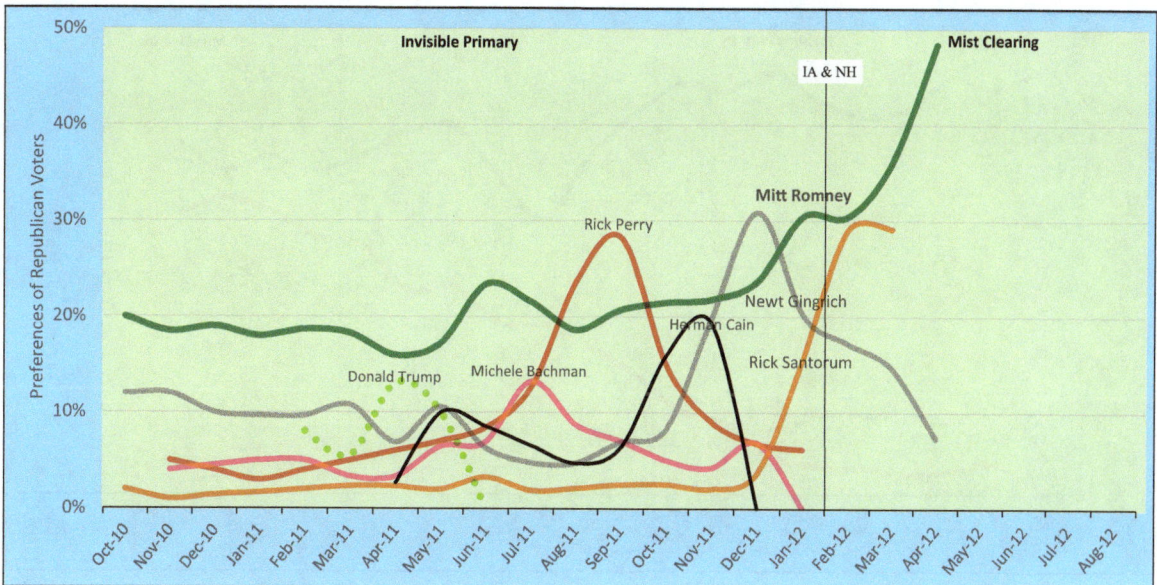

FIGURE 10.3a Republican Invisible Primary, 2012

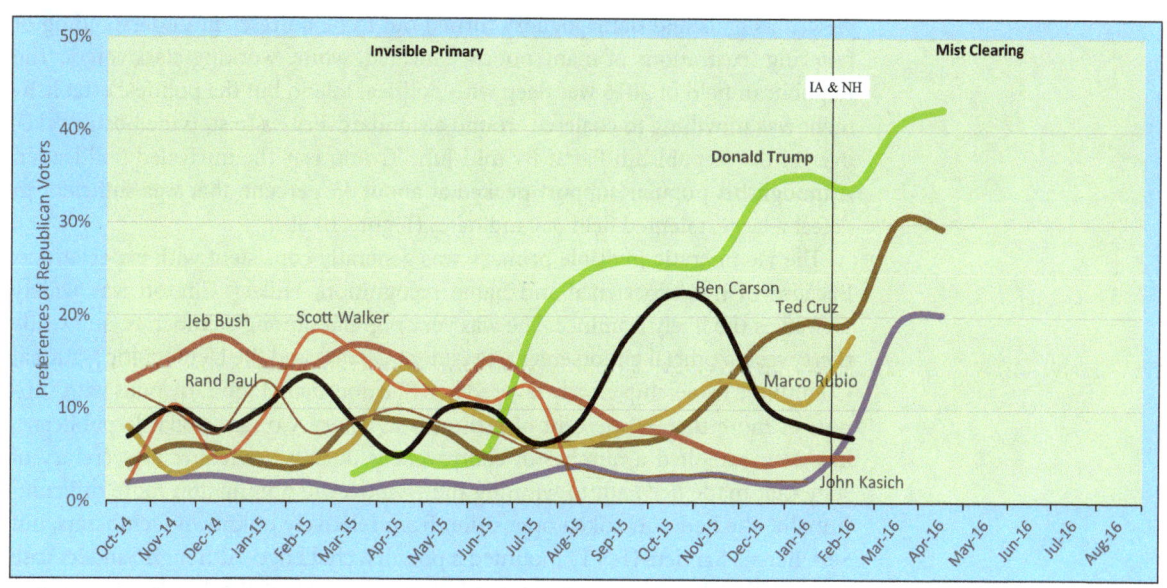

FIGURE 10.3b Republican Invisible Primary, 2016

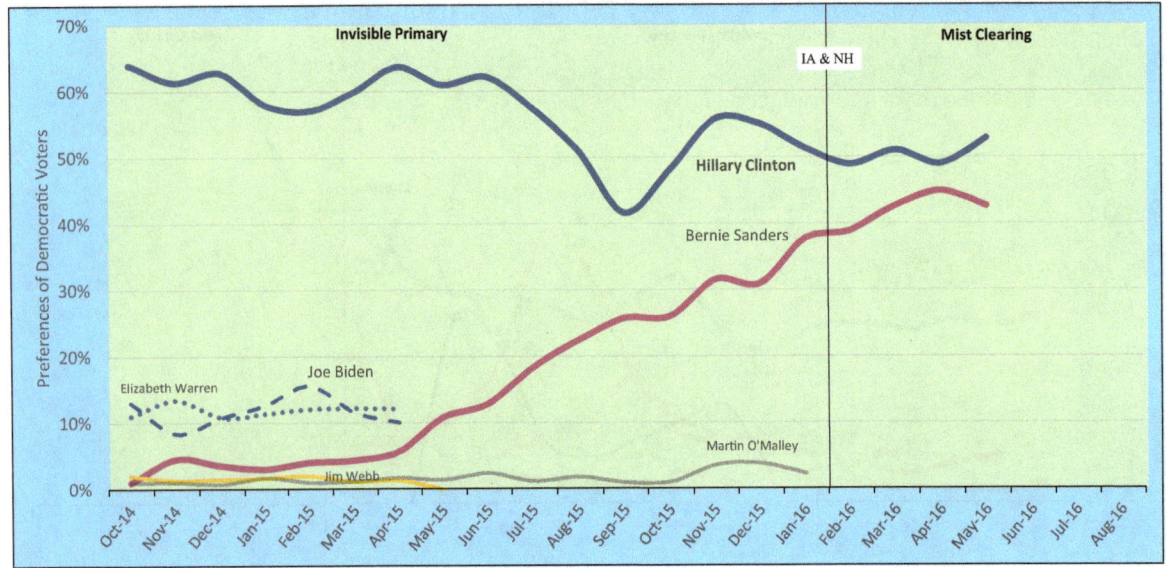

FIGURE 10.3c Democratic Invisible Primary, 2016

Source: Data from http://pollingreport.com/wh12rep.htm, http://pollingreport.com/wh16rep.htm, and http://pollingreport.com/wh16dem.htm.

viewed as gaffs and demagoguery turned out to be a prescient understanding of festering frustrations of many poorly educated, white, working-class voters. The Republican field of 2016 was deep with political talent, but the political establishment was unwilling to coalesce around a standard-bearer to stop the hostile takeover of the Republican Party. By mid-July, Trump was the unrivaled poll leader. Although his popular support peaked at about 35 percent, that was sufficient to defeat a large, talented field of candidates (Figure 10.3b).

The Democratic invisible primary was generally consistent with expectations. Because of her experience and name recognition, Hillary Clinton was widely viewed as the likely nominee. She was very popular among Democrats, and while there was no official endorsement, President Obama and the Democratic National Committee leadership clearly favored her. She dominated the early polls with support of more than 60 percent of Democratic voters. Congressional Republicans, however, exploited a number of controversies during her tenure as secretary of state that made her path to winning the Democratic nomination more difficult.[7] Initially, she had only token opposition from relatively unknown Democrats, but Sen. Bernie Sanders (I-VT) mounted a populist challenge. Although Sanders rose in the polls, Clinton's support among Democratic voters fell below 50 percent only briefly (see Figure 10.3c).

---

7 These include alleged negligence in responding to an attack on the U.S. diplomatic mission in Benghazi, Libya, on September 11, 2012, and sending classified e-mails on a privately maintained server.

The third indicator to identify the major contenders is endorsements from key members of the party establishment. These party insiders include federal and state elected officials (past presidents, governors, members of Congress, and state legislators), members of the party organization (state and local party officials), and other party notables such as celebrities, interest group leaders, and other party activists. Political scientists have generally dismissed endorsements as having little if any influence on election outcomes, including who wins a party's presidential nomination. Systematic research, however, provides persuasive evidence that the accumulation of endorsements in this "endorsement derby" (Cohen et al. 2001) reflects the results of a "long-running national conversation" among party insiders during the invisible primary. In the nine contested nominations from 1980 to 2000, the candidate preferred by party insiders won the nomination (Cohen et al. 2008a, 175–177).

The record in contests after 2000 is more mixed. In the 2004 Democratic contest, party elites were unable to reach a consensus. An unusually small percentage of party elites made endorsements, and three candidates attracted similar shares of the few that were made—Richard Gephardt had a slim plurality (around 25 percent), Howard Dean was a close second (around 23 percent), and John Kerry, the eventual nominee, finished a close third (Cohen et al. 2008a, 177). In the 2008 contests, Hillary Clinton "corralled about half of the party's public endorsements"; Obama, the eventual nominee, finished a distant second (Cohen et al. 2008b, 8). On the Republican side, McCain had a slim plurality over Romney. Romney was the clear winner in 2012, with Perry and Gingrich far behind (see Table 10.4), though the number of endorsements was low, suggesting that party elite consensus was not strong. In 2016, Hillary Clinton was the overwhelming choice of the Democratic Party establishment. In the Republican contest, the party establishment was unified in rejecting Donald Trump. But Trump was able to capture the nomination, because establishment support was divided among seven strong candidates—Bush and Rubio each had around 20 percent of the endorsements, while five others with significant experience as governors or senators attracted around 10 percent each. Although the Republican establishment was similarly divided in 2008, there was no effective outsider to take advantage of that division.

Initial Contests

The second phase of the nomination campaign consists of Iowa caucuses and the New Hampshire primary—the first official contests that begin choosing convention delegates. These initial contests are important *only* because they are first. The number of delegates at stake is small. In 2016, these two states combined had around 2 percent of the delegates at each convention. Moreover, Iowa and New Hampshire are not particularly representative of the demographic diversity in America. An Associated Press study (Ohlemacher 2007) ranked states according to how closely they looked like the nation on such demographic factors as race, age, income, education, industrial mix, immigration, and urban/rural residential patterns. Iowa ranked forty-first, and only West Virginia and Mississippi were less typical of America than New Hampshire. Which state looked most like America? Illinois.

TABLE 10.4 PRESIDENTIAL NOMINATION CANDIDATES' STANDINGS IN THE "ENDORSEMENT DERBY"

Democratic Candidates	Endorsements*	Republican Candidates	Endorsements*
2008			
Hillary Clinton	46.7%	**John McCain**	**28.7%**
Barack Obama	**29.5%**	Mitt Romney	26.3%
John Edwards	10.4%	Rudy Giuliani	17.0%
Bill Richardson	5.8%	Frank Thompson	15.4%
Chris Dodd	4.9%	Mike Huckabee	5.6%
Joe Biden	2.7%	Duncan Hunter	4.7%
5 others	0.0%	Sam Brownback	2.4%
		4 others	0.0%
2012			
Barack Obama	Unopposed	**Mitt Romney**	**56.0%**
		Rick Perry	11.6%
		Newt Gingrich	10.9%
		Ron Paul	8.6%
		Herman Cain	3.6%
		5 others (LT 3% each)	9.1%
2016			
Hillary Clinton	**95.1%**	Jeb Bush	24.1%
Joe Biden	2.3%	Marco Rubio	20.3%
Bernie Sanders	1.4%	Chris Christie	12.3%
Martin O'Malley	0.2%	Mike Huckabee	12.3%
		John Kasich	9.4%
		Ted Cruz	8.5%
		Rand Paul	7.1%
		6 others (LT 3% each)	6.2%
		Donald Trump	**0.0%**

Notes: * = Endorsements weighted by importance of the office.
Party nominee in bold.
Source: Data from Appleman (2008; 2012; 2016, http://www.p2016.org/candidates/natendorse16.html).

These contests provide the first major opportunity for candidates to generate some favorable national publicity, break out of the pack, and gain momentum for future contests. But they mainly serve to thin the field as weak candidates who fail to meet expectations drop out.

All candidates enter these contests, and the media devote much time to reporting how the contestants fared, granting favorable free publicity to the perceived winner. The perceived winner is not necessarily the candidate who finishes first but rather may be a less well-known candidate who does better than the pundits expected. The perceived winner gets headlines across the nation, becomes an instant topic of talk shows, and gains the image of a winner. This positive attention leads to a rise in the polls and additional campaign contributions.

In the 2012 Republican contest, for example, Rick Santorum was the surprise "winner" of the Iowa caucuses—after a recount, Santorum was declared the "winner" by 34 votes over front-runner Mitt Romney. A more objective interpretation is that the result was a tie, with Romney and Santorum each getting 25 percent and Ron Paul close with 21 percent. Indeed, Paul did better than his third-place finish suggests. After subsequent rounds of the caucus process—county conventions, congressional district conventions, and state convention—Ron Paul actually ended up with 21 of Iowa's delegates; Santorum got one, and Romney got none. But "winning" these early contests is not about precise vote counts or delegate counts—it's all about perceptions and headlines. Santorum's perceived victory in Iowa gave him a big boost in the polls. Romney scored a decisive victory in the New Hampshire primary a week later. Yet, anything short of a decisive win would have been viewed as a loss because, having been governor of neighboring Massachusetts, Romney was already known in New Hampshire. Bachman, Perry, and Huntsman dropped out after poor showings in these initial contests.

Similarly in 2016, media sources declared Hillary Clinton and Ted Cruz "winners" of the Iowa caucuses. Yet, in the Democratic contest, Clinton and Bernie Sanders were essentially tied with 49 percent each, and in the Republican contest there was a three-way tie with Cruz at 27.6 percent and Donald Trump and Marco Rubio at 24 and 23 percent. Sanders' 60 percent victory in New Hampshire confirmed that he presented a viable challenge to Clinton. Trump's first place finish with 35 percent in New Hampshire established him as the front-runner. But John Kasich kept his candidacy alive with a distant second place finish, while Cruz, Rubio, and Bush divided the remainder of the establishment vote with about 11 percent each. Christie and four others dropped out after poor showings in these initial contests.

Mist Clearing

The mist-clearing phase begins after the two initial contests. It is an ongoing process analogous to the lifting of an early morning fog, slowly bringing surroundings into focus (Kessel 1992, 9). This phase is characterized by a reduction in uncertainty as weaker candidates are sifted out in the contests that occur in the following weeks. Attention begins to focus on two or three major contenders. The criteria for assessing success shift from perceptions of who exceeded expectations to more objective indicators, such as number of contests won and delegate counts.

In 1980, several states began holding their primaries on a single day in early March. Because these states chose a significant portion of delegates to the national convention, this day was referred to as **Super Tuesday**. In subsequent elections, more states moved their nominating contests earlier, frontloading the process. Frontloading shortened the mist-clearing phase. In 2000 and 2004, for example, party nominations were for all practical purposes settled by Super Tuesday, six weeks after the

Super Tuesday The day in early March when several states hold their primaries. These states choose a significant portion of delegates to the national convention.

initial contests. Although no candidate had reached the magic number—that is, a majority of convention delegates—by this point, the front-runners had accumulated such commanding leads that there was little chance that anyone could win enough delegates in the remaining contests to stop them. The Republican process in 2012 was less frontloaded because Super Tuesday was not as "super-sized"— only 17.1 percent of delegates were chosen on Super Tuesday in 2012 compared to 41.5 percent in 2008. In 2016, however, 31.8 percent of Republican delegates were chosen on Super Tuesday. Democratic contests remained less frontloaded, with less than one-fourth of delegates chosen on Super Tuesday.

The accumulation of delegates is the most important indicator of success during the mist-clearing phase (see Figure 10.4). Romney led throughout this phase in 2012. Although Gingrich and Santorum won several later contests, their victories slowed but could not stop Romney's march toward the magic number—1,144 delegates—to win the nomination. Gingrich won the South Carolina primary on January 21, less than two weeks after New Hampshire. His only other victory was his home state of Georgia on Super Tuesday. Santorum scored three wins—the Colorado and Minnesota precinct caucuses and the Missouri primary—in early February. Winning these contests, however, was largely symbolic because they did not select any delegates bound to candidates. Such popular-vote victories in the initial

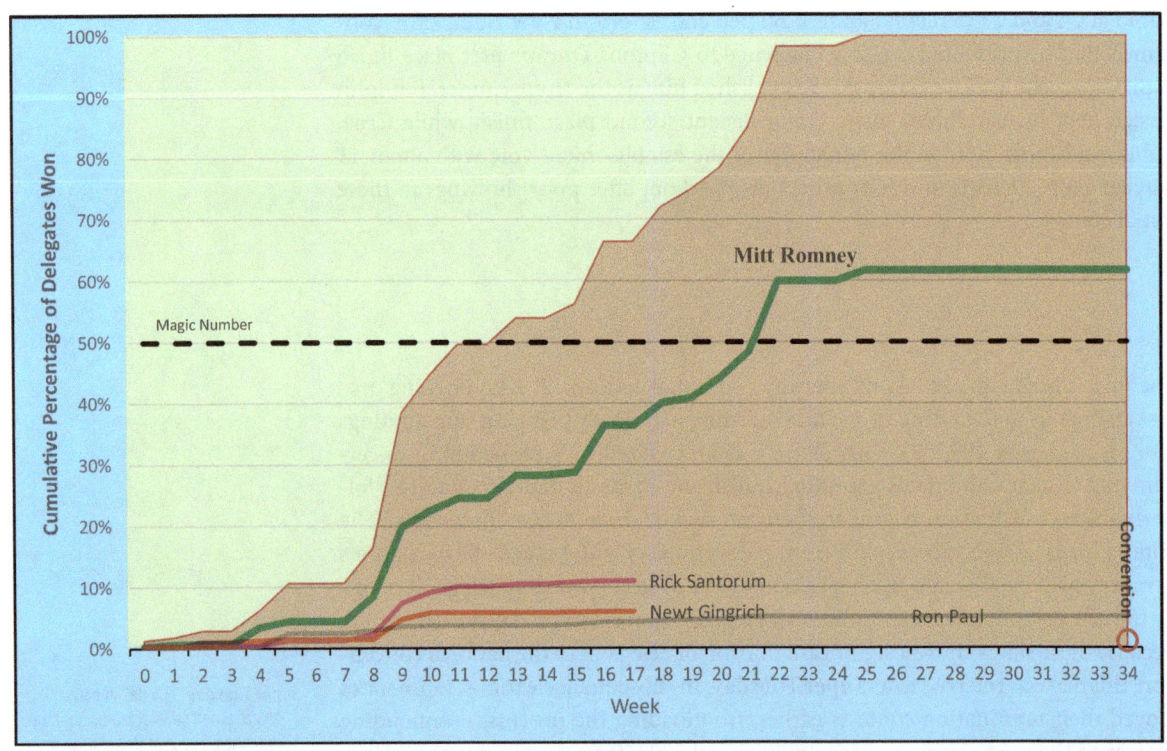

FIGURE 10.4a Mist Clearing: 2012 Republican Presidential Candidates' Delegate Accumulation

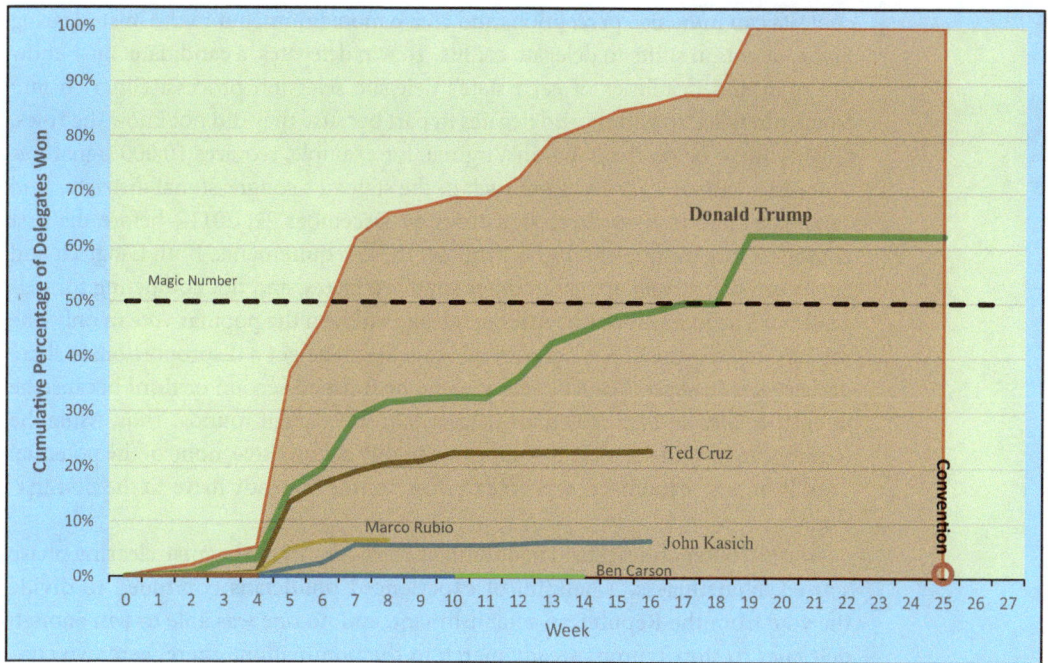

FIGURE 10.4b Mist Clearing: 2016 Republican Presidential Candidates' Delegate Accumulation

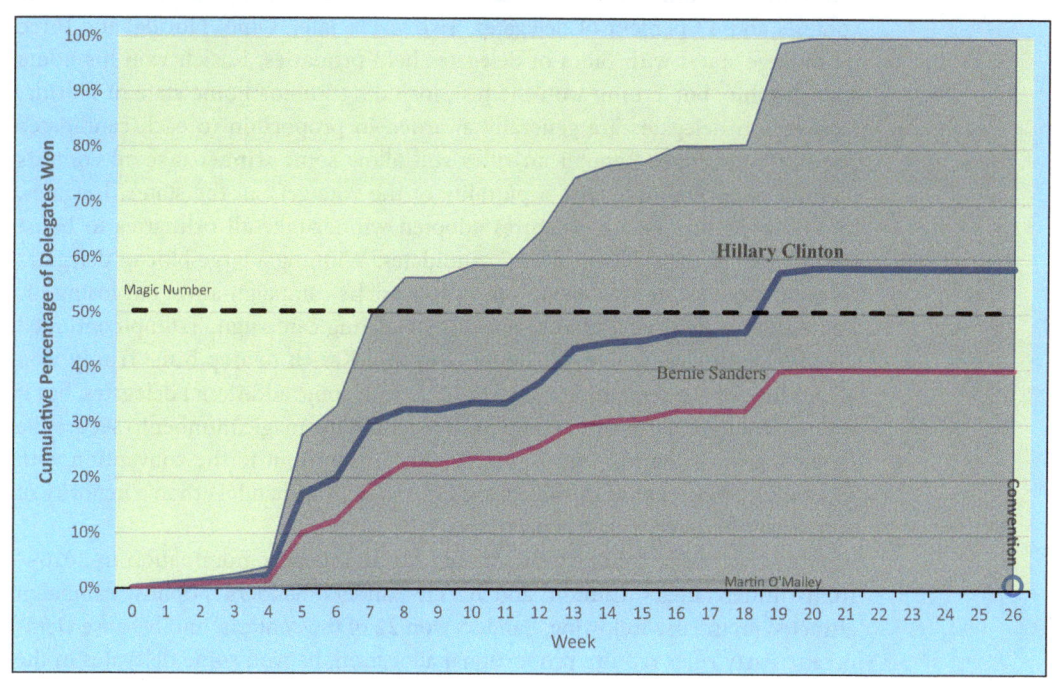

FIGURE 10.4c Mist Clearing: 2016 Democratic Presidential Candidates' Delegate Accumulation

Source: Data from Berg-Andersson (2008, 2012, 2016).

contests can influence perceptions and create momentum, but in the mist-clearing phase, attention shifts to delegate counts. To win delegates, a candidate must know the rules and deadlines of each state's delegate selection process. Gingrich and Santorum failed to win more delegates in part because they did not know the rules. Qualifying to be on the ballot in Virginia, for example, requires 10,000 signatures statewide, with at least 400 from each of the state's 11 congressional districts. And candidates had to have these signatures by December 22, 2011—before the first contests. Only Romney and Ron Paul met these requirements. Both Gingrich and Santorum had strong appeal in other southern states, and not competing for delegates in Virginia was costly. Although Ron Paul won the popular vote in only one minor contest—the U.S. Virgin Islands caucuses—he got a disproportionate share of delegates in several caucus states where he finished second or third because he knew the rules and competed for delegates in subsequent rounds. Thus, while the Republican nomination contest appeared highly competitive, none of the potential "Not Romney" candidates was able to stop Romney's steady drive to the nomination.

The 2016 Republican field had thinned considerably as the mist-clearing phase started. Nonetheless, a handful of experienced politicians continued to divide the vote from the Republican establishment, and no one was able to win enough delegates to stop Trump's steady march to the nomination. There were two contests, South Carolina and Nevada, before Super Tuesday. Trump won both with Rubio and Cruz essentially tied for second place. Bush dropped out after finishing fourth in the South Carolina primary. On Super Tuesday, Trump won most of the contests and 43 percent of delegates. Two weeks later, Ohio, Florida, and three more large states with blocs of delegates held primaries. Kasich won his home state of Ohio, but Trump won the rest, including Rubio's home state of Florida. Convention delegates are generally awarded in proportion to each candidate's popular vote share. Republican rules still allow some winner-take-all contests in which the candidate with a plurality of the vote gets all the state's delegates. The Ohio and Florida legislatures adopted winner-take-all primaries to boost the chances of their "favorite son" candidates. Winning a large bloc of delegates from his home state was enough to keep Kasich's campaign alive, but losing his home state convinced Rubio to end his struggling campaign. Trump continued his unorthodox campaign with only Cruz and Kasich to stop him. Trump won all but four of the remaining contests. Cruz won some additional delegates, but it was not enough to prevent Trump from reaching the magic number to secure the Republican nomination (see Figure 10.4b). Trump went to the convention with more than 60 percent of the delegates, even though he had less than a majority of votes cast (45 percent) in the primaries.

Only two viable candidates contested the Democratic nomination in 2016—front-runner Hillary Clinton, and Bernie Sanders. Sanders' populist campaign attracted an intense following. Sanders won 22 of the contests, and because Democratic Party rules require proportional allocation, he won some delegates in the contests where he finished second. Sanders repeatedly complained that the rules were rigged against him, but Clinton was the clear winner, with 55 percent of popular votes cast in the primaries and 56 percent of the delegates.

The National Convention

The national convention, composed of the delegates selected in the state primaries and caucuses, is the supreme governing authority of the party. The conventions meet for four days in presidential election years to nominate candidates for president and vice president and to conduct other party business.

Conventions do not choose the party's presidential nominee as they once did. The state primaries and caucuses select the presidential nominee, and the convention now acts as a ratifying body. Political scientists John Jackson and William Crotty observe that conventions have become "marketing devices for the parties, the candidates and the issues and images they want to sell the public in the general election" (1996, 63).

Although it is clear that modern conventions are carefully scripted to appeal to a mass television audience, conventions continue to have five major functions:

1. They officially nominate the party's candidates for president and vice president, which ratifies and legitimizes the results of the primaries and caucuses.
2. They approve a platform for the nominees to run on.
3. They provide a mechanism to encourage losing candidates and disparate party factions to unify for the general election.
4. They showcase the party and its candidates on national television and create a favorable image with the public.
5. They adopt rules to govern the party in the interim between elections.

The primary function of the national convention continues to be to formally choose the party's nominees for president and vice president. In recent nomination contests, the parties' conventions ratified the winner who secured a majority of the delegates in the primaries and caucuses. This official act *legitimizes* decisions of participants in primaries and caucuses about the presidential nominee.

Rules in both parties require delegates to vote for the candidate they are pledged to on the first ballot. If no candidate has secured a majority of delegates, they are free to switch to a different candidate on the next round of balloting. Between votes, the various delegations negotiate and cut deals until someone gets a clear majority of votes. This situation is referred to as a "brokered convention," a pejorative term meant to imply deals made by corrupt party bosses and smoke filled rooms. Neither party convention has required more than one ballot to nominate its presidential candidate. Although there was discussion among some "Never Trump" establishment Republicans about one of Trump's rivals winning enough delegates to deny him the nomination at the convention, these efforts were unsuccessful.

The convention also chooses the party's vice presidential nominee. The delegates typically ratify the presidential nominee's choice of a running mate. A number of considerations go into the choice of a running mate. Generally, there has been an attempt to balance the ticket with someone who differs in important ways from the presidential nominee, to unify the party and appeal to key segments of

An important function of the national convention is to promote party unity. Unable to differentiate themselves on policy, nomination campaigns sometimes become contentious and personal. Relations between Donald Trump and Senator Ted Cruz (R-TX) were particularly personal in the campaign for the 2016 Republican nomination. Cruz was given an opportunity to make a major speech at the convention in hopes that he would help unify the party. Yet hard feeling from the nomination campaign lingered. When Cruz addressed the delegates during the third day of the Republican National Convention in Cleveland, Wednesday, July 20, 2016, he congratulated Trump on winning the nomination, but withheld his endorsement, prompting boos from Trump's supporters.

© Matt Rourke/AP Photo

voters. The most common characteristics to balance are region, ideology, and political experience inside and outside of Washington, DC. In 2016, Republican nominee Donald Trump with no governing experience selected Indiana governor and former House member Mike Pence as his running mate. Pence also appealed to conservative evangelical Christians, a key part of the Republican base. In 2008, Barack Obama, a first-term senator from Illinois with no foreign policy experience, picked fellow senator Joe Biden from Delaware. Biden brought a great deal of seniority and experience as chair of the Senate Foreign Relations Committee.

A second important function of the national convention is adopting the platform, which is the central policy document of the party and a statement of its general philosophy. Platforms serve as campaign documents, and they provide a reasonably good indication of what a candidate will do as president. Although they do not deliver on all their promises, presidents attempt to follow through on the broad outlines of the party's basic document.

A third function of the national convention is to promote party unity. Candidates seeking a party nomination generally agree on policy. Unable to differentiate themselves on policy, nomination campaigns sometimes become contentious and personal. The partisan spirit at the convention gives the contestants an opportunity to put aside their personal disagreements and work together to defeat the other party's ticket. Promoting party unity was a major goal of the 2016 Democratic convention. Although some Sanders supporters expressed frustration at his loss, Sanders personally offered an enthusiastic endorsement and urged his supporters to work hard for Clinton's election. If disagreements prevent the party from unifying, its nominee will be in a weaker position in the general election. Byron Shafer (1988) has found that since 1968, the party with the most harmonious convention has been victorious over a party with a more contentious convention. Republicans, however, defied this tendency in 2016. Ted Cruz, the candidate who had the last chance to prevent Trump from reaching his magic number, was given an opportunity to make a major speech at the convention in hopes that he would help unify the party. Yet hard feeling from the nomination campaign lingered. Cruz congratulated Trump on winning the nomination, but withheld his endorsement, prompting boos from Trump's supporters and giving a boost to the "Never Trump" Republicans. Despite going into the general election campaign much less unified than Democrats, Trump eked out an electoral college victory while losing the popular vote.

THINKING ANALYTICALLY

CAN WE PREDICT WHO WILL WIN PARTY NOMINATIONS?

Unless an incumbent president is seeking reelection, numerous candidates seek their party's presidential nomination. Although competition is often limited to two or three "serious" candidates, that competition is vigorous, and the outcome may seem very much in doubt. In short, presidential nomination campaigns seem to be a "vast realm of uncertainty, unpredictability, and chaos. Unknown candidates rise out of nowhere to become front runners; 'can't miss' candidates suddenly see their best-laid plans come undone" (Mayer 1996, 44).

It turns out, though, that we have found indicators that predict quite well who wins presidential nominations. Yet winning the initial contests in Iowa and New Hampshire that get all the attention and hype does not predict the eventual nominee nearly as well as winning the invisible primary. It may seem a bit farfetched to suggest that we can identify the "winner" of a contest with no formal rules, no real votes cast, and no delegates selected. Political scientists, however, have that the leaders in money, the polls, and endorsements on the eve of the Iowa caucuses are good indicators of the invisible primary winner (Cohen et al. 2008a; Mayer 1996).

In the seven contested nominations for president from 1980 to 2000 (four Republican and three Democratic), only one money leader (former governor John Connally in 1980) and one poll leader (former senator Gary Hart in 1988) did not go on to win their party's nomination (86 percent correct predictions); the leader of the "endorsement derby" won all seven contested nominations. The winners in Iowa and New Hampshire, in contrast, fared no better than a coin toss—three of seven or 43 percent correct predictions (see accompanying table).

In the six contested nominations from 2004 to 2016, however, invisible primary variables did a poor job of predicting the nominees—two money leaders, two poll leaders (33 percent), and three endorsement leaders (50 percent) won their party's nomination. Initial contest winners fared only slightly better—three Iowa caucus winners (50 percent) and four New Hampshire primary winners (67 percent) won their party nominations. Across all contested nominations from 1980 to 2016, endorsement leaders won their party nomination 10 of 13 times (77 percent), and poll leaders won eight of 13 (62 percent). The other invisible primary indicator (money leader) and victories in the initial contests did no better than a coin toss.

Why have nominations become less predictable in the four most recent presidential elections? One explanation is luck and the small number of cases (or the small N, in scientific language). Seven contested nominations from 1980 to 2000 is enough to identify a systematic pattern if one exists (Cohen et al. 2008b, 13), but just barely. Idiosyncratic events often have a strong influence on political processes, and with a small number of observations, just one or two random events can obscure an underlying process. A limitation of using the results of the initial contests to predict who will win a party nomination is what some call the "your own backyard" effect—that is, candidates from Iowa and New Hampshire and adjacent states tend to have a built-in advantage in these contests. The winners of these initial Democratic contests in 1988 and 1992, for example, had this backyard advantage. Senator Tom Harkin from Iowa and Representative Richard Gephardt from neighboring Missouri won the Iowa caucuses, and former governor Paul Tsongas from neighboring Massachusetts and Bernie Sanders from neighboring Vermont won the New Hampshire primary, but all failed to win their party nomination. Thus, wins in Iowa and New Hampshire often do not tell us much about the strength of candidates in future contests. The primary indicators also have limitations. For example, Hillary Clinton led in the money primary in 2008 by raising a record $90 million. But Obama, the eventual nominee, was a close second with $80 million, which was nearly double the record-breaking $40 million raised by the money leader Howard Dean in 2004. And in 2016, Donald Trump won the Republican nomination with an unconventional and controversial campaign, but spent only a fraction of what the top four candidates spent.

PREDICTIONS OF PARTY PRESIDENTIAL NOMINEES

Year	Nominee	Invisible Primary "Winners"			Initial Contests Winners	
		Money Leader	Poll Leader	Endorsements Leader	IA Caucuses	NH Primary
Republicans						
1980	Reagan	Connally	Reagan	Reagan	Bush Sr.	Reagan
1988	Bush Sr.	Bush Sr.	Bush Sr.	Bush Sr.	R. Dole	Bush Sr.
1996	R. Dole	R. Dole	R. Dole	R. Dole	R. Dole	Buchanan
2000	G.W. Bush	G.W. Bush	G.W. Bush	G.W. Bush	G.W. Bush	McCain
2008	McCain	Romney	Giuliani	McCain	Huckabee	McCain
2012	Romney	Romney	Gingrich	Romney	Santorum	Romney
2016	Trump	Carson	Trump	J. Bush	Cruz	Trump
Democrats						
1984	Mondale	Mondale	Mondale	Mondale	Mondale	Hart
1988	Dukakis	Dukakis	Hart	Dukakis	Gephardt	Dukakis
1992	B. Clinton	B. Clinton	B. Clinton	B. Clinton	Harkin	Tsongas
2004	Kerry	Dean	Dean	Gephardt	Kerry	Kerry
2008	Obama	H. Clinton	H. Clinton	H. Clinton	Obama	H. Clinton
2016	H. Clinton	H. Clinton	H. Clinton	H. Clinton	H. Clinton (tie)	Sanders
Correct Predictions 1980–2000		86% (6/7)	86% (6/7)	100% (7/7)	43% (3/7)	43% (3/7)
Correct Predictions 2004–2016		33% (2/6)	33% (2/6)	50% (3/6)	50% (3/6)	67% (4/6)
Correct Predictions 1980–2016		54% (7/13)	62% (8/13)	77% (10/13)	46% (6/13)	54% (7/13)

Note: Entries are the candidates who were leaders in each of the indicators in contested nominations since 1980. Incorrect predictions are in red.

Source: Data from Mayer (1996, 49–51); Cohen et al. (2008b), Table 10.4; Federal Election Commission (http://www.fec.gov/); and http://pollingreport.com/.

The N of 13 for the entire period is still small. It's difficult to figure out whether the poor predictive power in six contested nominations since 2000 reflects a fundamental change or just random error. Marty Cohen et al. (2008b) present evidence that some fundamentals have changed. They find that the communications revolution—cable news, blogs, YouTube, and the related increase in visible campaign activity, especially debates—provides candidates more chances to make independent impressions on voters, thereby making it harder for parties to dominate the game. Trump's extensive use of Twitter in 2016 is consistent with this speculation.

Discussion Questions

1. Iowa and New Hampshire are small states with much less diverse populations than in most other states. Residents in Iowa and New Hampshire argue that their small size is a plus because candidates must get to know lots of actual voters there to have any chance to win. Do you think the experience of extended campaign interactions with actual voters produces better candidates?

2. The only reason Iowa and New Hampshire get to go first in the caucuses and primaries is because they cut to the front of line a long time ago. Do you think rotating which states go first would produce better candidates? Some have suggested having four or five regional primaries and rotating which region goes first. Do you think this would be a better system?

A fourth function of conventions is to present a favorable image on national television—what Stephen Wayne calls the "pep rally goal" (2000, 156). As reforms in delegate selection have reduced the chance that conventions will exercise independent choice, this pep rally function has assumed greater importance. According to Wayne, party leaders and the nominee now view the convention "primarily as a launching pad for the general election" (2000, 156). The pep rally goal has been paramount at both party conventions since 2000. Traditional party business, such as adopting rules and the platform and even the roll call where delegates cast their votes, has been relegated to the background.

The final function of the convention is to adopt the rules that govern the party. As the supreme governing authority of the party, the convention may affect the party's future operation through its rules. The elimination in 1936 of the Democratic Party rule requiring a two-thirds majority to nominate a candidate reduced the likelihood of a deadlocked convention. Another controversial rule used by Democrats until 1968 was the **unit rule**, in which a majority of a state delegation could require the entire delegation to vote the same way on nominations and other issues, thereby disenfranchising the minority.

Once the parties have chosen their nominees, attention turns to the general election.

ELECTING THE PRESIDENT

The presidency is the single greatest electoral prize in the United States, and it is the only office with a truly national constituency. The presidential election is the focus of more attention, more money, and more effort than any other election. The complex mechanism established to choose the president—the electoral college—is unique to the American political system.

The Electoral College

More Americans cast ballots for president than in any other election, yet the national popular vote does not choose the president. The race for the presidency is not a single contest for a national vote, but rather 51 separate elections in each state and the District of Columbia to choose slates of partisan electors. These electors choose the president according to rules and procedures specified in the Constitution.

The **electoral college**, a system "jerry-rigged out of odds and ends of parliamentary junk pressed together by contending interests" (Collier and Collier 1986, 303), reflects disagreement among the Founders about how to choose the executive. Some wanted direct popular election; others wanted Congress or the state legislatures to have the responsibility. The electoral college was the bargain struck to satisfy these competing preferences (Jackson and Crotty 1996, 104).

unit rule A rule that permitted a majority of a state's delegation to a political party's national convention to require that the entire state delegation vote the same way (or as a unit).

electoral college The institution (whose members are selected by whatever means the state legislature chooses) that is responsible for selecting the president of the United States.

The electoral college is not democratic, nor was it intended to be. Some of the Founders had a profound distrust of ordinary citizens' abilities to make sound judgments about choosing the president. Convention delegate George Mason, for example, argued that to allow the people to make such a choice made no more sense than "to refer a trial of colors to a blind man" (Benton 1986, 1128). Even Madison, Hamilton, and others who believed that the presidency ought to reflect the will of the people suggested that this popular will should be filtered through intermediaries who would have superior knowledge and judgment. As John Jay explained in *Federalist* Number 64, "the select assemblies [i.e., the electors] … will in general be composed of the most enlightened and respectable citizens." Yet only a handful of delegates opposed direct election in principle. The primary concern about direct election was more practical—delegates worried that voters would not have sufficient information about the candidates to make reasoned judgments because the long distances and slow communications in the new nation would make national campaigns difficult (G. Edwards 2019). The electoral college was a way to solve the communication problem but still give citizens indirect influence.

The 2000 presidential election dramatically illustrated the importance of counting electoral votes rather than the national popular vote. The 2016 election provides yet another illustration of what counts in electing the president, but it also exposes the fallacy of the Founders' belief that this more knowledgeable college of electors would exercise superior judgment than the unfiltered popular will in choosing principled and competent individuals to be president.

How the Electoral College Works

The electoral college is an awkward electoral process to choose the president. The Twelfth and Twenty-Third Amendments addressed some glitches, but the basic legal structure and requirements of the process remain relatively unaltered.

The Constitution calls for each state legislature to choose, by whatever means it desires, a number of electors equal to its total number of senators and House members.[8] The minimum number of electoral votes a state can have is three—every state has two senators and at least one representative in the House. Seven states—Alaska, Delaware, Montana, North Dakota, South Dakota, Vermont, and Wyoming—have the minimum. Larger states with more representatives have more electoral votes: California is the largest with 55 electoral votes. The total number of electoral votes is 538, the sum of 100 senators, 435 House members, and three votes for Washington, DC, as mandated by the Twenty-Third Amendment.

States choose their electors in November of presidential election years. The electors meet in their respective state capitals in December and, as clarified by the Twelfth Amendment, cast separate votes for president and vice president. These votes are transmitted to the nation's capital, to be opened and counted in a

---

8 Members of Congress and those who hold other national offices, however, are not eligible to serve as electors.

joint session of Congress in January. To be elected president or vice president, a candidate must receive an absolute majority of electoral votes—that is, 270 of the 538 votes. The incumbent vice president, who is the presiding officer of the Senate, announces the outcome before the joint session of Congress. One candidate usually receives a majority of the electoral votes, and the vice president officially declares that candidate to be president. This procedure sometimes produces some irony. In January 2001, Vice President Al Gore declared his opponent, George W. Bush, to be president.

If no presidential candidate gets a majority of electoral votes, the House of Representatives, voting by states, chooses the president from among the top three candidates. Each state has one vote; the state's representatives collectively agree on how to cast that vote. A candidate must receive 26 votes, a majority, to be elected. If no vice presidential candidate gets a majority of electoral votes, the Senate, voting as individuals, elects the vice president from among the top two candidates. An absolute majority, or 51 senators, is required to elect the vice president.

The original idea behind this convoluted process was to have politically savvy electors, typically chosen by state legislatures, exercise their independent judgment to select the president. If this was the intent, it was quickly dashed. In the first two presidential elections, most state legislatures chose electors, although four states used popular elections to select them. Regardless, there was no division: In 1789 and again in 1793, George Washington got every electoral vote cast. Consensus disappeared with Washington's decision to retire from public office and with the emergence of political parties. More states began having popular elections to choose electors. The Founders' original vision of a body of wise men insulated from the winds of public opinion who judiciously picked the nation's highest official faded.

In each state and Washington, DC, the political parties nominate a slate of partisan electors. Although citizens in each jurisdiction cast votes for president, voters are actually deciding which party's slate of electors will win the right to cast the state's electoral votes. These electors do not exercise independent judgment. Because the parties choose individuals who have proven their loyalty, unfaithful electors are rare. In the 41 presidential elections since 1856, only 17 electors voted for someone other than their party's candidate.[9]

Faithless electors have never changed the outcome of an election, and in many cases that is not their intent. In 2000, for example, Barbara Lett Simmons, a Gore elector from Washington, DC, left her ballot blank. But not because of dissatisfaction with Gore. Rather, she abstained to attract media attention to protest DC's lack of a voting representative in Congress. She would have voted for Gore if it made a difference (Stout 2000).

In 2016, there were seven faithless electors, an unusually large number. Some were an attempt to change the outcome. Concerns about Trump's competence and

---

9 This number does not include 63 electors in 1872 who did not vote for Democrat Horace Greeley, who died before electors cast votes. About half of the states have laws that bind electors to vote for their party's nominee.

fitness for office led some Republicans, including some Republican electors, to try to convince a sufficient number of them to vote against Trump to preclude a Trump presidency (Kruesi and Barrow 2016). Although a number of Republican electors expressed sympathy for the effort and a few resigned rather than vote for Trump, only two voted for someone else—one for Kasich, one for Ron Paul. The other five faithless electors were Democrats who were unhappy with Clinton's campaign—three voted for Colin Powell, a Republican and former secretary of state; one voted for Faith Spotted Eagle, a Native American activist in Washington State; and one voted for Bernie Sanders.

Thus, while faithless electors occasionally produce controversy, they are not the reason that the electoral college violates democratic principles.

How the Electoral College Violates Core Democratic Principles

The electoral college violates core democratic principles of political equality and sometimes majority rule. Although choosing electors by direct popular vote in each state rather than by the legislatures may be more democratic in that it gives ordinary people more influence, this reform does not prevent the electoral college from violating these core democratic principles.

The electoral college violates political equality because the value of a vote for president depends on where it is cast. To achieve political equality in the electoral college, each state's percentage of electoral votes must equal its percentage of the population. Recall that the number of representatives a state has in the House and Senate determines how many electoral votes it has. Because all states have two senators and at least one representative, no state can have fewer than three electoral votes. As a result, the smallest states have more voting weight and the largest states less weight relative to their populations (Table 10.5). California has about 12.1 percent of the nation's population, but only has 10.2 percent of the electoral college votes (55 of 538). Wyoming, on the other hand, has about 0.18 percent of the nation's population, but it has the minimum share of electoral votes (three of 538), which works out to be 0.56 percent. Proportionally speaking, this means California is underrepresented (−15.1 percent) in the electoral college, and Wyoming is vastly overrepresented (204.8 percent).

In addition, individuals' votes count more in some states than in others. In most cases, all of a state's electoral votes go to the candidate who wins a plurality of the popular votes. This winner-take-all feature means that the preferences of voters who supported a losing candidate are not represented in the electoral college. In 2016, for example, Hillary Clinton won about 61 percent of the popular vote in California and got all 55 of its electoral votes, while Donald Trump won a 49 percent plurality in Florida and got all 29 of its electoral votes. The preferences of nearly 5.5 million Trump voters in California and 4.5 million Clinton voters in Florida were not represented at all in their state's electoral vote. Moreover, a vote cast in a large state has a much smaller weight than votes cast in small states—one vote out of more than 13 million cast in California has much less weight than one out of 250,000 cast in Wyoming.

TABLE 10.5 ALLOCATION OF ELECTORAL VOTES, 2016

State	Electoral Votes	Population (millions)	% Under-/Over-Represented*	State	Electoral Votes	Population (millions)	% Under-/Over-Represented*
California	55	37.3	-15.4%	Oregon	7	3.8	4.7%
Texas	38	25.1	-13.4%	Oklahoma	7	3.8	6.9%
New York	29	19.4	-14.3%	Connecticut	7	3.6	12.2%
Florida	29	18.8	-11.7%	Iowa	6	3.0	12.8%
Illinois	20	12.8	-10.7%	Mississippi	6	3.0	15.8%
Pennsylvania	20	12.7	-9.8%	Arkansas	6	2.9	17.9%
Ohio	18	11.5	-10.6%	Kansas	6	2.9	20.5%
Michigan	16	9.9	-13.1%	Utah	6	2.8	24.3%
Georgia	16	9.7	-5.4%	Nevada	6	2.7	27.3%
North Carolina	15	9.5	-3.9%	New Mexico	5	2.1	39.1%
New Jersey	14	8.8	-8.8%	West Virginia	5	1.9	54.6%
Virginia	13	8.0	-6.9%	Nebraska	5	1.8	56.8%
Washington	12	6.7	2.2%	Idaho	4	1.6	46.2%
Massachusetts	11	6.5	-3.8%	Hawaii	4	1.4	68.4%
Indiana	11	6.5	-2.8%	Maine	4	1.3	72.5%
Arizona	11	6.4	-1.4%	New Hampshire	4	1.3	74.0%
Tennessee	11	6.3	-0.7%	Rhode Island	4	1.1	117.6%
Missouri	10	6.0	-4.4%	Montana	3	1.0	73.7%
Maryland	10	5.8	-0.8%	Delaware	3	0.9	91.4%
Wisconsin	10	5.7	0.7%	South Dakota	3	0.8	111.1%
Minnesota	10	5.3	-2.8%	Alaska	3	0.7	141.9%
Colorado	9	5.0	13.9%	North Dakota	3	0.7	155.5%
Alabama	9	4.8	7.8%	Vermont	3	0.6	174.6%
South Carolina	9	4.6	11.5%	DC	3	0.6	185.6%
Louisiana	8	4.5	1.1%	Wyoming	3	0.6	204.8%
Kentucky	8	4.3	5.6%				
				Totals	538	308.2	

Election of the president by the House of Representatives when no candidate has a majority in the electoral college also violates the principle of political equality. Because the House votes by state to select the president, the decision is not made according to the "one person, one vote" principle. The House has twice been called on to elect the president, in 1800 and 1824.[10]

---

[10] The Senate was called on to select the vice president in 1837. Martin Van Buren won a majority of electoral votes for president against four other candidates who received some electoral votes. But Democratic electors from Virginia withheld their votes from Van Buren's running mate, Richard M. Johnson, denying him a majority for vice president. The Senate elected Johnson vice president over the runner-up.

Nor does the electoral college ensure that the majority will rule. Six times in the nation's history the candidate elected president did not get the most popular votes: John Quincy Adams in 1824, Rutherford B. Hayes in 1876, Benjamin Harrison in 1888, John Kennedy in 1960,[11] George W. Bush in 2000, and Donald Trump in 2016. The electoral college may fail to choose the popular vote winner even if every elector votes for the candidate he or she was pledged to support. Table 10.6 illustrates a hypothetical election in which a candidate is on the ballot in only the 11 largest states. If this candidate wins the popular vote in these states by a one-vote margin and gets no votes in any other states, he or she would be elected president with 270 electoral votes. Although the other candidate would have more than 70 percent of the national popular vote, this popular candidate would get only 268 electoral votes from the other 39 states.

The mathematical advantage of the small states can also contribute to the popular winner losing in the electoral college. In the 2000 presidential election, for example, George W. Bush lost the popular vote nationwide, but he won a majority of electoral votes in part because of his success in the smallest states. Bush won 54 electoral votes from 13 of the 19 smallest states, where his popular vote total was about 2.7 million. More than twice as many people—5.7 million—voted for Al Gore in California to give him the same number of electoral votes.

The electoral college can fail to choose the candidate who gets the most votes because votes are aggregated state-by-state to choose electors. Allocating electoral votes on a winner-take-all basis in each state compounds the problem, but dividing electoral votes proportionately while continuing to aggregate votes state-by-state will not ensure election of the popular vote winner.

Proposals to Reform the Electoral College

These defects in the electoral college have led to several reform proposals. Attention has focused on three:

1. Direct popular election
2. The proportional plan
3. The district plan

Direct popular election would abolish the electoral college and voters would choose the president directly. Adopting this reform would require a constitutional

---

11 Kennedy is typically credited with a small popular vote victory over Nixon. But research by political scientists questions this result. Kennedy's name did not appear on the ballot in Alabama. Instead, only the names of Democratic electors appeared on the ballot, and six of the 11 chosen did not support Kennedy. Reports listing Kennedy as the popular vote winner nationwide count votes for any Democratic elector as popular votes for Kennedy, even though some clearly were not for Kennedy. If the popular vote in Alabama is apportioned based on how the electors voted, Nixon is the popular vote winner nationwide by a small margin (Gaines 2001).

direct popular election A proposal to abolish the electoral college and elect the president directly by national popular vote.

TABLE 10.6 HOW THE POPULAR VOTE WINNER CAN LOSE IN THE ELECTORAL COLLEGE

State	Electoral votes	Total votes cast in state* (millions)	Minimum votes needed to win state's electoral votes*
California	55	14.18	7.10
Texas	38	8.97	4.49
Florida	29	7.72	3.87
New York	29	9.42	4.72
Illinois	20	5.54	2.77
Pennsylvania	20	6.17	3.09
Ohio	18	5.50	2.75
Georgia	16	4.80	2.40
Michigan	16	4.11	2.06
North Carolina	15	4.74	2.38
New Jersey	14	3.87	1.94
Subtotal for 11 Largest States	270	75.02	37.59
Percent of Total	52.4%		**27.50%**
Other 39 States	268	61.65	
Total	538	136.67	

Notes: Popular vote totals are from 2016 presidential election. Votes needed to win state's electoral votes with only two candidates on the ballot is 50 percent plus 1 of votes cast in the state.

amendment. Although a majority of the public has consistently supported direct election for several decades (G. Edwards 2019), efforts to muster the two-thirds majorities in both houses of Congress to propose an amendment have been unsuccessful. Even if Congress were to propose such an amendment, ratification by three-fourths of state legislatures is unlikely.

The other two reforms would leave the electoral college in place, but electoral votes in each state would not be allocated on a winner-take-all basis. Either of these reforms could be implemented without amending the Constitution. Because the Constitution says that state legislatures can choose electors however they wish, any state legislature could choose to allocate electoral votes in proportion to the statewide popular vote or by congressional district.

The **proportional plan** would divide each state's electoral votes in proportion to the division of the popular vote. For example, a candidate receiving 40 percent of the popular vote in a state would get 40 percent of its electoral votes. Other features of the electoral college would remain, such as requiring a majority of electoral votes for a candidate to be elected and election by the House if no candidate receives a majority. Some states have considered this reform, but none has yet adopted it.

proportional plan A plan to revise the electoral college such that the number of electoral college votes given to candidates would be based on the proportion of the popular vote they obtained.

The **district plan** would return to the method some states used early in the nation's history. The district plan allocates one electoral vote to the presidential candidate who receives a plurality in a House district; the state's remaining two electoral votes go to the candidate who wins a plurality statewide. Thus, a state's electoral votes could be split if pluralities voted for the Democrat in some districts and for the Republican in others.

Maine and Nebraska have been using the district plan for some time, but until recently, neither state divided its electoral votes. Obama won a single electoral vote from one of Nebraska's three congressional districts in 2008, and Trump won a single electoral vote from one of Maine's two congressional districts in 2016.

If the goal of reform is to ensure that the winner of the national popular vote is elected president, only direct popular election achieves it. The electoral college failed to choose the popular vote winner in three of the 15 elections since 1960. The other reforms would have done no better and possibly worse.

Table 10.7 shows elections since 1960 in which one of the reforms would have failed to select the candidate who won the popular vote. The proportional plan likely would have failed to select the popular vote winner twice as often as the current system. In seven elections since 1960, minor party candidates could have received enough electoral votes to prevent any candidate from receiving a majority of electoral votes. If other features of the electoral college were maintained, these elections would have been decided by the House. The House probably would have chosen the popular vote winners, Carter and Clinton, in 1976 and 1992. Recall that if the House chooses the president, each state gets one vote, with a majority required (26 of 50) to elect the president. Thus, we need to look at the party split in each state delegation to see which party controls at least 26. Because 32 state delegations were mostly Democrats in these years, it's likely that the House would have chosen the Democrat. In the other five elections in which no candidate would have won a majority of electoral votes (1960, 1968, 1996, 2000, and 2016), the House probably would have elected the runner-up in the popular vote.

The district plan fares no better than the current electoral college. Nixon lost the electoral vote in 1960, but he would have won a majority if all states had used the district plan. In 2000 and 2016, the district plan would have produced the same result as the electoral college and the proportional plan—i.e., elect the runner-up. In 1976, the district plan would have produced the same result as the proportional plan and sent the election to the House. Although Carter probably would have been elected, failure to elect the popular vote winner outright would have created a great deal of turmoil. In 2000 and 2016, Bush and Trump still would have won a majority of electoral votes under the district plan. The district plan likely would have elected the runner-up in the popular vote in 2012 as well. Obama had a clear majority of the popular vote, and the electoral college and the proportional plan reflect that result. Yet if all states had used the district plan, Romney would have won a majority of electoral votes. This is the only case in which the candidate with a clear popular vote majority would not have been elected.

Moreover, neither the proportional plan nor the district plan would correct the violation of the democratic principle of political equality. The district plan

district plan A plan to revise the electoral college that would distribute a state's electoral college votes by giving one vote to the candidate who wins a plurality in each House district and two votes to the winner statewide.

TABLE 10.7 WINNER OF THE PRESIDENCY UNDER THE VARIOUS ELECTORAL COLLEGE REFORMS

Year	Candidates	Popular Vote	Electoral College		Proportional Plan		District Plan	
			Votes	Winner	Votes	Winner	Votes	Winner
1960	Nixon (R)*	49.55	219		266.1	Uncertain/ House	278	Nixon
	Kennedy (D)	49.46	303	Kennedy	265.6	**27 Dem**, 19 R, 4 tie	245	
	Byrd/others	0.99	15		5.3		14	
1968	Nixon (R)	43.2	301	Nixon	231.5	Uncertain/ House	289	Nixon
	Humphrey (D)	42.7	191		225.4	**27 Dem**, 19 Rep, 4 tie	192	
	Wallace (AI)/others	14.1	46		81.1		57	
1976	Carter (D)	50.1	297	Carter	269.7	Uncertain/ House	269	Uncertain/ House
	Ford (R)	48.0	240		258.0	**32 Dem**, 11 Rep, 7 tie	269	**32 Dem**, 11 Rep, 7 tie
	Others	1.9	0		10.2		0	
1992	B. Clinton (D)	43.0	370	B. Clinton	231.6	Uncertain/ House	324	B. Clinton
	Bush sr. (R)	37.5	168		203.3	**32 Dem**, 9 Rep, 9 tie	214	
	Perot (I)/others	19.5	0		103.1		0	
1996	B. Clinton (D)	49.2	379	B. Clinton	262.0	Uncertain/ House	345	B. Clinton
	Dole (R)	40.7	159		219.9	19 Dem, **28 Rep**, 3 tie	193	
	Perot (RF)/others	10.1	0		56.1		0	
2000	Gore (D)	48.4	266		264.0	Uncertain/ House	267	
	Bush (R)	47.9	271	Bush	265.0	18 Dem, **28 Rep**, 4 tie	**271**	Bush
	Nader (GR)/others	2.7	0		9.0		0	
2012	Obama (D)	51.1	332	Obama	272.2	Obama	262	
	Romney (R)	47.2	206		256.2		273	Romney
	Others	1.7	0		2.1		0	
2016	H. Clinton (D)	48.2	227		256.1	Uncertain/ House	246	
	Trump (R)	46.1	**304**	Trump	249.7	17 Dem, **32 Rep**, 1 tie	292	Trump
	Others	5.7	7		32.1		0	
Times Not Electing Popular Vote Winner		0	3		7 (5)		4 (3)	

Note: Kennedy is typically credited with a national popular vote victory in 1960. Footnote 11 explains why some political scientists believe that Nixon actually won the popular vote. Highlighted entries indicate cases in which the popular vote runner-up would have won.

Source: Adapted from Wayne 2004, 323–325, and updated by the authors.

consistently prevents equal weighting of votes because every state, regardless of population, gets two electoral votes for its two senators and awards two electoral votes to the statewide winner. Furthermore, since the electoral votes awarded by congressional district go to the plurality winner in the district, the preferences of voters who support the losing candidate in every district are not represented in the electoral vote. The proportional plan weights votes more equally, but this plan would often send the election to the House. Since voting is by state, small states have disproportionate influence—Wyoming, with about 600,000 people, has the same influence in electing the president as California, with over 37 million people. Thus, neither the proportional plan nor the district plan would reform the electoral college to ensure results consistent with core principles of democracy. Only direct popular election would ensure democratic results.

The electoral college system does have its defenders. Political scientist Judith Best argues, "the electoral vote system is a model of our federal Constitution … that creates one society out of many societies" (1996, 72). By making the presidency a race for states, it preserves the principle of federalism, the bedrock of the American political system. Although it presents an enormous obstacle to third-party candidates, it also helps promote a stable two-party system. And, echoing arguments in *Federalist* Number 68, defenders argue that electors chosen in each state provide a check on the tyranny of the majority. Demagogues who lack the competence to administer the distinguished office of president may be able to win in one state by appealing to voters' passions and prejudices, but to be elected they must attract the support of knowledgeable electors in many other states. Research by George Edwards (2019), however, shows that the electoral college has little to do with preserving federalism—equal representation in the Senate is more important on that score. Moreover, electors chosen by political parties cast votes to advance the party's candidates rather exercising reasoned judgement about candidates' character and competence as envisioned by the Founders.

The Campaign

Strategy and money are important components of a successful presidential campaign. Strategy is driven not just by the issues, but also by electoral rules.

The ultimate goal of presidential candidates is to get 270 electoral votes. Consequently, campaign efforts focus on states with a lot of electoral votes and on **swing states** in which the outcome could go either way. Although the presidential campaign is indeed a race for states, only a small number receive any attention from the candidates' campaigns. George Edwards (2019) observes that the most important indicator of which states get attention is how many times presidential candidates visit the state to campaign. Table 10.8 shows that in the four most recent presidential elections, presidential campaigns focused almost exclusively—over 90 percent of visits—on 13 states: Colorado, Florida, Iowa, Michigan, Missouri, Nevada, New Hampshire, New Mexico, North Carolina, Ohio, Pennsylvania, Virginia, and Wisconsin. Having a large number of electoral votes is not sufficient to

swing states States in which the outcome of a presidential race is unclear, and both candidates have a realistic chance of winning.

TABLE 10.8 RESIDENTIAL CANDIDATE CAMPAIGN STOPS

State	2004	2008	2012	2016	4 election total	Electoral votes*	Vote margin*
Ohio	OH (4)	OH (39)	OH (29)	OH (25)	OH (133)	GT 13	6.0%
Florida	FL (38)	FL (31)	FL (19)	FL (39)	FL (127)	GT 13	2.5%
Pennsylvania	PA (22)	PA (33)	PA (3)	PA (26)	PA (84)	GT 13	6.4%
Iowa	IA (19)	IA (5)	IA (12)	IA (12)	IA (48)	LT 7	6.7%
Wisconsin	WI (28)	WI (9)	WI (6)	WI (5)	WI (48)		3.7%
Colorado	CO (9)	CO (13)	CO (1)	CO (12)	CO (44)		6.0%
Virginia		VA (14)	VA (17)	VA (7)	VA (38)	GT 13	4.2%
North Carolina	NC (2)	NC (8)	NC (1)	NC (24)	NC (35)	GT 13	8.0%
New Hampshire	NH (7)	NH (8)	NH (7)	NH (1)	NH (32)	LT 7	4.6%
Michigan	MI (11)	MI (11)		MI (8)	MI (30)	GT 13	4.5%
Nevada	NV (5)	NV (7)	NV (7)	NV (7)	NV (26)	LT 7	4.7%
New Mexico	NM (8)	NM (9)		NM (1)	NM (18)	LT 7	5.2%
Missouri	MO (7)	MO (8)			MO (15)		5.5%
% of total	90.7%	94.7%	100.0%	91.7%	93.5%		
Total stops	216	206	111	192	725		

Note: States with greater than 13 electoral votes are the 11 largest with enough votes (270) to elect the president; states with less than 7 electoral votes are the 22 smallest. Vote margin is the popular vote difference in states with campaign appearances averaged across the four elections.

Source: Data from Edwards (2019).

get presidential candidates to campaign in a state. Of the 11 largest states, candidates campaigned only in the six that were competitive (an average margin of 5.3 percent). Presidential candidates largely ignored other large states, including California and Texas with the largest blocs of electoral votes (95 between them). No amount of campaigning would likely change the outcome in solid blue California or solid red Texas. Yet candidates made numerous visits to four of the smallest states (with a measly 21 electoral votes). Some of these elections were extremely close, and winning a handful of electoral votes in these competitive states could change the results.

Not only do the rules help determine where candidates will campaign, but they also determine to a considerable extent how they will campaign. Unlike the long invisible primary associated with the nomination campaign, the general election has tight time limits. After the parties' nominating conventions in 2016, there were only 16 weeks until the general election. This time limit determines the entire strategy of a campaign. As political scientists John Jackson and William Crotty put it, "all the strategic plans, all marshaling and deployment of resources, all the advertising, and every facet of the entire campaign effort works backward from the election date" (1996, 99). The time constraint places enormous pressure on the candidates and their organizations to get their messages out, mobilize their party bases, and attract undecided voters. The option of a front porch campaign in which the candidate stays at home rather than going out to engage the voters has long since receded into history.

Financing the Presidential Election

Running for president is an expensive proposition. In 2016, candidates spent a total of $1.5 billion and Super PACs supporting them spent an additional $0.62 billion. Yet, while lots of money is essential to be competitive, enormous spending is not sufficient to win. Hillary Clinton's blue team outspent Donald Trump's red team almost 2:1 ($795 million to $408 million) in a close, but ultimately losing, race (Center for Responsive Politics, https://www.opensecrets.org/pres16).

Numerous observers express legitimate concerns about the corrupting influence of money in politics, but efforts to regulate campaign spending must be balanced against constitutional guarantees of free speech and free association. Historically, restrictions on contributions to presidential campaigns have been ineffective. Congress enacted several laws in the first half of the twentieth century to prevent corporations and labor unions from contributing money to presidential elections, but channeling of money through intermediaries and political action committees (PACs) circumvented these laws. Candidates and political parties have also found loopholes in more recent efforts to regulate campaign contributions.

The Federal Election Campaign Act (FECA) regulates presidential campaign finance. Its key provisions include:

- Public financing of presidential campaigns and overall expenditure limits
- Contribution limits for candidates who accept public financing
- Public disclosure requirements
- Creation of the FEC to enforce the law

In 1976, the Supreme Court ruled that overall spending limits violated individuals' First Amendment free speech rights—that is, wealthy candidates have the right to spend as much of their own money as they wish on their campaigns. Limits on contributions and expenditures of candidates who accept public funds were upheld (*Buckley v. Valeo* 1976).

Candidates become eligible for public funds as soon as they raise at least $5,000 in contributions of $250 or less in each of 20 states, for a total of $100,000. Once qualified, they receive public funds on a dollar-for-dollar basis for the first $250 received from an individual. Those who accept public financing are bound by a spending limit. Candidates are not required to accept public financing and the spending limits that come with it.

Campaigns developed creative methods to avoid the spirit, if not the letter, of campaign finance laws. Campaign contributions can be characterized as either hard money or soft money. The contribution limits established by FECA applied to hard money—that is, money given to expressly support or oppose a candidate. FECA did not regulate soft money, which consists of contributions given to party organizations rather than to individual candidates. Parties use soft money for party building and for political purposes such as voter registration drives and to run issue ads advocating some cause or issue. Although political activities supported by soft money are not supposed to directly support or oppose a candidate, many observers viewed them as a loophole used to circumvent the contribution limits to indirectly benefit party standard-bearers.

In 2002, Congress passed the Bipartisan Campaign Reform Act (BCRA), better known as the McCain–Feingold Act, for its main Senate sponsors John McCain (R-AZ) and Russell Feingold (D-WI), to address the soft money problem. The BCRA banned soft money outright, and restricted "issue ads" run immediately before an election. This law also raised limits on hard money contributions during each election cycle to $2,000 from individuals and $5,000 from PACs. The law contained plenty of loopholes, however, and candidates took full advantage of them in the 2004 and 2008 presidential elections. In 2010, the Supreme Court struck down key provisions of the McCain–Feingold law. The Court ruled in *Citizens United v. Federal Election Commission* (2010) that the First Amendment prohibited limiting, let alone banning, corporate funding of independent political broadcasts in an election campaign. The ruling allows deep-pocketed advocacy groups and wealthy individuals to spend unlimited amounts of money through Super PACs discussed in Chapter 6.

Yet campaign finance legislation had important consequences for presidential nominations. Candidates could no longer turn to a few "fat cats" to bankroll their campaigns (unless they themselves are the fat cats). In the absence of a personal fortune, candidates had to raise many small individual contributions. This time-consuming logistical challenge rewards early starters.

Public campaign financing is also available in the general election. Nominees of the parties that received 25 percent or more of the popular vote in the previous presidential election—that is, the Democrats and Republicans—are eligible for full public financing; candidates of parties that received between 5 and 25 percent of the vote in the previous election are eligible to receive partial public financing. The major party candidates received equal funding, about $74 million, in 2004. Because candidates who accept public financing are limited to spending that amount, this law "leveled the playing field between the two major parties in the money available to support their" campaigns (Jackson and Crotty 1996, 186).

But the spending limit applies only if a candidate accepts public financing. In 2008, McCain accepted public financing, but Obama declined it, allowing the Democrat to spend a great deal more than the $84 million limit for candidates who accept public financing. In 2012 and 2016, neither major party nominee accepted public financing. With spending limits gone, 2012 was the most expensive election in history. The Obama campaign spent $683 million, and the Romney campaign spent $433 million. Including spending by the two parties and outside expenditures by Super PACs, the blue team spent $1.1 billion, and the red team spent $1.2 billion (http://www.opensecrets.org/pres12/). This may signal the end of public financing of presidential elections. In 2014, President Obama signed legislation to end the public funding of party conventions, and continued public financing of candidates is uncertain (Garrett 2014).

NOMINATING CANDIDATES FOR CONGRESS

Congressional elections differ from presidential elections in a number of ways—different rules for winning, smaller constituencies, shifting political jurisdictions, distinct advantages for incumbents. The Constitution leaves to the individual states the power to determine how parties nominate their candidates for the House and Senate.

Primary Laws

State parties nominate candidates for the Senate and House of Representatives in a direct primary or, at most, a primary and a runoff primary.[12] In most states, the candidate receiving a plurality wins the nomination. Ten states, primarily in the South, require a candidate to win a majority vote to win the nomination, and if no candidate receives a majority, a **runoff primary** is held between the two with the most votes. Southern states adopted the runoff primary because of one-party Democratic dominance following Reconstruction. With no viable Republican party to nominate candidates, winning the Democratic nomination was tantamount to election.

Each state's election law spells out how and when the primary is conducted. There are three types of primary elections: closed primary, open primary, and nonpartisan blanket primary. A little more than half of the states nominate congressional candidates in closed primaries, and most other states have open primaries. In both cases, voters are limited to casting votes in only one party's primary. Both open and closed primaries produce the same match-up: separate party nominees—one Democrat, one Republican, and one candidate from each minor party, if any—for the general election.

Washington and California use an unusual **top-two primary**. In this type of primary, candidates from all political parties run in the same primary. The top two vote-getters, which may be from the same party, face off in the general election.[13]

The Politics of Choosing Congressional Candidates

Although the politics of congressional nominations differ across states and regions, it is possible to identify some general patterns. First is the source of the candidates

---

runoff primary A second primary election held between the top two candidates if no candidate received a majority of the votes in the first primary.

top-two primary A type of election in which candidates from all political parties run in the same primary. The top two vote-getters, which may be from the same party, compete in a runoff in the general election.

---

12 A few states still use conventions as part of the nomination process, although the ability of the party organization to override the party in the electorate is limited in these cases.

13 Louisiana uses a related system, except technically there is no party primary. Instead, all candidates regardless of party appear on the general election ballot, often with multiple candidates from each party. A candidate who gets a majority of votes is elected to the office. If no candidate gets a majority, there is a runoff between the top two, which may be from the same party, to determine the winner.

themselves. Senatorial candidates traditionally have been members of the House of Representatives or state governors. Political scientist David Canon (1990) has shown that from 1913, when the Seventeenth Amendment instituted direct election of senators, to 1987, 34 percent of senators were former House members, and 20 percent were former governors. In the 115th Congress (2017–2018), 50 of the 100 senators had served in the U.S. House, 12 were former governors, and 3 were former lieutenant governors. The candidate pool of the House of Representatives is less structured, reflecting the lower prestige of the House relative to the Senate. In general, however, service in the state legislature or in local offices is a stepping stone to Congress. In the 115th Congress, about 228 members had served in their state legislature or held some other elected state office (e.g., lieutenant governor, state treasurer); another 38 had held a local elected office (e.g., mayor, city council, county sheriff). Since the 1930s, the proportion of House members with state legislative experience has increased (Canon 1990, 59).

Perhaps the most important generalization about congressional nominations is that incumbents seldom lose. Figure 10.5 shows the number of incumbent representatives and senators defeated in primaries. Since the 1950s, an average of five House incumbents have lost their bid for renomination, about 1.5 percent of those running. Although Senate races are more competitive than are House races in the general election, Senate incumbents rarely lose in the primary—only eight incumbent senators have been defeated in primaries in the last 38 years.

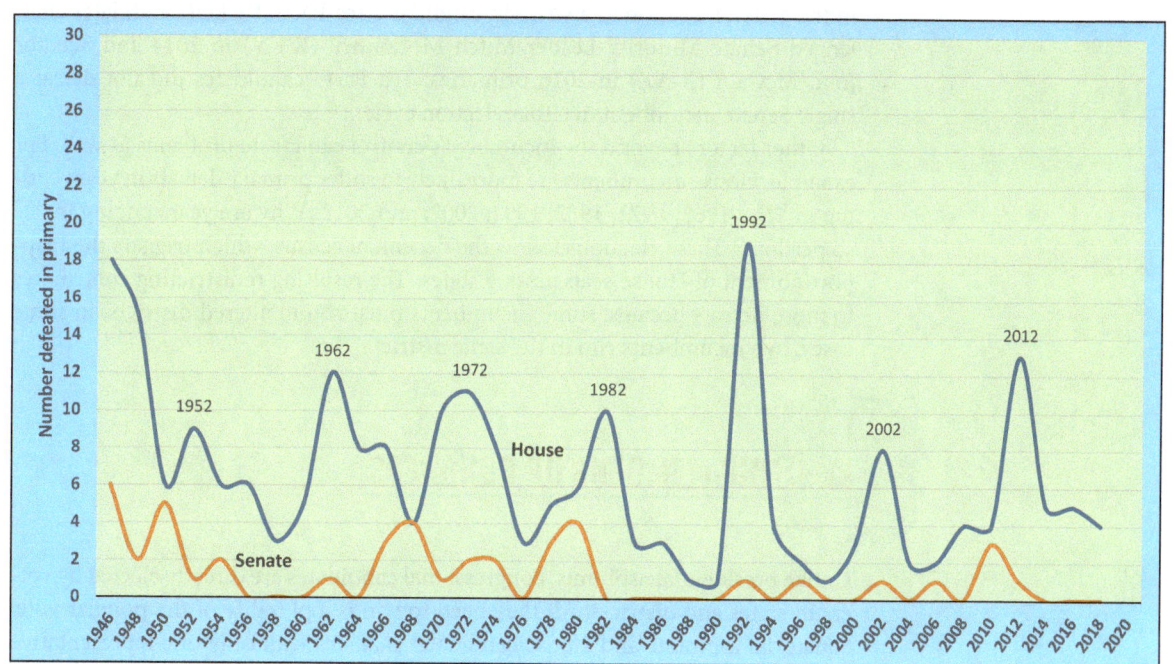

FIGURE 10.5 Incumbents Defeated in Primaries

Source: Ornstein et al. (2018, tables 2-3, 2-7, 2-8. https://www.brookings.edu/multi-chapter-report/vital-statistics-on-congress/).

In perhaps the biggest upset in the 2018 midterm-election, 28-year-old political newcomer, Alexandria Ocasio-Cortez defeated the incumbent Joseph Crowley in the Democratic primary in New York's 14th congressional district. Mr. Crowley, who was part of the House Democratic leadership, had not had a primary challenger since 2004. Here Representative-elect Ocasio-Cortez speaks to supporters after winning the general election in this heavily Democratic district.

© AP Photo

Unless there are indications that an incumbent is vulnerable, experienced candidates of the other party do not battle vigorously for the honor of going down to defeat in the general election. Previous campaign experience, close relationships with voters, greater knowledge of issues, and superior financial resources generally give veteran legislators enormous advantages over challengers. Although surmounting these obstacles is not impossible, it is rare.

Vigorous primary competition does occasionally occur. If the incumbent is perceived to be vulnerable or is not seeking reelection, competitive candidates are likely to jump into the nomination fray. Scandal, a weak showing in the previous election, or a voting record out of tune with the partisan base in the state or district can make an incumbent vulnerable. In 2010, for example, Senator Lisa Murkowski of Alaska lost her bid for the Republican nomination to a Tea Party-backed candidate, but she was reelected in the general election as a write-in candidate. Tea Party-backed candidates challenged Senate Minority Leader Mitch McConnell (R-KY) in 2014 and Senator John McCain (R-AZ) in 2016 primaries. Tea Party candidates did not defeat a single Senate incumbent in either election cycle.

Other factors beyond the incumbent's control can create problems as well. For example, House incumbents are more likely to suffer primary defeats in years ending in "2"—1962, 1972, 1982, 1992, 2002, and 2012. Why are years ending in "2" so perilous? These elections follow the decennial census, which triggers the reapportionment of House seats among states. The resulting redistricting contributes to more defeats because some incumbents must run in altered districts; in some cases, two incumbents run in the same district.

ELECTING MEMBERS OF CONGRESS

Unlike presidential aspirants, congressional candidates are directly elected by voters in states and districts. All they need to win is a plurality of the popular vote. Senatorial aspirants and House candidates in states with only one representative have a geographical constituency with stable boundaries—the entire state. The geographical boundaries of congressional districts in states with multiple House seats may change after each decennial census and reapportionment.

Apportionment

The Constitution provides for members of the House of Representatives to be apportioned among the states according to population. To keep the allocation of House seats current with changes in state populations, the Constitution requires a census—a national head count—every 10 years. The census has taken place each decade since 1790.

The Constitution does not establish a permanent size for the House of Representatives, leaving the matter to Congress. Following the 1790 census, membership of the House was set at 105. As both the population and the number of states grew, the size of the House gradually expanded until it reached 435 following the 1910 census. The size of the House was permanently fixed at 435 at that time (Jacobson 2009, 7).[14]

Apportioning seats in a legislature with a fixed size means that after each census, a state gains, loses, or retains seats depending on how its population changed in relation to the national average. The process of adjusting the number of House seats among the states to reflect population shifts is called **reapportionment**. Over the last several decades, population has been shifting away from the Northeast and Midwest to the South and West. From 1942 to 2012, for example, New York and Pennsylvania lost 18 and 15 House seats, respectively, whereas California gained 30 seats and Florida gained 21.

Congressional Districts

For congressional candidates, perhaps a more salient issue is not how many House seats a state gets, but how congressional constituencies are defined within a state. For the first half-century of the nation's existence, each state was free to determine how congressional seats were distributed internally. Many states elected their representatives at large, which means that all were elected statewide. This arrangement, in which more than one member is elected from the same constituency, is a **multimember district** election system. Another way to choose representatives is the **single-member district** system, in which the state is carved up into the number of districts equal to the number of representatives the state has in the House, and voters in each district choose one representative.

Since 1842, federal law has required representatives to be elected from single-member districts. After each reapportionment, state legislatures must redraw congressional district lines to accommodate changes in the number of seats and to reflect population shifts within the state. The process of redrawing the district lines within a state is called **redistricting**. In 31 of the 43 states with more than one House member, the state legislature is responsible for drawing congressional districts. To reduce political influence on redistricting, six states delegate primary responsibility for drawing congressional districts to an independent or bipartisan

reapportionment The process of adjusting the number of House seats among the states based on population shifts.

multimember district A method of selecting representatives in which more than one person is chosen to represent a single constituency.

single-member district A method of selecting representatives in which the voters in a district select a single representative.

redistricting The process of redrawing congressional district lines after reapportionment.

---

14 When Alaska and Hawaii were admitted into the Union in 1959, one seat for each of the new states was temporarily added to the House. After the 1960 census, the membership was reduced to 435.

redistricting commission, and another six states have an advisory commission or some other mechanism (National Conference of State Legislatures 2018).

The partisan stakes are high in redistricting, and they often result in **gerrymandering**, which means the drawing of district boundaries to benefit one interest and hinder another. The term was coined in honor of Elbridge Gerry, a Massachusetts governor who supposedly designed a district in 1812 shaped like a salamander in order to gain a partisan advantage (Figure 10.6). Gerrymanders can benefit several kinds of political interests:

1. Partisan gerrymanders benefit the majority party.
2. Incumbent gerrymanders benefit current officeholders regardless of party.
3. Racial gerrymanders benefit citizens of a particular race or deny representation to a particular race.

Gerrymandering is accomplished through a process of "packing and cracking." In packing, voters who support the disadvantaged interest are concentrated in as few legislative districts as possible, which means that minority candidates win those districts by overwhelming margins, but the number of seats they win is smaller than their share of the population. In cracking, such voters are spread out over many districts so that minority candidates are unlikely to win at all because their supporters are spread too thinly to muster a plurality in any district.

As a result of population shifts from rural areas to cities from the 1930s to the 1970s, the distribution of seats in the legislature did not fairly reflect the distribution of the population, and many state legislatures came to be **malapportioned**

gerrymandering The drawing of district lines in such a way as to help or hinder the electoral prospects of a specific political interest.

malapportioned A situation in which the distribution of legislative seats does not accurately reflect the distribution of the population.

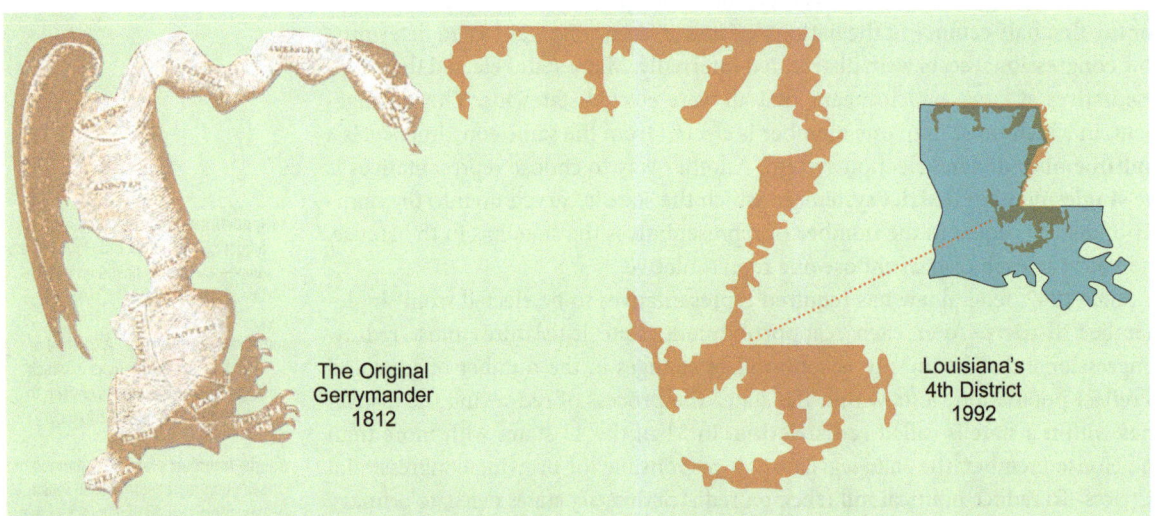

FIGURE 10.6 Gerrymandering, Then and Now

Source: Richard L. Engstrom and Jason Kirksey. 1998. "Race and Representational Districting in Louisiana." In *Race and Redistricting in the 1980s*, ed. Bernard Grofman. New York: Agathon Press.

(badly apportioned). Disparities in the populations of legislative districts were particularly pronounced in states whose constitutions granted towns and counties representation in the state legislature without regard to population. In 1960, for example, the most populous district of the California State Senate had 422 times more people than the smallest one. The ratio between the largest and smallest congressional districts in Texas was four to one. Yet neither state legislatures nor successive Congresses had an incentive to remedy the disparity. Changing the system required representatives from malapportioned and gerrymandered districts to risk their political careers.

Faced with the unwillingness of legislative bodies to remedy the situation, aggrieved parties turned to the courts for assistance. The basis for the court challenge was that the Constitution mandates reapportionment of congressional seats among the states after every census, and the Fourteenth Amendment's guarantee of equal protection of the law requires these new districts to be about equal in population. If legislative districts are not equal in size, then every person's vote does not have equal weight, denying them "equal protection of the law"—that is, malapportionment violates the core democratic value of political equality.

The federal courts initially declined to deal with unequally sized districts, on the grounds that legislative apportionment was a political question that courts did not have jurisdiction to decide; instead, the remedy of political questions lay with the state legislatures and Congress (*Colgrove v. Green* 1946). Then, in ***Baker v. Carr*** (1962), the Supreme Court overturned the political question doctrine, holding that legislative apportionment was a **justiciable issue** that the courts had jurisdiction to hear and decide.[15]

The ruling in *Baker* led to a number of landmark cases addressing the issue of political equality in legislative apportionment. In ***Wesberry v. Sanders*** (1964), the Supreme Court invalidated unequal congressional districts in Georgia. Citing constitutional provisions mandating that representatives be apportioned among the states according to population and that they be chosen by the people of the states, the Court ruled that "as nearly as practicable, one [person's] vote in a congressional election is to be worth as much as another's." The ruling established the principle of **one person, one vote**. It means that all legislative districts in a state must contain about equal numbers of people. The same year, in *Reynolds v. Sims* (1964), the Court extended the principle to state legislatures, holding that the equal protection of the laws clause of the Fourteenth Amendment requires that districts for both houses of a bicameral state legislature must be substantially equal in population.

These rulings, however, did not address gerrymandering. It is possible for a state legislature to distribute residents equally among districts but still benefit the majority party or an incumbent legislator. Perhaps the most controversial redistricting issue of recent years has been drawing district boundaries with the explicit goal

Baker v. Carr The 1962 case in which the Supreme Court overturned the political question doctrine, holding that legislative apportionment was a justiciable issue that the courts had jurisdiction to hear and decide.

justiciable issue An issue or topic over which the courts have jurisdiction or the power to make decisions.

Wesberry v. Sanders The 1964 case in which the Supreme Court invalidated unequal congressional districts, saying that all legislative districts must contain about equal numbers of people, establishing the principle of one person, one vote.

one person, one vote The idea, arising out of the 1964 Supreme Court decision of *Wesberry v. Sanders*, that legislative districts must contain about the same number of people.

---

15 It may seem strange that legislative apportionment was a political question in 1946 but not in 1962. As discussed in Chapter 15, the federal courts are political institutions that make public policy. The apportionment issue was always political. The Court was willing to deal with this political question in 1962; in 1946, it was not.

How to represent the interest of minorities in Congress remains the subject of debate. One side argues that ethnic minorities should be represented by members of their own ethnic group. The other side of the debate argues that a representative does not have to share racial, ethnic, gender, or other characteristics to represent those interests. Congressional Black Caucus Chairman Rep. Cedric Richmond (D-LA), right, speaks at a Congressional Tri-Caucus news conference on Capitol Hill in Washington, Wednesday, September 27, 2017, on injustice and inequality in America. The Congressional Tri-Caucus is composed of the Congressional Black Caucus, Congressional Hispanic Caucus and the Congressional Asian Pacific American Caucus. Also pictured from left are, Rep. Pramila Jayapal (D-WA), Rep. Sheila Jackson Lee (D-TX), and Rep. John Lewis (D-GA).

© Andrew Harnik/AP Photo

majority–minority districts Districts in which the majority of the population is composed of ethnic or racial minorities.

descriptive representation The view of representation that calls for the racial and ethnic makeup of Congress to reflect that of the nation.

substantive representation The concept of representation that states that officeholders do not have to be minorities to accurately represent minority interests.

of creating a majority block of ethnic minority voters within them. Following the 1990 census, a number of states in the South and Southwest drew up black-majority and Latino-majority districts, referred to as **majority–minority districts**. Both the U.S. Department of Justice and various civil rights groups supported such districts as a way to maximize the number of African American and Latino representatives in Congress.[16] The resulting districts often did not correspond to local political geography. Some divided towns and communities, and others sprawled across states in a bewildering pattern of spikes and curls that flicked out toward concentrations of minority populations and skirted predominantly white areas. For example, Louisiana's 4th Congressional District, shown in Figure 10.6, was designed to elect an African American to the House. The strange shape resulted from linking widely dispersed communities of African Americans into one district.

In subsequent lawsuits, federal courts began striking down some of these new districts. In the case of *Shaw v. Reno* (1993), the Supreme Court held that race may not be the sole criterion used in drawing congressional districts.

How best to represent the interests of minorities remains the subject of fierce debate. One side argues that ethnic minorities should be represented by members of their own ethnic groups. This view suggests that districts should be drawn to achieve **descriptive representation**, in which the racial makeup of Congress reflects the racial makeup of the nation. For example, if 12 percent of the population is African American, 12 percent of the representatives in Congress should be African American.

The other side of the debate contends that a representative does not have to be African American, Latino, Asian, or female to represent those interests. Rather, **substantive representation** of the basic interests of various groups is more important than descriptive representation. Political scientist Carol Swain (1995) argues that increasing the representation of African American interests by creating additional majority–minority districts is ineffective and shortsighted because there

---

16 *Gerrymandering* is a pejorative term. During the period between Reconstruction and the 1970s, racial gerrymanders were used to prevent the election of black representatives. Since drawing majority–minority districts is intended to help minorities overcome the barriers of past discrimination, referring to this practice as racial gerrymanders is misleading.

are a limited number of places where such districts can be drawn.[17] And there is evidence that packing so many African American voters into majority–minority districts may actually decrease their influence in Congress. Research found that when large numbers of African American voters were removed from the districts of white representatives during redistricting, the voting records of the representatives indicated less support of minority interests (Overby and Cosgrove 1996). After redistricting removed African American voters from their districts, several moderate southern Democrats who had often supported minority interests were defeated in the 1992 and 1994 elections by conservative Republicans who were less supportive (Hill 1995).

Some recent research presents evidence that descriptive representation does benefit minority interests. Electing more African American representatives increases African American influence in those bodies and leads to greater policy responsiveness to minority interests (Grose 2011). But the relationship depends on the degree of racial polarization. An increase in descriptive representation does not result in policies that are responsive to minority interests if the context is racially polarized, as it is in the South. In less racialized contexts, however, descriptive representation leads to more influence and policies that are responsive to African American interests (Preuhs 2006).

Overlapping Terms and Staggered Elections

Elections for president and Congress occur in even-numbered years. But the Constitution establishes overlapping terms and staggered elections: House members serve two-year terms; presidents serve four-year terms; senators serve six-year terms, but only one-third of Senate seats are up in any given election. Consider a recent cycle:

- In 2012 we elected the president, all 435 House members, and one-third of the senators.
- In 2014 we elected all 435 House members, and a different one-third of the senators; this is called a "midterm" because it is between presidential elections.
- In 2016 we elected the president, all 435 House members, and the other one-third of senators.
- In 2018 (another midterm), we elected all 435 House members, and the one-third of senators elected in 2012.

This system of elections was intended to make it difficult for one party to capture complete control of government, or to hold on to it if it did. Issues and political

---

17 In order to draw enough single-member districts to elect a Congress that will descriptively reflect the population, the various groups must be concentrated enough to combine into a district. In some states, African American and Latino populations are sufficiently concentrated to draw such districts. However, drawing a district that is majority female is not possible—even though women are a majority of the population.

trends are different in presidential election years than in midterms, and in any given election, two-thirds of the Senate won election two or four years earlier under different political circumstances.

A consequence of staggered elections with overlapping terms is that results in a presidential election influence the current and future elections for Congress. A prominent pattern in this cycle of alternating presidential and midterm elections is that the president's party (almost) always loses House seats in the midterm election. Figure 10.7 shows how many congressional seats the president's party gained or lost in elections since 1952. The president's party lost House seats in 88 percent (15 of 17) of midterms (see Figure 10.7a). This pattern of midterm seat losses is similar in the Senate, but not as strong—the president's party lost Senate seats in 65 percent (11 of 17) of midterms (see Figure 10.7b). In presidential election years, however, there is not a consistent pattern of gains and losses—the president's party picked up House seats almost two-thirds of the time (11 of 17 elections), but less than half the time (7 of 17) in the Senate.

The "surge and decline" theory (Campbell 1960) seeks to explain why the president's party loses seats in midterm elections. The basic idea is that turnout surges in presidential elections because presidential campaigns attract citizens to the polls who often don't vote (e.g., weak partisans and independents). These peripheral voters who turn out to vote for president may vote for the same party's House candidates. The surge helps some House candidates win as if they rode to victory on the winning presidential candidate's "coattails." As a result, the winning party tends to gain House seats in presidential election years. Without the president on the ballot in midterm elections two years later, turnout declines (an average of 16 percent), and members who rode to victory on the president's coattails lose. There are contrary cases, however. Large midterm seat losses in 1994 and 2018 followed elections in which the president's party lost seats.

This theory may help explain why the president's party loses House seats in midterm elections, but it does not explain why the pattern is weaker in the Senate. Six-year Senate terms with only one-third up at a time accounts for some of the difference. Two-year terms in the House mean that the same members are running in both the presidential and midterm elections. If the president has strong coattails and picks up lots of House seats as in 1964 and 2008, many of those new seats will be lost in the next midterm as in 1966 and 2010 (see Figure 10.7a). But when the president has strong coattails and picks up lots of Senate seats, those 33 seats are not up for election again until six years later. Political conditions change a lot in six years—a midterm and another presidential election have occurred, and the president those senators were elected with may no longer be in office. The two presidents who had large gains in the Senate and were still in office six years later experienced big losses. President Reagan's coattails in 1980 helped Republicans gain 12 seats and control of the Senate; Republicans lost eight seats and control of the Senate in 1986. President Obama's victory in 2008 helped add eight Democrats to the Senate; Democrats lost nine seats and control of the Senate in 2014.

These features of the American electoral system set broad limits of how many seats are gained or lost. Yet there is considerable variation within those broad limits. The surge and decline theory cannot account for the size of seat swings.

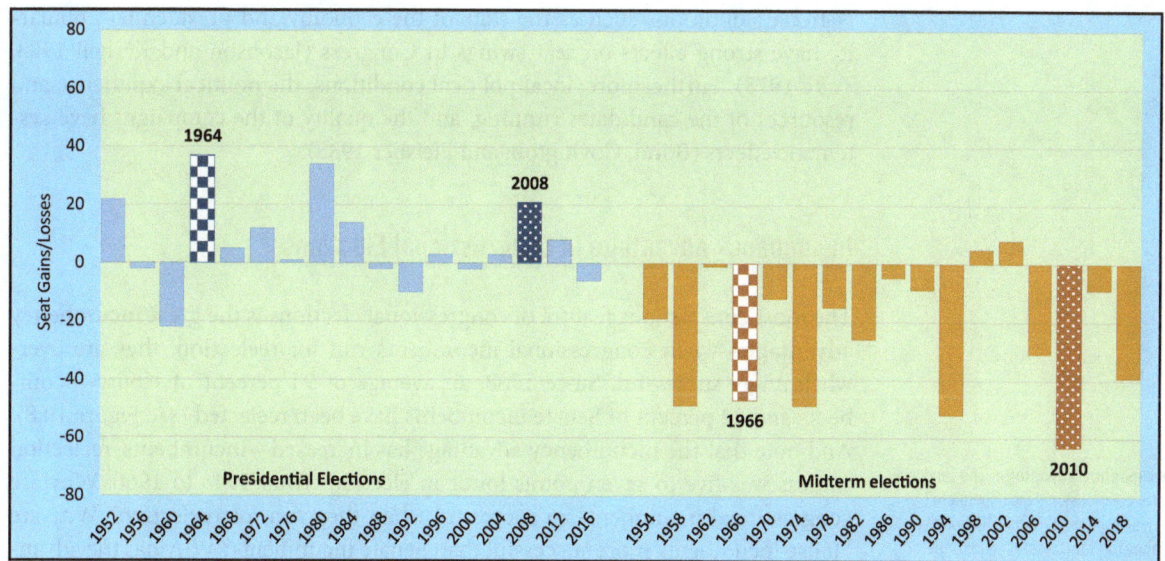

FIGURE 10.7a House Seats Gained and Lost by the President's Party, 1952–2018

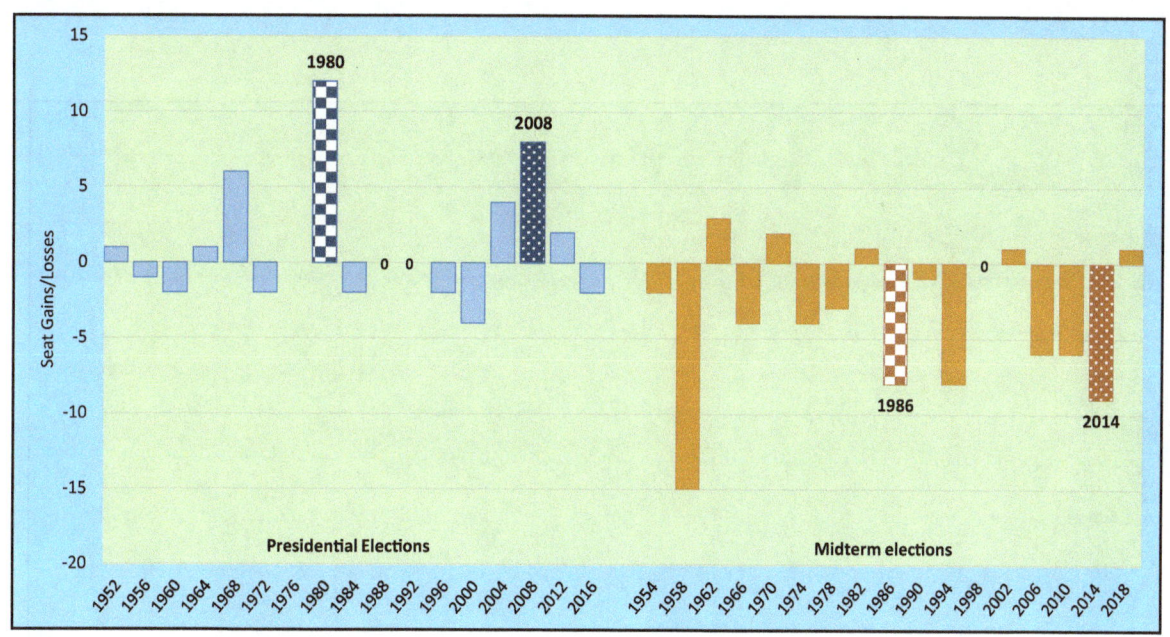

FIGURE 10.7b Senate Seats Gained and Lost by the President's Party, 1952–2018

Source: Data from Ornstein et al. (2018, table 2–3).

National conditions such as the state of the economy and presidential popularity have strong effects on seat swings in Congress (Jacobson and Kernell 1983; Tufte 1978). Furthermore, local political conditions, the political experience and resources of the candidates running, and the quality of the campaigns have systematic effects (Bond, Covington, and Fleisher 1985).

Incumbency Advantage in Congressional Elections

The most conspicuous feature of congressional elections is the great **incumbency advantage**—when congressional incumbents run for reelection, they are overwhelmingly successful. Since 1968, an average of 94 percent of House incumbents and 82 percent of Senate incumbents have been reelected (see Figure 10.8). And note that the incumbency advantage has increased—incumbents' reelection success was five to seven points lower in elections from 1946 to 1966. Why are congressional incumbents so successful when they run for reelection? Why are House incumbents more successful than Senate incumbents? Why has the advantage of incumbency increased since 1968? The reasons include the nature of congressional districts, resources, and relations with constituents, among others.

incumbency advantage The tendency for congressional incumbents to be overwhelmingly successful when they run for reelection due to the nature of congressional districts, resources, and relations with constituents, among other reasons.

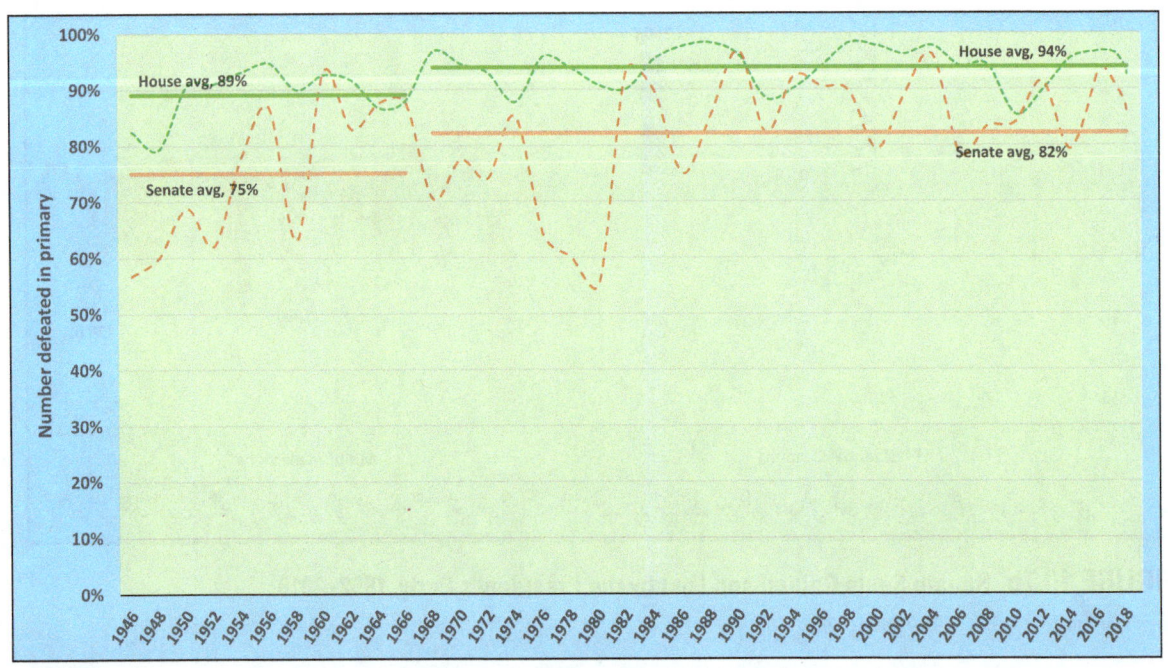

FIGURE 10.8 **Incumbency Advantage in House and Senate Elections**

Source: Ornstein et al. (2018, tables 2-7, 2-8, https://www.brookings.edu/multi-chapter-report/vital-statistics-on-congress/).

Districts, Challengers, and Resources

The political makeup of a district sets general limits of competition. Some districts are solidly Democratic or Republican, and some are more evenly balanced so that either party might win. Most House candidates run in districts drawn to have a distinct partisan tilt, whereas Senate candidates compete for votes of a more diverse and competitive statewide constituency.

Within the limits set by the nature of the district, several factors determine how competitive an election is likely to be. Most important is the quality of the challenger. Most House incumbents coast to easy, lopsided reelection victories because they run against challengers with no political experience who have little campaign money. Although having large sums of money does not guarantee victory, without adequate funding there is little chance of success. How much money does it take to run a competitive campaign? Political scientist Gary Jacobson estimates that "the minimum price tag for a competitive House campaign under average conditions today is probably [close] to $800,000" (2013, 54). Senate races are often more expensive, as much as 10 times more in large states. Whereas incumbents are able to raise and spend as much as they need, few challengers can raise enough money to be competitive.

The few challengers who can raise lots of money pose a serious threat to incumbents. But incumbents spend in response to the magnitude of the threat. Paradoxically, incumbents who spend the most money are the most likely to lose. This is because politically experienced challengers who are able to raise campaign money target vulnerable incumbents, who respond by spending huge amounts of money in losing campaigns. Humorist Will Rogers showed considerable foresight in 1931 when he quipped, "Politics has got so expensive that it takes lots of money to even get beat with nowadays" (quoted in Sterling 1979, 61).

Performance, Perks, and Pork-Barrel

What a representative does or fails to do over the course of the term can damage or improve his or her chances of reelection. Although they want to avoid it, a few incumbents are tarnished with scandal and suffer at the polls (J. Peters and Welch 1980; Welch and Hibbing 1997).

More typically, incumbents engage in activities intended to please their constituents and discourage vigorous challenges. Members work to bring pork-barrel benefits to their districts, and they use the perquisites of office to appeal to constituents. **Pork-barrel benefits** are government-sponsored projects that bring economic benefits to a member's state or district. *Pork-barrel* is a pejorative term first used in the mid-nineteenth century to describe projects viewed as a waste of tax dollars that serve no purpose other than to aid the reelection of a single incumbent. Examples include public works projects such as dams, roads, and government buildings; grants to local government or a university; and defense contracts.

pork-barrel benefits Government-sponsored projects that bring economic benefits to a Congress member's state or district. This is a pejorative term first used in the mid-nineteenth century to describe projects viewed as a waste of tax dollars that serve no purpose other than to aid the reelection of a single incumbent.

Perquisites, or **perks**, are benefits and support services that members need in order to do their jobs. These include an allowance to pay staff members to answer constituents' letters and help with their problems, the franking privilege that allows members to use their signatures instead of buying stamps to send mail to constituents, and a travel allowance so that representatives can make frequent trips home to stay in touch with constituents.

Perks are not supposed to be used to campaign, and there are legal regulations designed to prevent incumbents from using congressional staff or the frank for campaign activities. Nonetheless, critics suspect that pork-barrel projects and the use of perks provide incumbents with considerable electoral benefits. Political scientist David Mayhew suggests that members of Congress use their offices to make three basic kinds of appeals to constituents. The first is **advertising**, defined as "any effort to disseminate one's name among constituents ... to create a favorable image" (Mayhew 1974, 49). Advertising activities include sending out newsletters, making frequent visits to the district to talk to constituents, addressing high school commencements, and sending out infant-care booklets. The second is **credit claiming**, an effort to generate the belief that the representative is responsible for government actions that constituents find desirable, such as pork-barrel projects that benefit the district. The third is **position taking**, making public statements on issues that are pleasing to constituents.

These three activities are nonpartisan and are likely to win friends without making enemies. When a member of Congress votes on a controversial issue, the vote might make as many enemies as friends. But when a member helps a veteran who is having a problem with the Department of Veterans Affairs, it generates goodwill and contributes to the member's reputation as a good representative. Political scientists who have studied the electoral payoff of pork-barrel projects and the use of perquisites, however, have been unable to show that these activities make vulnerable members safe (Bickers and Stein 1996; Cain, Ferejohn, and Fiorina 1987; Feldman and Jondrow 1984).

Competitive House Races

The key to electoral competition is having two politically savvy candidates with adequate resources to run vigorous campaigns. If the first law of electoral politics is "you can't beat somebody with nobody," the corollary is "you're not likely to beat anybody with somebody nobody's ever heard of." As we have seen, incumbents are professional politicians who are well known in their districts and can raise the money necessary to mount a vigorous campaign. Incumbency advantage in House elections does not result from the absence of challengers, but rather from the absence of challengers that voters have heard of. The candidates who wage the most vigorous challenges are those who have experiences and attributes that make them known in the district and those who can raise enough campaign money to make voters aware of their positive qualities and the defects of the incumbent. Explaining why experienced and well-funded challengers emerge in some districts but not in others, therefore, is crucial to understanding the low level of competition in congressional elections.

perquisites (perks) The benefits and support activities that members of Congress receive in order to help them perform their job.

advertising The activities of members of Congress (such as sending out newsletters or visiting the district) designed to familiarize the constituency with the member.

credit claiming The efforts by members of Congress to get their constituents to believe they are responsible for positive government actions.

position taking Public statements made by members of Congress on issues of importance to the constituency.

Political scientists generally turn to rational choice theory in the study of elections. Gary Jacobson and Samuel Kernell (1983) proposed the "strategic politician theory" to explain variation in the emergence of experienced, well-funded challengers in congressional elections. National political conditions, such as the health of the economy and the president's popularity, influence elections. But national conditions do not directly affect voters' decisions on election day. Instead, the strategic politician theory suggests that voters' decisions are determined mainly by the alternatives available to them. Do voters have a choice between two candidates who run vigorous campaigns appealing for their votes, or do voters have to choose between a candidate they know (the incumbent) and one they have never heard of? The alternatives available to voters are the results of decisions made by political elites months before election day. Experienced politicians won't risk promising political careers in hopeless races for Congress, and campaign contributors won't waste money on a lost cause. Thus, these political elites act strategically and run for Congress when the chances of success look favorable. National conditions affect elites' assessment of the odds of success. If the president is popular and the economy is booming, the president's party will field more experienced, well-funded candidates; if national conditions are unfavorable to the president, the opposition party will field more. Because voters "favor attractive candidates who run well-financed campaigns," the party that fields more of these candidates nationally will win more seats held by the other party and lose fewer of its own (Jacobson and Kernell 1983, 2–3). There is strong empirical support for this thesis (Jacobson 1989; Jacobson and Kernell 1983).

But there is variation across congressional districts—that is, the party advantaged by favorable national conditions does not recruit high-quality candidates in all districts, and the disadvantaged party can still manage to recruit some high-quality candidates in spite of unfavorable national conditions. Bond, Covington, and Fleisher (1985) find that local political conditions and the incumbent's behavior influence how experienced, well-funded challengers assess the odds of success. An incumbent may be vulnerable because the congressional district has been greatly altered by redistricting, because he or she has lost touch with the district, or because his or her party affiliation or voting record does not match the preferences of most constituents. In such cases, a candidate with political experience and access to campaign money is likely to challenge the incumbent.

Some incumbents retire or die in each election cycle. Contests for **open seats** in which no incumbent is running are much more competitive. Both parties are likely to field experienced, well-funded candidates. In open-seat House races in 2016, for example, Democratic candidates spent an average of $1.61 million, and Republican candidates spent an average of $1.43 million (Ornstein et al. 2018, Table 3-2).

Incumbency in Senate Elections

Although incumbency is an advantage in Senate elections, it is a smaller advantage than in House races. Unlike House districts, the boundaries of Senate constituencies

open seats Legislative seats for which there is no incumbent running for reelection.

APPLYING THE FRAMEWORKS

STRATEGIC POLITICIANS: WHY HIGH SPENDING INCUMBENTS DO WORSE AT THE POLLS

Getting elected to Congress is an expensive proposition. In the 2016 congressional elections, the 379 House incumbents who won reelection spent an average of $1.5 million to hold on to their seats; the 8 losing incumbents spent an average of $2.9 million—almost twice as much—in failed reelection bids. That seems odd. Does spending more money really lose votes? Well, not exactly. But campaign spending does have different effects for incumbents and challengers. The rational choice model helps explain why. Let's look at the relationships.

For challengers, the relationship between campaign spending and winning votes is positive—that is, the more challengers spend, the better they do at the polls. A scatterplot of spending and vote share of challengers in elections since 1972 illustrates this positive relationship. The figure (top panel) shows two regression lines representing this relationship. Linear regression estimates the straight line that best fits the data. The linear regression line for challenger spending has a slope of 20.6. This model predicts that on average, for each $1 million challengers spend, their vote share increases 21 percent (or from 31 percent at zero spending to 51 percent at $1 million to 72 percent at $2 million). But notice that a straight line does not fit the data very well—there are lots of cases far away from the line, especially those challengers who

spend more than $1 million. The correlation, indicated by the R^2, is only 0.23.

But the effects of campaign spending are not linear. Rather, it's subject to diminishing returns—increasing spending from $1,000 to $200,000 gets you a big increase in votes; the same increase from $500,000 to

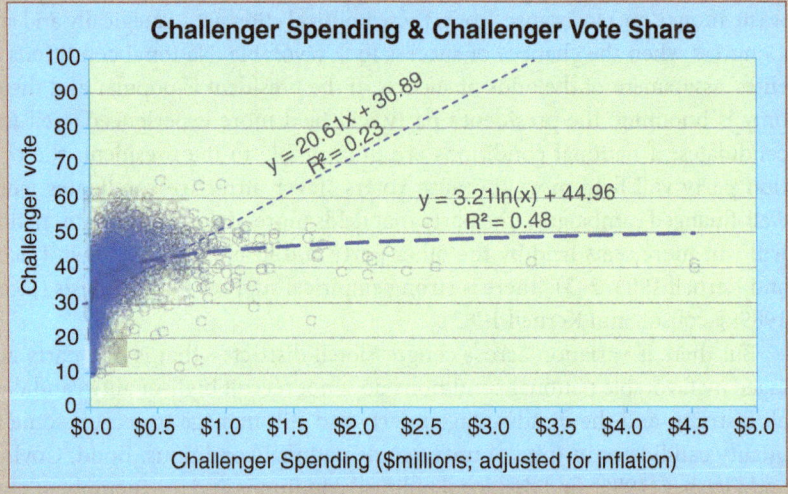

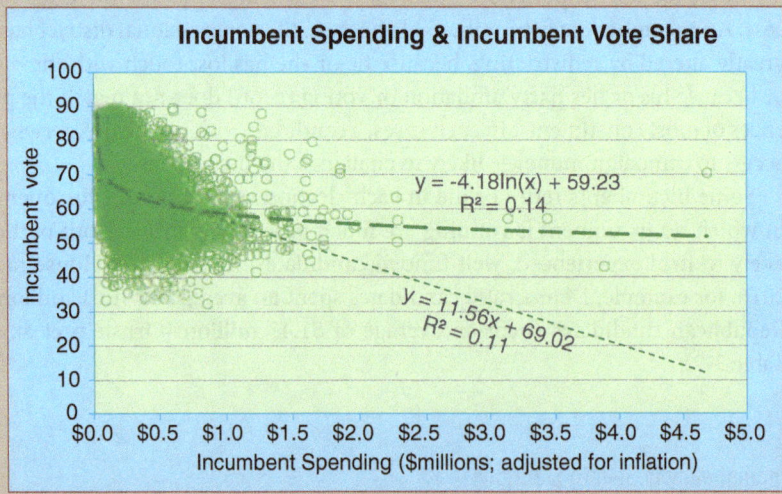

$700,000 results in a smaller increase; increasing from $1 million to $1.2 million increases vote share very little. A log function describes the relationship much better—it estimates a very steep slope at low levels of spending and then becomes almost flat at the highest levels. An indication that this non-linear log function is a better fit is the higher correlation—the R^2 is 0.48, indicating that in this model, spending explains about 48 percent of the variance in challengers' vote share.

The relationship between incumbent spending and vote share, in contrast, is negative—the more incumbents spend, the worse they do. The figure (bottom panel) shows the negative relationship. The relationship is not as strong as for challenger spending, but the diminishing returns log function describes the relationship a little better than a straight line. This negative relationship, however, does not mean incumbents are driving voters away by spending a lot of money.

So what's going on here? Why do incumbents do worse when they spend more money? The Strategic Politician Theory explains this seemingly perverse relationship (Jacobson 1989, 1990; Jacobson and Kernell 1983). The bottom line is that, for incumbents, spending lots of money is not a sign of strength, but a sign of weakness. Spending lots of money does not cause incumbents to lose votes, but incumbents who are in trouble raise and spend enormous sums of money in an (often unsuccessful) attempt to survive the election.

Most incumbents are positioned to win reelection with little difficulty: They have a proven record of running effective campaigns; they are well-known and well-liked by voters in their districts; and they can raise all the money they need to run another effective campaign because potential donors want to back a winner in order to make friends and gain access. Ambitious potential challengers who would pose the greatest threat to the incumbent—i.e., those who hold some other elective office—sit out the race because they know the costs are high and the odds of winning very low. Challengers who do enter the race are typically naïve political novices who don't know enough to realize they have no chance, or ambitious political novices who are using the campaign in pursuit of some future benefit. Such challengers are unable to raise the money necessary to run a competitive campaign because rational donors will not waste money on a hopeless cause. A rational strategy for a safe incumbent is to raise a big enough war chest to discourage experienced challengers, but not spend excessively—why waste campaign money if you don't need to? The result is that most incumbents coast to lopsided victories with relatively low campaign spending.

Yet, some incumbents are vulnerable. Some get enmeshed in a scandal; others benefited from favorable national political forces in a previous election that allowed them to win a district that typically votes for the other party's candidate. And sometimes there is a strong, national political tide that favors one party—if the president is unpopular and the economy is not doing well, the opposing party will recruit lots of experienced challengers and donors to supply the necessary campaign cash. Rational political elites identify and target vulnerable incumbents of the other party. Thus, incumbents who are most likely to lose spend the most money. It's the result of rational decisions all around.

Discussion Questions

1. The Supreme Court has ruled that campaign spending is free speech protected by the First Amendment (*Citizens United v. Federal Election Commission* 2010). Outside groups can spend unlimited amounts on political advertising as long as they don't coordinate with the candidates. As a result, total spending in recent elections has soared. How might spending by outside groups affect the calculations of strategic politicians—incumbents, challengers, and donors?

2. The enormous sums of money spent on political campaigns raises concerns that elected office is for sale to the highest bidder. If it were legal, do you think putting a cap on how much each side can spend would make congressional elections more competitive? Who would benefit more from a spending cap—challengers or incumbents?

(an entire state) cannot be manipulated to benefit a particular party or candidate. States also have a ready pool of ambitious, experienced House members, governors, and other statewide officeholders who want to be senators. These experienced politicians make formidable opponents because they have experience representing the same constituents as the incumbent senator and access to a campaign organization and campaign funds.

Other factors also contribute to greater vulnerability for senators. Because states are usually larger and more diverse than House districts, senators have a harder time developing the close personal bonds with their constituents that are common in the smaller House districts. Senate campaigns receive more media attention, which means that Senate challengers are likely to get more publicity and visibility than House challengers do. Together these factors make Senate races more competitive than are those of the House.

Anti-Incumbent Elections

While incumbents generally win reelection, public approval of the job Congress is doing is much lower. With historically low job approval (less than 15 percent approving from 2012 to 2018), it seems reasonable to expect that voters might be in the mood to "throw all the bums out." Indeed, some pundits predicted that the 2014 midterm would be an "anti-incumbent election" in which many incumbents of both parties would be defeated. This was not the first time political observers predicted that voters would take out their disgust on incumbents of both parties.

Yet, not a single midterm since 1946 satisfies the criteria for an anti-incumbent election. We do see several "wave elections" in which an unusually large number of incumbents were defeated, but voters flushed out incumbents mostly from one party, not both (see Table 10.9). There have been five midterm elections in which an above average number (mean = 30) of House incumbents lost; in every case, more than 85 percent of defeated incumbents were from one party. Although the 1982, 2006, and 2018 midterms do not qualify as wave elections because a below average number of incumbents lost, all defeated incumbents in 2006 and 2018 were Republicans, and 23 of 27 (85 percent) in 1982 were Republicans. There were four midterms in which an above average number (mean = 5) of Senate incumbents lost. In every case, incumbent losses were mostly from one party; in 1958 and 1986 all losing incumbents were Republicans. An average number of incumbent senators lost in 2006, 2014, and 2018, but all defeated incumbents were from one party in 2006 (Republicans) and 2014 (Democrats), and four of five were Democrats in 2018. Incumbency is a powerful advantage in congressional elections. In order "for an 'anti-incumbent' election to occur, Democratic voters would have to vote against Democratic nominees and Republican voters would have to vote against GOP nominees. That happens only in the rarest of cases" (Rothenberg 2014).

Financing Congressional Elections

Congressional candidates must raise all their funds from private sources. Although candidates for Congress are subject to the contribution limits and the ban on soft money

TABLE 10.9 MIDTERM WAVE ELECTIONS

Election	Democrats Defeated	Republicans Defeated	Total Defeats	Anti-Democratic Wave	Anti-Republican Wave
HOUSE					
1946	62	7	69	89.9%	
2010	54	4	58	93.1%	
1966	43	2	45	95.6%	
1958	6	34	40		85.0%
1994	37	0	37	100.0%	
2006	0	22	22		100.0%
2014	11	2	13	84.6%	
2018	0	29	29		100.0%
SENATE					
1946	11	2	13	84.6%	
1978	7	3	10	70.0%	
1958	0	10	10		100.0%
1986	0	7	7		100.0%
2006	0	5	5		100.0%
2014	5	0	5	100.0%	
2018	4	1	5	80.0%	

Source: Data from Ornstein et al. 2018, Table 2–10, 2–11; 2018 election results updated by the authors.

established by the BCRA of 2002, incumbents continue to have a significant advantage over challengers. They can raise more money than challengers because contributors are generally not motivated to give money to probable losers. Congressional candidates—incumbents and challengers—can also benefit from independent expenditures by Super PACs. Although they cannot coordinate with the candidate's campaign, Super PACs can raise and spend unlimited amounts of money from corporations, labor unions, and wealthy individuals to support or oppose particular candidates.

Raising a lot of money from a wide variety of donors, therefore, is essential to make a serious bid for a seat in Congress. Paul Herrnson (1995) observes that there are in effect two campaigns—a campaign for money and then the campaign for votes. Indeed, deciding whether a candidate is a serious contender or a "sacrificial lamb" often begins with an assessment of the campaign's bank balance. Often-quoted advice for those seeking congressional office is to "learn how to beg, and do it in a way that leaves you with some dignity" (Granat 1984).

The amount of money raised and spent on congressional campaigns is nothing short of staggering—about 906 candidates for the House and Senate spent over $1.42 billion in primary and general elections in the 2016 election cycle. Super PACs and other non-connected groups spent an additional $1.01 billion, bringing total spending to more than $2.4 billion. Where does this money come from? Well, more than two-thirds of it comes from the business sector. In 2016, business interests contributed about 68.9 percent of the money given to federal candidates, compared to only 4.3 percent from organized labor. Ideological groups provided a larger share of campaign money for federal races in 2016—about 9.4 percent of the total—than labor groups (https://www.opensecrets.org/overview/blio.php).

The relative contributions of the different sectors have changed significantly over the past decade. Ideological groups' share of spending on congressional campaigns, for example, has increased enormously. This sector's contributions increased from only 5.5 percent of the total in 2000 to 9.4 percent in 2016—a relative increase of over 70 percent. In contrast, the share of contributions from business and labor declined over this period. The relative decline in business contributions was a modest –8.5 percent, while labor contributions declined –21.8 percent.

Congressional campaigns are funded by contributions from individuals, PACs, parties, and the candidates themselves. Most of the money—more than half of the contributions to House candidates and more than 70 percent of the contributions to Senate candidates—is donated by individuals. Another important source of campaign money is PACs. In the 2015–2016 election cycle, PACs accounted for more than one-third of contributions to House candidates (36.8 percent) but only 17 percent of those to Senate candidates. Compared to senators, House members rely more on PAC contributions, because with a two-year term House members must campaign—for money and votes—all the time. Yet PACs are an important source of funding for both House and Senate candidates, and it is not difficult to understand why. The number of PACs and the amount of money available to them have grown considerably in the past 25 years. The remaining portion of campaign money comes from party committees and the candidates themselves. In recent elections, Super PACs and other outside groups that make independent expenditures have been much more prominent.

A variety of groups utilize PACs to channel their contributions to congressional candidates. Labor and ideology/single-issue groups channel over three-fourths of contributions through PACs. Business, lawyers, lobbyists, and the education and nonprofit groups, rely more heavily on individuals. Generally speaking, labor PACs tend to favor Democratic candidates—in the 2016 election, 88 percent of labor PAC money went to Democrats. Contributions from business are more evenly split between Republicans and Democrats (50 percent to each party in 2016), but there is considerable variation across different types of business. Contributions from energy and natural resources (oil and gas and mining), agribusiness, transportation, and construction went disproportionately (68–77 percent) to Republicans. Communications and electronics was the only type of business that contributed disproportionately (over 70 percent) to Democrats (https://www.opensecrets.org/overview/sectors.php). But the clearest bias of PACs is toward incumbents: Generally over 90 percent of PAC contributions went to incumbents in the 2016 congressional elections. The only types of PAC that showed less of an incumbent bias were labor and ideological/single-issue groups, which gave "only" two-thirds of their contributions to incumbents (https://www.opensecrets.org/overview/pac2cands.php?cycle=2016).

Thus, the rules of the game, campaign strategies, and available resources shape the outcome of both presidential and congressional campaigns. Winners of these contests tend to congratulate themselves for having conducted effective campaigns and praise the voters for having made wise choices. Losers are more likely to blame defeat on circumstances beyond their control: the superior financial resources of the opponent, the formidable obstacle of the opponent's incumbency, their minority party status, or other factors that even their best campaign efforts could not overcome.

CHAPTER TEN
Top 10 Takeaway Points

1. Elections to choose representatives in the United States consist of two steps: (1) nomination of candidates by political parties and (2) the general election where voters choose among the nominees selected by the parties.

2. Presidential candidates are nominated in national party conventions, a meeting of delegates from all the states. Delegates to the national party conventions are chosen by rank-and-file party members in caucuses/conventions held in the state or in state presidential primaries. Most convention delegates are selected through primary elections.

3. Presidential nomination contests generally progress through four stages: (1) the invisible primary, (2) the initial contests (Iowa caucuses and New Hampshire primary), (3) mist clearing, and (4) the national party convention.

4. The president is not elected by direct popular vote. Instead, the president is chosen by the electoral college, which consists of electors chosen from the 50 states and the District of Columbia. A state gets one electoral vote for each senator and House member, and the District of Columbia has three electoral votes. The total number of electoral votes is 538 (100 senators, 435 House members, and three votes for the District of Columbia). To be elected, a candidate must win a majority of electoral votes—that is, at least 270.

5. The electoral college has long been criticized because it violates the democratic principles of political equality and sometimes majority rule. Proposals to reform the electoral college include the proportional plan, the district plan, and direct popular election. Only direct election achieves political equality and guarantees majority rule.

6. Candidates for Congress are nominated by political parties in direct primaries in which rank-and-file voters choose the party nominees who will run in the general election. To be elected to Congress, a candidate must win a plurality of the popular vote in the congressional district or state.

7. Representation in the House is reapportioned among the states every 10 years following the national census to reflect changes in states' populations—that is, states that grow in population gain seats, and states that decline in population lose seats.

8. Redistricting is the process of redrawing the boundaries of congressional districts after seats have been reapportioned to the states. State legislatures are responsible for redistricting. The process is a political undertaking that often results in gerrymandered districts with boundaries drawn to benefit a particular interest.

9. The distinguishing feature of congressional elections is the incumbency advantage—in elections since 1968, averages of 94 percent of House incumbents and 82 percent of Senate incumbents who have run for reelection have been successful.

10. The primary reason incumbents have an advantage is that they typically run against unknown, politically inexperienced challengers who lack adequate funding to run a competitive campaign. Incumbents are generally able to raise more money than challengers are, but spending the most money does not guarantee victory. Incumbents who spend the most money are the ones most likely to lose, given that experienced challengers who can raise lots of money target incumbents who appear vulnerable.

CHAPTER TEN
Key Terms and Cases

advertising, 376
Baker v. Carr, 369
caucus, 327
caucus method, 331
closed primaries, 328
credit claiming, 376
descriptive representation, 370
direct popular election, 356
district plan, 358
election, 326
electoral college, 351
frontloading, 331
general election, 326
gerrymandering, 368
incumbency advantage, 374
invisible primary, 334
justiciable issue, 369
legislative caucus, 327
magic number, 332
majority–minority districts, 370
malapportioned, 368
multimember district, 367
national party convention, 327
nomination, 326
one person, one vote, 369
open primaries, 328
open seats, 377
perquisites (perks), 376
pork-barrel benefits, 375
position taking, 376
proportional plan, 357
reapportionment, 367
redistricting, 367
runoff primary, 364
single-member district, 367
state presidential primary, 331
substantive representation, 370
Super Tuesday, 343
swing states, 360
top-two primary, 364
unit rule, 351
Wesberry v. Sanders, 369

11 POLITICAL PARTICIPATION AND VOTING BEHAVIOR

KEY QUESTIONS

Why is voter turnout lower in the United States than in other Western democracies?

Why do some people participate in politics whereas others do not?

What explains why people vote the way they do?

© Elise Amendola/AP Photo

IN 2016, 90-year-old Christine Krucki failed to cast a ballot in a presidential primary for the first time since 1948. What ended the streak was not a waning desire to participate in the electoral process, but a new Wisconsin law requiring citizens to show a valid photo ID before being allowed to vote. Krucki didn't have one. She didn't have a Wisconsin-issued driver's license because she didn't drive. She didn't have a passport because she didn't do much in the way of international travel. She made several attempts to get a state-issued ID that would admit her to the polls, but ran into a bureaucratic brick wall. At one point she was turned down because the name on her birth certificate did not match her married name (Berman 2016). Krucki was far from the only Wisconsin resident who ran afoul of the voter ID law and found themselves unable to vote in 2016. Sean Reynolds, a 30-year-old Navy veteran, only had an out-of-state driver's license. Catelin Tindall, a 24-year-old graduate student, only had a school-issued ID. Sixty-six-year-old Gladys Harris only had her Social Security and Medicare cards, plus her county-issued buss pass (which actually did include a photo). None of these people—all U.S. citizens and legal residents of Wisconsin—got to vote (Cassidy and Mereno 2017).

Wisconsin's voter ID law and its impact on voter participation was, to put it mildly, controversial. By some estimates it made roughly 300,000 Wisconsin residents ineligible to participate in the 2016 election. No one knows for sure how many of those were people who actually wanted to vote but did not because of the new ID requirements, but it's certainly true that statewide voter turnout was lower than in the previous presidential election. In Milwaukee County alone, roughly 50,000 fewer voters went to the polls in 2016 compared to 2012. The controversy centered not just on how many citizens it discouraged from voting, but on who those citizens were: mostly poor, minority, and (at least by some accounts) more likely to vote Democrat. In a state that Donald Trump won by only 22,000 votes, the drop in turnout in places like heavily Democratic Milwaukee County kicked off a furious debate over whether the voter ID law gave Trump a leg up by suppressing turnout among groups more likely to vote for Democratic nominee Hillary Clinton. As the law was championed by Republican lawmakers and adamantly opposed by Democrats, these partisan battle lines were clearly drawn even before the law went into effect.

Republican supporters of the ID law pooh-poohed the charges of partisan voter suppression as unfounded sour grapes. Backers of the Wisconsin law and a wave of similar laws adopted in many other states in recent years argue they are just common-sense precautions to prevent voter fraud. Asking someone to show an ID to verify they are eligible to cast a ballot, supporters argue, hardly seems like a particularly onerous requirement to help ensure the integrity of the electoral process. Such supporters can point to a range of academic studies that have, for the most part, found voter ID laws have had a minimal impact on turnout rates (Highton 2017). Yet some of those same proponents have also explicitly said they support voter ID laws because they give Republicans a partisan electoral advantage (Wines 2016). Regardless of what voter ID laws actually do or do not do, there's no doubting that in places like Wisconsin where voter ID laws are followed by lower turnout rates, narrow victories, and stories of the Christine Kruckis of the world being unable to cast a ballot abound, the controversies will continue.

The bottom line is that in a democracy citizens need reasonable guarantees that their opportunity to contribute to decisions on "who gets what" is real and significant. If citizens are denied such opportunities, as in Christine Krucki's case, clearly their influence over decisions on who gets what is diminished. If casting a ballot is such a hassle that you simply can't be bothered, then obviously your vote does not count for anything.

In this chapter, we examine not just voting but also political participation in general and its crucial importance to democratic governance. What are the different forms of participation? Why do some people participate and others not? Why is voting the most common form of participation? Are there systematic patterns in who shows up to the polls and the choices they make? What explains how voters choose between candidates? The answers to these questions actually go a lot further in explaining the functioning of the political system and the legitimacy of government than the teething problems of new voting technology. Understanding what the people are doing, and why, is a prerequisite for judging whether elections—and the other forms of participation—are connecting the will of the people to the government.

THE CONCEPT OF POLITICAL PARTICIPATION

Political participation is the process of turning opinion into an action to influence "who gets what." In a representative democracy, political participation is a primary means of connecting the will of the people to the actions of government. If this connection is successfully made, participation helps uphold the core democratic principles of political freedom and majority rule. A hallmark of a democratic political system is that it counts heads rather than breaking them. If the will of the people is going to provide the fundamental basis for government action, then the people must participate in the political process.

Forms of Political Participation

Voting in elections is the most obvious way that citizens in representative democracies have to influence government. But political participation is not limited to voting. There are lots of ways to participate in politics. Political scientist Sidney Verba and colleagues (Verba and Nie 1987; Verba, Schlozman, and Brady 1995) identified four general categories:

- Voting, the most widespread and regularized form of participation
- Campaign activities, such as working for or contributing money to a party or a candidate and trying to persuade others to support a party or candidate
- Citizen-initiated contacts with government officials in which a person acts on a matter of individual concern (e.g., sending an e-mail or speaking to your representative at a public forum)
- Activities in which citizens act cooperatively to deal with social and political problems, including working with like-minded people in interest groups

political participation The translation of personal preference into a voluntary action designed to influence public policy.

If the will of the people is to be the basis for government action, then people must participate in the political process. Here canvassers for the Wisconsin Republican Party go door-to-door to drum up support for GOP candidates in the 2016 elections.
© Andy Manis/AP Photo

The Theoretical Basis of Political Participation

Verba argues that participating in these various activities is, more or less, rational: As the costs of participation increase, rates of participation decrease.

Cost here does not necessarily mean monetary cost (though that might be part of it). Rather, the term *cost* is used more broadly to indicate how easy or difficult it is to participate. For example, the costs of voting are relatively minor, and this tends to be the most popular form of political participation. Other activities—such as getting involved in civic organizations and interest groups, attending rallies, making monetary contributions, and running for office—require greater levels of time and effort; fewer people engage in these more costly forms of participation. Figure 11.1 shows that Americans' rates of participation in a variety of forms of nonvoting political participation decrease more or less directly with the costs involved. Only about 30 percent of citizens report contacting a government or elected official, 15 percent say they have attended a campaign event or made a small monetary donation to a campaign, 8 percent report volunteering to work in a political campaign, and only 4 percent say they have given a reasonably large sum of money (more than $250) to a political campaign. Even in low-profile, off-year elections, much higher proportions of citizens show up to vote. That's because there's little cost associated with voting—basically registering and perhaps standing in line a few minutes at your polling place. In contrast to the other forms of participation listed in Figure 11.1, voting simply takes less time, money, and effort.

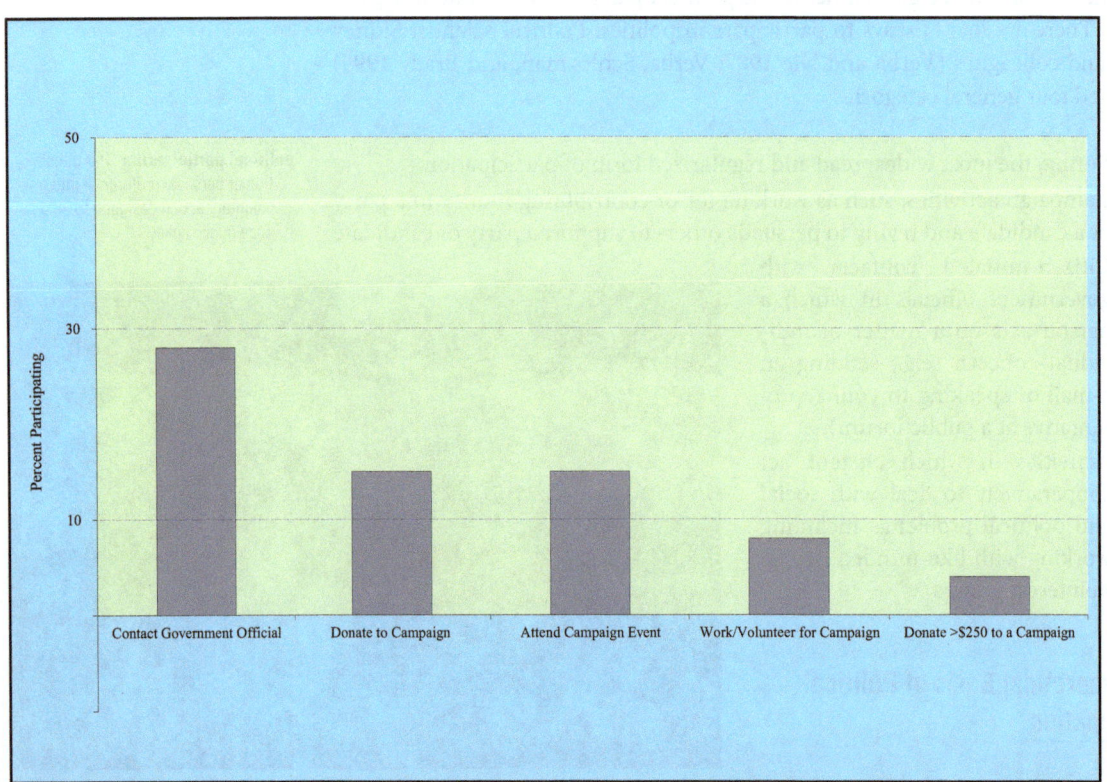

FIGURE 11.1 Different Forms of Political Participation

Source: Adapted from Michael Dimock, Caroll Doherty, Jocelyn Kiley, Vidya Krishnamurthy. "Beyond Red vs. Blue. The Political Typology. Section 10: 'Political Participation, Interest, and Knowledge.'" 2014. http://www.people-press.org/2014/06/26/section-10-political-participation-interest-and-knowledge/.

Is Political Participation in America High or Low?

Are voter turnout rates and/or the sort of participation rates reflected in Figure 11.1 high or low? Answering this question is harder than it seems because it requires a benchmark against which to measure the rates. In terms of one obvious benchmark—majority rule—these numbers appear low, with voting in presidential elections being the only activity that routinely attracts more than half of eligible citizens. In a large country such as the United States, though, even a small percentage translates into millions of people incurring costs to participate in politics.

Change over time is another useful benchmark to evaluate participation. There are mixed signs here. It is generally accepted that voting participation has declined over time. (We analyze this issue in more depth a little later in the chapter.) Other forms of participation, on the other hand, seem to have fluctuated or in some cases have even increased. For example, in the late 1960s about 13 percent of Americans reported contributing money to a political campaign, a figure that increased to 23 percent by the late 1980s, but seemed to have dipped to just below 20 percent over the past decade or so. Less than 20 percent of Americans reported attending a political meeting or rally in the late 1960s and 1980s, but 24 percent reported attending similar meetings in 2008 (A. Smith et al. 2009; Verba, Schlozman, and Brady 1995).

A third useful benchmark is comparison of Americans with citizens in other democracies. Figure 11.2 presents such a comparison. This figure shows voter turnout in legislative elections in nine industrialized democracies. The chart

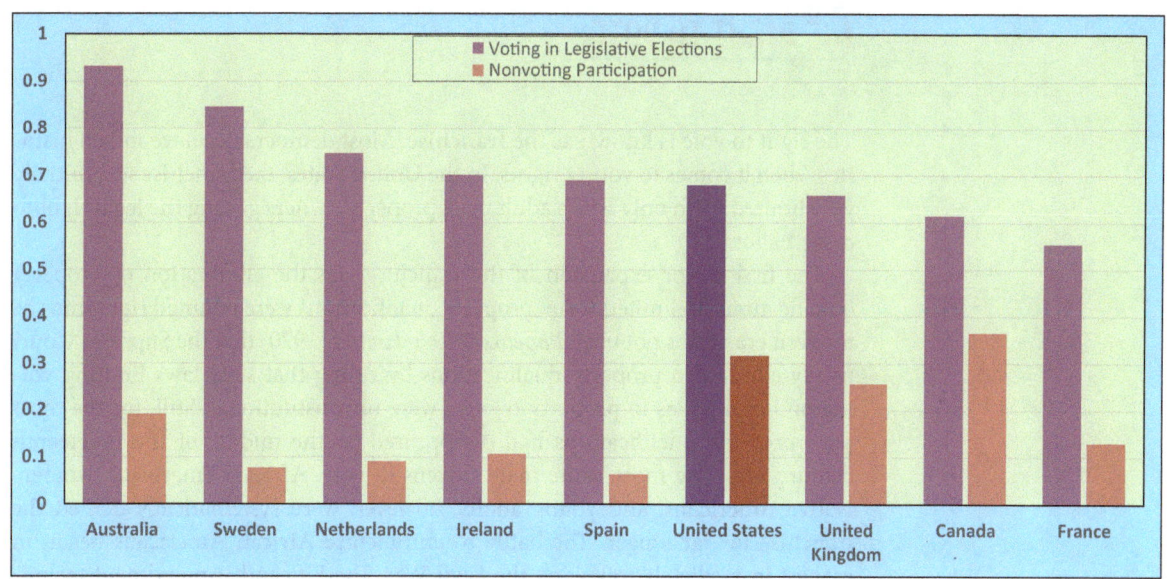

FIGURE 11.2 Political Participation Rates in Selected Representative Democracies

Note: Voting percentages are from most recent elections in each country.
Source: Data from the Institute for Democracy and Electoral Assistance, https://www.idea.int/data-tools/data/voter-turnout (voter turnout data); and Wattenberg (2007), table 1–8, "Nonvoting Political Participation in Established Democracies" (data on other forms of political participation).

clearly shows that voting participation in the United States is generally much lower than in other representative democracies. Lower voter turnout, however, does not necessarily mean that Americans are lazy compared to citizens in other democracies. Although Americans vote less, participation in activities other than voting (contributing money to political organizations, showing support for a party or candidate, and trying to persuade others) is higher than in most other democracies.

Why do Americans vote less? A likely answer is that the cost of voting is higher in the United States. For example, there are more barriers to voting in American elections compared to in other countries (for example, generally speaking, it is harder to register to vote in America than in other countries). This means Americans face higher costs to engage in this particular form of political participation. On the other hand, the costs associated with forms of participation such as contacting government officials and participating in community organizations are no higher, and in some cases considerably lower, in the United States than in comparable democracies.

Of all the basic forms of political participation, voting has the most visible connection to the core principles of democracy, and it is worth examining in some depth. Participating in elections allows people to participate in decision making about who gets what, and allows for direct expression of the will of the people. Exploring who has the right to participate in elections—in other words, the right to vote—provides an excellent starting point for judging the degree of political freedom within a democratic society.

THE RIGHT TO VOTE

The right to vote is known as the **franchise**. Most democracies have mixed histories when it comes to voting rights. In the United States, the franchise was initially very limited, with only white adult male property owners getting the legal right to cast a ballot.

The first major expansion of the franchise was the elimination of property qualifications. In limited form, property qualifications were retained right into the modern era; it was not until *Phoenix v. Kolodziejski* (1970) that the Supreme Court finally eliminated property qualifications by ruling that state laws limiting voting on bond issues to property owners were unconstitutional. Still, for the most part, property qualifications had disappeared by the middle of the nineteenth century, allowing most white male citizens to vote. African Americans, women, Native Americans, and young adults, however, were systematically denied the franchise for far longer. The battle to enfranchise African Americans began in earnest immediately following the Civil War. The Fifteenth Amendment technically granted African Americans the right to vote, although this right was stripped from many by state laws mandating poll taxes or literacy tests. It was not until the Voting Rights Act of 1965 that the franchise was fully and securely extended to African Americans.

franchise The constitutional or statutory right to vote.

Leaders of the early women's movement had hoped that the initial drive to gain African Americans the franchise would also benefit women. This was not the case, however, and women had to put up with widespread opposition to their political participation. In the late nineteenth and early twentieth centuries, business groups—such as textile manufacturers and brewers and distillers—opposed giving women the right to vote because they feared women would use their newfound political power to harm business interests. The Nineteenth Amendment, ratified in 1920, finally gave women universal voting rights by prohibiting federal and state governments from denying anyone voting rights on the basis of gender. And recall from Chapter 5 that Native Americans did not gain universal voting rights until Congress passed the American Indian Citizenship Act in 1924—more than 50 years after the Fifteenth Amendment (1870) formally enfranchised African American men and four years after the Nineteenth Amendment (1920) enfranchised women.

Young adults won the right to vote in the 1970s. The Constitution gives states the authority to set voting age requirements, and most states prior to the 1970s had set this age requirement at 21. Many young adults considered this to be unfair. During the Vietnam War, 18- and 19-year-olds were being drafted by the government and sent into combat. If they were old enough to fight and kill for their government, reasoned the generation of the 1960s, they should be old enough to vote. Congress responded to these arguments in 1970 by passing a law that reduced the voting age to 18 in national, state, and local elections. This law was challenged, however, and the Supreme Court ruled that although Congress had the authority to set the voting age in federal elections, it had no such rights for state and local elections (*Oregon v. Mitchell* 1970). It struck some as silly that an 18-year-old could vote for president but be considered too politically immature to vote for city dogcatcher. In March 1971 Congress proposed the Twenty-Sixth Amendment to secure the voting rights of all citizens 18 and older, which was duly submitted to the states and ratified with record speed (it took only four months for the required three-fourths of states to approve the amendment).

Eliminating property, race, gender, and age requirements extended the franchise to most adult citizens in the United States. Some barriers to voting still remain, although these strike most people as reasonable. Most states, for example, require voters to be U.S. citizens, residents of the jurisdiction where they want to cast a ballot, and registered to vote.

There are other restrictions on groups of people presumed to not have the intelligence or moral character necessary to cast a ballot. These include the mentally ill and convicted felons. In most states, felons are denied the right to vote even after they have served their sentences. This practice, though ruled constitutional by the Supreme Court, is increasingly controversial because such laws tend to disproportionately affect African Americans. Nationwide, roughly 7.5 percent of the African American population has been disenfranchised because of a felony conviction, which is about three times the overall disenfranchisement rate (Uggen, Larson, and Shannon 2016). The national numbers, however, mask a lot of state-by-state variation. Maine does not disenfranchise any citizens because of a past conviction. In Florida, 10 percent of the overall adult population, and 20 percent of the African American population, is disenfranchised due to a felony conviction.

Voter Turnout

Ironically, after struggles for two centuries to extend to all citizens the right to vote, fewer and fewer citizens seem interested in exercising that right. As Figure 11.3 shows, roughly 55 to 60 percent of those eligible cast ballots in presidential elections in recent decades. Voter turnout for congressional races in **midterm elections**—that is, the congressional elections held midway between presidential elections—is consistently well below 50 percent.

But is **voter turnout** really declining over time? Answering this question is more complicated than you might think. First, it must be clear what proportion of voters actually vote. Yet there is more than one way to calculate this proportion. A common practice is to calculate turnout rates based on the "voting-age population"—

midterm elections The congressional and gubernatorial elections that occur in the middle of a presidential term.

voter turnout The percentage of eligible voters who cast votes in an election.

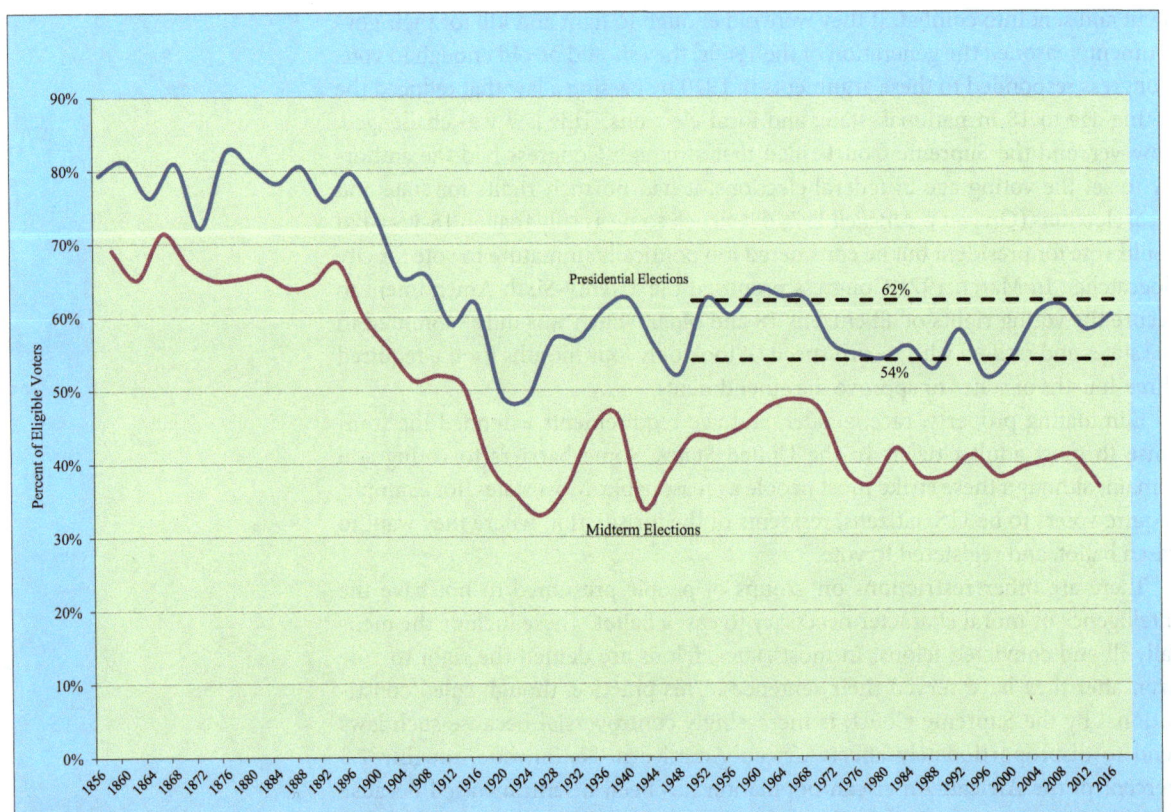

FIGURE 11.3 Voting Turnout, 1856–2016

Sources: Data from Stanley and Niemi (2013, Table 1-1); McDonald, Michael. 2017. "2016 November General Election Turnout Rates," United States Election Project, http://www.electproject.org/2016g.

that is, everyone of voting age who lives in one of the 50 states. But political scientists Michael McDonald and Samuel Popkin (2001) point out that not all residents older than the minimum voting age are eligible to vote—for example, non-citizens cannot vote, and most states do not allow felons to vote. A more accurate estimate is the percentage who vote out of the "voting-eligible population," which excludes from the calculation all those who are disqualified for some reason. Because the voting-age population includes people who cannot vote, it makes turnout look lower than it actually is. McDonald and Popkin argue that if ineligible people are excluded from the calculation, the apparent decline in turnout since 1968 is largely an illusion. Examining the different approaches to measuring turnout by looking at elections from 1980 to 2004 in individual states, Thomas Holbrook and Brianne Heidbreder (2010) find that the voting age approaches consistently underestimate turnout by two or three percentage points compared to the voting-eligible approach.

Second, regardless of what baseline we use, whether we see a decline in turnout depends a lot on where we start and where we stop. If we look at the trend for presidential elections from the 1950s forward, there seems to be not much change in turnout, which has stayed within a band of roughly eight percentage points (between 54 and 62 percent) during the past half-century (see Figure 11.3). Average turnout in presidential elections in the 1950s and early 1960s was a bit more than 60 percent of eligible voters. This dipped steadily to an average of about 55 percent in the 1990s, before once again rising to about 60 percent in more recent presidential contests. Yet if we go back to the nineteenth century, the typical twentieth- and twenty-first-century turnout rates of 55 to 60 percent look paltry compared to the 80 percent voting in elections around the time of the Civil War. Keep in mind, though, that the eligible electorate was more limited then—women, African Americans, and young people between 18 and 21 were excluded.

Different time periods and different measurement approaches may give different notions of how much or even whether turnout has declined. Yet regardless of these issues, the evidence is pretty clear that Americans are less likely to exercise their right to vote than are citizens in other democracies (see Figure 11.2). Why do proportionally fewer voters go to the polls in America? Political scientists have devoted considerable effort to explaining turnout and have arrived at two broad answers: (1) elements of the political system and (2) individual desire and ability to participate.

The Political System and Turnout

Particular aspects of the American political system that contribute to low turnout rates include voting laws, voter registration practices, the two-party system, and the scheduling and number of elections.

Voting Laws

In some countries (Australia, Belgium, and Italy are examples) voting is not optional. Citizens are required to vote by law and face fines, loss of voting rights, and social ostracism if they do not. In Italy, for example, the names of nonvoters

THINKING ANALYTICALLY

HOW WOULD YOU KNOW VOTER FRAUD IS A PROBLEM?

Do American elections have a voter fraud problem? Some people certainly seem to think so. President Donald Trump claimed that millions of people voted illegally in the 2016 election. As discussed in the text, concern about voter fraud is a primary justification for enacting voter ID laws. The federal government took the notion of voter fraud seriously enough that in 2017 it established a Commission on Election Integrity to investigate the problem. Roughly a third of the public believes there is a great deal of fraud in U.S. elections (Rourke 2016).

Is all this concern and worry justified? Is voter fraud a big enough problem to actually make a difference in an election outcome? Well, let's think analytically about the question. To figure out if we have a voter fraud problem, we first need to establish exactly what voter fraud is, and then figure out a way to measure it. This seems simple enough in concept. So, first things first, before we start trying to assess the degree of voter fraud we first need to know what we are measuring. What is voter fraud?

Let's take a fairly narrow definition and call voter fraud intentional, illegal interference with an election process by an individual voter. This definition is intended to keep our focus on the major concerns expressed about the problem of voter fraud, but note that this definition automatically excludes coordinated election interference campaigns by groups. What we are talking about are individuals going to the polls and knowingly and deliberately casting an illegal ballot. It turns out, there is more than one way to do that.

Under our definition, voter fraud can include double voting (voting twice in the same election), impersonating a voter (voting under someone else's name), and casting a ballot despite knowing you are ineligible (e.g., not being a United States citizen, not being properly registered, being registered in a different jurisdiction). One of the advantages of our definition is that many of these sorts of things are, at least in theory, relatively easy to measure because of the standard recordkeeping associated with elections in the United States. If John Smith of 22 Anywhere Lane votes twice, there's likely a public record of it. If he votes in Iowa, Nebraska, and Kansas, that can be tracked down. Similarly, some diligent record checking can pretty clearly establish if he is not a United States citizen, not a resident of the state he casts a ballot in, not properly registered, or is ineligible to vote because of a felony conviction.

There have actually been a wide variety of academic studies that have sought to measure exactly these types of voter fraud and they all seem to triangulate on the same conclusion: There is extremely little voter fraud occurring in U.S. elections. For example, one study looked at more than 2 million votes cast in Georgia elections, combing through this data to identify voters who were ineligible because of felony convictions or because they were deceased. Out of the more than 2 million ballots, the scholars verified that all but five were cast by eligible voters. And it was not clear that even those five were fraudulent; they just couldn't be verified with the available data (Hood and Gillespie 2012).

Another study went looking for double voting, looking at voter registration records to identify people who shared first and last names, and then digging down into county-level data to see if these were, for example, one person illegally registered to vote in two jurisdictions, or two different people who were properly and legitimately on their local voter rolls. This study concluded that a high-end estimate of double voting included perhaps 0.02 percent of votes cast in American elections, but was likely quite a bit less (Goel et al. 2017). Other studies have found fraudulent voting rates of 0.0003 percent in Missouri and 0.0002 percent in Wisconsin (Levitt 2007). In short, scholars have looked at tens of millions of ballots cast in the past 10 or 15 years and, as a general rule, had no problem in matching almost all of the ballots cast to a perfectly legitimate and eligible voter. It's not like voter fraud never happens; it just happens at such microscopic rates it is hard to imagine illegitimate votes having any impact on an election.

Even the ineligible voters scholars have managed to identify seem to be more likely the result of people making honest mistakes rather than intentionally committing fraud. People move to a new state and vote even though they do not meet residency requirements—that sort of thing. Jeffrey Gerrish, for example, voted in Virginia in 2016, even though he had just moved to Maryland. He only voted in the Virginia election (he didn't vote twice), but no longer met Virginia's residency requirements, so technically he cast an ineligible ballot. Gerrish's "voter fraud" briefly become national news in 2017 and drew the attention of the United States Senate because he was being nominated by President Trump for a position in his administration.

This was hardly the crime of the century; it's exactly the sort of thing scholars are most likely to find when they go looking for ineligible voters. In most instances nobody would care that much. But if people like Gerrish—someone tapped to represent an administration with deep concerns about voter fraud, and a lawyer to boot—unwittingly casts an ineligible ballot, it raises questions about who is actually behind the trifling numbers of ballots that scholars cannot associate with an eligible voter. Perhaps they are people with nefarious intent trying to swing an election. Or maybe, like Gerrish, they are otherwise law-abiding citizens who had no idea they did anything wrong.

Discussion Questions

1. Identify a recent election at any level of government and subtract the total number of votes of the losing candidate from those of the winning candidate. That number represents the "swing" needed to change the outcome of the election. How widespread would voter fraud have to be to generate such a swing? How could it be identified and prevented? Given the size of the swing, does it seem likely voter fraud played any role in the outcome of the election?

2. In spite of the available evidence, there is no doubt that many people believe voter fraud is widespread. Do such beliefs represent a problem for the integrity and legitimacy of the electoral process even if there is little empirical support for them? Why or why not?

---

are publicly posted. In the 1880s, Bavaria came up with an innovative way to encourage voting. In order for an election to be considered valid, two-thirds of eligible citizens had to cast ballots. If turnout fell below the two-thirds threshold, nonvoters were charged with the cost of putting on a new election (Robson 1923, 571–572).

Turnout where there are compulsory voting laws typically exceeds 70 percent and is often higher than 90 percent. Yet although turnout is clearly higher, it is obviously not universal. The punishments associated with compulsory voting laws, as well as the vigor with which they are enforced, undoubtedly vary considerably (Powell 1980, 9). Indeed, compulsory voting laws might more accurately be termed compulsory attendance laws; these laws require voters only to pick up a ballot, not to actually express a preference. In Australia, for example, voters rank-order their preferences on a ballot by putting numbers next to candidates. Many voters, however, cast a "donkey vote," which means they just put a "1" next to the first candidate, a "2" next to the second, and so on until the end of the ballot. In other words, the numbers they list on their ballots have no connection to their preferences. Donkey voting is seen as a form of protest against compulsory voting; it signals that a voter's chief preference was not to be forced to cast a ballot. This raises an important point: Compulsory voting reflects the notion of political participation as civic duty, but some question whether legally forcing citizens to vote is democratic. Individual liberty and political freedom in the United States imply not just the right to vote but also the right not to vote.

Voter Registration

Voter registration requires more effort in the United States than in other democracies. In European countries, it is common for 90 percent or more of those eligible to vote to actually be registered to vote. In the United States, registration rates are considerably lower. The reason for the difference is that in the United States, registering to vote is considered an individual responsibility; it is mostly left to citizens themselves to take the initiative to register. In other democracies, government takes on the responsibility of identifying potential voters and registering them to vote.

Several decades ago, political scientists argued that on the basis of their research, the burden of registration explained a big part of low voter turnout in the United States (Wolfinger 1991). The evidence underlying this argument is that turnout is much higher when it is calculated as the percentage of registered voters rather than the percentage of eligible voters. Persuaded by this logic, in 1993, Congress passed the National Voter Registration Act—the so-called motor voter law—requiring states to provide registration services when citizens go to renew their driver's license or seek other public services. This bill was controversial because, as a group, unregistered citizens tend to be poorer, less educated, and more likely to identify as Democrats. Republicans feared they would be at an electoral disadvantage if turnout increased in this group, though subsequent research suggests Republican fears were unfounded: The law increased registration rates but, at best, has had a modest impact on actual turnout (Knack and White 1998).

Registration laws and procedures vary from state to state. Minnesota and Wisconsin, for example, allow citizens to register on the day of election. Other states require voters to register at least a month before the election in order to vote in that election. Most states automatically cancel the registration of individuals who have not cast a ballot in a specified period of time (usually two to four years), thus forcing citizens to repeat the registration process if they do not vote on a regular basis.

States also vary in voter verification requirements. Some states card voters at the polls; that is, they require proof that the prospective registered voter is who he or she claims to be before allowing the voter to cast a ballot. Supporters of the most strict identification laws, which require a government-issued photo ID, argue that they help prevent election fraud and thus ensure the integrity of the ballot. Opponents argue that these laws create a burden on voters that is potentially disenfranchising. In 2008 the Supreme Court in *Crawford v. Marion County Election Board* upheld Indiana's voter ID law—one of the toughest in the nation. The court argued that any burdens created by ID requirements were counterbalanced by the law's potential to reduce voter fraud. Critics of the law and the court ruling argue that the net effect will be to make it harder for some people to vote. Some research has found no widespread decline in voter participation that can be attributed to such laws (Ansolabehere 2009). In recent years, however, state governments have passed a large number of laws that make it harder to register or to cast a ballot. In 2016, for example, voters in 32 states were required to show an ID before they could vote in-person at the polls. These sorts of regulations are not limited to ID laws but also include requirements mandating proof of citizenship before someone is allowed to register or vote, as well as other restrictions on registering and voting. Other states have made it harder to stay registered to vote if you move, if early voting opportunities have ended, and if the state has passed new laws disenfranchising those with criminal records. These changes tend to make it harder for the young, the poor, and minorities to register and cast a ballot, and some predict that the cumulative effect of these restrictions could start to noticeably lower turnout among these groups (Weiser and Norden 2011).

Thus far, academic studies have found no consistent, non-trivial impact of voter ID laws on turnout, though many of these laws are relatively new and their long-term effects are largely unknown. There is no doubt that voter ID laws are increasingly controversial, with opponents arguing they are little more than efforts at voter suppression, while proponents insist they are simply a prudent step to prevent voter fraud (see the Thinking Analytically box "How Would You Know Voter Fraud Is a Problem?" for further discussion of this debate).

The Two-Party System

Historically, some scholars argued that two-party systems may not offer voters a meaningful choice, leaving voters with less of an incentive to show up at the polls. This argument is rooted in rational choice theory and was most famously articulated by economist Anthony Downs (1957). He argued that in two-party systems, it is rational for parties to appeal to the average voter, which in the United States means appealing to a middle-of-the-road perspective on politics and policy.

It is perfectly rational for the parties to stake their ground in the middle of the political spectrum because that is where most voters' preferences lie. The problem is that if both parties are chasing the middle-of-the-road voter, they end up with overlapping appeals and make it hard for citizens to differentiate between them. If potential voters cannot see differences between parties or candidates, they will find it troubling to cast a ballot based on individual policy preferences. If this is the case, it is just as rational to go to the beach as to vote. As a Texas politician once said, "The only thing in the middle of the road are yella stripes and dead armadillos" (Hightower 1998).

In recent elections, however, Republicans and Democrats have been less likely to make similar appeals as they seek voters in the center. Indeed, the two major parties have become much more polarized, shifting away from the average voter and closer to the preferences of the more ideologically committed voters that characterize low-turnout primary elections (Masket 2011). Have the parties become less rational? Not really. What candidates have discovered is that it is often no use appealing to the middle-of-the-road voter in a primary election for the simple reason that low-turnout primary elections are not dominated by middle-of-the-road voters. Those who show up to vote in primary elections are more likely to be strong partisans or ideologues. If you want to win a primary election, obviously you have to appeal to those more extreme policy preferences. In rational choice terms, it is simply not rational to appeal to the voter on the 50-yard line in a primary election if most of the voters are to be found on the 10-yard or even 1-yard line of your side of the field. The end result is that Republican and Democratic primary winners start running in a general election from essentially their own goalposts, which are a long way from the middle of the political playing field. Even though candidates tend to move to the center in a general election, it is much harder to reach the middle if you start from so far away. When each party represents a clear ideological choice, it is a good thing for strong conservatives or liberals, but moderate voters in the middle may still end up feeling as if they have no meaningful choice to represent their preferences and may go to the beach anyway.

Election Schedules and Frequency

Presidential elections are held on Tuesdays, a workday for most Americans. Other democracies encourage voting by holding elections on Saturdays or Sundays. Holding national elections on weekends, or making election day a national holiday, would make it easier for working Americans to show up at the polls.

The reasons for holding federal elections on a weekday in November are purely historical, the timing being largely a product of nineteenth-century lifestyle conditions. At the time, the United States was a mostly rural agrarian nation, so elections were set for November because it didn't conflict with spring planting or the fall harvest, meaning farmers had the time to actually get to a ballot box. Tuesday was selected because most rural voters had to travel to the county seat to cast a ballot. That could easily take a day on foot or on horseback. Most people strictly observed Sunday as a day of rest, so Tuesday was arrived at to give voters Monday to get to the county seat before voting. Those lifestyle considerations are completely anachronistic today, yet election day remains a Tuesday. Some have suggested that it would be more fitting to hold national elections on November 11, Veterans Day. The argument here is that this would be an appropriate tribute to the members of the armed forces who have defended democracy and that it would highlight the importance of civic duty and participation (Wattenberg 1998).

It is not just the timing of elections but also the number that may depress voter turnout in America. Citizens in the United States are called on to vote much more often than in other democracies. The federal system means there are not just federal elections, but numerous elections

Voting requires more effort in the United States than in other democracies. It is harder to register to vote, and a slew of new laws places restrictions even on registered voters. Many states now require voters to show proof of identification in order to cast a ballot.

© Romy Varghese/Bloomberg/Getty Images

at the state and local levels too. Citizens in many states elect state agency heads, state and local judges, sheriffs, county officials, mayors, and city councils.

Electing candidates for these offices usually means at least two elections: a primary election and a general election. On top of that, elections are regularly held for special-purpose districts such as school districts, flood control districts, water districts, sewage districts, mosquito control districts, and park districts. In addition, voters are regularly called on to vote for proposed state constitutional amendments, ballot initiatives, and bond issues.

In short, there are a lot of elections, and the United States is far ahead of other democracies in the number of voting opportunities presented to citizens. U.S. voters may be exhausted by a virtually permanent election season. Like the mouse, they may beg, "Don't give me any more cheese; just let me out of the trap."

Individual Desire and Ability to Participate

The mix of reasons listed previously may help explain why voter turnout in the United States is lower compared to other democracies. What it does not explain is why turnout generally declined during the past 40 years, the past handful of election cycles excepted.

This decline is particularly puzzling because it has occurred at the same time as a number of reforms that, at least in theory, should have led to higher turnout. For example, although restrictive registration and voting laws keep voters away from the polls, some states have experimented with simpler registration laws, set up registration booths in shopping malls, and experimented with letting people register online. Yet, as registering to vote became easier, voter turnout went down.

The puzzle of voter turnout is tied to the fundamental question of political participation: Why do some people participate whereas others do not? There is no single, simple answer to this question. Research has identified a number of the key elements that affect an individual's desire and ability to participate:

- Socioeconomic status, which is simply the social and economic position a person occupies in society
- An individual's psychological engagement with politics
- The broader political and social context with which an individual is connected
- Resources necessary to participate—free time, money, and civic skills
- Group characteristics—age, gender, race

Socioeconomic Status

Perhaps the most important determinant of any form of political participation is **socioeconomic status (SES)**. Socioeconomic status is typically measured in terms

socioeconomic status (SES) The social background and economic position of a person.

of education, income, and occupation and serves as a baseline explanation of both the desire and the ability to participate.

Education seems to be especially important. Well-educated people tend to hold high-status positions (business executive, doctor, lawyer, and so on) and earn high incomes. They are likely to be aware of political matters and possess the confidence and intellectual tools to deal with them. They recognize their financial stake in politics (through taxes and fees), and they have professional, intellectual, and social skills that transfer easily to the political arena. In short, SES helps determine whether people have the ability to participate effectively in politics. Generally speaking, higher-SES citizens—those with high income, high education, and high-status occupations—are more likely to show up to the polls than low-SES citizens. But although SES clearly plays an important role in explaining why individuals do or do not vote, overall levels of SES do not necessarily track voter participation over time. Education and income levels, for example, rose across all levels of society in the four decades between the 1960s and the turn of the century even as the general trend in turnout drifted toward 50 percent in presidential elections. Shortly after the turn of the century, the recession began squeezing incomes, yet voter participation in the presidential elections actually went up, topping 60 percent for the first time since the 1960s (see Figure 11.3).

Psychological Engagement

People who believe that their opinions are important and that government will respect and respond to their views are said to believe in **political efficacy**. Individuals are more likely to participate if they feel efficacious, regardless of their SES (Milbrath and Goel 1977, 59). Though high-SES people have the skills necessary to participate, it is the psychological engagement with politics that provides the desire to participate.

Psychological engagement, or more accurately the lack of it, may play an important role in explaining voter turnout. **Political alienation** characterizes individuals with deep-seated feelings of isolation and estrangement from the political system (Finifter 1970; Milbrath and Goel 1977; Seeman 1959). Politically alienated citizens tend to have low levels of trust in government and feel the political system does not merit their participation. **Allegiant** individuals, in contrast, express high levels of trust in government.

Although it would seem to make sense that citizens with high levels of political efficacy would participate, and politically alienated citizens would not, the relationship between psychological engagement and voter turnout is not that clear-cut. Some argue that alienation and distrust translate into voter apathy, and, as alienation and distrust in government have increased, turnout has declined. Others, however, argue that this is a demonstration of "happy politics" (Eulau 1956), or the notion that people who are happy with the political process and who trust government to do the right thing simply see less of a need to participate. Logically, then, people who are unhappy with the government should be more likely to vote; their dissatisfaction with the status quo provides the motivation to go to the polls to try to change things.

political efficacy The belief that one's opinions are important and that government will respect and respond to one's views.

political alienation The feeling of being isolated from or not part of the political process and system.

allegiant Feeling great trust and support for the political system.

Psychological traits beyond efficacy may also play a role in influencing political participation. Recent research has found that an individual's personality can predict his or her level of political involvement. For example, people whose personalities are characterized by openness—they tend to consistently seek out information and engagement—tend to be more politically engaged (see Mondak et al. 2010). The finding that personality shapes political participation has also raised the possibility that biological factors influence political engagement. Personality traits are known to be heritable, and there is some evidence that individuals' political traits as well as their personality traits are based in the same set of genetic influences (Verhulst, Eaves, and Hatemi 2011).

Context

In addition to SES and psychological attributes, participation is affected by the context in which an individual lives. The broader social network, particularly organizational memberships and the neighborhood, is important in development of civic skills. Political scientists Robert Huckfeldt and John Sprague (1995) conducted an intensive study of political activity in 16 neighborhoods in South Bend, Indiana, during a presidential election. They found that people who live in neighborhoods that reflect and support their party identification are more likely to become politically active—not just voting, but also putting up yard signs, sporting bumper stickers, and making politics a topic of conversation.

Context, though, goes beyond the local level to include the broader impact of the political system and the experiences of the electorate as a whole. The **mobilization** hypothesis posits that "participation is a response to contextual cues and political opportunities" (Leighley 1995, 188). In other words, people are motivated to participate by their political environment. For example, political parties frequently mount "get out the vote" campaigns. These efforts, which may take the form of phone calls, media ads, or direct mail, are aimed at motivating people to actually cast a ballot. Even a simple text message reminding people to vote seems to be enough to significantly increase turnout in a given election (Dale and Strauss 2009). These sorts of mobilization efforts, though, have a mixed impact on participation. On the one hand, they undoubtedly encourage some people to get out and vote. On the other, they mostly tend to encourage certain types of people to get out and vote: the better-off, the

mobilization Efforts aimed at influencing people to vote in an election.

Political and social context helps influence levels of political participation. Neighborhoods where people put up political yard signs, sport political bumper stickers, and talk politics tend to have higher levels of political participation.

© Al Drago/CQ Roll Call/AP Photo

better-educated, and the better-informed. This is because the political elites who undertake the mobilization efforts—political parties, special interest groups, and the like—tend to target people who have resources to contribute (money or time), who have a particular partisan or ideological affiliation (these groups want to mobilize supporters, not opponents), or who are key members of social networks (i.e., people who can influence other people). That sort of targeting can certainly mobilize the better-off and better-connected, but it does little to boost the participation of a large mass of voters who do not have those traits (Rosenstone and Hansen 1993).

Rather than mobilization, others argue for the generational effect hypothesis of turnout. This view suggests that the key elements of social context driving voter turnout are the events and experiences that shape a generation's attitudes toward politics. The generation shaped by the Great Depression and World War II was more politically engaged because those events promoted a keen sense of the importance of politics and civic duty. The generations that followed experienced nothing equivalent to mass economic dislocation and a multiyear effort to fight a world war. This resulted in generational effect on turnout (Miller 1992). This might explain why turnout declined from the 1960s to the 1990s: Politics was simply seen as less important and less relevant to baby boomers and Generation Xers, and as the electorate came to be more dominated by these generational cohorts and their political context, turnout dropped off (Lyons and Alexander 2000). Currently, key elements of the social context that may shape long-term attitudes toward politics are economic hard times, long and bloody guerrilla wars in Iraq and Afghanistan, and bitter polarization between the major political parties over how to address these issues. Will this combine to prompt higher levels of political participation in the generation that follows the boomers and the Xers? It's too early to answer this question with confidence, but the generational hypothesis certainly suggests it is possible.

Resources

Verba, Schlozman, and Brady (1995) developed a resource-based model that is still widely accepted as one of the most comprehensive explanations of political participation. Their argument is that individuals need resources in order to participate and that three types of resources are important:

1. Free time after work, household duties, and school
2. Money
3. Civic skills, such as communication and organizational abilities

Voter turnout has important implications for democratic governance. Voting expresses the will of only those people who actually cast their ballots, and government policy favors those who participate.

© Bizuayehu Tesfaye/AP Photo

Individuals who have free time, above-average family income, and the ability to speak and write well or who are comfortable organizing and participating in meetings are more active and effective in politics (Verba, Schlozman, and Brady 1995). Different resources are required for different forms of participation. Contributing money to a campaign, for example, requires surplus income but not much time. Contacting a government official requires time and civic skills. These resources are distributed unequally across the population, which helps explain why some people are more likely to participate than others. But more importantly, the different resources are not equally associated with SES. Money is associated with high SES, by definition. Free time, however, is not; low-SES individuals have as much or more of it than people with high SES.

The connection between civic skills and SES is mixed. Individuals begin acquiring civic skills early in life from family and school. These skills develop throughout adult life in nonpolitical institutions such as the workplace, organizations, and churches and synagogues. High-SES individuals tend to have the civic skills to participate in activities requiring them, such as working in political campaigns or contacting government officials. They probably grew up in families that valued such activity, and as adults, they tend to have jobs and belong to organizations that allow them to practice writing, speaking, and organizing. But school offers opportunities to children from low-SES families to learn civic skills. For example, Verba, Schlozman, and Brady (1995) found that participation in student government contributes to an individual's civic skills. Furthermore, church attendance offers adults opportunities to develop civic skills. Church attendance is not associated with SES; individuals with low income and education have about as much opportunity to make speeches and organize meetings at church as do those with high SES. "In this way," conclude Verba and his associates, "the institutions of civil society operate, as Tocqueville noted, as the school of democracy" (Verba, Schlozman, and Brady 1995, 285).

Group Characteristics

Certain group characteristics—such as race and age—are also associated with participation. The relationship between age and participation is curvilinear: Participation is highest among middle-aged people (say, those aged 45 to 65) and much lower for the very young and very old. Middle-aged people tend to have the greatest stake in the political system, to be aware of how government affects their lives, and to have the resources necessary to participate. Very young citizens participate less in politics because they are less likely to see how politics and government affect them, and they lack other attributes that encourage participation. Young people, for example, may be just starting a career or may still be in school. Participation falls off among older people in part because of infirmities associated with aging. Some research indicates, however, that when differences in education and resources are accounted for, the decline in participation among the elderly is less pronounced. Retired people have the time to devote to politics, and many participate in organizations that provide them with pertinent information about politics and opportunities to develop civic skills.

APPLYING THE FRAMEWORKS

THE BIOLOGY OF POLITICAL PARTICIPATION

Two of the three theoretical frameworks we are highlighting throughout this book have obvious applications to the puzzle of why people do or do not vote. Behavioral frameworks point us toward the environment—people vote because they were socialized to have a sense of civic duty, because their social status gives them a high degree of political efficacy, because they have a sense of loyalty to a group or a political party, or simply because of their reaction to the issues or candidates at the center of a particular election. Rational choice models point us toward individual decision making—people vote because the potential benefits of voting outweigh the costs.

What about evolutionary and biological models, though? Can they tell us anything about why people decide to participate in politics? It turns out they can. A number of recent studies present evidence that variation in political participation is heritable, and there has even been some preliminary work identifying specific genes associated with greater probabilities of voting, though these are somewhat controversial (Deppe et al. 2013; Fowler, Baker, and Dawes 2008; Fowler and Dawes 2008).

At first glance, these sorts of studies seem a bit far-fetched. Is there really a gene for voting? Well, probably not in the strictest sense. But the sorts of things genes inarguably influence almost certainly do play a role in determining our levels of political participation. Take, for example, our stress levels.

Stress, for the human body, is heavily regulated by our neuroendocrine systems, particularly what's known as the hypothalamic-pituitary-adrenal (HPA) axis. The specifics of HPA axis functioning can get pretty complicated, and we won't bother with them here. The key thing for our purposes is that individuals vary in how their HPA axis responds to different stimuli in their environment. We can measure variation in HPA axis activation by looking at how much cortisol—the so-called "stress hormone"—a given individual is producing.

HPA axis activity and cortisol levels are influenced by a lot of things, but it is pretty uncontroversial to say that one of those influences is genetics. Specific genes have been implicated in making individual neuroendocrine stress systems more or less sensitive to whatever stressors are encountered in our daily lives. Okay, but what the heck does any of this have to do with political participation? Well, it has been pretty conclusively established by a long string of studies that individuals respond differently to social stressors. Some studies specifically suggest that higher HPA axis sensitivity (which is associated with higher cortisol levels) is correlated with the tendency to avoid socially stressful situations. That's relevant to us because politics in general and voting in particular can be socially stressful. Not only does voting mean you have to make a set of decisions (decision making can be stressful), you often have to go to a public place (a polling station) where it's likely politics is being discussed, a prospect that makes some people nervous.

A series of recent studies have found that voting is stressful in the sense that it raises cortisol levels (Neiman et al. 2015; Waismel-Manor, Ifergane, and Cohen 2011). This particularly seems to be the case for voting at the polls as opposed to voting at home with a mail-in ballot. Keep in mind the earlier point about individual variation in HPA axis sensitivity. What that variation suggests is that some people with less sensitive neuroendocrine systems will not find voting particularly stressful; they may even find it stimulating. Some people, on the other hand, might instinctively find participating in the unavoidably conflict-ridden world of politics a stress they can do without. They might avoid voting altogether.

If all this is the case, it suggests a fairly simple hypothesis: People with higher, naturally occurring cortisol levels will be less likely to vote. Exactly that hypothesis has been tested—twice—by a research group working with voters in Nebraska. Both times the researchers found a significant negative correlation between cortisol levels and the likelihood of voting (French et al. 2014; Neiman et al. 2015).

It would be wise to interpret these findings cautiously; no one is suggesting that whether you vote is determined solely by your cortisol levels. What these studies do collectively suggest is that political participation is one of a wide range of social behaviors that are influenced by individual variation in neuroendocrine systems. Those systems are in turn influenced by a whole bunch of things, including what we experienced growing up (did we grow up in a secure environment with a loving family, or did we suffer through insecurity and abuse?) and what we experienced as adults (traumatic experiences can induce long-term changes in our neuroendocrine systems). But yes, one of the things that clearly helps determine HPA axis functioning is our unique genetic makeup.

Note that while these new findings on political participation support the evolutionary and biological approach, they do not necessarily contradict the behavioral or the rational conceptual models. The cortisol studies make very clear the importance of the environment, which is the big focus of behavioral models. And just because you instinctually see politics as a stress you can do without does not mean you cannot rationally calculate that the payoff for participating outweighs whatever vague psychological discomfort it creates.

Discussion Questions

1. Think of different forms of political participation, e.g., voting, attending a rally, having a political discussion. Are some of these more likely to be socially stressful than others? Which are most socially stressful and why?
2. Besides a tendency toward getting stressed out by social conflict, might political participation be driven by other traits not traditionally considered causes of political engagement? How about personality? Risk tolerance or impulsiveness?

African Americans and Latinos also participate less than whites. This difference, however, results mostly from factors other than race, particularly education, income, and resources. When SES and resources are controlled for, participation of African Americans and Latinos is not significantly different from that of whites (Verba, Schlozman, and Brady 1995). On the other hand, voter turnout of Asian Americans, another growing ethnic minority, is lower than that of whites even after controlling for SES and other factors (Fraga 2016; Uhlaner, Cain, and Kiewiet 1989). For other types of participation, there is no significant difference between Asian Americans and whites once the effects of SES and other factors are taken into account (Leighley and Vedlitz 1999).

Voting and Democracy

Scholars have raised concerns that voter turnout—or the lack thereof—has important implications for democratic governance. If some groups participate less than others, are their preferences less likely to be accounted for in the democratic process? This concern is central to the elitist critique of the American system. How can government truly uphold the will of the people and act on majority preferences if a majority of people do not bother to cast a ballot?

Political scientists have approached this issue from a number of perspectives and are divided about the answer. For example, there is solid evidence that government is very responsive to broad currents of public opinion (Erikson, Wright, and McIver 1993). This suggests that people do not actually have to vote to have government respond to their preferences. It is also generally accepted that increasing turnout will not necessarily make a difference in election outcomes. On the other hand, it is also clear that the mobilization of various groups in the electorate is an important determinant of election outcomes (R. Jackson 1997). Disproportionate participation by higher-class citizens logically results in policies that favor their economic interests at the expense of lower-class citizens (Bennett and Resnick 1990; Gant and Lyons 1993; Hill and Leighley 1992; Leighley and Nagler 2007). In other words, voting expresses the will of only a portion of the people, and government policy favors those who participate.

MODELS OF VOTING BEHAVIOR

Explaining why people do or do not vote in an election is a complex undertaking. Yet explaining voter turnout is relatively simple compared to the challenge of explaining what happens once a voter enters the voting booth. Why do some people vote Republican and others Democrat? Why do some vote for liberal candidates and others for conservative candidates?

During the past half-century, three theories have dominated the search for an explanation of vote choice: the sociological model, the social-psychological model, and the rational choice model.

The Sociological Model

Researchers at Columbia University developed the sociological model to explain voting behavior in the 1940 presidential election. Initially, the Columbia researchers tried to explain voting choices as consumer preferences. The initial idea was that political candidates could be viewed as "products" offered by political parties and political campaigns as competing marketing efforts aimed at swaying voter preferences.

The consumer preference idea was a bust, mainly because researchers discovered that most voters decided who they were going to vote for well in advance of the advertising campaigns (Niemi and Weisberg 1993, 8). Casting about for an alternate explanation, the Columbia researchers noticed that sociological variables—a fancy term for the characteristics of groups—were strongly correlated with vote choice.

The result was the **sociological model** (sometimes called the Columbia model) of voting behavior. The sociological model uses group-level characteristics such as SES, religion, and place of residence to explain how people vote (Lazarsfeld, Berelson, and Gaudet 1944). At least in the 1940 election, this group-level approach worked well: Catholics, city dwellers, and people with low education, low income,

---

sociological model (Columbia model) A model explaining vote choice by considering factors such as religion, place of residence, and socioeconomic status.

and low-status occupations tended to vote for the Democratic candidate, Franklin Delano Roosevelt. Protestants, rural residents, and people higher up the socioeconomic chain tended to vote for the Republican candidate, Wendell Willkie.

The sociological model still provides a reasonable basis for explaining vote choice. Figure 11.4 shows the voting behavior of various sociological groups in recent elections. For example, people with low income and education have tended to vote Democratic, as do African Americans, Latinos, Catholics, and Jews. Republican candidates still get higher levels of support from whites, Protestants, and people with high income.

Yet as a comprehensive explanation of vote choice, the sociological model quickly fell from favor. Certain group characteristics—such as race, religion, and income—may be associated with differences in vote choice, but they do not always

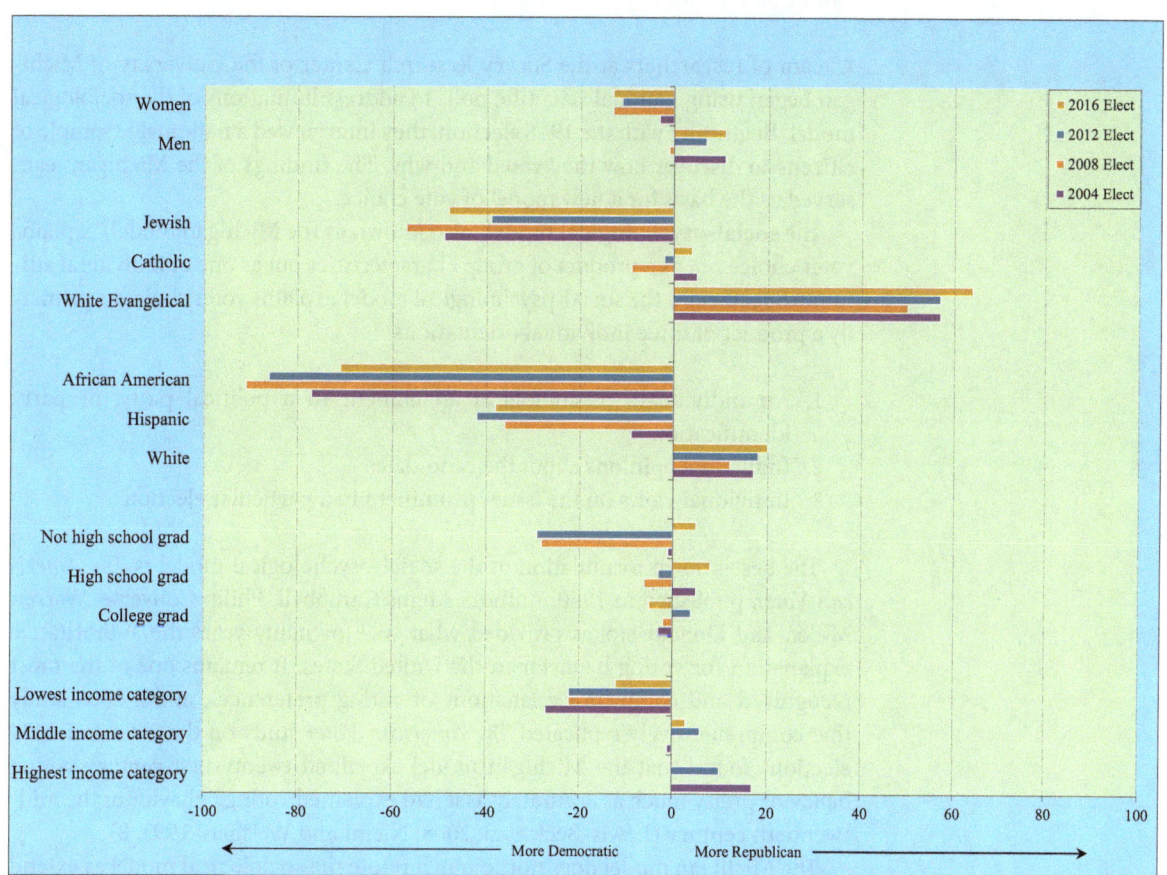

FIGURE 11.4 Voting Behavior of Sociological Groups

Source: Data from 2004 and 2008 exit polls reported by MSNBC (http://www.msnbc.msn.com/id/5297138/ and http://www.msnbc.msn.com/id/26843704); "National Exit Polls Table," *New York Times,* http://elections.nytimes.com/2008/results/president/national-exit-polls.html and http://elections.nytimes.com/2012/results/president/exit-polls; "Exit Polls 2012: How the Vote Has Shifted," *Washington Post,* http://www.washingtonpost.com/wp-srv/special/politics/2012-exit-polls/table.html; 2016 exit polling from CNN (http://www.cnn.com/election/results/exit-polls; and Stanley and Niemi (2013).

explain why those differences exist. Furthermore, group loyalties shift over time and are therefore not always reliable predictors of voting patterns. Certainly, there have been significant changes in group voting behavior since the Columbia study. The effects of education appear to be changing, for example. College graduates switched to favoring the Democrat in recent presidential elections, whereas less educated voters with a high school education or less switched to favoring the Republican (Trump) in 2016. And while the lowest-income voters still favor the Democrat, the highest-income voters split evenly between the parties in 2008 and 2016. Finally, the conclusions of the sociological model rested on a narrow research base: The sociological model was originally based on a limited sample of voters (taken from a single county in New York State). Other studies based on larger national samples had difficulty replicating the findings.

The Social-Psychological Model

A team of researchers at the Survey Research Center of the University of Michigan began using national scientific polls to address limitations of the sociological model. Beginning with the 1948 election, they interviewed a nationwide sample of citizens to discover how they voted and why. The findings of the Michigan team served as the basis for a new model of vote choice.

The **social-psychological model** (also known as the Michigan model) explains voter choice not as a product of group characteristics but as one of individual attitudes. Specifically, the social-psychological model explains voter choice as primarily a product of three individual orientations:

1. An individual's psychological attachment to a political party, or party identification
2. Individual opinions about the candidates
3. Individual views on the issues prominent in a particular election

The best-known formulation of the social-psychological model is *The American Voter*, published in 1960. Authors Angus Campbell, Philip Converse, Warren Miller, and Donald Stokes provided what was for many years the authoritative explanation for voting behavior in the United States. It remains one of the most recognized and complete explanations of voting preferences, and a 2008 study that comprehensively replicated *The American Voter* study on the 2000 and 2004 elections found that the Michigan model explained twenty-first-century voting behavior pretty much as accurately as it had explained voting behavior in the mid-twentieth century (Lewis-Beck et al. 2008; Niemi and Weisberg 1993, 8).

The Michigan model does not so much refute the sociological model as extend it. The Michigan researchers used the metaphor of a "funnel of causality" to explain voter choice (see Figure 11.5). Into the mouth or wide end of the funnel go factors such as SES, religion, gender, and race. These are the factors seen as driving an individual's party identification, and it is party identification that lies at the core of the social-psychological model. Other influences, such as the politics of parents

social-psychological model (Michigan model) A model explaining voter choice that focuses on individual attitudes.

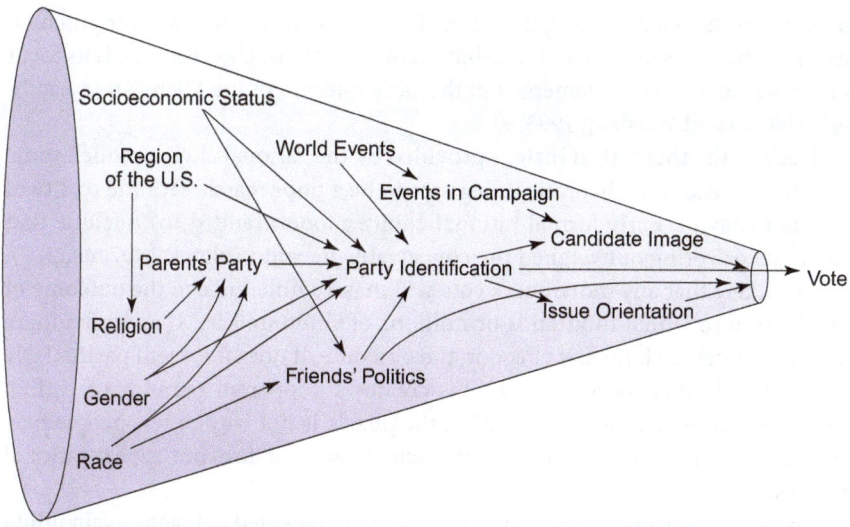

FIGURE 11.5 Funnel of Causality
Source: Luttbeg and Gant (1995, 13).

and friends and world events, also affect party identification. Party identification, in turn, shapes an individual's attitudes toward candidates and issues. These attitudes are what lead an individual, finally, to vote a certain way. At the tip or outlet of the funnel is the individual's actual vote, which is distilled from sociological factors into party identification and from party identification into a certain set of attitudes and opinions about candidates and issues. These final three factors—party identification, perception of candidate image, and issue orientation—play the biggest role in explaining vote choice.

The model thus explains party identification as something largely inherited from parents and the same group-level characteristics dominant in the sociological model. Party identification acts as a "brand" that orients voters toward particular candidates and issues and helps them make choices. The heart of the Michigan model is its focus on party identification and individual attitudes, a focus that continues to dominate explanations of voting behavior.

The Rational Choice Model

The Michigan model's primary competition as a comprehensive explanation of voter behavior is the **rational choice model**. This model argues that voting is the product of a rational cost–benefit calculation. Broadly speaking, rational choice means that individuals will vote if the benefits of doing so outweigh the costs and will cast their ballots for candidates who are closest to sharing their views on the issues.

Unlike the Columbia and Michigan models, rational choice offers fairly precise predictions of voter behavior. For example, as the costs of voting increase (e.g., a

rational choice model A model of voter choice that suggests that an individual will vote if the benefits of doing so outweigh the costs and will cast his or her ballot for candidates who are closest to sharing the individual's views on the issues.

long line at the polling place), the rational choice model predicts a lower probability of voting. A second major contribution of the rational choice model is its focus on issues "which were submerged in the early findings of the Michigan researchers" (Niemi and Weisberg 1993, 9).

Despite the theoretical insight provided by the rational choice model, some scholars consider its theoretical elegance to be a poor match with the reality of voting behavior. Early formal rational choice models tended to conclude that the costs of voting outweighed the conceivable benefit (Tullock 1967, chap. 7). It is unlikely that any individual's vote will make a difference to the outcome of an election in which thousands or millions of votes are cast. If an individual's vote is unlikely to have any effect on the outcome, it does not seem particularly rational to bother to vote at all. This creates an apparent paradox of voting: From the rational choice perspective, the puzzle is not why so few people participate but why so many bother to participate when it does not appear rational to do so.

To solve this paradox, rational choice scholars suggested that voters gain utility not just from the outcome of voting but also from the act of voting. If you believe voting is an important civic duty, voting becomes an important goal regardless of the outcome of the election (Riker and Ordeshook 1968). Critics saw some circular reasoning in this solution: People are rational, so if they vote, voting must be rational; and if voting is rational, then people who vote must also be rational. More refined rational choice approaches argue that voting is a low-cost, low-reward proposition, which means it doesn't take much to sway a citizen to vote (Aldrich 1993). In the vast majority of cases, it takes little effort to show up to the polls, and the payoff in terms of electoral outcomes or satisfaction in doing your civic duty is also pretty low. This means a lot of factors can push a rational individual into voting or not voting: mobilization efforts, the appeal of a particular candidate or ballot issue, and so on.

Rational choice models must also grapple with the information hurdles involved in political participation. To make rational voting decisions on the basis of issues, for example, voters need some minimal level of information about those issues. A good deal of research indicates that most Americans are poorly informed about politics. Because of such practical limitations to the rational choice model, the Michigan model in various modified forms continues to provide the most accepted explanations of voting behavior.

EXPLAINING VOTER CHOICE

According to the Michigan model, the three primary elements that go into a decision to vote for a particular candidate are party identification, candidate image, and issues. Although it is the combination of these elements that is thought to produce a final voting decision, scholars have long recognized that each plays a distinct role in shaping voter behavior.

Party Identification

The Michigan model argues that party identification is the most important determinant of vote choice (Campbell et al. 1960; Lewis-Beck et al. 2008). In contrast to candidate image and issues, party identification is a long-term influence on voting behavior, helping to shape vote choices across many elections.

Early research suggested that an individual's general psychological attachment to a political party begins in childhood and intensifies with age (Campbell et al. 1960, 165). Party identification is also important because voters use it as a form of shorthand or as a "cheat sheet." Voters rarely know everything about the specific issues a candidate supports or opposes. Indeed, they may not know anything at all about some candidates listed on a voting ballot. But most ballots are partisan ballots—they indicate the party affiliation of the candidates. Just knowing a candidate's political party can offer a rough-and-ready indication of what that candidate supports or opposes. So for a typical voter looking for guidance amid the complexities of personalities, issues, and events, a candidate's party label provides an important reference point. Party labels thus provide a quick and easy, if not 100 percent reliable, way of making judgments about a candidate.

Because of its central importance to explaining vote choice, political scientists have paid close attention to the partisan makeup of the electorate. It is generally recognized that levels of partisanship vary across time. In the 1950s, for example, 75 percent of the electorate identified themselves as Democrats or Republicans. According to the Pew Center, in 2016 roughly 60 percent of voters identified with one of the two major parties. (You can check out Pew's data on party identification trends at http://www.people-press.org/2016/09/13/party-identification-trends-1992-2016/.)

Some scholars see this downward shift in party identification patterns as heralding the rise of the independent voter, a view supported by an increase in split-ticket voting. Split-ticket voters vote for one party's candidate in one race and for the other party's candidate in another. In the 1950s, straight-ticket voting was common, and party "brand loyalty" was strong across the entire ballot. That pattern changed over the next 20 years as voters became more likely to split their votes between Republican presidents and Democratic congressional candidates, or vice versa (Nie, Verba, and Petrocik 1979). As we learned in Chapter 7, however, the decline of partisanship stalled in the 1970s. Most individuals who initially claim to be independent admit to favoring one party, and they vote just like weak partisans. Beginning in the 1990s, the electorate became noticeably more partisan, and straight-ticket voting increased. Party identification is probably more important in determining vote choice today than it was four or five decades ago (Abramson, Aldrich, and Rohde 2006, 194; Lewis-Beck et al. 2008, 127).

The partisan divide in the electorate has been made particularly clear in the red state–blue state divide of the past few presidential electoral cycles. Red states, mostly in the South and the middle of the country, reliably support Republican candidates. Blue states, mostly on the coasts, tend to back the Democratic nominee. Mapping electoral votes onto a map of the United States presents an image of a country starkly divided along geographically defined partisan lines (see Figure 11.6).

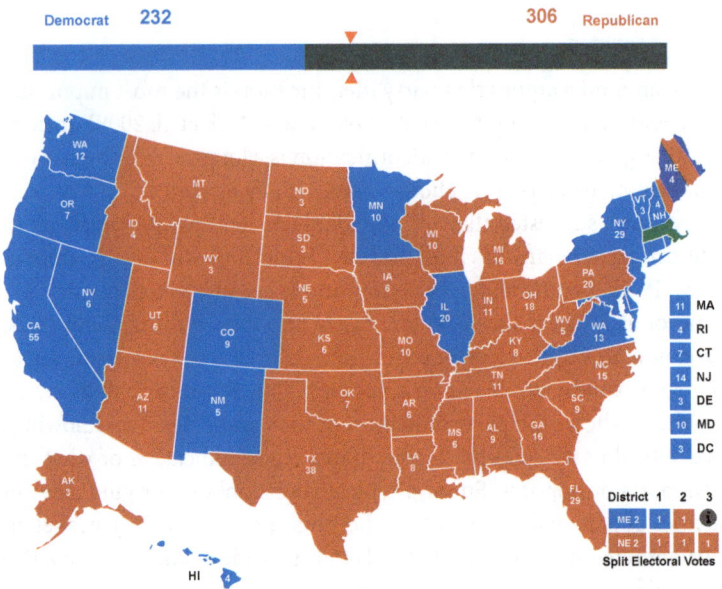

FIGURE 11.6 Red States–Blue States: Electoral Votes in the 2016 Presidential Election

This image is somewhat misleading; there are strong pockets of blue in the red states, and vice versa, and in 2016 some traditionally blue states (e.g., Michigan, Wisconsin) backed the Republican nominee. The starkest partisan divide, however, is not between states, but rather urban–rural—densely populated cites over 500,000, even in red states, vote for Democrats, while small towns and rural areas vote for Republicans. In 2016, Hillary Clinton won the largest cities in deep red Texas (Houston, San Antonio, Dallas, Austin, Fort Worth, and El Paso) and Tennessee (Nashville and Memphis). Trump won only one city over 500,000—Oklahoma City. In other words, although some states have electorates with disproportionate partisan loyalties, populations in some red and blue states are sharply divided between big cities and rural areas.

In some cases, however, the red or blue state maps reported in the popular media overstate the partisan division. Instead, purple—a mixing of red and blue—might be a more accurate depiction. The notion of purple states fits with research suggesting that party loyalties are not as fixed as the red state–blue state divide suggests. Early studies of voting behavior viewed party identification as a fixed and stable political characteristic (Campbell et al. 1960). But the swings over the past 40 or 50 years have convinced some political scientists that party loyalty is more fluid, with party affiliation shifting not just over the course of a lifetime but even within a single electoral season (Allsop and Weisberg 1988).

What explains such shifts in partisan loyalty? Research points to no single explanation but to a combination of factors. Key is the rise of candidate-centered (as opposed to party-centered) election campaigns and the rise of the electronic media. Candidates can make ideological and issue appeals directly to voters through television and radio ads, and this direct connection between candidate and voter may weaken party loyalties (Rapoport 1997). Another explanation is that party loyalty underwent a period of ideological and regional realignment in the 1970s and 1980s (Abramowitz and Saunders 1998). The argument here is that conservative Democrats, especially in the South, slowly shifted to the Republican Party, which traditionally reflects a more conservative ideology. (Southern states, remember, are reliably red states.)

The most recent research suggests that, once established, partisan loyalty is fairly resistant to change, though the intensity of party loyalty can wax and wane depending on a particular set of life experiences or on the context of a particular election. Roughly three in four voters express the same party identification from one presidential election to another. That means a quarter do shift party loyalty, but most of these are weak partisans to begin with (Lewis-Beck et al. 2008, 142). Regardless of what explains shifts in party loyalty, party identification has consistently remained the most reliable predictor of voter choice in presidential elections (Abramson, Aldrich, and Rohde 1999, 174).

Candidate Image

Voter perceptions of the qualities of a candidate are known as **candidate image** (Miller and Levitin 1976). Early studies viewed candidate image as an irrational basis for vote choice because these perceptions are often based on gut-level responses to things such as physical appearance, sense of humor, and family background. These factors were seen as a poor basis for making an informed, issue-based voting decision (Budesheim and DePaola 1994; Goren 1997).

Political scientists, however, also recognized that candidate image could play an incredibly important role in determining vote choice. The candidate viewed as a strong leader or as having high levels of integrity is more likely to gain the confidence of citizens and their votes, regardless of the person's knowledge and experience. The importance of candidate image has increased with the rise of television as the primary source of political information. Television is a passive and visual medium not well suited to in-depth coverage of policy issues and thus tends to elevate the importance of the personal and the symbolic (Carlin 1992; Patterson 1984). Not surprisingly, the personal and the symbolic have thus become a central focus of election campaigns. Television appearances and advertising are often centered on shaping image, because they are a way to resonate with viewers' values and emotions and to suitably project a presidential image (Carlin 1992; Kern and Just 1995; Schutz 1995).

In 2012 and 2016, for example, the major party presidential nominees had contrasting image problems. Obama, in 2012, was seen as empathetic, likable, and in touch with the concerns of regular folks, but lingering economic doldrums raised questions about his effectiveness as an executive. Supporters of Republican Mitt Romney championed his successful business career as evidence of his strengths as an executive, but they worried about his image as too calculating and too out of

candidate image Voters' perceptions of a candidate's qualities.

touch with the lives and concerns of the average Joe. In 2016 Republican nominee Donald Trump's campaign drew support from his image as a political outsider, a disrupter who would upend the status quo. The downside is that he was also widely viewed as inexperienced, reckless, and willing to share whatever was on his mind through an impolitic Tweet storm. In contrast, Democratic nominee Hillary Clinton was broadly seen as experienced and a steady hand, but her handling of an e-mail scandal reinforced a reputation for trying to cover up unpleasant news, for not being transparent or even truthful, an image problem she was never able to shake.

In contests for Congress, candidate image is even more important than in presidential contests. People tend to evaluate members of Congress primarily on personal characteristics and qualifications, as well as devotion to district services and local issues. Those who hold office are well aware of this and devote a lot of energy to burnishing their image and "bringing home the bacon" by getting federal dollars for projects and programs in their districts. In voting terms, this adds up to a huge advantage for incumbents (G. Jacobson 2001). Though voters tend to dislike the institution of Congress, they tend to like their own representatives (Hibbing and Theiss-Morse 1995, 45).

Issues

In their analysis of voting behaviors in the 1950s, Angus Campbell and his associates proposed a set of criteria to gauge the importance of issues on voting choices (Campbell et al. 1960). They argued that issues can influence a voting decision only if three conditions are present:

1. The voter must be aware that the issues exist.
2. The issues must be of personal concern to the voter.
3. The voter must perceive that one candidate better represents his or her own thinking on the issues.

When they analyzed voting decisions in the 1952 and 1956 presidential elections, Campbell and his colleagues found these criteria were rarely met: They judged that less than one-third of the electorate voted on the basis of issues. But subsequent research suggests there is more potential for issue-based voting than the highly influential work of Campbell's team suggests. For example, an analysis of the 2000 and 2004 presidential elections using the same Michigan model approach as Campbell and associates found polarization over issues to be an important component of voting behavior (Lewis-Beck et al. 2008).

In contrast to the mid-twentieth century, voters in the early twenty-first century seem to have more fundamental differences on issue preferences, and these differences are reflected in their votes. But it is not just a difference in political eras—the consensual 1950s versus the polarized 2000s—that makes issues important to voting behavior. A key factor is how issues play out in a campaign. If there are clear issue differences between the candidates, and if these issues are a central part of the campaign debate, then voters are more likely to pass the "issue test" suggested by Campbell and his colleagues regardless of what era the election takes place in (Abramson, Aldrich, and Rohde 1999, 132).

Some scholars view this issue test as an overly stringent basis for judging the importance of issues to vote choice. Morris Fiorina (1981) suggests that there are two basic types of issue voting. **Retrospective voting** is based on evaluations of the past performance of the candidate; if voters feel an incumbent has done a good job, they are inclined to support that incumbent at the polls. **Prospective voting** is based on how well a voter believes a candidate will perform once he or she is in office. In practice, voters make both retrospective and prospective judgments, but retrospective assessments seem to be stronger and more influential. In terms of issues, voters seem to use the performance of the incumbent "as a starting point for comparing the major contenders" (Abramson, Aldrich, and Rohde 1999, 57).

VOTING BEHAVIOR AND THE OPERATION OF THE AMERICAN POLITICAL SYSTEM

The political system must balance two necessary but often conflicting qualities: stability and change. Without stability and predictability, the political system would have difficulty making binding decisions about who gets what; without change and openness to new demands, the system risks becoming stagnant and illegitimate.

Elections help the political system achieve this delicate balance because they are driven by both long-term and short-term forces. Long-term forces such as party loyalty or incumbency advantage in congressional campaigns have similar effects across a number of elections; short-term forces such as dramatic events or hot new issues influence outcomes in one or two elections. The former produces stability: Most members of Congress, for example, serve multiple terms and provide institutional memory. The latter allows the system to adapt to new events and changing issues; for example, every election brings a significant number of new representatives to Congress, and occasionally this turnover results in the minority party becoming the majority party.

For the most part, long-term forces prevail in elections. An election in which the long-term partisan orientation of the electorate keeps the status quo, at least in terms of which party is in power, is known as a **maintaining election**. When long-term forces give way to short-term forces, what was the minority party prior to the election can become the majority party after the election—such elections are called **deviating elections**. If the subsequent election returns the traditional majority party to power, that election is called a **reinstating election**.

Maintaining, deviating, and reinstating elections are all part of the ebb and flow of democracy and represent long-term stability. Occasionally, however, an election brings about long-term change. The minority party wins an election, but it is not

retrospective voting Voting that is based on an individual's evaluation of the past performance of a candidate.

prospective voting Voting that is based on an individual's estimation of how well a candidate will perform duties in the future.

maintaining election An election in which the traditional majority party maintains power based on the long-standing partisan orientation of the voters.

deviating election An election in which the minority party is able to overcome the long-standing partisan orientation of the public based on temporary or short-term forces.

reinstating election An election in which the majority party regains power after a deviating election.

followed by a reinstating election; instead, the new majority stays in power for a number of elections. An election that brings about such a major political change is known as a **realigning election** or a critical election. Such elections are rare; they require a minority party to become the majority party and maintain that majority over the long term. Typically, realigning elections are a product of two forces: An event or crisis spawns issues that prompt blocs of voters to switch their party loyalties, and new voters are mobilized and disproportionately favor the minority party.

Realigning elections in U.S. history, however, are rare. The last undisputed realigning election was in 1932. In that year, the majority Republican Party was displaced by the Democratic Party for a long time. This realignment occurred because voters viewed Republicans as out of touch and not paying enough attention to the needs of immigrant and low-income groups who suffered mightily during the Great Depression. The latter event allowed the Democratic Party to put together a coalition of southerners, ethnic minorities, Catholics, Jews, the poor, urban blue-collar workers, and intellectuals. This coalition (known as the New Deal coalition) sustained the Democratic Party as the majority party in Congress, with relatively few interruptions, until the mid-1990s.

Contemporary Realignment?

Although there have been significant electoral changes over the last 30 years, there is no consensus about whether they add up to a realignment. The New Deal coalition has clearly collapsed, and that has benefited Republicans. Some argue that 1980 should be treated as a realigning election. In that year, Republican Ronald Reagan defeated incumbent Democrat Jimmy Carter, and Republicans made significant gains in the House and won the Senate outright. Most reject 1980 as a realigning election: Republicans failed to win control of both houses of Congress that year, and Democrats came back to win the White House with the election of Bill Clinton in 1992. Since then, Republicans and Democrats have swapped control of the White House and of both houses of Congress on multiple occasions.

What 1980 undoubtedly did make clear is that the New Deal coalition was fraying as a reliable basis of Democratic electoral power. In 1980, groups that traditionally had voted Democratic for 50 years shifted their support to the Republican nominee in large numbers. This shift was especially noticeable in the South, where voters began to realign their traditionally conservative ideology with Republican candidates. These changes laid the foundation for a 1990s Republican resurgence. In 1994 Republicans gained control of the House and Senate for the first time since 1953. Six years later, George W. Bush became the first Republican president in nearly 50 years to enjoy same-party control of both houses of Congress.

The Republican majority that emerged in the 1980s and 1990s, however, was never overwhelming. In the 2000 election, Bush won the presidency while actually losing the popular vote. Control of the U.S. Senate was so narrow in the early years of Bush's term that the defection of a single senator—Jim Jeffords of Vermont—from the Republican Party was enough to temporarily let Democrats regain control of the upper chamber. In the 2006 midterm elections, Democrats

realigning election An election in which the minority party is able to build a relatively stable coalition to win election, and this coalition endures over a series of elections.

ousted the GOP as the majority party and took control of both the House and the Senate. Republicans had a disastrous 2008 electoral campaign, as Democrats took the White House and majorities in both houses of Congress. Those majorities, however, were under almost immediate assault. In 2010 Republicans, who just two years earlier had been hammered at the ballot box, came back with a vengeance, slicing the Democratic majority in the U.S. Senate, retaking control of the House of Representatives, and scoring a string of smashing electoral victories at the state level. Yet Republican fortunes dipped again in 2012; not only did they fail to gain the White House, they lost seats in both houses of Congress. Though the GOP did retain its majority in the House, even here the news was not all good. Not only did Republicans see their House majority shrink, but in 2012 more people actually voted for Democratic House candidates than Republican House candidates. Republicans bounced back in 2014. They expanded their majority in the House, and they regained the majority in the Senate by winning nine Democratic-held seats. In 2016 the Democratic nominee again won the popular vote, but failed to win in the Electoral College, and while Republicans retained their control of both houses of Congress, Democrats chipped away at the size of their majorities. All this volatility from election cycle to election cycle seems to reflect only one consistent lesson: Voters are not particularly happy with either major political party.

CHAPTER ELEVEN
Top 10 Takeaway Points

1. Representative democracy rests on the notion that ordinary people have the right to influence decisions about who gets what. Participation in making those binding decisions upholds the core democratic principles of political freedom and majority rule.

2. There are several forms of political participation, including voting, campaign activities, citizen-initiated contacts with government officials, and local community activities. Voting is the most common and widespread form of political participation.

3. Voter turnout in America is lower than in other Western representative democracies, but participation in other forms of political activity is higher.

4. Voter turnout in the United States has generally declined over time, even as the franchise has expanded. Around the time of the Civil War (1860s), turnout was approximately 80 percent. In the 1950s and 1960s, it was more than 60 percent. Turnout in presidential elections during the 1980s and 1990s was below 60 percent. Turnout rose above 60 percent in recent presidential elections, but it is not clear whether this pattern will continue.

5. Turnout is lower in the United States because various elements of the U.S. election system impose higher barriers to voting than are found in other democracies. Elements of the American political system that might cause low turnout include voting laws, voter registration practices, the two-party system, and the scheduling and number of elections.

6. Some people participate in politics, and some people do not. An individual's desire and ability to politically participate are affected by socioeconomic status, psychological engagement with politics, political context, resources necessary to participate (free time, money, and civic skills), and group characteristics (age, gender, and race).

7. Political scientists are interested in explaining the choices voters make: For example, why do some people vote for Democrats and others vote for Republicans? Three theories have dominated the search for an explanation of vote choice: the sociological model, the social-psychological model, and the rational choice model. The sociological model uses group-level variables to explain voter behavior. The social-psychological model focuses on individual attitudes. The rational choice model views the decision to vote and the decision of whom to vote for as the product of an individual cost–benefit analysis.

8. Elections turn on both short-term forces (such as the candidates and issues associated with a particular election) and long-term forces (such as stable party loyalties within the electorate).

9. An election that brings about major political change over the long term is called a realigning election.

10. Significant electoral changes over the last 25 years have frayed the Democrats' New Deal coalition and aided Republicans, but there has been no long-term realignment to the GOP.

CHAPTER ELEVEN
Key Terms and Cases

allegiant, 402
candidate image, 415
deviating election, 417
franchise, 392
maintaining election, 417
midterm elections, 394
mobilization, 403

political alienation, 402
political efficacy, 402
political participation, 389
prospective voting, 417
rational choice model, 411
realigning election, 418
reinstating election, 417

retrospective voting, 417
social-psychological model (Michigan model), 410
socioeconomic status (SES), 401
sociological model (Columbia model), 408
voter turnout, 394

PART III

Official Decision Making

12 CONGRESS

KEY QUESTIONS

What does Congress do?

How is Congress organized?

How does the organization of Congress affect what it does?

© Ron Edmonds/AP Photo

AMERICANS DON'T LIKE THEIR CONGRESS very much. In the decade between 2007 and 2017 less than one in five Americans approved of the job Congress was doing (Gallup 2017). In 2017, nearly as many Americans expressed confidence in Russian President Vladimir Putin as in their own government (NPR/PBS 2017; Vice 2017), and only about a quarter of voters think members of Congress deserve to get reelected (Gallup 2016). This presents a paradox. Congress, especially the House of Representatives, is the governmental institution that is supposed to be the closest and most responsive to the will of the people. If most Americans are dissatisfied with the way "the people's branch" is doing its job, doesn't that imply that America's most democratic institution is failing? Maybe. Maybe not.

In general, Americans strongly disapprove of Congress, but have considerably higher opinions of their own representatives (see Figure 12.1). What could explain this? The short answer is that many people believe that there is broad agreement on the problems facing the nation and how to solve them. Their own representative shares their view, so it must be all those other bickering jerks in Congress that are preventing quick action to effectively address the nation's problems (Hibbing and Theiss-Morse 1995). This suggests that Americans lack a basic understanding of how Congress works. The 535 members of Congress have differing goals and preferences, and they work in an institution governed by rules that could be described as Byzantine. Moreover, our representatives actually contribute to popular misperceptions. Rather than educate constituents about how Congress works and why, they often pander to popular (and misinformed) perceptions. As political scientist Richard Fenno observed, "members run for Congress by running against Congress" (1978, 168).

As discussed in Chapter 9, the voice of the people on most issues is a jarring cacophony of conflict. There is no broad consensus on what government should do to solve the nation's problems, or even on what those problems are. Filtering these conflicting opinions through an institution as large and as complex as the U.S. Congress will not turn discord into harmony. Perhaps all the argument and debate in Congress is just a reflection of the

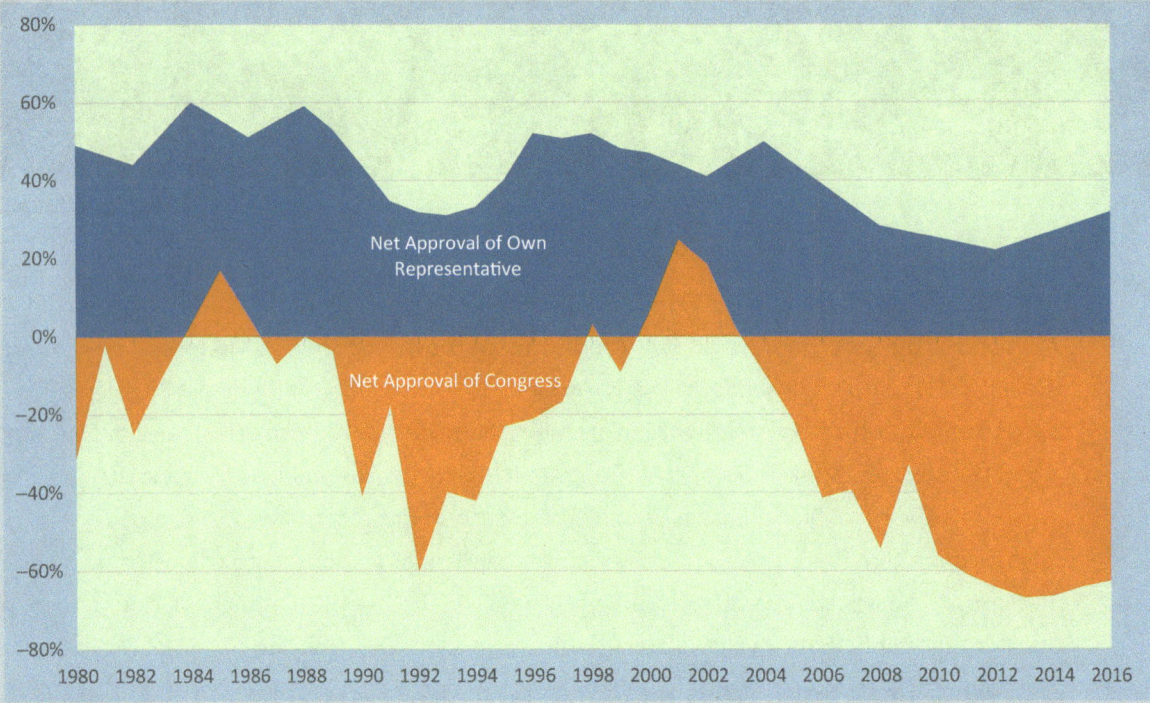

FIGURE 12.1 Americans Don't Like Their Congress but They Do Like Their Own Representative

Source: Approval of Congress: annual averages of all polls available in the year from Gallup Poll and various other news organizations and polling houses. Approval of respondents' own representative from the American National Election Study; approval of own representative interpolated for years between quadrennial ANES studies in 2004, 2008, 2012, and 2016.

diverse and often conflicting opinions in the public. If so, Congress does exactly what it was designed to do.

Some might be surprised by this conclusion. But Americans often fail to grasp the wide variety of functions Congress serves and how the institution connects its business to the broader political arena. In this chapter, we analyze what Congress is supposed to do, who does it, how it is done, and why. The chapter seeks to provide a foundation for judging whether Congress is fulfilling its democratic responsibilities.

THE CONCEPT OF THE U.S. CONGRESS

The U.S. Congress is a type of legislature. In general, a **legislature** can be defined as a deliberative council that has the authority to make and repeal laws. In representative democracies, ordinary citizens elect legislators to represent them. There are two general types of legislatures in representative democracies: (1) **parliamentary systems** in which the majority party in the legislature selects its leader to be chief executive, as in the British Parliament and prime minister; and (2) **presidential systems** in which citizens independently elect representatives in the legislature and the chief executive, as in the U.S. Congress and president.

Calling the American national legislature "Congress" follows the precedent of its historical antecedents—the First and Second Continental Congresses and the Congress under the Articles of Confederation. The term *congress* means "a coming together" (Ayto 1990, 131). Traditionally, the term referred to a meeting of representatives of independent organizations (e.g., trade unions, states, and nations) to discuss some problem. Hence, the Continental Congresses were meetings of delegates representing the colonies. The unicameral Congress under the Articles of Confederation represented sovereign states, not the people of those states. As political scientist Charles Stewart observes, this Congress was "an assembly of ambassadors" (2005, 8). Laws passed by Congress under the Articles were not binding on the people directly, but rather were requests to the states to take some action (which the states routinely ignored). The Congress created by the current Constitution does represent the people, and its laws are directly binding on the people. Nevertheless, representation is still tied to states—every state is guaranteed at least one representative in the House and two in the Senate (originally, senators were elected by state legislatures) and electors chosen by states elect the president. Moreover, the federal system retains the status of states as self-governing units, though federal laws take precedence over state constitutions and laws if there is a conflict. Continued use of the term for the bicameral Congress created by the current constitution recognizes the special status of states in this federal system.

Congress is both a representative institution and a policymaking institution. The purpose of Congress, therefore, is twofold: to represent the needs and interests of ordinary people and to translate those needs and wishes into laws that determine who gets what. To assess whether Congress is achieving this dual purpose, it is necessary to understand its responsibilities within the American political system.

legislature A deliberative council that has the authority to make and repeal laws. In representative democracies, ordinary citizens elect legislators to represent them.

parliamentary system An electoral system in which the party holding the majority of seats in the legislature selects the chief executive.

presidential system A political system in which the chief executive and the legislature are elected independently.

RESPONSIBILITIES OF CONGRESS

The national legislature is charged with a dizzying number of tasks. These tasks can be grouped into primary and secondary responsibilities. Primary responsibilities are performed on a continuous basis and consume the greatest share of members' time. Secondary responsibilities are not necessarily less important; these duties can be essential to achieving Congress's dual purpose. They are called secondary because they come up sporadically and constitute a smaller proportion of the legislator's workload.

Primary Responsibilities

Congress's two primary responsibilities are lawmaking and representing constituents.

Lawmaking

The legislature's foremost responsibility is enacting laws that address the major problems and concerns of American society. **Lawmaking** includes passing the laws and then overseeing government administration of those laws. For example, the Clean Air Act of 1990 "would have a direct impact on the lives of nearly all Americans" because it "was designed to improve the quality of the air we breathe. It would have wide-ranging impacts on health, transportation, and the economy" (R. Cohen 1995, 4). This particular legislation is instructive not only because of its substance but also because it shows Congress at its best and at its worst.

On the positive side, there was clear public support for cleaning up the air, and the legislative process managed to incorporate a diverse set of viewpoints on a divisive set of topics to produce a law that had strong majority support. This is no small achievement. Yet the process of lawmaking was agonizingly slow: The bill was 13 years in the making. Parochial protectionism, special interest meddling, and inter- and intra-party disagreements stalled the process at various points (see R. Cohen 1995). The Clean Air Act was not unique in this sense. Virtually every piece of major legislation has to run a similar gauntlet.

Passing laws to ameliorate social problems is a central function of Congress and an essential step in the policymaking process. The role Congress plays in the policymaking process, however, has changed over the course of the nation's history. The policymaking process (discussed in more detail in Chapter 16) involves several steps:

1. *Agenda setting:* Government identifies the list of issues and problems to which it will pay attention.

---

lawmaking A legislature's power to enact laws that address major problems and then to oversee government administration of those laws.

2. *Policy formulation and adoption:* Government considers various solutions and formally approves a particular one.
3. *Policy implementation:* Government translates the law into action.
4. *Policy evaluation:* Government and nongovernment actors assess the successes and problems of public policies (Ripley 1988, 48–55).

The goal of separation of powers in the Constitution was to make legislative and executive powers independent, which suggests that Congress would have primary responsibility for steps 1 and 2 in the policy process, and the president would have primary responsibility for steps 3 and 4. This division of responsibilities has become less clear-cut over time.

Congress continues to be a major agenda setter, but the legislative branch has come to expect the president to take the lead in initiating policy proposals. Since the 1950s, the president has initiated about one-third of the most important bills considered in Congress (Edwards and Barrett 2000, 122). Congress, of course, does not automatically pass the president's initiatives. Some presidential proposals do not pass, and those that do are often changed substantially as they work their way through the legislative process.

Congress has also delegated substantial lawmaking powers to the executive branch. Congress tends to pass laws that set broad goals and guidelines for dealing with a problem, while leaving the specifics of implementation to executive branch agencies. Filling in these details is known as rulemaking, a little-known form of lawmaking discussed in Chapter 14.

Although Congress has delegated significant legislative power to the executive branch, it has compensated by extending its lawmaking authority to the implementation of policies. The primary way Congress has extended its lawmaking power is through **legislative oversight of administration**, which refers to a variety of tools that Congress uses to control the administrative arm of government. Congressional oversight is often considered another primary function of Congress. Although it is certainly a vitally important activity, just as policymaking has come to mean more than passing laws, we believe oversight of the executive is better viewed as an essential part of lawmaking. Legislative oversight tools (discussed in more detail in Chapter 14) include the power to do the following:

- Create or abolish executive branch agencies
- Assign these agencies particular program responsibilities
- Provide or withhold funding for governmental programs
- Confirm or not confirm presidential appointments to the major administrative positions in the executive branch

legislative oversight of administration A variety of tools Congress uses to control administrative agencies, including creating or abolishing agencies, assigning program responsibilities, providing funds, and confirming presidential appointments.

Representation

The other primary responsibility of Congress is representation. **Representation** is a complex relationship that involves responding to constituents' needs and

representation The relationship between elected officials and the people who put them in office, involving the extent to which officials are responsive to the people.

demands and informing and educating the public. Political scientists Heinz Eulau and Paul Karps (1977) identify four types of responsiveness that illustrate some of the complexity of representation: policy responsiveness, service responsiveness, allocation responsiveness, and symbolic responsiveness.

The first and most obvious part of representation is **policy responsiveness**—that is, the extent to which the policymaking behavior of the representative is congruent with the preferences of constituents. In the most simplistic terms, representatives are supposed to vote the way their constituents want them to vote. Political science research finds that few citizens know how their representatives vote on issues before Congress. Absent clear expression of constituents' preferences, partisanship and ideology are the primary predictors of how members of Congress vote on roll calls.

Does this mean that members of Congress are failing as representatives? Not necessarily. Candidates who win election to Congress tend to reflect the politics and cultures of their constituencies. Consequently, representatives and constituents share many values, including party and policy preferences. Some districts are composed of voters who are mostly Democrats with preferences for liberal policies; these districts tend to elect liberal Democrats. Other districts are mostly Republicans with more conservative preferences, and they send conservative Republicans to Congress. On the most salient issues, representatives tend to follow constituency preferences. Constituents may know little about most policy proposals before Congress, but they are generally aware of high-profile policy issues. Failure to follow constituency preferences on these salient matters invites a negative response at the polls. Thus, there is likely to be substantial policy congruence between most representatives in Congress and their constituents.

A second component of representation is **service responsiveness**, which refers to the variety of tasks that legislators perform for constituents who request assistance in dealing with the federal government. For instance, an elderly constituent might want information about Social Security benefits, or the mayor of a small city may ask for help in applying for a federal grant for a water treatment facility. These activities are known as **casework**. In performing casework, members of Congress act as intermediaries between constituents and administrative agencies in the executive branch.

A third component of representation is **allocation responsiveness**. Members of Congress are notorious for using their position to see that their state or district gets a share of the benefits of government programs for roads, dams, government buildings, federal grants to local police and fire departments, support for agricultural commodities, and so on. Political scientists refer to such allocations as **distributive benefits**—that is, government expenditures and programs that concentrate benefits in specific geographical areas such as states or congressional districts but for which the costs are spread across the entire population (Evans 2004; Lowi 1969). These are also pejoratively called **pork-barrel benefits**, a term first used in this context in the mid-nineteenth century to describe projects viewed as a waste of tax dollars that serve no purpose other than to aid the reelection of a single incumbent. Although reelection is a primary reason that members of Congress pursue

---

policy responsiveness The amount of agreement between the people represented and their elected officials on policy issues.

service responsiveness Representation that takes the form of the tasks legislators perform based on the requests and needs of their constituents.

casework Activities of members of Congress to act as intermediaries and help private individuals who are having problems with the administrative agencies in the executive branch. These activities are service responsiveness.

allocation responsiveness Representation that takes the form of members of Congress ensuring that their district gets a share of federal benefits.

distributive benefits Government expenditures and programs that concentrate benefits in specific geographical areas such as states or congressional districts for which the costs are spread across the entire population. These benefits are allocation responsiveness.

pork-barrel benefits Government-sponsored projects that bring economic benefits to a Congress member's state or district. This is a pejorative term first used in the mid-nineteenth century to describe projects viewed as a waste of tax dollars that serve no purpose other than to aid the reelection of a single incumbent.

distributive programs, objectively identifying what is wasteful "pork" and what genuinely serves the public interest is a difficult task. By securing these allocations, a representative anticipates and responds to the needs of his or her constituency. Research by political scientist Diana Evans shows that leaders in Congress also use distributive benefits "as a sort of currency to purchase legislators' votes" in order "to build the majority coalitions necessary to pass broad-based, general interest legislation" (2004, 2).

The three types of representation discussed so far involve delivering some tangible benefit—a vote consistent with constituents' preferences, help with bureaucratic red tape, or government expenditures to assist the district. The fourth type of representation—symbolic responsiveness—draws attention to a psychological component of representation. **Symbolic responsiveness** includes activities that use broad "political symbols in order to generate and maintain trust or support" among constituents (Eulau and Karps 1977, 246). Members of Congress develop close, cordial relations with their constituents. They spend time in the district to show that they are part of the constituency and that they are "at home" there. Richard Fenno, one of the nation's foremost authorities on Congress, refers to these activities as **home style**, which is the way members of Congress present themselves to the various parts of their constituency and explain their Washington activities (Fenno 1978). Typically, members develop home styles that fit their constituencies. A member who represents a strongly partisan constituency, for example, might adopt a policy-oriented home style, whereas a member from a politically diverse constituency might adopt a home style that emphasizes constituency service.

Fenno found that "constituency" is a complex concept. Members of Congress view their constituencies like "a nest of concentric circles" (1978, 1): the geographical constituency, the reelection constituency, the primary constituency, and the personal constituency. The largest circle is the **geographical constituency**, which consists of everyone and everything within the boundaries of the member's House district. Nested within the geographical constituency is the **reelection constituency**, which is composed of the people in the district whom the member can count on for support. The **primary constituency** is a smaller number of the member's strongest, mostly partisan supporters. An even smaller number of intimate friends, advisors, and confidants are viewed as the **personal constituency**. A member's behavior will vary depending on which constituency he or she is interacting with.

Members of Congress sometimes have to choose between the preferences of constituents and positions taken by the national party. People march during a protest against the Republican bill in the U.S. Senate to replace President Barack Obama's healthcare law Tuesday, June 27, 2017, in Salt Lake City. Demonstrators with Utah's Disabled Rights Action Committee chanted and carried signs while blocking State Street Tuesday afternoon. Utah protesters criticized Utah Republican Senator Orrin Hatch for supporting the bill and say it will cut life-saving Medicaid services and other health protections.
© Rick Bowmer/AP Photo

symbolic responsiveness A congressional member's efforts to use political symbols to generate trust and support among the voters.

home style The way a member of Congress behaves, explains his or her legislative actions, and presents himself or herself in the home district.

geographical constituency Everyone and everything within the geographical boundaries of a congressional member's House district.

reelection constituency The people within a Congress member's House district who can be counted on for support.

primary constituency A member of Congress's strongest, mostly partisan supporters.

personal constituency A small number of intimate friends, advisors, and confidants who support a member of Congress.

The complexity of representation is especially evident when a member of Congress must choose between the preferences of constituents and the dictates of conscience or the best interests of the entire nation. A pork-barrel project might provide economic benefits and be strongly supported within the district, but what if it is an unnecessary drain on the federal treasury? Should a representative choose what the constituents clearly want or what serves the best long-run interests of the nation as a whole? Such conflicts are more common than most people realize, and they raise a basic question about the exact nature of representation. Edmund Burke, a British political philosopher and member of Parliament, argued that representatives should be **trustees** who use their own judgment to make the decisions they feel are appropriate for the interests first of the nation and then of their constituents. In contrast, representatives who adopt a **delegate** role simply do what their constituents want, regardless of whether those wants are in the public interest. These contrasting philosophies suggest different decisions: The delegate will vote for the pork-barrel project; the trustee will not (and may face the consequences during the next election). In reality, the philosophical divide is not quite so clear, and representatives often adopt a mix of both delegate and trustee roles; this type of representative is a **politico**.

Representation is a two-way concept. The four components of representation discussed so far view the relationship as one that flows from constituents to representative. Another aspect of representation focuses on the relationship that flows the other way, from representative to constituent. This aspect is the representative's duty to lead by informing and educating the public.

Scholars have long recognized that a central obligation of representatives is to inform the public about the major issues facing the country and the options for dealing with them (W. Wilson 1885). Thus, when Congress holds hearings on Social Security, pollution, drugs, or the U.S response to an international conflict, it is helping to educate and inform the American people about the problems on the nation's agenda and the policies that might deal with them. Such activities may be intended to produce an electoral advantage, but they also help inform citizens.

Performing the lawmaking and representative functions has important spillover effects. By serving the needs of constituents, lawmakers help develop loyalty and allegiance of the public to the political system. The give-and-take of the legislative process accommodates competing demands, which helps ensure that final decisions are acceptable to concerned parties. This accommodation helps legitimize the political system so that citizens in general are willing to abide by the rules and regulations developed by government. Political scientists have produced an enormous amount of research to explain how Congress works. It's not hard to figure out why. Congress is a complex institution with abundant data available over a long period of time to test important theories about politics. Theory building is an effort to simplify a complex process so we can understand how it works—to see the forest instead of a bunch of trees.

---

trustee A representative who uses his or her own judgment to make decisions promoting the best interests of the nation as a whole, with the particular interests of constituents remaining a secondary concern.

delegate A representative who makes legislative decisions based on the interests and views of his or her constituents, regardless of personal preference.

politico A representative whose philosophy of representation is a mix of both delegate and trustee. *See also* delegate and trustee.

APPLYING THE FRAMEWORKS

EXPLAINING WHY CONGRESS DOES WHAT IT DOES

How can we explain why members of Congress (MCs) do what they do? Early studies used sociological theory to explain congressional behavior. Two classic examples are Donald Matthews' (1960) study of the U.S. Senate and Richard Fenno's (1966) study of the House Appropriations Committee. Interviews with members indicated that several *norms*—expected patterns of behavior that members agree upon—allowed Congress to work smoothly. These include the apprenticeship norm (junior members remain in the background and learn from senior members), the deference norm (members defer to committee expertise), and the reciprocity norm (you do favors for colleagues and expect them to repay the favor). Members who fail to observe these norms—"mavericks"—lose the respect of their colleagues and are ineffective legislators (Fenno 1966; Matthews 1960).

Although sociological theories provided important insights, political scientists have found that rational choice theory offers more convincing explanations of congressional behavior. Rational choice models assume that MCs are motivated by three goals—reelection, power, good public policy—and they make choices intended to achieve these goals. Thus, members trade votes to get their pet projects adopted not because the norms of Congress prescribe this behavior, but because these are rational choices to achieve their goals (Hall 1996). There are several models of congressional behavior anchored in rational choice theory: the distributive model, the informational model, and the partisan model.

The Distributive Model
David Mayhew (1974) was the first political scientist to explicitly apply the rational actor model to analyze Congress. He assumes that MCs are "single-minded seekers of reelection" and asks what types of activity this goal implies (Mayhew 1974, 5). He highlights three activities intended to improve the odds of reelection: advertising, position taking, and credit claiming. *Advertising* includes sending newsletters to constituents and making frequent trips home to create a favorable image.

Position taking means making judgmental statements that will please constituents. Members choose topics to match the interests of constituents. Advertising and position taking are mostly symbolic representation and do not require any actual policymaking.

Credit claiming means taking credit for delivering government benefits. Distributive or "pork-barrel" projects are one way for members to make a credible claim that they are responsible for getting benefits for their constituents. This is why MCs seek membership on committees with jurisdiction over policies that are most important to their districts.

The Informational Model
Rational decision making requires information about the costs and benefits of alternative policies. MCs cannot be experts on every policy, so how do they get the information necessary to make rational choices? Keith Krehbiel (1991) suggests that rational legislators create committees with specialized knowledge to supply the necessary information. In this view, committees are agents of the chamber floor. Committees control what information is provided, so committees that are ideologically representative of the whole will provide the most useful information. Committee specialization and reciprocity, therefore, are not the result of norms or the need to enforce logrolls, but the result of a need for accurate information to cast rational votes.

The distributive and informational models do not account for political parties. In recent decades, partisanship has become a much more prominent aspect of Congress.

The Partisan Model
John Aldrich and David Rohde (Aldrich 2011; Aldrich and Rohde 2000; Rohde 1991) developed a partisan model of Congress called Conditional Party Government (CPG) theory (discussed in Chapter 7). They argue that achieving "party government" is *conditional* on the degree of ideological similarity among members

of the majority party. Reelection motivates CPG theory. How much party members agree on policy depends on what voters in their constituencies want. If partisan constituencies in different parts of the country have diverse preferences, representatives reflect that diversity. In this circumstance, party leaders cannot punish members who don't toe the party line, because forcing them to choose party over the folks back home threatens their reelection. But voter preferences may realign so that nearly all members represent similar constituencies.

When the "condition" of ideological similarity is met, the caucus adopts reforms to give party leaders more power to enact issues on the party's agenda on which there is consensus. Thus, the underlying power relationship between leaders and rank-and-file is bottom-up rather than top-down: Members empower leaders to take strong action to achieve party goals because they all represent similar electoral coalitions, and supporting the party does not threaten reelection. A consequence of conditional party government is party polarization. CPG theory focuses on the majority party—when policy preferences (or ideology) are homogeneous, the majority party becomes more internally cohesive. But if the majority party becomes more disciplined, the minority party is also likely to become more internally cohesive, and the parties move farther apart, or polarize. Another version of partisan theory is "cartel theory." Gary Cox and Mathew McCubbins (1993) view the majority party as a "legislative cartel" that uses its power to stack committees and control the policy agenda to increase the chances of its members' reelections. This model is consistent with CPG theory.

Discussion Questions

1. Consider a controversial issue Congress has grappled with recently—tax reform, a government shutdown, immigration, etc. Which of the theoretical models described above do you think does the better job of explaining the choices made by members of Congress in regards to that issue?
2. Consider a situation where a member of Congress wants to vote against a bill and his or her party has taken a strong stand for that bill. Examine this situation through each of the theories described above. Do they predict how this member of Congress will vote and why?

Secondary Responsibilities

Secondary responsibilities are essential for the overall functioning of the government or the legislative body. They are called secondary not because they are less important, but because they occur only occasionally. These tasks include impeachment, seating and disciplining members, and selecting leaders for the executive branch.

Impeachment

Congress has the power to remove executive and judicial officials of the federal government from their positions through the impeachment process. According to the Constitution, officials subject to removal by congressional action include "the president, the vice president, and all civil officers of the United States" (Article II, Section 4). Federal judges are the only other civil officers who are likely to be impeached; because they serve for life, there is no other practical way to remove them for wrongdoing. Although members of Congress and cabinet secretaries are subject to impeachment, other legal procedures exist to remove these officials for wrongdoing.

Removal through impeachment is a two-step process. The first step is impeachment by the House. To **impeach** means simply to charge or accuse. The House impeaches an official by passing articles of impeachment by a simple majority. The impeachment resolution serves as a formal charge of wrongdoing, similar to an indictment by a grand jury. If articles of impeachment pass, the process continues to the second stage: trial in the Senate. Members of the Senate sit as a jury to hear the evidence and decide whether to acquit the impeached official or remove him or her from office. The House sends "managers" to serve as prosecutors, and the impeached official is represented by defenders. Conviction and removal from office require a two-thirds vote of the Senate. As president of the Senate, the vice president normally presides over an impeachment trial. But if it is the president who has been impeached, the Constitution designates the chief justice of the Supreme Court to preside at the trial in the Senate. Having the vice president preside over a trial that could elevate him or her to the presidency would be an obvious conflict of interest.[1]

Grounds for impeachment include "treason, bribery, or other high crimes and misdemeanors" (Article II, Section 4). Treason and bribery are straightforward but are rarely the focus of impeachment proceedings. What constitutes "high crimes and misdemeanors" is the subject of some controversy. Kenneth W. Starr, the independent prosecutor whose investigation provided the basis for the impeachment of President Bill Clinton in 1998, once argued that an official could be impeached for poisoning a neighbor's cat (Gettinger 1998). Historically, the bar for impeachment has been set considerably higher, to include wrongdoing that threatens the basic functioning of government in the same way that treason or bribery would. Thus, impeachable offenses may not be limited to illegal acts. If a president were to move to a Middle Eastern country so that he could have several wives, such behavior would surely be impeachable, but it would not be illegal (Black 1974). On the other hand, even serious illegal acts are not necessarily sufficient grounds for removing a president from office. When Vice President Aaron Burr shot and killed Alexander Hamilton, Burr was indicted for murder in two states, but he never faced impeachment.

Impeachment is as much a political process as a legal one. As a member of Congress, Republican Gerald Ford of Michigan said that an impeachable offense is "whatever a majority of the House of Representatives considers it to be at a given moment in history" (Gettinger 1998, 565). Ford was ridiculed at the time, but the impeachment of President Clinton seemed to validate this definition; the House impeached Clinton on a largely partisan vote.

The Senate is likely to prevent the bar from being lowered too far. Senators have broader constituencies than House members, and the Senate has a special

---

[1] Senators take an oath to try the case impartially, but impeachment is a political process. Conflicts of interest are inevitable. In the impeachment trial of President Andrew Johnson in 1868, Senator Benjamin F. Wade (R-OH), president pro tempore of the Senate, took part in the trial and voted for conviction. Since there was no vice president, Wade was in line to become president. President Johnson's son-in-law, Senator David T. Patterson (D-TN), also participated; he voted to acquit. Senator Barbara Boxer (D-CA) participated in the Senate trial of President Clinton. Her daughter is married to Hillary Clinton's brother. In an ordinary judicial trial, individuals with such conflicts would be excluded.

impeach To charge or accuse.

President Bill Clinton was impeached by the House of Representatives in December 1998 on charges of perjury and obstruction of justice, and subsequently tried by the U.S. Senate. Clinton was acquitted in February 1999 when the Senate failed to muster the two-thirds majority required to convict and remove a federal official from office.

© Getty Images

status and responsibility under the Constitution that most senators take seriously. The supermajority vote (two-thirds rather than one-half plus one) required to convict and remove an official from office also reduces the chances that a president could be removed for solely partisan purposes.

Impeachment is rare. Only 17 officials have been impeached so far. Two presidents—Bill Clinton and Andrew Johnson—were formally impeached, though neither was removed from office. President Nixon resigned prior to the House vote on the articles of impeachment rather than face an almost-certain Senate trial. Most of the other impeached officials were federal judges; eight were convicted and removed from office.

Seating and Disciplining Members

Each chamber also has power over the seating and disciplining of its members. Thus, both the House and the Senate have the authority to judge the fairness of elections. Defeated candidates sometimes challenge the results of close elections on the grounds of voting irregularities. Although both chambers attempt to investigate and resolve such charges impartially, historically partisan interests have prevailed, with the majority party seating its candidate.

The House and the Senate can also **exclude** or refuse to seat individuals who win elections but do not meet the constitutional qualifications of being U.S. citizens, having residence in the state, and being at least 25 years old for House members and 30 years old for senators. Until 1969, each chamber occasionally used exclusion as a disciplinary tool against otherwise-qualified individuals who were disloyal, such as those who supported secession during the Civil War or who were charged with crimes or misconduct. The Supreme Court ended this practice in *Powell v. McCormack* (1969), ruling that a duly elected member could be excluded only for failure to meet constitutional qualifications.

Article I, Section 5 of the Constitution also authorizes both chambers to discipline sitting members for illegal or unethical behavior, though both are loath to exercise this power. Because most members do not relish the task of judging their colleagues, such formal actions are reserved for the most egregious cases. There are several penalties available, depending on the nature and seriousness of the wrongdoing: expulsion, censure or reprimand, and fine.

The most serious punishment, **expulsion**, requires a two-thirds vote and is rarely used. Several members were expelled in the 1860s for supporting the Confederacy

exclude The refusal of Congress to seat any candidate who wins election but does not meet the constitutional requirements to hold congressional office.

expulsion The ejection of a member of Congress from office.

in the Civil War, but aside from that, only one senator and one House member have been expelled from Congress. Senator William Blount of Tennessee was expelled in 1876 when it was discovered that he had a plan to provoke the Creek and Cherokee Indians to assist British efforts to conquer the Spanish territory of Florida. The House passed impeachment charges against him, but those charges were dropped because the expulsion had already removed him from office. The House member was Ozzie Myers of New York, who was expelled in 1980 for involvement in a bribery scandal.

The lesser penalties of censure or reprimand and fines require only a simple majority to pass. **Censures and reprimands** are verbal condemnations expressing public disapproval of the member's actions by his or her colleagues. Reprimands sometimes include a fine. In 1997, Speaker Newt Gingrich was reprimanded for violating House ethics rules and fined $300,000 (Katz 1998).

Selecting Leaders for the Executive Branch

Congress is also occasionally involved in matters of leadership selection for the executive branch. As discussed in Chapter 10, if no candidate for president or vice president receives a majority of the electoral votes, the issue is decided by the House in the case of the president, or the Senate in the case of the vice president. Under the Twenty-Fifth Amendment, if the vice presidency becomes vacant, both houses of Congress must approve the president's choice of a new vice president by majority vote. Notice that unlike presidential appointments to judicial and executive branch offices, which must be confirmed only by the Senate, appointment of a new vice president under the Twenty-Fifth Amendment requires approval of both houses of Congress. This procedure has been used twice. The first occasion was when President Richard Nixon nominated Representative Gerald Ford to become vice president after the resignation of Spiro Agnew in 1973. When Nixon resigned in 1974, Ford became president and nominated Nelson Rockefeller to be vice president.

The Senate also plays an important role in staffing positions in the executive branch and judiciary. The president appoints cabinet secretaries and other high-level executive branch personnel, foreign ambassadors, and federal judges with the "advice and consent" of the Senate. There is little Senate advising before the selection, but the consent provision means that the Senate must confirm the president's appointments to these offices by majority vote. Some nominations have run into trouble and have been defeated or withdrawn. However, the Senate has confirmed more than 96 percent of presidents' nominations, and a study found that nominations enjoy a "presumption of success" (Krutz, Fleisher, and Bond 1998). The Senate typically has been inclined to defer to the president's choice, and senators who are opposed to a particular nominee have had a difficult time overcoming this presumption of success. A more recent study suggests that the "presumption of success" does not hold to the same extent it once did, however. As the parties in Congress have become more polarized in recent decades, opponents increasingly

censures and reprimands Verbal condemnations of a member of Congress by the House or Senate, intended to punish bad behavior by expressing the public disapproval of the member's colleagues.

have used Senate rules to block nominations from getting to the floor for an up or down vote (Bond, Fleisher, and Krutz 2009).

Other Policy Responsibilities

Congress also becomes involved in specialized areas of public policymaking. Both houses join in initiating constitutional amendments. The Senate also has special powers in foreign policy: The Senate must ratify treaties negotiated by the president (by two-thirds vote) and confirm ambassadors to foreign countries appointed by the president (by a simple majority). Finally, Congress exercises legal jurisdiction over the District of Columbia.

MEMBERS OF CONGRESS AND THEIR WORLD

To grasp how and why Congress has such a broad social and political effect, it is important to understand not just what Congress does, but who drives the decisions of the legislature. How Congress executes responsibilities and how it shapes the broader social fabric are determined by the 535 men and women who are members of one of the world's most exclusive clubs.

Alexis de Tocqueville, the perceptive French observer of America during the Jacksonian period, referred to the "vulgar demeanor" of the American national legislature. The aristocrats who dominated European legislatures, he argued, were secure in their social positions, less tied to their constituents than to their parties, and more interested in big questions. American legislators derived their social position from service in the assembly, were more tied to their constituents than to their parties, and felt compelled to repeatedly confirm their importance and effectiveness whether there was any basis for such claims or not. Rather than tackle big questions, legislators in America focused on whatever issue was popular, regardless of its substantive merit. "The consequence," Tocqueville wrote, "is that the debates of that great assembly are frequently vague and perplexed and that they seem to drag their slow length along rather than to advance towards a distinct object" (Tocqueville [1835] 1955, 97). Does Tocqueville's analysis accurately portray Congress today? Who, exactly, are the people elected to Congress?

Backgrounds of National Legislators

Tocqueville noted that the national legislature was dominated by lawyers and businessmen, an observation that still holds true today. Although lawyers constitute less than 1 percent of the adult population in the United States, 218 members (about 41 percent) in the 115th Congress (2017–2018) listed law as their occupation. Fifty senators were lawyers, and the proportion of lawyers in the Senate has not fallen below 50 percent since the 1950s. Lawyers are somewhat less prevalent in the House—39 percent of House members in the 115th Congress—and lawyers have not constituted a majority of House members since the 95th Congress (1977–1978) (Manning 2018; Ornstein et al. 2018, tables 1–8, 1–11).

Why so many lawyers? For one thing, the tools of the lawyer's trade are verbal and argumentative facility, negotiation skills, and the ability to analyze statutes and administrative regulations—precisely the talents needed by those who legislate, control the administration, inform the public, and represent constituents. Lawyers are also professionals, which bestows social standing in the community, and their job is to help people with various kinds of problems. For these reasons, lawyers are often regarded as natural legislators.

Businesspeople now rival lawyers as the largest occupational group in Congress—208 (39 percent) members in the 115th Congress listed their occupation as business. People in business have some of the same attributes that provide lawyers with their advantages as legislators—they too tend to have relatively high social status in their communities, and they benefit from the high regard Americans have for entrepreneurs. And 238 members (44 percent) list public service and politics as their occupation.[2]

No other occupation rivals business, public service, or law in the national legislature. The remainder consists of an eclectic mix of educators, doctors, ministers, journalists, farmers, scientists, engineers, several professional entertainers, and four political scientists—Donna Shalala (D-FL), Daniel Lipinski (D-IL), Dave Loebsack (D-IA), and David Price (D-NC).

The similarities of the modern Congress to that of Tocqueville's time extend beyond the career background of its members. The legislature Tocqueville observed was dominated exclusively by white males. This exclusivity has diminished, but not the dominance. In 2010 the U.S. population was about 51 percent female, 13 percent African American, 16 percent Latino, 4.8 percent Asian American, and 0.9 percent Native American. In the House of Representatives in the 115th Congress, 19.3 percent of members were women, 10.6 percent were African American, 9.0 percent were Latino, 3.4 percent were Asian American, and two (0.37 percent) were Native American.[3] The Senate was even less representative of the nation—including only 22 women, three African Americans, five Latinos, three Asian Americans, and no Native Americans.

Although the numbers of women and ethnic minorities in Congress are low in comparison to their proportion in the electorate, they are high in comparison to the historical representation of women and minorities in Congress. These changes suggest that the future composition of Congress may be increasingly different.

Moreover, descriptive representation, in which the legislature reflects the gender and ethnic makeup of society, is only one of several types of representation. As

---

[2] Totals exceed 100 percent because most members list more than one occupation.
[3] This number includes only members who are on the rolls of federally recognized tribes. This does not include Senator Elizabeth Warren (D-MA), who has said that she grew up with family stories about her grandparents having some Cherokee or Delaware blood, but she is not listed on any tribal rolls. The claim provoked controversy during her Senate campaign in 2012, and continued in the 2016 presidential race when Donald Trump tagged her with the nickname "Pocahontas."

Jeannette Rankin.
© Bettmann/CORBIS

discussed in Chapter 10, substantive representation may be more important. Some argue that white male professionals can understand and represent the substantive interests of blue-collar workers, women, ethnic minorities, and the poor in the legislature.

Tenure and Career Patterns

Although the profile of the typical member of Congress has not changed much in the last 200 years, the profile of the typical congressional career has changed dramatically. The most obvious change is that serving in Congress is now a career. In the nineteenth century, a decade was an unusually long time for anyone to be a House member, and serving in the House as a lifetime member was virtually unknown. By the latter half of the twentieth century, the average member of the House of Representatives had been serving for about 10 years, and some members have served much longer (Hibbing 1991).

Tenure has increased for several reasons. Members of Congress are now more likely to run for reelection than they were in the past. In congressional elections since 1946, more than 90 percent of House members have run for reelection, and they are very successful when they run—an average of about 94 percent win reelection (see Figure 10.8). The reelection rate in the Senate is slightly lower—82 percent. Furthermore, government plays a much bigger role in social and economic life than it did before the twentieth century. Serving in Congress has evolved from a part-time job in a part-time body with limited responsibilities to a full-time job in a full-time body with enormous responsibilities (Hibbing 1991, 3).

The rise of congressional careerists may have fueled cynicism toward government. A common view is that the incumbency advantage allows career politicians to ignore the needs of ordinary people and serve the interests of powerful special interests in Washington. The popularity of term limits indicates that many voters are uncomfortable with public service becoming a career unto itself.

Political scientist John Hibbing (1991) conducted a comprehensive analysis of congressional careers. Consistent with the conventional wisdom, Hibbing found that the longer a representative serves in Congress, the less attention he or she pays to constituency matters. The number of trips to the district decreases, and district offices get fewer staffers. Yet he also found that the more senior members of Congress are more effective legislators; as representatives gain experience, they tend to become more active and successful legislators. First-term representatives might spend more time in the district with their constituents, but they are less likely to play a significant role in shaping legislation. Hibbing concluded that term limits are a bad idea and "would likely result in a devastating loss of legislative acumen, expertise, and activity" (1991, 180).

A study by Jeffery Mondak (1995) supports this conclusion. Mondak developed indicators of House members' competence and integrity. He found that members

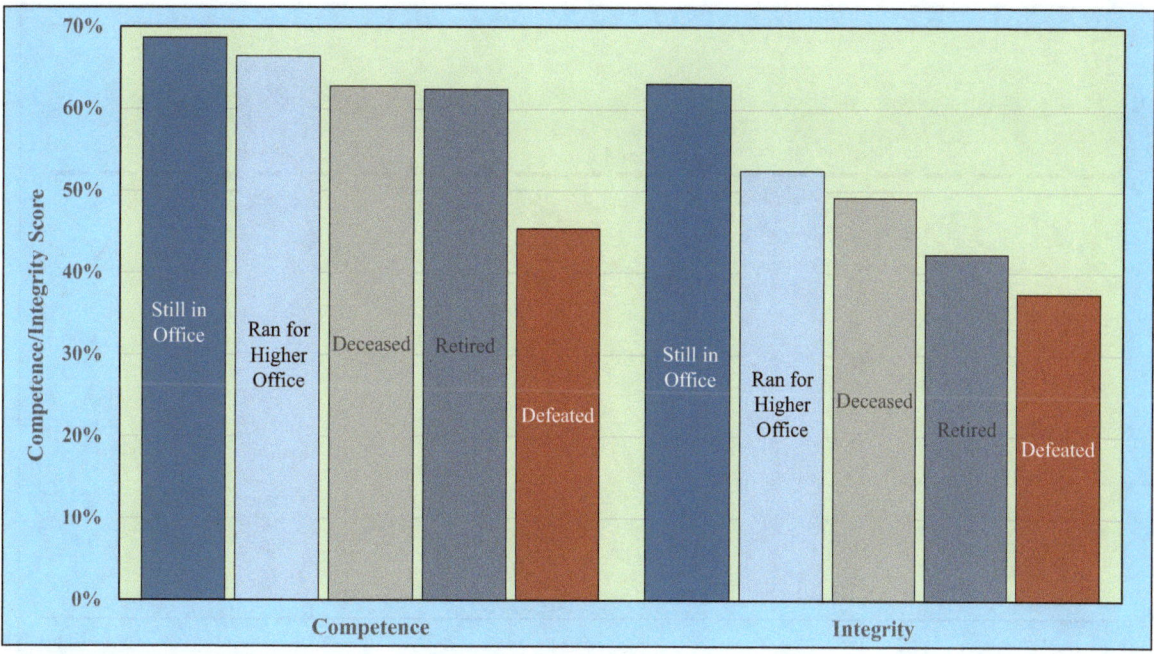

FIGURE 12.2 **Competence and Integrity of House Members**
Source: Data from Mondak (1995, 1057).

serving seven terms or more scored higher than members who retired or were defeated before the seventh term (Figure 12.2). Evidence from Mondak's study suggests that electoral defeats and retirements tend to filter out individuals less able to do the job well. In short, making experience and expertise a basis for disqualification from office is likely to deprive Congress of its most able legislators.

Although the length of service in Congress increased considerably from 1789 through the 1950s (Polsby 1968), this trend toward longer service has stabilized. As Figure 12.3 shows, the average length of service in both the House and the Senate has not changed much in the last five decades: The average tenure since 1953 is 10.7 years in both the House and Senate. The average in the House barely exceeded 12 years twice (in 1991 and 2009). The average in the Senate exceeded 12 years in four consecutive Congresses from 2003 to 2011, reaching a high of 14 years in the 111th Congress (2009–2010). Since 2013, the average tenure of senators fell below the average of 10.7 years. Thus, there continues to be substantial turnover in Congress, which casts out deadwood and brings in fresh blood.

Daily Life of a Member of Congress

Busy is the word to describe the typical workday of a member of Congress. One of the most accessible—and amusing—descriptions of a typical member's work routine was penned by the satirist P. J. O'Rourke (1991, 49–65). O'Rourke trailed a congressman

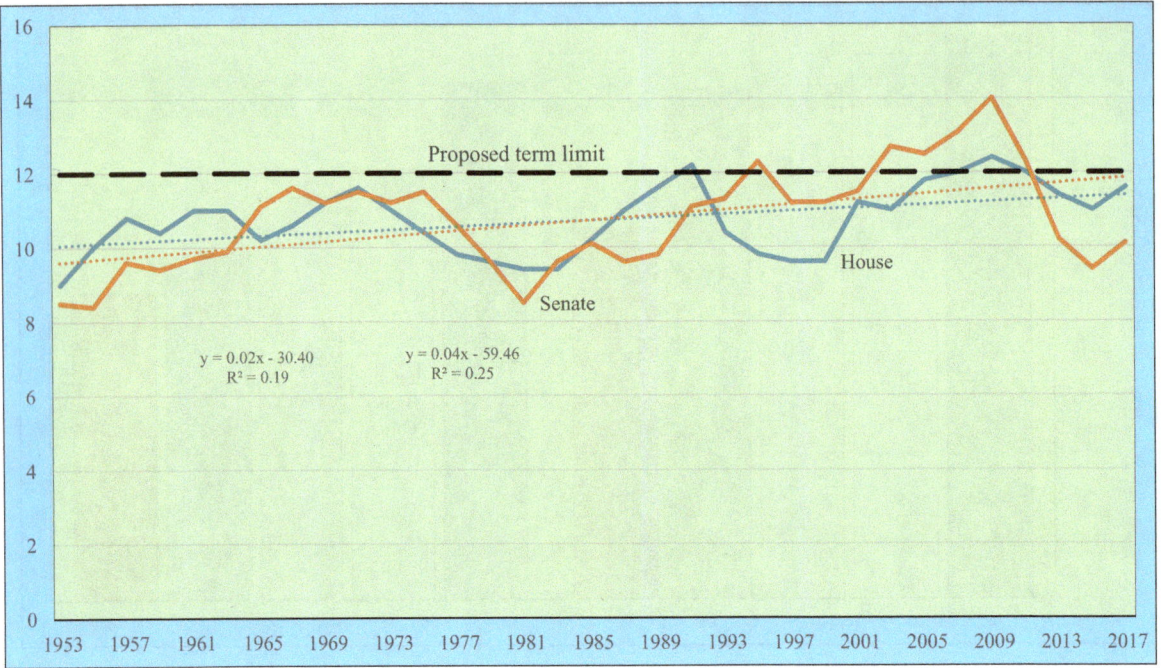

FIGURE 12.3 Average Length of Service in Congress

Source: Data from Ornstein et al. (2018, tables 1–6, 1–7). https://www.brookings.edu/multi-chapter-report/vital-statistics-on-congress/.

for 11 hours of one day. The day began with an 8:00 a.m. breakfast meeting, followed by an 8:30 a.m. breakfast meeting, followed by two committee meetings and a courtesy visit with a volunteer firefighting group from the congressman's district. There was no lunch break. In the afternoon, the congressman huddled with his staff for several hours to come up with coherent and defensible positions on an omnibus farm bill, the reauthorization of a commodities trading commission, a food safety act, a pesticide-control proposal, rural-development legislation, regular and supplemental appropriations bills, a number of foreign treaties, a proposed sale of fighter planes to South Korea, a housing bill, a proposal to close military bases, and a series of bills dealing with U.S. exports. There were 25 issues in all, representing roughly 10 percent of the items on the congressional calendar that week. The congressman had to balance the wishes of his constituents, the preferences of his party, the pressure of congressional leaders, the demands of the president, entreaties from lobbyists, and his own personal viewpoint for each issue. The congressman's position was likely to conflict with at least one of these on each of the 250 items on the calendar that week.

After two hours of trying to map defensible positions, the congressman was expected at a 4:00 p.m. meeting of party colleagues who were elected the same year he was (his "class"). From 5:30 to 9:00 p.m., he was expected at the National Fire and Emergency Services dinner, and from 6:00 to 8:00 p.m., he was supposed to accompany the governor of his state to another official function. O'Rourke did not stay to see how he managed to be in two places at one time: "I was completely exhausted by 7 and went home, leaving the congressman, 20 years my senior, looking as animated and energetic as a full school bus" (1991, 63). The congressman's staff assured O'Rourke that this had been a light day for their boss.

This description shows just one part of the job of serving in Congress. In reality, members of Congress live in two worlds. One is Washington, DC, the world of legislating and overseeing the executive agencies of the national government. This is the world that O'Rourke was describing. The other is the district, the world of listening to constituents in order to learn their wants and needs and to inform them of the issues before Congress.

A reelection-minded member of Congress needs to maintain close ties with his or her district. For those who live near the capital or at least on the eastern side of the country, this is not a heavy burden, and extended weekends in the district can be the norm.[4] Those who live farther away face a formidable commuting schedule. Even they typically go back to their districts at least two or three weekends a month; few travel home less than once a month. Once in the district, a member often has to hit the road, visiting various communities; attending high school graduations, civic meetings, and functions; and holding town hall meetings with constituents. Living in these two worlds is not easy. It frequently means extended separation from family, balancing time and resources between Washington and home, and the necessity of presenting a parochial face to constituents on home matters and a statespersonlike demeanor on questions of national import.

Congressional Pay and Perquisites

Compensation for members of Congress has been controversial since the beginning of the republic. On one side are legislators who have a heavy workload, grave responsibilities, and limited opportunities for earnings beyond their public paychecks. On the other side are voters skeptical about claims of financial distress from officials receiving what seems to be a generous salary.

The first Congress set legislative salaries at $6 a day. Even then, this was hardly a princely sum, and in 1816 Congress voted to raise its salary to $1,500 a year. The public response was swift and brutal; in the next election, 60 percent of House members were voted out of office. Congress quickly repealed the law, and legislators went back to the $6 a day stipend, which they raised shortly thereafter to $8. Congress learned early that voting itself a pay raise was electoral arsenic. Almost 40 years passed before it upped its compensation again. Annual salaries increased to $3,000 in 1855, to $5,000 a decade later, and then to $7,000 in 1873. Congressional salaries consistently lagged behind inflation; every attempt at adjustment prompted a backlash. The 1873 increase was so controversial that it was repealed a year later, but it still cost 96 members their seats in the next election (Harris 1995, 18).

The modern story of congressional compensation is little different. After Congress voted itself a modest increase in 1983 and again in 1984, public opposition

---

[4] Congress customarily transacts official business, roll calls, and the like on Tuesday, Wednesday, and Thursday.

began to grow against a third salary hike proposed in 1987. The raise passed, but in 1989 there was a huge public outcry against a further salary increase. In 1992, the requisite number of states finally ratified the Twenty-Seventh Amendment—203 years after it was proposed—requiring an election to intervene before members could receive a pay raise (discussed in more detail in Chapter 2).

Members attempted to insulate their salary from political controversy by making annual cost-of-living adjustments (COLAs) for themselves, federal judges, and other federal workers. Such increases take effect automatically, without a vote, which might attract less public attention and outrage. The 1989 law instituting these adjustments provided members with a cost-of-living increase equal to one-half of one percentage point below the inflation index. Since 1991, members have accepted annual adjustments 12 times and voted to forgo the increase 6 times (Brudnick 2008). In the 115th Congress (2017–2018), the salary for members of Congress was $174,000. Many people believe that this annual salary is more than adequate, since the median family income is roughly a third that of a member of Congress.

In addition to a paycheck, however, members of Congress receive a number of **perquisites** (colloquially called **perks**), or fringe benefits that go with the job. Such benefits include subsidized medical care, inexpensive insurance, a generous pension plan, free parking, and access to their own gym, cafeterias, and barber shop for nominal fees. Other perks help members do their jobs. Members of the House get a **members' representational allowance (MRA)** or more than $1 million per year to pay for office functions, official travel, and staff. Members use this money for office supplies and equipment for the Washington office, for setting up e-mail and web pages,[5] for leasing and equipping one or more offices in their districts so that constituents can contact them locally, and for frequent trips back home to the district.

The most expensive perk—and one of the most important—is salaries for aides to work in the Washington and district offices. Members can hire up to 18 full-time staff to assist in various tasks, including the following:

- An *administrative assistant* or chief of staff responsible for overall management of the office
- Several *legislative assistants*, each responsible for keeping the member briefed on specific policy areas
- A *legislative director* who supervises the legislative assistants
- An *appointment secretary* to screen and maintain the member's appointments
- A *press secretary* to handle press relations
- Several *legislative correspondents* to answer constituent mail
- One or more *caseworkers* to help constituents with their problems

District offices typically have only one or two staffers; caseworkers are often placed in the district office.

Another important perk is the **franking privilege**. The frank allows members of Congress to send mail that involves official business, such as answers to constituent

---

perquisites (perks) The benefits and support activities that members of Congress receive in order to help them perform their job.

members' representational allowance (MRA) An allowance of about $1 million per year that members of Congress receive to pay for official duties of representation and lawmaking (e.g., office functions, official travel, and staff). It cannot be used for personal or campaign expenses.

franking privilege The ability of members of Congress to send mail to their constituents free of charge by substituting a facsimile of their signature in place of a stamp.

---

5 Members' web pages can be found at http://thomas.loc.gov/.

THINKING ANALYTICALLY

ARE MEMBERS OF CONGRESS PAID TOO MUCH?

Members of Congress receive an annual salary of $174,000, roughly three times what the average American worker makes. That's a lot less than a Fortune 500 CEO or a major conference football coach, but it's still pretty good pay. And what's more, the Constitution (Article I, Section 6) authorizes senators and representatives to set their own compensation by law to be paid out of the U.S. treasury. That is, they ask us to hire them to represent us, but then the hired help gets to decide how much we have to pay them. Sounds like a sweet deal, doesn't it?

Well, maybe not. Most members of Congress would gladly give up the power to determine their own pay and let some independent panel decide what their work is worth. Every time Congress raises its salary, there is a public outcry, and many members lose their job in the next election. Voters and taxpayers can't understand why our hired help needs so much more to live on than the rest of us. How can we make sense of Congress members' salary and whether it is fair compensation? What are some consequences of their pay, and what is it comparable to?

Some argue that comparing congressional salaries to the average worker is not a relevant comparison. Former senator Fred Harris (1995) of Oklahoma noted that congressional salaries are often lower than salaries earned by individuals in jobs with comparable risks and responsibilities. The average salary of a Fortune 500 CEO is around $11 million and the average salary of a Division 1 football coach is about $1.6 million. Arguably, legislators have much greater responsibilities and just as little job security as people in those sorts of jobs, yet they receive a tiny fraction of those sorts of salaries. Moreover, members of Congress typically also must bear the expense of maintaining two residences—one in the capital and one in the district. Rep. Jim Moran represented a district in northern Virginia just outside of the beltway and so he commuted to work for the 24 years he served in Congress. He retired in 2014, saying he couldn't even afford his own home across the Potomac River on his $174,000 salary. Moran warned that keeping legislative compensation down means that only the wealthy would be able to afford to serve Congress (Parkinson and Portnoy 2014).

Moran may have been onto something. There are already a fair number of wealthy senators and representatives. It's difficult to get precise figures, but the Center for Responsive Politics estimates the net worth of members of Congress based on financial filing statements. In 2014, the typical member of Congress was a millionaire—median wealth was about $1.1 million—and the wealthiest legislators had fortunes stretching into the hundreds of millions of dollars (Tucker 2015). Yet, some members are not wealthy and live paycheck to paycheck like the rest of us. About 11 percent do not have significant assets (less than $100,000) beyond their salary and, in many cases, could significantly improve their take-home pay by going to work in the private sector.

Like it or not, serving in Congress is an important job with enormous responsibilities. The Framers of the Constitution recognized that members of Congress deserved compensation for their service. As with other jobs, it is reasonable that compensation should be commensurate with the importance of the work. The Constitution left it up to members of Congress to decide by law how much they should be paid. Deciding just exactly what would be commensurate is a judgment call that voters will ultimately get to make—and so far the voters' assessment is that their representatives are paid too much. But it's a judgment call that should be made by considering the arguments and evidence on both sides rather than on emotion.

Discussion Questions

1. The Constitution recognizes that members of Congress should be compensated for their service and authorizes Congress to set the amount by law. Do you agree that members of Congress should be compensated? What are the consequences of not compensating members of Congress?

2. Allowing Congress to determine its own pay is controversial. It makes voters angry every time Congress raises its pay. What are some other ways to determine how much members of Congress should be paid? Are there better ways than tax dollars to compensate members of Congress?

mail, under their signatures in lieu of postage. Since members get hundreds of letters each week, it would be unreasonable to expect them to pay for postage out of their salaries. Members also use the frank to send periodic newsletters to constituents.

These perks are paid for with tax money appropriated by Congress, and their purpose is to help representatives do their jobs by staying in touch with and responding to their constituents. Perks are not supposed to be used for political purposes, and Congress has adopted a number of rules intended to prevent members from using them in an election campaign (Committee on Standards of Official Conduct n.d.). For example, it is illegal for a representative either to assign staff members to work in the campaign or to send out campaign material using the frank. Mass mailings cannot be sent under the frank within 60 days of an election in which the member is a candidate. In practice, however, the line between representing and campaigning is blurry. Sometimes key staff members take a leave of absence to work in the campaign, and some do campaign work after hours on their own time. The perquisites of the office provide members with an undeniable political advantage; achieving widespread contact with the electorate is an expense that challengers must pay for with campaign money.

BICAMERALISM IN THE AMERICAN CONGRESS

A distinctive feature of Congress is that it has two separate and independent chambers. The Founders designed a **bicameral** legislature for several reasons, including the historical legacy from the British (the British Parliament is also bicameral) and the more immediate example of the colonial legislatures. Many of the latter were also bicameral, with the upper chamber appointed by the king or his representatives and the lower chamber composed of representatives elected by the colonists.

These traditions were not determinative. The national legislature under the Articles of Confederation, for example, was a **unicameral** (one-house) institution. The two-house legislature is mainly a product of the conflicts discussed in Chapters 2 and 3: the political struggle between large and small states and the legal battle over whether national legislators ought to represent sovereign states or individuals. Bicameralism was a compromise that settled both arguments. Bicameralism was also another way to fragment power, which the Founders believed would protect basic rights by making bargaining and compromise necessary.

The bicameral legislature serves two major purposes: (1) to represent different interests and (2) to foster deliberative, careful lawmaking. The Founders created the Senate to protect the interests of sovereign states and to safeguard property interests. The Founders expected the prestigious nature of a Senate seat to attract an aristocratic elite that would be insulated from popular control by indirect election and a long term in office.[6] In contrast, directly elected House members with two-year terms would reflect the interests of the many, the people who had little

bicameral A legislature with two chambers.

unicameral A legislature with one chamber.

---

6 Election of senators by state legislatures ended in 1913 with ratification of the Seventeenth Amendment.

in the way of worldly goods. Linked to the protection of states' rights and property interest was the belief that the Senate would serve as a check on hasty legislation passed in the House.

The Founders also had separate special functions in mind for the Senate and the House. The Senate was to confirm presidential nominees for major positions in the national government and play a major role in foreign policy through its "advice and consent" power on treaties negotiated by the executive with other countries. The House was entrusted with the special and traditional prerogative of lower chambers: originating bills to raise revenue. Although constitutional changes and political reforms over the course of more than 200 years have altered Congress, the House and the Senate remain separate and distinct legislative institutions. Table 12.1 summarizes some important differences.

TABLE 12.1 SELECT HOUSE–SENATE DIFFERENCES

	House	Senate
INSTITUTIONAL FEATURES		
Membership	Larger (435)	Smaller (100)
Term of office	Shorter (2 years)	Longer (6 years)
Minimum age for service	Younger (25 years)	Older (30 years)
Electoral arena	Smaller (district)	Larger (state)
Constituency	Narrower (less diverse)	Broader (more diverse)
Formal leadership	Speaker of the House	Vice president (president of the Senate)
Exclusive powers	Raise revenue	Advice and consent; ratify treaties
Committee consideration of bills	Difficult to circumvent committees	Easier to circumvent committee
Scheduling for floor consideration	Speaker; limited consultation with minority	Majority leader; broad consultation with minority leader
"Holds"	No practice of "holds"	Individual senators can place "holds" on bringing measures to the floor
Rules governing floor consideration	Rules Committee adopts *special rules* (approved by majority)	*Complex unanimous consent agreements* (requires unanimous consent)
Time for debate	Debate time restricted	Unlimited; senators can filibuster
Ending debate	Majority vote	Super-majority (60 votes) to invoke cloture
Quorum calls	Usually permitted only in connection with record votes	In order almost any time; used for delay
Amendments to bills	Number & type limited by *special rule*	Generally unlimited
Germaneness	Germaneness of amendments required	Germaneness of amendments *not* required
Decision rule for passing legislation	Majority rule	Super-majority; rules protect minority rights
INFORMAL		
Most powerful leader	Speaker	Majority leader
Level of comity	Lower	Somewhat higher
Reliance on staff	Lower	Higher
Policy focus	Policy specialists	Policy generalists
Degree of partisanship	Higher	Somewhat lower
Member accessibility	Higher	Lower

Source: Adapted from Moen and Copeland (1999) and Schneider (2008).

Leadership in the U.S. Senate

The U.S. Senate has two types of leaders: those designated by the Constitution and those who occupy party leadership positions. The first group exercises largely ceremonial powers and includes the vice president of the United States and the Senate president pro tempore. The second group includes the majority leader, minority leader, and party whips. There are differences in the amounts and types of power that these two types of leaders exercise in the Senate.

Article I, Section 3 of the Constitution designates the vice president as the **president of the Senate**. The vice president is entitled to preside over the chamber, exercising such parliamentary duties as recognizing speakers and ruling on points of procedure. The vice president can cast a ballot only to break a tie. Vice presidents do not have the opportunity to exercise this power very often—only 255 tie breaking votes have occurred since 1789, an average of about one per year. During eight years in office, Vice President Joe Biden (2009–2016) cast no tie-breaking votes, compared to eight tie-breaking votes by his predecessor, Vice President Richard Cheney (2001–2008) (U.S. Senate n.d.). Vice President Mike Pence (2017–present) cast a record six tie-breaking votes during his first year in office. Except in the rare instances when a tie-breaking vote is necessary, the vice president is not a powerful or important figure in the Senate. And the vice president typically does not preside over the Senate because senators tend to regard the vice president as an outsider, especially if the opposition party controls the Senate.

The Constitution also provides for a **president pro tempore** chosen by the members to preside over the Senate in the absence of the vice president. The party controlling the Senate picks its most senior member to occupy the post. This office is ceremonial and has no special influence. Because presiding over the Senate is generally of little importance, junior members of the majority party take turns exercising the responsibility.

The single most powerful person in the Senate is the **majority leader**, who is elected by members of the majority party. Majority leaders are typically people with considerable experience in the Senate, although long tenure is not always a requirement. For example, Lyndon Johnson (D-TX) gained the post after only one term in office; Johnson held the position from 1955 to 1961 and is generally considered one of the most powerful and effective majority leaders. Several others also won the post in their second term, including Democrats George Mitchell of Maine and Mike Mansfield of Montana and Republicans Bill Frist of Tennessee and Trent Lott of Mississippi.

Senate Minority Leader Charles Schumer (D-NY), left, leans in to speak to Senate Majority Leader Mitch McConnell (R-KY) before his speech at the McConnell Center's Distinguished Speaker Series Monday, February 12, 2018, in Louisville, Kentucky.

© Timothy D. Easley/AP Photo

president of the Senate The person who presides over the Senate and is responsible for many of the parliamentary duties such as recognizing speakers. The vice president of the United States holds this position.

president pro tempore The person chosen by the members to preside over the Senate in the absence of the vice president.

majority leader The person, chosen by the members of the majority party in the House and Senate, who controls the legislative agenda. In the Senate, the majority leader is the most powerful person in the chamber.

The majority leader has several tools with which to wield power in the Senate. Most important of these is control over the Senate's agenda. The majority leader knows which senators are for and against a bill and plays a key role in negotiating the rules and procedures under which bills will be debated and voted on. During consideration of legislation on the floor, the majority leader serves as floor leader to deal with the complex system of legislative procedures. The majority leader also influences other important matters, such as committee appointments, the location of government installations, and the distribution of prime office space.

The job of **minority leader** parallels that of majority leader: Elected by party colleagues, the minority leader usually has extensive Senate experience, and he or she is the floor leader who watches out for the minority's interest during consideration of bills on the floor and serves as the focal point of communication among senators of the minority party. The minority leader often works closely with the majority leader in legislative scheduling and influences the committee appointments of minority members. The minority leader's power, however, is less than that of the majority leader. The minority leader cannot bestow the same level of rewards and, as head of the minority party, has a numerical disadvantage in trying to influence what the chamber does (though, as we will see, the minority can use Senate rules to block action).

Both majority and minority leaders have assistants commonly referred to as **whips** (though both parties have started using the title "assistant majority [minority] leader"). The term is a legacy from the British Parliament, which in turn borrowed it from the sport of foxhunting. A whip, or "whipper-in," was responsible for keeping the hounds from leaving the pack during the chase of the fox. By analogy, a legislative whip's job is to keep the rank-and-file members from stepping out of the party line. He or she sees to it that they are present to vote on key legislative measures and that they know the party leader's desire. The whip's ability to fulfill this responsibility is limited. Unlike their counterparts in the British Parliament, party leaders in the U.S. Congress have few rewards and punishments with which to maintain party unity. In the Senate, each party's whip serves mainly as a communication link between the floor leader (a term applied to either the majority or the minority leader) and rank-and-file party members. Table 12.2 lists the leaders of the 116th Congress (2019–2020). The table was updated to reflect the new leaders who take over in January.

Leadership in the U.S. House of Representatives

The Constitution (Article I, Section 2) provides for a **Speaker of the House of Representatives**. Unlike the constitutionally designated leader of the Senate (the vice president), the Speaker of the House wields considerable power in Congress. The Speaker is the House's most powerful figure. Theoretically elected as an officer of the entire chamber, the Speaker is actually selected by the majority party, making him or her both a House officer and a party official. The Speaker presides over the House, has the power to recognize members who wish to speak, rules on procedural questions, and refers bills to committee. The Speaker may vote but usually does not exercise this prerogative except to break a tie.

minority leader The leader of the minority party in the House or Senate. Works with the majority leader to schedule legislation and leads the opposition party.

whips Assistants to the majority and minority party leaders in Congress who encourage rank-and-file members to support the party's positions. Whips make sure that rank-and-file members are present to vote on key legislative measures and that they know the party leader's desire.

Speaker of the House of Representatives The person who presides over the House. The Speaker is responsible for many of the parliamentary duties, such as recognizing speakers, and is the most powerful person in the chamber.

TABLE 12.2 CONGRESSIONAL LEADERS OF THE 116TH CONGRESS (2019–2020)

SENATE

President of the Senate Mike Pence (Vice President of the United States)

President Pro Tempore Chuck Grassley (R-IA)

Majority Leader Mitch McConnell (R-KY)	Minority Leader Charles E. Schumer (D-NY)
Asst. Majority Leader (Whip) John Thune (R-S.D.)	Asst. Minority Leader (Whip) Richard Durbin (D-IL)

HOUSE

Speaker Nancy Pelosi (D-CA)

Majority Leader Steny Hoyer (D-MD)	Minority Leader Kevin McCarthy (R-CA)
Majority Whip James Cyburn (D-SC)	Minority Whip Steve Scalise (R-LA)

The Speaker can generally use the same rewards as the Senate majority leader to influence colleagues: assistance in obtaining a favorable committee assignment, appointment to select committees, help with bills, and assistance in a tough political campaign. Like the Senate majority leader, the Speaker is the center of the chamber's internal communication network and serves as a central link with the White House and the Senate.

The position of Speaker became more powerful following the 1994 Republican takeover of Congress. The Republican-controlled House adopted reforms to curb the power of committees and committee chairs, and to centralize power in the hands of Republican Speaker Newt Gingrich. Subsequent speakers continued the pattern of strong, centralized leadership. Speaker Paul Ryan (R-WI), for example, played a dominant role in passing the 2017 Tax Reform bill. When Democrats regained majority control of the House in the 2018 elections, Nancy Pelosi (D-CA) was positioned to again become Speaker. She previously served as Speaker from 2007–2011, becoming the first woman to hold the office. Pelosi was credited with rescuing President Obama's stalled health-care reform bill in 2010. Although she faced some opposition in 2018 from Democrats who wanted younger leadership, she is expected to continue the pattern of strong Speakers.

Next in line behind the Speaker in the House leadership hierarchy is the majority leader. Chosen by the majority party caucus (Republicans call their caucus a "conference"), the majority leader often has strong ties with the Speaker, and the influence he or she wields depends largely on what the Speaker wants it to be. Generally, the majority leader assists the Speaker in scheduling legislation, distributes and collects information of concern to majority party members, and tries to persuade the rank and file to go along with the wishes of party leadership.

The nominee of the minority party caucus, who loses the election for Speaker, becomes the House minority leader. This role is essentially the same as it is in the Senate: to work with the majority leader in scheduling legislation and to lead the opposition party. Party whips have the same general function in the House as in the Senate.

The Committee System

Congress is a collegial rather than hierarchical institution. Power is widely dispersed, and leaders do not have the authority to command rank-and-file members to do their bidding. The committee system institutionalizes the diffusion of power by giving small groups of legislators disproportionate influence.

Standing committees are permanent panels with jurisdiction over particular issues and categories of legislation. The importance of standing committees in Congress is hard to overstate. Woodrow Wilson (1885) referred to them as "little legislatures." In both chambers, standing committees are the primary focus of legislative business, and they wield much power within their areas of jurisdiction. They are powerful for at least two reasons. First, committee members are more knowledgeable than nonmembers about legislation in their issue areas. In Congress, knowledge and expertise are important sources of power. Committee members are more knowledgeable than nonmembers because they have worked on the legislation in committee for a long time, they have attended committee hearings, and they have been kept informed of new developments by committee staff. Second, committee members are more interested in the legislation than the rank and file. Members of Congress with less expertise and less interest than committee members in the issue under discussion often defer to the recommendations of the committee reporting the bill.

Nancy Pelosi (D-CA) played a key role in Democrats regaining majority control of the House in 2018. Here she is cheered by a crowd of Democratic supporters during an election night event in Washington. She previously served as Speaker from 2007–2011, becoming the first woman to hold the office. She was credited with rescuing President Obama's stalled healthcare reform bill in 2010. Although she faced some opposition in 2018 from House Democrats who wanted younger leadership, she is expected to continue the pattern of strong Speakers.

© AP Photo/Jacquelyn Martin

Structure and Organization

Standing committees have jurisdiction over particular policy areas. Committee jurisdictions are defined in Senate and House rules and roughly correspond to the major organizational divisions of the executive branch. Senate and House committees are organized along parallel, though not identical, lines. There are 21 standing committees in the House and 19 in the Senate (see Table 12.3).

standing committees Permanent committees in Congress that are responsible for legislation in a specific policy area.

TABLE 12.3 COMMITTEES OF THE 115TH CONGRESS (2017–2018)

House Committees	Seats	Rep	Dem	Party Ratio	Over/under seat share	Dominant Member Goal	Rank
House Party Division	435	241	194	1.24			
Exclusive Committees							
Appropriations	52	30	22	1.36	0.12	prestige	3
Rules	13	9	4	2.25	1.01	prestige	4
Ways & Means	40	24	16	1.50	0.26	prestige	1
Energy & Commerce	55	31	24	1.29	0.05	policy	2
Financial Services	60	34	26	1.31	0.07	policy	6
Non-Exclusive Committees							
Budget	36	22	14	1.57	0.33	policy	11
Education & Workforce	40	23	17	1.35	0.11	policy	15
Foreign Affairs	47	26	21	1.24	0.00	policy	5
Homeland Security	30	18	12	1.50	0.26	policy	19
Judiciary	41	24	17	1.41	0.17	policy	8
Oversight & Government Reform	42	24	18	1.33	0.09	policy	14
Agriculture	46	26	20	1.30	0.06	constituency	16
Armed Services	62	34	28	1.21	-0.03	constituency	7
Natural Resources	43	25	18	1.39	0.15	constituency	13
Science, Space & Technology	39	22	17	1.29	0.05	constituency	18
Small Business	24	14	10	1.40	0.16	constituency	20
Transportation & Infrastructure	61	34	27	1.26	0.02	constituency	12
Veterans' Affairs	24	14	10	1.40	0.16	constituency	17
House Administration	9	6	3	2.00	0.76	unrequested	10
Exempt Committees							
Intelligence (Permanent Select)	22	13	9	1.44	0.20	unrequested	12
Ethics[a]	10	5	5	1.00	-0.24	unrequested	9

Senate Committees	Seats	Rep	Dem	Party Ratio	Over/under seat share	Dominant Member Goal	Rank
Senate Party Division	100	52	48[b]	1.08			
Super-A Committees							
Appropriations	31	16	15	1.07	-0.08	prestige/constituency	2
Armed Services	27	14	13	1.08	-0.05	prestige/policy/constituency	4
Finance	27	14	13	1.08	-0.13	prestige/policy/constituency	1
Foreign Relations	21	11	10	1.10	-0.1	prestige/policy	11

TABLE 12.3 continued

A Committees

Committee							
Agriculture, Nutrition, & Forestry	21	11	10	1.10	0	constituency	13
Banking, Housing, & Urban Affairs	25	13	12	1.08	-0.02	policy/constituency	15
Commerce, Science, & Transportation	27	14	13	1.08	-0.04	constituency	5
Energy & Natural Resources	23	12	11	1.09	-0.02	constituency	14
Environment & Public Works	21	11	10	1.10	0.16	constituency	12
Health, Education, Labor, & Pensions	23	12	11	1.09	0.08	policy	7
Homeland Security & Gov't'l Affairs	15	8	7	1.14	0.07	policy	6
Intelligence (Select)	19	10	9	1.11	-0.08	unrequested	9
Judiciary	21	11	10	1.10	0.03	policy	8
Small Business & Entrepreneurship	19	10	9	1.11	0.03	policy/constituency	16

B Committees

Budget	23	12	11	1.09	-0.02	policy	9
Rules & Administration	19	10	9	1.11	0.03	unrequested	3
Veterans Affairs	15	8	7	1.14	0.11	unrequested	10

C Committees

Indian Affairs	15	8	7	1.14	0.11	constituency	12
Ethics[a]	6	3	3	1.00	-0.22	unrequested	19

Notes:

a. House and Senate rules require an equal number of Democrats and Republicans on their Ethics committees.

b. Includes two Independents who caucus with Democrats.

Sources: Rules establishing committee categories are from Judy Schneider (2014a, 2014b); dominant goals of committee members adapted from Deering & Smith (1997); desirability rank from Stewart (2012).

Committee size varies considerably. The size of standing committees is determined at the beginning of a Congress. The seats on each standing committee are divided between the majority and minority party using the **party ratio**—that is, the ratio of majority to minority party members in the chamber—as a general guideline.

Party ratios on Senate committees closely reflect party strength in the chamber. In the 115th Congress, Senate Republicans outnumbered Democrats 52 to 48, resulting in a party ratio of 1.08. The ratio of Republicans to Democrats on most Senate committees matched this ratio closely.[7] Party ratios on House

party ratio The proportion of the seats that each political party controls in the House and the Senate.

---

7 The ethics committees are exceptions; they have an equal number of Republicans and Democrats.

committees, in contrast, are more likely to favor the majority, especially on committees crucial to achieving the party's policy priorities. The party ratio in the 115th House was 1.24 (241 Republicans to 194 Democrats), but Republicans took one or two extra seats on the three most prestigious exclusive committees—Appropriations, Ways and Means, and Rules (see Table 12.3). The Appropriations committee determines how much money the federal government can spend, and Ways and Means has jurisdiction over tax policy, Social Security, and Medicare. The Rules Committee formulates special rules (explained below) that determine which bills come to the floor for debate and which amendments will be offered. Taking extra seats on certain key committees is something the majority party does. Democrats followed this practice when they had a majority from 2007 to 2010. Remember that party discipline in the U.S. Congress is low compared to that in parliamentary democracies (see Chapter 7). Thus, regardless of which party is in the majority, it needs extra seats on key committees to have a working majority to pass party policies. The minority, of course, complains that underrepresentation on committees reduces their ability to influence legislation at this key stage of the process and "thereby deprives the electorate of the representation it sought in electing those Members" (Tong 2009, 5). This inequitable treatment of the minority may have contributed to the high levels of party conflict in recent Congresses and made it more difficult to find common ground.

Standing committees also have subcommittees with jurisdiction over smaller segments of policy. Subcommittees help Congress cope with a large workload, and they permit members to develop more specialized policy expertise.

Getting Assigned to a Committee

Party committees determine which members will fill the party's seats on the various congressional committees—that is, Republicans assign Republicans, and Democrats assign Democrats. Members request particular committee assignments, and party committees match up those requests with vacancies on the committees. As a general rule, members who want to continue serving on a committee are allowed to do so.[8] This practice fills most of the seats on the committees. Some continuing members, however, request to transfer to a more desirable committee, and new members need committee assignments. Demand always exceeds the supply of seats for some committees. In deciding who will get a contested seat, reelection is a major consideration. Seniority is also a consideration, especially in the Senate, where seniority is almost always the primary consideration when there is competition for a particular assignment. Some committees have a "state seat" tradition where the delegation from the state of the departing member claims that the vacancy should be filled by someone else from the state.

---

8 Some members may be denied reappointment to a committee if their party lost majority control and there are not enough seats for the minority on certain committees.

Committee Chairs

Traditionally, committee chairs were chosen on the basis of seniority. The relevant consideration was not seniority in Congress, but seniority on the committee among majority party members: That is, the practice was to appoint the committee member of the majority party with the longest continuous service on the committee. Automatic selection based on seniority insulated committee chairs from pressure from their party caucus and party leaders. In the Senate, committee seniority continues to serve as the primary basis for selecting committee chairs.

The House reforms adopted by Republicans in 1995 sought to place limits on such political power. Republicans ceased using seniority as the primary qualification for chairing a committee, as Speaker Gingrich skipped over the senior Republican on several key committees and handpicked trusted lieutenants as chairs. Democrats also ceased using seniority as the sole criterion for selecting committee chairs. And House Republicans have a party rule limiting committee chairs to three terms, which further weakened the seniority system.

Although these reforms weakened the role of seniority in selecting committee chairs in the House, they did not eliminate it. The competition to chair committees involves mostly senior members, so committee chairs are still relatively senior majority party members. But criteria such as competence, party loyalty, and especially a record of raising campaign money to help fellow majority party members have also become important considerations (Heberlig and Larson 2012). The Senate continues to rely primarily on seniority, though both parties have adopted rules that the chair "need not be the Member with the longest committee service" (J. Schneider 2006a, 7, 10).

Committee Rankings

Some committees are more important than others. There are some committees on which almost any member would like to serve; others on which almost no one wants to serve; and many that are desired by some but not others, depending on members' particular political and policy interests. There are two ways to rank the desirability of any given committee: (1) how the committee ranks based on what members say in House or Senate rules and in interviews; and (2) the preferences revealed by members' behavior as they transfer on and off committees. Both methods produce similar, but not identical, rankings.

The formal rules of the House and Senate create different categories of committees, and these categories show how members view the relative importance of committees. (Table 12.3 groups committees according to categories established in the rules.) Members of Congress generally have two major committee assignments, but the rules create different categories that restrict or expand on the two-committee baseline.

House rules divide committees into three categories: exclusive, nonexclusive, and exempt. Most House committees are in the nonexclusive category, and the rules permit members to serve on two of these major committees. Three **exclusive** committees—Appropriations, Rules, and Ways and Means—are the most powerful and prestigious committees in the House. House rules were amended to designate two additional committees—Energy and Commerce, and Financial Services—to the exclusive category. Members assigned to an exclusive committee typically receive no other major committee assignment. Restricting these members from serving on other major committees is formal recognition of the power and prestige of these committees. On the other hand, exempt committees—Ethics and Select Intelligence—are exempt from the two-committee limitation, allowing members to serve on these undesirable committees in addition to their two major committee assignments (J. Schneider 2014a).

Senate rules designate committees as "A," "B," or "C" level. Members may serve on two A committees, one B committee, and one or more C committees. Most Senate committees are in the A category, but four committees—Appropriations, Finance, Armed Services, and Foreign Relations—are called "Super-A" committees or the "Big Four." Senators generally serve on only one of the Big Four, though there are exceptions (J. Schneider 2014b).

Interviews with members of Congress also reveal differences in the importance and prestige of committees. Richard Fenno (1973) found that members seek committee assignments to pursue three goals: prestige and power, policy, and reelection. Committees can thus be classified as "prestige," "policy," or "constituency" committees according to which of the three goals is predominant. Some committees fulfill none of these goals, thereby forming an "unrequested committee" category (Deering and Smith 1997).

Interviews with members indicate that there are a small number of **prestige committees**, which are highly prized and which allow their members to wield tremendous power in Congress (Fenno 1973). In both chambers, the prestige committees include those dealing with major taxing and spending issues: Ways and Means (House), Finance (Senate), and Appropriations (House and Senate). Other prestige committees differ between the House and the Senate according to the particular rules and responsibilities of the chamber. In the House, the Rules Committee, which has special powers to control floor procedures, is a prestige committee. In the Senate, Appropriations, Finance, Foreign Relations, and Armed Services are prestige committees (Deering and Smith 1997, 64, 80). Notice that the "prestige committees" identified in interviews with members are also those codified in the House and the Senate rules as either exclusive or "Super-A" committees.

Most of the remaining standing committees are major policy and constituency committees. These committees have jurisdiction over important policy areas, but members' policy and reelection interests determine which committees are desirable for them. A representative from a New York City district dominated by financial institutions, for example, might want a seat on the Financial Services Committee, whereas a legislator from a district with a farm-based economy might need a seat on the Agriculture Committee to deal with legislation affecting agribusiness. Classifying Senate committees based on member goals is less clear than in the House (Deering and Smith 1997). Since the Senate is smaller than the House, senators

---

exclusive committees House committees—Appropriations, Rules, Ways and Means, Energy and Commerce, and Financial Services—whose members typically receive no other committee assignments.

prestige committees Congressional committees that are highly prized and allow their members to wield tremendous power in Congress.

tend to have more committee assignments. Almost every senator can put together a mix of assignments to cover all of his or her prestige, policy, and constituency goals, and on several committees no single goal is dominant. The prestige committees in the Senate are not exclusive—with 106 seats on these four committees, every senator can get a prestigious assignment.

Few members want to serve on the low-ranked "unrequested" committees (Deering and Smith 1997, 77). For example, in both chambers, members do not seek assignment to the Ethics Committee. A party leader in the House expressed members' distaste for sitting in judgment of their colleagues, saying that "anyone who wants a seat on [Ethics] doesn't deserve a seat on [Ethics]" (quoted in Deering and Smith 1997, 77).

Members' behavior as they transfer on and off committees also indicates which committees are most desirable: If a member gives up an assignment on the Agriculture Committee to move to the Ways and Means Committee, then it is reasonable to conclude that Ways and Means is more desirable to that member than Agriculture. The most desirable committees, then, are those that members transfer to but do not leave, and members leave the least desirable committees but will not give up an assignment to join them (Groseclose and Stewart 1998; Stewart and Groseclose 1999).

Charles Stewart (2012) used this technique to rank House and Senate committees from the 104th Congress (1995–1996) to the 112th Congress (2011–2012) (see Table 12.3). The findings are consistent with the other rankings in important ways. The prestigious committees tend to rank at the top; the unrequested ("Exempt" and "C") committees rank near the bottom. This method also allows us to see which policy and constituency committees are most desirable. In the House, Foreign Affairs and Armed Services, counterparts of "Super-A" committees in the Senate, are highly ranked. In the Senate, Commerce, Science, and Transportation are highly ranked.

House and Senate Differences

Although committees are a central organizational feature in both chambers, committees are more important and powerful in the House than in the Senate for several reasons. First, the larger membership of the House means that House members have fewer committee assignments (an average of about two) than senators (an average of over three); this scarcity makes committee assignments more highly valued in the House. Traditionally, the surest way to influence legislation in the House was to serve on a key committee, but high party polarization in recent years has tended to shift power away from committees to the Speaker on highly salient legislation. Because there are only 100 senators, these lawmakers have opportunities to develop power and influence independent of their committees. The relatively small membership means that senators can build personal relationships with more of their colleagues. In addition, the longer term and the representation of a statewide constituency make the Senate more prestigious than the House, and as a result, senators get more media attention and can develop bases of power outside the Senate, often even on a national scale.

Second, Senate rules allow individual senators opportunities to offer **nongermane amendments** that are not related to the bill under consideration, in some cases bypassing committee action. These amendments are commonly known as **riders** because they are attached to popular bills in an effort to get them a free ride through the legislative process. Riders are generally prohibited in the House.

Third, constituency differences create incentives for House members to become policy specialists and for senators to become policy generalists. Except for states that have only one House member, House constituencies are smaller and less diverse than Senate constituencies. With only a few interests dominating many House districts, a House member benefits from working on one or two committees with jurisdiction over policies important to a single district. Senators representing an entire state with a wide range of interests can benefit from serving on several committees.

RUNNING THE LEGISLATIVE OBSTACLE COURSE

American government textbooks typically include a diagram of how a bill becomes law. The generic diagram reproduced as Figure 12.4 follows a bill through the various obstacles it must overcome before becoming law: from introduction to committee referral, from committee consideration to floor action, from floor action to conference committee, from conference committee back to floor action, and from there to the White House—and back again if vetoed.

Political scientists consider such descriptions to be unrealistic portrayals of how Congress works. Barbara Sinclair (2012) shows that legislation is increasingly governed by what she terms "unorthodox lawmaking." Unorthodox lawmaking involves the use of special procedures and practices that have created "a number of different paths the legislation may follow" (Sinclair 2012, 10). These "modifications and innovations can be seen as responses to problems and opportunities the members—as individuals or collectively—confronted" (Sinclair 2012, 134).

Although the legislative process is no longer a linear progression from one point to the next, as depicted in the generic diagram, the fundamental nature of lawmaking remains an obstacle course characterized by multiple, sequential decision points. In order to pass, a bill must gain the approval of a group of legislators at each point. Only on the final floor votes does the majority have an opportunity to express its will, and even there a small minority determines which alternatives the majority will choose from. As a result, the legislative process is not really a process of majority rule. Rather, it is better described as a process of *minorities' consent* because, at each stage, a different minority of members has the power to stall or prevent the bill from going to the next decision point. The most important thing to remember about how a bill becomes law is that there are multiple points of access to the proposed legislation and thus plenty of opportunities for minority interests to slow the bill's progress or kill it outright.

---

nongermane amendments Amendments to a piece of legislation that are not related to the subject of the bill to which they are added.

riders A nongermane amendment that is added to a popular bill in hopes that the desirability of the proposed legislation will help the amendment pass.

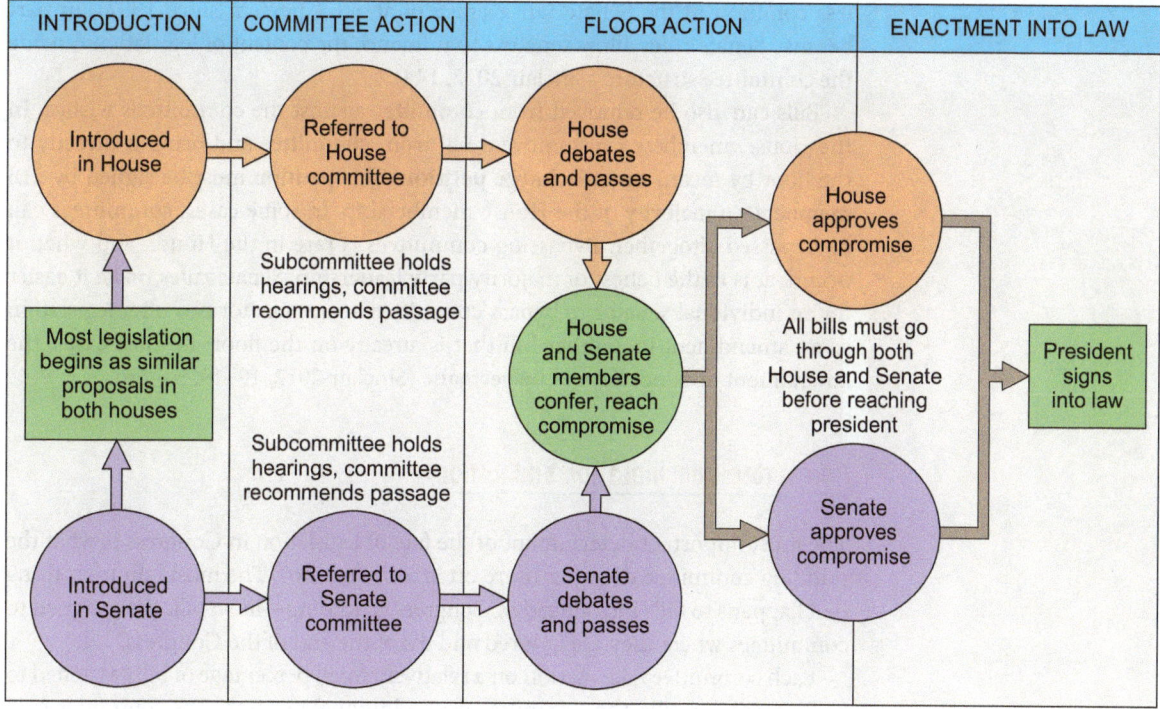

FIGURE 12.4 How a Bill Becomes Law

Bill Introduction and Committee Referral

Proposed legislation has numerous sources. Members introduce bills on behalf of the president, interest groups, or constituents. Only members of Congress can introduce bills into their respective chambers. In the House, members place a proposal into a wooden box called the hopper. Senators can introduce bills from the floor or submit them to Senate clerks.

After introduction, a bill is referred to the committee with jurisdiction over the particular issue or area it covers. Committee consideration can be long and complex: A bill is passed down to subcommittee and reported back to the full committee, and legislators negotiate and propose changes, while interested parties lobby for the version they favor.

Bills traditionally were referred to a single committee that had jurisdiction over that issue. As new issues became more prominent in the 1970s and 1980s (e.g., environmental protection, energy, and healthcare), legislation proposed to address these issues no longer fit within a single committee's jurisdiction. To deal with this problem, the House changed its rules in 1975 to permit a bill to be referred to more than one committee, a practice known as *multiple referral*. From the 100th to the 110th Congresses (1987–2010), about 20 percent of all bills and 34 percent of major bills were referred to more than one committee. Multiple referrals are much less common in the Senate (an average of about 4 percent since 1987), in part because Senate rules allow senators to influence the content of legislation outside the committee structure (Sinclair 2012, 144).

Bills can also be removed from committee against the committee's wishes. In the House, members can remove a bill from committee and bring it directly to the floor by means of a **discharge petition**. This petition must be signed by 218 members—a majority of the House membership. In some cases, committees can be bypassed altogether. Bypassing committees is rare in the House, and when it occurs, it is at the behest of majority party leadership. Senate rules make it easier for an individual senator to bypass committees—any senator can offer legislation as an amendment to another bill that is already on the floor; in most cases, the amendment does not have to be germane (Sinclair 2012, 18–19, 54–56).

Committee Consideration and Action

The most important determinant of the fate of legislation in Congress is what the standing committee does (or, more often, does not do). The most common thing that happens to bills introduced in Congress is nothing—most bills are assigned to committees where they are ignored and die at the end of the Congress.

Each committee takes action on a relatively small percentage of bills assigned to it. On these few bills, the committee does additional research. The committee staff studies the bill and provides information to the members. The committee will hold public hearings where interested parties (interest groups, members of the executive agency that administers the program, policy experts, and sometimes celebrities) provide information about the proposal. Committee hearings are typically highly scripted. The committee chair has substantial leeway to decide not only which bills get hearings, but also who the witnesses will be and what positions they will take. In addition to collecting information about the policy, hearings can also be used to test the breadth of political support—and sometimes to build support—for the legislation. Hearings that feature celebrities tend to attract media attention, which gives committee members an opportunity to get some free publicity.

After the hearings, the committee meets for the markup, where members literally mark up the bill, making changes deemed necessary. After the markup, the committee votes to report the bill to the floor for debate and a vote.

There is no doubt that standing committee action (or inaction) is the most important determinant of whether a bill passes or fails. And members of Congress certainly work hard to get a good committee assignment—that is, one that will help them achieve their goals. Given all this concern with committees, you might think that once members get the desired assignment, they work diligently on all the bills under the committee's jurisdiction. Richard Hall's (1996) study of participation on committees, however, found that participation was far from universal. The number of members participating varied from bill to bill, and it was largely a different subset of participants on each bill. He quips that his findings "reveal that the standing committees of Congress are not really standing committees; in most cases most of the committee members are standing somewhere else" (Hall 1996, 46).

discharge petition A procedure of the House of Representatives that permits a majority of the members of the House (218) to bring a bill out of committee for consideration on the floor.

From Committee to the Floor

Bills reported out of committee have a high probability of passage on the floor. Getting legislation reported from the committees to the floor for consideration and a vote, however, is more complex than it once was. It is not unusual, for example, for a bill to undergo "postcommittee adjustments"—that is, substantial alterations between the time it is reported by a committee and when it is scheduled for consideration on the chamber floor. Party leaders with the cooperation of the committee chair may lead efforts to forge changes to a bill, usually in an attempt to improve the chances of its passage on the floor (Sinclair 2012, 21–24, 57–58).

Furthermore, constraints are often placed on a bill before it gets to the floor for consideration. In the House, the Rules Committee determines what these constraints will be; in the Senate, they are set by the unanimous consent agreement (UCA). These procedural matters are critical in determining whether a bill will pass and in what form.

The House Rules Committee is powerful because it decides what bills come up for a vote, when they come up, and which amendments members will get to vote on. Once a House standing committee has completed its consideration of a proposed bill, it prepares a written report describing what the bill does, what amendments the committee has made, and why the bill should be passed. But before the committee's bill can go to the floor for debate and a vote, it must first go to the Rules Committee, which formulates a **special rule** that establishes the conditions under which the bill will be considered. The Rules Committee thus performs the role of a legislative traffic cop, regulating the flow of legislation from standing committees to the floor. There is no Senate committee that performs this role.

The rule formulated by the Rules Committee sets the date the bill will be brought up on the floor for debate and specifies the conditions of the debate. These conditions normally set time limits; specify which amendments, if any, can be offered; and set other rules that can significantly control the form of proposed legislation and its chances of passage. By controlling the order in which bills are considered, the Rules Committee kills some, while allowing others to be decided by majority vote. Some bills are considered under an **open rule** that permits any germane amendment (or sometimes a "modified open rule" requiring that amendments be preprinted in the *Congressional Record*); others come to the floor with a **closed rule** that prohibits all amendments. Frequently, bills come to the floor under a **structured rule** that permits only certain amendments, permits amendments to only parts of the bill, and sometimes specifies the order that amendments will be voted on (see Table 12.4).

The Speaker appoints a majority of the members, so the Rules Committee is a tool the majority party leadership uses to help meet policy objectives, keep debate under control, and prevent the minority party from scoring political points by offering amendments that would place majority party members in awkward positions. The majority must approve the rule before the House can consider the legislation. Losing a vote on a rule amounts to losing control of the chamber and is very embarrassing to the majority party leadership. Although rare, it does occasionally happen.

special rule A rule formulated by the House Rules Committee specifying the conditions under which a given bill will be considered on the House floor.

open rule A rule formulated by the House Rules Committee that permits any germane amendment to be considered on the floor.

closed rule The rule that prohibits amending a bill when it is on the floor of Congress for consideration.

structured rule A rule that permits only certain amendments to a bill.

TABLE 12.4 EXAMPLES OF HOUSE SPECIAL RULES FOR FLOOR CONSIDERATION OF BILLS

Rule for H.R. 2112-Agriculture, Rural Development, Food & Drug Administration and Related Agencies Appropriations Act, 2012

Adopted by record vote of 235-180 on Tuesday, June 14, 2011.

1. **Open rule.**
2. Provides for one hour of general debate equally divided [between majority and minority].
3. Waives all points of order against consideration of the bill.
4. Waives points of order against provisions . . . for failure to comply with [House rules].
5. Under the rules of the House the bill shall be read for amendment by paragraph.
6. Provides that the bill shall be considered for amendment under the five-minute rule.
7. Authorizes the Chair to accord priority in recognition to Members . . . .
8. Provides one motion to recommit with or without instructions.

Rule for H.R. 2842-Bureau of Reclamation Small Conduit Hydropower Development & Rural Jobs Act of 2011

Adopted by voice vote, after agreeing to the previous question by record vote of 232-177, on Tuesday, March 6, 2012.

1. **Modified open rule.**
2. Provides one hour of general debate equally divided [between majority and minority].
3. Waives all points of order against consideration of the bill.
4. Makes in order the amendment in the nature of a substitute [from] the Committee . . . .
5. Waives all points of order against the amendment in the nature of a substitute.
6. Makes in order only those amendments that are submitted for printing in the Congressional Record dated at least one day before the day of consideration . . . .

Rule for H.R. 2117-Protecting Academic Freedom in Higher Education Act

Adopted by record vote of 244-171 on Tuesday, February 28, 2012.

1. **Structured rule.**
2. Provides one hour of general debate equally divided [between majority and minority].
3. Waives all points of order against consideration of the bill.
4. Provides that the amendment in the nature of a substitute [from] the Committee . . . shall be considered as original text for the purpose of amendment . . . .
5. Waives all points of order against the committee amendment in the nature of a substitute.
6. Makes in order only . . . amendments printed in the Rules Committee report . . . . Each such amendment may be offered only . . . by a Member designated in the report, . . . shall not be subject to amendment, and shall not be subject to . . . division of the question.
7. Waives all points of order against the amendments printed in the report.
8. Provides one motion to recommit with or without instructions.

TABLE 12.4 Continued

Summary of Amendments to Be Made in Order:

Sponsor	Sponsor	Sponsor	Sponsor
1. Grijalva (AZ)	#8	Would retain the requirement that states . . . have a process to hear and take . . . action on student complaints . . .	(10 min.)
2. Foxx (NC)	#3	Would repeal a section of the credit hour regulation impacting clock hour programs.	(10 min.)
3. Polis (CO)	#6	Would link state authorization regulations to student outcomes.	(10 min.)
4. Bishop (NY)	#2	Would strike the prohibition on the Secretary of Educ. from . . . promulgating or enforcing any . . . rule defining the term "credit hour."	(10 min.)
5. Polis (CO)	#7	Would require the Secretary to present a plan to prevent waste, fraud, and abuse . . . of taxpayer dollars.	(10 min.)

Rule for H.R. 2560-Cut, Cap, and Balance Act of 2011

Adopted by record vote of 236–177, after agreeing to the previous question by record vote of 235–175, on Tuesday, July 19, 2011.

1. **Closed rule.**
2. Provides four hours of debate equally divided [between majority and minority].
3. Waives all points of order against consideration of the bill.
4. Provides that the bill shall be considered as read.
5. Waives all points of order against provisions in the bill.
6. Provides one motion to recommit.

Source: House Rules Committee. http://www.rules.house.gov/Default.aspx (accessed July 14, 2012).

If the rule passes, the House dissolves into the **Committee of the Whole**, a committee consisting of every member of the House. Its origins lie with a centuries-old British practice of getting the Speaker, who was a representative of the king, out of his chair so that the House of Commons could act independently of his scrutiny. The advantage of keeping this parliamentary fiction alive is that the Committee of the Whole has less burdensome rules governing debate and requires a smaller quorum than the House itself. While in Committee of the Whole, members debate the bill and consider amendments under constraints of the rule.

Once this process is completed, the Committee of the Whole reports the bill to the House, and the House votes on the bill. The House must approve amendments adopted in the Committee of the Whole, so opponents have a second chance to try to defeat them. Typically, the House votes on all amendments from the Committee of the Whole as a package, and passage is assured. But if the vote on an amendment in the Committee of the Whole was close, the losers in the first round may attempt to change the outcome on the House floor. Such efforts are rarely successful—"after all, the membership of the two bodies is identical" (Sinclair 2012, 44).

Thus, the simple-sounding act of voting on a bill is surrounded by complexities that can make it anything but straightforward. The floor vote is the place where

Committee of the Whole A parliamentary action whereby the House of Representatives dissolves into a committee consisting of every member of the House. This procedure is used to facilitate consideration of legislation because it has less burdensome rules governing debate and requires a smaller quorum than the House itself.

the majority has the opportunity to express its will, but the expression of majority will is limited by the rules governing consideration of the bill and may require multiple tries.

Power is more diffuse in the Senate than in the House. Senate rules and traditions disperse power to all senators. Perhaps the most important protection of individual prerogatives is the Senate rule permitting unlimited debate. The power of unlimited debate gives each senator the power to filibuster objectionable legislation and nominations favored by the majority. A **filibuster** is an effort by one or a few senators to delay action on a bill or nomination by making long speeches and using parliamentary tactics. The goal is to pressure the majority to give up and pull the bill from the floor or at least make changes to remove objectionable provisions.

Senators can signal their intention to filibuster by placing a "hold" on a bill. A **hold** is "a notice by a senator to his or her party leader of an intention to object to bringing a bill or nomination to the floor for consideration" (quoted in Oleszek 2008, 1). Holds are an informal tradition of the Senate, and the identity of the senator who placed the hold is secret. Certain provisions of the Honest Leadership and Open Government Act passed in 2007 attempted to end the practice of secret holds, but the practice persists because party leaders continued to honor them. In essence, a hold is a threat to filibuster, and merely the threat is often sufficient to deter the Senate majority leader from scheduling a vote on a bill or nomination.

A filibuster can be stopped if the Senate votes to invoke **cloture**—that is, end debate on a bill. Under Senate rules, it takes 60 votes to invoke cloture. This rule means that a minority of 41 senators can kill a bill by preventing a final vote.

Historically, filibusters were rare, but they have become much more common in recent decades. Once used by individual senators to block legislation they intensely opposed, filibusters have become part of a partisan strategy that the minority party uses to influence legislation (Binder and Smith 1997, 148; Koger 2010) and block confirmation of the president's judicial and executive branch nominations (Bond, Fleisher, and Krutz 2009).

Since the 1970s, filibuster activity (as indicated by the number of cloture votes) has increased precipitously (see Figure 12.5). The number of cloture votes in the 2010s soared to 171, more than twice the average for Congresses in the 2000s. The minority party in the Senate has begun using the 60-vote requirement to end filibusters as a way to block many presidential nominations. Because Democrats were blocking so many of President Bush's judicial nominees, in 2005 Majority Leader Bill Frist (R-TN) threatened to use the so-called "nuclear option"—a parliamentary procedure to end filibusters on nominations with a simple majority vote. The term is an analogy to the extreme devastation of nuclear weapons, as outraged Democrats threatened to use all prerogatives available under the rules to bring the Senate to a standstill. A compromise averted the threat, but both parties continued to use the 60-vote requirement to block presidential nominations when they were in the minority. In 2013, a Democrat-controlled Senate voted to end the 60-vote requirement and confirm executive branch judicial nominations, except for the Supreme Court, with a simple majority. In 2017, Republicans eliminated the exception for the Supreme Court and confirmed President Trump's nomination of

---

filibuster The effort by a senator to delay the chamber's business by making long speeches and using parliamentary tactics.

hold The formal request by a member of the Senate to be notified before a specific bill or presidential nomination comes to the floor.

cloture A procedure of the Senate to end a filibuster; invoking cloture requires votes of 60 senators.

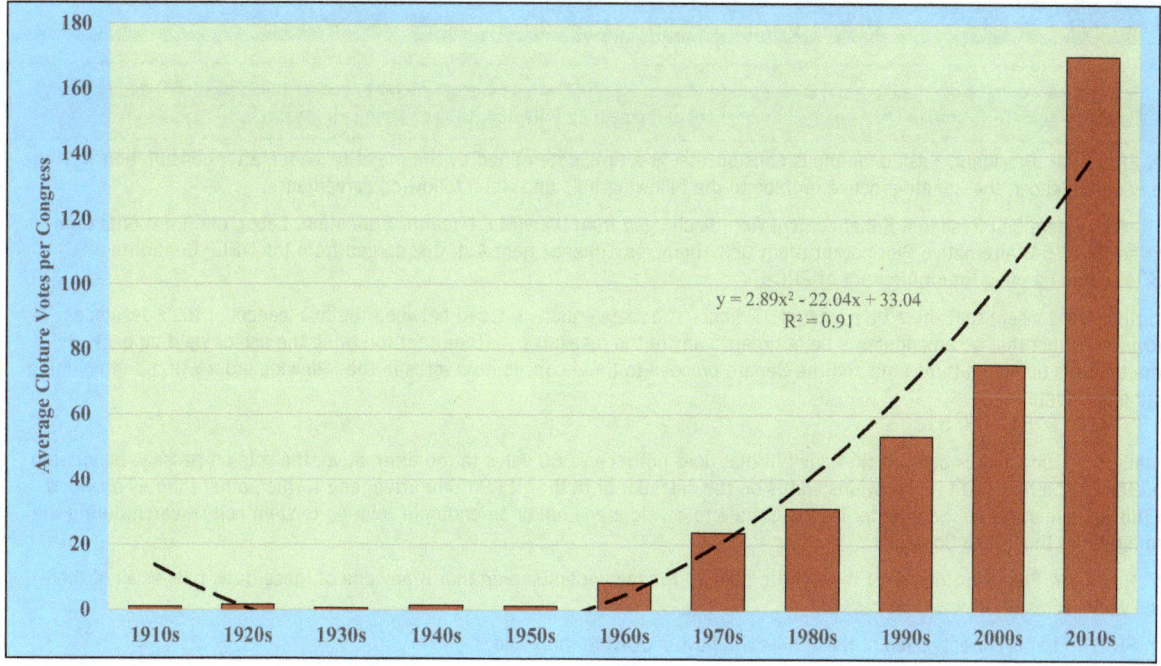

FIGURE 12.5 Increasing Filibuster Activity

Source: United States Senate, https://www.senate.gov/pagelayout/reference/cloture_motions/clotureCounts.htm.

Neil Gorsuch. The 60-vote requirement to end debates on legislation remains, but President Trump has advocated removing it as well.

Many bills are not filibustered. The Senate conducts much of its legislative business under **unanimous consent agreements (UCA)** negotiated by party leaders. These agreements define the procedures and conditions under which bills will be considered on the Senate floor. Unanimous consent agreements in the Senate perform a function similar to special rules from the Rules Committee in the House; they set limits on debate, specify which amendments will be in order, and set a schedule for the vote (see Table 12.5). But there is a big difference. Adoption of a special rule in the House requires a simple majority, and the majority party leadership rarely loses a vote on a rule. Unanimous consent in the Senate means just what it says: Any one senator can stop the agreement. An objection to a unanimous consent agreement is likely a threat to filibuster, which means that it might take 60 votes to pass the bill on the Senate floor.

Resolving House–Senate Differences

Even if a bill clears the many obstacles to passage in one chamber, both chambers must pass an identical proposal in order for it to become law. In some cases, differences can be worked out by informal contacts between the two chambers, or

unanimous consent agreement (UCA) An agreement between majority and minority party leaders on the procedures and conditions under which a bill will be considered in the Senate.

TABLE 12.5 AN EXAMPLE OF A UNANIMOUS CONSENT AGREEMENT

Following is an excerpt from the Congressional Record of June 29, 2006 where Senate Majority Leader Bill Frist (R-TN) and Minority Leader Harry Reid (D-NV) formalize a unanimous consent agreement on bills dealing with stem cell research.

Mr. FRIST. Mr. President, I ask unanimous consent that at a time determined by the majority leader, after consultation with the Democratic leader, the Senate proceed en bloc to the following bills under the following agreement:

H.R. 810, Stem Cell Research Enhancement Act, discharged from the HELP [Health, Education, Labor, and Pensions] Committee; S. 2754, Alternative Pluripotent Stem Cell Therapies Enhancement Act, discharged from the HELP Committee; S. 3504, Fetus Farming Prohibition Act of 2006.

I further ask consent that there be a total of 12 hours of debate equally divided between the two leaders or their designees; provided further that no amendments be in order to any of the measures; further, that following the use or yielding back of time the bills be read a third time and the Senate proceed to three consecutive votes in the following order with no intervening action or debate:
S. 3504, S. 2754, H.R. 810.

Finally, I ask unanimous consent that any bill that does not receive 60 votes in the affirmative, the vote on passage be vitiated and the bill be returned to its previous status on the calendar or in the HELP Committee; and further, other than as provided in this agreement, it not be in order for the Senate to consider any bill or amendment relating to stem cell research during the remainder of the 109th Congress.

Mr. REID. Mr. President, reserving the right to object, it is my understanding that if any one of these three bills or all of them receive 60 votes, they would be passed.

Mr. FRIST. That is correct. Each of these bills will have a 60-vote threshold.

Mr. REID. Mr. President, let me say, first of all, that I extend my appreciation to the distinguished majority leader.

This has been difficult. I know that. I would rather that we would just be going forward with H.R. 810, but we will take what we have. . . .

Again, I tell the leader how much I appreciate this and I speak for every Democrat and I speak for people throughout the country. I know this has not been easy.

The PRESIDING OFFICER. Is there objection?

Mr. REID. No objection.

The PRESIDING OFFICER. Without objection, it is so ordered.

Source: Congressional Record, U.S. Senate (June 29, 2006, pp. S7169–S7170).

---

one chamber might agree to accept the version passed by the other. Controversial measures, however, usually require a conference committee.

A **conference committee** is a temporary committee composed of House and Senate members that meets to reconcile differences between the House and Senate versions. Members of a conference committee are called *conferees*. Traditionally, conference committees consisted of just a few of the leading members of the committees that originally dealt with the bill. Modern conference committees have many more members. For example, the conference committee appointed to hammer out differences in the 1990 Clean Air Act discussed earlier contained 130 representatives from seven House committees and nine senators from two Senate committees (Sinclair 2012, 3). Members of a conference committee have broad discretion, and with a large membership, complex issues, and wide disparities between the House and Senate versions of a bill, the task of resolving differences is more complicated. Such conditions provide interests that lost out at earlier stages another chance to influence the legislation.

conference committee A temporary congressional committee made up of members of the House and Senate that meets to reconcile the differences in legislation that has passed both chambers.

To report legislation out of conference committee, a majority of each chamber's conferees must approve a common bill. The conference report is returned to the respective houses for an up or down vote. It cannot be amended, but it is subject to a filibuster in the Senate.

Conference committees play such an important role that they are sometimes called the "third house of Congress." Because conference committees are composed of the members of the House and Senate standing committees that first handled the bill, Kenneth A. Shepsle and Barry R. Weingast (1987) observe that standing committees have a second chance to enforce the deals made to get the bills passed. Shepsle and Weingast develop a theory suggesting that this "ex post veto" explains why standing committees are so powerful.

Once the bill passes both houses, it is sent to the president for signature or veto. Congress can override a presidential veto by a two-thirds vote in both chambers. Because getting two-thirds is difficult, vetoes are seldom overridden—only 7 percent have been overridden.

Congress's responsibilities, its members, and its operation combine into a process that is more complex and nuanced than many realize. As Sinclair points out, "if the textbook legislative process can be likened to climbing a ladder, the contemporary process is more like climbing a big old tree with many branches" (2012, 48). Some of the branches lead to passage, some lead to alteration, some entrap and entangle a proposal and halt its movement, and some give way altogether.

CHAPTER TWELVE
Top 10 Takeaway Points

1. Congress's primary responsibilities include lawmaking (passing laws and overseeing government agencies) and representation (responding to constituents' needs and informing the public about the major issues facing the country).

2. Secondary functions of Congress include impeaching and trying executive and judicial officials, seating and disciplining members, helping select leaders in the executive branch, and fulfilling specialized policy responsibilities such as ratifying treaties and confirming ambassadors to foreign countries.

3. Although there are more minorities and women in Congress today than in earlier decades, membership still does not reflect the diversity of today's American citizens.

4. During the last half of the twentieth century, serving in Congress became a career for many members. In the nineteenth century, a decade was an unusually long time for anyone to be a House member.

5. Members of Congress have heavy workloads, and there are enormous demands on their time and attention. Constituents, party leaders, the president, and interest groups often want different or contradictory things, and the member's own preferences may be different from those of these various groups.

6. The U.S. Congress has two chambers with two major purposes: (1) to represent different interests and (2) to foster deliberative, careful lawmaking. Both the House and the Senate are organized along party lines, although the specifics of each organization differ considerably.

7. Party leaders do not have the authority to command rank-and-file members to do their bidding, but they have a great deal of influence on the operation of Congress. The most powerful person in the Senate is the majority leader, chosen by members of the majority party, whose opposite in the minority party is the minority leader. The Speaker of the House of Representatives is the leader of and most powerful individual in the lower chamber. The Speaker is selected by the majority party and combines the powers shared in the Senate by the vice president and the Senate's majority leader.

8. Committees are the core organizational feature of Congress. Standing committees are the most important, being permanent panels with jurisdiction over particular issues and categories of legislation. Committees do research on proposed legislation, revise proposals to accommodate various interests, report the legislation out for consideration on the floor, and conduct oversight of the bureaucracy.

9. Some committees are more important and prestigious than others. The prestige committees in the House are Ways and Means, Appropriations, Rules, and Energy and Commerce; prestige committees in the Senate are Finance, Appropriations, Armed Services, and Foreign Relations.

10. The details of lawmaking are often highly complex, and traditional descriptions of how a bill becomes law oversimplify the legislative obstacle course. In both chambers, the rules and parliamentary maneuvering tend to favor those who want to prevent a bill from becoming law.

CHAPTER TWELVE
Key Terms and Cases

allocation responsiveness, 428
bicameral, 444
casework, 428
censures and reprimands, 435
closed rule, 459
cloture, 462
Committee of the Whole, 461
conference committee, 464
delegate, 430
discharge petition, 458
distributive benefits, 428
exclude, 434
exclusive committees, 454
expulsion, 434
filibuster, 462
franking privilege, 442
geographical constituency, 429
hold, 462
home style, 429
impeach, 433
lawmaking, 426
legislative oversight of administration, 427
legislature, 425
majority leader, 446
members' representational allowance (MRA), 442
minority leader, 447
nongermane amendments, 456
open rule, 459
parliamentary system, 425
party ratio, 451
perquisites (perks), 442
personal constituency, 429
policy responsiveness, 428
politico, 430
pork-barrel benefits, 428
president of the Senate, 446
president pro tempore, 446
presidential system, 425
prestige committees, 454
primary constituency, 429
reelection constituency, 429
representation, 427
riders, 456
service responsiveness, 428
Speaker of the House of Representatives, 447
special rule, 459
standing committees, 449
structured rule, 459
symbolic responsiveness, 429
trustee, 430
unanimous consent agreement (UCA), 463
unicameral, 444
whips, 447

13 THE PRESIDENCY

KEY QUESTIONS

Why has the power of the president grown?

What is the difference between the president and the presidency?

Does the president have enough power to do what people expect the president to do?

© J. Scott Applewhite/AP Photo

BY THE TIME PRESIDENT DONALD TRUMP finished his first year in office more than a third of his senior staffers had already quit, changed jobs, or been pushed out. In just 12 months, his administration chewed through two National Security Directors, four White House Communications Directors, the president's chief of staff, the chief White House strategist, a press secretary, the director and deputy director of the FBI, as well as two acting Attorneys General. The secretaries of State, Homeland Security, Veterans Affairs, and Health and Human Services came and went within 14 months of Trump's inauguration, and within the same timeframe the heads of two other cabinet agencies—Ben Carson at Housing and Urban Development and Scott Pruitt at the Environmental Protection Agency—became entangled in major ethics scandals.

Turnover and controversy is part and parcel of any presidential administration, but there is little historical precedent for the dizzying pace of personnel burn and churn in the Trump White House. Nine percent of President Barack Obama's "A Team," the 65 most influential and important staffers serving in the administration, left or switched jobs during his first year in office. The same figure for President George W. Bush was 6 percent. For Trump, it was an eye-popping 34 percent (Tenpas 2018). Some Trump appointees served so briefly they seemed to leave their jobs before really starting them. Michael Dubke resigned after serving only three months as White House Communications Director, Michael Flynn barely served three weeks as National Security Advisor, and that was two weeks longer than Anthony Scaramucci, who served an exciting, controversy-laced six days as one of Dubke's successors.

At least those three actually filled a job opening, however briefly. The president makes more than 600 appointments that require confirmation by the Senate. While many of those positions are less high profile than a cabinet secretary or press secretary, collectively they represent the team responsible for imposing the president's policy vision on the executive branch. This is why most presidents act as quickly as possible to get those positions filled, because these are the people who take the actions that constitute what the president wants the government to do. Presidents Obama, George W. Bush, Bill Clinton, and George

H. W. Bush had the vast majority in place within a year or so of being inaugurated. Well into his second year in office, President Trump had not even named a nominee for roughly a third of those positions (Washington Post 2018).

Trump came to office pledging to do things differently, and certainly made good on that pledge. An obvious difference separating him from his predecessors, as his administration's personnel ups and downs clearly demonstrate, is his management style. All presidents have their own management style, which reflects not just their philosophy of government but their personality. Larry Summers served in both the Obama and Clinton administrations and describes very different styles. Obama was disciplined, big picture, and kept the focus on moving his policy agenda forward. Meetings with Obama started on time and the president was ready with questions on how the issue at hand advanced his goals. In the Clinton White House, on the other hand, there was pretty much zero chance meetings started on time, maybe a one-in-three shot that the president had read the pre-meeting policy brief, but a very good possibility the president would say something like, "I was in the White House library reading the *Journal of Finance*, and there's some really interesting thinking about the role of dividends" (Fortune 2011). Clinton, in short, was less disciplined, but wonkish, a voracious consumer of information, very open to new ideas and willing to course correct on the basis of fresh data.

Presidents, in other words, are not just different in ideology, party, and policy ambitions, they are different in how they approach the job of being the nation's chief executive. Style makes a big difference. How does a president communicate with the public? What is their process for making big decisions? How do they run their administrative team? Are they a delegator? A micromanager? How do they deal with Congress? Are they an engaged dealmaker? An agenda-setting party leader? Or do they let party leaders in the legislature do their own thing with minimal input from the White House?

Presidents answer these questions very differently. Obama was known for being buttoned-down, somewhat aloof, and cerebral. George W. Bush, the first resident of the White House to hold an MBA, sought to impose a top-down corporate model onto the presidency (Crotty 2003). President Bill Clinton was seen as a backslapping policy nerd. President Donald Trump is seen as thriving on "chaos," with decisions and policy directions emerging from intramural feuding among rivals within his management team and not infrequently announced through stream-of-consciousness tweets (Wronski 2017).

Such style differences can have momentous consequences. How do you deal with a crisis? Immerse yourself in the details and weigh the pros and cons analytically? Make an executive the-buck-stops-here decision on the goal and leave the details to others? See what comes out of different White House factions duking it out over their differences? Tweet something and see what happens? This is important because the office of president of the United States is made up of two fundamental components: (1) the president as an individual and (2) the presidency as an institution. Trump, Obama, Bush, and Clinton all occupied the same office—they sat as the head of the same institution—but are very different individuals. To understand the presidency and its implications for how the nation reacts to particular crises or challenges, it is important to grasp the dual nature of the office.

To that end, this chapter examines the evolution of the institution of the presidency, the influence of the president as an individual, and the implications of the office's institutional structure for the performance of the chief executive.

THE CONCEPT OF THE U.S. PRESIDENCY

The president of the United States holds the most powerful office on the planet. He (or she) sits as chief executive in the American political system, commands the most awesome military machine in history, and exerts unequaled influence over national and international policy.

In general, an **executive** is a person or group that has administrative and supervisory responsibilities in an organization. The word derives from *execute*, which originally meant "to carry out" or "follow through to the end" (Ayto 1990, 212).[1] The title "president" traditionally referred to the individual who presides over an organization or legislative body to ensure orderly debate. We can find examples of the use of the title in early American governments—for example, John Hancock was "president of the Continental Congress of the United States of America," and Samuel Huntington was "president of the United States in Congress Assembled" under the Articles of Confederation. Although Hancock and Huntington were the first Americans to hold the title "president of the United States of America," neither had any *executive* authority. Rather, the title was used in the traditional sense of presiding over a legislative body, just as the vice president's constitutional responsibility to serve as president of the Senate is a legislative rather than executive power. The declaration of the Constitution of 1789 that "the executive Power shall be vested in a President of the United States of America" (Article II, Section 1) is generally credited as the first time the title was used for the chief executive of a republic who exercised executive powers.[2] Thus, the concept of the president as the chief executive of a nation is an innovation of the Constitution.

---

1 *OED Online*, s.v. "executive," adj. and n., http://www.oed.com/ (accessed October 25, 2012).

2 *OED Online*, s.v. "president," n., http://www.oed.com (accessed October 25, 2012); *Encyclopaedia Britannica*, s.v. "president," http://www.britannica.com/EBchecked/topic/475206/president (accessed March 5, 2013); *Online Etymology Dictionary*, s.v. "president," http://dictionary.reference.com/browse/president (accessed July 16, 2012).

executive A person or group that has administrative and supervisory responsibilities in an organization or government.

The president's powers and unique role within the political system have long created an uncomfortable paradox for the American political system—one that is closely related to the Madisonian dilemma discussed in Chapter 2: How do you create a presidency powerful enough to ensure things get done but not powerful enough to run the risk of tyranny? Setting up a chief executive and defining the office's powers and responsibilities were among the most difficult challenges of the Constitutional Convention. The problem was that "the delegates had exceedingly ambivalent feelings about what sort of an executive the new government should have" (Collier and Collier 1986, 284).

A clear deficiency of the Articles of Confederation was the absence of an executive branch. Convention delegates wanted an executive strong enough to provide clear national leadership and to serve as a real check on the legislative branch. Yet they also feared putting too much power into the hands of a single individual, which could lead to tyranny.

The delegates first agreed on what they did not want in an executive. They did not want a king (Alexander Hamilton was virtually alone in even considering resurrecting the British model). Rather than look to the United Kingdom for a model, the delegates looked to the states. Most states had weak executives dominated by state legislatures. In such a **weak-executive model**, the job of the chief executive is merely to implement the decisions of the legislature. A president in a weak-executive system would have limited terms, no veto power, and be allowed to exercise only the authority explicitly granted by Congress.

Yet a few states, notably New York and Massachusetts, had strong, independent governors. The **strong-executive model** meant an executive independent of the legislature, with important powers vested in the executive office. The strong-executive model suggested a president as a strong political actor independent of Congress, with veto power, the authority to appoint judges and diplomats, and primary responsibility for foreign affairs.

The Constitutional Convention ended up creating a strong presidency, but with clear constraints. The president was to be chosen by the electoral college rather than appointed by the legislature. The president would not serve at the pleasure of Congress but could be removed for treason, bribery, or high crimes and misdemeanors following impeachment by the House and conviction in the Senate. The Constitution gave the president specific grants of power, including command of the armed forces, the veto, the ability to issue executive pardons, and a very broad, undefined set of rights and responsibilities: "the executive power shall be vested in a President of the United States of America" (Article II, Section 1).

The delegates thus created a strong president but also placed clear limits on the president's power. The president cannot make law by decree; only Congress can pass laws. The president can veto legislation, but Congress can override the veto by a two-thirds vote of both chambers. The president can make appointments to the executive and judicial branches but only with Senate approval. The result is a powerful office, but one that is checked by other branches of government.

Several amendments make modest changes to the structure of the executive office formulated at the Constitutional Convention: the Twelfth Amendment, clarifying that electors cast separate votes for president and vice president; the

weak-executive model A model of the presidency in which the executive would have a limited term, no veto power, and be allowed to exercise only the authority explicitly granted by Congress.

strong-executive model A model of the presidency in which the powers of the executive office are significant and independent from Congress.

Twentieth, altering the beginning of the presidential term; the Twenty-Second, limiting a president to two terms; and the Twenty-Fifth, specifying the line of succession to the presidency. Despite these changes, the constitutional framework of the presidency has remained mostly intact for more than two centuries.

THE DEVELOPMENT OF THE PRESIDENCY

The presidency today is much more powerful than the office held by George Washington. Most of the changes in the presidency have come not from formal legal alterations but from informal custom and precedent. The power of the presidency, in short, derives in no small part from the legacy of the individuals who have occupied the office. Four factors explain the expansion of presidential power:

1. The energy associated with individual executives
2. Vague constitutional provisions that assertive presidents have used to broadly interpret their powers
3. Changing public expectations of the office
4. Congressional delegation of power and authority through law

A Single Executive

In *Federalist* Number 70, Alexander Hamilton used the term *energy* to describe a desirable characteristic of good government, especially in the executive branch. He saw decisiveness and dispatch as important qualities for a good executive. More than anything else, these traits have expanded presidential power.

A good example is the president's ability to make key decisions about committing American troops to military action. Although Congress has the constitutional authority to declare war, presidents have interpreted their power as commander in chief as giving them the right to place military units in combat situations without prior authorization from Congress. The last time Congress formally declared war was to authorize U.S. entrance into World War II in 1941. The major military conflicts the United States has been involved in since then—the Korean War, Vietnam War, and Iraq War—technically were not wars because Congress never made a formal declaration of hostilities. For example, Congress passed a joint resolution in 2002 authorizing the president to use U.S.

Although the Constitution gives Congress the power to declare war, it makes the president commander in chief of the armed forces. As commander in chief, the president has the ability to make important decisions about committing troops to military action. President Bush addresses the nation Tuesday, September 11, 2001, from the Oval Office of the White House in Washington, about the terrorist attacks at the World Trade Center and the Pentagon. Bush said, "Freedom itself has been attacked this morning by a faceless coward."

© Doug Mills/AP Photo

armed forces against Iraq, but this was not a formal declaration of war. Lee Hamilton, former chair of the House International Relations Committee, says, "In the exercise of its ... war-making power, Congress has basically ceded to the president over a period of years the decision in going to war" (quoted in Lehigh 2002, A27).

In addition to military action, the president retains a dominant role in foreign affairs. The power to negotiate treaties (which require Senate approval) and executive agreements (which do not), to initiate or break off diplomatic relations, and to choose representatives abroad make the president's voice the crucial one in foreign affairs.

Historian Arthur Schlesinger Jr. (1973) argues that such expansions of power have led to the creation of an "imperial presidency" that appropriates powers reserved to other branches by the Constitution. Presidents who have acted decisively and assertively have thus significantly expanded the power of the office.

Broad Constitutional Provisions

A key opportunity for assertive executives to expand their powers derives from the broad and indefinite opening sentence of Article II: "The executive power shall be vested in a President of the United States of America." This grant of authority allows bold and innovative ventures. Supplementing this provision are other clauses ripe for broad interpretation. For example, the president has responsibility for ensuring "that the laws be faithfully executed" (Article II, Section 3)—a clause that presidents have repeatedly used as legal justification for their actions.

Some presidents resisted the lure to expand their office. James Buchanan and William Howard Taft took a **restrictive view of presidential power**, arguing that the president could exercise only the powers specifically granted by the Constitution. In contrast, Theodore Roosevelt formulated the **stewardship doctrine**, arguing that the president is the steward of the people and should do anything required by the needs of the nation unless it is specifically prohibited by the Constitution. Abraham Lincoln subscribed to the **prerogative view of presidential power**, arguing that the oath of office required him both to preserve the Constitution and to take otherwise unconstitutional measures to ensure that the Constitution itself was well preserved. President George W. Bush took a similar position with respect to the war on terror.

Although earlier presidents could debate the extent of their powers, contemporary presidents do not have this luxury. People expect the president to deliver on a broad set of promises, so the president cannot choose to take the narrow role of caretaker. As political scientist Richard Neustadt put it, the modern president "may retain liberty, in Woodrow Wilson's phrase, 'to be as big a man as he can.' But nowadays he cannot be as small as he might like" (1960, 6).

Public Acceptance of Positive Government

Before the Great Depression began in 1929, government was viewed as having limited responsibility for regulating economic activity. The economic collapse

restrictive view of presidential power A view of presidential power that argues that the president can exercise only those powers listed in the Constitution.

stewardship doctrine A view of presidential power that states that the president is a steward of the people and should do anything the nation needs that is not prohibited by the Constitution.

prerogative view of presidential power A view of presidential power, promoted by Abraham Lincoln, that argues that the president is required to preserve the Constitution and take actions to do so that otherwise might be unconstitutional.

during the Great Depression and the social dislocation it caused changed this attitude. Many Americans welcomed President Franklin Roosevelt's New Deal and its bold government intervention into the social and economic patterns of the nation.

Since the 1930s, Americans have increasingly demanded that the government "do something" to ensure prosperity. Economic problems such as unemployment and inflation are now routinely seen as government's responsibility. Government is even expected to mitigate the pain and suffering caused by natural disasters such as hurricanes, tornadoes, floods, and earthquakes. Bold and effective responses to such crises have enhanced the influence of the presidency by creating a sense that the executive can move swiftly and decisively to solve or at least ameliorate such problems. Failure to respond effectively to such crises can diminish the president's leadership. For example, President Bush was on vacation in Crawford, Texas, when Hurricane Katrina struck the Gulf Coast in 2005. Perceptions that he was slow to recognize the magnitude of the crisis and that government's response was ineffective damaged Bush's image as a strong leader. Former White House press secretary Ari Fleischer said that it "turned out to be one of the most damaging events of his presidency" (Fletcher 2006). President Obama, in contrast, responded quickly and forcefully when Hurricane Sandy struck the New Jersey coast just days before the 2012 election.

This crisis and the increased governmental activity in response to it changed expectations about the proper role of government. Americans have come to accept the concept of **positive government**, a government that plays a major role in meeting or preventing most major crises or problems faced by society. The president is not solely responsible for the rise of positive government; Congress passed the laws and programs expanding governmental activity, and the courts turned away legal challenges to the expanded role. But the energy associated with a single executive makes the president the focal point of these expectations. Expectations of the president go beyond responding to a crisis. The president is routinely expected to manage the domestic economy to produce jobs and opportunity and to conduct foreign policy that promotes peace and democratic values while protecting the nation's economic and strategic interests. As Neustadt observed, Americans have transformed "into routine practice … the actions we once treated as exceptional" (1960, 6). The result has been a steady escalation of what the president is normally expected to achieve.

Congressional Delegation of Power

In many cases, Congress has specifically delegated additional power and resources to the executive branch. For example, Congress passed several laws in the twentieth century giving presidents an increased role in making budgetary decisions. Some scholars suggest that the legislative branch is too fragmented to be decisive on key policy matters. Thus, Congress followed the public and turned to the president to provide policy leadership. Nonetheless, Congress has not abdicated its authority to amend, change, or block presidential initiatives.

positive government The idea that government should play a major role in preventing or dealing with the crises that face the nation.

Contemporary Expectations of the President

Because of these factors, the public has come to expect all chief executives to be presidents of action. The president is held responsible for the economy and for addressing a wide array of social problems. He or she is expected to head the executive branch, conduct foreign policy, nominate federal judges, reflect and shape public opinion, and provide direction and leadership for Congress. The president is also expected to act as the chief partisan for a political party while remaining representative of all Americans.

Although the Founders settled on a single executive, the realities of managing broad expectations mean that the modern presidency has become a larger and more bureaucratic organization than in years past. The office of president now stands squarely at the center of the American political system. It has evolved into the center of policymaking, and it has experienced considerable bureaucratic expansion. About 1,700 individuals now make up the institution of the presidency. A broad variety of policy specialists and political advisors enhance the president's ability to meet the high expectations placed on the office. There are experts on everything from national security to agriculture and mass communications.

Yet although presidential power has grown, there is a question whether it has kept pace with rising expectations. The basic constitutional framework establishes a government of shared powers. If presidents have any hope of meeting the high expectations placed on the office, they must convince political actors in other branches and levels of government to take action. The American system of government makes the president dependent on the actions of others who have power independent of the presidency. This poses enormous difficulties when it comes to meeting the public's rising expectations. In the seminal behavioral analysis of the presidency, Richard Neustadt (1960, i) defined the problem in terms of personal influence: "what a President … can do, as one man among many, to carry his own choices through that maze of personalities and institutions called the government of the United States." Neustadt argued persuasively that to be successful, the president must rely on the powers of persuasion, bargaining, and compromise.

THE PRESIDENT AND THE PRESIDENCY

Americans tend to personalize the office of the president in terms of the current occupant, but this perspective ignores the complex organization that lies behind the individual. To fully understand the modern presidency, it is important to grasp how both the individual and the organization contribute to presidential performance.

Political science theory to explain the presidency is less developed than is theory about Congress or the judiciary. Developing and testing scientific models of the presidency is challenging for a number of reasons: There is a "small N" problem[3]—only 45 cases (presidents) in all to observe—with new cases added only every four or eight years; much of the president's behavior that we need to observe in order to test theories is hidden from public scrutiny; and although some useful information is in presidential papers, it can be decades before scholars can get access to it. Consequently, much of the scholarly analysis of the presidency has been descriptive or biographical. Nonetheless, political scientists have taken some modest steps toward a more scientific analysis of the presidency.

Neustadt's thesis that "presidential power is the power to persuade" can be viewed as relying loosely on a rational actor perspective. The president has policy goals but insufficient power to achieve those goals without the cooperation of other political actors—members of Congress, bureaucrats, and others—all of whom possess independent power to pursue their own goals. "The essence of the President's persuasive task," Neustadt argues, "is to convince [these powerful politicians] that what the White House wants of them is what they ought to do for their own sake and on their authority" (1960, 34). That is, the president must bargain with other political actors to change the cost–benefit calculations. Neustadt focused on the president's professional reputation as a skilled leader and his popularity with the public as key resources for influencing that cost–benefit calculation. Building on this informal theorizing, political scientists adapted bargaining games from the field of political economy to build formal rational actor models to explain key aspects of presidential power.

The President as an Individual

Some presidential scholars have turned to psychology for theoretical guidance, assuming that the way the president handles the powers and duties of office depends on individual personality and character. Family background and life experiences help determine self-confidence, psychological needs, values, and worldview. They also shape the political philosophy and the personal vision of presidential conduct.

Scholars such as Erwin Hargrove (1974) and James David Barber (1992) distinguish between active presidents and passive presidents. "Active presidents" invest a good deal of personal energy into the office, and their personal needs and skills translate well into political leadership. "Passive presidents" devote less time and effort to being president and have neither the inclination nor the ability to effectively exercise political power. Barber (1992) also distinguishes between "positive presidents," who gain personal satisfaction from serving as president, and "negative presidents," who serve because of compulsion or a sense of duty but derive little pleasure from the post.

This psychological approach to understanding the presidency has not proven particularly successful. There is little doubt that the background and personality of individual presidents affect their performance, but determining exactly how the former cause the latter is extraordinarily difficult. Part of the problem is context:

---

[3] "Small N" means that there is a small number of cases to observe.

APPLYING THE FRAMEWORKS

WHY PRESIDENTS VETO

Why do presidents veto bills? Well, the obvious answer is that presidents do not want them to become law. But why would Congress bother passing a bill in the first place if they know the president will veto it? Rational choice theory can help us explain this.

Game theory uses formal (mathematical and logical) models of rational actors to explain how and why people make decisions. These models are called "games," and a basic game that can be applied to a veto situation is what's known as a one-shot, take-it-or-leave-it (TILI) game. A TILI game has two players, in this case Congress and the president. Congress moves first and presents the president with a bill. The president can then "take it" (sign) or "leave it" (veto) depending on whether he benefits more from the new policy or more from the status quo. TILI assumes this is a one-shot game, in other words there's no opportunity to override the veto. This model predicts that there will be no vetoes because it is not rational for Congress to pay the costs of passing a bill (hearings, rounding up a majority, etc.) that bring no benefits if the president vetoes it.

This model isn't particularly realistic—presidents do veto and Congress can try to override—but it actually does help us explain some things. For example, when the president's party controls Congress, both branches of government are likely to have similar policy goals, so it is rational for Congress to incur the costs of passing legislation and rational for the president to sign it into law. That's not the case when there is divided government and the president and Congress are more likely to have very different policy goals. In other words, this model predicts, reasonably accurately, that we are likely to see more vetoes in periods of divided government than in unified government.

A more realistic game is the sequential veto bargaining (SVB) model (Cameron 2000). This model is considerably more complex, but the basic gist is easy enough to grasp. It assumes vetoes occur because Congress miscalculates what the president will accept, and that after a veto Congress has the option to attempt an override. Override attempts bring a third player into the game, a legislator (or legislators) who find themselves in the position of providing the key votes to determine whether the override attempt will pass or fail. This player is sometimes called the "veto pivot" (Krehbiel 1998). In the SVB game, if this third player prefers the bill to the status quo, they vote to override and the game ends (i.e., the bill becomes law).

A key insight from the SVB model is that if the override fails, the game can actually continue—this is where the "sequential veto bargaining" comes in. The veto and the override failure provide information and reduce uncertainty; in other words, everyone has a better sense of what the president and members of Congress will or will not support. Rational players can use that to bargain for votes by modifying the legislation. That increases the probability of getting the bill passed and reaping the rewards, thus making the costs of a second (or third, or fourth) try at getting the bill into law worthwhile.

The SVB model has been used to generate a wide range of hypotheses about vetoes, including: they will be rare events, they will mostly be used on minor rather than major bills, they will be used by presidents to extract concessions from Congress. Empirical tests have largely confirmed these hypotheses (Cameron 2000). The SVB and similar models have even provided insight to why Congress would pass bills when it is clear the president will veto them. Why would Congress incur those costs if there's no chance at the benefit? Because the benefit is not the passage of the bill, but the electoral payoff of getting the bill vetoed. In other words, instead of bargaining to get policy concessions, Congress passes a bill that is certain to be vetoed—veto bait—in order to create a campaign issue in the next election (Gilmour 1995, 2011; Groseclose and McCarty 2001).

The bottom line is that by thinking through the steps of rational decision making among a set of political actors seeking to maximize their own self-interests, it's possible to gain important insights into why those actors behave the way they do—even when that behavior (like passing a bill that has almost no chance of becoming a law) at first glance does not seem to make a whole lot of sense.

Discussion Questions

1. Following the 2014 elections, the United States had divided government, with Democratic President Barack Obama in the White House and Republicans controlling both houses of Congress. After the 2016 election, the United States had unified government, with Republican President Donald Trump in the White House and GOP majorities in both houses of Congress. Based on the discussion above, who would you predict issued more vetoes, Trump or Obama? How do the costs and benefits of the actors involved in veto decisions, i.e., the president and Congress, help explain your answer?
2. The take-it-or-leave-it (TILI) model is simple and makes unrealistic assumptions. Yet its main prediction—no veto for any bill passed by Congress—is actually 98 percent accurate. Only 2 percent of bills are vetoed. Is it really worth developing complex and sophisticated theories to explain that 2 percent? Why or why not?

What a president can accomplish is significantly affected by the type and magnitude of the problems the government faces at the time of their presidency and by the needs, interests, and preferences of the other actors who share power with the president. Rather than character traits causing job performance, the demands of the job instead reveal a president's character.

Furthermore, political scientists do not have professional training in psychological analysis. But such an analysis is controversial even for trained professionals. Guidelines adopted by several professional associations state that it is unethical for of psychologists and psychiatrists to give a professional opinion about public figures they have not examined in person, and from whom they have not obtained consent to discuss their mental health in public statements. This is known as the "Goldwater rule" named for Senator Barry Goldwater (R-AZ), the Republican nominee for president in 1964. The American Psychiatric Association adopted it after almost half of psychiatrists who responded to a magazine poll considered Goldwater psychologically unfit to be president. The issue arose again in 2017 when a number of psychologists published warnings that Donald Trump was mentally unfit to be president and urged that he be removed from office. This led additional professional associations to adopt guidelines against such armchair analysis.

The Presidency as an Organization

Over the course of history, presidents have used a variety of advisors and organizations to help manage their duties. One presidential advisor, the vice president, is explicitly provided for in the Constitution, although each president determines what role the vice president will play, if any. The cabinet and the Executive Office

THINKING ANALYTICALLY

DOES BUSINESS EXPERIENCE MAKE BETTER PRESIDENTS?

Americans like the idea of a president with business experience. Candidates running for the White House—think Donald Trump and Mitt Romney—are certainly quick to present their business credentials as an important qualification for holding high office. But does being a corporate CEO really make you a better government CEO? Well, to answer this question let's look at a pretty straightforward hypothesis: Business experience makes better presidents. To test this scientifically, we just need to define and measure two variables—(1) business experience and (2) presidential job performance.

Measuring business experience is straightforward—just look at each president's biography and see if he (or she) has business experience. We created a "Successful Business Experience" scale that put presidents into one of three categories: "Ran a failed business," "No business experience," "Ran a successful business."

Now we need a measure of presidential job performance. To be a valid scientific study, we need a measure based on objective criteria such as honesty, integrity, leadership ability, organizational and management skills, and the value of the president's accomplishments while in office. It's exceedingly difficult to define just exactly how to measure these qualities and construct a quantitative measure that will be reliable—one that other researchers could replicate. Fortunately, historians have been producing ratings of the best and worst presidents for a long time. We found 16 studies conducted between 1948 and 2011 that asked a sample of presidential scholars to rate presidents on a five-point scale—"Great," "Near Great," "Average," "Below Average," or "Failure"—using the value-neutral criteria just discussed. In much the same way letter grades are used to calculate your GPA, we averaged these assessments to calculate an overall "GPA" (Great President Average) ranging from 0.0 to 4.0.

We limit our analysis of business experience to the 27 presidents who served after 1860 (Silver 2014). Lincoln was the first president to own a business before entering politics, and this is the beginning of the period of continuous two-party competition between Democrats and Republicans. The table on the next page shows the rankings. We purposely exclude Trump and Obama because there are no evaluations of their administrations.

The figure below shows the results of our hypothesis test, which looks at the average GPA for presidents in each of the three categories. We find no support for the hypothesis that running a successful business makes better presidents. Indeed, the relationship is negative, indicating that presidents with successful business experience have *lower* ratings than others: The two presidents who ran failed businesses had an "A" average (GPA = 3.87); presidents with no business experience average a "C" (GPA = 2.20); the seven with successful businesses average a "D" (GPA = 1.44).

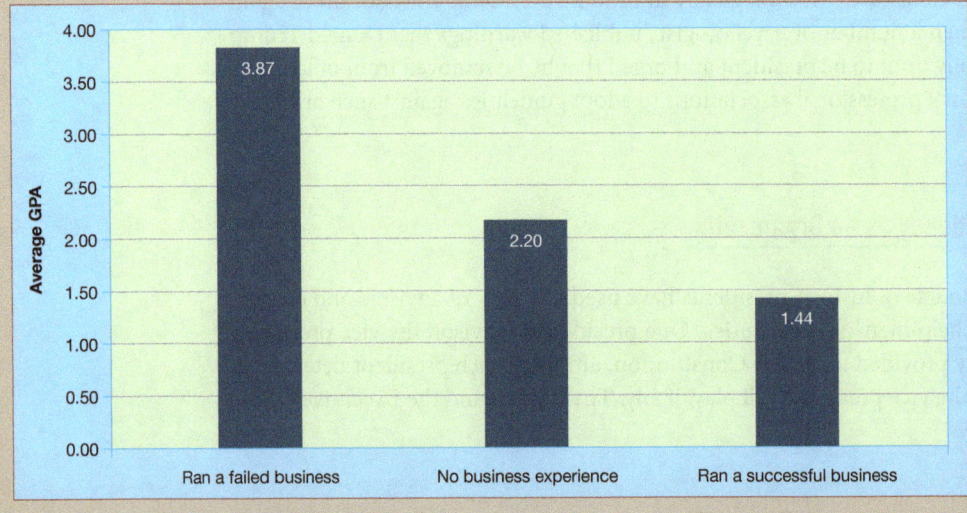

This result, of course, does not mean that running a failed business made them better presidents. We have a small number of cases, and one or two outliers can have a strong effect on the relationship. A more reasonable interpretation is that running a business, successful or otherwise, is simply not related to the job performance of presidents. Governments and for-profit businesses are different types of organizations with different goals. The skillset that helps achieve the goals in one sector does not necessarily transfer to the other sector.

Discussion Questions

1. Although business experience doesn't seem to matter, can you think of another variable that is strongly associated with being a highly rated president? (Hint: look at the far right column of the table.) Why is this variable so strongly associated with high ratings?
2. Can you think of any other measurable qualities or experiences that might screen out individuals who might be below average or failed presidents? How can we measure these qualities? Why would they make better presidents? Is there evidence to support this hypothesis?

OVERALL RATINGS OF PRESIDENTS FROM LINCOLN TO BUSH

	Rank	Average Rating	President	Party	Business Experience	Elected to Second Term
Great (A)	1	4.00	Abraham Lincoln	Rep	Yes (fail)	Yes
	1	4.00	Franklin D. Roosevelt	Dem	Yes	Yes
	5	3.88	Theodore Roosevelt	Rep		Yes
	6	3.81	Woodrow Wilson	Dem		Yes
	7	3.73	Harry S. Truman	Dem	Yes (fail)	Yes
Near great (B)	9	3.07	John F. Kennedy	Dem		Died in 1st term
	9	3.07	Dwight D. Eisenhower	Rep		Yes
	14	2.91	Ronald Reagan	Rep		Yes
	15	2.86	Lyndon B. Johnson	Dem		Yes
Average (C)	17	2.44	Grover Cleveland	Dem		Yes
	18	2.38	William McKinley	Rep		Yes
	19	2.33	Bill Clinton	Dem		Yes
	21	2.00	William Howard Taft	Rep		
	22	1.90	George H. W. Bush	Rep	Yes	
	24	1.81	Rutherford B. Hayes	Rep		
	25	1.79	Gerald Ford	Rep		
	26	1.63	Chester A. Arthur	Rep		
	27	1.57	Jimmy Carter	Dem	Yes	
Below average (D)	28	1.38	Calvin Coolidge	Rep		Yes
	29	1.36	Richard Nixon	Rep		Yes
	30	1.31	Herbert Hoover	Rep	Yes	
	31	1.25	Benjamin Harrison	Rep		
	33	1.00	George W. Bush	Rep	Yes	Yes
	36	0.75	James A. Garfield	Rep		Died in 1st term
	37	0.69	Ulysses S. Grant	Rep		Yes
Failure (F)	38	0.13	Andrew Johnson	Dem	Yes	
	41	0.00	Warren G. Harding	Rep	Yes	Died in 1st term

of the President (EOP) are authorized and funded by Congress. Other people play key advisory roles because of close personal ties to the president. John Kennedy relied on his brother Robert for advice, and George W. Bush frequently turned to his father, former president George H. W. Bush, for advice. Several presidents have turned to the first lady for political and policy advice. Donald Trump gave his daughter and son-in-law key advisory positions in the White House.

Irrespective of who is president, the presidency is a complex organization made up of many individuals. The major components of the presidency as an organization include the vice president, the cabinet, and the EOP. The individuals who serve in the executive branch often compete and struggle for access to the president, and some are more influential than others.

Vice President

Although the Constitution establishes the office of vice president and sets the same qualifications for the office as for the presidency, it lists no formal executive powers or responsibilities.[4] Historically, vice presidents have not been central policymakers, and ambitious politicians have shunned the office. John Nance Garner, who gave up the position of Speaker of the House to become Franklin Roosevelt's vice president in 1933, most famously summed up the disdain for the office by saying, "The vice presidency isn't worth a pitcher of warm piss" (Rees 1997, 254).

Some vice presidents have essentially been presidents-in-waiting, for when something arose to prevent the president from fulfilling the obligations of the office. The person with the "best job in the country," Will Rogers once quipped, "is the Vice President. All he has to do is get up every morning and say, 'How's the President?'" (quoted in Byrne 1988, 229). It has become common to describe the vice president as "just one heartbeat away from being president." Since 1960, two vice presidents have ascended to the presidency before the end of the president's term—Lyndon Johnson became president after the death of John F. Kennedy in 1963 and Gerald Ford after the resignation of Richard M. Nixon in 1974. The post has also been a stepping stone to the presidency. Richard Nixon and George H. W. Bush, for example, were vice presidents who then ran for and were elected president.

Vice presidents are not always condemned to ceremonial roles in the political backwaters. Vice President Spiro Agnew, for example, made harsh public attacks on critics of the Nixon administration. Vice presidents Nelson Rockefeller, Walter Mondale, George H. W. Bush, and Al Gore put their own stamps on the agendas and policies of the Ford, Carter, Reagan, and Clinton administrations (Berke 1999). Vice President Dick Cheney was so powerful that some wags quipped that George W. Bush was just a heartbeat away from being president. Despite the exaggeration in this political humor, close observers do consider Cheney to be "history's most powerful vice president" (Goldstein 2008, 384). Vice President Joe Biden carried

---

4 Article I, Section 3, gives the vice president some legislative responsibility as president of the Senate with the right to cast a vote to break a tie. But no formal executive power is granted unless the president dies, leaves office, or is disabled, in which case the vice president assumes the duties of the president.

on the growing power of the vice president. An experienced Washington observer argues, "The previous two vice presidents, Cheney and his predecessor, Al Gore, significantly changed that power dynamic. But on Biden's watch the 'OVP'—Office of the Vice President—has become something even more: almost a conjoined twin to the presidency" (Hirsh 2012).

Cabinet

The cabinet consists of the heads of the executive agencies and other officials designated by the president to serve as a council of advisors. The cabinet is more a product of law and historical accident than of constitutional design (Hart 1995). At the Constitutional Convention, Gouverneur Morris offered a detailed and elaborate plan for a Council of State to advise the president. Yet all that remained in the final draft was an indirect reference in Article II, Section 2: The president "may require the opinion, in writing, of the principal officer in each of the executive departments, upon any subject relating to the duties of their respective offices."

The first Congress created the Departments of War, Treasury, and State and the office of attorney general, but it established no formal advisory council. In 1789, George Washington attempted to use the Senate as an advisory council regarding a treaty with Native Americans, but senators refused to discuss the matter in his presence. Angered, Washington left the chamber and turned to the heads of the executive departments for advice. This was the first cabinet.

Every president since has had a cabinet, though its role has varied from one administration to the next. In general, the cabinet's role has declined over time. Reasons for this atrophy are varied. Cabinet secretaries sometimes become advocates for the bureaucratic agencies they head rather than promoting the president's priorities. The White House staff has grown so much that presidents have other sources of expert advice. Many White House staff members were part of the campaign team and were chosen for their demonstrated loyalty to the president. By contrast, cabinet members are not necessarily close to the president, and were appointed either out of electoral debt to some organized group or because the individual's expertise and experience lent credibility to the administration.

The cabinet consists of the heads of the executive agencies and other officials designated by the president to serve as a council of advisors. Cabinet members can serve the interests of the president above and beyond providing advice and use their positions to pursue the administration's agenda. Because they hold high-profile positions and are in close proximity to the president, their appointments are useful in strengthening ties to certain constituencies. Abraham Lincoln selected a strong cabinet that included all of his major rivals for the Republican presidential nomination: William H. Seward as secretary of state (center), Salmon P. Chase as secretary of the treasury (second from left), and Edward Bates as attorney general (far right). Here Lincoln reads them the Emancipation Proclamation on July 22, 1862.

© Bettmann/CORBIS

The decline of the cabinet as an advisory structure also reflects the evolution of the presidency as a distinct and separate entity within the executive branch. In the past 50 years, the boundary between the White House staff, who are loyal to the current president, and the career civil servants in the permanent departments and agencies of the federal government has become much sharper.

Despite this decline, cabinet members retain important and influential positions in the political system. The head of an executive agency such as the Department of Justice or the Department of Defense has enormous responsibilities and a strong position from which to influence both the policy governing the agency and the way that policy is implemented. Cabinet members can also serve the interests of the president beyond providing advice and using their positions to pursue the administration's agenda. Because they hold high-profile positions and are in proximity to the president, their appointments are useful in strengthening ties to certain constituencies. President Barack Obama, for example, appointed Senator Hillary Clinton, his primary rival for the nomination, to be secretary of state. The Democratic Party establishment had viewed Senator Clinton as the heir apparent, and Bill Clinton had used his influence as a past president and party leader to support her bid. By appointing her to this crucial and visible cabinet position, Obama helped soothe lingering disappointment with important Democratic Party constituencies. Obama also reappointed Robert Gates, President Bush's secretary of defense. Gates gave the young president credibility with the military, and his appointment signaled the president's desire to work with Republicans in a bipartisan way to solve some of the nation's most thorny problems. Donald Trump won the Republican nomination in 2016 running against the party establishment. He belittled current and former governors and senators who had been expected to be the serious contenders, as well as congressional leaders who criticized him. Although several cabinet appointments had no government experience, his appointment of Elaine Chao to be secretary of transportation may appeal to establishment Republicans. Chao served as George W. Bush's secretary of labor, and in other cabinet level positions in earlier administrations. And she is married to Senate Majority Leader Mitch McConnell (R-KY), a frequent target of Trump's displeasure with the Republican establishment.

Executive Office of the President

The president's closest and most influential advisors are in the **Executive Office of the President (EOP)**. Congress established the EOP in 1939 after the Brownlow Committee (a blue ribbon committee appointed by President Franklin D. Roosevelt) recommended organizational changes to make the executive branch more efficient. This office has grown in size and complexity over time. The EOP is not part of the cabinet, though cabinet secretaries are members of some of its units.

Among the various units in the EOP, the **White House Office** houses the president's most influential advisors. White House staffers include the chief of staff; the White House legal counsel; presidential speechwriters; the president's press secretary; assistants for domestic, foreign, and economic policy; and liaisons with

---

Executive Office of the President (EOP) The organizational structure in the executive branch that houses the president's most influential advisors and agencies. The most important include the White House Office, the Office of Management and Budget (OMB), the National Security Council, and the Council of Economic Advisers.

White House Office A section of the Executive Office of the President that houses many of the most influential advisors to the president, including the chief of staff; the White House legal counsel; presidential speechwriters; the president's press secretary; assistants for domestic, foreign, and economic policy; and liaisons with Congress, the public, and state and local governments.

Congress, the public, and state and local governments. This office also includes the president's personal staff, the vice president, and the first lady's staff.

Over the years, Congress has placed several other agencies under the EOP umbrella. The most important include the **Office of Management and Budget (OMB)**, the **National Security Council**, and the **Council of Economic Advisers**. As the EOP has expanded into a series of agencies with focused responsibilities, staffers have become increasingly specialized. After his first term in office, Franklin Roosevelt had fewer than 100 presidential assistants, most of them generalists with such titles as assistant to the president or counsel to the president. In recent administrations, the OMB alone had more than 500 employees, most of them with specialties in areas such as national security, human resources, or natural resources. With the growth and specialization of the White House Office, the presidency has taken on the trappings of a large bureaucratic organization. Political scientists Lyn Ragsdale and John Theis (1997) argue that the presidency has become "institutionalized" and that it has grown into a large, complex, permanent organization that all presidents must learn to manage once they take office.

First Lady

The role of the president's spouse has evolved over time. Originally, the first lady had mostly social duties, acting as a hostess and the like. But over the years, first ladies have become much more prominent as political and policy advisors, reflecting the changing role of women in society.[5]

Eleanor Roosevelt was one of the best-known politically active presidential spouses. She traveled widely to assess social and economic conditions, had her own newspaper column, and was a key member of Franklin Roosevelt's "kitchen cabinet," a group of individuals who were not members of the official cabinet and who fed the president's voracious appetite for information. Taking such a high-profile, nontraditional role was controversial, a problem other politically powerful first ladies encountered as well. President Jimmy Carter's reliance on his wife Rosalynn's advice led some to view her as "the second most powerful person in the United States" (Gutin 1994, 521). Bill Clinton appointed his wife, Hillary, to head a task force on healthcare reform and elevated the position of first lady to a more formal policy role than previous administrations had. Because they had influence and power without having been elected or formally appointed, both Rosalynn Carter and Hillary Clinton were controversial figures during their husbands' presidential terms.[6] President George W. Bush credited First Lady Laura Bush as the most important guiding force in his life, but

Office of Management and Budget (OMB) An agency of the Executive Office of the President that is responsible for assisting the president in creating the budget.

National Security Council A group of presidential advisors made up of the vice president, the attorney general, and cabinet officers chosen by the president to advise the president on national security issues; it is part of the Executive Office of the President.

Council of Economic Advisers An agency of the Executive Office of the President that is responsible for advising the president on the U.S. economy.

---

5 So far, there has been no first gentleman, and only two presidents were unmarried during their terms. Thomas Jefferson's wife died before he became president, and in his administration, hostess duties were performed by either his daughters or Dolley Madison, wife of Secretary of State James Madison. So far in the nation's history, James Buchanan has been the only bachelor president. During his administration, the official hostess was his niece, Harriet Lane.

6 Hillary Clinton has a political career in her own right. She was elected to the Senate from New York in 2000, becoming the first First Lady to win elective office. After losing her bid for the Democratic nomination for president in 2008, she was appointed secretary of state by President Obama.

Over the years first ladies have become much more prominent as political and policy advisors, reflecting the changing role of women in society. Eleanor Roosevelt had a very strong effect on this changing role. She traveled widely to assess social and economic conditions, had her own newspaper column, and was a key member of Franklin Roosevelt's "kitchen cabinet," a group of individuals who were not members of the official cabinet and who fed the president's voracious appetite for information. Here she tours conditions in a coal mine in Ohio in 1935 with mine officials and members of the United Mine Workers' union.

© Bettmann/CORBIS

her role as political and policy advisor was more behind the scenes and less controversial. Michelle Obama also adopted an uncontroversial role as first lady. Initially, she focused on supporting military families, helping working women balance career and family, and visiting schools to encourage national service. She engaged in a limited number of political activities, including publicly supporting the president's economic stimulus bill and hosting a White House reception for women's rights advocates to celebrate passage of the Lilly Ledbetter Fair Pay Act of 2009. Melania Trump did not immediately begin her duties as First Lady. Instead, she remained at their residence in Trump Tower until June 2018 so their 11-year-old son, Barron, could finish the school year. Her approach to the job of first lady is unlike any of her predecessors, adopting neither the traditional role of a high-profile hostess nor that of a policy advisor. She has remained low key when she accompanied her husband on foreign trips, and hosted a small number of social events.

Organization of the Presidency and Presidential Effectiveness

As the White House staff has grown, it has become more difficult to control and coordinate. More than four decades ago, political scientist Thomas Cronin observed, "The president needs help merely to manage his help. The swelling and continuous expansion of the presidency have reached such proportions that the president's ability to manage has been weakened rather than strengthened. Bigger has not been better" (1975, 118). Despite this warning, mismanagement of the White House staff has been blamed for a number of crises, ranging from an unsuccessful invasion of Cuba during the Kennedy administration to provision of funds to Nicaraguan rebels in contravention of a congressional mandate in the Reagan administration.

Presidents have tried various administrative arrangements to organize the White House staff so that it supports the president's agenda effectively without creating political quagmires. Most presidents use a **hierarchical model**, which sets up hierarchical lines of authority and delegates control through a chief of staff. Other presidents have tried a **spokes-of-the-wheel model**, where the president

hierarchical model A method of organizing the presidency that calls for clear lines of authority and that delegates responsibility from the president and through the chief of staff.

spokes-of-the-wheel model A method of organizing the presidency that calls for the president to be the center of activity, with numerous advisors reporting directly to the president.

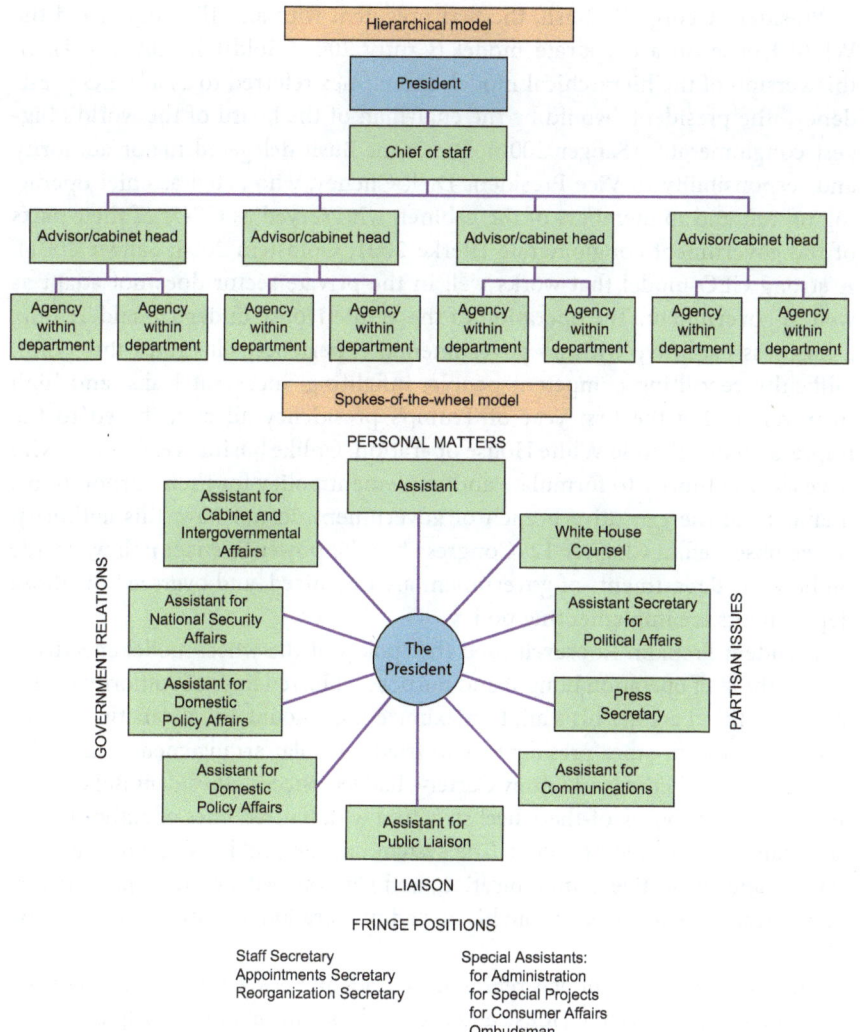

FIGURE 13.1 Two Models of Organizing the White House Staff

Sources: Hierarchical model adapted from George and George (1998, 209); spokes-of-the wheel model adapted from Campbell (1986, 85).

is in the middle, acting as the hub, and various presidential advisors representing the spokes of the wheel report directly to him. Figure 13.1 illustrates these models.

The hierarchical structure, with clear lines of authority going through a chief of staff, fit well with President Dwight Eisenhower's military experience. It was an efficient system that insulated Eisenhower from small details and allowed him to set general policy goals and build political support for them. President Richard Nixon also used a hierarchical model, with access to the president controlled by the chief of staff. Although the Nixon White House was efficient from a managerial standpoint, it insulated the president from the perspective and political insights of cabinet members and members of Congress.

President George W. Bush, the first president with an MBA, organized the White House on a corporate model (Crotty 2003; Goldstein 2008, 384). In this version of the hierarchical model, sometimes referred to as a "CEO presidency," the president "would be the chairman of the board of the world's biggest conglomerate" (Sanger 2001). President Bush delegated major authority and responsibility to Vice President Dick Cheney, who acted as chief operating officer, and to members of the cabinet, who served as CEOs of their parts of the government conglomerate (Berke 2001; Goldstein 2008; Sanger 2001). A strong CEO model that works well in the private sector does not adapt as well in government. The operation of the White House under Donald Trump, a business executive with no governmental experience, illustrates this point. Difficulty recruiting competent people, infighting, incessant leaks, and high turnover during the first year of Trump's presidency all contributed to the impression of a chaotic White House operation. Unlike business executives who have clear authority to formulate and implement policy for their corporations, members of the executive branch of government do not have this authority. As we observed in Chapter 12, Congress has the power to enact policy, decide on how the departments of government are organized, and oversee how those departments are implementing policy.

President Franklin Roosevelt used the spokes-of-the-wheel model effectively. He ran the staff operation himself and purposely blurred lines of authority to create competition among his staff, to maximize the amount and diversity of information. However, other presidents who tried a similar arrangement—e.g., John Kennedy, Gerald Ford, and Jimmy Carter—had less success. President Bill Clinton initially tried a spokes-of-the-wheel structure with blurred lines of authority and easy staff access to the president. The system created problems of slow decision making and ineffective communication, and Clinton switched to a more hierarchical arrangement two years into his first administration (G. Edwards and Wayne 2003).

The choice between models represents a tradeoff between the president's need for control over the White House and the need for information to help the president provide broad political leadership to adequately address the nation's problems. The hierarchical model maximizes control with clear lines of authority and responsibility. The problem is that it isolates the president; the president deals mostly with a small group of people who filter information from various sources and report to the president. Under the hierarchical model, the president may not receive information about the full range of opportunities and options available. The president does not keep tabs on lower-echelon assistants, who may take actions the president does not support.

The spokes-of-the-wheel model maximizes the amount and diversity of information available by giving the president access to more advisors. The problem is that the president can end up with too much information to process effectively and may be dragged into micromanaging minor details that could and should be handled by others. If the danger of the hierarchical system is that the president becomes isolated, the danger of the spokes-of-the-wheel system is that the president will be overwhelmed.

THE PRESIDENT'S PRIMARY CONSTITUTIONAL RESPONSIBILITIES

Article II, Sections 1 and 2 of the Constitution define the president's primary responsibilities. These include chief executive, commander in chief of the military, and chief diplomat.

Chief Executive

The executive power referenced in the opening sentence of Article II entails a number of activities. Organizing the presidency and being an effective manager, as discussed previously, are important executive duties. The president can also grant pardons and reprieves. The core of executive power involves implementation of the nation's laws.

Article II, Section 3 does not mandate that the president implements the laws but rather that the president "shall *take care* that the laws be faithfully executed" (emphasis added). In effect, the president is the chief bureaucrat because executing the laws is mainly the job of the federal bureaucracy. The president has the responsibility of making sure the federal bureaucracy is fulfilling its responsibilities as designated by law.

Administering this vast and varied operation is an enormous challenge. Many who implement the laws are not directly subordinate to the president; the president cannot fire or cut the salaries of individuals in the civil service. Others who serve at the president's discretion, such as cabinet secretaries, often develop political power bases independent of the president.

As chief executive, the president has the power to appoint individuals to fill the most important positions in the executive branch. But here too there are constraints, the most important of which is that appointments require confirmation by the Senate. Although the Senate eventually confirms over 90 percent of presidential nominations to executive branch agencies (cabinet, EOP, and major regulatory agencies), the length of time required for the Senate to act on these nominations has increased for recent presidents. Figure 13.2 shows the average number of months it took the Senate to process top-level executive branch nominations for the last nine presidents. During the Johnson, Nixon, Ford, and Carter presidencies, the Senate generally acted on executive branch nominations in about a month. For subsequent administrations, the time required to act on nominations increased exponentially, doubling to about two months for Reagan, the senior Bush, and Clinton in his first term and then doubling again to nearly four months from Clinton's second term to Obama.

Delaying confirmation of major executive branch officials an extra month or two also delays the president's ability "to take care that the laws be faithfully executed." But not only does it take longer for the Senate to act on executive branch

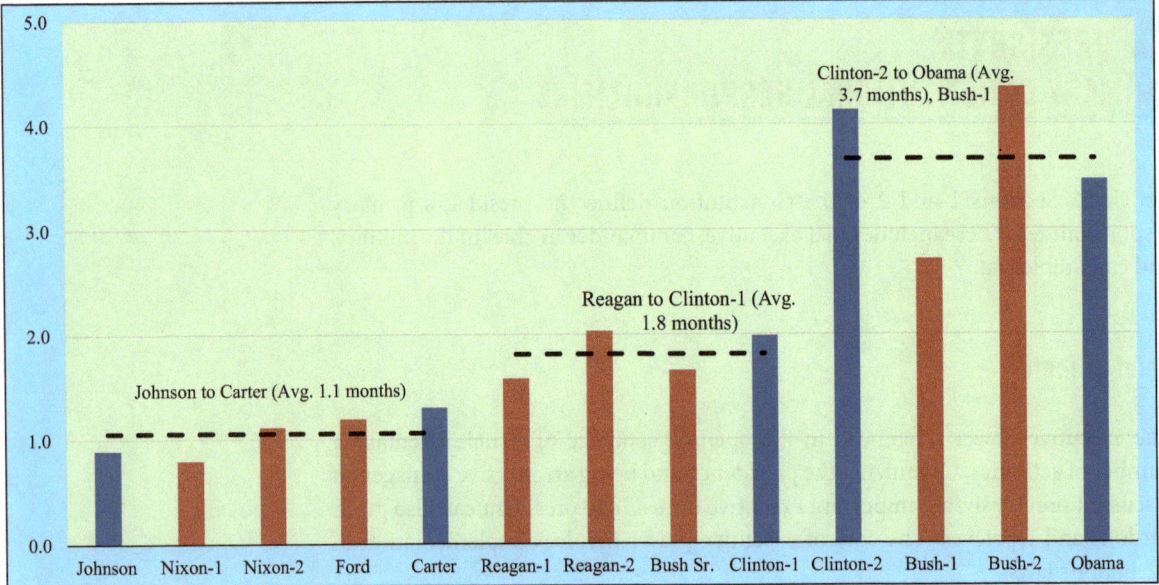

FIGURE 13.2 Length of the Confirmation Process for Executive Branch Nominations

Source: Data from Bond, Fleisher, and Krutz (2009); Obama nominations updated by the authors.

appointments, but also failure rates have increased (see Figure 13.3). For presidents before Reagan the failure rate for appointments to the cabinet, EOP, and regulatory agencies was less than 3 percent. The average doubled to almost 6 percent from the Reagan years to Clinton's first term. From Clinton's second term to Obama, the failure rate on top executive branch appointments jumped to an average of nearly 15 percent. Thus, recent presidents have to wait longer to put top administrative personnel in place, and they are less likely to get their first choice.

Furthermore, the president does not have the authority to determine the particular organization and structure of the executive branch. Instead, Congress determines the number of executive departments and frequently creates executive branch agencies that are insulated from the president. For example, the president appoints individuals to the Federal Reserve Board ("the Fed") and the Federal Election Commission (FEC), but members serve for fixed terms that overlap with the president's term, and these appointees cannot be removed except for wrongdoing.

Commander in Chief

Article II, Section 2 of the Constitution clearly states that "the President shall be commander-in-chief of the Army and Navy of the United States, and of the militia of the several states." Although this is a broad grant of power to the president, the extent of the power is the subject of some dispute. One view is that the president's

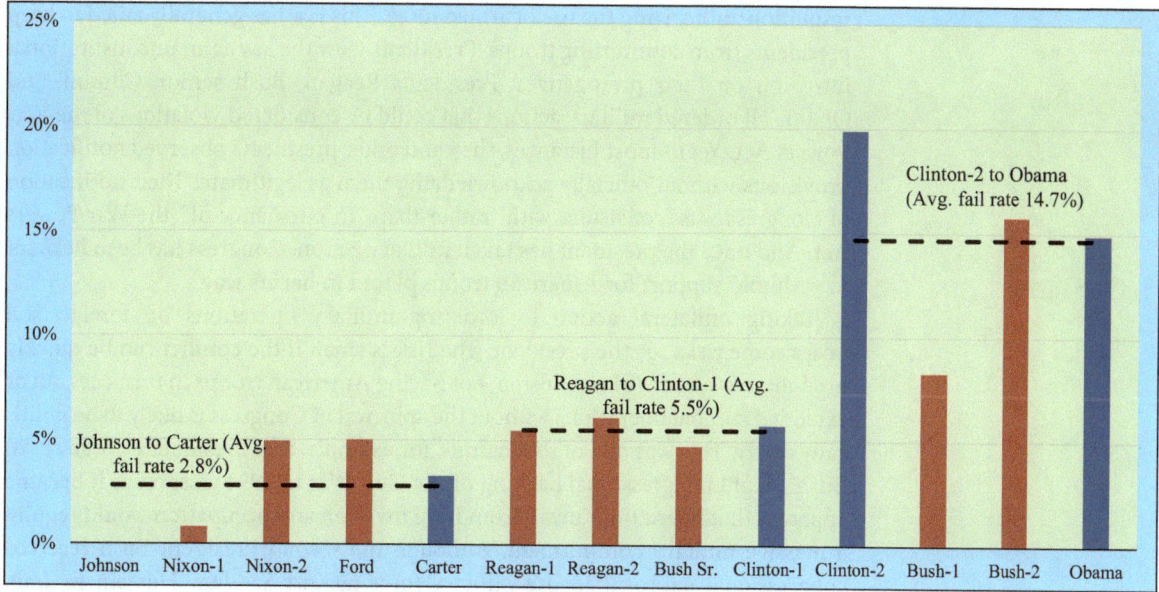

FIGURE 13.3 Failure Rates of Executive Branch Appointments

Source: Data from Bond, Fleisher, and Krutz (2009); Obama nominations updated by the authors.

power is limited to acting as civilian head of the military, with authority for the general policy direction and command of the armed forces. The other view is that this provision empowers the president to take direct operational command. George Washington's response to the Whiskey Rebellion that erupted in western Pennsylvania in 1794 set a precedent that seems to support this latter view. President Washington rode at the head of an army of state militias to suppress the insurrection. President Lincoln also asserted this view during the Civil War, and a number of other presidents, including Franklin Roosevelt, Harry Truman, Ronald Reagan, George H. W. Bush, Bill Clinton, George W. Bush, and Barack Obama, have acted as if they had direct operational command (G. Edwards and Wayne 2003, 487).

The president has greater autonomy in the exercise of the power as commander in chief than in the exercise of other executive powers. The Constitution grants Congress sole authority to declare war, and Congress passes laws establishing funding and regulating the military. Nonetheless, the president has the power—even the duty—to commit military forces to protect U.S. interests without having to wait for a formal declaration of war.

Attempts to limit the president's authority to commit troops without congressional approval have been largely unsuccessful. One important attempt to limit the power of the commander in chief is the War Powers Act of 1973. This law requires the president to consult "in every possible instance" with Congress before sending troops into action and to report such actions to Congress within 48 hours. Troops must be withdrawn after 60 days unless Congress declares war or passes a resolution authorizing the use of armed force. This law has generally failed to keep presidents from committing troops. Presidents view the law as an unconstitutional intrusion on their prerogatives. Presidents Reagan, Bush senior, Clinton, and Obama all ordered military actions that could be considered violations of the War Powers Act. Yet in most instances, they and other presidents observed notification provisions without officially acknowledging them as legitimate: Their notification of Congress was "consistent with" rather than "in pursuance of" the War Powers Act. And once the president has taken military action, Congress has been hesitant to withhold support for American troops placed in harm's way.

Taking unilateral action by ordering military operations on foreign soil poses some risks for the president. The risk is small if the conflict can be quickly brought to a successful conclusion, but having American troops in unsuccessful or extended combat operations without the approval of Congress is likely to be politically costly. This was one of the reasons, for example, that President George H. W. Bush sought congressional backing of the Gulf War in 1991 as soon as it became apparent that liberating Kuwait from Iraqi invasion and occupation would require a massive military commitment. Although the second President Bush received congressional approval to use military force against Saddam Hussein in Iraq, extended combat operations and questions regarding whether the invasion was justified eroded support for the war.

Chief Diplomat

The president's central role in foreign policy is a product of tradition and of the unique constitutional authority to "make treaties" subject to ratification by two-thirds of the Senate and to appoint ambassadors subject to confirmation by a majority in the Senate (Article II, Section 2). These constitutional provisions place the president at the center of foreign policy formulation, and presidents have interpreted these powers very broadly. George Washington, for example, assumed that the power to receive ambassadors also conferred the power to formally recognize other nations. Presidents have also used their powers as commander in chief to assert a primary role in foreign policy.

The president is the government official who negotiates treaties. Although the Constitution calls for the president to obtain the advice and consent of the Senate, Washington's attempt to seek advice from the Senate was unsuccessful, as noted earlier, and the Senate's role has been confined almost exclusively to deciding whether to consent. Presidents sometimes discuss controversial provisions of treaties with key senators in an effort to avoid difficulties with ratification, which requires a two-thirds vote. Sometimes, the Senate approves a treaty with reservations or amendments, necessitating further negotiations.

Since 1789, more than 90 percent of the hundreds of treaties submitted to the Senate have been approved—70 percent without any change. Of the treaties that failed, only about 20 were defeated on a floor vote; about 150 others were withdrawn by the president, mostly because they ran into resistance in the Senate. The most famous example of a treaty voted down on the Senate floor is the Treaty of Versailles, which ended World War I and established the League of Nations. It failed in large part because President Woodrow Wilson was unwilling to consult with key senators and to agree to compromises. In order to win approval of the Panama Canal Treaty in 1978, President Jimmy Carter agreed to a reservation added by the Senate stating that the United States had the right to use military force to keep the canal open if necessary (G. Edwards and Wayne 2003, 179).

The 90 percent approval rate, however, does not mean that presidents have an easy time winning approval of treaties they have negotiated. Although the Senate rarely turns down a treaty outright, treaties often languish for years in Senate committees that take no action to move them through the process. Presidents have responded to this difficulty by entering into **executive agreements** with other nations. These are treaties in all but name. An executive agreement takes the legal form of a contract between two nations, which does not require two-thirds approval from the Senate. As Figure 13.4 shows, presidents since Franklin Roosevelt (1933–1944) have negotiated many more executive agreements than treaties.

Although executive agreements account for more than 90 percent of all U.S. international agreements, this does not mean that presidents are using this device to usurp the Senate's power under the Constitution. Glen Krutz and Jeffrey Peake present persuasive evidence that the use of executive agreements "is a rational

executive agreements Agreements between the United States and other nations, negotiated by the president, that have the same weight as a treaty but do not require senatorial approval.

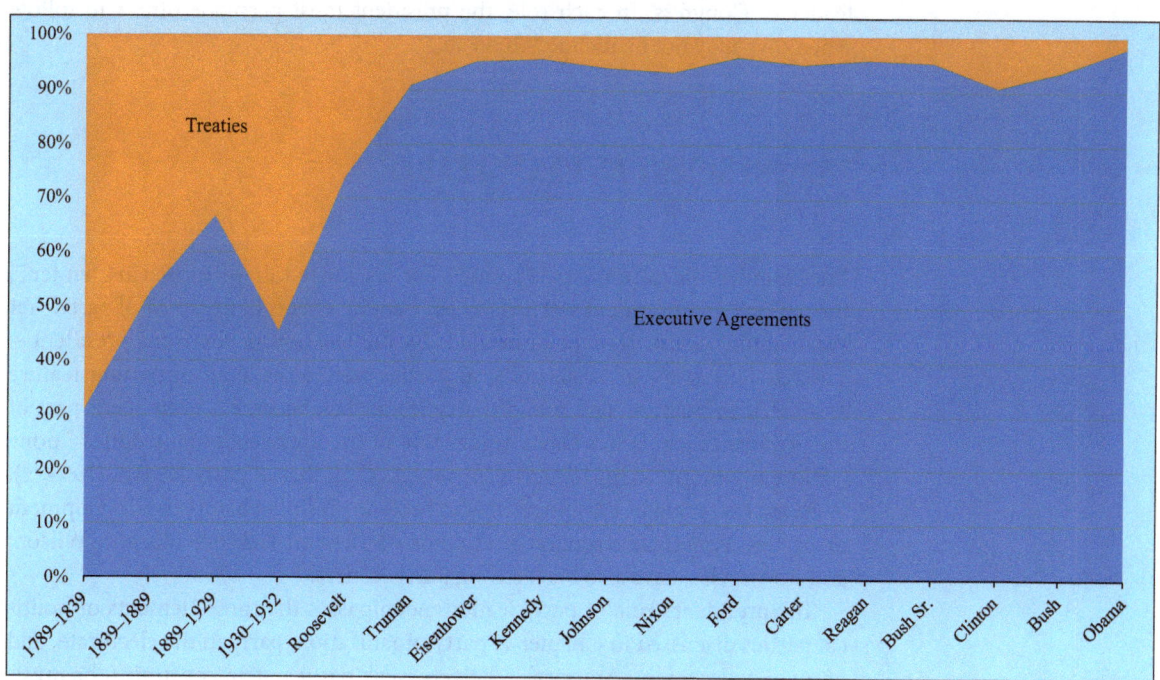

FIGURE 13.4 **Proportion of Treaties and Executive Agreements**

Source: Data from Stanley and Niemi (2013, 322); Krutz and Peake (2011); Peake (2018).

adaptation by [the president and Congress] to the complex foreign policy environment" (2009, 187). Most executive agreements involve minor, routine issues. If all of the hundreds of international agreements negotiated during each two-year Congress were submitted to the Senate as treaties for ratification, the Senate would be overwhelmed with minor issues and unable to deal with more consequential matters. Some executive agreements deal with weightier matters, and presidents typically submit these to Congress. The North American Free Trade Agreement (NAFTA), for example, was an executive agreement negotiated by President George H. W. Bush in 1992 to provide open markets among the United States, Canada, and Mexico. Although NAFTA did not require congressional approval, President Bush—and later President Clinton—recognized the political costs of not involving Congress in an agreement with such broad implications. Bush sent the agreement to both the Senate and the House in order to get legislation to implement NAFTA, and Congress approved the NAFTA legislation in 1993 (Ragsdale 1996, 290). NAFTA was not a treaty, so it did not require approval by a two-thirds vote in the Senate. But the enabling legislation—the law that put the agreement into effect—had to pass both houses by a simple majority. In this way, the House of Representatives sometimes plays a role in the treaty-making process—not in ratifying treaties, but in passing the legislation necessary to implement them.

The president's constitutional responsibilities as chief executive, commander in chief, and chief diplomat are well-known. We turn now to a discussion on three other presidential roles: leader of the political party, leader of public opinion, and leader of Congress. In each role, the president must persuade others to follow when they may not be inclined to do so.

THE PRESIDENT AS PARTY LEADER

The Founders did not anticipate political parties. Indeed, as we learned in Chapter 7, the nation's first president warned of the "baneful effects of the spirit of party." Yet Washington's warning went unheeded. By the election of the third president—Thomas Jefferson—in 1800, political parties were already an important feature of American politics. The role of party leader has become a permanent part of the president's job. James Davis argues that of the president's many duties, "none is more important to his longer-term success than that of party leader" (1994, 1). With the exception of Washington, who became president before the development of parties, America's strongest presidents—Jefferson, Jackson, Lincoln, Wilson, and Roosevelt—have also been strong party leaders.

The president's role of party leader encompasses the three elements of political parties discussed in Chapter 7: party organization, party in the electorate, and party in government. America's relatively weak party system constrains the president's ability to lead in each of these areas, and the effort devoted to party building varies from one president to the next.

Limitations on the President as Party Leader

Several features of American politics limit the president's ability to act as party leader. First is the traditional mistrust of parties, dating back to the founding. This suspicion promotes an inclination to be "president of all the people" and a fear that being too partisan is politically risky.

Constitutional fragmentation of powers also limits the president's ability to act as party leader. Federalism has led to national party organizations that are essentially confederations of 50 separate and autonomous state organizations. National party chairs and committees have little authority over state parties, and the president has little hope of centralizing control over such broad and often factious coalitions.

The separation of the national government into executive, legislative, and judicial branches further limits the president's party leadership. Although the president is the nominal head of the party, fellow partisans in other branches have not chosen the president as the leader and have limited influence over the president's policy positions. The reverse is also true: The president has little control over who wears the party's label in Congress and the policies the legislators support. House members and senators have to satisfy local constituencies, not the president, to get elected and reelected. The result is that although the president may be the most visible and influential player in defining the party's position on an issue, he or she will have competition from fellow party members who are officeholders in other branches and the states.

Finally, reforms of the 1880s and early 1900s, especially the decline of patronage and the rise of direct primaries, eroded party discipline and the role of party leaders. Rank-and-file voters, not party leaders, choose the party's standard-bearers in direct primaries. This reform bred independence within parties, and elected officials feel free to take positions contrary to the wishes of party leaders if it serves their reelection needs. Civil service reforms robbed the party of the patronage jobs and contracts distributed to party supporters in return for their electoral help. Thus, party leaders have neither the carrot (jobs for supporters) nor the stick (control of nominations) to secure party loyalty. As the head of the party, the president has not been immune from the weakened position the reforms assigned to party leaders. Even with such limitations, however, presidents must attend to party affairs if they are to be successful.

The President and Party Organization

As an organization, the national party is most active during presidential election years. Between elections, the national party's business is managed by a national party chair and a national committee made up of state party leaders. Although the president is recognized as the titular head of this organization, the president is not an officer of the party and has no formal authority.

Each president decides how much to emphasize the role of party leader. As an academic political scientist before he became president, Woodrow Wilson had a clear vision of the president's role as a strong party leader. He believed that political parties should be the vehicle of presidential leadership, and he envisioned presidents developing a direct relationship with citizens by rallying public opinion in support of administration proposals. As acknowledged party leader, the president would use the loyal support of fellow partisans to enact the administration's program. Franklin Roosevelt was also a strong party leader; he strategically stitched together a New Deal coalition of Democrats from the South and ethnic minorities from the North to transform the Democratic Party into a majority. Recent presidents, such as Ronald Reagan, Bill Clinton, George W. Bush, and Barack Obama made serious efforts to expand and build their national party bases.

Presidents can shape party organization even before they are elected to office. The candidate who controls a majority of delegates at the party's national convention usually controls most aspects of the convention, including choosing major officers, formulating the party platform, and selecting a running mate. This power offers an opportunity to put together a unified party base behind a set of clear proposals. It also has dangers. If significant numbers of the president's party disagree with the plans, they may fight the platform or force the convention to showcase candidates who opposed the winner. At the 1992 Republican convention, for example, President George H. W. Bush was forced to give more prominence and deference than he desired to supporters of rival Pat Buchanan. The result was public emphasizing of differences between factions in the Republican Party, which was not the preferred outcome of a party leader heading into a tough general election campaign.

The presidential candidate also names the national party chair, typically someone instrumental in securing the candidate's nomination. This power allows the president to influence the party organization between electoral cycles. Historically, the party chair was given a cabinet position, typically as postmaster general, a key source of patronage jobs. (This ended in 1970 when the Post Office Department became an independent government agency.) With the decline of patronage, party chairs are no longer given cabinet positions; the last to have one, Robert Hannegan, resigned his post in 1947.

The President and Electoral Activities

The president occupies a unique place within the electoral process. Many people would prefer the president to be above partisan bickering in the electoral arena, but the president can hardly avoid electoral activities. The presidency is, after all, an elective office, and as the de facto leader of a political party, a president also has some incentive to become involved in congressional campaigns.

Presidential Elections

One of the central difficulties the president faces as party leader is the presidential electoral process. Presidential campaigns are often candidate-centered, focusing on election of the candidate rather than the overall success of the party. The candidate's campaign organization is separate from the party, and its loyalty lies more with the candidate than with the party organization. Donald Trump won the Republican nomination while criticizing Republican elected officials and rejecting long-held Republican policy priorities such as supporting free trade.

This separation between candidate and party is increased by the rules governing the selection of presidential candidates. The need to wage primary battles to gain the majority of national convention delegates all but forces presidential candidates to engage in public disagreements with other candidates in the party. Party reforms (discussed in Chapter 10) have limited party leaders' control over nominations, and the party organization usually tries to remain neutral in the nomination battles. Winning a presidential nomination has much less to do with the leadership of the formal party organization than with the amount and type of media exposure a candidate receives, the campaign's finances, and the candidate's momentum (Bartels 1993). Since party officials have limited influence in the selection of a nominee, they feel less of a bond to the party's presidential candidate.

Congressional Elections

The president can choose to assist the electoral efforts of congressional candidates or to have little to do with them. Presidents sometimes choose a limited role in congressional campaigns out of fear of needlessly antagonizing opposition party members in Congress. Especially during divided government—a president of one party and a congressional majority of the other—the president is dependent on opposition votes to secure the administration's legislative priorities.

The rise of party-line voting in Congress since the 1980s (discussed in Chapter 12) has made it more difficult for the president to attract support from opposition party members (Fleisher and Bond 2000b). Although greater partisanship may amplify the benefits of unified government (i.e., a Congress controlled by the president's party), the president's ability to affect who ends up in Congress is limited. The large number of House seats limits significant presidential involvement to a fraction of them. Even popular presidents find it difficult to transfer their popularity to others, especially when they themselves are not on the ballot.

As discussed in Chapter 10, incumbents in Congress usually are in strong positions for reelection. In most congressional races, there is little point in expending effort on a candidate who has a high probability of winning regardless of the president's involvement. Moreover, campaign involvement depends not only on the president's desire and ability to help but also on the congressional candidate's perception of whether such support would be useful.

George Bush's and Barack Obama's experiences with midterm elections vividly demonstrate the limited effect presidents have on congressional elections. Bush engaged in a vigorous campaign to help elect more Republicans to the House and Senate in the 2002 midterm elections. These activities increased the narrow Republican majorities in Congress, but only in a handful of races. In the 2006 midterms, Bush's influence was limited by voter dissatisfaction with the war in Iraq. In 2008,

Bush's popularity was so low that GOP congressional candidates viewed him as a campaign liability. In the 2010 midterm elections, Republicans regained control of the House, picking up 63 seats, the largest gain for a party since the 1938 elections. The Republican sweep was due in large part to the unpopularity of President Obama's policies, especially healthcare reform (G. Jacobson 2013, 223–226).

THE PRESIDENT AS PUBLIC OPINION LEADER

Americans have varying attitudes about their government and their elected leaders. They also have different views about specific political and social problems and what should be done about them. The president is a central focus for all these views and attitudes. The chief executive is the symbol and personification of the state and is expected to inspire feelings of loyalty and patriotism, especially in times of crisis. Political opponents closed ranks behind Franklin Roosevelt after the Japanese bombing of Pearl Harbor in December 1941 and behind George W. Bush after the terrorist attacks of September 11, 2001.

As a symbol of the state, the presidency involves some of the ceremony and pomp associated with monarchy. Presidential inaugurations are similar to royal coronations, complete with a solemn oath taken in the midst of notables and the multitudes. Other ceremonial aspects of the office include the presidential seal, the music ("Hail to the Chief") that is played at official events, social duties such as entertaining foreign heads of state when they visit Washington, DC, and the lighting of the giant Christmas tree on the White House lawn. Such activities emphasize the chief executive's embodiment of the nation and its ideals.

Unlike monarchs in democracies such as the United Kingdom, the president not only reigns but also rules. Part of the president's job is to develop and implement policies that are binding on the entire populace. To achieve policy goals, the president needs to lead public opinion on important issues. At the same time, the president needs to be responsive to public opinion and to respect the limits that public attitudes place on presidential actions. It is a delicate balance.

One of the most important tools available to the president to shape public opinion is the high profile of the office. The public spotlight illuminates almost everything about the president, from stands on issues to reading habits and favorite foods. This public attention provides a bully pulpit, "a unique and imposing podium available only to the President as the one public official … elected by the nation as a whole and invested with all the trappings of his great office" (Mervin 1995, 19). Presidents seek to use this bully pulpit to establish close ties with a variety of publics in order to convert personal popularity into political effectiveness.

Such has not always been the case. The Founders envisioned a president removed from public passions rather than one who shapes and leads them. Insulation from public opinion was a central motivation in developing the electoral college. At least through the end of the nineteenth century, most presidents were somewhat detached from the public.

Going Public

Before becoming president, Woodrow Wilson (1885) argued that the president could remove the shackles imposed by the separation of powers and gain the leverage to act decisively by constructing broad public support for proposals. Modern presidents have come to act on it as a matter of routine. As we discussed earlier, Richard Neustadt (1960) argues that presidential power ultimately rests on the ability to persuade other political actors to do what the president wants. It is much easier to do that when the president has overwhelming public support.

According to Samuel Kernell (1997), contemporary presidents use public support not only as leverage with other political actors but also to evade those other actors. Kernell dubbed the strategy of taking a case directly to American citizens "**going public**." Presidents who go public make increased use of political rhetoric and create political spectacles in an effort to shape public beliefs. Going public is close to the leadership strategy envisioned by Wilson. Presidents make direct contact with the public to build public pressure to act on administration proposals in three ways: personal trips, managing communications with the media, and speeches.

Personal Trips

One of the earliest methods presidents used to communicate with the American public was a "grand tour." George Washington took a two-month trip through the South in 1791. This trip allowed him to assess the disposition of the people, and it reassured him that the new Federalist government was popular in the South. Modern presidents have continued this tradition. If nothing else, breaking from the confines of Washington, DC, to enjoy the adulation of crowds is reassuring to the president.

Modern presidents often find it helpful to extend their travels abroad. Economic summits, consultations with foreign heads of state, and visits to historical sites and memorials provide a chance to appear presidential and to capture the attention of a variety of publics. Contemporary presidents travel more than their predecessors. Harry Truman, for example, made only seven foreign appearances; Bill Clinton made 62 in his first two years in office (Ragsdale 1996, 170).

Although presidential trips offer opportunities to connect with various publics, they also have risks. Ironically, it was Woodrow Wilson who suffered one of the biggest failures of using personal trips to go public. When his case in favor of the Versailles peace treaty and the League of Nations met resistance in the Senate, he opted for the grand tour strategy to drum up support among the American people. Although he received some support in the West, he ran into a wall of indifference in the Midwest. His tour ended when he fell ill, and his efforts failed to move recalcitrant senators. President George W. Bush's "60 Stops in 60 Days" tour to promote his proposal to reform Social Security also failed to stem the tide of growing public opposition to the private account plan (Villalobos 2006).

There are costs even in a successful presidential trip. Grand tours divert time and attention from other aspects of a demanding job. In recent years, vice presidents and first ladies increasingly have been pressed into service and have journeyed

going public A political strategy in which the president appeals to the public in an effort to persuade Congress to support his or her political goals.

at home and abroad as presidential surrogates. Leading cabinet members are also frequently dispatched to explain administration policies to interest the public and to gauge reaction.

The Press

The press has been an important link between a president and the public. Early in our history, the press was partisan. The *Gazette of the United States* was the Federalists' party organ, whereas the *National Gazette* spoke for the Democratic-Republicans. During Andrew Jackson's presidency, federal officeholders were expected to subscribe to the party paper. The paper itself was given government contracts to print official notices. Today, the press is independent of political parties but still provides much of the raw material for public opinion.

Presidents recognize the importance of the press. Theodore Roosevelt initiated the practice of granting personal interviews and provided working quarters for reporters in the White House. Woodrow Wilson established the practice of inviting Washington correspondents to regular press conferences. Contemporary presidents have sophisticated press operations staffed with experts whose primary duty is to interact with and pass information to the news media.

Over the years, press conferences have evolved into important tools to influence public opinion and gauge the public mind. Presidents have used press conferences in different ways. Some, such as Warren Harding, Calvin Coolidge, and Herbert Hoover, required questions to be submitted in advance, a practice prompted by Harding's difficulty responding to a question about a treaty. Most presidents take spontaneous questions. The frequency of press conferences, though, varies. George H. W. Bush and Bill Clinton made themselves much more available to the press than Ronald Reagan and George W. Bush.

Some of this variation is almost certainly due to the extent that presidents feel at ease with formal press conferences. President Lyndon Johnson preferred to deal with small groups of reporters and experimented with informal, hastily called conferences in a variety of settings. Bill Clinton, on the other hand, was articulate and well versed in the complex details of policy, and he performed well in front of a crowd of rowdy reporters.

Presidents do not limit themselves to press conferences and interviews with the Washington press corps. John Kennedy invited newspaper editors and owners from around the nation to White House conferences where he discussed major public issues. Richard Nixon, who had a strained relationship with the White House press corps, experimented with a number of approaches, ranging from briefing members of selected news organizations to furnishing editorial writers with transcripts of his speeches and comments. Bill Clinton was a master of unscripted media appearances such as talk shows and televised "town meetings."

Much of the interaction between the White House and the press does not directly involve the president. Like other aspects of the modern presidency, the relationship between the media and the president has become highly formalized. Because presidents are concerned about the information the media present, the

White House Press Office filters much of the contact between the president and the press. The president's press secretary directs the press to the stories the administration wants covered and presents information that shows the administration in the most favorable light possible. The daily White House press briefing is a key platform for achieving these goals, and so are informal off-the-record communications by administration members. Some scholars claim that the result is "negotiating the news" (Cook 1998).

In contrast to his predecessors, Donald Trump has followed few, if any, of these practices.

Presidential Speeches

When presidents communicate directly with the public, they often do so by means of presidential addresses. Although presidents have always used speeches to educate and persuade the public about issues of importance, the advent of radio and television turned modern presidents into more visible public figures than their nineteenth-century predecessors. Contemporary presidents still address small audiences on particular issues or topics, but they can use television and radio to communicate with the entire nation.

There are two general types of presidential speeches. A presidential speech on a topic of national importance delivered directly to a national audience over radio or television during the prime evening listening and viewing hours is considered a major address. The president's inaugural address and the annual State of the Union address are major addresses that every president makes. In addition, presidents use major addresses to announce decisions to go to war, to inform the nation of a major international or economic crisis, and to outline their vision of the nation's future (Ragsdale 1996, 146–147).

A minor address is a speech on a substantive policy or political issue delivered to a specific audience, either in person or by use of a broadcast medium. A common example is a commencement address in which the president outlines a new policy proposal. Presidents also make speeches announcing policies at meetings of various business, labor, veterans, police, senior citizen, and professional groups (Ragsdale 1996, 150).

Presidents average about five major addresses and 12 minor addresses per year. Though major speeches are less frequent, they can help influence key elites. For example, national public addresses such as the State of the Union speech can positively shape editorials about the

Modern presidents often appeal directly to the people to get support for their policies. President Donald Trump speaks at the North Side Gymnasium in Elkhart, Indiana, Thursday, May 10, 2018.
© Carolyn Kaster/AP Photo

president. As "professional persuaders," newspaper editorialists can be important supporters of a president's proposals (Schaefer 1997).

The Limited Benefits of Going Public

Kernell (1997) provides clear evidence that modern presidents go public more often than their predecessors. The evidence that going public succeeds in raising the president's standing with the public, however, is limited to a small number of case studies.

Presidential scholar George Edwards (2003) conducted a systematic study of the effect of televised speeches by the four presidents before Barack Obama—Ronald Reagan, George H. W. Bush, Bill Clinton, and George W. Bush. Edwards compared presidential approval ratings in public opinion polls conducted immediately before and after major televised speeches. He found that the president's speeches seldom moved public opinion. Because of the margin of error in public opinion polls (discussed in Chapter 9), public approval must change about six percentage points for the difference to be considered statistically significant. Figure 13.5 shows the limited effects of going public. As Edwards observed, "significant changes [more than six points] rarely follow televised presidential addresses. Typically, changes in

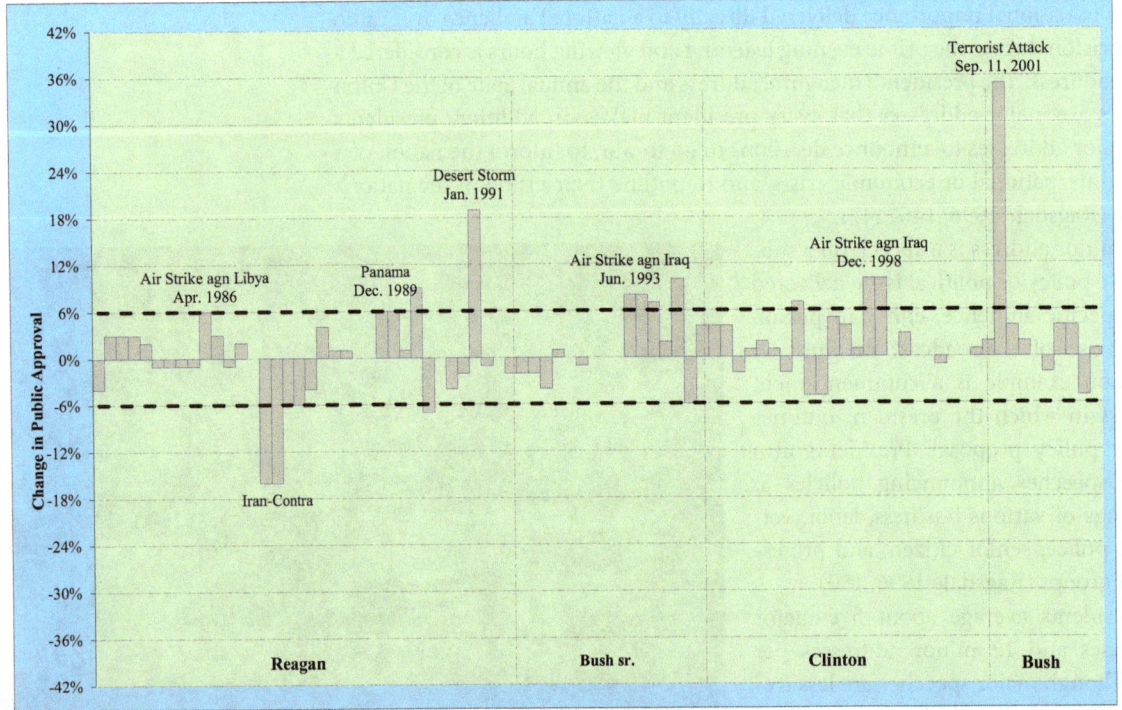

FIGURE 13.5 The Limited Effects of Going Public: Change in Presidential Approval after Televised Speeches

Source: Data from G. Edwards (2003), 30–32.

the president's ratings hardly move at all. Most changes are well within the margin of error—and many of them show a *loss* of approval" (2003, 29). Most of the significant increases followed a major military action; the largest improvement followed the terrorist attacks on September 11, 2001. These changes are more likely the result of the public rallying around the president during an international crisis than the result of a skilled use of the bully pulpit. About one-third of the significant changes are losses in presidential approval following the speech. This evidence indicates that the effects of going public are limited.

Presidential Approval Ratings

Although going public seldom succeeds, presidents try hard to influence the perceptions and attitudes of the American people. Public opinion polls on presidential job approval have been taken for more than 60 years. The results of these polls are commonly called "presidential popularity," and politicians and political scientists pay close attention to them. Figure 13.6 shows public job approval ratings

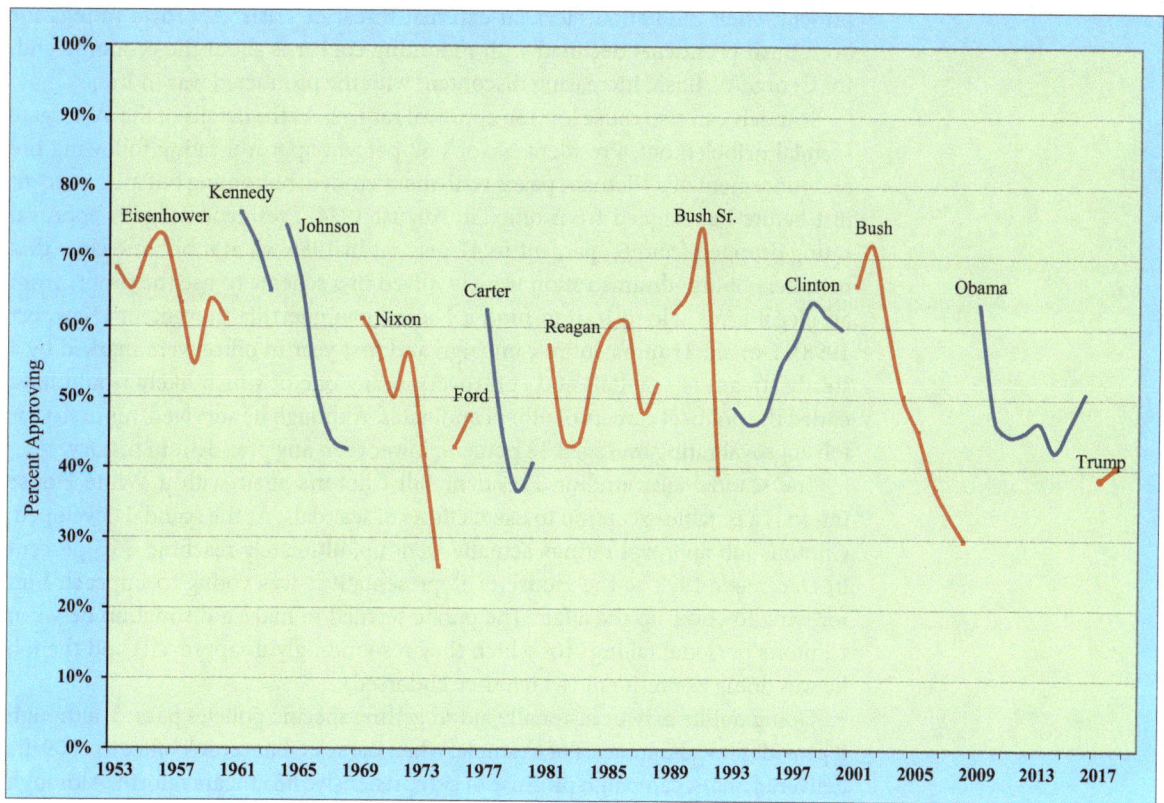

FIGURE 13.6 Presidential Job Approval

Source: Data from Gallup Polls.

from Dwight Eisenhower to Donald Trump. With few exceptions, presidents tend to enjoy their highest approval ratings during their first year or two in office. This honeymoon period dissipates as people become dissatisfied with specific decisions, and those who withheld their fire in the bipartisan spirit of support for a newly elected president feel freer to openly disagree with the administration. The tendency for public approval to decline creates pressure to use political capital quickly in order to advance a political agenda while the president has broad public support (Light 1983).

The annual averages show overall trends in presidential popularity but also large swings. Several forces significantly influence presidential popularity, but the effect of the president's activities are limited compared to other events over which the president has less control.

The economy, international crises, and scandal are three of the most important determinants of a president's approval rating. The annual averages in Figure 13.6 hide some short-term spikes. For example, George H. W. Bush's approval ratings briefly soared to 89 percent in February 1991 following victory during the first Gulf War. Ten years later, his son, President George W. Bush, had similarly astronomically high numbers following the terrorist attacks of September 11, 2001. In both cases, the levels of popularity reflected the "rally around the flag" effect often present when the nation faces an external threat or crisis. Approval ratings for both Bush presidents declined with mounting concerns about the economy and, for George W. Bush, increasing discontent with the protracted war in Iraq.

Scandals can also cause low job approval ratings. As the details of the Watergate scandal dribbled out, President Nixon's 62 percent approval rating following the announcement of a Vietnam peace settlement eroded, bottoming out at 25 percent just before he resigned from office in August 1974. President Reagan's approval rating dropped from 63 percent to 47 percent in 1986 when it became clear that members of his administration were involved in a scheme to use the profits from an illegal arms sale to Iran to fund a Nicaraguan guerrilla movement (Newport 1998). Donald Trump's entire campaign and first year in office were marked by a steady stream of scandals and controversies any one of which likely would have ended the political careers of other candidates. Although he survived, his first-year job approval rating averaged 38 percent, lower than any president in history.

The scandal surrounding President Bill Clinton's affair with a White House intern is a notable exception to usual effects of scandals. As the scandal developed, Clinton's job approval ratings actually went up, ultimately reaching 66.5 percent in December 1998 as the House of Representatives was voting to impeach him for lying to cover up the affair. The public seemed to make a distinction between Clinton's personal failings (of which they resoundingly disapproved) and the job he was doing as president (which they endorsed).

Going public may occasionally aid in getting specific policies passed, although it provides no guarantees. For example, when Barack Obama took office in 2009, he delivered on his campaign promise of comprehensive healthcare reform. Although passage of the Patient Protection and Affordable Care Act fulfilled a key campaign promise, an intense and unified Republican opposition managed to reverse the support Obama had received from independents in the election—independents split 51–43 for Obama (and presumably healthcare reform) in 2008 but voted for Republicans in 2010 by a margin of 56–37. Democratic losses occurred disproportionately among moderate Democrats (G. Jacobson 2013, 230).

These examples are telling reminders that while presidents are the most prominent actors in American politics, they are not the only ones trying to influence public opinion. The competition can be intense. All presidents use the bully pulpit, and some are effective communicators, but their ability to influence public opinion varies from issue to issue.

THE PRESIDENT AND CONGRESS

Although Congress has primary responsibility for making laws, the president plays a key role in influencing legislation. The Constitution gives the president significant formal powers to influence the legislative process, including the responsibility for sending messages and recommendations to Congress and the power to veto bills passed by Congress. In addition to formal powers, other practices have evolved that have further increased presidential involvement in the making of laws. Initiated by presidents who sought to exercise strong legislative leadership, these practices are now considered part of the political duties of office. The practicalities of politics mean that the president has little choice but to actively try to influence decisions made in the legislative branch. And although it is not explicitly spelled out, several presidents have claimed that the Constitution gives the chief executive unilateral power to act under certain circumstances—that is, sometimes the president deals with Congress by going around it. This section examines how formal legal power and evolved practices combine to determine presidential influence in Congress.

Messages and Recommendations

Article II, Section 3 of the Constitution mandates that the president "shall from time to time give to the Congress information on the state of the union, and recommend to their consideration such measures as he shall judge necessary and expedient." Since George Washington's administration, chief executives have followed the practice of annually presenting a message to Congress at the beginning of each regular session. Washington and John Adams gave their messages in person. Thomas Jefferson, a notoriously poor public speaker, sent his message in writing. Subsequent presidents followed Jefferson's practice until Woodrow Wilson surprised Congress and the nation by delivering a message in person shortly after he was inaugurated in 1913. Since then, all presidents, regardless of their oratorical skills, have appeared before Congress to deliver the annual State of the Union message.

Although the assembled senators and members of the House are the immediate target of the State of the Union speech, the president has other audiences in mind. In a sense, the message is addressed to all Americans, who can watch the

President Donald Trump delivers his State of the Union address to a joint session of Congress on Capitol Hill in Washington, Tuesday, January 30, 2018. Although the assembled senators and members of the House are the immediate target of the State of the Union speech, the president often seeks to reach a larger audience. The message is addressed to all Americans, who can watch the proceedings on television, and the speech is broadcast worldwide. In this speech, the president identifies the problems that the administration views as most pressing and suggests policies to address them.

© Susan Walsh/AP Photo

proceedings on television, and the message is broadcast worldwide as a matter of interest to U.S. allies and adversaries alike. In the speech, the president identifies the problems that the administration views as most pressing and suggests policies to address them. Modern presidents do not limit their recommendations to the State of the Union message. Woodrow Wilson initiated the practice of following the State of the Union address with written recommendations about specific policy topics.

Contemporary presidents go beyond making recommendations to actually developing specific bills. Even though Congress may (and usually does) change the administration proposals, the submission of a bill is designed to get Congress to focus on what the president thinks should be done about a problem. By the mid-twentieth century, presidents had become so adept at setting the legislative agenda that some scholars openly questioned whether Congress was too unwieldy to be capable of setting its own legislative priorities and needed the president to do it for them (Neustadt 1960). Later in the century, it became clear that Congress is able to independently set its own priorities. For example, the Democratic majority crafted a domestic legislative program without the assistance of President George H. W. Bush, and the Republican majority that won control of Congress after the 1994 elections set and pursued its own agenda without the assistance of President Bill Clinton. Political scientists George Edwards and Andrew Barrett (2000) found that a major presidential proposal rarely fails to get a hearing. Still, presidential proposals constitute only about a third of the legislative agenda; Congress initiates the other two-thirds.

Nonetheless, the public, the media, and even Congress expect the president to formulate, propose, and actively advance a legislative agenda to address the nation's problems. In fact, Congress has passed laws requiring the president to present proposals to the legislature. For example, the Budget and Accounting Act of 1921 made the executive responsible for formulating and proposing a budget for the federal government.

The Veto

Of the formal powers granted to the president by the Constitution, the veto is probably the most important tool for influencing legislation. The president has three options when presented with a bill passed by Congress:

1. Sign the bill into law.
2. Veto the bill by returning to the chamber where it originated with his objections; the bill dies unless a two-thirds majority in both chambers votes to pass the bill over the president's objection.
3. If the president takes no action within 10 days, the bill becomes law without the president's signature unless Congress has adjourned. If Congress has adjourned, the bill dies after 10 days if the president does not sign it. This is using a **pocket veto** to nullify the bill.

The Founders originally conceived of the veto as a defensive weapon the president could use to protect the executive from encroachment by a powerful legislature. In his classic analysis of presidential power, Neustadt (1960) suggested that a veto is a sign of weakness because it shows that the president failed to persuade Congress to adopt administration proposals. But the veto has evolved into a powerful tool to shape public policy. Because of the constitutionally mandated requirement of a supermajority to override, a veto represents a formidable obstacle to legislation. It gives even unpopular presidents without a party majority in Congress an effective way to influence the legislative process. Even as the Watergate scandal politically crippled Richard Nixon in 1973, Congress managed to override only one of his nine vetoes. Veto overrides are rare—across all presidents, only about 7 percent of vetoes are overridden.

The mere threat of a veto is a valuable tool to shape legislation (Cameron 2000). By making clear what features of a particular bill the administration finds objectionable and what must be done to make them acceptable, the president can shape the content of laws. The tactic does not always work. Especially if the opposition party has a majority, Congress may pass the bill as veto bait to use as a campaign issue (Gilmour 2011). The Democratic majority in 1992, for example, sent President George H. W. Bush several bills he had threatened to veto. In effect, they dared him to follow through on his threats, and when he did, Democrats used his opposition to the popular bills as fodder for political campaigns. Much of the time, though, the threat of a veto provides a lot of leverage in Congress. President Bill Clinton, for example, got budget bill concessions from the Republican majority in 1998 by threatening to veto the appropriations required to keep the government solvent and operating. Having suffered a political disaster when they forced a government shutdown three years earlier, the Republicans were willing to compromise with the president.

Presidential Success in Congress

In terms of the relationship between the executive and legislative branches, presidents succeed when Congress acts in accordance with their recommendations and fail when Congress takes a course of action opposed by the administration. One frequently used measure of presidential success is how often the president's position wins on the House or Senate floor.

Like other measures of presidential success, this one is imperfect. It measures success only on matters that come to a floor vote, and some issues never make it

pocket veto A maneuver in which the president allows a bill to die by taking no action within 10 days if Congress has adjourned.

that far. President Clinton's healthcare reform proposals, for example, never made it to a floor vote. But most significant issues do show up in House or Senate roll call votes, and these allow a reasonable basis on which to judge success or failure. Figure 13.7 shows the percentage of times the president got his way on House and Senate roll calls from 1953 to 2017.

This figure shows two important patterns. First, no president has enjoyed complete success or complete failure; all win some and lose some. This pattern is in stark contrast to parliamentary democracies, where losing an important vote in the legislature is a major embarrassment for the prime minister and may even lead to his or her resignation. Second, presidential success varies. It varies across presidential administrations as well as across chambers and over time within them. Political scientists seek to explain why some presidents win more than others do.

The Founders deliberately created a rivalry between the executive and the legislature by assigning important constitutional powers to each. By granting institutional rivals independent bases of political power, the Constitution also ensured that each would be capable of protecting and advancing its interests. The patterns

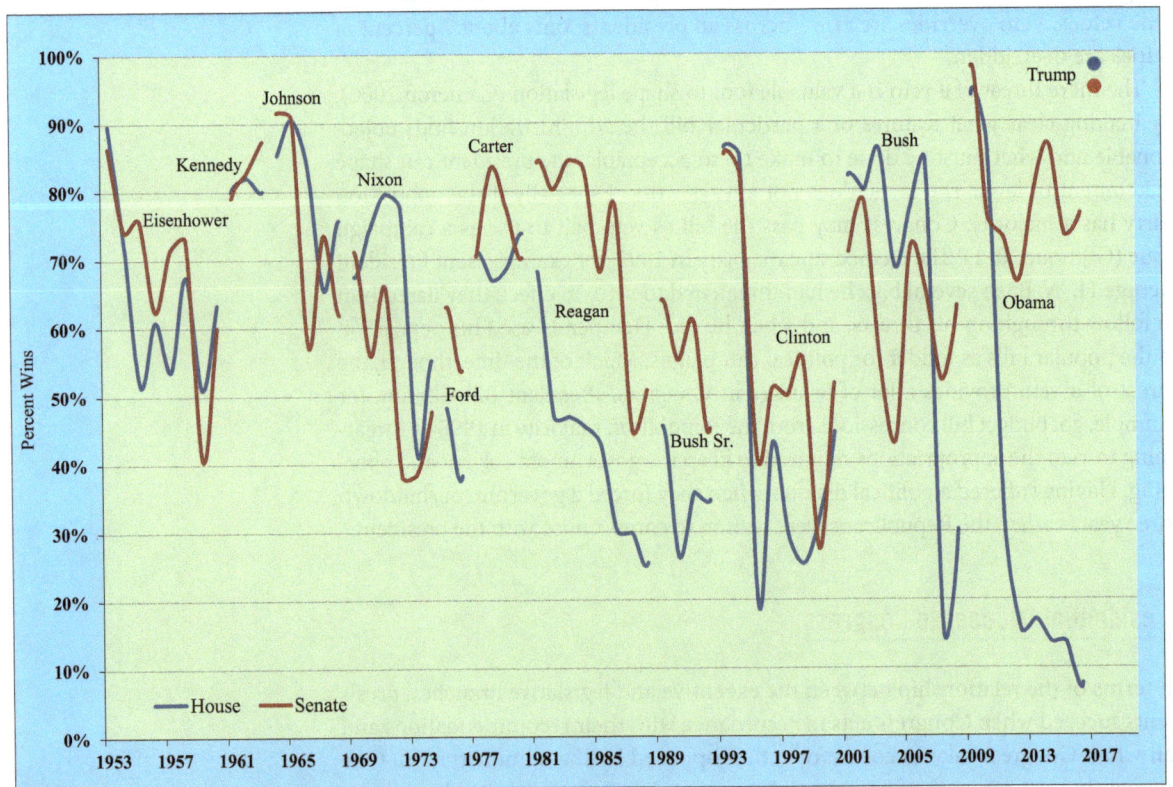

FIGURE 13.7 Presidential Success in the House and Senate

Sources: J. Cohen, Bond, and Fleisher (2013); updated by the authors from presidential roll calls identified by Congressional Quarterly, Inc.; 2017 estimates from Bond (2018).

in Figure 13.7 confirm that these expectations have been met. Members of the first Congress resisted Alexander Hamilton's attempts to advance his economic program, and senators and House members have resisted executive efforts to dominate legislative affairs ever since. But it is not only institutional differences that explain the variation in success rates. Other conditions that influence presidential success with Congress are electoral constituencies and cycles, party and ideology, presidential popularity, and the president's bargaining skill.

Electoral Constituencies and Cycles

The president and Congress have very different constituencies. Elected to represent a nationwide constituency, the president tends to see issues from a national perspective. Moreover, the president's diplomatic duties and role as commander in chief require an international perspective. Members of Congress, in contrast, tend to have a more parochial view. They are necessarily concerned with how their particular states or districts are affected. Different constituencies and electoral needs lead to different views of what is in the public interest. The inevitable result is conflict between the executive and legislative branches. The president wins some; Congress wins others.

The executive and legislative branches also operate under separate electoral cycles with overlapping terms. The timing of elections has a critical effect on relations between the president and Congress. In a presidential election year, the nation chooses the president, all 435 members of the House, and one-third of the Senate. If the president wins by a large margin, sympathetic House and Senate members may ride presidential coattails into office. Two-thirds of the senators, however, are holdovers from previous elections that they won without help from the president. And two years into the president's term, there is another election in which all 435 House seats and another third of Senate seats are up for election. Not being on the ballot, the president has less influence on these congressional races than on the races that took place two years earlier. As a result, most legislators are insulated from presidential influence.

Party and Ideology

Political science research consistently finds that party and ideology are the strongest determinants of how members of Congress vote. The primary reason is shared preferences—Republicans tend to agree on a wide range of policies, and Republican policy preferences differ from those of most Democrats. Because presidents are visible party leaders, party consistently exerts a crucial influence on presidential–congressional relations. Simply speaking, members of the president's party are likely to support administration positions because they agree with them, and members of the opposition party are less likely to agree. As a result, conflict between the president and Congress is more pronounced when different political parties control the two branches, a situation that has been common since World War II. Over the period since 1953, majority presidents have won an average of about 75 percent of roll calls in both the House and Senate. Minority presidents win less often in both chambers, but the disadvantage of minority status is less in the Senate—minority presidents win an average of 50 percent of Senate roll calls, but only 37 percent of House roll calls. Because partisanship is somewhat lower in the Senate than in the House (see Table 12.1), minority presidents may be better able to attract support from the opposition party in the Senate.

Ideology is also an important influence on roll call voting. As discussed in Chapters 1 and 9, an ideology is a consistent set of values, attitudes, and beliefs about the appropriate role of government in society (Campbell et al. 1960). Conservatives have different philosophies about the proper role of government than do liberals.

Party and ideology are related, but they are not the same thing. Democrats tend to be liberal, and Republicans tend to be conservative, but until the 1980s, both parties had factions of ideological misfits—conservative Democrats and liberal Republicans—who shared ideological ground with the rival party. These members were frequently cross-pressured: Their party pulled them in one direction and their ideological beliefs in another. Cross-pressured members of the president's party, therefore, tend to be less supportive of administration proposals, but cross-pressured members of the opposition party have often been an important source of support (Bond and Fleisher 1990). Minority presidents sometimes have won votes in Congress by forging ideological coalitions with members of the opposition party. President Ronald Reagan, for example, never enjoyed a Republican-controlled House of Representatives, and thus he always needed votes from Democrats to pass his legislative agenda. Reagan managed to achieve several key victories with votes from conservative Democrats.

Even members of the president's own party who face no inconsistencies between party and ideology oppose the administration on occasion. Members of Congress must satisfy state and district constituencies if they want to be reelected. If these local interests come into conflict with the president's national preferences, the White House cannot assume that party loyalty will win out. The president's fellow party members may find it politically advantageous to oppose administration positions if they are unpopular with the members' constituents. In 2017, Senators Susan Collins (R-ME) and Lisa Murkowski (R-AK) bucked President Trump and party leaders and provided crucial votes to defeat a bill to repeal "Obamacare" because certain provisions were harmful to their constituents.

Party Polarization

In the 1980s, the number of cross-pressured members in Congress began to decline, and they had all but disappeared by the 2000s (Fleisher and Bond 2004). Without conservative Democrats and liberal Republicans who often bucked their own party leaders and voted with the opposition, congressional parties polarized. **Party polarization** means that the parties diverge toward opposite extremes (or poles). With the departure of cross-pressured members, overlap in the center disappears, members in each party become more ideologically similar—Republicans

party polarization A distribution of preferences in which party means diverge toward opposite poles with little or no overlap in the center.

conservative, Democrats liberal—and the parties pull farther apart as the average Republican moves to the right, and the average Democrat moves left.

Party polarization has had a profound influence on presidential success in Congress. When parties are internally cohesive, members of the president's party are less likely to defect and vote with the opposition, but members of the opposition are also unlikely to defect and support the president. As a result, party polarization changes the effects of party control, but the effects are different in the House and Senate because the chambers have different rules.

House rules enable a cohesive majority to win. Thus, as members of Congress increasingly vote along party lines, majority party presidents win more often, and minority party presidents win less often (see Figure 13.8a). The slopes of the regression lines summarize how much presidential success will change if party votes increase one percent. The slope of the regression line for majority presidents is +0.29—if party polarization goes up 10 percent, the model predicts that majority presidents' success rate will increase about 2.9 percent. The slope of the regression line for minority presidents is –0.97, indicating that if party votes go up 10 percent, a minority president's success rate will decline about 10.0 percent. Because party polarization has opposite effects for majority and minority presidents, the majority party boost—that is, the difference in success rates of majority and minority presidents—grows as party voting increases. The majority party boost is about 14 percent more wins if polarization is low (around 35 percent) and about 52 percent if polarization is high (around 65 percent).

The Senate is a different story. Majority presidents have an advantage in the Senate, but the majority party boost is smaller than in the House. Given the tradition of somewhat muted partisanship in the Senate, this difference is not surprising. Although increasing party polarization extends to the Senate as well as the House, the effects on presidential success are much different in the Senate—as party voting increases, success rates of both majority and minority presidents decline (see Figure 13.8b). The decline in success rates is not large, but it is similar for both majority and minority presidents. In general, a 10 percent increase in party polarization reduces the success rates of both majority and minority presidents by about 2 percent. Because the slopes of the regression lines are similar, the majority party boost in the Senate is about the same (21–22 percent), regardless of the level of party polarization.

Why are the effects of party polarization so different in the Senate? The answer is that the minority party has started using rules unique to the Senate differently than in the past. Unlike the House, where rules empower the majority, Senate rules protect the minority. As party polarization increased, the minority party began to use these tools, especially the filibuster and the requirement of 60 votes to invoke cloture, to block action on legislation and nominations its members opposed. Thus, 60 votes has become the de facto threshold to pass any controversial legislation in the Senate (Binder and Smith 1997; Koger 2010).

Party polarization with a de facto 60-vote requirement has made passing controversial legislation in the Senate more difficult regardless of which party has a majority. Polarized parties reduce success rates of majority party presidents

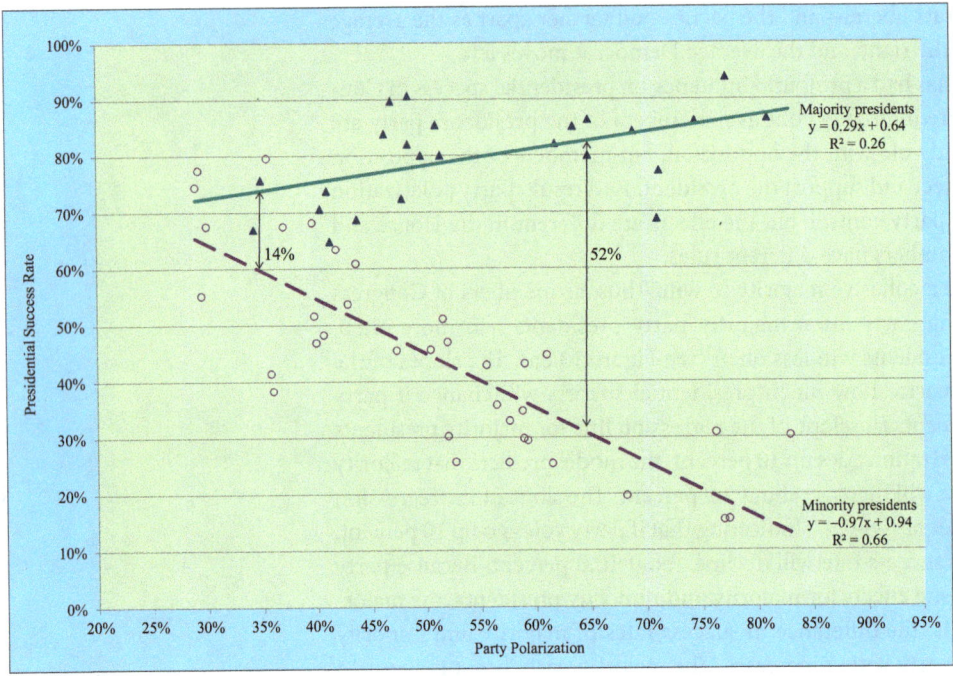

FIGURE 13.8a The Effects of Party Polarization on Presidential Success in the House

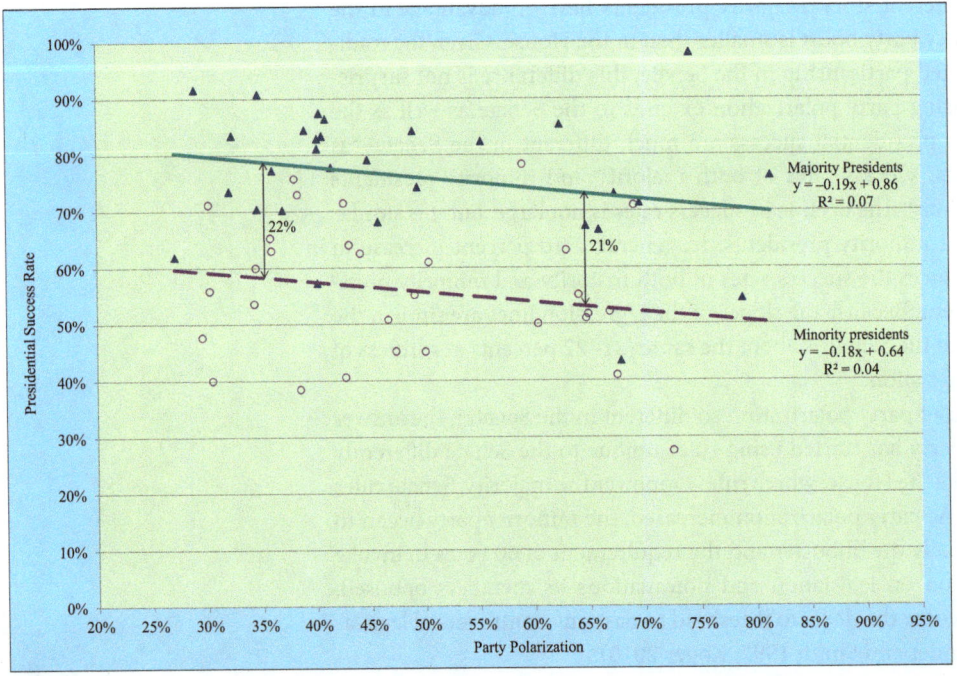

FIGURE 13.8b The Effects of Party Polarization on Presidential Success in the Senate

Source: Bond, Fleisher, and J. Cohen (2015); J. Cohen, Bond, and Fleisher (2013).

because a cohesive minority party exploits supermajoritarian rules to obstruct the president's initiatives, and there are few if any cross-pressured senators who might be inclined to defect from their party's filibuster to help the president. Party polarization tends to reduce the success of minority party presidents as well because there are fewer cross-pressured members who might be inclined to support the president, and the leader of a cohesive majority party is more likely to schedule floor votes that the president opposes (Bond, Fleisher, and J. Cohen 2015; J. Cohen, Bond, and Fleisher 2013).

Thus, party polarization has made party a stronger determinant of presidential success in Congress, especially in the House. For example, with cohesive Democratic majorities, President Obama had historically high success rates in 2009, winning 94 percent of House votes. After Republicans won control of the House in the 2010 midterm elections, his success rate took a nosedive to 31 percent. With cohesive Republican majorities remaining in control of the House, his success rate continued to plummet, so that by his last year in office he achieved another historic success rate—a record-breaking low of just 8 percent (see Figure 13.7).

Presidential Popularity

As elected representatives, members of Congress are supposed to be responsive to popular preferences. Consequently, they may be more likely to support administration proposals when the president has high public support. The belief that public approval affects presidential support in Congress is widely accepted by Washington insiders, and there is little doubt that popularity provides leverage on some occasions. Although public opinion may influence what issues Congress will consider, high public approval does not guarantee support.

Academic research has not been able to demonstrate that presidential popularity translates directly into desired legislative outcomes. Rather, systematic research generally finds that public approval has a positive, but marginal effect on success (Bond and Fleisher 1990; G. Edwards 1989). President George H. W. Bush's record in 1991 is a good example of the limits of presidential popularity. Despite astronomic public approval, Congress did not rally around Bush's policy agenda. His success rate on House roll call votes was only 43.

The expectation that members of Congress will respond to the president's popular support is based primarily on electoral considerations. The theory is that a legislator who opposes a popular president or supports an unpopular one becomes a target for electoral retribution by the voters. However, the electoral connection between the president and members of Congress has lessened somewhat with the weakening of presidents' electoral coattails (G. Jacobson 1990, 80–81). Furthermore, while some voters may use presidential popularity as a voting guide, few have sufficient knowledge to make the connection between their evaluation of the president and the voting behavior of their representative.

Moreover, presidential popularity is fluid, so using it as a guide in casting votes in Congress is risky. The president's popularity on election day may be very different than it was on the day of a roll call vote. Since presidential popularity at election time cannot be predicted with great accuracy, its utility in guiding an elected representative's roll call vote is limited. For these reasons, presidential popularity has only a marginal influence on legislators' decisions to support or oppose the president on roll call votes (Bond and Fleisher 1990; G. Edwards 1989).

Presidential Bargaining Skill

The president also has a certain amount of patronage to bring to the table in give-and-take with recalcitrant legislators. Although executive branch jobs have increasingly come under civil service regulations that require competitive examinations as the basis for hiring, the president still influences government contracts, grants, defense installations, and the like. Presidents have made sure that federal government contracts and grants were directed to key congressional districts and that legislators were given advance notice of them so that they could announce—and take credit for—the benefit to the district.

Presidents have also engaged in systematic lobbying efforts on behalf of legislative programs, essentially setting up special interest operations in the White House. Begun in earnest during the Eisenhower era, systematic lobbying varies somewhat from administration to administration. Such efforts usually include legislative liaisons from various executive departments, a central liaison unit in the White House Office, and the vice president. Some of these individuals concentrate on the House, others on the Senate, and they specialize in particular topics and issues. Executive branch lobbyists use the same general techniques as do lobbyists for interest groups, including direct contacts with representatives and indirect contact through congressional staff members, campaign contributors, defense contractors, newspaper editors, state and local party leaders, and others important to a legislator's constituency. They also join forces with private interest groups to work on legislation of mutual interest.

Political pundits, politicians, and some students of the presidency routinely assume that such efforts play a large role in determining presidential success in Congress. A prevailing belief is that strong legislative leadership is achieved by the skillful use of the tools at the president's disposal to persuade members of Congress to enact administration proposals. Evidence to support this belief comes mainly from in-depth case studies of specific bills. More systematic analyses of presidential support from members of Congress, such as those relying on roll call votes on many bills, give less support for this hypothesis (Bond and Fleisher 1990; G. Edwards 1989). Variation in presidential success rests more on party and ideology than on popularity, bargaining skill, and informal powers of persuasion. Success is also due to the political context of the time, which the president has limited ability to shape.

Yet some research shows that focusing only on roll call votes may underestimate the president's ability to influence legislative outcomes. Matthew Beckmann (2010, 108) argues that efforts to influence the roll call vote can be viewed as the endgame in the legislative process. But presidents can't win the endgame unless they are successful in the "early game" (i.e., getting a proposal through the legislative obstacle course to a floor vote). Beckmann's analysis replicates past research—presidents who "inherit a legislature filled with likeminded lawmakers typically find success on floor votes; those facing a Congress filled with opposition legislators do not" (2010, 108). Yet his analysis shows that presidential lobbying increases the odds of successfully negotiating the initial legislative obstacle course *and* of winning the floor vote that follows. And the president's "political capital"—a combination of public approval and economic growth—"amplifies or diminishes his effectiveness" (Beckmann 2010, 116).

Unilateral Powers

The conventional way presidents influence policy is to persuade Congress to enact the bills they want and to veto the ones they don't (Neustadt 1960). But presidents have another option—exercise unilateral powers. **Unilateral powers** are presidential directives that carry the weight of law even though they have not been formally endorsed by Congress. Examples include executive orders, signing statements, executive agreements, and national security directives (Howell 2005, 417). These actions not only represent an end run around Congress; they also stand on its head Neustadt's argument that persuasion is the core of presidential power. When they exercise these unilateral powers, "presidents simply set public policy and dare others to counter. As long as Congress lacks the votes (usually two-thirds of both chambers) to overturn him [or unless the courts find the action unconstitutional], the president can be confident that his policy will stand" (Howell 2005, 421).

The Constitution does not explicitly spell out unilateral, but presidents argue that Article II of the Constitution, which grants the broad "executive power," provides a legal basis for such actions. Unilateral powers also have historical precedent: Presidents of both parties have exercised unilateral powers to some extent since the beginning of the republic. Presidents since Ronald Reagan, however, have resorted to these devices with far greater frequency, in the process attracting widespread criticism from Congress and in the legal community. The controversy has escalated as recent presidents, especially George W. Bush and Barack Obama, increasingly used unilateral powers to achieve their policy goals.

Executive Orders

An **executive order** is a legally binding presidential order directing federal agencies and officials on how to implement laws or policies enacted by Congress. Many executive orders deal with routine administrative matters or symbolic proclamations. Others implement substantive public policies without input from Congress. A famous example is President Lincoln's Emancipation Proclamation in 1862.

Executive orders can be highly controversial when they go beyond or contradict congressional intent. Congress can amend the law to specify its interpretation,

unilateral powers Presidential directives that carry the weight of law even though they have not been formally endorsed by Congress.

executive orders Directives of the president that have the same weight as law but are not voted on by Congress.

but the president can veto such an amendment. Practically, what this means is that it may take a two-thirds vote of Congress to overturn an executive order. Executive orders can also be challenged in court, but the courts have overturned very few. A notable example is *Youngstown Sheet & Tube Co. v. Sawyer* (1952), in which the Supreme Court declared President Truman's executive order seizing the steel mills to avert a labor strike unconstitutional.

President Obama provoked considerable controversy in June of 2012 when he issued an executive order establishing the Deferred Action for Childhood Arrivals (DACA) program that allowed young immigrants who came to the US as children to apply for a deportation deferral. It affected millions of undocumented immigrants currently in the United States. Republicans were outraged. House Speaker John A. Boehner (R-OH) filed suit challenging this action, arguing that the President had changed the law, which was Congress's responsibility under the Constitution. The directive does not actually change the law, however. Instead, it is presented as an exercise of "prosecutorial discretion" in which an executive with limited resources sets priorities about who is to be prosecuted first (Rudalevige 2014). Although an executive order is a unilateral executive action that has the force of law, a subsequent president can unilaterally rescind it. Many of President Trump's 58 executive orders issued in his first year overturned Obama regulations.

Though every president has issued executive orders, presidents used them sparingly until the period between the Progressive Era, which began around the turn of the twentieth century, and the end of World War II. Presidents from Theodore Roosevelt (1901–1909) to Harry Truman (1945–1953) issued an average of over 200 executive orders per year, compared to averages of 26 or fewer in earlier periods (see Figure 13.9). The number of executive orders issued by presidents since World War II has stabilized around an average of about 56 per year.

Signing Statements

When signing a bill into law, the president can issue a written announcement of how he intends to interpret and apply the law. Such pronouncements are called **signing statements**. Specifically, they:

> (1) provide the president's interpretation of the language of the law, (2) announce constitutional limits on the implementation of some of its provisions, or (3) give directions to executive branch officials as to how to administer the new law in an acceptable manner. (Cooper 2005, 516–517)

Signing statements are controversial because the president sometimes claims that certain parts of the bill just signed into law are unconstitutional and will not be implemented. Some critics argue that this amounts to a line-item veto. The Constitution, however, provides only two options—veto the bill and send it back to Congress, or "faithfully execute" the law.

Signing statements were used as early as the James Monroe administration (1817–1825), but using them to modify laws to conform to presidential policy goals was not common before 1981 when Ronald Reagan became president (see Table 13.1).

signing statements Pronouncements of how the president intends to interpret and apply a law when he or she signs a bill into law.

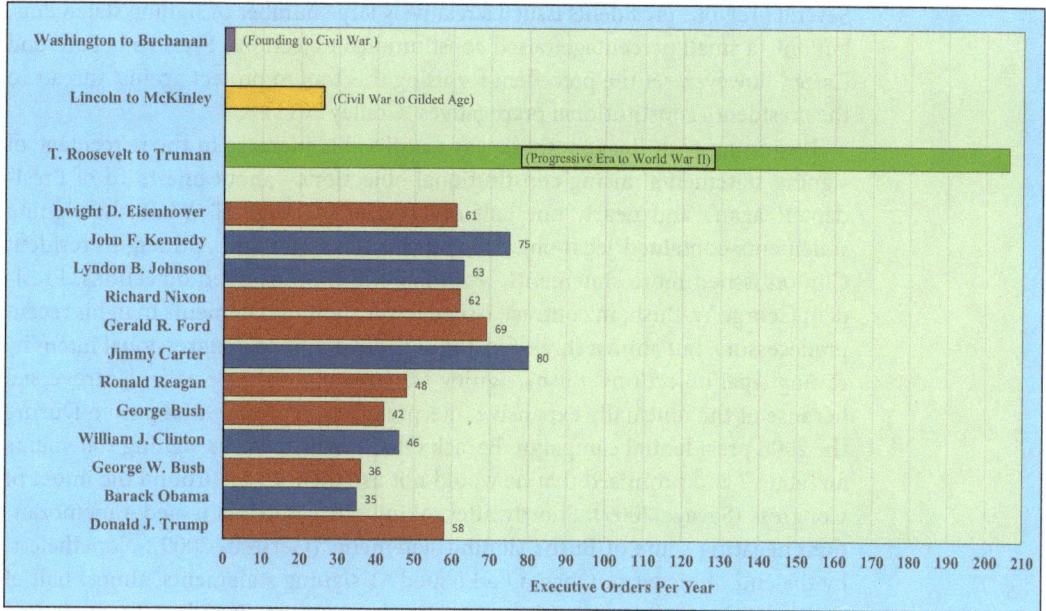

FIGURE 13.9 Executive Orders Per Year, From George Washington to Donald Trump

Source: Data from Peters and Woolley (1999–2018).

TABLE 13.1 PRESIDENTIAL SIGNING STATEMENTS

	Total Signing Statements	Percent with Constitutional Objections
Hoover	16	0.0%
Roosevelt	39	0.0%
Truman	106	0.9%
Eisenhower	142	1.4%
Kennedy	36	0.0%
Johnson	175	2.9%
Nixon	117	3.4%
Ford	137	3.6%
Carter	227	5.7%
Reagan	250	34.4%
Bush, Sr.	228	46.9%
Clinton	381	18.4%
Bush	162	72.8%
Obama	41	48.6%
Trump*	7	42.9%

Source: Data from Halstead 2007; Peters and Woolley (1999–2018); and Stanley and Neimi (2011), 251–252.

Note: Trump's signing statements in 2017.

Several previous presidents issued a relatively large number of signing statements, but only a small percentage raised constitutional objections. Presidents Ford and Carter, however, set the precedent for using this tool to protect against threats to the president's constitutional prerogatives (Conley 2011).

Beginning with Reagan, there was a noticeable increase in the percentage of signing statements raising constitutional objections—about one-third of President Reagan's and nearly one-half of President George H. W. Bush's signing statements contained legal objections to portions of a law. Although President Clinton issued more statements, less than one-fifth included objections. President George W. Bush, in contrast, issued fewer signing statements than his recent predecessors, but almost three-fourths of these modified congressional intent by raising legal objections. Bush's signing statements were especially controversial because of the unusually expansive interpretation of presidential power. During the 2008 presidential campaign, Barack Obama called Bush's signing statements an "abuse" and promised that he would not use them to get around the intent of Congress (Savage 2009). Shortly after taking office, Obama issued a memorandum negating some of Bush's signing statements (Gerstein 2009). Nonetheless, by the end of his term, Obama had issued 41 signing statements, almost half of which (49 percent) contained constitutional objections. President Trump issued only seven signing statements in 2017, but three (75 percent) contained constitutional objections.

National Security Directives

Presidents have more leeway to take unilateral action in the realm of foreign and national security policy than in the domestic arena, in large part because the president controls what information, if any, is available to Congress and the press (Howell 2005, 423–425). The growing tendency to use executive agreements rather than treaties and the president's power as commander in chief to unilaterally launch military action without a formal declaration of war—or sometimes without any prior authorization from Congress—are discussed earlier.

Another device presidents use to make national security policy without approval of Congress is the national security directive. A **national security directive**—called National Security Presidential Directives (NSPDs) in the Bush administration—is a type of executive order with the force of law authorizing federal agencies or officials to take some action to protect national security. President Bush relied heavily on national security directives in the conduct of the war on terror. For example, on May 4, 2007, he signed the National Security and Homeland Security Presidential Directive, which was designed to ensure that government would continue to function during a "catastrophic emergency." It authorized the president to coordinate "a cooperative effort among the executive, legislative, and judicial branches of the Federal Government" to take the place of the nation's regular government during the crisis. Both conservatives and liberals objected to this directive because the Constitution establishes three equal branches of government with no single branch having the power to coordinate the others, and because it did

national security directive A type of executive order with the force of law authorizing federal agencies or officials to take some action to protect national security.

not specify who had the power to decide the emergency was over and restore normal government function. Because such directives concern national security, the information (sometimes even the title) is often classified. One study estimates that the "titles of only about half" of President Bush's 54 National Security Presidential Directives had been made public, and there was "descriptive material or actual text in the public domain for only about a third" (Aftergood 2008). Sometimes, even members of Congress could not get access. For example, citing "national security concerns," the Bush White House denied Representative Peter DeFazio (D-OR), a member of the Homeland Security Committee, access to classified parts of the National Security and Homeland Security Presidential Directive.

CHAPTER THIRTEEN
Top 10 Takeaway Points

1. The office of president of the United States is made up of the president, an individual person, and the presidency, which is a complex institution.

2. The power of the president has grown because of (1) the energy associated with a single executive, (2) vague constitutional provisions that assertive presidents interpreted broadly to enhance presidential power, (3) rising public expectations, and (4) delegation of power and resources to the executive branch by Congress.

3. Presidential scholars suggest that an individual's background and psychological needs allow presidential character to be arrayed along two dimensions: the active–passive dimension is based on how much energy the president devotes to the exercise of power; the positive–negative dimension is based on the extent to which the president gains personal satisfaction from the exercise of power. This psychological perspective, however, has proved to be of limited use in explaining or predicting how presidents handle the job.

4. The major components of the presidency as an institution include the vice president, the cabinet, and the Executive Office of the President (EOP). The president's closest advisors are in the EOP. Historically, the vice president has not been particularly powerful, but recent vice presidents have held significant policymaking and advisory roles.

5. Article II of the Constitution defines the president's primary constitutional responsibilities: chief executive, commander in chief of the military, and chief diplomat.

6. In addition to the formal responsibilities of office, the president is also the party's most visible and prominent leader. Although the Founders did not anticipate this role, the strongest presidents have also been strong party leaders, and a president's ability to build and direct a strong party base is often important to the success of an administration's political agenda.

7. The president plays a critical role as a public opinion leader. The high profile of the presidential office and the constant public spotlight that goes with it provide the president with a unique and powerful opportunity to connect with the public. Recent presidents have increasingly adopted a strategy of going public—using speeches to take a case directly to American citizens in an effort to shape public beliefs and influence Congress. The benefits of going public, however, are limited; rarely does a presidential speech produce a significant change in the president's ratings. The economy, international crises, and scandal are three of the most important determinants of a president's approval rating.

8. Although Congress has primary responsibility for making laws, the president plays an important role in influencing legislation. All presidents have mixed success in getting their preferences approved by Congress. Differences in constituency, electoral cycles, partisanship, and ideology often give the president and Congress different legislative goals.

9. The strongest determinant of presidential success in Congress is whether Congress is controlled by the president's party. Increased partisanship in Congress since the 1990s has enhanced the benefits of majority control, especially in the House. The effects of public approval and bargaining skills on presidential success are limited.

10. Presidents interpret their constitutional powers to include some unilateral powers—executive orders, signing statements, executive agreements, and national security directives—that have the weight of law without congressional endorsement. Recent presidents have increasingly used these devices to achieve policies that Congress has not authorized or to alter laws passed by Congress that the president considers unconstitutional.

CHAPTER THIRTEEN
Key Terms and Cases

Council of Economic Advisers, 485
executive, 471
executive agreements, 493
Executive Office of the President (EOP), 484
executive orders, 515
going public, 499
hierarchical model, 486
National Security Council, 485
national security directive, 518
Office of Management and Budget, 485
party polarization, 510
pocket veto, 507
positive government, 475
prerogative view of presidential power, 474
restrictive view of presidential power, 474
signing statements, 516
spokes-of-the-wheel model, 486
stewardship doctrine, 474
strong-executive model, 472
unilateral powers, 515
weak-executive model, 472
White House Office, 484

14 THE BUREAUCRACY

KEY QUESTIONS

Why does a democracy need bureaucracy?

Where does bureaucracy get its power to make public policy?

How can the other three branches of government control the power of bureaucracy?

© The Union/AP Photo

TO MANY people, bureaucracy is a joke. Literally. Here's an example:

Q: How many government bureaucrats does it take to screw in a lightbulb?
A: Two. One to screw it in and one to screw it up.

We've all heard these sorts of wisecracks and one-liners about bureaucrats and bureaucracy. Bureaucracy is a place dedicated to passing a buck or spending it. Bureaucracy is a government system designed to allow 10 men to do the work of one. In a bureaucracy a penny saved is a penny burned. A government bureaucrat will help you fix the blame, not the problem. Poor guy, he's in a coma, which is sort of like having a government job.

Ha, ha. Bureaucracy has long been the target of jokes and putdowns and there's no doubt that some of this is good for a chuckle. The broadly shared contempt for bureaucracy that the humor reflects, however, is anything but funny. People mistrust bureaucracy and are quick to believe the worst: that bureaucracy is wasteful, inefficient, and wraps anything that moves in red tape. No matter how ridiculous the story—bureaucracy wants to regulate farm dust, prevent accidental drowning by requiring buckets to have holes in their bottoms—we are willing to believe it if it portrays a government agency doing something stupid, venal, or corrupt. The bottom line is that bureaucracy is held in such low esteem that many reasonable people don't just ridicule it, they are quite willing to accept, repeat, and invent patently fictitious horror stories to justify their disdain.

It's not surprising that citizens have such a visceral dislike of government bureaucracy; its portrayal in the mass media and popular culture is "typically scathing in nature" (Goodsell 1994, 8). Bureaucracy is blamed for everything from hampering the war on terror to bungling mail delivery. Reviled by politicians and citizens alike, bureaucracy is viewed as inefficient, wasteful, incompetent, and malfeasant. Thus it may come as something of a surprise to find that the vast majority of research on government bureaucracies (and there's a lot of it) generally finds them doing a good job under very difficult circumstances. That might be hard to believe, but (as we shall see) it is the general pattern that emerges from the empirical record. And that finding should be something of a relief. Why? Well, though this is understood by few and accepted by fewer, modern liberal democracies simply cannot function without bureaucracy. That's right. Democracy *needs* bureaucracy.

THE CONCEPT OF BUREAUCRACY

Bureaucracy can be defined as a system of public agencies that translate the intent of democratic institutions into action. These agencies, programs, and services are largely, though not exclusively, housed in the executive branches of government, and they do everything from fight wars (the Department of Defense) to repair potholes (municipal or county highway departments) to administer healthcare programs for senior citizens.

What this means is that bureaucracy, for better or worse, is largely responsible for the performance of pretty much the entire political system. The products of executives, legislatures, and courts—executive orders, laws, and rulings—represent what the government intends to do, not what it actually does.

Understanding the job of bureaucracy is important because democratic governments in the United States promise a great deal—law and order, equal opportunity public education, clean air, libraries, a safe food supply, basic healthcare; the list is long and growing. All these promises become the responsibilities of the public bureaucracy. Bureaucracy has to take the promise of a law and translate it into reality in order to have successfully done its job. Given this duty, bureaucracy is the part of government that is most involved in the daily lives of citizens. Political scientist Ken Meier (1993, 2) once described a day in the life of a typical American, starting with a breakfast of bacon and eggs (certified fit for consumption by the U.S. Department of Agriculture) and then continuing with a drive to work (the roads, the car, and the fuel all regulated or maintained by public agencies), a walk up a flight of stairs to the office (the stairs inspected by the Occupational Safety and Health Administration), and a climb into bed to sleep at the end of the day (on a mattress with a tag that may not be removed under penalty of law).

The bureaucracy is so involved in our daily lives that most people seem to notice only its absence. For example, the overwhelming majority of letters and packages mailed by the United States Postal Service (USPS) are delivered on time with no problems. Yet it is the small exception—the letter that goes astray—that gets people's attention. Maybe bureaucracy gets its poor reputation from its competence rather than its incompetence. This is not the typical perspective on bureaucracy, but as we shall see, it is almost certainly the more realistic one.

The job of bureaucracy is to make good on the promises of democratic governments. Whatever government decides to do—be it as mundane as building a road

bureaucracy The term used to refer to the agencies of the federal government. It also refers to an organizational framework and has negative connotations.

or as momentous as going to war—bureaucracy is the actual "doer." For instance, after approving a law to clean up inland waterways, legislators do not fan out to rivers and lakes and start taking water samples. The responsibility for determining what actions the government is obligated to undertake as a result of the law, and for then actually taking those actions, is passed on to a bureaucracy. This procedure sounds reasonable enough in the abstract. In practice, though, it means that bureaucracies deal with translating broad and vague intentions into specific actions. Congress passes laws to protect children from accidental harm and consumers from dangerous products. People like that. They are not so thrilled with childproof caps on medicine bottles, one of the specific actions mandated by the Consumer Safety Product Commission to put that general law into action. Those childproof caps do, in fact, save kids' lives by preventing accidental ingestion of medicines. For most people, though, they are simply a constant reminder of how government bureaucracy can make even the small things in life—like trying to get an aspirin out of its bottle—more of a headache.

First and foremost, then, bureaucracy is the management mechanism for government. Public agencies implement, manage, and monitor programs and policies authorized by law, executive order, and regulation. Public agencies take words on paper and translate them into action by issuing contracts, formulating programs, and engaging in any number of other activities, all designed to apply broad laws to specific circumstances.

Bureaucracy is not simply an implementer of policy, however, but rather is a policymaker in its own right. It is not simply the main means to deliver on the promises of democracy; it also helps make those promises. Bureaucracy makes policy in two broad ways. First, bureaucracies and bureaucrats are forced to make informal and formal choices about how to translate into action the broad desires of legislatures, executives, or courts and to apply those desires in specific instances. In the process of making these choices, bureaucrats can be viewed as making policy. For example, speed limits are set by law (usually by state legislatures). Yet in a practical sense, it is really the traffic cop who determines how fast a motorist can go before falling afoul of the law. The legislators, after all, are not on the highway; the police officer is. The ability of lower-level bureaucrats to informally set policy in this fashion is known as the power of the street-level bureaucrat (Lipsky 1980).

The second way in which bureaucracy makes policy is through active participation in the political process. Federal bureaucracies do not wait passively for Congress and the president to formulate policies in Congress and the White House. They help shape those decisions in a number of ways: by conducting evaluations of and analyzing problems, by providing expertise on potential responses to those problems, and by outright lobbying.

Thus, the bureaucracy can be considered a fourth branch of government. The characteristics and organization of that fourth branch of government significantly shape the nation's political system and how it delivers on the promise of democracy.

THE CHARACTERISTICS OF BUREAUCRACY

Agencies in the federal bureaucracy are enormously diverse, and at first glance, organizations as diverse as, say, the United States Navy and the Federal Deposit Insurance Corporation (FDIC) appear to have little in common. Yet virtually every public agency shares two common characteristics: (1) a broad mission to implement the decisions of government and (2) a common form of organizational structure. Organizational structure is crucial to understanding bureaucracy and how it goes about implementing government decisions. Indeed, to scholars who study the subject, this is what bureaucracy is—not a public agency or a program, but a specific type of organization.

The Weberian Model of Bureaucracy

The best-known description of the bureaucratic model of organization is attributed to Max Weber (Gerth and Mills 1946). Weber's model proposed five distinguishing characteristics of a bureaucracy:

1. *Division of labor.* In a bureaucracy, work is divided according to task specialization. For example, most large bureaucracies employ specialists in personnel, accounting, and data entry. In the public sector, specialists include virologists at the Centers for Disease Control and policy analysts at the Congressional Research Service.
2. *Hierarchy.* In a bureaucracy, there is a clear vertical chain of command, and authority flows downward from superiors to subordinate employees.
3. *Formal rules.* Bureaucracies operate according to standardized operating procedures.
4. *Maintenance of files and records.* Bureaucracies record their actions and keep the records.
5. *Professionalization.* Bureaucrats are appointed on the basis of their qualifications, and government bureaucracies develop a career civil service.

Microsoft, General Motors, and IBM all have this same set of characteristics. What separates public and private bureaucracies is not how they are organized but what they are organized to do. The purpose of most private bureaucracies is to make a profit. The purpose of a public bureaucracy is to implement laws and regulations—that is, to translate the expressed intentions of government into action. Given this purpose, there are several advantages to organizing public agencies along bureaucratic lines. For example, a formal framework of rules and procedures helps ensure stability, predictability, and impartiality in the way an agency carries out its mission.

The neutrality of bureaucracy is responsible, in part, for its unflattering reputation. Most Americans have endured the classic bureaucratic experience of waiting in line, filling out forms, and dealing with red tape. (The term *red tape*, by the way, originates from the red ribbons used to bind official documents in the nineteenth century; the ribbon is long gone, but *red tape* remains as a term describing excessive bureaucratic formality.) This is not the sort of process that makes an organization popular. Yet the rules and regulations associated with bureaucracy are designed to ensure equality. It does not matter if you are rich or poor, Democrat or Republican, black or white; when you go to get a driver's license, you have to meet the same qualification standards as everyone else. There is no cutting in line, and there are no exceptions to the testing requirement on the basis of social or political standing. Consider that a public bureaucracy's red tape is a sign of the core democratic principle of political equality in action. As discussed in earlier chapters, the core values enjoy almost universal support in the abstract; in practice, though, they can be downright irritating.

The Merit System

Another characteristic of bureaucracy that relates to the core principles of democracy is professionalization, which means that the people who staff public agencies are there on the basis of merit: They are hired and promoted on the basis of their qualifications and their job performance rather than on their political connections. Public agencies have not always used the merit system. In the **spoils system**, government jobs at all levels are rewards for people's loyalty to a politician or a party. Under such a system, a change of administration (as when a politician or party loses at the polls) results in an immediate large-scale turnover in the bureaucracy.

The spoils system dominated the public bureaucracy for much of the nineteenth and early twentieth centuries. Under the spoils system, getting a government job depended on whom rather than what you knew, and your job security extended only to the next election. The spoils system promoted corruption and incompetence, thoroughly politicizing the bureaucracy (Rosenbloom 1998, 211). It could (and did) lead to many breaches of the core principles of democracy. Bureaucracies operating under the spoils system were involved in everything from playing political favorites (which contradicts the principle of political equality) to rigging elections (which contradicts the principle of majority rule). Although the spoils system has been largely abandoned, a residue of it still exists. The president, for example, appoints the head of many executive agencies. In many cases, though, these appointments must be approved by the Senate, and the appointee must have some qualifications as a prerequisite for gaining that approval.

In contrast to the spoils system, the **merit system** bases government employment on competence rather than partisan fealty. A merit system staffs a bureaucracy by defining the skills and knowledge required to do a particular job and provides a way—typically a written examination—for prospective employees to demonstrate their ability to perform those tasks. A merit system is intended to create a career civil service of competent professionals to run public agencies. Of course, bureaucrats still have their own policy and political preferences, and a

spoils system A system of governing in which political positions and benefits are given to the friends of the winner.

merit system A system of governing in which jobs are given based on relevant technical expertise and the ability to perform.

THINKING ANALYTICALLY

WHY ADOPT A MERIT SYSTEM?

Merit systems have replaced spoils systems as the favored method for staffing government bureaucracies at both the federal and state levels. But why? Why would legislators pass laws that promote neutral competence and insulate executive agency employees from political influence?

There is, of course, an obvious answer to this question. Legislatures adopted merit systems in order to reduce corruption and patronage, to promote professionalism, and ensure government employees are qualified professionals rather than political hacks. These sorts of good government goals are hard to disagree with. Yet there's another side to this. If elected officials are rational, would they not want bureaucrats to support and advance their political agendas? Isn't such influence much easier to accomplish under a spoils system? After all, if a bureaucrat flaunts the president's political wishes under a spoils system, there's an easy remedy available: Fire the offender and hire someone willing to toe the party line. Wouldn't the president's party in Congress want him to do exactly that? In short, why would the legislature bother to pass laws to insulate bureaucrats against the very political influence they are seeking to wield?

It's an interesting question because legislatures—not just in the United States, but in Western democracies generally—have done exactly that. Why? Well, let's think about this analytically. What incentives do elected officials have to minimize political influence on bureaucracy by adopting merit systems? One answer is that in a representative democracy, a party that enjoys control of government today may be out of power at the next election. That raises the very real possibility that if government bureaucracy is doing the political bidding of your party today, it may reverse course and do the bidding of the opposition party tomorrow. And while you might be happy when the bureaucracy dances to your political tune, it will be painful when the political music changes. In other words, if politicians operate in a system where there is a reasonable chance they could lose the next election they have an incentive to insulate the bureaucracy. That will make it harder for them to exercise political influence over government agencies when they are in power, but it will also make it harder for political opponents to do the same thing when they are in power. That's a testable hypothesis: The greater the likelihood politicians will suffer electoral defeat, the higher the likelihood the government will adopt a merit system.

A group of political scientists did exactly this by looking at civil service reforms adopted by state governments and by cities (Ting et al. 2012). What they found is that such reforms tended to be adopted when two conditions existed: (1) a dominant political party had controlled government for an extended period of time and (2) electoral support for that party was declining. In other words, faced with the real possibility they could lose, the long-powerful majority political party acted to insulate the bureaucracy from future influence that might be coming from the opposition.

This provides empirical evidence that competitive elections provide a strong incentive for political parties to support merit systems. Neutral competence is preferable to political obedience if there is a reasonable chance it will not be your political party calling the bureaucracy to heel.

Discussion Questions

1. Should all patronage jobs in government bureaucracies be eliminated? Why or why not?
2. If the argument above is correct, does this imply that states controlled by dominant political parties whose electoral fortunes are rising will be tempted to reinstate spoils systems? Why or why not?

merit system does not entirely eliminate politics from the bureaucracy. Compared to a spoils system, however, a merit system greatly reduces the potential for incompetence, corruption, and naked partisanship.

The merit system was formally introduced into the federal bureaucracy by the Pendleton Act of 1883. This law was a direct product of the assassination of President James Garfield in 1881 by a disappointed (and mentally unstable) office seeker. This assassination sent shock waves through the political system, turned public opinion against the spoils system, and pushed Congress into considering radical reform of the bureaucracy (Brinkley 1993, 516–517). The Pendleton Act established the principle that government employment and promotion should be based on merit demonstrated through competitive examinations. This principle signaled the end of the spoils system and remains the primary means of staffing the bureaucracy today.

Neutral Competence

Generally speaking, the merit-based civil service system prizes technical competence in government employees above virtually anything else. Most importantly, the bureaucratic form of organization offers a way to install neutral competence into public agencies. **Neutral competence** means that public agencies make decisions based on expertise rather than political or personal considerations.

At least since Woodrow Wilson's administration, reformers have sought to separate the political and administrative functions of government. The general idea is that political functions should be performed by elected officials, not by bureaucrats. The president and Congress decide basic issues such as whether the government will wage war, agree to an international trade treaty, or provide or subsidize basic healthcare and, if so, under what conditions. These are all political decisions: They represent the outcomes of conflicts over what society ought to do. This conflict is processed by the political institutions of a representative democracy into a decision about what action, if any, government should take.

Implementing those decisions is seen as an administrative function and therefore the job of the administrative arm of government—in other words, of the bureaucracy. According to the principle of neutral competence, the bureaucracy does not decide policy or take sides in the political arena. It simply uses its expertise to ensure that policy decisions are implemented in the fashion intended by the institutions of representative democracy. If those institutions make decisions that uphold the core principles of democracy, the bureaucracy ensures that government upholds those values in deed as well as words.

In theory, the bureaucratic form of organization can help separate politics and administration. In practice, though, the record is mixed. As noted previously, the bureaucracy is actively involved in influencing the formation of policies, but as discussed later in this chapter, insulating the bureaucracy from politics is difficult, and there's some question whether it should even be attempted.

neutral competence The idea that agencies should make decisions based on expertise rather than political considerations.

The Bureaucrats

Like the agencies they serve, the roughly 2.7 million federal employees are also an astonishingly diverse group. Because of the merit system, the bureaucracy is largely staffed by people hired for their technical expertise rather than for their political or partisan loyalty. Government bureaucrats include doctors, nurses, lawyers, electricians, computer programmers, carpenters, clerical workers, and virtually every other occupational group imaginable. The term *bureaucrat* rarely conjures up the image of a creative arts therapist or a microbiologist, but the federal government employs hundreds of the former and thousands of the latter.

Generally speaking, all this expertise is put to productive use. The stereotype of the ineffective and incompetent bureaucracy is largely inaccurate. Public administration scholars generally conclude that government bureaucracies do a much better job than they get credit for (Goodsell 1994; Sclar 2000). For example, the American Customer Satisfaction Index (ACSI) was originally designed to assess customer satisfaction with various businesses but has been expanded to include a wide variety of federal agencies. Consumer satisfaction varies enormously from agency to agency, with many agencies rivaling or even exceeding the satisfaction scores of private sector counterparts. Other agencies tend to have very low satisfaction scores, but these scores may be as much a result of effective government bureaucracy as anything else. One of the lowest-ranked bureaucracies is the Treasury Department, the department that houses the Internal Revenue Service (IRS). The IRS is pretty good at getting money from people—that's its job—but it can hardly be expected to leave pleased "customers" in its wake (Fornell 2010). And even the Treasury Department gets 59 out of 100 on its satisfaction score (you can check out the latest scores for all agencies at http://www.theacsi.org/).

Not only do government employees by and large do a good job; they do it relatively inexpensively. Most federal employees are covered by what is known as the general schedule (GS) pay scale (see Table 14.1). There are 15 GS grades, which range in annual pay from a first-year GS-1 at $17,981 to a senior GS-15 with years of experience at $130,810. To put the pay of federal bureaucrats into perspective, a recent college graduate would most likely be hired as a GS-5, GS-6, or GS-7 depending on the area of expertise and qualifications. That means if you went to work for the federal government after graduation, your starting annual salary would most likely fall between $28,000 and $36,000. And if you do go to work for the federal government, it would not be wise to plan on big pay raises—or on any pay raises at all. In 2014 federal employees saw their first pay increase in nearly half a decade (their salaries were bumped up by a whopping 1 percent), and since then their salaries have increased at an annual rate of less than 2 percent.

The one stereotype of the bureaucracy that does hold true is a relative lack of diversity. The typical federal bureaucrat is a white male in his late forties who has worked for the government for 13.5 years. Roughly 64 percent of federal employees are white, and minorities tend to be concentrated in the middle and lower ranks of the bureaucracy. Females are also underrepresented—roughly 57 percent of federal employees are male. As a group, federal employees are also highly

TABLE 14.1 GENERAL SCHEDULE (GS) PAY SCALE, EFFECTIVE JANUARY 2014

Grade	Step 1	Step 2	Step 3	Step 4	Step 5	Step 6	Step 7	Step 8	Step 9	Step 10	WITHIN GRADE AMOUNTS
1	$17,981	$18,582	$19,180	$19,775	$20,373	$20,724	$21,315	$21,911	$21,934	$22,494	VARIES
2	20,217	20,698	21,367	21,934	22,179	22,831	23,483	24,135	24,787	25,439	VARIES
3	22,058	22,793	23,528	24,263	24,998	25,733	26,468	27,203	27,938	28,673	735
4	24,763	25,588	26,413	27,238	28,063	28,888	29,713	30,538	31,363	32,188	825
5	27,705	28,629	29,553	30,477	31,401	32,325	33,249	34,173	35,097	36,021	924
6	30,883	31,912	32,941	33,970	34,999	36,028	37,057	38,086	39,115	40,144	1,029
7	34,319	35,463	36,607	37,751	38,895	40,039	41,183	42,327	43,471	44,615	1,144
8	38,007	39,274	40,541	41,808	43,075	44,342	45,609	46,876	48,143	49,410	1,267
9	41,979	43,378	44,777	46,176	47,575	48,974	50,373	51,772	53,171	54,570	1,399
10	46,229	47,770	49,311	50,852	52,393	53,934	55,475	57,016	58,557	60,098	1,541
11	50,790	52,483	54,176	55,869	57,562	59,255	60,948	62,641	64,334	66,027	1,693
12	60,877	62,906	64,935	66,964	68,993	71,022	73,051	75,080	77,109	79,138	2,029
13	72,391	74,804	77,217	79,630	82,043	84,456	86,869	89,282	91,695	94,108	2,413
14	85,544	88,395	91,246	94,097	96,948	99,799	102,650	105,501	108,352	111,203	2,851
15	100,624	103,978	107,332	110,686	114,040	117,394	120,748	124,102	127,456	130,810	3,354

Source: U.S. Office of Personnel Management. https://www.opm.gov/policy-data-oversight/pay-leave/salaries-wages/2017/general-schedule/.

educated, with more than half holding college degrees (United States Office of Personnel Management 2016).

THE STRUCTURE OF AMERICAN BUREAUCRACIES

Federal government public agencies are organized into a rough hierarchy. If we confine the discussion to the executive branch (Congress and the courts have their own bureaucracies), there are five basic categories of public agency within this hierarchy. At the top are the Executive Office of the President and the cabinet departments. Below them come independent agencies, government corporations, and miscellaneous bureaus (see Figure 14.1).

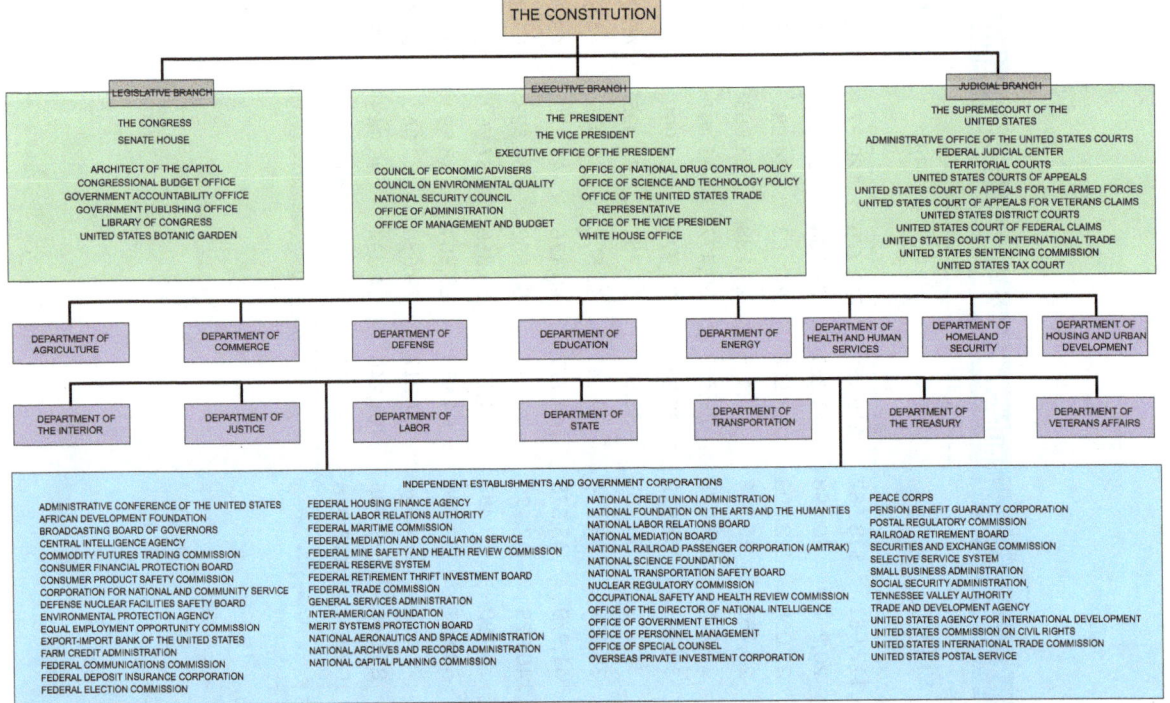

FIGURE 14.1 Organization of the U.S. Government

Source: https://www.gpo.gov/fdsys/pkg/GOVMAN-2017-08-02/pdf/GOVMAN-2017-08-02-The-Government-of-the-United-States-4.pdf.

The Executive Office of the President

At the top of the executive branch hierarchy is the **Executive Office of the President (EOP)**. This is the bureaucracy charged with collectively managing all of the executive branch bureaucracies for the president. The EOP is divided into several agencies with specific tasks. The White House Office consists of the key members of the president's staff who help with the day-to-day administrative responsibilities of the presidency. Also housed in the EOP are agencies specializing in particular policy areas, such as the Council of Economic Advisers and the National Security Council, as well as agencies with broader responsibilities. An example of the latter is the Office of Management and Budget (OMB), which provides a central location for all other agencies to submit program and budget requests and thus plays an important centralizing role in the federal bureaucracy.

Cabinet Departments

Just below the EOP in the bureaucratic hierarchy are the 15 **cabinet departments**, each headed by a cabinet secretary appointed by the president. Congress created each of these departments and has the power to determine their organization and internal operation. The first cabinet departments were State, War (which evolved into Defense), and Treasury, all created in 1789. The most recent is the Department of Homeland Security (DHS), created in 2002 in one of the most sweeping reorganizations of the federal bureaucracy in 50 years.

Cabinet departments are administrative agencies charged with carrying out government operations in general policy areas. These departments are the main institutions of the federal bureaucracy and are responsible for implementing most federal programs and policies. They have the highest profile of all the federal bureaucracies, and the people who run them are often known to the general public.

Cabinet departments are not monolithic and centralized bureaucracies. Many of them are more accurately described as holding companies. They serve as administrative umbrellas covering diverse programs and serving diverse clients. Each department is subdivided into smaller units. The Department of Justice (DOJ) is the largest law firm in the world, employing thousands of attorneys working in bureaus dedicated to antitrust efforts, civil rights protection, criminal prosecution, and other areas of the law. The DOJ also includes the FBI, the Drug Enforcement Agency, and the U.S. Marshals Service. In addition to lawyers and law enforcement agencies, the DOJ also includes the Federal Bureau of Prisons, which runs the federal prison system. All of these individual agencies may have considerable independence even though they are part of a single department. In fact, many of the individual agencies predate their departmental organizations and have proud and independent histories, some of which stretch back for centuries. The U.S. Coast Guard, for example, operated for more than 200 years before becoming a part of the DHS.

Executive Office of the President (EOP) The organizational structure in the executive branch that houses the president's most influential advisors and agencies. The most important include the White House Office, the Office of Management and Budget (OMB), the National Security Council, and the Council of Economic Advisers.

cabinet departments The 15 largest and most influential agencies of the federal bureaucracy.

Secretary of State Mike Pompeo holds a press conference after meeting with officials from North Korea to discuss a possible summit. The Department of State is a cabinet-level agency, and its chief is appointed by the president and given primary responsibility for executing the nation's foreign policy.

© Albin Lohr-Jones/Sipa/AP Photo

Independent Agencies

The central characteristic of **independent agencies** is their independence from cabinet departments: Unlike the Coast Guard or the FBI, they are not under the administrative control of a cabinet secretary. Independent agencies were created to operate outside the cabinet department umbrella for a number of reasons: For example, some did not seem to fit well within any existing department, and some were kept outside of cabinet departments in hopes of fostering fresh approaches to vexing policy problems. Putting agencies outside of cabinet departments also helps clarify policy intent. For example, if NASA were placed within a cabinet department, the most likely candidate would be the Department of Defense. But having the National Aeronautics and Space Administration (NASA) under the control of the military bureaucracy would indicate that the United States intends to use its space program for military rather than scientific and commercial purposes. With NASA operating as an independent agency, its mission is less likely to be seen as serving the military interests of the United States.

Although they generally have narrower areas of responsibility, independent agencies can rival the size and influence of the departments. NASA, for example, has roughly 18,000 employees. That is four times the roughly 4,400 people who work for the Department of Education.

Regulatory Agencies and Commissions

Regulatory agencies and commissions are specific types of independent agencies. They are part of the executive branch of government but are independent of cabinet departments. Examples include the Securities and Exchange Commission (SEC), which regulates stock and bond markets, and the Environmental Protection Agency (EPA), which regulates pollution. What separates regulatory agencies from other independent agencies is the focus of their responsibilities: Congress creates regulatory agencies to monitor and regulate specific areas of economic activity. The main reason for keeping regulatory agencies outside of cabinet departments is to provide them with a degree of insulation from political pressures. The idea is that policy areas such as industrial pollution should be regulated by a neutral referee who serves public rather than partisan interests.

The degree of insulation from political pressure varies. Some regulatory agencies, such as the EPA, are headed by a political appointee—someone who serves at the pleasure of the president. Others, such as the SEC, are headed by presidential

independent agencies Federal agencies that are not part of the cabinet-level executive departments.

regulatory agencies and commissions Agencies that are independent of cabinet departments and are created by Congress to monitor and regulate specific areas of economic activity.

appointees—in other words, they have to be nominated by the president and approved by Congress. Once appointed, however, commissioners serve a fixed term and cannot be removed if they make decisions the president disagrees with. Similarly, the Consumer Product Safety Commission is a regulatory agency headed by commissioners serving seven-year terms that overlap with presidential administrations; this overlap makes it more difficult for presidents to use their appointment powers to advance a particular set of interests or to promote a particular political agenda.

Regulatory agencies, or at least government regulations, have been a particular target of anti-bureaucracy criticism, with many arguing that when government regulates with too strong a hand, it ends up limiting individual liberty and acting as a drag on the economy. Conservatives in particular have championed **deregulation**, which means the simplification, loosening, or elimination of government rules (see this chapter's later section for a full discussion of rules and rulemaking). The basic idea is that government rules and regulations are a poor substitute for the natural discipline of free markets. Regulations restrict innovation, nimble decision making, and entrepreneurial activity; remove the regulations, and these activities are promoted, and everyone benefits. At least, that's the theory. In practice, most people are in favor of deregulation only until something goes really wrong; then everyone wants to know why government was asleep at the switch.

Government Corporations

Another set of organizations in the extended family of the federal bureaucracy consists of **government corporations**. These operate in a vague area somewhere between the public and private sectors. The general idea behind government corporations is to shift responsibility for a government task to a nonpartisan arena in hopes of keeping it insulated from politics to the greatest extent possible. Probably the best-known government corporation is the USPS (the postal service). Other examples include the FDIC, which insures bank deposits, and Amtrak, the nation's passenger rail service. In essence, government corporations are federally established businesses. They have narrow tasks and are run by bipartisan or nonpartisan boards. Most are designed to be self-supporting, although some receive at least some assistance from the federal government.

Other Bureaus

Besides the EOP, cabinet departments, independent agencies, and government corporations, there is a miscellaneous set of executive branch organizations that does not fit into any of these categories. This set includes **advisory committees**, which can be either permanent or temporary and which serve a number of purposes, ranging from providing agencies with technical expertise to providing a means for communicating citizen input to agency operations. In any given year, there are roughly 1,000 advisory committees salted throughout the federal bureaucracy.

deregulation The reduction or elimination of government rules and regulations that interfere with the efficient operation of market forces.

government corporations Federally established businesses that are narrow in focus and are in part self-supporting.

advisory committees Temporary or permanent organizations created to provide information and technical expertise to the bureaucracy.

There are also numerous boards, committees, and commissions that are temporary additions to the bureaucracy. These tend to be small, have well-defined tasks, and have few program responsibilities.

The Politics of Organization

Though we can classify public agencies and sort them into a rough pecking order, there really is no such thing as "the" federal bureaucracy. Rather than a single federal bureaucracy, there is actually a sprawling mass of individual agencies. The 2.7 million civilian employees of the federal government serve in 15 departments, 50 or so independent regulatory agencies, and numerous boards, commissions, and advisory committees. As we have seen, many of these bureaucracies are subdivided into smaller administrative units that have considerable independence. Rather than being a Big Brother, the bureaucracies are more like a vast extended family, replete with third cousins twice removed and siblings who are not talking to each other.

After reading about the confusing stew of departments, agencies, committees, bureaus, and commissions and their seemingly incoherent relationships with one another, you might be wondering whether the organization of the federal bureaucracy makes any sense. The short answer to that is simple: no. At least in terms of being organized to promote effective and efficient administration, the organization of the federal government is not particularly rational or logical.

Consider federal oversight of the banks. There is no single bureaucracy overseeing the regulation of these institutions. There are at least seven. These include two divisions of a cabinet department (the Office of the Comptroller of the Currency and the Financial Crimes Enforcement Network, both part of the Treasury Department), one independent agency (the National Credit Union Administration), one government corporation (the FDIC), one independent government commission (the Federal Trade Commission), one formal interagency body (the Federal Financial Institutions Examination Council), and the central banking system of the United States (the Federal Reserve System, which is headed by a presidentially appointed board of governors and includes 12 regional federal banks). The goals and responsibilities of these agencies overlap, yet there is little in the way of centralized or coordinated control over what they do, and one agency may be all but unaware of the activities of another.

The heads of federal agencies are often asked to report to Congress. Here National Security Agency Director Admiral Michael S. Rogers testifies before the U.S. Senate Committee on Intelligence.
© Ron Sachs/picture-alliance/dpa/AP Photo

Why does the federal bureaucracy contain such redundancy, overlap, and unclear lines of authority? Why, for heaven's sake, are there seven federal agencies regulating banks rather than one? Actually, there is a relatively simple answer to all these questions, one directly related to the purpose of bureaucracies: Bureaucracies are there to make good on the promises of democratic government, and the constituents of democratic governments often want their government to promise to do things that are not efficient, logical, or even particularly effective.

The reason for seven banking regulatory agencies is that the various sectors of the banking industry do not want to be regulated by a single agency. Credit unions and banks, for example, each wanted their own regulatory agency, each of which has a set of accompanying congressional committees. In other words, the bureaucracy regulating the financial industry is convoluted because it serves a set of political goals. Different sectors of the industry have lobbied government to give them different agencies that regulate different aspects of the business. A good example of this is the now defunct Office of Thrift Supervision (OTS), which regulated some of the biggest institutions implicated in the massive financial meltdowns of 2008–2009. The OTS had a reputation as a lax regulator, and this is exactly why big companies such as AIG supported the OTS and wanted to be regulated by them (AIG is a massive insurance company that required a massive taxpayer bailout to stay in business [National Public Radio 2009]). In hindsight the OTS regulatory regime was a bad idea; it might have been better to have a tougher regulatory agency watching outfits such as AIG. Had it been in existence, an agency such as the CFPB might have been more effective and more efficient. Yet that misses the point. The job of the bureaucracy is not to be effective or efficient, but to deliver on the promises of democratic governments. Whatever its considerable faults, the OTS was doing exactly that—in the 1990s and early 2000s, less federal regulation was what Congress was demanding, and with the OTS that is just what it got.

This basic rule of democratic governance—bureaucracy responds to the demands of elected government, no matter how silly or dangerous the demands—does not apply just to the financial industry. The pattern is repeated again and again. And it cannot be blamed on the catch-all villain of "special interests." All citizens, in some fashion, have vested interests in government agencies. You, or at least many of your peers, for example, probably want the Department of Education to keep guaranteeing student loans and offering student grants. This demand creates pressure on government—mainly from parents with college-age children—to make promises about higher education and financial aid. The result? A program run by a public agency with rules, regulations, red tape, and the rest of the bureaucratic machinery. (Those of you who have applied for a student loan will be intimately familiar with these details.)

THE POWER OF BUREAUCRACY

Although bureaucracy exists to implement the promises made by the elected branches of government, and the characteristics and organization of the federal bureaucracy reflect the politics of the democratic system, the federal bureaucracy does not simply passively respond to the executives and legislators. Bureaucracy is an independent policymaker. By our definition of politics (the authoritative allocation of values, or the process of deciding who gets what and when and how they get it), the bureaucracy is very much a political branch of government. Every day, bureaucracies make policy decisions about who gets what. Indeed, bureaucracy is a unique form of policymaking institution that combines all branches of government. Bureaucracies are executive branches of government, yet they also exercise legislative and judicial powers. How do they get this power, and how do they exercise it?

Rulemaking

Laws are often vague and provide bureaucracies with only minimal guidelines about the specific actions they must take. Vague laws give bureaucrats considerable discretion in deciding what these actions will be. Recognizing that these choices should not be made arbitrarily, Congress formally requires bureaucracies to follow a decision-making process that is very similar to the legislative process. This process is called rulemaking.

A **rule** is a statement by a federal agency that interprets a law and prescribes the specific action an agency will take to implement that law. **Rulemaking** is the process of deciding exactly what the laws passed by Congress mean. This process has been described as "the single most important function performed by agencies of government" (Kerwin 1994, xi). Once an agency approves a rule, the rule applies to everyone within the agency's jurisdiction and has the force of law. For all practical purposes, rules *are* law. Those annoying childproof caps, for example, are required by Consumer Product Safety Commission (CPSC) rules, and drug manufacturers are legally bound to follow them.

Rulemaking represents the formal process of making choices about what actions the government should undertake, and it amounts to a huge shadow lawmaking process most citizens know little to nothing about. Although it may be unsettling to acknowledge that unelected bureaucrats play a central role in shaping the law, in practical terms it is unavoidable. Passing a law is a difficult process and often requires much compromise. Congress often has more important priorities than thrashing out the minutiae of exactly how a program or policy is to be implemented. As a result, Congress passes laws that are vague about what they specifically obligate the government to do. For example, the Occupational Safety and Health Act was passed "to assure so far as possible every working man and woman in the nation safe and healthy work conditions." That law expresses a noble goal with which few would disagree. Yet how do we put this noble goal into action? What exactly should the government do to ensure that its citizens have a safe working environment? The answers to those questions come not from Congress but from the Occupational Safety and Health Administration (OSHA).

Bureaucracy's responsibility for fleshing out the messy details needed to implement vague laws helps explain how bureaucracy gets its negative image. Passing a law promoting safety in the workplace attracted considerable support in the

rule A statement of the bureaucracy that interprets the law or prescribes a specific action. These rules have the force of law.

rulemaking The process in which the bureaucracy decides what the laws passed by Congress mean and how they should be carried out.

abstract. In practice, OSHA was left to deal with a myriad of specifics, such as the minimum allowable thickness of ladder rungs and how much cotton dust a textile worker should be exposed to. Issuing a lengthy list of standards for manufacturing ladders seems more like petty bureaucratic meddling than work toward the grand cause of worker safety. Rulemaking is the "dirty work" of politics: detail-oriented, laborious, and necessary. Yet without these specifics, laws are just words on paper, not actions in the real world.

Few federal agencies have the authority to unilaterally issue rules. Rulemaking is governed by the Federal Administrative Procedures Act and other laws passed by Congress. At a minimum, agencies must give public notice of rules, allow interested parties an opportunity to comment on these rules, and publish the finished product in the *Federal Register*. Though the process is unknown to most citizens, most organized interest groups are well aware of the importance of rulemaking and actively participate in the process where their interests are involved. Bureaucracies take public input very seriously, and the rulemaking process is generally acknowledged to be open and to allow for conflicting interests to state their cases.

Bureaucracies have the difficult task of creating rules that will implement (the often vague) laws passed by Congress. The Consumer Product Safety Commission, for example, is charged with insuring safety standards on consumer products, including toys. The CPSC regulates everything from the size of parts that can be used in toys, to how loud a sound a toy can make, to what materials can be used to make the toy.

© Dominic Lipinski/Press Association/AP Photo

Adjudication

In making rules, bureaucracies act like legislatures; in judging them, they act like courts. **Adjudication** is a process designed to establish whether a rule has been violated. For example, the National Highway Traffic Safety Administration (NHTSA) uses adjudication to judge whether a particular type or model of automobile violates safety regulations and should be removed from the roads. If the NHTSA believes an automobile violates safety rules, it holds a hearing in which the manufacturer can present contesting evidence and arguments. If the agency deems a recall to be necessary, the manufacturer has an opportunity to negotiate the scope and wording of the recall.

Bureaucratic Lobbying

Bureaucratic policymaking is not only passive and reactive. Bureaucracies are also active in the initiation of new policies, and they actively participate in the broader political process. As the primary managers of policy, bureaucrats are in ideal positions to identify the problems and limitations of existing laws and programs, and

adjudication The process of determining whether a law or rule established by the bureaucracy has been broken.

they frequently recommend changes to the president and to the congressional committees with which they interact.

Bureaucracies' power to influence policy formation by legislatures and executives has two sources. First and foremost is their expertise. Knowledge is power, and bureaucracies are vast storehouses of information. The president and the Congress often rely on bureaucracy to collect and present the information needed to fashion policy, and by choosing what information to provide and how to present that information, bureaucrats can affect policy decisions.

The second source of power is close alliances with important clientele groups and the congressional committees that hold jurisdiction over the programs of interest to those clientele groups. The Department of Veterans Affairs, for example, has a powerful ally in the nation's veterans. Few legislators relish the prospect of taking a position that can be perceived as anti-veteran, and this provides a potent source of influence. Politicians and bureaucracy typically use this influence to advance common interests rather than wield it against each other. Some scholars argue that many important policy decisions are made in **iron triangles**, which are stable relationships among a clientele group, the bureaucracy managing the programs that affect that group's interests, and the congressional committees with jurisdiction over those programs. Each actor in this triangle has a shared set of interests, and they are able to work in harness to pursue common goals. Figure 14.2 shows how the basic relationships in an iron triangle work. Congress

iron triangles A term used to refer to the interdependent relationship among the bureaucracy, interest groups, and congressional committees.

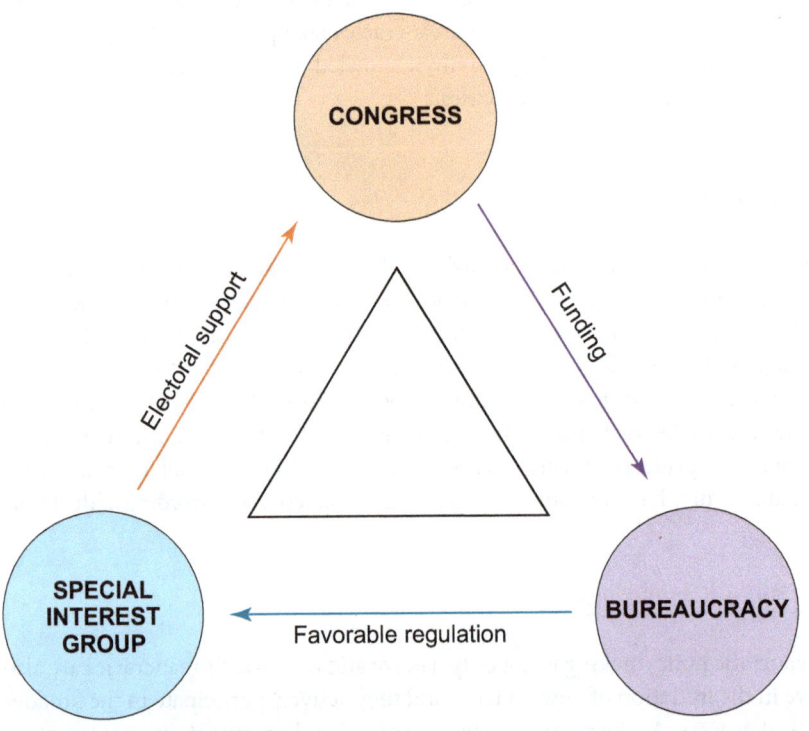

FIGURE 14.2 An Iron Triangle

provides a bureaucracy with generous funding and political power, the bureaucracy serves its clientele with favorable regulatory or program decisions, and the clientele serves as a special interest group that supports the electoral ambitions of lawmakers. Each corner of the triangle supports the goals and desires of another in a mutually reinforcing relationship. Though they were once seen as "governments within government" that were impervious to democratic control, political scientists have largely concluded that iron triangles are less autonomous and powerful than originally thought (F. Baumgartner and Jones 1993).

Political scientists have discovered that bureaucracies are more likely to operate in policy subsystems than in iron triangles. **Policy subsystems** are the "interaction of actors from different institutions interested in a policy area" (Sabatier 1988). In other words, they are networks of all the groups that share a particular policy interest. Unlike iron triangles, these networks may include executives, courts, a wide range of interest groups and legislative committees, and just about anyone or anything else that can get itself organized enough to participate in the process. These networks are not nearly as stable as iron triangles, and two actors who work together on one issue may oppose each other on another. Thus, the Sierra Club may champion an effort by the EPA to enforce the preservation of wildlife yet oppose the agency when it seeks to relax rules on power plant emissions.

CONTROLLING THE BUREAUCRACY

The discussion thus far shows that bureaucracy exists to make good on promises made by democratic governments, and to do this, federal agencies have been granted broad powers and been structured in a way that makes organizational sense for individual agencies and political sense for the overall bureaucracy. All of these characteristics combine to create a larger concern about the bureaucracy: control. Bureaucrats are appointed, not elected, yet we know that through the process of rulemaking, they for all practical purposes make law. If program or regulatory responsibilities are shared by two or four or six bureaucracies, whom do we hold responsible if something goes wrong?

One of the most consistent concerns about the bureaucracy is the need to ensure that it serves the purpose for which it was intended. We want bureaucracy to serve democracy, not to serve its own interests. This is the classic dilemma at the heart of studying bureaucracy: How do you make one of the most powerful institutions of government abide by the principles of democracy when that institution is not democratic? And make no mistake about it: Bureaucracies are *not* democratic. Glance back at the characteristics of the classic bureaucracy given earlier in this chapter. Bureaucracies are hierarchical and authoritarian; their personnel are not hired or fired by elections; their decisions are not put to a ballot. Every industrialized democracy has had to come to some sort of arrangement with the increasingly important role of the administrative arm of government. The trick

policy subsystems Networks of groups with an interest in a specific policy issue or area.

here is to make the bureaucracy accountable to the principles of democracy, rather than vice versa.

Theories of Bureaucratic Behavior

Theories of bureaucratic behavior highlight just how tough it can be to make the bureaucracy accountable to democratic principles. In seeking to explain the choices made by individual bureaucrats and the behavior of entire bureaucracies, political scientists have drawn heavily from the rational choice tradition. Assuming that bureaucrats are rational utility maximizers raises some disturbing implications for the political role of bureaucracies and highlights the need for effective control mechanisms.

Consider the highly influential theory of the budget-maximizing bureaucrat, formulated by William Niskanen (1971). Niskanen was seeking to answer this question: If bureaucrats are rational utility maximizers, what exactly are they seeking to maximize? He reasoned that a bureaucrat's personal utility, or satisfaction, is tied to the budget of the agency he or she works for. Agencies with bigger budgets mean bigger and more important programs, and that means more power, prestige, and opportunities for advancement. Niskanen's theory created a picture of bureaucracies as entities equivalent to corporations run by rational entrepreneurs. Just as rational business executives seek to make decisions that will maximize profit, so will bureaucrats seek to make decisions that maximize budgets. Niskanen's theory of the budget-maximizing bureaucrat thus suggests that bureaucrats will try to "sell" legislatures on the programs and public services they provide not because they serve the public interest, but because funding them serves the rational interests of bureaucrats. The result will be a bloated and expensive public sector, which is good for bureaucrats, but not so good for the taxpayer.

Gordon Tullock (1965) presented an alternative rational choice model of bureaucratic behavior. Tullock argued that bureaucrats maximize utility through career advancement, which is not necessarily achieved by increasing budgets. In Tullock's model, rational bureaucrats maximize utility by highlighting their successes and trying to hide their failures—because doing so increases chances of advancement. The implication here is not necessarily agencies with bloated bottom lines, but agencies that are dysfunctional and incompetent. If bureaucrats have an incentive to suppress information about poor performance and highlight information about successes, then legislatures will have an unrealistic picture of what agencies are doing and what they are capable of. Lacking accurate information about the real capabilities and performance of bureaucracy, Tullock argued, makes it hard for legislatures to figure out when bureaucracies are serving the public interest and when they are serving their own interests.

Rational choice theories of bureaucratic behavior thus highlight the need for effective control of bureaucracy because without effective controls, bureaucrats will serve their own interests rather than the public interest. Other theories of bureaucratic behavior, however, especially those in the social-psychological tradition, give a different picture of what motivates bureaucratic decision making. The most famous of these is Herbert Simon's theory of **bounded rationality**, formulated more than 70 years ago in his book *Administrative Behavior* (1947). Simon argues that actual humans bear little resemblance to the utility maximizers of classical rational choice models. Maximizing involves considering all possible options and weighing the costs and benefits of all of them to discover which one delivers maximum utility. But identifying alternatives involves costs (time and money), so it's unlikely that a decision maker could identify all of them. And even if one could identify all the alternatives, the information would be so vast and complex that no human being could possibly analyze and evaluate it. Thus, rather than maximize, Simon argues that people satisfice. **Satisficing** means considering possible alternatives until finding one that, in the person's view, is good enough to solve the problem at hand and then choosing it, even though it might not be the "best" possible solution. Because information is costly and people's ability to process it is limited, once a satisfactory solution is found, there is little incentive to continue searching.

Simon's model creates a very different picture of bureaucrats. It does not deny that bureaucrats try to act rationally, but argues that their ability to do so is constrained. Bounded rationality takes the psychological boundaries to our ability to be utility maximizers into account; we are not capable of true maximization because we have imperfect information. Instead, we use shortcuts and make decisions based on our values and habits rather than on a rational cost–benefit calculation. The implications of bounded rationality for our understanding of bureaucracy are profound. Consider budgets. Under Niskanen's model, a bureaucrat seeks to make his or her budget as large as possible. Under Simon's model, a bureaucrat is faced with the problem of coming up with a justifiable budget. To overcome that challenge, he or she starts with what worked in the past—last year's budget—and makes incremental adjustments up or down, based on perceived needs and political feasibility. Rather than portraying bureaucrats as people coldly calculating how to build independent empires to serve their own interests, Simon's model portrays them as individuals muddling through the problems they are given as best they can.

Viewed through the lens of bounded rationality, bureaucrats and bureaucracies seem less of a potential threat to the public interest and more as individuals and agencies trying to do a tough job with all the psychological baggage that comes with being human—limited attention spans, imperfect information, and a tendency to rely on personal values as much as on rational cost–benefit analysis when making choices. The result is some good decisions and some bad decisions. Control of the bureaucracy is still an issue from this perspective because public agencies still wield political power; they are delegated significant responsibilities and must be held accountable to democracy.

Controlling the bureaucracy and making it accountable requires two basic things. First, elected representatives and individual citizens must be able to effectively monitor the bureaucracy. Again, the organization of bureaucracy helps us here; bureaucracies operate by formal rules (which help make clear what they should and should not be doing), and they keep written records. Second, elected officials need a basic set of tools to influence bureaucracy.

bounded rationality Herbert Simon's theory that humans are not utility maximizers as suggested in classical rational choice models. Humans satisfice (see satisficing) rather than maximize.

satisficing Considering possible alternatives until finding one that is good enough to solve the problem at hand even though it might not be the "best" possible solution.

APPLYING THE FRAMEWORKS

CAN EVOLUTION TELL US ANYTHING ABOUT BUREAUCRACY?

Of the three prominent theoretical models used as running examples in this book, two have been extensively applied to the bureaucracy. One has barely been applied at all. Yet the theory that bureaucracy scholars have all but ignored may actually address some big questions left unanswered by the other two frameworks.

A good example of this is bureaucratic behavior, which represents one of the central explanatory challenges of bureaucracy scholarship. The key research question here is: Why do bureaucrats make the choices they do? Generating systematic answers to this question is considered critically important for at least a couple of reasons.

First, bureaucrats are in a unique position to have a big impact on the day-to-day lives of citizens. This is what's known as the power of the "street-level" bureaucrat, and the traffic cop example discussed in the text gives you an idea of what this power means. A traffic cop has a good deal of discretion over who to stop and who to ticket. How he or she exercises that power—in other words, what choices he or she makes—not only explains why you are paying a fine or losing your license, but also whether public programs and policies generally are being implemented and enforced as democratically elected legislatures intended.

Second, bureaucrats tend to have a lot of knowledge that legislators and citizens do not. They got their jobs, after all, on the basis of a merit system, meaning they have some technical competence or expertise that other people do not. They actually run the programs and policies and generally have a much better idea of what is working or not and why. The idea of the merit system is that this technical expertise and inside information will be used for the public good. Yet that same expertise can also be used to advance a bureaucracy's interests, or the interests of an individual bureaucrat, and these are not necessarily the same thing as the public good. This sort of situation is known as information asymmetry, which is just a fancy way of saying that bureaucrats know stuff that other people do not.

Rational choice frameworks have generally come to pretty gloomy conclusions about bureaucratic behavior. Starting from the assumption that bureaucrats are rational utility maximizers, it's a short step to theorizing that agency employees will routinely use information asymmetry to make self-interested choices (see discussion of William Niskanen and Gordon Tullock's research in the text). Behavioral theoretical models are not quite so pessimistic. They essentially conclude that bureaucrats will deal with information asymmetry by muddling through as best they can. They certainly might act self-interestedly, but if there is a strong agency culture of public service, or if the individual simply has strong professional or personal ethical rules, these are as likely to influence their choices as much as does their self-interest (see discussion of bounded rationality in the text).

But think about this. Rational choice theory tells us bureaucrats will use inside information to make self-interested choices. Bounded rationality tells us bureaucrats will sometimes use information asymmetry to their advantage, and sometimes they will not. This is not that helpful. What we really want to figure out is under what exact circumstances bureaucrats are likely to use information asymmetry to take advantage for themselves, and when they are likely to use that information for the benefit of others.

Scholars working with evolutionary models of behavior may have already figured this out. These folks have long been fascinated by how people make choices and have noted that while most people clearly have a streak of self-interest, they are also careful to be fair to others, even when it's not in their strict self-interest to do so. Why is such a weird mix of self-interest and altruism what triggers a decision to act self-interestedly versus a decision to act altruistically?

Evolutionary psychologists theorize that there are good reasons for this mix of nasty and nice in our natures. Evolutionarily speaking, it makes clear sense to act self-interestedly. If you know of a good hunting ground, a grove of fruit trees, or other source of food that will help you thrive and survive, keep it to yourself. You've got your larder, and to heck with the guy in the next cave over. Yet humans have also always been social creatures. Our survival has always depended on group collaboration and trust. On the evolutionary savannah, a lone naked ape is, in the technical terms of evolutionary theory, lunch. A group of them, especially if they act together, are the hunters rather than the hunted. Our survival, in short, has depended on being a valued member of a group.

The critical importance of sociality to the evolution of humans means we prize above most things our social reputation. We want to be seen as good guys, people who will help out the group. We will act in our own self-interests, but only if it does not harm our reputation as reliable social partners. This creates interesting hypotheses over exactly when people will or will not act self-interestedly under conditions of information asymmetry.

One study, for example, took a group of research subjects and gave them 15 tokens that could be cashed in after the study. The job of these subjects, termed "allocators," was to divide these tokens between themselves and another subject who would remain anonymous to them. This seems like a situation tailor-made for a self-interested choice. Take all the tokens, and to heck with the sucker who gets nothing. There was a twist, though. The allocators were told that the tokens were worth twice as much to them as they were to the recipient, and they were also told that the recipient had no idea of the differential value of the tokens. Under these conditions of information asymmetry, the allocators went for an even split of tokens. This meant they were acting self-interestedly but in a strange (for rational choice theory) sort of way. They didn't take all the tokens, which they could have. They got twice as much as the recipient, but the recipient got the impression the allocators were good guys, doing the right thing and going for an even split. This confirmed the predictions of evolutionary theory.

There was one more element to this study, though. It was rerun in exactly the same way, except allocators were told the tokens were worth twice as much to the recipient as they were to the allocator. Again, the recipient had no knowledge of the differential value of the tokens. Again, the allocators went for an even split. Effectively, this time allocators were not being rational at all—they consciously screwed themselves. They gave away twice as much to the recipient as they got themselves in order to maintain that good-guy appearance. Again, this confirmed the prediction of evolutionary theory—people prize that reputation as a good social collaborator even if it hurts to keep it.

These behavioral patterns would not be predicted by traditional rational choice or behavioral models. Yet the basic research focus here—how people make choices under conditions of information asymmetry—is exactly the problem rational choice and behavioral models of bureaucratic behavior have struggled to solve. Maybe it is time to apply evolutionary and biological frameworks to bureaucracy.

Discussion Questions

1. Think of the "street-level" bureaucrats you have interacted with recently (e.g., teachers, secretaries, police officers). Is their behavior, the actions and choices you observed them make, better explained by rational choice, bounded rationality, or the sort of evolutionary frameworks discussed above?
2. As discussed above, bureaucrats often have an asymmetric information advantage. In other words, they know more than the people they interact with. Are there rules or regulations that could help ensure that imbalance is not used to disadvantage citizens who interact with bureaucrats?

Monitoring Bureaucracy

The preferred method of making bureaucracy accountable to democracy is through a process called overhead democracy (Redford 1969; W. Wilson 1887). **Overhead democracy** is the idea that citizens can exercise indirect control over bureaucracy: Voters will hold elected officials accountable for their actions through their votes, and elected officials will hold bureaucracies accountable for their actions. Candidates who favor majority viewpoints will win office. To win reelection, these candidates must make some effort to keep the promises they made on the campaign trail. Thus, they have a built-in incentive to keep a close eye on the bureaucracies that will actually deliver on those promises. If the bureaucracy abuses its position and starts violating the core principles of democracy—if it plays favorites or denies people services to which they are entitled—an officeholder is expected to take action. If he or she does not, the officeholder will be voted out in favor of someone who will bring the bureaucracy to heel.

Overhead democracy is more complicated in practice than in theory (Meier 1993). It requires politicians to vigorously exercise their oversight responsibilities, systematically monitoring the bureaucracy to ensure that it is acting in accordance with democratically expressed wishes in much the same way that police officers patrol city streets to spot and deter crime. This process is called **police patrol oversight** (McCubbins and Schwartz 1984). The problem here is that for the individual politician, police patrol oversight rarely pays off. In the vast majority of cases, the agencies are doing pretty much what they are supposed and expected to do. Thus, a legislator's time is better spent crafting new laws, engaging in constituency service, or doing any of the other activities related to election.

Rather than engage in constant monitoring, Congress and its committees tend to rely on **fire alarm oversight**, which kicks into action once an alarm is raised (McCubbins and Schwartz 1984). There are many ways to raise an alarm about bureaucratic wrongdoing. Whistle-blowers (agency employees who bring attention to agency misdeeds), direct contact from constituents, and investigations by Congress's information-gathering agencies such as the General Accounting Office (GAO) all routinely raise alarms. Special interest groups are particularly effective at sounding alarms because they put a good deal of effort into monitoring the agencies that affect their interests. A high-profile failure or disaster can also trigger fire alarm oversight. For example, few people had heard of the Marine Minerals Service (MMS) prior to the massive BP oil spill in the Gulf of Mexico in 2010. The job of the MMS, an agency located in the Department of the Interior, is to manage the oil, gas, and other mineral resources in the nation's outer continental shelf. In order to drill for oil in the deep water of the outer continental shelf, companies need to get proper certification from the MMS, a process that includes vetting for safety and environmental impact. It was not until after the disastrous well blowout that spewed millions of gallons of crude oil into the Gulf, causing widespread environmental and economic damage in coastal states, that the president and Congress began questioning the MMS's cozy relationship with oil companies. After it came to light that there had been a number of questionable safety and environmental lapses prior to the blowout, the agency was castigated for lax oversight. The same

---

overhead democracy The idea that the bureaucracy is controlled through the oversight of elected officials, who are chosen by the people, thus giving the populace control over the bureaucracy.

police patrol oversight The active oversight of the bureaucracy by elected officials to make sure that the bureaucracy is acting according to the wishes of the people.

fire alarm oversight Oversight that becomes active only when there is evidence of bureaucratic wrongdoing.

complaint, though, might have been leveled at elected officials: This was a classic fire alarm scenario, with vigorous oversight of the MMS beginning after a catastrophe, not before. Obviously, the big problem with fire alarm oversight is that it is reactive rather than proactive. Relying on fire alarm oversight means Congress begins to tackle bureaucratic problems only after those problems have occurred.

Sometimes, the fire alarms Congress relies on to warn it of problems in the bureaucracy are kept silent. Failure to sound an alarm happens when the relationship between an interest group and a bureaucracy becomes a little too cozy. **Agency capture** describes a bureaucracy run for the benefit of those it is supposed to regulate; it occurs when the regulators appointed to an agency share the same professional and economic values as those they regulate. Some critics compare this to hiring foxes to guard the hen house. Even if regulators do not originally have ties to a regulated industry, over time they can come to identify with industry interests because interaction is so one-sided: Representatives of a regulated industry have frequent contacts with the agency and may develop cordial relationships with regulators there, whereas representatives of the broader public interest have only infrequent contacts with the agency. Agency capture upsets any notions of overhead democracy and raises questions about the bureaucracy's ability to uphold the core principles.

Although agency capture is recognized as a possibility by academics and fits well with popular beliefs on the influential role of special interests, systematic research has found relatively little hard evidence that it is a widespread problem. Though there certainly are examples of agencies coddling the regulated (think of the regulatory agencies literally designed around the interests of the finance industry and the MMS's close relationship with oil companies), it is actually much more common to find bureaucracies that are vigorously regulating the industries they are supposed to regulate (Meier 1995, 21). The real problem is not that interest groups capture agencies and run them for their own benefit but that interest groups sometimes have little incentive to raise an alarm that would trigger oversight. Why report or publicize negligent or inappropriate agency actions if you benefit from them? This is like making a bundle on insurance if the building burns down. What's the incentive to sound the alarm if you profit from the fire? AIG had little incentive to report OTS for lax oversight, just as BP had little incentive to complain that MMS was not rigorous enough in its permit process.

Even with its limitations, fire alarm oversight does demonstrate that there are forces providing incentives to monitor the bureaucracy and hold it accountable. Because it implements programs and policies, the bureaucracy is a natural focus for competing interests. Some argue that when they serve a range of clients and interest groups, bureaucracies help to responsibly represent and further those interests. As one scholar put it, "bureaucracies are not just passive actors who respond limply to external demand by politicians and groups. Rather, they integrate and transmit competing values from multiple overlapping constituencies" (Wood 1992).

This role is enhanced by laws that provide individual citizens with considerable monitoring powers and force bureaucratic decision making to be open and transparent. The Freedom of Information Act of 1967, for example, requires bureaucracies

agency capture A term used to describe when an agency seems to operate for the benefit of those whom it is supposed to regulate.

to respond to all reasonable public requests for documents. Other statutes called **sunshine laws** require that bureaucratic decisions be made in public meetings. These laws give individual citizens and interest groups the tools to keep tabs on what the bureaucracy does.

Influencing Bureaucracy

All branches of the federal government have at their disposal powerful tools to influence bureaucratic behavior. These tools range from the formal power to create and destroy public agencies to less formal techniques of persuasion that may be handled in an office visit or a telephone call. At least in terms of formal power, each branch of government has a different set of options for getting bureaucracies to follow their wishes.

The Congress and the Bureaucracy

Congress has the ultimate tool to control bureaucracy: legislation. Federal bureaucracies do not simply interpret the law; they are products of it. Congress has the constitutional authority to create or destroy federal agencies and to determine what programs and polices they administer.

Congress also controls bureaucracy through its power of the purse. Article I, Section 9 of the Constitution states that "no money shall be drawn from the treasury, but in consequence of appropriations made by law." This provision means that every federal agency's budget must be approved by Congress, and it is not unusual for Congress to use the appropriation process to place constraints or demands on the bureaucracy. The power of the purse is, in essence, a living embodiment of the golden rule: Who has the gold gets to make the rules.

A final way in which Congress controls the bureaucracy is through legislative vetoes. A **legislative veto** is a provision in a law that allows Congress to reject a proposed action by a public agency. Typically this process involves requiring an agency to inform Congress of proposed actions, and then Congress has the right to reject these proposals. Some legislative veto provisions require both houses of Congress to accept or reject rules, although some laws permit just one house, or even an individual committee, to accept or reject rules. The intent here is to give Congress some control over how laws are implemented.

Although the legislative veto is an effective check on the bureaucracy, it has its drawbacks. For one thing, it is not clear whether legislative vetoes are constitutional. The Constitution requires laws to be passed by a majority vote in both houses of Congress and presented to the president for signature or veto. It then becomes the president's responsibility to see "that the laws be faithfully executed." If Congress wants to modify a law, technically it must go through the full process of making a law. The Supreme Court ruled legislative vetoes unconstitutional because they cut the president out of the lawmaking process (*Immigration and Naturalization Service v. Chadha* 1983). Despite this ruling, Congress continues to use legislative vetoes.

sunshine laws Laws intended to keep the bureaucracy accountable to the people by requiring that agency meetings be open to the public.

legislative veto A measure that gives Congress the ability to reject an action or decision of the bureaucracy.

Another problem with the legislative veto is that it limits Congress's policy-making role. The legislative veto reduces Congress to a reactive body: It defines a broad goal through legislation and leaves the specifics to executive agencies. Though Congress can block the specifics it finds objectionable, in this process the legislature is reduced to telling the bureaucracy what it cannot do, rather than telling it what to do. The result is to delegate to the bureaucracy a powerful proactive role in determining public policy.

The President and the Bureaucracy

The president also has several powerful tools to control the bureaucracies. As chief executive, the president is technically the chief bureaucrat. The president is the overall boss of all executive agencies, and like most bosses, the president can exercise a good deal of influence over subordinates.

The most basic tool the president has for controlling bureaucracy is the **appointment power**, which allows the president to choose a wide range of subordinates. Although the elimination of the spoils system dramatically reduced the president's ability to preferentially staff the bureaucracy, the chief executive retains the power to appoint many of the nation's top bureaucrats. These include the secretaries of all cabinet departments, various deputies and undersecretaries, and a wide variety of top-ranking positions in non-cabinet agencies—roughly 3,000 officials in all.

The main advantage of appointment power is that it allows the president to put political allies and loyalists in key administrative positions. The power of appointment presumably puts the bureaucracy under closer control of the president. There are, however, two drawbacks to this system. One, these appointees often lack experience and tend to have short tenures. As many as a third of presidential appointees spend less than 18 months on the job. High turnover makes it hard for the president to provide consistent direction to a bureaucracy. Second, the appointees sometimes "go native," which means they end up becoming advocates of their agency's interests rather than the president's agenda.

Appointments can also generate a lot of controversy if a president is seen as using them as a means to a contested policy end or to openly serve a particular group's interest. For example, President Trump's 2017 appointment of Scott Pruitt to head the Environmental Protection Agency was opposed by many environmental groups. Pruitt, formerly Oklahoma's attorney general, was a longtime critic of the EPA, a skeptic of the evidence for climate change, and a leading opponent of environmental regulations. As head of the EPA he sought to scale back such regulation, cut his agency's budget, and reduce its number of employees. The moves were so extreme that Pruitt was accused of deliberately gutting the EPA in order to serve the interests of the fossil fuels industry (Dennis and Mufson 2017). In essence, this amounted to a charge that Pruitt and the Trump administration were pursuing agency capture as a policy goal—in other words they were running the EPA for the benefit of the fossil fuels industry. Regardless of the merits of that argument, there was little doubt that Pruitt's appointment had a profound impact on the EPA.

appointment power A power of the president that enables him or her to control the bureaucracy by selecting the people who will head its agencies.

The president does not have to rely solely on appointment power to control the bureaucracy. The president also has budgeting power, which, although different from the budgeting powers of Congress, can be just as effective. Only Congress has the power to approve a budget, but the president has the responsibility of proposing the budget. A president can thus reward or punish agencies by proposing increases or cuts in the annual budget proposal. Congress can change these proposals, but even then, the president can veto an appropriations bill to block agency funding (though such an action would be considered drastic). Even if the money is appropriated over a veto, the president has some limited powers of **impoundment**, or the ability to delay approved expenditures. A president who does not want to spend money appropriated by Congress can also seek to cancel the funding by sending a "rescission message" to Congress. If both houses approve the rescission, the funds are canceled. A president does not have complete control over agency budgets but has more than enough to make any agency wary of getting into a budgetary battle with the president.

The president also has the power to issue **executive orders**, directives that have the force of law even though they are not passed by Congress. These are the equivalent of presidential legislation and are often controversial. For example, early in his tenure President Trump signed an executive order banning the entry of immigrants from seven Muslim-majority nations for 90 days. The order was an attempt to keep campaign promises to promote strong borders and limit immigration, issues Congress had struggled to take action on. The order sparked protests and legal challenges because it was seen as deliberately seeking to unconstitutionally limit immigration on the basis of religious beliefs.

The Judiciary and the Bureaucracy

The courts have a few simple tools to control the bureaucracy. As the interpreters of law, judges can declare agency regulations, rules, or actions illegal if they fail to meet the constitutional litmus test. In assessing challenges to agency rules or actions, courts pose two broad questions. The first is whether the action is consistent with **legislative intent**. In other words, the court seeks to determine whether the agency's actions are authorized by the relevant law passed by Congress. The second question is whether the action violates **standards of due process**. Even if legislative intent is being followed, courts will seek to ensure that an agency is not depriving anyone of due process guarantees given by the Constitution or the law. For example, federal courts have probably done more than any other branch of the government in restricting local, state, and federal bureaucracies from discriminating in hiring, promotion, and provision of services (Meier 1993, 163–164). In checking for due process, the courts help ensure that bureaucracy abides by core democratic principles such as political equality.

It is important to note, though, that the interest of the courts is typically not whether a bureaucratic action is efficient, effective, or fair, or even whether it makes sense. Their concern is almost wholly with whether an action is legal.

---

impoundment The limited ability of the president to not spend money appropriated by Congress.

executive orders Directives of the president that have the same weight as law and are not voted on by Congress.

legislative intent The intention of Congress when it passes laws.

standards of due process The procedural guarantees provided to ensure fair treatment and constitutional rights.

REFORMING BUREAUCRACY

Because of their central role in the American political process, it is not surprising that bureaucracies are frequent targets of reform efforts. Pledges to change bureaucracy and make it run "more like a business" have been a perennial feature of American politics for more than a century.

Running Government Like a Business

Past efforts to reform the bureaucracy include the Hoover Commission, formed under the administration of Harry Truman and charged with identifying how to improve the efficiency and effectiveness of the bureaucracy. The Grace Commission was formed under the administration of Ronald Reagan and was charged with rooting out government inefficiency and wasteful programs. The National Performance Review was a program of President Bill Clinton's administration that was a sustained effort to "reinvent government." The notion behind reinventing government was to make government agencies more customer-oriented and more entrepreneurial (Osborne and Gaebler 1990). The administration of George W. Bush had no specific plan or program to make government more like a business, but he was the first MBA-holding businessman to become chief executive, and he staffed his administration with the elite of corporate America and ran a CEO-like White House. This was as likely a group as any to make government run more like a business. The Obama administration put forward no formal business-based bureaucratic reform program and was roundly criticized by various Republicans for not attempting to run government more like a business. A key element of President Trump's 2016 presidential campaign was his experience as a business executive, experience that he argued gave him the ability to make better deals on behalf of the American people than those who had little experience in the private sector.

The primary problem with this focus on trying to run government like a business is that government is not a business. All of the formal reform efforts mentioned in the previous paragraph ended up having very little

Contracting out is the process of hiring a private organization to provide a public service or program. Immigration and Customs Enforcement (ICE), for example, spends $2 billion a year to private companies who run immigration detention facilities to hold detainees like these.

© Ross D. Franklin/AP Photo

impact on how government is run. Business experience or credentials do not seem to make someone a better (or worse) elected executive than someone without those qualifications. Though there is a common belief that what works in the private sector will work just as well in the public sector, this belief is mostly wrong. Businesses are oriented toward efficiency and productivity, and their ultimate goal is to make money. Government agencies are oriented toward implementing the decisions of democratic governments. This basic mission is often an inherently inefficient proposition (remember all the agencies regulating the financial industry discussed earlier).

Businesses Running Government

Although efforts to make government run more like a business have, at best, had minimal success, there has been much more progress in having businesses run the government. In the past few decades, several Western democracies have sought ways to reduce the size and cost of the public sector while improving the efficiency and effectiveness of public programs. These efforts have resulted in the widespread practice of **contracting out**, or hiring a private organization rather than creating a government bureaucracy to deliver a public service.

The idea is to use the competitive leverage of the marketplace to make public policy more cost-effective. For example, the traditional approach to implementing a policy providing healthcare services to the poor meant creating a program and housing it in a bureaucracy. This approach also meant hiring people and providing facilities and other resources at the public expense. Contracting out involves paying a private healthcare company to provide the service and eliminates the trouble and expense of hiring more government employees or constructing new buildings.

Though contracting out sounds appealing in the abstract, in practice, it has raised a number of concerns. For example, contracting out creates an accountability problem. Political scientists who have studied traditional bureaucratic arrangements have mostly concluded that the bureaucratic tail does not wag the democratic dog (Wood and Waterman 1994). The relationship between Congress, the president, and the bureaucracy can be described by a **principal–agent model**. This model, derived from rational choice theory, is based on the idea of a relationship between a boss who wants some work done (the principal) and an employee who actually does the work (the agent). A number of studies have concluded that this model is pretty much how traditional bureaucracy works. In short, bureaucracy is responsive, not just to Congress and the president, but also to the courts, to media attention, and even to broader currents of public opinion (Wood and Waterman 1994).

Yet whereas traditional bureaucratic arrangements are responsive to democratic controls, it is not clear that the same is true for companies under government contract. Given a program or responsibility by an executive or a legislature, a public agency has three basic responses: work (make every effort to accomplish the policy), shirk (devote its efforts to something else), or sabotage (work to undermine the policy). In trying to ensure that agencies work rather than shirk

contracting out Hiring a private organization to deliver a public program or service.

principal–agent model A model explaining the relationship between Congress and the bureaucracy, which states that the relationship is similar to that between an employer who seeks to have work done (the principal) and an employee who does the work (the agent).

or sabotage, their principals (Congress and the president) are faced with an information problem. They often do not know the true abilities of a particular set of bureaucrats, and once they give them a job, it is difficult to assess how much effort the bureaucrats expend trying to do that job. These are known as the principal's problems of **adverse selection** (not knowing the abilities of an agent) and **moral hazard** (not knowing the effort of an agent). Adverse selection and moral hazard can make it difficult for a principal to judge whether an agency is working, shirking, or sabotaging a particular policy (Brehm and Gates 1997).

These problems multiply when a principal has multiple agents or an agent from whom it is hard to get information. Both of these scenarios are common in contracting out. Because contracts to deliver a public service are often given to more than one vendor, there is more opportunity for shirking. The result is not a single bureaucracy—required by law to keep records and maintain an open decision-making process—but a network of private organizations, all doing things slightly differently. Some have called this a "shadow bureaucracy," a layer of private companies that depend on government contracts. At the federal level, this shadow bureaucracy has roughly four times the number of workers than the entire public bureaucracy (Light 1999).

It is virtually impossible for government to control this shadow bureaucracy as tightly as it controls the public bureaucracy, and it is much harder to hold it accountable for its actions. Unlike public bureaucracies, for example, private companies often have private decision-making processes and are not required to keep the same sorts of paper trails as public bureaucracies. The logistics needed to keep up with all the contracting out is daunting. In 2016 the federal government's top 100 contractors entered into around 9.4 million contract actions worth roughly $262 billion (Federal Procurement Data System 2016). Keep in mind that these numbers are just for the 100 contractors that do the most business with the federal government. There are thousands of contractors engaging in millions more contract actions that add many billions of dollars to the top 100 figure. Keeping up with numbers like these in any sort of systematic way would require, well, a bureaucracy.

In addition to the accountability concerns, private sector organizations may not be any more effective or efficient than public bureaucracies. They also may increase rather than decrease the politics surrounding public programs. Big companies, for example, often seek to exert political pressure to reduce competitive bidding, which makes it harder to extract any cost savings. Using private companies also means dealing with profit motive incentives that may conflict with the public interest. Everyone has heard stories of the government paying inflated prices for all kinds of things, from screws to coffee makers. What usually gets left out of these stories is that it was a private company gouging the government by inflating prices and seeking to hide them, and a public bureaucracy exposed the fraud.

adverse selection A principal's lack of information about the abilities of an agent.

moral hazard A principal's lack of information about the effort of an agent.

CHAPTER FOURTEEN
Top 10 Takeaway Points

1. Bureaucracy can be thought of as public agencies and the public programs and services they run. Democracies need bureaucracy to translate the expressed intent of government into action.

2. Scholars of administration and organization use the term *bureaucracy* to describe a specific type of organization whose main characteristics are division of labor, hierarchy, formal rules, maintenance of files and records, and professionalization. Most large and complex organizations have these characteristics, not just public agencies.

3. Federal bureaucracies are organized in a loose hierarchy, but there is no centralized and coordinated control over all public agencies and programs. The responsibilities of federal agencies often overlap, and the agencies often have to report to multiple congressional committees. The structure of the federal bureaucracy is driven more by politics than by the need for organizational efficiency.

4. Bureaucracy wields considerable policymaking powers because it has to interpret laws and make choices about how to translate them into action. Among the most important of these is the power to make rules.

5. Rules are statements by a federal agency that interpret a law and prescribe the actions the agency will take to implement that law. Once finalized, rules have the power of law.

6. Rational choice models of bureaucracy suggest that control and accountability are critical issues for democratic political systems. Without effective accountability and control mechanisms, rational bureaucrats will serve their own interests at the expense of the public interest. Other theories of bureaucratic behavior suggest that rather than coldly calculating personal maximizing opportunities, bureaucrats search for "good enough" solutions for the problems they face. They rely on experience, habit, and values to make these decisions.

7. The size, responsibilities, and power of the federal bureaucracy also create a number of concerns about how to make it accountable to democratic authority. The preferred method of monitoring accountability is overhead democracy, the notion that voters will hold elected officials accountable for their actions and that public officials in turn will hold bureaucracies accountable for their actions.

8 Congress, the president, and the courts have a number of powerful tools to control bureaucracy and make it accountable. These include appointment of agency heads, legislative oversight, control of budgets, and judicial review.

9 Reform of the bureaucracy is a perennial part of the public agenda. Reform is difficult because many of the assumptions underlying these reform efforts are questionable. Government is not a business, and trying to run public programs like a business creates practical and political obstacles.

10 Bureaucracies are not run by democratic principles, but they play an important role in enforcing these principles for the political system. This is especially the case with political equality.

CHAPTER FOURTEEN
Key Terms and Cases

adjudication, 539
adverse selection, 553
advisory committees, 535
agency capture, 547
appointment power, 549
bounded rationality, 543
bureaucracy, 524
cabinet departments, 533
contracting out, 552
deregulation, 535
Executive Office of the President (EOP), 533
executive orders, 550
fire alarm oversight, 546
government corporations, 535
impoundment, 550
independent agencies, 534
iron triangles, 540
legislative intent, 550
legislative veto, 548
merit system, 527
moral hazard, 553
neutral competence, 529
overhead democracy, 546
police patrol oversight, 546
policy subsystems, 541
principal–agent model, 552
regulatory agencies and commissions, 534
rule, 538
rulemaking, 538
satisficing, 543
spoils system, 527
standards of due process, 550
sunshine laws, 548

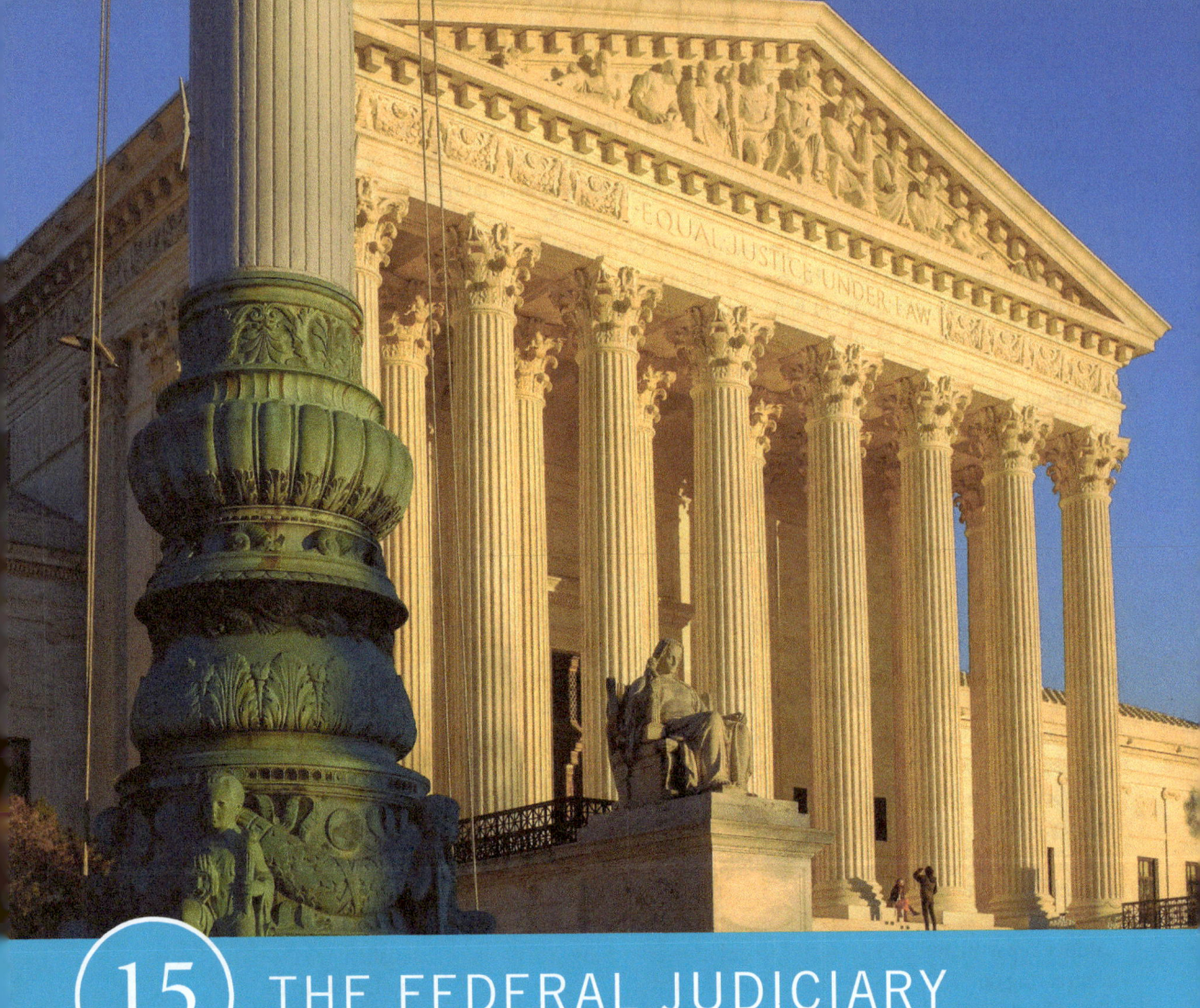

15 THE FEDERAL JUDICIARY

KEY QUESTIONS

Is judicial decision making unavoidably political decision making?

What is judicial review?

What are the democratic constraints on unelected judges' exercise of judicial power?

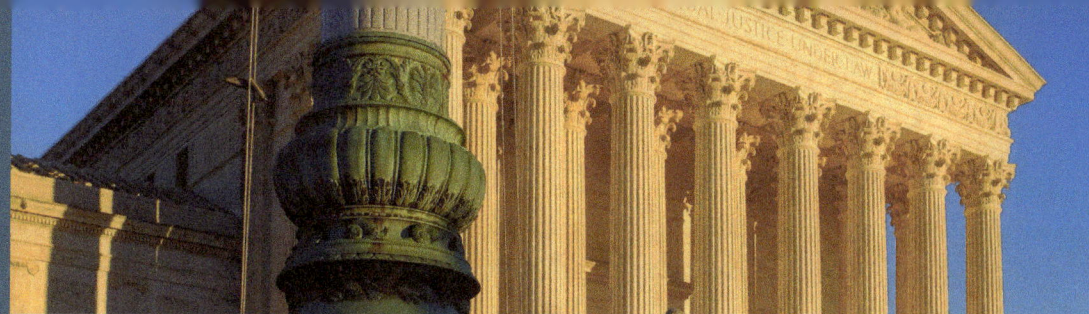

© Orhan Cam/Shutterstock

NEIL KATYAL was something of an unusual champion for Neil Gorsuch's nomination to the Supreme Court. Katyal is a left-leaning lawyer, he clerked for liberal Supreme Court Justice Stephen Breyer, and served as acting solicitor general for President Barack Obama. Gorsuch was nominated by President Donald Trump and is a favorite of the Federalist Society, a conservative group seeking to reform the judiciary. Yet Katyal was a prominent supporter of Gorsuch's elevation to the Supreme Court. He wrote op-eds backing Gorsuch and introduced him during his confirmation hearing in the United States Senate. Whatever their political differences, these guys clearly like and respect each other, and describe each other as friends.

So what do you do when a friend, one who played a prominent role in getting you appointed to the highest judicial post in the nation, appears to argue a case in your court? Gorsuch faced that question when hearing just his second case as a Supreme Court justice. As an appeals court judge, Gorsuch had often recused himself from cases being argued by lawyers who were friends or former colleagues. Not this time. Gorsuch, who asked an unusual number of questions for a rookie justice, asked Katyal nothing. He then voted (along with the rest of the court) in favor of Katyal's client (Mauro 2017).

While Gorsuch's decision not to recuse himself raised a few eyebrows, there is nothing necessarily wrong or improper here. The apex of the judicial system is a pretty small club, and lawyers who know or worked with justices will often appear before the Supreme Court. The problem is that most people think—or at least, would like to think—that judges are wise and neutral, applying the law impartially without prejudice or bias. Yet can you be fully objective if it is a friend making an argument before the bench? Especially if it was a friend who had stuck his neck out and angered his political tribe to advance your career? Might the friendship sway your decision, at least a little?

It is hard to ignore your beliefs and values when answering such questions. This is not simply a matter of bias or prejudice, but part and parcel of being a human being. The point here is not that Gorsuch is biased or unfit to be a Supreme Court justice—he is, virtually everyone agrees, a highly qualified jurist. Rather, the point is that Gorsuch, like all other judges, is human. Humans have likes and dislikes, with strong points of view on certain issues. Can we honestly expect judges to put this aside, to ignore their own feelings and beliefs simply because they wear a black robe to work?

Most Americans would like the answer to be yes. Judges are expected to make decisions based on the rule of law, not on partisan fealty, ideological prejudice, personal loyalty, or fear of political retribution. This is why judicial independence is a prized value in the American political system. Federal judges are appointed for life, and that job security is designed to allow judges to uphold the law, even when it means going against personal or popular expectations.

Yet Americans also want judges to be accountable for unpopular decisions. At some level, we recognize that judges are subject to the same range of opinions and biases that we all are, but we do not want judges caving in to political or personal pressure. We want them to stand firm for the core democratic principles embedded in law, even when it is the unpopular thing to do. On the other hand, we do not want them using their independence to play favorites from the bench. How do we reconcile independence with accountability?

This question is critical because the judiciary is a political branch of government. The job of a judge, after all, is to judge—in other words, to decide who gets what. Judges' decisions have affected how legislative districts can be drawn, where a child can attend school, and whether a woman has a right to an abortion. These are fundamentally political issues with plenty of room for disagreement about what is or is not constitutional or about what does or does not violate the core values of democracy.

Given the central role of courts as interpreters of the law, and recognizing that judges are political decision makers who are far from infallible, understanding the role of the judicial branch in the American political system is essential to assessing how well that system is delivering on the promise of democracy. When they interpret the Constitution, the courts are effectively deciding how to uphold that promise. This chapter provides a basic introduction to the federal judiciary. It covers the nature of judicial power in the political system, the organization and structure of federal courts, who staffs the federal bench, how judges are selected, the power judges hold, and how all this fits into and affects the promise of democracy.

THE CONCEPT OF THE FEDERAL JUDICIARY

The purpose of the federal judiciary in the United States is to serve as the ultimate umpire in the democratic political process. The term *judicial* is related to the concept of *just*, meaning "legal right" or fair (Ayto 1990, 309, 310).[1] Hence, a **judiciary** is a system of courts and judges concerned with administration of justice. The administration of justice involves resolving legal disputes, and to achieve justice, judges' decisions are supposed to be fair and impartial.

As we learned in Chapter 1, politics is a process to resolve conflict about who gets what, when, and how. A democratic government makes decisions consistent with the core democratic principles of political freedom, political equality, and majority rule. But how does a democracy resolve conflicts between core values? In the United States, it is the job of the judiciary to help resolve these conflicts, and the job is not easy. Judges are expected to simultaneously uphold the legitimate will of the majority as expressed in law and uphold political freedom and equality by protecting the liberties of minorities from infringement by tyrannical majorities.

How can judges make impartial decisions when the disputes they must resolve are fundamentally political? The short answer is that judicial power is political power. The Framers of the Constitution included provisions designed to insulate judges from political influences. Judges often claim that their decisions are not political and that they don't make the law; they merely *find* the law. Chief Justice John Marshall explained in 1824,

> Courts are the mere instruments of the law ... When they are said to exercise a discretion, it is ... exercised in discerning the course prescribed by law; and, when that is discerned, it is the duty of the court to follow it. Judicial power is never exercised for the purpose of giving effect to the will of the judge, always for the purpose of giving effect ... to the will of the law. (*Osborn v. Bank of the United States* 1824)

Political scientists refer to this claim as the "myth of judicial objectivity." It is a useful myth; it helps maintain the legitimacy of the courts and protects judicial independence. But it is a myth nonetheless. As we shall see, politics influences every aspect of the judicial process.

THE JURISDICTION OF FEDERAL COURTS

The term **judicial power** refers to the authority of courts to interpret and apply the law in particular cases. Judicial power is fundamentally political power. The

judiciary A system of courts and judges concerned with administration of justice.

judicial power The authority of courts to interpret and apply the law in particular cases.

---

1 *OED Online*, n.d. "judicial," adj. and n., http://www.oed.com/ (accessed October 25, 2012).

limits and conditions under which courts exercise this power—that is, the types of cases and controversies they can hear—constitute **jurisdiction**. The jurisdiction of federal courts is defined by the Constitution, by laws passed by Congress, and by the courts themselves.

Jurisdiction Defined in the Constitution

Article III, Section 2 of the Constitution sets the general jurisdiction of the federal courts:

> The judicial power shall extend to all cases, in law and equity, arising under this Constitution, the laws of the United States, and treaties ...; to controversies to which the United States shall be a party; to controversies between ... states; between a state and citizens of another state; between citizens of different states.

Two words used there, *cases* and *controversies,* mean that litigation heard by the federal courts must involve an actual dispute in which real people suffer real harm. In other words, courts do not decide hypothetical cases about the constitutionality of a statute. Federal judges cannot render advisory opinions about how or whether a particular law should be enforced. The judiciary is a powerful but passive political actor, exercising its powers only when someone who has actually been harmed by a law or a government act brings a constitutional issue before it by means of a lawsuit.

A case brought by a legitimate plaintiff can be heard by a federal court if it satisfies one of two general requirements. The first concerns the subject matter of the suit: It must be litigation involving the U.S. Constitution, a federal law, a treaty, or admiralty and maritime matters. Federal courts have jurisdiction to hear cases brought by private citizens challenging the constitutionality of state or federal laws. Criminal defendants who claim that they were denied individual rights protected by the Constitution can also have their cases heard in federal court.

The second requirement concerns the parties involved in the suit: The Constitution gives certain parties special status to file claims in federal courts. If the United States is suing or being sued, the federal courts can hear the case. The federal courts have jurisdiction over cases affecting ambassadors and other agents of foreign governments and over disputes between foreign governments or foreign citizens and a state or one of its citizens. Interstate conflicts also fall within the federal court's jurisdiction. These conflicts include litigation between the states, between citizens of different states, between citizens of the same state who claim lands under grants of different states, and between a state and a citizen of another state.

Of these cases, suits between citizens of different states are quite numerous and consume a great deal of time. To keep minor disputes out of federal courts, Congress has passed statutes requiring that cases involve at least $75,000 before federal courts have jurisdiction.

jurisdiction The types of cases a given court is permitted to hear.

Original and Appellate Jurisdiction

There are two general types of courts, each of which has jurisdiction over fundamentally different types of cases. **Courts of original jurisdiction** are the trial courts that hear cases the first time and make determinations of fact, law, and whether the plaintiff or the defendant wins. The federal district courts are courts of original jurisdiction in the federal court system; these district courts try cases involving alleged violations of federal criminal laws and certain civil lawsuits under federal court jurisdiction. **Courts of appellate jurisdiction** review the decisions of lower courts that are appealed. The U.S. circuit courts of appeal have jurisdiction to hear appeals of decisions made by federal district courts and certain government agencies.

Courts typically have either original or appellate jurisdiction. The U.S. Supreme Court is unique in that it has both. The Constitution gives the Supreme Court original jurisdiction in cases involving ambassadors, consuls, and other public ministers, and in cases in which a state is a party. Congress defines the Supreme Court's appellate jurisdiction.

The Power of Congress to Define Jurisdiction of Federal Courts

With few exceptions, Congress sets the jurisdictional boundaries of all federal courts. Congress can take the following actions:

- Forbid courts to handle a certain type of case.
- Allow state and federal courts to exercise concurrent jurisdiction (that is, allow both state and federal courts to hear a particular type of case).
- Assign exclusive jurisdiction; for example, cases involving violation of federal criminal law may be heard only in a federal court.

In addition to its power to allocate cases between federal and state courts, Congress also decides at which level in the federal judiciary a matter will be heard. Congress can establish lower courts, determine what cases they can hear, and regulate what matters initially tried in lower courts the Supreme Court can review.

Jurisdiction Determined by Judicial Interpretation

The courts themselves also can define their own power and jurisdiction. The most important power of federal courts in the American political system is the power of **judicial review**, or the authority to review lower-court decisions and to declare laws and actions of public officials unconstitutional. The Supreme Court asserted this power in the case of *Marbury v. Madison* (1803), discussed later in this chapter. Although the power of judicial review gives courts considerable influence in shaping public policy, where and how that power is exercised is constrained by both the Constitution and Congress.

courts of original jurisdiction Trial courts that hear cases for the first time and determine issues of fact and law.

courts of appellate jurisdiction Courts that review the decisions of lower courts.

judicial review The power to review decisions of the lower courts and to determine the constitutionality of laws and actions of public officials.

Marbury v. Madison The 1803 case in which the Court asserted the power of judicial review.

THE STRUCTURE AND ORGANIZATION OF FEDERAL COURTS

The Constitution leaves much of the structure and organization of federal courts to Congress. It calls for "one Supreme Court, and ... such inferior courts as the Congress may ... establish" (Article III, Section 1). Congress has created two additional levels of federal courts: district courts and courts of appeals. Congress has also established several specialized courts, such as the Court of Federal Claims and the U.S. Court of International Trade.

Congress determines by statute the number of judges serving on each court, including the Supreme Court. The Supreme Court has had nine justices since 1869, but the number has varied from as few as five in 1789 to as many as 10 in 1863. The number of lower-court judges is determined mainly by caseloads, so that areas with more cases filed have more judges.

The **Judicial Conference**, a committee of district and appellate court judges chaired by the chief justice of the Supreme Court, reviews the needs of the federal judiciary and makes recommendations to Congress to increase the number of judges to handle a growing caseload. Congress periodically responds to these requests and passes legislation creating new judgeships, but the last time Congress passed a comprehensive judgeship bill was 1990.

Although the need for more judges to handle an increasing caseload is the primary motivation for expanding the number of judgeships, political considerations inevitably come into play. One study shows that even if the need for new judges has been established, Congress is unlikely to create new judgeships if different parties control Congress and the presidency or if it is late in the president's term (Bond 1980). The motivations are purely political. Under divided government, the majority party in Congress is reluctant to give a president of the opposing party the chance to appoint fellow party members to new judgeships. In addition, if a presidential election is coming up, the opposing party in Congress delays creating new judgeships hoping that its candidate will win. The Judicial Conference recommended creating 57 new judgeships in 2017. Conditions for passage seem favorable—just after a presidential election with Republicans in control of Congress and the presidency—but there is no guarantee.

The District Courts

The U.S. district courts are trial courts of original jurisdiction. Although they hear certain classes of cases that are removed from state courts to federal jurisdiction and also enforce some of the actions of federal administrative agencies, these cases are not considered to have been appealed (Abraham 1993, 157–158).

The district courts are the workhorses of the federal judicial system. Approximately 90 percent of federal cases begin and end in the district courts. In these courts, spirited legal battles occur involving opposing attorneys, witnesses, and

---

Judicial Conference A committee of district and appellate judges chaired by the chief justice of the Supreme Court that reviews the needs of the federal judiciary and makes recommendations to Congress.

possibly a jury. (Parties in federal court often waive the right to a jury trial and have the judge make the decision.) A single judge presides over the courtroom.

District courts deal with a wide variety of matters. This is where the federal government brings antitrust suits and prosecutes people accused of breaking federal criminal laws. For example, Zacarias Moussaoui, suspected of being the "twentieth hijacker" in the September 11, 2001, terrorist attacks, was tried in a federal district court. Bankruptcy proceedings make up a large portion of district court dockets, and the courts also hear disputes between citizens of different states involving automobile accidents, breaches of contract, and labor cases.

This dizzying array of cases is heard by nearly 700 judges located in 94 district courts. Every state has at least one district, and 24 states have two, three, or four districts. No district crosses state lines. Each district court has at least one judge; the Southern District of New York has the most judges—28. The number of judges in a district is determined largely by caseload: Districts with heavy caseloads need more judges to process cases in a reasonable time.

Although district judges are officials of the federal government and enforce federal laws and the U.S. Constitution, they are oriented to states and localities (see Figure 15.1). Congress sets the number and boundaries of judicial districts, and the decision to draw districts that do not cross state lines has political implications. By political tradition, district court judges are selected from the states in which they serve, and they live there after appointment. Thus, federal district judges

District courts like this one from Albuquerque, New Mexico, deal with antitrust suits, people accused of breaking federal criminal laws, bankruptcy proceedings, and disputes between citizens of different states involving automobile accidents, breaches of contract, and labor cases—among many other matters. District judges are officials of the federal government and enforce federal laws and the U.S. Constitution, but they are oriented to states and localities.

© AP Photo/Richmond Times-Dispatch, Bob Brown

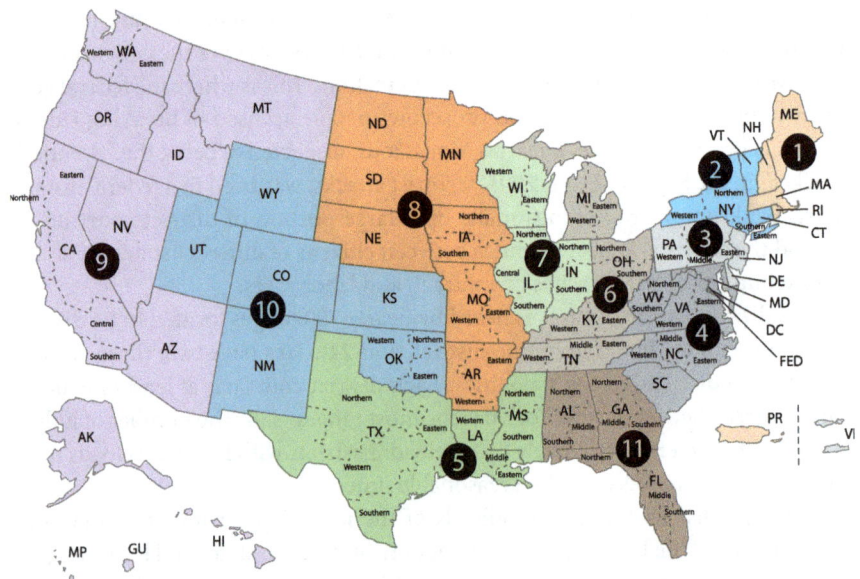

FIGURE 15.1 Federal District Courts and Courts of Appeals

Source: http://www.uscourts.gov/uscourts/images/CircuitMap.pdf.

have strong political and social ties to the states in which they serve (Richardson and Vines 1970, 93–98). District court judges occasionally hear cases in other districts to limit the influence of local political culture on the judge's decision. A classic example occurred in 1957 when a visiting North Dakota district court judge issued the injunction prohibiting Arkansas state officials from interfering with racial integration of Little Rock schools.

The Courts of Appeals

The U.S. courts of appeals have only appellate jurisdiction, and they serve as the major appellate tribunals in the federal court system. They review decisions in civil and criminal cases initially heard in federal district courts and the decisions of the independent regulatory agencies. Of the approximately 10 percent of cases decided by the district courts that are appealed, about 90 percent end in the federal courts of appeals. Thus, only a tiny proportion—about 1 percent—of federal cases go to the U.S. Supreme Court for final disposition.

There are nearly 200 appellate court judges serving on 13 courts of appeals, called circuits, located in various parts of the United States.[2] The size of the courts ranges from six to 28 judges depending on the caseload in the circuit. As shown

---

2 The courts of appeals were originally staffed by Supreme Court justices who would travel to various regions of the country to hear cases. This practice was called "making the circuit," and it is where the name came from.

in Figure 15.1, 11 of the appellate courts are arranged regionally, grouping three or more states into a circuit. A court of appeals hears appeals from the district courts located within its circuit. The Twelfth Circuit is the U.S. Court of Appeals for the District of Columbia, which covers the nation's capital. It is one of the most important courts of appeal because it deals with challenges to the rules and regulations issued by most federal government agencies. The Thirteenth Circuit is the Federal Circuit, which is also located in Washington, DC. Unlike all other circuits, however, its jurisdiction is not based on geography. This court has national jurisdiction to hear appeals from specialized federal courts (such as patent cases). Since appellate courts hear appeals from federal courts in several states, appellate court judges tend to be less closely tied to particular states and localities than their counterparts in district courts.

The courts of appeals are **collegial courts** in which a group of judges decides the case based on a review of the record of the lower-court trial. There is no jury at the appellate court level, and the appeals court does not make determinations of fact. Instead, the appellate court decides by majority vote whether the trial court made any legal or procedural errors that would justify a reversal or modification of the lower court's decision.

To expedite the considerable caseload, cases are usually decided by a panel of three judges, allowing several cases to be heard at the same time by different three-judge panels. The chief judge, who is the most senior judge under the age of 65, appoints the panels. Appointments are made randomly to even out workloads and to ensure that the same judges do not always sit together on the same panel. These procedures are intended to prevent a chief judge from stacking a panel with judges who will decide a case in a particular way. The U.S. Court of Appeals for the Eleventh Circuit uses a computerized random assignment process to set the composition of every panel a year in advance (Tarr 2003, 42).

On application of the parties involved in a suit or of the judges themselves, a case can be heard **en banc**—that is, by all of the judges in the circuit. This occurs in fewer than 5 percent of cases; it is restricted to questions of exceptional importance or cases in which the circuit court feels that a full tribunal is necessary to secure uniformity in its decisions or compliance with a controversial decision.

The U.S. Supreme Court

The U.S. Supreme Court sits at the top of the legal hierarchy, and it has both original and appellate jurisdiction (see Figure 15.2). In practice, it has almost complete discretion over the cases it hears, accepting mainly those that have broad implications for the law or government action. Congress determines the Supreme Court's appellate jurisdiction by law. There are two major sources of cases: (1) appeals from the U.S. courts of appeals and (2) appeals from the states' highest courts. Cases from the U.S. courts of appeals represent the final attempt to gain satisfaction by parties unhappy with decisions made in lower federal courts. Cases from state courts involve controversies that jump from state court systems to the federal court system.

collegial courts Courts in which groups of judges decide cases based on a review of the record of the lower-court trial.

en banc A procedure in which all the members of a U.S. court of appeals hear and decide a case.

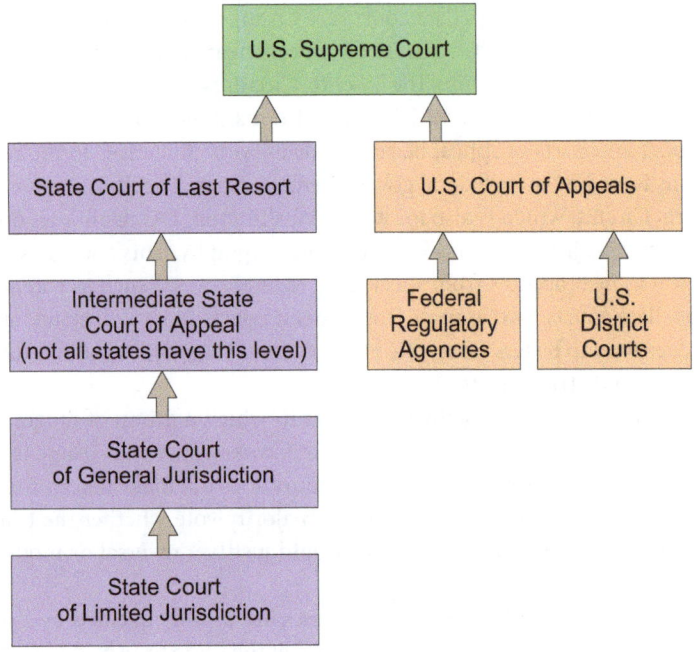

FIGURE 15.2 Structure of the U.S. Judicial System

Source: Adapted by the authors from "Comparing Federal & State Courts", http://www.uscourts.gov/about-federal-courts/court-role-and-structure/comparing-federal-state-courts

The Supreme Court is the only federal court that can hear appeals from a state court and then only if there is an important constitutional issue involved. Because of its federal structure (see Chapter 3), the United States has dual judicial systems: The federal courts deal with federal law, and the state courts with state law. Federal and state courts hold concurrent jurisdiction over some matters, so there is some overlap between the two systems, but state courts are not subordinate to federal courts. State courts enforce state laws using their own legal structure, procedures, and personnel, and they independently exercise the power of judicial review in both original and appellate jurisdictions. If a case involves state matters, it starts in state court and stays in the state court system until it is finally resolved. Each state judicial system has a court of last resort (a state supreme court or its equivalent) that represents the highest level to which a case involving a question of state law may be carried.

The only way a state court case can go beyond the state's court of last resort is if the case raises a federal question. Appeals of such cases go from the state court of last resort directly to the U.S. Supreme Court. For example, a criminal case that raises the issue of whether a state law restricting obscene materials violates an individual's First Amendment right of free speech raises an important federal question. Such a case could be appealed to the Supreme Court to rule on the constitutionality of the state law.

The justification for permitting appeals from the state supreme courts to the U.S. Supreme Court is that when state courts interpret their own constitutions, they are also interpreting the U.S. Constitution. A state constitution can provide its citizens greater protection of the basic rights guaranteed by the U.S. Constitution, but it cannot restrict those rights. Making the U.S. Supreme Court the final arbiter of all questions involving the U.S. Constitution helps ensure that its guarantees are uniformly interpreted and applied. In essence, this link makes the U.S. Supreme Court the ultimate umpire of the federal system.

The Supreme Court exercises discretion over its caseload by choosing relatively few cases for review each year. Of the approximately 7,000 cases appealed to the Supreme Court in a typical year, the Court will decide about 100–150 on the merits, meaning the Court will actually discuss the cases and vote on decisions. Only about 70–80 cases will get a full written opinion. Thus, more than 99 percent of cases are disposed of with no written explanation of the Court's reasoning in reaching that decision.[3] Generally, the Court picks cases that raise important constitutional issues or questions of substantial political importance, or on which different appellate circuits have issued conflicting rulings. The Court formally exercises its discretionary powers over what cases to hear by issuing a **writ of certiorari**,[4] which is granted according to the **rule of four**—that is, four of the nine justices must vote to review a case.

Like the courts of appeals, the Supreme Court is a collegial body, but it does not divide itself into separate panels to hear different cases. Justices have taken the position that the Constitution refers to one Supreme Court, not several, and that all judges should therefore participate in each case. The Court hears cases during a 36-week session from October to June. When the Court is in session, it hears oral arguments from attorneys representing opposing sides of the cases chosen for full hearings. Each side gets 30 minutes to make its case. This time limit is strictly enforced, but the justices frequently interrupt the presentations with questions. The Court occasionally allots more time for unusually complex and important cases. For example, the Court scheduled a total of six hours of oral arguments spread over three days on the case challenging the constitutionality of the healthcare reform law (*National Federation of Independent Business v. Sebelius* 2012).

Hearing oral presentations is a relatively small part of the Supreme Court's business; the overwhelming proportion of the Court's work takes place behind the scenes. The justices spend most of their time reading and studying cases and discussing them with their colleagues and their law clerks, who are recent graduates of the nation's top law schools.

The Court decides the cases it has heard in **conference**. Only the justices attend the conference; clerks and secretaries are not allowed in the room. The justices begin by shaking hands and taking their assigned seats around the conference table. The chief justice presides and sets the agenda. Part of the conference is

---

3 When the Court does not accept a case for review, the decision of the last court to rule stands.
4 A small number of cases get to the Supreme Court through other procedures, including through writ of appeal or by "extraordinary writ," such as habeas corpus. Although some of these cases can be appealed to the Supreme Court as a matter of right, in practice the Court has discretion about whether to hear these cases as well.

writ of certiorari An order from a higher court to a lower court ordering the lower court to turn over transcripts and documents of a case for review. The U.S. Supreme Court formally exercises its discretionary powers over what cases to hear by issuing a writ of certiorari, which is granted according to the rule of four.

rule of four Rule according to which four Supreme Court justices must agree to hear a case.

conference The meeting of Supreme Court justices where they decide which cases they will hear, and discuss and vote on the cases previously argued.

devoted to consideration of petitions for review; under the rule of four, four justices must vote to accept a case for full oral argument.

The next order of business is to discuss and vote on the cases previously argued before the Court. Traditionally, the chief justice speaks first, framing the issues presented by the case. The associate justice with the longest service on the court speaks next, and so on, with the most junior justice speaking last. The justices generally indicate how they will vote during their presentations in conference, although these votes are tentative and sometimes change during the opinion-writing stage.

After the most junior justice has spoken, the justices vote. The outcome of a case is decided by a majority vote, meaning that five of nine justices must support a position for it to become an official Court ruling. The most important decision following this vote is who gets to write the opinion announcing the Court's decision and the reasons behind it. If the chief justice votes with the majority, he or she decides who will write the opinion. If the case is a major one, the chief justice may assume the responsibility, as Chief Justice Roberts did in *National Federation of Independent Business v. Sebelius* (2012), upholding the constitutionality of most of the healthcare reform law. But opinions are usually assigned to spread the workload among the nine justices. If the chief justice is not on the prevailing side, the senior associate justice on the prevailing side makes the assignment.

The assignment of writing an opinion is often a delicate political decision. A controversial opinion may be assigned to the justice whose views are closest to those of the minority, the idea being that he or she may be able to win more justices over to the majority's side. This tactic can be helpful in a controversial case when a premium is placed on a unanimous or nearly unanimous Court to promote greater public acceptance.

The assignment of an opinion does not end the collegial process. Negotiation may continue as the opinion is drafted and redrafted so that a maximum number of justices will join it. The author may even adopt the suggestions and reasoning of other justices in order to attract their votes. But it is often not possible to settle differences. A unanimous decision expressed in a single opinion is often not possible, because cases heard by the Supreme Court are controversial, and the justices typically hold strong views.

The ability to forge a consensus on the Court has declined significantly since the early twentieth century. Until the 1930s, more than 80 percent of Supreme Court decisions were unanimous. Consensus on the Court declined sharply from the 1930s to the 1950s, leveling off at an average of about one-in-three unanimous decisions until the 1990s. In recent decades, the average rebounded slightly to about 45 percent, but remains considerably below levels in the early part of the twentieth century (see Figure 15.3). Moreover, rising party polarization since the 1990s that has had far-reaching effects on the presidency and Congress (see Chapter 13) extends to the Supreme Court as well. Evidence of a deepening division on the Court is the growing number of cases decided by one vote (5–4 or 4–3). Until the 1930s, cases decided by one vote were rare (about 2 percent). The frequency of closely divided opinions jumped to about 15 percent until the 1990s. The average

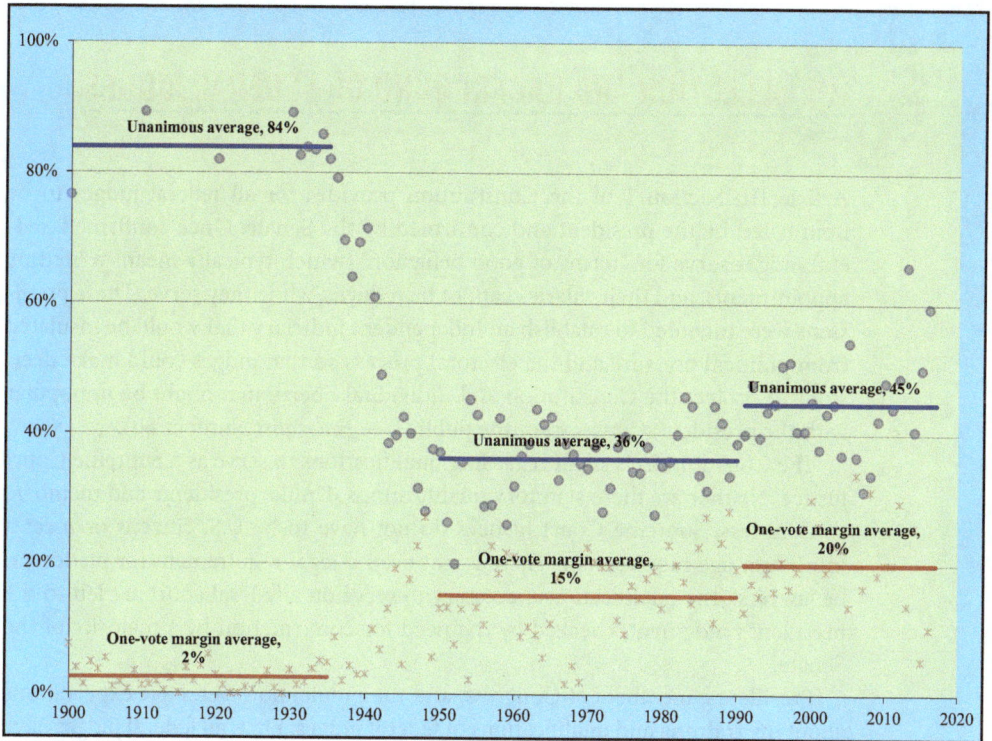

FIGURE 15.3 Unanimous and Closely Divided Supreme Court Decisions, 1900–2017

Source: Data from Epstein et al. (2012); data for 2010–2017 from http://www.scotusblog.com/statistics/.

climbed to 20 percent in recent decades, 10 times higher than levels in the early twentieth century.

There are four types of opinions. Most decisions are **majority opinions** in which five or more justices agree on both which side wins and the reason for the decision. **Concurring opinions** are sometimes written by justices who agree with the result reached by the majority opinion but not with the reasoning behind it. If a majority of justices cannot agree on both the outcome and the reasons, the case may be decided by a **plurality opinion** in which a majority support the outcome, but the lack of majority agreement on the reason may leave the meaning of the ruling unclear. **Dissenting opinions** are issued by justices in the minority; they disagree not only with the reasoning behind the Court's decision but also with the result. Dissenters do not always write dissenting opinions, but cases with dissenting opinions are much more common in recent decades—around 60 percent of cases, compared to around 8 percent in the early twentieth century (Epstein et al. 2012, table 3.2). The growing tendency to publicly express dissents is further evidence of growing polarization on the Court.

majority opinion A decision of the Supreme Court in which five or more of the justices are in agreement on the ruling on which party to the dispute should win a case and the reason that party should win.

concurring opinion An opinion written by a Supreme Court justice who agrees with the ruling of the Court but not the reason behind it.

plurality opinion A decision of the Supreme Court in which a majority of the Court agrees on a decision, but there is no majority agreement on the reason for the decision.

dissenting opinion An opinion written by a Supreme Court justice who is in the minority that presents reasons why the justices opposed the majority opinion.

THE SELECTION AND BACKGROUND OF FEDERAL JUDGES

Article III, Section 1 of the Constitution provides for all federal judges to be nominated by the president and confirmed by the Senate. Once confirmed, federal judges serve for "terms of good behavior" (which typically means a lifetime appointment), and their salaries cannot be reduced while they serve. These provisions were intended to establish an independent judiciary that would be insulated from political pressure and the electoral process so that judges could make decisions to protect the Constitution and individual liberty that might be unpopular with the president, Congress, or the public (see *Federalist* Number 80).

The Constitution is silent regarding qualifications to serve as a Supreme Court justice. Neither are there statutory qualifications. Unlike presidents and members of Congress, Supreme Court justices do not have to be U.S. citizens or meet a minimum age requirement. There is not even a legal requirement for justices to be lawyers. The qualifications necessary to serve on a federal court are left to the president's judgment, checked by the need for confirmation by a majority of the Senate.

Presidents, members of Congress, and the public, however, have expectations about the training and qualifications of federal judges. First, all federal judges have had legal training, and it is unimaginable that anyone without legal education would be appointed and confirmed.[5] For appointment to the Supreme Court, a degree from just any law school will not do. Graduates from the nation's most prestigious law schools dominate the list of Supreme Court justices: The 2017 Court had five graduates from Harvard, three from Yale, and one from Columbia.[6]

A second quality that federal judges have in common is a career in public service. Almost all Supreme Court justices engaged in public service or politics prior to their appointment. Through such activity, they developed ties to presidents and senators who later influenced their appointments. District court judges, for example, have been referred to as "lawyers who know a United States senator." As might be expected, one of the most prevalent kinds of previous public service is that connected with the courts themselves. Many federal judges have served as state judges or district attorneys, and judges serving in higher federal courts often served on lower federal courts.

Finally, although there are no legal age requirements, it is unlikely that the president would nominate individuals who are very young or very old. Viable

---

5 Early in the nation's history, individuals did not have to attend law school to be admitted to the bar. Instead, they would "read" the law under the tutorship of a member of the bar for several years. Only 59 of the 114 Supreme Court justices attended law school, and it was not until 1957 that all the justices had law degrees.

6 The elite education starts before law school. Most of the current Supreme Court justices got their undergraduate degrees at the same elite schools: Princeton (three), Stanford (two), Columbia (one), Harvard (one), and Cornell (one). Justice Clarence Thomas attended a Catholic school, Holy Cross, before going to Yale for his law degree.

candidates for appointment to the federal judiciary, especially the Supreme Court, are those who have distinguished careers in law, politics, and public service—and successful careers take time. But because presidents want to make appointments that will affect the Court for a long time, they are unlikely to select individuals of advanced age whose service may be cut short by illness or retirement.

A consequence of these expectations is that judicial appointees tend to be disproportionately white, male, and wealthy. As Figure 15.4 shows, President Jimmy Carter (1977–1980) was the first president to appoint significant numbers of women, African Americans, and Latinos to the federal courts (i.e., district courts and courts of appeal). Presidents who followed also increased diversity on the federal bench, but in varying degrees. President Bill Clinton made one of the more concerted efforts to increase diversity on the federal bench; during his two terms, Clinton appointed a larger percentage of women, African Americans, and Latinos than any of his predecessors. George W. Bush appointed somewhat fewer women and less than half as many African Americans as Clinton. But Bush appointed a larger percentage of Latinos than any previous president, and only Carter and Clinton appointed more African Americans. President Obama appointed more women to the federal judiciary than any of his predecessors—about 40 percent, plus both of his Supreme Court appointments were women. Obama's appointment of 18 percent African American and 11 percent Latino judges appointed is slightly higher than his immediate predecessors. Very few Asian Americans have been appointed to the federal bench. Presidents from Johnson to Bush appointed an average of less than 1 percent. In contrast, nearly 7 percent of President Obama's judicial appointments were Asian American. He nominated 11 Asian Americans during his first term. Among them was Goodwin Liu, the son of Taiwanese immigrants, who earned his law degree from Yale and became associate dean and professor of law at UC Berkeley School of Law. Obama nominated Liu to serve on the Ninth Circuit Court of Appeals. There was speculation that this appointment was meant to groom him for the Supreme Court (Santiago 2010). If so, the strategy failed. A Republican filibuster blocked a confirmation vote, and Liu withdrew in May 2011. Governor Jerry Brown appointed Liu to the Supreme Court of California.

Thus, the pool of prospective Supreme Court justices is limited to the small proportion of the population with legal training from (mostly) the elite universities, in the prime of distinguished careers in law and politics, and with the appropriate character and integrity. When appointments are made from among this relatively elite pool, political considerations inevitably influence presidents' choices. These political considerations include party affiliation and philosophy and balancing the representativeness of the Court.

Party Affiliation and Philosophy

The most important consideration in making appointments to the Supreme Court and the lower federal courts is the nominee's political party and philosophy. With few exceptions, presidents appoint individuals of their own political

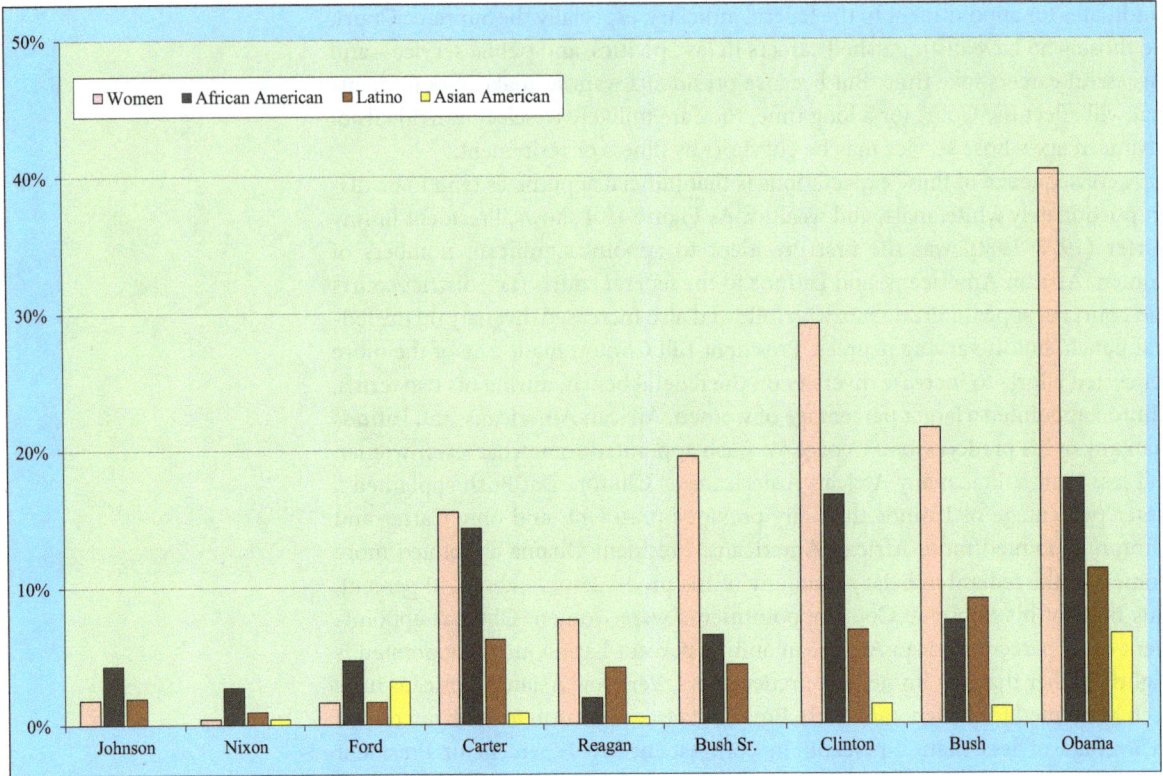

FIGURE 15.4 Appointments of Women and Minorities to the Federal Courts

Source: Data from Stanley and Niemi (2013, 278–280).

party who share their political philosophy. Of the 113 justices who have served on the Supreme Court, 90 percent have been of the same party as the president who appointed them. At least two considerations explain the importance of party in making appointments to the federal judiciary. First, old-fashioned patronage considerations lead presidents to appoint members of their own party. Federal judgeships are exceptional jobs: judges have power and prestige; they have great job security; and they are well paid.[7] Some of the individuals who have the requisite qualifications are Democrats, and others are Republicans; some are conservative, and others are liberal. When there are many highly qualified individuals who helped the president get elected, there is generally no incentive for a president to reward an equally well-qualified person of the opposite party and philosophy who worked against the president's election.

Second, policy considerations come into play. Presidents have term limits: They serve for four or eight years and then must leave office. But federal judges

---

[7] The chief justice of the Supreme Court earns $263,300, and associate justices earn $251,800; appellate court and district court judges earn $184,500 and $174,000, respectively (as of January 2017). These salaries are lower than those of lawyers at the nation's top law firms, which is where most federal judges would work if they were not judges. Many take significant cuts in pay to become federal judges.

appointed by the president serve for life. If presidents select wisely, their judicial appointees will be making important decisions that influence the course of public policy for decades after they have left office.

In the case of district court judges, another consideration comes into play. Nominations to U.S. district courts usually follow the practice of **senatorial courtesy**, which gives senators from the state where the vacancy occurs the power to influence who is appointed. Indeed, the practice actually turns the appointment process around in these cases. Because no district court boundary crosses state lines, senators from states with vacancies expect to recommend individuals who are qualified and available for the job. The president retains veto power, ruling out nominees who are politically offensive or who fail to meet minimum qualifications. But if the president fails to follow home state senators' recommendations, a slighted senator may object to the nomination and prevent it from coming to the floor for a confirmation vote. Traditionally, senatorial courtesy worked within a party, and opposite party senators could not block a nomination. The partisan nature of senatorial courtesy tended to reinforce same-party appointments. Only in unusual circumstances would a senator recommend that the president appoint someone of the opposite party.

The procedure changed during the Clinton administration. The Senate Judiciary Committee would not hold confirmation hearings on judicial nominees who did not have approval of both home state senators, regardless of party. This change allowed Republican senators to block many of President Clinton's judicial nominees. The practice of requiring one or both home state senators to approve district court nominees changed several times in subsequent years, depending on the party of the president and which party had a majority in the Senate (Edsall 2001; Masters 2001).

Senatorial courtesy is less of a consideration for appointments to appellate courts that hear cases from several states. There is, however, a tendency for each state in the circuit to get a certain number of judges, and the senators from those states do exercise some influence (Masters 2001). Senatorial courtesy does not come into play for appointments to the Supreme Court because the Court hears cases from the entire nation.

Cross-party appointments occur occasionally to further a political purpose. One such case occurred in 1985, when Republican senator Phil Gramm of Texas exercised senatorial courtesy to get President Ronald Reagan to appoint Texas Democratic representative Sam B. Hall to a federal judgeship. Gramm engineered this cross-party appointment in the hope that a Republican would win the special election in Hall's district, which was populated with conservative Democrats. Democrats held on to the seat, but political motivations accounted for this cross-party exercise of senatorial courtesy.

When presidents cross party lines for Supreme Court appointments, they typically choose individuals who share their political ideology. Republican president William Howard Taft, for example, appointed two southern Democrats, Horace Lurton and Joseph R. Lamar, to the Court in 1910 and 1911, respectively. Both men were Taft's personal friends and shared his conservative ideology. Taft also hoped that the appointment of Lurton, a Confederate Army veteran, would encourage

senatorial courtesy The practice that allows senators from states with federal district court vacancies to recommend individuals for the president to nominate. If the president fails to follow the home state senators' recommendations, a slighted senator may block the nomination from coming to the floor for a confirmation vote.

southern political leaders who held key leadership positions in Congress to help him get his legislative program passed (Abraham 1993, 67).

Balancing the Representativeness of the Court

Other political criteria are less important than party and come into play only sporadically. Concerns about balancing the representativeness of the Supreme Court occasionally influence appointments. The Supreme Court is not intended to be a representative institution. In fact, the Court is often in the position of declaring unconstitutional a law favored by the majority of Americans because it violates a fundamental individual right protected by the Constitution. Nevertheless, there is often a strong feeling that the Supreme Court should have justices of different regions, religions, races, and genders.

Geography

Early in the nation's history, geographical considerations were important in making Supreme Court appointments. Early presidents felt that having justices from the different regions of the country would help establish the legitimacy of the Court. As the nation expanded, presidents sometimes felt a political need to appoint justices from new states, as when Republican president Abraham Lincoln appointed Californian Steven J. Field, who was a Democrat, in 1863. Until 1891, Supreme Court justices had to ride the circuit to serve on the courts of appeals, which reinforced the need for justices from different regions (O'Brien 1996, 70).

In the twentieth century, geography became less important in Supreme Court appointments. The last time geography was a consideration in a Supreme Court appointment occurred in 1969 when President Nixon announced his intention to appoint a "southern strict-constructionist" to the Court. The term *strict-constructionist* was understood to mean a conservative who would resist and perhaps even reverse some of the Warren Court's liberal rulings. The focus on a southerner was meant to attract conservative white Democratic voters in the South to help build a new Republican majority. After the Senate rejected Nixon's first two nominations, both from the South, he appointed Harry Blackmun of Minnesota. Nixon did eventually get Lewis Powell of Virginia confirmed, but the Watergate Scandal which forced him to resign sidetracked his political goal of attracting conservative southern Democrats to the Republican Party.

Religion

Nearly 90 percent of Supreme Court justices have been Protestant. For much of the nation's history, there was a pattern of having a "Roman Catholic seat" and a "Jewish seat" on the Court (Abraham 1993, 65). Chief Justice Roger B. Taney was the first Catholic appointed, in 1835, and in 1916, Louis D. Brandeis became the first Jewish justice. Breaking the religion barrier was controversial. Brandeis, for example, was condemned as unfit to be a Supreme Court justice by former presidents of the American Bar Association. Anti-Semitism was barely concealed in the failed attempt to deny his appointment. He served a distinguished career and is generally recognized as one of the great Supreme Court justices.

Religion has become much less of a factor in the contemporary era, and there is no longer a demonstrable effort to ensure religious balance on the Court. There had been no Catholic on the Court for several years when President Dwight Eisenhower appointed William Brennan, a Democrat and a Catholic, in 1956. Brennan was a highly respected attorney, but the appointment of an eastern Catholic was seen as a potential help to Eisenhower in the upcoming election (Abraham 1993, 70). Five of the current justices are Catholic: Samuel Alito, Anthony Kennedy, John Roberts, Sonia Sotomayor, and Clarence Thomas. Neil Gorsuch, the most recent appointment, was raised Catholic, but is a member of an Episcopal church. The tradition of the Jewish seat was broken in 1970, when President Richard Nixon filled the vacancy created by the resignation of Abe Fortas with a Protestant, and he later named two other Protestants to the Court. As do all presidents, Nixon claimed that religion was irrelevant and that he was looking for the best-qualified person. There were no Jews on the Court again until the 1990s, when both of President Clinton's appointments, Ruth Bader Ginsburg and Stephen Breyer, were Jewish. There was no public controversy about religion in either case. President Obama's appointment of Elena Kagan to the Court in 2010 did generate some discussion about religion. Kagan identifies as a Conservative Jew. Although there was no objection to her religion per se, she replaced the sole remaining Protestant on the Court, retiring Justice John Paul Stevens. Thus, religion has not been a factor in the selection of Supreme Court justices for a long time.

Race and Ethnicity

Only two African Americans have served on the Supreme Court. The color barrier on the Court was broken in 1967, when President Lyndon Johnson appointed Thurgood Marshall, saying, "I believe it is the right thing to do, the right time to do it, the right man, and the right place." There is some indication that there is now an African American seat on the Court. When Justice Marshall retired in 1991, President George H. W. Bush appointed Clarence Thomas, who had the right credentials: He is conservative, he is Republican, and he has a law degree from Yale—and he is African American.

Another barrier fell in 2009 when President Obama appointed the first Latina, Sonia Sotomayor, to the Court. The politics are clear. Latinos are the largest ethnic group in the United States, and their political power is increasing. Latino votes

The Supreme Court is not intended to be a representative institution. In fact, the Court is often in the position of declaring unconstitutional a law favored by the majority of Americans because it violates a fundamental individual right protected by the Constitution. Nevertheless, there is often a strong feeling that the Supreme Court should have representatives of different regions, religions, races, and genders. In 1967 the color barrier on the Court was broken by the appointment of Thurgood Marshall (seen here) by President Lyndon Johnson. When Justice Marshall retired, he was replaced by Clarence Thomas, who is also African American.

© The Library of Congress

contributed to Obama's victories in several key states. Now that these race and ethnicity barriers have been broken, we may someday see an Asian American or Native American justice appointed.

Gender

Four women have served on the Supreme Court. The gender barrier fell in 1981, when President Ronald Reagan appointed Sandra Day O'Connor. Although she was eminently qualified for the job, having graduated near the top of her class at Stanford—where she and Chief Justice William Rehnquist had been classmates—the political motivation for this appointment was paramount. During the 1980 presidential campaign, women's groups criticized Reagan for his opposition to the proposed Equal Rights Amendment. In an attempt to reduce the growing gender gap, Reagan made a campaign promise: "One of the first Supreme Court vacancies in my administration will be filled by the most qualified woman I can find." Less than six months into his first year, Reagan fulfilled this campaign promise: O'Connor became a Supreme Court justice in 1981 and served 25 years. In 2005, President George W. Bush nominated White House counsel Harriet Miers to serve on the Supreme Court to fill the vacancy created by O'Connor's retirement. Miers' nomination was torpedoed by broad criticism, however, even from members of the president's own party, aimed at Miers' qualifications and commitment to conservative principles. She withdrew from consideration, and President Bush appointed Samuel Alito. President Clinton's first appointment to the Court was also a woman, Justice Ruth Bader Ginsburg. Sonia Sotomayor, appointed by President Obama in 2009, became the third female Supreme Court justice, and Elena Kagan became the fourth the following year. This was the first time that two consecutive appointments were women.

Supreme Court Justice Sonia Sotomayor is the Court's 111th justice, its first Hispanic justice, and its third female justice.

© Steve Petteway/Collection of the Supreme Court of the United States

Judicial Experience and Merit

It is rare for a president to ignore political considerations and make an appointment based exclusively on judicial experience and merit. Of course, no president wants to appoint an unqualified person to the Supreme Court, so in a sense merit is always the first consideration. In the rare instances when a president has nominated someone with questionable credentials, the Senate typically has blocked the appointment. With few exceptions, Supreme Court justices have been competent and intelligent.

The connection between judicial experience and merit is tenuous at best. Presidents, senators, and the American Bar Association frequently view service on a lower federal or state court as a prerequisite for "promotion" to the nation's highest court. However, the Supreme Court is unique, and it performs a very different role than trial courts or even courts of appeals. Lower courts deal with the details of the cases at hand: facts and evidence, guilt and innocence. The Supreme Court addresses disputes over the most fundamental issues of politics and society: the meaning of broad clauses in the Constitution and the basic rights of individuals and society. Experience as a trial judge is not necessarily relevant to resolving disputes over such fundamental questions. Justice Felix Frankfurter boldly asserted, "One is entitled to say without qualification that the correlation between prior judicial experience and fitness for the Supreme Court is zero" (1957, 781). Rather, the job of Supreme Court justice requires a "combination of philosopher, historian, and prophet" (Abraham 1993, 59).

Several great justices had no prior experience as judges, including Joseph Story (appointed 1812), Charles Evans Hughes (appointed 1910), Louis Brandeis (appointed 1916), Harlan Stone (appointed 1925), and Felix Frankfurter (appointed 1939). Among the "great" justices, only Oliver Wendell Holmes, Jr. (appointed 1902) and Benjamin Cardozo (appointed 1932) had extensive prior judicial experience, but as Frankfurter argued, their greatness "derived not from their judicial experience but from the fact they were … thinkers, and more particularly, legal philosophers" (Frankfurter 1957, 781).

There has been only one clear case in which a president ignored political concerns and appointed a justice solely on merit: Herbert Hoover's appointment of Benjamin Cardozo to the Court. Cardozo was a distinguished jurist widely admired in the legal community and the most qualified nominee to fill the court vacancy. Yet Cardozo was a liberal Democrat contrary to the conservative Republican politics of Hoover; he was a New Yorker when there were already two New Yorkers on the Court; and he was Jewish, but that "seat" was already occupied by Brandeis. Hoover compiled a short list of conservative, western Republicans to nominate and reluctantly added Cardozo's name at the bottom of the list. Hoover handed Republican senator William E. Borah of Idaho the list and asked for his advice. Borah replied, "Your list is all right, but you handed it to me upside down" (Abraham 1993, 69). Hoover appointed Cardozo.

Confirmation Politics in the Senate

Deciding who will wield the power of judicial review is an enormously important decision. The careers of federal judges often go well beyond those of the presidents who nominated them and the senators who confirmed them. In other words, selecting someone to exercise judicial power has implications far beyond the next election or administration. Because the makeup of the federal bench is one of a president's biggest legacies, it is not surprising that the **confirmation process** for federal judges—that is, the period between when a presidential nomination is received in the Senate and when the nominee is either confirmed or defeated—is a political process. The process has become even more politicized in recent decades.

The Senate takes its power to confirm judicial appointments seriously. Of the 146 Supreme Court nominees forwarded to the Senate, about one-fifth have failed. During the nation's first century, the Senate blocked Supreme Court nominations with some regularity; in the 106 years from the founding to 1894, 22 Supreme Court nominees failed. Appointments came a little easier for presidents during much of the nation's second century, and "the confirmation process was distinguished by

confirmation process The period between when a presidential nomination of a federal judge is received in the Senate and when the nominee is either confirmed or defeated.

THINKING ANALYTICALLY

DOES PRIOR JUDICIAL EXPERIENCE MAKE BETTER SUPREME COURT JUSTICES?

Some presidents, and certainly plenty of senators, seem to view judicial experience as an important prerequisite for serving on the Supreme Court. Some who have actually served on the court are not so sure. According to former Justice Felix Frankfurter, "the correlation between prior judicial experience and fitness for the Supreme Court is zero" (1957, 781).

Those are pretty radical differences. Which perspective is correct? Does experience as a judge make you a better Supreme Court justice or not? Let's think analytically about this. Essentially, this question poses a hypothesis about the relationship between two variables: (1) experience serving as a judge on a lower court and (2) how well individuals perform the job of Supreme Court justice. We can test that hypothesis if we can measure judicial experience and job performance as Supreme Court justices. Measuring judicial experience is easy—just look at each justice's biography and count up how many years he or she had been a judge before serving on the Supreme Court.

Measuring Supreme Court job performance, on the other hand, is difficult because of the subjective nature of how we interpret judicial decisions. Depending on whether you agree or disagree with those decisions, one person's wise jurist is another person's political hack. Ideally, what we want is some reasonable objective criteria of performance. Fortunately, a number of studies have attempted to do exactly that. The authors of these studies surveyed a sample of legal scholars—law school professors, political scientists, historians, and biographers—who teach and study constitutional law. These legal scholars were asked to rate Supreme Court justices using relatively value-neutral criteria like quality of judicial reasoning and clarity in communicating decisions on a five-point scale: "Great," "Near Great," "Average," "Below Average," or "Failure" (Blaustein and Mersky 1978; Comiskey 2006; Mersky and Bader 2004).[i] Notice that this scale is similar to the "A," "B," "C," "D," or "F" grading scale you are familiar with. The authors of the studies then averaged the legal scholars' evaluations of each justice to determine the most appropriate category, much like your professors average test scores to assign a course grade. We averaged the ratings from the different studies to construct an overall rating for 108 of the 113 Supreme Court justices.[ii]

There is evidence that the measure is valid and reliable. Across all of the studies, there was considerable agreement with very little change in ratings from one study to the next. The most common rating is "Average" (about 45 percent). This result does not mean that these were mediocre justices. Supreme Court justices are selected from an elite pool, and being average among the top legal minds in the nation is certainly not mediocrity. There is near consensus on the 15 (about 14 percent) standouts. And there are only four (about 4 percent) "Failures," suggesting that appointment with confirmation by the Senate works reasonably well.

The figure below shows the relationship between prior judicial experience and justices' ratings. Justice Frankfurter, of course, was not using "correlation" to indicate a statistical relationship, but the results are consistent with his claim that there is zero correlation between judicial experience and job performance on the Supreme Court. The correlation coefficient (Pearson's r) in this statistical analysis is -0.12, indicating a very weak negative relationship—high values of judicial experience are associated with lower ratings—and the correlation is not statistically different from zero. The slope of the regression line shows the weak negative relationship (-0.02), and it's not statistically significant.

---

i Comiskey (2006) used different, but comparable, labels: "Excellent," "Good," "Fair," "Poor," or "Failure."
ii The five most recent justices—Chief Justices John Roberts, Samuel Alito, Sonia Sotomayor, Elena Kagan, and Neil Gorsuch—were not included in these studies.

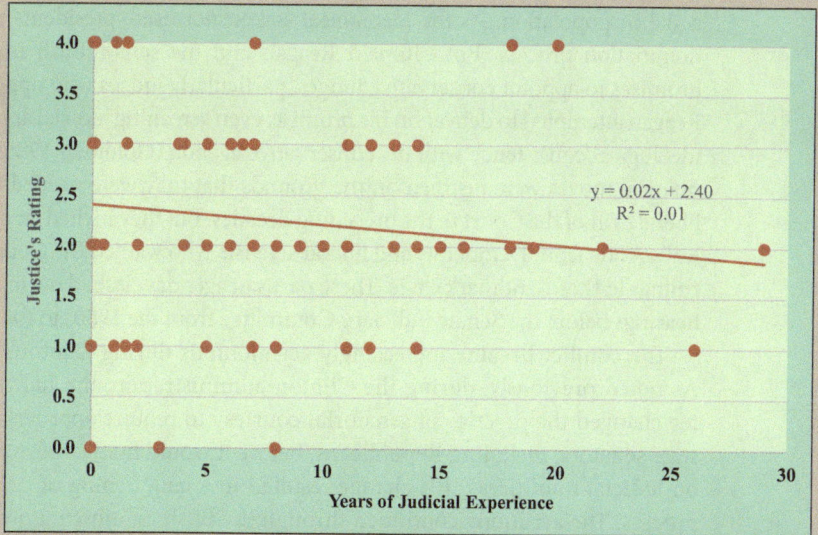

Discussion Questions

1. The Constitution does not contain any qualifications for federal judges like the age and citizenship requirements for the president and members of Congress. Do you think there should be qualifications to serve as a federal judge? What qualifications do you think would be appropriate? Why?

2. Do you think establishing qualifications would improve judicial decision making? What evidence would be required to show that qualifications improved decision making?

presidential prerogative to fill vacancies on the Supreme Court" (Silverstein 1994, 3). From 1895 to 1967, presidents made 45 nominations to the Supreme Court. Only one—John J. Parker in 1930—failed to gain confirmation. Since the late 1960s, the process of getting federal judges confirmed has become more politicized, and the Senate has once again become less deferential to presidents' preferences.

The shift from presidential prerogative to a more partisan and political process has its roots in procedural changes that took place in the mid-1950s. Before 1955, the only two Supreme Court nominees to testify before the Senate Judiciary Committee were Harlan Fiske Stone in 1925 and Felix Frankfurter in 1939. Nominees now must go before the committee to answer questions about their judicial philosophies and their opinions on specific legal issues. This practice has thrust Supreme Court nominees into political controversies as they are asked to publicly state their positions on, for example, abortion or affirmative action.

Because the Supreme Court has played an increasingly significant role in American political life in the past several decades, the political stakes in Supreme Court nominations have increased. It was the Supreme Court that decided that abortion was a private decision subject to limited regulation by government, that law enforcement agencies had to inform people taken into custody of their rights, that school-sponsored prayer and Bible reading in public schools violated the constitutional requirement of separation of church and state, and that legislative districts must be equal in population. As the ideological stakes increased, presidents politicized the nomination process. Both Ronald Reagan and the senior Bush made campaign promises to appoint conservative judges, particularly judges who opposed abortion. Reagan attempted to deliver on his promise, even screening judicial appointments for ideological consistency with his conservative agenda (Goldman 1985). Such openly political moves were justified on the grounds that they were needed to counter the liberal drift of the Court in the preceding decades. But they invited an opposing political agenda from Democrats and liberal activists who wanted the Court to defend its rulings in these landmark cases. These partisan agendas clashed during confirmation hearings before the Senate Judiciary Committee from the 1980s to the 2000s.

The conflict became increasingly acrimonious during Clinton's second term. As noted previously, during the Clinton administration, the Judiciary Committee changed the practice of senatorial courtesy to require approval of both home state senators, including Republicans, before it would hold confirmation hearings on judicial nominees. This change resulted in a lengthening of the confirmation process. The acrimony continued through the Bush administration as Democrats retaliated, and Republicans responded in kind to delay confirmation of Obama's judicial appointments. As Figure 15.5 shows, the average length of the confirmation process for Supreme Court and Circuit Court judges has increased exponentially since the 1960s. The average length of the confirmation process was about one and one half months in the 1960s and 1970s (Johnson to Carter); it more than doubled to almost four months during the 1980s and early 1990s (Reagan to the first Clinton term); and it doubled yet again to nearly nine months in the period from Clinton's second term to Obama.

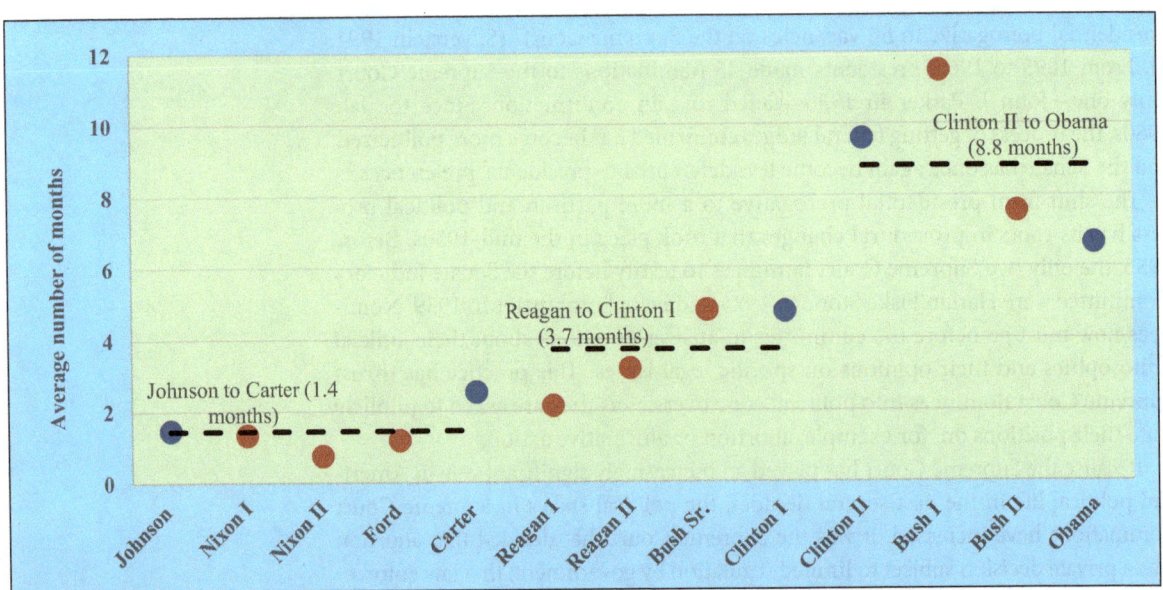

FIGURE 15.5 Increasing Length of the Confirmation Process for Judicial Nominations

Source: Data from Bond, Fleisher, and Krutz (2009); Obama nominations updated by the authors.

The longer confirmation process is symptomatic of more fundamental changes. Arguably, the most important change is the increasing rate at which judicial nominees fail to be confirmed. Before the Reagan administration, the average failure rate for Supreme Court and Circuit Court nominations was about 6 percent. From the Carter administration to Clinton's first term, the failure rate more than tripled to 18.6 percent, and then more than doubled to 42.8 percent from Clinton's second term to Obama (see Figure 15.6).

Moreover, the way nominations are defeated has changed. Typically, a nomination failed because the president withdrew it as controversy and opposition grew or because it was voted down in committee or on the Senate floor. Few nominations have been voted down (the last was Reagan's nomination of Judge Robert Bork to the Supreme Court in 1987). Most commonly, presidents have withdrawn controversial nominations before the Senate rejects them. For example, President Bush withdrew his nomination of Harriet Miers, his White House Counsel, in 2005. Although Miers was a highly respected lawyer (she was the first female president of the Texas Bar Association), both Republicans and Democrats questioned whether she had the intellectual credentials and experience necessary to serve on the Supreme Court.

Nominations can also fail because the Senate does not act on them before Congress adjourns. Historically, such failures were rare, occurring mainly in election years, when senators focus more on reelection than on Senate business. From 1965 to 1980, only nine nominations failed at the end of the session because of inaction, and seven of these were nominations made after the first quarter of a presidential election year. The number of judicial nominations failing at the adjournment of Congress began to increase during the Reagan and senior Bush presidencies,

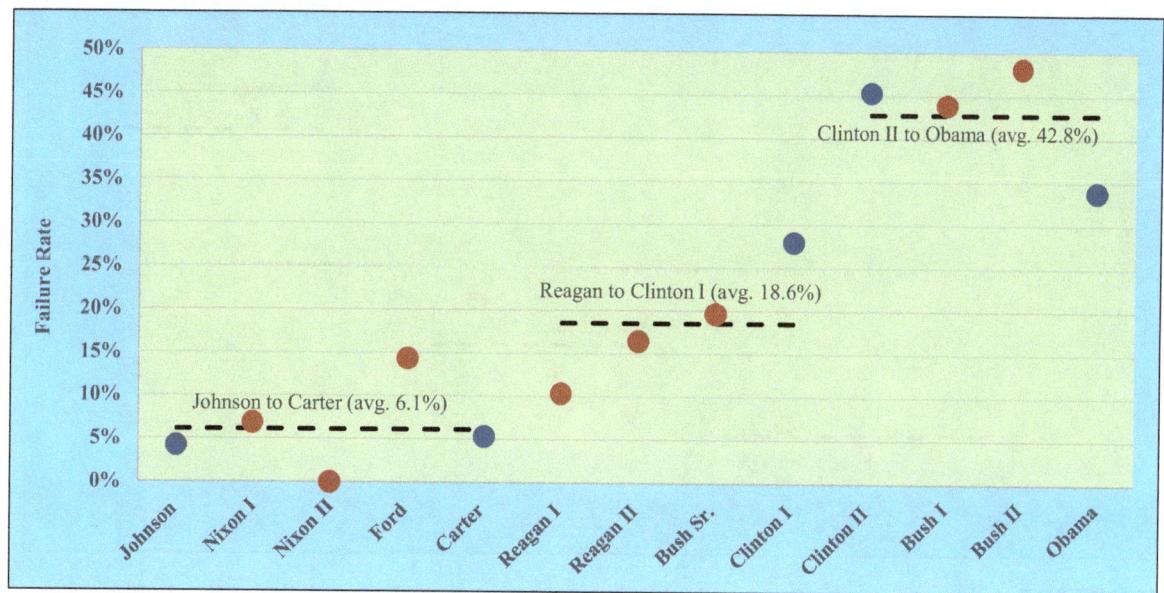

FIGURE 15.6 Increasing Failure Rates of Judicial Nominations

Source: Data from Bond, Fleisher, and Krutz (2009); Obama nominations updated by the authors.

though a few of them were late election year nominations. During the Clinton years, such failures increased dramatically—Clinton had more nominees defeated by delay than did the six preceding presidents combined. President Bush had similar numbers of judicial nominees defeated by stalling (see Figure 15.7). Delaying final action until Congress adjourns has become the most common way to defeat high-level judicial nominations.

This change seems to be the result of a political strategy in which opponents use Senate rules to block action on a nomination until Congress adjourns. The key to this strategy is the filibuster or the threat to filibuster by placing a "hold" on nominations. Recall from Chapter 10 that a hold is a request to party leaders that a senator has some concerns and wants to be notified before a bill or nomination comes to the floor. It is an implicit threat to filibuster if those concerns are not addressed. Senate rules do not explicitly authorize holds. Rather, the practice is one aspect of senatorial courtesy that party leaders usually observe—but not always.

Whether party leaders honor a hold and whether a senator will actually have to make good on a filibuster threat depend on the configuration of party control of the presidency and the Senate. Holds on nominations are most likely to come from members of the opposition party. If the opposition party controls the Senate, an actual filibuster is unlikely to be necessary because the majority leader will honor a "hold" and not bring the nomination to the floor. This was the situation in the 106th Congress (1999–2000) when President Clinton was unable to get a vote on numerous judicial nominations because the Senate majority leader, Trent Lott (R-MS), would not schedule a vote if there was a hold on the nominee. But if the president's party has a majority, filibusters are more likely. A majority leader from

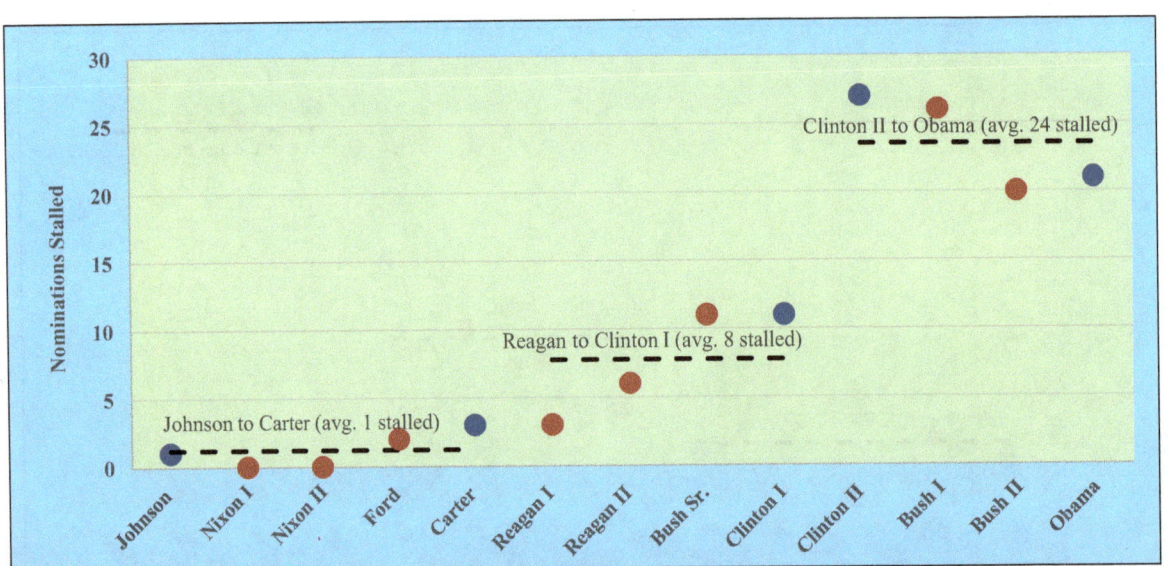

FIGURE 15.7 Increasing Use of Stalling the Confirmation Process to Defeat Judicial Nominations

Source: Data from Bond, Fleisher, and Krutz (2009); Obama nominations updated by the authors.

the president's party is likely to ignore holds placed by opposition party senators and bring nominations to the floor, forcing opponents to make good on the threat to filibuster. This was the situation in the 108th Congress (2003–2004) when Senate Majority Leader Bill Frist (R-TN) brought a number of President Bush's nominations to the floor, forcing Democrats to make good on filibuster threats.

Unable to muster 60 votes to invoke cloture, Senator Frist threatened to use a parliamentary maneuver to override the 60-vote requirement in Senate rules, and require only a simple majority to invoke cloture on filibusters of nominations. Republicans called the procedure the "constitutional option," arguing that filibusters of judicial nominees violated the Constitution. Democrats labeled it the "nuclear option" because the "explosive" conflict could potentially "incinerate" the Senate if they used other procedures to slow all Senate business. A compromise brokered by seven Republican and seven Democratic senators averted the crisis, temporarily.

The situation was similar in 2011, but the parties were on different sides of the issue. Majority Leader Harry Reid (D-NV) brought an Obama Court of Appeals nominee to the floor, forcing Republicans to filibuster. Democrats failed to muster the necessary 60 votes to invoke cloture, but the "nuclear option" was not off the table (Kane 2011). After Obama won reelection in 2012, the Democratic majority pulled the trigger and voted to require a simple majority to invoke cloture on filibusters of all nominations except for the Supreme Court. This cleared the way to confirm dozens of appellate court nominees that Republicans had blocked for years.

Republicans won back majority control of the Senate in the 2014 elections, which allowed them to prevent any more of Obama's judicial nominees from getting consideration in committee hearings or a floor vote—most notably, including a replacement for Justice Antonin Scalia, the intellectual anchor of the conservative bloc on the Court, who died in February of 2016. President Obama nominated DC Circuit Judge Merrick Garland to fill the vacancy. There were no doubts that Judge Garland was highly qualified, but his judicial record suggested that he would shift the ideological balance on the Court to the left. Republicans refused even to hold hearings, arguing the newly elected president should fill the vacancy.

Donald Trump's victory gave Republicans control of the White House as well as the Senate, which set the stage to invoke the "nuclear option" for all nominations. President Trump nominated Appeals Court Judge Neil Gorsuch. Judge Gorsuch was also well qualified, but his judicial record indicated that he would vote much the same as Scalia and not alter the ideological balance on the Court. Democrats filibustered the confirmation vote. When Republicans failed to get 60 votes to invoke cloture under current Senate rules, they voted to require a simple majority to invoke cloture on filibusters of all nominations. So ended the saga of the "nuclear option" on nominations, though the same parliamentary maneuver could be used to return to the 60-vote requirement to invoke cloture in the written rules of the Senate.[8]

---

8 The 60-vote requirement to invoke cloture on the legislation remains in place.

JUDICIAL DECISION MAKING

Presidents are periodically disappointed by the decisions of their appointees. President Eisenhower, for example, was bitterly disappointed by his appointment of Earl Warren as chief justice in 1953 (White 1982), calling it the "biggest damned-fool mistake I ever made." Given Warren's background as a "law and order" Republican and a prosecutor, Eisenhower was disappointed that he would become the leader of one of the most liberal, activist courts in the nation's history.[9] Under his leadership, the Supreme Court compiled a long list of decisions that attracted the wrath of conservatives. But once a justice is appointed and confirmed, there is little a president can do about that appointee's decisions. Years later, the Court's decision permitting a sexual harassment lawsuit to proceed against President Bill Clinton was unanimous, meaning that both of Clinton's appointees voted in favor of it. President Truman once observed that "packing the Supreme Court simply can't be done ... I've tried and it won't work" (quoted in Abraham 1993, 74).

Models of Judicial Decision Making

Political scientists who study the courts have turned to several models to explain judicial decision making. The traditional approach is the **legal model**, adapted from the law school tradition. This model argues that judges set aside their own values and make decisions based solely on legal criteria: the evidence, the law, legal precedents, and the Constitution. The legal model is grounded in sociological theory. From this framework, the law is a system operated by professionals (lawyers and judges) who perform different roles. These legal professionals must learn and follow formal legal rules and procedures when they are in court, as well as less formal norms that prescribe how the various roles should be performed both in and out of the courtroom. For example, lawyers are supposed to vigorously advocate the interests of their clients regardless of their personal feelings and keep communications with clients confidential. The judge's role is to be an impartial referee who makes sure the advocates on both sides follow the legal rules and norms; once the adversaries have presented their evidence and arguments, the judge makes an objective decision about which side wins based on the Constitution, laws, and precedents established by previous court decisions in similar cases. One version of the legal model articulated by Justice Owen Roberts is sometimes referred to as the **slot machine theory** of judicial decision making. Justice Roberts argued that when faced with a case challenging the constitutionality of a law, all a judge does is lay the constitutional provision involved beside the statute being challenged and "decide whether the latter squares with the former" (*United States v. Butler* 1936).

legal model A view of judicial decision making that argues that judges set aside their own values and make decisions based solely on legal criteria.

slot machine theory The view of judicial review that all judges do is lay the constitutional provision involved beside the statute being challenged and "decide whether the latter squares with the former."

---

9 However, studies of analyzing newspaper editorials prior to confirmation indicated that Warren had moderately liberal values (Epstein et al. 2012; Segal and Cover 1989).

According to Roberts, judges don't "make" law, but rather they "find" the law. More recently, another Justice Roberts expressed a similar view with a baseball analogy. At his Senate confirmation hearing to be chief justice, John Roberts summarized the legal model's view of the role of Supreme Court Justice: "I will remember that it's my job [role] to call balls and strikes and not to pitch or bat" (quoted in Epstein, Landes, and Posner 2013, 51). This perspective assumes there is always a right answer to resolve legal controversies, and the judge's job (role) is to mechanically calculate what the right answer is, similar to putting coins in a slot machine, then picking up and reporting what comes out.

The competing model is the **legal realist model**. Legal realists acknowledge that legal rules and norms determine judicial decisions in many—even most—cases, but they reject the mechanistic nature of legalism. Legal realists observe that judges are not computers, but rather human beings with personal preferences, including political and ideological biases, like the rest of us. Yet judges are not exactly the same as the rest of us. Instead, judges are professionals with rigorous legal and analytical training that teaches them to set aside subjective political preferences and to make decisions based on objective legal criteria. Most judges may believe that legal principles should be the basis of decisions, and they may make a sincere, professional effort to follow legal norms. Legal criteria may trump ideology in areas of law that are well settled—the finding that 35 to 40 percent of Supreme Court decisions are unanimous (see Figure 15.3) is evidence that legal criteria influence judicial decisions. But sometimes it's not feasible to just "follow the law." Some areas of law are not well-settled; new issues and controversies arise that don't fit neatly into established legal principles. These are cases where reasonable people disagree, and personal values (moral, religious, and yes, even party and ideology) inevitably influence the judge's decision. This does not mean, however, that judges are just "legislators in robes." Judges "make law" because they must fill in the gaps, but party and ideology do not influence judges' decisions in the same way they influence elected legislators. Members of Congress are chosen in partisan elections to represent the partisan interests of their constituents; if they don't, the voters can replace them in the next election. Federal judges are appointed for terms of good behavior, not to reflect the party and ideology of the president who appointed them, but to resolve disputes based on legal principles. Yet in cases without clear, controlling legal principles to guide them, judges evaluate the evidence through the lenses of non-legal values (including ideology). As a result, judges' votes often appear ideological because conservatives tend to be persuaded by certain types of evidence and arguments, while liberals are persuaded by different kinds of evidence and arguments.

Political scientists have extended the legal realist model with behavioral models that focus on attitudes. C. Herman Pritchett (1948) pioneered the behavioral study of the courts with a statistical analysis of voting blocs on the Supreme Court from 1937 to 1947. He argued that analyzing non-unanimous decisions reveals "information about [justices'] attitudes and their values" (xii). Building on this insight, Jeffrey Segal and Harold Spaeth (2002) developed the **attitudinal model**, suggesting that judges' decisions are largely, if not exclusively, determined by their personal ideological and policy preferences. While legal realists accepted that legal

legal realist model A model of judicial decision making that argues that personal values and ideologies affect a judge's decisions.

attitudinal model A model that suggests that judges' decisions are largely, if not exclusively, determined by their personal ideological and policy preferences.

norms—e.g., the facts of the case, the intent of the Framers, the plain meaning of words in the Constitution, and precedent—explained judicial decisions in many cases, proponents of the attitudinal model have largely rejected the sociologically based legal model as myth. Embracing a rational choice framework, attitudinalists argue that judges' use of objective-sounding legal doctrines does not explain their decisions, but rather are just excuses—smokescreens—to hide their policy values (Segal and Spaeth 2002; Spaeth 1979). With life tenure and little chance of removal, federal judges are just "politicians in robes," free to make rational decisions intended to maximize their own policy goals.

The attitudinal model assumes that judges' votes sincerely reflect their preferences. Lee Epstein and Jack Knight (1998) challenge this assumption, arguing that judges behave strategically. The **strategic model** (based on a type of rational choice model called game theory) indicates that sincere voting—that is, voting for the most preferred alternative—does not always maximize utility in the long run. Why? Well, basically because judges—even Supreme Court justices at the apex of judicial power—cannot achieve their goals without help from other actors with competing preferences. A Supreme Court justice must get at least four other justices to join in a majority opinion. And after the Court hands down its decision, other institutional actors—for example, the president, Congress, lower-court judges, and state officials—will have to take some action to implement the decision. To achieve their policy goals, therefore, judges must act strategically to get the help they need from other institutional actors. Thus, strategic behavior explains why, more than half the time, Supreme Court justices cast votes that do not reflect their personal preferences (Epstein and Knight 1998).

These debates have increased our understanding of judicial decision making, but conflict remains. But a more general theory that explains conditions under which ideology, legal principles, and other non-legal variables influence decisions on different types of courts would be an important advance. An interdisciplinary team of legal scholars (Epstein, Landes, and Posner 2013) has developed such a comprehensive rational choice model—the Labor-Market Model of judicial decision making (see Applying the Frameworks "The Labor-Market Model of Judicial Behavior").

Evidence of Political Influence on Judicial Decision Making

If judicial decisions were not influenced by judges' values, all the political maneuvering in the appointment and confirmation process would be wasted effort. Consistent with the legal model, judges invariably deny that personal political values influence their decisions. Legal training stresses that judges are supposed to be impartial. Most judges probably attempt to put aside their personal values and biases when they decide cases. Nonetheless, the empirical evidence from analyzing judges' behavior supports the legal realist and attitudinal models. Try as they may, the human beings who serve as judges do not become legal automatons when they put on judicial robes. When gray areas of the law are involved, judges' backgrounds and personal values influence which arguments and which parts of the

strategic model The view that sincere voting does not always maximize utility.

APPLYING THE FRAMEWORKS

THE LABOR-MARKET MODEL OF JUDICIAL BEHAVIOR

Why do judges make the decisions they do? Legal scholars have proposed three competing answers: the law, rational choices to maximize immediate policy goals, and strategic choices to maximize long-term policy goals. The Labor-Market Model of judicial behavior is a more comprehensive theory that incorporates legal, ideological, and other non-legal influences on decisions of federal court judges.

The Labor-Market Model views judges as workers in a labor market. It's a scientific model in that it is constructed to generate hypotheses about judicial behavior that are testable with data. The model begins with a general utility function. Utility is an abstract concept that refers to the satisfaction or happiness someone derives from their choices. A utility function is a formal statement of the benefits, costs, and constraints of choices made by a rational actor—a generic judge in this case—seeking to maximize satisfaction (utility). A formal statement of the Judicial Utility Function is:

$$U = U(S(t_j), EXT(t_j, t_{nj}), L(t_l), W, Y(t_{nj}), Z).$$

This may look a bit intimidating, but it's just a shorthand statement that says utility (U) is a function of six general factors. The table below (adapted from Solum [2014]) clarifies the types of variables associated with each factor.

Notice two things about this model. First, monetary benefits are part of the equation, but nonmonetary benefits (e.g., satisfaction derived from interesting and important work, public service, power, and prestige) have a much greater influence on overall satisfaction. Second, although the empirical analysis in this book focuses on the relative influence of the law versus policy, ideology is not part of the formal utility function. Achieving policy goals, however, is a product of the judge's external satisfaction derived from power.

This model generates hypotheses about the conditions under which law or politics will influence decisions. For example, proponents of the legal model point to unanimous decisions as proof that the law determines decisions. How can ideology explain votes if liberals and conservatives all vote the same way? The Labor-Market

SUMMARY OF THE JUDICIAL UTILITY FUNCTION

Symbol	Description
U	Judge's utility
$S(t_j)$	Internal satisfaction from doing an important job well, and social benefits and costs from interacting with colleagues. Productive working relationships add to utility, while animosities and conflict subtract from it
$EXT(t_j, t_{nj})$	External satisfaction from reputation, power, prestige, and celebrity produced by time spent on judicial and nonjudicial activities.
$L(t_l)$	Satisfaction derived from leisure time. For example, voting to reverse a lower court decision or writing dissenting opinions create more work (costs), which reduces leisure time.
W	Judicial salaries are a substantial benefit, but less important than other factors. Most federal judges could earn higher salaries in the private sector.
$Y(t_{nj})$	Other earned income from nonjudicial activities, such as writing books.
Z	The combined effect of all other variables, including activities to get promoted (auditioning) to a higher court or moving to a high-paid private sector job.

Model suggests a way to test this—analyze unanimous and non-unanimous Supreme Court decisions reversing an Appellate Court. This analysis finds that ideology plays a role in unanimous decisions, but the effect is small. For example, a Supreme Court dominated by conservatives is likely to reverse liberal decisions from the Appellate Courts (so ideology matters), but liberal justices go along quite often. Why would liberal justices vote to overturn a lower court decision they agree with? The Labor-Market Model explains why—there's a trade-off between the benefits of supporting your ideology and the costs of dissenting (it's more work to write a dissent, and dissents can damage collegial working relationships). Thus, decisions are unanimous when the ideological stakes are smaller than the costs of dissenting (Epstein, Landes, and Posner 2013, 136). In contrast, ideology has a large effect on non-unanimous Supreme Court decisions because ideological stakes are larger than the costs of dissenting.

Other empirical tests clarify the conditions under which the law or politics will prevail. The effects of ideology increase as we move up the judicial hierarchy—ideology is a prevalent influence on the Supreme Court; a factor sometimes on the Courts of Appeals, but legal criteria usually prevail; and the law dominates decisions of District Courts. The reason is that judicial power as well as discretion over which cases to hear increases as we move up the ladder. District Courts are trial courts that make the legal determination of facts, evidence, and who wins. The Circuit Courts of Appeals are required to hear appeals, and they have the power to reverse District Court decisions. Most reversals involve legal errors made by the district judge, but there are some opportunities for Appellate Court judges to advance their policy preferences. The Supreme Court has almost complete discretion over which appeals to hear, and the Court's decision is binding on lower courts. This hierarchy of power and discretion results in selection effects—cases that involve no legal ambiguity are resolved by the District Court through dismissal or summary judgment; cases that go to trial despite legal certainty are rarely appealed to Courts of Appeals; and the Supreme Court rarely grants certiorari to cases in which there is no legal ambiguity. As a result, the percentage of novel cases—those that present the greatest opportunity to make new law—is greatest at the Supreme Court.

So, which side is right—the legalists who argue that judges just apply the law, legal realists who argue that the law matters most of the time but ideology influences judicial decisions in cases where there is legal ambiguity, or the attitudinalists who argue that judges are "legislators in robes" who use their power to maximize their own ideological preferences? Well, it's pretty clear that they're all right some of the time. And that's a big contribution of the Labor-Market Model—it explains and empirically verifies the conditions under which the law or ideology prevail in judicial decision making. Attitudinalists' claim that the law plays no role in judicial decision making is a bit over the top. Even on the Supreme Court where the influence of ideology is most prevalent, this study shows that justices do pay more than lip service to the law. Yet even if a whopping 90 percent of cases are decided by legal criteria—leaving a mere 10 percent that are legalistically indeterminate—ideology still matters a lot. Cumulating that measly 10 percent over many years and many courts means that an immense number of decisions are determined by judges' ideology.

Discussion Questions

1. Do you think it is possible for judicial decisions to always follow the legal model? Why or why not?
2. If judges are just "legislators in robes," as the more stringent versions of the attitudinal model suggest, should federal judges be given lifetime appointments, or, like legislators, should they have to stand for review periodically?

evidence they find most persuasive as they consider the facts, the evidence, and the meaning of the law. As a result, Democratic judges tend to make more liberal decisions, and Republican judges tend to make more conservative decisions. These differences, however, are tendencies, and the influence of party and ideology generally is not as strong as for presidents and members of Congress.

Analyzing how judges vote, political scientists have found consistent evidence that attitudes influence judicial decisions. Although a judge's vote is not a direct indicator of attitudes, when there is disagreement, votes reveal information about preferences. If we find significant differences in how judges vote, then it is reasonable to infer that personal values influenced their decisions. Figure 15.8 shows how often Supreme Court justices cast liberal votes on non-unanimous civil liberties cases. The justices sort into three distinct voting blocs:

- On the left are four justices (Kagan, Sotomayor, Ginsburg, and Breyer) who voted on the liberal side of civil liberties questions over 60 percent of the time.
- On the right are three justices (Thomas, Scalia, and Alito) who voted liberal less than 33 percent of the time. Justice Gorsuch who replaced Scalia has cast too few votes to calculate a score, but he voted most consistently with Alito and Thomas in his first year.
- In the middle are Justice Kennedy and Chief Justice Roberts, who side with the liberal bloc about 40 percent of the time.

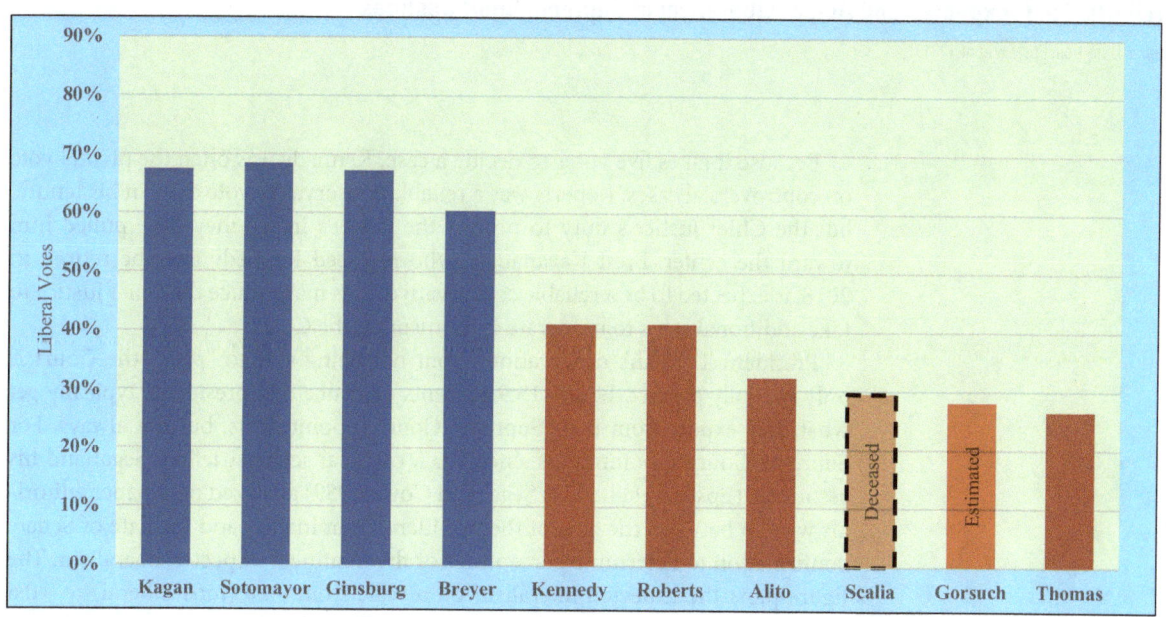

FIGURE 15.8 Civil Liberties Liberalism of Supreme Court Justices

Note: Liberalism is a composite average of liberal votes on cases involving civil rights, criminal procedure, and First Amendment is from Epstein et al. (2017). Gorsuch voted most consistently with Alito and Thomas in 2017; his liberalism estimated as average of Alito and Thomas.

Source: Data from Epstein et al. (2017).

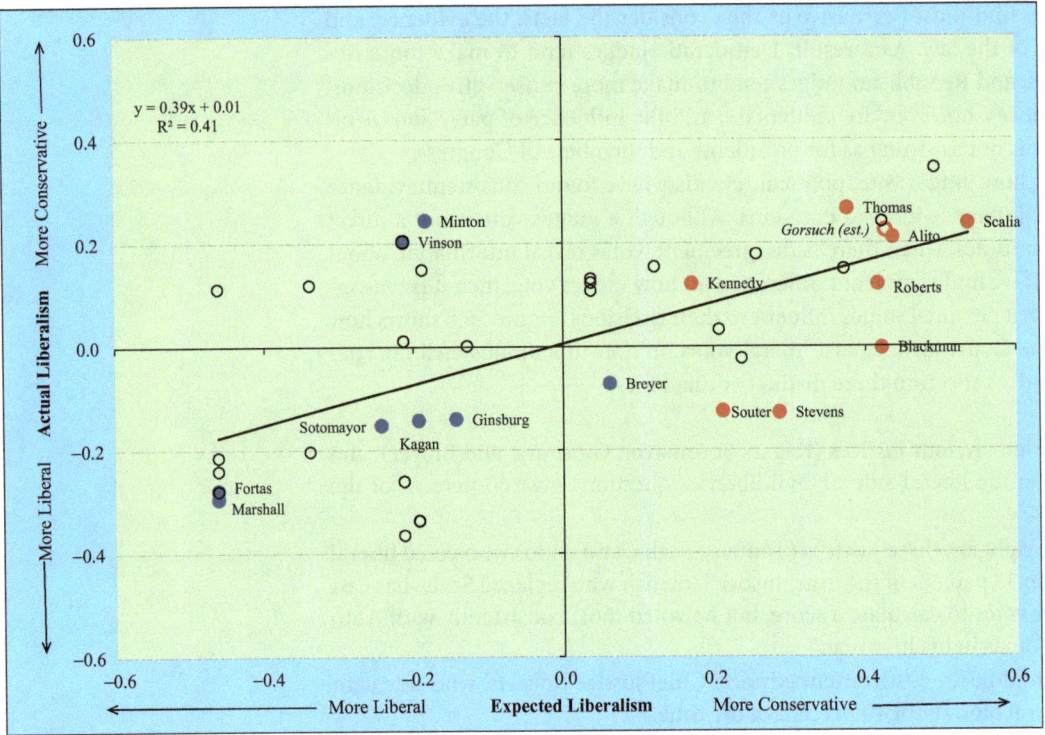

FIGURE 15.9 Expected and Actual Liberalism of Supreme Court Justices

Source: Data from Epstein et al. (2017).

Because it takes five votes to decide a case, Kennedy was often the pivotal vote on controversial cases. Roberts was a reliable conservative vote early in his tenure, but the Chief Justice's duty to protect the Court's image may have pulled him toward the center. Brett Kavanaugh, who replaced Kennedy after he retired in 2018, is expected to be a reliable conservative. This may induce the Chief Justice to take additional steps to moderate extremism on the Court.

President Truman's observation about not being able to "pack" the Court is only partially correct. Figure 15.9 presents evidence that presidents typically get what they expect from their Supreme Court appointments, but not always. For Supreme Court appointments since 1937, political scientist Jeffrey Segal and his associates (Epstein et al. 2017; Segal and Cover 1989) analyzed newspaper editorials written between the date of the president's nomination and the date of Senate confirmation to determine perceptions of the nominees' expected liberalism. The figure plots the expected liberalism on a scale from −0.6 (most liberal) to +0.6 (most conservative)[10] against the percentage of liberal votes the justices cast during

---

10 The scale is arbitrary. The zero point is the mean of all cases, and values are the relative distance above or below the mean.

their careers (re-scaled to range from −0.6 to +0.6 to simplify interpretation). The correlation between expected and actual liberalism is relatively high, with expectations expressed in newspaper editorials explaining about 41 percent of the variance in actual civil liberties liberalism.

President Truman's frustration is understandable—two of his appointees, Fred Vinson and Sherman Minton, voted much more conservatively than expected (see Figure 15.9). This analysis also reveals two Republican appointees, Souter and Stevens, who were more liberal than expected. Overall, however, justices generally vote as the presidents who appointed them might have predicted. For example, the three most conservative justices—Scalia, Thomas, and Alito, appointed by Republican presidents in hopes of moving the Court in a more conservative direction—have voted as expected. The first few votes cast by Justice Gorsuch, Scalia's replacement, have aligned most closely with Thomas and Alito. Similarly, the four current Democratic appointees—Sotomayor, Kagan, Ginsburg, and Breyer—have established moderately liberal records, and the justices from the Warren Court expected to be most liberal—Fortas and Marshall—voted as expected.

Partisan differences also show up in the behavior of lower federal court judges. Political scientists have found evidence that Democratic judges are more likely to make liberal decisions than are Republican judges (Carp, Stidham, and Manning 2004, 158–163).

Interest groups trying to advance their interests through the judicial process have become increasingly common in recent decades. Political scientists Gregory Caldeira and John Wright (1990, 783) find that the Court is open to a wide range of interests, and the Court's continued willingness to permit this participation is "tacit recognition that most matters before the justices have vast social, political, and economic ramifications." As discussed in Chapter 6, interest groups attempt to influence judicial decision making by filing amicus curiae briefs—that is, briefs filed by groups that are not actual parties to a case but that have an interest in the outcome. Political scientists have found evidence that amicus curiae briefs present new information not contained in the briefs of the actual parties in the case (i.e., the plaintiff and the defendant). The Court accepts arguments in these amicus curiae briefs fairly often, though not as often as it accepts the actual parties' arguments (Spriggs and Wahlbeck 1997).

JUDICIAL REVIEW IN A DEMOCRATIC SOCIETY

The Constitution is especially vague on the power of federal courts. It calls for judicial power to be exercised by a Supreme Court and lower courts created by Congress, and it sets up some basic jurisdictional guidelines. But the Constitution does not specify exactly what rights and responsibilities are encompassed by the term *judicial power*. The Founders seemed to expect the judiciary to play an important role in the political system, but they provided only a rudimentary sketch of what that role should be.

In *Federalist* Number 78, Alexander Hamilton did indicate that the federal courts would have the power to overturn laws that violated the Constitution. Hamilton argued that neither majorities of the people nor their elected representatives could be trusted to always respect the principles embedded in the Constitution. Hamilton saw the courts as a bulwark against the "turbulence and follies of democracy."

But this view was not universally held, and judicial review is not explicit in the Constitution. Rather, the Supreme Court itself claimed the power to review lower-court decisions, laws, and the actions of elected officials. It is hard to overstate the importance of judicial review to the role of the courts in the American political system. Judicial review means that the judiciary has the power to decide who gets what, when, and how—that is, the judiciary is a policymaking institution in its own right.

Judicial review is based on the recognition that the Constitution is superior to ordinary laws. Article VI established the Constitution as the "supreme law of the land," and all judges and elected officials take an oath to uphold the Constitution. To declare a governmental action unconstitutional and therefore invalid, the court must find that a legislature, an executive, or a judge has done something either prohibited or not authorized by the Constitution.

The power of a court to nullify actions of elected officials poses a greater threat to democracy than the power to invalidate the decisions of lower court judges. Few nations grant courts the power of judicial review as it is exercised in the United States. As a result, American courts have a more prominent role in the political system than do courts in other nations. Sooner or later, most important political conflicts end up in court, and the judicial branch in effect serves as the ultimate umpire to the democratic political process in the United States.

The Origins of Judicial Review

The Supreme Court famously asserted the power of judicial review in the case of *Marbury v. Madison* in 1803. The conflict at the heart of this case was a by-product of the election of 1800, when political power decisively shifted from the Federalists to Jefferson's Democratic-Republicans. Having lost control of both the executive and legislative branches of government, the lame-duck Federalist president, John Adams, and the Federalist Congress rapidly created new judgeships and filled the vacancies with Federalist loyalists. The Federalists hoped to retain significant influence in the third branch of government. Caught in the middle of these machinations was John Marshall, Adams' secretary of state. Not only was it Marshall's job to deliver the official commissions to the new judges who had been appointed and duly confirmed by the Senate, but he had been appointed chief justice of the Supreme Court as well.

The Federalists' attempt to pack the judiciary infuriated incoming president Thomas Jefferson. Once in office, he directed his secretary of state, James Madison, to withhold all the commissions Marshall had not yet delivered. Among these were commissions for 17 justices of the peace in the District of Columbia, one of whom was William Marbury. Without the commission, Marbury could not take his post, so along with several other disappointed Federalist appointees, he filed suit asking the Supreme Court to make Madison discharge his duty and deliver the commissions.

This suit, to put it mildly, put Marshall in a bind. To begin with, he was being asked to rule on his own dereliction of duty.[11] And that was the least of his problems. If he and the other Federalist justices ruled that Marbury was entitled to the commission, Jefferson would simply order Madison not to deliver it, demonstrating that the judiciary could not enforce its mandates. As a Federalist, Marshall favored a strong national government, including a powerful judiciary. Having a Supreme Court decision ignored would undermine this goal. On the other hand, to rule that Marbury had no right to the commission would validate Jefferson's and Madison's claim that the so-called midnight appointments were improper and would undercut the standing of the Federalists who had just taken the bench. In short, either option could disastrously weaken the Court that Marshall had just been appointed to lead.

Marshall's response was a stroke of political genius—and a classic example of strategic behavior predicted by the strategic model. Technically, what Marbury had petitioned the court for was a **writ of mandamus**, a court order requiring a public official to perform an official duty over which he or she has no discretion. Speaking on behalf of a unanimous Federalist Court, Marshall ruled that Marbury had a right to the commission and that the writ of mandamus was indeed the proper remedy to obtain it. But he also argued that the Supreme Court was not the proper tribunal to issue the writ. In making the ruling, Marshall struck down part of the Judiciary Act of 1789 that in effect had granted the Supreme Court the power to issue writs of mandamus in cases under its original jurisdiction.

To understand this legal controversy, it is important to remember that the Supreme Court has both original and appellate jurisdiction. The Constitution gives Congress authority to define the Court's appellate jurisdiction by statute. But the Court's original jurisdiction is specifically spelled out in the Constitution.[12] Because it is defined in the Constitution, the Court's original jurisdiction cannot be changed by statute; instead, changes can be made only by a constitutional amendment. Marshall said that the part of the Judicial Act that gave the Court the power to issue writs of mandamus was unconstitutional because it gave the Court powers of original jurisdiction beyond those set by the Constitution. In this ruling, Marshall claimed the power of judicial review for courts, saying that it is "the providence and duty of the judicial department to say what the law is."

---

11 Marshall probably should have recused himself from hearing this case. *Recuse* is from a Latin word meaning "to refuse." Judges usually refuse to participate in cases in which they have even the appearance of a conflict of interest or bias. Chief Justice Marshall was aware of this practice. He recused himself from participating in the decision in *Martin v. Hunter's Lessee* (1816) because he had appeared as counsel in an earlier phase of the case and had a financial interest in the property.

12 The Supreme Court can exercise original jurisdiction in cases affecting foreign ambassadors and consuls and those in which a state is a party. The Eleventh Amendment altered the provision that allows suits against a state by citizens of another state. This amendment overturned the decision in *Chisholm v. Georgia* (1793) that the Court had accepted and decided under its original jurisdiction.

writ of mandamus A court order requiring a public official to perform an official duty over which he or she has no discretion.

In effect, Marshall was saying that the meaning of the Constitution depends on how judges interpret it. Because the outcome (i.e., that Madison did not have to deliver the commissions) was the one Jefferson wanted, he did not challenge the ruling (Gunther 1980, 9–11), though Jefferson was surely outraged by this blatant judicial power grab.

The ruling had far-reaching effects. It raised the possibility that the Federalists could use the newfound power of judicial review to check the actions of the Democratic-Republican Congress and president. And most crucial of all, it established the power of the courts to declare acts of public officials invalid. *Marbury* did not settle all aspects of judicial review; for example, it was not until seven years later that the Court expanded this power to invalidate state laws. But it firmly planted the precedent, establishing the Court as a political institution of the highest order. The Supreme Court alone has the right to make final decisions about what the Constitution does and does not allow. This power means that the judiciary is a lawmaking institution, not simply a vehicle to resolve legal disputes.

John Marshall was the fourth chief justice. He is the author of the opinion in *Marbury v. Madison* (1803) establishing the power of judicial review. Because of his enormous influence on constitutional law and the development of an independent judiciary, he is generally considered the greatest Supreme Court justice.

© The Granger Collection, New York

Concepts of Judicial Review

How does a judge go about deciding whether a law or an executive order is unconstitutional? What role does the judge think judicial review should play in the political process? How do judges and how should judges interpret the Constitution?

There have been a number of famous answers to such questions. Roughly speaking, there are two primary perspectives on how judges should interpret the Constitution, and these lead to different views on the role of judicial review.

Originalism is the idea that justices should interpret the Constitution in terms of the original intentions of the Founders. This theory assumes that the meaning of the Constitution was fixed at the time of ratification, and the job of justices is to interpret the Constitution in terms of this original intent.

In contrast to the theory of originalism is the theory of the **living Constitution**. This assumes that the Constitution was meant to be a dynamic document whose meaning must account for contemporary social and political context. The basic argument of the living Constitution approach is that using the fixed ideas of a small seventeenth-century elite to decide key constitutional provisions as they relate to, say, freedom of speech or race relations will lead to wildly inappropriate decisions that many would perceive to be contrary to core principles of democracy. Many legal scholars view the living Constitution approach as a practical

originalism The idea that Supreme Court justices should interpret the Constitution in terms of the original intentions of the Framers.

living Constitution The theory that assumes the Constitution was meant to be a dynamic document whose meaning has to account for contemporary social and political context.

approach that helps make the Constitution a meaningful and relevant guide for judicial decision making. Originalist critics, however, argue that the living Constitution approach leads justices down a dangerous path, one where the meaning of key constitutional provisions becomes nothing more or less than the values of the judges making the decision.

Even if a judge concedes that personal values do play a role in judicial decision making, this does not solve the problem of deciding to what extent these values will affect rulings on constitutional issues. Justice Felix Frankfurter was one of the most articulate proponents of the "make law" perspective during the twentieth century, but he also hesitated to substitute his values for those of legislators and executives. For example, in a 1940 decision, *Minersville School District v. Gobitis*, Frankfurter held that a school board could expel students who refused to salute the flag, as required by Pennsylvania state law. Frankfurter argued that courts had no grounds to tell political authorities that they could not use this method to instill patriotism in children. Three years later, the Court overruled *Minersville*, with Frankfurter dissenting. In *West Virginia State Board of Education v. Barnette* (1943), Justice Robert Jackson argued that forcing students to salute the flag interfered with their right of free speech.

In one case, the Supreme Court exercised **judicial restraint**, meaning that it deferred policymaking authority to other branches and levels of government. Restraint is often associated with the originalist perspective. In the other, the Court exercised **judicial activism**, taking a more assertive role in determining public policy through broad constitutional interpretation. Judicial activism is typically associated with the living Constitution perspective. The tension between judicial restraint and judicial activism is an important political issue. Those who favor restraint argue that making law is properly a legislative function and that judges should not use the power of judicial review to legislate from the bench. Advocates of activism argue that legislatures sometimes pass laws that abrogate basic democratic values and constitutional rights. In such cases, the courts have not only the right but also the duty to act.

The power of judicial review introduced tensions over democratic values and the roles of the different branches of government that remain unresolved today. One reason the debate over activism versus restraint is so hard to resolve is that it is a conflict of political ideology rather than judicial philosophy. During the 1950s and 1960s, the Supreme Court led by Chief Justice Earl Warren handed down numerous landmark decisions on racial equality, freedom of speech and religion, rights of criminal defendants, and rights of privacy. Conservatives complained bitterly about liberal, activist judges "legislating" from the bench.

In the nearly half-century since Warren left the Court in 1969, Republican presidents have appointed 14 justices to the Supreme Court compared to four appointed by Democrats. Because conservatives generally advocate an originalist perspective, one might expect the Supreme Court to have exercised restraint. Yet the Court has remained activist, and it too has "thwarted the will of the majority." In *City of Boerne v. Flores* (1997), for example, it struck down the Religious Freedom Restoration Act, which passed both houses of Congress with only three dissenting votes. And in *Citizens United v. Federal Election Commission* (2010),

judicial restraint A view of Supreme Court decision making that calls for the Court to defer policymaking to the other branches of government.

judicial activism A view of Supreme Court decision making that calls for the Court to take an active role in policymaking through its interpretation of the Constitution.

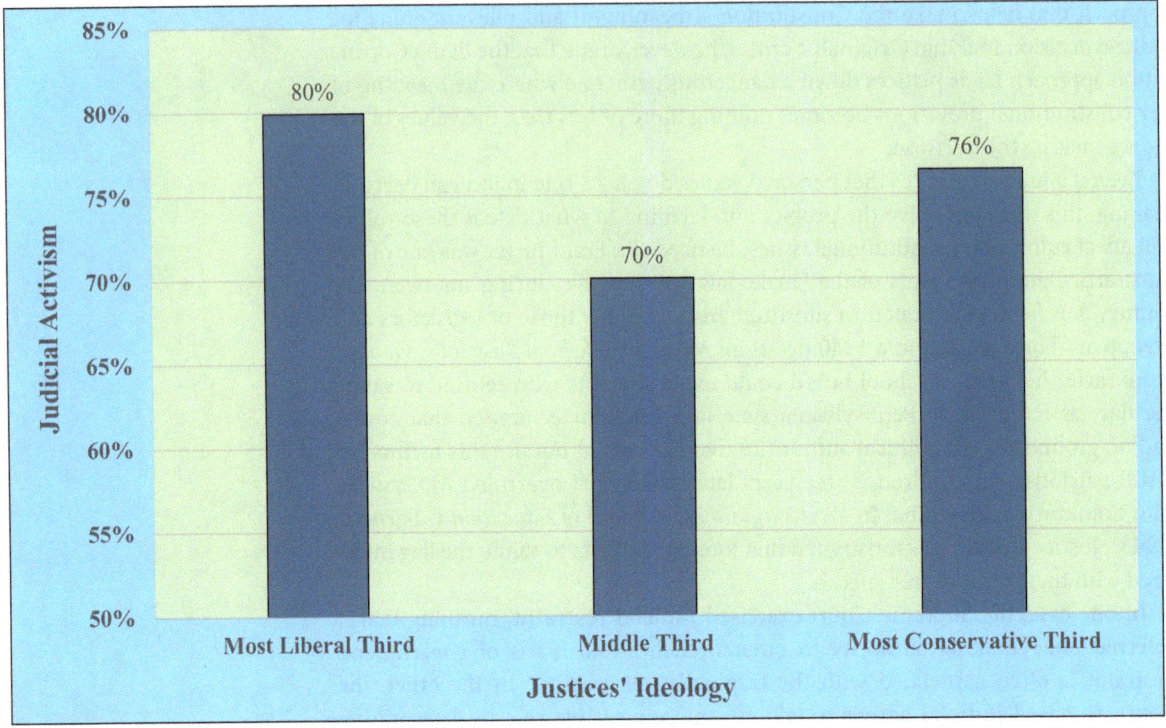

FIGURE 15.10 Supreme Court Justice's Ideological Extremism and Judicial Activism

Source: Data from Epstein et al. (2012, tables 6.4, 6.7, and 6.8).

a conservative majority struck down a 70-year-old precedent banning corporate and labor contributions to political campaigns. Activism is not a trait of a liberal ideology or a living Constitution perspective on constitutional interpretation any more than restraint is solely a trait of conservative ideology and an originalist perspective. Instead, as Figure 15.10 demonstrates, judicial activism tends to be supported by conservatives when it advances their ideological preferences and by liberals when it advances theirs; it is moderates who are more likely to exercise judicial restraint.

Patterns in the Exercise of Judicial Review

For the most part, the Supreme Court has exercised considerable restraint in the use of judicial review. The Court has struck down fewer than 200 federal laws and about 1,300 state laws, a tiny fraction of hundreds of thousands of laws passed in more than two centuries.[13]

---

[13] All state and federal judges take an oath to uphold the Constitution, so all courts have the power of judicial review. We focus on the Supreme Court because it has the most definitive say about what is constitutional.

The Supreme Court's use of judicial review has varied over the years. During some periods, the Court rarely used the power. For example, after *Marbury v. Madison* (1803), more than 50 years passed before the Supreme Court declared another federal law unconstitutional in *Dred Scott v. Sanford* (1857). In other periods of history, the Court has been much more active in its use of judicial review. In the two years from 1934 to 1936, for example, it declared 13 New Deal laws unconstitutional. The Court was more restrained in the 1940s and 1950s and then became more activist in the 1960s and 1970s (see Figure 15.11).

The issues of concern to the Supreme Court have also changed over the years. Subject matter naturally varies from case to case, but different themes have occupied the Supreme Court's attention in different eras of constitutional history. The issues have reflected both the major problems of American society at the time and the justices' own conceptions of the values they should protect through the power of judicial review.

The major issue facing the Supreme Court between 1789 and the Civil War was the relationship between the nation and the states. John Marshall, who was chief justice for much of this era, provided judicial support for a strong national government. The constitutional justification for the federal government's expansion during this time was a broad interpretation of the interstate commerce power and the "necessary and proper" clause. At the same time, state activities that restricted

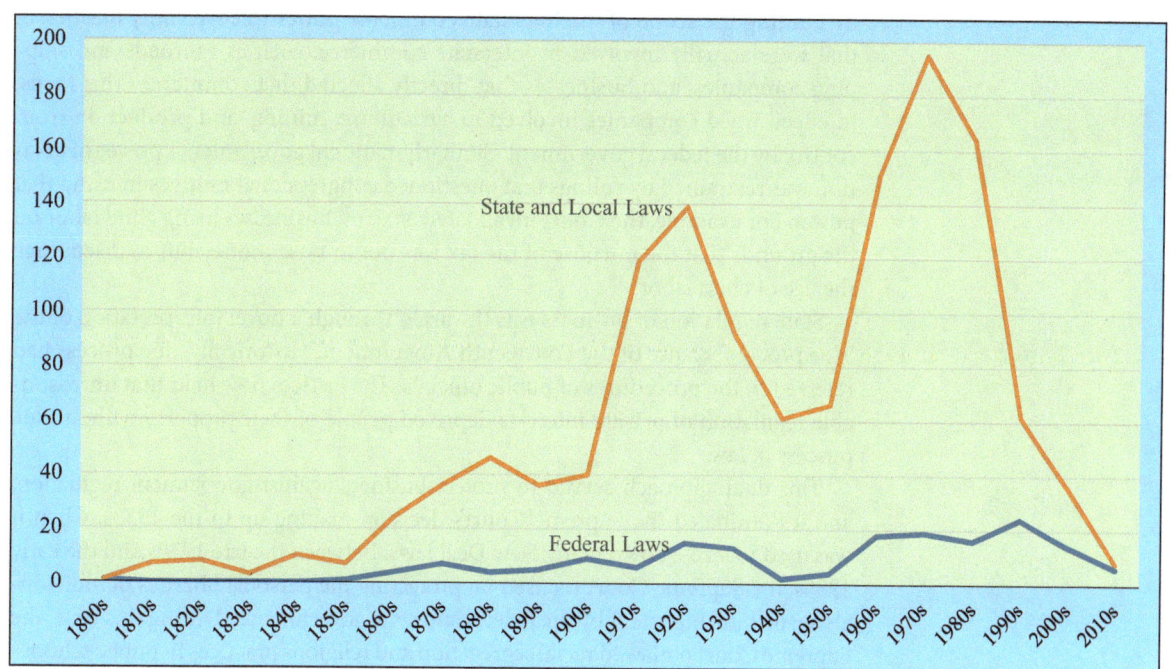

FIGURE 15.11 Federal and State Laws Declared Unconstitutional

Source: Adapted from Stanley and Niemi (2013, 289).

the powers of the national government were invalidated. Toward the end of this era, Roger Taney was appointed Chief Justice, and under his leadership the Court moderated its stand on the nation–state relationship. For example, it ruled that states could regulate interstate commerce if the regulation concerned local matters and did not affect a subject requiring uniform treatment throughout the United States. As a whole, however, this early era was a time of general support for the nation over the states in constitutional conflicts.

The pre-Civil War period was also characterized by judicial protection of private property. In fact, there was a connection between the nation–states and property rights issues. For the most part, the federal government was promoting business and commercial interests, whereas the states were more involved in trying to regulate them. Thus, judicial support for a strong national government that dominated the states also favored commercial interests. The exceptions tended to prove this rule. For example, Taney's decision in the *Dred Scott* case invalidated Congress's attempt to abolish slavery in the territories but showed Taney's solicitude for property owners—in this case, large landowners in the South.

The Civil War settled many nation–states issues, and the courts became preoccupied with the issues of business–government relations. Unlike the earlier era, however, both the national government and the states began regulating burgeoning industrial empires. Consequently, the justices did not need to favor one level of government over the other in order to accomplish the goal of protecting business against what they viewed as improper governmental interference.

The Supreme Court frustrated the national government's control of industry by limiting the scope of the interstate commerce power to cover only businesses that were actually involved in interstate commerce, such as railroads and shipping companies, and businesses that directly affected that commerce. This focus, in effect, freed companies involved in agriculture, mining, and production from control by the federal government. Similarly, national government's power of taxation was restrained by rulings that questioned congressional motives in using that power. For example, the Court invalidated a tax on businesses using child labor on the grounds that the purpose of the tax was not to raise money but to discourage the use of child labor.

State regulation of business was thwarted through a novel interpretation of the "due process" clause of the Fourteenth Amendment. Historically, due process had referred to the procedures of public officials. The justices now held that unreasonable regulation of private interests deprived people of their property without due process of law.

This dual approach served to protect business against government regulation, and it dominated the Supreme Court's decision making up to the 1930s, when it was used to strike down many New Deal laws. Between the late 1930s and the early 1980s, the Supreme Court focused on protecting the personal liberties of individuals against infringement by the federal and state governments. During this time, the Supreme Court outlawed racial segregation and religious practices in public schools, provided constitutional protection for the choice to have an abortion, and significantly expanded the protections of the First, Fourth, Fifth, Sixth, Eighth, and Fourteenth Amendments (these issues are covered in more depth in Chapters 4 and 5).

Conservatives strenuously opposed these liberal rulings, and Republican presidential candidates promised to appoint conservative justices who would exercise greater restraint. By 2008, Republican presidents had appointed seven of the nine Supreme Court justices. With the Supreme Court dominated by appointments from Republican presidents, a new conservative era on the Supreme Court was a reasonable expectation. To some extent, this expectation has been met. From the late 1980s on, the Supreme Court has shifted focus, but in a relatively limited way that has sometimes disappointed conservatives. Court rulings generally reflected the conservative backgrounds of the justices, but there was consistent support for liberal outcomes in civil liberties cases. In other words, the Supreme Court has been more likely to affirm than overturn the expansion of rights and liberties granted in earlier rulings (Lee, Sandstrum, and Weisert 1996). Two Republican appointees, Souter and Stevens, consistently joined with President Clinton's appointees, Ginsberg and Breyer, to form a liberal bloc. When Souter and Stevens retired, President Obama replaced them with Sonia Sotomayor and Elena Kagan, who have voted much the same to keep the liberal bloc intact (see Figure 15.9). The final Republican appointee, Kennedy, has established a record as a moderate conservative, and he sided with the liberal bloc on a number of cases. Rather than a solidly conservative court, the Court was deeply divided—the number of 5–4 decisions increased. The conservative side usually prevails, though there are important exceptions. In *Obergefell v. Hodges* (2015), a 5–4 majority held that same-sex couples had a constitutional right to marry, and all states must recognize same-sex marriages granted in other states. Justice Kennedy authored the majority opinion, joined by the four Democratic appointees—Ginsburg, Breyer, Sotomayor, and Kagan. But in a 2012 ruling upholding the constitutionality of key parts of the healthcare reform law (*National Federation of Independent Business v. Sebelius*), it was Chief Justice Roberts, usually a reliable conservative vote, who found a way to interpret the law to uphold the constitutionality of the individual mandate requiring everyone to have health insurance.

Constraints on the Exercise of Judicial Review

Giving unelected judges life tenure and the power to block actions of popularly elected branches of government challenges the basic democratic values of majority rule and popular sovereignty. Frequent exercise of judicial review would pose a significant threat to democracy. But the limited exercise of judicial review suggests that there are constraints on its use. Several mechanisms keep the Court from straying far from the popular will for too long.

Impeachment

Federal judges are subject to removal through the impeachment process. As discussed in Chapter 12, impeachment by the House and removal by a two-thirds vote in the Senate is both a legal and a political process. Article II, Section 4 of the Constitution establishes the grounds for impeachment and removal as "treason, bribery, or other high crimes and misdemeanors." Although political considerations inevitably come into play, Congress is unlikely to impeach judges without evidence of wrongdoing serious enough to merit impeachment. Yet if judges were to use the power of judicial review frequently and irresponsibly, Congress would scrutinize the judge's record and find grounds for impeachment and removal. Congress is the sole authority in impeachment, and these decisions are not subject to review by the courts.

Removal through impeachment is an extreme and infrequently used tool. No Supreme Court justice has been removed through the impeachment process. The House impeached one, Samuel Chase, in 1804, but he was acquitted in the Senate. That impeachment was politically motivated; Chase was a strong Federalist who behaved obnoxiously toward the Jeffersonian Democratic-Republicans in control of Congress. Although he remained on the Court until his death in 1811, he served with more contrition (Abraham 1993, 44). A total of 14 federal judges have been impeached, most as a result of allegations of corruption. Two impeached judges resigned before their trials in the Senate. Of the 12 who went on trial in the Senate, seven were removed. Most recent was in 2010, when Federal District Judge G. Thomas Porteous, Jr. was impeached and removed for accepting bribes and perjury (Federal Judicial Center n.d.).

Amendments to the Constitution

When the Court exercises judicial review, this review may be based on either legislative or constitutional interpretation. In a decision based on **legislative interpretation**, the Court interprets a statute passed by Congress and rules on the meaning or intent of the disputed section. If Congress disagrees with the Court's legislative interpretation, it can overturn the faulty interpretation by passing another law by a simple majority vote in both chambers. In a **constitutional interpretation**, the Court declares a law unconstitutional based on its interpretation of the Constitution. A constitutional interpretation cannot be overturned by a simple statute. But if the Court's interpretation of the meaning of the Constitution is contrary to the strongly held views of most Americans, the Constitution can be amended.

As discussed in Chapter 2, amending the Constitution is cumbersome and difficult. Nonetheless, seven of the 27 amendments overturned unpopular judicial interpretations of the Constitution. Four of these reversed rulings that had declared federal laws unconstitutional:

- The Thirteenth Amendment prohibiting slavery and the Fourteenth Amendment giving African Americans rights of citizenship overturned *Dred Scott v. Sanford* (1857).
- The Sixteenth Amendment overturned the Court's decision in *Pollock v. Farmers' Loan and Trust* (1895) that declared an income tax unconstitutional.
- The Twenty-Sixth Amendment lowering the voting age to 18 overturned *Oregon v. Mitchell* (1970), in which the Court struck down part of the federal law trying to extend voting rights to 18-year-olds by statute.

---

legislative interpretation A ruling of the Supreme Court in which the Court interprets on the meaning and intent of a statute passed by Congress. Congress can overturn a decision based on legislative interpretation by passing another law.

constitutional interpretation A ruling of the Supreme Court that declares a law unconstitutional based on the Court's interpretation of the Constitution. A constitutional interpretation cannot be overturned by a simple statute.

Three others changed practices that the Court had ruled were permitted under the Constitution:

- The Eleventh Amendment giving states immunity from suits in federal court overturned the decision in *Chisholm v. Georgia* (1793).
- The Nineteenth Amendment giving women the right to vote changed the ruling in *Minor v. Happersett* (1875) that held that the Fourteenth Amendment did not give women the right to vote.
- The Twenty-Fourth Amendment prohibiting poll taxes changed Court rulings that interpreted the Constitution to permit these practices.

Appointments

Federal judges have life tenure, but they are mortal. Periodic vacancies are created by death and retirement. On average, a new Supreme Court justice has been appointed about every two years. Only four presidents did not have an opportunity to fill vacancies on the Court. William Henry Harrison and Zachary Taylor died early in their terms, and Congress eliminated a seat that became vacant in 1866 to prevent Andrew Johnson from making the appointment. Jimmy Carter served a full term without getting a chance to appoint a Supreme Court justice. Most presidents get one or more opportunities to fill vacancies on the Supreme Court.

Because presidents and members of Congress are elected to office, their political values are likely to reflect those of society at a particular point in time. Presidents appoint individuals to the Court who share their political values, and the Senate is not likely to confirm individuals with views far out of the mainstream. Thus, through normal attrition, vacancies are filled with justices who better reflect contemporary views, and judicial interpretations of the Constitution are not likely to be greatly out of tune with the mainstream of American thought for too long.

There have been occasions, however, when the values represented on the Court have lagged behind contemporary thinking. Franklin Roosevelt, for example, was frustrated during his first term when the Supreme Court blocked his New Deal legislation. Justices serve life terms, and the salaries of sitting justices cannot be cut while they are in office. Congress and the president, however, don't have to sit idly by waiting for vacancy to open up. The Constitution leaves it to Congress to decide the number of seats on the Supreme Court. By passing a statute expanding the number of seats on the Court, Congress could give a president some vacant seats to fill. Indeed, this was the basis of President Roosevelt's "court-packing plan" of 1937. Roosevelt proposed legislation that would create one new justice for every Supreme Court member who had reached the age of 70 and had not retired. This court-packing proposal provoked a storm of protest and was defeated in Congress. But the threat may have triggered some change. Justice Owen Roberts, who had generally been aligned with four other justices who consistently voted to invalidate social and economic legislation, shifted sides and began voting to uphold these new laws. This shift—popularly known as the "switch in time that saved nine"—and a retirement in 1937 eliminated

Roosevelt's political need to expand the Court.[14] Nonetheless, Congress has the power to give the president new seats to fill if the Court's exercise of judicial review comes to be viewed as illegitimate.

Control of the Court's Appellate Jurisdiction

As discussed earlier, Congress sets the Supreme Court's appellate jurisdiction by statute. Since almost all cases in which the Court exercises judicial review come under its appellate jurisdiction, Congress can restrain the Court by altering its appellate jurisdiction. Following the outbreak of the Civil War, Congress passed legislation taking away the Supreme Court's appellate jurisdiction in certain habeas corpus proceedings—that is, a court order requiring government officials to bring a person being detained to court to determine whether the detention is lawful. Although members of Congress have introduced bills intended to reduce the Court's jurisdiction in response to a number of controversial rulings, efforts to restrict the Court's appellate jurisdiction usually fail. Even members of Congress who disagree with the Court's ruling may vote against such legislation because they believe the Court has the legitimate right to make the ruling. Yet if the Court strikes down too many laws favored by the majority, members of Congress could come to view the Court's exercise of judicial review as illegitimate and pass legislation restricting its appellate jurisdiction.

No Power to Initiate Policymaking

Courts are most definitely policymaking institutions, because they make authoritative decisions about who gets what, when, and how. The language and the process through which courts make policy, however, differ from the way legislatures, executives, and bureaucrats make policy.

Among the most important procedural differences between judicial and other types of policymaking is that courts cannot initiate the policymaking process. If a member of Congress sees the need for a new policy, he or she can start the process by introducing a bill that frames the issue in a particular way. The president and federal bureaucrats can propose policy changes. Courts, by contrast, must wait for others to bring cases to them. It is the parties to the case who frame the issues posed to the Court. Moreover, the rules of the judicial process require cases to involve real people who have suffered real and substantial harm. Persons who cannot show that they have been harmed by some governmental action do not have standing to sue. Although the Court has considerable discretion to choose which cases to hear, it still must choose from among the cases filed and answer the questions posed. Lack of the power of initiative is a significant constraint on judicial policymaking through judicial review.

---

14 Although some accounts attribute Justice Owen Roberts' switch to the court-packing plan, there is evidence that his change of philosophy occurred before the plan was proposed (Cushman 1998).

Lack of Enforcement Power

The Court's exercise of judicial review is further limited because it must rely on other public officials to enforce its decisions. While the first instance of judicial review in *Marbury v. Madison* (1803) was self-enforcing in that it required President Jefferson to do nothing, court decisions typically require public officials in another part of government to take some action. Take the case of school desegregation. In *Brown v. Board of Education* (1954, 1955), the Supreme Court ruled that segregated schools violated the equal protection clause of the Fourteenth Amendment and that the states must desegregate the schools "with all deliberate speed." Yet many parts of the South engaged in a strategy of "massive resistance," and when the school doors opened in the fall of 1956, very little had changed. President Eisenhower called out federal troops in 1957 to enforce the ruling in Little Rock, Arkansas. But it was not until nearly a decade later—when President Lyndon Johnson ordered federal education funds be withheld from schools that were still segregated, an action mandated by the Civil Rights Act of 1964—that significant progress was made toward integrating schools throughout the South.

When the Court declares a law unconstitutional, it is controversial. By definition, the Court is telling representatives of the majority that they cannot do something that the majority wants them to do. Because the Court is generally respected, and its legitimacy is unquestioned, even those who disagree with a decision believe that they are obligated to obey it. Federal and state judges and elected officials take an oath to support the Constitution, so there is considerable voluntary compliance with the Court's decisions, even unpopular ones. Frequent use of judicial review, however, could undermine the Court's legitimacy. The Court can do little if the president, members of Congress, and other public officials decide to ignore its rulings. As Hamilton observed in *Federalist* Number 58, the Court has the power of neither the sword nor the purse—the president is commander in chief of the armed forces, and Congress has the power to appropriate funds. Such considerations led legal scholar Alexander Bickel (1962) to label the judiciary "the least dangerous branch."

Self-Restraint

Finally, perhaps the most common and effective constraint on the exercise of judicial review is the self-restraint of the justices themselves. Judges' legal training teaches—and most of them sincerely believe—that it is not appropriate for them to routinely substitute their own views of good public policy for those of the elected branches of government. Justice Harlan Fiske Stone, who thought the Court was being too activist in *U.S. v. Butler* (1936), wrote,

> The only check on our own exercise of power is our own self-restraint ... Courts are not the only agency of government that must be assumed to have the capacity to govern ... For the removal of unwise laws from the statute books appeal lies not to the courts but to the ballot and to the process of democratic government.

The Court has adopted several self-imposed legal doctrines intended to restrain judicial power. These are the political question doctrine and the doctrines of standing to sue, ripeness, and mootness. The political question doctrine holds that courts do not have jurisdiction over certain issues that fall exclusively under the authority of the political branches (the president and Congress). The Court has modified the boundaries of issues reserved exclusively for other branches. In the case of *Baker v. Carr* (1962), for example, the Court held that federal courts had jurisdiction to hear disputes over reapportionment of congressional districts, a subject long considered a political question to be resolved by elected officials. Nonetheless, issues of foreign affairs and Congress's exclusive control over the impeachment and constitutional amendment processes continue to be beyond the Court's jurisdiction. Standing to sue (discussed previously) limits the Court by defining who can bring a case; the Court will hear cases brought only by someone who has suffered some actual harm. The remaining two doctrines deal with timing. The ripeness doctrine allows the Court to reject cases that are filed too early, before the issues and facts in question have clearly caused some real harm. The mootness doctrine means that the Court will not hear cases that are no longer a real controversy. Although they are sometimes ineffective, these doctrines are self-imposed limits on the Court's power.

CHAPTER FIFTEEN
Top 10 Takeaway Points

1. Most Americans want judges to be independent and to make decisions based on the rule of law rather than on partisan loyalty, ideological prejudice, or political pressure. But an independent judiciary is insulated from certain core democratic values, and Americans also want judges to be accountable for unpopular decisions.

2. The judiciary is a political branch of government. Interpreting the law is an inherently political process, and judges make decisions that authoritatively allocate values.

3. The jurisdiction of the federal courts is defined by the Constitution, by congressional statute, and by the courts themselves. Federal courts have jurisdiction over litigation involving the U.S. Constitution, federal law, treaties, and admiralty and maritime matters. They also have jurisdiction over cases affecting agents of foreign governments, suits that involve a state or U.S. citizen and a foreign citizen or government, and interstate litigation.

4. The most important power of the federal courts is the power of judicial review, which is the authority to review lower-court decisions and to declare

the laws and actions of public officials unconstitutional. This power is not explicitly spelled out in the Constitution but rather was originally claimed by the Supreme Court in *Marbury v. Madison* (1803).

5. The organization and structure of the federal courts is largely determined by Congress. The federal court system, broadly speaking, consists of three tiers: district courts, which are courts of original jurisdiction; U.S. courts of appeals, which have only appellate jurisdiction; and the U.S. Supreme Court, which has both original and appellate jurisdiction and sits at the top of both the federal and state court systems.

6. The Constitution does not specify any qualifications to be a federal judge. It simply mandates the nomination of all federal judges by the president and confirmation by the Senate. Once confirmed, federal judges serve for life.

7. Although there are no formal qualifications, presidents, senators, and the general public expect that federal judges should have legal training. In nominating federal judges, presidents take into account a wide variety of considerations besides legal background. The most important political considerations are party affiliation and political philosophy. Other political considerations that sometimes come into play include geography, religion, ethnicity, gender, and judicial experience and merit.

8. Although judges may strive to be politically neutral and impartial, there are many gray areas of the law, and it is virtually impossible for an individual's background and personal values not to play a role. Given the tenure of federal judges and the importance and wide-ranging effects of their decisions, the political stakes in the selection process are high.

9. The philosophy of judicial restraint emphasizes deferring policymaking authority to other branches and levels of government. Judicial activism promotes a more forceful role in determining public policy through constitutional interpretation. The tension between restraint and activism is a political conflict rather than a philosophical one. Ideologues on the left and the right are more likely than moderates to be activists. Whether liberals or conservatives advocate a philosophy of restraint or activism tends to depend heavily on their ideological preferences on a given issue.

10. Constraints on judicial power include the possibility of impeachment; amendments to the Constitution; turnover on the bench through death or voluntary retirement; Congress's power to set the jurisdiction of federal courts and to determine the number of justices; the Court's inability to initiate policymaking and its reliance on other branches of government to enforce its rulings; and the self-restraint of judges.

CHAPTER FIFTEEN
Key Terms and Cases

attitudinal model, 585
collegial courts, 565
concurring opinion, 569
conference, 567
confirmation process, 577
constitutional interpretation 600
courts of appellate jurisdiction, 561
courts of original jurisdiction, 561
dissenting opinion, 569
en banc, 565
judicial activism, 595
Judicial Conference, 562
judicial power, 559
judicial restraint, 595
judicial review, 561
judiciary, 559
jurisdiction, 560
legal model, 584
legal realist model, 585
legislative interpretation, 600
living Constitution, 594
majority opinion, 569
Marbury v. Madison, 561
originalism, 594
plurality opinion, 569
rule of four, 567
senatorial courtesy, 573
slot machine theory, 584
strategic model, 586
writ of certiorari, 567
writ of mandamus, 593

PART IV
Conclusion

16 CORE DEMOCRATIC PRINCIPLES AND PUBLIC POLICY

KEY QUESTIONS

What is public policy?

What are the key stages of the policy process, and how are decisions made in that process?

Does the American political system manage to uphold the three core democratic principles in the process of policymaking?

© Jacquelyn Martin/AP Photo

SENATOR JON TESTER (D-MT) received a copy of a proposed tax law late on November 29, 2017 and he was not happy. It was not that he disagreed with what was in the proposed law. It was more that he had no idea what was in it. The bill dropped off at his office was 479 pages long and edited in longhand with penmanship so bad that Tester couldn't make head or tails of whole paragraphs. Nonetheless, he was expected to cast a vote on a hugely complex reform of the tax code with far-reaching economic consequences on about an hour's notice. And he was supposed to do this using a document that he literally couldn't read. Tester, to put it mildly, was not amused. He put out a scathing video to express his displeasure that quickly went viral (type "John Tester hilarious reaction" into YouTube's search box if you want to see it for yourself).

The 2017 tax proposal was something of an extreme case, the result of enormous pressure on the majority Republican Party to get something done on taxes and get it done quickly. Lawmakers voting on bills with only a vague notion of their contents, however, happens more often than you might think. This is not because they are sloppy or lazy, it's because they have a lot to do. Crammed onto the congressional calendar in a single week can be everything from budgets to voter registration, immigration to net neutrality. Keeping all that straight and making informed decisions requires processing more information than the average human can handle. While any given Congress may pass only a few hundred laws, it's pretty typical for more than 10,000 bills and resolutions to be introduced. To put that into perspective, assume each one is a modest 15 pages long with 350 words to a page. That works out to more than 52 million words, the rough equivalent of plowing through something the length of this entire textbook every two or three days for two years straight.

Given those sort of numbers, it's easy to see why the average legislator might struggle to balance the several hundred issues clamoring for his or her attention at any one time. It is a major task simply to pare all this down into a manageable list of policy priorities, let alone get any of those priorities passed into law. And don't forget that on any one of those issues the president or party leaders might be pressuring a legislator to vote one way, while key constituencies in the home district might be pushing in a different direction. Focus on any one proposal and you are very likely to find different interests pushing for contradictory and mutually exclusive actions. Approving or rejecting any one of these actions may incur the heated displeasure of its supporters or opponents. If a policy decision actually emerges from this melee, it still has to be implemented, which likely will set off another round of argument and debate. Once it is implemented, someone somewhere will want it changed, and the clamor for government attention will rise again. Making public policy is a messy process, full of conflict and disagreement, and it never ends.

This messy, conflict-ridden, never-ending process of making public policy is also the ultimate test of the democratic process. Indeed, public policymaking can be viewed as a test of how well—or how poorly—core democratic principles are put into practice. Everything we have studied so far plays a part in making public policy—parties and interest groups, elections and legislatures, executives and judges, bureaucracies and the media, the Constitution and federalism, and all the rest of the machinery that makes up the political system.

As such, it is fitting to end this book with a chapter on how all these elements come together to tackle the fundamental undertaking of politics discussed in Chapter 1. The study of public policy, in essence, is the study of how all these elements combine to produce the "authoritative allocation of values" (Easton 1953, 143) or decisions about what we ought to do. Successfully combining all those elements, as Congress amply demonstrates, is a very tough task.

Public policy can be defined as a relatively stable, purposive course of action pursued by government officials or agencies (Anderson 2000, 4). This definition implies several important things about the concept of public policy. First, it implies that public policy is goal-oriented (purposive). In other words, public policies are undertaken to achieve some objective; they are not random or happenstance. In democratic societies, public policies are not the product of the whims or fancies of arbitrary rulers. They are the product of problems, issues, or demands that citizens expect or want the government to address.

Second, what makes public policy "public" is that it represents a goal undertaken by government. Nongovernmental groups also make policy. All businesses, for example, engage in purposive courses of action. Specifically, they systematically and deliberately choose courses of action they believe will result in a profit. Thus, they have sales policies, return policies, and customer policies. Yet these policies are not public policy. The government is the only institution that has the authority to make decisions about who gets what and to use coercion to make those decisions binding on everyone. Public policy is just that: the government's decision about who is getting what.

Finally, this definition implies a time element and a process; public policy is not just an action, but a relatively stable course of action. Public policy is more than a declared intent to do something; it also must involve some action that attempts to achieve the goal expressed or implied in the statement of intent. A campaign promise or even an actual law is a necessary part of a public policymaking process. These represent declarations of intent. However, our definition of public policy requires more. There must be some consistent follow-through to implement and enforce that promise or law.

THE CONCEPT OF PUBLIC POLICY

Public policy is nothing less than the business of translating the promise of democracy into the performance of democracy. Public policy encompasses the demands and expectations that citizens place on government and the government's response to these demands and expectations in the form of laws and public programs. For the political system to be democratic in practice as well as in theory, the core principles must be upheld throughout the entire process that produces the public policy. That process includes citizens and groups making demands on government, government formulating courses of action to respond to those demands, and the substantive response itself.

public policy A relatively stable, purposive course of action pursued by government officials or agencies.

Upholding those core democratic principles is an enormously difficult challenge because the key characteristic of public policymaking is conflict (Cobb and Elder 1983, 82–93). It is extraordinarily rare for the government to be faced with a demand, problem, or issue where there is a clear, universally approved response. Policymaking is easy if everyone knows what they want from government, and government can give everyone everything they want. Such consensus rarely happens.

Instead, public policy typically involves conflict between two or more groups over something they value. This can be something tangible such as budgets, tax cuts, healthcare benefits, or immigration quotas; or it can be intangible and symbolic such as whether individuals have the right to burn the flag. Symbolic policies do not generate less conflict just because they deal with intangibles. Compared to conflicts involving tangible benefits, symbolic policies actually can generate more strife because they often involve fundamental beliefs about what is right and what is wrong (Mooney 2001). Conflict over tangible benefits can often be resolved by splitting the difference—that is, through compromise. It is hard to split the difference on fundamental moral values. Consider the conflict over flag burning: a compromise that says protesters can burn only half the flag will satisfy neither side.

The study of public policy is astonishingly broad. It not only encompasses all of the institutions and processes we have covered in individual chapters in this book;

it also includes all the substantive issues at the heart of policy conflicts: education, welfare, the environment, economic stimulus, and more. The list of issues, large and small, is virtually endless. How is it possible to encompass all of this and come to some general conclusion about whether public policy in the United States reflects the core values of democracy?

THE STAGES OF POLICYMAKING

Political scientists who specialize in the study of public policy often impose order on their vast and sprawling topic by viewing public policymaking as a system made up of four distinct stages:

1. *Agenda setting,* which produces the list of issues and problems the government will pay attention to
2. *Policy formulation and adoption,* wherein the government considers the various alternatives to the issue at hand and formally approves a particular alternative
3. *Policy implementation,* in which the government translates the approved alternative into action
4. *Policy evaluation,* wherein government and nongovernment actors assess the successes and problems of public policies (Ripley 1988, 48–55)

The evaluation stage often leads to calls for changes in public policy, which takes the system back to the agenda-setting stage (see Figure 16.1).

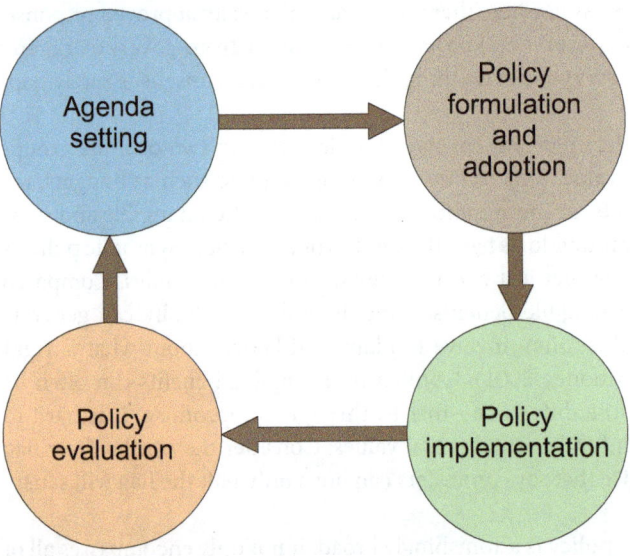

FIGURE 16.1 **Stages of Policymaking**

This stages approach provides us with a systematic way to evaluate how well—or how poorly—the various actors, institutions, and processes we have studied in this book translate the theory of democracy into the practical push-and-pull of making public policy. Once we have a reasonable understanding of this process, we will have a basis for assessing how well it reflects the core democratic values in action.

Agenda Setting

Government cannot attend to all the possible issues, problems, and demands that exist. Somehow a manageable list of issues on which government can focus must be created. This list is known as the **public agenda**, and it consists of the issues and problems that the government is actually paying attention to. But even if an issue or problem makes it to the public agenda, this does not mean a public policy will result. The public agenda is simply a list of topics included in the national debate about what government should (or should not) do at a given point in time.

Political scientists have devoted considerable effort to explaining how and why some policy issues make it onto the public agenda and others do not. The reason for this interest is not hard to fathom; the ability of a political system to deliver on the promise of democracy critically depends on the list of policy issues and alternatives a government actively considers. If the government is paying attention to issues and alternatives that few people support, it seems unlikely that core democratic principles such as majority rule and popular sovereignty are going to be upheld. Connecting the actions of government to the will of the people presumes that the government is considering actions that actually represent the will of the people.

Yet political scientists have long known that no political mechanism—certainly not any form of democracy—can guarantee that government will consider, much less pursue, policies that reflect the will of the people. This surprising conclusion is one of the more important contributions of rational choice theory to an understanding of politics and public policy. **Arrow's impossibility theorem**, formulated by economist Kenneth Arrow (1963), is a formal proof that no decision-making system can guarantee that the rank-ordered preferences of a group will reflect the rank-ordered preferences of the individuals who make up that group. The startling implication of Arrow's theorem for democratic systems is that there is no way they can, for certain, determine exactly what policies people want.

How can this be? Well, imagine that you and two friends want to order ice cream. You have to make a group decision on what flavor to order (only one flavor can be ordered for all three of you). The alternatives on the agenda are strawberry, chocolate, and vanilla. All three of you rank-order those preferences differently; one prefers chocolate to strawberry to vanilla, another vanilla to chocolate to strawberry, and the third strawberry to vanilla to chocolate. There is no single preferred alternative here. So, remembering the core democratic principles of majority rule, you all decide to take a vote on what flavor should be ordered by putting the flavors in direct, one-on-one electoral competition with each other.

public agenda All issues and problems that have the attention of the government at a particular point in time.

Arrow's impossibility theorem A formal proof that no decision-making system can guarantee that the rank-ordered preferences of a group will reflect the rank-ordered preferences of the set of rational individuals who make up that group.

The prestige, power, and visibility of the nation's chief executive give the president unrivaled ability to focus the public opinion and government on a particular set of issues. Here, President Barack Obama signs the healthcare reform bill he strongly advocated. Obama made the healthcare bill a top domestic priority.

© J. Scott Applewhite/AP Photo

Let's say chocolate and strawberry are voted on first. Assuming everyone votes rationally (i.e., to maximize their flavor preferences), in a vote of chocolate against strawberry, chocolate wins because two people prefer it over strawberry. Then you vote on chocolate over vanilla. Vanilla wins because two people prefer it over chocolate. The result of this voting is that the group has decided the following preference for ice cream flavor: vanilla over chocolate over strawberry. That vote, however, is not the will of the people in the group. Why? Well, let's retake the vote, but start by choosing between strawberry and vanilla. Now strawberry wins because two people prefer strawberry over vanilla. See what just happened? The group has the same set of alternatives, but because the choices were presented in a different order—in other words, because the agenda was framed differently—the preferences of the group were reversed by the voting process. Strawberry went from being ranked dead last in the original "flavor referendum" to being ranked first in the next vote. Arrow's theorem, in essence, demonstrates that this inability to aggregate individual preferences into group preferences is common to most mechanisms used to make group decisions. Those mechanisms, as the ice cream example demonstrates, include democratic processes.

An obvious implication of this theorem is that the person setting the agenda can influence group decisions. If you can control which choices are presented to the group (think chocolate over vanilla versus strawberry over vanilla), you can influence the preferred outcome of the group. In short, if you can determine what is on the public agenda, you can influence what policy alternatives government will adopt. Regardless of how an issue is framed, however, getting it on the public agenda does not guarantee a public policy will be made. It is absolutely certain, though, that a policy will never be made if it does not gain the attention of public authorities in the first place. Getting on the public agenda therefore represents the first critical stage in public policymaking. But how is this accomplished? Perhaps more importantly, who gets to set the agenda? And how are topics chosen from among the thousands of possibilities?

Agenda Setters

There are a number of actors both inside and outside the government struggling to get their particular interests and issues on the public agenda, although they have varying abilities to do this. Inside the government, the most powerful agenda setter is the president. The prestige, power, and visibility of the nation's chief executive give the president unrivaled ability to focus public opinion and the government's attention on a particular set of issues.

Close behind the president is Congress. Individual members of Congress cannot command the attention or set the agenda in the same fashion as the president. Yet representatives and senators are in a unique position to influence the public agenda because of the legal authority of Congress (a member of Congress must introduce a specific bill, and majorities in the House and Senate must approve it) and the public nature of the institution (Kingdon 1995, 21–44).

The courts play less of a role in agenda setting because they cannot initiate the process—they can only respond to issues that are litigated. But court decisions do occasionally add topics to the national agenda. For example, abortion policy was being openly debated in only a handful of states until 1973, when the Supreme Court's decision in *Roe v. Wade* (1973) propelled it onto the national agenda, where it has remained for decades. Outside the government, the key forces in agenda setting are interest groups, the media, political parties, elections, and public opinion. Of these, interest groups play the most important role in agenda setting, primarily because they expend considerable effort and resources trying to focus the attention of lawmakers on their interests. As we learned in Chapter 6, interest groups engage in a wide variety of lobbying efforts, all of them directed at gaining access to lawmakers so that their issue will be considered—that is, put on the agenda.

We also saw in Chapter 8 that the media play a powerful role in agenda setting (McCombs and Shaw 1972). The media role in agenda setting, though, differs from that of interest groups. Interest groups bring a sustained effort to a narrow set of interests. In contrast, the media shift focus rapidly. Only a few issues are powerful enough to generate sustained attention from the media. The pressure of a daily news cycle drives constant turnover in the issues that get prominent play in the media.

Theoretical frameworks anchored in rational choice view agenda setting as a competition between these various actors (the president, interest groups, etc.) to strategically frame the agenda so that it favors their policy preferences. For example, if immigration policy is framed as a choice between open borders and preventing potential terrorists from getting into the county, this pushes policy action toward tighter border security and immigration controls. If it is framed as a continuation of the great melting pot, the notion that America is and always has been a nation of immigrants, a place where anyone, regardless of color or creed, can pursue their dreams simply by committing to a shared set of values, this pushes policy action toward more progressive immigration policies.

Garbage Can Models of Agenda Setting

Other theories of agenda setting rely less on rational choice and more on behavioral theories. One of the best known of these social-psychological approaches to explaining agenda setting is a so-called garbage can model, formulated by John Kingdon (1995).

Garbage can models were originally formulated by a trio of researchers seeking to explain why decision making in large complex institutions (they originally

garbage can model A model that attempts to explain why decision making in large complex institutions often seems irrational.

examined universities) seemed so, well, irrational (M. Cohen, March, and Olsen 1972). They called such systems "organized anarchies." In organized anarchies, decision making is not the product of a rational cost–benefit calculation based on a clearly defined problem with a clear set of preferred outcomes. Instead, preferences are unclear, and solutions and problems are viewed as the product of independent processes. Organized anarchies produce a lot of solutions that are not particularly well suited to any pressing problem of the moment, and these are tossed into the metaphorical garbage can. Many problems never gain the attention of decision makers, and these also get tossed into the garbage can. These garbage cans, jumbles of problems and solutions, become useful when they happen to mix together a useful—or at least handy—solution to a problem that does gain the attention of decision makers. This mixing, called a "choice opportunity" in the jargon of the garbage can model, is used to emphasize the difference from rational choice models. Rather than maximizing preferences, decision makers rake through the "garbage" to see if they can find a solution that will connect to the problem they are paying attention to.

Kingdon (1995) saw a similar garbage can process at work in agenda setting in the U.S. political system. For example, consider the domestic production of corn-based ethanol as a solution. Toss it in the garbage can. Then say government gets concerned about the rising cost of gasoline (a problem); ethanol production can be fished out of the garbage can as a way to make us less dependent on oil imports (a solution). Say government is concerned about the environment (a problem); then ethanol can be pitched as a carbon-neutral fuel (a solution). If government is concerned about a sagging agricultural sector (a problem), corn-based ethanol might be seen as a basis for a good cash crop (a solution). If government is now concerned about unemployment (a problem), new ethanol plants might be pitched as a source of new jobs (a solution). You get the idea—the solution here is not necessarily the result of a rational analysis of the problem; it is something in the garbage can that policymakers can "find" whenever a range of problems present themselves.

For any of this "finding" to happen, of course, policymakers must be paying attention to the problem. Kingdon sought to systematically explain exactly how this happens.

Choosing Issues

In Kingdon's model, gaining a place on the public agenda means gaining the collective interest of policymakers. As a general rule of thumb, policymakers tend to focus on problems that they believe demand some sort of response or action on their part. This sort of focus is created when the various agenda-setting forces combine and produce one or more of the following: indicators, focusing events, and feedback.

Indicators are any measures that can be employed as systematic monitoring devices. A classic example is money. If gas prices spike, for example, the media pay attention, public opinion is aroused, sales of gas guzzlers fall, and policymakers are forced to pay attention to energy policy. Indicators are important because they send signals that a problem exists and that the government is expected to do something.

---

indicators Any measures that can be employed as systematic monitoring devices.

A **focusing event** is something that grabs attention immediately and puts an issue on the public agenda. The terrorist attacks on the World Trade Center on September 11, 2001, and Hurricane Harvey in 2017 are two classic examples. A similar example is the June 17, 2015, mass murder of nine black worshipers at Charleston, South Carolina's Emanuel African Methodist Episcopal Church, a black church with a long history of community organization for civil rights. A website belonging to the shooter, 21-year-old Dylann Roof, included photographs showing him with emblems associated with white supremacy, including the Confederate battle flag. After the shootings, the U.S. and South Carolina flags on the South Carolina Capitol building were lowered to half-staff out of respect for the victims, but in accordance with state law, the Confederate flag flying over the Capitol grounds was not lowered. This image triggered a national debate over whether the flag was a symbol of racism or of Southern heritage. Following sustained media coverage, Governor Nikki Haley (R-SC) reversed her position and called for the Confederate flag to be taken down. The legislature moved quickly to change the law. Less than a month after the shooting, the flag no longer flew over the State Capitol.

Feedback consists of the information policymakers routinely receive through government reports, hearings, the news, casework, meetings with lobbyists and government officials, and contact with constituents. Much of this information is unlikely to push an issue onto the public agenda. An irate constituent complaining about taxes, for example, does not suggest a major problem; that is simply a normal part of the background noise of a democratic political system.

Feedback helps select an issue for the public agenda when it signals that something is seriously different from how policymakers expect it to be. For example, feedback from constituents and military officials that U.S. troops were buying their own body armor because of army shortages prompted congressional focus on what, until then, had been a backwater military logistical issue (Lenz 2004).

Policy Formulation and Adoption

Once a problem or issue has the focused attention of policymakers, the policy process shifts to the **policy formulation and adoption** stage. Here the government considers various alternatives to the issue or problem at hand and works to formally approve one of those alternatives. The alternatives now under consideration are those that are on an institutional agenda. In contrast to the public agenda, which includes all the issues that are part of the broad public debate about what the government should do, an **institutional agenda** is a short list of actionable items being given serious consideration by policymaking institutions (Theodoulou 1995, 87).

Once elevated to the institutional agenda, the policy problem shifts from one of deciding what issues to address to one of choosing among the competing alternatives. Again, making this choice represents a significant challenge for government. An issue's placement on the institutional agenda does not automatically suggest a solution (F. Baumgartner and Jones 1993, 28). Poor educational performance, for

focusing event Something that grabs attention immediately and puts an issue on the public agenda.

feedback The information policymakers routinely receive through government reports, hearings, the news, casework, meetings with lobbyists and government officials, and contact with constituents.

policy formulation and adoption The stage in the policymaking process in which government considers various alternatives to the issue or problem at hand and formally approves one of those alternatives.

institutional agenda A short list of actionable items being given serious consideration by policymaking institutions.

The Confederate battle flag at full-staff on the South Carolina Capitol grounds. The mass murder of nine African Americans by a white gunman in the state focused attention on the issue of racist symbols in the South.

© Sean Rayford/Stringer/Getty Images

example, is a policy problem that has a near-permanent place on the institutional agendas of state and national governments. The range of possible responses to this problem includes more funding, tougher standards, a voucher system, and reform of teacher education. Each alternative has its champions and detractors. What alternative, or set of alternatives, should be chosen?

The garbage can model suggests that choices are a product of independently produced solutions and problems joining together at a particular point in time. Other decision-making models, however, not only suggest that there is more of an element of rational thought involved in making public policy; they actually prescribe how such rational decisions should be made. There are two general models of how rational decision makers should sort through policy alternatives and select the most appropriate response to the issue at hand. The first is based on classical rational choice theory and is known as **rational-comprehensive decision making**. In this model, a decision maker develops a comprehensive list of alternatives to the problem or issue, assesses the costs and benefits of each alternative, and then chooses the alternative that most effectively solves the problem or achieves the desired goal at the lowest cost (Chandler and Plano 1988, 127–131). The big advantage of the rational-comprehensive approach to policy formulation and adoption is that it considers all alternatives and is thus likely to hit on a policy that works to solve the problem at minimal cost. The big drawback is that it is not very practical. It assumes that policymakers have compatible objectives and complete information about the consequences of every potential alternative to achieving those objectives. This is very rarely the case. Policymakers often have different objectives for any given issue or policy problem, and they do not know all the possible consequences of every potential action. Even if they did, a comprehensive policy evaluation is enormously time-consuming; if the problem is to put out a raging forest fire, there is no time to collect and analyze information about all possible alternatives before the fire destroys the entire forest.

It is more practical for policymakers to engage in incremental decision making. **Incrementalism** describes an approach to the search for policy alternatives that involves looking at how similar problems or issues have been handled in the past, identifying a handful of alternative approaches to that issue or problem that are politically and financially feasible, and choosing the one that is the most "doable." Political scientist Charles Lindblom (1959) famously called this "the science of muddling through." Incrementalism reflects bounded rationality in action. As discussed in Chapter 14, bounded rationality views humans as imperfectly rational.

rational-comprehensive decision making A decision-making approach characterized by consideration of all alternatives to a problem or issue, an analysis of the costs and benefits of each alternative, and selection of the alternative with the most benefits at the least cost.

incrementalism A decision-making approach characterized by making current decisions that are small adjustments to past decisions.

Their ability to make rational decisions is "bounded," or constrained, by lack of information. Rather than search through all possible solutions to find the one that maximizes utility, a boundedly rational decision maker selects the first solution that is "good enough"—in other words, one that works (Simon 1947). As a practical matter, then, decision makers typically begin with what worked last time and expand their search from there in small steps until they hit on something that looks like it will solve the problem. The classic example of incremental decision making is budgeting. Federal and state government budgets are massive and complex—if policymakers started every budgeting cycle from scratch and went through a rational cost–benefit analysis for every dollar of planned spending, they would do little else. For example, suppose that Congress worked 365 days a year, seven days a week, and managed to consider all potential alternatives for spending every dollar, and they still justified and approved $1 billion in expenditures per day. At that rate, it would take them about a decade to generate an annual budget of a bit less than $4 trillion, which is roughly what annual federal budgets are running these days. The result would certainly be comprehensive but ultimately not very rational. The more practical alternative is to start with last year's budget and adjust it up or down to fit current circumstances or priorities. That's incrementalism and that's pretty much what you see with the federal budget, with each year being a minor adjustment up (or less often down) from the previous year (see Figure 16.2).

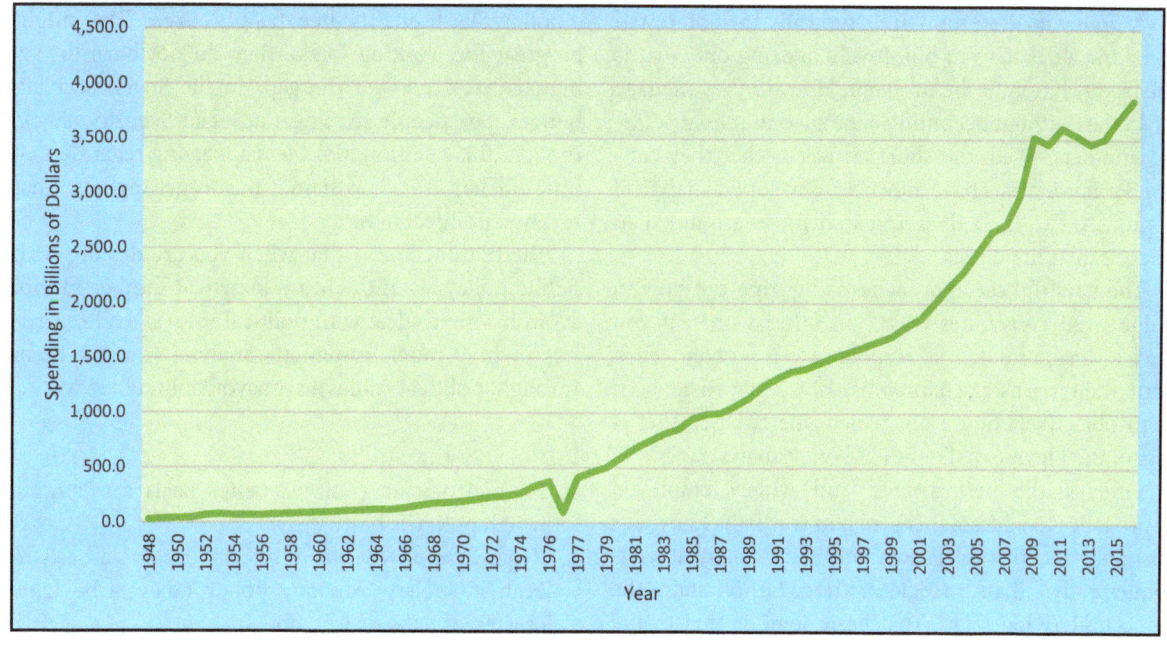

FIGURE 16.2 Federal Government Spending, 1948–2016

Source: Data from Office of Management and Budget (2017). "Historical Tables," https://www.whitehouse.gov/omb/historical-tables/.

THINKING ANALYTICALLY

THINKING LIKE A POLICY ANALYST

Policy analysts are basically professional analytical thinkers. Regardless of what policy issue they are grappling with, their task is centered on answering the same generic research question: What should we do?

This is because policy analysis is all about trying to figure out the best way to address a problem. Governments have to deal with all sorts of problems: How can we stimulate the economy? How can we make Social Security solvent for the long term? How can we fashion a fair immigration policy? While these problems are substantively different, they are all things that government are expected to do something about. What, though? What exact action should the government take to best address the problem?

There are multiple contradictory answers to these sorts of questions. Liberals will favor one thing, conservatives another. Partisans and stakeholder groups vigorously compete to make sure government action (or inaction) reflects their preferences. That's just democratic politics in action.

A policy analyst, though, is typically less interested in taking sides than in objectively figuring out what is the best solution to the problem. How do they manage to do that without becoming entangled in messy political conflicts? Well, the short answer is that they cannot. Policy analysts have, however, developed analytical approaches to keep their research more grounded in science than in politics.

The key to these approaches is figuring out how to judge what constitutes "best." In other words, if you have a range of potential responses to a problem, each with their partisan champions, how do you at least semi-objectively figure out which one is best? That is one of the biggest challenges of policy analysis.

One of the best known and widely employed approaches to address this problem is what is known as cost analysis. This refers to a family of analytical techniques rather than a single method, but all share the same underlying logic. That basic logic is tied to the concept of efficiency, which in very simplified terms can be thought of as "bang for the buck." Cost analysis views the best solution as the action that will produce the most of a desirable output for the least input. If this sounds like it's an application of generic rational choice thinking, kudos to you, because that's pretty much what it is.

Using the cost analysis approach, a policy analyst will look at a wide range of potential responses to a problem and systematically compare those solutions on the basis of efficiency. The most efficient solution is judged to be best, i.e., the action that does the most to address the target problem while promoting the public good.

The big problem with cost analysis is the concept it is using to judge what solution is best—efficiency. Is the efficient solution really always the best solution? Note that efficiency doesn't say anything about equity. It is quite possible for a highly efficient solution to result in big winners and big losers. An efficient solution to Social Security's long-term solvency problem might be a policy that limits the benefits of retirees. That might be great for working folks—they do not have to pay higher taxes to cover the gaps in the Social Security budget. For people living on a Social Security check, though, this solution looks less appealing regardless of how efficient it is. For them it means getting less. That means a political fight.

The bottom line is that when you are dealing with public policy, even the most analytical thinker cannot avoid having to deal with political values. And regardless of how much systematic analysis you put them through, political values are unavoidably subjective.

Discussion Questions

1. Is efficiency or equity a better basis for judging which policy is best? Why?
2. Regardless of what value is employed as a basis to evaluate policy, can any policy analysis be truly objective? Why or why not?

The big drawback of the incremental approach is that the cheapest or most effective alternative may not be chosen for the simple reason that it was never considered. The big advantage of the incremental approach is its sheer practicality for policymaking bodies trying to cram lots of issues onto their institutional agendas. The alternatives chosen might be second-best, but for the most part, they work.

Regardless of the particular approach, the actors who are most influential in defining the range of solutions to any given problem are not necessarily the same as those who drive agenda setting. Public opinion, for example, may help set the public agenda, but it rarely gives enough direction to define detailed ways of dealing with an issue or problem. Bureaucrats, on the other hand, have little influence on agenda setting but exercise considerable influence over the selection of policy alternatives (Kingdon 1995).

Bureaucrats are a powerful influence during the formulation and adoption stage of the policy process because of their expertise and their role in the political system. For example, if Congress is considering a law to promote clean water, members almost certainly will seek the input of experts from the Environmental Protection Agency (EPA). Not only will these experts provide important information on the impacts of the various policy alternatives; they also are in a unique position to assess the feasibility of these alternatives. Because they will be responsible for implementing whatever law is passed, EPA bureaucrats are best situated to tell Congress what is, or is not, likely to work.

Some actors remain influential throughout the agenda setting and formulation and adoption stages. Special interest groups, for example, will continue to lobby for their favored alternative. A member of Congress may consider how voting for a particular law will play with public opinion in his or her district. Yet the list of influential actors narrows as policy moves from the agenda-setting stage to the formulation and adoption stage, especially when the government actually moves to the point of selecting and formally approving a particular policy alternative.

The reason there is a limited range of actors at the formal adoption stage is simple: Only government has the power to authoritatively allocate values and make those decisions binding on everyone. Congress can pass a law; the president can issue an executive order; a public agency can approve a rule; a judge can make a ruling or issue a court order. Special interest groups, political parties, the media, and public opinion may influence the official decision makers throughout the process, but these nongovernmental actors do not have the authority to formally make public policy. Whatever influence nongovernmental actors exert at the formal adoption stage is indirect (Kingdon 1995).

Policy Implementation

Laws, executive orders, rules, and judicial decisions are a formal pronouncement of the intent to take purposive action, not the action itself. **Policy implementation** is the process of translating that intent into action (Sabatier and Mazmanian 1980). As the policy process shifts from the selection and adoption stage to the implementation stage, the cast of important policy actors once again gets shuffled.

policy implementation The process of translating government intent into government action.

Bureaucrats become, by far, the most important actors in this stage of the policy process. The reason is simple: Implementation is what public agencies are designed to do (Kerwin 1999).

Public agencies typically face a number of problems in translating the stated intent of the other institutions of government into action: laws with vague goals, laws with multiple or even contradicting goals, and inadequate resources to do the job. And though special interest groups, political parties, and governmental actors such as legislatures and executives play less of a role in implementation, they do not simply disappear from this stage of public policymaking. As the discussion on rulemaking in Chapter 14 highlights, public agencies are often subject to varying degrees of lobbying and political pressure as they go about trying to implement policy decisions.

There is typically a considerable distance between a formal declaration of intent and the action actually taken by government. What happens between formal adoption and action determines to a large extent whether a public policy will achieve its desired objectives. Political scientists have discovered that the success or failure of public policy is often determined by what happens during the implementation stage.

The classic political science study of implementation was undertaken by Jeffrey Pressman and Aaron Wildavsky (1973). This was a case study of a federal policy program aimed at alleviating unemployment in inner-city Oakland. The policy, at least at first glance, had all the ingredients for success: There was a clear goal, there was just one federal agency running the program, the program was amply funded, and there was near-universal agreement that creating jobs in the inner city was a worthy policy goal. But although just about everyone wanted the program to work, it was a miserable failure.

Pressman and Wildavsky concluded that a primary reason for the program's failure was how the implementation process was shaped by the federal system. The city of Oakland is a municipality in the state of California, but this was a federal program using (mostly) federal dollars. There was only one federal agency involved, but there were three levels of government (national, state, and local). As discussed in Chapter 3, the disadvantages of a federal system include a degree of inefficiency and complexity, and these disadvantages are particularly acute in attempts to implement a policy that requires the coordination of different levels of government.

Pressman and Wildavsky found that the multiple levels of government meant that a series of decision points had to be cleared before any action could be taken. In other words, before any money could be spent and before any action could be taken, it had to be approved by the federal, state, and local government units. The need to jump through these hoops had two major implications for implementation: (1) it made action—any action at all—much less likely and (2) it made it difficult to hold any specific unit accountable for any particular action.

To see why implementation is so difficult, consider a hypothetical implementation scenario in which any action to implement a federal policy has to go through 10 decision points at three levels of government (federal, state, and local). In other words, before there is any positive action to achieve the policy's objectives, 10 groups or people have to approve that particular action. In our hypothetical scenario, we will make everything easy (and a little unrealistic) by assuming that all of the people at each of these 10 decision points are more or less in agreement with the policy's goals and the actions that need to be taken in order to achieve them. Making it even easier, we will assume that whatever pressure is being applied from the political system—be it from legislators, public opinion, special interests, or whatever—this pressure is pushing for the same thing.

Surely under these ideal conditions, action will be undertaken and undertaken soon, right? Not necessarily. If the probability that an action is going to be approved is 90 percent at each of these decision points, the overall probability that the action will make it through all 10 stages drops to about 35 percent (this is the product of multiplying 0.9 by 0.9, 10 times). If it takes three days for a decision to be made by each group or person—a pretty reasonable time span if the action has to be carefully considered and meetings have to be scheduled—it will take a month for an action to be approved—that is, if it is approved. Even in ideal circumstances, that is no sure thing.

And if no action is taken, or an action turns out to be ineffective, inefficient, or just plain silly, who should be held accountable? Federal, state, or local authorities? The policy itself? Someone or something else? Could the problem be not enough resources or vague or competing goals? Political pressure to take one particular action over another? All of these can be real obstacles to successful implementation of any single policy. Studying the implementation process leads not just to an understanding of why policies fail but also to an appreciation of the enormous effort that goes into making them work.

Implementation can founder not just on decision points or on practical considerations such as funding; one of the biggest challenges is the nature of the goal or the problem being addressed. A policy to lower noise disturbances in neighborhoods adjacent to a university campus, for example, is much more doable than a policy to safely produce electricity from nuclear power plants. In the first example, the action needed to achieve the goal is clear: Reduce the number of fraternity parties, and you have less noise disturbance. What needs to be changed, whose behavior needs to change, and where they need to change it are all clear. Now consider the second policy. What needs to be changed? Whose behavior needs to be changed? What does it mean for nuclear energy to be "safe"? In this case, it is not clear what actions need to be taken

Public education policies address what many consider intractable problems. Partly because the goals of education policy are so contradictory and so hard to achieve, education policy is being constantly evaluated to assess what outcomes are produced by particular programs and to try and figure out how—or if—things can be done more effectively and efficiently. One formal way to do this is through standardized testing. Much attention has been paid to the results of these tests, but many suggest that they are a more accurate reflection of how well students have been trained to take the tests rather than an accurate reflection of their knowledge base.

© Christine Armario/AP Photo

APPLYING THE FRAMEWORKS

APPLYING THE FRAMEWORKS: THE NUDGE UNIT

Nudge, a 2008 book by economist Richard Thaler and legal scholar Cass Sunstein, argues that you need to understand human nature if you want to get people to make good choices. Strict rational choice theories do not help much with that; they simply assume humans are rational. Behavioral models are not much better. They say little about human nature beyond that we will try to muddle through and do the best we can in whatever circumstance we find ourselves in.

Psychologists working within an evolutionary framework have a lot more to say about human nature and how it relates to decision making. For one thing, they argue that the decision-making machinery of humans is not particularly rational; it's a jury-rigged contraption shaped mostly by evolution.

Evolution, they argue, has left us with not one, but two thinking systems. The first is automatic and rapid. If someone chucks a rock at your noggin, you do not calculate the velocity and mass of said rock and then weigh the pros and cons of evasive action. You duck. That automatic and reflexive response is the first system in action. It was shaped by evolution to make rapid decisions when doing so could mean life or death. That thinking system, though, does more than prevent us getting beaned by rocks. When you just *know* something is good or bad—you have a hunch, a gut feeling—that's this system in action.

The second system is what we'd all recognize as conscious thinking. Evolution designed this system so we could solve more complex problems, especially those related to social life. That doesn't mean, though, that this is our rational thinking system. It certainly can be employed this way, but we often use this system less for detached objective analysis than for trying to find reasons to support the first thinking system's decision. We "know," for example, that a tax reform proposal is good or bad because our first system tells us that. Our second system then goes looking to justify that gut feeling.

These two systems work differently and can conflict with each other. Part of the legacy of this evolutionary architecture is that humans have a lot of not particularly rational biases built into their decision-making patterns. How does this apply to policy? Well, *Nudge* suggests policymakers can take advantage of these biases to get people to behave in ways that support policy goals. For example, how do you get people to pay their taxes on time? One way to nudge people into doing this is to send them letters saying that most of their neighbors have already paid their taxes. The idea is that because of our evolutionary past humans are very susceptible to social pressure, and they are more likely to respond to social pressure than to a more rational appeal of "pay up or you will incur the cost of a fine."

Sounds simple? Maybe, but it works. In 2010 the United Kingdom government set up a specialized agency—the Behavioural Insights Team, also known as "The Nudge Unit"—with the specific task of incorporating these sorts of ideas into policy. The Nudge Unit was so successful it was spun off into an independent public policy consulting company that seeks to translate insights from social science research into improvements in public services (you can check out their website at: http://www.behaviouralinsights.co.uk/). By 2018 this company had offices and teams operating across the globe (including the United States), a success that suggests insights drawn from evolutionary frameworks can indeed improve public policy.

Discussion Questions

1. Some critics of *Nudge* argue its core idea is paternalistic, that it gives governments a guide on how to manipulate behavior. Is that necessarily bad? Public policies often *are* about getting people to make certain choices—pay their taxes, sign up for healthcare, etc. Are governments justified in using "nudge" research to achieve such objectives?
2. These days, behavioral social scientists (including many political scientists) with "nudge" expertise can be found at most major universities. Should state and local governments take advantage of this expertise to set up their own "nudge units"? Why or why not?

or even how to define the goal that is to be achieved. Consequently, successfully addressing that problem is much less likely. Implementation is extraordinarily difficult—maybe even impossible—if overarching policy goals are unlikely to be achieved regardless of what course of action is pursued (Sabatier and Mazmanian 1980).

Policy Evaluation

Despite the difficulties inherent in policy implementation, once a policy is formally approved and adopted, some purposive course of action is likely to be undertaken. A whole range of actors within the political system will be interested in what those actions are and what, if anything, they achieve.

The process of examining the consequences of public policy is known as **policy evaluation**. Policy evaluation is undertaken for any number of reasons. The obvious reason is to assess whether the policy worked. This reason is far from the only one, however. If a policy is not achieving its objectives, we might want to know why. Is it because the problem is simply too complex and the solution difficult to achieve? Was the policy poorly implemented? Starved of resources? Poorly managed? Even if a policy worked and achieved its stated goals, we might still be interested in figuring out whether there is a way to achieve those goals more effectively and efficiently. If the policy goals were achieved effectively and efficiently, we might want to know why in order to apply these lessons to other policy areas.

The various reasons for undertaking a policy evaluation serve the purposes of many different political actors. A special interest group might want to know how effectively a policy is serving its members' needs. The media might be interested in whether a program is wasting taxpayer dollars. The minority party may use evaluations to hold the majority party accountable for its policy failures, just as the majority party may use them to tout its policy successes.

For these reasons, public policies are constantly being evaluated. Evaluation can be done formally or informally and can be undertaken by a wide variety of actors, ranging from the public agency actually taking the actions to the media, interest groups, and academics. These actors all tend to use different approaches and have different goals for undertaking an evaluation, and they can come to very different conclusions about the same program or policy. Despite the wide variety of approaches, though, all policy evaluations can be classified into one of two broad categories: process evaluations and impact evaluations (Theodoulou 1995, 91).

Process evaluations assess whether a policy is being implemented according to its stated guidelines. If the policy is to reduce neighborhood noise by increasing police patrols, reducing response time to neighborhood complaints, and ticketing offenders for first offenses, then a process evaluation would look at the number of police patrols, the response time to noise complaints, and the ratio of tickets to warnings given to first offenders.

Impact evaluations assess policy outcomes. In other words, the goal in an impact evaluation is to see whether the policy has achieved its overall objectives.

policy evaluation The process of examining the consequences of public policy.

process evaluations Evaluations undertaken with the goal of assessing whether a program or policy is being implemented according to its stated guidelines.

impact evaluations Evaluations undertaken to assess the outcomes or effects of a policy or program.

In the preceding example, an impact evaluation would assess whether the actions that are the focus of a process evaluation—increased police patrols, faster response times, and citations for first offenders—actually contribute to a reduction in noise levels. Impact evaluations tend to come after process evaluations because it usually takes some time for a policy or program to produce a measurable change in outcomes. Process evaluations, on the other hand, can provide useful information on whether a policy is being implemented according to its guidelines as soon as the program gets underway.

Regardless of whether they are process or impact evaluations, reviews, reports, and analyses of public policy often lead to calls for change. Public policies that are adopted and implemented and that clearly achieve their stated goals do exist, but they are more the exception than the rule. A decision to build a bridge, for example, might fall into this category. The decision is made, funds are appropriated, plans are laid, contractors are hired, the bridge is built, and process and impact evaluations show an objective achieved in the time and manner expected.

A lot of public policy, however, is aimed at difficult or intractable problems. *Intractable* simply means the problem is complex, caused by many different factors, and hard to address within the confines of any single policy program—or even a whole group of them. Public education is a good example.

As already discussed, the underperformance or even outright failure of public schools is a staple of the public agenda. This is partially due to the intractable nature of the problems that public education policies address. It is hard enough just to define the goals of education policy. What constitutes a "quality education" or "equality of educational opportunity"? How do we know when these goals have been achieved? Some see tough academic standards as an education policy that will increase the quality of public education. Tough academic standards, though, may lead to higher dropout rates. Higher dropout rates may strike some as evidence of the failure of education policies.

Because the goals of education policy are so contradictory and so hard to achieve, education policy is being constantly evaluated to assess what outcomes are produced by particular programs and to figure out how or whether things can be done more effectively and efficiently. These evaluations are formal and informal, and they frequently lead to calls for policy change. Because public education affects so many people and because it consumes so many tax dollars, education issues are quick to get the attention of media, policymakers, special interest groups, and public opinion.

When this happens, evaluations shift the policy process back to the agenda-setting stage. What should we do about underperforming inner-city schools? A whole range of policy evaluations show that school voucher programs have not improved student achievement by much, if at all (Gill et al. 2001; K. Smith 2005). Does this mean vouchers do not work? Or does it mean that, to work, voucher programs should be expanded from relatively small-scale experiments involving small numbers of students? Should we expand the students eligible for vouchers? Scrap the voucher program and move back to neighborhood schools? What about setting tougher standards that will be more likely to increase achievement scores? What about after-school programs? Tougher teacher certification standards?

Evaluations constantly raise such questions, and these questions are inevitably followed by the political conflict that breaks out over the proposed answers.

PUBLIC POLICY AND CORE DEMOCRATIC VALUES

Now that we have some idea of how the various institutions and actors that make up the political system interact to make public policy, let us assess how that process upholds the core principles of democracy. In this final section of the book, we examine each of the core principles and provide an appraisal of how well (or poorly) they are reflected in the policymaking process.

Majority Rule

The first core principle we encountered in Chapter 1 was majority rule. Majority rule simply means that government follows the course of action preferred by most people. Majority rule can be defined (1) in terms of more than half of eligible citizens or voters preferring one particular policy or (2) as a plurality, which means no alternative has more than 50 percent support, but one alternative—the plurality choice—has more support than all the others.

Majority rule has a relatively good record in the policymaking process of the American political system. Large numbers of people express dissatisfaction with the policies of government, mostly saying they want middle-of-the-road government responses to problems. Yet political scientists find that government over the years has pretty consistently adopted a middle-of-the-road stance in making public policy. Americans often seem to be upset at government for giving them what they ask for (Hibbing and Theiss-Morse 2001). There are certainly people—sometimes even majorities—who disagree with specific substantive public policies. And most high-profile policy actions get varying levels of public support as they shift from adoption to implementation to evaluation. The wars in Iraq and Afghanistan, for example, began with high levels of public support that steadily dwindled with the expenditure of blood and treasure and a growing realization that many of the noble and idealistic goals justifying the conflicts were unlikely to be realized. Yet, overall, the evidence suggests that government does a pretty good job in addressing the policy preferences of its citizens. Given how divided public opinion is on most policy matters, an overall record indicating that there exists plurality, if not majority, support for government policies is no small feat.

For the system to remain true to core democratic values, though, majority rule needs to be balanced with minority rights. In this regard, the policymaking process in the United States has a much more mixed record. Historically, some public policies that were adopted and implemented were specifically aimed at robbing minorities of their rights as democratic citizens (for example, Jim Crow laws). Those sorts of egregious violations of minority rights are mostly a thing of the past. This is not to say that minority groups do not still have legitimate concerns. For example, the increasing prevalence of state-mandated voter ID laws raises real concerns about minority representation.

Political Freedom

As we learned in Chapter 1, government cannot respond to the will of the people if people are not free to express their wants and demands. The critical ingredients for this freedom are the right to criticize current governmental leaders and policies, the right to propose new courses of action for government to follow, the right to form and join interest groups, the right to discuss political issues free from government censorship, and the right of all citizens to seek and hold public office.

Of all the core democratic principles, political freedom is probably the easiest to recognize in the American policy process. From agenda setting to evaluation, the government's proposals and actions are discussed, analyzed, and criticized by just about everyone. Most people have an opinion on what the government should (or should not) do, and they are largely free to share that opinion as their means and abilities allow.

American citizens are free to speak in public places, write letters to the editor, contact public officials, join interest groups, circulate petitions, tweet, start a blog, or set up a Facebook page. Virtually all Americans, in short, have an opportunity and a venue to air their political views with little worry of government interference, restriction, or censorship. In some areas (states with ballot initiatives, for example), citizens even have the freedom to take public policy out of the government's hands entirely and make laws themselves. Americans also enjoy a free press and virtually unlimited access to information. Most government policy processes are, by law, transparent, meaning citizens can "see inside" government. In short, American citizens have all the necessary tools to enjoy a high degree of political freedom, and that freedom is widely exercised at every stage of the policy press.

However, as we learned in our discussion of the media in Chapter 8, being free to express an opinion or criticize a policy does not necessarily mean those views will reach their intended audience. If there is a downside to political freedom, it is that in the marketplace of public opinions and ideas, some voices are always going to speak more loudly than others. The danger to political freedom in the policymaking process is not really that minority or dissenting opinions will be silenced. Relatively speaking, the policy process is largely free of censorship of any kind—people are pretty much free to say what they want about the government and what it should do. No, the real danger is that minority or dissenting opinions will not be heard. Just about anyone can put up a website, but that does not mean anyone will actually find and read it.

Political Equality

Chapter 1 pointed out that political equality is the most complex and difficult core principle of democracy because it can take many forms (social equality, economic equality, equality under the law, or equality of opportunity). Essentially, political equality means that individual preferences are given equal weight.

If political freedom is the core democratic principle most readily translated from theory into policymaking practice, political equality provides an interesting contrast. Political equality is the principle the American political system has had the hardest time putting into practice. This difficulty is clearly evident in historical terms, as indicated by our discussion of civil liberties and civil rights in Chapters 4 and 5. For large parts of the republic's history, racial minorities, women, and other minority groups have been legally excluded from the policymaking process altogether.

Although such blatant inequalities are mostly a thing of the past, it is clear that some groups still enjoy more power and influence in the policymaking process. That power and influence translate into political inequality; in other words, the views and preferences of some count for more. The reasons for this are obvious. Economic inequality, for example, means different groups have different levels of influence in the policymaking process. Those with more money or more time or more organization are much better positioned to take advantage of the political freedoms the policymaking process affords. It is much easier (though far from guaranteed) to gain the attention of policymakers if you can underwrite campaign donations and pay for television and newspaper ads.

Chapter 1 also discussed the pluralist ideal of a democracy, where government is used as a means to settle conflicts and reach compromise among competing group interests and where all groups have enough political resources to successfully participate in the political process. In the pluralist ideal, groups are roughly equal, at least in the sense that they have the capability to defend their own interests through the policymaking process.

A number of studies have shown that this pluralist ideal is far from the reality of policymaking. For example, in a wide-ranging study of how policy is made, political scientists Anne Schneider and Helen Ingram (1997, 2005) argue that public policies always have target populations, or groups of people who will either receive benefits or pay costs as a result of a policy decision. Schneider and Ingram found that some groups are consistently viewed as those who deserve to receive the benefits of policy, whereas others are consistently viewed as those who deserve to bear the costs. These differences break down along traditional social fault lines such as race and class. Thus, for example, middle-class, white-collar workers are typically viewed as deserving of policy benefits. Criminals are viewed as deserving of policy costs.

This is important because framing a policy in terms of its target population can have a powerful impact. For example, take the substantive issue of crime. It is no longer acceptable in mainstream American politics to promote policies that are blatantly racist. Yet it is perfectly acceptable to push a tough line on crime. Quick, think of a criminal—what does a criminal look like? For most people, it is a he, and he is a young black male. This group has been targeted as deserving to bear the costs of crime. Don't white people who commit crimes also go to jail? Yes, but not with the same probability. And crimes that are more associated with the middle-class suburbs (for example, use of powdered cocaine) are punished less—and less harshly—than crimes associated more with the inner cities (use of crack cocaine). A celebrity with a drug problem typically goes to rehab; an inner-city youth goes to jail. Crime, some political scientists argue, is a policy shot through with racist undertones all the way from agenda setting to evaluation (Beckett 1997).

There are numerous other substantive policies wherein scholars have found similar inequalities among groups. Tax policy tends to favor the middle class. For example, being able to deduct interest paid on your mortgage is a nice tax benefit—but you get this benefit only if you are a homeowner. State and federal higher-education policies tend to disproportionately favor middle-class students and private colleges rather than public colleges. The latter tend to have higher minority enrollments (Alexander 1998). Inequality is clearly still a fact of the policymaking process.

CONCLUSION

Popular sovereignty requires the policy process to abide by all three core principles of democracy simultaneously. As we have learned throughout this book, that is a tough balancing act; in some cases it is downright impossible. Unsurprisingly, then, the performance of American democracy falls short of its promise. The institutions and processes that make up the policymaking process struggle to put the core principles into practice, especially political equality. Judged by the standards of theoretical perfection, however, it is not just the United States but every democracy that ever existed that falls short. Compared to other democracies, America generally has a worse record on the core principle of political equality, a better record on political freedom, and a roughly similar record on majority rule.

In terms of putting core principles into action and resolving the conflicts that inevitably occur between these principles, America should get reasonably high marks. The American political system has not completely reflected the core principles of democracy and still does not—something that should always be remembered. However, taken as a whole, the American political system has consistently tried to measure itself by those same principles—something that should never be forgotten.

CHAPTER SIXTEEN
Top 10 Takeaway Points

1. Public policy is a relatively stable, purposive course of action undertaken by public authorities. The process of making public policy and the policies themselves

are the ultimate test of how a political system implements the core principles of democracy.

2. The public policy process can be systematically ordered into four stages: agenda setting, policy formulation and adoption, policy implementation, and policy evaluation.

3. Agenda setting is the process of producing the list of issues and problems the government will address. Agenda setting can be viewed as a strategic game among rational actors or as a "garbage can" process where solutions and problems are produced independently and join together only when a particular problem has the focused attention of government.

4. Policy formulation and adoption is the process government undertakes to consider various alternatives to the issue or problem at hand and to formally approve one of those alternatives. Policy adoption can be viewed as a garbage can process in which the independent problems and solutions actually join together, as the result of rational decision making, or as the result of boundedly rational decision making.

5. Policy implementation is the process of attempting to translate the intent expressed in a formally approved policy into action.

6. Policy evaluation is the process of assessing the impact, effectiveness, and problems of a public policy. Policy evaluations often lead back to the agenda-setting stage.

7. With some important exceptions, the American political system has a fairly good record of upholding the core principle of majority rule. Though public opinion is mixed on most policy issues and is generally not positive about government performance, there is actually a high correlation between the policies people say they want from government and the policies government actually adopts and implements.

8. Political freedom is the core principle most easily observed in the policymaking process. Americans are free to express their views, share their opinions, and contact public authorities with relatively little censorship or restrictions.

9. Political equality is the core principle that the American political system has struggled the hardest to translate into practice. Even in the contemporary policymaking process, political scientists find that some groups are favored and others are not.

10. Overall, the American political system gets a mixed report card in its effort to sustain a policy process that is consistent with the core principles of

democracy. Despite some failures and difficulties, however, it is clear that the core principles of democracy—especially the principle of political freedom—remain guiding goals of the American political system.

CHAPTER SIXTEEN
Key Terms and Cases

Arrow's impossibility theorem, 613
feedback, 617
focusing event, 617
garbage can model, 615
impact evaluations, 625
incrementalism, 618
indicators, 616
institutional agenda, 617
policy evaluation, 625
policy formulation and adoption, 617
policy implementation, 621
process evaluations, 625
public agenda, 613
public policy, 612
rational-comprehensive decision making, 618

APPENDIX A

The Declaration of Independence

IN CONGRESS, July 4, 1776.

The unanimous Declaration of the thirteen united States of America, When in the Course of human events, it becomes necessary for one people to dissolve the political bands which have connected them with another, and to assume among the powers of the earth, the separate and equal station to which the Laws of Nature and of Nature's God entitle them, a decent respect to the opinions of mankind requires that they should declare the causes which impel them to the separation.

We hold these truths to be self-evident, that all men are created equal, that they are endowed by their Creator with certain unalienable Rights, that among these are Life, Liberty and the pursuit of Happiness.—That to secure these rights, Governments are instituted among Men, deriving their just powers from the consent of the governed.—That whenever any Form of Government becomes destructive of these ends, it is the Right of the People to alter or to abolish it, and to institute new Government, laying its foundation on such principles and organizing its powers in such form, as to them shall seem most likely to effect their Safety and Happiness. Prudence, indeed, will dictate that Governments long established should not be changed for light and transient causes; and accordingly all experience hath shewn, that mankind are more disposed to suffer, while evils are sufferable, than to right themselves by abolishing the forms to which they are accustomed. But when a long train of abuses and usurpations, pursuing invariably the same Object evinces a design to reduce them under absolute Despotism, it is their right, it is their duty, to throw off such Government, and to provide new Guards for their future security.—Such has been the patient sufferance of these Colonies; and such is now the necessity which constrains them to alter their former Systems of Government. The history of the present King of Great Britain is a history of repeated injuries and usurpations, all having in direct object the establishment of an absolute Tyranny over these States. To prove this, let Facts be submitted to a candid world.

He has refused his Assent to Laws, the most wholesome and necessary for the public good.

He has forbidden his Governors to pass Laws of immediate and pressing importance, unless suspended in their operation till his Assent should be obtained; and when so suspended, he has utterly neglected to attend to them.

He has refused to pass other Laws for the accommodation of large districts of people, unless those people would relinquish the right of Representation in the Legislature, a right inestimable to them and formidable to tyrants only.

He has called together legislative bodies at places unusual, uncomfortable, and distant from the depository of their public Records, for the sole purpose of fatiguing them into compliance with his measures.

He has dissolved Representative Houses repeatedly, for opposing with manly firmness his invasions on the rights of the people.

He has refused for a long time, after such dissolutions, to cause others to be elected; whereby the Legislative powers, incapable of Annihilation, have returned to the People at large for their exercise; the State remaining in the mean time exposed to all the dangers of invasion from without, and convulsions within.

He has endeavoured to prevent the population of these States; for that purpose obstructing the Laws for

Naturalization of Foreigners; refusing to pass others to encourage their migrations hither, and raising the conditions of new Appropriations of Lands.

He has obstructed the Administration of Justice, by refusing his Assent to Laws for establishing Judiciary powers.

He has made Judges dependent on his Will alone, for the tenure of their offices, and the amount and payment of their salaries.

He has erected a multitude of New Offices, and sent hither swarms of Officers to harrass our people, and eat out their substance.

He has kept among us, in times of peace, Standing Armies without the Consent of our legislatures.

He has affected to render the Military independent of and superior to the Civil power.

He has combined with others to subject us to a jurisdiction foreign to our constitution, and unacknowledged by our laws; giving his Assent to their Acts of pretended Legislation:

For Quartering large bodies of armed troops among us:

For protecting them, by a mock Trial, from punishment for any Murders which they should commit on the Inhabitants of these States:

For cutting off our Trade with all parts of the world:

For imposing Taxes on us without our Consent:

For depriving us in many cases, of the benefits of Trial by Jury:

For transporting us beyond Seas to be tried for pretended offences:

For abolishing the free System of English Laws in a neighbouring Province, establishing therein an Arbitrary government, and enlarging its Boundaries so as to render it at once an example and fit instrument for introducing the same absolute rule into these Colonies:

For taking away our Charters, abolishing our most valuable Laws, and altering fundamentally the Forms of our Governments:

For suspending our own Legislatures, and declaring themselves invested with power to legislate for us in all cases whatsoever.

He has abdicated Government here, by declaring us out of his Protection and waging War against us.

He has plundered our seas, ravaged our Coasts, burnt our towns, and destroyed the lives of our people.

He is at this time transporting large Armies of foreign Mercenaries to compleat the works of death, desolation and tyranny, already begun with circumstances of Cruelty & perfidy scarcely paralleled in the most barbarous ages, and totally unworthy of the Head of a civilized nation.

He has constrained our fellow Citizens taken Captive on the high Seas to bear Arms against their Country, to become the executioners of their friends and Brethren, or to fall themselves by their Hands.

He has excited domestic insurrections amongst us, and has endeavoured to bring on the inhabitants of our frontiers, the merciless Indian Savages, whose known rule of warfare, is an undistinguished destruction of all ages, sexes and conditions.

In every stage of these Oppressions We have Petitioned for Redress in the most humble terms: Our repeated Petitions have been answered only by repeated injury. A Prince whose character is thus marked by every act which may define a Tyrant, is unfit to be the ruler of a free people.

Nor have We been wanting in attentions to our British brethren. We have warned them from time to time of attempts by their legislature to extend an unwarrantable jurisdiction over us. We have reminded them of the circumstances of our emigration and settlement here. We have appealed to their native justice and magnanimity, and we have conjured them by the ties of our common kindred to disavow these usurpations, which, would inevitably interrupt our connections and correspondence. They too have been deaf to the voice of justice and of consanguinity. We must, therefore, acquiesce in the necessity, which denounces our Separation, and hold them, as we hold the rest of mankind, Enemies in War, in Peace Friends.

We, therefore, the Representatives of the united States of America, in General Congress, Assembled, appealing to the Supreme Judge of the world for the rectitude of our intentions, do, in the Name, and by Authority of the good People of these Colonies, solemnly publish and declare, That these United Colonies are, and of Right ought to be Free and Independent States; that they are Absolved from all Allegiance to the British Crown, and that all political connection between them and the State of Great Britain, is and ought to be totally dissolved; and that as Free and Independent States, they have full Power to levy War, conclude Peace, contract Alliances, establish Commerce, and to do all other Acts and Things which Independent States may of right do. And for the support of this Declaration, with a firm reliance on the protection of divine Providence, we mutually pledge to each other our Lives, our Fortunes and our sacred Honor.

Georgia:
Button Gwinnett
Lyman Hall
George Walton
North Carolina:
William Hooper
Joseph Hewes
John Penn
South Carolina:
Edward Rutledge
Thomas Heyward, Jr.
Thomas Lynch, Jr.
Arthur Middleton
Maryland:
Samuel Chase
William Paca
Thomas Stone
Charles Carroll of Carrollton

Virginia:
George Wythe
Richard Henry Lee
Thomas Jefferson
Benjamin Harrison
Thomas Nelson, Jr.
Francis Lightfoot Lee
Carter Braxton
Pennsylvania:
Robert Morris
Benjamin Rush
Benjamin Franklin
John Morton
George Clymer
James Smith
George Taylor
James Wilson
George Ross

Delaware:
Caesar Rodney
George Read
Thomas McKean
New York:
William Floyd
Philip Livingston
Francis Lewis
Lewis Morris
New Jersey:
Richard Stockton
John Witherspoon
Francis Hopkinson
John Hart
Abraham Clark
Rhode Island:
Stephen Hopkins
William Ellery

New Hampshire:
Josiah Bartlett
William Whipple
Matthew Thornton
Massachusetts:
John Hancock
Samuel Adams
John Adams
Robert Treat Paine
Elbridge Gerry
Connecticut:
Roger Sherman
Samuel Huntington
William Williams
Oliver Wolcott

APPENDIX B

The Articles of the Confederation (1781)

TO ALL TO WHOM these Presents shall come, we the undersigned Delegates of the States affixed to our Names send greeting. Whereas the Delegates of the United States of America in Congress assembled did on the fifteenth day of November in the Year of our Lord One Thousand Seven Hundred and Seventy seven, and in the Second Year of the Independence of America agree to certain articles of Confederation and perpetual Union between the States of New Hampshire, Massachusetts bay, Rhode Island and Providence Plantations, Connecticut, New York, New Jersey, Pennsylvania, Delaware, Maryland, Virginia, North Carolina, South Carolina and Georgia in the Words following, viz. "Articles of Confederation and perpetual Union between the states of New Hampshire, Massachusetts bay, Rhode Island and Providence Plantations, Connecticut, New York, New Jersey, Pennsylvania, Delaware, Maryland, Virginia, North Carolina, South Carolina and Georgia.

ARTICLE I.

The Style of this confederacy shall be "The United States of America."

ARTICLE II.

Each state retains its sovereignty, freedom and independence, and every Power, Jurisdiction and right, which is not by this confederation expressly delegated to the United States, in Congress assembled.

ARTICLE III.

The said states hereby severally enter into a firm league of friendship with each other, for their common defence, the security of their Liberties, and their mutual and general welfare, binding themselves to assist each other, against all force offered to, or attacks made upon them, or any of them, on account of religion, sovereignty, trade, or any other pretence whatever.

ARTICLE IV.

The better to secure and perpetuate mutual friendship and intercourse among the people of the different states in this union, the free inhabitants of each of these states, paupers, vagabonds and fugitives from Justice excepted, shall be entitled to all privileges and immunities of free citizens in the several states; and the people of each state shall have free ingress and regress to and from any other state, and shall enjoy therein all the privileges of trade and commerce, subject to the same duties, impositions and restrictions as the inhabitants thereof respectively, provided that such restriction shall not extend so far as to prevent the removal of property imported into any state, to any other state of which the Owner is an inhabitant; provided also that no imposition, duties or restriction shall be laid by any state, on the property of the united states, or either of them.

If any Person guilty of, or charged with treason, felony, or other high misdemeanor in any state, shall flee from Justice, and be found in any of the united states, he shall upon demand of the Governor or executive power, of the state from which he fled, be delivered up and removed to the state having jurisdiction of his offence.

Full faith and credit shall be given in each of these states to the records, acts and judicial proceedings of the courts and magistrates of every other state.

ARTICLE V.

For the more convenient management of the general interests of the united states, delegates shall be annually appointed in such manner as the legislature of each state shall direct, to meet in Congress on the first Monday in November, in every year, with a power reserved to each state, to recall its delegates, or any of them, at any time within the year, and to send others in their stead, for the remainder of the Year.

No state shall be represented in Congress by less than two, nor by more than seven Members; and no person shall be capable of being a delegate for more than three years in any term of six years; nor shall any person, being a delegate, be capable of holding any office under the united states, for which he, or another for his benefit receives any salary, fees or emolument of any kind.

Each state shall maintain its own delegates in a meeting of the states, and while they act as members of the committee of the states.

In determining questions in the united states, in Congress assembled, each state shall have one vote.

Freedom of speech and debate in Congress shall not be impeached or questioned in any Court, or place out of Congress, and the members of congress shall be protected in their persons from arrests and imprisonments, during the time of their going to and from, and attendance on congress, except for treason, felony, or breach of the peace.

ARTICLE VI.

No state without the Consent of the united states in congress assembled, shall send any embassy to, or receive any embassy from, or enter into any conference, agreement, or alliance or treaty with any King prince or state; nor shall any person holding any office of profit or trust under the united states, or any of them, accept of any present, emolument, office or title of any kind whatever from any king, prince or foreign state; nor shall the united states in congress assembled, or any of them, grant any title of nobility.

No two or more states shall enter into any treaty, confederation or alliance whatever between them, without the consent of the united states in congress assembled, specifying accurately the purposes for which the same is to be entered into, and how long it shall continue.

No state shall lay any imposts or duties, which may interfere with any stipulations in treaties, entered into by the united states in congress assembled, with any king, prince or state, in pursuance of any treaties already proposed by congress, to the courts of France and Spain.

No vessels of war shall be kept up in time of peace by any state, except such number only, as shall be deemed necessary by the united states in congress assembled, for the defence of such state, or its trade; nor shall any body of forces be kept up by any state, in time of peace, except such number only, as in the judgment of the united states, in congress assembled, shall be deemed requisite to garrison the forts necessary for the defence of such state; but every state shall always keep up a well regulated and disciplined militia, sufficiently armed and accoutered, and shall provide and constantly have ready for use, in public stores, a due number of field pieces and tents, and a proper quantity of arms, ammunition and camp equipage.

No state shall engage in any war without the consent of the united states in congress assembled, unless such state be actually invaded by enemies, or shall have received certain advice of a resolution being formed by some nation of Indians to invade such state, and the danger is so imminent as not to admit of a delay, till the united states in congress assembled can be consulted: nor shall any state grant commissions to any ships or vessels of war, nor letters of marque or reprisal, except it be after a declaration of war by the united states in congress assembled, and then only against the kingdom or state and the subjects thereof, against which war has been so declared, and under such regulations as shall be established by the united states in congress assembled, unless such state be infested by pirates, in which case vessels of war may be fitted out for that occasion, and kept so long as the danger shall continue, or until the united states in congress assembled shall determine otherwise.

ARTICLE VII.

When land-forces are raised by any state for the common defence, all officers of or under the rank of colonel, shall be appointed by the legislature of each state respectively by whom such forces shall be raised, or in such manner as such state shall direct, and all vacancies shall be filled up by the state which first made the appointment.

ARTICLE VIII.

All charges of war, and all other expenses that shall be incurred for the common defence or general welfare, and allowed by the united states in congress assembled, shall be defrayed out of a common treasury, which shall be supplied by the several states, in proportion to the value of all land within each state, granted to or surveyed for any Person, as such land and the buildings and improvements thereon shall be estimated according to such mode as the united states in congress assembled, shall from time to time direct and appoint. The taxes for paying that proportion shall be laid and levied by the authority and direction of the legislatures of the several states within the time agreed upon by the united states in congress assembled.

ARTICLE IX.

The united states in congress assembled, shall have the sole and exclusive right and power of determining on peace and war, except in the cases mentioned in the sixth article—of sending and receiving ambassadors—entering into treaties and alliances, provided that no treaty of commerce shall be made whereby the legislative power of the respective states shall be restrained from imposing such imposts and duties on foreigners, as their own people are subjected to, or from prohibiting the exportation or importation of any species of goods or commodities whatsoever—of establishing rules for deciding in all cases, what captures on land or water shall be legal, and in what manner prizes taken by land or naval forces in the service of the united states shall be divided or appropriated—of granting letters of marque and reprisal in times of peace—appointing courts for the trial of piracies and felonies committed on the high seas and establishing courts for receiving and determining finally appeals in all cases of captures, provided that no member of congress shall be appointed a judge of any of the said courts.

The united states in congress assembled shall also be the last resort on appeal in all disputes and differences now subsisting or that hereafter may arise between two or more states concerning boundary, jurisdiction or any other cause whatever; which authority shall always be exercised in the manner following. Whenever the legislative or executive authority or lawful agent state in controversy with another shall present a petition to congress, stating the matter in question and praying for a hearing, notice thereof shall be given by order of congress to the legislative or executive authority of the other state in controversy, and a day assigned for the appearance of the parties by their lawful agents, who shall then be directed to appoint by joint consent, commissioners or judges to constitute a court for hearing and determining the matter in question; but if they cannot agree, congress shall name three persons out of each of the united states, and from the list of such persons each party shall alternately strike out one, the petitioners beginning, until the number shall be reduced to thirteen; and from that number not less than seven, nor more than nine names as congress shall direct, shall in the presence of congress be drawn out by lot, and the persons whose names shall be so drawn or any five of them, shall be commissioners or judges, to hear and finally determine the controversy, so always as a major part of the judges who shall hear the cause shall agree in the determination: and if either party shall neglect to attend at the day appointed, without showing reasons, which congress shall judge sufficient, or being present shall refuse to strike, the congress shall proceed to nominate three persons out of each state, and the secretary of congress shall strike in behalf of such party absent or refusing; and the judgment and sentence of the court to be appointed, in the manner before prescribed, shall be final and conclusive; and if any of the parties shall refuse to submit to the authority of such court, or to appear to defend their claim or cause, the court shall nevertheless proceed to pronounce sentence, or judgment, which shall in like manner be final and decisive, the judgment or sentence and other proceedings being in either case transmitted to congress, and lodged among the acts of congress for the security of the parties concerned: provided that every commissioner, before he sits in judgment, shall take an oath to be administered by one of the judges of the supreme or superior court of the state, where the cause shall be tried, "well and truly to hear and determine the matter in question, according to the best of his judgment, without favor, affection or hope of reward;" provided also that no state shall be deprived of territory for the benefit of the united states.

All controversies concerning the private right of soil claimed under different grants of two or more states, whose jurisdictions as they may respect such lands, and the states which passed such grants are adjusted, the said grants or either of them being at the same time claimed to have originated antecedent to such settlement of jurisdiction, shall on the petition of either party to the congress of the united states, be finally determined as near as may be in the same manner as is before prescribed for deciding disputes respecting territorial jurisdiction between different states.

The united states in congress assembled shall also have the sole and exclusive right and power of regulating the alloy and value of coin struck by their own authority, or by that of the respective states—fixing the standard of weights and measures throughout the united states—regulating the trade and managing all affairs with the Indians, not members of any of the states, provided that the legislative right of any state within its own limits be not infringed or violated—establishing and regulating post offices from one state to another, throughout all the united states. and exacting such postage on the papers passing through the same as may be requisite to defray the expenses of the said office—appointing all officers of the land forces, in the service of the united states, excepting regimental officers—appointing all the officers of the naval forces, and commissioning all officers whatever in the service of the united states—making rules for the government and regulation of the said land and naval forces, and directing their operations.

The united states in congress assembled shall have authority to appoint a committee, to sit in the recess of congress, to be denominated "A Committee of the States," and to consist of one delegate from each state; and to appoint such other committees and civil officers as may be necessary for managing the general affairs of the united states under their direction—to appoint one of their number to preside, provided that no person be allowed to serve in the office of president more than one year in any term of three years; to ascertain the necessary sums of Money to be raised for the service of the united states, and to appropriate and apply the same for defraying the public expenses—to borrow money, or emit bills on the credit of the united states, transmitting every half year to the respective states an account of the sums of money so borrowed or emitted,—to build and equip a navy—to agree upon the number of land forces, and to make requisitions from each state for its quota, in proportion to the number of white inhabitants in such state; which requisition shall be binding, and thereupon the legislature of each state shall appoint the regimental officers, raise the men and clothe, arm and equip them in a soldier like manner, at the expense of the united states, and the officers and men so clothed, armed and equipped shall march to the place appointed, and within the time agreed on by the united states in congress assembled. But if the united states in congress assembled shall, on consideration of circumstances judge proper that any state should not raise men, or should raise a smaller number than its quota, and that any other state should raise a greater number of men than the quota thereof, such extra number shall be raised, officered, clothed, armed and equipped in the same manner as the quota of such state, unless the legislature of such state shall judge that such extra number cannot be safely spared out of the same, in which case they shall raise officer, clothe, arm and equip as many of such extra number as they judge can be safely spared. And the officers and men so clothed, armed and equipped, shall march to the place appointed, and within the time agreed on by the united states in congress assembled.

The united states in congress assembled shall never engage in a war, nor grant letters of marque and reprisal in time of peace, nor enter into any treaties or alliances, nor coin money, nor regulate the value thereof, nor ascertain the sums and expenses necessary for the defence and welfare of the united states, or any of them, nor emit bills, nor borrow money on the credit of the united states, nor appropriate money, nor agree upon the number of vessels of war, to be built or purchased, or the number of land or sea forces to be raised, nor appoint a commander in chief of the army or navy, unless nine states assent to the same: nor shall a question on any other point, except for adjourning from day to day be determined, unless by the votes of a majority of the united states in congress assembled.

The congress of the united states shall have power to adjourn to any time within the year, and to any place within the united states, so that no period of adjournment be for a longer duration than the space of six Months, and shall publish the Journal of their proceedings monthly, except such parts thereof relating to treaties, alliances or military operations as in their judgment require secrecy; and the yeas and nays of the delegates of each state on any question shall be entered on the Journal, when it is desired by any delegate; and the delegates of a state, or any of them, at his or their request shall be furnished with a transcript of the said Journal, except such parts as are above excepted, to lay before the legislatures of the several states.

ARTICLE X.

The committee of the states, or any nine of them, shall be authorized to execute, in the recess of congress, such of the powers of congress as the united states in congress assembled, by the consent of nine states, shall from time to time think expedient to vest them with; provided that no power be delegated to the said committee, for the exercise of which, by the articles of confederation, the voice of nine states in the congress of the united states assembled is requisite.

ARTICLE XI.

Canada acceding to this confederation, and joining in the measures of the united states, shall be admitted into, and entitled to all the advantages of this union: but no other colony shall be admitted into the same, unless such admission be agreed to by nine states.

ARTICLE XII.

All bills of credit emitted, monies borrowed and debts contracted by, or under the authority of congress, before the assembling of the united states, in pursuance of the present confederation, shall be deemed and considered as a charge against the united states, for payment and satisfaction whereof the said united states, and the public faith are hereby solemnly pledged.

ARTICLE XIII.

Every state shall abide by the determinations of the united states in congress assembled, on all questions which by this confederation are submitted to them. And the Articles of this confederation shall be inviolably observed by every state, and the union shall be perpetual; nor shall any alteration at any time hereafter be made in any of them; unless such alteration be agreed to in a congress of the united states, and be afterwards confirmed by the legislatures of every state.

AND WHEREAS it hath pleased the Great Governor of the World to incline the hearts of the legislatures we respectively represent in congress, to approve of, and to authorize us to ratify the said articles of confederation and perpetual union. KNOW YE that we the undersigned delegates, by virtue of the power and authority to us given for that purpose, do by these presents, in the name and in behalf of our respective constituents, fully and entirely ratify and confirm each and every of the said articles of confederation and perpetual union, and all and singular the matters and things therein contained: And we do further solemnly plight and engage the faith of our respective constituents, that they shall abide by the determinations of the united states in congress assembled, on all questions, which by the said confederation are submitted to them. And that the articles thereof shall be inviolably observed by the states we respectively represent, and that the union shall be perpetual. In Witness whereof we have hereunto set our hands in Congress. Done at Philadelphia in the state of Pennsylvania the ninth Day of July in the Year of our Lord one Thousand seven Hundred and Seventy-eight, and in the third year of the independence of America.

On the part and behalf of the State of New Hampshire:
JOSIAH BARTLETT
JOHN WENTWORTH JUNR.
August 8th 1778

On the part and behalf of The State of Massachusetts Bay:
JOHN HANCOCK
SAMUEL ADAMS
ELBRIDGE GERRY
FRANCIS DANA
JAMES LOVELL
SAMUEL HOLTEN

On the part and behalf of the State of Rhode Island and Providence Plantations:
WILLIAM ELLERY
HENRY MARCHANT
JOHN COLLINS

On the part and behalf of the State of Connecticut:
ROGER SHERMAN
SAMUEL HUNTINGTON
OLIVER WOLCOTT
TITUS HOSMER
ANDREW ADAMS

On the part and behalf of the State of New York:
JAMES DUANE
FRANCIS LEWIS
WM DUER
GOUV MORRIS

On the part and behalf of the State of New Jersey:
JNO WITHERSPOON
NATHANIEL SCUDDER
November 26, 1778

On the part and behalf of the State of Pennsylvania:
ROBT MORRIS
DANIEL ROBERDEAU
JOHN BAYARD SMITH
WILLIAM CLINGAN
JOSEPH REED
22nd July 1778

On the part and behalf of the State of Delaware:
THO McKEAN
February 12, 1779
JOHN DICKINSON
May 5th 1779
NICHOLAS VAN DYKE

On the part and behalf of the State of Maryland:
JOHN HANSON
March 1 1781
DANIEL CARROLL

On the part and behalf of the State of Virginia:
RICHARD HENRY LEE
JOHN BANISTER
THOMAS ADAMS
JNo HARVIE
FRANCIS LIGHTFOOT LEE

On the part and behalf of the State of North Carolina:
JOHN PENN
July 21st 1778
CORNs HARNETT
JNo WILLIAMS

On the part and behalf of the State of South Carolina:
HENRY LAURENS
WILLIAM HENRY DRAYTON
JNo MATHEWS
RICHD HUTSON
THOs HEYWARD Junr

On the part and behalf of the State of Georgia:
JNo WALTON
24th July 1778
EDWD TELFAIR
EDWD LANGWORTHY

APPENDIX C

Constitution of the United States

WE THE PEOPLE of the United States, in order to form a more perfect union, establish justice, insure domestic tranquility, provide for the common defense, promote the general welfare, and secure the blessings of liberty to ourselves and our posterity, do ordain and establish this Constitution for the United States of America

ARTICLE I

Section 1. All legislative powers herein granted shall be vested in a Congress of the United States, which shall consist of a Senate and House of Representatives.

Section 2. The House of Representatives shall be composed of members chosen every second year by the people of the several states, and the electors in each state shall have the qualifications requisite for electors of the most numerous branch of the state legislature.

No person shall be a Representative who shall not have attained to the age of twenty five years, and been seven years a citizen of the United States, and who shall not, when elected, be an inhabitant of that state in which he shall be chosen.

Representatives and direct taxes shall be apportioned among the several states which may be included within this union, according to their respective numbers, which shall be determined by adding to the whole number of free persons, including those bound to service for a term of years, and excluding Indians not taxed, three fifths of all other persons. The actual enumeration shall be made within three years after the first meeting of the Congress of the United States, and within every subsequent term of ten years, in such manner as they shall by law direct. The number of Representatives shall not exceed one for every thirty thousand, but each state shall have at least one Representative; and until such enumeration shall be made, the state of New Hampshire shall be entitled to choose three, Massachusetts eight, Rhode Island and Providence Plantations one, Connecticut five, New York six, New Jersey four, Pennsylvania eight, Delaware one, Maryland six, Virginia ten, North Carolina five, South Carolina five, and Georgia three.

When vacancies happen in the representation from any state, the executive authority thereof shall issue writs of election to fill such vacancies.

The House of Representatives shall choose their speaker and other officers; and shall have the sole power of impeachment.

Section 3. The Senate of the United States shall be composed of two Senators from each state, chosen by the legislature thereof, for six years; and each Senator shall have one vote.

Immediately after they shall be assembled in consequence of the first election, they shall be divided as equally as may be into three classes. The seats of the Senators of the first class shall be vacated at the expiration of the second year, of the second class at the expiration of the fourth year, and the third class at the expiration of the sixth year, so that one third may be chosen every second year; and if vacancies happen by resignation, or otherwise, during the recess of the legislature of any state, the executive thereof may make temporary appointments until the next meeting of the legislature, which shall then fill such vacancies.

No person shall be a Senator who shall not have attained to the age of thirty years, and been nine years a citizen of the United States and who shall not, when elected, be an inhabitant of that state for which he shall be chosen.

The Vice President of the United States shall be President of the Senate, but shall have no vote, unless they be equally divided.

The Senate shall choose their other officers, and also a President pro tempore, in the absence of the Vice President, or when he shall exercise the office of President of the United States.

The Senate shall have the sole power to try all impeachments. When sitting for that purpose, they shall be on oath or affirmation. When the President of the United States is tried, the Chief Justice shall preside: And no person shall be convicted without the concurrence of two thirds of the members present.

Judgment in cases of impeachment shall not extend further than to removal from office, and disqualification to hold and enjoy any office of honor, trust or profit under the United States: but the party convicted shall nevertheless be liable and subject to indictment, trial, judgment and punishment, according to law.

Section 4. The times, places and manner of holding elections for Senators and Representatives, shall be prescribed in each state by the legislature thereof; but the Congress may at any time by law make or alter such regulations, except as to the places of choosing Senators.

The Congress shall assemble at least once in every year, and such meeting shall be on the first Monday in December, unless they shall by law appoint a different day.

Section 5. Each House shall be the judge of the elections, returns and qualifications of its own members, and a majority of each shall constitute a quorum to do business; but a smaller number may adjourn from day to day, and may be authorized to compel the attendance of absent members, in such manner, and under such penalties as each House may provide.

Each House may determine the rules of its proceedings, punish its members for disorderly behavior, and, with the concurrence of two thirds, expel a member.

Each House shall keep a journal of its proceedings, and from time to time publish the same, excepting such parts as may in their judgment require secrecy; and the yeas and nays of the members of either House on any question shall, at the desire of one fifth of those present, be entered on the journal.

Neither House, during the session of Congress, shall, without the consent of the other, adjourn for more than three days, nor to any other place than that in which the two Houses shall be sitting.

Section 6. The Senators and Representatives shall receive a compensation for their services, to be ascertained by law, and paid out of the treasury of the United States. They shall in all cases, except treason, felony and breach of the peace, be privileged from arrest during their attendance at the session of their respective houses, and in going to and returning from the same; and for any speech or debate in either house, they shall not be questioned in any other place.

No Senator or Representative shall, during the time for which he was elected, be appointed to any civil office under the authority of the United States, which shall have been created, or the emoluments whereof shall have been increased during such time: and no person holding any office under the United States, shall be a member of either House during his continuance in office.

Section 7. All bills for raising revenue shall originate in the House of Representatives; but the Senate may propose or concur with amendments as on other Bills.

Every bill which shall have passed the House of Representatives and the Senate, shall, before it become a law, be presented to the President of the United States; if he approve he shall sign it, but if not he shall return it, with his objections to that house in which it shall have originated, who shall enter the objections at large on their journal, and proceed to reconsider it. If after such reconsideration two thirds of that house shall agree to pass the bill, it shall be sent, together with the objections, to the other house, by which it shall likewise be reconsidered, and if approved by two thirds of that house, it shall become a law. But in all such cases the votes of both houses shall be determined by yeas and nays, and the names of the persons voting for and against the bill shall be entered on the journal of each house respectively. If any bill shall not be returned by the President within ten days (Sundays excepted) after it shall have been presented to him, the same shall be a law, in like manner as if he had signed it, unless the Congress by their adjournment prevent its return, in which case it shall not be a law.

Every order, resolution, or vote to which the concurrence of the Senate and House of Representatives may be necessary (except on a question of adjournment) shall be presented to the President of the United States; and before the same shall take effect, shall be approved by him, or being disapproved by him, shall be repassed by two thirds of the Senate and House of Representatives, according to the rules and limitations prescribed in the case of a bill.

Section 8. The Congress shall have power to lay and collect taxes, duties, imposts and excises, to pay the debts and provide for the common defense and general welfare of the United States; but all duties, imposts and excises shall be uniform throughout the United States;

To borrow money on the credit of the United States;

To regulate commerce with foreign nations, and among the several states, and with the Indian tribes;

To establish a uniform rule of naturalization, and uniform laws on the subject of bankruptcies throughout the United States;

To coin money, regulate the value thereof, and of foreign coin, and fix the standard of weights and measures;

To provide for the punishment of counterfeiting the securities and current coin of the United States;

To establish post offices and post roads;

To promote the progress of science and useful arts, by securing for limited times to authors and inventors the exclusive right to their respective writings and discoveries;

To constitute tribunals inferior to the Supreme Court;

To define and punish piracies and felonies committed on the high seas, and offenses against the law of nations;

To declare war, grant letters of marque and reprisal, and make rules concerning captures on land and water;

To raise and support armies, but no appropriation of money to that use shall be for a longer term than two years;

To provide and maintain a navy;

To make rules for the government and regulation of the land and naval forces;

To provide for calling forth the militia to execute the laws of the union, suppress insurrections and repel invasions;

To provide for organizing, arming, and disciplining, the militia, and for governing such part of them as may be employed in the service of the United States, reserving to the states respectively, the appointment of the officers, and the authority of training the militia according to the discipline prescribed by Congress;

To exercise exclusive legislation in all cases whatsoever, over such District (not exceeding ten miles square) as may, by cession of particular states, and the acceptance of Congress, become the seat of the government of the United States, and to exercise like authority over all places purchased by the consent of the legislature of the state in which the same shall be, for the erection of forts, magazines, arsenals, dockyards, and other needful buildings;—and

To make all laws which shall be necessary and proper for carrying into execution the foregoing powers, and all other powers vested by this Constitution in the government of the United States, or in any department or officer thereof.

Section 9. The migration or importation of such persons as any of the states now existing shall think proper to admit, shall not be prohibited by the Congress prior to the year one thousand eight hundred and eight, but a tax or duty may be imposed on such importation, not exceeding ten dollars for each person.

The privilege of the writ of habeas corpus shall not be suspended, unless when in cases of rebellion or invasion the public safety may require it.

No bill of attainder or ex post facto Law shall be passed.

No capitation, or other direct, tax shall be laid, unless in proportion to the census or enumeration herein before directed to be taken.

No tax or duty shall be laid on articles exported from any state.

No preference shall be given by any regulation of commerce or revenue to the ports of one state over those of another: nor shall vessels bound to, or from, one state, be obliged to enter, clear or pay duties in another.

No money shall be drawn from the treasury, but in consequence of appropriations made by law; and a regular statement and account of receipts and expenditures of all public money shall be published from time to time.

No title of nobility shall be granted by the United States: and no person holding any office of profit or trust under them, shall, without the consent of the Congress, accept of any present, emolument, office, or title, of any kind whatever, from any king, prince, or foreign state.

Section 10. No state shall enter into any treaty, alliance, or confederation; grant letters of marque and reprisal; coin money; emit bills of credit; make anything but gold and silver coin a tender in payment of debts; pass any bill of attainder, ex post facto law, or law impairing the obligation of contracts, or grant any title of nobility.

No state shall, without the consent of the Congress, lay any imposts or duties on imports or exports, except what may be absolutely necessary for executing its inspection laws: and the net produce of all duties and imposts, laid by any state on imports or exports, shall be for the use of the treasury of the United States; and all such laws shall be subject to the revision and control of the Congress.

No state shall, without the consent of Congress, lay any duty of tonnage, keep troops, or ships of war in time of peace, enter into any agreement or compact with another state, or with a foreign power, or engage in war, unless actually invaded, or in such imminent danger as will not admit of delay.

ARTICLE II

Section 1. The executive power shall be vested in a President of the United States of America. He shall hold his office during the term of four years, and, together with the Vice President, chosen for the same term, be elected, as follows:

Each state shall appoint, in such manner as the Legislature thereof may direct, a number of electors, equal to the whole number of Senators and Representatives to which the state may be entitled in the Congress: but no Senator or Representative, or person holding an office of trust or profit under the United States, shall be appointed an elector.

The electors shall meet in their respective states, and vote by ballot for two persons, of whom one at least shall not be an inhabitant of the same state with themselves. And they shall make a list of all the persons voted for, and of the number of votes for each; which list they shall sign and certify, and transmit sealed to the seat of the government of the United States, directed to the President of the Senate. The President of the Senate shall, in the presence of the Senate and House of Representatives, open all the certificates, and the votes shall then be counted. The person having the greatest number of votes shall be the President, if such number be a majority of the whole number of electors appointed; and if there be more than one who have such majority, and have an equal number of votes, then the House of Representatives shall immediately choose by ballot one of them for President; and if no person have a majority, then from the five highest on the list the said House shall in like manner choose the President. But in choosing the President, the votes shall be taken by States, the representation from each state having one vote; a quorum for this purpose shall consist of a member or members from two thirds of the states, and a majority of all the states shall be necessary to a choice. In every case, after the choice of the President, the person having the greatest number of votes of the electors shall be the Vice President. But if there should remain two or more who have equal votes, the Senate shall choose from them by ballot the Vice President.

The Congress may determine the time of choosing the electors, and the day on which they shall give their votes; which day shall be the same throughout the United States.

No person except a natural-born citizen, or a citizen of the United States, at the time of the adoption of this Constitution, shall be eligible to the office of President; neither shall any person be eligible to that office who shall not have attained to the age of thirty five years, and been fourteen Years a resident within the United States.

In case of the removal of the President from office, or of his death, resignation, or inability to discharge the powers and duties of the said office, the same shall devolve on the Vice President, and the Congress may by law provide for the case of removal, death, resignation or inability, both of the President and Vice President, declaring what officer shall then act as President, and such officer shall act accordingly, until the disability be removed, or a President shall be elected.

The President shall, at stated times, receive for his services, a compensation, which shall neither be increased nor diminished during the period for which he shall have been elected, and he shall not receive within that period any other emolument from the United States, or any of them.

Before he enter on the execution of his office, he shall take the following oath or affirmation:—"I do solemnly swear (or affirm) that I will faithfully execute the office of President of the United States, and will to the best of my ability, preserve, protect and defend the Constitution of the United States."

Section 2. The President shall be commander in chief of the Army and Navy of the United States, and of the militia of the several states, when called into the actual service of the United States; he may require the opinion, in writing, of the principal officer in each of the executive departments, upon any subject relating to the duties of their respective offices, and he shall have power to grant reprieves and pardons for offenses against the United States, except in cases of impeachment.

He shall have power, by and with the advice and consent of the Senate, to make treaties, provided two thirds of the Senators present concur; and he shall nominate, and by and with the advice and consent of the Senate, shall appoint ambassadors, other public ministers and consuls, judges of the Supreme Court, and all other officers of the United States, whose appointments are not herein otherwise provided for, and which shall be by law: but the Congress may by law vest the appointment of such inferior officers, as they think proper, in the President alone, in the courts of law, or in the heads of departments.

The President shall have power to fill up all vacancies that may happen during the recess of the Senate, by granting commissions which shall expire at the end of their next session.

Section 3. He shall from time to time give to the Congress information of the state of the union, and recommend to their consideration such measures as he shall judge necessary and expedient; he may, on extraordinary occasions, convene both Houses, or either of them, and in case of disagreement between them, with respect to the time of adjournment, he may adjourn them to such time as he shall think proper; he shall receive ambassadors and other public ministers; he shall take care that the laws be faithfully executed, and shall commission all the officers of the United States.

Section 4. The President, Vice President and all civil officers of the United States, shall be removed from office on impeachment for, and conviction of, treason, bribery, or other high crimes and misdemeanors.

ARTICLE III

Section 1. The judicial power of the United States, shall be vested in one Supreme Court, and in such inferior courts as the Congress may from time to time ordain and establish. The judges, both of the supreme and inferior courts, shall hold their offices during good behaviour, and shall, at stated times, receive for their services, a compensation, which shall not be diminished during their continuance in office.

Section 2. The judicial power shall extend to all cases, in law and equity, arising under this Constitution, the laws of the United States, and treaties made, or which shall be made, under their authority;—to all cases affecting ambassadors, other public ministers and consuls;—to all cases of admiralty and maritime jurisdiction;—to controversies to which the United States shall be a party;—to controversies between two or more states;—between a state and citizens of another state;—between citizens of different states;—between citizens of the same state claiming lands under grants of different states, and between a state, or the citizens thereof, and foreign states, citizens or subjects.

In all cases affecting ambassadors, other public ministers and consuls, and those in which a state shall be party, the Supreme Court shall have original jurisdiction. In all the other cases before mentioned, the Supreme Court shall have appellate jurisdiction, both as to law and fact, with such exceptions, and under such regulations as the Congress shall make.

The trial of all crimes, except in cases of impeachment, shall be by jury; and such trial shall be held in the state where the said crimes shall have been committed; but when not committed within any state, the trial shall be at such place or places as the Congress may by law have directed.

Section 3. Treason against the United States, shall consist only in levying war against them, or in adhering to their enemies, giving them aid and comfort. No person shall be convicted of treason unless on the testimony of two witnesses to the same overt act, or on confession in open court.

The Congress shall have power to declare the punishment of treason, but no attainder of treason shall work corruption of blood, or forfeiture except during the life of the person attainted.

ARTICLE IV

Section 1. Full faith and credit shall be given in each state to the public acts, records, and judicial proceedings of every other state. And the Congress may by general laws prescribe the manner in which such acts, records, and proceedings shall be proved, and the effect thereof.

Section 2. The citizens of each state shall be entitled to all privileges and immunities of citizens in the several states.

A person charged in any state with treason, felony, or other crime, who shall flee from justice, and be found in another state, shall on demand of the executive authority of the state from which he fled, be delivered up, to be removed to the state having jurisdiction of the crime.

No person held to service or labor in one state, under the laws thereof, escaping into another, shall, in consequence of any law or regulation therein, be discharged from such service or labor, but shall be delivered up on claim of the party to whom such service or labor may be due.

Section 3. New states may be admitted by the Congress into this union; but no new states shall be formed or erected within the jurisdiction of any other state; nor any state be formed by the junction of two or more states, or parts of states, without the consent of the legislatures of the states concerned as well as of the Congress.

The Congress shall have power to dispose of and make all needful rules and regulations respecting the territory or other property belonging to the United States; and nothing in this Constitution shall be so construed as to prejudice any claims of the United States, or of any particular state.

Section 4. The United States shall guarantee to every state in this union a republican form of government, and shall protect each of them against invasion; and on application of the legislature, or of the executive (when the legislature cannot be convened) against domestic violence.

ARTICLE V

The Congress, whenever two thirds of both houses shall deem it necessary, shall propose amendments to this Constitution, or, on the application of the legislatures of two thirds of the several states, shall call a convention for proposing amendments, which, in either case, shall be valid to all intents and purposes, as part of this Constitution, when ratified by the legislatures of three fourths of the several states, or by conventions in three fourths thereof, as the one or the other mode of ratification may be proposed by the Congress; provided that no amendment which may be made prior to the year one thousand eight hundred and eight shall in any manner affect the first and fourth clauses in the ninth section of the first article; and that no state, without its consent, shall be deprived of its equal suffrage in the Senate.

ARTICLE VI

All debts contracted and engagements entered into, before the adoption of this Constitution, shall be as valid against the United States under this Constitution, as under the Confederation.

This Constitution, and the laws of the United States which shall be made in pursuance thereof; and all treaties made, or which shall be made, under the authority of the United States, shall be the supreme law of the land; and the judges in every state shall be bound thereby, anything in the Constitution or laws of any State to the contrary notwithstanding.

The Senators and Representatives before mentioned, and the members of the several state legislatures, and all executive and judicial officers, both of the United States and of the several states, shall be bound by oath or affirmation, to support this Constitution; but no religious test shall ever be required as a qualification to any office or public trust under the United States.

ARTICLE VII

The ratification of the conventions of nine states, shall be sufficient for the establishment of this Constitution between the states so ratifying the same.

Done in convention by the unanimous consent of the states present the seventeenth day of September in the year of our Lord one thousand seven hundred and eighty seven and of the independence of the United States of America the twelfth. In witness whereof we have hereunto subscribed our Names,

---

Virginia
G. Washington—Presidt. and deputy from Virginia
New Hampshire
John Langdon, Nicholas Gilman
Massachusetts
Nathaniel Gorham, Rufus King
Connecticut
Wm. Saml. Johnson, Roger Sherman
New York
Alexander Hamilton
New Jersey
Wil. Livingston, David Brearly, Wm. Paterson, Jona. Dayton
Pennsylvania
B. Franklin, Thomas Mifflin, Robt. Morris, Geo. Clymer, Thos. FitzSimons, Jared Ingersoll, James Wilson, Gouv Morris
Delaware
Geo. Read, Gunning Bedford jun, John Dickinson, Richard Bassett, Jaco. Broom
Maryland
James McHenry, Dan of St Thos. Jenifer, Danl Carroll
Virginia
John Blair—, James Madison Jr.
North Carolina
Wm. Blount, Richd. Dobbs Spaight, Hu Williamson
South Carolina
J. Rutledge, Charles Cotesworth Pinckney, Charles Pinckney, Pierce Butler
Georgia
William Few, Abr Baldwin

Bill of Rights

Amendments I Through X of the Constitution

AMENDMENT I

Congress shall make no law respecting an establishment of religion, or prohibiting the free exercise thereof; or abridging the freedom of speech, or of the press; or the right of the people peaceably to assemble, and to petition the government for a redress of grievances.

AMENDMENT II

A well regulated militia, being necessary to the security of a free state, the right of the people to keep and bear arms, shall not be infringed.

AMENDMENT III

No soldier shall, in time of peace be quartered in any house, without the consent of the owner, nor in time of war, but in a manner to be prescribed by law.

AMENDMENT IV

The right of the people to be secure in their persons, houses, papers, and effects, against unreasonable searches and seizures, shall not be violated, and no warrants shall issue, but upon probable cause, supported by oath or affirmation, and particularly describing the place to be searched, and the persons or things to be seized.

AMENDMENT V

No person shall be held to answer for a capital, or otherwise infamous crime, unless on a presentment or indictment of a grand jury, except in cases arising in the land or naval forces, or in the militia, when in actual service in time of war or public danger; nor shall any person be subject for the same offense to be twice put in jeopardy of life or limb; nor shall be compelled in any criminal case to be a witness against himself, nor be deprived of life, liberty, or property, without due process of law; nor shall private property be taken for public use, without just compensation.

AMENDMENT VI

In all criminal prosecutions, the accused shall enjoy the right to a speedy and public trial, by an impartial jury of the state and district wherein the crime shall have been committed, which district shall have been previously ascertained by law, and to be informed of the nature and cause of the accusation; to be confronted with the witnesses against him; to have compulsory process for obtaining witnesses in his favor, and to have the assistance of counsel for his defense.

AMENDMENT VII

In suits at common law, where the value in controversy shall exceed twenty dollars, the right of trial by jury shall be preserved, and no fact tried by a jury, shall be otherwise reexamined in any court of the United States, than according to the rules of the common law.

AMENDMENT VIII

Excessive bail shall not be required, nor excessive fines imposed, nor cruel and unusual punishments inflicted.

AMENDMENT IX

The enumeration in the Constitution, of certain rights, shall not be construed to deny or disparage others retained by the people.

AMENDMENT X

The powers not delegated to the United States by the Constitution, nor prohibited by it to the states, are reserved to the states respectively, or to the people.

Additional Amendments

AMENDMENT XI

(1798)

The judicial power of the United States shall not be construed to extend to any suit in law or equity, commenced or prosecuted against one of the United States by citizens of another state, or by citizens or subjects of any foreign state.

AMENDMENT XII

(1804)

The electors shall meet in their respective states and vote by ballot for President and Vice President, one of whom, at least, shall not be an inhabitant of the same state with themselves; they shall name in their ballots the person voted for as President, and in distinct ballots the person voted for as Vice President, and they shall make distinct lists of all persons voted for as President, and of all persons voted for as Vice President, and of the number of votes for each, which lists they shall sign and certify, and transmit sealed to the seat of the government of the United States, directed to the President of the Senate;—The President of the Senate shall, in the presence of the Senate and House of Representatives, open all the certificates and the votes shall then be counted;—the person having the greatest number of votes for President, shall be the President, if such number be a majority of the whole number of electors appointed; and if no person have such majority, then from the persons having the highest numbers not exceeding three on the list of those voted for as President, the House of Representatives shall choose immediately, by ballot, the President. But in choosing the President, the votes shall be taken by states, the representation from each state having one vote; a quorum for this purpose shall consist of a member or members from two-thirds of the states, and a majority of all the states shall be necessary to a choice. And if the House of Representatives shall not choose a President whenever the right of choice shall devolve upon them, before the fourth day of March next following, then the Vice President shall act as President, as in the case of the death or other constitutional disability of the President. The person having the greatest number of votes as Vice President, shall be the Vice President, if such number be a majority of the whole number of electors appointed, and if no person have a majority, then from the two highest numbers on the list, the Senate shall choose the Vice President; a quorum for the purpose shall consist of two-thirds of the whole number of Senators, and a majority of the whole number shall be necessary to a choice. But no person constitutionally ineligible to the office of President shall be eligible to that of Vice President of the United States.

AMENDMENT XIII

(1865)

Section 1. Neither slavery nor involuntary servitude, except as a punishment for crime whereof the party shall have been duly convicted, shall exist within the United States, or any place subject to their jurisdiction.

Section 2. Congress shall have power to enforce this article by appropriate legislation.

AMENDMENT XIV

(1868)

Section 1. All persons born or naturalized in the United States, and subject to the jurisdiction thereof, are citizens of the United States and of the state wherein they reside. No state shall make or enforce any law which shall abridge the privileges or immunities of citizens of the United States; nor shall any state deprive any person of life, liberty, or property, without due process of law; nor deny to any person within its jurisdiction the equal protection of the laws.

Section 2. Representatives shall be apportioned among the several states according to their respective numbers, counting the whole number of persons in each state, excluding Indians not taxed. But when the right to vote at any election for the choice of electors for President and Vice President of the United States, Representatives in Congress, the executive and judicial officers of a state, or the members of the legislature thereof, is denied to any of the male inhabitants of such state, being twenty-one years of age, and citizens of the United States, or in any way abridged, except for participation in rebellion, or other crime, the basis of representation therein shall be reduced in the proportion which the number of such male citizens shall bear to the whole number of male citizens twenty-one years of age in such state.

Section 3. No person shall be a Senator or Representative in Congress, or elector of President and Vice President, or hold any office, civil or military, under the United States, or under any state, who, having previously taken an oath, as a member of Congress, or as an officer of the United States, or as a member of any state legislature, or as an executive or judicial officer of any state, to support the Constitution of the United States, shall have engaged in insurrection or rebellion against the same, or given aid or comfort to the enemies thereof. But Congress may by a vote of two-thirds of each House, remove such disability.

Section 4. The validity of the public debt of the United States, authorized by law, including debts incurred for payment of pensions and bounties for services in suppressing insurrection or rebellion, shall not be questioned. But neither the United States nor any state shall assume or pay any debt or obligation incurred in aid of insurrection or rebellion against the United States, or any claim for the loss or emancipation of any slave; but all such debts, obligations and claims shall be held illegal and void.

Section 5. The Congress shall have power to enforce, by appropriate legislation, the provisions of this article.

AMENDMENT XV

(1870)

Section 1. The right of citizens of the United States to vote shall not be denied or abridged by the United States or by any state on account of race, color, or previous condition of servitude.

Section 2. The Congress shall have power to enforce this article by appropriate legislation.

AMENDMENT XVI

(1913)

The Congress shall have power to lay and collect taxes on incomes, from whatever source derived, without apportionment among the several states, and without regard to any census of enumeration.

AMENDMENT XVII

(1913)

The Senate of the United States shall be composed of two Senators from each state, elected by the people thereof, for six years; and each Senator shall have one vote. The electors in each state shall have the qualifications requisite for electors of the most numerous branch of the state legislatures.

When vacancies happen in the representation of any state in the Senate, the executive authority of such state shall issue writs of election to fill such vacancies: Provided, that the legislature of any state may empower the executive thereof to make temporary appointments until the people fill the vacancies by election as the legislature may direct.

This amendment shall not be so construed as to affect the election or term of any Senator chosen before it becomes valid as part of the Constitution.

AMENDMENT XVIII

(1919)

Section 1. After one year from the ratification of this article the manufacture, sale, or transportation of intoxicating liquors within, the importation thereof into, or the exportation thereof from the United States and all territory subject to the jurisdiction thereof for beverage purposes is hereby prohibited.

Section 2. The Congress and the several states shall have concurrent power to enforce this article by appropriate legislation.

Section 3. This article shall be inoperative unless it shall have been ratified as an amendment to the Constitution by the legislatures of the several states, as provided in the Constitution, within seven years from the date of the submission hereof to the states by the Congress.

AMENDMENT XIX

(1920)

The right of citizens of the United States to vote shall not be denied or abridged by the United States or by any state on account of sex.

Congress shall have power to enforce this article by appropriate legislation.

AMENDMENT XX

(1933)

Section 1. The terms of the President and Vice President shall end at noon on the 20th day of January, and the terms of Senators and Representatives at noon on the 3d day of January, of the years in which such terms would have ended if this article had not been ratified; and the terms of their successors shall then begin.

Section 2. The Congress shall assemble at least once in every year, and such meeting shall begin at noon on the 3d day of January, unless they shall by law appoint a different day.

Section 3. If, at the time fixed for the beginning of the term of the President, the President-elect shall have died, the Vice President-elect shall become President. If a President shall not have been chosen before the time fixed for the beginning of his term, or if the President-elect shall have failed to qualify, then the Vice President-elect shall act as President until a President shall have qualified; and the Congress may by law provide for the case wherein neither a President elect nor a Vice President-elect shall have qualified, declaring who shall then act as President, or the manner in which one who is to act shall be selected, and such person shall act accordingly until a President or Vice President shall have qualified.

Section 4. The Congress may by law provide for the case of the death of any of the persons from whom the House of Representatives may choose a President whenever the right of choice shall have devolved upon them, and for the case of the death of any of the persons from whom the Senate may choose a Vice President whenever the right of choice shall have devolved upon them.

Section 5. Sections 1 and 2 shall take effect on the 15th day of October following the ratification of this article.

Section 6. This article shall be inoperative unless it shall have been ratified as an amendment to the Constitution by the legislatures of three-fourths of the several states within seven years from the date of its submission.

AMENDMENT XXI

(1933)

Section 1. The eighteenth article of amendment to the Constitution of the United States is hereby repealed.

Section 2. The transportation or importation into any state, territory, or possession of the United States for delivery or use therein of intoxicating liquors, in violation of the laws thereof, is hereby prohibited.

Section 3. This article shall be inoperative unless it shall have been ratified as an amendment to the Constitution by conventions in the several states, as provided in the Constitution, within seven years from the date of the submission hereof to the states by the Congress.

AMENDMENT XXII

(1951)

Section 1. No person shall be elected to the office of the President more than twice, and no person who has held the office of President, or acted as President, for more than two years of a term to which some other person was elected President shall be elected to the office of the President more than once. But this article shall not apply to any person holding the office of President when this article was proposed by the Congress, and shall not prevent any person who may be holding the office of President, or acting as President, during the term within which this article becomes operative from holding the office of President or acting as President during the remainder of such term.

Section 2. This article shall be inoperative unless it shall have been ratified as an amendment to the Constitution by the legislatures of three-fourths of the several states within seven years from the date of its submission to the states by the Congress.

AMENDMENT XXIII

(1961)

Section 1. The District constituting the seat of government of the United States shall appoint in such manner as the Congress may direct:

A number of electors of President and Vice President equal to the whole number of Senators and Representatives in Congress to which the District would be entitled if it were a state, but in no event more than the least populous state; they shall be in addition to those appointed by the states, but they shall be considered, for the purposes of the election of President and Vice President, to be electors appointed by a state; and they shall meet in the District and perform such duties as provided by the twelfth article of amendment.

Section 2. The Congress shall have power to enforce this article by appropriate legislation.

AMENDMENT XXIV

(1964)

Section 1. The right of citizens of the United States to vote in any primary or other election for President or Vice President, for electors for President or Vice President, or for Senator or Representative in Congress, shall not be denied or abridged by the United States or any state by reason of failure to pay any poll tax or other tax.

Section 2. The Congress shall have power to enforce this article by appropriate legislation.

AMENDMENT XXV

(1967)

Section 1. In case of the removal of the President from office or of his death or resignation, the Vice President shall become President.

Section 2. Whenever there is a vacancy in the office of the Vice President, the President shall nominate a Vice President who shall take office upon confirmation by a majority vote of both Houses of Congress.

Section 3. Whenever the President transmits to the President pro tempore of the Senate and the Speaker of the House of Representatives his written declaration that he is unable to discharge the powers and duties of his office, and until he transmits to them a written declaration to the contrary, such powers and duties shall be discharged by the Vice President as Acting President.

Section 4. Whenever the Vice President and a majority of either the principal officers of the executive departments or of such other body as Congress may by law provide, transmit to the President pro tempore of the Senate and the Speaker of the House of Representatives their written declaration that the President is unable to discharge the powers and duties of his office, the Vice President shall immediately assume the powers and duties of the office as Acting President.

Thereafter, when the President transmits to the President pro tempore of the Senate and the Speaker of the House of Representatives his written declaration that no inability exists, he shall resume the powers and duties of his office unless the Vice President and a majority of either the principal officers of the executive department or of such other body as Congress may by law provide, transmit within four days to the President pro tempore of the Senate and the Speaker of the House of Representatives their written declaration that the President is unable to discharge the powers and duties of his office. Thereupon Congress shall decide the issue, assembling within forty-eight hours for that purpose if not in session. If the Congress, within twenty-one days after receipt of the latter written declaration, or, if Congress is not in session, within twenty-one days after Congress is required to assemble, determines by two-thirds vote of both Houses that the President is unable to discharge the powers and duties of his office, the Vice President shall continue to discharge the same as Acting President; otherwise, the President shall resume the powers and duties of his office.

AMENDMENT XXVI

(1971)

Section 1. The right of citizens of the United States, who are 18 years of age or older, to vote, shall not be denied or abridged by the United States or any state on account of age.

Section 2. The Congress shall have the power to enforce this article by appropriate legislation.

AMENDMENT XXVII

(1992)

No law varying the compensation for the services of the Senators and Representatives shall take effect until an election of Representatives shall have intervened.

APPENDIX D

Federalist Number 10

The Union as a Safeguard Against Domestic Faction and Insurrection

Author: James Madison

To the People of the State of New York:

    AMONG the numerous advantages promised by a well-constructed Union, none deserves to be more accurately developed than its tendency to break and control the violence of faction. The friend of popular governments never finds himself so much alarmed for their character and fate, as when he contemplates their propensity to this dangerous vice. He will not fail, therefore, to set a due value on any plan which, without violating the principles to which he is attached, provides a proper cure for it. The instability, injustice, and confusion introduced into the public councils, have, in truth, been the mortal diseases under which popular governments have everywhere perished; as they continue to be the favorite and fruitful topics from which the adversaries to liberty derive their most specious declamations. The valuable improvements made by the American constitutions on the popular models, both ancient and modern, cannot certainly be too much admired; but it would be an unwarrantable partiality, to contend that they have as effectually obviated the danger on this side, as was wished and expected. Complaints are everywhere heard from our most considerate and virtuous citizens, equally the friends of public and private faith, and of public and personal liberty, that our governments are too unstable, that the public good is disregarded in the conflicts of rival parties, and that measures are too often decided, not according to the rules of justice and the rights of the minor party, but by the superior force of an interested and overbearing majority. However anxiously we may wish that these complaints had no foundation, the evidence, of known facts will not permit us to deny that they are in some degree true. It will be found, indeed, on a candid review of our situation, that some of the distresses under which we labor have been erroneously charged on the operation of our governments; but it will be found, at the same time, that other causes will not alone account for many of our heaviest misfortunes; and, particularly, for that prevailing and increasing distrust of public engagements, and alarm for private rights, which are echoed from one end of the continent to the other. These must be chiefly, if not wholly, effects of the unsteadiness and injustice with which a factious spirit has tainted our public administrations.

    By a faction, I understand a number of citizens, whether amounting to a majority or a minority of the whole, who are united and actuated by some common impulse of passion, or of interest, adverse to the rights of other citizens, or to the permanent and aggregate interests of the community.

There are two methods of curing the mischiefs of faction: the one, by removing its causes; the other, by controlling its effects.

There are again two methods of removing the causes of faction: the one, by destroying the liberty which is essential to its existence; the other, by giving to every citizen the same opinions, the same passions, and the same interests.

It could never be more truly said than of the first remedy, that it was worse than the disease. Liberty is to faction what air is to fire, an aliment without which it instantly expires. But it could not be less folly to abolish liberty, which is essential to political life, because it nourishes faction, than it would be to wish the annihilation of air, which is essential to animal life, because it imparts to fire its destructive agency.

The second expedient is as impracticable as the first would be unwise. As long as the reason of man continues fallible, and he is at liberty to exercise it, different opinions will be formed. As long as the connection subsists between his reason and his self-love, his opinions and his passions will have a reciprocal influence on each other; and the former will be objects to which the latter will attach themselves. The diversity in the faculties of men, from which the rights of property originate, is not less an insuperable obstacle to a uniformity of interests. The protection of these faculties is the first object of government. From the protection of different and unequal faculties of acquiring property, the possession of different degrees and kinds of property immediately results; and from the influence of these on the sentiments and views of the respective proprietors, ensues a division of the society into different interests and parties.

The latent causes of faction are thus sown in the nature of man; and we see them everywhere brought into different degrees of activity, according to the different circumstances of civil society. A zeal for different opinions concerning religion, concerning government, and many other points, as well of speculation as of practice; an attachment to different leaders ambitiously contending for pre-eminence and power; or to persons of other descriptions whose fortunes have been interesting to the human passions, have, in turn, divided mankind into parties, inflamed them with mutual animosity, and rendered them much more disposed to vex and oppress each other than to co-operate for their common good. So strong is this propensity of mankind to fall into mutual animosities, that where no substantial occasion presents itself, the most frivolous and fanciful distinctions have been sufficient to kindle their unfriendly passions and excite their most violent conflicts. But the most common and durable source of factions has been the various and unequal distribution of property. Those who hold and those who are without property have ever formed distinct interests in society. Those who are creditors, and those who are debtors, fall under a like discrimination. A landed interest, a manufacturing interest, a mercantile interest, a moneyed interest, with many lesser interests, grow up of necessity in civilized nations, and divide them into different classes, actuated by different sentiments and views. The regulation of these various and interfering interests forms the principal task of modern legislation, and involves the spirit of party and faction in the necessary and ordinary operations of the government.

No man is allowed to be a judge in his own cause, because his interest would certainly bias his judgment, and, not improbably, corrupt his integrity. With equal, nay with greater reason, a body of men are unfit to be both judges and parties at the same time; yet what are many of the most important acts of legislation, but so many judicial determinations, not indeed concerning the rights of single persons, but concerning the rights of large bodies of citizens? And what are the different classes of legislators but advocates and parties to the causes which they determine? Is a law proposed concerning private debts? It is a question to which the creditors are parties on one side and the debtors on the other. Justice ought to hold the balance between them. Yet the parties are, and must be, themselves the judges; and the most numerous party, or, in other words, the most powerful faction must be expected to prevail. Shall domestic manufactures be encouraged, and in what degree, by restrictions on foreign manufactures? are questions which would be differently decided by the landed and the manufacturing classes, and probably by neither with a sole regard to justice and the public good. The apportionment of taxes on the various descriptions of property is an act which seems to require the most exact impartiality; yet there is, perhaps, no legislative act in which greater opportunity and temptation are given to a predominant party to trample on the rules of justice. Every shilling with which they overburden the inferior number, is a shilling saved to their own pockets.

It is in vain to say that enlightened statesmen will be able to adjust these clashing interests, and render them all subservient to the public good. Enlightened statesmen will not always be at the helm. Nor, in many cases, can such an adjustment be made at all without taking into view indirect and remote considerations, which will rarely prevail over the immediate interest which one party may find in disregarding the rights of another or the good of the whole.

The inference to which we are brought is, that the CAUSES of faction cannot be removed, and that relief is only to be sought in the means of controlling its EFFECTS.

If a faction consists of less than a majority, relief is supplied by the republican principle, which enables the majority to defeat its sinister views by regular vote. It may clog the administration, it may convulse the society; but it will be unable to execute and mask its violence under the forms of the Constitution. When a majority is included in a faction, the form of popular government, on the other hand, enables it to sacrifice to its ruling passion or interest both the public good and the rights of other citizens. To secure the public good and private rights against the danger of such a faction, and at the same time to preserve the spirit and the form of popular government, is then the great object to which our inquiries are directed. Let me add that it is the great desideratum by which this form of government can be rescued from the opprobrium under which it has so long labored, and be recommended to the esteem and adoption of mankind.

By what means is this object attainable? Evidently by one of two only. Either the existence of the same passion or interest in a majority at the same time must be prevented, or the majority, having such coexistent passion or interest, must be rendered, by their number and local situation, unable to concert and carry into effect schemes of oppression. If the impulse and the opportunity be suffered to coincide, we well know that neither moral nor religious motives can be relied on as an adequate control. They are not found to be such on the injustice and violence of individuals, and lose their efficacy in proportion to the number combined together, that is, in proportion as their efficacy becomes needful.

From this view of the subject it may be concluded that a pure democracy, by which I mean a society consisting of a small number of citizens, who assemble and administer the government in person, can admit of no cure for the mischiefs of faction. A common passion or interest will, in almost every case, be felt by a majority of the whole; a communication and concert result from the form of government itself; and there is nothing to check the inducements to sacrifice the weaker party or an obnoxious individual. Hence it is that such democracies have ever been spectacles of turbulence and contention; have ever been found incompatible with personal security or the rights of property; and have in general been as short in their lives as they have been violent in their deaths. Theoretic politicians, who have patronized this species of government, have erroneously supposed that by reducing mankind to a perfect equality in their political rights, they would, at the same time, be perfectly equalized and assimilated in their possessions, their opinions, and their passions.

A republic, by which I mean a government in which the scheme of representation takes place, opens a different prospect, and promises the cure for which we are seeking. Let us examine the points in which it varies from pure democracy, and we shall comprehend both the nature of the cure and the efficacy which it must derive from the Union.

The two great points of difference between a democracy and a republic are: first, the delegation of the government, in the latter, to a small number of citizens elected by the rest; secondly, the greater number of citizens, and greater sphere of country, over which the latter may be extended.

The effect of the first difference is, on the one hand, to refine and enlarge the public views, by passing them through the medium of a chosen body of citizens, whose wisdom may best discern the true interest of their country, and whose patriotism and love of justice will be least likely to sacrifice it to temporary or partial considerations. Under such a regulation, it may well happen that the public voice, pronounced by the representatives of the people, will be more consonant to the public good than if pronounced by the people themselves, convened for the purpose. On the other hand, the effect may be inverted. Men of factious tempers, of local prejudices, or of sinister designs, may, by intrigue, by corruption, or by other means, first obtain the suffrages, and then betray the interests, of the people. The question resulting is, whether small or extensive republics are more favorable to the election of proper guardians of the public weal; and it is clearly decided in favor of the latter by two obvious considerations:

In the first place, it is to be remarked that, however small the republic may be, the representatives must be raised to a certain number, in order to guard against the cabals of a few; and that, however large it may be, they must be limited to a certain number, in order to guard against the confusion of a multitude. Hence, the number of representatives in the two cases not being in proportion to that of the two constituents, and being proportionally greater in the small republic, it follows that, if the proportion of fit characters be not less in the large than in the small republic, the former will present a greater option, and consequently a greater probability of a fit choice.

In the next place, as each representative will be chosen by a greater number of citizens in the large than in the small republic, it will be more difficult for unworthy candidates to practice with success the vicious arts by which elections are too often carried; and the suffrages of the people being more free, will be more likely to centre in men who possess the most attractive merit and the most diffusive and established characters.

It must be confessed that in this, as in most other cases, there is a mean, on both sides of which inconveniences will be found to lie. By enlarging too much the number of electors, you render the representatives too little acquainted with all their local circumstances and lesser interests; as by reducing it too much, you render him unduly attached to these, and too little fit to comprehend and pursue great and national objects. The federal Constitution forms a happy combination in this respect; the great and aggregate interests being referred to the national, the local and particular to the State legislatures.

The other point of difference is, the greater number of citizens and extent of territory which may be brought within the compass of republican than of democratic government; and it is this circumstance principally which renders factious combinations less to be dreaded in the former than in the latter. The smaller the society, the fewer probably will be the distinct parties and interests composing it; the fewer the distinct parties and interests, the more frequently will a majority be found of the same party; and the smaller the number of individuals composing a majority, and the smaller the compass within which they are placed, the more easily will they concert and execute their plans of oppression. Extend the sphere, and you take in a greater variety of parties and interests; you make it less probable that a majority of the whole will have a common motive to invade the rights of other citizens; or if such a common motive exists, it will be more difficult for all who feel it to discover their own strength, and to act in unison with each other. Besides other impediments, it may be remarked that, where there is a consciousness of unjust or dishonorable purposes, communication is always checked by distrust in proportion to the number whose concurrence is necessary.

Hence, it clearly appears, that the same advantage which a republic has over a democracy, in controlling the effects of faction, is enjoyed by a large over a small republic,—is enjoyed by the Union over the States composing it. Does the advantage consist in the substitution of representatives whose enlightened views and virtuous sentiments render them superior to local prejudices and schemes of injustice? It will not be denied that the representation of the Union will be most likely to possess these requisite endowments. Does it consist in the greater security afforded by a greater variety of parties, against the event of any one party being able to outnumber and oppress the rest? In an equal degree does the increased variety of parties comprised within the Union, increase this security. Does it, in fine, consist in the greater obstacles opposed to the concert and accomplishment of the secret wishes of an unjust and interested majority? Here, again, the extent of the Union gives it the most palpable advantage.

The influence of factious leaders may kindle a flame within their particular States, but will be unable to spread a general conflagration through the other States. A religious sect may degenerate into a political faction in a part of the Confederacy; but the variety of sects dispersed over the entire face of it must secure the national councils against any danger from that source. A rage for paper money, for an abolition of debts, for an equal division of property, or for any other improper or wicked project, will be less apt to pervade the whole body of the Union than a particular member of it; in the same proportion as such a malady is more likely to taint a particular county or district, than an entire State.

In the extent and proper structure of the Union, therefore, we behold a republican remedy for the diseases most incident to republican government. And according to the degree of pleasure and pride we feel in being republicans, ought to be our zeal in cherishing the spirit and supporting the character of Federalists.

PUBLIUS.

Federalist Number 51

The Structure of the Government Must Furnish the Proper Checks and Balances Between the Different Departments

Author: James Madison

To the People of the State of New York:

TO WHAT expedient, then, shall we finally resort, for maintaining in practice the necessary partition of power among the several departments, as laid down in the Constitution? The only answer that can be given is, that as all these exterior provisions are found to be inadequate, the defect must be supplied, by so contriving the interior structure of the government as that its several constituent parts may, by their mutual relations, be the means of keeping each other in their proper places. Without presuming to undertake a full development of this important idea, I will hazard a few general observations, which may perhaps place it in a clearer light, and enable us to form a more correct judgment of the principles and structure of the government planned by the convention.

In order to lay a due foundation for that separate and distinct exercise of the different powers of government, which to a certain extent is admitted on all hands to be essential to the preservation of liberty, it is evident that each department should have a will of its own; and consequently should be so constituted that the members of each should have as little agency as possible in the appointment of the members of the others. Were this principle rigorously adhered to, it would require that all the appointments for the supreme executive, legislative, and judiciary magistracies should be drawn from the same fountain of authority, the people, through channels having no communication whatever with one another. Perhaps such a plan of constructing the several departments would be less difficult in practice than it may in contemplation appear. Some difficulties, however, and some additional expense would attend the execution of it. Some deviations, therefore, from the principle must be admitted. In the constitution of the judiciary department in particular, it might be inexpedient to insist rigorously on the principle: first, because peculiar qualifications being essential in the members, the primary consideration ought to be to select that mode of choice which best secures these qualifications; secondly, because the permanent tenure by which the appointments are held in that department, must soon destroy all sense of dependence on the authority conferring them.

It is equally evident, that the members of each department should be as little dependent as possible on those of the others, for the emoluments annexed to their offices. Were the executive magistrate, or the judges, not independent of the legislature in this particular, their independence in every other would be merely nominal.

But the great security against a gradual concentration of the several powers in the same department, consists in giving to those who administer each department the necessary constitutional means and personal motives to resist encroachments of the others. The provision for defense must in this, as in all other cases, be made commensurate to the danger of attack. Ambition must be made to counteract ambition. The interest of the man must be connected with the constitutional rights of the place. It may be a reflection on human nature, that such devices should be necessary to control the abuses of government. But what is government itself, but the greatest of all reflections on human nature? If men were angels, no government would be necessary. If angels were to govern men, neither external nor internal controls on government would be necessary. In framing a government which is to be administered by men over men, the great difficulty lies in this: you must first enable the government to control the governed; and in the next place oblige it to control itself. A dependence on the people is, no doubt, the primary control on the government; but experience has taught mankind the necessity of auxiliary precautions.

This policy of supplying, by opposite and rival interests, the defect of better motives, might be traced through the whole system of human affairs, private as well as public. We see it particularly displayed in all the subordinate distributions of power, where the constant aim is to divide and arrange the several offices in such a manner as that each may be a check on the other that the private interest of every individual may be a sentinel over the public rights. These inventions of prudence cannot be less requisite in the distribution of the supreme powers of the State.

But it is not possible to give to each department an equal power of self-defense. In republican government, the legislative authority necessarily predominates. The remedy for this inconveniency is to divide the legislature into different branches; and to render them, by different modes of election and different principles of action, as little connected with each other as the nature of their common functions and their common dependence on the society will admit. It may even be necessary to guard against dangerous encroachments by still further precautions. As the weight of the legislative authority requires that it should be thus divided, the weakness of the executive may require, on the other hand, that it should be fortified. An absolute negative on the legislature appears, at first view, to be the natural defense with which the executive magistrate should be armed. But perhaps it would be neither altogether safe nor alone sufficient. On ordinary occasions it might not be exerted with the requisite firmness, and on extraordinary occasions it might be perfidiously abused. May not this defect of an absolute negative be supplied by some qualified connection between this weaker department and the weaker branch of the stronger department, by which the latter may be led to support the constitutional rights of the former, without being too much detached from the rights of its own department?

If the principles on which these observations are founded be just, as I persuade myself they are, and they be applied as a criterion to the several State constitutions, and to the federal Constitution it will be found that if the latter does not perfectly correspond with them, the former are infinitely less able to bear such a test. There are, moreover, two considerations particularly applicable to the federal system of America, which place that system in a very interesting point of view.

First. In a single republic, all the power surrendered by the people is submitted to the administration of a single government; and the usurpations are guarded against by a division of the government into distinct and separate departments. In the compound republic of America, the power surrendered by the people is first divided between two distinct governments, and then the portion allotted to each subdivided among distinct and separate departments. Hence a double security arises to the rights of the people. The different governments will control each other, at the same time that each will be controlled by itself.

Second. It is of great importance in a republic not only to guard the society against the oppression of its rulers, but to guard one part of the society against the injustice of the other part. Different interests necessarily exist in different classes of citizens. If a majority be united by a common interest, the rights of the minority will be insecure. There are but two methods of providing against this evil: the one by creating a will in the community independent of the majority that is, of the society itself; the other, by comprehending in the society so many separate descriptions of citizens as will render an unjust combination of a majority of the whole very improbable, if not impracticable. The first method prevails in all governments possessing an hereditary or self-appointed authority. This, at best, is but a precarious security; because a power independent of the society may as well espouse the unjust views of the major, as the rightful interests of the minor party, and may possibly be turned against both parties. The second method will be exemplified in the federal republic of the United States. Whilst all authority in it will be derived from and dependent on the society, the society itself will be broken into so many parts, interests, and classes of citizens, that the rights of individuals, or of the minority, will be in little danger from interested combinations of the majority. In a free government the security for civil rights must be the same as that for religious rights. It consists in the one case in the multiplicity of interests, and in the other in the multiplicity of sects. The degree of security in both cases will depend on the number of interests and sects; and this may be presumed to depend on the extent of country and number of people comprehended under the same government. This view of the subject must particularly recommend a proper federal system to all the sincere and considerate friends of republican government, since it shows that in exact proportion as the territory of the Union may be formed into more circumscribed Confederacies, or States oppressive combinations of a majority will be facilitated: the best security, under the republican forms, for the rights of every class of citizens, will be diminished: and consequently the stability and independence of some member of the government, the only other security, must be proportionately increased. Justice is the end of government. It is the end of civil society. It ever has been and ever will be pursued until it be obtained, or until liberty be lost in the pursuit. In a society under the forms of which the stronger faction can readily unite and oppress the weaker, anarchy may as truly be said to reign as in a state of nature, where the weaker individual is not secured against the violence of the stronger; and as, in the latter state, even the stronger individuals are prompted, by the uncertainty of their condition, to submit to a government which may protect the weak as well as themselves; so, in the former state, will the more powerful factions or parties be gradually induced, by a like motive, to wish for a government which will protect all parties, the weaker as well as the more powerful. It can be little doubted that if the State of Rhode Island was separated from the Confederacy and left to itself, the insecurity of rights under the popular form of government within such narrow limits would be displayed by such reiterated oppressions of factious majorities that some power altogether independent of the people would soon be called for by the voice of the very factions whose misrule had proved the necessity of it. In the extended republic of the United States, and among the great variety of interests, parties, and sects which it embraces, a coalition of a majority of the whole society could seldom take place on any other principles than those of justice and the general good; whilst there being thus less danger to a minor from the will of a major party, there must be less pretext, also, to provide for the security of the former, by introducing into the government a will not dependent on the latter, or, in other words, a will independent of the society itself. It is no less certain than it is important, notwithstanding the contrary opinions which have been entertained, that the larger the society, provided it lie within a practical sphere, the more duly capable it will be of self-government. And happily for the REPUBLICAN CAUSE, the practicable sphere may be carried to a very great extent, by a judicious modification and mixture of the FEDERAL PRINCIPLE.

PUBLIUS.

APPENDIX E

Partisan Control of the Presidency, Congress, and the Supreme Court

Term	President	Party	Congress	Majority Party		Party of Appt. President	
				House	Senate	Supreme Court	
1789–1797	George Washington	Federalist	1st	(N/A)	(N/A)	6F	
			2nd	(N/A)	(N/A)		
			3rd	(N/A)	(N/A)		
			4th	(N/A)	(N/A)		
1797–1801	John Adams	Federalist	5th	(N/A)	(N/A)	6F	
			6th	Fed	Fed		
1801–1809	Thomas Jefferson	Democratic-Republican	7th	Dem-Rep	Dem-Rep	5F	1DR
			8th	Dem-Rep	Dem-Rep		
			9th	Dem-Rep	Dem-Rep		
			10th	Dem-Rep	Dem-Rep		
1809–1817	James Madison	Democratic-Republican	11th	Dem-Rep	Dem-Rep	3F	4DR
			12th	Dem-Rep	Dem-Rep		
			13th	Dem-Rep	Dem-Rep		
			14th	Dem-Rep	Dem-Rep		
1817–1825	James Monroe	Democratic-Republican	15th	Dem-Rep	Dem-Rep	2F	5DR
			16th	Dem-Rep	Dem-Rep		
			17th	Dem-Rep	Dem-Rep		
			18th	Dem-Rep	Dem-Rep		
1825–1829	John Quincy Adams	Democratic-Republican	19th	Admin	Admin	2F	5DR
			20th	Jack	Jack		
1829–1837	Andrew Jackson	Democrat	21st	Dem	Dem	2D 1F	4DR
			22nd	Dem	Dem		

(Continued)

				Majority Party		Party of Appt. President	
Term	President	Party	Congress	House	Senate		Supreme Court
			23rd	Dem	Dem		
			24th	Dem	Dem		
1837–1841	Martin Van Buren	Democrat	25th	Dem	Dem	7D	2DR
			26th	Dem	Dem		
1841–1841	William Henry Harrison	Whig	27th	Whig	Whig	7D	2DR
1841–1845	John Tyler	Whig	27th	Whig	Whig	7D	2DR
			28th	Dem	Whig		
1845–1849	James K. Polk	Democrat	29th	Dem	Dem	8D	1W
			30th	Whig	Dem		
1849–1850	Zachary Taylor	Whig	31st	Dem	Dem	8D	1W
1850–1853	Millard Fillmore	Whig	32nd	Dem	Dem	7D	2W
1853–1857	Franklin Pierce	Democrat	33rd	Dem	Dem	7D	2W
			34th	Rep	Dem		
1857–1861	James Buchanan	Democrat	35th	Dem	Dem	8D	1W
			36th	Rep	Dem		
1861–1865	Abraham Lincoln	Republican	37th	Rep	Rep	5D 1W	3R
			38th	Rep	Rep		
1865–1869	Andrew Johnson	Republican	39th	Union	Union	2D 1W	6R
			40th	Rep	Rep		
1869–1877	Ulysses S. Grant	Republican	41st	Rep	Rep	2D	7R
			42nd	Rep	Rep		
			43rd	Rep	Rep		
			44th	Dem	Rep		
1877–1881	Rutherford B. Hayes	Republican	45th	Dem	Rep	1D	8R
1881	James A. Garfield	Republican	47th	Rep	Rep	1D	8R
1881–1885	Chester A. Arthur	Republican	48th	Dem	Rep		9R
1885–1889	Grover Cleveland	Democrat	49th	Dem	Rep		9R
			50th	Dem	Rep		
1889–1893	Benjamin Harrison	Republican	51st	Rep	Rep	2D	7R
			52nd	Dem	Rep		
1893–1897	Grover Cleveland	Democrat	53rd	Dem	Dem	2D	7R
			54th	Rep	Rep		
1897–1901	William McKinley	Republican	55th	Rep	Rep	3D	6R
			56th	Rep	Rep		

(Continued)

APPENDIX E

Term	President	Party	Congress	Majority Party		Party of Appt. President	
				House	Senate	Supreme Court	
1901–1909	Theodore Roosevelt	Republican	57th	Rep	Rep	3D	6R
			58th	Rep	Rep		
			59th	Rep	Rep		
			60th	Rep	Rep		
1909–1913	William Howard Taft	Republican	61st	Rep	Rep	1D	8R
			62nd	Dem	Rep		
1913–1921	Woodrow Wilson	Democrat	63rd	Dem	Dem	2D	7R
			64th	Dem	Dem		
			65th	Dem	Dem		
			66th	Rep	Rep		
1921–1923	Warren G. Harding	Republican	67th	Rep	Rep	3D	6R
1923–1929	Calvin Coolidge	Republican	68th	Rep	Rep	2D	7R
			69th	Rep	Rep		
			70th	Rep	Rep		
1929–1933	Herbert Hoover	Republican	71st	Rep	Rep	2D	7R
			72nd	Dem	Rep		
1933–1945	Franklin D. Roosevelt	Democrat	73rd	Dem	Dem	5D	4R
			74th	Dem	Dem		
			75th	Dem	Dem		
			76th	Dem	Dem		
			77th	Dem	Dem		
			78th	Dem	Dem		
1945–1953	Harry S. Truman	Democrat	79th	Dem	Dem	9D	
			80th	Rep	Rep		
			81st	Dem	Dem		
			82nd	Dem	Dem		
1953–1961	Dwight D. Eisenhower	Republican	83rd	Rep	Rep	6D	3R
			84th	Dem	Dem		
			85th	Dem	Dem		
			86th	Dem	Dem		
1961–1963	John F. Kennedy	Democrat	87th	Dem	Dem	4D	5R
1963–1969	Lyndon B. Johnson	Democrat	88th	Dem	Dem	5D	4R
			89th	Dem	Dem		
			90th	Dem	Dem		
1969–1974	Richard M. Nixon	Republican	91st	Dem	Dem	4D	5R
			92nd	Dem	Dem		

(Continued)

Term	President	Party	Congress	Majority Party		Party of Appt. President	
				House	Senate	Supreme Court	
1974–1977	Gerald R. Ford	Republican	93rd	Dem	Dem	2D	7R
			94th	Dem	Dem		
1977–1981	Jimmy Carter	Democrat	95th	Dem	Dem	2D	7R
			96th	Dem	Dem		
1981–1989	Ronald Reagan	Republican	97th	Dem	Rep	2D	7R
			98th	Dem	Rep		
			99th	Dem	Rep		
			100th	Dem	Dem		
1989–1993	George Bush	Republican	101st	Dem	Dem	1D	8R
			102nd	Dem	Dem		
1993–2001	William Clinton	Democrat	103rd	Dem	Dem	2D	7R
			104th	Rep	Rep		
			105th	Rep	Rep		
			106th	Rep	Rep		
2001–2009	George W. Bush	Republican	107th	Rep	Dem	2D	7R
			108th	Rep	Rep		
			109th	Rep	Rep		
			110th	Dem	Dem		
2009–2017	Barack Obama	Democrat	111th	Dem	Dem	2D	7R
			112th	Rep	Dem	4D	5R
			113th	Rep	Dem		
			114th	Rep	Rep	4D	5R
2017–	Donald J. Trump	Republican	115th	Rep	Rep	4D	5R

REFERENCES

Abraham, Henry J. 1993. *The Judicial Process*. 6th ed. New York: Oxford University Press.

Abramowitz, Alan and Kyle Saunders. 1998. "Ideological Realignment in the U.S. Electorate." *Journal of Politics* 60 (August): 634–652.

Abramson, Paul R., John H. Aldrich, and David W. Rohde. 1999. *Change and Continuity in the 1996 and 1998 Elections*. Washington, DC: CQ Press.

Abramson, Paul R., John H. Aldrich, and David W. Rohde. 2006. *Change and Continuity in the 2004 Elections*. Washington, DC: CQ Press.

Aftergood, Steven. 2008. "The Next President Should Open Up the Bush Administration's Record." *Nieman Watchdog*, February 7. http://www.niemanwatchdog.org/index.cfm?fuseaction=ask_this.view&askthisid=321 (accessed September 19, 2010).

Ainsworth, Scott H. 1997. "The Role of Legislators in the Determination of Interest Group Influence." *Legislative Studies Quarterly* 22 (November): 517–533.

Aldrich, John H. 1993. "Rational Choice and Turnout." *American Journal of Political Science* 37 (February): 246–278.

Aldrich, John H. 2011. *Why Parties? A Second Look*. Chicago: University of Chicago Press.

Aldrich, John H. and David W. Rohde. 2000. "The Consequences of Party Organization in the House: The Role of the Majority and Minority Parties in Conditional Party Government." In *Polarized Politics: Congress and the President in a Partisan Era*, ed. Jon R. Bond and Richard Fleisher. Washington, DC: CQ Press.

Alexa. 2017. "The Top 500 Sites on the Web." http://www.alexa.com/topsites/category/News

Alexander, F. King. 1998. "Private Institutions and Public Dollars: An Analysis of the Effect of Federal Direct Student Aid on Public and Private Institutions of Higher Education." *Journal of Education Finance* 23 (Winter): 390–416.

Alford, John R., Carolyn L. Funk, and John R. Hibbing. 2005. "Are Political Orientations Genetically Transmitted?" *American Political Science Review* 99 (May): 153–168.

Alger, David. 1996. *The Media and Politics*. 2nd ed. Belmont, CA: Wadsworth.

Allard, Scott and Sheldon Danziger. 2000. "Welfare Magnets: Myth or Reality?" *Journal of Politics* 62(2): 350–368.

Allcott, Hunt and Matthew Gentzkow. 2017. "Social Media and Fake News in the 2016 Election." *National Bureau of Economic Research*. Working Paper 23089. http://www.nber.org/papers/w23089

Allsop, Dee and Herbert F. Weisberg. 1988. "Measuring Change in Party Identification in an Election Campaign." *American Journal of Political Science* 32 (November): 996–1017.

American National Election Studies. 2006. *The ANES Guide to Public Opinion and Electoral Behavior*. Ann Arbor: University of Michigan, Center for Political Studies. http://www.electionstudies.org/nesguide/nesguide.htm (accessed September 19, 2010).

Americans United for Affirmative Action. 1999. "Affirmative Action Timeline." http://www.aaua.org/timeline (accessed March 30, 1999).

Amnesty International. 2006. "The Death Penalty: Abolitionist and Retentionist Countries" (last updated May 15, 2006). http://web.amnesty.org/pages/deathpenalty—countries-eng (accessed June 13, 2006).

Anderson, Ashley, Dominique Brossard, Dietram Scheufele, Michael Xenos, and Peter Ladwig. 2013. "The 'Nasty Effect': Online Incivility and the Risk Perceptions of Emerging Technologies." *Journal of Computer-Mediated Communication* 19: 373–387.

Anderson, James. 2000. *Public Policymaking*. 4th ed. New York: Houghton Mifflin.

Ansolabehere, Stephen. 2009. "Effects of Identification Requirements on Voting: Evidence from the Experiences of Voters on Elections Day." *PS: Political Science and Politics* 42: 127–130.

Ansolabehere, S., S. Iyengar, A. Simon, and N. Valentino. 1994. "Does Attack Advertising Demobilize the Electorate?" *American Political Science Review* 88: 829–838.

Anspach, Nicolas M. 2017. "The New Personal Influence: How Our Facebook Friends Influence the News We Read."

Political Communication. http://www.tandfonline.com/doi/full/10.1080/10584609.2017.1316329.

Appleman, Eric M. 2008. "Early Endorsements by Congressmen, Senators and Governors." *Democracy in Action: P2008.* http://www.gwu.edu/~action/2008/cands08/endorse 08el.html.

Appleman, Eric M. 2012. "National Endorsements (pre-Iowa Caucuses)." *Democracy in Action: P2012.* http://www.p2012.org/candidates/natendorseprecaucus.html.

Appleman, Eric M. 2016. "National Endorsements—Republicans… to Jan. 13, 2016 only." *Democracy in Action: P2016.* http://www.p2016.org/candidates/natendorse16.html.

Arrow, Kenneth. 1963. *Social Choice and Individual Values.* New Haven, CT: Yale University Press.

Associated Press. 2009. "US Sn. Lindsey Graham Censured by SC County GOP." http://www.google.com/hostednews/ap/article/ALeqM5j5LOd06Q7MF-pkt9sNJ35kNoTM4w D9BTDPE81 (accessed November 30, 2009).

Association of American Medical Colleges. 2016. Press release, November 1. https://news.aamc.org/press-releases/article/applicant-enrollment-2016/

Austin-Smith, David. 1995. "Campaign Contributions and Access." *American Political Science Review* 89 (September): 566–581.

Ayto, John. 1990. *Dictionary of Word Origins.* New York: Arcade Publishing, Little, Brown.

Barber, Benjamin. 1996. *Jihad vs. McWorld: Terrorism's Challenge to Democracy.* New York: Ballantine Books.

Barber, James David. 1992. *The Presidential Character.* New York: Prentice-Hall.

Barone, Michael and Richard E. Cohen. 2007. *Almanac of American Politics 2008.* Washington, DC: National Journal.

Barone, Michael and Richard E. Cohen. 2015. *Almanac of American Politics 2016.* Washington, DC: National Journal.

Barone, Michael and Chuck McCutcheon. 2011. *Almanac of American Politics 2012.* Washington, DC: National Journal.

Bartels, Larry M. 1993. "Messages Received: The Political Impact of Media Exposure." *American Political Science Review* 87 (June): 267–285.

Barthel, Michael. 2016. "Newspapers: Fact Sheet". Pew Research Center. http://www.journalism.org/2016/06/15/newspapers-fact-sheet/?utm_content=buffereeb33&utm_medium=social&utm_source=plus.google.com&utm_campaign=buffer.

Barthel, Michael and Amy Mitchell. 2017. "Americans Attitudes About the News Media Deeply Divided Along Partisan Lines." Pew Research Center. http://www.journalism.org/2017/05/10/americans-attitudes-about-the-news-media-deeply-divided-along-partisan-lines/.

Baum, Matthew and Tim Groeling. 2008. "New Media and the Polarization of American Political Discourse." *Political Communication* 25: 345–365.

Baumgartner, Frank R. and Bryan D. Jones. 1993. *Agendas and Instability in American Politics.* Chicago: University of Chicago Press.

Baumgartner, Frank R. and Beth L. Leech. 1998. *Basic Interests: The Importance of Groups in Politics and in Political Science.* Princeton, NJ: Princeton University Press.

Baumgartner, Frank R. and Beth L. Leech. 2001. "Interest Niches and Policy Bandwagons: Patterns of Interest Group Involvement in National Politics." *Journal of Politics* 63 (November): 1191–1213.

Baumgartner, Frank R., Jeffrey M. Berry, Marie Hojnacki, David C. Kimball, and Beth L. Leech. 2009. *Lobbying and Policy Change: Who Wins, Who Loses, and Why.* Chicago: University of Chicago Press.

Baumgartner, Jody and Jonathan Morris. 2006. "The Daily Show Effect: Candidates, Efficacy and American Youth." *American Politics Research* 34: 341–367.

Bawn, Kathleen. 1999. "Constructing 'Us': Ideology, Coalition Politics, and False Consciousness." *American Journal of Political Science* 43 (April): 303–334.

Baybeck, Brady and William R. Lowry. 2000. "Federalism Outcomes and Ideological Preferences: The U.S. Supreme Court and Preemption Cases." *Publius* 30 (Summer): 73–97.

Beard, Charles A. 1913. *An Economic Interpretation of the Constitution of the United States.* New York: Macmillan.

Beauchamp, Nicholas. 2016. "Predicting and Interpolating State-Level Polls Using Twitter Textual Data." *American Journal of Political Science.* 61: 490–503.

Becker, Carl. 1922. *The Declaration of Independence: A Study in the History of Political Ideas.* New York: Harcourt, Brace.

Beckett, Katherine. 1997. *Making Crime Pay: Law and Order in Contemporary American Politics.* New York: Oxford University Press.

Beckmann, Matthew N. 2010. *Pushing the Agenda: Presidential Leadership in U.S. Lawmaking, 1943–2004.* Cambridge, UK: Cambridge University Press.

Bell, Roger. 1984. *Last Among Equals.* Honolulu: University of Hawaii Press.

Bennett, Stephen Earl and David Resnick. 1990. "The Implications of Nonvoting for Democracy in the United States." *American Journal of Political Science* 34 (August): 771–802.

Benson, T. 1996. "Rhetoric, Civility, and Community: Political Debate on Computer Bulletin Boards." *Communication Quarterly* 44: 359–378.

Benton, Wilbourne E., ed. 1986. *1787: Drafting the U.S. Constitution*. Vol. 2. College Station: Texas A&M University Press.

Berg-Andersson, Richard E. 2008. "Election 2008 Primary, Caucus, and Convention Phase." *The Green Papers*, http://www.thegreenpapers.com/P08/.

Berg-Andersson, Richard E. 2012. "Election 2012 Presidential Primaries, Caucuses, and Conventions." *The Green Papers*, http://www.thegreenpapers.com/P12/ (accessed March 2, 2013).

Berg-Andersson, Richard E. 2016. "Election 2016 Presidential Primaries, Caucuses, and Conventions." *The Green Papers*, http://www.thegreenpapers.com/P16/ (accessed August 18, 2016).

Berke, Richard L. 1999. "Weighing the Vice Presidential Factor in Gore's Feeble Showing in the Polls." *New York Times,* March 6, A7.

Berke, Richard L. 2001. "Bush Is Providing Corporate Model for White House." *New York Times,* March 11. http://www.nytimes.com/2001/03/11/politics/11GOVE.html (accessed October 23, 2004).

Berman, Ari. 2016. "A 90-Year-Old Woman Who's Voted Since 1948 Was Disenfranchised by Wisconsin's Voter-ID Law." *The Nation*. https://www.thenation.com/article/a-90-year-old-woman-whos-voted-since-1948-was-disenfranchised-by-wisconsins-voter-id-law/.

Berman, David R. and Tanis J. Salant. 1998. "Minority Representation, Resistance, and Public Policy: The Navajos and the Counties." *Publius* 28 (Autumn): 83–104.

Berry, William, Richard Fording, and Russel Hanson. 2003. "Reassessing the 'Race to the Bottom' in State Welfare Policy." *The Journal of Politics* 65 (2): 327–349.

Best, Judith A. 1996. *The Choice of the People: Debating the Electoral College*. Lanham, MD: Rowman & Littlefield.

Bibby, John F. 1996. *Politics, Parties, and Elections in America*. 3rd ed. Chicago: Nelson-Hall.

Bibby, John F. and L. Sandy Maisel. 1998. *Two Parties—Or More? The American Party System*. Boulder, CO: Westview Press.

Bickel, Alexander M. 1962. *The Least Dangerous Branch: The Supreme Court at the Bar of Politics*. Indianapolis, IN: Bobbs-Merrill.

Bickers, Kenneth N. and Robert M. Stein. 1996. "The Electoral Dynamics of the Federal Pork Barrel." *American Journal of Political Science* 40 (November): 1300–1326.

Binder, Sarah A. and Steven S. Smith. 1997. *Politics or Principle: Filibustering in the United States Senate*. Washington, DC: Brookings Institution.

Biskupic, Joan. 1999. "Disabled Pupils Win Right to Medical Aid." *Washington Post,* March 4, A1.

Black, Charles, Jr. 1974. *Impeachment: A Handbook*. New Haven, CT: Yale University Press.

Blaustein, Albert and Roy M. Mersky. 1978. *The First One Hundred Justices*. Hamden, CT: Archon Books.

Bond, Jon R. 1980. "The Politics of Court Structure: The Addition of New Federal Judges, 1949–1978." *Law and Politics Quarterly* 2 (April): 181–188.

Bond, Jon R. 2018. "President Trump Meet Professor Neustadt: Is Donald Trump a Threat to the Scientific Study of the Presidency?" Presented at the annual meeting of the Southern Political Science Association, New Orleans, LA, January 4–6, 2018.

Bond, Jon R. and Richard Fleisher. 1990. *The President in the Legislative Arena*. Chicago: University of Chicago Press.

Bond, Jon R., Cary Covington, and Richard Fleisher. 1985. "Explaining Challenger Quality in Congressional Elections." *Journal of Politics* 47 (May): 510–529.

Bond, Jon R., Richard Fleisher, and Jeffrey Cohen. 2015. "Presidential-Congressional Relations in an Era of Polarized Parties and a 60-Vote Senate." In *American Gridlock: Causes, Characteristics, and Consequences of Polarization*, ed. James A. Thurber and Antoine Yoshinaka. New York: Cambridge University Press.

Bond, Jon R., Richard Fleisher, and Glen S. Krutz. 2009. "Malign Neglect: Evidence That Delay Has Become the Primary Method of Defeating Presidential Appointments." *Congress and the Presidency* 36 (September–December): 226–243.

Boulard, Garry. 1999. "More News, Less Coverage?" *State Legislatures*, 25(6, June): 14–18.

Bradner, Eric. 2017. "Conway: Trump White House Offered 'Alternative Facts' on Crowd Size." *CNN*. https://www.cnn.com/2017/01/22/politics/kellyanne-conway-alternative-facts/index.html.

Brady, David W., Joseph Cooper, and Patricia Hurley. 1979. "The Decline of Party in the U.S. House of Representatives, 1887–1968." *Legislative Studies Quarterly* 4 (August): 381–407.

Brehm, John and Scott Gates. 1997. *Working, Shirking, and Sabotage*. Ann Arbor: University of Michigan Press.

Briffault, Robert. 1930. *Rational Evolution: The Making of Humanity*. New York: Macmillan.

Brinkley, Alan. 1993. *The Unfinished Nation*. New York: McGraw-Hill.

Broder, David S. 2000. *Democracy Derailed*. New York: Harcourt.

Browning, Graeme. 1996. "Please Hold for Election Results." *National Journal* 28 (November): 2517.

Brudnick, Ida A. 2008. "Salaries of Members of Congress: A List of Payable Rates and Effective Dates, 1789–2008." Congressional Research Service, February 21. Washington, DC: Library of Congress. http://www.senate.gov/reference/resources/pdf/97-1011.pdf (accessed May 21, 2010).

Budak, Ceren, Sharad Goel, and Justin M. Rao. 2016. "Fair and Balanced? Quantifying Media Bias Through Crowdsourced Content Analysis." *Public Opinion Quarterly* 80: 250–271.

Budesheim, Thomas Lee and Stephen J. DePaola. 1994. "Beauty or the Beast? The Effects of Appearance, Personality, and Issue Information on Evaluations of Candidates." *Personality and Social Psychology Bulletin* 20 (August): 339–349.

Burns, Alexander. 2017. "How Attorneys General Became Democrats' Bulwark Against Trump". *New York Times*. https://www.nytimes.com/2017/02/06/us/attorneys-general-democrats-trump-travel-ban.html

Business Insider. 2012. "These Six Corporations Control 90% of the Media in America." http://www.businessinsider.com/these-6-corporations-control-90-of-the-media-in-america-2012-6?IR=T

Byrne, Robert. 1988. *The 1,911 Best Things Anybody Ever Said*. New York: Fawcett Columbine.

Cain, Bruce, John Ferejohn, and Morris Fiorina. 1987. *The Personal Vote*. Cambridge, MA: Harvard University Press.

Caldeira, Gregory A. and John R. Wright. 1990. "Amici Curiae before the Supreme Court: Who Participates, When, and How Much?" *Journal of Politics* 52 (August): 782–806.

Cameron, Charles M. 2000. *Veto Bargaining: Presidents and the Politics of Negative Power*. Cambridge, UK: Cambridge University Press.

Campbell, Angus. 1960. "Surge and Decline: A Study of Electoral Change." *Public Opinion Quarterly* 24 (Autumn): 397–418.

Campbell, Angus, Philip Converse, Warren Miller, and Donald Stokes. 1960. *The American Voter*. New York: Wiley.

Campbell, Colin. 1986. *Managing the Presidency: Carter, Reagan, and the Search for Executive Harmony*. Pittsburgh, PA: University of Pittsburgh Press.

Canon, David T. 1990. *Actors, Athletes, and Astronauts: Political Amateurs in the United States Congress*. Chicago: University of Chicago Press.

Carlin, Diana Prentice. 1992. "Presidential Debates as Focal Points for Campaign Arguments." *Political Communication* 9 (January–March): 251–265.

Carp, Robert A., Ronald Stidham, and Kenneth L. Manning. 2004. *Judicial Process in America*. Washington, DC: CQ Press.

Carr, Robert K. 1947. *Federal Protection of Civil Rights: Quest for a Sword*. New York: Cornell University Press.

Cassidy, Christina and Ivan Mereno. 2017. "Wisconsin Voter ID Law Proved Insurmountable for Many Voters." *Milwaukee Journal Sentinel*. http://www.jsonline.com/story/news/politics/2017/05/14/wisconsin-voter-id-law-proved-insurmountable-many/321680001/

Center on Budget and Policy Priorities. 2016. "A Guide to Statistics on Historical Trends in Income Inequality." http://www.cbpp.org/research/poverty-and-inequality/a-guide-to-statistics-on-historical-trends-in-income-inequality.

Center for People and the Press. 2011. "Press Widely Criticized, But Trusted More Than Other Information Sources." http://www.people-press.org/2011/09/22/press-widely-criticized-but-trusted-more-than-other-institutions/ (accessed May 20, 2014).

Center for Responsive Politics. 2012a. "Super PACs." http://www.opensecrets.org/pacs/superpacs.php?cycle=2012 (accessed May 1, 2012).

Center for Responsive Politics. 2012b. "Types of Advocacy Groups." http://www.opensecrets.org/527s/types.php (accessed May 1, 2012).

Chaffee, Steven and Stacey Frank. 1996. "How Americans Get Political Information: Print Versus Broadcast News." *Annals of the American Academy of Political and Social Science* 546: 48–58.

Chandler, Ralph C. and Jack C. Plano. 1988. *The Public Administration Dictionary*. Santa Barbara, CA: ABC-CLIO.

Chin, Michelle L., Jon R. Bond, and Nehemia Geva. 2000. "A Foot in the Door: An Experimental Study of PAC and Constituency Effects on Access." *Journal of Politics* 62 (May): 534–549.

Chong, Dennis and James Druckman. 2007. "Framing Public Opinion in Competitive Democracies." *American Political Science Review* 101: 637–655.

Claasen, Ryan L. and Stephen P. Nicholson. 2013. "Extreme Voices: Interest Groups and the Misrepresentation of Issue Publics." *Public Opinion Quarterly* 77: 861–887.

Clark, Charles S. 1997. "Feminism's Future." *CQ Researcher* 7 (February): 169–192.

Clark, Peter and James Q. Wilson. 1961. "Incentive Systems: A Theory of Organizations." *Administrative Science Quarterly* 6 (September): 129–166.

Cobb, Roger W. and Charles D. Elder. 1983. *Participation in American Politics: The Dynamics of Agenda Building.* Baltimore, MD: Johns Hopkins University Press.

Coffey, Brian and Stephen Woolworth. 2003. "'Destroy the Scum, and Then Neuter Their Families.' The Web Forum as a Vehicle for Community Discourse?" *Social Science Journal* 41: 1–14.

Cohen, Bernard. 1963. *The Press and Foreign Policy.* Princeton, NJ: Princeton University Press.

Cohen, Jeffrey, Jon R. Bond, and Richard Fleisher. 2013. "Placing Presidential-Congressional Relations in Context: A Comparison of Barack Obama and His Predecessors." *Polity* 45 (January): 105–126.

Cohen, Marty, David Karol, Hans Noel, and John Zaller. 2001. "Beating Reform: The Resurgence of Parties in Presidential Nominations, 1980 to 2000." Paper presented at the annual meeting of the American Political Science Association, San Francisco, August 30–September 2.

Cohen, Marty, David Karol, Hans Noel, and John Zaller. 2008a. *The Party Decides: Presidential Nominations Before and After Reform.* Chicago: University of Chicago Press.

Cohen, Marty, David Karol, Hans Noel, and John Zaller. 2008b. "Political Parties in Rough Weather." *The Forum* 5(4): article 3. http://www.bepress.com/forum/vol5/iss4/art3.

Cohen, Michael D., James G. March, and Johan P. Olsen. 1972. "A Garbage Can Model of Organizational Choice." *Administrative Science Quarterly* 17 (March): 1–25.

Cohen, Richard E. 1995. *Washington at Work: Back Rooms and Clean Air.* Needham Heights, MA: Allyn & Bacon.

Coleman, John J. 1996. "Party Organizational Strength and Public Support for Parties." *American Journal of Political Science* 40 (August): 805–824.

Collier, Christopher and James Lincoln Collier. 1986. *Decision in Philadelphia: The Constitutional Convention of 1787.* New York: Ballantine Books.

Colomer, Josep M. 2005. "It's Parties That Choose Electoral Systems (or, Duverger's Laws Upside Down)." *Political Studies* 53 (March): 1–21.

Comiskey, Michael. 2006. "The Senate Confirmation Process and the Quality of U.S. Supreme Court Justices." *Polity* 38 (July): 295–313.

Committee on Political Parties. 1950. "Toward a More Responsible Two-Party System: A Report of the Committee on Political Parties." *American Political Science Review* 44 (September, Part 2, Supplement).

Committee on Standards of Official Conduct. n.d. "Members' Representational Allowance." U.S House of Representatives. http://ethics.house.gov/Subjects/Topics.aspx? Section=123 (accessed August 19, 2008).

Conley, Richard. 2011. "The Harbinger of the Unitary Executive? An Analysis of Presidential Signing Statements from Truman to Carter." *Presidential Studies Quarterly* 41 (September): 546–569.

Converse, Philip E. 1996. "The Advent of Polling and Political Representation." *PS: Political Science and Politics* 29 (December): 649–657.

Cook, Timothy. 1998. *Governing with the News: The News Media as a Political Institution.* Chicago: University of Chicago Press.

Cooper, Phillip J. 2005. "George W. Bush, Edgar Allan Poe, and the Use and Abuse of Presidential Signing Statements." *Presidential Studies Quarterly* 35 (September): 515–532.

Cotter, Cornelius P., James L. Gibson, John F. Bibby, and Robert Huckshorn. 1989. *Party Organizations in American Politics.* Pittsburgh, PA: University of Pittsburgh Press.

Cox, Gary W. and Mathew D. McCubbins. 1993. *Legislative Leviathan: Party Government in the House.* Berkeley: University of California Press.

Crispi, Irving. 1989. *Public Opinion, Polls, and Democracy.* Boulder, CO: Westview Press.

Cronin, Thomas E. 1975. *The State of the Presidency.* Boston: Little, Brown.

Crotty, William. 2003. "Presidential Policymaking in Crisis Situations: 9/11 and Its Aftermath." *Policy Studies Journal* 31: 451–464.

Cushman, Barry. 1998. *Rethinking the New Deal Court: The Structure of a Constitutional Revolution.* New York: Oxford University Press.

Dale, A. and A. Strauss. 2009. "Don't Forget to Vote: Text Message Reminders as a Mobilization Tool." *American Journal of Political Science* 5: 787–804.

D'Alessio, Dave and Mike Allen. 2000. "Media Bias in Presidential Elections: A Meta-analysis." *Journal of Communication* 50(4): 133–156.

Daniels, Jonathan. 1965. *They Will Be Heard: America's Crusading Newspaper Editors.* New York: McGraw-Hill.

Davis, James W. 1994. *The President as Party Leader.* New York: Praeger.

Day, Elizabeth. 2015. "#BlackLivesMatter: The Birth of a New Civil Rights Movement." *Guardian*, July 19. https://www.

theguardian.com/world/2015/jul/19/blacklivesmatter-birth-civil-rights-movement (last accessed March 18, 2018)

Death Penalty Information Center. 2012. *Facts About the Death Penalty*. Washington, DC: Death Penalty Information Center.

Deering, Christopher J. and Steven S. Smith. 1997. *Committees in Congress*. 3rd ed. Washington, DC: CQ Press.

Dennis, Brady, and Steven Mufson. 2017. "Thousands of Emails Detail EPA Head's Close Ties to Fossil Fuel industry." *Washington Post*. https://www.washingtonpost.com/news/energy-environment/wp/2017/02/22/oklahoma-attorney-generals-office-releases-7500-pages-of-emails-between-scott-pruitt-and-fossil-fuel-industry/?utm_term=.6dfafa6af20a.

Deppe, Kristen D., Scott F. Stoltenberg, Kevin B. Smith, and John R. Hibbing. 2013. "Candidate Genes and Voter Turnout: Further Evidence on the Role of 5-HTTLPR." *American Political Science Review* 107: 375–381.

DiMaggio, Paul, John Evans, and Bethany Bryson. 1996. "Have Americans' Social Attitudes Become More Polarized?" *American Journal of Sociology* 102 (November): 690–755.

Downie, Leonard and Robert G. Kaiser. 2002. *The News About News*. New York: Knopf.

Downs, Anthony. 1957. *An Economic Theory of Democracy*. New York: Harper & Row.

Doyle, Arthur Conan. 1890. *The Sign of the Four*. Project Gutenberg, 2008. http://www.gutenberg.org/files/2097/2097-h/2097-h.htm#chap01 (accessed February 25, 2012).

Duverger, Maurice. 1972. *Party Politics and Pressure Groups*, trans. David Wagoner. New York: Thomas Y. Crowell.

Easton, David. 1953. *The Political System*. New York: Knopf.

Edmondson, Brad. 1996. "How to Spot a Bogus Poll." *American Demographics* 18 (October): 10–15.

Edsall, Thomas B. 2001. "Democrats Press Bush for Input on Judges: Court Nominees Concern Senators." *Washington Post*, April 28, A04.

Edwards, George C., III. 1989. *At the Margins: Presidential Leadership of Congress*. New Haven, CT: Yale University Press.

Edwards, George C., III. 2003. *On Deaf Ears: The Limits of the Bully Pulpit*. New Haven, CT: Yale University Press.

Edwards, George C., III. 2019. *Why the Electoral College Is Bad for America*. 3rd ed. New Haven, CT: Yale University Press.

Edwards, George C., III. and Andrew Barrett. 2000. "Presidential Agenda Setting in Congress." In *Polarized Politics: Congress and the President in a Partisan Era*, ed. Jon R. Bond and Richard Fleisher. Washington, DC: CQ Press.

Edwards, George C., III. and Stephen J. Wayne. 2003. *Presidential Leadership: Politics and Policy Making*. 6th ed. Belmont, CA: Thomson/Wadsworth.

Ellsworth, Oliver. [1787] 1986. Letter to the *Connecticut Courant* (Hartford), December 17, 1787, signed "A Landholder" VII. In *The Debate on the Constitution: Federalist and Antifederalist Speeches, Articles, and Letters during the Struggle over Ratification*, part 1, ed. Bernard Bailyn, 521–525. New York: Library of America.

Epstein, Lee and Jack Knight. 1998. *The Choices Justices Make*. Washington, DC: CQ Press.

Epstein, Lee, William M. Landes, and Richard A. Posner. 2013. *The Behavior of Federal Judges: A Theoretical and Empirical Study of Rational Choice*. Cambridge, MA: Harvard University Press.

Epstein, L., Jeffrey A. Segal, Harold J. Spaeth, and Thomas G. Walker (eds.). 2012. *The Supreme Court Compendium: Data, Decisions, and Developments*. 5th ed. Washington, DC: CQ Press. doi:http://dx.doi.org/10.4135/9781608717620.

Epstein, Lee, Thomas G. Walker, Nancy Staudt, Scott Hendrickson, and Jason Roberts. 2017. "The U.S. Supreme Court Justices Database." November 1. http://epstein.wustl.edu/research/justicesdata.html

Erikson, Robert S. and Norman R. Luttbeg. 1973. *American Public Opinion: Its Origins, Content, and Impact*. New York: Wiley.

Erikson, Robert and Kent Tedin. 2014. *American Public Opinion*. 9th ed. New York: Routledge.

Erikson, Robert S., Gerald Wright, and John McIver. 1993. *Statehouse Democracy: Public Opinion and Policy in the American States*. New York: Cambridge University Press.

Erskine, H. 1970. "The Polls: Opinion of the News Media." *Public Opinion Quarterly* 34: 630–643.

Eulau, Heinz. 1956. "The Politics of Happiness: A Prefatory Note to Political Perspectives 1956." *Antioch Review* 16 (Fall): 259–264.

Eulau, Heinz and Paul D. Karps. 1977. "The Puzzle of Representation: Specifying Components of Responsiveness." *Legislative Studies Quarterly* 2 (August): 233–254.

Evans, Diana. 1996. "Before the Roll Call: Interest Group Lobbying and Public Policy Outcomes in House Committees." *Political Research Quarterly* 49 (June): 287–304.

Evans, Diana. 2004. *Greasing the Wheels: Using Pork Barrel Projects to Build Majority Coalitions in Congress*. New York: Cambridge University Press.

Federal Communications Commission. 2012. "Broadcast Station Totals as of December 31, 2011." http://hraunfoss.fcc.gov/edocs_public/attachmatch/DOC-311837A1.doc (accessed April 24, 2012).

Federal Election Commission. 2007. "Selected Presidential Reports for the 2007 October Quarterly." http://query.nictusa.com/pres/2007/Q3/.

Federal Election Commission. 2011a. "Coordinated Communications and Independent Expenditures" (first published in June 2007, updated February 2011). http://www.fec.gov/pages/brochures/indexp.shtml (accessed May 1, 2012).

Federal Election Commission. 2011b. "Selected Presidential Reports for the 2011 October Quarterly." http://query.nictusa.com/pres/2011/Q3/.

Federal Election Commission. 2015. "Selected Presidential Reports for the 2015 October Quarterly." http://docquery.fec.gov/pres/2015/Q3/

Federal Judicial Center. n.d. "Impeachments of Federal Judges." http://www.fjc.gov/history/home.nsf/page/judges_impeachments.html (accessed June 17, 2010).

Federal Procurement Data System. 2016. "Top 100 Contractors Report." https://www.fpds.gov/fpdsng_cms/index.php/en/reports/62-top-100-contractors-report

Feldman, Paul and James Jondrow. 1984. "Congressional Elections and Local Federal Spending." *American Journal of Political Science* 28 (February): 147–164.

Fenno, Richard. 1966. *The Power of the Purse: Appropriations Politics in Congress*. Boston: Little, Brown.

Fenno, Richard F., Jr. 1973. *Congressmen in Committees*. Boston: Little, Brown.

Fenno, Richard. 1978. *Home Style: House Members in Their Districts*. Boston: Little, Brown.

Ferguson, Andrew. 1995. "Disabling America." Excerpted in "Implementing the Disabilities Act." *CQ Researcher* 6 (December 1996): 1121.

Finifter, Ada W. 1970. "Dimensions of Political Alienation." *American Political Science Review* 64 (June): 389–410.

Fiorina, Morris. 1980. "The Decline of Collective Responsibility in American Politics." *Daedalus* 109 (Summer): 25–45.

Fiorina, Morris. 1981. *Retrospective Voting in American National Elections*. New Haven, CT: Yale University Press.

Fiorina, Morris. 1996. *Divided Government*. 2nd ed. Boston: Allyn & Bacon.

Fiorina, Morris. 2006. *Culture War? The Myth of a Polarized America*. New York: Longman.

Fiorina, Morris P. and Matthew Levendusky. 2006. "Disconnected: The Political Class Versus the People—Rejoinder." In *Red and Blue Nation? Volume I—Characteristics and Causes of America's Polarized Politics*, ed. Pietro S. Nivola and David W. Brady, 95–110. Washington, DC: Brookings Institution Press and Stanford: Hoover Institution Press.

Fleisher, Richard. 1993. "Explaining the Change in Roll-Call Voting Behavior of Southern Democrats." *Journal of Politics* 55 (May): 327–341.

Fleisher, Richard and Jon R. Bond. 2000a. "Congress and the President in a Partisan Era." In *Polarized Politics: Congress and the President in a Partisan Era*, ed. Jon R. Bond and Richard Fleisher, 1–8. Washington, DC: CQ Press.

Fleisher, Richard and Jon R. Bond. 2000b. "Partisanship and the President's Quest for Votes on the Floor of Congress." In *Polarized Politics: Congress and the President in a Partisan Era*, ed. Jon R. Bond and Richard Fleisher, 154–185. Washington, DC: CQ Press.

Fleisher, Richard and Jon R. Bond. 2004. "The Shrinking Middle in the US Congress." *British Journal of Political Science* 34 (July): 529–551.

Fletcher, Michael A. 2006. "Bush Starts 10-Day Texas Vacation: Shorter Summer Break Reflects Post-Katrina Criticism." *Washington Post*, August 4. http://www.washingtonpost.com/wp-dyn/content/article/2006/08/03/AR2006080300663.html (accessed September 25, 2006).

Fornell, Claes. 2010. "Citizen Satisfaction With Federal Government Services Dips Slightly." American Customer Satisfaction Index, January 26. http://www.theacsi.org/index.php?option=com_content&task=view&id=200&Itemid=62 (accessed June 1, 2010).

Fortune. 2011. "Inside the Oval Office: The Management Styles of Clinton and Obama." http://fortune.com/2011/07/25/inside-the-oval-office-the-management-styles-of-clinton-and-obama/.

Fowler, Anthony and Michele Margolis. 2014. "The Political Consequences of Uninformed Voters." *Electoral Studies* 34: 100–110.

Fowler, James and Christopher Dawes. 2008. "Two Genes Predict Voter Turnout." *Journal of Politics* 70(3): 579–594.

Fowler, James, Laura Baker, and Christopher Dawes. 2008. "Genetic Variation in Political Participation." *American Political Science Review* 102(2): 233–248.

Fraga, Bernard. 2016. "Candidates or Districts? Reevaluating the Role of Race in Voter Turnout." *American Journal of Political Science* 60: 97–122.

Frankfurter, Felix. 1957. "The Supreme Court in the Mirror of Justices." *University of Pennsylvania Law Review* 105 (April): 781–796.

Freedom House. 2006. "Freedom in the World 2006: Selected Data From Freedom House's Annual Global Survey of Political Rights and Civil Liberties." http://www.freedomhouse.org/uploads/pdf/Charts2006.pdf (accessed June 13, 2006).

French, Jeffrey A, Kevin B. Smith, John R. Alford, Adam Guck, Andrew K. Birnie, and John R. Hibbing. 2014. "Cortisol and Politics: Variance in Voting Behavior is Predicted by Baseline Cortisol Levels." *Physiology & Behavior* 133: 61–67.

Friedan, Betty. 1963. *The Feminine Mystique*. New York: Norton.

Gaines, Brian. 2001. "Popular Myths about Popular Vote–Electoral College Splits." *PS: Political Science and Politics* 34 (March): 71–75.

Gallup. 2016. "Anti-Incumbent Mood Toward Congress Still Going Strong." Gallup. http://news.gallup.com/poll/189215/anti-incumbent-mood-toward-congress-going-strong.aspx.

Gallup. 2017. "Congress and the Public." http://www.gallup.com/poll/1600/congress-public.aspx.

Gambino, Lauren. 2018. "'The Civil Rights Issue of Our Time': How Dreamers Came to Dominate U.S. Politics." *Guardian*, January 27, 2018. https://www.theguardian.com/us-news/2018/jan/27/the-civil-rights-issue-of-our-time-how-dreamers-came-to-dominate-us-politics/

Gant, Michael M. and William Lyons. 1993. "Democratic Theory, Nonvoting, and Public Policy: The 1972–1988 Presidential Elections." *American Politics Quarterly* 21 (April): 185–204.

Garrett, R. Sam. 2014. "Proposals to Eliminate Public Financing of Presidential Campaigns," January 8. Washington, DC: Congressional Research Service report R41604.

General Accounting Office. 2003. *Women's Earnings: Work Patterns Partially Explain Difference Between Men's and Women's Earnings*. Washington, DC: U.S. Government Printing Office.

George, Alexander L. and Juliette L. George. 1998. *Presidential Personality and Performance*. Boulder, CO: Westview Press.

Gerring, John. 1997. "Ideology: A Definitional Analysis." *Political Research Quarterly* 50: 957–994.

Gerstein, Josh. 2009. "Obama: Ignore Signing Statements." *Politico*, March 9. http://www.politico.com/news/stories/0309/19795.html (accessed May 31, 2010).

Gerth, H. H. and C. Wright Mills. 1946. *Max Weber: Essays in Sociology*. New York: Oxford University Press.

Gettinger, Stephen. 1998. "When Congress Decides a President's 'High Crimes and Misdemeanors.'" *Congressional Quarterly Weekly Report* 56 (March): 565–568.

Gibson, James L., Cornelius P. Cotter, John F. Bibby, and Robert J. Huckshorn. 1989. "Whither the Local Parties? A Cross-Sectional and Longitudinal Analysis of the Strength of Party Organizations." *American Journal of Political Science* 29 (February): 139–160.

Gilbert, Sophie. 2017. "The Movement of #MeToo: How a Hashtag Got Its Power." *The Atlantic*, October 16. https://www.theatlantic.com/entertainment/archive/2017/10/the-movement-of-metoo/542979/.

Gill, Brian, P. Michael Timpane, Karen E. Ross, and Dominic J. Brewer. 2001. *Rhetoric Versus Reality*. Santa Monica, CA: RAND.

Gilmour, John B. 1995. *Strategic Disagreement: Stalemate in American Politics*. Pittsburgh, PA: University of Pittsburgh Press.

Gilmour, John B. 2011. "Political Theater or Bargaining Failure: Why Presidents Veto." *Presidential Studies Quarterly* 41(3): 471–487.

Gintis, Herbert. 2007. "A Framework for the Unification of the Behavioral Sciences." *Behavioral and Brain Sciences* 30: 1–16.

Goel, Sharad, et al. 2017. "One Person, One Vote: Estimating the Prevalence of Double Voting in U.S. Presidential Elections." *Harvard Scholar*, January 13. scholar.harvard.edu/morse/publications/one-person-one-vote-estimating-prevalence-double-voting-us-presidential-elections.

Goldman, Sheldon. 1985. "Reaganizing the Judiciary: The First Term Appointments." *Judicature* 68 (April–May): 313.

Goldstein, Joel K. 2008. "The Rising Power of the Modern Vice Presidency." *Presidential Studies Quarterly* 38 (September): 374–389.

Goodsell, Charles. 1994. *The Case for Bureaucracy*. Chatham, NJ: Chatham House.

Goren, Paul. 1997. "Gut-Level Emotion and the Presidential Vote." *American Politics Quarterly* 25 (April): 203–229.

Granat, Diane. 1984. "Parties' Schools for Politicians Grooming Troops for Election." *CQ Weekly Report* 42 (May): 1036.

Gray, Virginia and David Lowery. 1996a. *The Population Ecology of Interest Representation: Lobbying Communities in the American States*. Ann Arbor: University of Michigan Press.

Gray, Virginia and David Lowery. 1996b. "A Niche Theory of Interest Representation." *Journal of Politics* 58 (February): 91–111.

Gray, Virginia and David Lowery. 1997. "Life in a Niche: Mortality Anxiety Among Organized Interests in the American States." *Political Research Quarterly* 50 (March): 25–47.

Greenstein, Fred. 1965. *Children and Politics.* New Haven, CT: Yale University Press.

Greenwald, Anthony, Debbie McGhee, and Jordan Schwartz. 1998. "Measuring Individual Differences in Implicit Cognition: The Implicit Association Test." *Journal of Personality and Psychology* 74(6): 1464–1480.

Grier, Kevin B., Michael C. Munger, and Brian E. Roberts. 1994. "The Determinants of Industry Political Activity, 1976–1986." *American Political Science Review* 88 (December): 911–926.

Groeling, Tim. 2008. "Who's the Fairest of Them All? An Empirical Test for Partisan Bias on ABC, CBS, NBC, and Fox News." *Presidential Studies Quarterly* 38(4): 631–657.

Groeling, Tim. 2013. "Media Bias by the Numbers: Challenges and Opportunities in the Empirical Study of Partisan News." *Annual Review of Political Science* 16: 129–151.

Grose, Christian R. 2011. *Congress in Black and White: Race and Representation in Washington and at Home.* New York: Cambridge University Press.

Groseclose, Tim. 2011. *Left Turn: How Liberal Media Bias Distorts the American Mind.* New York: St. Martin's Press.

Groseclose, Tim and Nolan McCarty. 2001. "The Politics of Blame: Bargaining Before an Audience." *American Journal of Political Science* 45 (January): 100–119.

Groseclose, Tim and Jeffrey Milyo. 2005. "A Measure of Media Bias." *Quarterly Journal of Economics* 120: 1191–1237.

Groseclose, Tim and Charles Stewart III. 1998. "The Value of Committee Seats in the House, 1947–91." *American Journal of Political Science* 42 (April): 453–474.

Gruszczynski, Mike and Michael W. Wagner. 2017. "Information Flow in the 21st Century: The Dynamics of Agenda-Uptake." *Mass Communication and Society* 20: 378–402.

Gunther, Gerald. 1980. *Constitutional Law.* Mineola, NY: Fountain Press.

Gutin, Myra G. 1994. "Rosalynn Carter in the White House." In *The Presidency and Domestic Policies of Jimmy Carter,* ed. Herbert D. Rosenbaum and Alexej Ugrinsky. Westport, CT: Greenwood Press.

Habermas, Jürgen. 1991. *The Structural Transformation of the Public Sphere: An Inquiry Into a Category of Bourgeois Society.* Cambridge, MA: MIT Press.

Hadley, Arthur T. 1976. *The Invisible Primary.* Englewood Cliffs, NJ: Prentice-Hall.

Haider-Markel, Donald P. and Kenneth J. Meier. 1996. "The Politics of Gay and Lesbian Rights: Expanding the Scope of the Conflict." *Journal of Politics* 58 (May): 332–349.

Haidt, Jonathan. 2012. *The Righteous Mind: Why Good People Are Divided by Politics and Religion.* New York: Vintage Books.

Hall, Richard L. 1996. *Participation in Congress.* New Haven, CT: Yale University Press.

Hamilton, James T. 2004. *All the News That's Fit to Sell.* Princeton, NJ: Princeton University Press.

Hargrove, Erwin C. 1974. *The Power of the Modern Presidency.* Philadelphia: Temple University Press.

Harris, Fred R. 1995. *In Defense of Congress.* New York: St. Martin's Press.

Hart, John. 1995. *The Presidential Branch: From Washington to Clinton.* 2nd ed. Chatham, NJ: Chatham House.

Hartranft, Dan. 2012. "Super PAC Spending Boosts Santorum." *OpenSecrets.org,* February 16. http://www.opensecrets.org/news/2012/02/super-pac-spending-boostssantorum.html (accessed June 25, 2012).

Heberlig, Eric S. and Bruce A. Larson. 2012. *Congressional Parties, Institutional Ambition, and the Financing of Majority Control.* Ann Arbor: University of Michigan Press.

Heldman, Carlin, Susan Carroll, and Stephanie Olson. 2005. "'She Brought Only a Skirt': Print Media Coverage of Elizabeth Dole's Bid for the Republican Presidential Nomination." *Political Communication* 22: 315–335.

Herman, Edward S. and Noam Chomsky. 2002. *Manufacturing Consent: The Political Economy of the Mass Media.* New York: Pantheon.

Herman, Edward S. and Robert W. McChesney. 1997. *The Global Media.* London: Cassell.

Herrnson, Paul S. 1995. *Congressional Elections: Campaigning at Home and in Washington.* Washington, DC: CQ Press.

Hibbing, John R. 1991. *Congressional Careers: Contours of Life in the U.S. House of Representatives.* Chapel Hill: University of North Carolina Press.

Hibbing, John R. and Elizabeth Theiss-Morse. 1995. *Congress as Public Enemy: Public Attitudes Toward American Political Institutions.* New York: Cambridge University Press.

Hibbing, John R. and Elizabeth Theiss-Morse. 1998. "The Media's Role in Public Negativity towards Congress: Distinguishing Emotional Reactions and Cognitive Evaluation." *American Journal of Political Science* 42 (April): 475–498.

Hibbing, John R. and Elizabeth Theiss-Morse. 2001. "Process Preferences and American Politics: What People Want Government to Be." *American Political Science Review* 95 (March): 145–154.

Hibbing, John R. and Elizabeth Theiss-Morse. 2003. *Stealth Democracy.* New York: Cambridge University Press.

Hibbing, John, Kevin Smith, and John Alford. 2014. *Predisposed: Liberals, Conservatives, and the Biology of Political Differences.* New York: Routledge.

Highton, Benjamin. 2017. "Voter Identification Laws and Turnout in the United States." *Annual Review of Political Science* 20: 149–167.

Hightower, Jim. 1998. *There's Nothing in the Middle of the Road But Yellow Stripes and Dead Armadillos*. New York: Harper Perennial.

Hill, Kevin A. 1995. "Does the Creation of Majority Black Districts Aid Republicans? An Analysis of the 1992 Congressional Elections in Eight Southern States." *Journal of Politics* 57 (May): 384–401.

Hill, Kevin A. and John E. Hughes. 1997. "Computer-Mediated Political Communication: The USENET and Political Communities." *Political Communication* 14 (January–March): 3–27.

Hill, Kim Quaile and Jan E. Leighley. 1992. "The Policy Consequences of Class Bias in State Electorates." *American Journal of Political Science* 36 (May): 351–365.

Hirsh, Michael. 2012. "Biden: Most Powerful VP Ever? Joltin' Joe Leads the Obama Attack on Romney." *National Journal*, April 26. http://www.nationaljournal.com/2012-presidential-campaign/biden-most-powerful-vp-ever 20120426 (accessed July 15, 2012).

Hofstetter, C. Richard, David Barker, James T. Smith, Gina M. Zari, and Thomas A. Ingrassia. 1999. "Information, Misinformation, and Political Talk Radio." *Political Research Quarterly* 52: 353–370.

Hojnacki, Marie and David C. Kimball. 1998. "Organized Interests and the Decision of Whom to Lobby in Congress." *American Political Science Review* 92 (December): 775–790.

Holbrook, Thomas and Brianne Heidbreder. 2010. "Does Measurement Matter? The Case of VAP and VEP in Models of Voter Turnout in the United States." *State Politics and Policy Quarterly* 10: 157–179.

Holland, Jesse J. 2016. "Census: Asians Remain Fastest-Growing Racial Group in US." *US News & World Report*. https://www.usnews.com/news/politics/articles/2016-06-23/census-asians-remain-fastest-growing-racial-group-in-us.

Hood, M. V. and William Gillespie. 2012. "'They Just Do Not Vote Like They Used to: A Methodology to Empirically Assess Election Fraud." *Social Science Quarterly*. onlinelibrary.wiley.com/doi/10.1111/j.1540-6237.2011.00837.x.

Howell, William G. 2005. "Unilateral Powers: A Brief Overview." *Presidential Studies Quarterly* 35 (September): 417–439.

Huckfeldt, R. Robert and John Sprague. 1995. *Citizens, Politics, and Social Communication: Information and Influence in an Election Campaign*. New York: Cambridge University Press.

Huckshorn, Robert J., James L. Gibson, Cornelius P. Cotter, and John F. Bibby. 1986. "Party Integration and Party Organizational Strength." *Journal of Politics* 48 (November): 976–991.

Humphries, Steve and Pamela Wright. 1992. *Out of Sight: The Experience of Disability, 1900–1950*. London: Northcote House.

Hurley, Patricia A. and Brinck Kerr. 1997. "The Partisanship of New Members in the 103rd and 104th Houses." *Social Science Quarterly* 78 (December): 992–1000.

Hutchings, Vincent. 2003. *Public Opinion and Democratic Accountability: How Citizens Learn About Politics*. Princeton, NJ: Princeton University Press.

Hutchinson, G. Evelyn. 1957. "Concluding Remarks." *Population Studies: Animal Ecology and Demography. Cold Spring Harbor Symposia on Quantitative Biology* 22: 415–427.

Isaak, Alan C. 1985. *Scope and Methods of Political Science*. 4th ed. Pacific Grove, CA: Brooks/Cole.

Iyengar, Shanto. 1997. "Media-Based Political Campaigns: Overview." In *Do the Media Govern?*, ed. Shanto Iyengar and Richard Reeves. Thousand Oaks, CA: SAGE.

Iyengar, Shanto and Donald Kinder. 1987. *News That Matters: Television and American Opinion*. Chicago: University of Chicago Press.

Jackson, John S. and William Crotty. 1996. *The Politics of Presidential Selection*. New York: HarperCollins.

Jackson, Robert A. 1997. "The Mobilization of U.S. State Electorates in the 1988 and 1990 Elections." *Journal of Politics* 59 (May): 520–537.

Jacobson, Gary C. 1989. "Strategic Politicians and the Dynamics of House Elections, 1946–1986." *American Political Science Review* 83 (September): 773–793.

Jacobson, Gary C. 1990. *The Electoral Origins of Divided Government: Competition in U.S. House Elections, 1946–1988*. Boulder, CO: Westview Press.

Jacobson, Gary C. 2001. *The Politics of Congressional Elections*. 5th ed. New York: Addison Wesley Longman.

Jacobson, Gary C. 2009. *The Politics of Congressional Elections*. 7th ed. New York: Pearson Longman.

Jacobson, Gary C. 2013. *The Politics of Congressional Elections*. 8th ed. New York: Pearson Longman.

Jacobson, Gary C. and Samuel Kernell. 1983. *Strategy and Choice in Congressional Elections*. 2nd ed. New Haven, CT: Yale University Press.

Jacobson, Louis. 1995. "Tanks on the Roll." *National Journal* 27 (July): 1767–1771.

Jefferson, Thomas. 1823. "Letter to Lafayette." *Thomas Jefferson Digital Archive*. University of Virginia Library.

http://etext.virginia.edu/jefferson/quotations/jeff1600.htm.

Jennings, M. Kent and Richard Niemi. 1975. "Continuity and Change in Political Orientations: A Longitudinal Study of Two Generations." *American Political Science Review* 69 (December): 1316–1335.

Johnson, Peter. 2004. "Survey: Profit Pressures Worry Most Journalists." *USA Today,* May 24, 3D.

Jones, Jeffrey M. 2014. "Americans' Support for Death Penalty Stable." *Gallup Poll: Politics*, October 23. http://www.gallup.com/poll/178790/americans-support-death-penalty-stable.aspx (accessed June 25, 2015).

Jones, Jeffrey M. 2016. "Democratic, Republican Identification Near Historical Lows," *Gallup..* http://www.gallup.com/poll/188096/democratic-republican-identification-near-historical-lows.aspx.

Jost, John T. 2006. "The End of the End of Ideology." *American Psychologist* 61 (October): 651–670.

Kahn, Kim Fridkin. 1992. "Does Being Male Help?" *Journal of Politics* 54 (May): 497–517.

Kahn, Kim Fridkin. 1996. *The Political Consequences of Being a Woman: How Stereotypes Influence the Content and Impact of Statewide Campaigns.* New York: Columbia University Press.

Kaminer, Wendy. 1999. "Taking Liberties." *American Prospect.* http://www.prospect.org/cs/articles?article=taking_liberties (accessed September 19, 2010).

Kane, Paul. 2011. "Senate Republicans Block Judicial Nominee Goodwin Liu." *Washington Post,* May 19. http://www.washingtonpost.com/politics/judicial-nominee-goodwinliu-faces-filibuster-showdown/2011/05/18/AF6ak76G_story.html (accessed August 1, 2012).

Kaplan, Jonas, Joshua Freedman, and Marco Iacoboni. 2007. "Us Versus Them: Political Attitudes and Party Affiliation Influence Neural Responses to Faces of Presidential Candidates." *Neuropsychologica* 45: 55–64.

Katz, Jeffrey. 1998. "Panel Drops Final Ethics Charges." *CQ Weekly Report* 56 (October): 2816.

Kern, Montague and Marion Just. 1995. "The Focus Group Method, Political Advertising, and the Construction of Candidate Images." *Political Communication* 12: 127–145.

Kernell, Samuel. 1997. *Going Public: New Strategies of Presidential Leadership.* 3rd ed. Washington, DC: CQ Press.

Kerwin, Cornelius. 1994. *Rulemaking.* Washington, DC: CQ Press.

Kerwin, Cornelius. 1999. *Rulemaking.* 2nd ed. Washington, DC: CQ Press.

Kesler, Erin, David Vance, and Viveca Novak. 2012. "Double-Duty Donors, Part II: Large Numbers of Wealthy Donors Hit Legal Limit on Giving to Candidates, Turn to Presidential Super PACs in Continuing Trend." Open Secrets.org. February 21. http://www.opensecrets.org/news/2012/02/double-duty-donors-part-ii-large-nu.html (accessed May 19, 2012).

Kessel, John H. 1992. *Presidential Campaign Politics.* 4th ed. Pacific Grove, CA: Brooks/Cole.

Key, V. O., Jr. 1964. *Politics, Parties, and Pressure Groups.* 5th ed. New York: Crowell.

King, David C. and Jack L. Walker. 1992. "The Provision of Benefits by Interest Groups in the United States." *Journal of Politics* 54 (May): 394–426.

Kingdon, John W. 1995. *Agendas, Alternatives, and Public Policies.* 2nd ed. New York: HarperCollins.

Klarman, Michael J. 2016. *The Framers' Coup: The Making of the United States Constitution.* New York: Oxford University Press.

Knack, Stephen and James White. 1998. "Did State Motor Voter Programs Help the Democrats?" *American Politics Quarterly* 26 (July): 344–356.

Koger, Gregory. 2010. *Filibustering: A Political History of Obstruction in the House and Senate.* Chicago: University of Chicago Press.

Krane, Dale and Heidi Koenig. 2005. "The State of American Federalism, 2004: Is Federalism Still a Core Value?" *Publius* 35 (Winter): 1–40.

Krehbiel, Keith. 1991. *Information and Legislative Organization.* Ann Arbor: University of Michigan Press.

Krehbiel, Keith. 1998. *Pivotal Politics.* Chicago: University of Chicago Press.

Krueger, Brian. 2002. "Assessing the Potential of Internet Political Participation in the United States." *American Politics Research* 30: 476–498.

Kruesi, Kimberlee and Bill Barrow. 2016. "Trump Foes Try to Beat Him at the Electoral College." The Associated Press. *Boston Globe,* November 20, 2016. https://www.bostonglobe.com/news/nation/2016/11/19/trump-foes-try-beat-him-electoral-college/LmroE1xEsv8bfpRIeMrrjO/story.html

Krutz, Glen S. and Jeffrey S. Peake. 2009. *Treaty Politics and the Rise of Executive Agreements: International Agreements in a System of Shared Powers.* Ann Arbor: University of Michigan Press.

Krutz, Glen S. and Jeffrey S. Peake. 2011. "President Obama, Congress and International Agreements: An Initial Assessment." Presented at the American Political Science Association annual meeting, Seattle, WA, August 31–September 4.

Krutz, Glen S., Richard Fleisher, and Jon R. Bond. 1998. "From Abe Fortas to Zoe Baird: Why Some Presidential Nominations Fail in the Senate." *American Political Science Review* 92 (December): 871–881.

Kuhn, David P. 2004. "Blogs: New Medium, Old Politics." CBS News, December 8. http://www.cbsnews.com/stories/2004/12/08/politics/main659955.shtml?tag=mncol;lst;1 (accessed August 10, 2006).

Kulish, Nicholas. 2017. "Iraqi Immigrant, Caught in a Trump Policy Tangle, Is Allowed to Stay," *New York Times*. https://www.nytimes.com/2017/01/28/us/iraqi-immigrant-donald-trump-airport-detention.html.

Lasswell, Harold D. 1938. *Politics: Who Gets What, When and How.* New York: McGraw-Hill.

Lazarsfeld, Paul F., Bernard Berelson, and Hazel Gaudet. 1944. *The People's Choice*. New York: Duell, Sloan and Pearce.

Lee, Emery G., III, Frances U. Sandstrum, and Thomas C. Weisert. 1996. "Context and the Court: Sources of Support for Civil Liberties on the Rehnquist Court." *American Politics Quarterly* 24 (July): 377–395.

Leech, Beth L. 2010. "Lobbying and Influence." In *The Oxford Handbook of American Political Parties and Interest Groups*, ed. L. Sandy Maisel and Jeffrey M. Berry, 534–551. Oxford, UK: Oxford University Press.

Lehigh, Scot. 2002. "President Needs OK by Congress for Iraq War." *Boston Globe*, August 23, A27.

Leighley, Jan E. 1995. "Attitudes, Opportunities and Incentives: A Field Essay on Political Participation." *Political Research Quarterly* 48 (March): 181–209.

Leighley, Jan E. 1996. "Group Membership and the Mobilization of Political Participation." *Journal of Politics* 58 (May): 447–463.

Leighley, Jan and Jonathan Nagler. 2007. "Unions, Voter Turnout, and Class Bias in the U.S. Electorate, 1964–2004. *Journal of Politics* 69: 430–441.

Leighley, Jan E. and Arnold Vedlitz. 1999. "Race, Ethnicity, and Political Participation: Competing Models and Contrasting Explanations." *Journal of Politics* 61 (November): 1092–1114.

Lenz, Ryan. 2004. "Soldiers in Iraq Buy Their Own Body Armor." *Guardian*. http://www.guardian.co.uk/worldlatest/story/0,1280,-3904926,00.html (accessed June 1, 2004).

Levinthal, Dave. 2012. "How Super PACs Got Their Name." *Politico*, January 10. http://www.politico.com/news/stories/0112/71285.html#ixzz1q0eZYeTs (accessed May 1, 2012).

Levitt, Justin. 2007. "The Truth About Voter Fraud." *Brennan Center for Justice*, NYU Brennan Center for Justice, November 9. www.brennancenter.org/publication/truth-about-voter-fraud.

Lewis-Beck, Michael, William Jacoby, Helmut Norpoth, and Herbert Weisberg. 2008. *The American Voter Revisited*. Ann Arbor: University of Michigan Press.

Light, Paul C. 1983. *The President's Agenda: Domestic Policy Choice From Kennedy to Carter (With Notes on Ronald Reagan)*. Baltimore, MD: Johns Hopkins University Press.

Light, Paul C. 1999. *The True Size of Government*. Washington, DC: Brookings Institution.

Lijphart, Arend. 1984. *Democracies: Patterns of Majoritarian and Consensus Government in Twenty-One Countries*. New Haven, CT: Yale University Press.

Lindblom, Charles. 1959. "The Science of Muddling Through." *Public Administration Review* 19 (Spring): 79–88.

Lippmann, Walter. 1922. *Public Opinion*. New York: Macmillan.

Lippmann, Walter. 1949. *Public Opinion*. New York: Free Press.

Lipsky, Michael. 1980. *Street-Level Bureaucracy*. New York: Russell Sage Foundation.

Liptak, Adam. 2013. "Supreme Court Invalidates Key Part of Voting Rights Act." *New York Times*. http://www.nytimes.com/2013/06/26/us/supreme-court-ruling.html (accessed September 8, 2014).

Lipton, Eric. 2016. "Trump Campaigned Against Lobbyists, but Now They're on His Transition Team." *New York Times*. https://www.nytimes.com/2016/11/12/us/politics/trump-campaigned-against-lobbyists-now-theyre-on-his-transition-team.html.

Lipton, Eric. 2017. "White House Moves to Block Ethics Inquiry Into Ex-Lobbyists on Payroll." *New York Times*. https://www.nytimes.com/2017/05/22/us/politics/trump-white-house-government-ethics-lobbyists.html.

Loveless, Tom. 1997. "The Structure of Public Confidence in Education." *American Journal of Education* 105 (February): 127–159.

Lowery, David. 2007. "Why Do Organized Interests Lobby? A Multi-Goal, Multi-Context Theory of Lobbying." *Polity* 39 (January): 29–54.

Lowery, David and Holly Brasher. 2004. *Organized Interests and American Government*. New York: McGraw-Hill.

Lowi, Theodore J. 1969. *The End of Liberalism: Ideology, Policy, and the Crisis of Public Authority*. New York: Norton.

Lowry, Robert C. 1997. "The Private Production of Public Goods: Organizational Maintenance, Managers' Objectives, and Collective Goals." *American Political Science Review* 91 (June): 308–323.

Luttbeg, Norman R. and Michael M. Gant. 1995. *American Electoral Behavior 1952–1992*. Itasca, IL: F. E. Peacock.

Lyman, Edward Leo. 1986. *Political Deliverance: The Mormon Quest for Utah Statehood.* Urbana: University of Illinois Press.

Lyons, William and Robert Alexander. 2000. "A Tale of Two Electorates: Generational Replacement and the Decline of Voting in Presidential Elections." *Journal of Politics* 62 (November): 1014–1034.

Maguire, Robert. 2012. "The Ties That Bind: Romney and the Super PACs." OpenSecrets.org. April 6. http://www.opensecrets.org/news/2012/04/the-coordinated-noncoordination-of.html (accessed May 19, 2012).

Maheshwari, Sapna. 2016. "How Fake News Goes Viral: A Case Study". *New York Times.* https://www.nytimes.com/2016/11/20/business/media/how-fake-news-spreads.html?mc=aud_dev&mcid=fb-nytimes&mccr=NovMidMC&mcdt=2016-11&subid=NovMidMC&ad-keywords=AudDevGate

Manheim, Jarol B. and Richard C. Rich. 1991. *Empirical Political Analysis: Research Methods in Political Science.* New York: Longman.

Manning, Jennifer E. 2018. "Membership of the 115th Congress: A Profile." CRS Report R44762. Washington DC: Congressional Research Service, January 17. https://www.senate.gov/CRSpubs/b8f6293e-c235-40fd-b895-6474d0f8e809.pdf. (accessed February 8, 2018).

Martin, N. G., L. J. Eaves, A. C. Heath, Rosemary Jardine, Lynn M. Feingold, and H. J. Eysenck. 1986. "Transmission of Social Attitudes." *Proceedings of the National Academy of Sciences* 15: 4364–4368.

Masket, Seth. 2011. *No Middle Ground.* Ann Arbor: University of Michigan Press.

Masket, Seth. 2016. *The Inevitable Party.* New York: Oxford University Press.

Masters, Brooke A. 2001. "Judgeship Hinges on Politics, Practice: Md. Liberals Keep Bush Pick Off List." *Washington Post,* May 13, C05.

Matthews, Donald R. 1960. *U.S. Senators and Their World.* Chapel Hill: University of North Carolina Press.

Mauro, Tony. 2017. "In Small World of SCOTUS Advocacy, Gorsuch Faces Early Recusal Choice." *National Law Journal.* https://www.law.com/supremecourtbrief/almID/1202783560121/.

Mayer, William G. 1996. "Forecasting Presidential Nominations." In *In Pursuit of the White House: How We Choose Our Presidential Nominees,* ed. William G. Mayer. Chatham, NJ: Chatham House.

Mayer, William G. and Andrew E. Busch. 2004. *The Frontloading Problem in Presidential Nominations.* Washington, DC: Brookings.

Mayhew, David. 1974. *Congress: The Electoral Connection.* New Haven, CT: Yale University Press.

McCombs Maxwell and Donald Shaw. 1972. "The Agenda-Setting Function of Mass Media." *Public Opinion Quarterly* 36 (Summer): 176–185.

McConnell, Allen and Jill Leibold. 2001. "Relations Among the Implicit Association Test, Discriminatory Behavior, and Explicit Measures of Racial Attitudes." *Journal of Experimental and Social Psychology* 37: 435–442.

McCool, Daniel. 1985. "Indian Voting." In *American Indian Policy in the Twentieth Century,* ed. Vine Deloria Jr., 105–134. Norman: University of Oklahoma Press.

McCubbins, Mathew D. and Thomas Schwartz. 1984. "Congressional Oversight Overlooked: Police Patrol Versus Fire Alarms." *American Journal of Political Science* 28 (February): 165–179.

McCullough, David. 2001. *John Adams.* New York: Simon & Schuster.

McDonald, Michael. 2017. "2016 November General Election Turnout Rates." United States Election Project. http://www.electproject.org/2016g.

McDonald, Michael P. and Samuel L. Popkin. 2001. "The Myth of the Vanishing Voter." *American Political Science Review* 95 (December): 963–974.

McGlen, Nancy E. and Karen O'Connor. 1983. *Women's Rights: The Struggle for Equality in the Nineteenth and Twentieth Centuries.* New York: Praeger.

McGuire, Robert A. 2003. *To Form a More Perfect Union: A New Economic Interpretation of the United States Constitution.* New York: Oxford University Press.

Meier, Kenneth J. 1993. *Politics and the Bureaucracy.* Pacific Grove, CA: Brooks/Cole.

Meier, Kenneth J. 1995. "The Policy Process." In *Regulation and Consumer Protection,* ed. Kenneth J. Meier and E. Thomas Garman. Houston, TX: Dame Publications.

Mersky, Roy M. and William D. Bader. 2004. *The First One Hundred Eight Justices.* Hamden, CT: Archon Books.

Mervin, David. 1995. "The Bully Pulpit, II." *Presidential Studies Quarterly* 25 (Winter): 19–23.

Messing, Solomon and Sean Westwood. 2014. "Selective Exposure in the Age of Social Media: Endorsements Trump Partisan Source Affiliation When Selecting News Online." *Communication Research* 41: 1042–1063.

Milbrath, Lester W. and M. L. Goel. 1977. *Political Participation: How and Why Do People Get Involved in Politics?* 2nd ed. Chicago: Rand McNally.

Miller, Warren E. 1992. "The Puzzle Transformed: Explaining Declining Turnout." *Political Behavior* 14 (March): 1–43.

Miller, Warren E. and Teresa E. Levitin. 1976. *Leadership and Change: Presidential Elections from 1952 to 1976.* Cambridge, MA: Winthrop.

Mills, K. 1997. "What Difference Do Women Journalists Make?" In *Women, Media, and Politics,* ed. Pippa Norris. New York: Oxford University Press.

Mitchell, Amy, Jeffrey Gottfried, and Katerina Eva Matsa. 2015. "Millennials and Political News." Pew Research Center. http://www.journalism.org/2015/06/01/millennials-political-news/.

Mitchell, Amy, Jeffrey Gottfried, Jocelyn Kiley, and Katerina Eva Matsa. 2014. "Political Polarization and Media Habits." Pew Research Center. http://www.journalism.org/2014/10/21/political-polarization-media-habits/.

Moen, Matthew C. and Gary W. Copeland. 1999. *The Contemporary Congress: A Bicameral Approach.* Belmont, CA: Wadsworth.

Mondak, Jeffery J. 1995. "Competence, Integrity, and the Electoral Success of Congressional Incumbents." *Journal of Politics* 57 (November): 1043–1069.

Mondak, J. J., M. V. Hibbing, D. Canache, M. A. Seligson, and M. R. Anderson. 2010. "Personality and Civic Engagement: An Integrative Framework for the Study of trait Effects on Political Behavior." *American Political Science Review* 104: 85–110.

Mooney, Christopher Z., ed. 2001. *The Public Clash of Private Values.* New York: Chatham House.

Morgan, Edmund S. 1992. *The Birth of the Republic.* Chicago: University of Chicago Press.

Morin, Richard. 2000. "The Big Picture Is Out of Focus." *Washington Post National Weekly Edition,* March 6–13, 21.

Morris, Fiorina, Samuel Abrams, and Jeremy Pope. 2008. "Polarization in the American Public: Misconceptions and Misreadings." *Journal of Politics* 70: 556–560.

Mount, Steve. 2006a. "Comparing the Articles and the Constitution." March 15. http://www.usconstitution.net/constconart.html (accessed March 15, 2018).

Mount, Steve. 2006b. "Constitutional Topic: The Constitution and Religion." March 15. http://www.usconstitution.net/consttop-reli.html (accessed March 15, 2018).

Mueller, John. 1973. *War, Presidents, and Public Opinion.* New York: Wiley.

Mullainathan, Sendhil and Andrei Schleifer. 2005. "The Market for News." *American Economic Review* 95 (4): 1031–1053.

National Conference of State Legislatures. 2018. "Redistricting Commissions: Congressional Plans", January 25. http://www.ncsl.org/research/redistricting/redistricting-commissions-congressional-plans.aspx.

National Public Radio. 2009. "The Watchmen." http://www.thisamericanlife.org/sites/default/files/382_transcript.pdf (accessed March 5, 2013).

Neiman, Jayme, Karl Giuseffi, Kevin Smith, Jeffrey French, Israel Waismel-Manor, and John Hibbing. 2015. "Voting at Home Is Associated with Lower Cortisol Than Voting at the Polls." *PLoS One.* http://journals.plos.org/plosone/article?id=10.1371/journal.pone.0135289.

Neiman, Jayme, Kevin Smith, Jeffrey French, Israel Waismel-Manor, and John Hibbing. 2013. "Can the Stress of Voting Be Reduced? A Test Within the Context of the 2012 U.S. Presidential Election." Paper presented at the annual meeting of the American Political Science Association, Chicago, IL.

Neustadt, Richard E. 1960. *Presidential Power.* New York: Wiley.

Newport, Frank. 1998. "History Shows Presidential Job Approval Ratings Can Plummet Rapidly." *Gallup Poll Monthly* 389 (February): 9–10.

Newspaper Association of America. 2010. "Total Paid Circulation." http://www.naa.org/TrendsandNumbers/Total-Paid-Circulation.aspx (accessed January 27, 2009).

Nichols, Tom. 2017. *The Death of Expertise.* New York: Oxford University Press.

Nie, Norman, Sidney Verba, and John Petrocik. 1979. *The Changing American Voter.* Cambridge, MA: Harvard University Press.

Niemi, Richard and Herbert Weisberg. 1993. *Classics in Voting Behavior.* Washington, DC: CQ Press.

Niskanen, William. 1971. *Bureaucracy and Representative Government.* Hawthorne, NY: Aldine de Gruyter.

Niven, David. 2002. *Tilt?* New York: Praeger.

NPR/PBS. 2017. "NPR/PBS Newshour/Marist Poll Results." http://maristpoll.marist.edu/npr-pbs-newshour-marist-poll/.

Numbers USA. 2002. "The 12 Top-Rated, Nationally Syndicated, Politically-Oriented Radio Talk Shows." June 2. http://www.numbersusa.com/text?ID_998 (accessed May 12, 2004).

O'Brien, David M. 1996. *Storm Center: The Supreme Court in American Politics.* 4th ed. New York: Norton.

Office of Management and Budget. 2017. "Historical Tables." http://www.whitehouse.gov/omb/budget/Historicals (accessed February 1, 2018).

Ohlemacher, Stephen. 2007. "Census Shows Early Primary States Are Far From 'Average.'" *Boston Globe,* May 17. http://www.boston.com/news/nation/washington/articles/2007/05/17/census_shows_early_primary_states_are_far_from_average/ (accessed September 19, 2010).

Oleszek, Walter J. 2008. "Senate Policy on 'Holds': Action in the 110th Congress." CRS Report for Congress, March 14. http://www.fas.org/sgp/crs/misc/RL34255.pdf (accessed May 24, 2010).

Olson, Elizabeth. 2016. "Women Make Up Majority of U.S. Law Students for First Time." *New York Times,* December 16, 2016. https://www.nytimes.com/2016/12/16/business/dealbook/women-majority-of-us-law-students-first-time.html.

Olson, Mancur. 1965. *The Logic of Collective Action.* Cambridge, MA: Harvard University Press.

Oremus, Will. 2013. "To Celebrate Spying on Google Users, the NSA Drew a Smiley Face." *Slate.com*. http://www.slate.com/blogs/future_tense/2013/10/30/nsa_smiley_face_muscular_spying_on_google_yahoo_speaks_volumes_about_agency.html (accessed March 12, 2015).

Ornstein, Norman J., Thomas E. Mann, Michael J. Malbin, and Andrew Rugg. 2018. *Vital Statistics on Congress*. Washington, DC: Brookings/AEI (updated May 21, 2018). https://www.brookings.edu/multi-chapter-report/vital-statistics-on-congress/ (accessed August 27, 2018).

O'Rourke, P. J. 1991. *A Parliament of Whores*. New York: Atlantic Monthly Press.

Osborne, David and Ted Gaebler. 1990. *Reinventing Government*. New York: Plume.

Overby, L. Marvin and Kenneth M. Cosgrove. 1996. "Unintended Consequences? Racial Redistricting and the Representation of Minority Interests." *Journal of Politics* 58 (May): 540–550.

Owen, Sue. 2013. "Gregg Abbott Says He Has Sued Obama Administration 25 Times." *Politifact*. http://www.politifact.com/texas/statements/2013/may/10/greg-abbott/greg-abbott-says-he-has-sued-obama-administration-/.

Parkinson, John and Steven Portnoy. 2014. "Should Members of Congress Make More Than Their $174K?" ABC News blogs, April 4, 2014. http://abcnews.go.com/blogs/politics/2014/04/should-members-of-congress-make-more-thantheir-174k/ (accessed May 20, 2014).

Patterson, Thomas E. 1984. *The Mass Media Election*. New York: Praeger.

Patterson, Thomas. 2017. "News Coverage of Donald Trump's First 100 Days." Shorenstein Center on Media, Politics and Public Policy, Harvard University. https://shorensteincenter.org/wp-content/uploads/2017/05/News-Coverage-of-Trump-100-Days-5-2017.pdf.

Peake, Jeffrey S. 2018. "Obama, Unilateral Diplomacy, and Iran: Treaties, Executive Agreements, and Political Commitments." In *Presidential Leadership and National Security: The Obama Legacy and Trump Trajectory*, ed. Richard S. Conley. New York: Routledge.

Peltason, J. W. 1961. *Fifty-Eight Lonely Men: Southern Federal Judges and School Desegregation*. New York: Harcourt, Brace & World.

Peltason, J. W. 1982. *Corwin and Peltason's Understanding the Constitution*. 3rd ed. New York: Holt, Rinehart & Winston.

Percy, Stephen. 1989. *Disability, Civil Rights, and Public Policy*. Tuscaloosa: University of Alabama Press.

Peters, Gerhard and John T. Woolley. 1999–2018. "Presidential Signing Statements." In *The American Presidency Project*, ed. John T. Woolley and Gerhard Peters. Santa Barbara, CA. http://www.presidency.ucsb.edu/signingstatements.php.

Peters, John G. and Susan Welch. 1980. "The Effects of Charges of Corruption on Voting Behavior in Congressional Elections." *American Political Science Review* 74 (September): 697–708.

Peterson, Paul E. 1995. *The Price of Federalism*. Washington, DC: Brookings Institution.

Peterson, Paul E. and Mark C. Rom. 1990. *Welfare Magnets: A New Case for a National Standard*. Washington, DC: Brookings Institution.

Pew Research Center. 2001. "Terror Coverage Boost News Media's Images." November 28. http://people-press.org/report/143/terror-coverage-boost-news-medias-images (accessed August 9, 2004).

Pew Research Center. 2009. "Press Accuracy Rating Hits Two Decade Low." http://www.people-press.org/2009/09/13/press-accuracy-rating-hits-two-decade-low/ (accessed April 26, 2012).

Pew Research Center. 2011. "Public Remains Divided Over the PATRIOT Act." http://pewresearch.org/pubs/1893/poll-patriot-act-renewal (accessed February 13, 2012).

Pew Research Center. 2012. "Cable Leads the Pack as Campaign News Source." http://www.people-press.org/2012/02/07/section-3-perceptions-of-bias-news-knowledge/ (accessed April 24, 2012).

Pew Research Center. 2015a. "Americans' Attitudes About Privacy, Security and Surveillance." http://www.pewinternet.org/2015/05/20/americans-attitudes-about-privacy-security-and-surveillance/ (accessed March 16, 2018).

Pew Research Center. 2015b. "What Americans Think About NSA Surveillance, National Security and Privacy." http://www.pewresearch.org/fact-tank/2015/05/29/what-americans-think-about-nsa-surveillance-national-security-and-privacy/ (accessed September 18, 2015).

Plano, Jack C. and Milton Greenberg. 2002. *The American Political Dictionary*. 11th ed. Belmont, CA: Thomson/Wadsworth.

Polsby, Nelson W. 1968. "The Institutionalization of the U.S. House of Representatives." *American Political Science Review* 62 (March): 144–168.

Polsby, Nelson and Aaron Wildavsky. 2000. *Presidential Elections: Strategies and Structures of American Politics*. 10th ed. New York: Chatham House.

Posner, Paul and Timothy Conlon. 2014. "The Future of Federalism in a Polarized Country." *Governing*. http://www.governing.com/columns/smart-mgmt/col-states-polarized-politics-variable-speed-federalism.html.

Powell, G. Bingham. 1980. "Voting Turnout in Thirty Democracies: Partisan, Legal, and Socio-Economic Influences." In *Electoral Participation: A Comparative Analysis*, ed. Richard Rose. Beverly Hills, CA: SAGE.

Pressman, Jeffrey L. and Aaron Wildavsky. 1973. *Implementation*. Berkeley: University of California Press.

Preston, Julia. 2017. "How the Dreamers Learned to Play Politics." *Politico Magazine*, September 9. https://www.politico.com/magazine/story/2017/09/09/dreamers-daca-learned-to-play-politics-215588.

Preuhs, Robert R. 2006. "The Conditional Effects of Minority Descriptive Representation: Black Legislatures and Policy Influence in the American States." *Journal of Politics* 69 (August): 585–599.

Pritchett, C. Herman. 1948. *The Roosevelt Court: A Study in Judicial Politics and Values, 1937–1946.* New York: Macmillan.

Pritchett, C. Herman. 1976. *The American Constitutional System.* New York: McGraw-Hill.

Puglisi, Riccardo. 2008. "Being the New York Times: The Political Behaviour of a Newspaper." Available at SSRN, http://ssrn.com/abstract=573801 or http://dx.doi.org/10.2139/ssrn.573801.

Ragsdale, Lyn. 1996. *Vital Statistics on the Presidency: Washington to Clinton.* Washington, DC: CQ Press.

Ragsdale, Lyn and John J. Theis, III. 1997. "The Institutionalization of the American Presidency 1924–92." *American Journal of Political Science* 41 (October): 1280–1318.

Rapoport, Ronald B. 1997. "Partisanship Change in a Candidate-Centered Era." *Journal of Politics* 59: 185–199.

Redford, Emmette S. 1969. *Democracy in the Administrative State.* New York: Oxford University Press.

Rees, Nigel. 1997. *Cassell Companion to Quotations.* London: Cassell.

Richardson, Richard J. and Kenneth N. Vines. 1970. *The Politics of Federal Courts.* Boston: Little, Brown.

Riker, William H. and Peter C. Ordeshook. 1968. "A Theory of the Calculus of Voting." *American Political Science Review* 62 (March): 25–42.

Ripley, Randall. 1988. *Policy Analysis in Political Science.* Chicago: Nelson-Hall.

Robson, William A. 1923. "Compulsory Voting." *Political Science Quarterly* 38 (December): 569–577.

Rogers, Will. 1974. *The Illiterate Digest*, ed. with intro by Joseph A. Stout Jr. Stillwater: Oklahoma State University Press.

Rohde, David W. 1991. *Parties and Leaders in the Post Reform House.* Chicago: University of Chicago Press.

Rom, Mark C., Paul E. Peterson, and Kenneth S. Scheve Jr. 1998. "Interstate Competition and Welfare Policy." *Publius* 28 (Summer): 17–37.

Rose, Shanna and Cynthia J. Bowling. 2015. "The State of American Federalism 2014–15: Pathways to Policy in an Era of Party Polarization." *Publius: The Journal of Federalism* 45(3): 351–379.

Rosenbloom, David H. 1998. *Public Administration: Understanding Management, Politics, and Law in the Public Sector.* 4th ed. New York: McGraw-Hill.

Rosenstone, Steven and John Mark Hansen. 1993. *Mobilization, Participation, and Democracy in America.* New York: Macmillan.

Rothenberg, Stuart. 2014. "Beware 'Anti-Incumbent' Election Hysteria." *Rothenberg Political Report*, June 25. http://rothenbergpoliticalreport.com/news/article/beware-anti-incumbent-election-hysteria (accessed December 4, 2014).

Rourke, Matt. 2016. "Views on the American Election and Perceptions of Voter Fraud." Associated Press–NORC Center for Public Affairs Research. http://www.apnorc.org/projects/Pages/HTML%20Reports/views-on-the-american-election-process-and-perceptions-of-voter-fraud-issue-brief.aspx#study.

Rudalevige, Andrew. 2014. "Five Points to Ponder on the Immigration Directives." *Washington Post*, The Monkey Cage. http://www.washingtonpost.com/blogs/monkey-cage/wp/2014/11/25/five-points-to-ponder-on-the-immigration-directives/ (accessed December 10, 2014).

Sabatier, Paul. 1988. "An Advocacy Coalition Framework of Policy Change and the Role of Policy-Oriented Learning Therein." *Policy Sciences* 21: 129–168.

Sabatier, Paul A. and Daniel Mazmanian. 1980. "The Implementation of Public Policy: A Framework for Analysis." *Policy Studies Journal* 8: 538–560.

Salisbury, Robert H. 1969. "An Exchange Theory of Interest Groups." *Midwest Journal of Political Science* 13 (February): 1–32.

Samuelson, Robert J. 2008. "Lobbying Is Democracy in Action." *Newsweek*, December 13. http://www.newsweek.com/id/174283 (accessed March 13, 2010).

Sanger, David E. 2001. "Look Sharp: Trying to Run a Country Like a Corporation." *New York Times*, July 8. http://www.nytimes.com/2001/07/08/weekinreview/08SANG.html (accessed October 23, 2004).

Santiago, Chris. 2010. "The First Asian-American Supreme Court Justice?" Race in America, *Change.org*, June 8. http://race.change.org/blog/view/the_first_asian-american_supreme_court_justice (accessed June 17, 2010).

Satija, Neena. 2017. "Texas vs. the Feds – A Look at the Lawsuits." *Texas Tribune.* https://www.texastribune.org/2017/01/17/texas-federal-government-lawsuits/.

Savage, Charlie. 2009. "Obama's Embrace of a Bush Tactic Riles Congress." *New York Times*, August 8. http://www.nytimes.com/2009/08/09/us/politics/09signing.html?_r=2 &hpw (accessed May 31, 2010).

Schaefer, Todd M. 1997. "Persuading the Persuaders: Presidential Speeches and Editorial Opinion." *Political Communication* 14 (January–March): 97–111.

Schattschneider, E. E. 1942. *Party Government*. New York: Rinehart.

Schattschneider, E. E. 1960. *The Semisovereign People: A Realist View of Democracy in America*. New York: Holt, Rinehart & Winston.

Schlesinger, Arthur M., Jr. 1973. *The Imperial Presidency*. Boston: Houghton Mifflin.

Schneider, Anne Larson and Helen Ingram. 1997. *Policy Design for Democracy*. Lawrence: University of Kansas Press.

Schneider, Anne and Helen Ingram, eds. 2005. *Deserving and Entitled: Social Constructions and Public Policy*. Albany: SUNY Press.

Schneider, Judy. 2006. "Committee Assignment Process in the U.S. Senate: Democratic and Republican Party Procedures." Congressional Research Service, CRS Report for Congress (RL30743) (updated November 3, 2006). http://www.senate.gov/reference/resources/pdf/RL30743.pdf (accessed May 24, 2010).

Schneider, Judy. 2008. "House and Senate Rules of Procedure: A Comparison." Congressional Research Service, CRS Report for Congress (RL30945) (updated April 16, 2008). http://assets.opencrs.com/rpts/RL30945_20080416.pdf.

Schneider, Judy. 2014a. "House Committees: Categories and Rules for Committee Assignments." CRS Report 98-151. Washington DC: Congressional Research Service, October 17, 2014. https://www.everycrsreport.com/files/20141017_98-151_2e7e947ded97a492e4146f366a20cfc0ddd928dd.pdf (accessed February 9, 2018).

Schneider, Judy. 2014b. "Senate Committees: Categories and Rules for Committee Assignments." CRS Report 98-183. Washington DC: Congressional Research Service, January 15, 2014. https://www.everycrsreport.com/files/20140115_98-183_f7757836e56ed515c64e97d-1a2614b2fdac6a937.pdf (accessed February 9, 2018).

Schumpeter, Joseph. 1942. *Capitalism, Socialism and Democracy*. New York: Harper and Brothers.

Schutz, Astrid. 1995. "Entertainers, Experts, or Public Servants? Politicians' Self-Presentation on Television Talk Shows." *Political Communication* 12: 211–221.

Sclar, Elliott D. 2000. *You Don't Always Get What You Pay For*. Ithaca, NY: Cornell University Press.

Sears, David and Nicholas Valentino. 1997. "Politics Matters: Political Events as Catalysts for Preadult Socialization." *American Political Science Review* 91 (June): 45–65.

Seeman, Melvin. 1959. "On the Meaning of Alienation." *American Sociological Review* 24 (December): 783–791.

Segal, Jeffrey A. and Albert D. Cover. 1989. "Ideological Values and the Votes of U.S. Supreme Court Justices." *American Political Science Review* 83: 557–565.

Segal, Jeffrey and Harold Spaeth. 2002. *The Supreme Court and the Attitudinal Model Revisited*. New York: Cambridge University Press.

Shafer, Byron E. 1988. *Bifurcated Politics: Evolution and Reform in the National Convention*. Cambridge, MA: Harvard University Press.

Shepsle, Kenneth A. and Barry R. Weingast. 1987. "The Institutional Foundations of Committee Power." *American Political Science Review* 81 (March): 85–104.

Sifry, Micah. 1998. "Low Tide for the Angry Middle." *The Nation* 267 (July): 16–20.

Silver, Nate. 2014. "Contemplating Obama's Place in History, Statistically." *FiveThirtyEight Politics*, January 23, 2013. http://fivethirtyeight.com/features/contemplatingobamas-place-in-history-statistically/ (accessed May 20, 2014).

Silverstein, Mark. 1994. *Judicious Choices: The New Politics of Supreme Court Confirmations*. New York: Norton.

Simon, Herbert. 1947. *Administrative Behavior*. New York: The Free Press.

Sinclair, Barbara. 2012. *Unorthodox Lawmaking: New Legislative Processes in the U.S. Congress*. 4th ed. Washington, DC: CQ Press.

Skocpol, Theda. 1999. "Associations Without Members." *American Prospect* 45: 1–8.

Smith, Aaron, Kay Lehman Schlozman, Sidney Verba, and Henry Brady. 2009. *The Internet and Civic Engagement*. Washington, DC: Pew Internet & American Life Project.

Smith, Kevin B. 1999. "Clean Thoughts and Dirty Minds: The Politics of Porn." *Policy Studies Journal* 27(4): 723–734.

Smith, Kevin B. 2005. "Data Don't Matter? Academic Research and School Choice." *Perspectives on Politics* 3(2): 285–299.

Smith, Kevin B., John Buntin, and Alan Greenblatt. 2004. *Governing States and Localities*. Washington, DC: CQ Press.

Smith, Richard A. 1995. "Interest Group Influence in the U.S. Congress." *Legislative Studies Quarterly* 20 (February): 89–139.

Sobieraj, Sarah and Jeffrey Berry. 2011. "From Incivility to Outrage: Political Discourse in Blogs, Talk Radio, and Cable News." *Political Communication* 28: 19–41.

Solum, Lawrence B. 2014. "The Positive Foundations of Formalism: False Necessity and American Legal Realism" (Book review of Lee Epstein, William M. Landes, and Richard A Posner, *The Behavior of Federal Judges: A Theoretical and Empirical Study of Rational*

Choice. Cambridge, MA: Harvard University Press). *Harvard Law Review* 127(8): 2464–2497.

Sommers, Samuel, Evan Apfelbaum, Kirstin Dukes, Negin Toosi, and Elsie Wang. 2006. *Analysis of Social Issues and Public Policy* 6: 39–55.

Spaeth, Harold J. 1979. *Supreme Court Policy Making: Explanation and Prediction.* San Francisco: W. H. Freeman.

Spitzer, Robert J. 1995. *The Politics of Gun Control.* Chatham, NJ: Chatham House.

Spitzer, Robert J. 1998. "Gun Control." In *Moral Controversies in American Politics: Cases in Social Regulatory Policy,* ed. Raymond Tatalovich and Byron W. Daynes. New York: Sharpe.

Spriggs, James F., II and Paul J. Wahlbeck. 1997. "Amicus Curiae and the Role of Information at the Supreme Court." *Political Research Quarterly* 50 (June): 365–386.

Spring, Joe. 1998. *American Education.* 8th ed. New York: McGraw-Hill.

Stanley, Harold W. and Richard G. Niemi. 2011. *Vital Statistics on American Politics 2011–2012.* Washington, DC: CQ Press.

Stanley, Harold W. and Richard G. Niemi. 2013. *Vital Statistics on American Politics 2013–2014.* Washington, DC: CQ Press.

Starr, Paul. 2010. "Governing in the Age of Fox News." *The Atlantic* 305 (January): 95–98.

Stelter, Brian. 2009. "Fox's Volley With Obama Intensifying." *New York Times,* October 11. http://www.nytimes.com/2009/10/12/business/media/12fox.html (accessed January 20, 2010).

Sterling, Bryan B., ed. 1979. *The Best of Will Rogers.* New York: Crown Publishers.

Stewart, Charles, III. 2005. "Congress and the Constitutional System." In *The Legislative Branch,* ed. Paul J. Quirk and Sarah A. Binder. New York: Oxford University Press.

Stewart, Charles, III. 2012. "The Value of Committee Assignments in Congress Since 1994." Presented at the annual meeting of the Midwest Political Science Association, Chicago, IL April 12–15.

Stewart, Charles, III and Tim Groseclose. 1999. "The Value of Committee Seats in the United States Senate, 1947–91." *American Journal of Political Science* 43 (July): 963–973.

Stout, David. 2000. "The 43rd President: The Electoral College; The Electors Vote, and the Surprises Are Few." *New York Times,* December 19, 2000. http://www.nytimes.com/2000/12/19/us/43rd-president-electoral-college-electors-vote-surprises-are-few.html

Strickland, Rennard J. 1992. "Native Americans." In *The Oxford Companion to the Supreme Court of the United States,* ed. Kermit L. Hall. New York: Oxford University Press.

Suskind, Rob. 2004. "Faith, Certainty and the Presidency of George W. Bush," *New York Times* Magazine, October 17. https://www.nytimes.com/2004/10/17/magazine/faith-certainty-and-the-presidency-of-george-w-bush.html

Svingen, Orlan J. 1987. "Jim Crow, Indian Style." *American Indian Quarterly* 11 (Autumn): 275–286.

Swain, Carol. 1995. *Black Faces, Black Interests: The Representation of African Americans in Congress.* Cambridge, MA: Harvard University Press.

Swanson, David L. 2000. "The Homologous Evolution of Political Communication and Civic Engagement: Good News, Bad News, and No News." *Political Communication* 17: 409–414.

Taber, Charles S., Damon Cann, and Simona Kucsova. 2009. "The Motivated Processing of Political Arguments." *Political Behavior* 31(2): 137–155.

Tanner, Michael and Charles Hughes. 2013. *The Work Versus Welfare Trade-Off.* Washington, DC: The Cato Instiute.

Tarr, G. Alan. 2000. *Understanding State Constitutions.* Princeton, NJ: Princeton University Press.

Tarr, G. Alan. 2003. *Judicial Process and Judicial Policymaking.* Belmont, CA: Thomson/Wadsworth.

Tenpas, Kathryn Dunn, 2018. "Why is Trump's Staff Turnover Higher than the 5 Most Recent Presidents?" *The Brookings Institution.* https://www.brookings.edu/research/why-is-trumps-staff-turnover-higher-than-the-5-most-recent-presidents/.

Tesh, Sylvia. 1984. "In Support of 'Single-Issue' Politics." *Political Science Quarterly* 99 (Spring): 27–44.

Theodoulou, Stella. 1995. "Making Public Policy." In *Public Policy: The Essential Readings,* ed. Stella Z. Theodoulou and Matthew A. Cahn. New York: Prentice Hall.

Theriault, Sean. 2013. *The Gingrich Senators: The Roots of Partisan Warfare in Congress.* New York: Oxford University Press.

Theriault, Sean and David W. Rohde. 2011. "The Gingrich Senators and Party Polarization in the U.S. Senate." *Journal of Politics* 73 (October): 1011–1024.

This American Life. 2015. "The Problem We All Live With." https://www.thisamericanlife.org/radio-archives/episode/562/transcript.

Thomsett, Michael C. and Jean Freestone Thomsett. 1994. *Political Quotations: A Worldwide Dictionary of Thoughts and Pronouncements from Politicians, Literary Figures, Humorists, and Others.* Jefferson, NC: McFarland.

Tierney, John. 2004. "The 2004 Campaign: Advertising; Using MRI's to See Politics on the Brain." *New York Times*, April 20, 2004. https://www.nytimes.com/2004/04/20/us/the-2004-campaign-advertising-using-mri-s-to-see-politics-on-the-brain.html

Ting, Michael, James Snyder, Jr, Shegeo Hirano, and Olle Folke. 2012. "Elections and Reform: The Adoption of Civil Service Systems in the U.S. States." *Journal of Theoretical Politics* 25: 363–387.

Tocqueville, Alexis de. [1835] 1955. *Democracy in America*. Vol. 2. New York: Vintage Books.

Tolbert, Caroline J. and Romona S. McNeal. 2003. "Unraveling the Effects of the Internet on Political Participation?" *Political Research Quarterly* 56(2): 175–185.

Tong, Lorraine H. 2009. "House Committee Party Ratios: 98th–111th Congresses." Congressional Research Service, March 30. http://www.fas.org/sgp/crs/misc/R40478.pdf (accessed May 21, 2010).

Tooby, John and Leda Cosmides. 1992. "The Psychological Foundations of Culture." In *The Adapted Mind*, ed. Jerome H. Barkow, Leda Cosmides, and John Tooby. New York: Oxford University Press.

Traugott, Michael W. and Paul J. Lavrakas. 2000. *The Voter's Guide to Election Polls*. 2nd ed. New York: Seven Bridges Press.

Tribe, Laurence H. 2004. "*Lawrence v. Texas*: The 'Fundamental Right' That Dare Not Speak Its Name." *Harvard Law Review* 117: 1894–1895.

Truman, David B. 1951. *The Governmental Process: Political Interests and Public Opinion*. 2nd ed. New York: Knopf.

Tucker, Will. 2015. "Personal Wealth: A Nation of Extremes, and a Congress Too." Center for Responsive Politics. https://www.opensecrets.org/news/2015/11/personal-wealth-a-nation-of-extremes-and-a-congress-too/.

Tufte, Edward R. 1978. *Political Control of the Economy*. Princeton, NJ: Princeton University Press.

Tullock, Gordon. 1965. *The Politics of Bureaucracy*. Washington, DC: Public Affairs Press.

Tullock, Gordon. 1967. *Toward a Mathematics of Politics*. Ann Arbor: University of Michigan Press.

Turner, Joel. 2007. "The Messenger Overwhelming the Message: Ideological Cues and Perceptions of Bias in Television News." *Political Behavior* 29(4): 441–464.

Uggen, Christopher, Ryan Larson, and Sarah Shannon. 2016. "6 Million Lost Voters: State-Level Estimates of Felony Disenfranchisement, 2016." *The Sentencing Project*. http://www.sentencingproject.org/wp-content/uploads/2016/10/6-Million-Lost-Voters.pdf.

Uhlaner, Carole J., Bruce E. Cain, and Roderick Kiewiet. 1989. "Political Participation of Ethnic Minorities in the 1980s." *Political Behavior* 11 (September): 195–231.

Unah, Isaac. 2012. "Race and Death Sentencing." In *New Directions in Judicial Politics*, ed. Kevin T. McGuire. New York: Routledge.

United States Office of Personnel Management. 2016. "Profile of Civilian Non-Postal Employees." https://www.opm.gov/policy-data-oversight/data-analysis-documentation/federal-employment-reports/reports-publications/profile-of-federal-civilian-non-postal-employees/.

U.S. Census Bureau. 2008. "Statistical Abstract of the United States." http://www.census.gov/compendia/statab/cats/income_expenditures_poverty_wealth.html (accessed November 25, 2008).

U.S. Census Bureau. 2011. "The Hispanic Population: 2010." http://www.census.gov/prod/cen2010/briefs/c2010br-04.pdf (accessed March 2, 2012).

U.S. Department of Justice. 2000. "Enforcing the ADA: Looking Back on a Decade of Progress." June 27. http://www.usdoj.gov/crt/ada/pubs/10thrpt.htm#anchor37661 (accessed October 26, 2000).

U.S. Senate. n.d. "Votes." Statistics and Lists. http://www.senate.gov/reference/common/generic/Votes.htm (accessed September 27, 2010).

Vedantam, Shankar. 2006. "How the Brain Helps Partisans Admit No Gray." *Washington Post*, July 31, A2.

Verba, Sidney and Norman Nie. 1987. *Political Participation in America*. New York: Harper & Row.

Verba, Sidney, Kay Lehman Schlozman, and Henry E. Brady. 1995. *Voice and Equality: Civic Voluntarism in American Politics*. Cambridge, MA: Harvard University Press.

Verhulst, Brad, Lindon Eaves, and Peter Hatemi. 2011. "Correlation Not Causation: The Relationship Between Personality Traits and Political Ideologies." *American Journal of Political Science* 56: 34–51.

Vice, Margaret. 2017. "Publics Worldwide Unfavorable Toward Putin, Russia." Pew Research Center. http://www.pewglobal.org/2017/08/16/publics-worldwide-unfavorable-toward-putin-russia/.

Villalobos, Jose D. 2006. "When Made to Choose: Cross-Pressured Republican Senators and George W. Bush's Private Account Plan." In *A Dialogue on Presidential Challenges and Leadership*, ed. Thomas M. Kirlin and Jay M. Parker, 25–37. Washington, DC: Center for the Study of the Presidency.

Waismel-Manor, Israel, Gal Ifergane, and Hagit Cohen. 2011. "When Endocrinology and Democracy Collide: Emotions, Cortisol and Voting at National Elections." *European Neuropsychopharmacology* 21(11): 789–795.

Walsh, Mary Williams. 2017. "Puerto Rico Declares a Form of Bankruptcy." *New York Times*. https://www.nytimes.com/2017/05/03/business/dealbook/puerto-rico-debt.html.

Washington, George. 1796. *Washington's Farewell Address 1796*. Retrieved from the Yale University Law School, Lillian Goldman Law Library, Avalon Project website: http://avalon.law.yale.edu/default.asp.

Washington Post. 2018. "Tracking How Many Key Positions Trump Has Filled So Far," May 7. https://www.washingtonpost.com/graphics/politics/trump-administration-appointee-tracker/database/?utm_term=.340d0d314d88.

Wattenberg, Martin P. 1998. "Politics: Should Election Day Be a Holiday?" *Atlantic Monthly* 1 (October): 42.

Wattenberg, Martin P. 2007. "Comments on Chapter 1." In *Red and Blue Nation? Volume 2: Consequences and Correction of America's Polarized Politics*, ed. Pietro S. Nivola and David W. Brady, 42. Washington, DC: Brookings Institution Press.

Wayne, Stephen. 2000. *The Road to the White House 2000*. Boston: Bedford/St. Martin's Press.

Wayne, Stephen. 2004. *The Road to the White House 2004*. Belmont, CA: Wadsworth/Thompson.

Weaver, David, Randal Beam, Bonnie Brownlee, Paul Voakes, and G. Cleveland Wilhoit. 2006. *The American Journalist in the 21st Century*. Mahwah, NJ: Lawrence Erlbaum.

Weber, Paul J. and Barbara A. Perry. 1989. *Unfounded Fears: Myths and Realities of a Constitutional Convention*. Westport, CT: Greenwood Press.

Weiser, Wendy and Lawrence Norden. 2011. "Voting Law Changes in 2012." New York: Brennan Center for Justice at NYU School of Law.

Welch, Susan and John R. Hibbing. 1997. "The Effects of Charges of Corruption on Voting Behavior in Congressional Elections, 1982–1990." *Journal of Politics* 59 (February): 226–239.

White, G. Edward. 1982. *Earl Warren: A Public Life*. New York: Oxford University Press.

Wiecek, William. 1992. "Declaration of Independence." In *The Oxford Companion to the Supreme Court of the United States*, ed. Kermit L. Hall. New York: Oxford University Press.

Wildavsky, Aaron. 1965. "The Goldwater Phenomenon: Purists, Politicians, and the Two-Party System." *Review of Politics* 27 (July): 386–413.

Williams, David. 2003. *The Mythic Meanings of the Second Amendment*. New Haven, CT: Yale University Press.

Wilson, James Q. 1962. *The American Democrat*. Chicago: University of Chicago Press.

Wilson, Woodrow. 1885. *Congressional Government: A Study in American Politics*. Boston: Houghton Mifflin.

Wilson, Woodrow. 1887. "The Study of Administration." *Political Science Quarterly* 2 (March): 197–222.

Wines, Michael. 2016. "Some Republicans Acknowledge Leveraging Voter ID Laws for Political Gain." *New York Times*. https://www.nytimes.com/2016/09/17/us/some-republicans-acknowledge-leveraging-voter-id-laws-for-political-gain.html.

Wolfinger, Raymond E. 1991. "The Politics of Voter Registration Reform." In *Registering Voters: Comparative Perspectives*, ed. John C. Courtney. Cambridge, MA: Harvard University Center for International Affairs.

Wolfley, Jeanette. 1991. "Jim Crow, Indian Style: The Disenfranchisement of Native Americans." *American Indian Law Review* 16 (Spring): 167–202.

Wood, B. Dan. 1992. "Modeling Federal Implementation as a System: The Clean Air Case." *American Journal of Political Science* 36 (February): 4–67.

Wood, B. Dan and Richard W. Waterman. 1994. *Bureaucratic Dynamics: The Role of Bureaucracy in a Democracy*. Boulder, CO: Westview Press.

Worsnop, Richard L. 1996. "Implementing the Disabilities Act." *CQ Researcher* 6 (December): 1107–1127.

Wright, John R. 1990. "Contributions, Lobbying, and Committee Voting in the U.S. House of Representatives." *American Journal of Political Science* 84 (June): 417–438.

Wronski, Laura. 2017. "The No. 1 Word Business Owners Use to Describe Trump's Management Style." CNBC. https://www.cnbc.com/2017/09/25/business-owners-describe-president-trump-management-style.html.

Zaller, John R. 1992. *The Nature and Origins of Mass Opinion*. New York: Cambridge University Press.

Zhuravskaya, Ekaterina. 2010. "Federalism in Russia." *Centre for Economic and Financial Research at New Economic School*. http://www.cefir.ru/papers/WP141.pdf (accessed March 15, 2012).

Ziegert, Jonathan and Paul Hanges. 2005. "Employment Discrimination: The Role of Implicit Attitudes, Motivation and a Climate for Racial Bias." *Journal of Applied Psychology* 90(3): 553–562.

Zink, James R. 2009. "The Language of Liberty and Law: James Wilson on America's Written Constitution." *American Political Science Review* 103 (August): 442–455.

GLOSSARY

absolute majority Fifty percent plus one of all members or all eligible voters.

absolutist approach The view of the First Amendment that states that the Founders wanted it to be interpreted literally so that Congress should make "no laws" about the expression of views.

ad hoc federalism The process of adopting a state- or nation-centered view of federalism on the basis of political convenience.

adjudication The process of determining whether a law or rule established by the bureaucracy has been broken.

adverse selection A principal's lack of information about the abilities of an agent.

advertising The activities of members of Congress (such as sending out newsletters or visiting the district) designed to familiarize the constituency with the member.

advisory committees Temporary or permanent organizations created to provide information and technical expertise to the bureaucracy.

affirmative action Governmental actions designed to help minorities compete on an equal basis and overcome the effects of discrimination in the past.

agency capture A term used to describe when an agency seems to operate for the benefit of those whom it is supposed to regulate.

agenda setting The process of selecting the issues or problems that government will pay attention to.

allegiant Feeling great trust and support for the political system.

allocation responsiveness Representation that takes the form of members of Congress ensuring that their district gets a share of federal benefits.

Americans with Disabilities Act (ADA) Specifically extended to citizens with disabilities, the civil rights and protections that were the cornerstone of the 1964 Civil Rights Act. It largely codified existing laws and regulations and extended them to the private sector.

amicus curiae brief A legal brief filed by someone or some organization who holds an interest in a case but is not an actual party.

Anti-Federalists The group of people who opposed a stronger national government than what existed under the Articles of Confederation and opposed the ratification of the Constitution.

appointment power A power of the president that enables him or her to control the bureaucracy by selecting the people who will head its agencies.

Arrow's impossibility theorem A formal proof that no decision-making system can guarantee that the rank-ordered preferences of a group will reflect the rank-ordered preferences of the set of rational individuals who make up that group.

Articles of Confederation The first constitution of the United States.

attitudinal model A model that suggests that judges' decisions are largely, if not exclusively, determined by their personal ideological and policy preferences.

autocracy A form of government in which the power to make authoritative decisions and allocate resources is vested in one person.

bad tendency rule An approach to determining whether an action should be protected under the First Amendment that considers whether the action would have a tendency to produce a negative consequence.

Baker v. Carr The 1962 case in which the Supreme Court overturned the political question doctrine, holding that legislative apportionment was a justiciable issue that the courts had jurisdiction to hear and decide.

balancing test The view of freedom of expression that states the obligation to protect rights must be balanced with the impact on society of the action in question.

Barron v. Baltimore The 1833 Supreme Court case that explicitly confirmed that the Bill of Rights applied only to the national government.

biased sample A group of poll respondents that does not accurately represent the target population and provides inaccurate estimates of the true opinions and attitudes of the target population.

bicameral A legislature with two chambers.

Bipartisan Campaign Reform Act (BCRA) A law that limited hard-money contributions during each election cycle to $2,000 from individuals and $5,000 from PACs, and banned soft money.

#BlackLivesMatter movement A modern civil rights movement formed to protest police brutality and killings of African Americans; noteworthy features include: effective use of Twitter's hashtags, inclusion of those who were marginalized in earlier black liberation movements (women, lesbian, gay, bisexual, transgender, and queer), and a localized organizational structure with no recognizable leader who speaks for the movement.

block grants A type of federal grant that provides funds for a general policy area but offers state and local governments' discretion in designing the specific programs.

bounded rationality Herbert Simon's theory that humans are not utility maximizers as suggested in classical rational choice models. Humans satisfice (*see* satisficing) rather than maximize.

Brandenburg v. Ohio The 1969 case that upheld a KKK member's right to controversial speech, which supported lawbreaking in the abstract, because it contained no incitement to commit an "imminent or specific" crime, establishing the imminent lawless action test.

Brown v. Board of Education The 1954 case in which a unanimous Court overturned the "separate but equal" precedent set by *Plessy v. Ferguson* and declared that separate educational facilities are inherently unequal.

bureaucracy The term used to refer to the agencies of the federal government. It also refers to an organizational framework and has negative connotations.

by-product theory The theory that most people will not engage in collective action with the sole aim of producing public goods. Instead, groups build membership by offering selective benefits available only to group members.

cabinet departments The 15 largest and most influential agencies of the federal bureaucracy.

candidate image Voters' perceptions of a candidate's qualities.

casework Activities of members of Congress to act as intermediaries and help private individuals who are having problems with the administrative agencies in the executive branch. These activities are service responsiveness.

categorical grants A type of federal grant that provides money for a specific policy activity and details how the programs are to be carried out.

caucus A meeting of members of a political party.

caucus method A method of selecting the delegates to a political party's national convention by permitting the state conventions to select representatives from their states.

censures and reprimands Verbal condemnations of a member of Congress by the House or Senate, intended to punish bad behavior by expressing the public disapproval of the member's colleagues.

check and balance The idea that each branch of the federal government should assert and protect its own rights but must also cooperate with the other branches. Each branch is to serve as a limit on the others' powers, balancing the overall distribution of power.

Citizens United v. Federal Election Commission A 2010 Supreme Court case holding that corporations, labor unions, and mega-wealthy individuals have a First Amendment right to spend unlimited amounts of money from their general treasuries to convince people to vote for or against some candidate.

civil disobedience Deliberately disobeying laws viewed as morally repugnant.

civil liberties The freedoms and protections against arbitrary governmental actions given to the people in a democratic society.

civil rights The obligations placed on government to protect the freedom of the people.

Civil Rights Act of 1964 The landmark law that outlawed racial segregation in schools and public places and barred discrimination in employment based on sex.

"clear and present danger" test An approach to determining whether an action should be protected under the First Amendment that considers "whether the words used are used in such circumstances and are of such a nature as to create a clear and present danger that they will bring about the substantive evils that Congress has a right to prevent."

closed primaries Elections to choose a party's nominees for the general election that are open only to party members.

closed rule The rule that prohibits amending a bill when it is on the floor of Congress for consideration.

cloture A procedure of the Senate to end a filibuster; invoking cloture requires votes of 60 senators.

coalition building A means of expanding an interest group's influence that involves working with other groups.

collective action Action in which a group of people work together for the provision of public goods.

collegial courts Courts in which groups of judges decide cases based on a review of the record of the lower-court trial.

Committee of the Whole A parliamentary action whereby the House of Representatives dissolves into a committee consisting of every member of the House. This procedure is used to facilitate consideration of legislation because it has less burdensome rules governing debate and requires a smaller quorum than the House itself.

concurrent powers The powers listed in the Constitution as belonging to both the national and state governments.

concurring opinion An opinion written by a Supreme Court justice who agrees with the ruling of the Court but not the reason behind it.

conditional party government When members of the majority party caucus in Congress achieve consensus on policy issues, they adopt reforms that strengthened party leaders' ability to promote party unity to enact the party's legislative agenda on which there is a consensus.

confederation A political system in which the central government receives no direct grant of power from the people and can exercise only the power granted to it by the regional governments.

conference The meeting of Supreme Court justices where they decide which cases they will hear, and discuss and vote on the cases previously argued.

conference committee A temporary congressional committee made up of members of the House and Senate that meets to reconcile the differences in legislation that has passed both chambers.

confidence level The chance, measured in percent, that the results of a survey will fall within the boundaries set by the margin of error.

confirmation process The period between when a presidential nomination of a federal judge is received in the Senate and when the nominee is either confirmed or defeated.

Connecticut Compromise (Great Compromise) A proposal at the Constitutional Convention that called for a two-house legislature with a House of Representatives apportioned on the basis of population and a Senate representing each state on an equal basis.

constituency The group of people served by an elected official or branch of government.

constitution A document or unwritten set of basic rules that provides the basic principles that determine the conduct of political affairs.

constitutional interpretation A ruling of the Supreme Court that declares a law unconstitutional based on the Court's interpretation of the Constitution. A constitutional interpretation cannot be overturned by a simple statute.

contracting out Hiring a private organization to deliver a public program or service.

cooperative federalism The idea that the distinction between state and national responsibilities is unclear and that the different levels of government share responsibilities in many areas.

Council of Economic Advisers An agency of the Executive Office of the President that is responsible for advising the president on the U.S. economy.

courts of appellate jurisdiction Courts that review the decisions of lower courts.

courts of original jurisdiction Trial courts that hear cases for the first time and determine issues of fact and law.

credit claiming The efforts by members of Congress to get their constituents to believe they are responsible for positive government actions.

crossover sanction Conditions placed on grant money that have nothing to do with the original purpose of the grant.

custom and usage The term used to describe constitutional change that occurs when practices and institutions not specifically mentioned in the Constitution evolve in response to political needs and alter the structure, functions, or procedures of the political system

Declaration of Independence A document written by Thomas Jefferson that lays the foundation of American constitutional theory. Jefferson justifies the struggle for independence with a republican theory of government based on the concepts of natural rights and popular sovereignty.

de facto discrimination Discrimination that exists in fact, in real life, or in practice.

de jure discrimination Discrimination that is set forth in law.

delegate A representative who makes legislative decisions based on the interests and views of his or her constituents, regardless of personal preference.

delegate model of representative democracy The idea that the job of elected leaders is to make decisions solely based on the views of the majority of the people.

democracy A form of government in which all the citizens have the opportunity to participate in the process of making authoritative decisions and allocating resources.

deregulation The reduction or elimination of government rules and regulations that interfere with the efficient operation of market forces.

descriptive representation The view of representation that calls for the racial and ethnic makeup of Congress to reflect that of the nation.

deviating election An election in which the minority party is able to overcome the long-standing partisan orientation of the public based on temporary or short-term forces.

devolution The return of policy power and responsibility to the states from the national government.

direct democracy A form of democracy in which ordinary citizens, rather than representatives, collectively make government decisions.

direct lobbying Direct contact by lobbyists with government officials in an effort to influence policy.

direct popular election A proposal to abolish the electoral college and elect the president directly by national popular vote.

direct primary The selection of a political party's candidate for the general election by vote of ordinary citizens.

direction The idea of public opinion being either positive or negative (favorable or unfavorable) on an issue.

discharge petition A procedure of the House of Representatives that permits a majority of the members of the House (218) to bring a bill out of committee for consideration on the floor.

dissenting opinion An opinion written by a Supreme Court justice who is in the minority that presents reasons why the justices opposed the majority opinion.

distributive benefits Government expenditures and programs that concentrate benefits in specific geographical areas such as states or congressional districts for which the costs are spread across the entire population. These benefits are allocation responsiveness.

District of Columbia v. Heller The 2008 case in which the Supreme Court struck down the Washington, DC, ban on the possession of handguns and for the first time held that the Second Amendment protects an individual's right to possess a firearm for lawful purposes such as self-defense.

district plan A plan to revise the electoral college that would distribute a state's electoral college votes by giving one vote to the candidate who wins a plurality in each House district and two votes to the winner statewide.

divided government When one party controls the presidency and another controls Congress.

Dream Movement A civil rights movement to protect "Dreamers," undocumented immigrants mostly from Latin America who arrived in the United States as children and have known no other country.

dual federalism The idea that the national and state governments are sovereign, with separate and distinct jurisdictions.

Duverger's Law The tendency, as documented by French sociologist Maurice Duverger, for the single-member district plurality system to favor a two-party system.

economic equality The idea that each individual should receive the same amount of material goods, regardless of his or her contribution to society.

election A collective decision-making process in which citizens choose an individual to hold and exercise the powers of public office. Elections are the primary mechanism that representative democracies use to achieve popular sovereignty.

electoral college The institution (whose members are selected by whatever means the state legislature chooses) that is responsible for selecting the president of the United States.

electronic media Consists of television, radio, movies, video and audio recordings, and the Internet.

elite opinion The attitudes or beliefs of those people with influential positions within society.

elitist A term used to describe a society in which organized, influential minority interests dominate the political process.

empirical Questions and debates that can be answered by careful observation. Systematic empirical observation is the foundation of science and the scientific method.

en banc A procedure in which all the members of a U.S. court of appeals hear and decide a case.

enabling act A resolution passed by Congress authorizing residents of a territory to draft a state constitution as part of the process of adding new states to the Union.

enumerated powers The powers specifically listed in the Constitution as belonging to the national government.

equality of opportunity The idea that every individual has the right to develop to the fullest extent of his or her abilities.

equality under the law The idea that the law is supposed to be applied impartially, without regard for the identity or status of the individual involved.

establishment clause A clause in the First Amendment of the Constitution that states that government cannot establish a religion.

Everson v. Board of Education The 1947 case in which the Court for the first time directly articulated the principle of separation of church and state, concluding that transportation expenditures to parochial schools did not support any religious activity but rather assisted families and were therefore allowable.

exchange theory The theory that interest groups form as a result of a deal—an exchange—between a group entrepreneur and an unorganized interest that may be underrepresented or not represented at all.

exclude The refusal of Congress to seat any candidate who wins election but does not meet the constitutional requirements to hold congressional office.

exclusionary rule The rule derived from the Fourth and Fourteenth Amendments that states that evidence obtained from an unreasonable search or seizure cannot be used in federal trials.

exclusive committees Four House committees—Appropriations, Energy and Commerce, Rules, and Ways and Means—whose members typically receive no other committee assignments.

executive A person or group that has administrative and supervisory responsibilities in an organization or government.

executive agreements Agreements between the United States and other nations, negotiated by the president, that have the same weight as a treaty but do not require senatorial approval.

Executive Office of the President (EOP) The organizational structure in the executive branch that houses the president's most influential advisors and agencies. The most important include the White House Office, the Office of Management and Budget (OMB), the National Security Council, and the Council of Economic Advisers.

executive orders Directives of the president that have the same weight as law and are not voted on by Congress.

executive privilege An inherent power of the president to withhold confidential communications from Congress and the courts if disclosure would violate separation of powers or interfere with the president's ability to discharge the powers and duties of the executive branch.

expulsion The ejection of a member of Congress from office.

faction In James Madison's terms, "a number of citizens, whether amounting to a majority or a minority of the whole, who are united and actuated by some common impulse of passion, or of interests, adverse to the right of other citizens, or to the permanent and aggregate interests of the community."

fake news Stories presented as real news articles that are intentionally and verifiably false. Also used as an epithet to discredit valid but critical news stories.

false consensus The tendency of people to believe their views are normal or represent common sense and therefore are shared by most people.

Federal Election Campaign Act (FECA) A 1971 act that allowed unions and corporations to form political action committees to raise and contribute campaign funds to candidates.

federalism A political system in which regional governments share power with a central or national government, but each level of government has legal powers that are independent of the other. This division of power between the national and state governments attempts to balance power by giving independent sources of authority to each and allowing one level of government to serve as a check on the other.

Federalist **Papers** A series of 85 political essays written by James Madison, Alexander Hamilton, and John Jay with the intent of persuading New Yorkers to ratify the proposed Constitution. They remain the single best source for understanding the justifications for the political institutions and processes the Constitution established.

Federalists The group of people who supported the adoption of the Constitution and favored a stronger national government.

feedback The information policymakers routinely receive through government reports, hearings, the news, casework, meetings with lobbyists and government officials, and contact with constituents.

filibuster The effort by a senator to delay the chamber's business by making long speeches and using parliamentary tactics.

fire alarm oversight Oversight that becomes active only when there is evidence of bureaucratic wrongdoing.

focusing event Something that grabs attention immediately and puts an issue on the public agenda.

framing Emphasizing certain aspects of a story to make them more important.

franchise The constitutional or statutory right to vote.

franking privilege The ability of members of Congress to send mail to their constituents free of charge by substituting a facsimile of their signature in place of a stamp.

free exercise of religion The First Amendment guarantee that individuals are free to choose religious beliefs and practice them as they see fit or to not practice any religion at all.

free rider A person who makes the strictly rational choice to enjoy the benefits of public goods without incurring the costs of providing them, thus presenting a dilemma to the community as a whole.

frontloading The tendency of states to move their primaries earlier in the season in order to gain more influence over the presidential selection process.

"full faith and credit" The provision in the Constitution that requires states to honor the civil obligations (wills, birth certificates, and other public documents) generated by other states. Note: States apparently are not required to recognize marriages under "full faith and credit."

garbage can model A model that attempts to explain why decision making in large complex institutions often seems irrational.

gatekeeper A person or institution that controls access to something.

general election The process by which voters choose their representatives from among the parties' nominees.

general revenue sharing A type of federal grant that returns money to state and local governments with no requirements as to how it is spent.

genocide The killing of an entire race of people.

geographical constituency Everyone and everything within the geographical boundaries of a congressional member's House district.

gerrymandering The drawing of district lines in such a way as to help or hinder the electoral prospects of a specific political interest.

Gideon v. Wainwright The 1963 case in which the Supreme Court ruled that state courts are required under the Sixth and Fourteenth Amendments of the Constitution to provide counsel in criminal cases for defendants who cannot afford to hire their own lawyer.

going public A political strategy in which the president appeals to the public in an effort to persuade Congress to support his or her political goals.

good faith exception An exception to the exclusionary rule that allows evidence obtained in a search with a flawed warrant to be admissible as long as the law officer believed the warrant was valid at the time of the search.

government The institution that has the authority to make binding decisions for all of society.

government corporations Federally established businesses that are narrow in focus and are in part self-supporting.

grandfather clause A provision in election laws used in conjunction with literacy tests to prevent African Americans from voting. People whose ancestors were entitled to vote in 1866 (i.e., whites) were exempt from passing the literacy test, but African Americans, whose ancestors were slaves, had to pass the literacy test in order to vote. This clause was ruled unconstitutional in 1915.

grants-in-aid A form of national subsidy to the states designed to help them pay for policies and programs that are the responsibility of states rather than the national government.

Griswold v. Connecticut The 1965 case ruling that Connecticut could not prohibit the use of contraceptives by married couples, enumerating a right of privacy. Although the Constitution contains no explicit right of privacy, the Court argued that various guarantees in the First, Third, Fourth, Fifth, and Ninth Amendments create "zones of privacy" that the government has no right to invade.

group entrepreneur Someone who invests resources (such as time, money, and organizational skill) to create and build an organization that offers various types of benefits (material, solidary, and purposive) to entice others to join the group.

hard money Campaign contributions made directly to candidates and regulated by law.

hard news Stories that focus on factual information about important decisions or events.

hierarchical model A method of organizing the presidency that calls for clear lines of authority and that delegates responsibility from the president and through the chief of staff.

hold The formal request by a member of the Senate to be notified before a specific bill or presidential nomination comes to the floor.

home style The way a member of Congress behaves, explains his or her legislative actions, and presents himself or herself in the home district.

hypothesis An "educated guess" that logically must be either true or false and can be empirically tested.

ideology A consistent set of values, attitudes, and beliefs about the appropriate role of government in society.

imminent lawless action test As decided in *Brandenburg v. Ohio*, speech is protected if it contains no incitement to commit an "imminent or specific" crime. This test replaced the old "clear and present danger" test and protects a broader range of speech.

impact evaluations Evaluations undertaken to assess the outcomes or effects of a policy or program.

impeach To charge or accuse.

implied powers Those powers belonging to the national government that are suggested in the Constitution's "necessary and proper" clause.

impoundment The limited ability of the president to not spend money appropriated by Congress.

incorporation doctrine The idea that the specific protections provided in the U.S. Bill of Rights are binding on the states through the "due process" clause of the Fourteenth Amendment.

incrementalism A decision-making approach characterized by making current decisions that are small adjustments to past decisions.

incumbency advantage The tendency for congressional incumbents to be overwhelmingly successful when they run for reelection due to the nature of congressional districts, resources, and relations with constituents, among other reasons.

independent agencies Federal agencies that are not part of the cabinet-level executive departments.

indicators Any measures that can be employed as systematic monitoring devices.

indirect lobbying The use of intermediaries by lobbyists to speak to government officials, with the intent to influence policy.

inevitable discovery exception An exception to the exclusionary rule that states that evidence obtained from an illegal search may be used in court if the evidence eventually would have been discovered through legal means.

inherent powers (prerogative powers) Powers that are not listed or implied by the Constitution but that rather have been claimed as essential to the functioning of government or a particular office.

initiative An election in which ordinary citizens circulate a petition to put a proposed law on the ballot for the voters to approve.

institutional agenda A short list of actionable items being given serious consideration by policymaking institutions.

instrumentation The process of designing survey questionnaires.

intensity How strongly people hold the beliefs or attitudes that comprise public opinion.

interest group A group organized around a set of views or preferences and who engage in collective action to influence others in order to promote or protect those preferences.

interstate rendition The obligation of states to return people accused of a crime to the state from which they fled.

invisible primary The period of time between the election of one president and the first contest to nominate candidates to run in the general election to select the next president.

iron triangles A term used to refer to the interdependent relationship among the bureaucracy, interest groups, and congressional committees.

issue public A section of the public with a strong interest in a particular issue.

Jim Crow laws Laws designed to prevent African Americans from voting.

judicial activism A view of Supreme Court decision making that calls for the Court to take an active role in policymaking through its interpretation of the Constitution.

Judicial Conference A committee of district and appellate judges chaired by the chief justice of the Supreme Court that reviews the needs of the federal judiciary and makes recommendations to Congress.

judicial power The authority of courts to interpret and apply the law in particular cases.

judicial restraint A view of Supreme Court decision making that calls for the Court to defer policymaking to the other branches of government.

judicial review The power to review decisions of the lower courts and to determine the constitutionality of laws and actions of public officials.

judiciary A system of courts and judges concerned with administration of justice.

jurisdiction The types of cases a given court is permitted to hear.

justiciable issue An issue or topic over which the courts have jurisdiction or the power to make decisions.

lawmaking A legislature's power to enact laws that address major problems and then to oversee government administration of those laws.

Lawrence v. Texas The 2003 case ruling that the government had no right to regulate or control consensual personal relationships. This case overruled *Bowers v. Hardwick*, which had allowed states to make engaging in homosexual sex a crime.

leak The revealing of information that officials want kept secret.

legal model A view of judicial decision making that argues that judges set aside their own values and make decisions based solely on legal criteria.

legal realist model A model of judicial decision making that argues that personal values and ideologies affect a judge's decisions.

legislative caucus A method of selecting political party candidates that calls for party members in the state legislature to select candidates for statewide office and party members in the House of Representatives to select a party's candidates for president and vice president.

legislative intent The intention of Congress when it passes laws.

legislative interpretation A ruling of the Supreme Court in which the Court interprets on the meaning and intent of a statute passed by Congress. Congress can overturn a decision based on legislative interpretation by passing another law.

legislative oversight of administration A variety of tools Congress uses to control administrative agencies, including creating or abolishing agencies, assigning program responsibilities, providing funds, and confirming presidential appointments.

legislative veto A measure that gives Congress the ability to reject an action or decision of the bureaucracy.

legislature A deliberative council that has the authority to make and repeal laws. In representative democracies, ordinary citizens elect legislators to represent them.

libel To make false or defaming statements about someone in print or the media.

liberal democracy A representative democracy, such as the United Kingdom or the United States, that has a particular concern for individual liberty. The rule of law and a constitution constrain elected representatives and the will of the majority from using their power to take away the rights of minorities.

literacy tests Reading or comprehension tests that citizens are required to pass to demonstrate their fitness to vote.

living Constitution The theory that assumes the Constitution was meant to be a dynamic document whose meaning has to account for contemporary social and political context.

lobbying Activity of a group or person that attempts to influence public policymaking on behalf of the individual or the group.

lobbyists Individuals whose job it is to contact and attempt to influence governmental officials on behalf of others.

logrolling The exchange of support on issues between groups that do not have common interests in order to gain mutual advantage.

Madisonian dilemma The problem of limiting self-interested individuals who administer stronger governmental powers from using those powers to destroy the freedoms that government is supposed to protect.

magic number The number of delegates needed at a political party's national convention for a candidate to be nominated as the party's candidate for the presidency; this number equals 50 percent plus one of all delegates at the convention.

maintaining election An election in which the traditional majority party maintains power based on the long-standing partisan orientation of the voters.

majority leader The person, chosen by the members of the majority party in the House and Senate, who controls the legislative agenda. In the Senate, the majority leader is the most powerful person in the chamber.

majority–minority districts Districts in which the majority of the population is composed of ethnic or racial minorities.

majority opinion A decision of the Supreme Court in which five or more of the justices are in agreement on the ruling on which party to the dispute should win a case and the reason that party should win.

majority rule The principle under which government follows the course of action preferred by most people.

malapportioned A situation in which the distribution of legislative seats does not accurately reflect the distribution of the population.

Mapp v. Ohio The 1961 case that extended the exclusionary rule to state trials.

Marbury v. Madison The 1803 case in which the Court asserted the power of judicial review.

margin of error The amount that sample responses are likely to differ from those of the population within very tight boundaries that are known as the confidence level.

mass media All the means used to transmit information to masses of people.

material benefits Tangible rewards gained from membership in an interest group.

McCulloch v. Maryland An 1819 court case involving a dispute over whether the central government had the power to create a national bank.

McDonald v. Chicago A 2010 case in which the Supreme Court ruled that the Second Amendment right of an individual to "keep and bear arms" applies to the states as well as the federal government.

media bias The tendency to present an unbalanced perspective so that information is conveyed in a way that consistently favors one set of interests over another.

members' representational allowance (MRA) An allowance of about $1 million per year that members of Congress receive to pay for official duties of representation and lawmaking (e.g., office functions, official travel, and staff). It cannot be used for personal or campaign expenses.

merit system A system of governing in which jobs are given based on relevant technical expertise and the ability to perform.

#MeToo Movement A movement using social media to destigmatize survivors of sexual violence, and highlight the prevalence of sexual harassment and assault in society.

midterm elections The congressional and gubernatorial elections that occur in the middle of a presidential term.

minority leader The leader of the minority party in the House or Senate. Works with the majority leader to schedule legislation and leads the opposition party.

minority rights The full rights of democratic citizenship held by any group numerically inferior to the majority. These fundamental democratic rights cannot be taken away—even if a majority wishes to do so—without breaking the promise of democracy.

Miranda v. Arizona The 1966 case that established a criminal suspect's right against self-incrimination and right to counsel during police interrogation.

misinformation The belief that incorrect information is true.

mixed government The idea that government should represent both property and the number of people.

mobilization Efforts aimed at influencing people to vote in an election.

moral hazard A principal's lack of information about the effort of an agent.

multimember district A method of selecting representatives in which more than one person is chosen to represent a single constituency.

multiparty system A political system in which three or more political parties effectively compete for political office, and no one party can win control of all.

national party convention A nomination method in which delegates selected from each state attend a national party meeting to choose the party's candidates for president and vice president.

National Security Council A group of presidential advisors made up of the vice president, the attorney general, and cabinet officers chosen by the president to advise the president on national security issues; it is part of the Executive Office of the President.

national security directive A type of executive order with the force of law authorizing federal agencies or officials to take some action to protect national security.

neutral competence The idea that agencies should make decisions based on expertise rather than political considerations.

new federalism A movement to take power away from the federal government and return it to the states.

New Jersey plan A proposal presented at the Constitutional Convention that called for a one-house legislature with equal representation for each state.

news Accounts of timely and specific events.

news media Organizations and journalists that cover the news.

nomination The process through which political parties winnow down a field of candidates to a single one who will be the party's standard-bearer in the general election.

nongermane amendments Amendments to a piece of legislation that are not related to the subject of the bill to which they are added.

normative Theories or statements that seek to prescribe how things should be valued, what should be, what is good or just, and what is better or worse.

null hypothesis A statement positing that there is no relationship between the variables being observed. It is the opposite of the research hypothesis.

nullification The act of declaring a national law null and void within a state's borders.

Obergefell v. Hodges A 2015 Supreme Court ruling that marriage is a fundamental right protected by the Constitution that must be extended to same-sex couples.

objective journalism An approach to journalism that places emphasis on reporting facts rather than on analysis or a partisan point of view.

Office of Management and Budget (OMB) An agency of the Executive Office of the President that is responsible for assisting the president in creating the budget.

oligarchy A form of government in which the power to make authoritative decisions and allocate resources is vested in a small group of people.

one-party system A political system in which representatives of one political party hold all or almost all of the major offices in government.

one person, one vote The idea, arising out of the 1964 Supreme Court decision of *Wesberry v. Sanders*, that legislative districts must contain about the same number of people.

open primaries Elections to select a party's candidate for the general election that are open to independents and, in some cases, to members of other parties.

open rule A rule formulated by the House Rules Committee that permits any germane amendment to be considered on the floor.

open seats Legislative seats for which there is no incumbent running for reelection.

originalism The idea that Supreme Court justices should interpret the Constitution in terms of the original intentions of the Framers.

overhead democracy The idea that the bureaucracy is controlled through the oversight of elected officials, who are chosen by the people, thus giving the populace control over the bureaucracy.

parliamentary system An electoral system in which the party holding the majority of seats in the legislature selects the chief executive.

partisanship A psychological attachment to a political party.

party discipline Requiring political party members in public office to promote or carry out the party's agenda and punishing those who do not.

party in the electorate The component of a political party that is made up of the people in the public who identify with a political party.

party in government The component of a political party that is made up of elected and appointed government officeholders who are associated with a political party.

party organization The component of a political party that is composed of the party professionals who hold official positions in the party.

party polarization A distribution of preferences in which party means diverge toward opposite poles with little or no overlap in the center.

party professionals Party activists whose incentives for participating in party activities are primarily material and social in nature.

party ratio The proportion of the seats that each political party controls in the House and the Senate.

party vote A vote in which a majority of Democrats vote on one side and a majority of Republicans vote on the other.

passive resistance A nonviolent technique of protest that entails resisting government laws or practices that are believed to be unjust.

perquisites (perks) The benefits and support activities that members of Congress receive in order to help them perform their job.

personal constituency A small number of intimate friends, advisors, and confidants who support a member of Congress.

Plessy v. Ferguson An 1896 Supreme Court decision ruling that separate public facilities for people of different races satisfied the Fourteenth Amendment's equal protection clause, provided the facilities were "equal."

pluralist explanation (of interest groups) The idea that interest groups form in reaction to problems created by particular social or economic events.

pluralistic A term used to describe a society in which power is widely distributed among diverse groups and interests.

plurality The largest percentage of a vote, when no one has a majority.

plurality opinion A decision of the Supreme Court in which a majority of the Court agrees on a decision, but there is no majority agreement on the reason for the decision.

pocket veto A maneuver in which the president allows a bill to die by taking no action within 10 days if Congress has adjourned.

police patrol oversight The active oversight of the bureaucracy by elected officials to make sure that the bureaucracy is acting according to the wishes of the people.

police power The authority of the states to pass laws for the health, safety, and morals of their citizens.

policy evaluation The process of examining the consequences of public policy.

policy formulation and adoption The stage in the policy-making process in which government considers various alternatives to the issue or problem at hand and formally approves one of those alternatives.

policy implementation The process of translating government intent into government action.

policy-motivated activists Party activists whose incentives for participating in party activities are primarily purposive and social. They are dedicated to implementing certain principles in public policies, and they are less willing to compromise those principles than are party professionals.

policy responsiveness The amount of agreement between the people represented and their elected officials on policy issues.

policy subsystems Networks of groups with an interest in a specific policy issue or area.

political action committees (PACs) Organizations specifically created to raise money and make political contributions on behalf of an interest group.

political alienation The feeling of being isolated from or not part of the political process and system.

political bias The tendency to favor a political party or ideological point of view.

political culture A set of shared beliefs that includes broad agreement about basic political values, agreement about the legitimacy of political institutions, and general acceptance of the process government uses to make policy.

political efficacy The belief that one's opinions are important and that government will respect and respond to one's views.

political equality The idea that individual preferences should be given equal weight.

political machine A political organization characterized by a reciprocal relationship between voters and officeholders. Political support is given in exchange for government jobs and services. Headed by a "party boss," political machines and party bosses maintain their power and control over government offices with techniques such as control over nominations, patronage, graft and bribery, vote buying, and election-rigging.

political participation The translation of personal preference into a voluntary action designed to influence public policy.

political party An organization that nominates and runs candidates for office under its own label.

political patronage The giving of government jobs to people based on their party affiliation and loyalty.

political science The systematic study of government, political institutions, processes, and behavior.

political socialization The process through which a younger generation learns political values from previous generations.

politico A representative whose philosophy of representation is a mix of both delegate and trustee. *See also* delegate and trustee.

politics The process of making binding decisions about who gets what or whose values everyone is going to live by.

poll taxes A technique used to keep certain groups from voting by charging a fee to vote.

popular sovereignty The idea that the highest political authority in a democracy is the will of the people.

pork-barrel benefits Government-sponsored projects that bring economic benefits to a Congress member's state or district. This is a pejorative term first used in the mid-nineteenth century to describe projects viewed as a waste of tax dollars that serve no purpose other than to aid the reelection of a single incumbent.

position taking Public statements made by members of Congress on issues of importance to the constituency.

positive government The idea that government should play a major role in preventing or dealing with the crises that face the nation.

preemption Congress expressly giving national laws precedence over state and local laws.

preferred freedoms doctrine The idea that the rights provided in the First Amendment are fundamental and as such the courts have a greater obligation to protect those rights than others.

prerogative view of presidential power A view of presidential power, promoted by Abraham Lincoln, that argues that the president is required to preserve the Constitution and take actions to do so that otherwise might be unconstitutional.

president of the Senate The person who presides over the Senate and is responsible for many of the parliamentary duties such as recognizing speakers. The vice president of the United States holds this position.

president pro tempore The person chosen by the members to preside over the Senate in the absence of the vice president.

presidential system A political system in which the chief executive and the legislature are elected independently.

press The print and electronic media that are partially or wholly devoted to collecting and reporting news in the United States.

prestige committees Congressional committees that are highly prized and allow their members to wield tremendous power in Congress.

primary constituency A member of Congress's strongest, mostly partisan supporters.

principal–agent model A model explaining the relationship between Congress and the bureaucracy, which states that the relationship is similar to that between an employer who seeks to have work done (the principal) and an employee who does the work (the agent).

print media Media consisting of newspapers, magazines, and books.

prior restraint The prohibition or censoring of a news story prior to publication or broadcast.

process evaluations Evaluations undertaken with the goal of assessing whether a program or policy is being implemented according to its stated guidelines.

propaganda model The idea that mainstream media are biased toward corporate and conservative interests because most mainstream media are corporately owned.

proportional plan A plan to revise the electoral college such that the number of electoral college votes given to candidates would be based on the proportion of the popular vote they obtained.

proportional representation A method of selecting representatives in which representation is given to political parties based on the proportion of the vote obtained. This method has the effect of encouraging multiple parties.

prospective voting Voting that is based on an individual's estimation of how well a candidate will perform duties in the future.

public agenda All issues and problems that have the attention of the government at a particular point in time.

public good A benefit that is provided to everyone and cannot be withheld from those who did not participate in its provision.

public opinion The sum of individual attitudes or beliefs about an issue or question.

public policy A relatively stable, purposive course of action pursued by government officials or agencies.

public sphere A forum where information on matters important to civic life can be freely accessed and exchanged.

purposive benefits Benefits that interest group members derive from feeling good about contributing to a worthy cause in an effort to improve the lot of society in general, not just the individual concerns of the group's members.

push poll A type of public opinion poll that intentionally uses leading or biased questions in order to manipulate the responses.

random sample A method of selecting a sample (subset of the population) in which every person in the target population has an equal chance of being selected.

rational Making choices that maximize benefits and minimize costs.

rational choice model A model of voter choice that suggests that an individual will vote if the benefits of doing so outweigh the costs and will cast his or her ballot for candidates who are closest to sharing the individual's views on the issues.

rational-comprehensive decision making A decision-making approach characterized by consideration of all alternatives to a problem or issue, an analysis of the costs and benefits of each alternative, and selection of the alternative with the most benefits at the least cost.

realigning election An election in which the minority party is able to build a relatively stable coalition to win election, and this coalition endures over a series of elections.

reapportionment The process of adjusting the number of House seats among the states based on population shifts.

redistricting The process of redrawing congressional district lines after reapportionment.

reelection constituency The people within a Congress member's House district who can be counted on for support.

reference groups Groups that influence the political attitudes of non-group members.

referendum An election in which a state legislature refers a proposed law to the voters for their approval.

regulatory agencies and commissions Agencies that are independent of cabinet departments and are created by Congress to monitor and regulate specific areas of economic activity.

reinstating election An election in which the majority party regains power after a deviating election.

representation The relationship between elected officials and the people who put them in office, involving the extent to which officials are responsive to the people.

representative democracy Defined as a system of government where ordinary citizens do not make governmental decisions themselves but choose public officials—representatives of the people—to make decisions for them.

republican form of government A form of government in which the government operates with the consent of the governed through some type of representative institution.

research question a statement of information or knowledge being sought. A research question assumes there is no known universally correct answer and that alternative answers need to be given fair consideration.

responsible party model A concept that describes democracies with competitive parties in which one party wins control of the government based on its policy proposals, enacts those proposals once it is in control, and stands or falls in the next election based on its performance in delivering on its promises.

restrictive view of presidential power A view of presidential power that argues that the president can exercise only those powers listed in the Constitution.

retrospective voting Voting that is based on an individual's evaluation of the past performance of a candidate.

riders A nongermane amendment that is added to a popular bill in hopes that the desirability of the proposed legislation will help the amendment pass.

right to privacy An individual's right to be free of government interference without due cause or due process.

Roe v. Wade The 1973 case in which the Court reaffirmed the right of privacy enumerated in Griswold, balancing the mother's right to privacy against the state's interest in protecting an unborn fetus.

role theory A behavioral model of politics based on the assumption that human beings have a psychological need for predictability in their relations with each other.

rule A statement of the bureaucracy that interprets the law or prescribes a specific action. These rules have the force of law.

rule of four Rule according to which four Supreme Court justices must agree to hear a case.

rulemaking The process in which the bureaucracy decides what the laws passed by Congress mean and how they should be carried out.

runoff primary A second primary election held between the top two candidates if no candidate received a majority of the votes in the first primary.

salience The prominence or visibility of an issue or question and how important the issue is to the public.

satisficing Considering possible alternatives until finding one that is good enough to solve the problem at hand even though it might not be the "best" possible solution.

Schenck v. United States The 1919 case that articulated the "clear and present danger" test.

science A method of acquiring knowledge through the formulation of hypotheses that can be tested through empirical observation in order to make claims about how the world works and why.

selective benefits Benefits provided by interest groups that are available to members only.

senatorial courtesy The practice that allows senators from states with federal district court vacancies to recommend individuals for the president to nominate. If the president fails to follow the home state senators' recommendations, a slighted senator may block the nomination from coming to the floor for a confirmation vote.

separate but equal A practice in southern states to comply with the Fourteenth Amendment's "equal protection" clause by passing laws requiring separate but equal accommodations for blacks and whites in public facilities. The Supreme Court ruled such laws unconstitutional in 1954.

separation of church and state The idea that neither national nor state governments may pass laws that support one religion or all religions or give preference to one religion over others.

separation of powers The idea that each branch of government is authorized to carry out a separate part of the political process.

service responsiveness Representation that takes the form of the tasks legislators perform based on the requests and needs of their constituents.

Shays' Rebellion An armed revolt by farmers in western Massachusetts who were resisting state efforts to seize their property for failure to pay taxes and debts.

signing statements Pronouncements of how the president intends to interpret and apply a law when he or she signs a bill into law.

simple majority Fifty percent plus one of those participating or of those who vote.

single-issue groups Groups that take extreme, uncompromising positions on only one specific issue (e.g., abortion, guns, LGBTQ rights, the environment).

single-member district A method of selecting representatives in which the voters in a district select a single representative.

single-member district plurality (SMDP) system A method of selecting representatives in which a nation or state is divided into separate election districts and voters in each district choose one representative. The candidate in each district with a plurality of the vote wins the seat. This method tends to hinder the development of third parties.

slander To make false or defamatory oral statements about someone.

slot machine theory The view of judicial review that all judges do is lay the constitutional provision involved beside the statute being challenged and "decide whether the latter squares with the former."

social equality The idea that people should be free of class or social barriers and discrimination.

social media Websites and computer applications that allow users to share content and participate in virtual social networks.

social-psychological model (Michigan model) A model explaining vote choice that focuses on individual attitudes.

socioeconomic status (SES) The social background and economic position of a person.

sociological model (Columbia model) A model explaining voter choice by considering factors such as religion, place of residence, and socioeconomic status.

soft money Campaign contributions given to political parties rather than directly to candidates.

soft news Stories characterized by opinion, human interest, and often entertainment value.

solidary benefits Satisfaction gained from membership in interest groups such as friendship and a sense of belonging to a group or meeting people with similar interests.

sovereignty The legitimate authority in a government to wield coercive power to authoritatively allocate values.

Speaker of the House of Representatives The person who presides over the House. The Speaker is responsible for many of the parliamentary duties, such as recognizing speakers, and is the most powerful person in the chamber.

special rule A rule formulated by the House Rules Committee specifying the conditions under which a given bill will be considered on the House floor.

spoils system A system of governing in which political positions and benefits are given to the friends of the winner.

spokes-of-the-wheel model A method of organizing the presidency that calls for the president to be the center of activity, with numerous advisors reporting directly to the president.

stability The likelihood of changes in the direction of public opinion.

standards of due process The procedural guarantees provided to ensure fair treatment and constitutional rights.

standing committees Permanent committees in Congress that are responsible for legislation in a specific policy area.

state presidential primary A method of selecting delegates to a political party's national convention in which the voters directly elect delegates.

stewardship doctrine A view of presidential power that states that the president is a steward of the people and should do anything the nation needs that is not prohibited by the Constitution.

straight-ticket voters People who vote for the same party's candidates across different offices.

strategic framing Giving prominence in media stories to who is gaining or losing on an issue.

strategic model The view that sincere voting does not always maximize utility.

straw polls Unscientific polls based on nonrandom samples.

strong-executive model A model of the presidency in which the powers of the executive office are significant and independent from Congress.

structured rule A rule that permits only certain amendments to a bill.

substantive representation The concept of representation that states that officeholders do not have to be minorities to accurately represent minority interests.

suffrage The right to vote.

sunshine laws Laws intended to keep the bureaucracy accountable to the people by requiring that agency meetings be open to the public.

Super PAC A type of political committee that can raise unlimited sums of money from corporations, unions, associations, and wealthy individuals to independently support or oppose political candidates. Unlike traditional PACs, Super PACs may not contribute directly to or coordinate with political candidates' campaigns.

Super Tuesday The day in early March when several states hold their primaries. These states choose a significant portion of delegates to the national convention.

"supreme law of the land" The idea that the U.S. Constitution, laws passed by Congress, and the treaties made by the federal government are supreme, and state constitutions and laws are subordinate to them.

swing states States in which the outcome of a presidential race is unclear, and both candidates have a realistic chance of winning.

symbolic responsiveness A congressional member's efforts to use political symbols to generate trust and support among the voters.

test case A lawsuit filed to test the constitutionality of some government policy.

Texas v. Johnson The 1989 case in which the Supreme Court ruled that burning the American flag was a form of expression that had constitutional protection.

theory A potential explanation of how the world works.

third parties Minor political parties that periodically appear but have little success in winning office.

top-two primary A type of election in which candidates from all political parties run in the same primary. The top two vote-getters, which may be from the same party, compete in a run-off in the general election.

trustee A representative who uses his or her own judgment to make decisions promoting the best interests of the nation as a whole, with the particular interests of constituents remaining a secondary concern.

trustee system of democracy The idea that the job of elected leaders is to make decisions based on their own expertise and judgment, and not just make decisions based on the wishes and preferences of constituents.

two-party system A political system in which only two political parties have a realistic chance of controlling the major offices of government.

unanimous consent agreement (UCA) An agreement between majority and minority party leaders on the procedures and conditions under which a bill will be considered in the Senate.

unfunded mandates Federal mandates for which the federal government does not pay any associated costs.

unicameral A legislature with one chamber.

unilateral powers Presidential directives that carry the weight of law even though they have not been formally endorsed by Congress.

unit rule A rule that permitted a majority of a state's delegation to a political party's national convention to require that the entire state delegation vote the same way (or as a unit).

unitary system A political system in which the power is concentrated in the national government, and the regional governments can exercise only those powers granted them by the central government.

utility The amount of enjoyment an individual receives from a given situation or outcome.

Virginia plan The first major proposal presented at the 1787 Constitutional Convention that formed the basis of the Constitution. It called for a bicameral legislature with a popularly elected lower house and an upper house nominated by state legislatures.

voter turnout The percentage of eligible voters who cast votes in an election.

Voting Rights Act of 1965 Act authorizing the federal government to ensure that eligible voters were not denied access to the ballot, actively protecting the Fifteenth Amendment's promise of voting rights for African Americans.

weak-executive model A model of the presidency in which the executive would have a limited term, would have no veto power, and would be allowed to exercise only the authority explicitly granted by Congress.

Weeks v. United States The 1914 case that said that evidence obtained through an unreasonable search and seizure cannot be used in federal trials.

Wesberry v. Sanders The 1964 case in which the Supreme Court invalidated unequal congressional districts, saying that all legislative districts must contain about equal numbers of people, establishing the principle of one person, one vote.

whips Assistants to the majority and minority party leaders in Congress who encourage rank-and-file members to support the party's positions. Whips make sure that rank-and-file members are present to vote on key legislative measures and that they know the party leader's desire.

White House Office A section of the Executive Office of the President that houses many of the most influential advisors to the president, including the chief of staff; the White House legal counsel; presidential speechwriters; the president's press secretary; assistants for domestic, foreign, and economic policy; and liaisons with Congress, the public, and state and local governments.

writ of certiorari An order from a higher court to a lower court ordering the lower court to turn over transcripts and documents of a case for review. The U.S. Supreme Court formally exercises its discretionary powers over what cases to hear by issuing a writ of certiorari, which is granted according to the rule of four.

writ of mandamus A court order requiring a public official to perform an official duty over which he or she has no discretion.

CASES INDEX

Note: page numbers in **bold type** refer to Tables.

Abington Township v. Schempp, 374 U.S. 203 (1963) 124
Alberts v. California, 354 U.S. 476 (1957) 131
Alden v. Maine, 527 U.S. 706 (1999) 105
Angersinger v. Hamlin, 407 U.S. 25 (1972) 139
Arizona Christian School Tuition Org v. Winn, 131 S. Ct. 1436, 563 U.S. __ (2011) 126, 127
Arizona v. United States, 567 U.S. __ (2012) 164
Ashcroft v. Free Speech Coalition, 535 U.S. 234 (2002) 133
Associated Press v. Walker, 388 U.S. 130 (1967) 134

Baker v. Carr, 369 U.S. 186 (1962) 369, 604
Barron v. Baltimore, 32 U.S. 243 (1883) 119
Benton v. Maryland, 395 U.S. 784 (1969) **121**
Berghuis v. Thomkins, 560 U.S. 370 (2010) 140
Board of Education Kiryas Joel Village v. Grumet, 512 U.S. 687 (1994) 124
Board of Trustees v. Garrett, 531 U.S. 356 (2001) 178
Bowers v. Hardwick, 478 U.S. 186 (1986) 136
Brandenburg v. Ohio, 395 U.S. 444 (1969) 130
Brown v. Board of Education, 347 U.S. 483 (1954) 136, 153, 209, 603
Buck v. Bell, 274 U.S. 200 (1927) 151
Buckley v. Valeo, 434 U.S. 1 (1976) 216, 362

Cantwell v. Connecticut, 310 U.S. 296 (1940) **121**, 123, 126
Chicago, Burlington & Quincy RR v. Chicago, 166 U.S. 266 (1897) **121**
Chisholm v. Georgia, 2 U.S. (2 Dall.) 419 (1793) 59, 593n12, 601
Citizens United v. Federal Election Commission, 558 U.S. 50 (2010) 130–131, 217, 363, 595–596
City of Boerne v. Flores, 521 U.S. 507 (1997) 595
Coleman v. Miller, 307 U.S. 433 (1939) 70

Colgrove v. Green, 328 U.S. 433 (1946) 369
Cox Broadcasting v. Cohn, 420 U.S. 469 (1975) 135
Coyle v. Smith, 211 U.S. 559 (1911) 92
Crawford v. Marion County Election Board, 553 U.S. 181 (2008) 398
Curtis Publishing Company v. Butts, 388 U.S. 130 (1967) 134

De Jonge v. Oregon, 299 U.S. 253 (1937) **121**
Dennis v. United States, 341 U.S. 494 (1951) 129
District of Columbia v. Heller, 554 U.S. 570 (2008) 120–122
Doe v. Bolton, 410 U.S. 179 (1973) 134–135
Dred Scott v. Sanford, 60 U.S. 393 (1857) 597, 598, 600
Duncan v. Louisiana, 391 U.S. 145 (1968) **121**

Eisenstadt v. Baird, 405 U.S. 438 (1972) 134
Engel v. Vitale, 370 U.S. 421 (1962) 124
Everson v. Board of Education, 330 U.S. 1 (1947) **121**, 123–124, 125
Federal Election Commission v. Wisconsin Right to Life, 551 U.S. 449 (2007) 217
Fiske v. Kansas, 274 U.S. 380 (1927) **121**
Furman v. Georgia, 408 U.S. 238 (1972) 140

Gibbons v. Ogden, 22 U.S. 1 (1824) 88
Gideon v. Wainwright, 372 U.S. 335 (1963) **121**, 139
Gitlow v. New York, 268 U.S. 652 (1925) 120, **121**
Good News Club v. Milford Central School District, 533 U.S. 98 (2001) 127
Gregg v. Georgia, 428 U.S. 153 (1976) 140, 141, 142
Griswold v. Connecticut, 381 U.S. 479 (1965) **121**, 134
Guinn v. United States, 238 U.S. 347 (1915) 152–153

Hamilton v. Regents of the U. of California, 293 U.S. 245 (1934) **121**
Heart of Atlanta Motel v. United States, 379 U.S. 241 (1964) 88

Illinois v. Gates, 462 U.S. 213 (1984) 138
Immigration and Naturalization Service v. Chadha, 462 U.S. 919 (1983) 548
In re Oliver, 33 U.S. 257 (1948) **121**

Jacobellis v. Ohio, 378 U.S. 184 (1964) 131
Johnson v. Zerbst, 304 U.S. 458 (1938) 139

Katzenbach v. McClung, 379 U.S. 294 (1964) 88
Klopfer v. North Carolina, 386 U.S. 213 (1967) **121**

Lamb's Chapel v. Center Moriches School District, 508 U.S. 385 (1993) 127
Lawrence v. Texas, 539 U.S. 577 (2003) 136, 178
Ledbetter v. Goodyear Tire and Rubber Co, 550 U.S. 618. (2007) 173
Lee v. Weisman, 505 U.S. 577 (1992) 124
Lewis v. United States, 455 U.S. 55 (1980) 120
Locke v. Davey, 540 U.S. 712 (2004) 127

Malloy v. Hogan, 378 U.S. 1 (1964) **121**
Mapp v. Ohio, 367 U.S. 643 (1961) **121**, 138
Marbury v. Madison, 5 U.S. 137 (1803) 74, 561, 592–594, **594**, 597, 603
Martin v. Hunter's Lessee, 14 U.S. 304 (1816) 593n11
McConnell v. Federal Election Commission, 540 U.S. 93 (2003) 130
McCulloch v. Maryland, 17 U.S. 316 (1819) 59, 88
McDonald v. Chicago, 561 U.S. (2010) 120, **121**, 122
Michigan v. Mosley, 423 U.S. 96 (1975) 139
Miller v. California, 413 U.S. 15 (1973) 132, 133
Mills v. Board of Education of the District of Columbia, 348 F. Supp. 866 (1972) 176–177
Minersville School District v. Gobitis, 310 U.S. 586 (1940) 126, 595
Minor v. Happersett, 88 U.S. 162 (1875) 601
Miranda v. Arizona, 384 U.S. 436 (1966) 139, 140

Missouri ex rel. Gaines v. Canada, 305 U.S. 337 (1938) 153

Murphy v. Waterfront Commission, 378 U.S. 52 (1964) **121**

National Federation of Independent Business v. Sebelius, 567 U.S. __ (2012) 567, 568, 599

Near v. Minnesota, 283 U.S. 697 (1931) **121**

New York Times v. Sullivan, 376 U.S. 254 (1964) 133–134

New York Times v. United States, 403 U.S. 713 (1971) 274

New York v. Quarles, 467 U.S. 144 (1984) 139

Nix v. Williams, 467 U.S. 431 (1984) 138

Obergefell v. Hodges, 576 U.S. __ (2015) 179, 295, 599

Oregon v. Mitchell, 400 U.S. 112 (1970) 393, 600

Osborn v. Bank of the United States, 22 U.S. (9 Wheat.) 738 (1824) 559

Parker v. Gladden, 385 U.S. 363 (1967) **121**

Pennsylvania Association for Retarded Children (PARC) v. Pennsylvania, 343 F. Supp. 279 (1971) 176

Phoenix v. Kolodziejski, 399 U.S. 204 (1970) 392

Pierce v. United States, 252 U.S. 239 (1920) 129

Planned Parenthood v. Casey, 505 U.S. 833 (1992) 135

Plessy v. Ferguson, 163 U.S. 537 (1896) 153

Pointer v. Texas, 380 U.S. 400 (1965) **121**

Pollock v. Farmers' Loan and Trust, 157 U.S. 429 (1895) 600

Pollock v. Williams, 322 U.S. 4 (1944) 149

Powell v. Alabama, 287 U.S. 45 (1932) **121**

Powell v. McCormack, 395 U.S. 489 (1969) 434

Printz v. United States, 538 U.S. 1036 (1997) 105

Regents of the University of California v. Bakke, 438 U.S. 265 (1978) 157

Reno v. ACLU, 521 U.S. 844 (1997) 132, 275

Reynolds v. Sims, 377 U.S. 844 (1964) 369

Reynolds v. United States, 98 U.S. 145 (1879) 126

Ricci v. DeStefano, 557 U.S. 557 (2009) 158

Robinson v. California, 370 U.S. 660 (1962) **121**

Roe v. Wade, 410 U.S. 113 (1973) 134–135, 195, 208, 615

Roth v. United States, 354 U.S. 476 (1957) 131, 132

Santa Fe Independent School District v. Doe, 530 U.S. 290 (2000) 124

Schenck v. United States, 249 U.S. 47 (1919) 129

Schuette v. Coalition to Defend Affirmative Action, 572 U.S. __ (2014) 148, 158

Scott v. Illinois, 440 U.S. 367 (1979) 139

Shaw v. Reno, 509 U.S. 630 (1993) 370

Shelby v. Holder, 570 U.S. __ (2013) 156

Smith v. Allwright, 321 U.S. 649 (1944) 224

Snyder v. Phelps, 562 U.S. __ (2011) 129–130

Standing Bear v. Crook (1879) 165–166

Stone v. Graham, 449 U.S. 39 (1980) 124

Texas v. Johnson, 491 U.S. 397 (1989) 129

U.S. v. Miller, 307 U.S. 174 (1939) 120

United States v. American Library Association, 539 U.S. 194 (2004) 132

United States v. Butler, 297 U.S. 1 (1936) 584, 603

United States v. Jones, 565 U.S. __ (2012) 135

United States v. Leon, 468 U.S. 897 (1984) 138

United States v. Lopez, 514 U.S. 549 (1995) 90

United States v. Miller, 425 U.S. 435 (1976) 135

United States v. Morrison, 529 U.S. 1062 (2000) 89

United States v. Windsor, 570 U.S. __ (2013) 179

United Steelworkers of America v. Weber, 443 U.S. 193 (1979) 157

Virginia v. Black, 538 U.S. 343 (2003) 130

Wallace v. Jaffree, 472 U.S. 38 (1985) 124

Washington v. Glucksberg, 521 U.S. 702 (1997) 135

Washington v. Texas, 388 U.S. 14 (1967) **121**

Webster v. Reproductive Health Services, 492 U.S. 490 (1989) 135

Weeks v. United States, 232 U.S. 383 (1914) 138

Wesberry v. Sanders, 376 U.S. 1 (1964) 369

West Virginia State Board of Education v. Barnette, 319 U.S. 624 (1943) 126, 595

White v. Register, 412 U.S. 755 (1973) 163

Wickard v. Filburn, 317 U.S. 111 (1964) 88

Wolf v. Colorado, 338 U.S. 25 (1949) **121**

Youngstown Sheet & Tube Co. v. Sawyer, 343 U.S. 579 (1952) 516

Zelman v. Simmons-Harris, 536 U.S. 539 (2002) 125–126, 127

NAME INDEX

Note: page numbers in *italic type* refer to Figures and photographs

Abbott, Gregg 78, 79
Adams, John 43n1, 46, 278, 505, 592
Agnew, Spiro 435, 482
Albright, Madeleine 173
Aldrich, John 228, 250, 431
Alito, Samuel 575, 576, 589, 591
Allen, Mike 282
Anspach, Nicholas 264–265
Anthony, Susan B. 168, 169
Aristotle 25
Arrow, Kenneth 613
Arthur, John 179

Bachman, Michelle 338, 343
Barber, Benjamin 17
Barber, James David 477
Barrett, Andrew 506
Bates, Edward *483*
Baum, Matthew 286
Baumgartner, Frank 197, 198, 215
Beard, Charles A. 48
Beckmann, Matthew 514–515
Best, Judith 360
Beutler, Jaime Herrera 205
Beyoncé *279*
Bibby, John 237
Bickel, Alexander 603
Biden, Joe 348, 446, 482–483
Blackman, Harry 135, 574
Blitzer, Wolf *334*
Blount, William 435
Boehner, John 516
Bond, Jon R. 377
Booker, Cory 156
Borah, William E. 577
Bork, Robert 581
Bowser, Muriel *95*
Boxer, Barbara 433n1
Brady, David 250
Brady, Henry E. 404–405
Brandeis, Louis D. 86, 574–575, 577
Brandenberg, Clarence 130
Brennan, William 575
Breyer, Stephen 557, 575, 589, 591, 599
Brown, Jerry 571

Brown, Michael 161
Bryan, William Jennings 240
Buchanan, James 474, 485n5
Buchanan, Pat 496
Budak, Ceren 281–282
Burke, Edmund 430
Burke, Tarana 175
Burr, Aaron 72, 433
Busch, Andrew 331
Bush, George H. W. 105, 202, 469–470, 482, 489, 491, 492, 494, 496, 500, 502, *502*, 504, 506, 507, 513, 518, 575, 580, 581
Bush, George W. 3, 73–74, 98, 106, 240, 281, 314, 315–316, 333, 353, 358, 418, 462, 469, 470, 471, *473*, 474, 475, 482, 484, 485, 488, 491, 492, 496, 497–498, 499, 500, 502, *502*, 504, 515, 518–519, 551, 571, 576, 580, 581, 582, 583
Bush, Jeb *334*, 337–338, 341, 343
Bush, Laura 485–486

Cain, Herbert 338
Caldiera, Gregory 591
Califano, Joseph Jr. 177
Callender, James 278, 288
Campbell, Angus 30, 410, 416–417
Canon, David 365
Cardozo, Benjamin 577
Carson, Ben *334*, 337, 338, 469
Carswell, G. Harrold 171
Carter, Jimmy 177, 358, 418, 482, 485, 488, 489, 493, 518, 571, 581, 601
Carter, Rosalynn 485
Chao, Elaine 484
Charles II, King 53
Chase, Salmon P. *483*
Chase, Samuel 600
Cheney, Dick 74, 446, 482, 483, 488
Christie, Chris *334*, 343
Cleveland, Grover 232
Clinton, Bill 67, 105, 106, 179, 281, 297, 358, 418, 433, 434, *434*, 469, 470, 471, 482, 485, 488, 489, 490, 491, 492, 494, 496, 499, 500, 502, *502*, 504, 506, 507, 508, 518, 551, 571, 573, 576, 580, 581, 582, 584, 599

Clinton, George 49
Clinton, Hillary *168*, 173, 205, 242, *243*, 244–245, 269, *288*, 306, 307, 325, 331n4, 336–337, 340, 341, 343, 346, 348, 349, 362, 414, 416, 484, 485
Cohen, Bernard 271, 272
Cohen, Marty 334, 350
Colberg, Stephen 268–269
Cole, Tom 167
Coleman, John 254
Collins, Susan 205, 510
Colomer, Josep 235
Connally, John 349
Converse, Phil 410
Conway, Kellyanne 259
Coolidge, Calvin 500
Cooper, Joseph 250
Cooper, Phillip J. 516
Cotter, Cornelius P. 255
Covington, Cary 377
Cox, Gary 432
Cronin, Thomas 486
Crossley, Archibald 292
Crotty, William 347, 361
Cruz, Ted *334*, 337, 343, 346, 348
Cueller, Henry 205
Cullors, Patrisse 161

D'Alessio, Dave 282
Darrow, Clarence 152
Darweesh, Hameed Khalid 113, 114, *114*
Davey, Joshua 127
Davis, James 494
Dean, Howard 341, 349
DeFazio, Peter 519
DeVos, Betsy *123*
Dewey, John 152
Douglass, Frederick 168
Downie, Leonard 273
Downs, Anthony 34, 223, 399
Du Bois, W. E. B. 152
Dubke, Michael 469
Dundy, Elmer 166
Durbin, Richard 164
Duverger, Maurice 235

I-703

Easton, David 5
Edmondson, Brad 307–308
Edwards, George 360, 502–503, 506
Eisenhower, Dwight D. 101, 154, 487, 504, 514, 575, 584, 603
Ellsworth, Oliver 53
Epstein, Lee 586
Eulau, Heinz 428
Evans, Diana 215, 428

Faith Spotted Eagle 354
Feingold, Russell 116, 217, 362
Fenno, Richard 423, 428, 431, 454
Ferraro, Geraldine A. 172
Field, Stephen J. 574
Fiorina, Carly *334*
Fiorina, Morris 24, 222, 244, 250, 417
Fitz-Pegado, Lauri 204
Fleischer, Ari 475
Fleisher, Richard 377
Flynn, Michael 469
Ford, Gerald 177, 433, 435, 482, 488, 489, 518
Fortas, Abe 575, 591
Frankfurter, Felix 128, 577, 578, 579, 595
Franklin, Benjamin 43n1, 51, 56
Fremont, John 228
Friedan, Betty 171
Friedman, Brandon 114
Frist, Bill 446, 462, 583

Gallup, George 292, 299
Gandhi, Mahatma 155
Garfield, James 529
Garland, Merrick 583
Garner, John Nance 482
Garza, Alicia 160–161
Gates, Robert 484
Gephardt, Richard 341, 349
Gerrish, Jerry 397
Gerry, Elbridge 50, 368
Gingrich, Newt 253, 336, 338, 341, 344, 346, 435, 448, 453
Ginsburg, Ruth Bader 173, 575, 576, 589, 591, 599
Gintis, Herbert 35
Goel, Sharad 281–282
Goldwater, Barry 479
Gonzalez, Emma 203
Gore, Al 240, 353, 482, 483
Gorsuch, Neil 463, 557–558, 583, 589, 591
Graham, Lindsey 95
Gramm, Phil 573
Gray, Virginia 196, 199
Greeley, Horace 353n9
Greenwald, Anthony 159
Groeling, Tim 281, 286
Groseclose, Tim 280, 281

Habermas, Jürgen 261
Haidt, Jonathan 116
Haley, Nikki 617
Hall, Richard 458
Hall, Sam B. 573
Hamilton, Alexander 49, 57, 88, 89, 99, 222, 228, 352, 433, 472, 509, 592, 603
Hamilton, Lee 474
Hancock, John *44,* 471
Hannegan, Robert 496
Harding, Warren 232, 500
Hargrove, Erwin 477
Harkin, Tom 349
Harris, Fred 443
Harris, Gladys 337
Harris, Kamala 156
Harris, Mark 366
Harrison, William Henry 228, 601
Hart, Gary 349
Hatch, Orrin *428*
Hayes, Rutherford B. 150
Heidbreder, Brianne 395
Henry, Patrick *47,* 49, 50, 57
Herrnson, Paul 381
Heston, Charlton 207
Hibbing, John 438
Hickel, Walter 237
Hitler, Adolf 6
Hobbes, Thomas 25, 43
Holbrook, Thomas 395
Holmes, Oliver Wendell Jr. 128, 129, 577
Hoover, Herbert 500, 577
Huckfeldt, Robert 403
Hughes, Charles Evans 577
Humphrey, Hubert 239
Huntington, Samuel *44*
Hurley, Patricia 250
Hussein, Saddam 492

Ingram, Helen 629

Jackson, Andrew 99, 228, 328, 494, 500
Jackson, John 347, 361
Jackson, Robert 595
Jacobson, Gary 375, 377
Jay-Z 279
Jay, John 57, 352
Jefferson, Thomas 43, *44,* 72, 88, 118, 123, 222, 234n4, 262, 278, 485n5, 494, 505, 592, 593, 594
Jeffords, Jim 418
Johnson, Andrew 74, 433n1, 434, 601
Johnson, Lyndon 101, 155, 156, 157, 232, 446, 482, 489, 500, 571, 575, *575,* 603
Johnson, Richard M. 355n10

Kagan, Elena 173, 575, 576, 589, 591, 599
Kaiser, Robert 273

Kaminer, Wendy 136
Karps, Paul 428
Kasich, John *334,* 343, 346, 354
Katyal, Neil 557
Kavanaugh, Brett 590
Kennedy, Anthony 575, 590, 599
Kennedy, John F. 155, 170–171, 482, 488, 500
Kennedy, Robert 482
Kernell, Samuel 377, 499, 502
Kerry, John 341
Key, V. O. 226, 228
King, Angus 237, 242n8
King, Martin Luther Jr. 154, 155, *155*
Kingdon, John 615, 616
Knight, Jack 586
Krehbiel, Keith 431
Krucki, Christine 337, 338
Krutz, Glen 493–494

La Follette, Robert 239, 240
Lamar, Joseph R. 573
Landon, Alf 303
Lane, Harriet 485n5
LaPierre, Wayne 202
Lasswell, Harold D. 5
Ledbetter, Lilly 173, 486
Lee, Richard Henry 49
Leech, Beth 197, 198
Lijphart, Arend 231
Lincoln, Abraham 231, 292, 474, *483,* 491, 494, 515, 574
Lindblom, Charles 618
Lipinski, Daniel 437
Lippman, Walter 272, 299
Liu, Goodwin 571
Livingston, Bob 204
Livingston, Robert 43n1
Locke, John 25, 43
Loebsack, Dave 437
Lott, Trent 446, 582
Lowery, David 196, 199
Lowi, Theodore 195
Luton, Horace 573–574

Machiavelli, Niccolò 25–26
Madison, Dolley 485n5
Madison, James 25, 49, *50,* 51, 52, 57–58, 60, 61, 64, 71, 86, 87, 89, 119, 123, 189, 210, 222, 223, 228, 234n4, 352, 485n5, 592–594
Maisel, L. Sandy 237
Malcolm, Ellen 196
Manchin, Joe 205
Mansfield, Mike 446
Marbury, William 592–594
Marshall, John 57, 99, 559, 591, 592, 593–594, *594,* 597
Marshall, Louis 41

Marshall, Thurgood 575, *575*
Martin, Luther 50
Martin, Nick 319
Martin, Trayvon 160
Mason, George 123, 352
Matthews, Donald 431
Mayer, William 331
Mayhew, David 367, 431
McCain, John 217, 288, 336, 341, 362, 366
McCombs, Maxwell 271
McConnell, Mitch 366, *446*, 484
McCubbins, Mathew 432
McCulloch, James 88
McDonald, Michael 395
McGuire, Robert 48–49
Meier, Ken 524
Meyers, Seth 269
Miers, Harriet 576, 581
Milano, Alyssa 175, *207*
Mill, John Stuart 25
Miller, Warren 410
Milyo, Jeffrey 281
Minton, Sherman 591
Miranda, Ernesto 139, 140, *140*
Mitchell, George 446
Mondak, Jeffery 438–439
Mondale, Walter 482
Monroe, James 57, 516
Montesquieu, Charles 62
Moran, Jim 443
Morris, Gouverneur 51, 483
Mott, Lucretia 168
Moussaoui, Zacarias 563
Mullin, Markwayne 167
Murdoch, Rupert 276
Murkowski, Lisa 366, 510
Myers, Ozzie 435

Nader, Ralph 240, *240*
Neustadt, Richard 474, 475, 476, 477, 499, 507, 515
Nichols, Tom 3–4
Niskanen, William 542, 543, 544
Niven, David 280
Nixon, Richard *68*, 103, 172, 177, 232, 239, 240, 274, 356n11, 358, 434, 435, 482, 487, 489, 500, 504, 507, 574, 575

O'Connor, Sandra Day 173, 576
O'Rourke, P. J. 439–441
Obama, Barack 78, 106, 108, 109, 164, 205, 273, 306, 314, 316, 333, 336, 340, 341, 348, 349, 358, 363, 372, 415, *428*, 469, 470, 471, 475, 480, 484, 485n5, 489, 490, 491, 492, 496, 497, 498, 502, *502*, 504–505, 513, 515, 516, 518, 551, 557, 571, 575, 576, 580, 581, 583, 599, *614*
Obama, Michelle 486

Obergefell, James 179
Ocasio-Cortez, Alexandria *366*
Ochs, Albert 278
Olson, Mancur 192, 195

Parker, John J. 579
Parks, Rosa 154
Patterson, David T. 433n1
Paul, Alice 170
Paul, Rand *334*
Paul, Ron 343, 346, 354
Peake, Jeffrey 493–494
Pelosi, Nancy 172, 448, *449*
Pence, Mike 348, 446
Perot, Ross 236, 237, 238
Perry, Rick 336, 338, 341, 343
Peterson, Esther 171
Phelps, Fred 129–130
Plato 25
Pompeo, Mike *534*
Popkin, Samuel 395
Porteous, G. Thomas Jr. 600
Powell, Colin 354
Powell, Lewis 574
Pressman, Jeffrey 622
Price, David 437
Pritchett, C. Herman 61, 585
Pruitt-Martin, Mah'ria 147–148
Pruitt, Scott 469, 549
Putin, Vladimir 423

Quesada, Vicente Fox 231

Ragsdale, Lyn 485
Rankin, Jeannette *438*
Rao, Justin 281–282
Reagan, Ronald 104–105, 253, 372, 418, 482, 489, 490, 491, 492, 496, 500, 502, *502*, 510, 515, 516, 518, 551, 573, 576, 580, 581
Rehnquist, William 576
Reid, Harry 583
Reynolds, Sean 337
Rice, Condoleezza 173
Roberts, John 156, 568, 575, 585, 590, 599
Roberts, Owen 584–585, 601, 602n14
Rochelle, Portia *216*
Rockefeller, Nelson 435, 482
Rogers, Michael S. 536
Rogers, Will 66, 210, 375, 482
Rohde, David 250, 431
Romney, Mitt 306, 336, 338, 343, 344, 346, 358, 363, 415–416, 480
Roof, Dylann 617
Roosevelt, Eleanor 485, *486*
Roosevelt, Esther 170
Roosevelt, Franklin D. 74, 101, 154, 232, 238, 303, 409, 475, 482, 484, 485, 488, 491, 493, 494, 496, 498, 601–602

Roosevelt, Theodore 239, 240, 474, 500, 516
Roper, Elmo 292
Rosenthal, Alan 277
Rubio, Marco *334*, 337, 341, 343, 346
Ryan, George 143
Ryan, Paul 448

Salisbury, Robert 195
Samuelson, Robert J. 185
Sanders, Bernie 242n8, *310*, 331n4, 337, 340, 343, 346, 348, 349, 354
Santorum, Rick 336, 338, 343, 344, 346
Scalia, Antonin 583, 589, 591
Scaramucci, Anthony 469
Schafly, Phyllis 172
Schattschneider, E. E. 187, 222
Schlesinger, Arthur Jr. 474
Schneider, Anne 629
Scholzman, Kay Lehman 404–405
Schumer, Charles *446*
Schurz, Carl 165
Scott, Tim 156
Segal, Jeffrey 585, 590
Seward, William H. *483*
Shaw, Donald 271
Shays, Daniel 49
Sheekey-Church, Colleen *191*
Shepsie, Kenneth A. 465
Sherman, Roger 43n1
Silver, Nate 306
Simmons, Barbara Lett 353
Simon, Herbert 543
Sinclair, Barbara 456, 465
Snyder, Albert 130
Snyder, Matthew 130
Sotomayor, Sonia 173, 575–576, *576*, 589, 591, 599
Souter, David 591, 599
Spaeth, Harold 585
Speier, Jackie 175
Sprague, John 403
Stalin, Joseph 6
Stanton, Elizabeth Cady 168, 169
Starr, Kenneth W. 433
Stevens, John Paul 575, 591, 599
Stewart, Charles 425, 455
Stewart, Jon 269
Stewart, Potter 131–132
Stokes, Donald 410
Stone, Harlan Fiske 577, 579, 603
Stone, Lucy 169
Story, Joseph 577
Summers, Larry 470
Sumner, Charles 91
Sunstein, Cass 624
Suskind, Ron 3
Swain, Carol 370
Swanson, David 286

NAME INDEX

Taft, William Howard 92, 239, 474, 573–574
Taney, Roger B. 99, 574, 598
Taylor, Zachary 601
Tester, Jon 609
Thaler, Richard 624
Theis, John 485
Thomas, Clarence 570n6, 575, *575*, 589, 591
Thurmond, J. Strom 239, 240
Tilden, Samuel J. 150
Tindall, Catelin 337
Tocqueville, Alexis de 186, 436, 437
Tribe, Laurence 136
Truman, David 194
Truman, Harry 154, 176, 491, 499, 516, 551, 584, 590, 591
Trump, Donald J. 78, 109, 113–114, *133*, 164, 165, 185, 242, 244–245, 259, 268, *268*, 269, 272, 273, 284, 307, 314, 316, 325, 334, *334*, 337, 338, 340, 341, 343, 346, 347, 348, 349, 350, 353–354, 358, 362, 396, 414, 416, 437n3, 462, 463, 469, 470, 479, 480, 482, 484, 488, 497, 501, *501*, 504, *506*, 510, 516, 518, 549, 550, 551, 557, 583
Trump, Melania 486
Tsongas, Paul 349
Tucker, Eric 259
Tullock, Gordon 542, 544
Tweed, William Magear "Boss" 253–254, 327

Unah, Isaac 141

Van Buren, Martin 355n10
Ventura, Jesse 237, 238
Verba, Sidney 389–390, 404–405
Vinson, Fred 591

Wade, Benjamin F. 433n1
Walker, Scott 338
Wallace, George 239, 240
Wang, Sam 306
Warren, Earl 153, 574, 584, 584n9, 591, 595
Warren, Elizabeth 437n3
Washington, Booker T. 152
Washington, George 47, 49, 50, 51, 56, 57, 73, 88, 119, 122, 222, 223, 228, 229, 278, 353, 473, 483, 491, 492, 494, 499, 505
Wayne, Stephen 351
Weber, Max 526
Weicker, Lowell 237
Weingast, Barry R. 465
Weinstein, Harvey 175
Wildavsky, Aaron 622
Willkie, Wendell 409
Wilson, Darren 161
Wilson, James 51, 61
Wilson, Woodrow 74, 232, 239, 449, 474, 493, 494, 495–496, 499, 500, 505, 506, 529
Wright, Fielding 239, 240
Wright, John 591

Young, Arthur 61

Zaller, John 299
Zimmerman, George 160
Zuckerberg, Mark *276*

SUBJECT INDEX

Note: page numbers in *italic type* refer to Figures and photographs; those in **bold type** refer to Tables.

9/11 terrorist attacks *see* September 11, 2001 terrorist attack

A committees **451**, 454, 455
AARP (American Association of Retired Persons) 189–190, 194, 202, 210
ABC 281
abortion 6, 18, 336, 558; female candidates and 283; interest groups 195, 200, 201, 206, 215, 217, 224, 227; public opinion 294–295, *295*, 296, 297, *297*, 303, 310, 319; Supreme Court and 134–135, 195, 208, 579, 580, 598, 615
absolute majority 8, 332, 353
absolutist approach 128
access issues 176, *176*
accountability 87, 103, 241, 244, 245, 256, 554; and private sector 552–553
accumulation of delegates 344, *344–345*, 346
ACSI (American Customer Satisfaction Index) 530
active presidents 477
ad hoc federalism 106
ADA (Americans with Disabilities) Act 1990 177–178
adjudication 539
Administrative Behavior (Simons) 543
adverse selection 553
advertising: mass media revenue from 263, 276–277; negative 131; political 131, *361*, 376, 408, 415, 431
advisory committees 535
AFDC (Aid to Families with Dependent Children) program 105
affirmation, as substitute for oath 53
affirmative action 148, 156–161, *158*
Afghanistan war 106, 129, 297, 316, 404; federal spending 97–98; public opinion 273–274, *274*, 627
AFL-CIO 217
African Americans: affirmative action *148*, 156–161, *158*; citizenship rights 600; civil liberties 117; civil rights 149, 150–161, *155*, *158*; college education 158, *158*, 160; in Congress 437; and the Democratic Party 234, 252–253; descriptive representation 370–371; earnings and college education comparison with whites 158, *158*, 160; Jim Crow laws 156, 166, 627; judicial appointments 571; media bias 283; police brutality and killings 160–161; political participation 407; population statistics 19; race relations revolution 153–155; racial segregation 152–153; Supreme Court appointments 575, *575*; voting rights 150, 152, 156, 252–253, 392, 393–394; *see also* NAACP (National Association for the Advancement of Colored People); slavery
age: discrimination 150; and political participation 405
agency capture 547
agenda setting: by Congress 426, 427, 615; garbage can models of 615–616, 618; mass media 271–271, 615; public policy 612, 613–617, *614*
aggregating interests 242
Agriculture Committee 454, 455
Aid to Families with Dependent Children (AFDC) program 105
AIG company 537, 547
AIM (American Indian Movement) 167
Alabama 124, 154, 163
Alaska 94, 352, 366, 367n14
Alien and Sedition Acts 1798 275
alienation, political 402
allegiant individuals 402
allocation responsiveness 428
"alternative facts" 3, 259–260
alternatives, simplification of 242–243
amendments to the Constitution: Eighteenth 68, 72, 652; Eighth **121**, 137, 140, 598, 650; Eleventh 71, 593n12, 601, 650; Equal Rights Amendment (ERA) 68n5, 70, 170, 171, 172, 576; Fifteenth 71, 99, 119, 150, 156, 166, 168, 392, 393, 651; Fifth 120, **121**, 134, 137, 139, 598, 649; First 115, 120, **121**, 123, 124, 125, 126, 127–128, 129, 130, 132, 134, 149, 166, 185, 186, 216, 217, 274, 275, 293, 362, 566, 598, 649; formal 66–72, *68*, **69**; Fourteenth 71, 74, 99, 119–120, **121**, 138, 153, 157, 179, 209, 216, 369, 598, 600, 601, 604, 651; Fourth 115, **121**, 134, 135, 137, 138, 598, 649; and judicial review 600–601; Nineteenth 71, 166, 170, 393, 601, 652; Ninth **121**, 134, 650; Second 120–122, **121**, 207, 649; Seventeenth 71, 652; Seventh 120, 650; Sixteenth 72, 96, 600, 652; Sixth **121**, 137, 138, 139, 598, 649; and the Supreme Court 600–601; Tenth 90, 91, 105, 650; text of 649–654; Third 134, 649; Thirteenth 70, 71, 99, 119, 600, 651; Twelfth 71–72, 352, 472, 650–651; Twentieth 71, 72, 473, 652–653; Twenty-Fifth 71, 435, 473, 654; Twenty-First 68, 72, 653; Twenty-Fourth 71, 601, 654; Twenty-Second 71, 473, 653; Twenty-Seventh 69, 72; Twenty-Sixth *68*, 71, 150, 393, 600, 654; Twenty-Third 68n5, 71, 94, 352, 653–654
America *see* United States
American Agricultural Movement 206
American Anti-Slavery Society 168
American Association of Retired Persons (AARP) 189–190, 194, 202, 210
American Bar Association 190, 203, 575, 576
American Civil Liberties Union 217
American Customer Satisfaction Index (ACSI) 530
American Enterprise 201
American Farm Bureau Federation 194, 207, 224
American flag 129, 130, 595
American Independent Party 239
American Indian Citizenship Act 1924 393
American Indian Movement (AIM) 167
American Indians *see* Native Americans
American Medical Association 190, 202, 203, 207
American Psychiatric Association 479

I-707

American Recovery and Reinvestment Act (ARRA) 103
American Revolution 44, 45, 47–48, 61, 122; *see also* Revolutionary War
American Voter, The (Campbell) 30, 410
American Women Suffrage Association 169
Americans Elect 237
Americans with Disabilities (ADA) Act 1990 177–178
amicus curiae briefs 209, 591
Amtrak 535
analytical thinking 4, *4,* 27–28, 30–31
Anti-Federalists 50, 53, 71, 79, 83, 90, 99, 119, 234; ratification process 47, *47,* 49, 53, 56–57
anti-incumbent elections 380
Anti-Masonic Party 237, 328n3
anti-Semitism: Supreme Court appointments 575
anti-slavery movement: and women's civil rights 168
apathy, voter 402
appellate jurisdiction, courts of 561, 564, 565, 573, 588, 593, 602; *see also* courts of appeals; Supreme Court
appointment power 535, 549–550
apportionment 69–70, 367, 369; legislative 369, 369n15; *see also* reapportionment
apprenticeship norm 431
Appropriations Committee **450,** 452, 454
approval ratings, presidential *315,* 315–316, *502, 503,* 503–505
Architectural Barriers Act 1968 176
Arizona 108, 126, 127; immigration policy 108, 163–164; statehood 92; *see also Miranda v. Arizona* (Table of Cases)
Arkansas 92, *564, 603*
Armed Services Committee **450,** 454
arms, right to bear 120–122
ARRA (American Recovery and Reinvestment Act) 103
Arrow's impossibility theorem 613–614
Article I of Constitution 73, 87, 110, 149, 165, 434, 443, 446, 447, 482n4, 548
Article II of Constitution 53, 72, 73, 432, 433, 471, 472, 474, 483, 489, 490, 492, 505, 515, 519, 599
Article III of Constitution 560, 562, 570
Article IV of Constitution 60, 91, 92, 93
Article VI of Constitution 53, 95, 123, 592
Articles of Confederation 80, 82, 83; comparison with Constitution **54–55;** Congress under 425, 444; deficiencies in 59–60, 472; overview 44–45; revision of 49, 50, 53, 56; text 636–641
Asian Americans 19, 407, 437, 571, 576
attitude congruency bias 279
attitudinal model of judicial decision making 595–586
Australia 231, 395, 397

authority, government, and individual liberties 115–116, 118
autocracy 6, 7, 25, 42, 80

B committees **451,** 454
baby boomer generation 404
bad tendency rule 129
balancing test 128
ballot initiative 12, *14,* 148, 158, 179, 401, 628
banks: federal oversight of 536–537; privacy rights 135
Barden-LaFollette Act 1943 176
bargaining skill, presidential 509, 514–515, 520
Bavaria 397
BCRA (Bipartisan Campaign Reform Act; McCain-Feingold Act) 2002 130, 217, 363, 381
behavioral models 31, 34–35; bureaucratic behavior 544; judicial decision making 595; political interest 32; political participation 406; public opinion 308–309
bias *see* media bias
biased samples 303
bicameral legislature 52, 444
bicameralism in Congress 425, 444–449, **445,** *446,* **448,** *449,* **450–451,** 451–456
Big Four committees 454
Bill of Rights 59, 118–119, 120, **121,** 122; text of 649–654
bills to law process *see* legislative process
biological models 31, 35; misapplication of 151; political interest 32; processing of political information 263; public opinion 317–320; *see also* evolutionary and biological models
biology, and civil liberties 117
Bipartisan Campaign Reform Act (BCRA; McCain-Feingold Act) 2002 130, 217, 363, 381
bisexual *see* LGBTQ (lesbian, gay, bisexual, transgender, and questioning/queer) citizens
Black Muslims 155
Black Panthers 155
#BlackLivesMatter movement 160–161
Blacks *see* African Americans
Blaine amendment 127
blanket primary 364
block grants 102
blogs 288
blue states 413–414, *414*
bounded rationality 543, 544, 618–619
BP oil spill, Gulf of Mexico 546–547
BPW (National Federation of Business and Professional Women) 170, 171
Brady Campaign to Prevent Gun Violence 190
Brady Law 1993 215

bribery 216, 433, 472, 600
British Parliament 44, 203, 245, 425, 430, 444, 447
broad constitutional provisions 474
Brookings Institute 201
Brownloe Committee 484
Budget and Accounting Act 1921 506
budgets: budget-maximising bureaucrat model 542, 543; budgetary powers 550; federal 67, *97, 102,* 104, *104,* 506; OMB (Office of Management and Budget) 485, 533
bureaucracy 523–524; American structure *532,* 532–537, *534, 536*; bureaucrats 530, **531,** 532; characteristics of 526–530, **531,** 532; concept of 524–525; and Congress 548–549; control of 541–550; influencing 548–550; and the judiciary 550; merit system 527–529, 544; monitoring 546–548; neutral competence 529; policy formulation and adoption phase 621; policy implementation 622; power of 537–541, *539,* 540; and the president 549–550; reform of *551,* 551–553; spoils system 527, 549; theories of bureaucratic behavior 542–543; Weberian model of 526–527
business experience, and the president/ presidency 480, *481*
business sector: and government 552–553; political finance 381–382; state regulation of 598
businesspeople in Congress 437
by-product theory 195

C committees 454
cabinet *483,* 483–484; cabinet departments 533, *534*
California 108, 367, 369, 574, 622; affirmative action policy 155, 157; obscenity rulings 131, 132; population 19, 91, 354, 360; presidential elections 325, 329, 352, 354, 356, 360, 361, 364
California Democratic Party 217
campaign support 208
campaigns: finance laws 216–217; mass media 265–266; as political participation 389, 390, *390*; presidential **361,** 361–363
Canada 81, 153, 231, 494, 664
candidate image 410, 411, *411,* 412, 415–416
capital punishment 140–143, *142*
career patterns, Congress 438–439, *439*
carrying capacity 196
"cartel theory" 432
cases 560
casework 428
categorical grants 101–102
categorical groups 188

Cato Institute 201
caucuses/caucus method 327, 331, 332, 333, 343, 347, 448
CBS 268–269, 276, 281
cell phones: public opinion polls 303–304, 306
censures and reprimands 435
Center for American Progress 201
CEO presidency 488, 501
CFPB (Consumer Financial Protection Bureau) 537
Chamber of Commerce of the United States 194, 207
check and balance 15, 23, 63
chief diplomat, president as 492–494, *493*
chief executive, president as 489–490
chief justice 433, 562, 567–568, 572n7
child labor 598
child pornography 132–133
"choice opportunity" 616
Christian Crusade 172
churches: and civic skills 405
citizen-initiated contacts with governments 389, 390, *390*
civic engagement 287–288
civic skills 404–405
civil disobedience 154
civil liberties 7–8, 71, 113–114, 629; biology and 117; and civil rights 149; concept of 115–118; criminal procedures 136–143; freedom of expression 127–134, *133*; freedom of religion 122–127, *123*; restrictions on the government 118–122, **121**; right to privacy 134–136
civil rights 7–8, 147–148, 629; African Americans 149, 150–161, *155, 158*; and civil liberties 149; concept of 149–150; Latinos 150, 161–165, *162, 164*; LGBTQ citizens 150, 178–179; Native Americans 150, 165–167; people with disabilities 150, 175–178, *176*; population statistics 19; Social Darwinism and eugenics 151; women 150, 167–175, *168, 169, 174*
Civil Rights Act 1957 155, 164
Civil Rights Act 1964 155–156, 171, 177, 603; 1972 amendments 172
Civil War 74, 93, 109, 168, 395, 435, 491, 602; civil rights after 86, 154, 234, 392; nation-state relationship issues 597–598; secession 82, 99, 434; slavery 52, 70, 94, 99, 119, 150
Clean Air Act 1990 426, 464
"clear and present danger" test 129
climate change 549
closed primaries 328
closed rule 459
closed shop 193
cloture 462, 583
CNN *270*, 271, 283

coalition building by interest groups 206–207
coalition governments 235
Coast Guard 533, 534
coercion 6
collective action 187, 191, 192–193, 194, 198, 228, 229, 241
college education: African Americans 158, *158*, 160; Latinos 162, *162*; women 174, *174*
collegial courts 565
Colorado 344, 368
Columbia Journalism Review 276
Columbia model (sociological model of voting behavior) 408–410, *409*
commander in chief, president as 473, 490–492
Commission on the Status of Women 170, 171
Committee of the Whole 461
Committee on Fair Employment Practices 1941 154
committee system 449, **450–451**, 451–456; conference committee 464–465; legislative process 458–459, **460–461**, 461–465, *463*, **464**
Common Cause 191
Communications Act 1934 275
Communications Decency Act 132, 275
Communist Party 237, 238
competence, of public opinion 299–300
complexity, and federalism 86–87
compulsory voting 395, 397
concurrent powers 90–91
concurring opinions 569
conditional party government (CPG) 252, 431–432
Confederate flag 617, *618*
Confederate States of America (CSA) 99
confederation 80, *80*
Confederation, Articles of *see* Articles of Confederation
conference, Supreme Court cases heard in 567–568
conference committee 464–465
confidence level 304
confirmation process 577; length of process 489–490, *490*; politics of in the Senate 577, 579–583, *580, 581, 582*
conflict, and public policy 611
conflict resolution 244–245
Congress 423–424, *424*; African American members 156; agenda setting 615; bicameralism 425, 444–449, **445**, *446*, **448**, *449*, **450–451**, 451–456; and bureaucracy 548–549; committee system 449, **450–451**, 451–456; competition for control of 232, *233*; concept of 425; constituencies 509; delegation of power 475; ethnic and gender analysis

of members 437; female members 173; impact of population change on representation 18–19; Latino members 163; legislative process 456–459, *457*, **460–461**, 461–465, *463*, **464**; length of service 438–439, *440*; majority party members 243; members and their world 436–444, *438, 439, 440*; minority party members 243; partisan control of **663–666**; partisanship 250–251, *251*; party polarization 511, *512*, 513; pay and perquisites 441–444; policymaking process 426–427; power of definition of federal courts 561; powers of 73, 87; and the president/presidency 505–511, *506, 508, 512*, 513–516, *517*, **517**, 518–519; presidential bargaining skill 514–515; presidential popularity 513–514; presidential success in 507-5-9, *508*; press freedom 275; purpose of 425; racial composition of 370–371; redistricting 367–368; responsibilities of 426–436, *429, 434*; separation of powers 63; Supreme Court's appellate jurisdiction 565, 602; tenure and career patterns 438–439, *439*; war declarations 473–474; *see also* congressional behavior; divided government; House of Representatives; Senate; unified government
Congress of Racial Equality 155
congressional behavior: distributive model 431; informational model 431; partisan model 431–432
Congressional elections 325–326; anti-incumbent 380; candidate image 416; Congressional districts 367–371, *368, 370*; election process 366–372, *368, 370, 373, 374*, 374–380, **381**; financing 378–379, 380–383; general election 326; incumbency advantages *374*, 374–380, *378*, 416, 497; nominations 326; overlapping terms and staggered elections 371–372, *373, 374*, 509; politics of candidate choice 364–366, *365, 366*; and the presidency 497–498; primary laws 364; voter turnout 394, *394*
Congressional Union 1913 170
Connecticut 52, 53, 70, 123, 134
Connecticut Compromise (Great Compromise) 52
conservatives 20, 21, *21*
constituencies 214, 252, 351; Congress 366, 367, 375, 377, 380, 428, 432, 433, 455; House/Senate differences 455–456; separation of 63, 65
Constitution: addition of new states 93–94; Article I 73, 87, 110, 149, 165, 434, 443, 446, 447, 482n4, 548; Article II 53, 72, 73, 432, 433, 471, 472, 474, 483, 489, 490,

492, 505, 515, 519, 599; Article III 560, 562, 570; Article IV 60, 91, 92, 93; Article VI 53, 95, 123, 592; changes to 66–74, *68*, **69**, 92; comparison with Articles of Confederation **54–55**; concept of 42–43; Constitutional Convention 49–53, **54–55**, 56–57, 472, 483; custom and usage 72–73; "elastic" clause 87; electoral college 352–353; executive interpretation 73–74; federalism 63–65, 83; formal amendments 66–72, *68*, **69**; fragmentation of power 62–65, *64*; historical antecedents 43–46, *44*; interstate commerce clause 88–89; judicial interpretation 74; judicial review 591–592; jurisdiction 560; legislative interpretation 74; living 594–595; major deficiencies in Articles of Confederation 59–60; mixed government *65*, 65–66; overview of 41–42; and public opinion 293; ratification process 53, 56–57, 118–119; rational choice explanation of 48–49; and religion 52–53; as representative government 62; and state powers, rights, and obligations 90–93, 95; Supreme Court as final arbiter 567; text of 642–648; as a written document 61–62

Constitutional Convention 49–53, **54–55**, 56–57, 472, 483
constitutional interpretation 600
Consumer Financial Protection Bureau (CFPB) 537
Consumer Product Safety Commission (CPSC) 525, 535, 538, *539*
context, and political participation *403*, 403–404, *404*
Continental Congress 49, 50, 56; Second 43
contraception: and privacy rights 134
"Contract with America" 253
contracting out 552–553
controversies 560
convention 327–328
conventions *see* national conventions
cooperative federalism 100–103, *102*
core democratic values 627–630
corporate model of presidential organization 488
correlation 27, 28
cortisol 32
Council of Economic Advisers 485, 533
counsel, right to 138–139
courts: agenda setting 615; *see also* collegial courts; courts of appeals; district courts; federal courts; judiciary; Supreme Court
courts of appeals 588; structure and organization *564*, 564–565
courts of appellate jurisdiction 561, 564, 588, 593, 602; appointments to 573; *see also* courts of appeals; Supreme Court

courts of original jurisdiction 561, 562, 565, 593; *see also* district courts; Supreme Court
CPG (conditional party government) 252, 431–432
CPSC (Consumer Product Safety Commission) 525, 535, 538, *539*
credit claiming 376, 431
crime 629–630
criminal law: capital punishment 140–143, *142*; interstate obligations 92–93; right against self-incrimination 139–140; right to counsel 138–139
criminal procedure 136–138
crosses, burning of 130
crossover sanction 103
CSA (Confederate States of America) 99
Cuban missile crisis 486
culture, political 309–310
custom and usage 72–73

DACA (Deferred Action for Childhood Arrivals) program 164, 165, 516
Daily Kos 282, 288
"Daily Show" effect 269
de facto discrimination 160
de jure discrimination 157
decision making: rational-comprehensive decision making 618; *see also* judicial decision making
Declaration of Independence 43–44, *44*, 50, 117; text 633–635
Declaration of Rights, Virginia 119
Defense of Marriage Act (DOMA) 1996 179
Delaware 56, 348, 352
delegate model of representative democracy 299
delegates 430; accumulation of 344, *344–345*, 346; allocation of 329; selection method and timing 329, 331–32, *332*, *333*
democracy: case for 22–23; core principles 8–11, 13–15, 42, 61, 354–356, **355**, *357*; definition 6; diversity and difference 18, 19–20; dynamics of 18–20, *19*; false consensus 21–22; ideology and partisanship 20–21; major criticisms of 23–24; as process 7; trustee system of 299; *see also* direct democracy; representative democracy
Democratic Party 21, *230*; and African Americans 234, 252–253; brain imaging research 35, 263; and contemporary realignment 418–419; effect of minor parties on 239, 240; and ideology 510; national convention **330**, 331, 333, 348; national-level competition *233*, 234–237; New Deal Coalition 418, 496; nineteenth century 228–229; presidential elections

332, **335**, 336–337, **337**, *340*, 340–341, **342**, 343, 344, *345*, 346–347, 348, 349, **350**, 351; response to Trump administration 244; southern faction 224; two-thirds majority rule 351; unit rule 351; and voter behavior 399–400, 409, *409*, 410, 413–414, *414*
Democratic-Republican Party 222, 228, 229, *230*, 234, 500, 592
democratic substance 7–8
Department of Education 534
Department of Homeland Security (DHS) 533
Department of Justice (DOJ) 533
Department of State *534*
Department of Veteran Affairs 540
dependent variable 27; and the death penalty 141
deregulation 535
descriptive representation 370
desegregation *92*
deviating elections 417
devolution 104
direct democracy 12, 60
direct lobbying 204–205
direct popular election 351, 356–357, 358, 360
direct primary 254, 263, 265, 328–329, 331, 364
direction, of public opinion 294
disabilities, people with 150, 175–178, *176*
discharge petition 458
discipline, party 245, 246, 253, 452, 495
disconfirmation bias 279
discrimination: age 150; de facto 160; de jure 157; disability 175, 177–178; gender 155, 156, 167, 171, 172, 173–174; racial 88, 148, 150, 151, 152, 155, 156, 157, 158, 166, 171; religious 127, 150; sexuality 178
disenfranchisement 86, 152, 156, 393–394
disgust reactions 318–319
Disney 276
dissenting opinions 569
distributive benefits 428–429, 431
distributive model of congressional behavior 431
district courts 588; nomination and appointment of judges 573; structure and organization 562–564, *563*, *564*
District of Columbia 164; *see also* Washington DC
district plan 358, **359**, 360
districts, Congressional 367–371, *368*, *370*
diversity and difference 18, 19–20, 85–86; and the bureaucracy 530, 532
divided government 243, 244, 246, 250, *251*
division of labor 526
division of powers, in federalism 82, 87–95
Dixiecrat Party (States' Rights Democratic Party) 239, 240

DOJ (Department of Justice) 533
DOMA (Defense of Marriage Act) 1996 179
donkey voting 397
double voting 396
Dream Act 164
Dream Movement *164*, 164–165
Drudge Report 280, 282
Drug Enforcement Agency 533
dual federalism 98–100
Ducks Unlimited 196
"due process" clause 598
Duverger's Law 235

economic depression, 1780s 46
economic equality 10
Economic Interpretation of the Constitution of the United States (Beard) 48–49
Economic Theory of Democracy, An (Downs) 34
education: gender gap 174, *174*; people with disabilities 176–177; and political participation 401–402; racial segregation 153, 209; sex discrimination 172; *see also* college education
Education Amendment Act 1972 172
Education for All Handicapped Children Act 1975 177
EEOC (Equal Employment Opportunity Commission) 171
Eighteenth Amendment 68, 72, 652
Eighth Amendment **121**, 137, 140, 598, 650
"elastic" clause of the Constitution 87
elderly people: civil rights 150; *see also* age
elections 14, *15*, 325–326; agenda setting 615; campaign finance regulation 216–218; direct primaries 328–329; electoral rules 234–236; general election 326, 363; limitation of political speech before 130–131, 217; local 243n9; mass media 261; nominations 326, 327–329; nonpartisan 243n9n, 254; overlapping terms 371–372, *373*, 374, 509; and the president 496–498; public campaign financing 362–363; rational choice theories 377, 411–412; schedules and frequency 400–401; staggered 371–372, *373*, 374, 509; wave elections 380, *381*; *see also* Congressional elections; presidential elections
electoral college 72–73, 235–236, 351–352; direct popular election 355–356; district plan 358, **359**, 360; proportional plan 357, 358, **359**, 360; reform proposals 356–358, **359**, 360; violation of core democratic principles 354–356, **355, 357**; working system 352–254
electronic media 260; *see also* free press; mass media
Eleventh Amendment 71, 593n12, 601, 650

elite opinion 300
elitism 24
Emancipation Proclamation 1862 *483*, 515
Emanuel African Methodist Episcopal Church mass shooting 283
Emily's List 196
empirical questions 26, 30
Employment Act 1946 74
en banc 565
enabling act 92, 93
endorsement derby 341, **342**, 349
energy 473
Energy and Commerce Committee **450**, 454
enforced sterilization 151
England: religious tests 63
enumerated powers 73, 87, 88
Environmental Protection Agency (EPA) 534, 541, 549
EOP (Executive Office of the President) 479, 482, 484–485, 532, 533
EPA (Environmental Protection Agency) 534, 541, 549
Equal Employment Opportunity Commission (EEOC) 171
Equal Opportunity Act 1972 171
Equal Pay Act 1963 171
Equal Rights Amendment (ERA) 68n5, 70, 170, 171, 172, 576
equality of opportunity 10–11
equality under the law 9–10
ERA (Equal Rights Amendment) 68n5, 70, 170, 171, 172, 576
Espionage Act 129
establishment clause 123
Ethics Committee **450**, 455
ethnic minorities: and the bureaucracy 531; population growth 19, 20; racial discrimination 88, 148, 150, 151, 152, 155, 156, 157, 158, 166, 171; and redistricting 370; and Supreme Court appointments *575*, 575–576; voting rights 13
eugenics 151
evolutionary and biological models: bureaucratic behavior 544–545; misapplication of 151; political participation 406–407; public opinion 309; *see also* biological models
exchange theory 195–196
exclusion 434
exclusionary rule 138
exclusive committees **450**, 453–454
executive agreements *493*, 493–494
executive branch 471, 514; delegation of lawmaking powers from Congress 427; failure rates of appointments 490, *491*; length of confirmation process 489–490, *490*; selection of leadership for 435–436; and the separation of powers 63, *64*

executive interpretation of Constitution 73–74
Executive Office of the President (EOP) 479, 482, 484–485, 532, 533
executive orders 515–516, *517*, 550
executive privilege 73–74
expression, freedom of 127–128; general approaches 128; libel and slander *133*, 133–134; obscenity 131–133; specific tests 128–131; unprotected speech 131–134, *133*
expulsion 434–435
extraordinary writ 567n4

Facebook 175, 264–265, 208, 286
factions 58, 86, 189, 223; comparison with political parties 224
Fair Housing Amendments Act 1988 177
fair trial, right to 138–139
fake news 3, 259, 269
false consensus 21–22
falsifiable hypothesis 27
families, and political socialization 311, 313
Farewell Address, George Washington 222, 223
FBI 533
FCC (Federal Communications Commission) 188, 275
FDIC 535, 536
FEC (Federal Election Commission) 213, 216, 490
FECA (Federal Election Campaign Act) 1971 216, 217
Federal Administrative Procedures Act 539
federal budget 67, *97*, *102*, 104, *104*, 506
Federal Bureau of Prisons 533
federal bureaucracy *see* bureaucracy
Federal Communications Commission (FCC) 188, 275
federal courts 561; jurisdiction of 559–561; structure and organization 562–569, *563, 564, 566, 569*
Federal Election Campaign Act (FECA) 1971 216, 217
Federal Financial Institutions Examination Council 536
federal government *see* government
federal judges *see* judges
federal judiciary *see* judiciary
Federal Register 539
Federal Reserve Board ("the Fed") 490
Federal Reserve System 536
Federal Trade Commission 536
federalism 78–79; advantages of 83–96; context 79–83, *80, 81, 82*; cooperative federalism 100–103, *102*; disadvantages of 86–87; division of power in 82, 87–95; dual federalism 98–100; evolution of 96–109, *97, 102, 104*; future relations 109–110; national government powers

87–89; new federalism 103–109, *104*; overview 81–83, *82*; power conflict 95; rationale for 83–87; state government powers 89–95, *90, 92, 95*
Federalist, The 57–58, 64, 86, 89, 189, 223, 360, 473, 603, 655–662
Federalist Society 557
Federalists 47, 49, 50, 52, 56, 57, 79, 89–90, 99, 118, 119, 222, 234, 500, 592; political party 228, 229, *230*, 275
feedback 617
felons, disenfranchisement of 393–394
Feminine Mystique, The (Friedan) 171
Fifteenth Amendment 71, 99, 119, 150, 156, 166, 168, 392, 393, 651
Fifth Amendment 120, **121**, 134, 137, 139, 598, 649
files and records, bureaucracies 526
filibuster 462–463; Supreme Court confirmation process *582*, 582–583
Financial Crimes Enforcement Network 536
Financial Services Committee **450**, 454
financing: by business 381–382; campaign laws 216–217; Congressional elections 378–379, 380–383; presidential elections 362–363; public campaign financing 362–363
fire alarm oversight 546
First Amendment 23, 115, 120, **121**, 123, 124, 125, 126, 127–128, 129, 130, 132, 134, 149, 166, 185, 186, 216, 217, 274, 275, 293, 362, 566, 598, 649
First Continental Congress 425
first gentleman 485n5
first ladies 499–500
first lady 485–486, *486*
FISA (Foreign Intelligence Surveillance Act) 73
flags: American 129, 130, 595; Confederate 617, *618*
floor action 456
Florida 140, 393–394
focusing event 617
Foreign Intelligence Surveillance Act (FISA) 73
foreign policy 492–494, *493*
Foreign Relations Committee **450**, 454
formal rules in bureaucracies 526, 543
Fourteenth Amendment 71, 74, 99, 119–120, **121**, 138, 153, 157, 179, 209, 216, 369, 598, 600, 601, 604, 651
Fourth Amendment 115, **121**, 134, 135, 137, 138, 598, 649
Fox News 269, *270,* 271, 273, 276, 280, 281, 282, 283
fragmentation of power, in the Constitution 62–65, *64*
framing 272
France 61, 82, 154

franchise (right to vote) 392–394; *see also* disenfranchisement
franking privilege 442, 444
free exercise of religion 123; *see also* religious freedom
free expression 9
free press 260; agenda setting 271–271; concept of 261–269, *267, 268, 270*, 271–273; government control *274,* 274–275; information and education role 262–266; media bias 277–284, *279*; private control 275–277, *276*; threats to 273–277, *274, 276*; trust and information 269, *270,* 271; watchdog/public advocate role 272–273
Free Republic 282
free riders 192, 193–194
free time, and political participation 404–405
freedom *see* political freedom
freedom of expression *see* expression, freedom of
Freedom of Information Act 1967 547–548
freedom of religion *see* religious freedom
French Socialist Party 224
frontloading 331, *333,* 343–344
"full faith and credit" 92
functionalism 228
functions of government 42, 59
"funnel of causality" 410, 411, *411*

game theory 478, 586
GAO (General Accounting Office) 546
garbage can model of agenda setting 615–616, 618
gatekeepers 285–287
gay citizens: gay rights movement 178–179; *see also* LGBTQ (lesbian, gay, bisexual, transgender, and questioning/queer) citizens
Gazette of the United States, The 500
gender: earnings gap 20; judicial appointments 571; and Supreme Court appointments 576, *576*
gender bias, in mass media 283–284
gender discrimination 155, 156, 167, 171, 172, 173–174
General Accounting Office (GAO) 546
general elections 326, 363; *see also* elections
general revenue sharing 101
general schedule (GS) pay scale 530, **531**
Generation X 404
generational effect hypothesis 404
genocide 165
genome-wide association studies (GWAS) 318
geographical constituency 429
geography, and Supreme Court appointments 574
Georgia 140, 163

gerrymandering 368, *368,* 369–370
GI Bill of Rights 162
Gilded Age 100
"Gingrich Senators" 253
going public 499; limited benefits of 502, 502–503; personal trips 499–500; presidential speeches *501,* 501–502, *502*; and the press 500–501
"Goldwater rule" 479
good faith exception 138
"good losers" 245
government: and business sector 552–553; civil liberty restrictions on 118–122, **121**; coalition 235; CPG (conditional party government) 252, 431–432; definition 6; divided 243, 244, 246, 250, *251*; functions of 42, 59; mixed *65*, 65–66; party in 226, 250–255, *251, 252*; positive 474–475; representative 62; republican form of 60–61, 91; responsiveness to public opinion 407–408; structure of 42, 59, 60; unified 243, 244; unitary 82; *see also* state governments
government accountability 244
government authority 115–116, 118
government contractors 552, 553
government corporations 535
government expenditure 96–98, *97,* 619, *619*
government responsiveness 243–244
Grace Commission 551
grading scale 27
grandfather clause 152–153
grants-in-aid 100–101, 102–103, *104,* 104–105
Great Britain: African Americans 154; American revolution against 44, 45, 46, 47–48, 61, 80, 118, 122; exit from EU (Brexit) 306; Nudge Unit 624; Parliament 44, 203, 245, 425, 430, 444, 447; political system 13, 45, 62, 82, 245, 472, 498; religion 17; two-party system 231; *see also* United Kingdom
Great Compromise (Connecticut Compromise) 52
Great Depression, 1930s 96, 98, 100, 106, 161, 303, 404, 418, 474–475
Great Recession 2008-2009 98, 108
Great Society programs 101, 103
Green Party 240, *240*
group characteristics, and political participation 405, 407
group entrepreneur 195
groups: categorical 188; reference 314; single issue 200, 211, *212,* 217–218, 285; *see also* interest groups
GS (general schedule) pay scale 530, **531**
Guadalupe Hidalgo, Treaty of 161
Gulf of Mexico 546–547
Gulf War, 1991 492, 504
gun control *203,* 215

Gun-Free School Zones Act 1990 90
GWAS (genome-wide association studies) 318

habeas corpus 602
Handgun Control, Inc. 215
"happy politics" 402
hard money 216, 362
hard news 277
Hawaii 94, 107, 307n14
Heritage Foundation 201
hierarchical model of presidential organization 486, *487*, 487–488
hierarchy, and bureaucracy 526
high crimes and misdemeanors 433, 472, 600
Hispanics *see* Latinos
holds: on legislation 462; on Supreme Court nominations 582
home style 429
homosexuality 178; and privacy rights 135–136; *see also* gay citizens; LGBTQ (lesbian, gay, bisexual, transgender, and questioning/queer) citizens
Honest Leadership and Open Government Act 2007 462
Hoover Commission 551
House Appropriations Committee 431, 452
House of Representatives 423; apportionment 367; Committee of the Whole 461; competence and integrity of members 438–439, *439*; constituency size 13; differences from Senate **445**; elections 325–326, 371–372, *373*, 374, *374*, 376–377, 378–379, 380, *381*, 382; ethnic and gender analysis of members 437; leadership in 447–449, **448**; legislative process 459, **460–461**, 463–465; length of service 438–439, *440*; membership cap 70; party polarization 511, *512*, 513; party ratios on committees 451–452; politics of candidate choice 365, *365*, 366; presidential success in 507-5–9, *508*; reapportionment 367; redistricting 253; role in presidential elections 353, 355, 358, *359*, 435; seating and disciplining of members 434–435; special rules for floor consideration of bills **460–461**; standing committees **450**, 453–454, 455, 456; treaty-making 494
House Rules Committee 452, 454, 459, 463
HPA (hypothalamic-pituitary axis) 406–407
Huffington Post 282
Hurricane Harvey, 2017 617
Hurricane Katrina, 2005 283, 316, 475
Hurricane Sandy, 2012 475
hypothesis 27, 29

"I Have A Dream" speech (Martin Luther King Jr.) 155, *155*
IAT (Implicit Association Test) 159–160

ICE (Immigration and Customs Enforcement) *551*
Idaho 107
ideology 20–21; and party 509–510; and public opinion 310–311, *312*
Illinois 138, 139, 348
immigration 108; Latino 163–164; "Muslim ban" 113–114, 550; undocumented immigrants 163–164, 516
Immigration and Customs Enforcement (ICE) *551*
imminent lawless action test 130
impact evaluations 625–626
impeachment 432–434, 472; federal judges 599–600
Implicit Association Test (IAT) 159–160
implied powers 73, 87, 88
impossibility theorem (Arrow) 613–614
impoundment 550
income levels, and political participation 401–402
incorporation doctrine 120
incrementalism 618–619, 621
incumbency advantages in Congressional elections *374*, 374–380, *378*, 416, 497
independent agencies 534
independent variable 27, 141
independents 246, 247, *248*, 249
India: federal system 83
Indian tribes *see* Native Americans
Indiana 163, 398
indicators 616
indirect lobbying 204, 205–207
individual liberties 9, 13, 115–116, 118; *see also* civil liberties
Individuals with Disabilities Education Act 1992 177
inefficiency, and federalism 86–87
inevitable discovery exception 138
influentials 23
information: mass media role 262–266; processing of political 263; trust and 269, *270*, 271
information utility 264
informational model of congressional behavior 431
inherent (prerogative) powers 73
initial contests 333, 341–343, 349, **350**; *see also* Iowa caucus; New Hampshire primary
initiative 12
Instapundit 288
Instapundit 288
institutional agenda 617
Institutional Revolutionary Party (PRI) 231
institutional theory 141
institutions, role in representative democracy 42–42
instrumentation 305
intelligent design 124–125

intensity of public opinion 296–297
interest 223; aggregation of 242
interest groups 15, 185–187; agenda setting 615; biological theory and 199–200; campaign support 208; coalition building 206–207; comparison with political parties 223–224; concept of 187–190, *189*; definition 187; goals of 188–189; membership *189*, 189–190, 201–202; motivation for joining 190–194, *191*; origins and growth of 194–201, **197**, *198*; policy formulation and adoption phase 621; policy implementation 622; political participation 389, 390, *390*; political resources 201–203, *203*; political tactics 203–209, **206**, *207*; power and regulation of 209–218, *212*, **214**, **216**; and the Supreme Court 591
Internet: and civil engagement 287–288; as news source 267, *267*, 268; and obscenity 132; and public opinion 316; regulation of 275
interstate commerce clause of the Constitution 88–89
interstate rendition 93
intractable problems 626
invisible primary, presidential elections 334, 336–338, **337**, *339*, *340*, 340–341, **342**, 349
Iowa 18, 86, 341, 360
Iowa caucus 331, 341, 343
Iraq war 315, 316, 474, 492, 497, 627
iron triangles *540*, 540–541
IRS (Internal Revenue Service) 530
issue publics 300–301
issues: choice of in public policy 616–617; and voting behavior 410, 411, *411*, 412, 416–417
Italy 395, 397

Jehovah's Witnesses 126
Jim Crow laws 86, 156, 166, 627
John Birch Society 172
journalism: objective 278; *see also* mass media; media bias
Judaism, and Supreme Court appointments 574–575, 577
judges: confirmation politics in Senate 577, 579–583, *580*, *581*, *582*; experience and merit 576–577, 578–579; gender 576, *576*; geography 574; impeachment 599–600; party affiliation and philosophy 571–574; race and ethnicity 575, 575–576; religion 574–575; selection, appointment and background of 570–583, *572*, *575*, *579*, *580*, *581*, *582*, 601–602; self-restraint 603–604
judicial: definition 559
judicial activism 595–596, *596*

Judicial Conference 562
judicial decision making 584; Labor-Market Model 586, 587–588; models of 584–586; political influence on 586, *589*, 589–591, *590*
judicial interpretation 74, 561
judicial power 559–560
judicial restraint 595
judicial review 74, 561, 591–592; concepts of 594–596, *596*; constraints on 599–604; and impeachment 599–600; origins of 592–594, *594*; patterns in exercise of 596–599, *597*
judiciary 557–558; and the bureaucracy 550; concept of 559; definition 559; and the separation of powers 63, *64*
jurisdiction: appellate 561, 564, 565, 573, 588, 593, 602; Congress power of definition 561; defined in Constitution 560; definition 560; of federal courts 559–561; and judicial interpretation 561; original 561, 562, 565, 593
justice, and democracy 7
justiciable issue 369

Kaiser Aluminum Chemical Corporation 157
Kansas 18, 70, 86, 109, 209
Kentucky 93n1, 124
KKK (Ku Klux Klan) 130

Labor-Market Model of judicial decision making 586, 587–588
landslide presidential elections 232, 232n3, 303, 325
Late Night 269
Late Show, The 268–269
Latinos 571; civil rights 150, 161–165, *162*, *164*; college education 162, *162*; in Congress 437; earnings and college education comparison with whites 162, *162*; political participation 407; population statistics 161; and redistricting 370; Supreme Court appointments 575–576; undocumented immigrants 163–164
lawmaking: responsibilities of Congress 426–427; *see also* legislative process
lawyers, in Congress 436–437
leaders/leadership: executive branch selection 435–436; House of Representatives 447–449, **448**; majority leader *446*, 446–447; minority leader 447; party leaders 485–496, 2450246; Senate *446*, 446–447, **448**; *see also* president/presidency
League of Nations 493, 499
League of United Latin American Citizens (LULAC) 161–162
League of Women Voters 171

leak 274
legal model of judicial decision making 584
legal realist model of judicial decision making 585
legislative apportionment 369, 369n15
legislative cartel 432
legislative caucus 327
legislative intent 550
legislative interpretation of Constitution 74, 600
legislative oversight of administration 427
legislative process 456, *457*; bill introduction and committee referral 457–458; committee consideration and action 458–459, **460–461**, 461–465, *463*, **464**
legislative veto 548
legislature 425; and the separation of powers 63, *64*; *see also* Congress; House of Representatives; Senate
LGBTQ (lesbian, gay, bisexual, transgender, and questioning/queer) citizens: civil rights 150, 178–179; same-sex marriage 178–179, 295–296, *296*, 599
libel 133–134
liberal democracies 13, 16–17, 235
liberals 20, 21, *21*
Libertarian Party 237–238
life tenure 63, 586, 599, 601
Lilly Ledbetter Fair Pay Act 2009 173–173, 486
literacy tests 152, 153, 156, 392
Literary Digest 303
little legislatures 449
Little Rock, Arkansas *92*, 564, 603
living Constitution 594–595
Livingston Group 204
lobbying/lobbyists 185, 203, 211, 212, 213; biological theories of 199–200; bureaucratic 539–540, *540*; in court 208–209; direct and indirect 204–206; growth of 197–198, *198*; professional 204; systematic lobbying by presidents 514; *see also* interest groups
local elections 243n9
logrolling 207
Louisiana 70, 140, 158, 240, 364n13, *368*, 370
LULAC (League of United Latin American Citizens) 161–162
lynching 152

MADD (Mothers Against Drunk Driving) *191*
Madisonian dilemma 58, 114, 472
magazines, as news sources 260, 261, 264, 267, 282, 285
magic number 332–333, 344, *345*, 346, 348
Maine 93n1, 358, 393
maintaining elections 417
majority: absolute majority 8, 332, 353; simple majority 8; supermajority 434; three-fourths 67, 68, 357, 393; two-thirds 60, 67, 67n4, 68, 71, 172, 357, 433, 434, *434*, 436, 465, 472, 492, 493, 494, 507, 515, 516, 599
majority leader *446*, 446–447
majority-minority districts 253, 370, 371
majority opinions 569
majority rule 8–9, 11, 16–17, 34, 61; and public policy 627–628; and state constitutions 45
malapportioned 368–369
MALDEF (Mexican American Legal Defense and Educational Fund) 163–164, 167
March for Our Lives *203*
margin of error 304–305, **305**
Marine Minerals Service (MMS) 546–547
marriage: plural 94, 126; same-sex 178–179, 295–296, *296*, 599
mass media 259–261; agenda setting 271–271, 615; free press concept 261–269, *267*, *268*, *270*, 271–273; gatekeepers 285–287; government control 274, 274–275; information and civic engagement 287–288; information and education role 262–266; media bias 277–284, *279*; political socialization 316–317; private control 275–277, *276*; public sphere changes 285–288, *288*; threats to free press 273–277, *274*, *276*; trust and information 269, *270*, 271; watchdog/public advocate role 272–273
mass shootings 283
Massachusetts 46, 49, 56, 472
Massachusetts Bay Colony 122
material benefits 190, 191
mavericks 431
McCain-Feingold Act (BCRA; Bipartisan Campaign Reform Act) 2002 130, 217, 363, 381
ME TOO Congress (Member and Employer Training and Oversight on Congress) Act 2017 175
measurement 27
media *see* mass media
media bias 277–278; measurement of 280, 281–282; negativity bias 284; political 278–283, *279*; race and gender 283–284
Member and Employer Training and Oversight on Congress (ME TOO Congress) Act 2017 175
members' representational allowance (MRA) 442
mentally ill people, disenfranchisement 393
merit system 254, 527–529, 544
#MeTooMovement 175, *207*
Mexican American Legal Defense and Educational Fund (MALDEF) 163–164, 167

Mexican-American War 1848 161
Mexican Americans 161–162; see also Latinos
Mexico 231
Michigan 69, 148, 157, 360
Michigan model 29–30, 34, 69
midterm elections 371–372, *373*, 374, 380, 497–498; voter turnout 394, *394*
military action, power to authorise 473–474, 491–492
military services: racial segregation 164
military veterans 175–176
Minnesota 225, 238, 344, 398
minor parties 236, 237–238; effects of 239–241, *240*
minorities: political exclusion of 23; see also ethnic minorities
minorities' consent 456
minority leader 447
minority rights 8–9, 34, 61, 627–628
misdemeanors and high crimes 433, 472, 600
misinformation 268
Mississippi 158, 240, 341
Missouri 109, 135, 147, 153, 161, 344, 360, 396
mist clearing phase 343–344, *344, 345,* 346
mixed government *65,* 65–66
MMS (Marine Minerals Service) 546–547
mobilization 403–404
moderates 21, *21*
monarchs/monarchy 6, 60, 62, 222, 498
money: and political participation 404–405; see also financing
money primary 336–337, **337**
Montana 109, 352
Moral Foundations 117
moral hazard 553
Mormons/Mormon Church 94, 126
Mothers Against Drunk Driving (MADD) *191*
motor voter law (National Voter Registration Act 1993) 398
MRA (members' representational allowance) 442
MSNBC 282, 283
multimember districts 367
multiparty system 231, 235
multiple referrals 457–458
"Muslim ban" on immigration 113–114, 550

"myth of judicial objectivity" 559
NAACP (National Association for the Advancement of Colored People) 152, 153, 154, 163, 167, 209, 314
NAFTA (North America Free Trade Agreement) 494
NARAL (National Abortion and Reproductive Rights Action League) 195, 200

NARF (Native American Rights Fund) 167
NASA (National Aeronautics and Space Agency) 534
nation-state relationship 597–598
National Abortion and Reproductive Rights Action League (NARAL) 195, 200
National Academy of Sciences 202
National Action Party (PAN) 231
National Aeronautics and Space Agency (NASA) 534
National American Woman Suffrage Association 169
National Association for the Advancement of Colored People (NAACP) 152, 153, 154, 163, 167, 209, 314
National Association of Manufacturers 194–195
National Coalition of Latino Clergy and Christian Leaders 163
National Commission on Architectural Barriers 1968 176
national conventions 327–328; allocation of delegates 329; delegate selection method and timing 329, 331–32, *332, 333*; Democratic Party 329, **330,** 333, 348; presidential elections 347–348, 351; Republican Party 329, **330,** 333
National Credit Union Administration 536
National Federation of Business and Professional Women (BPW) 170, 171
National Gazette 500
national government see government
National Highway Traffic Safety Administration (NHTSA) *191,* 539
National Organization for Women (NOW) 171, 203
National Performance Review 551
National Public Radio (NPR) 281, 282
National Rifle Association (NRA) 190–191, 195, 202, 207, 215, 217, 285
National Right to Life Committee (NRLC) 195, 200, 217
National Security Agency (NSA) 73, 116, 136
National Security and Homeland Security Presidential Directive 518, 519
National Security Council 485, 533
national security directives 518
National Security Presidential Directives (NSPDs) 518–519
National Urban League 154
National Voter Registration Act 1993 398
National Woman Suffrage Association 169
National Women's Party (NWP) 170
Native American Rights Fund (NARF) 167
Native Americans 150, 165–167, 166, 393, 437, 576
NBC 269, 281
NCLB (No Child Left Behind) 106, 109
Nebraska 122, 157, 225, 254

negative electioneering 266, 317
negativity bias 284
neutral competence 529
Nevada 346, 360
New Deal 100, 475, 598, 601
New Deal coalition 418, 496
New England 99
new federalism 103–109, *104*
New Hampshire 50, 59, 341, 343, 360
New Hampshire primary 331, 341, 343
New Jersey 56, 69, 123–124, 475
New Jersey plan 52
New Mexico 360
New Orleans: Hurricane Katrina 2005 283
New York 19, 45, 46, 56, 57, 88, 124, 327, 367, 472, 563, 577
New York Times 268, *270,* 271, 278, 281, 282, 283
news: hard and soft 277; rational choice of source 264–265; see also mass media
News Corporation 276, 285
news media 261; see also free press; mass media
newspapers, as news source 267, *267,* 268
Newsweek 183, 285
NHTSA (National Highway Traffic Safety Administration) *191,* 539
niche theory 196, 199–200
Nineteenth Amendment 71, 166, 170, 393, 601, 652
Ninth Amendment **121,** 134, 650
No Child Left Behind (NCLB) 106, 109
nomination procedure 327–329; presidential elections 326, 329, **330,** 331–334, *332, 333, 334,* **335,** 336–338, **337,** *339, 340,* 340–344, *342, 344, 345,* 346–351, *348,* **350**
"non-response bias" in opinion pools 306
nongermane amendments 456
nonpartisan blanket primary 364
nonpartisan elections 243n9n, 254
Normandy, Missouri 147–148
normative 25
norms 218, 228, 245, 337, 431, 584, 585
North America Free Trade Agreement (NAFTA) 494
North Carolina 93n1, 140, 141, 360
North Dakota 352, 564
Northwest Ordinance 1787 100
NOW (National Organization for Women) 171, 203
NPR (National Public Radio) 281, 282
NRA (National Rifle Association) 190–191, 195, 202, 207, 215, 217, 285
NRLC (National Right to Life Committee) 195, 200, 217
NSA (National Security Agency) 73, 116, 136
NSPDs (National Security Presidential Directives) 518–519

nuclear option 462, 583
Nudge (Thaler and Sunstein) 624
Nudge Unit, UK 624
null hypothesis 29, 31
nullification 99, 109
NWP (National Women's Party) 170

Oakland, California 622
Obamacare healthcare reform (Patient Protection and Affordable Care Act) 297, 316, *429*, 498, 504–505, 510, *614*
objective journalism 278
obscenity 131–133
Occupational Safety and Health Act 538
Occupational Safety and Health Administration (OSHA) 538–539
Office of Management and Budget (OMB) 485, 533
office of president *see* president/presidency
Office of the Comptroller of the Currency 536
Office of Thrift Supervision (OTS) 537
Ohio 130, 131, 138, 179, 346, 360
oil spill, BP, Gulf of Mexico 546–547
Oklahoma 92, 93, 108, 152–153, 165, 329
oligarchy 6, 7
OMB (Office of Management and Budget) 485, 533
one-party system 231
one person, one vote 369
open primaries 328
open rule 459
open seats 377
operationalize 27
opinion polls *see* public opinion/public opinion polls
opposition parties 15
Oregon 329
organized anarchies 616
original jurisdiction, courts of 561, 562, 565, 593; *see also* district courts; Supreme Court
originalism 594, 595
OSHA (Occupational Safety and Health Administration) 538–539
ostracism 193
OTS (Office of Thrift Supervision) 537
overhead democracy 546
overlapping terms, Congress 371–372, *373*, *374*, 509

PACs (political action committees) 211–214, *212*, **214**, 216, 217, 363, 382; *see also* Super PACs
PAN (National Action Party) 231
Panama Canal Treaty, 1978 493
parliamentary systems 231, 235, 245, 251, 253, 310, 425; British Parliament 44, 203, 245, 425, 430, 444, 447
participation *see* political participation

parties *see* political parties
partisan model of congressional behavior 431–432
partisanship 21; Congress 250–251, *251*; independents 246, 247, *248*, 249; Senate 253; straight-ticket voters 246, *249*, 249–250; strong partisans 246, 247, *247*
party discipline 245, 246, 253, 452, 495
party elites 341
party identification (PID) 246; and voting behavior 410, 411, *411*, 412, 413–415, *414*
party in government 226; strength of 250–255, *251*, *252*
party in the electorate 226; strength of 246–247, *247*, *248*, *249*, 249–250
party leaders 245–246; president as 494–498
party organization 226; and the president 485–496; strength of 253–255
party polarization 251–252, 510–511, *512*, 513
party professionals 227, 229
party ratio 451–452
party strength 246–247, *247*, *248*, *249*, 249–255, *251*, *252*
party vote 251, *252*
passive presidents 477
passive resistance 155
Patient Protection and Affordable Care Act (Obamacare healthcare reform) 297, 316, *429*, 498, 504–505, 510, *614*
PATRIOT Act 115–116
Pearl Harbor attack, 1941 498
peers, and political socialization 314
Pendelton Act 1883 529
Pennsylvania 56–57, 124–125, 135, 325, 360, 367, 491, 595
Pentagon Papers 274
"pep rally goal" 351
perquisites (perks) 376, 442, 444
personal constituency 429
personal trips, by the president 499–500
personality traits, and political participation 403
physician-assisted suicide 135
PID (party identification) 246; and voting behavior 410, 411, *411*, 412, 413–415, *414*
plural marriage 94, 126
pluralist theory 194–195, 628
pluralistic system 22–23, 24
plurality 8, 14, 235, 236; SMDP (single member district plurality) 235
plurality opinions 569
pocket veto 507
polarization, party 251–252, 510–511, *512*, 513
police patrol oversight 546
police power 90; killing of African Americans 160–161

policy *see* public policy
policy analysts 620
policy evaluation 427, 612, 625–627
policy experimentation, and federalism 86
policy formulation and adoption 427, 612, 617–621, *619*
policy implementation 427, 612, 621–625, *623*
policy-motivated activists 227, 229
policy responsiveness 428
policy subsystems 541
policymaking stages *612*, 612–617, *614*, *618*, *623*
political action committees (PACs) 211–214, *212*, **214**, 216, 217, 363, 382; *see also* Super PACs
political activists 23
political alienation 402
political bias, and mass media 278–283, *279*
political culture 309–310
political efficacy 402
political elites 23, 24
political equality 9–11, 61, 628–630
political freedom 9, 11, 61, 628
political ideology *see* ideology
political influence 10
political interest 32–33
political machine 227, 253–254
political participation 337–338; biology of 406–407; concept of *389*, 389–392, *390*, *391*; and context *403*, 403–404, *404*; election schedules and frequency 400–401; forms of 389; group characteristics 405, 407; individual desire and ability to participate 401–407, *403*, *404*; parties' facilitation of 241–243; and psychological engagement 402–403; public opinion 293, 320–321; resources 404–405; socioeconomic status (SES) 401–402; theoretical basis of 389–390, *390*; two-party system 399–400; U.S. and international comparisons *391*, 391–392; U.S. rate of *391*, 391–392; voter behavior and American political system 417–419; voter choice explanations 412–417, *414*; voter identification laws 388; voting behavior models 408–412, *409*, *411*; voting rights 392–408, *394*, *400*, *403*, *404*
political parties 14–15, 222, 223; agenda setting 615; aggregating interests in 242; comparison with interest groups and factions 223–224; concept of 223–229; definition 223; development of 72; endurance of 225–226; functions of 241–246, *243*; and ideology 509–510; incentives for association with 226–227, 229; membership 224; minor 237–241, *240*; organization, and the president 485–496; party in government 226; party in the electorate 226; party organization

226; policy implementation 622; president as party leader 494–498; rationale for 228–229; responsible party model 245–246, 250, 252; strength of 246–247, *247, 248, 249,* 249–255, *251, 252*; two-party competition in American politics 229, *230,* 231–232, *233,* 234–241, *240*; *see also* Anti-Masonic Party; Democratic Party; Democratic-Republicans; Dixiecrat Party; partisanship; Republican Party; Socialist Labor Party; Socialist Party
political patronage 254
political question doctrine 369, 604
political resources 23, 187, 201–203, 629
political science 25; roots of 25–26; scientific method 26–30; theoretical frameworks in 31–35; *see also* analytical thinking; behavioral models; biological models; evolutionary and biological models; rational choice models
political socialization 311; events and experiences 314–316, *315*; and the family 311, 313; and the mass media 316–317; and peers 314; and schools 313–314, *314*; *see also* public opinion/public opinion polls
political tactics 203–209, **206,** *207*
politico 430
politics: definition 5–6; process and substance 7–8
poll taxes 152
polls *see* public opinion/public opinion polls
polygamy 126
popular election *see* direct popular election
popular sovereignty 7, 630
population biology 199–200
population ecology 196
population growth in U.S. 18–19, *19*
Populist Party 238, 240
pork-barrel benefits 375, 376, 428–429, 430, 431
pornography 132–133
position taking 376, 431
positive government 474–475
power: dispersal of, in federalism 83; division of, in federalism 82, 87–95; fragmentation of, in the Constitution 62–65, *64*
powers: budgetary 550; concurrent 90–91; Congressional 73, 87; Constitution, and state powers, rights, and obligations 90–93, 95; enumerated 73, 87, 88; implied 73, 87, 88; inherent (prerogative) 73; national government 87–89; presidential unilateral powers 515–516, **517,** *517,* 518–519; state government 89–95, *90, 92, 95*; veto 478–479, 506–507
prayer, in public schools 67, *123,* 124, 127, 319, 579

preemption 104
preferred freedoms doctrine 128
prerogative (inherent) powers 73
prerogative view of presidential power 474
president/presidency 469–471, 476–477; agenda setting 614; as an individual 477, 479; as an organization 479, 482; approval ratings *315,* 315–316, *502, 503,* 503–505; bargaining skill 509, 514–515, 520; broad constitutional provisions 474; and the bureaucracy 549–550; business experience and 480, *481*; as chief diplomat 492–494, *493*; as chief executive 489–490; as commander in chief 473, 490–492; competition for 232, *233*; concept of 471–473; and Congress 505–511, *506, 508, 512,* 513–516, *517,* **517,** *518–519*; congressional delegation of power 475; constituencies 509; contemporary expectations of 476; development of 473–476; electoral activities 496–498; executive privilege 73–74; going public 499–503, *501, 502*; impeachment 432–434, *433*; messages and recommendations 505–506, *506*; organization and effectiveness 486–488, *487*; partisan control of **663–666**; as party leader 494–498; and party organization 485–496; party polarization 510–511, *512,* 513; personal trips 499–500; popularity, in Congress 513–514; and positive government 474–475; and the press 500–501; primary constitutional responsibilities 489–494, *490, 491, 493*; as public opinion leader 498–404, *501, 502, 503*; single executive concept 473–474; speeches *501,* 501–502, *502*; unilateral powers 515–516, **517,** *517,* 518–519; veto power 478–479, 506–507
president pro tempore 446
presidential elections 496–497; campaign **361,** 361–363; candidate image 415–416; election process 351–358, **355, 357,** 360–367, **361,** *362, 366*; electoral college 351–358, **355, 357,** *359,* 360; endorsement derby 341, **342,** 349; financing 362–363; general election 326, 363; House of Representatives role in 353, 355, 358, **359**; initial contests 341–343; invisible primary 334, 336–338, **337,** *339, 340,* 340–341, **342,** 349; landslides 232, 232n3, 303, 325; mist clearing phase 343–344, *344, 345,* 346; money primary 336–337, **337,** 349; national convention 347–348, 351; national convention delegate allocation and selection 329, 331–332, *332, 333*; negativity bias in media 284; nomination procedure 326, 329, **330,** 331–334, *332,*

333, 334, **335,** 336–338, **337,** *339, 340,* 340–344, *342, 344, 345,* 346–351, *348,* **350**; overlapping terms and staggered elections 371–372, *373,* 374; prediction of nomination winners 349–350, **350**; public campaign financing 362–363; public opinion polls 2016 306–307
presidential oath of office 53
presidential popularity 513–514
presidential system 235–236, 425
President's Commission on the Handicapped 176
press 261; and the president 500–501; *see also* free press; mass media
pressure groups 212; *see also* interest groups; lobbying/lobbyists
prestige committees 454
presumption of success 435
PRI (Institutional Revolutionary Party) 231
primaries 331, *332*; blanket primary 364; closed primaries 328; Congressional elections 364; direct primary 254, 263, 265, 328–329, 331, 364; endorsement derby 341, **342,** 349; invisible primary 334, 336–338, **337,** *339, 340,* 340–341, **342,** 349; money primary 336–337, **337,** 349; nonpartisan primary 364; open primaries 328; runoff primary 364; two-top primary 364
primary constituency 429
primary responsibilities of Congress 426–430, *429*
principal-agent model 552
print media 260; *see also* free press; mass media
prior restraint 274
privacy rights 134–136
private control of mass media 275–277, *276*
private property rights 17, 58, 61, 598
PRLDEF (Puerto Rican Legal Defense and Education Fund) 163
pro tempore president 446
probable cause 138
procedures of government 12, 59, 60
process evaluations 625, 626
professional lobbying/lobbyists 204
professionalization, and bureaucracy 526, 527
Progressive Party 238–239
Prohibition Party 237
propaganda model 280
property qualifications for franchise 392
proportional plan 357, 358, **359,** 360
proportional representation 235
Proposition 209 157
prospective voting 417
Protestants, Supreme Court appointments 574
psychological engagement 402–403
psychology, and presidents 477, 479

public advocate 272–273
public agenda 36, 170, 271–272, 613–617, 621, 626
public campaign financing 362–363
public education policies 623, 626
public goods 192
public officials: and libel suits 133–134; role in representative democracy 42–42
public opinion/public opinion polls 292–294, 627; accuracy of polls 306–307; agenda setting 615; bases of 213, 308–311, 310, 313–320, 314, 315; biological models of 317–320; competence of 299–300; concept of 294–298, 295, 296, 297, 298; and Congress 513–514; direction 294; elite opinion and issue publics 300–301; government responsiveness to 407–408; ideology 310–311, 312; intensity 296–297; interpretation of polls 301–308, 302305; margin of error 304–305, **305**; and participation 320–321; policy formulation and adoption phase 621; political culture 309–310; political socialization 311, 313–317, 314, 315; and positive government 474–475; question order 300, 307–308; question wording 300, 305, 306; salience 297–298, 298; sampling methods 302–304; shaping of 207–208; stability 294–296, 296
public policy 609–611; agenda setting 612, 613–617, 614; concept of 611–612; and core democratic values 627–630; definition 610, 612; and majority rule 627–628; policy evaluation 612, 625–627; policy formulation and adoption 612, 617–621, 619; policy implementation 612, 621–625, 623; and political equality 628–630; and political freedom 628
public sphere 261, 273
Puerto Rican Legal Defense and Education Fund (PRLDEF) 163
Puerto Rico 93–94
purposive benefits 191, 192
push polls 300

question order, public opinion polls 300, 307–308
question wording, public opinion polls 300, 305, 306

race: and amendments to the Constitution 71; and political participation 405, 407; and Supreme Court appointments 575, 575–576; *see also* ethnic minorities
Race IATs (Implicit Association Tests)
race relations revolution 153–155; government's response to 155–156
racial attitudes, measurement of 159–160
racial bias 283

racial discrimination 88, 148, 150, 151, 152, 155, 156, 157, 158, 166, 171
racial segregation 152–153
radio, as news source 267, 267, 268
"rally around the flag" effect 504
random sample 302, 306
rape victims, and privacy rights 135
ratchet effect 96
ratification: amendments 67, 69, 156, 172; Anti-Federalists 47, 47, 49, 53, 56–57; Constitution 53, 56–57, 118–119; treaties 492
rational 190
rational choice models 31, 33–34, 199, 228, 245; agenda setting 615; bureaucratic behavior 542–543, 544; choice of news source 264–265; congressional behavior 431–432; Constitution 48–49; elections 377, 411–412; judicial decision making 586; political interest 32; political participation 407; public opinion 308; two-party system 399–400; voting behavior 411–412; wave elections 380, 381
rational-comprehensive decision making 618
rationality, bounded 543, 544, 618–619
Real ID Act 106
realigning elections 418
realist political theory 25–26
reality-based community 3, 4, 5
reapportionment 67, 232n2, 366, 367, 369, 604; *see also* apportionment
reciprocity norm 431
Reconstruction period 99, 154, 156, 231, 364, 370n16
record-keeping, bureaucracies 526
recuse 593n11
red states 413–414, 414
red tape 527
redistribution 10, 106–106
redistricting 156, 253, 366, 367–368, 369–370, 371
reelection constituency 429
reference group 314
referendum 12
Reform Party 238
regression analysis 27, 28, 28
regulatory agencies and commissions 534–535
Rehabilitation Act 1973 177
reinstating elections 417–418
relationship (scientific research)
relationship (scientific research), strength of 27–28, 28
religion: limited role of on Constitution 52–53; prohibition against establishment of 123, 123–126; religious freedom 122–123, 126–127; religious tests 63, 113–114; and representative democracy 17; and

schools 67, 123, 123–126, 127, 319, 579; and Supreme Court appointments 574–575
Religious Freedom Restoration Act 595
representation, responsibilities of Congress 427–430, 429
representative democracy 13, 59, 60; central beliefs of 16; core democratic principles 13–15; delegate model of 299; election rules 235; fallacies associated with 16–17; role of public officials and institutions 42–42; types of legislature 425
representative government 62
republican form of government 60–61, 91
Republican National Committee 217
Republican Party 21, 230; brain imaging research 35, 263; and contemporary realignment 418–419; effect of minor parties on 239, 240; and ideology 510; national convention 329, **330**, 333; national-level competition 234–237; nineteenth century 228–229; presidential elections 332, 333, 334, **335**, **337**, 337–338, 339, 340, 341, **342**, 343, 344, 344, 345, 346, 348, 349, **350**; Tea Party faction 224, 336, 338, 366, 448; and voter behavior 409, 409, 410, 413–414, 414; *see also* Democratic-Republican Party
research question 26
residential segregation 152
resources: political 23, 187, 201–203, 629; and political participation 404–405
responsible party model 245–246, 250, 252
responsiveness 243–244, 407–408, 428, 429
restrictive view of presidential power 474
retrospective voting 417
revenue sharing, general 101
reverse discrimination 157
Revolutionary War 46, 47, 80, 122
Rhode Island 41, 45, 49, 56
Richmond, Virginia 563
right to privacy 134–136
rights: African Americans 149, 150–161, 155, 158; Bill of Rights 59, 118–119, 120, **121**, 122, 649–654; ERA (Equal Rights Amendment) 68n5, 70, 170, 171, 172, 576; Latinos 150, 161–165, 162, 164; privacy rights 134–136; private property rights 17, 58, 61, 598; against self-incrimination 139–140; women 150, 167–175, 168, 169, 174; *see also* civil rights; voting rights
role theory 227, 228, 245
Roman Catholicism, Supreme Court appointments 574, 575
Roth test 132
rule, defined 538
rule of four 567, 568

rulemaking 427, 538–539, 622
Rules Committee 450, 452, 454, 459
runoff primary 364
Russian Federation 83

salience, in public opinion 297–298, *298*
same-sex marriage 178–179, 295–296, *296*, 599
sampling error 304; *see also* margin of error
sampling methods, public opinion polls 302–304
sanction, crossover 103
satisficing 543
scandals, and presidential approval ratings 504
schools: civic skills 405; political socialization 313–314, *314*; racial segregation 148, 603; religion 67, *123*, 123–126, 127, 319, 579
science, defined 26
scientific method 26–30
SEC (Securities and Exchange Commission) 534–535
secession 82, 99, 434
Second Amendment 120–122, **121**, 207, 649
Second Congress (1791-1793) 222
Second Continental Congress 43, 425
secondary responsibilities of Congress 432–436, *434*
secret ballot 254
segregation, racial 152–153
Select Intelligence committee 454
selective benefits 193–194
self-incrimination, right against 139–140
Senate: confirmation politics and the judiciary 577, 579–583, *580*, *581*, *582*; differences from House of Representatives **445**; elections 326, 365, *365*, 366, 371–372, *373*, 374, 375, 377, 380, *381*, 382; equal representation of states 91; ethnic and gender analysis of members 437; executive branch and judiciary leadership staffing 435–436; impeachment 433–434; leadership in *446*, 446–447, **448**; legislative process 462–465; length of service 438–439, *440*; party polarization 511, *512*, 513; party ratios on committees 451; presidential success in 507–5–9, *508*; role in vice presidential elections 435; seating and disciplining of members 434–435; and the separation of powers 63; standing committees **450–451**, 454–455, 456
Senate Judiciary Committee 573, 580
senatorial courtesy 573, 580
separate but equal doctrine 153
separation of church and state 123–124
separation of constituency 63, 65
separation of powers 62–63

September 11, 2001 terrorist attack 315, *473*, 498, 503, 504, 563, 617; and civil liberties 115–116
sequential veto bargaining (SVB) model 478
service responsiveness 428
SES (socioeconomic status) 401–402, 403, 405, 407, 408, 410
Seventeenth Amendment 71, 652
Seventh Amendment 120, 650
sexual harassment: #MeTooMovement 175
sexual orientation: civil rights 178–179; *see also* LGBTQ (lesbian, gay, bisexual, transgender, and questioning/queer) citizens
sexually explicit materials 132–133
"shadow bureaucracy" 553
Shay's Rebellion 49
Sierra Club 192, 196, 202, 541
signing statements 516, **517**, 518
simple majority 8, 60, 67, 68n5, 433, 435, 436, 462, 463, 494, 583, 600
single executive, president as 473–474
single-issue groups 200, 211, *212*, 217–218, 285
single-member district 367
single member district plurality (SMDP) 235
Sixteenth Amendment 72, 96, 600, 652
Sixth Amendment **121**, 137, 138, 139, 598, 649
slander 133
slavery 52, 70, 149, 150; Civil War 52, 70, 94, 99, 119, 150
slope of a regression line 27, 28, *28*
slot machine theory of judicial decision making 584–585
SMDP (single member district plurality) 235
Smith-Fess Act 1920 175
Smith-Sears Veterans' Rehabilitation Act 1918
Social Darwinism 151
social equality 10, 162
social media 175, 259, 260; agenda setting 272; and civil engagement 287–288; lack of gatekeepers 286; as news source 264, 267, *267*; and public opinion *207*, 208; *see also* free press; mass media
social-psychological model of voting behavior (Michigan model) 410–411, *411*, 412–413, 416
social-psychological models: bureaucratic behavior 542–543; voter behavior 29 (*see also* Michigan model)
Social Security Act 1935 74, 176
Socialist Labor Party 238
Socialist Party 237, 238
socio-structural theory 141
socioeconomic status (SES) 401–402, 403, 405, 407, 408, 410

sociological model of voting behavior (Columbia model) 408–410, *409*
sodomy 135
soft money 217, 362–363, 380–381
soft news 277
solidarity benefits 190–191
South Bend, Indiana 403
South Carolina 95, 99, 163, 240, 344, 346, 617, *618*
South Dakota 167, 352
Southern Christian Leadership Conference 155
sovereignty 6; *see also* popular sovereignty
Spain 47
Speaker of the House of Representatives 447–448, **448**
special interest groups *see* interest groups
special rule 459
speeches, presidential *501*, 501–502, *502*
spoils system 527, 549
spokes-of-the-wheel model of presidential organization 486–487, *487*, 488
stability 244–245, 294–296, *296*
staggered elections 371–372, *373*, 374, 509
"standard social science model" 34
standards of due process 550
standing committees 449, **450–451**, 452, 453–455; structure and organization 449, 451–452
standing to sue 602, 604
state courts 566, 567
state governments 53, 59, 80, 86; addition of new states 93–94; civil liberty restrictions 119–122, **121**; civil rights 119–120, *121*, 132, 139, 149, 151, 393, 398, 598; comparative method 84–85; constitutions 45–46, 90; equal representation in Senate 91; expenditure 96–98, *97*, 98, 619; and federal government 63–64, 78–79, 81, 98, 99–100, 108, 109; nation-state relationship 597–598; obligations 92–93, 99, 105, 106; powers 89–91, *90*, 95; and religion 123, 124, 125, 127; rights 91–92, *92*; status of in federal system 425
State of the Union address 501–502, 505–506, *506*
state presidential primary 331
statehood 91–92, 93–94
States' Rights Democratic Party (Dixiecrat Party) 239, 240
stereotyping of Native Americans 167
sterilization, enforced 151
stewardship doctrine 474
straight-ticket voters 246, *249*, 249–250
strategic framing 284
strategic model of judicial decision making 586
Strategic Politician Theory 377, 379
straw polls 303

strength of a relationship (scientific research) 27–28, *28*
stress, biology of 406–407
strict-constructionist 574
strong-executive model 472
strong partisans 246, 247, *247*
structure of government 42, 59, 60
structured rule 459
student government, and civic skills 405
Student Nonviolent Coordinating Committee 155
substantive representation 370, 438
suffrage 168; *see also* voting rights
suicide, physician-assisted 135
sunshine laws 548
"Super-A" committees 454, 455
Super PACS 131, 211, 217, 336, 362, 381
Super Tuesday 343–344
supermajority vote 434
Supreme Court 95; abortion issues 579, 580, 598; civil liberties liberalism *589*, 589–590; and the Declaration of Independence 44; dual federalism 99; expected and actual liberalism of justices *590*, 590–591; and the interstate commerce clause of the Constitution 88–89; judicial review power 74; original and appellate jurisdiction 561, 565; partisan control of **663–666**; representativeness of 574–576, *575, 576*; and state powers 90; structure and organization 565–569, *566, 569*; *see also* Table of Cases
"supreme law of the land" 95
surge and decline theory 372
surveillance, state 115–116, 135, 136
SVB (sequential veto bargaining) model 478
Sweden 81
swing states 360
Switzerland 13
symbolic responsiveness 429

taxation: and ethnic minorities 52, 149, 152, 156, 166; government power of 59, 72, 87, 89, 91, 96; and religion 123–124, 125, 126–127
Tea Party faction 224, 336, 338, 366, 448
telephone samples 303–304, 306
television: as dominant medium 266–267, *267*; as news source 267, *267,* 268; and presidential elections 351
Tennessee 93n1, 414
Tenth Amendment 90, 91, 105, 650
terms of good behavior 570, 585
terrorism/terrorist attacks: PATRIOT Act 115–116; September 11, 2001 terrorist attack 115–116, 315, *473,* 498, 503, 504, 563, 617; *see also* war on terror
test case 208–209
testable hypothesis 27

Texas 78, 93, 108, 134, 140, 156, 158, 163, 361, 369, 414
Texas Democratic Party 224
theory 29, 30
theory of formal legal rationality 141
think tanks 201
Third Amendment 134, 649
"third house of Congress" 465
third parties 235, 236, 237–240, 360; *see also* minor parties
Thirteenth Amendment 70, 71, 99, 119, 600, 651
three-fourths majority 67, 68, 357, 393; *see also* Supermajority
TILI (one-shot, take-it-or-leave-it) game 478
Time Warner 276, 285
town meetings 12, 500
transgender citizens *see* LGBTQ (lesbian, gay, bisexual, transgender, and questioning/queer) citizens
treason 433, 472, 599
Treasury Department 530, 536
treaties 44, 60, 73, 90, 95, 474, 492–493, *493*
Treaty of Guadalupe Hidalgo 161
Treaty of Versailles 492–493, 499
trust, and mass media 269, *270,* 271
trustee system of democracy 299
trustees 430
truthiness 3
Tuesday: elections on 400; Super Tuesday 343–344
Twelfth Amendment 71–72, 352, 472, 650–651
Twentieth Amendment 71, 72, 473, 652–653
Twenty-Fifth Amendment 71, 435, 473, 654
Twenty-First Amendment 68, 72, 653
Twenty-Fourth Amendment 71, 601, 654
Twenty-Second Amendment 71, 473, 653
Twenty-Seventh Amendment 69, 72
Twenty-Sixth Amendment *68,* 71, 150, 393, 600, 654
Twenty-Third Amendment 68n5, 71, 94, 352, 653–654
twin research 317–318, 319–320
Twitter 175, 208, 259, 264, 272, 287, 288
two-party system 231, 235; American politics 229, *230,* 231–232, *233,* 234–241, *240*; and political participation 399–400; *see also* political parties
"two-speed federalism" 108
two-thirds majority 60, 67, 67n4, 68, 71, 172, 357, 433, 434, *434,* 436, 465, 472, 492, 493, 494, 507, 515, 516, 599
two-top primary 364

UAW (United Automobile Workers) 191
UCA (unanimous consent agreement) 459, 463, **464**

undocumented immigration 163–164, 516
unfunded mandates 106
unicameral legislature 44, 444
unified government 243, 244
unilateral powers of president 505, 515–516, **517**, *517,* 518–519
unintentional mobilization 210
union shop 193
unit rule, Democratic Party 351
unitary system 81, *81*
United Auto Workers 207
United Automobile Workers (UAW) 191
United Kingdom: as a liberal democracy 13; Nudge Unit 624; political parties 245; referendum to leave EU, 2016 306; unitary government 82; *see also* Great Britain
United Nations (UN) 80
United States Postal Service (USPS) 524, 535
unorthodox lawmaking 456
unprotected speech, and civil liberties 131–134, *133*
unwritten constitution 62
Urban Institute 201
U.S. Civil Rights Commission 154
U.S. Coast Guard 533
U.S. Commission on Civil Rights 172
U.S. Constitution *see* Constitution
U.S. Marshals Service 533
USPS (United States Postal Service) 524, 535
Utah 94, 163
utility 33, 48, 191; and the act of voting 412; bureaucratic behavior 542, 543; information utility 264

variable 27
Vermont 93n1, 242n8, 329, 349, 352
Versailles, Treaty of 492–493, 499
veto power 478–479, 506–507; legislative veto 548
vice president 482–483; nominees 347–348; personal trips 499–500; Senate role 446, 471
Vietnam War 150, 274, 297, 393, 473, 504
Violence Against Women Act 1994 89, 172
Virginia 56, 57, 93n1, 119, 123, 346, 355n10, 360, 397
Virginia plan 51, 52
Virginia Statute for Religious Freedom 123
Vocational Rehabilitation Act 1954 176
volunteering 160, 226, 265, 390
voter apathy 402
voter fraud 396–397
voter identification and verification 387–388, 396, 398–399
voter registration 398–399
voter turnout *394,* 394–401, *400,* 401, 407–408; generational effect hypothesis 404; mobilization hypothesis 403–404

voting 389, 390; biological aspects of 406–407; costs of 389, 390, 411–412; and democracy 407–408
voting behavior 408; and the American political system 417–419; candidate image 410, 411, *411*, 412, 415–416; explanations of 412–417, *414*; Michigan model of 29–30, 34; rational choice model 411–412; social-psychological model 410–411, *411*; sociological model 408–410, *409*
voting laws 395, 397
voting rights 392–408, *394, 400, 403, 404*; African Americans 150, 152, 156, 252–253, 392, 393–394; political participation 392–408, *394, 400, 403, 404*; women 13, 71, 166, 168–170, *169*, 393, 601; young people *68*, 71, 150, 393, 600
Voting Rights Act 1965 156, 166, 252–253, 392
voucher system 618

Wall Street Journal 281
war on terror 474, 518, 523; *see also* terrorism/terrorist attacks

War Powers Act 1973 491–492
Washington (state) 78, 127, 157
Washington DC 67, 68n5, 71, 94, *95*, 104, 105
Washington Post 273, 282
Washington Times 280
Watergate scandal 504, 507, 574
wave elections 380, *381*
Ways and Means Committee **450,** 452, 454, 455
WBC (Westboro Baptist Church) 129–130
weak-executive model 472
Weberian model of bureaucracy 526–527
welfare spending 105, 107
West Virginia 93n1, 341
Westboro Baptist Church (WBC) 129–130
Whig party 228
whips 447
Whiskey Rebellion, 1794 491
White House Office 484–485, 533
White House Press Office 501
Wilson-Patterson Index 27
Wisconsin 178, 325, 328, 360, 387–388, 396, 398
women: and the bureaucracy 531; civil rights 150, 167–175, *168, 169, 174*; college education 174, *174*; in Congress 437; education gap 174, *174*; gender discrimination 155, 156, 167, 171, 172, 173–174; historical background *168*, 168–170, *169*; judicial appointments 571; pay gap 20, 173, *174*; and Supreme Court appointments 576, *576*; voting rights 13, 71, 166, 168–170, *169,* 393, 601
World Anti-Slavery Convention, London, 1840 168
World War I 170
World War II 101
writ of appeal 567n4
writ of certiorari 567
writ of habeas corpus 165–166
writ of mandamus 593
write-in votes 236n6
Wyoming 91, 94, 169, 329, 352, 354, 360

yardstick 27
Young Americans for Freedom 172
young people 405; voting rights *68,* 71, 150, 393, 600

zones of privacy 134